The Cambridge Handbook of Infant Development

This multidisciplinary volume features many of the world's leading experts of infant development, who synthesize their research on infant learning and behavior, while integrating perspectives across neuroscience, socio-cultural context, and policy.

It offers an unparalleled overview of infant development across foundational areas such as prenatal development, brain development, epigenetics, physical growth, nutrition, cognition, language, attachment, and risk. The chapters present theoretical and empirical depth and rigor across specific domains of development, while highlighting reciprocal connections among brain, behavior, and social-cultural context.

The handbook simultaneously educates, enriches, and encourages. It educates through detailed reviews of innovative methods and empirical foundations and enriches by considering the contexts of brain, culture, and policy. This cutting-edge volume establishes an agenda for future research and policy, and highlights research findings and application for advanced students, researchers, practitioners, and policy-makers with interests in understanding and promoting infant development.

JEFFREY J. LOCKMAN is the Lila L. and Douglas J. Hertz Chair of Psychology at Tulane University, USA, and past-editor of the journal *Child Development*.

CATHERINE S. TAMIS-LEMONDA is Professor of Applied Psychology at New York University, USA.

The Cambridge Handbook of Infant Development

Brain, Behavior, and Cultural Context

Edited by

Jeffrey J. Lockman
Tulane University

Catherine S. Tamis-LeMonda
New York University

CAMBRIDGE
UNIVERSITY PRESS

CAMBRIDGE
UNIVERSITY PRESS

University Printing House, Cambridge CB2 8BS, United Kingdom

One Liberty Plaza, 20th Floor, New York, NY 10006, USA

477 Williamstown Road, Port Melbourne, VIC 3207, Australia

314–321, 3rd Floor, Plot 3, Splendor Forum, Jasola District Centre,
New Delhi – 110025, India

79 Anson Road, #06-04/06, Singapore 079906

Cambridge University Press is part of the University of Cambridge.

It furthers the University's mission by disseminating knowledge in the pursuit of
education, learning, and research at the highest international levels of excellence.

www.cambridge.org
Information on this title: www.cambridge.org/9781108426039
DOI: 10.1017/9781108351959

First published 2020

Printed in the United Kingdom by TJ International Ltd, Padstow Cornwall

A catalogue record for this publication is available from the British Library.

ISBN 978-1-108-42603-9 Hardback
ISBN 978-1-108-44439-2 Paperback

For Ben (JJL) and Lila (CTL) — the infants who have inspired us.

Contents

Illustrations

Tables

Contributors

KAREN E. ADOLPH, New York University, USA

YEOJIN AMY AHN, University of Miami, USA

EVIN AKTAR, Leiden University, the Netherlands

DIMA AMSO, Brown University, USA

ERIN M. ANDERSON, Northwestern University, USA

LORRAINE E. BAHRICK, Florida International University, USA

RACHEL BARR, Georgetown University, USA

MARC H. BORNSTEIN, Institute of Fiscal Studies, UK, and Eunice Kennedy Shriver National Institute of Infant Health and Human Development, USA

ANDREW J. BREMNER, University of Birmingham, UK

NATALIE H. BRITO, New York University, USA

FRANCES A. CHAMPAGNE, University of Texas at Austin, USA

LAURA K. CIRELLI, University of Toronto, Canada

STEFANIA CONTE, University of South Carolina, USA

OR DAGAN, Stony Brook University, USA

RANJAN DEBNATH, University of Maryland, USA

GIANLUCA ESPOSITO, Nanyang Technological University, Singapore, and University of Trento, Italy

TERJE FALCK-YTTER, Uppsala University, Sweden

JENNIFER ORLET FISHER, Temple University, USA

CATHERINE A. FORESTELL, College of William and Mary, USA

NATHAN A. FOX, University of Maryland, USA

ROBERTA MICHNICK GOLINKOFF, University of Delaware, USA

J. KILEY HAMLIN, University of British Columbia, Canada

HARLENE HAYNE, University of Otago, New Zealand

JANE S. HERBERT, University of Wollongong, Australia

SUSAN J. HESPOS, Northwestern University, USA

KATHY HIRSH-PASEK, Temple University, USA

JUSTINE HOCH, New York University, USA

SWAPNAA JAYARAMAN, Indiana University, USA

EMILY JONES, Birkbeck, University of London, UK

HOSHINORI KANAZAWA, University of Tokyo, Japan

YASUO KUNIYOSHI, University of Tokyo, Japan

MICHELLE LAMPL, Emory University, USA

DANI LEVINE, Temple University, USA

ROBERT LICKLITER, Florida International University, USA

JEFFREY J. LOCKMAN, Tulane University, USA

DAPHNE MAURER, McMaster University, Canada

JULIE A. MENNELLA, Monell Chemical Senses Center, USA

DANIEL S. MESSINGER, University of Miami, USA

SAMANTHA MITSVEN, University of Miami, USA

JACQUELYN MOFFITT, University of Miami, USA

SANTIAGO MORALES, University of Maryland, USA

NORA S. NEWCOMBE, Temple University, USA

LISA M. OAKES, University of California, Davis, USA

KORALY PÉREZ-EDGAR, Pennsylvania State University, USA

JAYA RACHWANI, New York University, USA

REBECCA K. REH, University of British Columbia, Canada

JOHN E. RICHARDS, University of South Carolina, USA

SYLVIA N. RUSNAK, Georgetown University, USA

ABRAHAM SAGI-SCHWARTZ, University of Haifa, Israel

VIRGINIA C. SALO, Vanderbilt University, USA

MIRANDA SITCH, University of British Columbia, Canada

ELIZABETH G. SMITH, Cincinnati Children's Hospital, USA

LINDA B. SMITH, Indiana University, USA

CATHERINE S. TAMIS-LEMONDA, New York University, USA

JAMES T. TODD, Florida International University, USA

SANDRA E. TREHUB, University of Toronto, Canada

KRISTEN TUMMELTSHAMMER, Brown University, USA

ALISON K. VENTURA, California Polytechnic State University, USA

ANNE S. WARLAUMONT, University of California, Los Angeles, USA

JANET F. WERKER, University of British Columbia, Canada

YASUNORI YAMADA, University of Tokyo, Japan

Preface

When the two of us agreed to work on *The Cambridge Handbook of Infant Development*, our vision was to produce a collection of essays that would integrate perspectives across traditionally disparate areas, pose new directions for research, and enrich policy and practice. We recognized that this was a tall order. Yet, thanks to our contributors – *the* premier experts in infancy and human development, spanning disciplines and the globe – the Handbook has achieved its intended purpose. The end product is a state-of-the-art essential guide to contemporary research and theory on infant development.

The Cambridge Handbook of Infant Development spans a broad range of topics, including physical growth, brain development, health, and nutrition; cognitive, language, perception–action, social, and emotional development; and media and cultural influences in early development. Each chapter provides theoretical and empirical depth and rigor, while highlighting reciprocal connections among brain, behavior, and cultural context, and bridging the long-standing divide between basic research and real-world application. Thus, the Handbook simultaneously educates, enriches, and encourages. It educates through in-depth reviews of innovative methods and empirical foundations. It enriches an understanding of learning and development by considering the contexts of brain, culture, and policy. And it encourages new directions for research and policy by highlighting gaps between the current knowledge base and where research and practice need to go.

This definitive reference will appeal to academics, professionals, policy makers, and graduate and advanced undergraduate students from psychology, education, human development, pediatrics, nursing, occupational therapy, speech and hearing, and physical therapy. We hope that you are inspired by this collection of essays, and find them to be as educational, enriching, and encouraging as we did.

Jeffrey J. Lockman and Catherine S. Tamis-LeMonda

PART I

Foundations

1 Embodied Brain Model for Understanding Functional Neural Development of Fetuses and Infants

Yasunori Yamada, Hoshinori Kanazawa, and Yasuo Kuniyoshi

Early functional neural development is increasingly recognized as important for revealing the developmental origins of human cognitive-motor function and related disorders. Previous studies focusing on fetuses and neonates have revealed sophisticated behaviors and cognitive repertoires, indicating that fetuses begin learning through sensorimotor experience even inside the uterus. Despite accumulating evidence supporting the importance of sensorimotor experience in neural development as early as the fetal period, the developmental mechanisms by which intrauterine sensorimotor experience guides cortical learning, including factors in prenatal experience that are needed for normal development, remain unclear. However, investigating causal links between sensorimotor experience and cortical learning is particularly challenging in human fetuses owing to technical and ethical difficulties. Therefore, computational approaches based on comprehensive biological data about nervous system, body, and environment have been developed to probe mechanisms underlying early functional brain development. In this chapter, we show how an embodied approach focusing on interactions among brain, body, and environment offers opportunities to explore relations between functional neural development and sensorimotor experience.

1.1 The Origins of Cognitive/Motor Development and Learning

Developmental science has revealed the cognitive/motor abilities of infants (Adolph & Berger, 2006; Piaget, 1952; Rochat, 2009; Tomasello, 2009; von Hofsten, 2007). Many studies have reported that some amazing abilities can be observed in infants soon after birth, including neonatal imitation (Meltzoff & Moore, 1977), recognition of the difference between self- and other-derived stimulation in the rooting reflex (Rochat & Hespos, 1997), predictive mouth movements when sucking a pacifier (Rochat, 2009), orientation towards sound (Clifton, Morrongiello, Kulig, & Dowd, 1981), hand–eye coordination in reaching (van der Meer, 1997; von Hofsten, 1982), and leg movement adjustment in response to visual stimulation (Barbu-Roth et al., 2014). These findings indicate that human infants are not born as a *tabula rasa* (i.e., blank slate), but come into the world with various cognitive, motor, perceptual, and social abilities.

From this early competence perspective, fetal development has been investigated as well. Ultrasound imaging and observational studies reveal that the sensory systems except for vision are already functionally mature in the fetal period (Purves, 2012). Additionally, visual perception has been reported; fetuses can feel light and show a preference to engage with face-like stimuli in the third trimester of pregnancy (Gerhard, 2013; Reid et al., 2017). Collectively, these studies suggest that fetuses already sense the world with multiple sensory organs and adapt their movements accordingly. Further, spontaneous movements and somatosensory responses can be observed as early as 8 weeks before the formation of a spinal reflex circuit (Bradley & Mistretta, 1975; Lüchinger, Hadders-Algra, van Kan, & de Vries, 2008). Ultrasound imaging studies show that fetuses show structured movements (Butterworth & Hopkins, 1988; Kurjak et al., 2003; Reissland, Francis, Aydin, Mason, & Schaal, 2014), predictive mouth opening during hand–mouth coordination (Myowa-Yamakoshi & Takeshita, 2006), and planned hand movements (Zoia et al., 2007), suggesting that even fetuses possess sophisticated behaviors and cognitive repertoires (Reissland et al., 2014; Rochat, 2011).

Moreover, fetuses learn from sensorimotor experiences. For example, fetuses distinguish their own mother's voice and rhythms (DeCasper, Lecanuet, Busnel, Granier-Deferre, & Maugeais, 1994; Kisilevsky et al., 2003), recognize music heard prenatally during the neonatal period (James, Spencer, & Stepsis, 2002), and distinguish the taste/smell of amniotic fluid (Hepper, 1996; Schaal, Marlier, & Soussignan, 1998). Although few human studies have addressed motor learning based on prenatal sensorimotor experience, there have been multiple animal studies on this topic, including investigations of coordinated peristaltic movements in zebrafish embryos (Warp et al., 2012), motor learning in fetal/neonatal rats (Brumley & Robinson, 2013; Granmo, Petersson, & Schouenborg, 2008; Robinson, Kleven, & Brumley, 2008), and spontaneous movement and somatotopic map formation in rats and human preterm infants (Khazipov et al., 2004; Milh et al., 2006)). These reports suggest that cognitive/motor development (learning) based on sensorimotor–environment interactions starts during the early fetal phase.

1.1.1 A Key to Understanding Developmental Disorders: Clinical, Epidemiological, and Policy Perspectives

With reference to clinical, epidemiological, and policy considerations, a deeper understanding of early human development would inform prevention and intervention. Neurodevelopmental disorders, such as autism spectrum disorder (ASD) and attention-deficit hyperactivity disorder (ADHD), have recently increased in prevalence and have received considerable attention (Fombonne, 2009; Gaugler et al., 2014). Long-term follow-up studies have shown that perinatal environmental factors and diverse genetic factors influence the risk of developmental disorders later in life (Gaugler et al., 2014). Related studies suggest that even preterm infants without apparent brain injuries experience motor, cognitive, and learning difficulties and are at a greater risk of developmental disorders than their term-born counterparts (Larroque et al., 2008). Additionally, functional connectivity studies document differences between preterm infants and full-term neonates at term-equivalent ages, suggesting that preterm infants follow different trajectories of brain development from those of full-term neonates (Fuchino et al., 2013; Smyser et al., 2010). These studies suggest that abbreviated intrauterine periods and early exposure to extrauterine environments contribute to developmental disorders in later life. However, the causal links between sensorimotor experiences and atypical brain development remain unknown.

Additionally, care for preterm infants at high risk has been a challenge. In neonatal intensive care units, clinical staffs or caregivers often implement positioning or swaddling methods that are designed to provide a sense of containment similar to the intrauterine environment. In contrast, novel clinical techniques and devices such as artificial wombs (Partridge et al., 2017), which have been developed to support extremely premature infants, provide different forms of developmental care and may be associated with improved longer-term developmental outcomes. Although some studies report positive effects of early intervention with respect to reduced mortality or cognitive outcome (Lawn, Mwansa-Kambafwile, Horta, Barros, & Cousens, 2010; Ludington-Hoe, 2013), meta-analyses and systematic reviews report mixed evidence regarding the effects of early developmental intervention programmes on long-term cognitive or motor outcomes (Sizun & Westrup, 2004; Spittle, Orton, Doyle, & Boyd, 2007; Wallin & Eriksson, 2009). Thus, in the case of preterm human infants, the impact of developmental care on neuronal development remains controversial (Ohlsson & Jacobs, 2013). To improve current developmental care, research on the mechanisms underlying early functional brain development, including the types of prenatal experience that contribute to normal development, is needed.

1.1.2 Large-Scale Datasets for Understanding Human Brain Development: Neuroscience Perspectives

To date, knowledge about the process of fetal brain development has been mainly gained through histological/immunochemical studies using human fetal specimens at a microscopic level (Gerhard, 2013; Kanold & Luhmann, 2010; Tau & Peterson, 2010). In addition, recent methodological advances in neuroimaging such as diffusion tensor imaging and high-angular resolution diffusion tractography allow investigators to study the architecture of the human fetal brain (Dubois, Hertz-Pannier, Dehaene-Lambertz, Cointepas, & Le Bihan, 2006; Takahashi, Folkerth, Galaburda, & Grant, 2011; Takahashi, Hayashi, Schmahmann, & Grant, 2014). In Europe, the Developing Human Connectome Project launched in 2013 aims to create a dynamic map of human brain connectivity from 20 to 44 weeks post-conceptional age, which will link imaging, clinical, behavioral, and genetic information (Developing Human Connectome Project, n.d.). This longitudinal project plans to investigate the relation between developmental change in brain structure and neurodevelopmental disease. Additionally, the BRAIN Initiative project published an open-source atlas of gene expression across the developing brain using laser microdissection or DNA microarray technology (Miller et al., 2014). The creation of this open database of gene expression in the brain has made it possible to conduct allied investigations when new discoveries regarding developmental disorders and psychiatric disorders occur. Although these large-scale datasets of the prenatal human brain help to elucidate typical and atypical trajectories of human brain formation, investigations of brain structure alone do not directly address how sensorimotor experiences, arising from brain, body, and environment interactions, influence and guide brain development.

1.1.3 Sensorimotor Experiences of Embodied Interactions

We define the interactions among the brain, body, and environment as "embodied interactions." The term "embodied interactions" has been used to emphasize the role of "the body" with the environment when considering intelligence, including cognitive-motor function and its development. This concept has also been used to understand differences in brain function related to intelligence. Ideas relating to embodiment have developed in various fields, including philosophy, cognitive science, psychology, and robotics (Gallagher & Zahavi, 2007; Gibson, 1979; Merleau-Ponty & Smith, 1996; Varela, Rosch, & Thompson, 1992). In the field of developmental science, Thelen and Smith (1994) proposed a "dynamic systems approach," which argued that the development of thinking was part of a larger integrated system involving the development of the body and action as well as the brain. Byrge, Sporns, and Smith (2014) proposed a network-based account of developmental process in terms of nested dependencies and interdependent timescales of change within structural and functional brain networks. Consistent with these embodied approaches, studies to explain early human development from the perspective of complex body, nervous system, and environment interactions have been undertaken.

For instance, in the field of robotics, Brooks (1991) provided empirical evidence that intelligence can be constructed by using sensorimotor interactions in the environment even without detailed representations of the world as internal models. In keeping with this idea, embodiment cognitive science has tried to understand intelligence as an embodied system that dynamically utilizes the structure of the body and the environment (Pfeifer & Scheier, 2001). Furthermore, a novel field called "developmental robotics," which is based on embodiment notions in cognitive science, has emerged and focuses on mechanisms that underlie the development of intelligence (Asada, MacDorman, Ishiguro, & Kuniyoshi, 2001; Kuniyoshi, 1994; Kuniyoshi & Berthouze, 1998; Lungarella, Metta, Pfeifer, & Sandini, 2003; Weng et al., 2001) and other developmental phenomena such as reaching (Caligiore, Parisi, & Baldassarre, 2014; Pitti, Mori, Yamada, & Kuniyoshi, 2010), body image (Hoffmann et al., 2010; Sasaki, Yamada, Tsukahara, & Kuniyoshi, 2013), joint attention (Nagai, Hosoda, Morita, & Asada, 2003), and imitation (Demiris, Rougeaux, Hayes, Berthouze, & Kuniyoshi, 1997; Kuniyoshi, Cheng, & Nagakubo, 2003; Kuniyoshi, Yorozu, Inaba, & Inoue, 2003). These studies reveal how embodied interactions that exploit body and environmental constraints enable various behaviors to emerge and how incremental developmental processes can be explained with just simple control and learning rules.

We next show how an embodied approach focusing on brain, body, and environment interactions engendered by sensorimotor experience can be used to understand the mechanisms that underlie functional neural development in human fetuses and infants. We first describe the development of the nervous system (spinal cord and cortex) from the fetal to the infancy stage. Second, we explain development and learning based on sensorimotor experiences occurring from the embryonic to the infancy stage. Third, we present novel, integral embodied brain models of the human fetus and infant and show how these models provide insights into the mechanisms by which sensorimotor experience influences and is influenced by functional neural development.

1.2 Development of the Human Embryo and Fetus

In this section, we highlight the functional development of the sensory modalities, bodily movements, and nervous system during the early fetal and infancy periods, particularly in relation to learning based on sensorimotor experience.

1.2.1 Development of Sensory Modalities

To consider learning based on sensorimotor experiences in the embryonic and fetal periods, we first explain the development of the sensory modalities. Although it takes most sensory organs several years to fully mature after birth, sensory systems begin to work functionally even in the fetal period (Vauclair, 2012). Here, we consider the development of tactile perception, proprioception, equilibrium sensation, taste, olfaction, auditory, and vision during the fetal period.

Relative to all the sensing modalities, somatosensory perception such as tactile perception and proprioception matures earliest. With regard to tactile perception, Hooker (1952) reported developmental differences in tactile sensation after aborted fetuses were stimulated with a von Frey hair. Before 7 weeks after conception, the fetus did not respond to tactile stimulation. After 7 weeks post-conception, the fetus responded to tactile stimulation on the lip. At 10.5 weeks after conception, the fetus responded to hand, foot, and upper limb stimulation. At 11 weeks after conception, the fetus responded to stimulation on the face and all limbs. Approximately 14 weeks after conception, the fetus responded to stimulation on the whole body except for the top of the head and back.

Proprioception is the sense of self-movement and body position and its developmental emergence has been mainly investigated through study of muscle spindles. The muscle spindle is embedded in skeletal muscle fibres and senses information related to muscle length and its change. The structure of the muscle spindle appears at 11 weeks after conception and matures by 30 weeks after conception (Cuajunco, 1940). The stretch reflex, which is the most representative monosynaptic reflex induced by an afferent signal from the muscle spindle, is reported to mature by 25 weeks (Hakamada, Hayakawa, Kuno, & Tanaka, 1988). Although there is no study investigating when sensory feedback of the muscle spindle begins to induce the reflex in the human fetus, several studies suggest that it begins to work and affect neural learning in the spinal nervous system from around the end of first trimester (Clancy, Darlington, & Finlay, 2001; Robinson et al., 2008; Sarnat, 2003). For example, Sarnat (2003) suggested that the human fetus at its earliest stages can register proprioceptive feedback based on findings that: (i) the stretch reflex emerges at the same time as the formation of muscle spindle in the rat fetus, and (ii) sensory branches reach to the anterior horn of the spinal cord at 8 weeks in the human fetus. In addition, the rat fetus shows motor learning based on proprioceptive feedback at embryonic day 19 (Robinson et al., 2008). Because this period in the rat fetus is estimated to be equivalent to 11–13 weeks after conception in the human fetus (Clancy et al., 2001), these findings also suggest the beginning of proprioceptive feedback in the human fetus.

In the visual system, basic structures such as the eyeball and retina start to form by 7 weeks after conception; the optic nerve reaches the cerebral cortex at 16 weeks after conception (Bremner, Lewkowicz, & Spence, 2012). Although the maturation of these structures continues throughout infancy (Bremner et al., 2012), some visual function has been reported in the early fetal stage. Preterm infants showed eye tracking for visual stimulation from 22 to 28 weeks after conception and cortical activity in response to a flash of light (Bremner et al., 2012). Moreover, a recent study reported that the human fetus looked towards face-like stimulation projected through the uterine wall in the middle of third trimester (Reid et al., 2017).

The sense of equilibrium starts to function at 8 weeks after conception and functionally matures by 25 weeks after conception (Hakamada et al., 1988). In this phase, we can observe the righting reflex, which reflects the functioning of the vestibular sensory system (Bremner et al., 2012). Stimulation to the vestibular system in the fetus and preterm infant may affect state regulation, which plays an essential role in early functional development.

Gustatory and olfactory organs start to function approximately 14 weeks after conception (Vauclair, 2012). Regarding the auditory system, the cochlea is formed 9 weeks after conception and matures functionally at 24 weeks (Bremner et al., 2012). For example, some studies report that the fetus begins to respond to sounds at 24 weeks after conception, whereas others report auditory evoked cortical responses in preterm infants at 21 weeks after conception (Bremner et al., 2012). Regarding these three sensory modalities, many studies have suggested the possibility of fetal learning based on sensory experiences (James, 2010).

In summary, the central nervous system is capable of receiving almost all sensory inputs from peripheral organs in the third trimester. Further, somatosensory perception is the first of all the sensing modalities to mature and already begins to function in the early fetal period.

1.2.2 Development of Fetal and Infantile Bodily Movements

One of the earliest studies of fetal movement was done by Wilhelm Preyer in 1885. He noticed stepping-like movements by fetuses that were removed from the womb (Robinson & Kleven, 2005). After his original study, many researchers investigated fetal behaviors, especially behavioral responses to stimulation. Such attempts were carried out extensively from 1925 to 1940, which is known as "The golden age of behavioral embryology" (Robinson & Kleven, 2005). Due to technical and ethical difficulties associated with human studies, most studies were conducted on animals such as rodents and pigs. Researchers investigated movements of embryos and fetuses outside their mother's body with intact umbilical cords (Robinson et al., 2008). Results showed that fetal movements in response to chemical and tactile stimulation were coordinated and structured. In addition to behavioral responses to stimulation, researchers found that animal embryos and fetuses exhibit spontaneous movements without overt stimulation. Spontaneous movements were actively investigated especially around the 1960s. For example, Hamburger, Wenger, and Oppenheim (1966) studied early spontaneous movements in the chick embryo and quantitative changes in spontaneous movements during development. In addition, they reported that movements can be observed even in embryonic isolation of the spinal cord from the brain. These animal studies showed that embryos and fetuses generate various types of movements including structured behavioral responses to stimuli as well as spontaneous movements.

Observational studies of movements by human fetuses in the intrauterine environment became more feasible with techniques such as ultrasonic measurement. In 1982, de Vries, Visser, and Precthl conducted a systematic longitudinal observation of fetal motility for 11 pregnancies during the first 20 weeks of gestation. They reported that 16 distinct movement patterns could be observed by 15 weeks of gestation. Regarding the emergence of spontaneous bodily movements, recent studies indicate that these movements emerge as early as muscles function (Lüchinger et al., 2008). Specifically, spontaneous movements started from 7 weeks and 2 days after conception in an in-vitro fertilized fetus (Hadders-Algra, 2007; Lüchinger et al., 2008). The formation of the reflective arc in the spinal cord occurs at 8 weeks (Okado, 1984), indicating that spontaneous fetal movements emerge prior to maturation of the nervous system (Hadders-Algra, 2007).

Spontaneous movements have been characterized qualitatively in terms of "complexity" (the spatial variation of movement), "variation" (the temporal variation of the movement), and "fluency" (the presence of smooth, supple, and graceful movements) (Hadders-Algra et al., 2004; Prechtl, 1990). Clinical studies reveal that atypical variation in these qualitative features of spontaneous movement can be associated with neurological dysfunction, including cerebral palsy and neurodevelopmental disorders in later life (Groen, de Blécourt, Postema, & Hadders-Algra, 2005). In neonates and infants, spontaneous movements have also been described quantitatively by using marker-based motion capture systems and accelerometers (Vaal, van Soest, Hopkins, Sie, & van der Knaap, 2000). In such studies, researchers find that infants with brain injuries or at risk for neurological dysfunction evidence disorganized limb trajectories characterized by chaoticity and fractal properties (Ohgi, Morita, Loo, & Mizuike, 2007; Stephen et al., 2012).

1.2.3 Neural Development Related to Sensory-Motor Learning

Next, we consider the development of the nervous system during the embryo, fetal, and perinatal periods. We emphasize neural learning via sensorimotor experiences and focus on the spinal circuit and cerebral cortex.

1.2.3.1 *Development of the Spinal Nervous System*

The spinal nervous system relays afferent signals from peripheral sensory organs to the central nervous system, including the primary sensory and motor cortex. It is also the final pathway of the motor system, conducting efferent signals from the motor cortex to muscle. The most representative monosynaptic reflex named the stretch reflex is induced by α and γ motor neurons in this system. The former activates skeletal muscle, and the latter activates muscle spindles. Various other spinal circuits, which comprise several excitatory and inhibitory interneurons, process information from afferent and efferent signals to and from the peripheral organs and the central nervous system. The spinal cord integrates and relays the afferent signals of somatosensory inputs, leading to complex motor responses including reflexes and locomotion behaviors.

From morphological studies, muscle spindle afferents start to reach the motor neuron pools by 8 weeks and project to the ventral horn in the intermediate zone between 11 and 19 weeks. Because the human fetus starts to move as early as 7 to 8 weeks (Lüchinger et al., 2008), efferent output of alpha motor neurons also starts to reach the muscle at the similar time period (Sarnat, 2003). Although the development of interneuronal connectivity remains poorly understood, the neuromuscular loop for the stretch reflex emerges and matures by 25 weeks (Hakamada et al., 1988). Among the descending inputs to spinal circuits, the corticospinal tract, which is the descending pathway from the motor cortex to alpha motoneurons, has been most actively investigated. Morphological studies demonstrate that corticospinal axons have reached their most distant destination by 24 weeks post-conceptional age (Eyre, Miller, Clowry, Conway, & Watts, 2000; Sarnat, 2003). Following a waiting period of up to a few weeks, there is extensive innervation of spinal neurons, including motor neurons. Neurophysiological studies also provide evidence for prenatal and neonatal functional corticospinal projections (Eyre et al., 2000; Kanazawa et al., 2014).

The spinal circuit consists of excitatory and inhibitory interneurons, like all circuits. Early in development, GABAergic and glycinergic interneurons drive depolarization of postsynaptic neurons, while they act as inhibitory neurons and produce hyperpolarization after maturation (Ben-Ari, Gaiarsa, Tyzio, & Khazipov, 2007; Blaesse, Airaksinen, Rivera, & Kaila, 2009). These interneurons with recurrent connections exhibit a spontaneous rhythmic activity before the formation of the afferent and efferent projections, which is thought to play an important role in generating spontaneous bodily movements (Blankenship & Feller, 2010). Animal studies have shown that developmental changes in movement patterns generated by the spinal circuits proceed in progressive phases (Yvert, Branchereau, & Meyrand, 2004). Initially, activities of all hindlimb muscle groups are synchronized, followed by a phase in which left–right alternation of the limbs increases, proceeding finally to a pattern of intermuscular coordination within individual limbs (e.g., flexor–extensor alternation). In part, this phasic progression has been explained by a switch in signaling sign of the GABAergic and glycinergic interneurons because these inhibitory neurons are responsible for patterning the interneuron and motor output that directs left–right and flexor–extensor alternation in adult mammalian species (Grillner & Jessell, 2009). Although little is known about how the spinal circuit generates spontaneous rhythmic activity and how it changes developmentally, these networks are usually referred to as central pattern generators (CPGs) or neural oscillators. They are considered the neural basis of spontaneous bodily movements of fetuses and infants, and for locomotion behaviors as well (Hadders-Algra, 2007).

Recent animal studies have reported activity-dependent neural development and learning in the spinal circuit. Observations of spontaneous activity suggest that such activity could play essential roles in the maturation of the nervous system including neuron differentiation, migration, synaptic formation, and maturation of neuromuscular junction (Gonzalez-Islas & Wenner, 2006; Hanson, Milner, & Landmesser, 2008; Spitzer, 2006). In addition, recent studies on mice suggest that proprioceptive sensory feedback is required for the formation of antagonistic circuits at the level of premotor interneurons (Tripodi, Stepien, & Arber, 2011). The finding that even the distribution of premotor neurons is affected by activity-dependent factors suggests that the development of functional neural circuits is dependent on both genetic and activity-dependent factors.

Bodily movements generated by spontaneous activity in the spinal circuit have also attracted attention due to their important role in neural development and learning. Studies on neonatal rats have shown that spontaneous movements play an essential role in the formation of a body representation in the spinal nervous system as well as in the spinal circuit for the withdrawal reflex (Granmo et al., 2008; Petersson, Granmo, & Schouenborg, 2004; Petersson, Waldenström, Fåhraeus, & Schouenborg, 2003). Other studies have documented the important role of bodily movements in the formation of spinal circuits engendering locomotion behaviors. For example, studies on the zebrafish embryo have shown that spontaneous movements are needed for the proper development of coordinated patterns of activity in the motor system (Warp et al., 2012). Studies on *Drosophila* larvae also have revealed the essential role of the movements for maturation of a spinal circuit engendering coordinated crawling-like behavior (Crisp, Evers, & Bate, 2011; Suster & Bate, 2002). Interestingly, these studies also suggest that adequate patterns of activity may be required for the normal maturation of the spinal circuit since synchronized stimulation leads to delay or prevents it. Likewise, Robinson et al. (2008) showed that fetal rats can modify patterns of interlimb coordination based on sensorimotor experience and feedback before birth. Collectively, these studies show that the development of spinal circuits is highly dependent on activity from the earliest stages of development. They also suggest that sensorimotor experience plays an essential role in the formation of the spinal circuits that are used to perceive sensory information and control movements, including reflex movements and locomotion behaviors.

1.2.3.2 *Development of the Cortex*
Next, we describe cortical development by focusing on neocortex, which is a distinctive feature of the mammalian brain. Cortical neurons are mainly generated from neural progenitors through cell proliferation, migration, and differentiation. In the human fetus, cortical neurons proliferate between 10 weeks and 22 weeks from the ventricular zone. Neuronal migration peaks between 12 and 20 weeks and is largely complete by 26–29 weeks. The number of neurons peaks at 28 weeks, and approximately half of these cells decrease with apoptosis and naturally occurring cell death by adolescence. The synaptic density

of the cerebral cortex increases at a growth rate of 4% per week from 26 to 28 weeks. With gradual acceleration, synaptogenesis peaks at 34 weeks and continues to generate 40,000 synapses per second during the neonatal period. In general, developmental events occur earliest in primary motor and sensory cortices before maturation of the higher-order association cortices (Gogtay et al., 2004; Kanold & Luhmann, 2010; Kinney, Brody, Kloman, & Gilles, 1988; Tau & Peterson, 2010; Toga, Thompson, & Sowell, 2006).

The layer structure of neocortex is formed gradually by the neuronal migration and differentiation between 10 and 34 weeks after conception (Bayatti et al., 2007). During layer formation, a transient neocortical structure named the subplate layer can be observed. The emergence and dissolution of the subplate layer plays an important role in patterning subsequent synaptic connections (Ghosh, Antonini, McConnell, & Shatz, 1990; McConnell, Ghosh, & Shatz, 1989) and cortical connectivity (Allendoerfer & Shatz, 1994). Although the contribution of the subplate for functional cortical development is not fully understood, subplate neurons may be required for the functional maturation of thalamocortical connections, which provide a structural substrate for sensory-driven cortical activities (Ghosh et al., 1990; McConnell et al., 1989). Through thalamocortical connections, afferent sensory feedback is inputted to the cortex from the third trimester of pregnancy, which helps guide the patterning of cortical connectivity and the formation of sensory response properties (Kostović & Judaš, 2010). In this period, spike-timing-dependent plasticity (STDP), an activity-dependent synaptic modification, is thought to already be functional, especially in primary sensory cortices, based on observations of the developing neocortex of newborn rats and mice (Banerjee et al., 2009; Larsen, Rao, Manis, & Philpot, 2010; Meliza & Dan, 2006; Narayanan & Ghazanfar, 2014). The subplate neurons also help to regulate the maturation of cortical inhibition and the molecular machinery required to establish a balance of excitation and inhibition activities (Kanold & Shatz, 2006).

Recent studies also report activity-dependent neural development and learning in cortex. Neural activities resulting from intrinsic and experiential factors guide the patterning of neural pathways and the establishment of sensory response properties as early as the prenatal period (Akerman, Smyth, & Thompson, 2002; Sretavan, Shatz, & Stryker, 1988). For instance, many studies of the visual system have shown that spontaneous and visually evoked activity is necessary for the development of various receptive field properties and visual feature maps (White, Coppola, & Fitzpatrick, 2001). Likewise, with respect to the somatosensory system, imaging studies suggest that sensory feedback from spontaneous fetal movements plays an important role in the establishment of body representations in the primary somatosensory cortex (Milh et al., 2006; Narayanan & Ghazanfar, 2014).

In addition, preterm infants without apparent brain injuries are increasingly recognized as being at greater risk than their term-born counterparts for sensorimotor/cognitive impairments and neurodevelopmental disorders

(Larroque et al., 2008). Recent imaging studies of preterm infants also have shown atypical variation in structural and functional connectivity within and between brain regions, including the somatosensory area, which persist beyond the period of childhood (Ball et al., 2013; Mullen et al., 2011). Further, the atypical experiences of human preterm infants might affect functional neural development. One such type of experience is premature exposure to the extrauterine environment. Because change from the intrauterine to extrauterine environment alters sensorimotor experience, neural learning might be affected. Additionally, several studies have reported that preterm infants show atypical changes in spontaneous movements, characterized by low complexity and/or variability (Groen et al., 2005; Hadders-Algra, 2004; Koyanagi et al., 1993; Prechtl, 1984). While these qualitative changes in bodily movements have been suggested to result from neurodevelopmental disorders, atypical bodily movements of preterm infants may also influence statistical regularities in sensory feedback, which in turn might affect neural learning and development.

Further, while many studies have reported vulnerability of subplate neurons resulting from factors related to preterm birth such as hypoxia-ischemia, lesions of the subplate in preterm infants are suggested to have long-term effects on structural and functional cortical development leading to subsequent deficits of motor and cognitive functions (Kostović & Judaš, 2010; McQuillen, Sheldon, Shatz, & Ferriero, 2003). Additionally, excitation/inhibition (E/I) neuron imbalance in the cortex is known to be related to neurodevelopmental disorders such as ASD (Rubenstein, 2010; Rubenstein & Merzenich, 2003). Because subplate neurons play an important role in the maturation of inhibitory neurons and the establishment of E/I balance (Kanold & Shatz, 2006), atypical cortical E/I balance may adversely affect brain development during the perinatal period.

1.3 Embodied Approach for Understanding Functional Neuronal Development

Functional neural development begins as early as the fetal period and is influenced by sensorimotor experiences via embodied interactions. But the mechanisms by which sensorimotor experience guides functional neural development in the human fetus and infant remain unclear due to technical and ethical difficulties. To deepen our understanding of these mechanisms, we have developed an approach using an embodied brain model. This model incorporates models of the body, nervous system, and environment to simulate embodied interactions. In this approach, we validate the biological relevance of our model by comparing simulated outcomes with biological observations. We also test potential causal mechanisms that underlie functional neural development. Our computational approach allows us to systematically manipulate each factor constituting sensorimotor experience, which is difficult to do in human studies, and conduct detailed analyses to examine the resulting effects. We believe that this computational approach can help disentangle the complex relation between functional neural development and sensorimotor experience. In this section, we first provide an overview of the basic properties of our embodied brain model, and then show how it can lead to new insights about functional neural development in the human fetus and infant.

1.3.1 Embodied Brain Model

Our goal was to develop a model that simulated embodied interactions via spontaneous whole-body movements in the intrauterine and extrauterine environment, and neural learning via sensory feedback that results from embodied interactions. To this end, we developed an embodied brain model based on multiple sources of biological data about the nervous system, physical body, and environment (Figures 1.1 and 1.2). The model of the human fetus incorporates a cortex, spinal circuit, and musculoskeletal body with sensory receptors for somatosensory (proprioception and tactile) perception within a model of an intrauterine environment consisting of a uterine wall and amniotic fluid. In the experiments for the postnatal period, we added visual perception and simulated embodied interactions in an extrauterine environment. For a full description of the model, please see our original paper (Yamada et al., 2016).

We constructed a musculoskeletal body model with size, weight, and muscle force parameters corresponding to target gestational ages by incorporating the following data sets (Figure 1.1): (i) magnetic resonance imaging (MRI) of historical specimens of a human fetus; (ii) computed tomography scan data from a fetal skeleton replica; (iii) measurement data related to growth curves of length and weight of body parts and cross-sectional area of muscles; and (iv) experimental data related to muscle dynamics, proprioception, and tactile perception. The model simulates 21 rigid body parts connected by 20 joints with 36 degrees of freedom, 390 muscles with proprioceptive receptors for the muscle spindles and Golgi tendon organs, and 3,000 tactile mechanoreceptor models in the entire body. To simulate the three-dimensional rigid-body dynamics, we used the Open Dynamics Engine, which is a widely used open-source physics engine (www.ode.org).

The fetal model is placed inside a uterine environment model consisting of a uterine membrane and amniotic fluid. In this intrauterine condition, the fetal model receives forces from the uterine membrane, amniotic fluid, and physical contact between the body parts in addition to gravity and buoyancy forces. Simultaneously, pressures on the skin surface resulting from interactions with the uterine membrane, amniotic fluid resistance, and physical contact are calculated and input into the tactile models. For the tactile model, to simulate tactile sensation in our rigid-body model, we modeled Merkel cells, which are

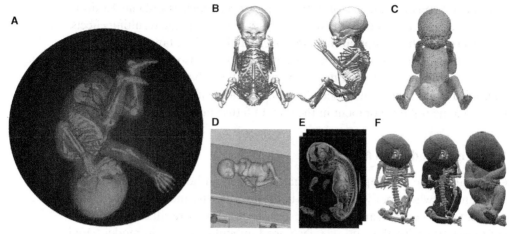

Figure 1.1. *Overview of the embodied brain model of a human fetus. (A, B) Fetal body model in the intrauterine and extrauterine condition. (C) MRI of the fetal specimen with a menstrual age of 206 days. (D) Fetal skeleton, muscles, and skin extracted from the MRI. (E) Fetal musculoskeletal model. Each line is a uniaxial muscle actuator in the body. (F) Tactile sensors throughout the body. The distribution is based on human two-point discrimination data. Source: Reprinted from Yamada et al. (2016, fig. 1 and supplementary fig. 1), with permission.*

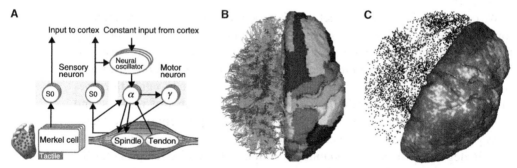

Figure 1.2. *Overview of the nervous model. (A) Spinal circuit model. The arrows and filled circles represent the excitatory and inhibitory connections, respectively. S0 represents sensory interneurons. (B) Representative tractography and parcellation of preterm infant brain MRI scans. (C) A snapshot of the simulated cortical activities. Source: Reprinted from Yamada et al. (2016, figs. 1 and 2, see also supplementary videos), with permission.*

mechanoreceptors that mainly detect continuous pressure. To simulate the extrauterine environmental condition, we placed the body model on a flat, rigid bed (Figure 1.1D). The model is only subject to the forces of gravity and physical contact between body parts and the flat, rigid bed.

The neural model consists of a spinal circuit model and a cortical model (Figure 1.2). The spinal circuit model generates muscle commands with basic neuromuscular loops and relays sensory feedback related to proprioception and tactile perception to the cortical model (Figure 1.2A). This spinal circuit has neural oscillators, α and γ motor neurons, and sensory interneurons that are based on experimental data (He, Maltenfort, Wang, & Hamm, 2001).

The cortical model includes 2.6 million spiking neurons and 5.3 billion synaptic connections (Figures 1.2B and 1.2C). The cortical connectivity and axonal conductance delays were determined based on MRI and diffusion tensor imaging extracted from 15 preterm human infants. The cell bodies of the model neurons were also allocated according to the voxels of the gray matter surface extracted from the MRI data. We input proprioception and tactile feedbacks to Brodmann's areas 3a and 3b in the post-central gyrus, and visual feedback to the primary visual cortex. The spiking dynamics of each neuron are simulated with a leaky integrate-and-fire neural model with conductance-based excitatory and inhibitory synapses. Activity-dependent plasticity is also modeled with an STDP rule based on observations of the developing neocortex (Larsen et al., 2010). The biological relevance of the cortical model was validated by comparing multiple statistical and dynamical features of intrinsic cortical activity in the resting state. Our cortical model exhibits autonomous, self-sustained activities with no external inputs with the following distinctive properties observed *in vivo*: low firing rates of individual neurons that approximate lognormal distributions (Hromádka, DeWeese, & Zador, 2008), irregular neuronal firing following a Poisson distribution (Softky & Koch, 1993), a network balance between excitation and inhibition (Haider, Duque, Hasenstaub, & McCormick, 2006), greater depolarizations of the average membrane potentials relative to the resting potentials (Teramae, Tsubo, & Fukai, 2012), correlations between structural and functional connectivity across cortical regions (Honey, Kötter, Breakspear, & Sporns, 2007; van den Heuvel et al., 2014), and responsiveness to single spikes (Cheng-yu, Poo, & Dan, 2009).

1.3.2 Underlying Mechanisms of Spontaneous Bodily Movements

Bodily movement patterns constrain sensorimotor experiences and consequently influence statistical regularities in sensory feedback that affect neural learning. Thus, to investigate neural learning based on sensorimotor experience, the evaluation of whether simulated movements can capture the features of human fetal movements is critical. Because spinal circuits for generating spontaneous movements remain unknown, we started to build a minimal spinal circuit model based on experimentally supported interneuronal connectivity. Therefore, we first investigated whether such a minimal model would reproduce the distinctive properties of whole-body spontaneous movements (see Yamada et al., 2016).

In the computer simulation, we introduced random inputs to the motor neurons of the fetal model inside the uterus at the beginning of the simulation.

After this procedure, the model generated self-sustained whole-body movements in a closed-loop manner using proprioceptive sensory feedback (supplementary video S1 of Yamada et al., 2016). We analyzed these movements and confirmed that the simulated movements exhibited normal behavioral features that have been reported in human studies in terms of the following qualitative and quantitative aspects: the participation of multiple body parts (complexity) (Hadders-Algra et al., 2004; Prechtl, 1990), continuously varying combinations of body-part movement direction (variation) (Prechtl, 1990; Shirado, Konyo, & Maeno, 2007), well-coordinated and self-organized patterns (fluency) (Prechtl, 1990, 2001), and chaotic and fractal properties in limb movements (Gima et al., 2011; Waldmeier et al., 2013). Therefore, we could confirm the biological relevance of the simulated bodily movements, which is a prerequisite for investigating neural learning via sensorimotor experiences. Note that the biologically plausible dynamic properties are not directly built into the model but autonomously emerge from the overall interactions between the model components based on anatomical and physiological data.

Next, we introduce our hypotheses and results regarding the underlying mechanisms for generating spontaneous movements. As mentioned, we employed a minimal spinal circuit model with only basic neuromuscular loops, such as the stretch reflex and Alpha-Gamma linkage. The spinal circuit model independently controls each muscle within an elementary circuit including a neural oscillator and is considered the neural basis of spontaneous movements. In other words, the spinal circuit model has no interneuronal connectivity for regulating inter-muscle coordination. Through the computer simulation with our embodied model, we found that even such a minimal spinal circuit model could generate whole-body movements that match typical patterns and quantitative indices from biological observations. Based on these results, we made the following hypotheses: the movement of one muscle would influence other muscles due to their physical constraints, and such embodied coupling enables the generation of spontaneous bodily movements with high variability and complexity as well as good coordination. For example, the movement of one muscle will change the configuration of other muscles, which in turn will alter their sensory inputs (Figure 1.3A). Neural oscillators are mutually entrained by exploiting such dynamic coupling via embodied interactions and enables the exploration of various sensorimotor experiences. In other words, the structure of embodied coupling via physical constraints may have enough information to generate bodily movements and the spinal circuit may just need to exploit it through embodied interaction. That may be why our simple spinal circuit model without interneuronal connectivity for regulating inter-muscle coordination could reproduce the distinct properties of variation, complexity and coordination.

To support our hypotheses, we performed further analyses of simulated bodily movements (Yamada & Kuniyoshi, 2012b). We first quantified embodied coupling by measuring information transfer from motor commands to proprioceptive sensory feedback between all muscle pairs by using transfer

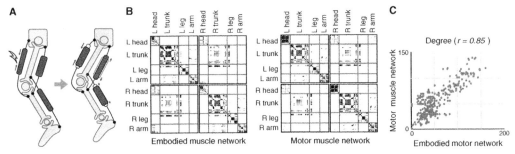

Figure 1.3. *Embodied couplings underlying bodily spontaneous movements. (A) Example of embodied coupling. Motor command to increase the contraction of one muscle will change joint angle and then alter sensory signals of other muscles related to their length and tension. (B) Embodied and motor muscle networks during spontaneous bodily movements. (C) Example of significant correlation between two networks in terms of degree measure. The degree is the most basic graph measure and is used for measuring similarities between different networks. The degree is equal to the number of links connected to a node.*

entropy ("embodied muscle network" in Figure 1.3B). We also characterized simulated bodily movements by calculating the pairwise correlation between muscle activities and then investigated whether the embodied couplings could explain emergent bodily movements ("motor muscle network" in Figure 1.3B). Consequently, we found several graph theoretic measures that showed significant correlations between them (Figure 1.3C). These results support our hypothesis that spontaneous movements are generated based on the structure of embodied coupling via physical constraints. To gain deeper insight, we also investigated the structure of these embodied couplings by using network analysis techniques. Interestingly, we found that these couplings exhibited not only body-part specific modular architecture but also small-world organization, one of the network types characterized by high global and local transport efficiency. The small-world organization is thought to play an important role in efficient distributed information processing as well as the emergence of diverse and complex spatiotemporal dynamics (Sporns, 2010; Watts & Strogatz, 1998). From this perspective, such specific structural properties of embodied coupling via physical constraints could provide a substrate for diverse and complex explorative dynamics in the spontaneous bodily movements of human babies.

1.3.3 Learning Spinal Circuit and Motor Development Via Embodied Interactions

Next, we introduce our results on how sensorimotor experiences evoked by bodily movements could guide neural learning for the formation of the spinal

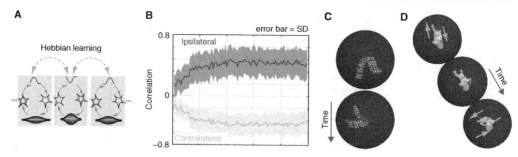

Figure 1.4. *(A) Spinal circuit model with activity-dependent plastic connections between. (B) Time evolution of average pairwise correlations among the outputs of alpha motor neurons comparing ipsilateral and contralateral muscle pairs during learning periods in the simulation using the zebrafish embryo model. (C, D) Examples of movement patterns after learning. The zebrafish embryo model learned left–right alternating movements and the human fetal model learned left–right alternation of the legs, using the same nervous model and learning rule.*

circuit engendering movement changes (Yamada & Kuniyoshi, 2012a). Our hypothesis is that spontaneous movements exploiting embodied coupling enable exploration and entrainment of a variety of embodied interactions, which could provide a scaffold for neural learning, especially for primitive behaviors such as locomotion.

We simulated spinal circuit learning using both zebrafish embryo and human fetus models, which normally undergo 22 fertilization hours and 20 gestational weeks, respectively. We used the same spinal circuit model and activity-dependent plasticity rule based on Hebbian learning for two different body models (Figure 1.4A). The zebrafish model was used for comparing the results with those *in vivo* studies, because of the limited data that can be compared with the simulated results of the human fetus model.

First, we calculated how the correlations of motor neurons across each ipsilateral and contralateral change over learning time in the zebrafish embryo model and compared them with biological data. Consequently, we found that ipsilateral motor neurons changed from weak to strong correlations over time (Figure 1.4B). In contrast, contralateral motor neurons became increasingly anti-correlated (Figure 1.4B). For qualitative changes in movements, we observed a transition from movements within a single hemi-segment to undulatory left–right alternating movements over time (Figure 1.4C). These results were consistent with the results of the experimental study on zebrafish embryos (Warp et al., 2012). In the learned spinal circuit model, we found strong contralateral inhibitory connections. A previous experimental study on zebrafish embryos indicated that the formation of contralateral inhibition plays an essential role in the learning of left–right alternating movements (Grillner, 2006; Warp et al., 2012), and our results support this hypothesis. Next, we investigated the learning results in the human fetus model. We performed cross-correlations using a canonical correlation analysis between the position of the two legs and compared it before and after learning. We found a statistically significant increase in left–right alternation of the legs over time (Figure 1.4D).

Taken together, the results of the zebrafish embryo and human fetus models suggest that spontaneous bodily movements exploiting embodied coupling enable the exploration of embodied interactions with specific statistical regularities, which lead to the learning of spinal circuits engendering locomotion behaviors. In addition, this developmental mechanism might be applied to other vertebrate animals as shown in our computer simulations.

1.3.4 Learning Body Representations in Primary Somatosensory Cortex

Next, we tried to gain insights into the mechanisms underlying the learning of body representations via bodily movements using our embodied neural modeling approach (Yamada, Fujii, & Kuniyoshi, 2013; Yamada et al., 2016). Specifically, we simulated cortical learning not only in typical conditions but also in several atypical conditions that could be observed in preterm infants. Through systematic comparisons, we sought to determine whether and how these conditions influence cortical learning. Here, we used only a part of our cortical model corresponding to the primary somatosensory area (Figure 1.5A). We will introduce the results obtained using the entire cortical model in a later section.

We first simulated neural learning via embodied interactions in the intra-uterine environmental condition and investigated its biological relevance. More specifically, we investigated whether the learned neural model could show body-part-specific functional responses and structural synaptic connectivity in terms of the following body parts: head, arm, trunk, and leg.

For the functional responses, we first investigated whether the model reproduced key response properties to somatosensory inputs from specific single body parts (Kaas, 1983; Penfield & Boldrey, 1937). Specifically, we compared the firing rates of each neuron among different body-part inputs. We found that on average more than 80% of the neurons exhibited significantly higher firing rates when receiving sensory inputs from one specific body part (Figure 1.5B). We also investigated the neural response properties for specific movement kinematics reported in experimental studies (Bosco & Poppele, 2001; Kalaska, Cohen, Prud'Homme, & Hyde, 1990). We found that approximately half of the arm-specific neurons in the learned network with proprioceptive sensory input showed high firing rates at specific localized three-dimensional hand positions (Figure 1.5C).

We next investigated whether the learned neural network could have structural synaptic connectivity with input segregation and modular architecture according to body parts, which has also been reported in biological studies

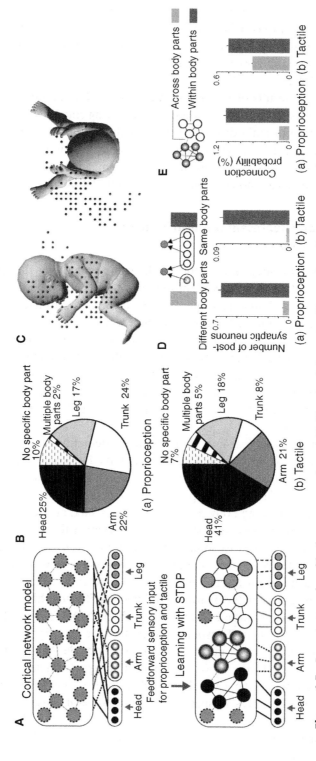

Figure 1.5. *Learning results of body representations. (A) Sketch of the cortical network model based on STDP. (B) Average ratio of neurons that significantly respond to specific single body parts. (C) Three-dimensional positions of the left hand where neurons showed significant high activities. (D) The number of common postsynaptic neurons comparing input pairs of the same body group with those of different body groups. (E) Probabilities of synaptic connections across and within body parts.*

(Huffman & Krubitzer, 2001; Rausell, Bickford, Manger, Woods, & Jones, 1998). The input segregation is measured by comparing synaptic projections from the same and different body parts. In our simulation, we found that synaptic projections from the same body parts have more shared postsynaptic neurons than do those from different body parts (Figure 1.5D). In contrast, the modular architecture is measured by comparing probabilities of synaptic connections across and within body parts. To this end, we first subdivided the neuron groups according to the body parts in which each neuron exhibits a significant response to inputs and investigated connection probabilities within and across the neuron groups. We found that within-group connection probabilities were higher than across-group probabilities in all four groups (Figure 1.5E).

Taken together, our results resembled those observed in experimental studies in terms of the above functional and structural measures. Next, by using the embodied model, we investigated the impact of changes in learning conditions on the learned body representations.

1.3.5 Influence of Atypical Conditions and Context in Preterm Infants

We investigated the following types of atypical learning conditions that could be related to preterm infants: (i) an environmental change from intrauterine to extrauterine conditions, (ii) a decrease in variation and complexity of bodily movement patterns (Beccaria et al., 2012; Hadders-Algra, 2007), and (iii) an E/I imbalance in their cortices (Pitcher et al., 2012; Rubenstein & Merzenich, 2003). To compare the effects of the learning conditions, we quantitatively measured the learning results in terms of functional responses and structural synaptic connectivity. Specifically, for the functional responses, we compared the ratio of neurons exhibiting body-part-specific responses. For structural synaptic connectivity, we measured modularity and input segregation with regard to the body parts (Girvan & Newman, 2002; Newman, 2004).

As an example, we explain how environmental change alters sensorimotor experiences and then influences the learning of body representations. In the experiments, we simulated change from intrauterine to extrauterine conditions. In the intrauterine environment, the fetal model received forces from the uterine membrane, amniotic fluid, and physical contact between body parts in addition to gravity and buoyancy forces. In contrast, in the extrauterine environment, the model was subject to only the force of gravity and physical contact forces between the body parts and the flat, rigid bed.

To compare the sensory signals resulting from the intrauterine and extrauterine embodied interactions, we calculated pairwise Pearson's correlation coefficients for the sensory signals within and across the body parts. We then found that intrauterine embodied interactions produced a substantial increase in correlations between the tactile sensors within body parts and a decrease in correlations between the proprioception sensors across body parts

(Figure 1.6A). Considering the above results, the spatially continuous pressure exerted by the amniotic fluid resistance and the uterine membrane could be the primary contribution to the increased correlations within body parts in terms of the tactile sensory feedback. In contrast, regarding proprioception, the increased correlations across body parts outside the uterus reflected the effects of the movements of each body part on other body parts; for example, the contact of the limbs with the ground could change the ground reaction force on other body parts.

We then investigated whether and how the difference between sensory signals changes the learning of cortical body representations. Consequently, we found that extrauterine learning significantly decreased functional and structural properties of body representations in both sensory modalities (Figure 1.6B). These results clearly show how different environmental conditions could induce different statistical regularities in sensory feedback via embodied interactions, and then affect neural learning.

We also briefly consider the results for cortical learning in other atypical conditions. For movement patterns, variation and complexity in spontaneous bodily movements have been qualitatively measured and suggest a relationship with developmental disorders later in life (Gaugler et al., 2014; Groen et al., 2005; Hadders-Algra, 2004). In this regard, variation is considered to be of the temporal variety, and complexity is considered to reflect the spatial variation of movements. Accordingly, we decreased variation by using repeatedly specific movement patterns and reducing variation of movement patterns, while decreasing complexity by fixing a part of the joints and reducing the number of those participating in the movements. Using this method, we modulated variation and complexity of the bodily movements in a step-by-step manner and investigated their impacts on learning, respectively. Similar to the extrauterine environment condition, each change in bodily movements negatively influenced cortical learning of body representation for both functional and structural measures. The decrease in variation led to increased correlations across the body parts due to the biased and small number of movement repertories (Figure 1.7A). In contrast, the decrease in movement complexity causes two different changes (Figure 1.7B): (i) increased spike correlations of the sensory neurons across body parts due to increases in similar movements across body parts for tactile perception, and (ii) decreased spike co-occurrence within the time window required for activity-dependent plasticity due to decreased number of body parts participating in the movements together for proprioception. Both changes in sensor signals reduce the difference between body parts and thus would negatively impact the learning of body representations. Previously, these peculiar movement patterns were thought to result from abnormalities in neural development, but whether they affect neural development remains unknown. Through a series of experiments and analyses, we suggest a new hypothesis: These peculiar movement patterns may change sensorimotor experiences in a different manner in the

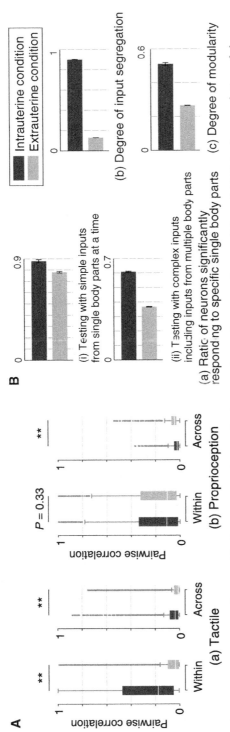

Figure 1.6. *Learning of cortical body representations under intrauterine and extrauterine conditions. (A) Pairwise correlation of the sensory feedbacks within and across body parts during simulated whole-body movements. (B) Functional and structural measures of the learned body representations for tactile perception.*

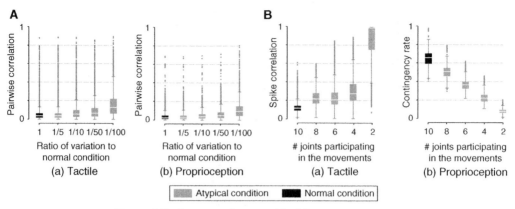

Figure 1.7. *Impacts of atypical bodily movements on somatosensory feedbacks. (A and B) Impacts of the reduced variation and complexity of bodily movements, respectively.*

extrauterine environmental condition and discourage neural learning of cortical body representation during the perinatal period.

The last atypical condition is E/I imbalance in the cortices. Patients with schizophrenia and ASD show different E/I balances from typical development (Hashimoto et al., 2008; Rubenstein, 2010; Rubenstein & Merzenich, 2003). To simulate this condition, we decreased inhibitory synaptic strength, which was a constant parameter throughout learning in our computer simulation, while synaptic strength for excitatory-to-excitatory connections had activity-dependent plasticity based on STDP. In this setup, we found different effects on learning of body representations from those in the other two atypical conditions. The elevated E/I ratio did not disturb the learning of body representations in all structural and functional measures used above. But it decreased the number of learned input patterns, with responses becoming dominated by a small number of input patterns and body parts (Figure 1.8). For this reason, reducing inhibition increased the number of neurons responding to sensory inputs and thus reduced the learning capacity of the cortical network. Although there is no study directly investigating the relation between E/I imbalance and body representations, some studies showed E/I imbalance in the cortices of people with neurodevelopmental disorders such as ASD (Rubenstein, 2010; Rubenstein & Merzenich, 2003), while others showed disruption of body representations in primary motor cortex in children with ASD (Nebel et al., 2014). Our prediction of a causal link between E/I imbalance and biased body representation in primary somatosensory area can be tested in future studies.

1.3.6 Implications for Policy and Context

Our results using the embodied brain model provide initial insights into the mechanistic links between sensorimotor experiences via embodied interactions and the cortical learning of body representations. Using comparative

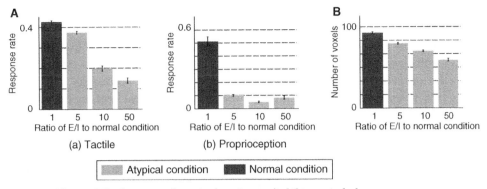

Figure 1.8. *Impacts of cortical excitatory/inhibitory imbalance on functional response properties of the network. (A) Ratio of the sensory input patterns that the network learned to significantly response. (B) The number of three-dimensional positions where neurons showed significant high activities after learning.*

experiments related to multiple kinds of atypical variations observed in pre-term infants, we showed how each could change sensorimotor experiences and lead to immature functional neural development. These insights are possible because the computational approach allows for systematic manipulations and detailed analyses that are difficult or impossible in human studies. For the developmental care of preterm infants in neonatal intensive care units, caregivers often implement positioning or swaddling methods that are designed to provide a sense of containment similar to the intrauterine environment (Als et al., 1986; Symington & Pinelli, 2006; Wallin & Eriksson, 2009). However, the effect of developmental care on neuronal development remains unexplored, and the developmental benefits are still controversial (Ohlsson & Jacobs, 2013). As shown in this chapter, the approach using the embodied brain model can provide insights into the mechanisms underlying early functional neural development. This model also holds promise for investigating how different environmental conditions and interventions influence sensorimotor experiences and cortical learning. These insights are made possible by the uniqueness of the embodied brain model – that is, a unified platform that models the nervous system, body, and environment. From this perspective, our embodied brain model might be useful for not only exploring the origin of neurodevelopmental disorders but also improving current developmental care.

1.3.7 Simulating Cortical Learning of Body Representations Using the Entire Cortical Model

Here, we present experimental results using our entire cortical model (Yamada et al., 2016). First, we show that we can obtain consistent results showing that atypical conditions could negatively influence the learning of body representations. Next, we demonstrate how these differences in cortical learning could affect other learning processes in later developmental periods, especially focusing on multisensory integration. By using these experimental results, we consider how our embodied brain model can lead to insights into the mechanisms underlying incremental developmental processes.

With the embodied brain models, we simulated cortical learning in the same intrauterine and extrauterine environmental conditions used in the above experiments. We first investigated the properties of responses to somatosensory inputs from the head, arm, trunk, and leg. We also investigated how somatosensory input from each body part propagated over time in the cortical models that had learned under the intrauterine and extrauterine embodied interactions. The somatosensory inputs spread over a wider range of cortical regions in the model that learned under the intrauterine as compared to the extrauterine condition (see fig. 4a in Yamada et al., 2016). We next compared cortical responses to multiple patterns of somatosensory inputs from each body part. Consequently, we identified cortical regions that responded significantly to a single body part in the learned cortical models in both intrauterine and extrauterine conditions (see fig. 4b in Yamada et al., 2016). Compared to extrauterine learning, intrauterine learning significantly increased the number of cortical regions that responded to specific single body parts for all tested body regions. As previously shown, extrauterine embodied interactions produced a substantial decrease in correlations between the tactile sensors within body parts and an increase in correlations between proprioception sensors across body parts (Figure 1.6A). The experimental results using the entire cortical model also showed that changes in such statistical regularities in somatosensory feedback resulting from extrauterine sensorimotor experiences could cause immature cortical learning of body representations.

1.3.8 The Effect of Immature Cortical Learning of Body Representation on Multisensory Integration

We next introduce our results using the entire cortical model to explain how the embodied brain model could lead to insights into the mechanisms underlying incremental developmental processes. Developmental studies have indicated that learning about one's own body through tactile and proprioceptive perceptions is considered a prerequisite for the development and integration of other senses, such as vision and audition (Cascio, 2010). We thus examined how differences in cortical learning of body representations in typical and atypical conditions could affect subsequent neural learning about multisensory integration (see Yamada et al., 2016).

In our experimental procedure, we first simulated embodied interactions using the human fetus model with parameters appropriate for 32 weeks of gestational age (GA) in the intrauterine and extrauterine environment conditions. After the simulation experiments, we investigated the two cortex models, and confirmed that extrauterine embodied interactions relative to intrauterine ones caused immature cortical learning of body representations, as shown in the previous section. Using these two cortical models, we then investigated the effects on subsequent visuo-somatosensory integration during the postnatal period. Specifically, we extracted the two cortex models learned under intrauterine and extrauterine conditions and embedded them in neonate body models with parameters appropriate for 40 weeks of GA. We generated arm movements in the right arm using motor commands during simulated whole-body movements under an extrauterine condition in which the body was laid on a flat bed, and investigated cortical responses to somatosensory and visual feedback. We then investigated the cortical regions that significantly responded to simultaneous visual-somatosensory inputs but not to separate inputs. Consequently, we found that the number of cortical regions responding to the simultaneous cross-modal inputs significantly increased in the cortical model that learned under the intrauterine condition compared to the extrauterine condition (see figs. 4e and 4f in Yamada et al., 2016).

In our computer simulations, we showed that early exposure to extrauterine environments could change statistical regularities in sensory feedback and then negatively affect learning of cortical body representations. Importantly, it also might affect subsequent developmental processes such as multisensory integration, even if environmental conditions do not differ at that time. In other words, intrauterine embodied interactions could provide a scaffold for subsequent developmental processes including multisensory integration in postnatal periods via cortical learning of body representations during the fetal period. Several studies have suggested that the development of body representation provides a foundation for the subsequent development of higher cognitive functions and multisensory integration (Cascio, 2010; Goldman & de Vignemont, 2009). In developmental science, this cascading process has been recognized as an important characteristic for understanding development (Byrge et al., 2014; Lungarella et al., 2003). However, the neuronal mechanisms underlying such developmental cascades have not been investigated in depth. Our computational approach offers a unique opportunity to explore the mechanisms by which multiple functions emerge and build on one another during development.

1.4 Conclusion

In this chapter, we introduced a new approach using an embodied brain model to understand functional neural development via sensorimotor experiences starting from the fetal period. We demonstrated how this approach could open new avenues for exploring causal links between sensorimotor experiences and functional neural learning. Our embodied brain approach offers new opportunities for understanding the origins of neurodevelopmental disorders and the effects of interventions by specifying the neural mechanisms by which prenatal and postnatal contexts influence interactions of the body, environment, and nervous system.

References

Adolph, K. E., & Berger, S. E. (2006). Motor development. *Handbook of Child Psychology*, 2, 161–213.

Akerman, C. J., Smyth, D., & Thompson, I. D. (2002). Visual experience before eye-opening and the development of the retinogeniculate pathway. *Neuron*, 36(5), 869–879.

Allendoerfer, K. L., & Shatz, C. J. (1994). The subplate, a transient neocortical structure: Its role in the development of connections between thalamus and cortex. *Annual Review of Neuroscience*, 17(1), 185–218.

Als, H., Lawhon, G., Brown, E., Gibes, R., Duffy, F. H., McAnulty, G., & Blickman, J. G. (1986). Individualized behavioral and environmental care for the very low birth weight preterm infant at high risk for bronchopulmonary dysplasia: Neonatal intensive care unit and developmental outcome. *Pediatrics*, 78(6), 1123–1132.

Asada, M., MacDorman, K. F., Ishiguro, H., & Kuniyoshi, Y. (2001). Cognitive developmental robotics as a new paradigm for the design of humanoid robots. *Robotics and Autonomous Systems*, 37(2–3), 185–193.

Ball, G., Srinivasan, L., Aljabar, P., Counsell, S. J., Durighel, G., Hajnal, J. V., ... Edwards, A. D. (2013). Development of cortical microstructure in the preterm human brain. *Proceedings of the National Academy of Sciences*, 110(23), 9541–9546.

Banerjee, A., Meredith, R. M., Rodríguez-Moreno, A., Mierau, S. B., Auberson, Y. P., & Paulsen, O. (2009). Double dissociation of spike timing-dependent potentiation and depression by subunit-preferring NMDA receptor antagonists in mouse barrel cortex. *Cerebral Cortex*, 19(12), 2959–2969.

Barbu-Roth, M., Anderson, D. I., Després, A., Streeter, R. J., Cabrol, D., Trujillo, M., ... Provasi, J. (2014). Air stepping in response to optic flows that move toward and away from the neonate. *Developmental Psychobiology*, 56(5), 1142–1149.

Bayatti, N., Moss, J. A., Sun, L., Ambrose, P., Ward, J. F., Lindsay, S., & Clowry, G. J. (2007). A molecular neuroanatomical study of the developing human neocortex from 8 to 17 postconceptional weeks revealing the early differentiation of the subplate and subventricular zone. *Cerebral Cortex*, 18(7), 1536–1548.

Beccaria, E., Martino, M., Briatore, E., Podestà, B., Pomero, G., Micciolo, R., ... Calzolari, S. (2012). Poor repertoire general movements predict some aspects of development outcome at 2 years in very preterm infants. *Early Human Development*, 88(6), 393–396.

Ben-Ari, Y., Gaiarsa, J. -L., Tyzio, R., & Khazipov, R. (2007). GABA: A pioneer transmitter that excites immature neurons and generates primitive oscillations. *Physiological Reviews*, 87(4), 1215–1284.

Blaesse, P., Airaksinen, M. S., Rivera, C., & Kaila, K. (2009). Cation-chloride cotransporters and neuronal function. *Neuron*, 61(6), 820–838.

Blankenship, A. G., & Feller, M. B. (2010). Mechanisms underlying spontaneous patterned activity in developing neural circuits. *Nature Reviews Neuroscience*, *11*(1), 18.

Bobet, J., & Stein, R. B. (1998). A simple model of force generation by skeletal muscle during dynamic isometric contractions. *IEEE Transactions on Biomedical Engineering*, *45*(8), 1010–1016.

Boivin, M. J., Kakooza, A. M., Warf, B. C., Davidson, L. L., & Grigorenko, E. L. (2015). Reducing neurodevelopmental disorders and disability through research and interventions. *Nature*, *527*(7578), S155.

Bosco, G., & Poppele, R. (2001). Proprioception from a spinocerebellar perspective. *Physiological Reviews*, *81*(2), 539–568.

Bradley, R. M., & Mistretta, C. M. (1975). Fetal sensory receptors. *Physiological Reviews*, *55*(3), 352–382.

Bremner, A. J., Lewkowicz, D. J., & Spence, C. (2012). *Multisensory development*. Oxford: Oxford University Press.

Brooks, R. A. (1991). Intelligence without representation. *Artificial intelligence*, *47*(1–3), 139–159.

Brumley, M. R., & Robinson, S. R. (2013). Sensory feedback alters spontaneous limb movements in newborn rats: Effects of unilateral forelimb weighting. *Developmental Psychobiology*, *55*(4), 323–333.

Butterworth, G., & Hopkins, B. (1988). Hand–mouth coordination in the new-born baby. *British Journal of Developmental Psychology*, *6*(4), 303–314.

Byrge, L., Sporns, O., & Smith, L. B. (2014). Developmental process emerges from extended brain–body–behavior networks. *Trends in Cognitive Sciences*, *18*(8), 395–403.

Caligiore, D., Parisi, D., & Baldassarre, G. (2014). Integrating reinforcement learning, equilibrium points, and minimum variance to understand the development of reaching: A computational model. *Psychological Review*, *121*(3), 389.

Cascio, C. J. (2010). Somatosensory processing in neurodevelopmental disorders. *Journal of Neurodevelopmental Disorders*, *2*(2), 62.

Cheng-Yu, T. L., Poo, M. -M., & Dan, Y. (2009). Burst spiking of a single cortical neuron modifies global brain state. *Science*, *324*(5927), 643–646.

Clancy, B., Darlington, R., & Finlay, B. (2001). Translating developmental time across mammalian species. *Neuroscience*, *105*(1), 7–17.

Clifton, R. K., Morrongiello, B. A., Kulig, J. W., & Dowd, J. M. (1981). Newborns' orientation toward sound: Possible implications for cortical development. *Child Development*, *52*(3), 833–838.

Crisp, S. J., Evers, J. F., & Bate, M. (2011). Endogenous patterns of activity are required for the maturation of a motor network. *Journal of Neuroscience*, *31*(29), 10445–10450.

Cuajunco, F. (1940). Development of the neuromuscular spindle in human fetuses. *Contributions to Embryology*, *28*, 97–128.

de Vries, J. I., Visser, G. H., & Prechtl, H. F. (1982). The emergence of fetal behaviour. I: Qualitative aspects. *Early Human Development*, *7*(4), 301–322.

DeCasper, A. J., Lecanuet, J. -P., Busnel, M. -C., Granier-Deferre, C., & Maugeais, R. (1994). Fetal reactions to recurrent maternal speech. *Infant Behavior and Development*, *17*(2), 159–164.

Demiris, J., Rougeaux, S., Hayes, G., Berthouze, L., & Kuniyoshi, Y. (1997). *Deferred imitation of human head movements by an active stereo vision head.* Paper presented at 6th IEEE International Workshop on Robot and Human Communication, RO-MAN'97 SENDAI, Sendai, Japan.

The Developing Human Connectome Project. Retrieved from www.developing connectome.org.

Dubois, J., Hertz-Pannier, L., Dehaene-Lambertz, G., Cointepas, Y., & Le Bihan, D. (2006). Assessment of the early organization and maturation of infants' cerebral white matter fiber bundles: A feasibility study using quantitative diffusion tensor imaging and tractography. *Neuroimage, 30*(4), 1121–1132.

Eyre, J., Miller, S., Clowry, G., Conway, E., & Watts, C. (2000). Functional corticospinal projections are established prenatally in the human foetus permitting involvement in the development of spinal motor centres. *Brain, 123*(1), 51–64.

Fombonne, E. (2009). Epidemiology of pervasive developmental disorders. *Pediatric Research, 65*(6), 591.

Fuchino, Y., Naoi, N., Shibata, M., Niwa, F., Kawai, M., Konishi, Y., ... Myowa-Yamakoshi, M. (2013). Effects of preterm birth on intrinsic fluctuations in neonatal cerebral activity examined using optical imaging. *PloS one, 8*(6), e67432.

Gallagher, S., & Zahavi, D. (2007). *The phenomenological mind: An introduction to philosophy of mind and cognitive science.* London: Routledge.

Gaugler, T., Klei, L., Sanders, S. J., Bodea, C. A., Goldberg, A. P., Lee, A. B., ... Reichert, J. (2014). Most genetic risk for autism resides with common variation. *Nature Genetics, 46*(8), 881.

Gerhard, D. (2013). Neuroscience. 5th edition. *Yale Journal of Biology and Medicine, 86*(1), 113–114.

Ghosh, A., Antonini, A., McConnell, S. K., & Shatz, C. J. (1990). Requirement for subplate neurons in the formation of thalamocortical connections. *Nature, 347*(6289), 179.

Gibson, J. (1979). The theory of affordances. In J. Gibson (Ed.), *The ecological approach to visual perception* (pp. 127–143). Boston, MA: Houghton Mifflin.

Gima, H., Ohgi, S., Morita, S., Karasuno, H., Fujiwara, T., & Abe, K. (2011). A dynamical system analysis of the development of spontaneous lower extremity movements in newborn and young infants. *Journal of Physiological Anthropology, 30*(5), 179–186.

Girvan, M., & Newman, M. E. (2002). Community structure in social and biological networks. *Proceedings of the National Academy of Sciences, 99*(12), 7821–7826.

Gogtay, N., Giedd, J. N., Lusk, L., Hayashi, K. M., Greenstein, D., Vaituzis, A. C., ... Toga, A. W. (2004). Dynamic mapping of human cortical development during childhood through early adulthood. *Proceedings of the National Academy of Sciences, 101*(21), 8174–8179.

Goldman, A., & de Vignemont, F. (2009). Is social cognition embodied? *Trends in Cognitive Sciences, 13*(4), 154–159.

Gonzalez-Islas, C., & Wenner, P. (2006). Spontaneous network activity in the embryonic spinal cord regulates AMPAergic and GABAergic synaptic strength. *Neuron, 49*(4), 563–575.

Granmo, M., Petersson, P., & Schouenborg, J. (2008). Action-based body maps in the spinal cord emerge from a transitory floating organization. *Journal of Neuroscience*, *28*(21), 5494–5503.

Grillner, S. (2006). Biological pattern generation: The cellular and computational logic of networks in motion. *Neuron*, *52*(5), 751–766.

Grillner, S., & Jessell, T. M. (2009). Measured motion: Searching for simplicity in spinal locomotor networks. *Current Opinion in Neurobiology*, *19*(6), 572–586.

Groen, S. E., de Blécourt, A. C., Postema, K., & Hadders-Algra, M. (2005). General movements in early infancy predict neuromotor development at 9 to 12 years of age. *Developmental Medicine and Child Neurology*, *47*(11), 731–738.

Hadders-Algra, M. (2004). General movements: A window for early identification of children at high risk for developmental disorders. *Journal of Pediatrics*, *145*(2), S12–S18.

(2007). Putative neural substrate of normal and abnormal general movements. *Neuroscience & Biobehavioral Reviews*, *31*(8), 1181–1190.

Hadders-Algra, M., Mavinkurve-Groothuis, A. M., Groen, S. E., Stremmelaar, E. F., Martijn, A., & Butcher, P. R. (2004). Quality of general movements and the development of minor neurological dysfunction at toddler and school age. *Clinical Rehabilitation*, *18*(3), 287–299.

Haider, B., Duque, A., Hasenstaub, A. R., & McCormick, D. A. (2006). Neocortical network activity *in vivo* is generated through a dynamic balance of excitation and inhibition. *Journal of Neuroscience*, *26*(17), 4535–4545.

Hakamada, S., Hayakawa, F., Kuno, K., & Tanaka, R. (1988). Development of the monosynaptic reflex pathway in the human spinal cord. *Developmental Brain Research*, *42*(2), 239–246.

Hamburger, V., Wenger, E., & Oppenheim, R. (1966). Motility in the chick embryo in the absence of sensory input. *Journal of Experimental Zoology*, *162*(2), 133–159.

Hanson, M. G., Milner, L. D., & Landmesser, L. T. (2008). Spontaneous rhythmic activity in early chick spinal cord influences distinct motor axon pathfinding decisions. *Brain Research Reviews*, *57*(1), 77–85.

Hashimoto, T., Bazmi, H. H., Mirnics, K., Wu, Q., Sampson, A. R., & Lewis, D. A. (2008). Conserved regional patterns of GABA-related transcript expression in the neocortex of subjects with schizophrenia. *American Journal of Psychiatry*, *165*(4), 479–489.

He, J., Maltenfort, M. G., Wang, Q., & Hamm, T. M. (2001). Learning from biological systems: Modeling neural control. *IEEE Control Systems*, *21*(4), 55–69.

Hepper, P. G. (1996). Fetal memory: Does it exist? What does it do? *Acta Paediatrica*, *85*, 16–20.

Hoffmann, M., Marques, H., Arieta, A., Sumioka, H., Lungarella, M., & Pfeifer, R. (2010). Body schema in robotics: A review. *IEEE Transactions on Autonomous Mental Development*, *2*(4), 304–324.

Honey, C. J., Kötter, R., Breakspear, M., & Sporns, O. (2007). Network structure of cerebral cortex shapes functional connectivity on multiple time scales. *Proceedings of the National Academy of Sciences*, *104*(24), 10240–10245.

Hooker, D. (1952). *The prenatal origin of behavior*. Lawrence: University of Kansas Press.

Hromádka, T., DeWeese, M. R., & Zador, A. M. (2008). Sparse representation of sounds in the unanesthetized auditory cortex. *PLoS biology*, *6*(1), e16.

Huffman, K. J., & Krubitzer, L. (2001). Area 3a: Topographic organization and cortical connections in marmoset monkeys. *Cerebral Cortex*, *11*(9), 849–867.

James, D. K. (2010). Fetal learning: A critical review. *Infant and Child Development: An International Journal of Research and Practice*, *19*(1), 45–54.

James, D. K., Spencer, C., & Stepsis, B. (2002). Fetal learning: A prospective randomized controlled study. *Ultrasound in Obstetrics & Gynecology*, *20*(5), 431–438.

Kaas, J. H. (1983). What, if anything, is SI? Organization of first somatosensory area of cortex. *Physiological Reviews*, *63*(1), 206–231.

Kalaska, J., Cohen, D., Prud'Homme, M., & Hyde, M. (1990). Parietal area 5 neuronal activity encodes movement kinematics, not movement dynamics. *Experimental Brain Research*, *80*(2), 351–364.

Kanazawa, H., Kawai, M., Kinai, T., Iwanaga, K., Mima, T., & Heike, T. (2014). Cortical muscle control of spontaneous movements in human neonates. *European Journal of Neuroscience*, *40*(3), 2548–2553.

Kanold, P. O., & Luhmann, H. J. (2010). The subplate and early cortical circuits. *Annual Review of Neuroscience*, *33*, 23–48.

Kanold, P. O., & Shatz, C. J. (2006). Subplate neurons regulate maturation of cortical inhibition and outcome of ocular dominance plasticity. *Neuron*, *51*(5), 627–638.

Khazipov, R., Sirota, A., Leinekugel, X., Holmes, G. L., Ben-Ari, Y., & Buzsáki, G. (2004). Early motor activity drives spindle bursts in the developing somatosensory cortex. *Nature*, *432*(7018), 758.

Kinney, H. C., Brody, B. A., Kloman, A. S., & Gilles, F. H. (1988). Sequence of central nervous system myelination in human infancy: II. Patterns of myelination in autopsied infants. *Journal of Neuropathology & Experimental Neurology*, *47*(3), 217–234.

Kisilevsky, B. S., Hains, S. M., Lee, K., Xie, X., Huang, H., Ye, H. H., … Wang, Z. (2003). Effects of experience on fetal voice recognition. *Psychological Science*, *14*(3), 220–224.

Kostović, I., & Judaš, M. (2010). The development of the subplate and thalamocortical connections in the human foetal brain. *Acta Paediatrica*, *99*(8), 1119–1127.

Koyanagi, T., Horimoto, N., Maeda, H., Kukita, J., Minami, T., Ueda, K., & Nakano, H. (1993). Abnormal behavioral patterns in the human fetus at term: Correlation with lesion sites in the central nervous system after birth. *Journal of child neurology*, *8*(1), 19–26.

Kuniyoshi, Y. (1994). *The science of imitation-towards physically and socially grounded intelligence.* Paper presented at the Special Issue TR-94001, Real World Computing Project Joint Symposium, Tsukuba-shi, Ibaraki-ken.

Kuniyoshi, Y., & Berthouze, L. (1998). Neural learning of embodied interaction dynamics. *Neural Networks*, *11*(7–8), 1259–1276.

Kuniyoshi, Y., Cheng, G., & Nagakubo, A. (2003). Etl-humanoid: A research vehicle for open-ended action imitation. *Robotics Research*, *6*, 67–82.

Kuniyoshi, Y., Yorozu, Y., Inaba, M., & Inoue, H. (2003). *From visuo-motor self-learning to early imitation: A neural architecture for humanoid learning.* Paper presented at the 2003 IEEE International Conference on Robotics and Automation (Cat. No. 03CH37422), Taipei, Japan.

Kurjak, A., Azumendi, G., Veček, N., Kupešic, S., Solak, M., Varga, D., & Chervenak, F. (2003). Fetal hand movements and facial expression in normal pregnancy studied by four-dimensional sonography. *Journal of Perinatal Medicine*, *31*(6), 496–508.

Larroque, B., Ancel, P. -Y., Marret, S., Marchand, L., André, M., Arnaud, C., ... Thiriez, G. (2008). Neurodevelopmental disabilities and special care of 5-year-old children born before 33 weeks of gestation (the EPIPAGE study): A longitudinal cohort study. *Lancet*, *371*(9615), 813–820.

Larsen, R. S., Rao, D., Manis, P. B., & Philpot, B. D. (2010). STDP in the developing sensory neocortex. *Frontiers in Synaptic Neuroscience*, *2*, 9.

Lawn, J. E., Mwansa-Kambafwile, J., Horta, B. L., Barros, F. C., & Cousens, S. (2010). "Kangaroo mother care" to prevent neonatal deaths due to preterm birth complications. *International Journal of Epidemiology*, *39*(suppl. 1), i144–i154.

Lüchinger, A. B., Hadders-Algra, M., van Kan, C. M., & de Vries, J. I. (2008). Fetal onset of general movements. *Pediatric Research*, *63*(2), 191.

Ludington-Hoe, S. M. (2013). Kangaroo care as a neonatal therapy. *Newborn and Infant Nursing Reviews*, *13*(2), 73–75.

Lungarella, M., Metta, G., Pfeifer, R., & Sandini, G. (2003). Developmental robotics: A survey. *Connection Science*, *15*(4), 151–190.

McConnell, S. K., Ghosh, A., & Shatz, C. J. (1989). Subplate neurons pioneer the first axon pathway from the cerebral cortex. *Science*, *245*(4921), 978–982.

McQuillen, P. S., Sheldon, R. A., Shatz, C. J., & Ferriero, D. M. (2003). Selective vulnerability of subplate neurons after early neonatal hypoxia-ischemia. *Journal of Neuroscience*, *23*(8), 3308–3315.

Meliza, C. D., & Dan, Y. (2006). Receptive-field modification in rat visual cortex induced by paired visual stimulation and single-cell spiking. *Neuron*, *49*(2), 183–189.

Meltzoff, A. N., & Moore, M. K. (1977). Imitation of facial and manual gestures by human neonates. *Science*, *198*(4312), 75–78.

Merleau-Ponty, M., & Smith, C. (1996). *Phenomenology of perception*. Delhi: Motilal Banarsidass Publishers.

Milh, M., Kaminska, A., Huon, C., Lapillonne, A., Ben-Ari, Y., & Khazipov, R. (2006). Rapid cortical oscillations and early motor activity in premature human neonate. *Cerebral Cortex*, *17*(7), 1582–1594.

Miller, J. A., Ding, S. -L., Sunkin, S. M., Smith, K. A., Ng, L., Szafer, A., ... Aiona, K. (2014). Transcriptional landscape of the prenatal human brain. *Nature*, *508*(7495), 199.

Mullen, K. M., Vohr, B. R., Katz, K. H., Schneider, K. C., Lacadie, C., Hampson, M., ... Ment, L. R. (2011). Preterm birth results in alterations in neural connectivity at age 16 years. *Neuroimage*, *54*(4), 2563–2570.

Myowa-Yamakoshi, M., & Takeshita, H. (2006). Do human fetuses anticipate self-oriented actions? A study by four-dimensional (4D) ultrasonography. *Infancy*, *10*(3), 289–301.

Nagai, Y., Hosoda, K., Morita, A., & Asada, M. (2003). A constructive model for the development of joint attention. *Connection Science*, *15*(4), 211–229.

Narayanan, D. Z., & Ghazanfar, A. A. (2014). Developmental neuroscience: How twitches make sense. *Current Biology*, *24*(19), R971–R972.

Nebel, M. B., Joel, S. E., Muschelli, J., Barber, A. D., Caffo, B. S., Pekar, J. J., & Mostofsky, S. H. (2014). Disruption of functional organization within the primary motor cortex in children with autism. *Human Brain Mapping*, *35*(2), 567–580.

Newman, M. E. (2004). Fast algorithm for detecting community structure in networks. *Physical review E*, *69*(6), 066133.

Ohgi, S., Morita, S., Loo, K. K., & Mizuike, C. (2007). A dynamical systems analysis of spontaneous movements in newborn infants. *Journal of Motor Behavior*, *39*(3), 203–214.

Ohlsson, A., & Jacobs, S. E. (2013). NIDCAP: A systematic review and meta-analyses of randomized controlled trials. *Pediatrics*, *131*(3), e881–e893.

Okado, N. (1984). Ontogeny of the central nervous system: Neurogenesis, fibre connection, synaptogenesis and myelination in the spinal cord. In H. F. R. Prechtl (Ed.), *Continuity of neural functions from prenatal to postnatal life* (pp. 31–45). London: Spastics International Medical Publications.

Partridge, E. A., Davey, M. G., Hornick, M. A., McGovern, P. E., Mejaddam, A. Y., Vrecenak, J. D., ... Weiland, T. R. (2017). An extra-uterine system to physiologically support the extreme premature lamb. *Nature Communications*, *8*, 15112.

Penfield, W., & Boldrey, E. (1937). Somatic motor and sensory representation in the cerebral cortex of man as studied by electrical stimulation. *Brain*, *60*(4), 389–443.

Petersson, P., Granmo, M., & Schouenborg, J. (2004). Properties of an adult spinal sensorimotor circuit shaped through early postnatal experience. *Journal of Neurophysiology*, 92, 280–288.

Petersson, P., Waldenström, A., Fåhraeus, C., & Schouenborg, J. (2003). Spontaneous muscle twitches during sleep guide spinal self-organization. *Nature*, *424*(6944), 72.

Pfeifer, R., & Scheier, C. (2001). *Understanding intelligence*. Cambridge, MA: MIT Press.

Piaget, J. (1952). *The origins of intelligence in children*. Madison, CT: International Universities Press.

Pitcher, J. B., Schneider, L. A., Burns, N. R., Drysdale, J. L., Higgins, R. D., Ridding, M. C., ... Robinson, J. S. (2012). Reduced corticomotor excitability and motor skills development in children born preterm. *Journal of Physiology*, *590*(22), 5827–5844.

Pitti, A., Mori, H., Yamada, Y., & Kuniyoshi, Y. (2010). *A model of spatial development from parieto-hippocampal learning of body-place associations*. Paper presented at the 10th International Conference on Epigenetic Robotics, Sweden.

Prechtl, H. F. R. (1984). Continuity and change in early neural development. In H. F. R. Prechtl (Ed.), *Continuity of neural functions from prenatal to postnatal life* (pp. 1–15). London: Spastics International Medical Publications.

Prechtl, H. F. R. (1990). Qualitative changes of spontaneous movements in fetus and preterm infant are a marker of neurological dysfunction. *Early Human Development*, *23*(3), 151–158.

(2001). General movement assessment as a method of developmental neurology: New paradigms and their consequences. *Developmental Medicine & Child Neurology*, *43*(12), 836–842.

Purves, D. (2012). *Neuroscience*: Oxford: Oxford University Press.

Rausell, E., Bickford, L., Manger, P. R., Woods, T. M., & Jones, E. G. (1998). Extensive divergence and convergence in the thalamocortical projection to monkey somatosensory cortex. *Journal of Neuroscience, 18*(11), 4216–4232.

Reid, V. M., Dunn, K., Young, R. J., Amu, J., Donovan, T., & Reissland, N. (2017). The human fetus preferentially engages with face-like visual stimuli. *Current Biology, 27*(12), 1825–1828. e1823.

Reissland, N., Francis, B., Aydin, E., Mason, J., & Schaal, B. (2014). The development of anticipation in the fetus: A longitudinal account of human fetal mouth movements in reaction to and anticipation of touch. *Developmental Psychobiology, 56*(5), 955–963.

Robinson, S. R., & Kleven, G. A. (2005). Learning to move before birth. In B. Hopkins & S. Johnson (Eds.), *Prenatal development of postnatal functions (Advances in Infancy Research series)* (Vol. 2, pp. 131–175). Westport, CT: Praeger.

Robinson, S. R., Kleven, G. A., & Brumley, M. R. (2008). Prenatal development of interlimb motor learning in the rat fetus. *Infancy, 13*(3), 204–228.

Rochat, P. (2009). *The infant's world.* Cambridge, MA: Harvard University Press.

(2011). The self as phenotype. *Consciousness and Cognition, 20*(1), 109–119.

Rochat, P., & Hespos, S. J. (1997). Differential rooting response by neonates: Evidence for an early sense of self. *Infant and Child Development, 6*(3–4), 105–112.

Rubenstein, J. L. (2010). Three hypotheses for developmental defects that may underlie some forms of autism spectrum disorder. *Current Opinion in Neurology, 23*(2), 118–123.

Rubenstein, J. L. & Merzenich, M. M. (2003). Model of autism: Increased ratio of excitation/inhibition in key neural systems. *Genes, Brain and Behavior, 2*(5), 255–267.

Sarnat, H. B. (2003). Functions of the corticospinal and corticobulbar tracts in the human newborn. *Journal of Pediatric Neurology, 1*(1), 3–8.

Sasaki, R., Yamada, Y., Tsukahara, Y., & Kuniyoshi, Y. (2013). *Tactile stimuli from amniotic fluid guides the development of somatosensory cortex with hierarchical structure using human fetus simulation.* Paper presented at the 2013 IEEE Third Joint International Conference on Development and Learning and Epigenetic Robotics (ICDL), Osaka, Japan.

Schaal, B., Marlier, L., & Soussignan, R. (1998). Olfactory function in the human fetus: Evidence from selective neonatal responsiveness to the odor of amniotic fluid. *Behavioral Neuroscience, 112*(6), 1438.

Shirado, H., Konyo, M., & Maeno, T. (2007). Modeling of tactile texture recognition mechanism. *Nihon Kikai Gakkai Ronbunshu, C Hen/Transactions of the Japan Society of Mechanical Engineers, Part C, 73*(9), 2514–2522.

Sizun, J., & Westrup, B. (2004). Early developmental care for preterm neonates: A call for more research. *Archives of Disease in Childhood: Fetal and Neonatal Edition, 89*(5), F384–F388.

Smyser, C. D., Inder, T. E., Shimony, J. S., Hill, J. E., Degnan, A. J., Snyder, A. Z., & Neil, J. J. (2010). Longitudinal analysis of neural network development in preterm infants. *Cerebral Cortex, 20*(12), 2852–2862.

Softky, W. R., & Koch, C. (1993). The highly irregular firing of cortical cells is inconsistent with temporal integration of random EPSPs. *Journal of Neuroscience, 13*(1), 334–350.

Spittle, A., Orton, J., Doyle, L. W., & Boyd, R. (2007). Early developmental intervention programs post hospital discharge to prevent motor and cognitive impairments in preterm infants. *Cochrane Database of Systematic Reviews, 2,* CD005495. doi: 005491-CD005495. 005471.

Spitzer, N. C. (2006). Electrical activity in early neuronal development. *Nature, 444*(7120), 707.

Sporns, O. (2010). *Networks of the brain.* Cambridge, MA: MIT Press.

Sretavan, D. W., Shatz, C. J., & Stryker, M. P. (1988). Modification of retinal ganglion cell axon morphology by prenatal infusion of tetrodotoxin. *Nature, 336*(6198), 468.

Stephen, D. G., Hsu, W. -H., Young, D., Saltzman, E. L., Holt, K. G., Newman, D. J., ... Goldfield, E. C. (2012). Multifractal fluctuations in joint angles during infant spontaneous kicking reveal multiplicativity-driven coordination. *Chaos, Solitons & Fractals, 45*(9–10), 1201–1219.

Suster, M. L., & Bate, M. (2002). Embryonic assembly of a central pattern generator without sensory input. *Nature, 416*(6877), 174.

Symington, A. J., & Pinelli, J. (2006). Developmental care for promoting development and preventing morbidity in preterm infants. *Cochrane Database Systematic Review, 4,* CD001814.

Takahashi, E., Folkerth, R. D., Galaburda, A. M., & Grant, P. E. (2011). Emerging cerebral connectivity in the human fetal brain: An MR tractography study. *Cerebral Cortex, 22*(2), 455–464.

Takahashi, E., Hayashi, E., Schmahmann, J. D., & Grant, P. E. (2014). Development of cerebellar connectivity in human fetal brains revealed by high angular resolution diffusion tractography. *Neuroimage, 96,* 326–333.

Tau, G. Z., & Peterson, B. S. (2010). Normal development of brain circuits. *Neuropsychopharmacology, 35*(1), 147.

Teramae, J. -N., Tsubo, Y., & Fukai, T. (2012). Optimal spike-based communication in excitable networks with strong-sparse and weak-dense links. *Scientific Reports, 2,* 485.

Thelen, E., & Smith, L. B. (1994). *A dynamic systems approach to the development of cognition and action.* Cambridge, MA: MIT Press.

Toga, A. W., Thompson, P. M., & Sowell, E. R. (2006). Mapping brain maturation. *TRENDS in Neurosciences, 29*(3), 148–159.

Tomasello, M. (2009). *The cultural origins of human cognition*: Cambridge, MA: Harvard University Press.

Tripodi, M., Stepien, A. E., & Arber, S. (2011). Motor antagonism exposed by spatial segregation and timing of neurogenesis. *Nature, 479*(7371), 61.

Vaal, J., van Soest, A., Hopkins, B., Sie, L., & van der Knaap, M. (2000). Development of spontaneous leg movements in infants with and without periventricular leukomalacia. *Experimental Brain Research, 135*(1), 94–105.

van den Heuvel, M. P., Kersbergen, K. J., de Reus, M. A., Keunen, K., Kahn, R. S., Groenendaal, F., ... Benders, M. J. (2014). The neonatal connectome during preterm brain development. *Cerebral Cortex, 25*(9), 3000–3013.

van der Meer, A. L. (1997). Keeping the arm in the limelight: Advanced visual control of arm movements in neonates. *European Journal of Paediatric Neurology, 1*(4), 103–108.

Varela, F. J., Rosch, E., & Thompson, E. (1992). *The embodied mind: Cognitive science and human experience.* Cambridge, MA: MIT Press.

Vauclair, J. (2012). *Developpment du jeune enfant, Motricite, Perception, Cognition.* Paris: Belin.

von Hofsten, C. (1982). Eye–hand coordination in the newborn. *Developmental Psychology, 18*(3), 450.

(2007). Action in development. *Developmental Science, 10*(1), 54–60.

Waldmeier, S., Grunt, S., Delgado-Eckert, E., Latzin, P., Steinlin, M., Fuhrer, K., & Frey, U. (2013). Correlation properties of spontaneous motor activity in healthy infants: A new computer-assisted method to evaluate neurological maturation. *Experimental Brain Research, 227*(4), 433–446.

Wallin, L., & Eriksson, M. (2009). Newborn individual development care and assessment program (NIDCAP): A systematic review of the literature. *Worldviews on Evidence-Based Nursing, 6*(2), 54–69.

Warp, E., Agarwal, G., Wyart, C., Friedmann, D., Oldfield, C. S., Conner, A., … Isacoff, E. Y. (2012). Emergence of patterned activity in the developing zebrafish spinal cord. *Current Biology, 22*(2), 93–102.

Watts, D. J., & Strogatz, S. H. (1998). Collective dynamics of "small-world" networks. *Nature, 393*(6684), 440.

Weng, J., McClelland, J., Pentland, A., Sporns, O., Stockman, I., Sur, M., & Thelen, E. (2001). Autonomous mental development by robots and animals. *Science, 291*(5504), 599–600.

White, L. E., Coppola, D. M., & Fitzpatrick, D. (2001). The contribution of sensory experience to the maturation of orientation selectivity in ferret visual cortex. *Nature, 411*(6841), 1049.

Yamada, Y., Fujii, K., & Kuniyoshi, Y. (2013). *Impacts of environment, nervous system and movements of preterms on body map development: Fetus simulation with spiking neural network.* Paper presented at the Development and Learning and Epigenetic Robotics (ICDL), 2013 IEEE Third Joint International Conference, Osaka, Japan.

Yamada, Y., Kanazawa, H., Iwasaki, S., Tsukahara, Y., Iwata, O., Yamada, S., & Kuniyoshi, Y. (2016). An embodied brain model of the human foetus. *Scientific Reports, 6*, 27893.

Yamada, Y., & Kuniyoshi, Y. (2012a). *Embodiment guides motor and spinal circuit development in vertebrate embryo and fetus.* Paper presented at the Development and Learning and Epigenetic Robotics (ICDL), 2012 IEEE International Conference, San Diego, California.

Yamada, Y., & Kuniyoshi, Y. (2012b). *Emergent spontaneous movements based on embodiment: Toward a general principle for early development.* Paper presented at the Post-Graduate Conference on Robotics and Development of Cognition, Lausanne, Switzerland.

Yvert, B., Branchereau, P., & Meyrand, P. (2004). Multiple spontaneous rhythmic activity patterns generated by the embryonic mouse spinal cord occur within a specific developmental time window. *Journal of Neurophysiology, 91*(5), 2101–2109.

Zoia, S., Blason, L., D'Ottavio, G., Bulgheroni, M., Pezzetta, E., Scabar, A., & Castiello, U. (2007). Evidence of early development of action planning in the human foetus: a kinematic study. *Experimental Brain Research, 176*(2), 217–226.

2 Infant Physical Growth

Michelle Lampl

Physical growth is a fundamental feature of an infant's first year, evident as the average neonate triples their weight and becomes 50% taller, rapidly outgrowing clothing while uttering their first words, enduring eruption of their first teeth, and taking their first steps. This remarkable transition in form continues a journey that began roughly 270 days earlier (Jukic, Baird, Weinberg, McConnaughey, & Wilcox, 2013) when a 0.5 micron fertilized egg cell initiated a series of differentiation, proliferation, and expansion events. Within days of consolidating the genetic material from maternal and paternal germ cells, the new zygotic genome becomes activated (Braude, Bolton, & Moore, 1988), replacing a sole reliance on proteins from the mother's egg and reproductive tract. The first cell undergoes successive mitotic cycles resulting in cell proliferation within the original membrane formed by the fusion of the sperm and egg. By the end of the first week, the contiguous mass of new cells is compressed by the emergence of a fluid-filled cavity, creating an inner cell mass within the membrane. At this stage, amid only a few hundred cells, cell differentiation commences (Chen, Wang, Wu, Ma, & Daley, 2010). Even before implantation in the uterus, tissue destinies are inaugurated and the size of the developing individual is forecast based on the number of cells in the inner mass (Fleming et al., 2004). These innermost cells embark upon the path to become the fetus, while the outer membrane cells pursue their destiny to form the placenta. Uterine wall implantation of this membrane-bounded cell mass, known as the blastocyst, initiates physical growth of the embryo as maternal uterine fluids provide nourishment. By 9 weeks after fertilization, with tissue specificity, nascent organ structure and functionalities emerging, the embryo phase gives way to the fetal phase and the foundation for infant physical growth is established (Fleming et al., 2004).

Observations from *in vitro* fertilization (IVF) and assisted reproductive treatment (ART) studies reveal previously unappreciated influences on subsequent infant physical growth from an even earlier time point, the maternal preconceptual environment. Associations between specific IVF culture media and infant weight across the first 2 years of life (Kleijkers et al., 2014) imply that long before women become pregnant, their body's health has an impact on the next generation. Maternal body composition, a reflection of a woman's development, eating behavior, nutrition, and general health, influences her ovarian follicles. Years before conception, the nascent ova develop strategies for nutrient sensing, including epigenetic methylation and ribosomal biogenesis. Subsequently expressed by fertilized ova, these mechanisms influence embryonic and fetal growth trajectories of somatic organs, such as the liver and kidney (Fleming et al., 2018; Velazquez et al., 2018).

In this way, physical growth of the infant body continues a process set in motion even prior to conception, when energetic mechanisms are initiated that will become refined and embodied during the embryonic and fetal periods. Under the watchful eye of biological clocks, organs form according to an ordered morphological sequence followed by all individuals. The functional units of the kidneys (nephrons), for example, have completed growth by about 36 gestational weeks of age. If this process is attenuated, the individual will have diminished kidney functional potential for life. The time-specific opportunities during which functional anatomical units emerge and grow are known as "critical periods." Infancy represents a critical period for physical growth, as it is a time during which the functional destinies of many body systems are established. The intrauterine environment has a strong effect on how this unfolds, accounting for 18% to 70% of the total variance among individuals' infant growth rates in the first 3 to 6 months (Livshits, Peter, Vainder, & Hauspie, 2000).

Remarkably, for all of its overt manifestations, we know relatively little about what controls the magnitude and timing of physical growth. While the precise mechanistic details remain to be described, it is clear that infant physical growth follows fundamental principles of cell biology under the guidance of chronobiology.

2.1 Infant Physical Growth: Definitions and Perspectives

2.1.1 Size Versus Growth

Everyday usage of the word "growth" conveys the concept of "getting bigger." Accurate scientific usage requires further specification: *growth is an increase in size* documented by serial measurements of individuals across time. Infant physical growth is an aspect of a developmental biological program governing the timed emergence and expansion of the body's anatomical units, encompassing activities at the cellular, organ, and tissue levels. While growth is often imputed from a single measurement, one assessment only provides information on size – how big an individual is at one time point. Size is a static state, a summary of past growing. Birthweight, for example, represents the accumulation of all tissues arising from a single cell by the time of birth, summarizing all cell proliferative and differentiation processes. While often used as a proxy for "fetal physical growth," birth weight is not fetal *growth*. Neonates who emerge long and lean have experienced very different fetal growth journeys from those who are born short and plump. These phenotypes embody biological processes that may portend very different long-term health outcomes (Barker, 1995). This is because the milieu in which cells emerge impacts the size, composition, and functioning of the tissues they become, and the paths by which organs and tissues expand are developmental histories for lifelong health (Barker, 1995).

Growth is a *process* that involves the expansion of both cell numbers and cell size. Cell numbers increase through the start and stop of mitotic cell cycles, while cells increase in size through fluid dynamics, protein, and fat-content accrual. These activities may be influenced by perturbations that either accelerate or interrupt cell cycle rates and expansion processes. When inhibitions lead to lengthy interruptions and size deficits, amelioration may prompt "catch-up" growth as cells undergo rapid proliferation and/or expansion. Understanding the biological influences impacting how infants *grow*, rather than merely cataloguing how *big* infants are, permits successful interventions that support infant growth and health, in both the short term and across the life span.

2.1.2 Developmental Timing

The infant physical growth process is characterized by the continued construction of neonatally nascent architectural units, coupled to their expansion. Reiterative cross talk between the external environment and internal processes up- and down-regulate gene expression to influence molecular and cellular activities. These, in turn, determine the formation of cell lineages for morphogenesis, coordinate cell division and expansion, and guide the maturation of metabolic and nutrient uptake pathways that enable the synthesis and expansion of tissues (Lampl & Schoen, 2017). By the time of birth, when infant physical growth in the extrauterine world commences, many anatomical parts have been built and growth trajectories have been established. Some organs' functional units are already complete (such as the kidneys), while others remain to be established (aspects of the immune system). For some organs, such as adipose tissue, infant physical growth involves processes of increasing both cell number and cell size (Arner, 2018). For other organs and tissues, no further cell proliferation occurs and infant physical growth solely reflects the expansion of cell size. For example, the majority of skeletal muscle fibers are formed by mid-gestation with subsequent muscle growth focused on hypertrophy. Infancy is a critical period for skeletal muscle cell nuclei expansion and protein anabolism. Disruptions during these critical times result in muscle mass deficits that are not likely recoverable (Fiorotto & Davis, 2018).

While the sequence of emerging anatomical development is common across infants, each individual infant increases in size according to their own unique pace with some individuals growing relatively more rapidly during the same time frames. In this way, infants of the same age attain different sizes by unique paths.

2.2 How Infant Physical Growth Is Known: Measurement

Formal study of infant physical growth involves measurement of body dimensions with specialized toolkits, techniques, and sampling protocols for serial measurements of individuals over time (Himes, 2006). Seeking anatomical accuracy, some twentieth-century studies employed radiographs to record individual skeletal components and dental development (McCammon, 1970). Recent decades have relied on noninvasive anthropometric tools to assess the size and shape of the living infant (e.g., weight; total body and limb lengths and breadths; head, torso, and limb circumferences) with tools ranging from a common measuring tape and balance scale to specially designed calipers and digitized equipment that requires careful maintenance. The validity and reproducibility of measurements depend on the accuracy of the instrument, the skill of the measurer, contributions from infant physiology, and the volitional cooperation of the infant. The biological accuracy of our descriptions of the growth process depends on the measurement sampling frequency. Traditional monthly or quarterly infant assessments cannot identify a growth process that progresses nonlinearly or at pulsatile intervals in smaller time frames.

Clinical assessment of infant physical growth (weight, length, head circumference, and the derived variables weight-for-length and body mass index [BMI]) is part of the American Academy of Pediatrics Recommendations for Preventive Pediatric Health Care (www.aap.org) at birth, 3–5 days of age, monthly to 6 months, 9 months, and 12 months of age.

2.2.1 Infant Weights

Infant weights are measured by simple devices under field conditions, including slings and bathroom-type scales for measuring infants alone or in tandem with their mothers with infant weight inferred by subtraction from maternal weight. High-sensitivity digital scales are used for weighing infants in a research environment, estimating weight to the nearest gram. Quality control issues include maintenance of the scale itself (particularly portable devices), the presence of infant clothing, infant state (including diurnal/circadian effects), and time since last ingestion and excretion: pre- and post-feeding and pre- and post-urinary or fecal excretion state can account for notable variability in a small infant's weight (Rose, Parker, Jefferson, & Cartmell, 2015).

Weight gain patterns in the first 3 to 4 months primarily reflect maternal and placental prenatal factors, with additive genetic influences ranging from 50% to 90% emerging between 5 or 6 months to 2 years of age (Demerath et al., 2007; L. Johnson, Llewellyn, van Jaarsveld, Cole, & Wardle, 2011; Livshits et al., 2000; van Dommelen, de Gunst, van der Vaart, & Boomsma, 2004) to join environmental influences on infant weight due to postnatal nutritional access and content, and infant appetite and energy expenditure variability as motoric developmental differences influence activity patterns (Adolph & Robinson, 2015).

The systematic measurement of infant weight, initiated in mid-nineteenth-century France by Alfred Donné, promoted the "medicalization" of childcare (La Berge, 1991) and concerns with infant feeding adequacy. A legacy of this era is the reliance on weight as a mainstay of protocols assessing the general health of infants and persists in clinical, community-, and national-level surveys as a proxy for infant physical growth without considered reflection.

Weight summarizes tissues and organ mass, reflects hydration status, and is a nonspecific marker of energy balance between consumption and expenditure at any age. Weight gain is not specific to the developmental acquisition of mass. For health monitoring, infant underweight and low weight-for-length remain central health-associated metrics among populations facing challenging social or ecological environments, such as those experiencing extreme impoverishment or conflict, contemporaneous poor nutrition, or illness. In contrast, increasing weight-for-age in infancy, once seen as the marker of healthy growth, is now appreciated as a potential health risk as weight gain, absent knowledge of the constituents of weight, can reflect adiposity rather than lean body mass (associated with potential health benefits) (Adair et al., 2013). The need to clarify infant weight gain according to body composition has become a high research priority and the use of weight as the single proxy for assessing growth is discouraged.

2.2.2 Infant Body Composition

Infant body composition has been estimated most frequently by a distinction between fat mass (FM) and fat-free mass (FFM). Assessment of these tissue compartments has relied on indirect estimation using anthropometric measures of limb and torso circumferences together with subcutaneous skinfolds. An anthropometric (nonstretch) measurement tape assesses circumferences, with repeatability and reproducibility related to the user's tension on the tape, measurement position (e.g., distance from bony landmarks for limb measures; umbilical and pelvic markers for waist and hips), mechanical factors that contribute to soft tissue or organ distensibility (e.g., respiratory phase for chest circumference; food consumption and time since intake for waist circumference), and other physiological factors (e.g., hydration status for circumferences and skinfolds). Subcutaneous fat is assessed as double folds of skin and underlying subcutaneous adipose tissue, raised away from other tissue by the examiner in a pinch action (Cameron, 1984). This adipose-bearing "skinfold" thickness is measured with jaw calipers designed with a calibrated pressure spring over an operating range that varies according to manufacturer. A reliable measurement of subcutaneous fat depends on correct anatomical acquisition of the tissue to be measured, optimal positioning of the calipers, skill on the part of the researcher (acquiring only fat tissue, free of underlying muscle), status of the infant (young infants do not necessarily have well-defined body tissue compartments), and a consistent time between compression and measurement to minimize errors due to compressibility.

Recent research interest in infant fat and lean tissue growth confronts practical challenges for data collection, including specialized equipment requiring infant assessment in designated research units, variable degrees of constraint, and biological exposures. These methods all infer body composition based on tissue chemistry, density, or conductivity characteristics. Deuterium dilution involves the infant consuming isotopically labeled water (D_2O), from which lean body mass is estimated by inference (Fabiansen et al., 2017). Densitometric methods use the fact that lean mass is denser than fat mass to estimate tissue composition. Ultrasound devices rely on the characteristics of sound waves: transducers are placed on the infant's body at specific locations from which sound is transmitted to the tissue beneath. As the beam contacts the tissue interface between fat and underlying muscle, a portion of the beam is reflected back to the device; the reflection time differentiates tissues and allows for a measure of fat (Wagner, 2013). Tissue percentages are calculated based on water or air displacement for known mass. Air displacement plethysmography (ADP), embodied by the PEAPOD ™, requires an infant to weigh between 1 kg and 8 kg and remain still while lying alone in a closed chamber for approximately 7 minutes (de Cunto et al., 2014; Demerath & Fields, 2014), hence it is principally useful in research studies of younger infants. Alternatively, bioelectrical impedance analysis (BIA) assesses conductance (fat is essentially anhydrous and therefore a poor electrical conductor, resulting in higher impedance with greater fat mass). This approach has been investigated as an option for infants as they outgrow the PEAPOD ™, but does not outperform anthropometrics at this time. Bone densities are studied with dual energy X-ray absorptiometry (DEXA) and state-of-the-art imaging methods permitting organ-level anatomic resolution include magnetic resonance imaging (MRI). All of these methods require subject restraint and exposure to variable levels of radiation. Their use is limited in infancy.

A strong correlation between ultrasound and anthropometrically assessed subcutaneous tissue measurements supports the noninvasive anthropometric approach as the technique of choice for infant screening assessments at this time (Brei et al., 2015). Overall, knowledge about infant body composition growth remains limited and evidentiary gaps include the nature and extent of both individual and ethnic variability in tissue patterns (Fields, Demerath, Pietrobelli, & Chandler-Laney, 2012).

2.2.3 Infant Fat Pattern Development

Infant fat pattern development is important to clarify as associations between infant growth, body composition, and adult disease risks are epidemiologically evidenced. Both adipocyte cell number and size increase during the first year of life, with a decline in cell number proliferation thereafter (Arner, 2018; Knittle, Timmers, Ginsberg-Fellner, Brown, & Katz, 1979). More specifically, it is the first 4 months of life that appear to be a critical period, when adipose tissue density increases by about 50% (Kabir & Forsum, 1993). Both ultrasound and MRI assessments describe this tissue as predominantly subcutaneous fat (Brei et al., 2015), superseded by preperitoneal fat thereafter (Holzhauer et al., 2009).

2.2.4 Infant Lean Body Mass Patterns

Infant lean body mass patterns are likewise not well characterized, but for the observation that a steady increase in fat-free mass occurs across the first year (Butte, Hopkinson, Wong, Smith, & Ellis, 2000). Infancy is a critical period for muscle growth characterized by rapid deposition of protein in muscle fibers (Davis & Fiorotto, 2009). The long-term implications of these patterns are unclear but metabolic distinctions in fat depots and the importance of muscle for metabolic health identifies infancy as a critical period for the developmental origins of health.

There is little predictability between tissue compartments, and neither weight and BMI nor weight-for-length are reliable proxies for overall adiposity, or subcutaneous versus visceral fat, specifically (Bell et al., 2018; Breij, Abrahamse-Berkeveld et al., 2017; Breij, Kerkhof et al., 2017; Roy et al., 2019). In some studies, increasing birth weight accompanies lower subcutaneous fat, implying a positive correlation between weight and lean body mass. On average, the neonate's birth weight is composed of about 14% fat, which increases to 25%–30% of weight by 4–6 months of age with gender, feeding, and age effects. At birth, boys tend to have greater fat-free mass and lower fat mass, relative to girls. As body tissues are characterized by metabolic differences, these gender and age patterns may contribute to individual variability in energy utilization and this, in turn, may underlie individual variability in growth patterns.

2.2.5 Total Body Length Measures

Total body length measures are assessed on recumbent infants during the first 2 years of life. This is a notoriously fraught variable, often subject to offhand measurements in delivery rooms, clinics, and survey environments, where a measurement tape stretched close to the infant's body suffices as an estimate. Total infant body length assessment in research settings requires two observers and a recumbent infant length measuring board (Cameron, 1984). After lying the infant on their back, one observer steadies the infant's head at the fixed headboard in the Frankfort plane (head at a 90 degree angle to the horizontal), while the second observer applies gentle pressure to fully extend the infant's legs and slides the footboard to meet the sole of the feet. Reproducibility within and between well-trained observers with proper equipment and a compliant infant is less than 0.2 cm, compared to 2.0 cm with a single observer and a tape measure. Observer errors contribute to: (1) overestimation of length due to incorrect infant head placement and asymmetric positioning of the infant's body, (2) underestimation of length due to compression of the legs by the footboard; and infant body tension, back arching, knee flexure, hydration state, and time since recumbence can add as much as several centimeters error due to the compressive spine and joint tissues as infants begin to sit and stand. Rigorous attention to these error components in planning measurement protocols and data analysis is not always appreciated. Intervention study practices of converting actual measurements to categories above and below a size cut-off are at particular risk of confounding study outcomes.

A total body length measurement summarizes skull height, thoracic and lumbar spinal length, pelvic height, and the lower-limb long bones with their associated hip, knee, and ankle joint tissues, as well as bones of the foot. Distinctive population differences in upper and lower body length ratios are well described with sources for these differing morphologies attributed to both genetic and environmental influences, some of which may have their onset before birth and influence subsequent infant length growth patterns (Buschang, 1982).

Growth of the upper body in infancy is estimated as crown-rump length, assessed as full body length, but with the footboard pressed against the buttocks. The pliability of the fatty tissue on the buttocks results in poor replicability and inter-observer differences average 0.5 cm. Estimates of the "lower body" are derived by subtracting crown-rump length estimates from total body length.

Measurements of the lower leg (from the flexed knee to the heel) are acquired by a caliper, a knemometer, with reported precision to the micrometer. Considering the compression/relaxation effects across joints, soft-tissue expansions and contractions reflecting circadian and diurnal physiology, and hydration effects, it is likely that knemometric measurements are capturing confounding effects to a far greater extent than is appreciated, resulting in assessments that are not simply limb-length estimates of "limb growth."

Alternative approaches to the recumbent stretching method have been explored, including photographic approaches. To date, these methods perform significantly less well than research-quality recumbent length measurements (Conkle et al., 2018).

2.2.6 Head Circumference

Head circumference among infants is traditionally assessed noninvasively as the maximal occipital frontal circumference (OFC) with a nonstretch measuring tape (Cameron, 1984). It is a relatively simple measurement to take with high reproducibility within and between observers (<0.1 cm) (T. S. Johnson, Engstrom, & Gelhar, 1997). A head circumference measurement encompasses the thickness of the skull and its contents: the brain, cerebrospinal fluid, and vascular structures. Among neonates, head circumference comprises the anatomy of six bony plates abutted by areas of unmineralized dura. This anatomy permits the skull plates to both overlap, thereby assisting the fetus in passage through the birth canal, and expand, allowing for rapid postnatal brain growth.

Head circumference growth reflects brain volume expansion (Bartholomeusz, Courchesne, & Karns, 2002; Bray, Shields, Wolcott, & Madsen, 1969; Lindley, Benson, Grimes, Cole, & Herman, 1999) as the skull passively follows volumetric increase in the cerebral hemispheres (Amiel-Tison, Cosselin, & Infante-Rivard, 2002). Infancy continues a critical period of brain growth, initiated *in utero* with neuronal cell proliferation, white matter tract, nascent axon and dendrite outgrowth, glial formation and differentiation, and early myelination (van Dyck & Morrow, 2017). From 28 weeks gestation to term, head circumference increases by nearly 50%, approximating 35% of adult size by birth (Knickmeyer et al., 2008). Thereafter, the postnatal growth trajectory is characterized by increasing neural connectivity, cellular proliferation and arborization, gliogenesis and increasing myelination, as well as synaptogenesis and pruning. Some 70% of adult size is achieved by 1 year of age (Amiel-Tison et al., 2002, Knickmeyer et al., 2008; van Dyck and Morrow, 2017).

Brain growth is a hallmark of healthy growth in the first year of life with a 100% increase in total brain volume, including two-fold expansions in lateral ventricle and cerebellar volume, and nearly 50% expansion of hemispheric gray matter (Knickmeyer et al., 2008). By the second birthday, 80% to 90% of adult volume is achieved. This pattern embodies the altricial nature of humans at birth, and the importance of postnatal experience and learning to shape brain connectivity and circuitry during this critical period (van Dyck & Morrow, 2017). The malleable neonatal skull undergoes suture closure through bone formation in the midline sphenoid and metopic sutures, followed by the anterior fontanelle (Idriz, Patel, Renani, Allan, & Vlahos, 2015; Pindrik, Ye, Ji, Pendleton, & Ahn, 2014) with interindividual variation in maturational ages ranging from 3 to 19 months (Pindrik et al., 2014; Teager, Constantine, Lottering, & Anderson, 2018).

Rapid infant head growth rates may provide an opportunity for catch-up growth as prenatal constraints (intrauterine growth retardation due to poor maternal nutrition or health, exposure to smoking, drugs, or other toxins, for example) are alleviated (de Brito et al., 2017), but this is likely limited as cell lines with critical developmental periods restricted to prenatal life are irremediable (Bhardwaj et al., 2006).

Genetic influences on head size emerge during development. Head size tends to run in families (Martínez-Abadías et al., 2009; Weaver & Christian, 1980) with morphological variation achieved through variability in head growth trajectories. Heritability, or the variation among individuals in a population attributable to genes, is low in early infancy due to postnatal recovery from prenatal head growth tempos (Smith et al., 1976), increasing to nearly 90% among some samples of 4–5-month-old infants (Smit et al., 2010). Boys have bigger heads than girls, matching their overall larger body size and greater lean mass (Knickmeyer et al., 2014; Raymond & Holmes, 1994), and variation in growth rates according to ethnicity is well described among healthy babies (Janssen et al., 2007; Natale & Rajagopalan, 2014).

2.2.6.1 *Neuroscience*

Scientific interest in infant head circumference growth increased following reports of altered head growth trajectories among infants presenting with developmental pathologies, including autism spectrum disorder (ASD) (Courchesne et al., 2001). A subsequent review of studies found no clear predictability but for an association between abnormally slow or fast head growth and increased likelihood for the expression of developmental issues in the socioemotional, cognitive, or motor domains (Dupont et al., 2018). While simple anthropometry provides no insight into the cell-level processes responsible, perturbations in brain growth and development may be inferred from the gross measurement of head circumference (Courchesne et al., 2018). MRI studies describe overgrowth (or hyperexpansion) of the cortical surface preceding brain volume expansion and the emergence of ASD behavioral features (Hazlett et al., 2017). These observations suggest that the normal sequence of development is for neural progenitor cell proliferation to be followed by elimination, and failure to refine neural circuit connections alters the normal experience-dependent neuronal development (Courchesne et al., 2001; Piven, Elison, & Zylka, 2018). These observations point to the importance not only of growth, but the cessation of growth and the opportunity to refine structure, as part of normal infant physical growth. Overall, more work is needed to define how the normal expansion of whole-brain functional connectivity undergoes nuanced alterations in functional circuits related to social and sensorimotor function as it unfolds in individuals (Chen et al., 2018).

Many studies focused on infant samples report altered head growth size and imply functional deficits deriving from prenatal exposures (drug and tobacco, for example). Few reports have attended specifically to the head circumference growth patterns after exposure in individual infants. For example, smaller head circumferences during infancy are associated with *in utero* alcohol exposure at the group level (Day et al., 1990). Investigations of specific relationships between head circumference growth rates, brain volumes, and cognitive scores after prenatal alcohol exposure in individuals, however, lack definitive associations (Treit et al., 2016). Whether these results are sample specific or more generalizable is not clear, but identify that absence of head circumference deficits after prenatal exposures does not exclude toxin effects at the cellular level.

Specific attention to infant head circumference growth patterns emerged following the startling appearance of microcephaly associated with exposure to the Zika virus teratogen (de Araújo et al., 2016). Infant head circumference measurements took on importance as a diagnostic tool as it became clear that viral exposure resulted in decreased head growth from 5 months of age, despite the absence of effects at birth (van der Linden et al., 2016). While functional outcomes have yet to be clarified, the reliable and efficient measurement of head circumference remains an important screening tool.

Overall, measurements of head circumference offer a good proxy for both head and brain growth in infancy with the caveat that this does not hold for developmental anomalies, such as synostoses, which may result in unusual skull shapes. Here, the estimate is improved by the addition of cranial height as measured ear to ear over the vertex in addition to head circumference (Martini, Klausing, Lüchters, Heim, & Messing-Jünger, 2018).

2.2.6.2 Culture and Infant Head Circumference Assessment
The inclusion of head circumference measurements at US well-child visits across the first year identifies extremes in head size, either micro- or macro-cephalic status (<3rd or 5th centiles; >95th or 97th centiles for age), that can reflect genetic, anatomical, or infectious etiology for which early detection and intervention may offer the child benefits for ensuing neurocognitive disorders with lifelong consequences (van Dyck & Morrow, 2017). The screening practice includes the caveats that (1) large intra- and interindividual variations are to be expected, thus concerns should only be raised when measurements exceed the 95% confidence intervals of size for age to avoid unnecessary alarm; and (2) diagnostic utility is found in serial assessments, not isolated measurements (Illingworth & Lutz, 1965).

The US focus on early clinical detection for intervention and prevention is not shared by the UK, where recommendations for routine measurements of infant head circumference have been limited to the time around birth and 8 weeks of age (www.growthcharts.rcpch.ac.uk). Low rates of hydrocephalus, concerns about false positives due to high variability in infant head growth rates, and poor sensitivity and specificity in head growth rates to predict childhood cognitive test scores (Wright & Emond, 2015) have led to a proposed revision in the UK, which limits measures to the first 2 to 5 days after birth (after any molding associated with birth was resolved) and once before the age of 6 months. These national-level screening differences reflect risk/benefit judgments that embody sociocultural perspectives, reasonable expectations for head circumference measurement predictions, and values associated with societal responsibilities.

2.2.7 Culture and Infant Head Shape Growth: Implications for Policy

Infant head shape has been a focus for the expression of cultural aesthetics for millennia. Intentional cranial deformation of the infant skull has been practiced among a wide range of populations (Dingwall, 1931; Karasik, Tamis-LeMonda, Ossmy, & Adolph, 2018; Tubbs, Salter, & Oakes, 2006) using caps, scarves, and other forms of mechanical restraint on the pliable infant skull to achieve the conical skull as a feminine ideal (Dingwall, 1931; Tubbs et al.,

2006). Recognition that skull growth restrictions were associated with infant pain led to outcries against the practice of infant head molding for the purpose of fashion in some nineteenth-century communities (Dingwall, 1931).

In other populations, altered head shapes accompany the exigency of carrying infants on cradle boards. The application of tight swaddling clothes that rigidly secure the infant head against a board was a common practice historically and remains part of a few local cultures today (Karasik et al., 2018). The biology of positional plagiocephaly (skull deformation due to persistent positioning) emerged into present day US cultural consciousness following the American Academy of Pediatrics supine sleeping position campaign, launched in 1992, to decrease the risk of sudden infant death syndrome (SIDS) (Laughlin, Luerssen, Dias, & American Academy of Pediatrics Committee on Practice and Ambulatory Medicine 2011; Persing, James, Swanson, Kattwinkel, & American Academy of Pediatrics Committee on Practice and Ambulatory Medicine, 2003). As infants spent more time on their backs, the pliability of the cranium resulted in occipital flattening similar to that associated with the practice of cradle boarding.

Increasing parental concerns about their infants' flattened occiputs could have been met with reassurance, given the lack of knowledge regarding functional consequences of sleeping practices. In the United States, however, parental worries were met with the emergence of a series of cranial orthotics. The Food and Drug Administration (FDA) ruled that these devices should be classified as class II medical devices, thereby restricting them to prescription use for reasonable assurance of safety and effectiveness (FDA Fed Reg 63:146, 1998). It was determined that the infant helmet could be applied among infants 3 to 18 months of age with moderate to severe plagiocephaly, and be worn up to 23 hours a day. All available helmets work similarly, exerting mechanical pressure on an infant's cranium to promote cranial symmetry. Pediatric recommendations for helmet therapy were published in 2016 (American Academy of Pediatrics, 2016).

The need for, and benefit from, infant cranial orthotics is a matter of both medical and sociocultural risk/benefit considerations. It is important to distinguish between pathologies associated with disturbed brain and/or cranio-facial growth, including craniosynostosis (abnormal fusion of the cranial bones that can put pressure on the growing brain), and the alterations in head shape secondary to sleep position. The former may portend functional alterations as part of underlying developmental pathology while the latter reflects mechanical skull plasticity resulting in a morphological variant.

Efficacy of helmet application, as judged by cranial sphericity, has shown mixed results associated with age of application, duration of follow-up, and underlying causality. Prospective studies have reported rounder occipital regions among helmeted infants compared to unhelmeted peers, but the clinical significance and long-term outcome of these changes are unclear (Lipira et al., 2010). A Dutch study among healthy infants showed no significant difference by 24 months of age in terms of head shape among infants receiving helmet therapy and those who did not, leading the authors to discourage the use of helmet therapy among healthy infants (van Wijk et al., 2014). These results were countered by the American Academy of Pediatrics (2014) for methodological weaknesses, including helmet fit and maintenance, specificity of outcome measures, and a focus on a sample of healthy infants.

This debate raises questions about the natural history of infant head shape among healthy children, in addition to confronting cultural ideas about head shape normality. Positional molding in the first year of life need not lead to permanent shape alterations, as demonstrated by outcomes at age 5 among healthy children who were plagiocephalic as infants (van Vlimmeren et al., 2017). Concerns about perfectly circular skull morphology as a sign of "normality" are not founded on scientific evidence of any association between head "sphericity" and superior or inhibited cognitive powers at this time, due solely to sleep positioning. While there are reports of developmental lags among children with increasing plagiocephaly, the causal pathways are not entirely clear. Infants who spend a considerable part of each day confined to infant car seats, mechanical swings, or other devices that restrict their position and movement, likely experience less time physically active, in social interaction, or exploring the environment and expanding their motoric development (Collett et al., 2011; Karasik et al., 2018).

Excluding congenital craniofacial anomalies, there is no "correct shape" for the human head and human variability in head size and shape is anthropologically well documented (Martinez-Abadias et al., 2009), with no predictive functional implications (Treit et al., 2016). Judging successful outcome of cranial orthotic application on the basis of infant head roundness, cephalic index (maximum breadth/maximum length) and/or parental aesthetic satisfaction (Kelly et al., 2018; Lee, Kim, & Kwon, 2018) is in line with the many historical examples of infant head molding for cultural appeal. Parental concerns that so-called infant "flat head syndrome" may, if left untreated, lead to a permanent skull deformity, has no evidentiary support of harm to date in terms of either practical or psychological outcomes. At this time, the monetary burden of the orthotics (Lam et al., 2017) raises questions regarding whether the medicalization of head shape "deformity" due to sleeping position serves a health imperative or a modern day cultural aesthetic.

Circumferences of other individual body components have less frequently been the object of infant physical growth research records. *Chest circumference*, assessed with a tape measure at the level of the nipples, is a difficult serial measurement to achieve with high reliability due to inspiratory and expiratory cycles. It has been reported to be a good indicator for suboptimal prenatal conditions (Hadush, Berhe, & Medhanyie, 2017) and to have high accuracy predicting both birth weight in general (Pomeroy, Stock, Cole, O'Callaghan, & Wells, 2014) and low birth weight, specifically (Goto, 2011), an advantage in low-resource settings absent of scales and trained staff. Increased chest circumference has been reported to be both a good proxy for rapid weight gain in the first 3 to 4 months and a predictor of obesity at 3 years of age (Akaboshi, Kitano, Kan, Haraguchi, & Mizumoto, 2012). While infrequently considered, changes in the shape and size of the chest and abdomen are one of the most significant features of infant physical growth across the first year. The lungs launch their functional respiratory phase only after birth when they undergo significant growth. Accompanied by rib expansion, these growth changes transform the neonatal pyramidal thorax into a barrel shape with functional effects, shifting breathing from predominantly diaphragmatic to thoracic, and postural adjustments occur as the infant becomes upright (Bastir et al., 2013).

2.3 The Meaning of Infant Size in Cultural Context

Parents are commonly interested in whether their baby will follow in the footsteps of the taller or shorter side of the family, and clinicians want to be sure that babies are developing normally. Many people, from grandmothers to health professionals, want to ensure that infants are getting enough to eat and infant size is the most frequently used proxy for making this inference. For the most part, as long as infants "look healthy" and "get bigger" across time, parents are reassured that their babies are doing well and they themselves are doing a good job of caring for them. But just how big each infant is "supposed to be" to allay worries on the part of both parents and health care workers differs by culture, group, and historical time.

Most parents have ideas about the satisfactory status of their child by observation: Regardless of what anyone tells them, they collect their own data as they compare their child to others. They worry about "scrawny legs" with concerns analogous to those they experience when their infant's expanding motor and verbal abilities lag relative to other babies. Variability in infant size is a subject of social discourse. While many people believe that whether an infant is "skinny" or "plump" is obvious to the eye, not all people agree about what these states look like, what is actually desirable, or what is "normal." Cultural beliefs are embedded in concerns about infant size with some people valuing a "fat baby" as a "healthy baby" while others worry about what "chubby" thighs portend for their child as an adult.

For decades, a primary interest in monitoring infant size was to screen for "small" babies in need of intervention because early growth of the body, particularly the brain, has significance for lifelong well-being. Infants in the United States began to weigh more after the 1970s (L. Johnson et al., 2011), and in recent years screening interests have turned to the identification of "heavy" babies in response to an epidemic of obesity, starting at ever earlier ages. Objective characterization of who is "small" and "big" requires answering the question of "compared to whom?" To provide a frame of reference, measurements taken on large numbers of infants are collected at prescribed ages and analyzed to provide statistical distributions of size for age. These tools are known as growth references.

2.3.1 Growth References: Defining Small and Big

Growth references are optimally generated from, and then applied to, children of similar backgrounds living in comparable environments with shared feeding style and health phenotype to address questions of whether a child is *actually* "short," "skinny," or "chubby" compared to others like themselves. These caveats are important because infant size is influenced by genetic predisposition, biological age (gestational age in young infants), pregnancy history, postnatal feeding style, illness, and ecology, with effects from altitude and food availability, safety and conflict, as well as lifestyle variables captured by family socioeconomic level and maternal education. Each of these variables has the potential to mediate an infant's access to resources, ranging from nutrients to psychological well-being and health care. It is important to note that growth references do not impute value judgments on what size is desirable for an infant. They simply describe the size of infants in the sample. Just as adults around the world vary in size, so do infants (Eveleth & Tanner, 1990).

2.3.1.1 *Methods: Sampling for References*
The characteristics of the infants providing the data define the utility of any reference. National references have been developed by many countries to describe their infant population (Himes, 2006). Some of these are purely descriptive and include measurements from a diverse sample of children; others have selective inclusion and exclusion criteria based on health status or ethnicity, for example. In order to better understand the status of infants with known distinctive growth characteristics, unique growth references have been developed for assessing the size of preterm, low birth weight (1500–2500 g), and very low birth weight (<1500 g) infants, as well as those with genetically based growth disorders or other clinical conditions whose pathology perturbs growth.

National-level references require sampling strategies to collect representative samples, a significant challenge depending on the size of the country and the infrastructure to support such an endeavor. It is notable that while a number of locally based longitudinal growth studies of healthy infants were carried out in the United States in the 1900s (in Denver, Dayton, and Iowa City, for example) (Himes, 2006), there were no national survey data available for infant size until the end of the twentieth century. The 1978 references produced by the US National Center for Health Statistics (NCHS), and subsequently recommended by the World Health Organization (WHO) for international application (the NCHS/WHO, CDC/WHO [Center for Disease Control], or NCHS/CDC/WHO growth references) (Kuczmarski et al., 2002; World Health Organization, 2006), comprised infant measurements drawn from the longitudinal research study carried out at the Fels Institute in Dayton, Ohio. This is a sample of largely Caucasian, middle-class male and female infants born between 1929 and 1975 who were predominantly formula fed. The number of subjects contributing to the references ranged from 150 to 480 within each age category (1, 3, 6, 9, and 12 months of age) (Hamill, Drizd, Johnson, Reed, & Roche, 1977). The need for an expanded sample of infants came to the fore as a product of rising global interest in infant size as a monitor of infant health, and attention to the importance of breastfeeding. On both accounts, the small sample of formula-fed Ohio infants was deemed an inappropriate reference.

By the year 2000, the small NCHS/CDC/WHO sample of infants was augmented by a more nationally representative data set and a new US reference was released. This was known as the "CDC growth reference" (Kuczmarski et al., 2002) and represented the size of American infants born across the United States between 1963 and 1994, weighing more than 1,500 g at birth from a wide array of socioeconomic levels and ethnicities, with breastfeeding percentages matching those in practice. By this time, national infant growth studies had been completed in many countries and these locally generated references were becoming used in lieu of the American-sourced NCHS/WHO/CDC international references (Eveleth & Tanner, 1990; Himes, 2006), as they were found to better characterize their local populations.

2.3.1.2 Methods: Data Analysis
Once data have been collected, descriptive statistics of individuals' measurements are calculated such that for each age at which measures were taken, percentile distributions (e.g., the 5th, 10th, 50th, 90th, and 95th percentiles) are generated. These data are prepared in tables with the sizes for age at each percentile presented in columnar form to provide a reference for any infant to be compared to their peers (Hamill et al., 1977).

2.3.1.3 Methods: Data Presentation
A practical difficulty of categorical, tabulated data is their utility for individuals at ages between the protocol assessment targets. This requires data interpolation of both size and age. Historically, this was accomplished visually by hand-drawing a connect-the-dots graph so as to fill in missing data between sequential monthly data, permitting size for any age to be estimated. This crude approach has been replaced by formal mathematical curve-fitting procedures. Commonly, a polynomial spline function has been used to mathematically derive points to "stand in" for missing data between the ages when data were actually collected. The resulting interpolated graphic, in which mathematically derived sizes for age have been imputed by a curvilinear fit, connects the percentiles of size across age (e.g., 50th percentiles at each sequential month) and is known as a "growth chart" of size-for-age.

2.3.1.4 Methods: Growth Chart Use
Growth references answer the question of how big an infant is relative to their peers. The graphic curve format permits measurements taken on individual infants at each health visit, regardless of age, to be easily visualized in terms

of relative size, providing easy monitoring and rapid screening. In this way, infants who are "small for age" (often defined as less than the 3rd or 5th percentile) and "large for age" (greater than the 95th or 97th percentile) are easily identified from those who are "appropriate for age." Commonly, no immediate actions are taken for the small and large infants, but they are followed closely and reassessed to determine if further diagnostic procedures and/or intervention is needed.

A point of debate for several decades has been whether these comparisons should be made with reference to local infants of similar background or infants more globally. This decision is influenced by the availability of local data, the purpose of the comparison, and scientific evidence for the role of genetics in infant growth. One view posits that there is a need for a universal standard identifying "how big infants should be" at each age to better guide interventions in support of each child reaching their "optimal growth potential."

2.3.2 Growth Standards: Cultural and Policy Viewpoints on How Big Infants Should Be

In 1997 the WHO launched the collaborative collection of data from six global communities with inclusion criteria that limited enrollment to infants from families with socioeconomic status that did not constrain growth (defined by infant weight and height, and morbidity statistics), living at low altitude with access to safe water, born from singleton pregnancies of 37 to 42 weeks gestation in which there was no maternal smoking, and of mothers who agreed to adhere to WHO feeding recommendations (predominant breastfeeding to 4 months and partial breastfeeding to 12 months of age) with availability to breastfeeding support and counseling on complementary feeding. Data on 888 infants from Brazil (67 infants), Ghana (228 infants), India (173 infants), Norway (148 infants), Oman (153 infants), and the United States (119 infants) measured longitudinally in their first year (de Onis et al., 2006) were analyzed as previously described: Statistical distributions of size-for-age were calculated by month and a curve-fitting procedure interpolated sizes for intervening ages. Known as the Multicentre Growth Reference Study (MRGS), the resulting charts were proposed as a standard, or the size-for-age that infants should be when born and raised under optimal circumstances. The underlying assumption of the proposed global standard was that all humans are genetically alike (Martorell, 2017), and will grow alike when exposed to optimal environmental circumstances. The MGRS/WHO charts have been widely used since their publication.

The adoption of the MGRS/WHO as a single gold standard is not free of controversy on both theoretical and evidentiary grounds. The claim of a recent pan-human genome has been replaced by evidence documenting a much older common origin than previously assumed (Scerri et al., 2018), making claims of logical similarities in growth timing patterns far less likely. Aside from monogenic height disorders, direct genetic links to the magnitude of infant length/height growth are neither clear nor simple (Livshits et al., 2000). Phenotypic size reflects age-based gene expression patterns (Demerath et al., 2007; Helgeland et al., 2018) and involves many genes with small but additive effects at the level of growth-related cellular processes. This is an optimal system framework, permitting flexibility and adaptive options for infant growth to proceed in changing environments, and is expressed as variation in infant growth worldwide that is greater than the 888 subject MGRS database embodies. Research analyses suggest that infant health in local populations may be better served by local references/standards when available (Natale & Rajagopalan 2014).

2.3.2.1 *Growth Charts: Limitations*

Common clinical practice plots individuals' serial measurements on growth charts at health checkups, providing a fine screening tool: If an individual of average weight at 6 weeks of age is at the 3rd percentile by 3 months of age, attention to potential causes should be raised. The graphical growth chart curve (both references and standard) is frequently misunderstood, however, and employed as a diagnostic tool in a scope beyond their appropriate use. Individuals' serial growth measurements are frequently inspected for "tracking" along a percentile line with the expectation that the graph represents a model of *growing*, assuming that the connecting curves are growth *rates* applicable to *individuals*. This is incorrect. The growth chart curves are simply mathematically generated interpolations of size, not tracks prescribing individual growth trajectories. Research has shown that it is quite common for infants to change percentile rankings across the first year of life. This is because individuals do not grow alike, but follow personalized growth rates. More than 60% of infants "cross" two percentile lines either up or down in weight-for-length in the first 6 months of life, and one in five do so for length between 6 months and 2 years of age (Mei, Grummer-Strawn, Thompson, & Dietz, 2004). Some of this jostling across percentile lines reflects postnatal regression to the mean (Cameron, Preeze, & Cole, 2005), as infants adjust their growth rates after birth, sometimes being relatively tall or short, depending on when and how much they grow. Those individuals who were held back *in utero* "catch up" once released from prenatal constraints, while others "slow down" their pace of growth. Many of these "centile-crossing" growth trajectories reflect the normal variation in individual growth rates as they unfold through growth biology (Lampl & Thompson, 2007).

2.4 Individual Growth Biology: How Babies Grow

Individual infants do not grow little by little each day as the growth chart curve implies. Infant physical growth occurs only episodically, in growth spurts. Both elongation of the skeleton, as assessed by total body length, and expansion in head circumference are documented to change within time spans of one day (Lampl & Johnson, 2011a, 2011b; Lampl, Veldhuis, & Johnson, 1992). These dynamic growth events, or saltations, are separated by days to weeks of no measurable size changes. This "saltatory" growth pattern underlies the infant's morphological transformation in size over the first year, propelling body dimensions by episodic leaps in cellular proliferation and expansion events. This means that the overall growth across the first year, or some 25 cm in length and 10 cm in head circumference (de Onis et al., 2006; Kuczmarski et al., 2002), is accrued in a series of intermittent growth spurts. Individuals grow episodically by 0.3 cm to 1.2 cm saltations in length and 0.1 cm to 0.7 cm in head circumference within a day, separated by intervals ranging from one day to several weeks of no growth. This is a very different biological process than the slow growth of less than 1 mm a day implied by the mathematically derived growth curves (Roche & Guo, 1992). Identifying how individuals grow requires sampling at appropriate time density. The evidence documenting saltation and stasis growth emerged from a protocol of daily infant measurement. It is not knowable from weekly or monthly measures as the increments become attenuated across time as growth rate estimates (change per day) obscure the unique temporal features of the growth saltations.

The anatomical sources of head growth saltations are not precisely known at this time, but are to be found in neural developmental patterns. The growth saltations in length occur as the cells responsible for long-bone elongation, chondroblasts, pass through their cellular life stages from recruitment, clonal proliferation, and hypertrophy in organized units at the site of bone growth, the growth plates. These areas, found at either end of the long bones of the arms and legs just adjacent to joints, are the action sites where growth unfolds. Saltations occur as a coordinated volumetric expansion of clonal chondroblast units hydraulically expand at the growth plate, resulting in bone elongation. The expanded, hypertrophic chondrocytes secrete an architectural protein matrix upon which bone-forming cells, osteoblasts, then deposit bone matrix. Sequential generations of chondroblasts embark on their developmental journey from recruitment and proliferation to hypertrophy, affecting bone elongation through sequential saltatory growth spurts. Environmental influences modify both when and how much growth occurs through effects on specific cell functions, enhancing or inhibiting both the number of cells that contribute to the hypertrophic cohort and the amount of volumetric expansion (Lampl & Schoen, 2017). Whether the timing of growth saltations is cell line in origin (Ramanathan et al., 2014) or centrally regulated by neural chronobiology remains to be clarified.

2.4.1 Culture

The scientific documentation that individual growth proceeds by saltation and stasis in which saltatory increments sum to size attained (Lampl et al., 1992) is not part of pediatric clinical culture. It is not, however, news to most parents, who are well aware of the sudden emergence of "outgrown" clothing – pants, socks, and shoes that fit yesterday – and the irregular disruptions in the biobehavioral state of their infants, including inconsolable crying, fussiness, fits of hunger, and altered sleep patterns.

2.4.2 Neuroscience: Interfacing Physical Growth

There are a number of physiological conversations between the brain, the skeleton, and soft tissues orchestrating and responding to infant physical growth. Hormonal pathways broker energetics to fuel growth and establish bone–brain collaborations, while emerging developmental skills navigate their realization within the context of the growing infant body.

2.4.2.1 Brain Talks to Bone

Neural pathways originating in the hypothalamus were long assumed to be the principal control point over normal growth by inference from hormonal-based pathologies among children of short stature (Mehta & Hindmarsh, 2002). The primacy of hypothalamic/pituitary hormones as master growth controls has been eclipsed by cell-level processes. It is now clear that it is the prerogative of bone growth cells, sensitive to signals regarding available energy and resources, to locally execute the activities associated with building the skeleton (Lampl & Schoen, 2017). Centrally regulated hormones are part of a network of cross-talking signals, together with tissue-based cytokines, that have endocrine, paracrine, and autocrine roles in the biological system influencing infant growth. Information regarding energetic state and resource availability for undergoing a bone growth saltation, for example, is exchanged at network hubs where hypothalamic monitors overseeing anabolic state through appetite and satiety, sleep state and immune status, translate into both permissive and inhibitory signals for saltatory growth events. This is exemplified by associations between sleep frequency and duration, and infant skeletal growth, with increasing naps and longer sleep duration preceding growth in length (Lampl & Johnson, 2011a). Likewise, potential limitations on the timeliness of a growth saltation are signaled by dysregulated cortisol levels under psychosocial stresses, illustrated by stunted infant physical growth in the context of family conflict (Montgomery, Bartley, & Wilkinson, 1997), child abuse, and neglect, institutional rearing (Dobrova-Krol, van IJzendoorn, Bakermans-Kranenburg, Cyr, & Juffer, 2008), and maternal postnatal depression (Avan, Richter, Ramchandani, Norris, & Stein, 2010).

2.4.2.2 Bone Talks to Brain

The skeleton is no mere static structure but is an endocrine organ, acting by way of the hormone osteocalcin, which is uniquely secreted by osteoblasts, cells that are up-regulated during bone growth (Karsenty, 2017). Osteocalcin is required for establishing cognitive function in early development. It crosses the blood–brain barrier to bind G protein-coupled receptor 158 (Gpr158) on neurons in the brainstem, ventral tegmental area, and hippocampus, promoting the synthesis of monoamine neurotransmitters such as serotonin, dopamine, and norepinephrine, while inhibiting GABA (Obri, Khrimian, Karsenty, & Oury, 2018; Oury et al., 2013). The Gpr158 receptors represent a nexus of stress, depression, and synaptic plasticity. Absence of osteocalcin is associated with increased anxiety-like behavior and depression, along with deficits in exploratory behavior, spatial learning, and memory (Oury et al., 2013). In this way, healthy bone growth supports normal brain development, specifically favoring learning and memory.

The *dynamically growing body* is the context in which developmental skills emerge. Perceptual-motor skill (PMS) acquisition and performance, a consequence of motor cortex maturation (Newell & Wade, 2018), is regulated by a complex interplay of biomechanics, neuropsychology, and cognition (Adolph & Franchak, 2017), and occurs within a dynamically changing anatomy. Abrupt physical growth of the limbs has implications for the three-dimensional stability of developing motor skills, posing challenges for infants who thought they had gotten their balance yesterday and are suddenly faced with readjustment (Adolph & Franchak 2017), adapting to changes in inertia to preserve motor proficiency (Chester & Jensen, 2005; Jensen, 1981; Schneider, Zernicke, Ulrich, Jensen, & Thelen, 1990), while they struggle to develop their muscular strength. This may challenge problem-solving skills more generally, identifying a unifying developmental synergy between infant physical growth and broader competencies.

2.5 Policy

With the vision of building a healthy body to last a lifetime, scientific evidence identifies the following opportunities for goals and action steps in support of achieving healthy infant growth rather than bigger size.

2.5.1 Promote Comprehensive Understanding of Individual Variability in Infant Growth

Infants neither grow alike nor according to any growth chart's curvilinear growth centile shapes. Infants experience personalized growth rates through episodic growth saltations according to their unique timing patterns. Nutrient intakes differ across days, and when we feed infants is at least as important as what and how much. Steps to support healthy growing require awareness of growth phenotypes and variable, infant-responsive eating schedules need to be embraced. In lieu of labeling deviation from scheduled feeds as a feeding problem, supporting a feeding pattern that matches babies' changing metabolic needs is called for in recognition that appetites fluctuate, increasing during saltatory growth and declining during stasis. This has health consequences during infancy's sensitive period for expanding adipose cell number with overfeeding, specific protein requirements for muscle cell expansion, and entrainment of appetite.

2.5.2 Support Parents in Supporting Their Infant's Growth

Parents rely on the advice of pediatricians and childcare workers. Education on infant growth biology needs to be improved to empower parents to act on behalf of their children.

2.5.3 Improve Regulatory Oversight of Infant Growth Claims

Infant health is increasingly a target of business opportunities and product claims of beneficial effects as gaged by infant growth abound. There is widespread misuse of "growth" as an outcome and a supportive claim in poorly designed research. Expert panels unencumbered by conflicts of interest are needed to review the scientific evidence behind statements such as "proven to help babies grow," which is frequently loosely construed to be valid if subjects "get bigger." A specific example is a need for policies overseeing the evidentiary base supporting the health claim properties of liquid-based nutritional supplements, as these are outside of the specific guidelines of the FDA. Healthy babies grow and get bigger. In a time of obesity, simply growing babies bigger is often equivalent to driving weight gain and can do more harm than good (Lampl, Mummert, & Schoen, 2016).

2.5.4 Align Practice and Research Educating Pediatricians and Infant Health Workers

A tendency to misunderstand the purpose of growth charts and other models of infant size attainment requires education to refrain health worker misinterpretation and interventions. A focus on the median as the target for "normal" is common and prompts worry on the part of parents, and erroneous goalsetting on the part of infant health care workers. The specific use of weight growth charts to prompt feeding intervention when individual infants cross centiles at a well-baby visit needs to be curtailed.

The flexibility in the biological underpinnings of the physical growth process results in the remarkable variation in size found worldwide as cells differentiate and grow into the functional organism during infancy. Policies in recognition of variation are needed.

References

Adair, L. S., Fall, C. H. D., Osmond, C., Stein, A. D., Martorell, R., Ramirez-Zea, M., … COHORTS Group (2013). Associations of linear growth and relative weight gain during early life with adult health and human capital in countries of low and middle income: Findings from five birth cohort studies. *Lancet, 382*(9891), 525–534.

Adolph, K. E., & Franchak, J. M. (2017). The development of motor behavior. *Wiley Interdisciplinary Reviews. Cognitive Science, 8* (1–2).

Adolph, K. E., & Robinson, S. R. (2015). Motor development. In L. S. Liben & U. Muller (Eds.), *Handbook of child psychology and developmental science* (7th ed., Vol. 2: Cognitive processes (pp. 114–157). New York, NY: Wiley.

Akaboshi, I., Kitano, A., Kan, H., Haraguchi, Y., & Mizumoto, Y. (2012). Chest circumference in infancy predicts obesity in 3-year-old children. *Asia Pacific Journal of Clinical Nutrition, 21*(4), 495–501.

American Academy of Pediatrics (2014). Study on helmet therapy suffers from several weaknesses. *AAP News, 35*(11), 5–5.

(2016). Systematic review and evidence-based guidelines for the management of patients with positional plagiocephaly. *Pediatrics, 138*(5), e20162802.

Amiel-Tison, C., Gosselin, J., & Infante-Rivard, C. (2002). Head growth and cranial assessment at neurological examination in infancy. *Developmental Medicine and Child Neurology, 44*(9), 643–648.

Arner, P. (2018). Fat tissue growth and development in humans. *Nestle Nutrition Institute Workshop Series, 89*, 37–45.

Avan, B., Richter, L. M., Ramchandani, P. G., Norris, S. A., & Stein, A. (2010). Maternal postnatal depression and children's growth and behaviour during the early years of life: exploring the interaction between physical and mental health. *Archives of Disease in Childhood, 95*(9), 690–695.

Barker, D. J. P. (1995). Fetal origins of coronary heart disease. *British Medical Journal, 311*(6998), 171–174.

Bartholomeusz, H. H., Courchesne, E., & Karns, C. M. (2002). Relationship between head circumference and brain volume in healthy normal toddlers, children, and adults. *Neuropediatrics, 33*(5), 239–241.

Bastir, M., García Martínez, D., Recheis, W., Barash, A., Coquerelle, M., Rios, L., … O'Higgins, P. (2013). Differential growth and development of the upper and lower human thorax. *PLoS ONE, 8*(9), e75128.

Bell, K. A., Wagner, C. L., Perng, W., Feldman, H. A., Shypailo, R. J., & Belfort, M. B. (2018). Validity of body mass index as a measure of adiposity in infancy. *Journal of Pediatrics, 196*, 168–174.

Bhardwaj, R. D., Curtis, M. A., Spalding, K. L., Buchholz, B. A., Fink, D., Björk-Eriksson, T., … Frisén, J. (2006). Neocortical neurogenesis in humans is restricted to development. *Proceedings of the National Academy of Sciences, 103*(33), 12564–12568.

Braude, P., Bolton, V., & Moore, S. (1988). Human gene expression first occurs between the four- and eight-cell stages of preimplantation development. *Nature, 332*(6163), 459–461.

Bray, P. F., Shields, W. D., Wolcott, G. J., & Madsen, J. A. (1969). Occipitofrontal head circumference: An accurate measure of intracranial volume. *Journal of Pediatrics, 75*(2), 303–305.

Brei, C., Much, D., Heimberg, E., Schulte, V., Brunner, S., Stecher, L., ... Hauner, H. (2015). Sonographic assessment of abdominal fat distribution during the first year of infancy. *Pediatric Research, 78*(3), 342–350.

Breij, L. M., Abrahamse-Berkeveld, M., Acton, D., de Lucia Rolfe, E., Ong, K. K., & Hokken-Koelega, A. C. S. (2017). Impact of early infant growth, duration of breastfeeding and maternal factors on total body fat mass and visceral fat at 3 and 6 months of age. *Annals of Nutrition & Metabolism, 71*(3–4), 203–210.

Breij, L. M., Kerkhof, G. F., de Lucia Rolfe, E., Ong, K. K., Abrahamse-Berkeveld, M., Acton, D., ... Hokken-Koelega, A. C. S. (2017). Longitudinal fat mass and visceral fat during the first 6 months after birth in healthy infants: Support for a critical window for adiposity in early life. *Pediatric Obesity, 12*(4), 286–294.

Buschang, P. H. (1982). Differential long bone growth of children between two months and eleven years of age. *American Journal of Physical Anthropology, 58*(3), 291–295.

Butte, N. F., Hopkinson, J. M., Wong, W. W., Smith, E. O., & Ellis, K. J. (2000). Body composition during the first 2 years of life: An updated reference. *Pediatric Research, 47*(5), 578–585.

Cameron, N. (1984). *The measurement of human growth*. London: Routledge.

Cameron, N., Preece, M. A., & Cole, T. J. (2005). Catch-up growth or regression to the mean? Recovery from stunting revisited. *American Journal of Human Biology, 17*(4), 412–417.

Chen, H., Wang, J., Uddin, L. Q., Wang, X., Gui, X., Lu, F., ... Wu, L. (2018). Aberrant functional connectivity of neural circuits associated with social and sensorimotor deficits in young children with autism spectrum disorder. *Autism Research, 11*(12), 1643–1652.

Chen, L., Wang, D., Wu, Z., Ma, L., & Daley, G. Q. (2010). Molecular basis of the first cell fate determination in mouse embryogenesis. *Cell Research, 20*(9), 982–993.

Chester, V. L., & Jensen, R. K. (2005). Changes in infant segment inertias during the first three months of independent walking. *Dynamic Medicine, 4*(1), 9.

Collett, B. R., Starr, J. R., Kartin, D., Heike, C. L., Berg, J., Cunningham, M. L., & Speltz, M. L. (2011). Development in toddlers with and without deformational plagiocephaly. *Archives of Pediatrics & Adolescent Medicine, 165*(7), 653–658.

Conkle, J., Suchdev, P. S., Alexander, E., Flores-Ayala, R., Ramakrishnan, U., & Martorell, R. (2018). Accuracy and reliability of a low-cost, handheld 3D imaging system for child anthropometry. *PloS One, 13*(10), e0205320.

Courchesne, E., Karns, C. M., Davis, H. R., Ziccardi, R., Carper, R. A., Tigue, Z. D., ... Courchesne, R. Y. (2001). Unusual brain growth patterns in early life in patients with autistic disorder: An MRI study. *Neurology, 57*(2), 245–254.

Courchesne, E., Pramparo, T., Gazestani, V. H., Lombardo, M. V., Pierce, K., & Lewis, N. E. (2018). The ASD living biology: From cell proliferation to clinical phenotype. *Molecular Psychiatry, 24*(1), 88–107.

Day, N. L., Richardson, G., Robles, N., Sambamoorthi, U., Taylor, P., Scher, M., … Cornelius, M. 1990). Effect of prenatal alcohol exposure on growth and morphology of offspring at 8 months of age. *Pediatrics, 85*(5), 748–752.

Davis, T. A., & Fiorotto, M. L. (2009). Regulation of muscle growth in neonates. *Current Opinion in Clinical Nutrition and Metabolic Care, 12*(1), 78–85.

de Araújo, T. V. B., Rodrigues, L. C., de Alencar Ximenes, R., de Barros Miranda-Filho, D., Ramos Montarroyos, U., Lopes de Melo, A. P., … Turchi Martelli, C. M. (2016). Association between Zika virus infection and microcephaly in Brazil, January to May, 2016: Preliminary report of a case-control study. *Lancet: Infectious Diseases, 16*(12), 1356–1363.

de Brito, M. L., Nunes, M., Bernardi, J. R., Bosa, V. L., Goldani, M. Z., & da Silva, C. H. (2017). Somatic growth in the first six months of life of infants exposed to maternal smoking in pregnancy. *BMC Pediatrics, 17*(1), 67.

de Cunto, A., Paviotti, G., Ronfani, L., Travan, L., Bua , J., Cont, G., & Demarini, S. (2014). Can body mass index accurately predict adiposity in newborns? *Archives of Disease in Childhood: Fetal and Neonatal Edition, 99*(3), F238–239.

de Onis, M., de, Onyango, A. W., Borghi, E., Garza, C., & Yang, H. (2006). Child growth standards and the National Center for Health Statistics/WHO international growth reference: Implications for child health programmes. *Public Health Nutrition, 9*(7), 942–947.

Demerath, E. W., Choh, A. C., Czerwinski, S. A., Lee, M., Sun, S. S., Chumlea, W. C., … Towne, B. (2007). Genetic and environmental influences on infant weight and weight changes: The Fels Longitudinal Study. *American Journal of Human Biology, 19*, 692–702.

Demerath, E. W., & Fields, D. A. (2014). Body composition assessment in the infant. *American Journal of Human Biology, 26*(3), 291–304.

Dingwall, E. J. (1931). *Artificial cranial deformation: A contribution to the study of ethnic mutilations.* London: J. Bale & Danielsson.

Dobrova-Krol, N. A., van IJzendoorn, M. H., Bakermans-Kranenburg, M. J., Cyr, C., & Juffer, F. (2008). Physical growth delays and stress dysregulation in stunted and non-stunted Ukrainian institution-reared children. *Infant Behavior & Development, 31*(3), 539–553.

Dupont, C., Castellanos-Ryan, N., Séguin, J. R., Muckle, G., Simard, M. -N., Shapiro, G. D., … Lippé, S. (2018). The predictive value of head circumference growth during the first year of life on early child traits. *Scientific Reports, 8*(1), 9828.

Eveleth, P. B., & Tanner, J. M. (1990). *Worldwide variation in human growth.* Cambridge, UK: Cambridge University Press.

Fabiansen, C., Yaméogo, C. W., Devi, S., Friis, H., Kurpad, A., & Wells, J. C. (2017). Deuterium dilution technique for body composition assessment: Resolving methodological issues in children with moderate acute malnutrition. *Isotopes in Environmental and Health Studies, 53*(4), 344–355.

Fields, D. A., Demerath, E. W., Pietrobelli, A., & Chandler-Laney, P. C. (2012). Body composition at 6 months of life: Comparison of air displacement plethysmography and dual-energy X-ray absorptiometry. *Obesity, 20*(11), 2302–2306.

Fiorotto, M. L., & Davis, T. A. (2018). Critical windows for the programming effects of early-life nutrition on skeletal muscle mass. *Nestle Nutrition Institute Workshop Series, 89*, 25–35.

Fleming, T. P., Kwong, W. Y., Porter, R., Ursell, E., Fesenko, I., Wilkins, A., ... Eckert, J. J. (2004). The embryo and its future. *Biology of Reproduction, 71*(4), 1046–1054.

Fleming, T. P., Watkins, A. J., Velazquez, M. A., Mathers, J. C., Prentice, A. M., Stephenson, J., ... Godfrey, K. M. (2018). Origins of lifetime health around the time of conception: Causes and consequences. *Lancet, 391*(10132), 1842–1852.

Goto, E. (2011). Meta-analysis: Identification of low birthweight by other anthropometric measurements at birth in developing countries. *Journal of Epidemiology, 21*(5), 354–362.

Hadush, M. Y., Berhe, A. H., & Medhanyie, A. A. (2017). Foot length, chest and head circumference measurements in detection of low birth weight neonates in Mekelle, Ethiopia: A hospital based cross sectional study. *BMC Pediatrics, 17*(1), 111.

Hamill, P. V., Drizd, T. A., Johnson, C. L., Reed, R. B., & Roche, A. F. (1977). NCHS growth curves for children birth–18 years: United States. *Vital and Health Statistics Series 11: Data from the National Health Survey,* 165(i–iv), 1–74.

Hazlett, H. C., Gu, H., Munsell, B. C., Kim, S. H., Styner, M., Wolff, J. J., ... Piven, J. (2017). Early brain development in infants at high risk for autism spectrum disorder. *Nature, 542*(7641), 348–351.

Helgeland, O., Vaudel, M., Juliusson, P. B., Holmen, O. L., Juodakis, J., Bacelis, J., ... Njølstad, R. (2018). Genome-wide association study reveals a dynamic role of common genetic variation in infant and early childhood growth. *bioRxiv,* November 25. http://dx.doi.org/0.110/478255.

Himes, J. H. (2006). Long-term longitudinal studies and implications for the development of an international growth reference for children and adolescents. *Food and Nutrition Bulletin, 27*(Suppl. 4), S199–211.

Holzhauer, S., Zwijsen, R. M. L., Jaddoe, V. W. V., Boehm, G., Moll, H. A., Mulder, P. G., ... Witteman, J. C. M. (2009). Sonographic assessment of abdominal fat distribution in infancy. *European Journal of Epidemiology, 24*(9), 521–529.

Idriz, S., Patel, J. H., Renani, S. A., Allan, R. A., & Vlahos, I. (2015). CT of normal developmental and variant anatomy of the pediatric skull: Distinguishing trauma from normality. *Radiographics, 35*(5), 1585–1601.

Illingworth, R. S., & Lutz, W. (1965). Head circumference of infants related to body weight. *Archives of Disease in Childhood, 40*(214), 672–676.

Janssen, P. A., Thiessen, P., Klein, M. C., Whitfield, M. F., Macnab, Y. C., & Cullis-Kuhl, S. C. (2007). Standards for the measurement of birth weight, length and head circumference at term in neonates of European, Chinese and South Asian ancestry. *Open Medicine, 1*(2), e74–288.

Jensen, R. K. (1981). The effect of a 12-month growth period on the body moments of inertia of children. *Medicine and Science in Sports and Exercise, 13*(4), 238–242.

Johnson, L., Llewellyn, C. H., van Jaarsveld, C. H. M., Cole, T. J., & Wardle, J. (2011). Genetic and environmental influences on infant growth: Prospective analysis of the Gemini twin birth cohort. *PloS One, 6*(5), e19918.

Johnson, T. S., Engstrom, J. L., & Gelhar, D. K. (1997). Intra- and interexaminer reliability of anthropometric measurements of term infants. *Journal of Pediatric Gastroenterology and Nutrition, 24*(5), 497–505.

Jukic, A. M., Baird, D. D., Weinberg, C. R., McConnaughey, D. R., & Wilcox, A. J. (2013). Length of human pregnancy and contributors to its natural variation. *Human Reproduction, 28*(10), 2848–2855.

Kabir, N., & Forsum, E. (1993). Estimation of total body fat and subcutaneous adipose tissue in full-term infants less than 3 months old. *Pediatric Research, 34*(4), 448–454.

Karasik, L. B., Tamis-LeMonda, C. S., Ossmy, O., & Adolph, K. E. (2018). The ties that bind: Cradling in Tajikistan. *PLOS ONE, 13*(10), e0204428.

Karsenty, G. (2017). Update on the biology of osteocalcin. *Endocrine Practice, 23*(10), 1270–1274.

Kelly, K. M., Joganic, E. F., Beals, S. P., Riggs, J. A., McGuire, M. K., & Littlefield, T. R. (2018). Helmet treatment of infants with deformational brachycephaly. *Global Pediatric Health, 5*. https://doi.org/10.1177/2333794X18805618.

Kleijkers, S. H. M., van Montfoort, A. P. A., Smits, L. J. M., Viechtbauer, W., Roseboom, T. J., Nelissen , E. C., … Dumoulin, J. C. (2014). IVF culture medium affects post-natal weight in humans during the first 2 years of life. *Human Reproduction, 29*(4), 661–669.

Knickmeyer, R. C., Gouttard, S., Kang, C., Evans, D., Wilber, K., Smith, J. K., … Gilmore, J. H. (2008). A structural MRI study of human brain development from birth to 2 years. *Journal of Neuroscience, 28*(47), 12176–12182.

Knickmeyer, R. C., Wang, J., Zhu, H., Geng, X., Woolson, S., Hamer, R. M., … Gilmore, J. H. (2014). Impact of sex and gonadal steroids on neonatal brain structure. *Cerebral Cortex, 24*(10), 2721–2731.

Knittle, J. L., Timmers, K., Ginsberg-Fellner, F., Brown, R. E., & Katz, D. P. (1979). The growth of adipose tissue in children and adolescents: Cross-sectional and longitudinal studies of adipose cell number and size. *Journal of Clinical Investigation, 63*(2), 239–246.

Kuczmarski, R. J., Ogden, C. L., Guo, S. S., Grummer-Strawn, L. M., Flegal, K. M., Mei, Z., … Johnson, C. L. (2002). 2000 CDC growth charts for the United States: methods and development. *Vital and Health Statistics Series 11: Data from the National Health Survey, 246*, 1–190.

La Berge, A. F. (1991). Mothers and infants, nurses and nursing: Alfred Donné and the medicalization of child care in nineteenth-century France. *Journal of the History of Medicine and Allied Sciences, 46*(1), 20–43.

Lam, S., Luerssen, T. G., Hadley, C., Daniels, B., Strickland, B. A., Brookshire, J., & Pan, I. W. (2017). The health belief model and factors associated with adherence to treatment recommendations for positional plagiocephaly. *Journal of Neurosurgery Pediatrics, 19*(3), 282–288.

Lampl, M., & Johnson, M. L. (2011a). Infant growth in length follows prolonged sleep and increased naps. *Sleep, 34*(5), 641–650.

(2011b). Infant head circumference growth is saltatory and coupled to length growth. *Early Human Development, 87*(5), 361–368.

Lampl, M., Mummert, A., & Schoen, M. (2016). Promoting healthy growth or feeding obesity? The need for evidence-based oversight of infant nutritional supplement claims. *Healthcare, 4*(4), 84. https://doi.org/10.3390/healthcare4040084

Lampl, M., & Schoen, M. (2017). How long bones grow children: Mechanistic paths to variation in human height growth. *American Journal of Human Biology, 29*(2), e22983.

Lampl, M., & Thompson, A. L. (2007). Growth chart curves do not describe individual growth biology. *American Journal of Human Biology, 19*(5), 643–653.

Lampl, M., Veldhuis, J. D., & Johnson, M. L. (1992). Saltation and stasis: A model of human growth. *Science, 258*(5083), 801–803.

Laughlin, J., Luerssen, T. G., Dias, M. S., & American Academy of Pediatrics Committee on Practice and Ambulatory Medicine (2011). Prevention and management of positional skull deformities in infants. *Pediatrics, 128*(6), 1236–1241.

Lee, H. S., Kim, S. J., & Kwon, J. -Y. (2018). Parents' perspectives and clinical effectiveness of cranial-molding orthoses in infants with plagiocephaly. *Annals of Rehabilitation Medicine, 42* 5), 737–747.

Lindley, A. A., Benson, J. E., Grimes, C., Cole, T. M., & Herman, A. A. (1999). The relationship in neonates between clinically measured head circumference and brain volume estimated from head CT-scans. *Early Human Development, 56*(1), 17–29.

Lipira, A. B., Gordon, S., Darvann, T. A., Hermann, N. V., van Pelt, A. E., Naidoo, S. D., ... Kane, A. A. (2010). Helmet versus active repositioning for plagiocephaly: A three-dimensional analysis. *Pediatrics, 126*(4), e936–945.

Livshits G., Peter I., Vainder M., & Hauspie, R. (2000) Genetic analysis of growth curve parameters of body weight, height and head circumference. *Annals Human Biology, 27*(3):299–312.

Martínez-Abadías, N., Esparza, M., Sjøvold, T., González-José, R., Santos, M., & Hernández, M. (2009). Heritability of human cranial dimensions: Comparing the evolvability of different cranial regions. *Journal of Anatomy, 214*(1), 19–35.

Martini, M., Klausing, A., Lüchters, G., Heim, N., & Messing-Jünger, M. (2018). Head circumference: A useful single parameter for skull volume development in cranial growth analysis? *Head & Face Medicine, 14*(1), 3.

Martorell, R. (2017). Improved nutrition in the first 1000 days and adult human capital and health. *American Journal of Human Biology, 29*(2). doi: 10.1002/ajhb.22952.

McCammon, R. W. (1970). *Human growth and development.* Oxford: Charles C. Thomas.

Mehta, A., & Hindmarsh, P. C. (2002). The use of somatropin (recombinant growth hormone). in children of short stature. *Paediatric Drugs, 4*(1), 37–47.

Mei, Z., Grummer-Strawn, L. M., Thompson, D., & Dietz, W. H. (2004). Shifts in percentiles of growth during early childhood: Analysis of longitudinal data from the California Child Health and Development Study. *Pediatrics, 113*(6), e617–627.

Montgomery, S., Bartley, M., & Wilkinson, R. (1997). Family conflict and slow growth. *Archives of Disease in Childhood, 77*(4), 326–330.

Natale, V., & Rajagopalan, A. (2014). Worldwide variation in human growth and the World Health Organization growth standards: A systematic review. *British Medical Journal: Open, 4*(1), e003735.

Newell, K. M., & Wade, M. G. (2018). Physical growth, body scale, and perceptual-motor development. *Advances in Child Development and Behavior, 55*, 205–243.

Obri, A., Khrimian, L., Karsenty, G., & Oury, F. (2018). Osteocalcin in the brain: From embryonic development to age-related decline in cognition. *Nature Reviews. Endocrinology, 14*(3), 174–182.

Oury, F., Khrimian, L., Denny, C. A., Gardin, A., Chaouni, A., Goedden, N., ... Karsenty, G. (2013). Maternal and offspring pools of osteocalcin influence brain development and functions. *Cell, 155*(1), 228–241.

Persing, J., James, H., Swanson, J., Kattwinkel, J., & American Academy of Pediatrics Committee on Practice and Ambulatory Medicine (2003). Prevention and management of positional skull deformities in infants. *Pediatrics, 112*(1), 199–202.

Pindrik, J., Ye, X., Ji, B.G., Pendleton, C., & Ahn, E. S. (2014). Anterior fontanelle closure and size in full-term children based on head computed tomography. *Clinical Pediatrics, 53*(12), 1149–1157.

Piven, J., Elison, J. T., & Zylka, M. J. (2018). Toward a conceptual framework for early brain and behavior development in autism. *Molecular Psychiatry, 23*(1), 165.

Pomeroy, E., Stock, J. T., Cole, T. J., O'Callaghan, M., & Wells, J. C. K. (2014). Relationships between neonatal weight, limb lengths, skinfold thicknesses, body breadths and circumferences in an Australian cohort. *PLOS One, 9*(8), e105108.

Ramanathan, C., Xu, H., Khan, S. K., Shen, Y., Gitis, P. J., Welsh, D. K., ... Liu, A. C. (2014) Cell type-specific functions of period genes revealed by novel adipocyte and hepatocyte circadian clock models. *PLoS Genet, 10*(4), e1004244. doi:10.1371/journal.pgen.1004244.

Raymond, G. V., & Holmes, L. B. (1994). Head circumference standards in neonates. *Journal of Child Neurology, 9*(1), 63–66.

Roche, A. F., & Guo, S. (1992). Development of reference data for increments in variables related to growth. *American Journal of Human Biology, 4*(3), 365–371.

Rose, C., Parker, A., Jefferson, B., & Cartmell, E. (2015). The characterization of feces and urine: A review of the literature to inform advanced treatment technology. *Critical Reviews in Environmental Science and Technology, 45*(17), 1827–1879.

Roy, S. M., Fields, D. A., Mitchell, J. A., Hawkes, C. P., Kelly, A., Wu, G. D., ... McCormack, S. E. (2019). Body mass index is a better indicator of body composition than weight-for-length at age 1 month. *Journal of Pediatrics, 204*, 77–83.

Scerri, E. M. L., Thomas, M. G., Manica, A., Gunz, P., Stock, J. T., Stringer, C., ... Chikhl, L. (2018). Did our species evolve in subdivided populations across Africa, and why does it matter? *Trends in Ecology and Evolution, 33*(8), 582–594.

Schneider, K., Zernicke, R. F., Ulrich, B. D., Jensen, J. L., & Thelen, E. (1990). Understanding movement control in infants through the analysis of limb intersegmental dynamics. *Journal of Motor Behavior, 22*(4), 493–520.

Smit, D. J. A., Luciano, M., Bartels, M., van Beijsterveldt, C. E. M., Wright, M. J., Hansell, N. K., ... Boomsma, D. I. (2010). Heritability of head size in Dutch and Australian twin families at ages 0–50 years. *Twin Research and Human Genetics, 13*(4), 370–380.

Smith, D. W., Truog, W., Rogers, J. E., Greitzer, L. J., Skinner, A. L., McCann, J. J., & Harvey, M. A. (1976). Shifting linear growth during infancy: Illustration of genetic factors in growth from fetal life through infancy. *Journal of Pediatrics, 89*(2), 225–230.

Teager, S. J., Constantine, S., Lottering, N., & Anderson, P. J. (2018). Physiologic closure time of the metopic suture in South Australian infants from 3D CT scans. *Child's Nervous System, 35*(2), 329–335.

Treit, S., Zhou, D., Chudley, A. E., Andrew, G., Rasmussen, C., Nikkel, S. M., … Beaulieu, C. (2016). Relationships between head circumference, brain volume and cognition in children with prenatal alcohol exposure. *PloS One, 11*(2), e0150370.

Tubbs, R. S., Salter, E. G., & Oakes, W. J. (2006). Artificial deformation of the human skull: A review. *Clinical Anatomy, 19*(4), 372–377.

Velazquez, M. A., Sheth, B., Smith, S. J., Eckert, J. J., Osmond, C., & Fleming, T. P. (2018). Insulin and branched-chain amino acid depletion during mouse preimplantation embryo culture programmes body weight gain and raised blood pressure during early postnatal life. *Biochimica et Biophysica Acta. Molecular Basis of Disease, 1864*(2), 590–600.

van der Linden, V. (2016). Description of 13 infants born during October 2015–January 2016 with congenital Zika virus infection without microcephaly at birth. *Morbidity and Mortality Weekly Report, 65*(47), 1343–1348.

van Dommelen P., de Gunst, M. C., van der Vaart, A. W., & Boomsma, D. I. (2004). Genetic study of the height and weight process during infancy. *Twin Research, 7*(6), 607–616.

van Dyck, L. I., & Morrow, E. M. (2017). Genetic control of postnatal human brain growth. *Current Opinion in Neurology, 30*(1), 114–124.

van Vlimmeren, L. A., Engelbert, R. H., Pelsma, M., Groenewoud, H. M., Boere-Boonekamp M. M., & van der Sanden, M. (2017). The course of skull deformation from birth to 5 years of age: A prospective cohort study. *European Journal of Pediatrics, 176*(1), 11–21.

van Wijk, R. M., van Vlimmeren, L. A., Groothuis-Oudshoorn, C. G. M., van der Ploeg, C. P. B., Ijzerman, M. J., & Boore-Boonekamp, M. M. (2014). Helmet therapy in infants with positional skull deformation: Randomised controlled trial. *British Medical Journal, 348*, g2741.

Wagner, D. R. (2013). Ultrasound as a tool to assess body fat. *Journal of Obesity, 2013*, 1–9.

Weaver, D. D., & Christian, J. C. (1980). Familial variation of head size and adjustment for parental head circumference. *Journal of Pediatrics, 96*(6), 990–994.

World Health Organization (2006). *WHO child growth standards: Length/height-for-age, weight-for-age, weight-for-length, weight-for-height and body mass index-for-age: Methods and development.* Geneva: WHO.

Wright, C. M., & Emond, A. (2015). Head growth and neurocognitive outcomes. *Pediatrics, 135*(6), e1393–1398.

3 Dynamic Epigenetic Impact of the Environment on the Developing Brain

Frances A. Champagne

3.1 Introduction

Development is a dynamic process shaped by the interactions between genes and environments. Within the field of developmental biology, the complex interactions between genes and their products that create the foundation for cellular differentiation and the formation of the nervous system have been well described. Advances in molecular biology have permitted increasing precision in the characterization of the cascade of molecular changes that link genes to specific developmental endpoints. However, beyond addressing questions regarding the processes linking a gene to a phenotypic outcome, description of these molecular changes has also provided insight into the ways in which the environment induces lasting biological effects. Though environments – particularly characteristics of the social world around us – are typically viewed as a separate and distinct influence from genes, there is increasing understanding of the interplay between genes and environments. Within the evolving field of epigenetics, the modification of gene regulatory mechanisms has been demonstrated as a consequence of a broad range of environmental conditions (Baccarelli & Bollati, 2009; Champagne, 2016). These modifications have implications for the expression of genes that shape neurodevelopment, health, and behavior, and have been hypothesized to be the mediators between the environment and phenotypic outcomes (Cortessis et al., 2012). The malleability of epigenetic mechanisms in early development, coupled with the knowledge of early life sensitive periods, has resulted in increasing integration of epigenetics in the study of infancy.

The broad application of epigenetics within developmental biology, environmental sciences, psychology, and psychiatry has highlighted the converging biological pathways through which experiences, particularly those occurring early in development, can exert a lasting impact on health and behavior. A critical question that emerges from this work is how diverse forms of experience, including social, nutritional, and physical, are able to induce molecular-level changes. There is also increasing speculation that the multigenerational transmission of environmental influences involves epigenetic mechanisms (Champagne, 2008; Nilsson, Sadler-Riggleman, & Skinner, 2018). Within this context, epigenetics can account for both the direct effects of environmental exposures occurring within an individual's life span and for the propagation of these effects across generations. The notion that biological and behavioral traits are shaped by our ancestors has traditionally emerged from genetic studies. However, the introduction of epigenetics into discussions of inheritance allows for a broader, more inclusive, and dynamic perspective on the mechanisms that shape our similarity and dissimilarity to our ancestors and descendants (Champagne, 2016; Danchin et al., 2011).

The implications of the ever-expanding "epigenetic perspective" for developmental science, medicine, and public health are becoming increasingly realized. In this chapter, the historical context of the field of epigenetics and modern notions regarding epigenetic mechanisms will be described followed by a more in-depth look at how epigenetics has been integrated into studies of early life experiences occurring prenatally and during infancy. Though much of the mechanistic work in this field is conducted in animal models, the emerging work in humans will be emphasized. The role of epigenetic mechanisms in the transmission of environmentally induced changes in brain and behavior will be explored and the potential implications of these multigenerational effects for public policy will also be addressed. This chapter will also consider the role of sociocultural context, namely how individual, family, and community-level experiences shape infancy, and the need for improved understanding of proximal and distal epigenetic influences that lead to the biological embedding within the brain of early life experiences.

3.2 Evolving Concepts in Gene–Environment Interactions: The Epigenetic Perspective

The concept of gene–environment interactions has become ingrained within the developmental sciences and more broadly in the biological and social sciences. The general principle of a gene–environment interaction is that genes may predict phenotypic outcomes – such as behavior, growth, or health – but the predictive utility of genes is moderated by the types of environments to which an individual is exposed. For example, a gene variant (e.g., having gene A vs. gene B) may significantly predict hyperactivity if a child has been raised in a highly stressful environment, but this gene variant may not predict hyperactivity when an individual has been raised in a highly nurturing environment. Gene–environment interactions also provide insights into the conditions under which an environment would impact phenotypic outcomes. In the case of the hyperactivity example, increasingly stressful environments are more likely to increase hyperactivity in individuals with a certain genetic variant (e.g., gene A) whereas individuals who have a different genetic variant (e.g., gene B) are buffered from the effects of stressful environments.

The simple theoretical conclusion of studies indicating a gene–environment interaction is that the prediction of phenotypic outcomes is likely to be enhanced by knowing about both the genetic and environmental characteristics of an individual. However, the study of gene–environment interactions is methodologically far from simple and can yield effects that are challenging to replicate due in part to the broad definitions of gene (e.g., twin studies, candidate genes, genome-wide DNA sequencing) and environment (e.g., socioeconomic status, exposure to trauma, nutrition) and the occurrence of correlations between genes and environmental exposures (Jaffee & Price, 2007). Consistent with the theoretical example of hyperactivity, psychosocial factors (early life social adversity) have been found to interact with the presence of gene variants considered candidate genes for attention-deficit hyperactivity disorder (ADHD) in the prediction of ADHD (Nigg, Nikolas, & Burt, 2010). Though this effect may not always be observed (see Gould, Coventry, Olson, & Byrne, 2018), the presence of a gene–environment interaction raises many questions regarding the interplay between the world around us and our biology.

The notion that knowledge of genetic characteristics is insufficient to predict the diversity of phenotypic outcomes during development is the foundation of epigenetics. The term "epigenetics" was originally coined by the developmental biologist Conrad Waddington (1905–75) to describe the very dynamic process through which genes and their products interact (Noble, 2015; Waddington, 1940). By introducing the concept that there was a biological feature of genes above the genome (using the Greek prefix "epi" meaning upon or above), epigenetics provides a way of thinking about development that embraces the complexity of events occurring from fertilization through to infancy. As a developmental biologist, Conrad Waddington was all too familiar with the phenomenon of cellular differentiation – a process through which genetically identical cells acquire unique phenotypic characteristics. Beyond acquisition of characteristics, epigenetics also contributes to a better understanding of how these characteristics are maintained. Epigenetics is currently defined as the study of heritable phenotype changes that do not involve alterations in the DNA sequence (Dupont, Armant, & Brenner, 2009). Cells that differentiate do not revert to their ancestral states of undifferentiated stem cells. Cells retain their differentiated state and when they divide they transmit this state to the cells they produce (Mohn & Schübeler, 2009). Thus, the epigenetic state of cells is heritable during the process of mitosis. There are many questions raised by the role of epigenetics in cellular differentiation. Though the genetic state of a cell is determined by the combined genomes of mother and father at the time of fertilization, what determines the epigenetic state of a cell? To answer this question, it is necessary to reintroduce the environment as a critical factor that regulates development. During the past two decades, it has become apparent that the environment of a cell – and of the organism in which the cell resides – is an epigenetic modulator (Feil & Fraga, 2012; Meaney, 2010). Environments shape the epigenetic characteristics of the genome and these

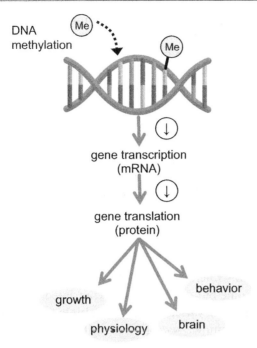

Figure 3.1. *DNA methylation and regulation of phenotypic outcomes. DNA methylation involves a chemical modification to DNA whereby a methyl group (Me) is added to cytosines within the DNA sequence. This epigenetic modification typically results in reduced gene expression through transcriptional silencing. As a consequence of reduced transcription, translation of mRNA to protein is reduced with broad phenotypic consequences.*

characteristics impact genome function with consequences for the development of the organism. Genes and environments interact through epigenetics.

Advances in molecular biology have provided the tools needed to translate the theoretical notion of epigenetics and gene–environment interactions into biological processes that explain how genes are regulated. Within studies of epigenetic mechanisms, there are currently three general types of molecular changes that impact gene regulation and are malleable in response to environmental experiences: DNA methylation, histone modifications, and noncoding RNA. Among the nucleotides that create the DNA sequence, cytosines can become chemically modified through the addition of a methyl group (see Figure 3.1). This process is referred to as DNA methylation and serves a critical role in cellular differentiation (Razin & Riggs, 1980). The methylation of cytosines within DNA can lead to long-term gene silencing (Razin, 1998), though the location of the methylated DNA and other contextual factors may determine the ultimate impact that DNA methylation has on gene expression (Guibert & Weber, 2013; Jones, 2012).

In addition to DNA methylation, epigenetic regulation of genes can be achieved through chemical modification of histone proteins and altered expression of noncoding RNAs. DNA is wrapped around a cluster of histone proteins and it is this DNA-histone complex that allows the very dense compacting of DNA in the cell nucleus. Like all proteins, histones can become chemically modified. Due to the close interactions between DNA and the histones, these chemical modifications can impact the likelihood that gene expression will occur. Histone modifications can result in both increases and decreases in gene expression – with the prediction of gene regulatory effects dependent on the type and location within the protein of the modification (Cheung, Allis, & Sassone-Corsi, 2000; Jenuwein & Allis, 2001).

In the case of noncoding RNAs, the epigenetic regulation of gene function can occur both at the level of transcription (DNA to mRNA) and translation (mRNA to protein). Though we typically think of DNA as being an instruction manual to build proteins, a considerable portion of the genome does not serve this role. Noncoding RNAs are RNA molecules that are encoded by the genome but do not become translated into proteins (Eddy, 2001). These molecules are varied and have multiple functions relating to gene regulation. For example, microRNAs (miRNAs) – small noncoding RNAs – inhibit mRNA production and also target existing mRNA for degradation.

Collectively, DNA methylation, histone modifications, and noncoding RNAs create the epigenetic landscape that Conrad Waddington had conceived of as the fundamental process of development (Baedke, 2013). The malleability of this epigenetic landscape by the environment illustrates the occurrence of gene–environment interactions at the level of biology – an interplay that is both dynamic and stable allowing for phenotypic variation to emerge and persist.

3.3 Epigenetic Impact of Fetal Environments on the Developing Brain

The prenatal period is a time of rapid brain development and sets the stage for later emerging outcomes in infancy and beyond. Prenatal maternal exposure to toxins, variation in nutritional environments, and stress can impact the developing fetal brain either through direct exposure to the environmental agent or indirectly via dysregulation of placental function or maternal physiology (Monk, Spicer, & Champagne, 2012). These pathways are not mutually exclusive and it is likely the case that disruption to fetal development and infant outcomes is the product of additive and interactive direct and indirect exposure effects (see Figure 3.2). These outcomes are associated with and in some cases shown to be mediated by environmentally induced epigenetic changes.

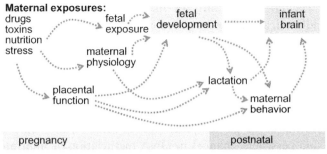

Figure 3.2. *Complex pathways through which prenatal maternal environmental exposures impact the infant brain. Maternal environmental exposures occurring during pregnancy can impact the infant brain through both direct exposure-induced epigenetic changes in the fetal brain and indirect pathways involving epigenetic effects in the placenta and altered maternal physiology and behavior that extends into the postnatal period. Interplay between the fetus, placenta, and mother contribute to changes in infant brain development.*

3.3.1 Drug and Toxin Exposure

Consistent with a growing literature on *in utero* drug and toxin exposure effects in animal models, studies in humans indicate that these exposures are associated with epigenetic changes in the placenta, fetus, and infant. Longitudinal studies illustrate the consequences of maternal smoking during pregnancy for child development, physical and psychological health, including increased hyperactivity (Melchior et al., 2015), conduct disorder (Talati, Wickramaratne, Wesselhoeft, & Weissman, 2017), and asthma (Hu et al., 1997). Analyses of genome-wide DNA methylation levels indicate that maternal smoking during pregnancy results in broad changes to DNA methylation in the placenta, fetal cord blood, and buccal cell samples in children at 3–6 years of age (Shorey-Kendrick et al., 2017), though the consequences of these changes for outcomes in infancy are unclear. Analyses from the Avon Longitudinal Study of Parents and Children (ALSPAC) similarly demonstrate the impact of both maternal smoking and alcohol consumption on cord blood DNA methylation levels and identifies these epigenetic changes as a critical intermediary between the prenatal environment and subsequent substance use risk in adolescence (Cecil et al., 2016). Maternal levels of the endocrine disrupting chemical bisphenol A (BPA) are associated with altered DNA methylation levels within the brain-derived neurotrophic factor (*BDNF*) gene in cord blood samples taken at the time of birth, such that high levels of maternal BPA are associated with increased *BDNF* DNA methylation. The *BDNF* gene plays a critical role in neural plasticity and facilitates emotional and cognitive development. This epigenetic effect of *in utero* BPA on *BDNF* is only observed in males – an indication of sex differences in the epigenetic effects of exposures – and may explain the particular vulnerability of males to BPA-associated behavioral changes in childhood, including increased emotionally reactive and aggressive behaviors (Kundakovic et al., 2015; Perera et al., 2012).

3.3.2 Prenatal Nutrition

In humans, exposure to extreme reductions in caloric intake during pregnancy induces metabolic and neurodevelopmental abnormalities in offspring (Susser & Lin, 1992) and persistent changes in DNA methylation of imprinted genes (Heijmans et al., 2008). The impact of timing of exposure is highlighted by these studies and the epigenetic changes observed are associated with famine exposure in the preconception and early pregnancy period. Imprinted genes may be particularly susceptible to environmentally induced epigenetic disruption due to the particular dynamics of their regulation and these genes play a critical role in placental function, brain development and somatic growth (Wilkinson, Davies, & Isles, 2007). During fetal development, folate is an essential resource needed for neural tube closure and supplementation of maternal diets with folate preconception and during pregnancy has been associated with a marked reduction in neurodevelopmental abnormality (Wilson et al., 2003). Increased dietary folate during pregnancy alters levels of DNA methylation within imprinted genes within the placenta and fetal cord blood (Pauwels et al., 2016; Tserga, Binder, & Michels, 2017). Obesity and a high-fat diet are associated with impaired placental function and genome-wide changes in DNA methylation and hydroxymethylation (a chemical variant of methylation) within placental tissue (Mitsuya et al., 2017). Epigenetic changes associated with maternal obesity are also observed in blood samples from newborn infants (Sharp et al., 2017) and maternal BMI is associated with epigenetic age acceleration – a DNA methylation-based metric of biological aging – in children, suggesting a biological burden incurred by maternal weight/diet (Horvath, 2013; Simpkin et al., 2016).

3.3.3 Maternal Stress

There is an expansive literature on the effects of maternal stress during pregnancy on offspring development in animals and humans, with outcomes being observed prenatally and persisting across the life span. During infancy, outcomes associated with prenatal stress can include poorer sleep quality, increased anxiety, and reduced cognitive ability. One of the challenges posed by this literature is the very broad definition of stress. Animal studies tend to rely on physical or social stressors but can also include food restriction and immune challenge. These exposures may vary in their predictability, chronicity, severity, and timing during pregnancy (Weinstock, Fride, & Hertzberg, 1988). Similarly, human studies of prenatal stress include measures of self-report perceived stress, elevated glucocorticoids, exposure to trauma, exposure to famine, and maternal psychopathology (primarily anxiety and depression). There are likely unique effects on offspring development specific to exposure type and diverse pathways through which each of these exposures lead to biological change in offspring (Wadhwa, Entringer, Buss, & Lu, 2011). However, a common outcome of broadly defined prenatal stress is preterm birth – suggestive of disruption to the *in utero* environment (Hobel, Goldstein, & Barrett, 2008; Staneva, Bogossian, Pritchard, & Wittkowski, 2015; Torche & Kleinhaus, 2012). Preterm birth is a risk factor for poorer neurodevelopmental outcomes, including a heightened risk of autism spectrum disorder (ASD), attention deficits, and cognitive impairment (Schieve et al., 2016). These deficits may be the consequence of altered connectivity between brain regions and a delayed maturation of white matter tracts (Rogers, Lean, Wheelock, & Smyser, 2018).

Epigenetic changes within the placenta, fetus, and infant as a consequence of both prenatal stress and preterm birth have been observed. Perceived psychosocial stress during pregnancy is associated with increased DNA methylation of the *HSD11B2* gene in the placenta. The *HSD11B2* gene encodes for an enzyme that inactivates stress hormones and buffers the fetus from elevated maternal glucocorticoids. Increased DNA methylation of this gene may lead to elevated exposure of the fetus to stress hormones.

This placental epigenetic change is also associated with delays in fetal neurodevelopment indicated by reduced autonomic coupling between fetal movement and heart rate. Moreover, mediation analyses indicate that stress-associated placenta epigenetic changes statistically mediate the effects of maternal stress on offspring brain development (Monk et al., 2016). Trauma and chronic stress exposure during pregnancy are associated with altered DNA methylation within the *BDNF* gene in mother's blood, placenta, and fetal cord blood (Kertes et al., 2017). Maternal depression during pregnancy is associated with altered DNA methylation in the cord blood of neonates (Non, Binder, Kubzansky, & Michels, 2014; Oberlander et al., 2008) and in buccal cells of 3-month-old infants (Braithwaite, Kundakovic, Ramchandani, Murphy, & Champagne, 2015), which may have consequences for the stress reactivity of infants. Unfortunately, the pharmacological treatment of depression, particularly using selective serotonin reuptake inhibitors (SSRIs), is also associated with epigenetic (Gurnot et al., 2015), neurodevelopmental (Millard, Weston-Green, & Newell, 2017), and functional outcomes in offspring (Brown et al., 2016), highlighting the need for careful evaluation of treatment approaches for mood disorders during pregnancy that benefit the mother without potential harm to the fetus. Among infants born preterm as a consequence of prenatal adversity, epigenetic changes, such as increased DNA methylation of the *NR3C1* gene (which encodes for the glucocorticoid receptor) in buccal cells correlates with poorer neurodevelopment (Lester et al., 2015). Collectively, this growing body of literature illustrates the complex pathways through which prenatal stress can impact development and the role of epigenetics in predicting exposure and outcomes. A challenge for these studies and the broader literature on environmentally induced epigenetic changes is bridging the link between exposure-induced epigenetic variation and consequent outcomes observed in brain and behavior.

3.4 Social Environments in Infancy: Epigenetics of Adversity and Resilience

The social context of development can have enduring effects on a child. Initial observations of the association between parent–offspring separation, infant distress, and impairments in the parent–offspring social relationship (Bowlby & World Health Organization, 1952) have been coupled with decades of work in humans, primates, and rodents illustrating the impact of mother–infant social interactions on brain development and behavior. Mammalian development during postnatal development is shaped by variation in the quality and frequency of caregiver contact. In humans, deprivation of postnatal parental care through institutionalization results in increased rates of symptoms of ASD, poorer social engagement, attentional deficits, and hyperactivity (Sonuga-Barke et al., 2017). These effects are associated with duration of deprivation, such that infants exposed to less than 6 months of institutional rearing and then fostered into nurturing homes display fewer deficits in functioning. Brain changes associated with institutional rearing include significant reductions in prefrontal cortex and hippocampal volume (Hodel et al., 2015), increased positive coupling of activity between the ventral striatum and prefrontal cortex (Fareri et al., 2017), and broad changes in connectivity within brain networks critical for cognitive functioning (Stamoulis, Vanderwert, Zeanah, Fox, & Nelson, 2017). Comparison of children who remain institutionalized and those who are placed in nurturing foster homes indicates that deficits in social and cognitive functioning can be ameliorated (Almas et al., 2012; Troller-Renfree, McDermott, Nelson, Zeanah, & Fox, 2015). Disruptions to the early child–parent relationship in the form of abuse and neglect increase risk of psychopathology, alter immune and neuroendocrine function, and impact brain structure and function (Bernard, Frost, Bennett, & Lindhiem, 2017; Busso et al., 2017; D'Elia et al., 2018; McLaughlin & Lambert, 2017). Variation in maternal caregiving – particularly sensitivity to infant cues – can similarly impact developmental trajectories in infants such that reduced maternal sensitivity is associated with increased likelihood of socially inhibited behavior, aggressive play behavior, and elevated levels of internalizing behavior (Hane, Henderson, Reeb-Sutherland, & Fox, 2010).

The role of epigenetics in the long-term effects of early social interactions was first established in rodents. Decreased postnatal pup licking and grooming by rat dams is associated with increased glucocorticoid response to stress, behavioral inhibition, poorer cognitive performance, and increased aggressive social behavior (Caldji et al., 1998; Liu, Diorio, Day, Francis, & Meaney, 2000;

Liu et al., 1997; Parent & Meaney, 2008). Cross-fostering studies confirm that these phenotypic outcomes are predicted by the postnatal rearing environment and are associated with altered expression and protein levels of hippocampal glucocorticoid receptors (Francis, Diorio, Liu, & Meaney, 1999; Liu et al., 1997). Within hippocampal tissue from rat pups there is increased DNA methylation of the *Nr3c1* gene in offspring that receive low levels of care (Weaver et al., 2004). Increased *NR3C1* DNA methylation is also observed in human postmortem hippocampal tissue of individuals with a history of childhood maltreatment (McGowan et al., 2009). Genome-wide DNA methylation assays reveal that effects of childhood maltreatment are not specific to the *NR3C1* gene promoter and include both hypomethylation and hypermethylation at hundreds of gene promoters within the hippocampus (Labonté et al., 2012).

Epigenetic biomarkers have been observed in peripheral tissue samples (e.g., blood, buccal cells, saliva) associated with exposure to a broad range of childhood experiences. Childhood adversity, including low socioeconomic status, parental mental and physical illness, and parental death are associated with altered DNA methylation in peripheral cells in children, adolescents, and adults (Bush et al., 2018; Houtepen et al., 2018; Papale, Seltzer, Madrid, Pollak, & Alisch, 2018). Overall increases in DNA methylation are observed in blood cells from children raised in institutional care compared to children raised by their biological families (Naumova et al., 2012). Maternal depression is associated with global DNA methylation changes in infants (Cicchetti, Hetzel, Rogosch, Handley, & Toth, 2016). In adulthood, increased DNA methylation of the *NR3C1* gene in blood samples is related to the severity of exposure to childhood emotional abuse (Farrell et al., 2018). Among 3–5-year-olds, childhood maltreatment (abuse/neglect) is associated with altered DNA methylation of the FK506 binding protein 5 (*FKBP5*) gene – which plays a critical role in the neuroendocrine response to stress – and these effects interact with degree of contextual stressors such as separation from a caregiver, housing instability, and neighborhood violence (Parade et al., 2017). The experience of sexual abuse in childhood is predictive of epigenetic age acceleration in buccal cells in adulthood (Lawn et al., 2018). Low socioeconomic status during childhood is also associated with epigenetic age acceleration in blood cells and this effect can be ameliorated if there is an upward trajectory of socioeconomic status across the life span (Fiorito et al., 2017).

The growing literature on the epigenetic effects of childhood exposure to social adversity is accompanied by increasing evidence that epigenetic changes observed at birth or during infancy can predict childhood outcomes. It should be noted, however, that correlations between exposures and epigenetic outcomes or epigenetic variation and neurobehavioral outcomes does not necessarily indicate a particular mechanistic pathway linking exposure to altered brain development. The interpretation of the meaning of peripheral epigenetic biomarkers in humans must be tempered with caution when making predictions about brain function and behavior. Placental DNA methylation profiling reveals associations between DNA methylation at a variety of genomic locations and newborn neurobehavioral outcomes, such as attention, arousal, and movement (Paquette et al., 2016, 2014). Among preterm infants, increased DNA methylation of *NR3C1* and decreased methylation of *HSD11B2* in buccal cells is associated with increased neurobehavioral risk assessment likely related to alterations in the stress reactivity of infants (Lester et al., 2015). DNA methylation within the oxytocin receptor gene (*OXTR*) is predictive of behavioral resilience (reduced likelihood of conduct disorder in childhood) to prenatal and postnatal adversity (Milaniak et al., 2017). Infant attachment (secure vs. disorganized) is a significant predictor of childhood outcomes and can buffer infant/child development from the effects of exposure to contextual adversity. Genome-wide DNA methylation analyses have revealed that infant attachment accounts for over 11% of variation in DNA methylation and that combining measures of infant attachment and child genetic makeup is the best strategy for predicting DNA methylation profiles (Garg et al., 2018). Though the mediating role of epigenetic changes such as DNA methylation in the link between environments and infant/child outcomes has yet to be established, these studies clearly point to the importance of gene–environment interplay in shaping both risk and resilience.

3.5 Across Generations: The Evolving Concept of Epigenetic Inheritance

Exploration of genetic influences on infant development have focused on both the emergence of traits and the implications of genes for stability and change in phenotype across generations. This same broad focus has extended to epigenetic variation that is associated with both exposures to salient environmental cues and phenotypic variation. Unlike DNA – which has a well-described system of generational transmission – epigenetic variation has a less clear path as an inherited biological signal. However, there is growing evidence for the phenomenon of intergenerational and transgenerational effects of environmental exposures on neurodevelopment and behavior that is increasingly identifying epigenetic mechanisms as important mediators of this transmission (Champagne, 2016). Studies of prenatal maternal exposure to toxins/drugs, nutritional variation, and stress are illustrative of an intergenerational transmission from mother to offspring – though in these cases, the fetus may have direct exposure. The indirect exposure routes associated with the prenatal period, such as changes to placental function, altered maternal physiology, and even continued impact of the exposure on maternal postpartum brain and behavior provide some insight into the mechanism of intergenerational effects in the matriline (Champagne, 2008). In mammals, females provide the context of development through internal fertilization, gestation, and reliance on lactation as a primary form of infant feeding. Environmental conditions that impact these contexts of early development are well poised to exert lasting epigenetic effects in offspring. Studies in rodents suggest that these maternal effects can also be propagated to the next generation. Maternal exposure to stress, social isolation, or environmental enrichment (e.g., increased opportunities for physical and social interactions) in rodents is predictive of variation in postpartum maternal LG (Champagne & Meaney, 2006, 2007), which shapes the epigenome of offspring and may account for phenotypic outcomes in offspring (Champagne et al., 2006; McGowan et al., 2011; Weaver et al., 2004). In particular, maternal LG alters the level of DNA methylation within the estrogen receptor alpha gene (*Esr1*) within the developing hypothalamus of female offspring such that low levels (compared to high levels) of maternal LG are associated with increased *Esr1* DNA methylation and epigenetic silencing of the *Esr1* gene (Peña, Neugut, & Champagne, 2013). This epigenetic effect of maternal care emerges during infancy, persists into adulthood, and influences the maternal behavior of females toward their own offspring – creating another generation of neonates exposed to varying levels of maternal LG and a mechanism for multigenerational transmission of phenotypes associated with variation in the experience of maternal care (Champagne, 2008). In rodents, other maternal conditions, such as diet and exposure to glucocorticoids (Moisiadis, Constantinof, Kostaki, Szyf, & Matthews, 2017; Winther et al., 2019), have similarly been shown to impact phenotypes in granddaughters – though the role of maternal care or other elements of maternal reproductive investment in this transmission have yet to be determined.

The transmission of environmental effects across generations is not limited to maternal exposures and there is intriguing evidence – drawn primarily from rodent studies – that the preconception experiences of fathers can exert intergenerational and transgenerational effects on offspring development through epigenetic transmission. In mice and rats, paternal preconception exposure to cocaine (Vassoler, White, Schmidt, Sadri-Vakili, & Pierce, 2013), bisphenol A (Fan et al., 2018), stress (Rodgers, Morgan, Bronson, Revello, & Bale, 2013), and a high-fat diet (Ng et al., 2010) (among many other exposures) is associated with phenotypic characteristics in offspring, grand-offspring, and beyond through the patriline – the descendants of exposed males and their offspring. The presence of these effects in mating systems where exposed males have limited contact with the female mate and no contact with offspring is suggestive that a sperm-mediated transmission of environmentally induced biological changes may mediate these effects (see Figure 3.3). In accordance with this hypothesis, epigenetic changes – including altered DNA methylation, histone modifications, and expression of noncoding RNAs – are observed in sperm of exposed males, including humans (Ben Maamar et al., 2018; Curley, Mashoodh, & Champagne, 2011). Studies in mice demonstrate that manipulation of these epigenetic modifications in the developing embryo can recapitulate the growth and neurodevelopmental effects in offspring that are observed following paternal exposures (Gapp et al., 2014). This paternal epigenetic

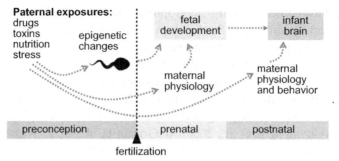

Figure 3.3. *Complex pathways through which paternal preconception environmental exposures impact the infant brain. Paternal environmental exposures occurring during preconception can impact the infant brain through exposure-induced epigenetic changes in sperm that are recapitulated in the fetal and infant brain. Fathers can also exert a developmental influence through their impact on maternal physiology and behavior during the prenatal and postnatal period – which also induces epigenetic changes in the fetus and infant.*

inheritance hypothesis is further supported by evidence that epigenetic changes observed in sperm following paternal environmental exposures in rodents are also observed in the brain of offspring (Dias & Ressler, 2014; Franklin et al., 2010). In humans, there is certainly evidence for the intergenerational impact of fathers, though the mechanism of inheritance is less clear (Bowers & Yehuda, 2016). High levels of dietary intake of methyl donors (methionine, folate, betaine, choline) in human males is associated with increased blood levels of DNA methylation in both the exposed male and in cord blood samples from their offspring, suggesting a epigenetic transmission in humans that may impact developmental outcomes (Pauwels et al., 2016).

3.6 Sociocultural Context of Families, Individuals, and the Epigenome

The focus on proximal factors (toxins, drugs, diet, parent–infant interactions) that influence development and the epigenetic transmission of traits across generations offers a very narrow view on the cause–effect relationships that contribute to individual differences in risk and resilience. Though this view creates testable hypotheses and identifies targets for intervention, it does obscure the broader context in which these proximal variables reside and the interdependencies between proximal predictors of outcomes and context. For example, low socioeconomic status is associated with several individual- and family-level environmental exposures, including nutritional deficits, elevated toxin exposure, family conflict, housing insecurity, and harsh parenting. These more proximal influences have been shown to impact development and it is assumed that socioeconomic status induces epigenetic and phenotypic changes via these individual- and family-level exposures. However, epigenetic analyses indicate that socioeconomic status has a unique epigenetic effect that is broader (impacting more genetic loci) and generally nonoverlapping with the epigenetic effects of family adversity (Bush et al., 2018). Disentangling the routes through which distal and proximal influences exert an epigenetic effect poses a significant challenge but may ultimately improve our capacity to predict the emergence of risk versus resilience among individuals exposed to early life adversity. The utility of this approach is demonstrated by findings that maltreatment is only predictive of *FKBP5* DNA methylation when there is also heightened stress in the family context – such as housing instability and elevated neighborhood violence (Parade et al., 2017). Similarly, cultivating high levels of self-control during development is a predictor of better educational attainment but can also incur a significant biological "cost" in the form of epigenetic age acceleration among individuals from communities characterized by high exposure to discrimination and low socioeconomic status (Miller, Yu, Chen, & Brody, 2015).

The role of contextual variables for the transmission of environmentally induced epigenetic changes across generations also requires careful consideration. Though experimental studies in rodents allow us to control genetic and environmental conditions as a strategy for creating optimal conditions for characterizing cause–effect relationships, these manipulations also create an artificial context for development and reproduction. Demonstrations of epigenetic inheritance may also be restricted to these artificial contexts – or modulated by genetic and environmental factors under more naturalistic conditions. For example, paternal preconception stress effects on offspring that have been observed in mice can be modulated by the quality of the prenatal nutritional environment and postnatal mother–infant interactions (Mashoodh, Habrylo, Gudsnuk, Pelle, & Champagne, 2018). Developmental and multigenerational trajectories may be reinforced or redirected dependent on the prevailing ecological conditions at different periods within the life span. These sociocultural contexts will be particularly important to consider when describing the intergenerational and multigenerational impact of environments in humans. Stress-induced epigenetic transmission, for example, may be reinforced across generations through lack of social mobility and continued exposure to poverty, discrimination, and neighborhood violence. Conversely, epigenetic shifts that predict better health outcomes may be observed when individuals have opportunities to transition into elevated socioeconomic strata (Fiorito et al., 2017).

3.7 Epigenetics and Public Policy

Integration of epigenetics into studies of environmental effects on infant development have provided insights into epigenetic plasticity and the profound epigenetic consequences of adversity. Though much of the current literature on epigenetic effects focuses on adversity, epigenetic plasticity in response to interventions is being increasingly demonstrated. For example, prenatal effects of smoking on DNA methylation and asthma risk can be significantly ameliorated using vitamin C supplementation during pregnancy (Shorey-Kendrick et al., 2017). Family-based interventions that reduce harsh parenting can result in epigenetic age deceleration (Brody, Yu, Chen, Beach, & Miller, 2016). Fostering increased sensory and socioemotional contact between mothers and preterm infants results in improved neurodevelopment and reduced ASD risk (Welch et al., 2015, 2017). Though the epigenetic effects of this intervention strategy are currently unknown, there are likely long-term changes in DNA methylation associated with the experience of these caregiver interactions. Characterization of the epigenetic effects of the environment can strengthen arguments for policy measures that facilitate prevention and intervention strategies. The emerging data on both proximal and distal contextual determinants of epigenetic and neurodevelopmental variation argue for policy changes that address individual-, family-, and community-level adversity. Our increased appreciation of epigenetic transmission across generations may also inform the timescale of program/intervention evaluation. A small epigenetic shift in one generation may accumulate over subsequent generations – leading to either increased risk or increased resilience that could ultimately be observed at a population level.

3.8 Conclusions/Future Directions

The interplay between genes and environments is a fundamental feature of development and advances in our understanding of epigenetic mechanisms and their malleability have promoted a more integrated perspective on this interplay. In humans, evidence for epigenetic effects of prenatal and postnatal environments and their association with infant outcomes is continuing to grow, extending to global epigenomic outcomes and multigenerational effects. Though epigenetic analyses in humans are not typically conducted in the brain, the value of epigenetic biomarkers in peripheral tissues for predicting neurodevelopmental outcomes is evident. Future directions of this work include bridging the mechanistic gap between the occurrence of peripheral epigenetic changes and brain structure/function, expanding our understanding of the epigenetic consequences of nurturing/healthy environments, and integrating sociocultural/contextual factors into the analyses of environmentally induced epigenetic changes emerging during infancy and childhood.

References

Almas, A. N., Degnan, K. A., Radulescu, A., Nelson, C. A., Zeanah, C. H., & Fox, N. A. (2012). Effects of early intervention and the moderating effects of brain activity on institutionalized children's social skills at age 8. *Proceedings of the*

National Academy of Sciences of the United States of America, 109(Suppl. 2), 17228–17231. https://doi.org/10.1073/pnas.1121256109

Baccarelli, A., & Bollati, V. (2009). Epigenetics and environmental chemicals. *Current Opinion in Pediatrics, 21*(2), 243–251.

Baedke, J. (2013). The epigenetic landscape in the course of time: Conrad Hal Waddington's methodological impact on the life sciences. *Studies in History and Philosophy of Science Part C: Studies in History and Philosophy of Biological and Biomedical Sciences, 44*(4, Part B), 756–773. https://doi.org/10.1016/j.shpsc.2013.06.001

Ben Maamar, M., Sadler-Riggleman, I., Beck, D., McBirney, M., Nilsson, E., Klukovich, R., ... Skinner, M. K. (2018). Alterations in sperm DNA methylation, non-coding RNA expression, and histone retention mediate vinclozolin-induced epigenetic transgenerational inheritance of disease. *Environmental Epigenetics, 4*(2), dvy010. https://doi.org/10.1093/eep/dvy010

Bernard, K., Frost, A., Bennett, C. B., & Lindhiem, O. (2017). Maltreatment and diurnal cortisol regulation: A meta-analysis. *Psychoneuroendocrinology, 78*, 57–67. https://doi.org/10.1016/j.psyneuen.2017.01.005

Bowers, M. E., & Yehuda, R. (2016). Intergenerational transmission of stress in humans. *Neuropsychopharmacology: Official Publication of the American College of Neuropsychopharmacology, 41*(1), 232–244. https://doi.org/10.1038/npp.2015.247

Bowlby, J., & World Health Organization. (1952). *Maternal care and mental health : A report prepared on behalf of the World Health Organization as a contribution to the United Nations programme for the welfare of homeless children* (2nd ed.). Geneva: World Health Organization.

Braithwaite, E. C., Kundakovic, M., Ramchandani, P. G., Murphy, S. E., & Champagne, F. A. (2015). Maternal prenatal depressive symptoms predict infant NR3C1 1F and BDNF IV DNA methylation. *Epigenetics, 10*(5), 408–417. https://doi.org/10.1080/15592294.2015.1039221

Brody, G. H., Yu, T., Chen, E., Beach, S. R. H., & Miller, G. E. (2016). Family-centered prevention ameliorates the longitudinal association between risky family processes and epigenetic aging. *Journal of Child Psychology and Psychiatry, and Allied Disciplines, 57*(5), 566–574. https://doi.org/10.1111/jcpp.12495

Brown, A. S., Gyllenberg, D., Malm, H., McKeague, I. W., Hinkka-Yli-Salomäki, S., Artama, M., ... Sourander, A. (2016). Association of selective serotonin reuptake inhibitor exposure during pregnancy with speech, scholastic, and motor disorders in offspring. *JAMA Psychiatry, 73*(11), 1163–1170. https://doi.org/10.1001/jamapsychiatry.2016.2594

Bush, N. R., Edgar, R. D., Park, M., MacIsaac, J. L., McEwen, L. M., Adler, N. E., ... Boyce, W. T. (2018). The biological embedding of early-life socioeconomic status and family adversity in children's genome-wide DNA methylation. *Epigenomics, 10*(11), 1445–1461. https://doi.org/10.2217/epi-2018-0042

Busso, D. S., McLaughlin, K. A., Brueck, S., Peverill, M., Gold, A. L., & Sheridan, M. A. (2017). Child abuse, neural structure, and adolescent psychopathology: A longitudinal study. *Journal of the American Academy of Child & Adolescent Psychiatry, 56*(4), 321–328.e1. https://doi.org/10.1016/j.jaac.2017.01.013

Caldji, C., Tannenbaum, B., Sharma, S., Francis, D., Plotsky, P. M., & Meaney, M. J. (1998). Maternal care during infancy regulates the development of neural systems mediating the expression of fearfulness in the rat. *Proceedings of the National Academy of Sciences of the United States of America, 95*(9), 5335–5340.

Cecil, C. A. M., Walton, E., Smith, R. G., Viding, E., McCrory, E. J., Relton, C. L., … Barker, E. D. (2016). DNA methylation and substance-use risk: A prospective, genome-wide study spanning gestation to adolescence. *Translational Psychiatry, 6*(12), e976. https://doi.org/10.1038/tp.2016.247

Champagne, F. A. (2008). Epigenetic mechanisms and the transgenerational effects of maternal care. *Frontiers in Neuroendocrinology, 29*(3), 386–397. https://doi.org/10.1016/j.yfrne.2008.03.003

(2016). Epigenetic legacy of parental experiences: Dynamic and interactive pathways to inheritance. *Development and Psychopathology, 28*(4 Pt. 2), 1219–1228. https://doi.org/10.1017/S0954579416000808

Champagne, F. A., & Meaney, M. J. (2006). Stress during gestation alters postpartum maternal care and the development of the offspring in a rodent model. *Biological Psychiatry, 59*(12), 1227–1235. https://doi.org/10.1016/j.biopsych.2005.10.016

(2007). Transgenerational effects of social environment on variations in maternal care and behavioral response to novelty. *Behavioral Neuroscience, 121*(6), 1353–1363. https://doi.org/10.1037/0735-7044.121.6.1353

Champagne, F. A., Weaver, I. C. G., Diorio, J., Dymov, S., Szyf, M., & Meaney, M. J. (2006). Maternal care associated with methylation of the estrogen receptor-alpha1b promoter and estrogen receptor-alpha expression in the medial preoptic area of female offspring. *Endocrinology, 147*(6), 2909–2915. https://doi.org/10.1210/en.2005-1119

Cheung, P., Allis, C. D., & Sassone-Corsi, P. (2000). Signaling to chromatin through histone modifications. *Cell, 103*(2), 263–271.

Cicchetti, D., Hetzel, S., Rogosch, F. A., Handley, E. D., & Toth, S. L. (2016). Genomewide DNA methylation in 1-year-old infants of mothers with major depressive disorder. *Development and Psychopathology, 28*(4 Pt. 2), 1413–1419. https://doi.org/10.1017/S0954579416000912

Cortessis, V. K., Thomas, D. C., Levine, A. J., Breton, C. V., Mack, T. M., Siegmund, K. D., … Laird, P. W. (2012). Environmental epigenetics: prospects for studying epigenetic mediation of exposure–response relationships. *Human Genetics, 131*(10), 1565–1589. https://doi.org/10.1007/s00439-012-1189-8

Curley, J. P., Mashoodh, R., & Champagne, F. A. (2011). Epigenetics and the origins of paternal effects. *Hormones and Behavior, 59*(3), 306–314. https://doi.org/10.1016/j.yhbeh.2010.06.018

Danchin, É., Charmantier, A., Champagne, F. A., Mesoudi, A., Pujol, B., & Blanchet, S. (2011). Beyond DNA: Integrating inclusive inheritance into an extended theory of evolution. *Nature Reviews. Genetics, 12*(7), 475–486. https://doi.org/10.1038/nrg3028

D'Elia, A. T. D., Matsuzaka, C. T., Neto, J. B. B., Mello, M. F., Juruena, M. F., & Mello, A. F. (2018). Childhood sexual abuse and indicators of immune activity: A systematic review. *Frontiers in Psychiatry, 9*, 354. https://doi.org/10.3389/fpsyt.2018.00354

Dias, B. G., & Ressler, K. J. (2014). Parental olfactory experience influences behavior and neural structure in subsequent generations. *Nature Neuroscience, 17*(1), 89–96. https://doi.org/10.1038/nn.3594

Dupont, C., Armant, D. R., & Brenner, C. A. (2009). Epigenetics: Definition, mechanisms and clinical perspective. *Seminars in Reproductive Medicine*, *27*(5), 351–357. https://doi.org/10.1055/s-0029-1237423

Eddy, S. R. (2001). Non–coding RNA genes and the modern RNA world. *Nature Reviews Genetics*, *2*(12), 919–929. https://doi.org/10.1038/35103511

Fan, Y., Tian, C., Liu, Q., Zhen, X., Zhang, H., Zhou, L., ... Zhu, M. (2018). Preconception paternal bisphenol A exposure induces sex-specific anxiety and depression behaviors in adult rats. *PloS One*, *13*(2), e0192434. https://doi.org/10.1371/journal.pone.0192434

Fareri, D. S., Gabard-Durnam, L., Goff, B., Flannery, J., Gee, D. G., Lumian, D. S., ... Tottenham, N. (2017). Altered ventral striatal-medial prefrontal cortex resting-state connectivity mediates adolescent social problems after early institutional care. *Development and Psychopathology*, *29*(5), 1865–1876. https://doi.org/10.1017/S0954579417001456

Farrell, C., Doolin, K., O' Leary, N., Jairaj, C., Roddy, D., Tozzi, L., ... O'Keane, V. (2018). DNA methylation differences at the glucocorticoid receptor gene in depression are related to functional alterations in hypothalamic-pituitary-adrenal axis activity and to early life emotional abuse. *Psychiatry Research*, *265*, 341–348. https://doi.org/10.1016/j.psychres.2018.04.064

Feil, R., & Fraga, M. F. (2012). Epigenetics and the environment: Emerging patterns and implications. *Nature Reviews. Genetics*, *13*(2), 97–109. https://doi.org/10.1038/nrg3142

Fiorito, G., Polidoro, S., Dugué, P. -A., Kivimaki, M., Ponzi, E., Matullo, G., ... Vineis, P. (2017). Social adversity and epigenetic aging. A multi-cohort study on socioeconomic differences in peripheral blood DNA methylation. *Scientific Reports*, *7*(1), 16266. https://doi.org/10.1038/s41598-017-16391-5

Francis, D., Diorio, J., Liu, D., & Meaney, M. J. (1999). Nongenomic transmission across generations of maternal behavior and stress responses in the rat. *Science*, *286*(5442), 1155–1158.

Franklin, T. B., Russig, H., Weiss, I. C., Gräff, J., Linder, N., Michalon, A., ... Mansuy, I. M. (2010). Epigenetic transmission of the impact of early stress across generations. *Biological Psychiatry*, *68*(5), 408–415. https://doi.org/10.1016/j.biopsych.2010.05.036

Gapp, K., Jawaid, A., Sarkies, P., Bohacek, J., Pelczar, P., Prados, J., ... Mansuy, I. M. (2014). Implication of sperm RNAs in transgenerational inheritance of the effects of early trauma in mice. *Nature Neuroscience*, *17*(5), 667–669. https://doi.org/10.1038/nn.3695

Garg, E., Chen, L., Nguyen, T. T. T., Pokhvisneva, I., Chen, L. M., Unternaehrer, E., ... Mavan Study Team. (2018). The early care environment and DNA methylome variation in childhood. *Development and Psychopathology*, *30*(3), 891–903. https://doi.org/10.1017/S0954579418000627

Gould, K. L., Coventry, W. L., Olson, R. K., & Byrne, B. (2018). Gene–environment interactions in ADHD: The roles of SES and chaos. *Journal of Abnormal Child Psychology*, *46*(2), 251–263. https://doi.org/10.1007/s10802-017-0268-7

Guibert, S., & Weber, M. (2013). Functions of DNA methylation and hydroxymethylation in mammalian development. *Current Topics in Developmental Biology*, *104*, 47–83. https://doi.org/10.1016/B978-0-12-416027-9.00002-4

Gurnot, C., Martin-Subero, I., Mah, S. M., Weikum, W., Goodman, S. J., Brain, U., ... Hensch, T. K. (2015). Prenatal antidepressant exposure associated with

CYP2E1 DNA methylation change in neonates. *Epigenetics, 10*(5), 361–372. https://doi.org/10.1080/15592294.2015.1026031

Hane, A. A., Henderson, H. A., Reeb-Sutherland, B. C., & Fox, N. A. (2010). Ordinary variations in human maternal caregiving in infancy and biobehavioral development in early childhood: A follow-up study. *Developmental Psychobiology, 52*(6), 558–567. https://doi.org/10.1002/dev.20461

Heijmans, B. T., Tobi, E. W., Stein, A. D., Putter, H., Blauw, G. J., Susser, E. S., … Lumey, L. H. (2008). Persistent epigenetic differences associated with prenatal exposure to famine in humans. *Proceedings of the National Academy of Sciences of the United States of America, 105*(44), 17046–17049. https://doi.org/10.1073/pnas.0806560105

Hobel, C. J., Goldstein, A., & Barrett, E. S. (2008). Psychosocial stress and pregnancy outcome. *Clinical Obstetrics and Gynecology, 51*(2), 333–348. https://doi.org/10.1097/GRF.0b013e31816f2709

Hodel, A. S., Hunt, R. H., Cowell, R. A., van den Heuvel, S. E., Gunnar, M. R., & Thomas, K. M. (2015). Duration of early adversity and structural brain development in post-institutionalized adolescents. *NeuroImage, 105*, 112–119. https://doi.org/10.1016/j.neuroimage.2014.10.020

Horvath, S. (2013). DNA methylation age of human tissues and cell types. *Genome Biology, 14*(10), R115. https://doi.org/10.1186/gb-2013-14-10-r115

Houtepen, L. C., Hardy, R., Maddock, J., Kuh, D., Anderson, E. L., Relton, C. L., … Howe, L. D. (2018). Childhood adversity and DNA methylation in two population-based cohorts. *Translational Psychiatry, 8*(1), 266. https://doi.org/10.1038/s41398-018-0307-3

Hu, F. B., Persky, V., Flay, B. R., Zelli, A., Cooksey, J., & Richardson, J. (1997). Prevalence of asthma and wheezing in public schoolchildren: Association with maternal smoking during pregnancy. *Annals of Allergy, Asthma & Immunology: Official Publication of the American College of Allergy, Asthma, & Immunology, 79*(1), 80–84. https://doi.org/10.1016/S1081-1206(10)63090–6

Jaffee, S. R., & Price, T. S. (2007). Gene–environment correlations: A review of the evidence and implications for prevention of mental illness. *Molecular Psychiatry, 12*(5), 432–442. https://doi.org/10.1038/sj.mp.4001950

Jenuwein, T., & Allis, C. D. (2001). Translating the histone code. *Science, 293*(5532), 1074–1080. https://doi.org/10.1126/science.1063127

Jones, P. A. (2012). Functions of DNA methylation: Islands, start sites, gene bodies and beyond. *Nature Reviews Genetics, 13*(7), 484–492.

Kertes, D. A., Bhatt, S. S., Kamin, H. S., Hughes, D. A., Rodney, N. C., & Mulligan, C. J. (2017). BNDF methylation in mothers and newborns is associated with maternal exposure to war trauma. *Clinical Epigenetics, 9*, 68. https://doi.org/10.1186/s13148-017-0367-x

Kundakovic, M., Gudsnuk, K., Herbstman, J. B., Tang, D., Perera, F. P., & Champagne, F. A. (2015). DNA methylation of BDNF as a biomarker of early-life adversity. *Proceedings of the National Academy of Sciences of the United States of America, 112*(22), 6807–6813. https://doi.org/10.1073/pnas.1408355111

Labonté, B., Suderman, M., Maussion, G., Navaro, L., Yerko, V., Mahar, I., … Turecki, G. (2012). Genome-wide epigenetic regulation by early-life trauma. *Archives of General Psychiatry, 69*(7), 722–731. https://doi.org/10.1001/archgenpsychiatry.2011.2287

Lawn, R. B., Anderson, E. L., Suderman, M., Simpkin, A. J., Gaunt, T. R., Teschendorff, A. E., ... Howe, L. D. (2018). Psychosocial adversity and socio-economic position during childhood and epigenetic age: Analysis of two prospective cohort studies. *Human Molecular Genetics*, *27*(7), 1301–1308. https://doi.org/10.1093/hmg/ddy036

Lester, B. M., Marsit, C. J., Giarraputo, J., Hawes, K., LaGasse, L. L., & Padbury, J. F. (2015). Neurobehavior related to epigenetic differences in preterm infants. *Epigenomics*, *7*(7), 1123–1136. https://doi.org/10.2217/epi.15.63

Liu, D., Diorio, J., Day, J. C., Francis, D. D., & Meaney, M. J. (2000). Maternal care, hippocampal synaptogenesis and cognitive development in rats. *Nature Neuroscience*, *3*(8), 799–806. https://doi.org/10.1038/77702

Liu, D., Diorio, J., Tannenbaum, B., Caldji, C., Francis, D., Freedman, A., ... Meaney, M. J. (1997). Maternal care, hippocampal glucocorticoid receptors, and hypothalamic-pituitary-adrenal responses to stress. *Science*, *277*(5332), 1659–1662.

Mashoodh, R., Habrylo, I. B., Gudsnuk, K. M., Pelle, G., & Champagne, F. A. (2018). Maternal modulation of paternal effects on offspring development. *Proceedings. Biological Sciences*, *285*(1874). https://doi.org/10.1098/rspb.2018.0118

McGowan, P. O., Sasaki, A., D'Alessio, A. C., Dymov, S., Labonté, B., Szyf, M., ... Meaney, M. J. (2009). Epigenetic regulation of the glucocorticoid receptor in human brain associates with childhood abuse. *Nature Neuroscience*, *12*(3), 342–348. https://doi.org/10.1038/nn.2270

McGowan, P. O., Suderman, M., Sasaki, A., Huang, T. C. T., Hallett, M., Meancy, M. J., & Szyf, M. (2011). Broad epigenetic signature of maternal care in the brain of adult rats. *PloS One*, *6*(2), e14739. https://doi.org/10.1371/journal.pone.0014739

McLaughlin, K. A., & Lambert, H. K. (2017). Child trauma exposure and psychopathology: Mechanisms of risk and resilience. *Current Opinion in Psychology*, *14*, 29–34. https://doi.org/10.1016/j.copsyc.2016.10.004

Meaney, M. J. (2010). Epigenetics and the biological definition of gene x environment interactions. *Child Development*, *81*(1), 41–79. https://doi.org/10.1111/j.1467-8624.2009.01381.x

Melchior, M., Hersi, R., van der Waerden, J., Larroque, B., Saurel-Cubizolles, M. -J., Chollet, A., ... EDEN Mother–Child Cohort Study Group. (2015). Maternal tobacco smoking in pregnancy and children's socio-emotional development at age 5: The EDEN mother–child birth cohort study. *European Psychiatry: The Journal of the Association of European Psychiatrists*, *30*(5), 562–568. https://doi.org/10.1016/j.eurpsy.2015.03.005

Milaniak, I., Cecil, C. A. M., Barker, E. D., Relton, C. L., Gaunt, T. R., McArdle, W., & Jaffee, S. R. (2017). Variation in DNA methylation of the oxytocin receptor gene predicts children's resilience to prenatal stress. *Development and Psychopathology*, *29*(5), 1663–1674. https://doi.org/10.1017/S0954579417001316

Millard, S. J., Weston-Green, K., & Newell, K. A. (2017). The effects of maternal antidepressant use on offspring behaviour and brain development: Implications for risk of neurodevelopmental disorders. *Neuroscience and Biobehavioral Reviews*, *80*, 743–765. https://doi.org/10.1016/j.neubiorev.2017.06.008

Miller, G. E., Yu, T., Chen, E., & Brody, G. H. (2015). Self-control forecasts better psychosocial outcomes but faster epigenetic aging in low-SES youth. *Proceedings of the National Academy of Sciences of the United States of America*, *112*(33), 10325–10330. https://doi.org/10.1073/pnas.1505063112

Mitsuya, K., Parker, A. N., Liu, L., Ruan, J., Vissers, M. C. M., & Myatt, L. (2017). Alterations in the placental methylome with maternal obesity and evidence for metabolic regulation. *PloS One*, *12*(10), e0186115. https://doi.org/10.1371/journal.pone.0186115

Mohn, F., & Schübeler, D. (2009). Genetics and epigenetics: Stability and plasticity during cellular differentiation. *Trends in Genetics: TIG*, *25*(3), 129–136. https://doi.org/10.1016/j.tig.2008.12.005

Moisiadis, V. G., Constantinof, A., Kostaki, A., Szyf, M., & Matthews, S. G. (2017). Prenatal glucocorticoid exposure modifies endocrine function and behaviour for 3 generations following maternal and paternal transmission. *Scientific Reports*, *7*(1), 11814. https://doi.org/10.1038/s41598-017-11635-w

Monk, C., Feng, T., Lee, S., Krupska, I., Champagne, F. A., & Tycko, B. (2016). Distress during pregnancy: Epigenetic regulation of placenta glucocorticoid-related genes and fetal neurobehavior. *American Journal of Psychiatry*, *173*(7), 705–713. https://doi.org/10.1176/appi.ajp.2015.15091171

Monk, C., Spicer, J., & Champagne, F. A. (2012). Linking prenatal maternal adversity to developmental outcomes in infants: The role of epigenetic pathways. *Development and Psychopathology*, *24*(4), 1361–1376. https://doi.org/10.1017/S0954579412000764

Naumova, O. Y., Lee, M., Koposov, R., Szyf, M., Dozier, M., & Grigorenko, E. L. (2012). Differential patterns of whole-genome DNA methylation in institutionalized children and children raised by their biological parents. *Development and Psychopathology*, *24*(1), 143–155. https://doi.org/10.1017/S0954579411000605

Ng, S. -F., Lin, R. C. Y., Laybutt, D. R., Barres, R., Owens, J. A., & Morris, M. J. (2010). Chronic high-fat diet in fathers programs β-cell dysfunction in female rat offspring. *Nature*, *467*(7318), 963–966. https://doi.org/10.1038/nature09491

Nigg, J., Nikolas, M., & Burt, S. A. (2010). Measured gene-by-environment interaction in relation to attention-deficit/hyperactivity disorder. *Journal of the American Academy of Child & Adolescent Psychiatry*, *49*(9), 863–873. https://doi.org/10.1016/j.jaac.2010.01.025

Nilsson, E. E., Sadler-Riggleman, I., & Skinner, M. K. (2018). Environmentally induced epigenetic transgenerational inheritance of disease. *Environmental Epigenetics*, *4*(2), dvy016. https://doi.org/10.1093/eep/dvy016

Noble, D. (2015). Conrad Waddington and the origin of epigenetics. *Journal of Experimental Biology*, *218*(6), 816–818. https://doi.org/10.1242/jeb.120071

Non, A. L., Binder, A. M., Kubzansky, L. D., & Michels, K. B. (2014). Genome-wide DNA methylation in neonates exposed to maternal depression, anxiety, or SSRI medication during pregnancy. *Epigenetics*, *9*(7), 964–972. https://doi.org/10.4161/epi.28853

Oberlander, T. F., Weinberg, J., Papsdorf, M., Grunau, R., Misri, S., & Devlin, A. M. (2008). Prenatal exposure to maternal depression, neonatal methylation of human glucocorticoid receptor gene (NR3C1) and infant cortisol stress responses. *Epigenetics*, *3*(2), 97–106.

Papale, L. A., Seltzer, L. J., Madrid, A., Pollak, S. D., & Alisch, R. S. (2018). Differentially methylated genes in saliva are linked to childhood stress. *Scientific Reports*, *8*(1), 10785. https://doi.org/10.1038/s41598-018-29107-0

Paquette, A. G., Houseman, E. A., Green, B. B., Lesseur, C., Armstrong, D. A., Lester, B., & Marsit, C. J. (2016). Regions of variable DNA methylation in human placenta associated with newborn neurobehavior. *Epigenetics*, *11*(8), 603–613. https://doi.org/10.1080/15592294.2016.1195534

Paquette, A. G., Lester, B. M., Koestler, D. C., Lesseur, C., Armstrong, D. A., & Marsit, C. J. (2014). Placental FKBP5 genetic and epigenetic variation is associated with infant neurobehavioral outcomes in the RICHS cohort. *PloS One*, *9*(8), e104913. https://doi.org/10.1371/journal.pone.0104913

Parade, S. H., Parent, J., Rabemananjara, K., Seifer, R., Marsit, C. J., Yang, B. -Z., … Tyrka, A. R. (2017). Change in FK506 binding protein 5 (FKBP5) methylation over time among preschoolers with adversity. *Development and Psychopathology*, *29*(5), 1627–1634. https://doi.org/10.1017/S0954579417001286

Parent, C. I., & Meaney, M. J. (2008). The influence of natural variations in maternal care on play fighting in the rat. *Developmental Psychobiology*, *50*(8), 767–776. https://doi.org/10.1002/dev.20342

Pauwels, S., Ghosh, M., Duca, R. C., Bekaert, B., Freson, K., Huybrechts, I., … Godderis, L. (2016). Dietary and supplemental maternal methyl-group donor intake and cord blood DNA methylation. *Epigenetics*, *12*(1), 1–10. https://doi.org/10.1080/15592294.2016.1257450

Peña, C. J., Neugut, Y. D., & Champagne, F. A. (2013). Developmental timing of the effects of maternal care on gene expression and epigenetic regulation of hormone receptor levels in female rats. *Endocrinology*, *154*(11), 4340–4351. https://doi.org/10.1210/en.2013-1595

Perera, F., Vishnevetsky, J., Herbstman, J. B., Calafat, A. M., Xiong, W., Rauh, V., & Wang, S. (2012). Prenatal bisphenol A exposure and child behavior in an inner-city cohort. *Environmental Health Perspectives*, *120*(8), 1190–1194. https://doi.org/10.1289/ehp.1104492

Razin, A. (1998). CpG methylation, chromatin structure and gene silencing-a three-way connection. *EMBO Journal*, *17*(17), 4905–4908. https://doi.org/10.1093/emboj/17.17.4905

Razin, A., & Riggs, A. D. (1980). DNA methylation and gene function. *Science*, *210*(4470), 604–610.

Rodgers, A. B., Morgan, C. P., Bronson, S. L., Revello, S., & Bale, T. L. (2013). Paternal stress exposure alters sperm microRNA content and reprograms offspring HPA stress axis regulation. *Journal of Neuroscience: The Official Journal of the Society for Neuroscience*, *33*(21), 9003–9012. https://doi.org/10.1523/JNEUROSCI.0914-13.2013

Rogers, C. E., Lean, R. E., Wheelock, M. D., & Smyser, C. D. (2018). Aberrant structural and functional connectivity and neurodevelopmental impairment in preterm children. *Journal of Neurodevelopmental Disorders*, *10*(1), 38. https://doi.org/10.1186/s11689-018-9253-x

Schieve, L. A., Tian, L. H., Rankin, K., Kogan, M. D., Yeargin-Allsopp, M., Visser, S., & Rosenberg, D. (2016). Population impact of preterm birth and low birth weight on developmental disabilities in US children. *Annals of Epidemiology*, *26*(4), 267–274. https://doi.org/10.1016/j.annepidem.2016.02.012

Sharp, G. C., Salas, L. A., Monnereau, C., Allard, C., Yousefi, P., Everson, T. M., … Relton, C. L. (2017). Maternal BMI at the start of pregnancy and offspring epigenome-wide DNA methylation: Findings from the pregnancy and childhood epigenetics (PACE) consortium. *Human Molecular Genetics*, *26*(20), 4067–4085. https://doi.org/10.1093/hmg/ddx290

Shorey-Kendrick, L. E., McEvoy, C. T., Ferguson, B., Burchard, J., Park, B. S., Gao, L., … Spindel, E. R. (2017). Vitamin C prevents offspring DNA methylation changes associated with maternal smoking in pregnancy. *American Journal of Respiratory and Critical Care Medicine*, *196*(6), 745 755. https://doi.org/10.1164/rccm.201610-2141OC

Simpkin, A. J., Hemani, G., Suderman, M., Gaunt, T. R., Lyttleton, O., Mcardle, W. L., … Smith, G. D. (2016). Prenatal and early life influences on epigenetic age in children: A study of mother–offspring pairs from two cohort studies. *Human Molecular Genetics*, *25*(1), 191–201. https://doi.org/10.1093/hmg/ddv456

Sonuga-Barke, E. J. S., Kennedy, M., Kumsta, R., Knights, N., Golm, D., Rutter, M., … Kreppner, J. (2017). Child-to-adult neurodevelopmental and mental health trajectories after early life deprivation: The young adult follow-up of the longitudinal English and Romanian Adoptees study. *Lancet*, *389*(10078), 1539–1548. https://doi.org/10.1016/S0140-6736(17)30045-4

Stamoulis, C., Vanderwert, R. E., Zeanah, C. H., Fox, N. A., & Nelson, C. A. (2017). Neuronal networks in the developing brain are adversely modulated by early psychosocial neglect. *Journal of Neurophysiology*, *118*(4), 2275–2288. https://doi.org/10.1152/jn.00014.2017

Staneva, A., Bogossian, F., Pritchard, M., & Wittkowski, A. (2015). The effects of maternal depression, anxiety, and perceived stress during pregnancy on preterm birth: A systematic review. *Women and Birth: Journal of the Australian College of Midwives*, *28*(3), 179–193. https://doi.org/10.1016/j.wombi.2015.02.003

Susser, E. S., & Lin, S. P. (1992). Schizophrenia after prenatal exposure to the Dutch Hunger Winter of 1944–1945. *Archives of General Psychiatry*, *49*(12), 983–988.

Talati, A., Wickramaratne, P. J., Wesselhoeft, R., & Weissman, M. M. (2017). Prenatal tobacco exposure, birthweight, and offspring psychopathology. *Psychiatry Research*, *252*, 346–352. https://doi.org/10.1016/j.psychres.2017.03.016

Torche, F., & Kleinhaus, K. (2012). Prenatal stress, gestational age and secondary sex ratio: The sex-specific effects of exposure to a natural disaster in early pregnancy. *Human Reproduction*, *27*(2), 558–567. https://doi.org/10.1093/humrep/der390

Troller-Renfree, S., McDermott, J. M., Nelson, C. A., Zeanah, C. H., & Fox, N. A. (2015). The effects of early foster care intervention on attention biases in previously institutionalized children in Romania. *Developmental Science*, *18*(5), 713–722. https://doi.org/10.1111/desc.12261

Tserga, A., Binder, A. M., & Michels, K. B. (2017). Impact of folic acid intake during pregnancy on genomic imprinting of IGF2/H19 and 1-carbon metabolism. *FASEB Journal: Official Publication of the Federation of American Societies for Experimental Biology*, *31*(12), 5149–5158. https://doi.org/10.1096/fj.201601214RR

Vassoler, F. M., White, S. L., Schmidt, H. D., Sadri-Vakili, G., & Pierce, R. C. (2013). Epigenetic inheritance of a cocaine-resistance phenotype. *Nature Neuroscience*, *16*(1), 42–47. https://doi.org/10.1038/nn.3280

Waddington, C. H. (1940). *Organisers & genes*. Cambridge, UK: Cambridge University Press.

Wadhwa, P. D., Entringer, S., Buss, C., & Lu, M. C. (2011). The contribution of maternal stress to preterm birth: Issues and considerations. *Clinics in Perinatology, 38*(3), 351–384. https://doi.org/10.1016/j.clp.2011.06.007

Weaver, I. C. G., Cervoni, N., Champagne, F. A., D'Alessio, A. C., Sharma, S., Seckl, J. R., … Meaney, M. J. (2004). Epigenetic programming by maternal behavior. *Nature Neuroscience*, *7*(8), 847–854. https://doi.org/10.1038/nn1276

Weinstock, M., Fride, E., & Hertzberg, R. (1988). Prenatal stress effects on functional development of the offspring. *Progress in Brain Research*, *73*, 319–331. https://doi.org/10.1016/S0079-6123(08)60513-0

Welch, M. G., Firestein, M. R., Austin, J., Hane, A. A., Stark, R. I., Hofer, M. A., … Myers, M. M. (2015). Family nurture intervention in the neonatal intensive care unit improves social-relatedness, attention, and neurodevelopment of preterm infants at 18 months in a randomized controlled trial. *Journal of Child Psychology and Psychiatry, and Allied Disciplines*, *56*(11), 1202–1211. https://doi.org/10.1111/jcpp.12405

Welch, M. G., Stark, R. I., Grieve, P. G., Ludwig, R. J., Isler, J. R., Barone, J. L., & Myers, M. M. (2017). Family nurture intervention in preterm infants increases early development of cortical activity and independence of regional power trajectories. *Acta Paediatrica*, *106*(12), 1952–1960. https://doi.org/10.1111/apa.14050

Wilkinson, L. S., Davies, W., & Isles, A. R. (2007). Genomic imprinting effects on brain development and function. *Nature Reviews. Neuroscience*, *8*(11), 832–843. https://doi.org/10.1038/nrn2235

Wilson, R. D., Davies, G., Désilets, V., Reid, G. J., Summers, A., Wyatt, P., … Genetics Committee and Executive and Council of the Society of Obstetricians and Gynaecologists of Canada (2003). The use of folic acid for the prevention of neural tube defects and other congenital anomalies. *Journal of Obstetrics and Gynaecology Canada, 25*(11), 959–973.

Winther, G., Eskelund, A., Bay-Richter, C., Elfving, B., Müller, H. K., Lund, S., & Wegener, G. (2019). Grandmaternal high-fat diet primed anxiety-like behaviour in the second-generation female offspring. *Behavioural Brain Research*, *359*, 47–55. https://doi.org/10.1016/j.bbr.2018.10.017

4 Brain Development in Infants

Structure and Experience

John E. Richards and Stefania Conte

The development of the brain in humans following birth is one of the most remarkable changes in human growth. The structure, myelination, and connectivity of the brain are relatively primitive at birth. Much of the development of the size, shape, and connectivity occurs after birth and before the end of the second year of life. The brain appears in size and shape similar to the adult brain at 2 years of age. The brain continues to change and develops over the entire life span, although the changes after 2 years appear to be more quantitative and gradual than the changes in the first 2 years. Some of the brain changes are from intrinsic growth factors governed by maturational factors, whereas other brain changes are affected by individual experiences and background setting. The interplay of intrinsic and extrinsic forces shapes the brain through the life span.

The current chapter will present some of the remarkable changes in brain development in the first 2 years. These will include the overall size of the brain and head, a process called synaptogenesis in which synaptic connectivity is established, and myelination of the axonal structures of the brain. We will present examples where specific environmental experiences directly affect brain growth and development. We also will mention the effects that overall background environment has on brain development – focusing on the effects of environmental deprivation and poverty on brain development outcome.

4.1 Major Periods of Brain Development

Brain development can be roughly categorized into five major periods. These are prenatal, first 2 years, age 2 through early adolescence, young and middle adulthood, and late adulthood. These periods are characterized by different emphases of brain development and major developmental accomplishments. Most of the changes in the brain during these periods are quantitative in nature and involve gradual changes over several years. However, there are some sensitive periods during which environmental factors have their strongest influences on developmental changes. This suggests a stage-like progression for some aspects of brain development. For example, during the infancy period there is a rapid synaptic growth (synaptogenesis, synaptic proliferation).

Synaptic growth during this period produces the largest number of synapses found during the entire life span and is stage-like in nature. This is followed by synaptic pruning guided by individual experiences and environmental conditions. The synaptic pruning is gradual and continues through childhood until adolescence. The periods also differ on the rate and duration of change. Some periods (e.g., prenatal, infancy) have rapid changes in a relatively short duration compared to the life span, whereas others (second year through adolescence, adulthood) are characterized by slow steady growth or decline of specific brain processes over a relatively long duration.

Brain development in these five periods is covered by several reviews (Lyall, Savadjiev, Shenton, & Kubicki, 2016; Sowell, Thompson, & Toga, 2004; Stiles & Jernigan, 2010). The major accomplishments of the prenatal period include the neurogenesis of nearly all neurons in the brain by mid-gestation, the migration of cells and axons from the early neural tube structure to cortical and neocortical layers, the completion of the major fiber pathways, and the emergence of the lobes of the brain (i.e., occipital lobe, frontal lobe, parietal lobe). The accomplishments during the infancy period include nearly doubling of the brain from the newborn size to 80% of the adult size by age 2; cortical thickness reaches 97% of adult levels by age 2 (Lyall et al., 2016). It is often hypothesized that evolutionary pressures resulted in primate brains and heads at birth matching the size of the maternal birth canal with subsequent substantial postnatal growth necessary to reach the mature brain size (Rosenberg & Trevathan, 2002). Over evolution the size of the mature brain has increased at a greater rate than the size of the maternal birth canal, resulting in extensive postnatal growth and environmental adaptability (DeSilva & Lesnik, 2008). This change in brain size is accomplished by the proliferation of glial cells into nonneuron brain tissue and migration of those cells to cortical areas, a surge in synaptogenesis during the infancy period, and the growth and increase in myelin. The change in overall head size during this period is affected by the unseamed bone plates at birth becoming seamed and expanding to contain the growing brain. The period of time from age 2 through adolescence is accompanied by selective synaptic pruning based on experience, gradual increases in gray matter and white matter volume, increases in myelination, and accompanying changes in head volume. The periods after adolescence through the end of the life span tend to show gradual changes in the brain over the extended period of adulthood. There is continuing myelination though not to the degree found in the childhood years. There is a gradual and selective loss of gray matter and white matter throughout adulthood, though overall brain weight and volume are relative stable until the 50s and then gradually decline (Sowell et al., 2004).

An example marking the periods of brain development is illustrated by Figure 4.1. Figure 4.1 shows the changes in head volume and brain volume from 2 weeks through 89 years. These data are from the "Neurodevelopmental MRI Database" (Richards, Sanchez, Phillips-Meek, & Xie, 2016; Richards,

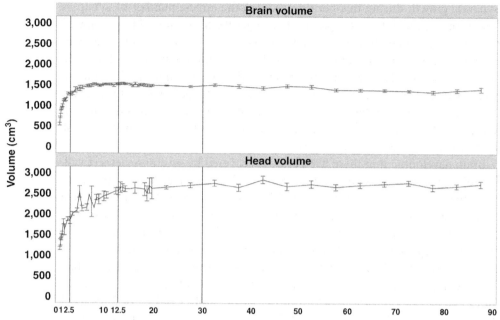

Figure 4.1. *Postnatal changes in head volume and brain size from birth through 85 years. Note the rapid development during the first 2 years, gradual development from ages 2 through early adolescence, relative stable levels in adolescence and early adulthood, and graduate decreases in brain volume over adulthood.*
Source: Data from the "Neurodevelopmental MRI Database" (Richards, Sanchez et al., 2015; Richards & Xie, 2015), with the brain volume data coming from approximately 6,000 MRI volumes of individual participants and the head volume data coming from approximately 2,000 participants.

& Xie, 2015), which is a database of MRIs from over 6,000 participants. The figure shows rapid increase in head and brain volume in the first 2 years, gradual increases from years 2 through adolescence, a leveling of volume through adolescence, and a decline in brain volume in adults. The changes in head size reflect the growth of the skull and the growth of the brain, whereas the changes in brain size reflect glial proliferation, increases, and then decreases in synaptic connectivity and gray matter density, and myelination.

4.2 Gray Matter Development, Thickness, Overall Levels, Synaptogenesis

There are two major developments of brain neurons during infancy. These are the proliferation of synapses and myelination. These occur in addition to other changes in brain weight and volume caused by proliferation of nonneuronal processes (e.g., glial cells are nonneuronal cells in the brain that support neural processes; cerebrospinal fluid [CSF]). The current section will review the growth of gray matter due to synaptic proliferation, synaptic pruning, and volumetric studies of gray matter volume in the brain.

The proliferation of synapses between the axonal terminals of neurons and the dendrites of surrounding neurons during the postnatal period is referred to as synaptogenesis. The neural axonal processes may already be in place at birth or may grow through the layers of the cortex. One method to study synaptic growth is invasive surgery or sacrifice with nonhuman primates (Bourgeois, 1997; Bourgeois & Rakic, 1993). A limit of nonhuman primate studies for the study of humans is the inexact parallel between the stages of growth in nonhuman primates and humans. This is particularly true for the temporal lobes and the prefrontal cortex. These are larger proportionally to the rest of the brain in mature humans than in mature nonhuman primates and show extended development patterns in humans.

A second method for studying synaptic growth is human autopsy studies (Conel, 1939–67; Huttenlocher, 1990, 1994; Huttenlocher & Dabholkar, 1997; Shankle, Romney, Landing, & Hara, 1998). A series of studies of postmortem samples by Conel published from 1939 through 1967 examined the cytoarchitecture and neuroanatomy of the cortical layers of the human cerebral cortex. Four general findings from these studies are: progressive growth of axonal fibers through the layers of the cerebral cortex, exuberant synaptic growth (synaptogenesis), regressive synaptic pruning, and hetero-synchronous synaptogenesis/pruning across regions of the brain. Figure 4.2A shows the layers of the visual cortex at three different ages and the inputs/output from this area to other visual areas. There is a progressive growth of axonal fibers through the layers of the visual cortex differentially from the visual areas across age. This differential growth may act as the limiting factor for visual behavior controlled by these visual areas. Synaptogenesis accompanies the growth of the axons through the cortical layers. Figure 4.2B shows results from the Conel series demonstrating synaptic growth through the proliferation of axonal and dendrite processes for three different areas (auditory cortex, Broca's area, fusiform gyrus) at different ages. These figures show a rapid increase in the density of the axon terminals and dendrites at all cortical layers. About two-thirds of the change in the synaptic cytoarchitectonic structure occurs between birth and 15 months (Shankle et al., 1998). The exuberant growth found in synaptogenesis is followed by a systematic elimination of up to 50% of these connections resulting from synaptic pruning as a result of experience (Stiles & Jernigan, 2010). The rapid growth in the first 2 years is followed by regionally selective decreases in the number of neuronal processes (Conel, 1951, 1967). Finally, these studies find differential synaptogenesis and synaptic pruning for regions of the cortex. Figure 4.3 shows changes in synaptic density for the visual cortex, auditory cortex, and prefrontal cortex (Huttenlocher, 1994; Huttenlocher & Dabholkar, 1997). The age profile differs markedly for these three areas in the

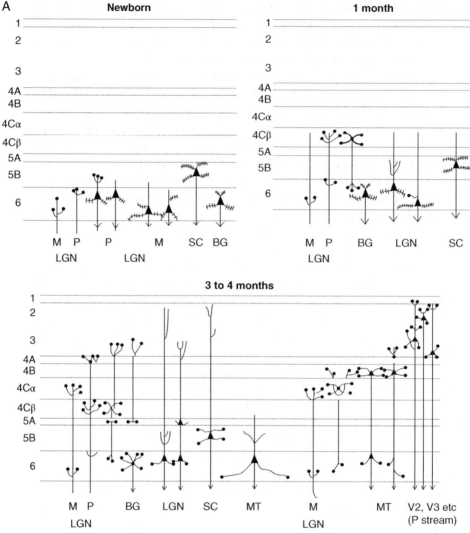

Figure 4.2A. *Postnatal development of human cerebral cortex. The overall complexity of cortical neurons increases from birth to about 2–4 years, with sensorimotor areas showing peak maturation before association areas. Figures show the layers in the primary visual cortex by different cell types at birth, 1 month, and 3 to 4 months of age.*

Note: LGN = lateral geniculate nucleus; BG = basal ganglia; SC = superior colliculus; MT = middle temporal visual area, V5; V2, V3 = visual areas 2 and 3.

Source: Adapted from Conel (1939–67).

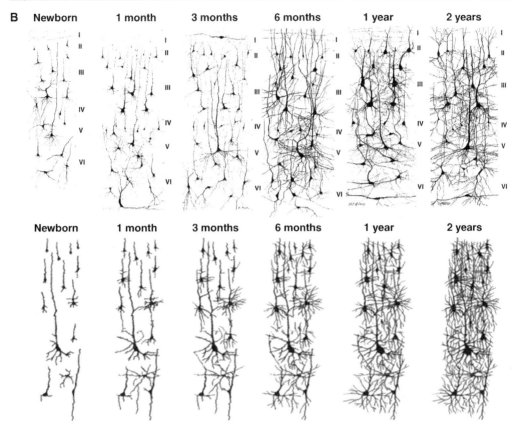

Figure 4.2B. *(Top) Postnatal development of human cerebral cortex around Broca's area as taken from camera lucida drawings of Golgi-Cox preparations. (Bottom) The development of neuronal morphology in human primary auditory cortex. Dendritic complexity shows an increase during postnatal development corresponding to later-described increases in synaptic densities.*
Source: Adapted from Conel (1939–67) (top) and Kolb and Fantie (1989) and Kral (2007) (bottom).

age at which the peak occurs and the type of decline through adulthood. The pattern of synaptic growth and decline generally occurs earliest in sensorimotor and primary sensory areas and latest in the temporal lobes and prefrontal cortex.

Spatial and temporal changes in gray and white matter tissues can be studied by using magnetic resonance imaging (MRI) techniques. MRI functioning is based on nuclear magnetic resonance of protons within tissues and it is often divided into structural MRI and functional MRI (fMRI). Specifically, structural MRI measures the response of hydrogen molecules to a perturbation while in a magnetic field. Thus, it constitutes a noninvasive tool to obtain high-resolution images of anatomical location and morphological characteristics of brain areas (Symms, Jager, Schmierer, & Yousry, 2004). On the other hand, functional imaging techniques provide dynamic physiological information of specific activity in the brain. fMRI uses the blood-oxygen-level dependent (BOLD) contrast to detect changes in brain activity associated with blood flow. The BOLD technique is based on the fact that neuronal activity and regulation of blood flow and oxygenation are linked in the brain. Thus, when an area of the brain is in use, blood flow to that region also increases. Both MRI and fMRI are useful techniques to detect structural and functional changes in gray matter. However, MRI can be used to measure the self-diffusion of water by means of specific sequence of acquisition, namely diffusion-weighted imaging (DWI), which quantifies the diffusion coefficients in the brain. A special kind of DWI is diffusion tensor imaging (DTI). This technique uses fractional anisotropy values to produce probability maps of the distribution of white matter in the brain. Thus, this technique may be useful to investigate white matter changes during development. Further information about imaging techniques used to track white matter can be found in the following section of the current chapter.

The introduction of MRI in the last 20 years as a neuroimaging tool has resulted in a burgeoning literature on gray matter development. Reviews of this work are presented in several places (Lyall et al., 2016; O'Hare, 2008; Sowell et al., 2004; Stiles & Jernigan, 2010; Toga, Thompson, & Sowell, 2006). Structural MRI and "voxel-based morphometry" (VBM) provide a precise quantitative view of brain development (Lyall et al., 2016). MRI information is not as precise at the neuronal level as invasive and autopsy studies, but provides quantitative volumetric analysis at the gyrus and lobar levels not provided by invasive and autopsy studies (Lyall et al., 2016; Sowell et al., 2004).

The MRI studies show increases in gray matter volume through adolescence and then a gradual decline in gray matter from adolescence through adulthood. An example using structural MRIs for voxel-based morphometry (VBM) is shown in Figure 4.3B. This figure shows the changes from birth through 85 years in volume for gray matter, white matter volume, and other matter. These data are from the "Neurodevelopmental MRI Database" (Richards, Sanchez et al., 2016; Richards, & Xie, 2015). This analysis was done by segmenting the brain by assigning the probability for each voxel in an MRI volume for being gray matter, white matter, or other matter, and summing the probability X volume from each voxel. There were rapid increases in gray matter and white matter in the first 2 years followed by less rapid development from 2 years through adolescence. The increase in gray matter volume paralleled the synaptic density increase due to synaptogenesis found with postmortem studies (e.g., cf. Figures 4.3A and 4.3B; Huttenlocher, 1990, 1994). The increase in gray matter volume through adolescence was followed by a decline in brain volume in adolescence and throughout adulthood. The decrease in

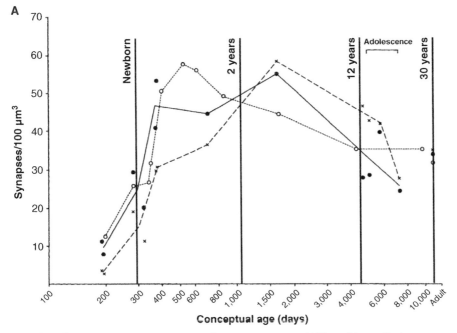

Figure 4.3A. *Mean synaptic density in synapses/100 μm³ in auditory,
calcarine, and prefrontal cortex at various ages.*
*Note: Open circles = visual cortex (area 17), filled circles = auditory cortex;
x = prefrontal cortex (middle frontal gyrus). The first four periods of brain
growth are shown by lines at newborn, 2 years, 12 years, and 30 years.
Source: Adapted from Huttenlocher and Dabholkar (1997).*

gray matter volume is assumed to be a result of the cortical thinning caused by
synaptic pruning, though the parallel between gray matter volume decreases
measured by MRI and synaptic pruning measured with invasive methods is
inexact. The changes in gray matter and white matter shown in these graphs
help define the five periods of brain development.

The change in brain structure in the first few years, like the changes in synapses due to synaptogenesis and synaptic pruning, occur differentially over
brain regions. An example of this comes from a recent study of cortical development in children from 1 to 6 years of age (Remer et al., 2017). They used structural MRIs to quantify cortical thickness, surface area, mean curvature, and
gray matter volume across 34 cortical areas. Figure 4.3C shows the changes for
two cortical areas, rostral anterior cingulate, and parahippocampal-fusiform
gyrus, across these measures. Cortical thinning increased across all ages at the
same time as cortical surface and gray matter volume increased. These changes
occurred at different rates across the 34 brain regions. These changes in gray
matter continue through adulthood.

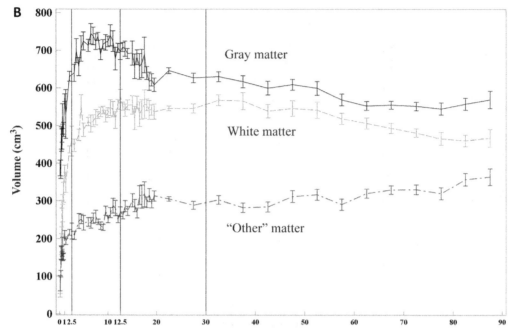

Figure 4.3B. *Postnatal changes in gray matter (black), white matter (light gray), and "other matter" (dark gray) volume from birth through 85 years. Note the rapid development of the GM and WM in the first 2 years, the decline of GM volume in the second and third periods, and the gradual decrease in WM and GM volume throughout adulthood. Since the overall head size does not change, the "other matter" appears to grow since the neural matter (WM, GM) are decreasing.*
Source: Data are from the "Neurodevelopmental MRI Database" (Richards, Sanchez et al., 2016; Richards & Xie, 2015), with the GM/WM volume data coming from approximately 4,000 MRI volumes of individual participants. Adapted from Richards & Xie (2015) with updated data.

4.3 White Matter Development: WM from VBM, Myelin from Advanced Methods

The second major characteristic of brain neuronal development in infancy is myelination. Like axonal and synaptic proliferation, this process is a major contributor to brain volume changes. However, unlike the rise of synaptic connectivity and subsequent synaptic pruning in infancy and childhood, myelin changes flow primarily in the increasing direction during the first half of life span without significant regressive decline. Myelination like gray matter has been studied with animal models, autopsy studies, and MRI. Unlike gray matter measurement, current MRI methods provide an accurate measure of myelin concentration in the brain better than invasive methods, particularly for human developmental studies (Lebel & Deoni, 2018). The growth of myelin is

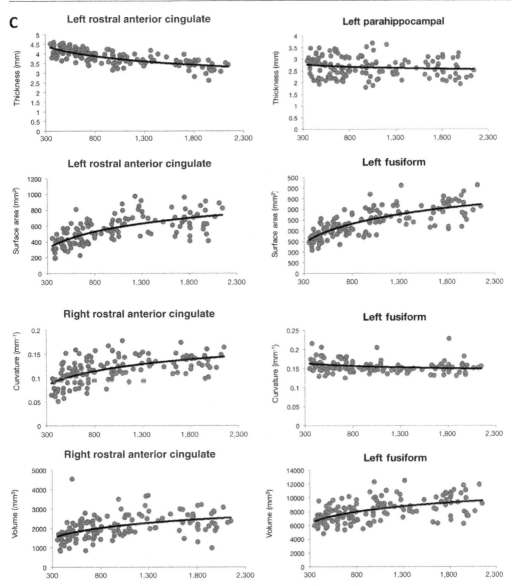

Figure 4.3C. *Region-specific cortical thickness, surface area, curvature, and gray matter volume trajectories for a selection of anatomical regions. Points correspond to subject-specific thickness value and the line corresponds to the trend line of best fit from BIC analysis. X-axis is age in days. The original figures did not have the left fusiform (face area) for cortical thickness so the adjacent left-parahippocampal area (place area) is shown. Similarly, the original figures 1 and 2 included the left rostral anterior cingulate, whereas figures 3 and 4 included the right rostral anterior cingulate (emotional processing).*
Source: Adapted from Remer et al. (2017, figs. 1–4).

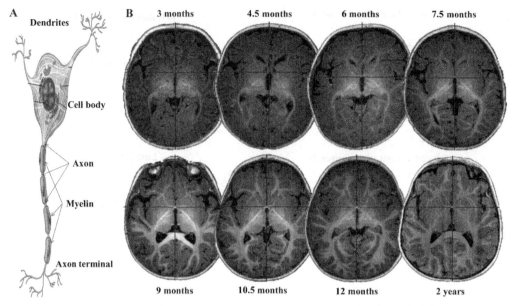

Figure 4.4. *(A) Cartoon drawing of a "typical" neuron with unmyelinated dendrites, cell body, and axon terminal, and the myelin sheath covering the axon. (B) How white matter increases over age. The MRIs are shown at the same axial level, and the crosshairs are centered on the anterior commissure. The myelination changes are shown by the increasing level of white matter tracts; notice the changes in myelination at the center of the crosshairs on the anterior commissure. Source: Brain images are from the Neurodevelopmental MRI Database (Richards, Sanchez et al., 2016).*

used as an explanatory mechanism for how changes in the brain affect cognitive development through adolescence (Klingberg, 2008, 2010; Nagy, Westerberg, & Klingberg, 2004; O'Muircheartaigh et al., 2014). The current section will review the changes in brain white matter that reflect myelination.

Myelin is a fatty substance that in mature neurons covers the axons of many neurons, especially those in fiber tracts. Figure 4.4A has a cartoon drawing of a typical neuron with an unmyelinated portion (cell body, dendrites, axonal terminal) and whose axon is covered with the myelin sheath. The myelin sheath consists of nonneuronal glial cells, specifically the myelin-producing oligodendrocytes, and contains relatively large amounts of fatty tissue (Lyall et al., 2016). Since fatty tissue reflects light, myelin appears "white" when viewed in autopsied brains. Myelination of the axon results in less noisy and quicker transmission, making the communication between neurons more efficient. Figure 4.4B shows MRIs with an axial cut for infants from 3 months to 2 years. The "white" color in T1-weighted MRIs represents a longer MRI T1 delay time of white matter over gray matter. The longer delay time is represented as voxels with larger numbers – displayed as white in MRI pictures. The 3-month MRI volume in both figures shows myelinated fiber tracts in the

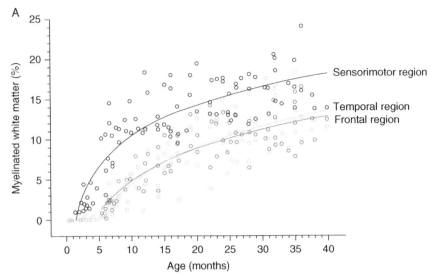

Figure 4.5A. *Plot of age-related increase in relative content of myelinated white matter for the 100 studied children. For the sensorimotor region (black), the logarithmic curve showed white matter volume 2.38 5.60 * ln (age) (adjusted R2 0.74, p 0.0001); for the temporal region (light gray), white matter volume 10.48 6.52 * ln (age) (adjusted R2 0.66, p 0.0001); and for the frontal region (dark gray), white matter volume 8.43 5.78 * ln (age) (adjusted R2 0.72, p 0.0001).*
Source: Adapted from Pujol et al. (2006).

sensorimotor cortex and from the lateral geniculate nucleus to the occipital lobe. The white matter figure tracts increase rapidly with the most rapid development in the second half of the first year and the entire second year.

The MRI studies of white matter development have used three main techniques. First, volumetric studies of white matter and gray matter are intertwined in voxel-based morphometry (VBM). Figure 4.3B, described earlier for gray matter volume development, shows VBM results for changes in white matter from birth through 85 years. The increase in white matter volume in the first 2 years was very rapid, followed by a steady increase in volume through early adolescence, a seeming plateau in adolescence and adulthood, followed by a gradual decline in the later years of adulthood. Unlike gray matter, which shows rapid increases followed by synaptic pruning, the changes in white matter are continuous and occur only in the forward manner with little regressive decline in volume. Like gray matter, white matter volume shows hetero-synchronous development across brain regions. Figure 4.5A shows the results from children ranging in ages from 1 to 40 months from a volumetric study of white matter from sensorimotor, temporal, and frontal regions. The sensorimotor regions show the earliest increases and plateau followed by temporal and frontal regions. These differential changes in brain regions reflect similar changes in the MRI volumes displayed in Figure 4.4B.

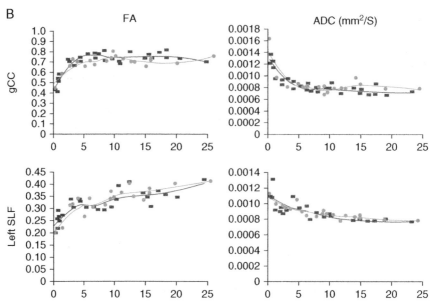

Figure 4.5B. *Changes in fractional anisotropy (FA) and apparent diffusion coefficient (ADC) for the genu of the corpus callosum (gCC) and the left superior longitudinal fasciculus (SLF). The two figures show the changes in size. Gray dots and lines denote the values of females, while black markers (filled squares) and lines denote males.*
Source: Adapted from Uda et al. (2015).

The second method for measuring myelination is "diffusion tensor imaging" (DTI). The DTI method uses the magnetic field of the MRI to force changes in brain tissue along spatial pathways. The ease at which the magnetic flow occurs is measured by "fractional anisotropy" (FA). White matter fiber tracts contain a relatively large amount of magnetic water molecules constrained within the fiber bundles by the myelin sheath. Thus, diffusion of magnetic flow is through fiber tracts that have this structural characteristic, and thus are myelinated fiber pathways. The level of FA is presumed then to be a measure of the structural intactness of the fiber bundles. The DTI method for measuring myelination with MRI more closely reflects the measurement of tissue properties than volumetric methods, or than MRI methods of synapse development.

The measure of changes in FA with age has been used extensively to study the development of myelination in the large myelinated fiber bundles of the brain (Lyall et al., 2016; Sowell et al., 2004; Stiles & Jernigan, 2010). For example, Uda et al. (2015) used DTI to study changes in FA in participants from 2 months through early adulthood. Figure 4.5B shows some of their results. Figure 4.5B shows the increase in FA in the genu of the corpus callosum and the superior longitudinal fasciculus and a monthly decelerating growth through about 6 years. The increase in FA was accompanied by decreases in

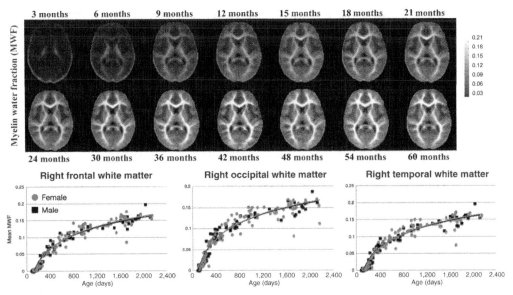

Figure 4.6. *(Top) Matched axially oriented slices through the mean myelin water fraction (MWF) for 3 months to 5 years. (Bottom) Change in MWF for an early region (occipital) and two late regions (frontal, temporal). Source: Adapted from Deoni et al., 2012 (top) and Deoni et al. (2015) (bottom).*

measures of diffusion. The increase in FA and decrease in diffusion measures imply the growth of myelination fiber bundle tracts across these ages.

A third MRI method to study myelination uses the characteristics of the MRI sequence to estimate the concentration of myelin. Deoni and colleagues have developed an MRI sequence that is claimed to be a direct measure of myelin concentration called "myelin water fraction" (MWF) (Spader et al., 2013). The technique is called "multicomponent relaxometry" (MCR) and uses an MRI sequence called "multicomponent driven equilibrium single-pulse observation of T1 and T2," (MCDESPOT; Dean, O'Muircheartaigh, Dirks, Waskiewicz, Lehman et al., 2015; Deoni, Peters, & Rutt, 2005; Deoni, Rutt, Arun, Pierpaoli, & Jones, 2008; Deoni, Rutt, & Peters, 2003, 2006). The MWF is calculated on each voxel in the MRI volume giving a whole-head quantification of myelination. This measure is presumed to measure myelin content directly rather than the volume of white matter (VBM) or the flow of magnetic signals (DTI).

The McDESPOT MCR technique has been used to map the development of myelination in children from 3 months of age through about 5 years (Dean et al., 2014; Dean et al., 2016; Dean, O'Muircheartaigh, Dirks, Waskiewicz, Walker et al., 2015; Deoni, Dean, O'Muircheartaigh, Dirks, & Jerskey, 2012; Deoni et al., 2011; Deoni, Dean, Remer, Dirks, & O'Muircheartaigh, 2015; Lebel & Deoni, 2018). An excellent review of this work is Lebel and Deoni (Lebel & Deoni, 2018). Figure 4.6 (top panel) shows axial slices of the myelin water fraction (MWF) in average templates from ages 3 months through 5 years (Deoni et al., 2012). The MWF showed rapid increases in the first 2 years and the largest increase occurred in the second year, similar to the axial MRI volume cuts in Figure 4.4. Figure 4.6 (bottom panel) shows a figure of the quantitative changes in MWF and T1 relaxation time for children ranging in age from about 1 to 6 years (Deoni et al., 2015) or 3 months to 5 years (Deoni et al., 2012). The somatosensory and motor areas and visual areas (e.g., pre-central gyrus and occipital lobe in Figure 4.6 bottom panel) showed the fastest myelination patterns showing myelination by about 1 year of age, whereas temporal and frontal areas (e.g., inferior temporal gyrus, inferior frontal gyrus, temporal, and frontal lobes) showed more gradual and protracted trajectories lasting through 5 to 6 years.

4.4 Brain Development and Experience: Face Processing

Brain development is a result of intrinsic maturation and genetic factors dynamically interacting with environmental input and experience. The earliest views of human development hypothesized that brain development was a maturational unfolding of genetic potential without much regard for the role of experience. More recent views have documented the important role of experience on brain development. The most current perspective is that brain development is a complex interaction between genetic-maturational factors and experience (Greenough, Black, & Wallace, 1987; Stiles, 2017). The current section will discuss some manners in which experience affects brain changes using the development of face processing as an example. We discuss face processing primarily because this is a research area in which we have special expertise. However, the developmental changes in face processing occurring during the second 6 months of life and during the second year have several analogs in other domains and cognitive abilities (e.g., audition, speech and language, motor development, sustained attention, joint attention, and social interactions).

One way in which experience affects brain development is to provide the basis for synaptic pruning following the exuberant period of synaptogenesis. The dramatic changes in brain synaptic density during the first year would suggest that this is a time when experience-expectant processes (Greenough et al., 1987) would have a large influence on selective brain growth. "Experience-expectant" refers to brain development that occurs as a result of common experience of humans such as the presence of faces, or other humans, and colors. This development would not occur without the experience but generally occurs in all members of the species due to common experiences. Experience-dependent processes result from individuals' unique experiences to define neural and behavioral changes and do not necessarily include temporal developmental constraints. Species-specific environmental input changes the brain architecture and synaptic connections among neurons, so as to determine a relatively stable cortical specialization in the adult brain (Bick, Zeanah, Fox, & Nelson, 2018; Greenough et al., 1987). Several studies conducted with newborns and infants showed that over the course of the first 12 months of life there is a rapid development of face processing. We hypothesize that, at the neural level, the pruning of synaptic connections due to face stimuli input defines the set of connections that will survive into childhood and beyond.

The development of responses to face stimuli in the first year illustrates the interplay between intrinsic factors, which are independent from experience, and environmental input, which may act through experience-expectant mechanisms or experience-dependent mechanisms. The responses to faces at birth and during the first 3 to 6 months are hypothesized to be dominated by subcortical brain areas that are relatively mature at birth (e.g., CONSPEC; M. H. Johnson, & Morton, 1991; M. H. Johnson, Senju, & Tomalski, 2014; Morton & Johnson, 1991). Low-level, domain-general, perceptual processes guide infants' response and preference to stimuli by orienting their visual attention towards structural and featural properties that both faces and other stimuli possess (Simion & Giorgio, 2015; Simion, Leo, Turati, Valenza, & Dalla Barba, 2007). Cortical circuits in the ventral visual pathway begin their synaptogenesis around 3 months of age and last through the first year. These cortical circuits become selectively tuned through synaptic pruning toward the most experienced category of stimuli, e.g., human faces (e.g., CONLERN; M. H. Johnson et al., 2014; Simion & Giorgio, 2015; Simion et al., 2007). Faces are considered to have first-order configuration representing the featural arrangements of the face (e.g., two eyes arranged above the nose and mouth) and second-order configuration representing the distances and geometric arrangement of the face (e.g., distance between eyes, a triangle for the eyes and nose). The specialization hypothesized by the CONLERN model is evident in the emergence of a sensitivity to first- and second-order configural properties of the human face (Maurer, Le Grand, & Mondloch, 2002).

The age changes in the response to faces, hypothesized to be a result of experience affecting brain areas involved in face processing, are paralleled by face-sensitive event-related-potential (ERP) components (see Hoehl & Peykarjou, 2012). The infant N290 ERP component is a negative deflection in averaged ERP that occurs about 280 to 320 ms following stimulus onset in inferior lateral-posterior occipito-temporal scalp regions. This component begins around 9 months of age to show sensitivity to face stimuli with which experience has occurred; including human versus nonhuman primate faces (de Haan, Pascalis, & Johnson, 2002; Halit, de Haan, & Johnson, 2003); own-race versus other race faces (Balas, Westerlund, Hung, & Nelson, 2011; Vogel, Monesson, & Scott, 2012); familiar versus unfamiliar faces (Guy, Richards, Tonnsen, & Roberts, 2017; Guy, Zieber, & Richards, 2016; Scott & Nelson, 2006); and faces versus objects (Conte, & Richards, 2019; Guy et al., 2016; Richards, Guy, Zieber, Xie, & Roberts, 2016; Xie & Richards, 2016).

Figure 4.7 shows the development of the N290 ERP component from 4.5 through 12 months of age in response to faces (adult male or female faces) and to other objects (novel toys, familar toys, upright houses; Richards, Guy et al., 2016; Conte, Richards, Guy, Xie, & Roberts, 2020). Figure 4.7 (top panel) shows a significant change in the form of the N290 over these recording ages, as well as changes in N290 amplitude and face-object discriminability (Figure 4.7 bottom panel). Studies with infants using cortical source analysis have concluded that the N290 is generated in the middle fusiform gyrus (Conte et al. 2020; Guy et al., 2016; M. H. Johnson et al., 2005; Richards, Guy et al., 2016; Richards, Guy, Zieber, Xie, & Roberts, 2017). There is an adult ERP component that is very similar to the infant N290 called the N170 (Eimer, Gosling, Nicholas, & Kiss, 2011), which cortical source analysis has localized in the middle or posterior fusiform gyrus (Gao, Conte, Richards, Xie, & Hanayik, 2019). This area in adults is known as the "fusiform face area" (FFA; Kanwisher, McDermott, & Chun, 1997; Kanwisher & Yovel, 2006). The FFA represents the first region in the brain's serial processing that responds to face configuration. The findings of the N290 ERP development imply that face-sensitive brain areas show developmental changes over the age range when the cortical face areas are thought to be developing.

An evidence of the cortical face processing ability at the end of the first year of life is the emergence of the so-called "face inversion" effect. The face inversion effect refers to the impairment in processing faces when presented inverted. This is attributed to difficulty in accessing configural information in inverted faces (Valentine, 1988). Infants at 3 months respond to changes in configural properties similarly in upright and inverted faces (Bhatt, Bertin, Hayden, & Reed, 2005; Hayden, Bhatt, Reed, Corbly, & Joseph, 2007). Infants by 5 to 7 months respond to featural spacing (second-order configuration) changes of upright but not inverted faces. By the end of the first year, infants' face-processing system is specialized to process upright faces in a manner similar to adults (Cashon & Holt, 2015).

The age changes in the behavioral response to face inversion are loosely paralleled by age changes in face-sensitive ERP components. Figure 4.8 shows a study that presented infants at 3 or 12 months of age with upright or inverted faces (Halit et al., 2003). The N290 was larger for inverted than for upright faces at 12 but not at 3 months of age. Some studies have manipulated specific face experiences that infants have and evaluated the effect on these ERP inversion effects. It has been shown that visual experience with individual representations of unfamiliar faces, i.e., monkey faces, during a period between 6 and 9 months, resulted in the discrimination of monkey faces at 9 months (Scott & Monesson, 2009). Three months of individual-level training between 6 and 9 months of age with books depicting monkey faces also led to an occipital-temporal ERP inversion effect on the N290 and P400 ERP components in 9-month-old infants (Scott & Monesson, 2010). The inversion effect for monkey faces was not present prior to training, implying that the acquired

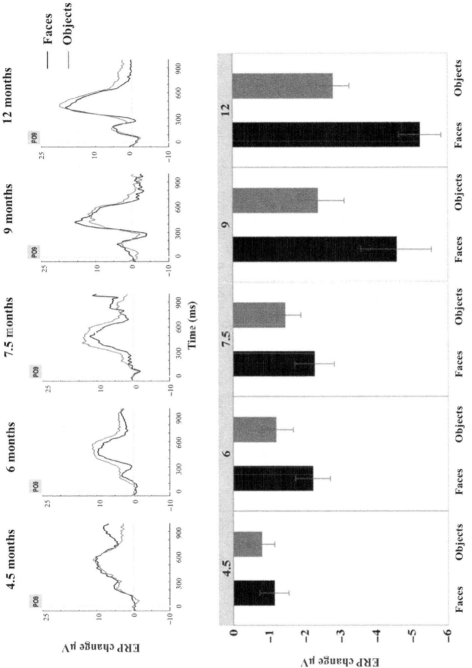

Figure 4.7. Changes in the N290 from 4.5 to 12 months of age. (Top) The activity segmented at the onset of the face and object stimuli for the lateral inferior temporal occipital electrode, PO9. (Bottom) Mean amplitude of the N290 ERP component to faces and objects across ages.

Source: Adapted from Conte et al., 2020; Richards, Guy et al., 2016; Richards et al., 2017.

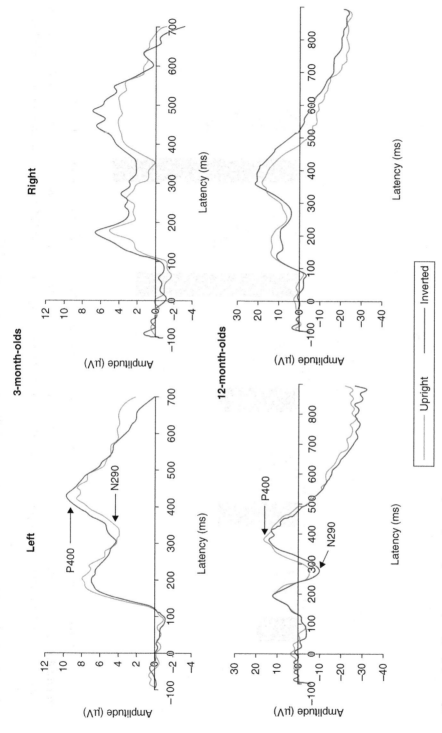

Figure 4.8. *Grand-averaged waveforms for upright and inverted human faces in 3- and 12-month-old infants at left and right posterior temporal channels (respectively electrode 32 and 44 of the Geodesic 63-channels net). Please note amplitude scale differences. Source: Adapted from Halit et al. (2003).*

experience drives the specialization of neural regions underlying face processing. These results are consistent with the view that the infant face processing system in the brain is broadly tuned in the first months, but becomes more narrowly specialized through the influence of significant experiences.

The potential for changes in brain areas supporting face processing exists beyond the infancy period. These changes may occur when synaptogenesis and wide-scale synaptic pruning are no longer occurring. These are labeled experience-dependent processes (Greenough et al., 1987). An example of this is the differentiation of the fusiform gyrus (FFG) into a "fusiform face area" (FFA; Baldauf & Desimone, 2014; Kanwisher et al., 1997) and "visual word form area" ("VWFA"; Dehaene, Le Clec'H, Poline, Le Bihan, & Cohen, 2002; Reinholz & Pollmann, 2005). The FFA is likely defined by 12 months of age and is represented equally in left and right hemispheres in the FFG (Conte et al., 2020; Richards, Guy et al., 2016; Richards et al., 2017). Exposure to school-based reading and writing experiences result in a VWFA in the left FFG that responds more strongly to visual words than other stimuli (Cantlon, Pinel, Dehaene, & Pelphrey, 2011; Cohen et al., 2000; Dehaene et al., 2010; Reinholz & Pollmann, 2005). As the VWFA activity in the left FFG increases with increases in reading performance, the activation to faces in the left FFG (left FFA) diminishes and the right FFG becomes the dominant FFA in adults (Dehaene et al., 2010). These gradual changes are found in other brain systems as well, e.g., changes in myelination due to specific training experiences in older children and adolescents (Klingberg, 2008, 2010; Nagy et al., 2004). The rapid organizational changes in the brain during the infancy period are replaced by gradual experience-dependent brain changes in children and adults.

4.5 Brain Development and Experience: Social Context, Environment, and Poverty

The prior section reviewed the role of experience in brain development, by looking at evidence from the domain of face processing. The typical developmental trajectory for face development was presented as an experience-expectant process in which typical exposure to faces during the period of exuberant synaptic growth leads to the development of brain structures with relatively stable properties. These structures can be modified in later periods by idiosyncratic individual experiences leading to experience-dependent changes in the brain. These changes in faces as a result of experience are similar to changes in several other domains in the infancy period (e.g., language, motor development, attention). The lack of these experiences may produce atypical trajectories of structural and functional brain development. An example of the influence of atypical negative experiences on brain development are findings that broad environmental deficits lead to widespread atypical suboptimal brain development.

An example of a broad environmental deficit that affects brain development are studies showing that early institutional care results in structural and functional brain deficits compared to typical familial care (foster care, adoptive, biological). Many studies have shown that children raised in institutional settings have a wide range of social and cognitive deficits with long-lasting consequences (Bick & Nelson, 2017; McLaughlin, Sheridan, & Nelson, 2017). For example, studies have compared children raised in institutional settings with children placed in foster care, adoptions, or children raised in biological families. There are long-term deficits in cognitive and neuropsychological functioning lasting through adolescence for children raised in institutional settings (e.g., attention, memory, executive function; Bick et al., 2018; Pollak et al., 2010) and deficits that are partially ameliorated by placement in foster care or adoption at an early age (e.g., attachment security, Smyke, Zeanah, Fox, Nelson, & Guthrie, 2010).

The most interesting evidence for the effect of institutional care on brain functioning and development comes from the "Bucharest Early Intervention Project" (BEPI; Bick & Nelson, 2017; Bick et al., 2018; Zeanah et al., 2003). Fox, Nelson, Zeanah and colleagues conducted a 12-year longitudinal study of infants and toddlers living in institutional care. Some children were randomly placed in foster care as a part of the study. The institutional-only group were compared to the foster care group, and control groups of adopted and biological-parent raised children. The several reports from this study found cognitive and neuropsychological effects of the psychosocial deprivation due to the institutional care (Bick et al., 2018). There were negative effects of institutionalization on overall measures of brain activity. Marshall and colleagues (Marshall, Fox, & CoreGroup, 2004) examined baseline resting EEG in the BEIP groups at ages between 5 and 31 months. EEG power in alpha, beta, and theta bands has been explored as index of neuronal maturation. Specifically, previous studies consistently reported that an excess of spectral power in low-frequency bands (e.g., theta) and a deficit of power at high-frequency bands (e.g., alpha and beta) is associated with disorders in attention, arousal and alertness (Marshall, Bar-Haim, & Fox, 2002), and learning (Barry, 2004). Marshall et al. (2004) found several differences in baseline theta and alpha in the institutionalized group (IG) and never-institutionalized group (NIG). Figure 4.9A shows that relative theta power was larger in the IG than the NIG children. The larger theta power was interpreted as an index of brain dysfunction or immaturity. Some of the IG children were assigned to foster care or adoption (FCG) whereas others were left in institutional care ("care as usual," CAUG). The CAUG, FCG, and NIG children were assessed at later ages (42 months, 8 years, 12 years). It was found that the EEG differences found between IG and NIG children at the early ages were ameliorated as a function of placement duration. First, an inverse relation was found between the amount of time spent in foster care and the subsequent theta activity recorded at 42 months (Marshall, Reeb, Fox, Nelson, & Zeanah, 2008). Second, the

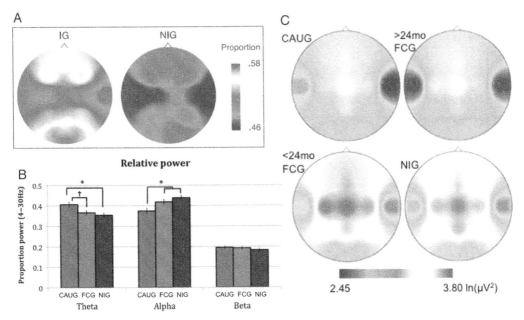

Figure 4.9. *(A) The distribution of relative theta power, expressed as the proportion of theta power band (3–5 Hz) relative to the total power in the EEG power spectrum at a given electrode site, for the institutionalized group (IG) and the never-institutionalized group (NIG). (B) Mean absolute and relative power from the theta (4–7 Hz), alpha (8–13 Hz), and beta (15–30 Hz) bands for the care-as-usual group (CAUG), foster care intervention (FCG), and never-institutionalized community controls (NIG). * p < .05, † p < .10. (C) Distribution of alpha power across the scalp at 8 years of age for children who remained in the institution (i.e., the care-as-usual group), children placed into foster care after 24 months (>24 months FCG), children placed in foster care before 24 months (<24 months FCG), and children reared with their biological parents, (i.e., the never-institutionalized group). Source: Adapted from Marshall et al. (2004) (A), Vandervert et al. (2016) (B), and Vanderwert et al. (2010) (C).*

FCG children who were placed in foster care before they were 2 years old showed patterns of brain activity that were more similar to NIG children than those placed in foster care after they turn 2 (Marshall et al., 2008). Third, the differences in EEG power spectrum were erased when tested at 8 years or 12 years of age. Figure 4.9C shows that alpha power was smaller in the IG and >24mo-FCG children than in the <24-mo-FCG and NIG children at 8 years of age (Vanderwert, Marshall, Nelson, Zeanah, & Fox, 2010). The differences in theta and alpha between the IG, FCG, and NIG groups persisted when the children were recorded at 12 years of age (Figure 4.9B; Vanderwert, Zeanah, Fox, & Nelson, 2016).

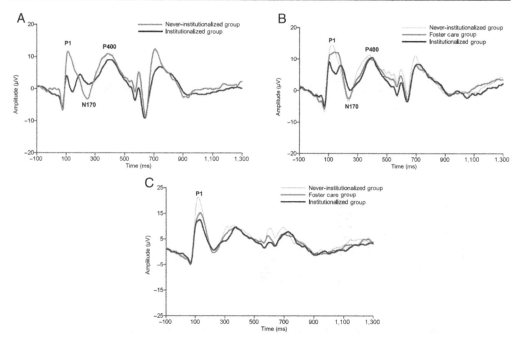

Figure 4.10. *Grand-averaged ERP waveforms of the IG and NIG at the baseline assessment (A), the 30-month post-intervention assessment (B), and the 42-month post-intervention assessment (C) over the right occipital electrode (collapsed across conditions). The x-axis represents latency in milliseconds (ms), and the y-axis represents amplitude in microvolts (μV). Note: ERP = event-related potential; IG = institutionalized group; FCG = foster care group; NIG = never-institutionalized group. Source: Adapted from Moulson et al. (2009).*

It is reasonable to assume that institutional care might adversely affect the development of the neural system underlying face processing specifically. This might occur because of the lack of consistent caregiver–infant interactions than it would occur in typical family situations. The development of face-specific areas in the brain was shown in the prior section to be an experience-expectant process that required the exposure to faces. The institutional-care children could result in a pattern of cortical hypoarousal as a result of the lack of exposure to faces compared to the typical family setting. Parker and Nelson (Parker, Nelson, & Group, 2005a, 2005b) found that institutionalized children showed cortical hypoarousal compared to noninstitutionalized children in response to pictures of familiar, unfamiliar, and emotional faces. Moulson et al. (Moulson, Westerlund, Fox, Zeanah, & Nelson, 2009) examined the amplitude of face-sensitive ERP components during passive viewing of familiar and unfamiliar faces. Figure 4.10 shows smaller amplitude and longer latency of P1 ERP component in the IG compared to the NIG children when tested at the first baseline period, and apparent reduced amplitude of the N170 ERP component for the IG children (Figure 4.10A). Amplitude differences in these two groups in the P1 and N170 persisted over time (Figure 4.10B). The FCG children, who had been moved into foster care subsequent to the first baseline period, had nearly complete recovery of the P1 and N170 ERP components. The differences between groups in the amplitude of the P1 ERP component continued through 42 months, though the N170 at this age was not significantly different for the IG, FCG, and NIG children. The foster care intervention, if started before 24 months of age, provided positive experience that largely ameliorated the effects of the negative environment found in the institutional setting.

There was evidence of widespread changes in cortical white matter and gray matter as a function of institutionalization in the BEIP study. A study of the BEIP with children at 8 years using structural MRI found smaller gray matter volume in the institutionalized groups (CAUG, FCG) compared to the noninstitutionalized group (NIG), and larger white matter volume in both the FCG and NIG children than the CAUG children (Sheridan, Fox, Zeanah, McLaughlin, & Nelson, 2012). These findings and several of the EEG/ERP findings suggest that long-term deficits in brain development resulting from institutional care may be ameliorated by an improvement in the environmental setting.

It is not just the unusual conditions of institutional care that have deleterious effects on brain development. Children born into families of low socioeconomic status (SES) are exposed to several of developmental risk factors, ranging from context of biological risk exposure (e.g., food insecurity, environmental contaminants, infectious disease) to psychosocial disadvantages (e.g., chaotic living arrangements, community violence), which affect the achievement of early developmental milestones and result in poorer neurocognitive outcomes when compared to peers from homes with greater resources (Hackman & Farah, 2009; Jensen, Berens, & Nelson, 2017; S. B. Johnson, Riis, & Noble, 2016). Psychological or environmental stress is related to poverty conditions and is likely one mediator of the effect of poverty on neural development. It has been reported that stress correlates with volumetric variations in the prefrontal cortex (Hanson et al., 2012; McEwen & Gianaros, 2010) and hippocampal volume (Hanson, Chandra, Wolfe, & Pollak, 2011; Luby et al., 2013). These brain changes act synergistically with deprived educational opportunities to produce deficits in cognitive functions such as executive functioning, memory and language (Jensen et al., 2017; Pavlakis, Noble, Pavlakis, Ali, & Frank, 2015).

Several studies have investigated the correlation between poverty and brain volume (Leijser, Siddiqi, & Miller, 2018). For example, in one study infants from low- and high-income families had similar overall brain volume, but significant and widening differences in gray matter volumes (Hanson et al., 2013). Figure 4.11 (bottom panel) shows the effect of SES level on overall gray matter volume and gray matter volume in frontal and parietal areas. These

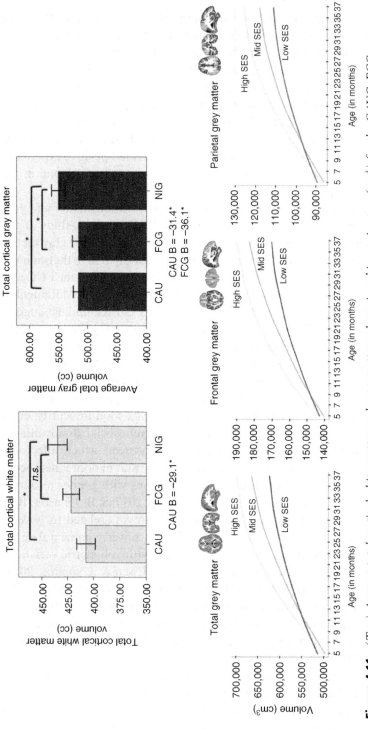

Figure 4.11. *(Top) Average total cortical white matter and gray matter volume in cubic centimeters (cm^3) for the CAUG, FCG, and NIG; error bars are ± 1 SEM. (Bottom) Growth trajectories of total gray matter, frontal lobe, and parietal lobe gray matter for children from high- (light gray lines), mid- (dark gray lines) and low- (black lines) SES families.*
Source: Adapted from Sheridan et al. (2012) (top) and Hanson et al. (2013) (bottom).

levels were similar during the first year, and then showed widening differences through the second year and following. The influence of SES seems to become stronger with increasing exposure to less favorable SES factors. In a multisite longitudinal study Hair et al. (Hair, Hanson, Wolfe, & Pollak, 2015) reported that children from families with low SES (below 1.5 times the federal poverty level) showed atypical gray matter volumes in hippocampus, frontal, and temporal lobes and low scores on standardized test of achievement. Overall, being exposed to an impoverished environment during the period of postnatal brain growth is associated with atypical brain development and leads to behavior problems that affect scholastic and occupational success.

4.6 Toward a Social Policy for Optimal Brain and Brain-Behavior Development

This section will conclude with some general recommendations for societal responsibilities for optimal development based on the characteristics of brain development. There are several obvious roles for societal structure and intervention based on our review of some of the effects of experiences on brain development. The experience-expectant process implies that typical species-specific exposure is necessary to guarantee a typical development in many cognitive domains. For instance, studies with institutionalized children imply that social interactions typically found in familial settings are necessary for children to process face configuration correctly. We presume that an atypical developmental trajectory results from inadequate quantity or quality of face-social experiences in the institutionalized infants, not the setting per se. However, overall brain activity may become muted from unspecific experiential factors in institutional settings or other disadvantaged settings. Nutrition, stimulation, and health might diminish the synaptogenesis itself resulting in insensitivity to the appropriate experience due to lack of synapses. The more gradual processes of experience-dependent activity leading to further brain specialization are necessary to provide adaption for idiosyncratic environmental characteristics. The developmental changes in face processing occurring during the second 6 months of life and during the second year have several analogs in other domains and cognitive abilities (e.g., audition, speech and language, motor development, sustained attention, joint attention, social interactions). It would be useful to delineate the experience-expectant sequelae and developmental ages for the effects of experiences on brain development, with the ultimate aim to develop a full catalog of recommendations in this regard.

The role of negative experience-dependent effects on brain development also has obvious societal implications. In addition to the specific effects of institutionalization, there are general effects of poverty on brain development. The poverty effects are likely mediated by a wide range of risk factors with additive or synergistic influences (Fox, Levitt, & Nelson, 2010; Jensen et al.,

2017; Leijser et al., 2018). The influences specifically related to brain development include nutrition (e.g., food insecurity or insufficiency), health (infectious disease, environmental teratogens, access to health care), and psychosocial stimulation (inferior childcare, underemployment resulting in inaccessible parenting, parental education deficiencies). Children in poverty not only have fewer environmental resources leading to the lack of brain development, but increased environmental stressors (teratogens, stress, housing) leading to damage to brain systems that is reflected in atypical brain development. The effects of poverty on brain development are found in high-income developed countries (Western, educated, industrialized, rich, democratic, WEIRD), but are exacerbated in poor countries with inadequate food, poor health, poverty living conditions, and psychosocial stress. The liberal humanitarian impulse to provide assistance to these non-WEIRD countries is needed to provide more optimal brain development that bridges national boundaries.

References

Balas, B., Westerlund, A., Hung, K., & Nelson III, C. A. (2011). Shape, color and the other-race effect in the infant brain. *Developmental Science, 14*(4), 892–900. doi:10.1111/j.1467-7687.2011.01039.x

Baldauf, D., & Desimone, R. (2014). Neural mechanisms of object-based attention. *Science, 344*(6182), 424–427. doi:10.1126/science.1247003

Barry, R. J., Clarke, A. R., McCarthy, R., Selikowitz, M., Rushby, J. A., & Ploskova, E. (2004). EEG differences in children as a function of resting-state arousal level. *Clinical Neurophysiology, 115*, 402–408.

Bhatt, R., Bertin, E., Hayden, A., & Reed, A. (2005). Face processing in infancy: Developmental changes in the use of different kinds of relational information. *Child Development, 76*(1), 169–181.

Bick, J., & Nelson, C. A. (2017). Early experience and brain development. *Wiley Interdisciplinary Reviews: Cognitive Science, 8*(1–2), e1387. doi:10.1002/wcs.1387

Bick, J., Zeanah, C. H., Fox, N. A., & Nelson, C. A. (2018). Memory and executive functioning in 12-year-old children with a history of institutional rearing. *Child Development, 89*(2), 495–508. doi:10.1111/cdev.12952

Bourgeois, J. P. (1997). Synaptogenesis, heterochrony and epigenesis in the mammalian neocortex. *Acta Paediatric Supplement, 422*, 27–33.

Bourgeois, J. P., & Rakic, P. (1993). Changes of synaptic density in the primary visual cortex of the macaque monkey from fetal to adult stage. *Journal of Neuroscience, 13*(7), 2801–2820. doi:10.1523/JNEUROSCI.13-07-02801.1993

Cantlon, J. F., Pinel, P., Dehaene, S., & Pelphrey, K. A. (2011). Cortical representations of symbols, objects, and faces are pruned back during early childhood. *Cerebral Cortex, 21*(1), 191–199. doi:10.1093/cercor/bhq078

Cashon, C. H., & Holt, N. A. (2015). Developmental origins of the face inversion effect. In B. B. Janette (Ed.), *Advances in child development and behaviour* (Vol. 48, pp. 117–150). Philadelphia, PA: Elsevier.

Cohen, L., Dehaene, S., Naccache, L., Lehéricy, S., Dehaene-Lambertz, G., Hénaff, M. -A., & Michel, F. (2000). The visual word form area: Spatial and temporal characterization of an initial stage of reading in normal subjects and posterior split-brain patients. *Brain*, *123*(2), 291–307. doi:10.1093/brain/123.2.291

Conel, J. L. (1939–67). *Postnatal development of the human cerebral cortex* (Vols. 1–8). Cambridge, MA: Harvard University Press.

   (1951). *The postnatal development of the human cerebral cortex. Vol. 6: The cortex of the six-month infant*. Cambridge, MA: Harvard University Press.

   (1967). *The postnatal development of the human cerebral cortex. Vol. 8: The cortex of the six-year-old child*. Cambridge, MA: Harvard University Press.

Conte, S., & Richards, J. E. (2019). *The development of face-sensitive cortical processing in early Infancy*. Paper presented at the Society for Research in Child Development, Baltimore, MD.

Conte, S., Richards, J. E., Guy, M. W., Zieber, N., Xie, W., & Roberts. J.E. (2020). Face-sensitive brain responses in the first year of life. *NeuroImage*, 211, 116602. https://doi.org/10.1016/j.neuroimage.2020.116602

de Haan, M., Pascalis, O., & Johnson, M. H. (2002). Specialization of neural mechanisms underlying face recognition in human infants. *Journal of Cognitive Neuroscience*, *14*(2), 199–209. doi:10.1162/089892902317236849

Dean, D. C., III, O'Muircheartaigh, J., Dirks, H., Travers, B. G., Adluru, N., Alexander, A. L., & Deoni, S. C. L. (2016). Mapping an index of the myelin g-ratio in infants using magnetic resonance imaging. *Neuroimage*, *132*, 225–237. doi:10.1016/j.neuroimage.2016.02.040

Dean, D. C., III, O'Muircheartaigh, J., Dirks, H., Waskiewicz, N., Lehman, K., Walker, L., … Deoni, S. C. L. (2014). Modeling healthy male white matter and myelin development: 3 through 60 months of age. *Neuroimage*, *84*, 742–752. doi:10.1016/j.neuroimage.2013.09.058

   (2015). Estimating the age of healthy infants from quantitative myelin water fraction maps. *Human Brain Mapping*, *36*(4), 1233–1244. doi:10.1002/hbm.22671

Dean, D. C., III, O'Muircheartaigh, J., Dirks, H., Waskiewicz, N., Walker, L., Doernberg, E., … Deoni, S. C. L. (2015). Characterizing longitudinal white matter development during early childhood. *Brain Structure & Function*, *220*(4), 1921–1933. doi:10.1007/s00429-014-0763-3

Dehaene, S., Le Clec'H, G., Poline, J.-B., Le Bihan, D., & Cohen, L. (2002). The visual word form area: A prelexical representation of visual words in the fusiform gyrus. *Neuroreport*, *13*(3), 321–325.

Dehaene, S., Pegado, F., Braga, L. W., Ventura, P., Nunes Filho, G., Jobert, A., … Cohen, L. (2010). How learning to read changes the cortical networks for vision and language. Supplemental Info. *Science, 330*(6009), 1359–1364. doi:10.1126/science.1194140

Deoni, S. C. L., Dean, D. C., III, O'Muircheartaigh, J., Dirks, H., & Jerskey, B. A. (2012). Investigating white matter development in infancy and early childhood using myelin water faction and relaxation time mapping. *Neuroimage*, *63*(3), 1038–1053. doi:10.1016/j.neuroimage.2012.07.037

Deoni, S. C. L., Dean, D. C., III, Remer, J., Dirks, H., & O'Muircheartaigh, J. (2015). Cortical maturation and myelination in healthy toddlers and young children. *Neuroimage, 115*, 147–161. doi:10.1016/j.neuroimage.2015.04.058

Deoni, S. C. L., Mercure, E., Blasi, A., Gasston, D., Thomson, A., Johnson, M., … Murphy, D. G. M. (2011). Mapping infant brain myelination with magnetic resonance imaging. *Journal of Neuroscience*, *31*(2), 784–791. doi:10.1523/JNEUROSCI.2106–10.2011

Deoni, S. C. L., Peters, T. M., & Rutt, B. K. (2005). High-resolution T1 and T2 mapping of the brain in a clinically acceptable time with DESPOT1 and DESPOT2. *Magnetic Resonance in Medicine*, *53*(1), 237–241. doi:10.1002/mrm.20314

Deoni, S. C. L., Rutt, B. K., Arun, T., Pierpaoli, C., & Jones, D. K. (2008). Gleaning multicomponent T1 and T2 information from steady-state imaging data. *Magnetic Resonance in Medicine*, *60*(6), 1372–1387. doi:10.1002/mrm.21704

Deoni, S. C. L., Rutt, B. K., & Peters, T. M. (2003). Rapid combined T1 and T2 mapping using gradient recalled acquisition in the steady state. *Magnetic Resonance in Medicine*, *49*(3), 515–526. doi:10.1002/mrm.10407

(2006). Synthetic T1-weighted brain image generation with incorporated coil intensity correction using DESPOT1. *Magnetic Resonance Imaging*, *24*(9), 1241–1248. doi:10.1016/j.mri.2006.03.015

DeSilva, J. M., & Lesnik, J. J. (2008). Brain size at birth throughout human evolution: A new method for estimating neonatal brain size in hominins. *Journal of Human Evolution*, *55*(6), 1064–1074. https://doi.org/10.1016/j.jhevol.2008.07.008

Eimer, M., Gosling, A., Nicholas, S., & Kiss, M. (2011). The N170 component and its links to configural face processing: A rapid neural adaptation study. *Brain Research*, *1376*, 76–87. doi:10.1016/j.brainres.2010.12.046

Fox, S. E., Levitt, P., & Nelson, C. A. (2010). How the timing and quality of early experiences influence the development of brain architecture. *Child Development*, *81*(1), 28–40. doi:10.1111/j.1467-8624.2009.01380.x

Gao, C., Conte, S., Richards, J.E., Xie, W., & Hanayik, T. (2019). The neural sources of N170: Understanding timing of activation in face-selective areas. *Psychophysiology*, *56*(6), e1336.

Greenough, W. T., Black, J. E., & Wallace, C. S. (1987). Experience and brain development. *Child Development*, *58*(3), 539–559.

Guy, M. W., Richards, J. E., Tonnsen, B. L., & Roberts, J. E. (2017). Neural correlates of face processing in etiologically-distinct 12-month-old infants at high risk of autism spectrum disorder. *Developmental Cognitive Neuroscience*, *29*, 61–71. doi:10.1016/j.dcn.2017.03.002

Guy, M. W., Zieber, N., & Richards, J. E. (2016). The cortical development of specialized face processing in infancy. *Child Development*, *87*(5), 1581–1600. doi:10.1111/cdev.12543

Hackman, D. A., & Farah, M. J. (2009). Socioeconomic status and the developing brain. *Trends in Cognitive Sciences*, *13*(2), 65–73. https://doi.org/10.1016/j.tics.2008.11.003

Hair, N. L., Hanson, J. L., Wolfe, B. L., & Pollak, S. D. (2015). Association of child poverty, brain development, and academic achievement. *JAMA Pediatrics*, *169*(9), 822–829. doi:10.1001/jamapediatrics.2015.1475

Halit, H., de Haan, M., & Johnson, M. H. (2003). Cortical specialisation for face processing: Face-sensitive event-related potential components in 3- and 12-month-old infants. *Neuroimage*, *19*(3), 1180–1193. doi:10.1016/S1053-8119(03)00076-4

Hanson, J. L., Chandra, A., Wolfe, B. L., & Pollak, S. D. (2011). Association between income and the hippocampus. *PLoS One*, *6*(5), e18712. doi:10.1371/journal.pone.0018712

Hanson, J. L., Chung, M. K., Avants, B. B., Rudolph, K. D., Shirtcliff, E. A., Gee, J. C., ... Pollak, S. D. (2012). Structural variations in prefrontal cortex mediate the relationship between early childhood stress and spatial working memory. *Journal of Neuroscience, 32*(23), 7917–7925. doi:10.1523/JNEUROSCI.0307-12.2012

Hanson, J. L., Hair, N., Shen, D. G., Shi, F., Gilmore, J. H., Wolfe, B. L., & Pollak, S. D. (2013). Family poverty affects the rate of human infant brain growth. *PLoS One, 8*(12), e80954. doi:10.1371/journal.pone.0080954

Hayden, A., Bhatt, R. S., Reed, A., Corbly, C. R., & Joseph, J. E. (2007). The development of expert face processing: are infants sensitive to normal differences in second-order relational information? *Journal of Experimental Child Psychology, 97*(2), 85–98. doi:10.1016/j.jecp.2007.01.004

Hoehl, S., & Peykarjou, S. (2012). The early development of face processing: What makes faces special? *Neuroscience Bulletin, 28*(6), 765–788. doi:10.1007/s12264-012-1280-0

Huttenlocher, P. R. (1990). Morphometric study of human cerebral cortex development. *Neuropsychologia, 28*(6), 517–527.

(1994). Synaptogenesis, synapse elimination, and neural plasticity in human cerebral cortex. In C. A. Nelson (Ed.), *Threats to optimal development, the Minnesota symposia on child psychology* (Vol. 27, pp. 35–54). Hillsdale, NJ: Lawrence Erlbaum Associates.

Huttenlocher, P. R., & Dabholkar, A. S. (1997). Regional differences in synaptogenesis in human cerebral cortex. *Journal of Comparative Neurology, 387*(2), 167–178. doi:10.1002/(SICI)1096–9861(19971020)387:2<167::AID-CNE1>3.0.CO;2 Z

Jensen, S. K. G., Berens, A. E., & Nelson, C. A., III (2017). Effects of poverty on interacting biological systems underlying child development. *Lancet Child & Adolescent Health, 1*(3), 225–239. doi:10.1016/S2352-4642(17)30024-X

Johnson, M. H., Griffin, R., Csibra, G., Halit, H., Farroni, T., de Haan, M., ... Richards, J. (2005). The emergence of the social brain network: Evidence from typical and atypical development. *Development and Psychopathology, 17*(3), 599–619. doi:10.1017/S0954579405050297

Johnson, M. H., & Morton, J. (1991). *Biology and cognitive development: The case of face recognition.* Oxford: Basil Blackwell.

Johnson, M. H., Senju, A., & Tomalski, P. (2014). The two-process theory of face processing: Modifications based on two decades of data from infants and adults. *Neuroscience Biobehaviour Review.* doi:10.1016/j.neubiorev.2014.10.009

Johnson, S. B., Riis, J. L., & Noble, K. G. (2016). State of the art review: Poverty and the developing brain. *Pediatrics, 137*(4). doi:10.1542/peds.2015-3075

Kanwisher, N., McDermott, J., & Chun, M. M. (1997). The fusiform face area: A module in human extrastriate cortex specialized for face perception. *Journal of Neuroscience, 17*(11), 4302–4311.

Kanwisher, N., & Yovel, G. (2006). The fusiform face area: A cortical region specialized for the perception of faces. *Philosophical Transactions of the Royal Society B: Biological Sciences, 361*(1476), 2109–2128. doi:10.1098/rstb.2006.1934

Klingberg, T. (2008). White matter maturation and cognitive development during childhood. In C. A. Nelson & M. Luciana (Eds.), *Handbook of developmental cognitive neuroscience* (2nd ed., pp. 237–244). Cambridge, MA: MIT Press.

(2010). Training and plasticity of working memory. *Trends in Cognitive Science, 14*(7), 317–324. doi:10.1016/j.tics.2010.05.002

Kolb, B., & Fantie, B. (1989). Development of the child's brain and behavior. In C. R. Reynolds & E. Fletcher-Janzen (Eds.), *Handbook of clinical child neuropsychology* (pp. 17–39). New York, NY: Plenum Press.

Kral, A. (2007). Unimodal and cross-modal plasticity in the "deaf" auditory cortex. *International Journal of Audiology, 46*(9), 479–493.

Lebel, C., & Deoni, S. (2018). The development of brain white matter microstructure. *Neuroimage, 182*, 207–218. https://doi.org/10.1016/j.neuroimage.2017.12.097

Leijser, L. M., Siddiqi, A., & Miller, S. P. (2018). Imaging evidence of the effect of socioeconomic status on brain structure and development. *Seminars in Pediatric Neurology, 27*, 26–34. doi:https://doi.org/10.1016/j.spen.2018.03.004

Luby, J., Belden, A., Botteron, K., Marrus, N., Harms, M. P., Bapp, C., … Barch, D. (2013). The effects of poverty on childhood brain development: The mediating effect of caregiving and stressful life events. *JAMA Pediatrics, 167*(12), 1135–1142. doi:10.1001/jamapediatrics.2013.3139

Lyall, A. E., Savadjiev, P., Shenton, M. E., & Kubicki, M. (2016). Insights into the brain: Neuroimaging of brain development and maturation. *Journal of Neuroimaging in Psychiatry & Neurology, 1*(1), 10–19. doi:10.17756/jnpn.2016-003

Marshall, P. J., Bar-Haim, Y., & Fox, N. A. (2002). Development of the EEG from 5 months to 4 years of age. *Clinical Neurophysiology, 113*(8), 1199–1208.

Marshall, P. J., Fox, N. A., & CoreGroup, T. B. (2004). A comparison of the electroencephalogram between institutionalized and community children in Romania. *Journal of Cognitive Neuroscience, 16*(8), 1327–1338. doi:10.1162/0898929042304723

Marshall, P. J., Reeb, B. C., Fox, N. A., Nelson, C. A., III, & Zeanah, C. H. (2008). Effects of early intervention on EEG power and coherence in previously institutionalized children in Romania. *Development and Psychopathology, 20*(3), 861–880. doi:10.1017/S0954579408000412

Maurer, D., Le Grand, R., & Mondloch, C. J. (2002). The many faces of configural processing. *Trends in Cognitive Sciences, 6*(5), 6.

McEwen, B. S., & Gianaros, P. J. (2010). Central role of the brain in stress and adaptation: Links to socioeconomic status, health, and disease. *Annals of the New York Academy of Sciences, 1186*(1), 190–222. doi:10.1111/j.1749-6632.2009.05331.x

McLaughlin, K. A., Sheridan, M. A., & Nelson, C. A. (2017). Neglect as a violation of species-expectant experience: Neurodevelopmental consequences. *Biological Psychiatry, 82*(7), 462–471. doi:10.1016/j.biopsych.2017.02.1096

Morton, J., & Johnson, M. H. (1991). CONSPEC and CONLERN: A two-process theory of infant face recognition. *Psychological Review, 63*, 1743–1753.

Moulson, M. C., Westerlund, A., Fox, N. A., Zeanah, C. H., & Nelson, C. A. (2009). The effects of early experience on face recognition: An event-related potential study of institutionalized children in Romania. *Child Development, 80*(4), 1039–1056.

Nagy, Z., Westerberg, H., & Klingberg, T. (2004). Maturation of white matter is associated with the development of cognitive functions during childhood. *Journal of Cognitive Neuroscience, 16*(7), 1227–1233. doi:10.1162/0898929041920441

O'Hare, E. D., & Sowell, E. R. (2008). Imaging developmental changes in gray and white matter in the human brain. In C. A. Nelson & M. Luciana (Eds.),

Handbook of developmental cognitive neuroscience (2nd ed., pp. 23–38). Cambridge, MA: MIT Press.

O'Muircheartaigh, J., Dean, D. C., III, Ginestet, C. E., Walker, L., Waskiewicz, N., Lehman, K., … Deoni, S. C. L. (2014). White matter development and early cognition in babies and toddlers. *Human Brain Mapping*, *35*(9), 4475–4487. doi:10.1002/hbm.22488

Parker, S. W., Nelson, C. A., & Group, T. B. E. I. P. C. (2005a). An event-related potential study of the impact of institutional rearing on face recognition. *Development and Psychopathology*, *17*, 621–639.

(2005b). The impact of early institutional rearing on the ability to discriminate facial expressions of emotion: An event-related potential study. *Child Development*, *76*(1), 54–72. doi:10.1111/j.1467-8624.2005.00829.x

Pavlakis, A. E., Noble, K., Pavlakis, S. G., Ali, N., & Frank, Y. (2015). Brain imaging and electrophysiology biomarkers: Is there a role in poverty and education outcome research? *Pediatric Neurology*, *52*(4), 383–388. https://doi.org/10.1016/j.pediatrneurol.2014.11.005

Pollak, S. D., Nelson, C. A., Schlaak, M. F., Roeber, B. J., Wewerka, S. S., Wiik, K. L., … Gunnar, M. R. (2010). Neurodevelopmental effects of early deprivation in postinstitutionalized children. *Child Development*, *81*(1), 224–236. doi:10.1111/j.1467-8624.2009.01391.x

Pujol, J., Soriano-Mas, C., Ortiz, H., Sebastián-Gallés, N., Losilla, J. M., & Deus, J. (2006). Myelination of language-related areas in the developing brain. *Neurology*, *66*(3), 339–343. doi:https://doi.org/10.1212/01.wnl.0000201049.66073.8d

Reinholz, J., & Pollmann, S. (2005). Differential activation of object-selective visual areas by passive viewing of pictures and words. *Brain Research: Cognitive Brain Research*, *24*(3), 702–714. doi:10.1016/j.cogbrainres.2005.04.009

Remer, J., Croteau-Chonka, E., Dean, D. C., III, D'Arpino, S., Dirks, H., Whiley, D., & Deoni, S. C. L. (2017). Quantifying cortical development in typically developing toddlers and young children, 1–6 years of age. *Neuroimage*, *153*, 246–261. https://doi.org/10.1016/j.neuroimage.2017.04.010

Richards, J. E., Guy, M., Zieber, N., Xie, W., & Roberts, J. E. (2016). *Brain changes in response to faces in the first year.* Poster presented at the International Conference on Infant Studies, New Orleans, LA.

(2017). *Brain changes in response to faces in the first year.* Paper presented at the Society for Research in Child Development, Austin, TX.

Richards, J. E., Sanchez, C., Phillips-Meek, M., & Xie, W. (2016). A database of age-appropriate average MRI templates. *Neuroimage*, *124*(Pt. B), 1254–1259. doi:10.1016/j.neuroimage.2015.04.055

Richards, J. E., & Xie, W. (2015). Brains for all the ages: Structural neurodevelopment in infants and children from a life-span perspective. In J. Benson (Ed.), *Advances in Child Development and Behaviour* (Vol. 48, pp. 1–52). Philadelphia, PA: Elsevier.

Rosenberg, K., & Trevathan, W. (2002). Birth, obstetrics and human evolution. *BJOG: An International Journal of Obstetrics and Gynaecology*, *109*(11), 1199–1206. https://doi.org/10.1016/S1470-0328(02)00410-X

Scott, L. S., & Monesson, A. (2009). The origin of biases in face perception. *Psychological Science*, *20*(6), 676–680. doi:10.1111/j.1467-9280.2009.02348.x

(2010). Experience-dependent neural specialization during infancy. *Neuropsychologia*, *48*(6), 1857–1861. doi:10.1016/j.neuropsychologia.2010.02.008

Scott, L. S., & Nelson, C. A. (2006). Featural and configural face processing in adults and infants: A behavioral and electrophysiological investigation. *Perception*, *35*(8), 1107–1128. doi:10.1068/p5493

Shankle, W. R., Romney, A. K., Landing, B. H., & Hara, J. (1998). Developmental patterns in the cytoarchitecture of the human cerebral cortex from birth to 6 years examined by correspondence analysis. *Proceedings of the National Academy of Sciences of the United States of America*, *95*(7), 4023–4028.

Sheridan, M. A., Fox, N. A., Zeanah, C. H., McLaughlin, K. A., & Nelson, C. A. (2012). Variation in neural development as a result of exposure to institutionalization early in childhood. *Proceedings of the National Academy of Sciences of the United States of America*, *109*(32), 12927–12932. doi:10.1073/pnas.1200041109

Simion, F., & Giorgio, E. D. (2015). Face perception and processing in early infancy: inborn predispositions and developmental changes. *Frontiers in Psychology*, *6*, 969. doi:10.3389/fpsyg.2015.00969

Simion, F., Leo, I., Turati, C., Valenza, E., & Dalla Barba, B. (2007). How face specialization emerges in the first months of life. *Progressive Brain Research*, *164*, 169–185. doi:10.1016/S0079-6123(07)64009-6

Smyke, A. T., Zeanah, C. H., Fox, N. A., Nelson, C. A., & Guthrie, D. (2010). Placement in foster care enhances quality of attachment among young institutionalized children. *Child Development*, *81*(1), 212–223. doi:10.1111/j.1467-8624.2009.01390.x

Sowell, E. R., Thompson, P. M., & Toga, A. W. (2004). Mapping changes in the human cortex throughout the span of life. *Neuroscientist*, *10*(4), 372–392. doi:10.1177/1073858404263960

Spader, H. S., Ellermeier, A., O'Muircheartaigh, J., Dean, D. C., III, Dirks, H., Boxerman, J. L., … Deoni, S. C. L. (2013). Advances in myelin imaging with potential clinical application to pediatric imaging. *Neurosurgical Focus*, *34*(4), e9. doi:10.3171/2013.1.FOCUS12426

Stiles, J. (2017). Principles of brain development. *Wiley Interdisciplinary Reviews: Cognitive Science*, *8*(1–2). doi:10.1002/wcs.1402

Stiles, J., & Jernigan, T. L. (2010). The basics of brain development. *Neuropsychology Review*, *20*(4), 327–348. doi:10.1007/s11065-010-9148-4

Symms, M., Jager, H. R., Schmierer, K., & Yousry, T. A. (2004). A review of structural magnetic resonance neuroimaging. *Journal of Neurology, Neurosurgery, and Psychiatry*, *75*(9), 1235–1244. doi:10.1136/jnnp.2003.032714

Toga, A. W., Thompson, P. M., & Sowell, E. R. (2006). Mapping brain maturation. *Trends in Neurosciences*, *29*(3), 148–159. doi:10.1016/j.tins.2006.01.007

Uda, S., Matsui, M., Tanaka, C., Uematsu, A., Miura, K., Kawana, I., & Noguchi, K. (2015). Normal development of human brain white matter from infancy to early adulthood: A diffusion tensor imaging study. *Journal of Developmental Neuroscience*, *37*(2), 182–194. doi:10.1159/000373885

Valentine, T. (1988). Upside-down faces: A review of the effect of inversion upon face recognition. *British Journal of Psychology*, *79*(Pt. 4), 471–491.

Vanderwert, R. E., Marshall, P. J., Nelson, C. A., Zeanah, C. H., & Fox, N. A. (2010). Timing of intervention affects brain electrical activity in children exposed to severe psychosocial neglect. *PLoS One*, *5*(7), e11415. doi:10.1371/journal. pone.0011415

Vanderwert, R. E., Zeanah, C. H., Fox, N. A., & Nelson, C. A. (2016). Normalization of EEG activity among previously institutionalized children placed into foster care: A 12-year follow-up of the Bucharest Early Intervention Project. *Developmental Cognitive Neuroscience*, *17*, 68–75. https://doi.org/10.1016/j.dcn.2015.12.004

Vogel, M., Monesson, A., & Scott, L. S. (2012). Building biases in infancy: The influence of race on face and voice emotion matching. *Developmental Science*, *15*(3), 359–372. doi:10.1111/j.1467-7687.2012.01138.x

Xie, W., & Richards, J. E. (2016). Effects of interstimulus intervals on behavioral, heart rate, and event-related potential indices of infant engagement and sustained attention. *Psychophysiology*, *53*(8), 1128–1142. doi:10.1111/psyp.12670

Zeanah, C. H., Nelson, C. A., Fox, N. A., Smyke, A. T., Marshall, P., Parker, S. W., & Koga, S. (2003). Designing research to study the effects of institutionalization on brain and behavioral development: The Bucharest Early Intervention Project. *Development and Psychopathology*, *15*(4), 885–907.

5 Development During Infancy in Children Later Diagnosed with Autism Spectrum Disorder

Terje Falck-Ytter and Emily Jones

5.1 Introduction

Autism spectrum disorder (ASD) is a heritable, heterogeneous, and common neurodevelopmental condition defined by impairments in social communication alongside restricted and repetitive behaviors (RRB). ASD is a moving target; its definition has changed dramatically over the years. The first comprehensive clinical descriptions of the condition were given by Leo Kanner and Hans Asperger more than 70 years ago (Asperger, 1944; Kanner, 1943), but it was not before 1980, with the publication of the third edition of the *Diagnostic and Statistical Manual* (DSM) of the American Psychiatric Association that the term autism was introduced as a formal category. At that time, only one criterion related to social interaction was listed (pervasive lack of responsiveness to other people). Today, in the latest (fifth) version of the DSM, ASD is defined by several possible symptoms within the broad domains of social communication impairments and RRB, highlighting that ASD is seen as a highly heterogeneous condition. Clinically, another outstanding and blurring factor is the high rates of co-occurring conditions (e.g., with intellectual disability, attention-deficit hyperactivity disorder [ADHD], language disorder, motor problems). ASD is also etiologically diverse, with a primary role for a range of genetic factors but also potential interactions with environmental exposures.

Over the last decades, there has been a strong interest in increasing our knowledge about early development in ASD to enable earlier detection and novel support strategies. Further, because ASD is very likely to reflect atypicalities in to the early development of the brain, longitudinal studies of infants are required to fully understand its emergence.

Early research addressed early development in ASD using retrospective designs. For example, in one of the earliest systematic studies of this type, Hoshino et al. (1982) compared 85 autistic children to 65 children with developmental delays and 150 typically developing controls. Based on interviews with the parents, the study identified early (< 2 years) behavioral signs that were either specific to ASD or shared among the two clinical groups (the identified specific signs included atypicalities in social communication, perception, and sleep). However, a general concern with such retrospective designs is that they rely on parent report of "historical" and quite personal events, which may be biased. To address this, some researchers have collected more objective material such as videos of the child recorded by the parents during infancy (e.g., Baranek, 1999). While this mitigates some of the biases of report-based retrospective studies, they introduce several other issues such as problems with comparable video recordings for analysis. The field generally now seems to have converged on the view that the most promising research approach is to study infant siblings prospectively. The sharp increase in research focusing on early development during the last 15 years is largely due to the demonstration that it is feasible and fruitful to study infant siblings of children with the condition in prospective longitudinal studies (Zwaigenbaum et al., 2005). Therefore, before continuing, we will now briefly summarize some key characteristics of these "infant sib studies."

5.1.1 The Infant Sibling Design

The primary strength of the infant sibling design is that it allows for systematic, longitudinal and (relatively) unbiased assessment of specific constructs putatively related to ASD. Such data are needed to inform our theories of neurodevelopmental trajectories "leading to" the diagnosis and to identify the developmental periods with maximal endo phenotypic homogeneity (Figure 5.1), which may enable us to develop screening tools or biological markers with improved sensitivity and specificity (an endo-phenotype can be defined as an underlying trait, e.g., at the level of brain structure or function, useful for explaining the condition of interest). Typically, a sib study recruits infants with an older sibling with ASD, with a first assessment before the infant's first birthday. The probability of receiving an ASD diagnosis among full siblings is between 10% and 20%, a very high figure seen in light of the general prevalence of ASD (1–2%). A low-risk control group consisting of infant siblings of typically developing children is most often included as well. Infants are typically assessed on a dense longitudinal protocol including a mixture of brain-based and behavioral measures, with clinical symptomatology and cognitive and adaptive function assessed in person and through parent questionnaire at outcome. Categorical diagnostic judgments made by experienced clinicians based on gold-standard instruments like the Autism Diagnostic Observation Schedule and the Autism Diagnostic Interview – Revised are typically complemented by continuous measures, including but not restricted to measures of autistic traits.

In the categorical analysis, the researcher typically compares three main outcome groups: (1) high-risk siblings with ASD diagnosis at follow-up, (2) low-risk infants (without ASD diagnosis), and (3) high-risk infants without ASD diagnosis. The latter group is sometimes divided into two: one with no developmental concerns and one with developmental problems other than ASD.

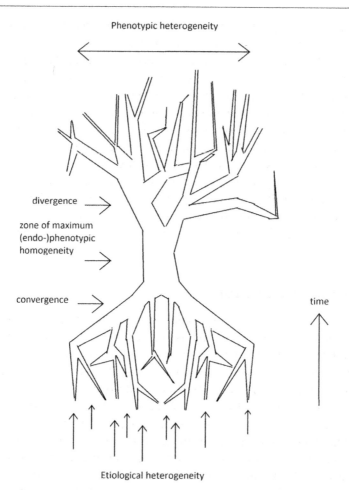

Figure 5.1. *Variable heterogeneity in ASD as a function of developmental time. Emerging evidence suggests that diverse (genetic and environmental) etiological factors converge on a smaller set of key neurodevelopmental processes in the early development of ASD. Subsequently, these key processes are likely to interact with secondary risk/protective factors, transactional processes, and stochastic events, causing increased phenotypic variability and ultimately the complex picture of ASD we see today in the clinics. Infant sibling studies can play a key role in describing these developmental processes and their potential causes, and identifying the measures and time periods associated with maximum (endo-)phenotypic homogeneity.*

The low-risk group is important to establish the typical developmental course of the constructs studied. The subgroups within the high-risk sample share many characteristics due to all having an older sibling with ASD; hence these contrasts naturally control for several confounding factors that may explain differences between the low-risk and the high-risk group more generally.

The infants sibling design is not without limitations and challenges (for a review, see Zwaigenbaum et al., 2007). First, it is a passive observational approach that can illuminate developmental pathways only in a descriptive sense. Although the longitudinal design is helpful for identifying new causal hypotheses, other research designs (such as intervention studies) are needed to actually test these ideas. Second, there is a risk that siblings of children with ASD are not representative of the broader ASD population. A proportion of cases with ASD can be caused by *de novo* mutations that do not run in families, and at an etiological level these cases may differ from familial cases included in infant sib studies. On the other hand, different etiological factors may converge on common developmental pathways and thus differences in distal etiological causes may not threaten the generalizability of the key findings of the study (Figure 5.1). Third, it may be that the families who choose to participate in an infant sibling study are different from the ones that do not (i.e., the majority of the population of interest). Fourth, the infant sibling design is very resource demanding and even after years of expensive data collection, one may still have only a modestly sized group of children with ASD in the study. Needless to say, although the design is powerful, it is not immune to the general issues such as risk for spurious findings. The timescale these projects operate on typically extends the duration of research grants, placing high burden on research leaders attracting new funding without having to change all parameters of any existing study protocol.

5.2 Early Development in ASD: A Review of the Literature

With these strengths and challenges in mind, we now turn to the main part of the review, which summarizes and discusses findings related to different domains implicated in the early development of ASD. We focus primarily on findings from prospective studies of infant siblings of children with ASD. Due to space limitations, the review is selective; readers wanting a more in-depth discussion of specific points should read the original works and consult previous reviews on the topic (e.g., Jones, Gliga, Bedford, Charman, & Johnson, 2014; Varcin & Jeste, 2017). We finish the chapter by discussing what we see as key future directions for the field, as well as some ethical, sociocultural, and policy-related issues.

5.2.1 Sensory Processing and Responses to Basic Sensory Stimulation

In Kanner's seminal 1943 paper on (what later should be termed) autism, there are examples of what appears to be sensory hypersensitivity in the toddlers and older children he described (e.g., special interest in light reflections, intolerance to touch). Some 70 years later, in the latest edition of the DSM (DSM-5), sensory hyper- and hyposensitivity was included as a formal symptom that can count toward the diagnosis of ASD, included in the RRB domain. In line with the late inclusion of sensory symptoms in the diagnostic criteria, research within infants has been limited to date but is of increasing interest given its translational relevance.

Parental reports of perceptual sensitivity (a temperamental measure) at 6 months and early parent concerns about sensory problems (but not social or communicative problems) predict later ASD diagnosis (Clifford et al., 2013; Sacrey et al., 2015). Qualitative studies also support the notion of sensory atypicalities preceding the onset of an ASD diagnosis (Bryson et al., 2007; Dawson, Osterling, Meltzoff, & Kuhl, 2000). Notably, Jones, Dawson, and Webb (2017) reported a positive relation between sensitivity in infancy and later attentional capture by faces (operationalized as early components of the ERP response) in the total sample of low- and high-risk infants; in an older sample this pattern also related to *better* social functioning. Thus, the relation between sensory sensitivity and social function may be more complex than it first appears; this area needs more study.

A recent study investigated the pupillary light reflex (PLR) in infants at risk (Nyström et al., 2018; Figure 5.2). The PLR is a low-level sensory measure, reflecting the regulation of the amount of light reaching the retina. In older patients with ASD, the PLR is generally weaker than in controls. However, Nyström et al. found that at 9–10 months of life, the PLR was stronger (greater amplitude) in infants who went on to receive an ASD diagnosis in toddlerhood. Although more study is needed to elucidate the exact mechanisms explaining this result, it is notable that in older children, the amount of constriction is correlated with the amount of sensory atypicalities (Daluwatte, Miles, Sun, & Yao, 2015). Other recent eye-tracking studies have found reduced attention to audiovisual synchrony in infants with later ASD, possibly indicating problems with multisensory processing in this group (Falck-Ytter et al., 2018). Although relatively little is known about the neural correlates of altered sensory processing in infancy, brain atypicalities emerging early in development are likely to reflect or cause atypicalities in sensory processing, as the sensory networks are formed during this period and depend on the integrity of the underlying neural systems. Future work should explore how observations like structural atypicalities in visual sensory cortices at 6 months (Hazlett et al., 2017) and atypical connectivity patterns at 14 months (Orekhova et al., 2014; Figure 5.2) may relate to sensory phenotypes (see also Section 5.2.7 Structural Brain Development).

5.2.2 Motor Development

Landa and Garrett-Mayer (2006) reported data from the Mullen Scales of Early Learning (MSEL) collected within a longitudinal sibling study, indicating that broad gross and fine motor atypicalities assessed with this scale are initially subtle, but that both become increasingly discriminative over the course

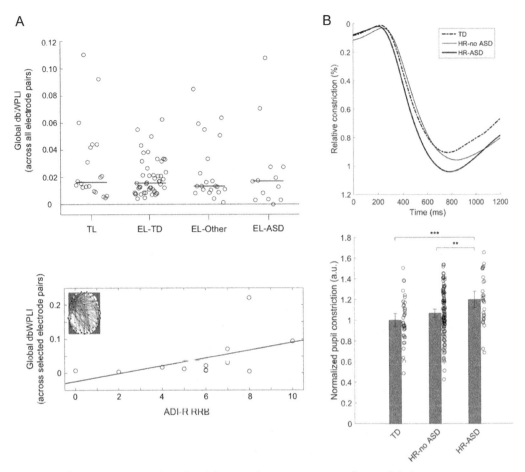

Figure 5.2. *(A) Alpha band (7–8 Hz) connectivity in infants; global dbWPLI (debiased weighted phase lag index) averaged across all electrode pairs was similar across the groups of 14-month-old infants with typical likelihood (TL) and elevated likelihood (EL) for autism, with a typical developmental outcome (EL-TD), meeting criteria for autism (EL-ASD), and other outcomes (EL-other) at 36 months of age; circles represent individual infants, horizontal lines represent group medians (A, top panel). Within the EL-ASD group, elevated infant global dbWPLI averaged across front-central electrode pairs (inserted, based on a previous study by Orekhova et al., 2014) associated with increased severity of restricted and repetitive behaviors (RRB) measured by the Autism Diagnostic Interview – Revised (ADI-R) at 36 months (Spearman's rho = 0.60, p = .037 (A, bottom panel). (B) Pupillary light reflex in infants; averaged normalized pupil constriction across epochs within groups of 9- to 10-month-old infants with typical development (TD = dashed line) and high risk for autism without and with a diagnosis of autism (HR-no ASD = thin solid line, and HR-ASD = thick solid line resp.) at 36 months of age (B, top panel). The normalized constriction of the pupil in the HR-ASD group differed from both the TD and HR-no ASD groups (means and error bars with 95% CI) (B, bottom panel). Source: (A) Printed with permission by R. Haartsen; (B) printed with permission by P. Nyström.*

of the second year of life in children with later ASD diagnosis. Based on the same measure as well as a parent report measure of motor function, Estes et al. (2015) noted that infants with later ASD and high symptom levels showed poorer gross motor functioning than low-risk infants already at 6 months.

More recently, researchers have started to look beyond the results on broad measures such as the MSEL, focusing instead on more specific motor functions. For example, based on a small sample of infants at risk, Flanagan, Landa, Bhat, and Bauman (2012) found that head lag during pull-to-sit at 6 months was associated with increased risk of ASD diagnosis at 3 years of age. Interestingly, this result is consistent with a very early retrospective parent report study by Ornitz, Guthrie, and Farley (1977), which also reported delays in the age at which the child first held her head erect (steady) when in an upright position. These results are important, because posture and head stability constrain the ability of the infant to attend to and interact with the environment, including other people. Increased head lag during pull-to-sit could also reflect problems with anticipation of future events. One study that was based on retrospective video analysis found that at 4–6 months of age (Brisson, Warreyn, Serres, Foussier, & Adrien-Louis, 2012), infants with later ASD less often opened their mouth before the hand/spoon arrived there than a control infant with typical development. While this study suffered from both a small sample and lack of adequate control groups (such as high-risk infants without ASD), it is consistent with the idea that processes linked to motor anticipation could be an early sign of ASD. In addition to addressing the question of specificity in terms of developmental outcomes, future research should continue to study more specific aspects of motor planning, control, and execution in infants at risk (Brisson et al., 2012; Ekberg, Falck-Ytter, Bölte, & Gredebäck, 2015; Flanagan et al., 2012).

One intriguing recent study showed that while infants with a typical developmental outcome showed a boost in their language skills around the onset of walking, infants with later ASD did not (West, Leezenbaum, Northrup, & Iverson, 2019). Vulnerabilities in communication were also noted prior to walking onset, but children with ASD appeared to lag increasingly further behind after this milestone was reached. The authors suggest that walking may afford a typically developing child more opportunity to interact with other people; but may allow a child with ASD to increasingly withdraw. Such processes could be interpreted in line with an adaptive account of ASD, which proposes that the behavioral symptoms of ASD represent adaptations to earlier atypical neural processing, including the construction of ecological niches that may better suit the child's individual processing style (Johnson, Jones, & Gliga, 2015).

5.2.3 Attention, General Cognition, and Emerging Executive Function

Based on observational and eye-tracking data (Elison et al., 2013; Elsabbagh, Fernandes et al., 2013; Zwaigenbaum et al., 2005), Keehn, Mueller, and

Townsend (2013) suggested that problems with visual disengagement – the ability to shift visual attention between areas of interest – could cause problems in both social and nonsocial domains. Indeed, problems with visual disengagement are among the most replicated infant markers of ASD. Still, the findings are not entirely consistent when it comes to the onset of this putative atypicality in ASD and how the dependent variables are defined (Elison et al., 2013; Elsabbagh, Fernandes et al., 2013). Attentional atypicalities may also not be limited to disengagement. For example, Wass et al. (2015) found that when viewing a static image, infants with later ASD showed shorter dwell times than low-risk controls with later typical development. The high-risk group without ASD fell in between those two other groups. This result indicates there may be broad low-level differences in attentional and oculomotor processes in infants with later ASD.

Estes et al. (2015) studied general cognitive development in terms of the MSEL in a large sample of infants at risk. It was found that at 6 months, only the infants with the most clear ASD symptoms later on differed from LR infants, and only in the domains of visual reception and gross motor function. At 12 months, specific group differences were more pronounced and included the overall developmental score (early learning composite score) and language scores. At 24 months, all aspects of the MSEL (language, motor, visual) were highly significantly altered in infants with later ASD. This indicates that cognitive development starts from a similar baseline but progresses more slowly in this group, leading to pronounced average group differences in toddlerhood (although individual variability is large). A similar pattern of gradual group differentiation emerged in a European sample (Bussu et al., 2018), although fine motor differences were somewhat more pronounced early on in the latter study.

So far, there is very little available research on emerging executive function (EF) in infants at risk for ASD. One exception is St. John et al. (2016) who studied the A-not-B task in infants at risk for ASD; this task reflects – at least in part – individual differences in simple inhibition. It was found that performance improved less in the high-risk group compared to the low-risk group between 12 and 24 months of age, but this effect was not linked to later diagnostic status. Surprisingly better fine motor skill was associated with *worse* performance on the A-not-B task in the HR-ASD infants, while in the low-risk group, the association was in the opposite (and expected) relation. This is the first study to investigate EF-related tasks in infants at risk – more research using more comprehensive testing batteries is clearly needed to elucidate the early development of EF in ASD. As some infant sibling studies broaden their focus to also encompass infants at risk for ADHD, mapping early development in different areas of EF development (including motivational and emotional aspects) will be important (see also Section 5.3 New Directions for Research). One recent study examined the relation between look durations in infancy and later variation in executive functioning, finding that slower developmental change in the duration of individual looks to faces was apparent in high-risk relative to low-risk infants, and predicted poorer later executive functioning (Hendry et al., 2018).

5.2.4 Social Attention and Processing of Basic Social Information

Social attention refers to the general tendency to prioritize social information over nonsocial information. According to one hypothesis, early problems with social attention – due to atypical development of subcortical neural pathways – cause infants with later ASD to orient less to faces and therefore get less learning opportunities in the social domain early in life (Johnson, 2005). The available evidence does not seem to support this idea however, as young infants with later ASD appear to orient to faces just as efficiently as other children (Elsabbagh, Gilga et al., 2013; Jones & Klin, 2013).

While basic orienting to faces appears intact, there are, however, several reports suggesting that social attention is generally attenuated in young infants with later ASD, most typically reported in terms of looking time to faces and people (Chawarska, Macari, & Shic, 2013; Chawarska et al., 2014). A general difficulty in interpreting these findings is that they are not based on experimental manipulations that can isolate the effect of specific information. So, while social attention is reduced in a descriptive sense, it is still largely unknown why. As we will see later on, functional brain imaging studies may provide some new clues as to whether these atypicalities reflect atypical brain activation patterns to social stimuli, specifically.

Biological motion refers to the movement signatures of living animals. It is considered an important type of social information, and the ability to detect and process it has evolutionary roots. So far, only one study has assessed preference for biological motion in infants with later ASD, and this study found no difference between groups on this measure (Falck-Ytter et al., 2018). In contrast, toddlers with ASD have been found to have a weaker preference for biological motion (Falck-Ytter, Rehnberg, & Bölte, 2013; Klin, Lin, Gorrindo, Ramsay, & Jones, 2009). One possibility is that preference for biological motion is initially at typical levels in most children with ASD, but subsequently declines, potentially reflecting that the nature of the processes that drive this behavior change over time (even in typically developing infants).

Elsabbagh et al. (2012) used an event-related potential (ERP) paradigm to test whether infants with later ASD differ in terms of their brain responses to other people's gaze shifts. They contrasted gaze shifts away versus toward the infant, and found that infants who later received a diagnosis showed attenuated sensitivity to this shift, particularly in a late component (P400) often associated with more semantic aspects of face processing. Further, examining responses to faces versus objects revealed a difference in latency of this component (faster responses to faces). This pattern was also noted in a separate study (Jones, Dawson, & Webb, 2017), and may be considered consistent with reduced attention engagement to faces during infancy in ASD.

Lloyd Fox, Blasi et al. (2017) conducted a study of brain activation in response to social versus nonsocial stimuli using functional near-infrared spectroscopy (fNIRS) in 4–6-month-old infants at risk for ASD. They contrasted social videos with nonsocial images and vocal sounds with nonvocal sounds (both presented in the context of social videos). The study suffered from very small sample size, but found some noteworthy preliminary results: The infants with later ASD showed an attenuated hemodynamic response to vocal sounds, which was in stark contrast to all other groups and conditions. Even in the visual domain, social stimuli appeared to elicit less strong responses, but this contrast was confounded with motion differences making conclusions less clear-cut. These results are noteworthy because they indicate what appears to be a selective disruption in the processing of basic *social* stimuli, and that this atypicality generalizes over modalities. Blasi et al. (2015) reported a similar result on partially the same group using fMRI (auditory stimulation only), but only comparing high-risk versus low-risk groups.

5.2.5 Social Interaction and Nonverbal Communication

Social interaction appears relatively intact in the first few months for infants with later ASD. For example, perturbations of social interaction as studied in the "still face" paradigm appear to have the same effects on interaction in infants with and without later ASD (Rozga et al., 2011). Similarly, tasks like the Autism Observational Schedule for Infants (which assess a broad range of social behaviors) do not appear to strongly discriminate infants with later ASD at 6 months (Gammer et al., 2015). Researchers have also studied more specific behavioral constructs that are critical for social interaction. For example, the term "joint attention" refers to the triadic sharing of attention between two individuals and an object or event. In typical development, infants increasingly engage in such behaviors towards the end of their first year of life, and the ability to do so plays a unique role in the development of social cognition and language. In terms of responding to other people's joint attention bids in infants with later ASD, the evidence is rather mixed, with some studies reporting an association between reduced gaze following at ages between 12 and 18 months and later symptomatology (Brian et al., 2008; Landa, Holman, & Garrett-Mayer, 2007; Rozga et al., 2011; Sullivan et al., 2007; Yoder, Stone, Walden, & Malesa, 2009) while other studies fail to find such an association (Bedford et al., 2012; Chawarska et al., 2014; Ibanez, Grantz, & Messinger, 2013; Macari et al., 2012). In contrast, there seems to be more clear evidence for impaired tendency to initiate joint attention between 8 and 18 months as a predictor of later ASD (Ibanez et al., 2013; Landa et al., 2007; Macari et al., 2012; Rozga et al., 2011; Thorup et al., 2018; but see Chawarska et al., 2014).

Researchers have also studied the interactions between infants and more familiar partners, like their parents. Such work indicates that infants with later ASD show relatively typical interactions with their parents at 6 months, but by 12 months show reduced levels of mutuality in the interaction, positive affect, and attentiveness (Wan et al., 2012). This work is consistent with other evidence that broad metrics of social interaction appear typical in early development, but rapidly diverge towards the end of the first year of life. A longitudinal study of social attention in infants from 6 to 24 months showed a similar pattern, with infants initially looking at the face of an examiner at similar levels in typical development and later ASD groups, and a pattern of gradual decline in social attention over the next 18 months in the ASD group (Ozonoff et al., 2010; see also the previous section).

5.2.6 Verbal Communication

Several prospective studies of high-risk infants have identified delays in understanding language by 12 months of age in infants later diagnosed with ASD (Mitchell et al., 2006; Zwaigenbaum et al., 2005). These results are borne out by laboratory measures in which an examiner tests whether a child understands phrases like "give it to me" (with gesture), "give it to mommy" (with no gesture), and "no!" (Landa & Garrett-Mayer, 2006; Zwaigenbaum et al., 2005), in which infants with later ASD typically show delays at 12–14 months (though these may be comparable to those seen in infants with language delays but no ASD).

In parallel with poor language comprehension, language production is also atypical in infants that develop ASD. One intriguing large study recently investigated both receptive and expressive language in high-risk infants. Specifically, Lazenby et al. (2016) analyzed data from 346 12-month-olds (43 of whom had later ASD) and found delays in both receptive and expressive language on observational measures, and in single-word comprehension by parent report (but not production, possibly due to a floor effect). However, when analyzing patterns of use of single words, the authors found that there were several words that infants with later ASD were more likely to produce than other comparison groups without later ASD (such as "block," "hello," "bite," "bye," and "uncle"). This may reflect idiosyncratic patterns of early word learning, rather than the typical pattern of culturally shaped acquisition seen in control groups.

Other studies have identified atypicalities in even more subtle aspects of vocal communication. For example, Paul, Fuerst, Ramsay, Chawarska, and Klin (2011) investigated the phonemic content of speech produced by infants at risk for ASD. Data showed that at each age, infants with later ASD showed delays in the production of the most advanced consonant type produced by typically developing infants of that age. Specifically, high-risk infants later diagnosed with ASD or who had other sociocommunicative delays produced fewer "middle" consonant types at 6 months, fewer "late" consonant types at 9 months, and a lower total number of different consonant types at 12 months than high-risk infants with typical outcomes. Thus, these findings may suggest difficulty with each new stage of language production in infants with later ASD, although the specificity to ASD is unclear. However, not all studies observe early language delays in infants later diagnosed with ASD (e.g., Hudry et al., 2014), and so considering heterogeneity within the population is important.

An important future direction for this area is to understand the neural mechanisms that may underpin early language delays within autism, and whether these are the same or distinct from those observed in infants with other language delays. Swanson et al. (2017) compared structural brain development in infants with an older sibling with ASD who were later diagnosed with ASD relative to those with early signs of language delay. Consistent with previous reports, behavioral data indicated poorer language function at 12 months in infants later identified with ASD or language delay. The volume of key subcortical structures at 12 months was associated with 24-month language skills in a different way across outcome groups, indicating that there were differential brain–behavior relations in infants with later ASD and language delay. For example, smaller amygdala and thalamic volumes in infancy were associated with more normative outcome language profiles in infants with later language delays, but not infants with later ASD. The authors conclude that there may be different neural mechanisms and background genetic and environmental etiologies in the two outcome groups.

5.2.7 Structural Brain Development

Fine-grained insights into structural brain development can be yielded by neuroimaging techniques such as magnetic resonance imaging (MRI). This technique uses magnetic fields to produce an image of the brain that can be used to quantify important features such as gray matter (the cell bodies, dendrites, and axon terminals of neurons), white matter (axons connecting different regions of gray matter to each other), and cerebrospinal fluid (CSF). Although challenging to acquire, a number of research groups have successfully collected MRI data in babies during natural sleep or mild sedation.

Research with MRI has yielded a number of nuanced insights into early structural brain development in infants at high risk for ASD (Wolff, Jacob, & Elison, 2018). First, one study has delineated patterns of early overgrowth of gray matter regions that are somewhat consistent with earlier reports of accelerated head growth from circumference measures in infancy (e.g., Webb et al., 2007). Hazlett et al. (2017) analysed MRI data taken from the US multisite Infant Brain Imaging Study at 6, 12, and 24 months, and used both traditional and machine-learning analyses to describe patterns of gray matter development in this cohort. Results showed that there was a hyperexpansion of the cortical surface area between 6 and 12 months that subsequently predicted a more rapid increase in brain volume between 12 and 24 months. Regions with a particularly large expansion in surface area included primary visual areas, and frontal and temporal areas of the "social brain." Individual differences in the degree of overgrowth were linked to the emergence and severity of social difficulties related to ASD. Another measure that could contribute to early increased head circumference is an excess of cerebrospinal fluid (CSF) in the subarachnoid space. Two recent studies have shown that infants with later ASD had significantly greater extra-axial CSF volume at 6 months that persisted through development (Shen et al., 2017; Shen et al., 2013). The accumulation seemed most pronounced in the frontal cortex. Although the implication of these findings remains unclear, the presence of excess extra-axial fluid has been anecdotally associated with seizures or motor delays. Further exploration of the mechanistic relationship between excess CSF and later ASD is necessary to understand the implication of these findings.

Finally, researchers have also identified early alterations in brain connectivity associated with later ASD. For example, Wolff et al. (2017) have examined patterns of connectivity within targeted cortical, cerebellar, and striatal white matter pathways. Longitudinal analyses indicate that higher fractional anisotropy (a measure of white matter reflects fiber density, axonal diameter, and myelination) of the genu of the corpus callosum at 6 months significantly predicted later sensory responsiveness and repetitive behaviors within the group of infants with a later ASD diagnosis. The corpus callosum is the primary white matter tract that links the left and right hemispheres of the brain, and the genu is the part closest to the frontal cortex. The result suggests that in addition to the structural atypicalities observed in the same cohort (Hazlett et al., 2017), alterations in how brain regions communicate with each other could underpin the later emergence of behavioral challenges associated with ASD. Indeed, increases in whole-brain EEG functional connectivity at 12 months have been dimensionally related to later restricted and repetitive behaviors in two separate cohorts of infant siblings (Orekhova et al., 2014). Further, the strongest relations were with connectivity predominately over fronto-temporal regions. Thus, in early development, increased communication between brain regions may relate to later sensory and repetitive features of the autistic phenotype.

5.2.8 Robustness and Replicability

One key challenge facing the field as it matures is to begin to complement exploratory studies that generate new leads with robust replications in large samples with preregistered analytic plans. There remain few examples of replications in the field, though there are some exceptions. For example, Shen and colleagues recently replicated their earlier report of increased CSF in infants with later ASD in a new cohort (Shen et al., 2017; Shen et al., 2013); Braukmann et al. (2018) replicated earlier reports of reduced specialization for social stimuli in the temporal lobe in a new cohort of 5-month-old high-risk infants (Lloyd-Fox et al., 2013); and Haartsen, Jones, Orekhova, Charman, and Johnson (2019) have recently replicated the observation that increased connectivity at 12 months predicts dimensional measures of later restrictive and repetitive behaviors (Orekhova et al., 2014). Increased efforts to replicate results in other samples will be an important step towards refining our understanding of early ASD. Preregistration of analytic plans will also be another crucial step forward in helping us to rigorously avoid common problems that affect all research fields, including p-hacking, fishing, and implicit bias.

5.3 New Directions for Research

As this chapter shows, the infant sibling studies published over the last 15 years have increased our knowledge about early ASD in important ways. We now know that early signs of ASD are first rather subtle, and barely noticeable for the naked eye (even a trained clinician's eye), but that underneath the surface, at the level of brain structure and function, atypical processes unfold that predict the later development of core ASD symptoms or a full clinical diagnosis. Early signs are not only found in one domain, rather they involve different areas such as motor function, sensory processing, and early processing of social information. Against this background, it is increasingly difficult to argue that ASD is related to a specific or localized disruption to a specific brain function, such as atypicalities within the "social brain network." Distributed atypicalities in more general aspects of brain development appear to be more suitable to explain the pattern of results.

At the same time, clearly, more work lies ahead of us. Few findings have been replicated and we thus lack a validated model of the key processes involved in the early development of ASD. Thus, as is the case also in ASD research more generally, the picture is quite fragmented and incomplete. This should not be seen as a failure of the past work, but rather as a reflection of the complexity of the subject and the fact that it is still early days for this research field. In the next sections we discuss a few directions we believe should be considered in future efforts.

5.3.1 Comparing Results from Sibling Studies with Results from Other Types of Research

Animal models have several strengths as a means of studying ASD. For example, they allow the causality of particular processes to be probed through pharmacological manipulations, optogenetic techniques that can turn particular pathways on or off in precise brain regions, and the application of environmental risk factors (like maternal immune activation) to strains with the same genetic background. Further, they afford more possibilities to link precise genetic or neurobiological mechanisms to phenotypic changes. However, it is unclear whether the phenotypes studied as "autism-like" in animal models (like preference for a novel mouse, or repetitive grooming) are or are not mechanistically similar to symptoms of autism in humans (Kas et al., 2014).

Further, the role of postnatal experience may be very different in rodents, who reach maturity faster and have a much less protracted postnatal developmental trajectory in critical brain regions like the frontal cortex. Thus, we need to combine insights from both animal models and human infancy to gain a full understanding of autism. Ways forward include using tasks that can be administered in the same way across species (e.g., basic sensory processing tasks like neural responses to sounds); increasing the use of developmental animal models where trajectories are traced over time, rather than simply focusing on the end state of development (e.g., Molenhuis, de Visser, Bruining, & Kas, 2014); and testing which neurocognitive features observed in siblings are also present in populations with more homogenous genetic profiles (e.g., infants with known genetic syndromes and mouse models of those syndromes, see below), which may provide insight into links to specific etiologies.

The study of infants with older siblings with ASD has been a fruitful way to begin to characterize factors that may relate to the emergence of symptoms. However, infant siblings represent "multiplex" cases of autism – autism that runs in families. Around 10% of ASD is thought to occur in families who already have a family member with a confirmed diagnosis; the majority of cases occur in families that do not have a clear family history. Some genetic and epidemiological evidence suggests that multiplex and simplex routes to ASD may be associated with partly different etiologies (e.g., Leppa et al., 2016). Thus, we need ways to examine whether insights from multiplex infants generalize to infants with other background risk factors for ASD. One promising avenue is to study infants with genetic conditions that are known to significantly raise the risk of an ASD diagnosis. These include tuberous sclerosis (TS), fragile X syndrome, and neurofibromatosis type 1 (NF1). Rates of ASD diagnosis within children with these disorders can be up to 50% (Jeste & Geschwind, 2014). Thus, prospective longitudinal studies of infants with these syndromes are feasible. NF1 and TS are particularly intriguing, because they are typically identified pre- or neonatally, enabling longitudinal studies starting from birth. For example, early results from a case series of infants with NF1 indicate early language and motor delays that resemble but are more extreme than those in infants with later ASD from multiplex families (Kolesnik et al., 2017). Other disorders like fragile X syndrome are of interest too (e.g., Hogan et al., 2017). However, this syndrome is typically diagnosed through the presence of developmental delays. This could mean that only the most severely affected cases are included in a study, yielding a biased sample. Although this work is just beginning, it holds great promise for identifying neurocognitive processes that may be shared by infants with different routes to ASD. Further, since infants with these genetic syndromes are theoretically more etiologically homogenous, insights could be more easily tied to particular pathophysiological underlying mechanisms (Jeste & Geschwind, 2014).

A different approach to bringing in genetics used by some researchers in the field is to align a sibling study with an infant twin study, comparing trait similarity in identical and fraternal twins. The strength of this (behavioral genetic) approach is that it allows researchers to establish the overall contribution of genes and environments to putative antecedent markers for ASD.

While initial studies focused primarily on analyzing infant data with respect to ASD outcome only, a range of groups have begun to compare early markers of ASD with markers of other common neurodevelopmental conditions. This can help to delineate neurocognitive mechanisms that are specific to particular phenotypic outcomes from those that are more general markers of developmental problems (Jones et al., 2014). One such approach is to measure traits of both ASD and commonly co-occurring conditions within the cohort of infants with older siblings with ASD, and contrast the relation between infant predictors of the different phenotypic traits. Conditions like ADHD and anxiety have an increased incidence in both individuals with ASD and their family members (Hallett, Ronald, Rijsdijk, & Happé, 2012; Ronald, Edelson, Asherson, & Saudino, 2010). Recently, Shepherd et al. (2019) examined whether early temperamental profiles might overlap or be distinct in relation to later symptoms of ASD, ADHD, and anxiety in a longitudinal analysis of infant siblings followed to age 7. Results indicated that higher infant activity levels predicted elevated ADHD traits independently of ASD; while higher levels of infant fear predicted both later anxiety and ASD. A second approach is to study cohorts of infants at familial risk for ASD in parallel with infants with familial risk for other conditions, like ADHD (Johnson, Gliga, Jones, & Charman, 2014). This can allow researchers to disentangle whether neurocognitive paths to symptoms of conditions like ADHD are similar or distinct in cohorts of infants with different background risk profiles. Given that etiological factors for different psychiatric conditions are to a large extent general (not diagnosis specific), it will be interesting to map the degree of similarity of the developmental paths of these cohorts. Taken together, broadening our approaches beyond autism will enable us to begin to realize the potential of prospective studies to use developmental trajectories to refine our diagnostic categories.

5.3.2 Increasing Robustness and Replicability Through Large-Scale Multisite Studies

Given the heterogeneity of ASD, building large samples is essential to enabling better powered analyses that allow the potential stratification (identification of subgroups) of different developmental paths (illustrated in Figure 5.1). To date, the majority of studies in the field focus on examining group-level effects that relate to ASD as a single category. However, it is becoming increasingly recognized that group-level insights do not necessarily apply at the level of the individual. While the heterogeneity within the ASD population is likely to have a strong biological basis, sociocultural factors may influence how the core symptoms are expressed and their consequences for psychological well-being and participation in society (see also Section 5.4 Ethical, Sociocultural, and Policy Perspectives).

Some researchers have begun to use techniques such as machine learning to determine the degree to which particular measures might be predictive at the individual level (Bussu et al., 2018; Hazlett et al., 2017). Others have focused on potential stratification factors like gender; for example, Bedford et al. (2016) found that a variety of markers were significantly associated with later ASD in male but not female infants (a similar result was obtained in Falck-Ytter et al., 2018). However, such analyses require even greater power than traditional group-based approaches, and thus large samples will be needed to move further in this direction. Given the prevalence of ASD and the longitudinal nature of infant sibling studies, building particularly large sample sizes requires a multi-site approach but this does require significant investment of resources (such as the US IBIS study, or the Eurosibs consortium, www.eurosibs.eu).

Early development in ASD is likely to involve cascading effects operating at several levels within the individual and in interaction with the environment. Thus, it is important that new studies are not only sufficiently sized, they should also include measures that can capture key aspects of this intricate interplay. For example, transactional processes – i.e., dynamic, bidirectional processes occurring between the child and the parent – may provide leads on feasible treatment options, as such negative feedback loops that potentially can be canceled through a change in the behavior of the parent (Green et al., 2017). Note that this does not imply that the parent is the ultimate cause of the loop; the process may reflect, for example, evocative gene–environment interplay (Kennedy et al., 2017).

5.3.3 Toward Causation: Embedding Intervention in the Sibling Design

Recently, several groups have developed therapeutic models based around boosting the social cues available to infants who may struggle to benefit from a typical interaction style (Green et al., 2017; Jones, Dawson, Kelly, Estes, & Webb, 2017). Early data suggest that such approaches could produce boosts in social attention (Jones, Dawson, Kelly et al., 2017) and longer-term gains in social communication skills (Green et al., 2017). These models can be viewed as "environmental enrichment" approaches that provide scaffolds for communication that can be conceptually compared to putting in ramps for someone who uses a wheelchair to ambulate.

With greater progress in genetics and neurobiology the field will likely consider medication-based treatment options. At the same time, pharmacological intervention is unlikely to be ethically defendable to conduct in infants at risk for ASD in the foreseeable future. Less invasive approaches such as dietary supplementation may be more realistic and can provide mechanistic insights. For example, recent data from typically developing infants suggest that impaired auditory sensory gating (the ability to filter out redundant or repeated sensory information) soon after birth is associated with social withdrawal and behavioral impairments at 2 years of age (Ross et al., 2016). Molecular genetic analyses in combination with prenatal dietary intervention in this study implicated the cholinergic system in the atypical sensory responses, and this neurotransmitter system is known to play a key role in the maturation of inhibitory neurons (GABA) in critical periods of development. The specific genetic allele targeted in this study as well as the GABA system more generally is implicated in ASD, meaning that this and similar approaches could be relevant also in high-risk cohorts. That the study found dietary supplementation (choline) to moderate the effect of common allelic risk variants also provides a general example of gene–environment interaction related to early brain development in human infants.

5.4 Ethical, Sociocultural, and Policy Perspectives

The ethical issues associated with studies of infant siblings of children with ASD need to be taken very seriously. For example, some parents of infant siblings of children with ASD are concerned about the development of their youngest child, and the exposure to the various aspects of the study, including advertisement material, may potentially increase this worry. Similarly, "at-risk" terminology may increase worry (for participating and nonparticipating families alike), and can make families feel stigmatized. For this reason it is important to emphasize in all communications around this type of study, that most infant siblings do not develop ASD. The research team also needs to have routines for how to respond if concrete concerns are reported by the parents, or if the team themselves think there is reason for concern. Exactly how these situations are dealt with differs between studies (Bölte et al., 2016), but the key point is to have a well-thought-out strategy for this, grounded in general ethical standards and local cultural norms, and make sure families understand how the particular study deals with these issues at enrollment.

As our understanding of the early mechanisms leading to ASD deepens, the field must move to develop new therapeutic and support strategies for families. The hope is that one can develop interventions that boost adaptive skills and prevent the emergence of longer-term cascading difficulties (like anxiety, depression, or seizures). Without anything to offer in terms of treatment options, early detection is likely to create profound stress.

It is important that we recognize the complex ethical questions associated with early intervention. Autism is a spectrum, and comes with both strengths and weaknesses. Many autistic people have spoken profoundly and eloquently about the centrality of their autism to how they view themselves, and in no sense is a "treatment" a relevant concept in this context. Other autistic people do not have the communication skills to express these viewpoints, and across the spectrum many autistic people have real needs that society should be addressing. It is important to recognize that the way in which we think about therapies and the language we use to describe them must reflect the views and needs of this whole community. It is particularly challenging to ensure that the views of "the community" do indeed reflect the full community, and not just those with the skills or desire to express themselves vocally. These issues are particularly pertinent in infancy, where (commonly neurotypical) parents must choose the strategies they use with their child.

The majority of insights about early autism thus come from populations that are Caucasian, relatively affluent, and living in relatively industrialized, high-income contexts (the United States and Western Europe). The extent to which this knowledge may generalize to other populations remains unclear. There are several barriers that contribute to this picture. First, research teams require expertise in both infancy and autism, and those expertise distributions tend to be more common in the United States and Western Europe. Second, running large longitudinal protocols requires significant resources and investment, and appropriately scaled grants are not available across much of the world. It is important to broaden our approach for several reasons. Populations in other regions may be exposed to significantly higher levels of the environmental risk factors that have been hypothesized to contribute to autism, providing both the opportunity to understand their effects and an obligation to determine which risk factors should be the target of global eradication efforts. Further, it is possible that early manifestations of autism are modulated by cultural experience. If we view autism as a difference in the way the brain specializes in response to the environment, different social environments could produce subtly different early signs. Finally, there may be critical interactions between vulnerability and family resources. Families with higher levels of individual or societal resources may be better able to support their children relative to those in lower-income settings. We must understand these interactions in order to develop culturally appropriate support packages. One way forward is to increase partnerships between researchers in different settings and cultures. For example, one partnership between researchers in the Gambia and the UK has begun to trace early brain development in low-resource settings in order to identify early markers of environmental risk factors like undernutrition (Lloyd-Fox, Begus et al., 2017). Such collaborations are an important way to build the body of knowledge and expertise required to begin to broaden our understanding of autism across national barriers.

Being both expensive and complex and generating results of substantial general interest and with potential clinical implications, high-risk sibling studies are highly dependent on, and may also influence, policy. As ASD is a common condition associated with significant social costs, some countries prioritize funding research in this area. Maintaining and increasing the level of funding critically depends on the field's ability to produce robust, replicable results, and to communicate these broadly. High-risk infant sibling studies also rely on and benefit from a close collaboration with clinical services, and even here, policy makers should facilitate win–win arrangements, for example by establishing mechanisms for increased interaction between academia and other sectors (e.g., health care).

While most results so far have not had an immediate clinical relevance, this situation may change quickly (Hazlett et al., 2017). Particularly, if (or perhaps rather: when) sensitive and specific infant predictors of later ASD are identified, policy makers need to address the delicate question of what to do with this information (fund more research into early intervention, incorporate the new measures into screening programs, nothing?). If, in the future, it is possible to reliably predict later ASD diagnoses already in infancy or even prenatally but the age at which one can get help and support remains as it is today, this is likely to create substantial frustration and worry in the affected families. Although this situation could be avoided in principle by very proactive actions by policy makers, a more realistic view is perhaps that some "tension" between the current and the wanted state of affairs is needed to create the impetus for more research and development of clinical services. Finally, as results get more relevant for individualized medicine approaches, commercial use of results is likely to increase, creating new options for academia–industry collaboration.

5.5 Conclusion

Given that longitudinal studies of infants at risk are very resource demanding, a justified question is: is it worth the effort? Being the devil's advocate, one may point out that some of the general conclusions we adhere to today, such as the fact that onset patterns of ASD are heterogeneous and involve multiple domains (including but not restricted to social function), were the exact main conclusions of the retrospective report described at the outset of our chapter (Hoshino et al., 1982). This study was published more than 30 years ago, before anyone had come up with the idea of studying infant siblings. At the same time, we clearly have a much more detailed picture of the most relevant developmental processes now than one had at that time (Jones et al., 2014; Varcin & Jeste, 2017). Moreover, some distinct theoretical positions have been tested (not seldom with a negative result; Elsabbagh, Gilga et al., 2013; Falck-Ytter et al., 2018; Jones & Klin, 2013). Arguably, the single most important advance is the demonstration of atypical structural and functional brain development during infancy in individuals with ASD (Wolff et al., 2018). If coupled with other informative designs and approaches, the infant sibling design will be an increasingly valuable source of information about ASD, related conditions, and the large variability in human development more generally.

References

Asperger, H. (1944). Die "Autistischen Psychopathen" im Kindesalter. *Archiv für Psychiatrie und Nervenkrankheiten, 117*, 76–136.

Baranek, G. T. (1999). Autism during infancy: A retrospective video analysis of sensory-motor and social behaviors at 9–12 months of age. *Journal of Autism and Developmental Disorders, 29*(3), 213–224.

Bedford, R., Elsabbagh, M., Gliga, T., Pickles, A., Senju, A., Charman, T., & Johnson, M. (2012). Precursors to social and communication difficulties in infants at-risk for autism: Gaze following and attentional engagement. *Journal of Autism and Developmental Disorders, 42*(10), 2208–2218. doi:10.1007/s10803-012-1450-y

Bedford, R., Jones, E. J., Johnson, M. H., Pickles, A., Charman, T., & Gliga, T. (2016). Sex differences in the association between infant markers and later autistic traits. *Molecular Autism, 7*(1), 21.

Blasi, A., Lloyd-Fox, S., Sethna, V., Brammer, M. J., Mercure, E., Murray, L., ... Johnson, M. H. (2015). Atypical processing of voice sounds in infants at risk for autism spectrum disorder. *Cortex, 71*, 122–133.

Bölte, S., Tomalski, P., Marschik, P. B., Berggren, S., Norberg, J., Falck-Ytter, T., ... Roeyers, H. (2016). Challenges and inequalities of opportunities in european psychiatry research. *European Journal of Psychological Assessment, 34*(4), 270–277.

Braukmann, R., Lloyd-Fox, S., Blasi, A., Johnson, M. H., Bekkering, H., Buitelaar, J. K., & Hunnius, S. (2018). Diminished socially selective neural processing in 5-month-old infants at high familial risk of autism. *European Journal of Neuroscience, 47*(6), 720–728.

Brian, J., Bryson, S. E., Garon, N., Roberts, W., Smith, I. M., Szatmari, P., & Zwaigenbaum, L. (2008). Clinical assessment of autism in high-risk 18-month-olds. *Autism, 12*(5), 433–456. doi:10.1177/1362361308094500

Brisson, J., Warreyn, P., Serres, J., Foussier, S., & Adrien-Louis, J. (2012). Motor anticipation failure in infants with autism: A retrospective analysis of feeding situations. *Autism, 16*(4), 420–429.

Bryson, S. E., Zwaigenbaum, L., Brian, J., Roberts, W., Szatmari, P., Rombough, V., & McDermott, C. (2007). A prospective case series of high-risk infants who developed autism. *Journal of Autism and Developmental Disorders, 37*(1), 12–24. doi:10.1007/s10803-006-0328-2

Bussu, G., Jones, E. J., Charman, T., Johnson, M. H., Buitelaar, J., & Team, B. (2018). Prediction of autism at 3 years from behavioural and developmental measures in high-risk infants: A longitudinal cross-domain classifier analysis. *Journal of Autism and Developmental Disorders, 48*, 2418–2433.

Chawarska, K., Macari, S., & Shic, F. (2013). Decreased spontaneous attention to social scenes in 6-month-old infants later diagnosed with autism spectrum disorders. *Biological Psychiatry, 74*(3), 195–203. doi:10.1016/j.biopsych.2012.11.022

Chawarska, K., Shic, F., Macari, S., Campbell, D. J., Brian, J., Landa, R., ... Bryson, S. (2014). 18-month predictors of later outcomes in younger siblings of children with autism spectrum disorder: A baby siblings research consortium study.

Journal of the American Academy of Child and Adolescent Psychiatry, 53(12), 1317–1327. doi:10.1016/j.jaac.2014.09.015

Clifford, S. M., Hudry, K., Elsabbagh, M., Charman, T., Johnson, M. H., & Team, B. (2013). Temperament in the first 2 years of life in infants at high-risk for autism spectrum disorders. *Journal of Autism and Developmental Disorders, 43*(3), 673–686.

Daluwatte, C., Miles, J., Sun, J., & Yao, G. (2015). Association between pupillary light reflex and sensory behaviors in children with autism spectrum disorders. *Research in Developmental Disabilities, 37*, 209–215.

Dawson, G., Osterling, J., Meltzoff, A. N., & Kuhl, P. (2000). Case study of the development of an infant with autism from birth to two years of age. *Journal of Applied Developmental Psychology, 21*(3), 299–313.

Ekberg, T. L., Falck-Ytter, T., Bölte, S., & Gredebäck, G. (2015). Reduced prospective motor control in 10-month-olds at risk for autism spectrum disorder. *Clinical Psychological Science, 4*(1), 129–135. https://doi.org/10.1177/2167702615576697

Elison, J. T., Paterson, S. J., Wolff, J. J., Reznick, J. S., Sasson, N. J., Gu, H. B., … Network, I. (2013). White matter microstructure and atypical visual orienting in 7-month-olds at risk for autism. *American Journal of Psychiatry, 170*(8), 899–908. doi:10.1176/appi.ajp.2012.12091150

Elsabbagh, M., Fernandes, J., Webb, S. J., Dawson, G., Charman, T., Johnson, M. H., & British Autism Study of Infant Siblings Team (2013). Disengagement of visual attention in infancy is associated with emerging autism in toddlerhood. *Biological Psychiatry, 74*(3), 189–194. doi:10.1016/j.biopsych.2012.11.030

Elsabbagh, M., Gliga, T., Pickles, A., Hudry, K., Charman, T., Johnson, M. H., & Team, B. (2013). The development of face orienting mechanisms in infants at-risk for autism. *Behavioural Brain Research, 251*, 147–154. doi:10.1016/j.bbr.2012.07.030

Elsabbagh, M., Mercure, E., Hudry, K., Chandler, S., Pasco, G., Charman, T., … Team, B. (2012). Infant neural sensitivity to dynamic eye gaze is associated with later emerging autism. *Current Biology, 22*(4), 338–342. doi:10.1016/j.cub.2011.12.056

Estes, A., Zwaigenbaum, L., Gu, H., John, T. S., Paterson, S., Elison, J. T., … Schultz, R. T. (2015). Behavioral, cognitive, and adaptive development in infants with autism spectrum disorder in the first 2 years of life. *Journal of Neurodevelopmental Disorders, 7*(1), 24.

Falck-Ytter, T., Nyström, P., Gredebäck, G., Gliga, T., Bölte, S., & Team E (2018). Reduced orienting to audiovisual synchrony in infancy predicts autism diagnosis at 3 years of age. *Journal of Child Psychology and Psychiatry, 59*(8), 872–880. doi:10.1111/jcpp.12863

Falck-Ytter, T., Rehnberg, E., & Bölte, S. (2013). Lack of visual orienting to biological motion and audiovisual synchrony in 3-year-olds with autism. *Plos One, 8*(7). doi:e6881610.1371/journal.pone.0068816

Flanagan, J. E., Landa, R., Bhat, A., & Bauman, M. (2012). Head lag in infants at risk for autism: A preliminary study. *American Journal of Occupational Therapy, 66*(5), 577–585.

Gammer, I., Bedford, R., Elsabbagh, M., Garwood, H., Pasco, G., Tucker, L., … Team, B. (2015). Behavioural markers for autism in infancy: Scores on the Autism Observational Scale for infants in a prospective study of at-risk siblings. *Infant Behavior and Development*, *38*, 107–115.

Green, J., Pickles, A., Pasco, G., Bedford, R., Wan, M. W., Elsabbagh, M., … Cheung, C. (2017). Randomised trial of a parent-mediated intervention for infants at high risk for autism: Longitudinal outcomes to age 3 years. *Journal of Child Psychology and Psychiatry*, *58*(12), 1330–1340.

Hallett, V., Ronald, A., Rijsdijk, F., & Happé, F. (2012). Disentangling the associations between autistic-like and internalizing traits: A community based twin study. *Journal of Abnormal Child Psychology*, *40*(5), 815–827.

Haartsen, R., Jones, E. J. H., Orekhova, E., Charman, T., & Johnson, M. H. (2019), Functional EEG connectivity in infants associates with later circumscribed interests in autism: A replication study. *Translational Psychiatry*, *9*(1), 1–14.

Hazlett, H. C., Gu, H., Munsell, B. C., Kim, S. H., Styner, M., Wolff, J. J., … Botteron, K. N. (2017). Early brain development in infants at high risk for autism spectrum disorder. *Nature*, *542*(7641), 348–351.

Hendry, A., Jones, E. J., Bedford, R., Gliga, T., Charman, T., & Johnson, M. H. (2018). Developmental change in look durations predicts later effortful control in toddlers at familial risk for ASD. *Journal of Neurodevelopmental Disorders*, *10*(1), 3.

Hogan, A. L., Caravella, K. E., Ezell, J., Rague, L., Hills, K., & Roberts, J. E. (2017). Autism spectrum disorder symptoms in infants with fragile X syndrome: A prospective case series. *Journal of Autism and Developmental Disorders*, *47*(6), 1628–1644.

Hoshino, Y., Kumashiro, H., Yashima, Y., Tachibana, R., Watanabe, M., & Furukawa, H. (1982). Early symptoms of autistic children and its diagnostic significance. *Psychiatry and Clinical Neurosciences*, *36*(4), 367–374.

Hudry, K., Chandler, S., Bedford, R., Pasco, G., Gliga, T., Elsabbagh, M., … Charman, T. (2014). Early language profiles in infants at high-risk for autism spectrum disorders. *Journal of Autism and Developmental Disorders*, *44*(1), 154–167.

Ibanez, L. V., Grantz, C. J., & Messinger, D. S. (2013). The development of referential communication and autism symptomatology in high-risk infants. *Infancy*, *18*(5), 687–707. doi:10.1111/j.1532-7078.2012.00142.x

Jeste, S. S., & Geschwind, D. H. (2014). Disentangling the heterogeneity of autism spectrum disorder through genetic findings. *Nature Reviews Neurology*, *10*(2), 74.

Johnson, M. H. (2005). Subcortical face processing. *Nature Reviews Neuroscience*, *6*(10), 766–774.

Johnson, M. H., Gliga, T., Jones, E., & Charman, T. (2014). Annual research review: Infant development, autism, and ADHD – early pathways to emerging disorders. *Journal of Child Psychology and Psychiatry*, *56*(3), 228–247. https://doi.org/10.1111/jcpp.12328

Johnson, M. H., Jones, E. J., & Gliga, T. (2015). Brain adaptation and alternative developmental trajectories. *Development and Psychopathology*, *27*(2), 425–442.

Jones, E. J. H., Dawson, G., Kelly, J., Estes, A., & Jane Webb, S. (2017). Parent-delivered early intervention in infants at risk for ASD: Effects on electrophysiological and habituation measures of social attention. *Autism Research*, *10*(5), 961–972.

Jones, E. J. H., Dawson, G., & Webb, S. (2017). Sensory hypersensitivity predicts enhanced attention capture by faces in the early development of ASD. *Developmental Cognitive Neuroscience, 29*, 11–20.

Jones, E. J. H., Gliga, T., Bedford, R., Charman, T., & Johnson, M. H. (2014). Developmental pathways to autism: A review of prospective studies of infants at risk. *Neuroscience and Biobehavioral Reviews, 39*, 1–33. doi:10.1016/j.neubiorev.2013.12.001

Jones, W., & Klin, A. (2013). Attention to eyes is present but in decline in 2–6-month-old infants later diagnosed with autism. *Nature, 504*(7480), 427. doi:10.1038/nature12715

Kanner, L. (1943). Autistic disturbances of affective contact. *Nervous Child, 2*, 217–250.

Kas, M. J., Glennon, J. C., Buitelaar, J., Ey, E., Biemans, B., Crawley, J., … Talpos, J. (2014). Assessing behavioural and cognitive domains of autism spectrum disorders in rodents: Current status and future perspectives. *Psychopharmacology, 231*(6), 1125–1146.

Keehn, B., Mueller, R. -A., & Townsend, J. (2013). Atypical attentional networks and the emergence of autism. *Neuroscience and Biobehavioral Reviews, 37*(2), 164–183. doi:10.1016/j.neubiorev.2012.11.014

Kennedy, D. P., D'Onofrio, B. M., Quinn, P. D., Bölte, S., Lichtenstein, P., & Falck-Ytter, T. (2017). Genetic influence on eye movements to complex scenes at short timescales. *Current Biology, 27*(22), 3554–3560.

Klin, A., Lin, D. J., Gorrindo, P., Ramsay, G., & Jones, W. (2009). Two-year-olds with autism orient to non-social contingencies rather than biological motion. *Nature, 459*(7244), 257–261.

Kolesnik, A. M., Jones, E. J. H., Garg, S., Green, J., Charman, T., & Johnson, M. H. (2017). Early development of infants with neurofibromatosis type 1: A case series. *Molecular Autism, 8*(1), 62.

Landa, R., & Garrett-Mayer, E. (2006). Development in infants with autism spectrum disorders: A prospective study. *Journal of Child Psychology and Psychiatry, 47*(6), 629–638.

Landa, R. J., Holman, K. C., & Garrett-Mayer, E. (2007). Social and communication development in toddlers with early and later diagnosis of autism spectrum disorders. *Archives of General Psychiatry, 64*(7), 853–864.

Lazenby, D. C., Sideridis, G. D., Huntington, N., Prante, M., Dale, P. S., Curtin, S., … Dobkins, K. (2016). Language differences at 12 months in infants who develop autism spectrum disorder. *Journal of Autism and Developmental Disorders, 46*(3), 899–909.

Leppa, V. M., Kravitz, S. N., Martin, C. L., Andrieux, J., Le Caignec, C., Martin-Coignard, D., … Cantor, R. M. (2016). Rare inherited and de novo CNVs reveal complex contributions to ASD risk in multiplex families. *American Journal of Human Genetics, 99*(3), 540–554.

Lloyd-Fox, S., Begus, K., Halliday, D., Pirazzoli, L., Blasi, A., Papademetriou, M., … Moore, S. (2017). Cortical specialisation to social stimuli from the first days to the second year of life: A rural Gambian cohort. *Developmental Cognitive Neuroscience, 25*, 92–104.

Lloyd-Fox, S., Blasi, A., Elwell, C. E., Charman, T., Murphy, D., & Johnson, M. H. (2013). Reduced neural sensitivity to social stimuli in infants at risk for autism. *Proceedings of the Royal Society B: Biological Sciences, 280*(1758), 9. doi:10.1098/rspb.2012.3026

Lloyd-Fox, S., Blasi, A., Pasco, G., Gliga, T., Jones, E., Murphy, D., ... Johnson, M. (2017). Cortical responses before 6 months of life associate with later autism. *European Journal of Neuroscience, 47*(6), 736–749.

Macari, S. L., Campbell, D., Gengoux, G. W., Saulnier, C. A., Klin, A. J., & Chawarska, K. (2012). Predicting developmental status from 12 to 24 months in infants at risk for autism spectrum disorder: A preliminary report. *Journal of Autism and Developmental Disorders, 42*(12), 2636–2647. doi:10.1007/s10803-012-1521-0

Mitchell, S., Brian, J., Zwaigenbaum, L., Roberts, W., Szatmari, P., Smith, I., & Bryson, S. (2006). Early language and communication development of infants later diagnosed with autism spectrum disorder. *Journal of Developmental and Behavioral Pediatrics, 27*(2), S69-S78.

Molenhuis, R. T., de Visser, L., Bruining, H., & Kas, M. J. (2014). Enhancing the value of psychiatric mouse models: Differential expression of developmental behavioral and cognitive profiles in four inbred strains of mice. *European Neuropsychopharmacology, 24*(6), 945–954.

Nyström, P., Gliga, T., Nilsson Jobs, E., Gredebäck, G., Charman, T., Johnson, M., ... Falck-Ytter, T. (2018). Enhanced pupillary light reflex in infancy is associated with autism diagnosis in toddlerhood. *Nature Communications, 9*(1). doi:10.1038/s41467-018-03985-4

Orekhova, E. V., Elsabbagh, M., Jones, E. J., Dawson, G., Charman, T., & Johnson, M. H. (2014). EEG hyper-connectivity in high-risk infants is associated with later autism. *Journal of Neurodevelopmental Disorders, 6*(1), 40.

Ornitz, E. M., Guthrie, D., & Farley, A. H. (1977). The early development of autistic children. *Journal of Autism and Childhood Schizophrenia, 7*(3), 207–229.

Ozonoff, S., Iosif, A. M., Baguio, F., Cook, I. C., Hill, M. M., Hutman, T., ... Young, G. S. (2010). A prospective study of the emergence of early behavioral signs of autism. *Journal of the American Academy of Child and Adolescent Psychiatry, 49*(3), 256–266. doi:10.1016/j.jaac.2009.11.009

Paul, R., Fuerst, Y., Ramsay, G., Chawarska, K., & Klin, A. (2011). Out of the mouths of babes: Vocal production in infant siblings of children with ASD. *Journal of Child Psychology and Psychiatry, 52*(5), 588–598.

Ronald, A., Edelson, L. R., Asherson, P., & Saudino, K. J. (2010). Exploring the relationship between autistic-like traits and ADHD behaviors in early childhood: Findings from a community twin study of 2-year-olds. *Journal of Abnormal Child Psychology, 38*(2), 185–196. doi:10.1007/s10802-009-9366-5

Ross, R. G., Hunter, S. K., Hoffman, M. C., McCarthy, L., Chambers, B. M., Law, A. J., ... Freedman, R. (2016). Perinatal phosphatidylcholine supplementation and early childhood behavior problems: Evidence for CHRNA7 moderation. *American Journal of Psychiatry, 173*(5), 509–516.

Rozga, A., Hutman, T., Young, G. S., Rogers, S. J., Ozonoff, S., Dapretto, M., & Sigman, M. (2011). Behavioral profiles of affected and unaffected siblings of children with autism: Contribution of measures of mother–infant interaction and nonverbal communication. *Journal of Autism and Developmental Disorders, 41*(3), 287–301.

Sacrey, L. -A. R., Zwaigenbaum, L., Bryson, S., Brian, J., Smith, I. M., Roberts, W., … Novak, C. (2015). Can parents' concerns predict autism spectrum disorder? A prospective study of high-risk siblings from 6 to 36 months of age. *Journal of the American Academy of Child and Adolescent Psychiatry, 54*(6), 470–478.

Shen, M. D., Kim, S. H., McKinstry, R. C., Gu, H., Hazlett, H. C., Nordahl, C. W., … Swanson, M. R. (2017). Increased extra-axial cerebrospinal fluid in high-risk infants who later develop autism. *Biological Psychiatry, 82*(3), 186–193.

Shen, M. D., Nordahl, C. W., Young, G. S., Wootton-Gorges, S. L., Lee, A., Liston, S. E., … Amaral, D. G. (2013). Early brain enlargement and elevated extra-axial fluid in infants who develop autism spectrum disorder. *Brain, 136*(9), 2825–2835.

Shephard, E., Bedford, R., Milosavljevic, B., Gliga, T., Jones, E. J. H., Pickles, A., … Bolton, P. (2019). Early developmental pathways to childhood symptoms of attention-deficit hyperactivity disorder, anxiety and autism spectrum disorder. *Journal of Child Psychology and Psychiatry*, 60(9), 963–974.

St. John, T., Estes, A. M., Dager, S. R., Kostopoulos, P., Wolff, J. J., Pandey, J., … Botteron, K. (2016). Emerging executive functioning and motor development in infants at high and low risk for autism spectrum disorder. *Frontiers in Psychology*, 7, 1016.

Sullivan, M., Finelli, J., Marvin, A., Garrett-Mayer, E., Bauman, M., & Landa, R. (2007). Response to joint attention in toddlers at risk for autism spectrum disorder: A prospective study. *Journal of Autism And Developmental Disorders, 37*(1), 37.

Swanson, M. R., Shen, M. D., Wolff, J. J., Elison, J. T., Emerson, R. W., Styner, M. A., … Paterson, S. (2017). Subcortical brain and behavior phenotypes differentiate infants with autism versus language delay. *Biological Psychiatry: Cognitive Neuroscience and Neuroimaging, 2*(8), 664–672.

Thorup, E., Nystrom, P., Gredeback, G., Bölte, S., Falck-Ytter, T., & EASE Team (2018). Reduced alternating gaze during social interaction in infancy is associated with elevated symptoms of autism in toddlerhood. *Journal of Abnormal Child Psychology*, 46(7), 1547–1561.

Varcin, K. J., & Jeste, S. S. (2017). The emergence of autism spectrum disorder: Insights gained from studies of brain and behaviour in high-risk infants. *Current Opinion in Psychiatry, 30*(2), 85–91.

Wan, M. W., Green, J., Elsabbagh, M., Johnson, M., Charman, T., & Plummer , F. (2013). Quality of interaction between at-risk infants and caregiver at 12–15 months is associated with 3-year autism outcome. *Journal of Child Psychology and Psychiatry, 54*(7), 763–771.

Wass, S. V., Jones, E. J. H., Gliga, T., Smith, T. J., Charman, T., & Johnson, M. H. (2015). Shorter spontaneous fixation durations in infants with later emerging autism. *Scientific Reports*, 5, 8284. doi:10.1038/srep08284

Webb, S. J., Nalty, T., Munson, J., Brock, C., Abbott, R., & Dawson, G. (2007). Rate of head circumference growth as a function of autism diagnosis and history of autistic regression. *Journal of Child Neurology, 22*(10), 1182–1190.

West, K. L., Leezenbaum, N. B., Northrup, J. B., & Iverson, J. M. (2019). The relation between walking and language in infant siblings of children with autism spectrum disorder. *Child Development, 90*(3), e356–e372.

Wolff, J. J., Jacob, S., & Elison, J. T. (2018). The journey to autism: Insights from neuroimaging studies of infants and toddlers. *Development And Psychopathology, 30*(2), 479–495.

Wolff, J. J., Swanson, M. R., Elison, J. T., Gerig, G., Pruett, J. R., Styner, M. A., … Estes, A. M. (2017). Neural circuitry at age 6 months associated with later repetitive behavior and sensory responsiveness in autism. *Molecular Autism, 8*(1), 8.

Yoder, P., Stone, W. L., Walden, T., & Malesa, E. (2009). Predicting social impairment and ASD diagnosis in younger siblings of children with autism spectrum disorder. *Journal of Autism and Developmental Disorders, 39*(10), 1381–1391. doi:10.1007/s10803-009-0753-0

Zwaigenbaum, L., Bryson, S., Rogers, T., Roberts, W., Brian, J., & Szatmari, P. (2005). Behavioral manifestations of autism in the first year of life. *International Journal Of Developmental Neuroscience, 23*(2–3), 143–152.

Zwaigenbaum, L., Thurm, A., Stone, W., Baranek, G., Bryson, S., Iverson, J., … Sigman, M. (2007). Studying the emergence of autism spectrum disorders in high-risk infants: Methodological and practical issues. *Journal of Autism and Developmental Disorders, 37*(3), 466–480.

PART II

Perceptual Development

6 Visual Development

Daphne Maurer

Newborns can see – but only if they are awake with an object right in front of them that is large with elements of high contrast against the background, like the mother's face. Improvements come rapidly after birth with the maturation of the retina and the visual cortex to which it connects, allowing better input to higher visual areas that underlie the perception of whole objects and their movement. Nevertheless, missing visual input near birth because of dense cataracts in one or both eyes alters the developmental trajectory, even when treatment occurs within the first few months of life. Thus, the early visual input, despite its limitations, is critical for setting up the neural architecture for later refinement.

This chapter begins with a description of the limitations on the newborn's visual world and their source in immaturities in the retina and visual cortex. Variations in diet affect the postnatal development of the retina and hence lead to cross-cultural variations in the quality of visual input. Although the long-term consequences of these cross-cultural differences are unknown, we do know that when input is more seriously limited by visual deprivation, deficits in both low-level (acuity, peripheral vision) and high-level (motion, faces) processing emerge later. Those effects will be illustrated by using motion and face perception as examples of how changing neural limitations alter the effective visual world of the baby and of how, in turn, environmental variations ranging from complete visual deprivation to culturally biased visual input, can affect that neural development.

6.1 Newborns' Visual Perception: Low-Level Vision

6.1.1 Acuity

To assess an adult's vision, the adult is asked to read letters of decreasing size and the measure of acuity is the smallest letters the adult can recognize accurately. To measure newborns' vision, the test is adapted to take advantage of infants' preference to look at something patterned over something plain (Fantz, 1963; Fantz, Ordy, & Udelf, 1962): the baby is shown a gray field with a gray patch to one side (to the right or left) and a patch of black-and-white stripes to the other side. When the stripes are large, the baby rapidly orients toward and fixates them. As the stripes get smaller, the looking preference – for stripes sometimes on the right and sometimes on the left – diminishes until the baby responds randomly. The measure of vision is the smallest size of stripe for which the baby shows a reliable preference. Newborns respond to stripes only if they are about 40 times larger than the limit for adults with normal vision, a size larger than the top line of most eye charts. Over the next 6 months there is a rapid 8-fold improvement, so that the baby responds to lines like those forming the 20/100 line of an adult eye chart. Over the next 6–7 years, there is gradual improvement to adult thresholds for detecting thinner lines and for the harder task of recognizing them when they form a letter surrounded by other letters (Ellemberg, Lewis, Liu, & Maurer, 1999; Mayer et al., 1995). The implication is that initially only large objects will be visible to the baby, and within them, only large details.

6.1.2 Contrast Sensitivity

Not only must the details be large, they must also be of high contrast. Newborns' sensitivity to contrast has been tested with a method similar to the acuity test, but now, during each block, the stripes remain the same size over trials, but their contrast is systematically reduced. Then in another block, the same test is performed with stripes of a different size. For each size of stripe, the measure is the lowest contrast at which the baby reliably fixates the stripes (Brown, Lindsey, Cammenga, Giannone, & Stenger, 2015; Brown, Opoku, & Stenger, 2018). For the large sizes of stripe to which the newborn responds, contrast has to be more than 100 times greater than in adults with normal vision (Brown et al., 2015). Over the next few months, babies begin to respond to thinner stripes and to lower contrasts but adult-like sensitivity is not achieved until around age 7 (Banks & Salapatek, 1978; Drover, Earle, Courage, & Adams, 2002; Ellemberg et al., 1999). The implication is that infants can see only high-contrast features of objects, such as the eyes and hairline of a face, but not its nose, and likely the mouth only if its contrast is heightened by showing the teeth or the application of makeup.

The initially poor vision of the newborn arises largely from an immature retina. In adults, the perception of fine detail and low contrast is mediated by the fovea, the central region of the retina that is densely packed with cones that efficiently transmit light. In newborns, the transmission is estimated to be 350 times less efficient than in adults (Banks & Bennett, 1988) because the foveal cones are wider and shorter and, therefore, spaced further apart, preventing the resolution of fine detail and efficient light transmission from their inner to outer segments; they are also intermingled with, and covered by, outer ganglion cells that block light transmission. Computational modeling indicates that retinal immaturities account for much, but not all, of newborns' limited acuity and contrast sensitivity (Banks & Bennett, 1988; Candy, Crowell, & Banks, 1998).

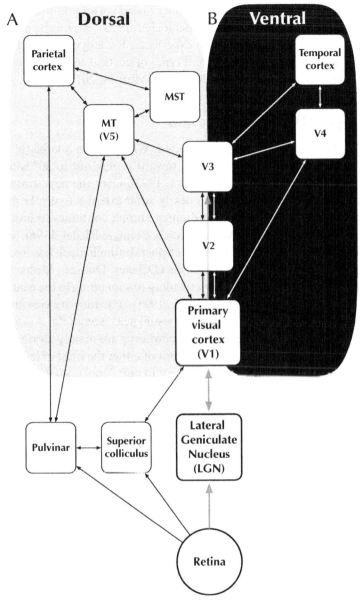

Figure 6.1. *The most principal pathways from the retina to the visual cortices.*

The remaining limitations likely arise from immaturities in the pathway from the retina through the lateral geniculate nucleus to the primary visual cortex (V1) (see Figure 6.1): neurons in the lateral geniculate nucleus and the primary visual cortex are less sensitive than in adults, at least in the monkey (Blakemore, 1990; Blakemore & Vital-Durand, 1986; Kiorpes, 2016; Movshon & Kiorpes, 1993), and synaptic density in the human primary visual cortex continues to increase until about 8 months after birth (Huttenlocher, 1990), later to be pruned back to adult levels, presumably based on experience. Underlying these changes are shifts in the predominance of different types of cortical receptors that mediate excitatory versus inhibitory responses (Siu & Murphy, 2018).

6.1.3 Peripheral Vision and Stereopsis

Newborns' peripheral vision is also limited. When shown a large (6°) flashing light in the periphery, newborns orient toward it only out to 30° while adults can detect it past 100° (Lewis & Maurer, 1992). Over the next 4 months, the visual field expands rapidly to reach nearly adult extent for such large stimuli. However, sensitivity to smaller and dimmer stimuli continues to improve into middle childhood (Bowering, Maurer, Lewis, Brent, & Riedel, 1996). Moreover, throughout infancy, babies respond to peripheral stimuli much less frequently if the stimulus is static rather than flickering (Delaney, Dobson, Mohan, Harvey, & Harvey, 2004), if they are already attending to something in the central visual field ("sticky fixation": Hood & Atkinson, 1993), or if they are viewing monocularly while the stimulus is in their nasal visual field (across the nose) (Lewis & Maurer, 1992). The consequence is that newborns are mainly aware of objects only if they are large and in a tunnel in front of either the right or left eye. These limitations in peripheral vision arise, at least in part, from immaturities between the primary visual cortex and the networks controlling eye movements (Maurer & Lewis, 1998). Only objects dead ahead functionally stimulate both eyes – and initially those two eyes work independently. It is not until several months after birth that the inputs from the two eyes fuse into a binocular image (3 months) and begin to mediate the perception of three-dimensional depth (4 months: stereopsis) (E. E. Birch, Gwiazda, & Held, 1982; Braddick, Wattam-Bell, Day, & Atkinson, 1983; Gwiazda, Bauer, & Held, 1989). Mom's face is processed independently by each eye as she leans over her newborn's crib but out of sight once she moves even a little bit off to the side.

6.2 Importance of Early Visual Experience for the Development of Low-Level Vision

Despite these limitations, early visual experience is critical for later visual development. The clearest evidence comes from children who were born with cataracts in both eyes that blocked all patterned visual input until the cataracts were removed surgically and the eyes fit with compensatory contact lenses (Maurer, Lewis, Brent, & Levin, 1999). At the time that the treated infants can first see, their acuity is like that of a normal newborn, even when treatment occurs 2–8 months after birth. Thus, the rapid improvement in babies with normal eyes immediately after birth must depend on visual experience: it fails to occur when that experience is missing because of cataracts. Treated infants show rapid recovery that normalizes visual acuity by 12 months of age (Lewis, Maurer, & Brent, 1995). Nevertheless, deficits in all aspects of low-level vision emerge later: Adults treated during infancy for bilateral congenital cataracts later have abnormal acuity, contrast sensitivity, peripheral vision, and stereopsis, even when treatment occurred before 2 months of age (E. E. Birch, Cheng, Stager, Weakley, & Stager, 2009; Bowering, Maurer, Lewis, & Brent, 1993; Bowering et al., 1996; Ellemberg, Lewis, Maurer, Lui, & Brent, 1999; Tytla, Lewis, Maurer, & Brent, 1993). These "sleeper effects" that emerge later (Maurer, Mondloch, & Lewis, 2007) indicate that early visual experience – at a time when infants' vision is poor – is, nevertheless, critical for setting up the visual neural architecture for later refinement.

The outcome is worse when the baby was born with a cataract in only one eye. Vision in the treated eye – acuity, contrast sensitivity, and peripheral vision – are worse than in eyes treated for bilateral congenital cataracts, unless there had been extensive patching of the "good" eye throughout early childhood (Lewis & Maurer, 2009). This pattern indicates that during infancy the two eyes – which begin by functioning independently – compete for cortical connections, and when one eye sends better input – because it is a normal eye – and the other eye sends weaker input – because there is no patterned input before removal of a cataract and then less sharp input after treatment – one eye will develop better vision at the expense of the affected eye. However, even the good eyes in children treated for monocular congenital cataract later have subtle deficits in acuity (Lewis, Maurer, Tytla, Bowering, & Brent, 1992). Thus, visual experience in the perinatal period that is balanced between eyes is critical if the child is to later develop normal vision in both eyes. When the input is monocular, both the deprived eye and the "normal" eye fail to develop optimal vision.

On the other hand, extra-visual experience because of premature birth does not lead to any advantage: Acuity and binocular vision develop based on gestational age, rather than the number of months of postnatal experience (Weinacht, Kind, Mönting, & Gottlob, 1999). On many measures, premature babies even lag behind, especially if they were born very early, for example, before 30 weeks gestation (Hou et al., 2011). The overall pattern suggests that the visual cortex is experience-expectant after 40 weeks of gestation – that the cortex evolved to profit from visual experience during a critical period near birth, when many types of neurotransmitter have become functional (Siu & Murphy, 2018).

6.3 Cultural Variations: Effect of Diet on the Development of Low-Level Vision

Cultural variations in diet may influence the baby's visual development because of the influence of long-chain polyunsaturated fatty acids in the mother's diet during pregnancy, in the mother's breast milk, or included as an additive to the baby's formula. Critical are docosahexaenoic acid (DHA) and arachidonic acid (ARA). These fatty acids support neural development during the last trimester of pregnancy and the early months of development, greatly increasing their concentration in gray matter over this period (E. E. Birch et al., 2007; Hoffman, Boettcher, & Diersen-Schade, 2009). DHA has an especially high concentration in retinal photoreceptors and appears to affect both myelination and synaptic formation throughout the nervous system. Infants cannot generate adequate DHA and ARA endogenously and must obtain it from breast milk or from supplemented formula, supplementation that became common only after 2002. Preterm infants fed formula containing long-chain fatty acids show better retinal development (as indexed by the electroretinogram) (D. G. Birch, Birch, Hoffman, & Uauy, 1992) and better visual acuity (especially when indexed by visually evoked responses) than preterm babies fed unsupplemented formula (E. E. Birch, Birch, Hoffman, & Uauy, 1992). Even full-term babies fed supplemented formula have visual acuity that is better than that of age-matched babies fed formula without the supplement and as good as babies fed human breast milk (Hoffman et al., 2009). Comparisons of groups fed in different ways postnatally reveal differences in visual acuity as late as 4 years after birth (E. E. Birch et al., 2007). Although these differences are small and there is considerable overlap in acuity between groups, in animal (rodent) models the changes effected in neurotransmitters from inadequate diets are not reversible after weaning (Kodas et al., 2004).

The levels of ARA and DHA in breast milk vary cross-culturally over a 4-fold and 18-fold range, respectively (Brenna et al., 2007). Levels are higher in societies where fish is a regular part of the diet (e.g., Japan, Canadian Arctic, Philippines) than in societies where eating fish is rare (e.g., Pakistan, Europe, the United States, and the rest of Canada). A causal relation is suggested by the finding that the concentration of DHA in maternal blood is directly related to the amount of oily fish that she consumes (Williams, Birch, Emett, & Northstone, 2001). Moreover, maternal consumption of oily fish during the pregnancy is related to the infant's later visual development, presumably through fetal exposure to DHA: Children 3.5 years old whose mothers ate oily fish at least once every 2 weeks during pregnancy had better stereo (3-D) vision than those whose mothers never ate oily fish, even after controlling for postnatal diet (Williams et al., 2001).

Together, the evidence on the effect of diet suggests that there may be considerable variation cross-culturally in retinal and visual cortical development and the fine visual resolution they come to mediate. Newborns are known to differ in the quality of the visual input they receive with which to build their cortical circuitry – the quality is lower for babies born preterm or with peripheral visual perturbations like cataracts. Additional differences may arise from variations in provision of ARA and DHA through the maternal diet prenatally, breast milk postnatally, and/or the composition of formula. Not only will such variation influence the initial visual input made available through retinal processing but it may affect the ultimate acuity achieved: One can speculate that the distribution of visual acuities (with any necessary optical correction) may be shifted toward finer values in cohorts living in countries where the eating of oily fish during pregnancy and breast-feeding have always been common (e.g., high Canadian Arctic, Philippines) than in cohorts where this is uncommon and/or formulas had not yet been supplemented with fatty acids. Although this pattern has been documented for stereoacuity at 3.5 years of age (see above), the prediction about the distribution of adult acuities is speculative because there has been no study that compared the distributions in different geographic regions or across different time periods.

6.4 Higher-Level Vision: Motion Processing

6.4.1 Newborns' (In)Sensitivity to Direction of Motion

Newborns fail most tests of sensitivity to motion, whether tested for sensitivity to the direction of motion with visually evoked potentials or with preferential looking. For example, when shown a stimulus with uniformly moving dots versus a stimulus in which a form is defined by dots moving in a direction opposite the background, infants show no preference to look at the motion-defined form before 7 weeks of age and then do so only for a restricted range of velocities, namely, dots moving about 5–10 deg/second (Wattam-Bell, 1996b). This is the same age at which sensitivity to direction of motion is first evident in visually evoked potentials (Braddick, Birtles, Wattam-Bell, & Atkinson, 2005; Wattam-Bell, 1991). Even so, babies do not show evidence of discriminating between two directions of uniform motion until after 9–12 weeks of age (Armstrong, Maurer, Ellemberg, & Lewis, 2011; Wattam-Bell, 1996a): after habituation to one direction of motion, before that age they do not show renewed interest when the direction is shifted by 180°. Newborns' preference for moving over stationary stimuli, therefore, likely is a preference for the flicker induced by the moving stimuli when the infant maintains fixation on a selective part of it. The slow development of sensitivity to direction of motion contrasts with the earlier development of sensitivity to the orientation of stationary stimuli, whether measured with habituation/dishabituation (Maurer & Martello, 1980) or visually evoked potentials (Braddick et al., 2005). The limitations in sensitivity to motion likely reflect immaturities in the primary visual cortex and the retinal input it receives (see above) since it is the first cortical way station where individual neurons are tuned to direction.

6.4.2 Surprising Exceptions: Sensitivity to Evolutionarily Important Global Patterns of Movement

Despite apparent insensitivity to direction of motion, from birth infants prefer to look at certain overall patterns of movement, specifically those signaling that an object is going to strike the baby's face and those signaling that the movement comes from a biological organism. For example, they fixate a video of a striped ball moving toward them in preference to one moving away or one on a trajectory that will miss the face (Orioli, Filippetti, Gerbino, Dragovic, & Farroni, 2018). The sensitivity to collision is likely based on sensitivity to the optical expansion of a stimulus as it approaches the face, filling more and more of the visual field, modulated by sensitivity to whether the expansion is symmetrical (as it will be if the object is on a trajectory colliding with the face) or not (as it will be if the trajectory will miss the face).

Another exception is sensitivity to *biological motion*, the special trajectories of motion formed by the joints of biological organisms, which is commonly tested by point light displays in which the baby sees only the movement trajectories of lights affixed to those joints. From birth, babies look longer at a pattern of dots moving like a biological organism (such as a walking hen) than a pattern with the same dots moving in random directions or inverted, or a pattern of rigid nonbiological motion (a rotating object) (Bardi, Regolin, & Simion, 2011; Simion, Regolin, & Bulf, 2008). However, the preference disappears if the biologically moving display is pitted against a display with the dots scrambled spatially (Bardi et al., 2011) or against randomly moving dots following the same pattern of translation (e.g., moving sideways to the left) (Bidet-Ildei, Kitromilides, Orliaguet, Pavlova, & Gentaz, 2014). Both results suggest that the initial preference is based on some innate sensitivity to certain patterns of movement that are present in moving human organisms but that are not human-specific.

What this means for the newborn's perception is that modulation attracts attention – the flickering input on the retina induced by limited scanning (Salapatek & Kessen, 1966) of moving stimuli – with special sensitivity to modulation coming toward the baby's face or from a biological organism. Initially the baby will perceive local motion within an object – such as moving lips as the mother talks or changes her facial expression – only as change, not as movement in a particular direction. Nevertheless, the change will attract the baby's attention and hence bias the baby's visual experience. The initial sensitivities ensure that young infants will preferentially attend to human adults over inanimate objects in their environment because adults frequently move into the baby's field of view and do so with the signature movement patterns of a biological organism, enhanced by being on an approaching trajectory.

When 7-week-old infants are shown dots moving coherently in a pattern of expansion (looming, signaling collision), or spiraling inward or outward compared to randomly moving dots, there is selective fMRI activation for the coherent motion in areas active under the same conditions in adults, namely throughout the dorsal stream, including likely areas V3 and MT and their projections to the parietal cortex (see Figure 6.1; Biagi, Crespi, Tosetti, & Morrone, 2015). One possibility is that during early infancy, input reaches these higher cortical areas not via V1 as it does in adults, but mainly via the retinal-pulvinar pathway, as has been documented anatomically in the developing marmoset (Warner, Kwan, & Bourne, 2012). With age, the pulvinar input to the marmoset's MT diminishes as V1 input increases in magnitude. That type of reorganization is supported by evidence in humans that the topography of visually evoked potentials induced by global motion is different at 4–5 months of age from that shown in adults (Wattam-Bell et al., 2010).

Similarly, the early preferences for biological motion may be mediated by pathways that largely bypass the primary visual cortex yet innervate higher motion processing systems, including MT/MST and STS (biological motion). (See Figure 6.1 for a schematic drawing of the motion visual pathways; STS is a more central hub receiving input from several dozen structures, including MT and MST.) Later sensitivity may reflect the increased influence of input through the primary visual cortex to these higher cortical areas. Just such a reorganization is suggested by research on newborns' preference to look at upright biological motion over an inverted version with the frames in reverse order. Unlike newborns (Simion et al., 2008), 2-month-olds fail to show a looking preference for the upright version, with the preference re-emerging from 3 months of age (Sifre et al., 2018). This apparently U-shaped developmental trajectory may represent early sensitivity mediated by an early experience-expectant mechanism that is largely subcortical (Sifre et al., 2018) and biased for certain patterns of local motion typically made by moving limbs (Bardi et al., 2011), without any sensitivity to the biological form itself (Chang & Troje, 2009). Only later may an experience-dependent and cortically mediated mechanism emerge that is sensitive to those configural cues and affected by learning (Chang & Troje, 2009).

6.5 Importance of Early Visual Experience for the Development of Motion Processing

Children who missed early visual input because of dense cataracts in one or both eyes later have only small deficits in processing the direction of motion in sine wave gratings when local cues are sufficient and no global integration is required (Ellemberg et al., 2005). However, when global integration is required because only some dots are moving coherently in the same direction while the rest move randomly (e.g., in a random dot kinematogram testing sensitivity to the direction of global motion), adults treated for congenital cataract have significant deficits even when the deprivation began at birth and lasted only a few months. When tested as adults, those treated for bilateral congenital cataracts have greatly elevated thresholds, such that roughly 50% of the dots have to move coherently for them to detect the direction while adults with normal vision can do so with fewer than 10% of the dots moving coherently. This is another example of a sleeper effect (Maurer et al., 2007): Visual deprivation early in life – before the capability is manifest in babies with normal eyes – prevents *later* normal development of processing of global motion. No such deficit is evident in patients treated for dense bilateral cataracts that developed postnatally between 1 and 10 years of age: Despite acuity deficits secondary to the visual deprivation, their sensitivity to global motion is completely normal (Ellemberg, Lewis, Maurer, Brar, & Brent, 2002; see also Fine et al., 2003). This pattern supports the hypothesis that some aspects of sensitivity to global motion depend on postnatal experience, as does visual acuity, but that the timing of the needed experience varies from a short critical period for global motion to a much longer one for visual acuity. Similar tests of sensitivity to global form also reveal deficits, although they are smaller than the deficits for global motion (Lewis et al., 2002), suggesting more damage to the dorsal pathway (Figure 6.1A) than the ventral pathway (Figure 6.1B).

Despite the deficits in sensitivity to global motion, patients treated for bilateral congenital cataracts are normal at detecting the presence of biological motion (compared to motion with the trajectories spatially scrambled), even when moving masking dots are superimposed on the stimulus (Hadad, Maurer, & Lewis, 2012). Like adults with normal vision, they can still detect which of two patterns contains the biological motion when more than 70 masking dots are superimposed (Hadad et al., 2012). Similar to the findings on normal development, this pattern suggests that more than one mechanism is at work: an early developing experience-expectant mechanism that allows the newborn to pick out biological motion and that continues to be able to mediate that behavior after early visual deprivation, and two later developing experience-dependent mechanisms that mediate sensitivity to the *direction* of global motion and the *form* of the moving organism. The first mechanism is evident at birth and even after early visual deprivation, dependent only on there having been normal development in the womb without the necessity of *visual* experience; the second are manifest only postnatally and only when there has been patterned visual input. Unclear from these experiments is whether the visual experience must involve exposure to moving stimuli (for global motion) and pattern elements (for global form). However, studies of kittens raised without exposure to moving stimuli – because the environment was lit by stroboscopic light – suggest that experience with moving stimuli may be necessary. After strobe rearing, cats have normal sensitivity to orientation but can discriminate opposite directions of motion only at high contrast and they have fewer cortical neurons tuned to direction (Humphrey & Saul, 1998; Pasternak & Leinen, 1986).

Further insights arise from comparisons to children treated for unilateral congenital cataracts who, as described above, have larger deficits than patients treated for bilateral congenital cataracts in basic visual capabilities like acuity, contrast sensitivity, and peripheral vision. They, too, manifest deficits in integrating local signals into a global perception of motion or of form, but, unlike bilateral patients, their thresholds are only slightly elevated compared to adults with normal eyes (Ellemberg et al., 2002; Lewis et al., 2002). Thus, the integrative processes mediated by the dorsal pathway (see Figure 6.1A) for motion processing and by the ventral pathway for form processing (see Figure 6.1B) can develop almost normally when there was normal visual input through one eye throughout life. Neurons in the visual cortical pathway in areas beyond the primary visual cortex are predominantly binocular, with larger receptive fields than in primary visual cortex and less spatial resolution. The consequence is that input from just one eye before treatment and from a second eye with poor acuity after treatment may be sufficient to induce nearly normal development for these higher visual areas but be inadequate for tuning the neurons in primary visual cortex that mediate basic low-level visual capabilities.

What goes wrong in children treated for bilateral congenital cataract that prevents such recovery, especially in dorsal stream areas? One possibility is that, in the absence of visual input, those areas start responding to input from other sensory modalities, as happens in the congenitally blind (Renier, de Volder, & Rauschecker, 2014), and continue to do so after treatment. Indeed, as in the congenitally blind, there is activation in the dorsal *visual* cortex, around area V3, when adults treated for bilateral congenital cataracts do *auditory* processing (Collignon et al., 2015). Unlike adults with normal vision, in such patients, a motion aftereffect induced by sound transfers to vision (Guerreiro, Putzar, & Röder, 2016): After hearing a sound that increases in loudness to simulate an approaching object, adults treated for bilateral congenital cataracts, unlike controls, perceived a pattern of squares to be increasing in size as if they were approaching the face. That transfer suggests that the auditory input to the visual cortex may be functional. Input from one eye during the period of deprivation may be sufficient to prevent such rewiring in children treated for unilateral congenital cataract. If this interpretation is correct, then during normal development, visual input during infancy is not only setting up the visual cortical architecture for later refinement, it is also preserving the dorsal visual pathway as a visual processor.

Getting this visual experience early – because of premature birth, however, is not beneficial. Even in the absence of any detectable neurological problems, during infancy, such children show delays in developing visually evoked potentials to changes in the direction of motion (Birtles, Braddick, Wattam-Bell, Wilkinson, & Atkinson, 2007) and, during middle childhood, they have elevated thresholds for seeing global motion (Taylor, Jakobson, Maurer, & Lewis, 2009). Enhancing the diet of preterm babies promotes better neurological growth, including white matter growth, and normalizes the directionally selected visually evoked potential recorded at 5 months corrected age (Blakstad et al., 2015). The deficits in motion processing contrast with normal visually evoked potentials to changes in orientation during infancy (Birtles et al., 2007) and, in middle childhood, normal thresholds for discriminating changes in orientation (MacKay et al., 2005) and in seeing static global form (Taylor et al., 2009). The pattern is consistent with "dorsal vulnerability" (Atkinson et al., 1999), that is, especial vulnerability of the dorsal pathway through the primary visual cortex to areas V3 and V5 (MT/MST; see Figure 6.1) that mediates the processing of motion compared to less vulnerability of the ventral pathway to the ventral extrastriate cortex (e.g., V4 and fusiform face area in temporal cortex; see Figure 6.1) that mediates the processing of form and its properties. When some abnormality affects the development of higher levels of the visual cortex, be it visual deprivation, prematurity, brain damage, or genetic disorders like fragile X or Williams syndrome, it is the dorsal stream that is more likely to be affected adversely (Braddick & Atkinson, 2011). Nevertheless, the pattern of deficits is not hierarchical – they do not increase monotonically from lower to higher cortical areas or from low-level to higher-level visual processing: Like children treated for bilateral congenital cataracts, babies born premature have (almost) normal sensitivity to biological motion, a capability that requires integration of form and motion information (Taylor et al., 2009) and that is mediated by a complex network of dorsal and ventral pathway structures, including the superior temporal sulcus (STS; Giese & Poggio, 2003).

6.6 Higher-Level Vision: Face Processing

6.6.1 Detecting Faces

The immaturities in newborns' acuity and contrast sensitivity result in severe limits on the information they can perceive in a face, especially if it is more than a foot away. One simulation (von Hofsten et al., 2014) shows faces at that distance preserve the shape of the head framed by hair, but very few details about the internal features, which look merely like dark blobs. At 2 feet, even the dark blobs begin to disappear. Picking up information about the internal features is further limited by the newborn's bias to scan the external contour of the face (the dark transition from face to hair) (Hainline, 1978; Haith, Bergman, & Moore, 1977), rarely looking at the internal features. Nevertheless, already at birth, or perhaps even during the last trimester of pregnancy (Reid et al., 2017), infants have some sensitivity to face-like properties in the arrangement of the internal features. Within the first hour after birth, they look preferentially toward faces over other visual stimuli with the same amount of visible energy (Johnson, Dziurawiec, Ellis, & Morton, 1991; Mondloch et al., 1999), especially if the face is oriented frontally with direct gaze (Farroni, Menon, & Johnson, 2006). The preference is based only on very low spatial frequencies (de Heering et al., 2008) and may be mediated in part by peripheral vision (Morton & Johnson, 1991; Johnson, Senju, & Tomalski, 2015).

Newborns' preference to look at face-like stimuli does not appear be an attraction specifically to faces but rather an attraction to stimulus properties like being top-heavy (having more elements in the top half), having congruent structure (the outer contour is widest where the internal features are also widest), and having positive polarity (black elements on a white background) (Cassia, Turati, & Simion, 2004; Simion & Giorgio, 2015). A looking preference is manifest whenever a schematic drawing containing these properties is pitted against other drawings without them and the preference may be mediated subcortically through the superior colliculus (see Figure 6.1; Johnson, 2005; Johnson et al., 2015), rather than the ventral cortical pathway that will come to mediate face processing (see Figure 6.1). The looking preference generalizes to nonface-like schematic drawings (Cassia et al., 2004) and to monkey faces (Di Giorgio, Leo, Pascalis, & Simion, 2012). Regardless of the basis for the preference, however, it assures that the newborn infant is biased to attend to faces over other stimuli in the environment and will prefer to look at an upright human face rather than an inverted face because only the former has the requisite properties.

6.6.2 Learning About Individual Faces

Already at birth, newborns can learn about faces they encounter repeatedly, like those of their parents. When tested with habituation in the lab, after repeated exposure to the face of one unfamiliar woman, they show recovered interest for a different unfamiliar woman and can do so even after sleeping for 2 hours (Cecchini et al., 2017) and even when required to generalize from *en face* to 3/4 view (Turati, Bulf, & Simion, 2008). Not surprisingly, they show evidence of recognizing the mother's face within a few days after birth (Pascalis, de Schonen, Morton, Deruelle, & Fabre-Gremet, 1995), even when the cumulative exposure is just a few hours (Bushnell, 2001), at least if it has been accompanied by the mother's voice (Sai, 2005). Newborns' recognition of individual faces is likely to be based on scanning the external features of the face (Haith et al., 1977) and noting something about very blurry internal features from peripheral vision: When the images of mom and the contrasting stranger wear identical scarves, evidence of recognition disappears (Pascalis et al., 1995; see Turati, Macchi Cassia, Simion, & Leo, 2006 for similar results for the discrimination of two strangers' faces). Nevertheless, information about individual faces is fed into developing cortical pathways.

By 3 months of age, acuity and contrast sensitivity have improved sufficiently to allow many more details of faces to be visible. Perhaps as a consequence, babies now scan the internal features of faces, shifting among them rapidly, with a bias to come back repeatedly to the eyes (Haith et al., 1977; Maurer & Salapatek, 1976). By 3 months, the baby has also developed the cognitive ability to average faces across presentations to form a prototype to which future encounters are compared (de Haan, Johnson, Maurer, & Perrett, 2001).

Forming a prototype is a prerequisite for the formation of the multidimensional face space that underlies adults' efficient processing of faces (Rhodes & Jeffery, 2006). The possibly related ability to process faces holistically, rather than piecemeal, develops at the same age (Turati, Di Giorgio, Bardi, & Simion, 2010). The consequence of these developments is that babies' accumulating experience can be organized across viewpoints and facial expressions. At the same time, the baby develops more complex face preferences, looking preferentially at faces with more face-like structure even when the comparison stimuli are matched on the originally preferred basic structural properties like top-heaviness (Turati, Valenza, Leo, & Simion, 2005).

6.7 Cultural Biases in the Tuning of Early Face Processing

6.7.1 Face Input

The face input that tunes infants' face processing is not a representative sample of the world, but rather restricted initially to people who resemble the baby's mother. Those faces are predominantly female, own race, and of adult age, even in a city as multicultural as Toronto (Sugden, Mohamed-Ali, & Moulson, 2014). Cameras mounted on the heads of young infants indicate that they see faces more often than objects, that the faces are usually upright and facing them at a close distance, and that a small handful of faces are present repeatedly and for a relatively long duration (Jayaraman & Smith, 2018; Sugden et al., 2014; Sugden & Moulson, 2017). This biased experience combines with the infant's attentional bias toward face-like structure to guarantee that developing cortical systems receive upright face input and that the input promotes learning to recognize a few individual faces. After the first 3 months, the exposure changes to more often involve hands or other body parts, rather than the face, such that face exposure when a person is present decreases by a factor of 3 between 3 and 18 months of age (Jayaraman, Fausey, & Smith, 2017).

Given the female bias (70% of faces overall in Sugden et al., 2014), it is not surprising the infants' face processing at 3 months is more discriminating for female than male faces, unless the baby is being reared by a male rather than female caretaker (Quinn, Yahr, Kuhn, Slater, & Pascalils, 2002). This difference for male and female faces emerges by 3 months of age but only for same-race faces, that is, faces of the type to which the baby has been exposed (Quinn et al., 2008). At this age, infants show a looking preference for both female and for own-race faces over male and other-race faces (Bar-Haim, Ziv, Lamy, & Hodes, 2006; Kelly et al., 2005; Kelly, Liu et al., 2007; Quinn et al., 2002). At 3 months, babies do not yet seem to integrate the processing of internal and external features of faces (Cashon & Cohen, 2004) or to be sensitive to differences in the spacing of the internal features (Bhatt, Bertin, Hayden, & Reed, 2005), both of which are fundamental components of adults' expertise in face processing (Maurer, Le Grand, &

Mondloch, 2002). These skills are only evident by 4–6 months of age (Ferguson, Kulkofsky, Cashon, & Casasola, 2009; Hayden, Bhatt, Reed, Corbly, & Joseph, 2007), initially for all faces, be they upright or inverted, own or other race.

6.7.2 Perceptual Narrowing: Tuning to Human Species and Own Race

Over the first year of life, babies' face processing improves (see previous section) but at the same time becomes specialized for the categories of faces that are most commonly seen, namely, upright human faces matching the baby's ethnicity. This phenomenon – termed perceptual narrowing – has been well documented for both species (human vs. nonhuman primate) and for ethnicity (matching that of the baby or not).

6.7.3 Species

At birth, babies have no looking preference for human over monkey faces (Di Giorgio et al., 2012) and as late as 6 months, babies can discriminate as readily between two monkey faces as between two human faces (Pascalis, de Haan, & Nelson, 2002). At 9–12 months, however, babies fail to show discrimination between monkey faces when tested with the same paradigm, while continuing to "pass" for human faces (Fair, Flom, Jones, & Martin, 2012; Pascalis et al., 2002; Pascalis et al., 2005). A similar pattern has been documented for sheep faces (Simpson, Varga, Frick, & Fragaszy, 2011). Evidence of discrimination can be recovered by extending the exposure time (Fair et al., 2012) or by giving the baby experience looking at individually named pictures of monkeys (Pascalis et al., 2005; Scott & Monesson, 2009). Nevertheless, it is evident that toward the end of the first year of life, biased exposure to human faces leads babies to improve their skill at individuating human faces while their skill at doing so for nonhuman faces is attenuated.

6.7.4 Race

At birth, babies have no looking preference for faces matching their own ethnicity (and hence the ethnicity of the faces to which they are most likely to be exposed), but by 3 months they already have a looking preference for "own-race" faces, unless they are being raised in an environment in which they are exposed to both the "own" and the "other" category on which they are tested (Bar-Haim et al., 2006; Kelly, Liu et al., 2007). As with monkey faces, initially babies can discriminate as readily between other-race as own-race faces but by 9 months they fail the same tests with other-race faces (Heron-Delaney et al., 2011; Kelly, Quinn et al., 2007; Kelly et al., 2009; Sugden & Marquis, 2017; Vogel, Monesson, & Scott, 2012). As with species, the other-race discrimination failures can be overcome by encouraging babies to attend to their features by, for example, exposing the baby to named individuals of the rarely encountered race (Anzures et al., 2012; Heron-Delaney et al., 2011) or using spatial cuing to encourage babies to attend to the location where the other-race face appears (Markant, Oakes, & Amso, 2016).

6.7.5 Other Domains

Perceptual narrowing occurs across a number of domains over the first year of life (Maurer & Werker, 2014) in each case biasing the baby's discriminations to the categories the baby has experienced. This happens for speech distinctions in the language the baby hears versus other languages; for human versus animal voices; and for matching talking faces to the accompanying sound track. Although the timing of the narrowing may differ across domains, they have in common the attunement of the baby's perceptual categories to stimuli emanating from his/her own cultural group. The baby learns to recognize members of his/her own "tribe" and to treat members of other groups simply as "other." In fact, by 6 months, babies match the sound of a nonnative language with an other-race face (Uttley et al., 2013).

6.8 Importance of Early Visual Experience for the Development of Face Processing

Perceptual narrowing provides evidence that changes in face processing are driven by the statistics of the faces that the baby encounters during the first year of life. When the baby fails to see any faces during early infancy – because bilateral congenital cataracts block all patterned input to both eyes – developmental changes in face processing fail to occur both during infancy and later in development. When the babies can first see after the cataracts are removed and the eyes given corrective contact lenses, they select face-like patterns matching the preferences of normal newborns, rather than age mates with postnatal visual experience (Mondloch, Lewis, Levin, & Maurer, 2013), just as is the case with their visual acuity (Maurer et al., 1999). In other words, neither more complex face preferences nor better acuity emerge in the absence of visual input. Unlike acuity, the improvements in face preferences after treatment are not accelerated but take the normal number of months of visual experience: for example, only after 3 months of visual experience do face preferences begin to match those of 3-month-old babies with normal eyes (Mondloch, Lewis et al., 2013). By late infancy, the ability of infants treated for bilateral congenital cataracts to detect facial structure appears to be normal and this normality is corroborated when they are tested as adults: They have normal accuracy and response times to distinguish intact and scrambled facial structure (Mondloch, Segalowitz et al., 2013). Nevertheless, event-related potentials reveal that the neural network underlying this normal adult performance is altered: The adults deprived of visual experience in infancy demonstrate the normally larger N170 to a face than to a scrambled image but its amplitude is roughly double that of controls and it occurs after a significantly longer latency. A similarly increased amplitude is evident for the P100 and the response to scrambled faces. The amplified response to photographs of faces is correlated with the duration of the initial deprivation. Thus, normal visual experience is necessary for the postnatal changes in face preferences *and* for their normal efficient neural processing.

Patients treated for bilateral congenital cataract show later deficits in other aspects of face processing. When asked to indicate whether or not two faces are the same, they are as good as controls when the faces differ only in the shape of the external contour or only in the shape of the eyes and mouth, but make more errors than controls when the only difference is the location of the eyes and mouth, a cue termed "spacing" or "second-order relations" (Le Grand, Mondloch, Maurer, & Brent, 2001; Mondloch, Le Grand, & Maurer, 2003; Mondloch, Robbins, & Maurer, 2010).This is the condition in which adults with normal eyes are experts – as long as faces are upright, that is, as long as they match the condition to which experience is biased from early infancy (Maurer et al., 2002). When the accuracy plummets for adults with normal vision because the faces are inverted or the same spacing differences are introduced into monkey faces, adults treated for bilateral congenital cataracts perform normally (Maurer et al., 2002; Robbins, Nishimura, Mondloch, Lewis, & Maurer, 2010. Thus, early visual experience appears to be necessary to set up the neural circuitry for later refinement of sensitivity to spacing specifically in upright human faces, an ability that normally emerges during infancy (Bhatt et al., 2005) and improves into middle childhood (Mondloch, Le Grand, & Maurer, 2002). Studies of adults treated for unilateral congenital cataract suggest that it is early input to the right hemisphere that is especially important (Le Grand, Mondloch, Maurer, & Brent, 2003). fMRI data suggest that it is connectivity within the extended face network centered in the temporal cortex (see Figure 6.1) that is altered by early visual deprivation (Grady, Mondloch, Lewis, & Maurer, 2014).

The difficulty of adults treated for bilateral congenital cataract in perceiving subtle differences in the spacing of the features of upright human faces may be related to their piecemeal processing of facial features, unlike the more holistic processing of adults with normal vision. A sensitive test of holistic processing is the "composite face effect": The task is to decide whether the top halves of two faces are the same while ignoring their different bottom halves. Holistic processing makes it difficult – unless it is broken by misaligning the top and bottom halves or inverting the face (Mondloch & Maurer, 2008; Young, Hellawell, & Hay, 2013). Adults treated for bilateral congenital cataracts, however, are good at the task even with upright aligned faces: their superior accuracy to controls indicates that they do not process faces holistically (de Heering & Maurer, 2014; Le Grand, Mondloch, Maurer, & Brent,

2004). Thus, even though holistic face processing normally emerges postnatally (Nakato, Kanazawa, & Yamaguchi, 2018; Turati et al., 2010), it fails to emerge in babies who missed early experience with faces because of congenital cataracts – another sleeper effect (Maurer et al., 2007). Critical to the difference between babies with normal eyes and those treated for congenital cataracts may be the timing of first exposure to faces (different neurotransmitters present when exposure is delayed by treatment for cataracts), the initial density of faces as the learning takes place (higher in early infancy than later after treatment because parents' behavior changes), and/or the blurriness of the input as the initial representations are formed (blurred in newborns with normal eyes and poor acuity vs. rapidly improving acuity in treated infants) (Jayaraman et al., 2017; Vogelsang et al., 2018).

Babies whose visual experience with faces is altered by being born premature also follow an abnormal developmental trajectory. At birth, they do not show the standard preferences for face-like stimuli (Pereira et al., 2017) and at 6–10 months corrected age, the brain's response to the mother's face is smaller in the right frontotemporal cortex than in controls and not normally differentiated from the response to a stranger's face (Frie, Padilla, Ådén, Lagercrantz, & Bartocci, 2016). Thus, extra exposure to faces in the preterm nursery at an earlier-than-normal time appears not to be beneficial and may even interfere with the normal development of face processing.

6.9 Summary and Policy Implications

Newborns' vision is limited to large stimuli of high contrast in the central visual field. Nevertheless, that type of visual input is necessary for the system to be refined later for low-level visual sensitivity (acuity, contrast sensitivity, and peripheral vision), as well as for higher-level integrative perceptual processing (of global motion, global form, and facial identity). In the absence of visual input, development, at least of acuity and of face processing, the only two tested longitudinally, appears to be in stasis and the input received after treatment is not sufficient to offset the delay. One reason may be the encroachment of input from other sensory modalities during the visual deprivation, input that forms functional synapses that remain after the cataracts are removed. When the deprivation is monocular rather than binocular, such encroachment may be prevented. When the perturbation is premature birth, the extra and early visual experience appears not to aid visual development.

In the child with normal eyes, patterned visual input near the time of normal birth appears to be critical to set up the neural pathways for later refinement. Delayed input is inadequate, as is the mistimed input in the preterm nursery. The timing may be so critical because of changes in excitatory versus inhibitory neurotransmitters and their balance, as well as in myelination, which make experiential effects more likely at certain points in development (Hensch & Quinlan, 2018; Siu & Murphy, 2018).

The implication of these findings is that any condition or treatment that blocks early visual input is to be avoided when possible. If it is necessary – like patching an eye after surgery or covering the eyes during photo treatment for jaundice – the period of deprivation should be as short as medically allowed and relieved, when possible, by periods of visual stimulation (e.g., a 2-hour break from jaundice treatment with the blindfold off). When visual input cannot be normal, it would be wise to begin therapeutic compensation during infancy, rather than wait until deficits emerge later in development.

The evidence on perceptual narrowing indicates that early visual experience affects the tuning of every baby's visual processing to match the characteristics of faces and speech most often experienced. That experience appears almost always to be biased toward the baby's own ethnic group. By the end of the first year of life, the baby has improved ability to discriminate among speech sounds and faces from the own-race group but has begun to process speech and faces from other groups at the categorical ("speech" or "face") level, no longer processing enough details to make individual discriminations. This perceptual bias may form the basis for, or at least contribute to, later prejudice. It can be overcome by exposure to individuated other-race faces. Although such individuated training is effective even later in development (Sangrigoli, Pallier, Argenti, Ventureyra, & de Schonen, 2005; Ventureyra, Pallier, & Yoo, 2004), retuning during infancy may be easier and might be more durable.

There is reason to suspect that there are other cross-cultural differences in visual processing that arise from variations in the mother's diet during the pregnancy and breastfeeding and in the composition of any formula. Such differences have been documented for certain polyunsaturated fats but possible differences arising from mineral or vitamin deficiencies, maternal malnutrition, vegetarian versus paleo diets, etc. have not been investigated. Any such effects could lead to generational as well as cross-cultural differences in visual processing. They are likely to be subtle – showing up as small changes in distributions, such as more adults with 20/10 vision when the early diet included substance X – and hence may easily go unnoticed. They could be manifest not only as cross-cultural differences but also differences within a country where the diet varies across geographical regions (e.g., coastal vs. inland, plains vs. mountains).

In summary, the newborn baby emerges from the womb able to see the stimuli right in from of him/her that are large and of high contrast: the mother's face usually first and foremost. Her face continues to dominate the baby's experience over the next few months, along with the faces of the father and close relatives and friends. Because these are usually of the same ethnicity as the baby and mother, the baby's processing begins to be tuned to upright, human faces that are female and own race. As the baby begins to see more details and the visual field expands, the baby picks up more information from faces and other objects in the environment. Still, he/she is learning to recognize "my tribe" and by the end of the first year of life, treats faces and speech that are less often encountered as "other." Underlying this attunement are cortical changes that support more complex visual processing acting on the types of experience the baby encounters. Through this process, the baby's acculturation begins.

If the process is altered by mistiming from premature birth or visual deprivation, the cortical changes do not proceed normally, preventing the later development of normal low-level and high-level vision. More subtle changes may be induced by variations in the nutrients to which the baby's developing cortical system is exposed. Combined, these alterations indicate that we have evolved so that visual experience at the expected time, when the right stew of neurochemicals are active, will tune cortical pathways to allow the optimal refinement of vision and its adaptation to our particular visual environment.

References

Anzures, G., Wheeler, A., Quinn, P. C., Pascalis, O., Slater, A. M., Heron-Delaney, M., … Lee, K. (2012). Brief daily exposures to Asian females reverses perceptual narrowing for Asian faces in Caucasian infants. *Journal of Experimental Child Psychology, 112*(4), 484–495. doi:10.1016/j.jecp.2012.04.005

Armstrong, V., Maurer, D., Ellemberg, D., & Lewis, T. L. (2011). Sensitivity to first- and second-order drifting gratings in 3-month-old infants. *Iperception, 2*(5), 440–457. doi:10.1068/i0406

Atkinson, J., Braddick, O., Lin, M. H., Curran, W., Guzzetta, A., & Cioni, G. (1999). Form and motion: Is there a dorsal stream vulnerability in development? *Investigative Ophthalmology & Visual Science, 40*, S395.

Banks, M., & Bennett, P. (1988). Optical and photoreceptor immaturities limit the spatial and chromatic vision of human neonates. *Journal of the Optical Society of America, 5*(12), 2059–2079.

(1978). Acuity and contrast sensitivity in 1-, 2-, and 3-month-old human infants. *Investigative Ophthalmology & Visual Science, 17*, 361–365.

Bar-Haim, Y., Ziv, T., Lamy, D., & Hodes, R. M. (2006). Nature and nurture in own-race face processing. *Psychological Science, 17*(2), 159–163.

Bardi, L., Regolin, L., & Simion, F. (2011). Biological motion preference in humans at birth: Role of dynamic and configural properties. *Developmental Science, 14*(2), 353–359.

Bhatt, R. S., Bertin, E., Hayden, A., & Reed, A. (2005). Face processing in infancy: Developmental changes in the use of different kinds of relational information. *Child Development, 76*(1), 169–181. doi:10.1111/j.1467-8624.2005.00837.x

Biagi, L., Crespi, S. A., Tosetti, M., & Morrone, M. C. (2015). BOLD response selective to flow-motion in very young infants. *PLoS Biol, 13*(9), e1002260. doi:10.1371/journal.pbio.1002260

Bidet-Ildei, C., Kitromilides, E., Orliaguet, J. P., Pavlova, M., & Gentaz, E. (2014). Preference for point-light human biological motion in newborns: Contribution of translational displacement. *Developmental Psychology*, *50*(1), 113–120. doi:10.1037/a0032956

Birch, D. G., Birch, E. E., Hoffman, D. R., & Uauy, R. D. (1992). Retinal development in very-low-birth-weight infants fed diets differing in omega-3 fatty acids. *Investigative Ophthalmology & Visual Science*, *33*(8), 2365–2376.

Birch, E. E., Birch, D. G., Hoffman, D. R., & Uauy, R. (1992). Dietary essential fatty acid supply and visual acuity development. *Investigative Ophthalmology & Visual Science*, *33*, 3242–3253.

Birch, E. E., Cheng, C., Stager, D. R., Weakley, D. R., & Stager, D. R. (2009). The critical period for surgical treatment of dense congenital bilateral cataracts. *Journal of American Association for Pediatric Ophthalmology and Strabismus*, *13*(1), 67–71.

Birch, E. E., Garfield, S., Castañeda, Y., Hughbanks-Wheaton, D., Uauy, R., & Hoffman, D. (2007). Visual acuity and cognitive outcomes at 4 years of age in a double-blind, randomized trial of long-chain polyunsaturated fatty acid-supplemented infant formula. *Early Human Development*, *83*(5), 279–284. doi:10.1016/j.earlhumdev.2006.11.003

Birch, E. E., Gwiazda, J., & Held, R. (1982). Stereoacuity development for crossed and uncrossed disparities in human infants. *Vision Research*, *22*(5), 507–513.

Birtles, D. B., Braddick, O. J., Wattam-Bell, J., Wilkinson, A. R., & Atkinson, J. (2007). Orientation and motion-specific visual cortex responses in infants born pre-term. *Neuroreport*, *18*, 1975–1979. doi:10.1097/WNR.0b013e3282f228c8

Blakemore, C. (1990). Maturation of mechanisms for efficient spatial vision. In C. Blakemore (Ed.), *Vision: Coding and efficiency* (pp. 254–266). Cambridge, UK: Cambridge University Press.

Blakemore, C., & Vital-Durand, F. (1986). Organization and post-natal development of the monkey's lateral geniculate nucleus. *Journal of Physiology*, *380*(1), 453–491.

Blakstad, E. W., Strømmen, K., Moltu, S. J., Wattam-Bell, J., Nordheim, T., Almaas, A. N., … Nakstad, B. (2015). Improved visual perception in very low birth weight infants on enhanced nutrient supply. *Neonatology*, *108*(1), 30–37. doi:10.1159/000381660

Bowering, E. R., Maurer, D., Lewis, T. L., & Brent, H. P. (1993). Sensitivity in the nasal and temporal hemifields in children treated for cataract. *Investigative Ophthalmology & Visual Science*, *34*(13), 3501–3509.

Bowering, E. R., Maurer, D., Lewis, T. L., Brent, H. P., & Riedel, P. (1996). The visual field in childhood: Normal development and the influence of deprivation. *Developmental Cognitive Neuroscience Technical Report*, *96*, 1–33.

Braddick, O., & Atkinson, J. (2011). Development of human visual function. *Vision Research*, *51*(13), 1588–1609. doi:10.1016/j.visres.2011.02.018

Braddick, O., Birtles, D., Wattam-Bell, J., & Atkinson, J. (2005). Motion- and orientation-specific cortical responses in infancy. *Vision Research*, *45*(25–26), 3169–3179. doi:10.1016/j.visres.2005.07.021

Braddick, O., Wattam-Bell, J., Day, J., & Atkinson, J. (1983). The onset of binocular function in human infants. *Human Neurobiology*, *2*(2), 65–69.

Brenna, J. T., Varamini, B., Jensen, R. G., Diersen-Schade, D. A., Boettcher, J. A., & Arterburn, L. M. (2007). Docosahexaenoic and arachidonic acid concentrations in human breast milk worldwide. *American Journal of Clinical Nutrition, 85*(6), 1457–1464.

Brown, A. M., Lindsey, D. T., Cammenga, J. G., Giannone, P. J., & Stenger, M. R. (2015). The contrast sensitivity of the newborn human infant. *Investigative Ophthalmology & Visual Science, 56*(1), 625–632. doi:10.1167/iovs.14-14757

Brown, A. M., Opoku, F. O., & Stenger, M. R. (2018). Neonatal contrast sensitivity and visual acuity: Basic psychophysics. *Translational Vision Science & Technology, 7*(3), 18. doi:10.1167/tvst.7.3.18

Bushnell, I. W. R. (2001). Mother's face recognition in newborn infants: Learning and memory. *Infant and Child Development, 10*(1–2), 67–74. doi:10.1002/icd.248

Candy, T. R., Crowell, J. A., & Banks, M. S. (1998). Optical, receptoral, and retinal constraints on foveal and peripheral vision in the human neonate. *Vision Research, 38*(24), 3857–3870.

Cashon, C. H., & Cohen, L. B. (2004). Beyond U-shaped development in infants' processing of faces: An information-processing account. *Journal of Cognition and Development, 5*(1), 59–80.

Cassia, V. M., Turati, C., & Simion, F. (2004). Can a nonspecific bias toward top-heavy patterns explain newborns' face preference? *Psychological Science, 15*(6), 379–383. doi:10.1111/j.0956-7976.2004.00688.x

Cecchini, M., Iannoni, M. E., Aceto, P., Baroni, E., Di Vito, C., & Lai, C. (2017). Active sleep is associated with the face preference in the newborns who familiarized with a responsive face. *Infant Behaviour and Development, 49*, 37–45. doi:10.1016/j.infbeh.2017.06.004

Chang, D. H., & Troje, N. F. (2009). Characterizing global and local mechanisms in biological motion perception. *Journal of Vision, 9*(5), 8.1–810. doi:10.1167/9.5.8

Collignon, O., Dormal, G., de Heering, A., Lepore, F., Lewis, T. L., & Maurer, D. (2015). Long-lasting crossmodal cortical reorganization triggered by brief postnatal visual deprivation. *Current Biology, 25*(18), 2379–2383. doi:10.1016/j.cub.2015.07.036

de Haan, M., Johnson, M. H., Maurer, D., & Perrett, D. I. (2001). Recognition of individual faces and average face prototypes by 1- and 3-month-old infants. *Cognitive Development, 16*(2), 659–678.

de Heering, A., & Maurer, D. (2014). Face memory deficits in patients deprived of early visual input by bilateral congenital cataracts. *Developmental Psychobiology, 56*(1), 96–108. doi:10.1002/dev.21094

de Heering, A., Turati, C., Rossion, B., Bulf, H., Goffaux, V., & Simion, F. (2008). Newborns' face recognition is based on spatial frequencies below 0.5 cycles per degree. *Cognition, 106*(1), 444–454. doi:10.1016/j.cognition.2006.12.012

Delaney, S. M., Dobson, V., Mohan, K. M., Harvey, M. A., & Harvey, E. M.(2004). The effect of flicker rate on nasal and temporal measured visual field extent in infants. *Optometry and Vision Science, 81*(12), 922–928.

Di Giorgio, E., Leo, I., Pascalis, O., & Simion, F. (2012). Is the face-perception system human-specific at birth. *Developmental Psychology, 48*(4), 1083–1090. doi:10.1037/a0026521

Drover, J. R., Earle, A. E., Courage, M. L., & Adams, R. J. (2002). Improving the effectiveness of the infant contrast sensitivity card procedure. *Optometry and Vision Science, 79*(1), 52–59.

Ellemberg, D., Lewis, T. L., Defina, N., Maurer, D., Brent, H. P., Guillemot, J. -P., & Lepore, F. (2005). Greater losses in sensitivity to second-order local motion than to first-order local motion after early visual deprivation in humans. *Vision Research, 45*(22), 2877–2884. doi:10.1016/j.visres.2004.11.019

Ellemberg, D., Lewis, T. L., Liu, C. H., & Maurer, D. (1999). Development of spatial and temporal vision during childhood. *Vision Research, 39*(14), 2325–2333.

Ellemberg, D., Lewis, T. L., Maurer, D., Brar, S., & Brent, H. P. (2002). Better perception of global motion after monocular than after binocular deprivation. *Vision Research, 42*(2), 169–179.

Ellemberg, D., Lewis, T. L., Maurer, D., Lui, C. H., & Brent, H. P. (1999). Spatial and temporal vision in patients treated for bilateral congenital cataracts. *Vision Research, 39*(20), 3480–3489.

Fair, J., Flom, R., Jones, J., & Martin, J. (2012). Perceptual learning: 12-month-olds' discrimination of monkey faces. *Child Development, 83*(6), 1996–2006. doi:10.1111/j.1467-8624.2012.01814.x

Fantz, R. L. (1963). Pattern vision in newborn infants. *Science, 140*(3564), 296–297.

Fantz, R. L., Ordy, J. M., & Udelf, M. S. (1962). Maturation of pattern vision in infants during the first six months. *Journal of Comparative and Physiological Psychology, 55*, 907–917.

Farroni, T., Menon, E., & Johnson, M. H. (2006). Factors influencing newborns' preference for faces with eye contact. *Journal of Experimental Child Psychology, 95*(4), 298–308. doi:10.1016/j.jecp.2006.08.001

Ferguson, K. T., Kulkofsky, S., Cashon, C. H., & Casasola, M. (2009). The development of specialized processing of own-race faces in infancy. *Infancy, 14*(3), 263–284. doi:10.1080/15250000902839369

Fine, I., Wade, A. R., Brewer, A. A., May, M. G., Goodman, D. F., Boynton, G. M., … MacLeod, D. I. (2003). Long-term deprivation affects visual perception and cortex. *Nature Neuroscience, 6*(9), 915–916.

Frie, J., Padilla, N., Ådén, U., Lagercrantz, H., & Bartocci, M. (2016). Extremely preterm-born infants demonstrate different facial recognition processes at 6–10 months of corrected age. *Journal of Pediatrics, 172*, 96–102.e1. doi:10.1016/j.jpeds.2016.02.021

Giese, M. A., & Poggio, T. (2003). Neural mechanisms for the recognition of biological movements. *Nature Reviews Neuroscience, 4*(3), 179–192.

Grady, C. L., Mondloch, C. J., Lewis, T. L., & Maurer, D. (2014). Early visual deprivation from congenital cataracts disrupts activity and functional connectivity in the face network. *Neuropsychologia, 57*, 122–139. doi:10.1016/j.neuropsychologia.2014.03.005

Guerreiro, M. J. S., Putzar, L., & Röder, B. (2016). Persisting cross-modal changes in sight-recovery individuals modulate visual perception. *Current Biology, 26*(22), 3096–3100. doi:10.1016/j.cub.2016.08.069

Gwiazda, J., Bauer, J., & Held, R. (1989). Binocular function in human infants: Correlation of stereoptic and fusion-rivalry discriminations. *Journal of Pediatric Ophthalmology and Strabismus, 26*(3), 128–132.

Hadad, B.-S., Maurer, D., & Lewis, T. L. (2012). Sparing of sensitivity to biological motion but not of global motion after early visual deprivation. *Developmental Science, 15*(4), 474–481. doi:10.1111/j.1467-7687.2012.01145.x

Hainline, L. (1978). Developmental changes in visual scanning of face and nonface patterns by infants. *Journal of Experimental Child Psychology, 25*(1), 90–115.

Haith, M. M., Bergman, T., & Moore, M. J. (1977). Eye contact and face scanning in early infancy. *Science, 198*(4319), 853–855.

Hayden, A., Bhatt, R. S., Reed, A., Corbly, C. R., & Joseph, J. E. (2007). The development of expert face processing: Are infants sensitive to normal differences in second-order relational information? *Journal of Experimental Child Psychology, 97*(2), 85–98. doi:10.1016/j.jecp.2007.01.004

Hensch, T. K., & Quinlan, E. M. (2018). Critical periods in amblyopia. *Visual Neuroscience, 35*, E014. doi:10.1017/S0952523817000219

Heron-Delaney, M., Anzures, G., Herbert, J. S., Quinn, P. C., Slater, A. M., Tanaka, J. W., ... Pascalis, O. (2011). Perceptual training prevents the emergence of the other race effect during infancy. *PloS one, 6*(5), e19858.

Hoffman, D. R., Boettcher, J. A., & Diersen-Schade, D. A. (2009). Toward optimizing vision and cognition in term infants by dietary docosahexaenoic and arachidonic acid supplementation: A review of randomized controlled trials. *Prostaglandins, Leukotrienes and Essential Fatty Acids, 81*(2–3), 151–158. doi:10.1016/j.plefa.2009.05.003

Hood, B., & Atkinson, J. (1993). Disengaging visual attention in the infant and adult. *Infant Behaviour and Development, 16*, 405–422.

Hou, C., Norcia, A. M., Madan, A., Tith, S., Agarwal, R., & Good, W. V. (2011). Visual cortical function in very low birth weight infants without retinal or cerebral pathology. *Investigative Ophthalmology & Visual Science, 52*(12), 9091–9098. doi:10.1167/iovs.11–7458

Humphrey, A. L., & Saul, A. B. (1998). Strobe rearing reduces direction selectivity in area 17 by altering spatiotemporal receptive-field structure. *Journal of Neurophysiology, 80*(6), 2991–3004.

Huttenlocher, P. (1990). Morphometric study of human cerebral cortex development. *Neuropsychologia, 28*(6), 517–527.

Jayaraman, S., Fausey, C. M., & Smith, L. B. (2017). Why are faces denser in the visual experiences of younger than older infants? *Developmental Psychology, 53*(1), 38–49. doi:10.1037/dev0000230

Jayaraman, S., & Smith, L. B. (2018). Faces in early visual environments are persistent not just frequent. *Vision Research, 157*, 213–221. doi:10.1016/j.visres.2018.05.005

Johnson, M. H. (2005). Subcortical face processing. *Nature Reviews Neuroscience, 6*(10), 766–774. doi:10.1038/nrn1766

Johnson, M. H., Dziurawiec, S., Ellis, H., & Morton, J. (1991). Newborns' preferential tracking of face-like stimuli and its subsequent decline. *Cognition, 40*(1–2), 1–19.

Johnson, M. H., Senju, A., & Tomalski, P. (2015). The two-process theory of face processing: Modifications based on two decades of data from infants and adults. *Neuroscience Biobehavioral Review, 50*, 169–179. doi:10.1016/j.neubiorev.2014.10.009

Kelly, D. J., Liu, S., Ge, L., Quinn, P. C., Slater, A. M., Lee, K., ... Pascalis, O. (2007). Cross-race preferences for same-race faces extend beyond the African versus

Caucasian contrast in 3-month-old infants. *Infancy, 11*(1), 87–95. doi:10.1080/15250000709336871

Kelly, D. J., Liu, S., Lee, K., Quinn, P. C., Pascalis, O., Slater, A. M., & Ge, L. (2009). Development of the other-race effect during infancy: Evidence toward universality? *Journal of Experimental Child Psychology, 104*(1), 105–114. doi:10.1016/j.jecp.2009.01.006

Kelly, D. J., Quinn, P. C., Slater, A. M., Lee, K., Ge, L., & Pascalis, O. (2007). The other-race effect develops during infancy: Evidence of perceptual narrowing. *Psychological Science, 18*(12), 1084–1089.

Kelly, D. J., Quinn, P. C., Slater, A. M., Lee, K., Gibson, A., Smith, M., … Pascalis, O. (2005). Three-month-olds, but not newborns, prefer own-race faces. *Developmental Science, 8*(6), F31–F36.

Kiorpes, L. (2016). The puzzle of visual development: Behavior and neural limits. *Journal of Neuroscience, 36*(45), 11384–11393. doi:10.1523/JNEUROSCI.2937-16.2016

Kodas, E., Galineau, L., Bodard, S., Vancassel, S., Guilloteau, D., Besnard, J. C., & Chalon, S. (2004). Serotoninergic neurotransmission is affected by n-3 polyunsaturated fatty acids in the rat. *Journal of Neurochemistry, 89*(3), 695–702. doi:10.1111/j.1471-4159.2004.02401.x

Le Grand, R., Mondloch, C. J., Maurer, D., & Brent, H. P. (2001). Neuroperception: Early visual experience and face processing. *Nature, 410*(6831), 890.

(2003). Expert face processing requires visual input to the right hemisphere during infancy. *Nature Neuroscience, 6*(10), 1108–1112. doi:10.1038/nn1121

(2004). Impairment in holistic face processing following early visual deprivation. *Psychological Science, 15*(11), 762–768.

Lewis, T. L., Ellemberg, D., Maurer, D., Wilkinson, F., Wilson, H. R., Dirks, M., & Brent, H. P. (2002). Sensitivity to global form in glass patterns after early visual deprivation in humans. *Vision Research, 42*(8), 939–948.

Lewis, T. L., & Maurer, D. (1992). The development of the temporal and nasal visual fields during infancy. *Vision Research, 32*(5), 903 911.

(2009). Effects of early pattern deprivation on visual development. *Optometry and Vision Science, 86*(6), 640–646. doi:10.1097/OPX.0b013e3181a7296b

Lewis, T. L., Maurer, D., & Brent, H. P. (1995). Development of grating acuity in children treated for unilateral or bilateral congenital cataract. *Investigative Ophthalmology & Visual Science, 36*(10), 2080–2095.

Lewis, T. L., Maurer, D., Tytla, M. E., Bowering, E. R., & Brent, H. P. (1992). Vision in the "good" eye of children treated for unilateral congenital cataract. *Ophthalmology, 99*(7), 1013–1017.

MacKay, T. L., Jakobson, L. S., Ellemberg, D., Lewis, T. L., Maurer, D., & Casiro, O. (2005). Deficits in the processing of local and global motion in very low birthweight children. *Neuropsychologia, 43*(12), 1738–1748. doi:10.1016/j.neuropsychologia.2005.02.008

Markant, J., Oakes, L. M., & Amso, D. (2016). Visual selective attention biases contribute to the other-race effect among 9-month-old infants. *Developmental Psychobiology, 58*(3), 355–365. doi:10.1002/dev.21375

Maurer, D., Le Grand, R., & Mondloch, C. J. (2002). The many faces of configural processing. *Trends in Cognitive Sciences, 6*(6), 255–260.

Maurer, D., & Lewis, T. L. (1998). Overt orienting toward peripheral stimuli: Normal development and underlying mechanisms. In J. Richards (Ed.), *Cognitive neuroscience of attention: A developmental perspective* (pp. 51–102). Mahwah, NJ: Lawrence Erlbaum Associates.

Maurer, D., Lewis, T. L., Brent, H. P., & Levin, A. V. (1999). Rapid improvement in the acuity of infants after visual input. *Science, 286*(5437), 108–110.

Maurer. D., & Martello, M. (1980). The discrimination of orientation by young infants. *Vision Research, 20*, 201–204.

Maurer, D., Mondloch, C. J., & Lewis, T. L. (2007). Sleeper effects. *Developmental Science, 10*(1), 40–47. doi:10.1111/j.1467-7687.2007.00562.x

Maurer, D., & Salapatek, P. (1976). Developmental changes in the scanning of faces by young infants. *Child Development, 47*, 523–527.

Maurer, D., & Werker, J. F. (2014). Perceptual narrowing during infancy: A comparison of language and faces. *Developmental Psychobiology, 56*(2), 154–178. doi:10.1002/dev.21177

Mayer, D. L., Beiser, A. S., Warner, A. F., Pratt, E. M., Raye, K. N., & Lang, J. M. (1995). Monocular acuity norms for the Teller Acuity Cards between ages one month and four years. *Investigative Ophthalmology & Visual Science, 36*(3), 671–685.

Mondloch, C. J., Le Grand, R., & Maurer, D. (2002). Configural face processing develops more slowly than featural face processing. *Perception, 31*(5), 553–566. doi:10.1068/p3339

Mondloch, C. J., Le Grand, R., & Maurer, D. (2003). Early visual experience is necessary for the development of some – but not all – aspects of face processing. In O. Pascalis & A. Slater (Eds.), *The development of face processing in infancy and early childhood* (pp. 99–117). New York, NY: Nova Science.

Mondloch, C. J., Lewis, T. L., Budreau, D. R., Maurer, D., Dannemiller, J. L., Stephens, B. R., & Kleiner-Gathercoal, K. A. (1999). Face perception during early infancy. *Psychological Science, 10*(5), 419–422.

Mondloch, C. J., Lewis, T. L., Levin, A. V., & Maurer, D. (2013). Infant face preferences after binocular visual deprivation. *International Journal of Behavioral Development, 37*(2), 148–153. doi:10.1177/0165025412471221

Mondloch, C. J., & Maurer, D. (2008). The effect of face orientation on holistic processing. *Perception, 37*(8), 1175. doi:10.1068/p6048

Mondloch, C. J., Robbins, R., & Maurer, D. (2010). Discrimination of facial features by adults, 10-year-olds, and cataract-reversal patients. *Perception, 39*(2), 184–194. doi:10.1068/p6153

Mondloch, C. J., Segalowitz, S. J., Lewis, T. L., Dywan, J., Le Grand, R., & Maurer, D. (2013). The effect of early visual deprivation on the development of face detection. *Developmental Science, 16*(5), 728–742. doi:10.1111/desc.12065

Morton, J., & Johnson, M. H. (1991). CONSPEC and CONLERN: A two-process theory of infant face recognition. *Psychological Review, 98*, 164–181.

Movshon, J. A., & Kiorpes, L. (1993). Biological limits on visual development in primates. In K. Simons (Ed.), *Early visual development: normal and abnormal* (pp. 296–305). New York, NY: Oxford University Press.

Nakato, E., Kanazawa, S., & Yamaguchi, M. K. (2018). Holistic processing in mother's face perception for infants. *Infant Behaviour and Development*, *50*, 257–263. doi:10.1016/j.infbeh.2018.01.007

Orioli, G., Filippetti, M. L., Gerbino, W., Dragovic, D., & Farroni, T. (2018). Trajectory discrimination and peripersonal space perception in newborns. *Infancy*, *23*(2), 252–267. doi:10.1111/infa.12207

Pascalis, O., de Haan, M., & Nelson, C. A. (2002). Is face processing species-specific during the first year of life? *Science*, *296*(5571), 1321–1323.

Pascalis, O., de Schonen, S., Morton, J., Deruelle, C., & Fabre-Gremet, M. (1995). Mother's face recognition by neonates: A replication and an extension. *Infant Behaviour and Development*, *18*, 79–85.

Pascalis, O., Scott, L. S., Kelly, D. J., Shannon, R. W., Nicholson, E., Coleman, M., & Nelson, C. A. (2005). Plasticity of face processing in infancy. *Proceedings of the National Academy of Sciences of the United States of America*, 102(14), 5297–5300.

Pasternak, T., & Leinen, L. J. (1986). Pattern and motion vision in cats with selective loss of cortical directional selectivity. *Journal of Neuroscience*, 6(4), 938–945.

Pereira, S. A., Pereira Junior, A., Costa, M. F., Monteiro, M. V., Almeida, V. A., Fonseca Filho, G. G., … Simion, F. (2017). A comparison between preterm and full-term infants' preference for faces. *Journal of Pediatrics (Rio J)*, 93(1), 35–39. doi:10.1016/j.jped.2016.04.009

Quinn, P. C., Uttley, L., Lee, K., Gibson, A., Smith, M., Slater, A. M., & Pascalis, O. (2008). Infant preference for female faces occurs for same- but not other-race faces. *Journal of Neuropsychology*, 2(Pt. 1), 15–26.

Quinn, P. C., Yahr, J., Kuhn, A., Slater, A. M., & Pascalils, O. (2002). Representation of the gender of human faces by infants: a preference for female. *Perception*, *31*(9), 1109–1121.

Reid, V. M., Dunn, K., Young, R. J., Amu, J., Donovan, T., & Reissland, N. (2017). The human fetus preferentially engages with face-like visual stimuli. *Current Biology*, *27*(12), 1825–1828.e3. doi:10.1016/j.cub.2017.05.044

Renier, L., de Volder, A. G., & Rauschecker, J. P. (2014). Cortical plasticity and pre-served function in early blindness. *Neuroscience and Biobehaviour Reviews*, *41*, 53–63. doi:10.1016/j.neubiorev.2013.01.025

Rhodes, G., & Jeffery, L. (2006). Adaptive norm-based coding of facial identity. *Vision Research*, *46*(18), 2977–2987. doi:10.1016/j.visres.2006.03.002

Robbins, R. A., Nishimura, M., Mondloch, C. J., Lewis, T. L., & Maurer, D. (2010). Deficits in sensitivity to spacing after early visual deprivation in humans: A comparison of human faces, monkey faces, and houses. *Developmental Psychobiology*, *52*(8), 775–781. doi:10.1002/dev.20473

Sai, F. Z. (2005). The role of the mother's voice in developing mother's face preference: Evidence for intermodal perception at birth. *Infant and Child Development*, *14*(1), 29–50. doi:10.1002/icd.376

Salapatek, P., & Kessen, W. (1966). Visual scanning of triangles by the human newborn. *Journal of Experimental Child Psychology*, *3*(2), 155–167.

Sangrigoli, S., Pallier, C., Argenti, A. M., Ventureyra, V. A., & de Schonen, S. (2005). Reversibility of the other-race effect in face recognition during childhood. *Psychological Science*, *16*(6), 440–444.

Scott, L. S., & Monesson, A. (2009). The origin of biases in face perception. *Psychological Science*, *20*(6), 676–680. doi:10.1111/j.1467-9280.2009.02348.x

Sifre, R., Olson, L., Gillespie, S., Klin, A., Jones, W., & Shultz, S. (2018). A longitudinal investigation of preferential attention to biological motion in 2- to 24-month-old infants. *Scientific Reports*, *8*(1), 2527. doi:10.1038/s41598-018-20808-0

Simion, F., & Giorgio, E. D. (2015). Face perception and processing in early infancy: Inborn predispositions and developmental changes. *Frontiers in Psychology*, *6*, 969. doi:10.3389/fpsyg.2015.00969

Simion, F., Regolin, L., & Bulf, H. (2008). A predisposition for biological motion in the newborn baby. *Proceedings of the National Academy of Sciences of the United States of America*, *195*, 809–813.

Simpson, E. A., Varga, K., Frick, J. E., & Fragaszy, D. (2011). Infants experience perceptual narrowing for nonprimate faces. *Infancy*, *16*, 318–330.

Siu, C. R., & Murphy, K. M. (2018). The development of human visual cortex and clinical implications. *Eye Brain*, *10*, 25–36. doi:10.2147/EB.S130893

Sugden, N. A., & Marquis, A. R. (2017). Meta-analytic review of the development of face discrimination in infancy: Face race, face gender, infant age, and methodology moderate face discrimination. *Psychological Bulletin*, *143*(11), 1201–1244. doi:10.1037/bul0000116

Sugden, N. A., Mohamed-Ali, M. I., & Moulson, M. C. (2014). I spy with my little eye: Typical, daily exposure to faces documented from a first-person infant perspective. *Developmental Psychobiology*, *56*(2), 249–261. doi:10.1002/dev.21183

Sugden, N. A., & Moulson, M. C. (2017). Hey baby, what's "up"? One- and 3-month-olds experience faces primarily upright but non-upright faces offer the best views. *Quarterly Journal of Experimental Psychology (Hove)*, *70*(5), 959–969. doi:10.1080/17470218.2016.1154581

Taylor, N. M., Jakobson, L. S., Maurer, D., & Lewis, T. L. (2009). Differential vulnerability of global motion, global form, and biological motion processing in full-term and preterm children. *Neuropsychologia*, *47*(13), 2766–2778. doi:10.1016/j.neuropsychologia.2009.06.001

Turati, C., Bulf, H., & Simion, F. (2008). Newborns' face recognition over changes in viewpoint. *Cognition*, *106*(3), 1300–1321. doi:10.1016/j.cognition.2007.06.005

Turati, C., Di Giorgio, E., Bardi, L., & Simion, F. (2010). Holistic face processing in newborns, 3-month-old infants, and adults: Evidence from the composite face effect. *Child Development, 81*(6), 1894–1905. doi:10.1111/j.1467-8624.2010.01520.x

Turati, C., Macchi Cassia, V., Simion, F., & Leo, I. (2006). Newborns' face recognition: Role of inner and outer facial features. *Child Development, 77*(2), 297–311. doi:10.1111/j.1467-8624.2006.00871.x

Turati, C., Valenza, E., Leo, I., & Simion, F. (2005). Three-month-olds' visual preference for faces and its underlying visual processing mechanisms. *Journal of Experimental Child Psychology*, *90*(3), 255–273. doi:10.1016/j.jecp.2004.11.001

Tytla, M. E., Lewis, T. L., Maurer, D., & Brent, H. P. (1993). Stereopsis after congenital cataract. *Investigative Ophthalmology & Visual Science*, *34*(5), 1767–1773.

Uttley, L., de Boisferon, A. H., Dupierrix, E., Lee, K., Quinn, P. C., Slater, A. M., & Pascalis, O. (2013). Six-month-old infants match other-race faces with a non-native language. *International Journal of Behavioral Development, 37*(2), 84–89. doi:10.1177/0165025412467583

Ventureyra, V. A. G., Pallier, C., & Yoo, H. -Y. (2004). The loss of first language phonetic perception in adopted Koreans. *Journal of Neurolinguistics, 17*(1), 79–91. doi:10.1016/S0911-6044(03)00053-8

Vogel, M., Monesson, A., & Scott, L. S. (2012). Building biases in infancy: The influence of race on face and voice emotion matching. *Developmental Science, 15*(3), 359–372. doi:10.1111/j.1467-7687.2012.01138.x

Vogelsang, L., Gilad-Gutnick, S., Ehrenberg, E., Yonas, A., Diamond, S., Held, R., & Sinha, P. (2018). Potential downside of high initial visual acuity. *Proceedings of the National Academy of Sciences of the United States of America, 115*(44), 11333–11338. doi:10.1073/pnas.1800901115

von Hofsten, O., von Hofsten, C., Sulutvedt, U., Laeng, B., Brennen, T., & Magnussen, S. (2014). Simulating newborn face perception. *Journal of Vision, 14*(13), 16. doi:10.1167/14.13.16

Warner, C. E., Kwan, W. C., & Bourne, J. A. (2012). The early maturation of visual cortical area MT is dependent on input from the retinorecipient medial portion of the inferior pulvinar. *Journal of Neuroscience, 32*(48), 17073–17085. doi:10.1523/JNEUROSCI.3269-12.2012

Wattam-Bell, J. (1991). Development of motion-specific cortical responses in infancy. *Vision Research, 31*(2), 287–297.

    (1996a). Visual motion processing in one-month-old infants: Habituation experiments. *Vision Research, 36*(11), 1679–1685.

    (1996b). Visual motion processing in one-month-old infants. Preferential looking experiments. *Vision Research, 36*(11), 1671–1677.

Wattam-Bell, J., Birtles, D., Nyström, P., von Hofsten, C., Rosander, K., Anker, S., … Braddick, O. (2010). Reorganization of global form and motion processing during human visual development. *Current Biology, 20*(5), 411–415. doi:10.1016/j.cub.2009.12.020

Weinacht, S., Kind, C., Mönting, J. S., & Gottlob, I. (1999). Visual development in preterm and full-term infants: A prospective masked study. *Investigative Ophthalmology & Visual Science, 40*(2), 346–353.

Williams, C., Birch, E. E., Emmett, P. M., & Northstone, K. (2001). Stereoacuity at age 3.5 y in children born full-term is associated with prenatal and postnatal dietary factors: A report from a population-based cohort study. *American Journal of Clinical Nutrition, 73*(2), 316–322. doi:10.1093/ajcn/73.2.316

Young, A. W., Hellawell, D., & Hay, D. C. (2013). Configurational information in face perception. *Perception, 42*(11), 1166–1178.

7 Infant Visual Attention

Dima Amso and Kristen Tummeltshammer

From the moment infants open their eyes, they are confronted with a continuous stream of objects, people, sounds, and events that comprise their world. Some are adaptive to attend to and others are not (Gibson, 2000; Werchan & Amso, 2017). They will rely heavily on these observations to build the internal representations that will shape their future behavior. In this chapter, we review the development of infant visual attention, and the role this development plays in the remarkable achievements of infancy.

By just 2 months of age, infants have over 200 hours of visual exposure and have produced more than 2,500,000 eye movements (Haith, 1980). Even the youngest infants must employ selection mechanisms to extract a subset of the rich multisensory environment for further processing. Here we describe what is known about the development of visual attention, how it is tested in infancy, and how it is shaped by differences in early life experience.

"Attention" is a broad term used to describe a complex set of processes that enables us to filter the information available to our senses, selecting some information while simultaneously ignoring or inhibiting competing information. Selection enables cognitive resources to be focused on certain items or locations (and away from others) to facilitate processes such as perception, memory, and goal-relevant action (Carrasco, 2011; Desimone & Duncan, 1995; Markant, Worden, & Amso, 2015). An accepted mechanistic framework for selective attention is *biased competition* (Desimone & Duncan, 1995), in which attention is a bias or a resource allocation to one of many competing stimuli. In this sense, attention is not a singular construct but a domain-general computation over any competing input. Attention can operate in response to external input from various sensory modalities, as well as internally to select among competing goals, rules, and the contents of working memory. Many have used the metaphor that visual attention is like a *spotlight*, enhancing contrast sensitivity, acuity, and perceptual processing of selected information (Carrasco, 2011). Although we focus largely on visual attention and the neural mechanisms that support it, the principles and processes we discuss are thought to operate in a similar way across other competing inputs.

In this chapter we review the literature on how visual attention has been measured, what is currently known about its development and neural circuitry, and how the study of attention might inform policy and practice. We begin with a brief introduction to labels that have been used to describe attention constructs. These share the principle of resource allocation to one stimulus in favor of competing others, but vary in the type of information managed. Posner and Petersen's classic model (Posner & Petersen, 1990) describes three attention systems: alerting, orienting, and executive attention. *Alerting* refers to a state of heightened arousal or readiness in response to the abrupt onset of an external stimulus. *Orienting* refers to the shifting of attention to an item or location in the environment, either overtly (with an eye or head movement) or covertly (without a physical movement). *Executive attention* refers to processes that resolve competition among multiple stimuli, and includes switching, inhibition, and control processes. Colombo (2001) divided Posner and Petersen's *orienting* process into two distinct functions: *spatial attention* and *object-based attention*. Spatial attention involves directing attention to a particular location in space and enhances processing of information presented at the attended location. *Object-based attention* involves directing attention to particular objects or features of objects (such as color or shape). Moreover, attention is not only modulated by spatially distributed eye movements, but also by sustaining focus on the processing of events at the attended location. The maintenance of *sustained attention* is modulated by the structural and featural characteristics of the attended information, such as stimulus complexity and regularity, with increasing amounts of variability required to maintain infants' attention across the first year (e.g., Courage, Reynolds, & Richards, 2006). In the following section, we describe the methods that have been used to measure these various attention constructs.

7.1 Measuring Infant Attention

There are inherent challenges to measuring and studying cognitive processes in infants and these challenges pose problems in particular for understanding the development of visual attention. The human infant is not able to produce verbal or complex behavioral responses and cannot be given instructions on how to perform a given task; thus, most empirical studies rely on some measure of look duration or visual preference to assess infant attention (Aslin, 2007). However, as we review below, looking times are complex and often reflect learning and memory, as well as visual attention processes.

7.1.1 Looking-Time Measures

In the past, researchers were limited to measuring coarse aspects of infants' looking behavior – evaluating the direction of the eyes (and head) to determine whether and when infants looked at a particular image, object, or person. The use of looking-time measures in infants was first developed by Fantz (1956), based on the robust and reliable finding that infants' looking to a stimulus decreases with repeated exposure and recovers when a new stimulus is introduced. When the same stimulus, or a set of highly similar stimuli, is presented in repetition, infants exhibit a predictable and quantifiable decrement in looking time and are more likely to disengage from the stimulus display with each subsequent presentation (e.g., Cohen & Cashon, 2003). This decreased responsiveness is known as *habituation*, and the recovery of response to a new stimulus is *dishabituation*.

The speed with which an infant habituates to a particular stimulus is thought to reflect the efficiency of the infant's information processing, as disengagement from the stimulus suggests that the infant has fully processed it and committed it to memory. Fantz (1963) also noted that infants exhibited preferences for some visual stimuli over others (e.g., patterns, faces) and looked longer to these stimuli when exploring their visual environment. This nonrandom distribution of infant looking time suggested that it could be a useful and reliable index of infants' perceptual and cognitive processing abilities, broadly construed.

Infants' sensitivity to differences between visual events can also be measured using preferential looking (i.e., if infants prefer one display to another, then they have necessarily detected a difference between the two displays) and violation of expectation paradigms. The preferential looking method takes advantage of infants' spontaneous preferences; it does not require training, as infants will naturally look longer at events they prefer, such as their mother's face compared to a stranger's face (Bushnell, 2001) or biological motion compared to scrambled motion (Simion, Regolin, & Bulf, 2008).

In violation of expectation paradigms, infants look longer at events that are impossible or inconsistent with their prior expectations (due to "core knowledge" about how the world works [e.g., Baillargeon, 2002]; or due to previous experience gained outside the context of an experiment). Longer looking due to violation of expectations has been used to evaluate a variety of phenomena, such as infants' understanding of object permanence (e.g., Baillargeon, 1987), physical laws (e.g., Spelke, Katz, Purcell, Ehrlich, & Breinlinger, 1994), goal directed actions (e.g., Somerville, Woodward, & Needham, 2005), and social relationships (e.g., Kuhlmeier, Wynn, & Bloom, 2003).

Because of the ubiquity of these looking-time measures in infant research, looking and attending have sometimes been used interchangeably. However, looking time is not a uniquely visual attention metric; rather it likely reflects a conglomeration of psychological processes, such as information processing, learning rates, memory, and visual preference (Aslin, 2007). For example, in different scenarios, longer looking time could indicate increased interest or attraction to a stimulus, recognition of the stimulus, or even surprise that the stimulus has appeared.

Despite these differences in interpretation, it is generally agreed that time spent looking at a stimulus is related to time needed to collect information and assemble a mental representation of that stimulus; in the case of visual stimuli, looking time is intricately tied to visual processing (Colombo, Mitchell, Coldren, & Freeseman, 1991). Infants can be categorized as "short lookers" or

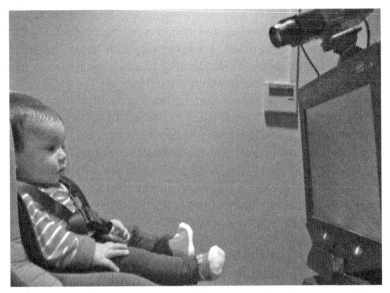

Figure 7.1. *An infant participating in an eye-tracking experiment. The infant is seated in a car seat, positioned in front of the eye tracker.*

"long lookers" to reflect their relative processing speeds, with "short lookers" showing faster response latencies to new peripheral stimuli and broader spatial distributions of gaze than "long lookers" (Jankowski, Rose, & Feldman, 2001). Short-looking patterns have been associated with improved stimulus processing in infancy (Jankowski et al., 2001), as well as better executive functions at 11 years (Rose, Feldman, & Jankowski, 2012).

In sum, looking times have historically been used to consider attention development, but indeed reflect several processes in infancy. In the following sections, we review how developments in eye tracking (S. P. Johnson, Amso, & Slemmer, 2003), heart-rate monitoring (Richards & Casey, 1992), event-related potentials (ERPs; Reynolds, Guy, & Zhang, 2011), and near-infrared spectroscopy (NIRS; Lloyd-Fox, Blasi, & Elwell, 2010) have opened new possibilities for examining infants' attention more precisely.

7.1.2 Eye-Tracking Tools for Measuring Infant Attention

Eye trackers are advanced physiological measuring systems that estimate the point of gaze and motion of the eye relative to the head, allowing researchers to record exactly where participants look on a stimulus display (Holmqvist et al., 2011). Corneal reflection eye trackers are typically used in infant research because they are remote, wireless systems that can compensate for small amounts of head and body movement (Figure 7.1).

Eye tracking offers many advantages as an experimental technique: First, it is noninvasive and simple to use with infant participants, and is able to tolerate head and body movements with minimal data loss. Second, eye tracking offers substantial increases in accuracy and precision over traditional video recording, as looking behavior is sampled at a faster rate with higher spatial resolution (Aslin, 2012). Thus it enables observation of gaze behaviors that are time critical (such as the distinction between an anticipatory or reactive look) or space critical (such as scanning the edges or internal features of a stimulus), which could not be obtained with traditional video recording. Third, eye tracking provides real-time gaze data, affording the experimenter greater control, and removes the need for offline human coding, which is time consuming and less precise.

Continuously sampled eye movements can be separated into two components: saccades and fixations (Holmqvist et al., 2011). Fixations are periods during which the eyes remain relatively stable in a particular location, enabling visual encoding and processing to occur. The duration of fixations is typically associated with cognitive processes such as attention, information processing, and memory encoding, similar to looking time. Saccades are the ballistic eye movements that occur between fixations, when the eyes are rapidly moved from one point to the next and visual sensitivity is suppressed. The latency and trajectory of saccades are typically linked to processes such as disengagement, attention switching, and anticipation.

Attentional control of saccadic eye movements involves connections between visual regions (primary visual cortex (V1), secondary visual area (V2), fourth visual area (V4), the parietal cortex, and the frontal eye fields (FEF), the superior colliculus and the basal ganglia. A pathway from the retina to the superior colliculus is the first component of the system to be operational, with evidence of function of this pathway in newborns, whereas the development of projections from V1 and the middle temporal area to the superior colliculus is completed later (M. H. Johnson, 1990). Input from the FEF allows for more voluntary anticipatory looking after 3 months of age, while a role for the prefrontal cortex (PFC) in saccade planning emerges from 6 months of age (Canfield & Haith, 1991).

7.1.3 Heart Rate as a Physiological Measure of Sustained Attention

The development of sustained attention has been examined using heart-rate markers in young infants as a physiological index of attentional engagement during periods of looking (Richards & Casey, 1992). Specifically, periods of increased sustained attention (i.e., marked by resistance to distraction, slower and less accurate shifts away from the attended stimulus) are accompanied by decreased heart rate (Casey & Richards, 1988). The heart rate stays below pre-stimulus level as long as the infant is attentive, and is followed by an increase as infants prepare for and terminate attention. Heart-rate deceleration during sustained attention increases from 3 to 6 months, along with some developing visual processing measures such as the time required for infants to acquire familiarity with stimulus characteristics (Frick & Richards, 2001).

7.1.4 EEG and Near-Infrared Spectroscopy

The introduction of novel neuroimaging tools and statistical methods has provided some precision to the study of the neural architecture underlying attention development. Electroencephalography (EEG) methods have been used to study the temporal dynamics of neural signals relevant to visual attention orienting. EEG is a noninvasive, painless method for recording the electrical activity of the human brain from the surface of the scalp. The main advantage of EEG is its high temporal resolution; changes in the brain's neural activation can be measured with millisecond precision as they unfold over time. However, its spatial resolution is relatively poor, as electrical conduction through neural tissue, skull, and scalp create substantial blurring of the surface distribution of the voltage and make it difficult to localize the source of neural activity.

Event-related potentials (ERPs) can be obtained from continuous EEG recordings by averaging segments that are "time locked" to a discrete stimulus or event (deBoer, Scott, & Nelson, 2007). The resulting signal deflections reflect specific aspects of sensory and cognitive processing associated with that particular stimulus or event. Thus, ERPs offer an opportunity to study the neural processes underlying observed behavior or even to study responses that cannot be observed with behavioral measures (e.g., predictive processes in the absence of anticipatory eye movements).

In infant ERP research, the component most clearly related to visual attention is the negative central (Nc) component. The Nc is a high-amplitude, negatively polarized component that occurs from 400 to 800 ms following the presentation of a salient stimulus. This ERP component is maximal over frontal and central scalp areas and tends to be larger for novel or "oddball" stimuli (Courchesne, Ganz, & Norcia, 1981; Reynolds & Richards, 2005). Richards (2003) found that the Nc component was greater in amplitude during periods of sustained attention (as indicated by HR deceleration) in a sample of 4.5- to 7.5-month-old infants. The Nc component has been found to increase in amplitude as the infant ages and may reflect increased attention-related activity in the prefrontal cortex during infancy (Reynolds & Richards, 2005).

Near-infrared spectroscopy (NIRS) allows better spatial precision and is relevant for understanding cortical attention networks. NIRS uses infrared light to measure cortical activity precisely beneath the locus of the measuring optodes and emitters. As light migrates from sources to detectors, the attenuation (or loss) of this light will be due to absorption and scattering effects within the skin, skull, and underlying brain tissue (Jöbsis, 1977; Lloyd-Fox et al., 2010). Since blood oxyhemoglobin (HbO_2) and deoxyhemoglobin (HHb) have different absorption properties of near-infrared light, changes in their concentration can be measured as a proxy for blood flow and used to index brain function. Stimulus onset and neural activity induces an increase in the concentration of HbO, which is accompanied by a lesser decrease in HHb concentration. This vascular response, known as the hemodynamic response function (HRF), varies according to the evoking stimuli as well as the underlying neural activity. In this way, functional brain activation can be measured in awake, behaving infants. NIRS systems are inexpensive and portable, and can accommodate a degree of movement from infants. However, the main limitation of NIRS is that it depends on the penetration of light through the brain, and therefore can only be used to measure the cortical surface.

Looking time, as well as eye tracking, heart rate, and EEG/fNIRS tools are almost always paired with paradigms that index aspects of visual attention. We sample some of the most commonly used visual attention paradigms in the following section.

7.1.5 Common Tasks in Infant Visual Attention Research

From the previous sections, it is clear that studies of visual attention may focus on spatial attention, object-based attention, executive attention, or sustained attention. Here we describe commonly used tasks that have allowed for the examination of these constructs in infancy.

Stimuli that direct attention to a particular location in space are called *spatial cues*. The ability to overtly orient, or move the eyes, to peripheral cues develops rapidly from birth. However, there are task dynamics using spatial cues that enable measuring of attentional shifts in the absence of eye movements (i.e., covert orienting). In spatial cueing paradigms, infants' attention is directed to a central location, and a spatial cue can flash briefly to the right or left of that central location. If the flashed cue is too brief to elicit an eye movement, but it is nonetheless registered by visual attention orienting systems, the cued location will experience an attentional bias relative to competing locations (e.g., Markant & Amso, 2013). Orienting to a target that subsequently appears in this cued location is *facilitated*, or faster, relative to a target presented in a different location. The facilitation of orienting to a previously cued location is evident by 3–4 months of age (M. H. Johnson, Posner, & Rothbart, 1991). The length of time between the cue and the target is critical. If the time interval is longer, on the order of 600–2000 ms, then orienting to the cued location becomes *suppressed*, or slower, as attention is now biased to the competing location (Posner, Rafal, & Choate, 1985). This phenomenon, called inhibition of return (IOR), is evident in infants by 6 months (Markant & Amso, 2013, 2016; Richards, 2000). IOR plays an important role in visual search, as a strategy that prevents perseverative return to a previously attended location in which a target did not rapidly occur and instead promotes orienting to novel locations (Klein, 2000).

Visual search tasks, in which a target is presented among multiple distracters, are also used to examine attention orienting. When the target differs from the distracters by only a single feature, it is said to pop out; however, when the target differs by a conjunction of features (such as a red T among red and green Ts and Ls), search is effortful and search times increase with the number or

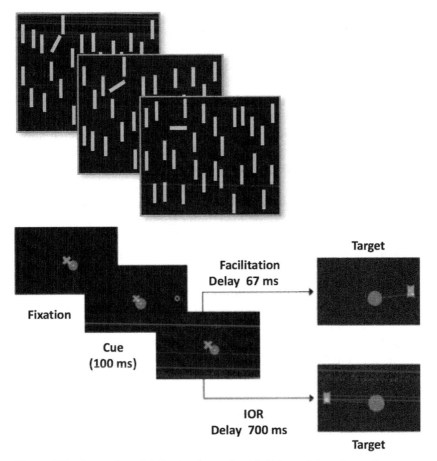

Figure 7.2. *Examples of (A) visual search and (B) spatial cueing tasks presented to infants.*
Source: Adapted from Amso and Johnson (2006) and Markant and Amso (2013).

similarity of distracters in the scene. Very early in infancy, visual pop-out search can be used to assess which stimulus features automatically capture attention (e.g., Dannemiller, 2005). For example, when 2- and 4.5-month-old infants were presented with a single oscillating target in a field of static bars, Dannemiller (2005) observed a strong pop-out effect in the 4.5-month-olds but not yet in the 2-month-old infants. The moving target captured the older infants' attention, and they were able to successfully inhibit looking at the nonmoving distracters, providing evidence of significant development in orienting between 2 and 4.5 months. Similarly, Amso and Johnson (2006) observed that 3-month-old infants effectively selected both a moving target in a field of nonmoving targets, and an oriented bar in a field of vertical bars above chance. Performance on the moving target search was significantly better than on the more difficult orientation-based search. Frank, Amso, and Johnson (2014) showed developmental improvement in both search tasks from 3 to 10 months of age.

Visual attention orienting in cluttered natural scenes has recently been assessed through the use of *free viewing tasks* (e.g., Amso, Haas, & Markant, 2014). Infants are presented with either animated or naturalistic scenes and eye tracking is used to assess the influence of scene characteristics on how attention is allocated in these natural visual search scenarios. For example, Amso et al. (2014) showed that young infants do not preferentially orient to faces that are presented in cluttered natural scenes. Indeed, orienting to faces embedded in cluttered images improved in infancy. Moreover, the data showed that infants were not "bottom-up" driven, meaning that they did not reflexively orient to the most visually salient location in natural scenes. Rather, this bottom-up processing developed along with visual development throughout infancy. As color and motion processing improved, for example, so did infants' ability to detect items that were distinct from their surround based on color and movement.

Executive attention development has been examined in infancy using the *anti-saccade task* (M. H. Johnson, 1995). This spatial cueing task involves infants learning a rule through trial and error. In the anti-saccade task, infants must inhibit saccades to a cue that appears on the screen and instead orient to a target stimulus that appears on the opposite side of the screen. M. H. Johnson (1995) found that while 4-month-olds initially made only prosaccades – all their eye movements were directed toward the cued location even though the target appeared on the opposite side – there was a rise in the number of anti-saccades across trials, indicating increasing executive attention control.

An additional means of assessing sustained attention is with *free play tasks* that allow infants to interact independently and spontaneously with toys (e.g., Lawson & Ruff, 2004; Ruff, Lawson, Parrinello, & Weissberg, 1990). Active learning and information gathering are indexed by the duration of infants' focused exploration (i.e., closely concentrating and examining toys), while the amount of time infants spend distracted and unfocused is indicative of inattention and linked to later attention deficits (Ruff et al., 1990).

Using the tools and tasks described thus far, the scientific community has made progress in understanding the development of infant visual attention. A summary of the basic findings is offered below.

7.2 A Review of Infant Attention Development

7.2.1 Attention Development in the First Postnatal Year

The information offered to this point allows us to now consider what is known about the development of visual attention chronologically, from both behavioral and neural studies. Visual attention in the fetus is complicated by stimulus presentation and available imaging techniques. Research from DiPietro, Bornstein, Hahn, Costigan, and Achy-Brou (2007) has examined the role of heart-rate variability *in utero* on subsequent cognitive development. They found that increased heart-rate variability during the third trimester was an important predictor of cognitive development, including visual attention, into the second year of life. In a recent study, Reid et al. (2017) used 4-D ultrasound to examine fetal head turns to faces, a visual object class. They projected either inverted face-like stimuli (three dots that form an upside-down triangle, two dots on top and one on the bottom) or upright face-like stimuli (three dots that form a right-side-up triangle with one on top and two on the bottom) through the uterine wall and found that fetuses in the third trimester preferred the upright face-like stimuli. This study is remarkable in its methodological contribution and also for providing evidence that a bias towards dot configurations that resemble facial feature configurations is present before exposure to faces.

Posner and Petersen's (1990) alerting network, arguably functional at birth, includes the locus coeruleus and right parietal and frontal regions and is modulated by the neurotransmitter noradrenaline. Alertness, the ability to attain and maintain an alert, attentive state, is observed in newborn infants. Changes in infants' regulation of waking and sleep cycles contribute to a gradual increase in alertness over the first 12 weeks of life. At birth, visual attention orienting is believed to be primarily involuntary. Direct pathways from the retina to the superior colliculus drive newborn fixations toward high-contrast edges and motion (M. H. Johnson et al., 1991). Newborn eye-movement control may be *obligatory* (M. H. Johnson, 1990), in that very young infants often find it difficult to look away from attractive targets. This behavior, called "sticky fixation," has been taken as evidence of limited eye-movement disengagement ability (Hood, 1995).

According to Posner and Petersen (1990), the orienting network includes the frontal eye fields (FEF), superior parietal junction, superior temporal junction, superior colliculus, and pulvinar. Orienting is modulated by the neurotransmitter acetylcholine. M. H. Johnson (1990) provided evidence that cortical maturation underlies the development of visual attention orienting in infancy. In particular, he argued that early orienting processes are reflexive, or subcortically mediated, and that there is a transition from stimulus-based exogenous orienting to more endogenous or cortically mediated volitional control over eye movements (Colombo, 2001; M. H. Johnson, 1990). This transition is due, in part, to the gradual development of oculomotor control and changes in the local and long-range connectivity of visual cortical regions. In an adapted spatial cueing task, M. H. Johnson et al. (1991) trained 2-, 3-, and 4-month-old infants using abstract visual stimuli as central cues: one stimulus cued the appearance of a target on the right side of the screen, while the other cued a target on the left side. At test, when targets appeared on both sides of the screen, they found that only 4-month-olds oriented preferentially to the correctly cued side. Furthermore, a few studies have demonstrated longer response latencies when the central cue remained in view compared to when it was extinguished before the peripheral target's onset, indicating that disengagement and inter-stimulus shifting continue to develop more gradually (the gap-overlap task: Hood, Willen, & Driver, 1998).

Between 3 and 6 months, continued development is seen in the voluntary control of eye movements with the functional onset of the posterior orienting system, which includes the posterior parietal areas, pulvinar, and frontal eye fields (M. H. Johnson et al., 1991; Posner & Peterson, 1990). This system is involved in disengaging fixation and initiating voluntary saccades, resulting in a marked increase in infants' ability to shift attention among multiple competing stimuli. Infants' average look durations drop significantly to a wide range of stimuli from 3 to 6 months of age (Courage et al., 2006). Rapid changes are observed in other aspects of eye-movement control, including the ability to continuously track a moving object. At 3–4 months, infants show more smooth pursuit, fixate moving targets more accurately, and are able to track faster-moving targets (Rosander, 2007; von Hofsten & Rosander, 1997). Improvements in smooth pursuit and in orienting to peripheral cues in the gap-overlap task are reflective of significant changes in oculomotor control between birth and 4 months.

The second half of the first postnatal year is dominated by changes in spatial and object-based attention. As noted, after a longer delay (e.g., >600 ms), spatial cueing can result in a suppressed or slower response to a target that appears in the cued location. This IOR effect reflects the inhibition of returning attention to a previously attended location to encourage orienting to new locations (Klein, 2000). Although there is some evidence of IOR in newborns (Simion, Valenza, Umiltà, & Barba, 1995; Valenza, Simion, & Umiltà, 1994) when overt shifts of attention can be made, covert-shifting IOR appears to emerge at 5–6 months of age (Richards, 2000) and is stable by 9 months (Markant & Amso, 2013, 2016).

Object-based attention refers to the selection and shifting of attention to one of multiple objects or object features at the expense of others. An object is defined as a set of perceptually grouped visual features that adhere to Gestalt principles such as proximity, good continuation, and closure. When attention selects a whole object, its constituent features (e.g., color, location, motion) benefit from further processing in support of learning and memory (e.g., Schoenfeld, Hopf, Merkel, Heinze, & Hillyard, 2014). In this way, infants can learn to recognize and act appropriately on an object even if seen rapidly or if only one part of it is visible.

Object-based attention has been assessed in infants by presenting a cue on one of two identical bars. After a delay, infants see a target appear in either the cued location or in one of two uncued locations: on the cued object ("invalid same object") or on the uncued object ("invalid different object"). Though both uncued locations were equidistant from the cue, 8-month-old infants were faster to detect targets in the same-object displays relative to targets in the different-object displays (Bulf & Valenza, 2013).

While there is some evidence of attentional control in infants as young as 4 months (e.g., M. H. Johnson, 1995), there is substantial development in executive attention processes across early childhood and into adolescence (Hwang, Velanova, & Luna, 2010; Konrad et al., 2005). Executive attention has been described as resolving competition between bottom-up features of the environment, such as saliency and novelty, and top-down influences, such as one's goals, expectations, and prior knowledge (Posner, 2004). With effortful control of attention through disengagement, inter-stimulus shifting, and inhibition of automatic responses, older infants gradually exhibit more goal-based or rule-based allocation. A few studies have provided evidence of increasing top-down influences on attention in the second half of the first postnatal year (Tummeltshammer & Amso, 2017). For example, when Tummeltshammer and Amso (2017) presented 6- and 10-month-old infants with repeated and novel visual search arrays, they found that infants were able to use visual context as a top-down cue, orienting faster to targets that appeared in the repeated arrays.

From 6 months, infants also demonstrate the ability to sustain attention for longer periods while inhibiting looks to distracters. Oakes, Kannass, and Shaddy (2002) observed that when playing with toys, 10-month-old infants were less distracted by an external stimulus when engaged in deeper processing of those toys than when they were less engaged. At 6 months, infants show similar levels of distraction in different states of engagement, suggesting that infants' ability to control their attentional focus – and resist distraction during information processing – shows developmental change during this time.

7.2.2 Feedforward and Feedback Cortical Connections

Amso and Scerif (2015) recently framed visual attention development as emergent from the development of cortical visual processing. This conceptual framework relies on a biased competition lens. The development of behavior, functional connectivity, and gray matter volume has been described as proceeding from caudal regions to more rostral regions, along a cortical hierarchy that processes increasingly complex aspects of stimuli, space, and even abstract rules for action (Amso & Scerif, 2015). Visual processing areas mature early in development, followed by the maturation of parietal and temporal regions, which are responsible for integrating information received from feedforward connections. The last to mature are prefrontal cortical regions, which modulate the activity of some lower visual areas, including V1, via feedback, or top-down signals (Gilbert & Sigman, 2007).

Amso and Scerif (2015) proposed a framework that embeds visual attention development into the emerging functionality of this hierarchical organization of visual pathways. For example, the lower visual areas responsible for attending to specific features develop prior to the parietal and temporal regions that support spatial and object-based attention; importantly, the cumulative development of visual areas feeding forward into higher-level regions acts as a catalyst for top-down attentional modulation of these same visual pathways. Furthermore, these regions send feedback signals that modulate the activity and local connectivity of lower visual areas, enhancing the processing of attended information and shaping perceptual learning across development.

Consider a visual search display where an infant must select a moving red target embedded in multiple red static distractors. Very young infants with limited motion processing will not experience the moving stimulus as particularly different from the surround and it will not pop out, as Dannemiller (2005) observed in 2-month-olds. As motion processing improves by 4.5 months, moving stimuli will drive a pop-out effect and a rapid eye movement. Now consider a visual search display where an infant must select a moving red target from among multiple red *and* green static distractors. In order to select a moving red target in this conjunction search, infants must be sensitive to both motion and color. If they are insensitive to color because red/green color processing is still developing, then the moving target will simply pop out because the red and green distractors will not compete with it and the search will be easy. If color processing is strong, then the target and distractor colors will compete and attention is needed to bias competition to the target. In this way, as visual processing develops, there is increased demand to select among additive competing visual inputs.

Amso and Scerif (2015) argued that changes in visual attention development are driven by visual processing demands, making visual attention an emergent process of adaptation to the cumulative development of visual features in infancy. This is only part of the rich developmental story. It is also important to note that the literature suggests that eye-movement control and body kinematics constrain infant attention development. In turn, visual attention development is interactive with learning, memory, and decision making. We review these findings in turn.

7.3 Attention Interacts with Other Developing Systems

7.3.1 Vision and Eye-Movement Control

During the first year of life, basic features of the visual system such as acuity, binocular disparity, and oculomotor control undergo significant development, meaning that an infant's visual processing differs from an adult's in a number of fundamental ways (Colombo, 2001; Colombo & Cheatham, 2006). Vision is poor in newborn humans, and most visual skills improve rapidly during the first 6 months. Acuity is estimated at 20/800 for most newborns but improves quickly over the next few months, as does contrast sensitivity (Atkinson, Braddick, & Moar, 1977). Full motion sensitivity is noted by 6 months, whereas it is known that infants are sensitive to orientation shifts as early as 6 weeks after birth (Braddick, Wattam-Bell, & Atkinson, 1986).

Evidence of infants' sensitivity to low-level visual features can be seen in their eye movements from birth (e.g., Fantz, 1963; Salapatek & Kessen, 1966). Even when scanning a novel input, infants' eye movements are not random, but depend on the distribution of visual features (Fantz, 1956; Frank, Vul & Johnson, 2009; Schlesinger & Amso, 2013). Low-level visual features such as luminance, contrast, edges, color saturation, and motion tend to influence gaze behavior in infants more strongly than adults (Frank et al., 2009). Frank et al. (2009) showed infants video clips of a Charlie Brown cartoon; they found that 3-month-olds' eye movements were better captured by low-level image salience, while more high-level semantic factors (such as the presence of a face) influenced looking behavior to a greater extent in 6- and 9-month-olds.

Comparing infants' spontaneous eye-movement patterns over the first few months of life reveals that fixations are initially longer and more concentrated, and become more distributed and controlled by 3–4 months (Bronson, 1990; Salapatek & Kessen, 1966). With the introduction of even the tiniest amounts of noise to the visual environment (e.g., flicker), infants' eye movements become less stable (Bronson, 1990). Although even very young infants fixate objects, they tend to scan their edges and angles rather than internal features and struggle to track smoothly moving objects (Haith, 1980). Further, infants' visual acuity will not reach adult levels until 7–8 months, at about the same time as their ability to integrate depth cues such as relative size and interposition.

7.3.2 Body Kinematics and Posture

Overt attention, which involves turning one's head and eyes to bring a stimulus, object, or feature of the environment into focus, relies on the physical abilities involved in holding one's head upright, making effortful and voluntary head turns, and voluntarily controlling eye movements. Motor control over the head and eyes, as well as their coordination, undergoes significant developmental change in infancy (Bertenthal & von Hofsten, 1998), which opens up novel exploratory and attentional strategies for young infants.

Observation of infants in naturalistic settings has offered key insights into how infants deploy, control, select, and inhibit attention as they reach for objects, navigate environments, and interact with others. Using head-mounted eye trackers, Franchak and Adolph (2010) documented changes in visual attention across developmental changes in motor abilities. They found that children and adults attended differently to obstacles as they walked around a space. This suggests that different motor skill and confidence may require more or less need for visual attention in order to avoid obstacles during walking. Further, Kretch, Franchak, and Adolph (2014) found that crawling and walking infants directed their gaze differently at caregivers as they approached them. When infants were crawling, their view was of mostly the floor and they had to stop crawling to sit up and look at objects or their caregiver. In contrast, when infants were walking, they could look continuously at their caregiver, other objects, or their destination without stopping. Thus, changes in locomotor ability corresponded to changes in the visual environment of the child and their visual attention strategies.

These data show that visual attention development does not occur in isolation. We next offer support for the idea that visual attention development impacts and is impacted by other information-processing systems.

7.3.3 Attention and Learning/Memory

Studies of infant looking behavior indicate that the way infants distribute their attention to a stimulus can have critical consequences for learning (Amso & Johnson, 2006; Jankowski et al., 2001). For example, when presenting infants with a visually ambiguous display (a rod divided by a central box), S. P. Johnson, Slemmer, and Amso (2004) found that infants who oriented to the object parts and their movement were more likely to perceive the central rod in an adult-like manner (complete or broken) than infants who scanned the display randomly. In this way, efficient attention-guided orienting has been shown to support both object and face perception (Amso, Fitzgerald, Davidow, Gilhooly, & Tottenham, 2010; Amso & Johnson, 2006; Emberson & Amso, 2012; S. P. Johnson et al., 2004).

Studies have shown that orienting attention with spatial cues may enhance infants' processing and memory for events at the cued location (Jankowski et al., 2001; Reid, Striano, Kaufman, & Johnson, 2004; Striano, Chen, Cleveland, & Bradshaw 2006). When Jankowski et al. (2001) familiarized 5-month-old infants with arrays of shapes, only a subset of infants were able to successfully discriminate familiar from novel arrays at test. However, when they presented the arrays with a "spotlight" that illuminated each shape one at a time, they found a consistent novelty preference across all infants at test, indicating that the "spotlight" cue had enhanced infants' processing of the arrays.

Learning can in turn shape how infants orient attention. For example, infants who live with pets distribute their looking differently to images of dogs and cats than do infants who do not live with pets (Hurley & Oakes, 2015; Markant & Amso, 2016). In this way, the strategies that infants use to guide their attention to a stimulus may reflect their prior learning. To the extent that daily experience is different across cultures, one may expect that the specific items and categories that benefit from an attention bias will be specific to individuals' social or cultural contexts.

Developmental changes in infant memory are also intricately tied to infants' visual attention capacities; for example, infants must rely on visual short-term memory (VSTM) to represent visual input through brief disruptions during blinks and saccades. Studies in which infants must detect the changing item in a multielemental array have shown that visual short-term memory increases substantially in the second half of the first year, as infants are able to encode more items and bind features to locations (Káldy & Leslie, 2003; Ross-Sheehy, Oakes, & Luck, 2003). Using a spatial cueing task, Markant and Amso (2013) showed that items encoded on selective attention IOR trials, that engage simultaneous distractor suppression, but not simple facilitation or no-cueing trials (where no distractor suppression was engaged), were subsequently remembered better by 9-month-old infants. The idea is that engaging suppression reduces distractor interference during target encoding, resulting in a more robust target representation for subsequent memory.

7.3.4 Joint Attention, Social Development, and Decision Making

One type of spatial cue that has been studied in depth is attention to others' eye gaze. Human adults orient automatically to shifts in others' eye gaze, and the ability to follow gaze is a critical component of many aspects of social interaction, such as joint attention, imitation, communication, and coordinated action. Human infants also use others' gaze to direct spatial attention, orienting faster to visible targets that appear in the direction of an adult's gaze (Farroni, Massaccesi, Pividori, & Johnson, 2004). Infants follow faces to look at objects from 4 months of age, and are sensitive to the relationship between the direction of gaze and the object's location (Hoehl, Reid, Mooney, & Striano, 2008; Senju, Csibra, & Johnson, 2008). The speed and robustness of gaze following develops over the first year as infants shift attention with greater spatial precision, make anticipatory looks in the direction of gaze, and search for targets out of sight (Csibra & Volein, 2008).

Joint attention occurs when two social partners look at the same object or location; it has been shown to be critical to early learning and the development of social skills (Mundy & Newell, 2007). The frequency with which infants engage in joint attention is related to their language acquisition, depth of information processing, as well as with individual differences in childhood measures of IQ, self-regulation, and social competence (Mundy et al., 2007). Furthermore, impairments in spontaneously initiating joint attention are characteristic of autism spectrum disorders (ASDs) (Mundy, 2003). Engaging in joint attention is thought to involve both the anterior and posterior attention networks, which integrate the internal monitoring of one's own control of gaze direction, and its relations to goal-directed behavior, with external monitoring of the relations between others' gaze direction and their behavior (Mundy & Newell, 2007).

Yu and Smith (2016) demonstrated how joint attention impacts of the development of sustained attention abilities in the first year of life. Using head-mounted eye tracking to record moment-by-moment gaze data from both parents and infants, they observed that infants were more likely to extend their duration of visual attention to an object if the parent also attended to the same object (Yu & Smith, 2016).

This section highlights how infants' visual attention development interacts with other developing systems within the child. It is also the case that visual attention is impacted by factors external to the infant. Next, we review the evidence that the development of visual attention systems is shaped by social, cultural, and biological variables.

7.4 Social, Cultural, and Biological Factors That Drive Individual Differences in Infant Attention Development

Infant visual attention development is an early and critical means of information gathering and learning with long-term impact on subsequent development. For example, visual attention at 3 months predicts cognitive function at 2 years of age (Lewis & Brooks-Gunn, 1981) and adolescent intelligence (Sigman, Cohen, & Beckwith, 1997). Infant social attention has predictive value for social cognition in preschool (Wellman, Phillips, Dunphy-Lelii, & LaLonde, 2004). Infant visual attention allocation has predictive value for autism risk (Zweigenbaum et al., 2005) and language development in infants at risk for autism (Young, Merin, Rogers, & Ozonoff, 2009). As such, understanding the individual differences that impact its developmental course is important for understanding foundations of child development. In this section, we discuss how early one-on-one social interactions with caregivers, the general characteristics of the home environment, societal experiences and exposures, and biological factors can all shape infant visual development.

7.4.1 Infants of Depressed Mothers or Fathers

Early interactions with caregivers offer important opportunities to direct visual attention in infancy. Postpartum depression is one of the most common complications post-pregnancy. Maternal depression is associated with stronger alerting responses to external stimuli (e.g., a bell, rattle, or light) in newborns as well as higher levels of the adrenocorticotropic hormone (ACTH), which regulates the production of the stress hormone cortisol (Lancaster et al., 2010). Children of depressed mothers demonstrate attentional deficits and impaired cognitive performance (Weissman, Leckman, Merikangas, Gammon, & Prusoff, 1984). In the first few months, infants of depressed mothers have shown inferior orienting, suggesting lesser sensitivity to maternal cues (Abrams, Field, Scafidi, & Prodromidis, 1995). Infants and their depressed mothers show less mutual attentiveness and less time in collaborative joint attention than those in dyads with nondepressed mothers (Field, Healy, & Leblanc, 1989). During interactions, depressed mothers more frequently directed infants' attention toward and away from toys (Breznitz & Friedman, 1988), with the result being that infants focused on more objects but for shorter durations.

These differences in how attention is directed have an impact on learning and memory. For example, Bornstein, Mash, Arterberry, and Manian (2012) examined object perception in 5-month-old infants of depressed mothers relative to nondepressed mothers. After a period of familiarization with an object, they showed infants with the same object presented in the familiar or in a novel perspective. They found that infants of depressed mothers did not discriminate between object views.

Studies are not clear about whether maternal depression and anxiety impact attention to threat. This is generally tested by examining how visual attention is distributed to faces, a class of objects, exhibiting different emotion. For example, Leppänen, Cataldo, Bosquet Enlow, and Nelson (2018) showed developmental change in attention bias to threat (fearful, angry faces) but not evidence of a relation to maternal depression or anxiety. However, Aktar et al. (2016) found that the relation with the father's and/or mother's depression and attention to objects paired with threat faces was moderated by the infant's own temperamental predisposition to sadness.

7.4.2 Are Infant Attention Mechanisms Culturally Specific or Universal?

As mentioned above, the way that attention is distributed to an object, location, or event is based on a biased competition computation, the winner of which is selected while the distractors are suppressed (Desimone & Duncan, 1995). Amso and Scerif (2015) argued that visual development is one way in which this bias changes over time. But what makes an object more or less likely to receive this bias? There are individual differences in experience, for example as a result of parental depression or material wealth, that make some objects likely to be selected by one person but not another. These effects of *what* attention selects could theoretically extend to entire groups of people who have similar experiences as a result of where they live, the people they encounter, or the activities they commonly engage in. Thus, while the circuitry that makes the attentional bias possible is likely universal, the items and events that this neural circuitry selects should be driven by the experiences of the individual and are culturally relevant.

A key example of this is the "other-race effect" (ORE) in which older, but not younger, infants orient attention differently when viewing relatively familiar, own-race faces compared to relatively unfamiliar, other-race faces (Pascalis, de Haan, & Nelson, 2002). The ORE is likely a product of repeated exposure to own-race faces (Sugita, 2008) and can be reduced in infancy with increased exposure to other-race faces (Fair, Flom, Jones, & Martin, 2012). Further, the effect can be mitigated by exposure to diverse communities (Ellis, Xiao, Lee, & Oakes, 2017) and differs in monoracial and biracial infants (Gaither, Pauker, & Johnson, 2012). The ORE may arise from a loss of perceptual sensitivity to other-race features, the development of scanning strategies that specifically benefit own-race faces (Wheeler et al., 2011), and/or a process of perceptual learning in which face processing becomes more attuned to experienced faces (Fair et al., 2012).

Another possibility is that frequent experience with own-race faces may elicit increased selective attention engagement, which has been shown to enhance the quality of early vision, contrast sensitivity, acuity, and perceptual processing of selected information (Carrasco, 2011). According to this explanation, selectively biasing attention to any face, regardless of race, should improve online visual processing and subsequent discrimination and create the type of asymmetries seen in the ORE. Markant, Oakes, and Amso (2016) tested this hypothesis in a spatial cueing experiment. They presented 9-month-old infants with all the same faces, but some infants were biased to attend to own-race faces while others were biased to attend to other-race faces. Indeed, infants showed stronger discrimination of and memory for the race of the faces that they had been biased to attend, regardless of whether those faces were from their own race or another race.

What remains unclear is how the attention bias to own-race faces arises from repeated exposure in infancy. One possibility is that own-race faces are assigned some emotional significance over repeated exposures, and attention resources become biased due to the faces' association with positive or negative valence (Scott & Monesson, 2010). For example, when own- and other-race faces were paired with laughing or crying sounds, 9-month-old infants showed the ORE and a race-specific ERP response to the face/sound association (Vogel, Monesson, & Scott, 2012). This result provides evidence that the emotional valence of experienced faces may influence the development of attention biases towards own-race faces.

7.4.3 Infant Attention and Socioeconomic Status

A widely used means of leveraging differences in early experience is socioeconomic status (SES). SES reflects a family's social standing and parent education, occupation, and income (McLloyd, 1998). SES effects are not specific to poverty, but occur across the entire income distribution (Amso & Lynn, 2017). Extensive evidence has documented differences in home environments across SES in material object stimulation, exposure to complex language, provision of learning opportunities, and parent–child interactions (Bradley & Corwyn, 2002; Hart & Risley, 1995). Markant, Ackerman, Nussenbaum, and Amso (2016) found that SES does not predict spatial attention facilitation or IOR in 9-month-old infants. However, SES did impact memory performance in the same infants only in the facilitation-orienting condition. When infants were forced to use IOR because of the temporal dynamics of the cue-target pairing, the effect of SES on memory disappeared. These data suggest that inhibitory attention may compensate for the impact of SES on memory.

Amso et al. (2014) found that family SES predicted attention orienting to faces in cluttered natural scenes, suggesting a role of SES on object-based attention. A longitudinal study (6, 9, and 12 months) in infants from varying SES homes (Clearfield & Jedd, 2012) showed that high-SES infants outperformed low-SES infants on focused attention and inattention as the number and the complexity of toy objects they presented to infants increased. Yet another study (Tacke, Bailey, & Clearfield, 2015) showed that high- but not low-SES infants used information learned from object or surface exploration to recognize opportunities for exploration. Taken together, these data indicate that the availability of experiences or material enrichment offered by SES may affect the development of object-based attention in infancy.

7.4.4 Infant Attention and Preterm Birth

On the extreme end of SES are families living in poverty, which is an important risk factor for preterm birth (Kramer et al., 2001). The majority of infants born preterm and early term (gestational age <32 weeks) show decreased attention, learning, and memory compared to full-term infants (e.g., Rose, Feldman & Jankowski, 2001, 2012) and these deficits persist through childhood and adolescence (e.g., Grunau, Whitfield, & Fay, 2004).

Rose et al. (2001) observed that infants born preterm with very low birth weight (<1750 g) had longer look durations, slower shift rates, more off-task behavior, and lower attention to novelty than infants born full term. One possible explanation for these deficits is preterm infants' exposure to stresses in the neonatal intensive care unit (NICU) may alter development of the stress response during a time of rapid neurodevelopment and nervous system vulnerability (Grunau, Weinberg, & Whitfield, 2004). Indeed, Grunau, Whitfield et al. (2004) found that 8-month-old infants born at extremely low gestational age (<28 weeks) had higher cortisol levels in response to visual novelty than full-term infants.

7.5 Summary and Clinical and Policy Implications

Because of its role as a bottleneck for sensory input, attention is a candidate for targeted interventions that may mitigate the risk for adverse health outcomes and alter the trajectory of neurodevelopmental disorders. Visual attention processes are impaired in a variety of neurodevelopmental disorders including ASDs, fragile X, and attention-deficit hyperactivity disorder (ADHD). In some cases, the described developmental trajectories of visual attention processes can be used to predict whether an infant at familial risk for disorders will deviate from typical trajectories (Jones & Klin, 2013). For example, Elsabbagh et al. (2009) found reduced attentional disengagement in the infant siblings of children with ASD in comparison to siblings of children without ASD. Similarly, infants at risk for ADHD have been shown to have some differences in sensory processing as measured by ERP that later related to ADHD symptomology (externalizing behavior, attentional problems; Hutchinson, de Luca, Doyle, Roberts, & Anderson, 2013). In this way visual attention processes are starting to serve as biomarkers of need for early intervention.

Engaging visual attention may also benefit interventions designed to improve learning and memory in at-risk populations, perhaps as a result of low SES, and also relevant to education policy. Different forms of visual attention are differentially susceptible to environmental influence. For example, we discussed that object-based but not spatial attention has been shown to be susceptible to SES influences. From a policy perspective, these data highlight the need for opportunities for variable rich visual experiences with objects, books, and faces in infancy. Moreover, Markant, Ackerman et al. (2016) showed that engaging spatial selective attention at item encoding can mitigate the effects of SES on subsequent memory. Markant and Amso (2014) showed that engaging visual spatial selective attention at item encoding can mitigate individual differences in IQ on subsequent memory in children. Thus, visual attention can additionally serve as a protective mechanism. Future work can determine the value of visual attention interventions designed to improve learning and memory processes both in at-risk groups and also in the design of educational strategies.

References

Abrams, S. M., Field, T., Scafidi, F., & Prodromidis, M. (1995). Newborns of depressed mothers. *Infant Mental Health Journal, 16*(3), 233–239.

Aktar, E., Mandell, D. J., de Vente, W., Majdandžić, M., Raijmakers, M. E., & Bögels, S. M. (2016). Infants' temperament and mothers', and fathers' depression predict infants' attention to objects paired with emotional faces. *Journal of Abnormal Child Psychology, 44*(5), 975–990.

Amso, D., Fitzgerald, M., Davidow, J., Gilhooly, T., & Tottenham, N. (2010). Visual exploration strategies and the development of infants' facial emotion discrimination. *Frontiers in Psychology, 1*, 180.

Amso, D., Haas, S., & Markant, J. (2014). An eye-tracking investigation of developmental change in bottom-up attention orienting to faces in cluttered natural scenes. *PLoS One, 9*(1), e85701.

Amso, D., & Johnson, S. P. (2006). Learning by selection: Visual search and object perception in young infants. *Developmental Psychology, 42*, 1236–1245. doi: 10.1037/0012-1649.42.6.1236

Amso, D., & Lynn, A. (2017). Distinctive mechanisms of adversity and socioeconomic inequality in child development: A review and recommendations for evidence-based policy. *Policy Insights from the Behavioral and Brain Sciences, 4*(2), 139–146.

Amso, D., & Scerif, G. (2015). The attentive brain: Insights from developmental cognitive neuroscience. *Nature Reviews Neuroscience*, *16*(10), 606.

Aslin, R. N. (2007). What's in a look? *Developmental Science*, *10*(1), 48–53. doi: 10.1111/j.1467-7687.2007.00563.x

(2012). Infant eyes: A window on cognitive development. *Infancy*, *17*(1), 126–140. doi: 10.1111/j.1532-7078.2011.00097.x

Atkinson, J., Braddick, O., & Moar, K. (1977). Development of contrast sensitivity over the first 3 months of life in the human infant. *Vision Research*, *17*(9), 1037–1044.

Baillargeon, R. (1987). Object permanence in 3½- and 4½-month-old infants. *Developmental Psychology*, *23*(5), 655–664. doi: 10.1037/0012-1649.23.5.655

(2002). The acquisition of physical knowledge in infancy: A summary in eight lessons. In U. Goswami (Ed.), *The Blackwell handbook of childhood cognitive development* (Vol. 1, pp. 46–83). Malden, MA: Blackwell.

Bertenthal, B., & von Hofsten, C. (1998). Eye, head and trunk control: The foundation for manual development. *Neuroscience & Biobehavioral Reviews*, *22*(4), 515–520.

Bornstein, M. H., Mash, C., Arterberry, M. E., & Manian, N. (2012). Object perception in 5-month-old infants of clinically depressed and nondepressed mothers. *Infant Behavior and Development*, *35*(1), 150–157.

Braddick, O. J., Wattam-Bell, J., & Atkinson, J. (1986). Orientation-specific cortical responses develop in early infancy. *Nature*, *320*(6063), 617–619.

Bradley, R., & Corwyn, R. (2002). Socioeconomic status and child development. *Annual Review of Psychology*, *53*, 371–399. doi: 10.1146/annurev.psych.53.100901.135233

Breznitz, Z., & Friedman, S. L. (1988). Toddlers' concentration: Does maternal depression make a difference? *Journal of Child Psychology and Psychiatry*, *29*(3), 267–279.

Bronson, G. W. (1990). Changes in infants' visual scanning across the 2- to 14-week age period. *Journal of Experimental Child Psychology*, *49*, 101–125.

Bulf, H., & Valenza, E. (2013). Object-based visual attention in 8-month-old infants: Evidence from an eye-tracking study. *Developmental Psychology*, *49*(10), 1909–1918. doi: 10.1037/a0031310

Bushnell, I. W. R. (2001). Mother's face recognition in newborn infants: Learning and memory. *Infant and Child Development*, *10*(1–2), 67–74. doi: 10.1002/icd.248

Canfield, R. L., & Haith, M. M. (1991). Young infants' visual expectations for symmetric and asymmetric stimulus sequences. *Developmental Psychology*, *27*, 198–208.

Carrasco, M. (2011). Visual attention: The past 25 years. *Vision Research*, *51*(13), 1484–1525.

Casey, B. J., & Richards, J. E. (1988). Sustained visual attention in young infants measured with an adapted version of the visual preference paradigm. *Child Development*, *59*(6), 1514–1521.

Clearfield, M. W., & Jedd, K. E. (2012). The effects of socio-economic status on infant attention. *Infant and Child Development*, *22*(1), 53–67. doi: 10.1002/icd.1770

Cohen, L. B., & Cashon, C. H. (2003). Infant perception and cognition. In R. M. Lerner, M. A. Easterbrooks, & J. Mistry (Eds.), *Handbook of psychology: Developmental psychology* (Vol. 6, pp. 65–89). Hoboken, NJ: John Wiley & Sons.

Colombo, J. (2001). The development of visual attention in infancy. *Annual Review of Psychology*, *52*(1), 337–367. doi: 10.1146/annurev.psych.52.1.337

Colombo, J., & Cheatham, C. L. (2006). The emergence and basis of endogenous attention in infancy and early childhood. *Advances in Child Development and Behavior*, *34*, 283.

Colombo, J., Mitchell, D. W., Coldren, J. T., & Freeseman, L. J. (1991). Individual differences in infant visual attention: Are short lookers faster processors or feature processors? *Child Development*, *62*(6), 1247–1257. doi: 10.1111/j.1467–8624.1991.tb01603.x

Courage, M. L., Reynolds, G. D., & Richards, J. E. (2006). Infants' attention to patterned stimuli: Developmental change from 3 to 12 months of age. *Child Development*, *77*(3), 680–695.

Courchesne, E., Ganz, L., & Norcia, A. M. (1981). Event-related brain potentials to human faces in infants. *Child Development*, *52*(3), 804–811.

Csibra, G., & Volein, A. (2008). Infants can infer the presence of hidden objects from referential gaze information. *British Journal of Developmental Psychology*, *26*, 1–11.

Dannemiller, J. L. (2005). Motion popout in selective visual orienting at 4.5 but not at 2 months in human infants. *Infancy*, 8(3), 201–216.

de Boer, T., Scott, L. S., & Nelson, C. A. (2007). Methods for acquiring and analyzing infant event-related potentials. In M. de Haan (Ed.), *Infant EEG and event-related potentials* (pp. 5–37). New York, NY: Psychology Press.

Desimone, R., & Duncan, J. (1995). Neural mechanisms of selective visual attention. *Annual Reviews of Neuroscience*, *18*, 193–222. doi: 10.1016/j.cub.2014.02.049

DiPietro, J. A., Bornstein, M. H., Hahn, C. S., Costigan, K., & Achy-Brou, A. (2007). Fetal heart rate and variability: Stability and prediction to developmental outcomes in early childhood. *Child Development*, *78*(6), 1788–1798.

Ellis, A. E., Xiao, N. G., Lee, K., & Oakes, L. M. (2017). Scanning of own- versus other-race faces in infants from racially diverse or homogenous communities. *Developmental Psychobiology*, *59*(5), 613–627. doi: 10.1002/dev.21527

Elsabbagh, M., Volein, A., Holmboe, K., Tucker, L., Csibra, G., Baron-Cohen, S., … Johnson, M. H. (2009). Visual orienting in the early broader autism phenotype: Disengagement and facilitation. *Journal of Child Psychology and Psychiatry*, *50*(5), 637–642.

Emberson, L. L., & Amso, D. (2012). Learning to sample: Eye tracking and fMRI indices of changes in object perception. *Journal of Cognitive Neuroscience*, *24*, 2030–2042. doi: 10.1162/jocn_a_00259

Fair, J., Flom, R., Jones, J., & Martin, J. (2012). Perceptual learning: 12-month-olds' discrimination of monkey faces. *Child Development*, *83*(6), 1996–2006.

Fantz, R. L. (1956). A method for studying early visual development. *Perceptual and Motor Skills*, *6*, 13–15. doi: 10.2466/pms.1956.6.g.13

    (1963). Pattern vision in newborn infants. *Science*, *140*(3564), 296–297. doi: 10.1126/science.140.3564.296

Farroni, T., Massaccesi, S., Pividori, D., & Johnson, M. H. (2004). Gaze following in newborns. *Infancy*, *5*, 39–60.

Field, T., Healy, B., & LeBlanc, W. G. (1989). Sharing and synchrony of behavior states and heart rate in nondepressed versus depressed mother–infant interactions. *Infant Behavior and Development*, *12*(3), 357–376.

Franchak, J. M., & Adolph, K. E. (2010). Visually guided navigation: Head-mounted eye-tracking of natural locomotion in children and adults. *Vision Research, 50*(24), 2766–2774. doi: 10.1016/j.visres.2010.09.024

Frank, M. C., Amso, D., & Johnson, S. P. (2014). Visual search and attention to faces during early infancy. *Journal of Experimental Child Psychology, 118*(1), 13–26. doi: 10.1016/j.jecp.2013.08.012

Frank, M. C., Vul, E., & Johnson, S. P. (2009). Development of infants' attention to faces during the first year. *Cognition, 110*, 160–170.

Frick, J. E., & Richards, J. E. (2001). Individual differences in infants' recognition of briefly presented visual stimuli. *Infancy, 2*(3), 331–352. doi: 10.1207/S15327078IN0203_3

Gaither, S. E., Pauker, K., & Johnson, S. P. (2012). Biracial and monoracial infant own-race face perception: An eye-tracking study. *Developmental Science, 15*(6), 775–782.

Gibson, E. (2000). Perceptual learning in development: Some basic concepts. *Ecological Psychology, 12*(4), 295–302. doi: 10.1207/S15326969ECO1204_04

Gilbert, C. D., & Sigman, M. (2007). Brain states: Top-down influences in sensory processing. *Neuron, 54*(5), 677–696.

Grunau, R. E., Weinberg, J., & Whitfield, M. F. (2004). Neonatal procedural pain and pre-term infant cortisol response to novelty at 8 months. *Pediatrics, 114*(1), e77-e84.

Grunau, R. E., Whitfield, M. F., & Fay, T. B. (2004). Psychosocial and academic characteristics of extremely low birth weight (≤ 800 g) adolescents who are free of major impairment compared with term-born control subjects. *Pediatrics, 114*(6), e725-e732.

Haith, M. M. (1980). *Rules that babies look by: The organization of newborn visual activity*. Hillsdale, NJ: Lawrence Erlbaum Associates.

Hart, B., & Risley, T. R. (1995). *Meaningful differences in the everyday experiences of young American children*. Baltimore, MD: Paul H. Brookes.

Hoehl, S., Reid, V. M., Mooney, J., & Striano, T. (2008). What are you looking at? Infants' neural processing of an adult's object-directed eye gaze. *Developmental Science, 11*, 10–16.

Holmqvist, K., Nyström, M., Andersson, R., Dewhurst, R., Jarodzka, H., & van de Weijer, J. (2011). *Eye tracking: A comprehensive guide to methods and measures*. Oxford: Oxford University Press.

Hood, B. M. (1995). Visual selective attention in the human infant: A neuroscientific approach. In C. Rovee-Collier & L. Lipsitt (Eds.), *Advances in infancy research* (Vol. 9, pp. 163–216). Norwood, NJ: Ablex.

Hood, B. M., Willen, J. D., & Driver, J. (1998). Adult's eyes trigger shifts of visual attention in human infants. *Psychological Science, 9*(2), 131–134. doi: 10.1111/1467-9280.00024

Hurley, K. B., & Oakes, L. M. (2015). Experience and distribution of attention: Pet exposure and infants' scanning of animal images. *Journal of Cognition and Development, 16*(1), 11–30. doi: 10.1080/15248372.2013.833922

Hutchinson, E. A., de Luca, C. R., Doyle, L. W., Roberts, G., & Anderson, P. J. (2013). School-age outcomes of extremely preterm or extremely low birth weight children. *Pediatrics, 131*(4), e1053–e1061. doi: 10.1542/peds.2012-2311

Hwang, K., Velanova, K., & Luna, B. (2010). Strengthening of top-down frontal cognitive control networks underlying the development of inhibitory control: A functional magnetic resonance imaging effective connectivity study. *Journal of Neuroscience, 30*(46), 15535–15545. doi: 10.1523/JNEUROSCI.2825-10.2010

Jankowski, J. J., Rose, S. A., & Feldman, J. F. (2001). Modifying the distribution of attention in infants. *Child Development, 72*(2), 339–351. doi: 10.1111/1467-8624.00282

Johnson, M. H. (1990). Cortical maturation and the development of visual attention in early infancy. *Journal of Cognitive Neuroscience, 2*, 81–95. doi: 10.1162/jocn.1990.2.2.81

(1995). The inhibition of automatic saccades in early infancy. *Developmental Psychobiology, 28*, 281–291. doi: 10.1002/dev.420280504

Johnson, M. H., Posner, M. I., & Rothbart, M. K. (1991). Components of visual orienting in early infancy: Contingency learning, anticipatory looking, and disengaging. *Journal of Cognitive Neuroscience, 3*, 335–344. doi: 10.1162/jocn.1991.3.4.335

Johnson, S. P., Amso, D., & Slemmer, J. A. (2003). Development of object concepts in infancy: Evidence for early learning in an eye-tracking paradigm. *Proceedings of the National Academy of Sciences, 100*(18), 10568–10573. doi: 10.1073/pnas.1630655100

Johnson, S. P., Slemmer, J. A., & Amso, D. (2004). Where infants look determines how they see: Eye movements and object perception performance in 3-month-olds. *Infancy, 6*, 185–201.

Jones, W., & Klin, A. (2013). Attention to eyes is present but in decline in 2–6-month-old infants later diagnosed with autism. *Nature, 504*(7480), 427.

Jöbsis, F. F. (1977). Noninvasive, infrared monitoring of cerebral and myocardial oxygen sufficiency and circulatory parameters. *Science, 198*, 1264–1267.

Káldy, Z., & Leslie, A. M. (2003). Identification of objects in 9-month-old infants: integrating "what" and "where" information. *Developmental Science, 6*, 360–373.

Klein, R. M. (2000). Inhibition of return. *Trends in Cognitive Sciences, 4*(4), 138–147.

Konrad, K., Neufang, S., Thiel, C. M., Specht, K., Hanisch, C., Fan, J., … Fink, G. R. (2005). Development of attentional networks: An fMRI study with children and adults. *NeuroImage, 28*(2), 429–439.

Kramer, M. S., Goulet, L., Lydon, J., Seguin, L., McNamara, H., Dassa, C., … Koren, G. (2001). Socio-economic disparities in preterm birth: Casual pathways and mechanisms. *Pediatric and Perinatal Epidemiology, 15*(Suppl. 2), 104–123.

Kretch, K. S., Franchak, J. M., & Adolph, K. E. (2014). Crawling and walking infants see the world differently. *Child Development, 85*(4), 1503–1518. doi: 10.1111/cdev.12206

Kuhlmeier, V., Wynn, K., & Bloom, P. (2003). Attribution of dispositional states by 12-month-olds. *Psychological Science, 14*(5), 402–408. doi: 10.1111/1467-9280.01454

Lancaster, C. A., Gold, K. J., Flynn, H. A., Yoo, H., Marcus, S. M., & Davis, M. M. (2010). Risk factors for depressive symptoms during pregnancy: A systematic review. *American Journal of Obstetrics and Gynecology, 202*, 5–14. doi: 10.1016/j.ajog.2009.09.007

Lawson, K. R., & Ruff, H. A. (2004). Early focused attention predicts outcome for children born prematurely. *Journal of Developmental & Behavioral Pediatrics, 25*(6), 399–406.

Leppänen, J. M., Cataldo, J. K., Bosquet Enlow, M., & Nelson, C. A. (2018). Early development of attention to threat-related facial expressions. *PLoS One*, *13*(5), e0197424. doi: 10.1371/journal.pone.0197424

Lewis, M., & Brooks-Gunn, J. (1981). Visual attention at three months as a predictor of cognitive functioning at two years of age. *Intelligence*, *5*(2), 131–140.

Lloyd-Fox, S., Blasi, A., & Elwell, C.E. (2010). Illuminating the developing brain: The past, present and future of functional near infrared spectroscopy. *Neuroscience & Biobehavioral Reviews*, *34*(3), 269–284.

Markant, J., Ackerman, L. K., Nussenbaum, K., & Amso, D. (2016). Selective attention neutralizes the adverse effects of low socioeconomic status on memory in 9-month-old infants. *Developmental Cognitive Neuroscience*, *18*, 26–33.

Markant, J., & Amso, D. (2013). Selective memories: Infants' encoding is enhanced in selection via suppression. *Developmental Science*, *16*, 926–940.

(2014). Leveling the playing field: Attention mitigates the effect of IQ on memory. *Cognition*, *131*(2), 195–204.

(2016). The development of selective attention orienting is an agent of change in learning and memory efficacy. *Infancy*, *21*(2), 154–176.

Markant, J., Oakes, L. M., & Amso, D. (2016). Visual selective attention biases contribute to the other-race effect among 9-month-old infants. *Developmental Psychobiology*, *58*(3), 355–365.

Markant, J., Worden, M. S., & Amso, D. (2015). Not all attention orienting is created equal: Recognition memory is enhanced when attention orienting involves distractor suppression. *Neurobiology of Learning and Memory*, *120*, 28–40. doi: 10.1016/j.nlm.2015.02.006

McLoyd, V. C. (1998). Socioeconomic disadvantage and child development. *American Psychologist*, *53*(2), 185–204. doi: 10.1037/0003-066X.53.2.185

Mundy, P. (2003). Annotation: The neural basis of social impairments in autism – the role of the dorsal medial-frontal cortex and anterior cingulate system. *Journal of Child Psychology and Psychiatry*, *44*(6), 793–809.

Mundy, P., Block, J., Delgado, C., Pomares, Y., van Hecke, A. V., & Parlade, M. V. (2007). Individual differences and the development of joint attention in infancy. *Child Development*, *78*(3), 938–954.

Mundy, P., & Newell, L. (2007). Attention, joint attention, and social cognition. *Current Directions in Psychological Science*, *16*(5), 269–274.

Oakes, L. M., Kannass, K. N., & Shaddy, D. J. (2002). Developmental changes in endogenous control of attention: The role of target familiarity on infants' distraction latency. *Child Development*, *73*(6), 1644–1655. doi: 10.1111/1467–8624.00496

Pascalis, O., de Haan, M., & Nelson, C.A. (2002). Is face processing species-specific during the first year of life? *Science*, *296*, 1321–1323.

Posner, M. I. (Ed.). (2004). *Cognitive neuroscience of attention*. New York, NY: Guilford Press.

Posner, M. I., & Petersen, S. E. (1990). The attention system of the human brain. *Annual Review of Neuroscience*, *13*, 25–42. doi: 10.1146/annurev.ne.13.030190.000325

Posner, M. I., Rafal, R. D., & Choate, L.S. (1985). Inhibition of return: Neural basis and function. *Cognitive Neuropsychology*, *2*, 211–228.

Reid, V. M., Dunn, K., Young, R. J., Amu, J., Donovan, T., & Reissland, N. (2017). The human fetus preferentially engages with face-like visual stimuli. *Current Biology*, *27*(12), 1825–1828.

Reid, V. M., Striano, T., Kaufman, J., & Johnson, M. H. (2004). Eye-gaze cueing facilitates neural processing of objects in 4-month-old infants. *NeuroReport*, *15*, 2553–2555.

Reynolds, G. D., Guy, M. W., & Zhang, D. (2011). Neural correlates of individual differences in infant visual attention and recognition memory. *Infancy*, *16*(4), 368–391. doi: 10.1111/j.1532-7078.2010.00060.x

Reynolds, G. D., & Richards, J. E. (2005). Familiarization, attention, and recognition memory in infancy: An event-related potential and cortical source localization study. *Developmental Psychology*, *41*(4), 598.

Richards, J. E. (2000). Localizing the development of covert attention in infants with scalp event-related potentials. *Developmental Psychology*, *36*(1), 91–108. doi: 10.1037/0012-1649.36.1.91

(2003). Attention affects the recognition of briefly presented visual stimuli in infants: An ERP study. *Developmental Science*, *6*(3), 312–328. doi: 10.1111/1467-7687.00287

Richards, J. E., & Casey, B. J. (1992). Development of sustained visual attention in the human infant. In B. A. Campbell & H. Hayne (Eds.), *Attention and information processing in infants and adults: perspectives from human and animal research* (pp. 30–60). Hillsdale, NJ: Lawrence Erlbaum Associates.

Rosander, K. (2007). Visual tracking and its relationship to cortical development. *Progress in Brain Research*, *164*, 105–122. doi: 10.1016/S0079-6123(07)64006-0

Rose, S. A., Feldman, J. F., & Jankowski, J. J. (2001). Attention and recognition memory in the 1st year of life: A longitudinal study of preterm and full-term infants. *Developmental Psychology*, *37*(1), 135.

(2012). Implications of infant cognition for executive functions at age 11. *Psychological Science*, *23*(11), 1345–55.

Ross-Sheehy, S., Oakes, L. M., & Luck, S. J. (2003). The development of visual short-term memory capacity in infants. *Child Development*, *74*, 1807–1822.

Ruff, H. A., Lawson, K. R., Parrinello, R., & Weissberg, R. (1990). Long-term stability of individual differences in sustained attention in the early years. *Child Development*, *61*(1), 60–75.

Salapatek, P., & Kessen, W. (1966). Visual scanning of triangles by the human newborn. *Journal of Experimental Child Psychology*, *3*, 155–167.

Schlesinger, M., & Amso, D. (2013). Image free-viewing as intrinsically motivated exploration: Estimating the learnability of center-of-gaze image samples in infants and adults. *Frontiers in Psychology*. doi: 10.3389/fpsyg.2013.00802

Schoenfeld, M. A., Hopf, J. M., Merkel, C., Heinze, H. J., & Hillyard, S. A. (2014). Object-based attention involves the sequential activation of feature-specific cortical modules. *Nature Neuroscience*, *17*(4), 619–624.

Scott, L. S., & Monesson, A. (2010). Experience-dependent neural specialization during infancy. *Neuropsychologia*, *48*(6), 1857–1861.

Senju, A., Csibra, G., & Johnson, M. (2008). Understanding the referential nature of looking: Infants' preference for object-directed gaze. *Cognition*, *108*, 303–319.

Sigman, M., Cohen, S. E., & Beckwith, L. (1997). Why does infant attention predict adolescent intelligence? *Infant Behavior and Development*, *20*(2), 133–140.

Simion, F., Regolin, L., & Bulf, H. (2008). A predisposition for biological motion in the newborn baby. *Proceedings of the National Academy of Sciences*, *105*(2), 809–813. doi: 10.1073/pnas.0707021105

Simion, F., Valenza, E., Umiltà, C., & Barba, B. D. (1995). Inhibition of return in newborns is temporo-nasal asymmetrical. *Infant Behavior and Development*, *18*(2), 189–194.

Sommerville, J. A., Woodward, A. L., & Needham, A. (2005). Action experience alters 3-month-old infants' perception of others' actions. *Cognition*, *96*(1), B1–B11. doi: 10.1016/j.cognition.2004.07.004

Spelke, E. S., Katz, G., Purcell, S. E., Ehrlich, S. M., & Breinlinger, K. (1994). Early knowledge of object motion: Continuity and inertia. *Cognition*, *51*(2), 131–176. doi: 10.1016/0010-0277(94)90013-2

Striano, T., Chen, X., Cleveland, A., & Bradshaw, S. (2006). Joint attention social cues influence infant learning. *European Journal of Developmental Psychology*, *3*, 289–299.

Sugita, Y. (2008). Face perception in monkeys reared with no exposure to faces. *Proceedings of the National Academy of Sciences*, *105*(1), 394–398.

Tacke, N. F., Bailey, L. S., & Clearfield, M. W. (2015). Socio-economic status (SES) affects infants' selective exploration. *Infant and Child Development*, *24*(6), 571–586. doi: 10.1002/icd.1900

Tummeltshammer, K., & Amso, D. (2017). Top-down contextual knowledge guides visual attention in infancy. *Developmental Science*, 21(4), 1–9. doi: 10.1111/desc.12599

Valenza, E., Simion, F., & Umiltà, C. (1994). Inhibition of return in newborn infants. *Infant Behavior and Development*, *17*(3), 293–302.

Vogel, M., Monesson, A., & Scott, L.S. (2012). Building biases in infancy: The influence of race on face and voice emotion matching. *Developmental Science*, *15*(3), 359–372.

von Hofsten, C., & Rosander, K. (1997). Development of smooth pursuit tracking in young infants. *Vision Research*, *37*(13), 1799–1810.

Weissman, M. M., Leckman, J. F., Merikangas, K. R., Gammon, G. D., & Prusoff, B. A. (1984). Depression and anxiety disorders in parents and children: Results from the Yale Family Study. *Archives of General Psychiatry*, *41*(9), 845–852.

Wellman, H. M., Phillips, A. T., Dunphy-Lelii, S., & LaLonde, N. (2004). Infant social attention predicts preschool social cognition. *Developmental Science*, *7*(3), 283–288.

Werchan, D. M., & Amso, D. (2017). A novel ecological account of prefrontal cortex functional development. *Psychological Review*, *124*(6), 720–739. doi: 10.1037/rev0000078

Wheeler, A., Anzures, G., Quinn, P. C., Pascalis, O., Omrin, D. S., & Lee, K. (2011). Caucasian infants scan own- and other-race faces differently. *PloS One*, *6*(4), e18621.

Young, G. S., Merin, N., Rogers, S. J., & Ozonoff, S. (2009). Gaze behavior and affect at 6 months: Predicting clinical outcomes and language development in typically developing infants and infants at risk for autism. *Developmental Science*, *12*(5), 798–814

Yu, C., & Smith, L. B. (2016). The social origins of sustained attention in one-year-old human infants. *Current Biology*, *26*(9), 1235–1240. doi: 10.1016/j.cub.2016.03.026

Zweigenbaum, L., Bryson, S., Rogers, T., Roberts, W., Brian, J., & Szatmari, P. (2005). Behavioral manifestations of autism in the first year of life. *International Journal of Developmental Neuroscience*, *23*(2–3), 143–152.

8 Infants' Perception of Auditory Patterns

Laura K. Cirelli and Sandra E. Trehub*

Unlike visual patterns, which are typically distributed in space, auditory patterns are necessarily distributed in time. As a result, listeners must allocate their attention over time, implicating memory processes as they track global as well as local features of patterns. Because of the cognitive and experiential limitations of infants, one might expect their perception of auditory patterns to differ drastically from that of adults. There are notable adult–infant differences, of course, but there are also parallels, which stem largely from infants' holistic approach to auditory pattern processing and their biological predispositions.

Differences between infants and adults are most noticeable in basic aspects of auditory perception (e.g., detection thresholds, discrimination of simple sounds). We provide a brief review of these basic abilities in infancy because several authoritative accounts are available elsewhere (e.g., Abdala & Keefe, 2012; Lasky & Williams, 2005; Werner, 2017). Our principal focus is on infants' processing of auditory patterns, which is central to understanding auditory perception in the contexts of everyday life. Foremost among the challenges of infant listeners is the separation of target auditory signals from the complex sound mixtures that simultaneously bombard their ears – a process known as *auditory scene analysis*. Arguably, the two most important domains of auditory pattern processing for infants, both of which have critical sociocultural ramifications, are speech, which is addressed by Reh and Werker in this volume (Chapter 21), and music, which is highlighted in this chapter. In fact, music perception is the realm that best exemplifies infants' relational processing of pitch and temporal patterns. Although the available research in this domain is largely restricted to Western infants, the findings are largely generalizable across cultures despite possible variations in the developmental timetable.

8.1 Basic Auditory Abilities

Auditory events produce compressions and rarefactions in the air, which normally pass through the outer ear and cause vibrations in the middle

* The authors acknowledge support from the Social Sciences and Humanities Research Council of Canada and the Natural Sciences and Engineering Research Council of Canada.

ear. These vibrations, which are transferred through membranes, bones, and fluids, are amplified as they reach the cochlea, where they are converted into electrochemical signals. The electrochemical signals are transmitted to auditory areas of the brainstem and midbrain before being relayed to the auditory cortex via the thalamus (see Lasky & Williams, 2005 for further details).

8.1.1 The Auditory System: Anatomical, Physiological, and Neural Development

The peripheral and central auditory system develops more rapidly than the visual system, the former receiving external as well as internal input in the prenatal period. Because the ear is filled with fluid prenatally, sounds are transmitted to the inner ear largely by bone conduction (Sohmer, Perez, Sichel, Priner, & Freeman, 2001). Fetal responses to sound have been documented by 25 weeks of gestational age (e.g., Birnholz & Benacerraf, 1983), but responsiveness increases substantially by 35 weeks when the cochlea is relatively mature, the vibrating bones of the middle ear are ossified, and the relevant neural pathways are online (see Lasky & Williams, 2005 for a review).

The auditory cortex undergoes rapid growth in the early postnatal months. By 3 months of age, peak synaptic density is achieved (Huttenlocher & Dabholkar, 1997), and the process of axon myelination begins (Pujol et al., 2006). Axonal maturation may be achieved in deep layers of the auditory cortex by 4 months of age, but it reportedly continues in superficial layers into early adolescence (Moore & Guan, 2001). Recent evidence suggests, however, that axonal maturation is adult-like in all cortical layers by 9 months of age (Pundir et al., 2012), with synaptic pruning continuing into early adulthood (Pundir et al., 2016). In fact, adult-like cortical responses to rich, naturalistic auditory patterns (e.g., sung lullabies) are evident by 3 months of age (Wild et al., 2017).

Early exposure to sound influences the time course of specialization in the auditory cortex. The effects of noise on cochleotopic organization of the auditory cortex are evident in a number of species, with continuous (E. F. Chang & Merzenich, 2003) and pulsed white noise (Zhang, Bao, & Merzenich, 2002) delaying and disrupting auditory cortical specialization. Although congenital deafness delays the onset of such specialization in the human brain, suitable prostheses (e.g., hearing aids, cochlear implants) before the end of the putative sensitive period – by 3.5 years of age, according to some estimates – result in reorganization and age-appropriate neural responses within 6 to 8 months (Sharma, Dorman, & Kral, 2005). Moreover, there is increasing consensus that earlier interventions for congenital deafness (i.e., by 6 months of age) foster optimal outcomes (Papacharalampous, Nikolopoulos, Davilis, Xenellis, & Korres, 2011; Yoshinaga-Itano, 1999). Early intervention requires early diagnosis, which has spurred the adoption of hearing screening in the newborn period or by 1 month of age in many countries (World Health Organization, 2010). Interestingly, early visual deprivation (i.e., congenital blindness) results in auditory enhancement, including superior discrimination thresholds for speech and music (Arnaud, Gracco, & Ménard, 2018).

8.1.2 Auditory Perception in the Prenatal Period

The soundscape within the womb differs dramatically from that at birth (Parga et al., 2018), partly because infants have access to internal as well as external sounds and partly because of the predominance of bone conduction. Intrauterine recordings of external sounds, either by hydrophone placement in the uterus or electronic stethoscope on the maternal abdomen, reveal significant attenuation of high- and mid-frequency sounds, but little attenuation of frequencies below 1,000 Hz (Parga et al., 2018; Richards, Frentzen, Gerhardt, McCann, & Abrams, 1992), which makes vowel sounds more salient than consonant sounds and fundamental frequency contours more salient than spectral information (S. L. Smith, Gerhardt, Griffiths, Huang, & Abrams, 2003). Internal sounds are subject to lesser attenuation than external sounds, resulting in an 8 dB enhancement for the maternal voice relative to other voices (Richards et al., 1992). Note, however, that maternal bowel noise remains the most prominent sound in the womb in terms of its incidence and intensity (Parga et al., 2018).

Although knowledge of basic auditory abilities in the fetal period is limited, there is evidence of sensitivity to frequency change (e.g., Draganova et al., 2005) and auditory learning, especially in relation to complex patterns. For example, fetuses differentiate their mother's voice from other voices (Kisilevsky et al., 2009), as indicated by fetal heart rate. Because sounds are low-pass filtered in the uterine environment (i.e., high-frequency sounds attenuated substantially), fetal recognition of the mother's voice is likely to be based on its pitch and rhythmic patterning rather than its timbre or voice quality. In fact, the salience of pitch contours is evident in 1-month-old infants' distinctive cardiac responses to a descending melodic contour, but only for those who had repeated prenatal exposure to that contour (Granier-Deferre, Bassereau, Ribeiro, Jacquet, & DeCasper, 2011).

8.1.3 Auditory Perception in Infancy

Infants detect and differentiate a wide range of sound frequencies (Olsho, Koch, & Halpin, 1987), but their resolution is well below that of adults. They also exhibit enhanced processing of sounds between 2,000 and 4,000 Hz (Olsho, Koch, Carter, Halpin, & Spetner, 1988). By 6 months of age infants' and adults' thresholds differ considerably less at high frequencies than at lower frequencies (Trehub, Schneider, & Endman, 1980). Development continues to proceed more rapidly in the high-frequency range than for low and middle frequencies, with maximal sensitivity attained by 5 years of age for 10,000 Hz stimuli, 8 years of age for stimuli between 2,000 and 4,000 Hz, and 10 years of

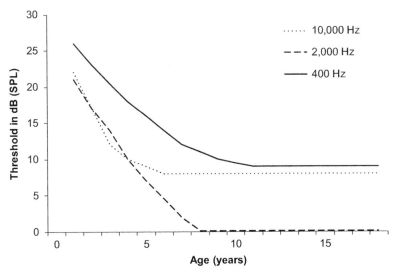

Figure 8.1. *Thresholds for high-, middle-, and low-frequency bands at different ages.*
Source: Values are estimated from Trehub et al. (1988).

age for stimuli between 400 and 1,000 Hz (see Figure 8.1) (Trehub, Schneider, Morrongiello, & Thorpe, 1988).

Infants' temporal resolution is also deficient relative to that of adults (Werner, Marean, Halpin, Spetner, & Gillenwater, 1992), but 6-month-olds detect gaps as small as 12 milliseconds in the context of 500 Hz Gaussian tone bursts (Trehub, Schneider, & Henderson, 1995). Nevertheless, infants' resolution of pitch and timing is sufficient for the processing of complex auditory patterns such as speech, music, and environmental sounds at conventional (i.e., suprathreshold) amplitude levels. In principle, infants' deficiency in selective attention (Bargones & Werner, 1994) could pose problems for pattern processing. However, on the view that our perceptual systems are designed to search for regularities in the environment (Jones, 1976), infants may fare well as pattern processors despite their sensory and cognitive limitations.

8.1.4 Analysis of Auditory Scenes

Perceiving the soundscapes of everyday life and understanding their significance depend on parsing simultaneously occurring sounds into separate units or *auditory objects* (i.e., simultaneous grouping), grouping the units into *streams* that unfold over time (i.e., sequential grouping of speech sequences, melodies, environmental sounds), and linking the streams to specific sources – persons, objects, or events. The process of separating the disparate components of a complex auditory environment and integrating or maintaining the coherence of separate streams is known as *auditory scene analysis* (Bregman, 1990).

Auditory scene analysis involves Gestalt principles such as proximity (i.e., the grouping of elements based on their proximity to one another), similarity (i.e., grouping based on the similarity of elements), and closure (i.e., grouping based on completion of a form or entity). For example, sounds that are close in frequency (proximity) and those with the same timbre (similarity) are grouped together (i.e., integrated) and segregated from other sounds that differ in those respects (Rose & Moore, 2000). A soft sound occluded by bursts of a louder sound will be heard as continuous rather than intermittent (closure) (Cooke & Brown, 1993). These principles are thought to operate in an automatic or bottom-up manner (Bregman, 1990) in conjunction with maturational changes in the auditory system (Werner, 2017). Other aspects of auditory scene analysis, such as the recognition of a familiar voice in a background of other voices, are influenced by attention and experience (Sussman & Steinschneider, 2009).

8.1.4.1 *Auditory Object Perception*

Because natural sounds contain energy at the fundamental frequency (perceived as the pitch of those sounds) and at higher frequencies, or *overtones*, their identification as unified auditory objects depends on the integration of those frequencies. For pitched sounds, which are relevant for communicative signals such as speech or music, the overtones are integer multiples of the fundamental frequency. For example, a complex sound with a fundamental frequency of 200 Hz has overtones at 400 Hz, 600 Hz, 800 Hz, and so on. Note that these frequency components of a complex sound are related by simple or small-integer ratios (e.g., 400 and 200 Hz are related by a 2:1 ratio, and 600 and 400 Hz are related by a 3:2 ratio). The relative intensity of these harmonics as well as their attack and decay contribute to the perception of timbre. Adults perceive concurrent sounds at harmonic frequencies as a single auditory object, but slight mistuning of a single harmonic creates the percept of two sound sources (Lin & Hartmann, 1998). Note that the mistuned harmonic would be related to the fundamental frequency by a complex or large-integer ratio.

It is unclear whether automatic integration of harmonic frequencies is present from birth. Newborns exhibit event-related responses to mistuning for some stimuli but not others (Bendixen et al., 2015). Moreover, 4-month-olds but not 2-month-olds show differential electroencephalographic (EEG) responses to mistuned harmonics, and the response becomes more adult-like in subsequent months (Folland, Butler, Payne, & Trainor, 2015). In line with these findings, infants as young as 4 months of age perceive a stimulus with in-tune harmonics as a single auditory event (i.e., linking it to a single bouncing ball) and one with mistuned harmonics as two events (i.e., linking it to two bouncing balls) (N. A. Smith, Folland, Martinez, & Trainor, 2017).

These relations among the components of natural, single sounds also influence the perception of simultaneous combinations of pitched tones, or harmonic intervals. In addition to the unison (two sounds with the same fundamental frequency, or 1:1 fundamental frequency ratio) and octave (2:1 ratio),

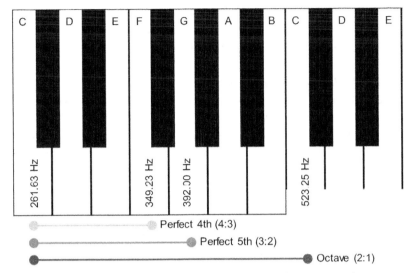

Figure 8.2. *Keyboard beginning on middle C and ending on E in the subsequent octave. Some adjacent white notes are separated by 2 semitones, as between C and D, and others are separated by 1 semitone, as between E and F.*

the perfect fifth (7 semitones or 3:2 ratio) and perfect fourth (5 semitones or 4:3 ratio) intervals occur in many musical cultures (Sachs, 1943) (See Figure 8.2).

Across cultures group singing commonly occurs in unison (i.e., at the same pitch level) except that men and women typically sing an octave apart because of differences in their vocal anatomy. The aforementioned tone combinations with small-integer frequency ratios (unison, octave, perfect fifth, perfect fourth) are considered *consonant* or pleasant sounding by Western music theorists and by musically trained or untrained Western listeners (Plomp & Levelt, 1965). These tone combinations exhibit *harmonicity* because of overlapping overtones or harmonics of the upper and lower tones. The coincident overtones may enhance pitch clarity, facilitating the processing of these tone combinations. By contrast, the nonoverlapping overtones of tone combinations with fundamental frequencies related by large-integer ratios (e.g., 6 semitones or 45:32) can generate interference on the basilar membrane, resulting in rapid amplitude fluctuations that tend to be perceived as *dissonant* or unpleasant by Western listeners (Plomp & Levelt, 1965).

Perhaps because of differences in pitch clarity and ease of processing, infants differentiate the so-called *consonant* tone combinations from the *dissonant* combinations (Plantinga & Trehub, 2014; Trainor & Heinmiller, 1998; Zentner & Kagan, 1996), and they detect changes to consonant intervals more readily than comparable changes to dissonant intervals (Schellenberg & Trehub, 1996). In fact, infants categorize tone combinations on the basis of qualities linked to their classification as consonant or dissonant (Schellenberg &

Trainor, 1996). Newborns' evoked responses are also consistent with the differentiation of consonant and dissonant intervals (Virtala, Huotilainen, Partanen, Fellman, & Tervaniemi, 2013).

8.1.4.2 *Auditory Stream Segregation*

Once auditory objects are isolated from competing sound sources, they must be tracked over time. Adults' perception of sequentially unfolding streams is typically explored with tasks that cannot be used with infants. Nevertheless, there is suggestive evidence that infants segregate auditory streams on the basis of differences in frequency (N. A. Smith & Trainor, 2011) and timbre (McAdams & Bertoncini, 1997).

Stream segregation on the basis of spatial separation (Darwin & Hukin, 1999) is more challenging for infants. Although infants can localize sounds, they require greater sound separation than adults to do so. Adult–infant differences in minimum audible angle (i.e., the minimum sound separation required for localization) narrow considerably between 2 months and 2 years of age, disappearing altogether by about 5 years of age (Litovsky, 1997).

Infants are typically exposed to speech in the context of other sounds that mask some acoustic elements of the target signal (i.e., energetic masking) or that are acoustically distinct but potentially distracting (i.e., informational masking) because of limited control of attention (Bargones & Werner, 1994). As early as 5 months of age infants perceive speech – a familiar word or their own name, for example – in a background of other talkers or non-speech sounds (Bernier & Soderstrom, 2018; Newman, 2005). Like adults, they have greater success with familiar voices (e.g., the mother's voice) than with unfamiliar voices (Newman, 2005). When infants succeed in focusing on the target voice, however, they typically require a signal-to-noise ratio of 5 to 10 dB (i.e., signal 5 to 10 dB greater than the noise) in contrast to a signal-to-noise ratio of –5 to –10 dB (i.e., noise 5 to 10 dB greater than the signal) for adults with comparable stimuli. Noise has adverse effects on infant learning as well as perception (Erickson & Newman, 2017; McMillan & Saffran, 2016). Moreover, the adverse effects of noise on speech perception persist well beyond infancy into the teen years (Wightman & Kistler, 2005), which implies a protracted developmental course for selective attention and strategic listening.

Perceiving a target voice in the context of other vocal or nonvocal sounds is facilitated by timbral similarity or difference (i.e., spectral features of the voice), spatial separation (Broadbent, 1952), word and talker familiarity (Newman, 2005), as well as talker-specific differences in timing (Remez, Fellowes, & Nagel, 2007) and pitch patterning (Bergeson & Trehub, 2007). For infants, tracking their mother's voice is likely to be facilitated by the unique timbre or spectral shape (Piazza, Iordan, & Lew-Williams, 2017) and by the unique melodic patterns (Bergeson & Trehub, 2007) in her infant-directed speech.

8.1.5 Sound–Meaning Associations

Auditory (nonspeech) patterns can have meanings that are discernible, even for infants. Everyday observations reveal infants' anticipatory responses to the sound of approaching footsteps or the ring of a doorbell. These associations have comparable specificity to word meanings. Infants also exhibit broader or more general links between sounds and meanings. Just as 4-month-olds link *bubu* with round objects and *kiki* with spiky objects (Ozturk, Krehm, & Vouloumanos, 2013), they also link high and low pitch with high and low spatial locations (Walker et al., 2010). At 6 but not 4 months of age, infants link ascending frequency sweeps (300–1,700 Hz) with small objects and descending frequency sweeps with large objects (Fernández-Prieto, Navarra, & Pons, 2015), the age differences implicating experience or maturation. With static (unvarying frequency) rather than dynamic tones, however, 10-month-olds fail to link pitch and size, but they link high-pitched tones to bright objects rather than dark ones (Haryu & Kajikawa, 2012).

8.2 Music Processing: Model System for Auditory Pattern Perception

Music may be the ideal model system for the study of auditory pattern perception because it is universal, complex, and rule-governed in its vertical (simultaneous or harmonic) and horizontal (sequential or melodic) dimensions (Bregman, 1990; Dowling & Harwood, 1986). Like language, music has critical communicative and social implications, although its meanings are much less specific and transparent than those of language. Just as the human capacity for language in different historical and cultural contexts gives rise to distinctive languages, the capacity for music generates different musical systems that share certain features and functions (Savage, Brown, Sakai, & Currie, 2015). Note that the social power and broadcast range of music are dramatically increased by the possibility of coordinated, simultaneous productions by two or more persons in contrast to the turn-taking of conventional linguistic communication.

Some acoustic features are more prominent and more highly specified in music (e.g., pitch contours, precise relative pitch and timing) than in speech (Zatorre & Baum, 2012). Although the boundaries of music are fuzzy, members of a culture generally agree on the auditory patterns that constitute music. Music listening necessarily involves the perception of form or structure (Dowling & Harwood, 1986), which depends on "primitive" (bottom-up) processes as well as learned schemas that arise from incidental or deliberate exposure.

The indefinite, nonreferential meanings of music and the primary reliance of music perception on holistic or relational processing make this realm especially suitable for study with naive or immature listeners. It has become clear, moreover, that the implicit musical knowledge of musically untrained listeners is comparable in many respects to that of highly trained listeners (Bigand & Poulin-Charronnat, 2006), which implies that the requisite learning results from incidental exposure. In addition, parents throughout the world sing to infants (Trehub & Gudmundsdottir, 2019; Trehub & Trainor, 1998), and they do so with a special song repertoire and performing style that are identifiable across cultures (Mehr, Singh, York, Glowacki, & Krasnow, 2018; Trehub, Unyk, & Trainor, 1993a, 1993b). Finally, because music is inherently social and commonly transmitted orally across generations (Rubin, 1995), its structure is likely to be tailored, over time, to the processing capacities of listeners (Trehub, 2015).

8.2.1 Analysis of Musical Scenes

The melody line of music, whether vocal or instrumental, may have instrumental or vocal accompaniment. Cues from frequency proximity and timbre similarity facilitate the separation of those auditory streams (melody vs. accompaniment) while linking them as parts of the same auditory object (i.e., the musical performance). Interestingly, the EEG responses of 3- and 7-month-old infants parallel those of adults (Fujioka, Trainor, & Ross, 2008) in revealing separate memory traces for the high and low tones (often called high and low voices) of polyphonic stimuli and greater salience for high tones (Marie & Trainor, 2013, 2014), which typically carry the main melody line.

8.2.2 Temporal Processing

Grouping processes are implicated in organizing and maintaining the coherence of single streams of music. The temporal organization of music is hierarchical, involving the beat or pulse – the level at which we usually tap or clap to music, the meter – the repeating pattern of strong and weak beats (e.g., differentiating a march from a waltz) – and the rhythm, involving the relative durations of notes and silences. Infants' sensitivity to the temporal organization of speech and the influence of language-specific exposure on that sensitivity is considered elsewhere in this volume (see Reh & Werker, Chapter 21).

Newborns are sensitive to the beat of music (Winkler, Háden, Ladinig, Sziller, & Honing, 2009) and to the tempo of tone sequences (Háden, Honing, Török, & Winkler, 2015), as revealed by their EEG responses during sleep. A few months later, awake, alert infants discriminate small tempo changes but only for patterns that are intermediate in tempo (inter-onset intervals of 600 milliseconds) (Baruch & Drake, 1997). They differentiate contrasting rhythms or tone groupings (H. W. Chang & Trehub, 1977b) and, by 7 months of age, their relational processing of rhythm is evident in their recognition of specific rhythms (e.g., XX XX vs. XXX X) across changes in tempo (Trehub &

Thorpe, 1989). Even when tones in a sequence are of equal duration (e.g., XXXOOO), 6- to 9-month-olds group those tones on the basis of similar frequency, intensity, and timbre, with the consequence that temporal disruptions (e.g., small silent increments) within a group of tones (XXXO OO) are more readily detected than those between groups (XXX OOO) (Thorpe & Trehub, 1989). Similarly, pauses within a musical phrase are more readily detected than pauses between phrases (Krumhansl & Jusczyk, 1990).

Metrical regularity also influences infants' perception of musical patterns. For example, infants more readily detect pitch and timing changes to metrically regular patterns than to nonmetric patterns (Bergeson & Trehub, 2006; Trehub & Hannon, 2009). By 7 months of age, they exhibit neural entrainment to the beat as they listen to simple rhythmic sequences (Cirelli, Spinelli, Nozaradan, & Trainor, 2016). They also move rhythmically to rhythmic sound patterns such as music, but their movements are not aligned with the sounds (Zentner & Eerola, 2010). Despite claims that infants' movements exhibit some degree of tempo flexibility in the sense of faster movement to faster music (Rocha & Mareschal, 2017; Zentner & Eerola, 2010), faster movement may result from heightened arousal. In fact, rudimentary synchronization to music is not achieved until about 4 years of age (McAuley, Jones, Holub, Johnston, & Miller, 2006). By 8 months of age, however, infants seem to recognize synchronous movement in others, differentiating adult dancing that is synchronized with the beat from unsynchronized dancing (Hannon, Schachner, & Nave-Blodgett, 2017).

Infants' perception of rhythm is influenced by passive movement experienced in the course of listening. If 7-month-olds are bounced to an ambiguous drum rhythm (i.e., one without duration or intensity accents) on every second or third beat, they subsequently listen preferentially to a pattern in duple meter (accents on every second beat) or triple meter (accents on every third beat), corresponding to the previous pattern of bouncing (Phillips-Silver & Trainor, 2005). Real or simulated movement (i.e., through vestibular activation) has comparable consequences for adults' perception of rhythm (Phillips-Silver & Trainor, 2007).

8.2.2.1 *Cross-Cultural Perspectives on Temporal Processing*
Incidental exposure to music, which varies cross-culturally, affects metrical processing in the first year of life. By 4 months of age, Western infants listen preferentially to music with simple metrical structures that are characteristic of Western music, and Turkish infants listen equally long to simple and complex metrical structures, both of which are present in Turkish music (Soley & Hannon, 2010). Despite their early listening bias, Western 6-month-olds are equally adept at detecting metrical changes in the context of music with simple and complex metrical structures, in contrast to Western adults, who fail to detect the latter changes (Hannon & Trehub, 2005a). Perceptual narrowing is evident by 12 months of age, as revealed by infants' difficulty with

foreign metrical structures (Hannon & Trehub, 2005b). Nevertheless, 2 weeks of passive exposure to music with foreign metrical structures is sufficient for 12-month-olds but not adults to overcome that difficulty. In other words, 12-month-olds remain perceptually flexible listeners and learners even after the onset of culture-specific learning. Moreover, active, multimodal exposure to music and movement enhances 9-month-olds' temporal processing of music and speech, as reflected in neural measures (Zhao & Kuhl, 2016).

8.2.3 Pitch Processing

Relative pitch processing is fundamental to the perception of music. For example, a melody retains its identity despite changes in pitch level (i.e., all component pitches changed) so long as the relations between adjacent pitches (i.e., pitch intervals) remain unchanged. Intervals, which are irrelevant to speech, involve precise pitch distances between notes. Contours are relevant to music as well as speech, but they are defined much more precisely in music. In music, every change in pitch direction is relevant to the contour, in contrast to speech, where coarse intonation shape defines the contour and brief changes in pitch direction are ignored. To illustrate differences in pitch precision across domains, consider a small pitch deviation from the standard version of a song, which would render it out of tune and unpleasant; comparable pitch deviations in speech are irrelevant and often unnoticed (Zatorre & Baum, 2012).

Melodic contour is critical to infants' perception of melodies. After brief familiarization with a melody (i.e., several repetitions), 5- to 11-month-old infants perceive transformations that alter the contour as novel and those that preserve the contour, even with altered pitch level and intervals, as familiar (e.g., Trehub, Thorpe, & Morrongiello, 1987). In fact, infants' perception of contour is so robust that they detect a contour change when the standard and comparison melodies are separated by as much as 15 seconds (H. W. Chang & Trehub, 1977a) or when the 6-tone standard and comparison melodies differ by a single tone (Trehub, Thorpe, & Morrongiello, 1985).

In some circumstances, infants detect interval changes even when the contour remains unchanged. For example, 6-month-old infants detect small (single-semitone) changes to consonant melodic intervals but not to dissonant melodic intervals (Schellenberg & Trehub, 1996), in line with the relative difficulty of those discriminations for adult listeners (Schellenberg & Trehub, 1994). For adults and children, processing priorities for some harmonic (simultaneous) tone combinations have been attributed to their similarity to the harmonics of natural single sounds, with their smooth sound quality (Tramo, Cariani, Delgutte, & Braida, 2001), but these factors are irrelevant to melodic intervals. Exposure to consonant melodic intervals, which are prevalent in Western music, may contribute to adults' and children's performance, but they are less likely to account for the performance of infants, who are no better at detecting out-of-key notes than in-key notes in a melody (Trainor & Trehub, 1992). In fact, sensitivity to key membership (i.e., the pitches that belong in a key) does not emerge before 4 or 5 years of age (Corrigall & Trainor, 2010).

8.2.3.1 *Cross-Cultural Perspectives on Pitch Processing*

Musicologists consider melodic intervals as entirely arbitrary and culturally determined (Blacking, 1992), but biologically based constraints could favor some intervals (e.g., those considered consonant) over others. Interestingly, the perfect fifth interval (pitch distance of 7 semitones), which is considered highly consonant, is prominent in traditional music from a number of non-Western cultures (e.g., Morton, 1980). Moreover, there is suggestive evidence that this interval plays an anchoring role in melodies, even for 7- to 11-month-old infants, who more readily detect changes to melodies with prominent perfect fifth intervals than those without them (e.g., Trainor & Trehub, 1993).

Although the octave is ubiquitous across musical cultures, different cultures carve up the octave in different ways, resulting in pitch collections or scales that are the raw material for melodies. Interestingly, scales across cultures typically have steps (i.e., pitch distances between one pitch level and the next) that are unequal, like the whole steps (e.g., *do* to *re* or C to D) and half steps (e.g., *ti* to *do* or B to C) in the Western musical scale (see Figure 8.2), which are hypothesized to promote ease of processing and memorability (Dowling & Harwood, 1986). Although adults exhibit more accurate detection of small pitch deviations to the familiar major scale than to an invented scale with unequal or equal steps, 9-month-old infants detect small pitch deviations in the context of either scale with unequal steps but not in an equal-step scale (Trehub, Schellenberg, & Kamenetsky, 1999). The findings are consistent with inherent processing advantages for unequal scale steps in early development and processing advantages for familiar scale structure later on.

Despite infants' predominant focus on pitch relations, they encode absolute aspects of pitch in the context of specific stimuli or tasks. For example, 7-month-old infants exhibit long-term memory for the pitch level of a *sung* lullaby (Volkova, Trehub, & Schellenberg, 2006). Although infants also show long-term recognition of an *instrumental* melody (English folk song), there is no indication that they remember its pitch level (Plantinga & Trainor, 2005). Infants' enhanced memory for the details of vocal melodies is consistent with adults' memory advantage for vocal over instrumental melodies (Weiss, Trehub, & Schellenberg, 2012). The use of lullabies, an ecologically valid song form that is putatively universal and identifiable across cultures (Mehr et al., 2018; Trehub et al., 1993a), may also contribute to enhanced encoding. Infants' memory for specific songs is especially enduring. After a week or two of exposure to a novel song at 5 months of age, infants remember it several months later, distinguishing it from another song with the same words and rhythm (Mehr, Song, & Spelke, 2016).

8.2.4 Song and Coordinated Movement as Sociocultural Signals

The distinctive maternal style of speech to infants (Broesch & Bryant, 2015; Fernald, 1992) has its counterpart in a distinctive style of singing to infants, which features higher pitch level, slower tempo, greater emotional expressiveness, and greater temporal regularity relative to singing when an infant is absent or out of view (Nakata & Trehub, 2011; Trainor, 1996; Trehub, Plantinga, & Russo, 2016; Trehub et al., 1997). In face-to-face contexts, which is the norm for Western mother–infant interaction (often without physical contact), mothers exhibit distinctive facial expressions, smiling considerably more when singing than when speaking to infants (Trehub et al., 2016) and typically singing lively play songs. In many non-Western cultures, mothers have almost constant physical contact with infants, carrying them in slings during the day, sleeping with them at night, and engaging in less face-to-face interaction than their Western counterparts (Trehub & Gudmundsdottir, 2019). These non-Western mothers generally sing lullabies rather than play songs, which infants experience in conjunction with body contact and movement.

Research on the consequences of infant-directed singing is largely limited to Western infants. Just as audio-recordings of infant-directed speech are more effective than adult-directed speech in *capturing* infant attention (e.g., Fernald, 1985), audio-recordings of infant-directed singing are more effective than self-directed singing in capturing infant attention (Trainor, 1996). Infant-directed singing is also more effective than infant-directed speech in *sustaining* infants' attention, maintaining their composure, and delaying the onset of distress (Corbeil, Trehub, & Peretz, 2016). Moreover, audiovisual recordings of infant-directed singing are considerably more effective than infant-directed speech in capturing and maintaining infants' attention and engagement (Costa-Giomi, 2014; Nakata & Trehub, 2004).

The meanings of musical patterns, which are primarily connotative and context-bound (Cross, 2011), have special relevance for infants. When mothers sing to their prelinguistic infants, they are using a communication system that is every bit as potent, if not more so, than speech. Mothers heighten the salience of their songs to infants in many ways. As noted, they smile when they sing, highlighting their positive affect, and they use feedback from infants to fine-tune their emotional expressiveness (Trehub et al., 2016). Their use of a very small song repertoire and their almost identical performances of the same songs on different occasions (Bergeson & Trehub, 2002) contribute to the memorability and meaning of those songs, which become symbols of dyadic identity. Like adults, infants engage in predictive listening, experiencing surges of pleasure as an unfolding song fulfills their expectations on the basis of its familiarity. Unlike adults, however, they do not derive pleasure from the fulfillment of expectations based on musical conventions (Salimpoor, Zald, Zatorre, Dagher, & McIntosh, 2015). As the first line of "Twinkle, Twinkle, Little Star" concludes, for example, infants are pleased by hearing the expected sound "star" at the expected pitch level because of their repeated exposure to this song. By contrast, an out-of-tune rendition of an unfamiliar Western song would not evoke unpleasantness, as it would for adults, because infants lack implicit knowledge of Western tonality.

Mothers' stereotyped song performances undoubtedly contribute to their greater efficacy than maternal speech in ameliorating distress and high arousal in 8- and 10-month-olds (Cirelli & Trehub, 2020; Ghazban, 2013). Although play songs are more effective than lullabies in reducing the distress of Western infants (Ghazban, 2013), lullabies may be more effective in cultures where they have precedence over play songs. For nondistressed infants, mothers' playful song renditions heighten their attention and engagement, and mothers' soothing renditions reduce arousal for singers as well as listeners (Cirelli, Jurewicz, & Trehub, in press).

The songs that mothers sing repeatedly to infants become important affiliative signals. One consequence is that 5-month-old infants are more favorably disposed toward an unfamiliar adult who sings one of the mother's songs rather than a contrasting song (Mehr et al., 2016). Moreover, 14-month-olds exhibit more prosocial behavior toward an unfamiliar woman after she sings a song from the mother's repertoire rather than an unfamiliar song (Cirelli & Trehub, 2018). Sometime between their first and second birthday, infants begin singing some of their mother's songs, and they do so with surprising proficiency, maintaining the target pitch range and contours (Gudmundsdottir & Trehub, 2018). Their ability to sing provides them with a potent tool for self-regulation. One example of such self-regulations is toddlers' solo singing in the crib (Sole, 2017), which eases the separation from the primary caregiver and the transition to sleep.

Coordinated movement to music (i.e., dance), which occurs throughout the world (e.g., Savage et al., 2015), promotes social cohesion (McNeill, 1995), even for those as young as 14 months of age. For example, unfamiliar adults who bounce to music in synchrony with 14-month-old infants receive more help from the infants than do adults who bounce out of synchrony (Cirelli, Einarson, & Trainor, 2014). Adults' synchronous bouncing, like their singing of familiar songs, may mark them as in-group members rather than out-group members (Cirelli, 2018).

8.3 Policy Implications

Links of music to well-being in infancy and throughout the life span (Trehub & Cirelli, 2018) have potential public policy implications, especially for dyads in challenging circumstances. We offer a small sampling of circumstances that are potentially amenable to interventions involving parental singing. Depressed mothers or those who lack adequate social or material support are less sensitive to infants' nutritional, interpersonal, and safety needs than mothers without such challenges (Field, 2010; Shaw, Isaia, Schwartz, & Atkins, 2019). Obviously, maternal singing would not eliminate the underlying difficulties, but it could be a useful complement to appropriate community-based interventions. In fact, interventions involving singing and movement have been linked to gradual increases in dyadic engagement, even for mothers with severe postnatal depression (Fancourt & Perkins, 2018; van Puyvelde et al., 2014).

Prematurely born infants and their parents are another population of interest because of medical circumstances that necessitate extended separation of parents and infants, the challenging environment of neonatal intensive care units (NICUs), and the stress of uncertain developmental outcomes (e.g., Anderson & Patel, 2018). Maternal singing to infants in the NICU enhances infant autonomic stability and reduces maternal anxiety (Arnon et al., 2014), in line with reductions in maternal arousal that have been observed in mothers with normally developing infants (Cirelli et al., in press). Aside from its potential for arousal reduction in mother and infant, such singing could enhance maternal self-efficacy in a context in which parents are typically excluded from infant care.

The American Academy of Pediatrics, aiming to promote word learning, literacy, and family relationships, has urged its members to recommend reading aloud to infants from birth (Rich, 2014). It might be prudent to add singing to the Academy's list of recommended parenting activities based on its efficacy in alleviating infant distress (Cirelli & Trehub, 2020; Ghazban, 2013) and its arousal-regulatory effects on mothers and infants (Cirelli et al., in press). Sensitive responsiveness to infant distress is predictive of subsequent attachment security and self-regulation (Leerkes, Blankson, & O'Brien, 2009; McElwain & Booth-Force, 2006), and singing is likely to be at least as successful as reading aloud in enhancing family relationships.

Finally, because of the challenges posed by noise for infant listeners and learners (Erickson & Newman, 2017), background music or chatter should be used prudently (i.e., not too much) in home or care environments that provide the foundation for early social and cognitive development. Policies such as these could be promoted by professional associations of public health nurses, social workers, pediatricians, and others who have contact with caregivers and infants.

8.4 Conclusion

Despite infants' limitations in processing isolated sounds or sound features, they are remarkably proficient at perceiving complex auditory patterns such as music or speech, especially when those patterns are presented in quiet backgrounds. Infants' focus on relative pitch and timing allows them to perceive the equivalence of melodies presented at different pitch levels (e.g., Trehub et al., 1987) and the equivalence of rhythms presented at different tempos (Trehub & Thorpe, 1989). For reasons that remain unclear, they exhibit enhanced processing of simultaneous and sequential tone combinations that feature intervals considered consonant rather than dissonant by Western adults (Schellenberg & Trehub, 1996). Their memory for melodies, especially for vocal renditions, is detailed (Volkova et al., 2006) and unusually enduring (Mehr et al., 2016).

Early and continuing exposure to culturally typical auditory patterns, including speech, music, and other sounds, supports auditory cortical development in infancy as well as listening and learning skills that are relevant to their sociocultural niche. The pattern-perception skills that have been observed in Western infants are presumed to be independent of culture. However, infants' equivalent processing of simple and complex metrical rhythms at 6 months of age (Hannon & Trehub, 2005a) in conjunction with favored processing of simple metrical rhythms by 12 months of age (Hannon & Trehub, 2005b) provides an unambiguous instance of their transition from culture-general to culture-specific processing of musical structure. Rapid culture-specific tuning to temporal structure and slow culture-specific tuning to pitch structure (e.g., Corrigall & Trainor, 2010) are interesting in view of the centrality of pitch patterning in music and the centrality of temporal patterning in speech (Shannon, Zeng, Kamath, Wygonski, & Ekelid, 1995; Zatorre, Belin, & Penhune, 2002). The complexity of pitch structure and simplicity of temporal structure in music, especially in Western music, may contribute to the observed differences in acquisition.

It is clear that music plays a critical role in caregiving and in social and emotional development more generally. Mothers' songs to infants are appropriately considered bonding rituals that promote mutual gaze, reciprocal attachment, and overall well-being (Cirelli, Trehub, & Trainor, 2018; Trehub & Russo, in press). Moreover, such songs have implications beyond the dyad, influencing infants' social engagement with others (Cirelli & Trehub, 2018; Mehr et al., 2016).

Although the ingredients of optimal auditory environments for infants remain unclear, the harmful ingredients have become clearer, such as noise that masks critical auditory input, or factors that interfere with primary caregivers' ability to provide suitable auditory input for infants. Interventions aimed at ameliorating these circumstances are warranted.

References

Abdala C., & Keefe D. H. (2012) Morphological and functional ear development. In L. Werner, R. Fay, & A. Popper (Eds.) *Human auditory development* (pp. 19–60). New York, NY: Springer International.

Anderson, D. E., & Patel, A. D. (2018). Infants born preterm, stress, and neurodevelopment in the neonatal intensive care unit: Might music have an impact? *Developmental Medicine & Child Neurology, 60*, 256–266.

Arnaud, A., Gracco, V., & Ménard, L. (2018). Enhanced perception of pitch changes in speech and music in early blind adults. *Neuropsychologia, 117*, 261–270.

Arnon, S., Diamant, C., Bauer, S., Regev, R., Sirota, G., & Litmanovitz, I. (2014). Maternal singing during kangaroo care led to autonomic stability in preterm infants and reduced maternal anxiety. *Acta Paediatrica*, *103*, 1039–1044.

Bargones, J. Y., & Werner, L. A. (1994). Adults listen selectively: Infants do not. *Psychological Science*, *5*, 170–174.

Baruch, C., & Drake, C. (1997). Tempo discrimination in infants. *Infant Behavior and Development*, *20*, 573–577.

Bendixen, A., Háden, G. P., Németh, R., Farkas, D., Török, M., & Winkler, I. (2015). Newborn infants detect cues of concurrent sound segregation. *Developmental Neuroscience*, *37*, 172–181.

Bergeson, T. R., & Trehub, S. E. (2002). Absolute pitch and tempo in mothers' songs to infants. *Psychological Science*, *13*, 72–75.

(2006). Infants perception of rhythmic patterns. *Music Perception*, *23*, 345–360.

(2007). Signature tunes in mother's speech to infants. *Infant Behavior and Development*, *30*, 648–654.

Bernier, D. E., & Soderstrom, M. (2018). Was that my name? Infants' listening in conversational multi-talker backgrounds. *Journal of Child Language*, *45*, 1439–1449.

Bigand, E., & Poulin-Charronnat, B. (2006). Are we "experienced listeners"? A review of the musical capacities that do not depend on formal musical training. *Cognition*, *100*, 100–130.

Birnholz, J. C., & Benacerraf, B. R. (1983). The development of human fetal hearing. *Science*, *222*, 516–518.

Blacking, J. (1992). The biology of music making. In H. Myers (Ed.), *Ethnomusicology: An introduction* (pp. 301–314). New York, NY: Norton.

Bregman, A. S. (1990). *Auditory scene analysis: The perceptual organization of sound.* Cambridge, MA: MIT Press.

Broadbent, D. E. (1952). Listening to one of two synchronous messages. *Journal of Experimental Psychology*, *44*, 51–55.

Broesch, T. L., & Bryant, G. A. (2015). Prosody in infant-directed speech is similar across Western and traditional cultures. *Journal of Cognition and Development*, *16*, 31–43.

Chang, E. F., & Merzenich, M. M. (2003). Environmental noise retards auditory cortical development. *Science*, *300*, 498–502.

Chang, H. W., & Trehub, S. E. (1977a). Auditory processing of relational information by young infants. *Journal of Experimental Child Psychology*, *24*, 324–331.

(1977b). Infants' perception of temporal grouping in auditory patterns. *Child Development*, *48*, 1666–1670.

Cirelli, L. K. (2018). How interpersonal synchrony facilitates early prosocial behavior. *Current Opinion in Psychology*, *20*, 35–39.

Cirelli, L. K., Einarson, K. M., & Trainor, L. J. (2014). Interpersonal synchrony increases prosocial behavior in infants. *Developmental Science*, *17*, 1003–1011.

Cirelli, L. K., Jurewicz, Z. B., & Trehub, S. E. (in press). Effects of maternal singing style on mother–infant arousal and behavior. *Journal of Cognitive Neuroscience*.

Cirelli, L. K., Spinelli, C., Nozaradan, S., & Trainor, L. J. (2016). Measuring neural entrainment to beat and meter in infants: Effects of music background. *Frontiers in Neuroscience*, *10*, 229.

Cirelli, L. K., & Trehub, S. E. (2018). Infants help singers of familiar songs. *Music & Science*, *1*, doi:2059204318761622.

(2020). Familiar songs reduce infant distress. *Developmental Psychology*, *56*(5), 861–868. doi: 10.1037/dev0000917

Cirelli, L. K., Trehub, S. E., & Trainor, L. J. (2018). Rhythm and melody as social signals for infants. *Annals of the New York Academy of Sciences*, *1423*, 66–72.

Cooke, M. P., & Brown, G. J. (1993). Computational auditory scene analysis: Exploiting principles of perceived continuity. *Speech Communication*, *13*, 391–399.

Corbeil, M., Trehub, S. E., & Peretz, I. (2016). Singing delays the onset of infant distress. *Infancy*, *21*, 373–391.

Corrigall, K. A., & Trainor, L. J. (2010). Musical enculturation in preschool children: Acquisition of key and harmonic knowledge. *Music Perception*, *28*, 195–200.

Costa-Giomi, E. (2014). Mode of presentation affects infants' preferential attention to singing and speech. *Music Perception*, *32*, 160–169.

Cross, I. (2011). The meanings of musical meanings: Comment on "Towards a Neural Basis of Processing Musical Semantics" by Stefan Koelsch. *Physics of Life Reviews*, *8*, 116–119.

Darwin, C. J., & Hukin, R. W. (1999). Auditory objects of attention: The role of interaural time-differences. *Journal of Experimental Psychology: Human Perception and Performance*, *25*, 617–629.

Dowling, W. J., & Harwood, D. L. (1986). *Music cognition*. New York, NY: Academic Press.

Draganova, R., Eswaran, H., Lowery, C. L., Murphy, P., Huotilainen, M., & Preissl, H. (2005). Sound frequency change detection in fetuses and newborns: A magnetoencephalographic study. *NeuroImage*, *28*, 354–361.

Erickson, L. C., & Newman, R. S. (2017). Influences of background noise on infants and children. *Current Directions in Psychological Science*, *26*, 451–457.

Fancourt, D., & Perkins, R. (2018). Effect of singing interventions on symptoms of postnatal depression: Three-arm randomised controlled trial. *British Journal of Psychiatry*, *212*, 119–121.

Fernald, A. (1985). Four-month-old infants prefer to listen to motherese. *Infant Behavior and Development*, *8*, 181–195.

(1992). Meaningful melodies in mothers' speech to infants. In H. Papousek, U. Jurgens, & M. Papousek (Eds.), *Nonverbal vocal behaviour* (pp. 262–282). Cambridge, UK: Cambridge University Press.

Fernandez-Prieto. I., Navarra, J., & Pons, F. (2015). How big is this sound? Crossmodal association between pitch and size in infants. *Infant Behavior and Development*, *38*, 77–81.

Field, T. (2010). Postpartum depression effects on early interactions, parenting, and safety practices: A review. *Infant Behavior and Development*, *33*, 1–6.

Folland, N. A., Butler, B. E., Payne, J. E., & Trainor, L. J. (2015). Cortical representations sensitive to the number of perceived auditory objects emerge between 2 and 4 months of age: Electrophysiological evidence. *Journal of Cognitive Neuroscience*, *27*, 1060–1067.

Fujioka, T., Trainor, L. J., & Ross, B. (2008). Simultaneous pitches are encoded separately in auditory cortex: An MMNm study. *NeuroReport*, *19*, 361–366.

Ghazban, N. (2013). *Emotion regulation in infants using maternal singing and speech* (Unpublished doctoral dissertation). Ryerson University, Toronto, Canada.

Granier-Deferre, C., Bassereau, S., Ribeiro, A., Jacquet, A. Y., & Decasper, A. J. (2011). A melodic contour repeatedly experienced by human near-term fetuses elicits a profound cardiac reaction one month after birth. *PLoS ONE, 6,* e17304.

Gudmundsdottir, H., & Trehub, S. (2018). Adults recognize toddlers' song renditions. *Psychology of Music, 46,* 281–291.

Háden, G. P., Honing, H., Török, M., & Winkler, I. (2015). Detecting the temporal structure of sound sequences in newborn infants. *International Journal of Psychophysiology, 96,* 23–28.

Hannon, E. E., Schachner, A., & Nave-Blodgett, J. E. (2017). Babies know bad dancing when they see it: Older but not younger infants discriminate between synchronous and asynchronous audiovisual musical displays. *Journal of Experimental Child Psychology, 159,* 159–174.

Hannon, E. E., & Trehub, S. E. (2005a). Metrical categories in infancy and adulthood. *Psychological Science, 16,* 48–55.

(2005b). Tuning in to musical rhythms: Infants learn more readily than adults. *Proceedings of the National Academy of Sciences, 102,* 12639–12643.

Haryu, E., & Kajikawa, S. (2012). Are higher-frequency sounds brighter in color and smaller in size? Auditory-visual correspondences in 10-month-old-infants. *Infant Behavior and Development, 35,* 727–732.

Huttenlocher, P. R., & Dabholkar, A. S. (1997). Regional differences in synaptogenesis in human cerebral cortex. *Journal of Comparative Neurology, 387,* 167–178.

Jones, M. R. (1976). Time, our lost dimension: Toward a new theory of perception, attention, and memory. *Psychological Review, 83,* 323–355.

Kisilevsky, B. S., Hains, S. M., Brown, C. A., Lee, C. T., Cowperthwaite, B., Stutzman, S. S., … Wang, Z. (2009). Fetal sensitivity to properties of maternal speech and language. *Infant Behavior and Development, 32,* 59–71.

Krumhansl, C. L., & Jusczyk, P. W. (1990). Infants' perception of phrase structure in music. *Psychological Science, 1,* 70–73.

Lasky, R. E., & Williams, A. L. (2005). The development of the auditory system from conception to term. *NeoReviews, 6,* 141–152.

Leerkes, E. M., Blankson, A. N., & O'Brien, M. (2009). Differential effects of maternal sensitivity to infant distress and nondistress on social-emotional functioning. *Child Development, 80,* 762–775.

Lin, J. Y., & Hartmann, W. M. (1998). The pitch of a mistuned harmonic: Evidence for a template model. *Journal of the Acoustical Society of America, 103,* 2608–2617.

Litovsky, R. Y. (1997). Developmental changes in the precedence effect: Estimates of minimum audible angle. *Journal of the Acoustical Society of America, 102,* 1739–1745.

Marie, C., & Trainor, L. J. (2013). Development of simultaneous pitch encoding: Infants show a high voice superiority effect. *Cerebral Cortex, 23,* 660–669.

(2014). Early development of polyphonic sound encoding and the high voice superiority effect. *Neuropsychologia, 57,* 50–58.

McAdams, S., & Bertoncini, J. (1997). Organization and discrimination of repeating sound sequences by newborn infants. *Journal of the Acoustical Society of America, 102,* 2945–2953.

McAuley, J. D., Jones, M. R., Holub, S., Johnston, H. M., & Miller, N. S. (2006). The time of our lives: Life span development of timing and event tracking. *Journal of Experimental Psychology: General, 135*, 348–367.

McElwain, N. L., & Booth-Laforce, C. (2006). Maternal sensitivity to infant distress and nondistress as predictors of infant–mother attachment security. *Journal of Family Psychology, 20*, 247–255.

McMillan, B. T., & Saffran, J. R. (2016). Learning in complex environments: The effects of background speech on early word learning. *Child Development, 87*, 1841–1855.

McNeill, W. H. (1995). *Keeping together in time: Dance and drill in human history.* Cambridge, MA: Harvard University Press.

Mehr, S. A., Singh, M., York, H., Glowacki, L., & Krasnow, M. M. (2018). Form and function in human song. *Current Biology, 28*, 356–368.

Mehr, S. A., Song, L. A., & Spelke, E. S. (2016). For 5-month-old infants, melodies are social. *Psychological Science, 27*, 486–501.

Moore, J. K., & Guan, Y. L. (2001). Cytoarchitectural and axonal maturation in human auditory cortex. *Journal of the Association for Research in Otolaryngology, 2*, 297–311.

Morton, D. (1980). Thailand. In S. Sadie (Ed.), *The new Grove dictionary of music and musicians* (Vol. 18, pp. 712–722). London: Macmillan.

Nakata, T., & Trehub, S. E. (2004). Infants' responsiveness to maternal speech and singing. *Infant Behavior and Development, 27*, 455–464.

(2011). Expressive timing and dynamics in infant-directed and non-infant-directed singing. *Psychomusicology: Music, Mind and Brain, 21*, 130–138.

Newman, R. S. (2005). The cocktail party effect in infants revisited: Listening to one's name in noise. *Developmental Psychology, 41*, 352–362.

Olsho, L. W., Koch, E. G., Carter, E. A., Halpin, C. F., & Spetner, N. B. (1988). Pure-tone sensitivity of human infants. *Journal of the Acoustical Society of America, 84*, 1316–1324.

Olsho, L. W., Koch, E. G., & Halpin, C. F. (1987). Level and age effects in infant frequency discrimination. *Journal of the Acoustical Society of America, 82*, 454–464.

Ozturk, O., Krehm, M., & Vouloumanos, A. (2013). Sound symbolism in infancy: Evidence for sound-shape cross-modal correspondences in 4-month-olds. *Journal of Experimental Child Psychology, 114*, 173–186.

Papacharalampous, G. X., Nikolopoulos, T. P., Davilis, D. I., Xenellis, I. E., & Korres, S. G. (2011). Universal newborn hearing screening, a revolutionary diagnosis of deafness: Real benefits and limitations. *European Archives of Otorhinolaryngology, 268*, 1399–1406.

Parga, J. J., Daland, R., Kesavan, K., Macey, P. M. Zeltzer, L., & Harper, R. M. (2018). A description of externally recorded womb sounds in human subjects during gestation. *PLoS ONE, 13*, e0197045.

Pujol, J., Soriano-Mas, C., Ortiz, H., Sebastián-Gallés, N., Losilla, J. M., & Deus, J. (2006). Myelination of language-related areas in the developing brain. *Neurology, 66*, 339–343.

Pundir, A. S., Hameed, L. S., Dikshit, P. C., Kumar, P., Mohan, S., Radotra, B., … Iyengar, S. (2012). Expression of medium and heavy chain neurofilaments in the developing human auditory cortex. *Brain Structure and Function, 217*, 303–321.

Pundir, A. S., Singh, U. A., Ahuja, N., Makhija, S., Dikshit, P. C., Radotra, B., … Iyengar, S. (2016). Growth and refinement of excitatory synapses in the human auditory cortex. *Brain Structure and Function*, *221*, 3641–3674.

Phillips-Silver, J., & Trainor, L. J. (2005). Feeling the beat: Movement influences infant rhythm perception. *Science*, *308*, 1430–1430.

(2007). Hearing what the body feels: Auditory encoding of rhythmic movement. *Cognition*, *105*, 533–546.

Piazza, E. A., Iordan, M. C., & Lew-Williams, C. (2017). Mothers consistently alter their unique vocal fingerprints when communicating with infants. *Current Biology*, *27*, 3162–3167.

Plantinga, J., & Trainor, L. J. (2005). Memory for melody: Infants use a relative pitch code. *Cognition*, *98*, 1–11.

Plantinga, J., & Trehub, S. E. (2014). Revisiting the innate preference for consonance. *Journal of Experimental Psychology Human Perception & Performance*, *40*, 40–49.

Plomp, R., & Levelt, W. J. (1965). Tonal consonance and critical bandwidth. *Journal of the Acoustical Society of America*, *38*, 548–60.

Remez, R. E., Fellowes, J. M., & Nagel, D. S. (2007). On the perception of similarity among talkers. *Journal of the Acoustical Society of America*, *122*, 3688–3696.

Rich, M. (2014, June 24). Pediatrics group to recommend reading aloud to children from birth. *New York Times*. Retrieved from www.nytimes.com/2014/06/24/us/pediatrics-group-to-recommend-reading-aloud-to-children-from-birth.html.

Richards, D. S., Frentzen, B., Gerhardt, K. J., McCann, M. E., & Abrams, R. M. (1992). Sound levels in the human uterus. *Obstetrics & Gynecology*, *80*, 186–190.

Rocha, S., & Mareschal, D. (2017). Getting into the groove: The development of tempo-flexibility between 10 and 18 months of age. *Infancy*, *22*, 540–551.

Rose, M. M., & Moore, B. C. (2000). Effects of frequency and level on auditory stream segregation. *Journal of the Acoustical Society of America*, *108*, 1209–1214.

Rubin, D. C. (1995). *Memory in oral traditions: The cognitive psychology of epic, ballads, and counting-out rhymes*. New York, NY: Oxford University Press.

Sachs, C. (1943). The road to major. *Musical Quarterly*, *29*, 381–404.

Salimpoor, V. N., Zald, D. H., Zatorre, R. J., Dagher, A., & McIntosh, A. R. (2015). Predictions and the brain: How musical sounds become rewarding. *Trends in Cognitive Sciences*, *19*, 86–91.

Savage, P. E., Brown, S., Sakai, E., & Currie, T. E. (2015). Statistical universals reveal the structures and functions of human music. *Proceedings of the National Academy of Sciences*, *112*, 8987–8992.

Schellenberg, E. G., & Trainor, L. J. (1996). Sensory consonance and the perceptual similarity of complex-tone harmonic intervals: Tests of adult and infant listeners. *Journal of the Acoustical Society of America*, *100*, 3321–3328.

Schellenberg, E. G., & Trehub, S. E. (1994). Frequency ratios and the perception of tone patterns. *Psychonomic Bulletin & Review*, *1*, 191–201.

(1996). Natural musical intervals: Evidence from infant listeners. *Psychological Science*, *7*, 272–277.

Shannon, R. V., Zeng, F. G., Kamath, V., Wygonski, J., & Ekelid, M. (1995). Speech recognition with primarily temporal cues. *Science*, *270*, 303–304.

Sharma, A., Dorman, M. F., & Kral, A. (2005). The influence of a sensitive period on central auditory development in children with unilateral and bilateral cochlear implants. *Hearing Research, 203*, 134–143.

Shaw, R., Isaia, A., Schwartz, A., & Atkins, M. (2019). Encouraging parenting behaviors that promote early childhood development among caregivers from low-income urban communities: A randomized static group comparison trial of a primary care-based parenting program. *Maternal and Child Health Journal, 23*, 39–46.

Smith, N. A., Folland, N. A., Martinez, D. M., & Trianor, L. J. (2017). Multisensory object perception in infancy: 4-month-olds perceive a mistuned harmonic as a separate auditory and visual object. *Cognition, 164*, 1–7.

Smith, N. A., & Trainor, L. J. (2011). Auditory stream segregation improves infants' selective attention to target tones amid distracters. *Infancy, 16*, 655–668.

Smith, S. L., Gerhardt, K. J., Griffiths, S. K., Huang, X., & Abrams, R. M. (2003). Intelligibility of sentences recorded from the uterus of a pregnant ewe and from the fetal inner ear. *Audiology and Neurotology, 8*, 347–353.

Sohmer, H., Perez, R., Sichel, J. Y., Priner, R., & Freeman, S. (2001). The pathway enabling external sounds to reach and excite the fetal inner ear. *Audiology and Neurotology, 6*, 109–116.

Sole, M. (2017). Crib song: Insights into functions of toddlers' private spontaneous singing. *Psychology of Music, 45*, 172–192.

Soley, G., & Hannon, E. E. (2010). Infants prefer the musical meter of their own culture: A cross-cultural comparison. *Developmental Psychology, 46*, 286–292.

Sussman, E., & Steinschneider, M. (2009). Attention effects on auditory scene analysis in children. *Neuropsychologia, 47*, 771–785.

Thorpe, L. A., & Trehub, S. E. (1989). Duration illusion and auditory grouping in infancy. *Developmental Psychology, 25*, 122–127.

Trainor, L. J. (1996). Infant preferences for infant-directed versus noninfant-directed playsongs and lullabies. *Infant Behavior and Development, 19*, 83–92.

Trainor, L. J., & Heinmiller, B. M. (1998). Infants prefer to listen to consonance over dissonance. *Infant Behavior, 21*, 77–88.

Trainor, L. J., & Trehub, S. E. (1992). A comparison of infants' and adults' sensitivity to Western musical structure. *Journal of Experimental Psychology: Human Perception and Performance, 18*, 394–402.

(1993). What mediates infants' and adults' superior processing of the major over the augmented triad? *Music Perception, 11*, 185–196.

Tramo, M. J., Cariani, P. A., Delgutte, B., & Braida, L. D. (2001). Neurobiological foundations for the theory of harmony in Western tonal music. *Annals of the New York Academy of Sciences, 930*, 92–116.

Trehub, S. E. (2015). Cross-cultural convergence of musical features. *Proceedings of the National Academy of Sciences, 112*, 8809–8810.

Trehub, S. E., & Cirelli, L. K. (2018). Precursors to the performing arts in infancy and early childhood. *Progress in Brain Research, 237*, 225–242.

Trehub, S. E., & Gudmundsdottir, H. R. (2019). Mothers as singing mentors for infants. In G. F. Welsh, D. M. Howard, & J. Nix (Eds.), *The Oxford handbook of singing* (pp. 455–469). Oxford: Oxford University Press.

Trehub, S. E., & Hannon, E. E. (2009). Conventional rhythms enhance infants' and adults' perception of musical patterns. *Cortex*, *45*, 110–118.

Trehub, S. E., Plantinga, J., & Russo, F. A. (2016). Maternal vocal interactions with infants: Reciprocal visual influences. *Social Development*, *25*, 665–683.

Trehub, S. E., & Russo, F. A. (in press). Infant-directed singing from a dynamic multimodal perspective: Evolutionary origins, cross-cultural variation, and relation to infant-directed speech. In F. Russo, B. Ilari, & A. Cohen (Eds.), *Routledge companion to interdisciplinary studies in singing: Vol 1*. New York, NY: Routledge.

Trehub, S. E., Schellenberg, E. G., & Kamenetsky, S. B. (1999). Infants' and adults' perception of scale structure. *Journal of Experimental Psychology: Human Perception and Performance*, *25*, 965–975.

Trehub, S. E., Schneider, B. A., & Endman, M. (1980). Developmental changes in infants' sensitivity to octave-band noises. *Journal of Experimental Child Psychology*, *29*, 282–293.

Trehub, S. E., Schneider, B. A., & Henderson, J. L. (1995). Gap detection in infants, children, and adults. *Journal of the Acoustical Society of America*, *98*, 2532–2541.

Trehub, S. E., Schneider, B. A., Morrongiello, B. A., & Thorpe, L. A. (1988). Auditory sensitivity in school-age children. *Journal of Experimental Child Psychology*, *46*, 273–285.

Trehub, S. E., & Thorpe, L. A. (1989). Infants' perception of rhythm: Categorization of auditory sequences by temporal structure. *Canadian Journal of Psychology*, *43*, 217–229.

Trehub, S. E., Thorpe, L. A., & Morrongiello, B. A. (1985). Infants' perception of melodies: Changes in a single tone. *Infant Behavior and Development*, *8*, 213–223.

(1987). Organizational processes in infants' perception of auditory patterns. *Child Development*, *58*, 741–749.

Trehub, S. E., & Trainor, L. (1998). Singing to infants: Lullabies and play songs. *Advances in Infancy Research*, *12*, 43–78.

Trehub, S. E., Unyk, A. M., Kamenetsky, S. B., Hill, D. S., Trainor, L. J., Henderson, J. L., & Saraza, M. (1997). Mothers' and fathers' singing to infants. *Developmental Psychology*, *33*, 500–507.

Trehub, S. E., Unyk, A. M., & Trainor, L. J. (1993a). Adults identify infant-directed music across cultures. *Infant Behavior and Development*, *16*, 193–211.

(1993b). Maternal singing in cross-cultural perspective. *Infant Behavior and Development*, *16*, 285–295.

van Puyvelde, M., Rodrigues, H., Loots, G., de Coster, L., Du Ville, K., Matthijs, L., ... Pattyn, N. (2014). Shall we dance? Music as a port of entrance to maternal-infant intersubjectivity in a context of postnatal depression. *Infant Mental Health Journal*, *35*, 220–232.

Virtala, P., Huotilainen, M., Partanen, E., Fellman, V., & Tervaniemi, M. (2013). Newborn infants' auditory system is sensitive to Western music chord categories. *Frontiers in Psychology*, *4*, 492.

Volkova, A., Trehub, S. E., & Schellenberg, E. G. (2006). Infants' memory for musical performances. *Developmental Science*, *9*, 583–589.

Walker, P., Bremner, J. G., Mason, U., Spring, J., Mattock, K., Slater, A., & Johnson, S. P. (2010). Preverbal infants' sensitivity to synaesthetic cross-modality correspondences. *Psychological Science*, *21*, 21–25.

Weiss, M. W., Trehub, S. E., & Schellenberg, E. G. (2012). Something in the way she sings: Enhanced memory for vocal melodies. *Psychological Science*, *23*, 1074–1078.

Werner, L. A. (2017). Ontogeny of human auditory system function. In K. S. Cramer, A. Coffin, R. R. Fay, & A. N. Popper (Eds.), *Auditory development and plasticity* (pp. 161–192). New York, NY: Springer International.

Werner, L. A., Marean, G. C., Halpin, C. F., Spetner, N. B., & Gillenwater, J. M. (1992). Infant auditory temporal acuity: Gap detection. *Child Development*, *63*, 260–272.

Wightman, F. L., & Kistler, D. J. (2005). Informational masking of speech in children: Effects of ipsilateral and contralateral distracters. *Journal of the Acoustical Society of America*, *118*, 3164–3176.

Wild, C. J., Linke, A. C., Zubiaurre-Elorza, L., Herzmann, C., Duffy, H., Han, V. K., ... Cusack, R. (2017). Adult-like processing of naturalistic sounds in auditory cortex by 3- and 9-month old infants. *NeuroImage*, *157*, 623–634.

Winkler, I., Háden, G. P., Ladinig, O., Sziller, I., & Honing, H. (2009). Newborn infants detect the beat in music. *Proceedings of the National Academy of Sciences*, *106*, 2468–2471.

World Health Organization (2010). *Newborn and infant hearing screening: Current issues and guiding principles for action*. Geneva: WHO Press.

Yoshinaga-Itano, C. (1999). Benefits of early intervention for children with hearing loss. *Otolaryngology Clinics of North America*, 32, 1089–1102.

Zatorre, R. J., & Baum, S. R. (2012). Musical melody and speech intonation: Singing a different tune. *PLoS Biology*, *10*, e1001372.

Zatorre, R. J., Belin, P., & Penhune, V. B. (2002). Structure and function of auditory cortex: music and speech. *Trends in Cognitive Sciences*, *6*, 37–46.

Zentner, M., & Eerola, T. (2010). Rhythmic engagement with music in infancy. *Proceedings of the National Academy of Sciences*, *107*, 5768–5773.

Zentner, M. R., & Kagan, J. (1996). Perception of music by infants. *Nature*, *383*, 29.

Zhang, L. I., Bao, S., & Merzenich, M. M. (2002). Disruption of primary auditory cortex by synchronous auditory inputs during a critical period. *Proceedings of the National Academy of Sciences*, *99*, 2309–2314.

Zhao, T. C., & Kuhl, P. K. (2016). Musical intervention enhances infants' neural processing of temporal structure in music and speech. *Proceedings of the National Academy of Sciences*, *113*, 5212–5217.

9 The Development of Touch Perception and Body Representation

Andrew J. Bremner*

Touch occupies a greater extent of our bodies than all other senses put together (see Gallace & Spence, 2014, for a rich characterization of touch). The skin, our organ of cutaneous touch, is thought to account for 16–18% of body mass (Montagu, 1978). As such, touch can certainly be considered *the* bodily sense, being distributed not just in our haptic organs (typically our hands; see Radman, 2013), but throughout and covering our bodies. Partly as a result of this, touch is pervasive in sensory experience. It is also our first sense: At 7 weeks of gestation, a human fetus will move if its lips are touched (Hooker, 1952). Given the pervasive nature of touch and its primacy in early development, it is reasonable to assume that tactile perception has great importance to the developing (and also the mature) organism. And yet it is surprising to note a significant lack of interest in touch in developmental psychologists' consideration of perceptual development. In a small literature survey of article titles, Bremner and Spence (2017) report that tactile development seems to be considered only once in PsycINFO titles (between 1956 and 2015) for every eight articles (at the very least) that addressed visual development.

In this chapter I will lay out the literature concerning the emergence of tactile perception in human infancy. I will focus on the development of three key contributions of touch: (i) haptics (i.e., active tactile sensing of the external environment); (ii) affective touch (i.e., the role tactile input plays in affective and interpersonal contexts); and (iii) self/body sensing (i.e., the role of cutaneous touch and proprioception in specifying the body's shape and layout in space), with a particular focus on this latter. Throughout, I will draw out directions for future research. In summing up, I will, in line with the cross-cutting themes of this handbook, pose questions about sociocultural roles in tactile perceptual development as well as the implications of touch development research for policy.

It is useful at this point to indicate three particular themes considered throughout the chapter. First, as one of the aims of this handbook (not to

* The author would like to acknowledge helpful discussions with his collaborators, especially J. J. Begum Ali, Dorothy Cowie, Frances Le Cornu Knight, Giulia Orioli, Silvia Rigato, Charles Spence, Rhiannon Thomas, and Jiale Yang.

mention a current theme in the discipline), I will consider the development of touch perception at both biological and behavioral levels of explanation, and reporting research that uses both behavioral and physiological indices. Second, I will not consider touch in isolation. Even if we might tend to introspect that we *see*, *hear*, *touch*, *taste*, and *smell* the world around us in separate sensory acts, touch is no exception to the multisensory principle by which humans perceive (Stein, 2012). Our sense of touch is substantially affected by visual, auditory, and olfactory information (see Gallace & Spence, 2014), and so a consideration of the development of such multisensory interactions is going to be crucial to our understanding of the development of tactile perception (Bremner, Lewkowicz, & Spence, 2012).

Lastly, I will consider the development of touch perception from the perspective of the sense as conveying information that has been both passively received and actively obtained. I make this distinction as part of a functional taxonomy of touch. One way to define touch is in terms of the physiological receptors that it makes use of. Like vision, hearing, and all of our sensory systems, touch is mediated by a specialized set of receptor cells that transduce information in our skin, muscles, and joints (e.g., information about mechanical distortions, temperature, etc.) into meaningful information about ourselves and the world around us. But this kind of account can feel problematically reductive. When we think more carefully about the ways we use (and feel) touch it is quite apparent that it is more than a network of receptors. As a case in point, it is common among scientists and the wider public to think of touch not as a passive sense, but as the *active* contact we make between our skin and objects in order to search out, encode, and recognize objects, surfaces, and their features. Throughout this chapter I will attempt to clarify the extent to which the tactile perceptual abilities researchers have studied are relatively active or passive in nature. I will argue that there is value to thinking about the development of touch perception as the acquisition of *both* an active sensorimotor perceptual system (Gibson, 1966), and an ability to perceive and interpret a more passively presented sensory experience. As we shall see, the distinction between active and passive modes of touch may be particularly relevant to the study of tactile perceptual development, given the altricial nature of human newborns, and because of the period of rapid changes in sensorimotor functioning that they go through in the first months of life.

9.1 The Neural Substrates of Touch and Their Ontogeny

As already discussed, touch occupies a greater extent of our bodies than all other senses put together. Strikingly, however, despite a comparable number of receptors, the tactile system has much lower bandwidth than vision and hearing when it comes to transducing information for perception. Nonetheless, as Gallace and Spence (2014) have argued, it would be an error to rate the importance of a sense modality purely on the basis of how much information it can carry; surely the type and salience of that information matters just as much.

The broad definition of touch includes not just cutaneous sensation, but also interoception and proprioception. Interoceptors are located in the internal organs and provide information (typically unconscious) that is used to maintain organ function, homeostasis, digestion, and respiration (for a review of what we know about interoception in adults see Craig, 2009). Proprioception provides information about how our body and limbs are arrayed, or moving, in space (the latter is sometimes also referred to as kinesthesis), and is mediated by receptors that are found in the muscles, tendons, and joints.

To limit the scope of this chapter, I will not discuss the development of the more interoceptive aspects of touch. Little is yet known in fact (although see Maister, Tang, & Tsakiris, 2017), despite a notable interest in interoceptive processes in regard to certain developmental disorders (e.g., Murphy, Brewer, Catmur, & Bird, 2017; Quattrocki & Friston, 2014). I will cover proprioceptive aspects of touch as they play crucial roles alongside cutaneous touch both in the formation of body representations, and in the context of haptics.

Cutaneous tactile sensations are determined by the activation of several different classes of receptors scattered throughout the skin surface including Meissner's corpuscles, Merkel's disks, Pacinian corpuscles, Ruffini's end organs, and free nerve endings. These various receptor types are differentially sensitive to different kinds of stimulus, including pressure (low, high, sustained), temperature, pain, itch, vibration, and so on. As with the eyes, tactile sensitivity and acuity is certainly not uniform across the receptor (body) surface, with higher levels in some areas compared to others. For instance, the lips are particularly sensitive to pressure, and the fingertips have particularly high spatial resolution. The lower leg is not really well known for either of these skills. Proprioceptive tactile sensations are transduced by proprioceptors: Muscle spindles provide information about muscle length, and Golgi tendon organs in the tendons provide information about muscle stretch. Tactile signals are transmitted to the primary somatosensory cortex where areas on the body with greatest tactile innervation (and typically greatest tactile sensitivity and acuity) are represented across greater portions of the cortex, giving rise to the somatosensory homunculus made famous by Penfield and Rasmussen (1950).

However, not everything we feel and would identify as touch is determined by signals entering our brain in somatosensory cortex, or even signals arising from the stimulation of the tactile receptors. As is now well established across all sense modalities, numerous cross-modal interactions influence tactile perception (see Gallace & Spence, 2014). For example, the perceived dryness of our skin can been greatly altered by changing the sound that we hear when running our hands together (the "parchment skin illusion"; Jousmäki & Hari, 1998). In perhaps the most famous of all multisensory illusions, the "rubber hand illusion" (Botvinick & Cohen, 1998), seeing a fake hand being stroked in synchrony with felt touches on the real (hidden hand) induces powerful feelings of ownership over the fake hand. Here, visual information about a hand and strokes applied to it fool us by overriding the veridical information about hand position coming from proprioception. Researchers have even demonstrated that olfactory cues influence tactile perception: What a person smells while touching fabric influences their perception of its softness (Demattè, Sanabria, Sugarman, & Spence, 2006).

The first sensations we experience are tactile. Cutaneous and trigeminal somatosensory receptors mature at around 4–7 weeks of gestation (Humphrey, 1964), and somatosensory function follows soon thereafter. At 7 weeks of gestation, the fetus will move if its lips are touched (Hooker, 1952). Grasping and rooting reflex responses are reported to have been observed from as early as 12 weeks of gestation (Humphrey, 1964). Thalamic connections to the subplate zone underneath the cortex occur ~2 weeks earlier to somatosensory than to frontal and occipital areas (Krsnik, Majić, Vasung, Huang, & Kostović, 2017), and somatosensory cortical responses are observed very soon after at about 23–24 weeks gestational age (GA; Nevalainen, Lauronen, & Pihko, 2014). Given the primacy of touch sensory physiology in early development, it is reasonable to assume that tactile perception has great importance to the developing (and also the mature) organism. Indeed, some have argued that the differential timing of these separate sensory systems facilitates perceptual development by reducing, in the initial stages, the amount of sensory information that the developing fetus has to assimilate and combine (Turkewitz, 1994). Accepting this, touch might well be seen as the sensory scaffold on which multisensory perceptual development is constructed.

9.2 The Early Development of Haptic Sensing

The use of touch to sense objects and their properties is an "active" perceptual system known as haptic touch. Despite the more limited ability of fetuses and newborn infants to use their bodies and limbs to explore objects in a systematic manner, some aspects of behavior that resemble haptic abilities are present from very early stages of development. Consider, for example, the situation in which your eyes are closed and an object is placed in your outstretched hand. The near-immediate response is to enclose the object with the fingers – helping to determine the shape and size of that which we hold. Thus, we do not simply feel these properties as presented to the skin – we use proprioceptive information from our hand in order to infer the shape of the object (see Lederman & Klatszky, 2009). In this way, haptic perception allows us to gain information about objects and surfaces; information concerning both their substance (hardness, weight, temperature, texture, etc.) and structural properties (size, shape, and volume; Kahrimanovic, Bergmann Tiest, & Kappers, 2010).

When an object is placed in the hand, newborns will press down on it with their fingers (referred to as the palmar grasp reflex). This also happens with the toes when objects are presented to the soles of the feet (the plantar grasp reflex). Furthermore, in the first 6 months of life, there is a strong tendency to use the hand to bring objects to the mouth for exploration, although this declines substantially in preference for manual exploration thereafter (see Rochat & Senders, 1991). As well as some limited ability to make the appropriate contact with objects with their hands, newborns are able to encode some tactile properties in this way. For instance, Jouen and Molina (2005) demonstrate that the palmar grasp reflex is modulated by the textural properties of objects placed in the hand. Streri, Lhote, and Dutilleul (2000) have used haptic habituation to show that newborns can discriminate objects on the basis of their shapes (prism vs. cylinder). After habituating to one of these objects held in the hand (habituation was identified by a decline in manual inspection of the object below a certain criterion – i.e., earlier release of the object from the hand), newborns would then show a novelty preference for the object that had not been presented in habituation. A similar ability has also been demonstrated more recently in preterm infants as young as 28 gestational weeks (Marcus, Lejeune, Berne-Audéoud, Gentaz, & Debillon, 2012).

Despite these early competencies, with only the grasp reflex and rooting/mouthing at their disposal it seems likely that newborns will be more limited in the aspects of objects that they can encode at this stage. Indeed, Bushnell and Boudreau (1993), who undertook a literature survey of the development of both manual exploratory abilities and haptic perceptual competencies, proposed that the development of manual exploratory abilities across infancy should bootstrap the emergence of more sophisticated haptic perceptual abilities. Referring to Lederman and Klatzky's (2009) classification of optimal "exploratory procedures" for haptic perception of certain object properties (e.g., enclosure of the object with the hands for extracting size/volume, unsupported holding of the object to extract weight, or contour following to extract shape), Bushnell and Boudreau (1993) argue that there is a close developmental link between the ability to produce a given exploratory procedure, and the ability to differentiate an object haptically according to the properties that exploratory procedure yields.

One study has found some evidence for Bushnell and Boudreau's (1993) proposal within individual children. Exploratory procedures for haptic perception are largely developed and adult-like by 3 years of age (Kalagher & Jones, 2011b). However, shape perception is one of the last skills to develop haptically according to Bushnell and Boudreau (1993), and Kalagher and Jones (2011a) report that children under 5 years of age were less likely to produce the enclosure exploratory procedures required for shape encoding (according to Lederman & Klatzky, 2009). Those children who produced these behaviors were more likely to be able to match the haptically felt shape to a corresponding visual shape in a cross-modal matching task.

Another question researchers have asked is to what extent representations formed through haptic exploration are available or transferable to other representational modalities. Can, for example, the newborn infant make a cross-modal match concerning an object between touch and vision? Since the 1970–1980s it has been clear that haptic-visual cross-modal matching is available rather early in postnatal development, and while there has been some difficulty replicating oral–visual transfer at 1 month (Maurer, Stager, & Mondloch, 1999; Meltzoff & Borton, 1979), there is rather more evidence for manual–visual transfer in newborns (see Streri, 2012).

Nonetheless, Rose, Gottfried, and Bridger (1981), have also demonstrated that between 6 and 12 months infants become progressively more efficient at cross-modal encoding and recognition (see Rose, 1994). An account of the development of visual-haptic transfer that rests on the role of sensory experience is also suggested by more recent work with congenitally blind adults who have been restored to sight by the removal of cataracts. Held et al. (2011) found that an ability to make visual tactile cross-modal matches is not available straight away in these patients (despite abilities to make visual–visual and tactile–tactile matches), but is learned over a period of several days following the onset of visual experience. Could it be that newborns learn the correspondences they are successful at (see Streri, 2012) very quickly? More research is needed to determine this.

There is also a requirement for more research into visual-haptic coordination abilities that go beyond the ability to transfer information between the senses. For instance, we can ask how infants come to coordinate vision and haptics to enhance their multisensory perceptual identification of objects and surfaces. When adults are presented with multiple cues to the same stimulus dimension their estimates tend to combine estimates from the component modalities that are weighted according to their relative reliabilities (Ernst & Banks, 2002). For instance, visual size is often the most reliable cue to the size of an object, and so adults tend to weight it more highly than haptic cues. And because this optimal weighting of touch and vision determines the combined estimate, adults perform significantly better when *both* visual and haptic cues are presented. However, we know next to nothing about infants' ability to combine such cues across modalities. Nonetheless, research with older children and children with sensory impairments indicates some important developmental changes in these kinds of perceptual abilities (Gori, Del Viva, Sandini, & Burr, 2008; Gori, Sandini, Martinoli, and Burr, 2010).

In summary, haptic perception is a key skill at our disposal from early in postnatal development and even before. Indeed, the ability to make links between what we sense about objects with our hands and what we see appears to be something that develops early with fairly minimal experience (Held et al., 2011; Streri, 2012). Nonetheless, by its nature haptic perception is an active tactile process, mediated by sensorimotor skills. And so as infants' and children's motor skills progress, their ability to explore objects haptically and form more accurate and transferable representations of them also improves (Kalagher & Jones, 2011a).

9.3 The Early Development of Affective and Interpersonal Aspects of Touch in Brain and Behavior

Some of the most salient examples of pleasant and comforting sensations are mediated by touch, as are some of the most unpleasant painful feelings. Given the precedence of touch in prenatal sensory ontogeny, it seems reasonable to suppose that touch is important in mediating early affective experience.

Recent research on cortical responses to painful stimulation in newborn infants is beginning to reveal the details of how the neural basis of pain perception develops. Functional magnetic resonance imaging (fMRI) reveals that the majority of the brain regions that encode the sensory and affective components of pain in adults are activated by noxious stimuli in full-term newborns (Goksan et al., 2015). However, while cortical responses to noxious stimuli have been observed in preterm newborns from as early as 28 weeks gestational age (Bartocci, Bergqvist, Lagercrantz, & Anand, 2006), recent studies show that there is a switch in their neural response to touches around 35 weeks gestational age, when nonspecific "neural bursts" are replaced by evoked potentials that differentiate noxious and nonnoxious tactile stimulation for the first time (Fabrizi et al., 2011). As well as mediating noxious stimuli, touch also provides positive affective content, concerning, for instance, the proximity of a caregiver or other social partner. Providing an affective motivation for maintaining physical contact with a caregiver may be a particularly important function of touch in the early stages of development, potentially foundational in the establishment of reciprocal attachment between infant and caregiver (see, e.g., Harlow & Zimmerman, 1959). Indeed, there is now evidence that newborn infants show cortical activity in both somatosensory and socio-affective brain regions (postcentral gyrus and posterior insular cortex) in response to "gentle" touches (Tuulari et al., 2019).

But what are the precise parameters of the tactile stimuli that infants might (hypothetically) find pleasant and seek out? The discovery of a new class of tactile fibers in humans, known as C-Tactile (CT) afferents (e.g., see Löken, Wessberg, Morrison, McGlone, & Olausson, 2009), may be one answer to this question. These fibers, found in the hairy skin, respond optimally when the skin is stroked at a speed of about 1–10 cm/sec, i.e., a touch that resembles a caress. More recently, research has indicated that this "social touch" neural channel also responds preferentially to stimuli at human body temperature as opposed to room temperature (Ackerley et al., 2014).

Are infants sensitive to these properties of social touch? Fairhurst, Löken, and Grossmann (2014) have established that 9-month-olds' heart-rates declined more to strokes of 3 cm/s, with trends for increased heartrate following slower (0.3 cm/s) or faster (30 cm/s) stroking. The infants also showed greatest interest in the 3 cm/s stroking condition. Of course, 9 months is a reasonable length of time in which infants may have been able to learn about which kinds of touch are particularly associated with interpersonal scenarios, so it is difficult to be completely sure that this specific response is related to an innate physiology for preferential processing (and seeking of) interpersonal touch. More recently, there has been a rush of publications that have attempted to establish cortical signatures of affective touch in younger infants using optical imaging techniques. Unfortunately, the picture arising from these studies is fairly confused, at least in part due to a proliferation of different ways by which researchers have attempted to operationalize cortical responses to affective touch. Studying 2-month-olds, Jönsson et al. (2018) report that the insula (implicated in affective sensory processing in adults) responds to the difference between "affective" slow stroking and fast stroking stimulation to the forearm. By contrast, Kida and Shinohara (2013), studying only prefrontal cortical responses, find that there is greater activation of anterior prefrontal areas in response to affective touch in 10-month-old infants as compared to 3- to 6-month-olds (in this case affective touch was operationalized as the difference between touch to the palm of the hand – i.e., not in a region innervated by CT afferents – from a piece of velvet fabric, as opposed to a wooden rod). To complicate the matter further, Pirazzoli, Lloyd-Fox, Braukman, Johnson, and Gliga (2019), studying 5-month-olds, find no difference in cortical responses to touch to the upper arm from a spoon versus a human finger, and Miguel, Lisboa, Gonçalves, and Sampaio (2019) find no evidence of differential cortical responses to gentle stroking by a brush versus pressure applied by a wooden rod on the forearm in 7-month-olds. If we are to make sense of the origins of brain responses to affective touch, it is clear that we need a more structured approach, including a better-shared definition of what kinds of stimuli should give rise to affective touch responses in infants (considering the full gamut of relevant sensory features, i.e., the velocity of stroking, the objects delivering their touch, their temperature, and so on), as well as the areas of skin to which the touches should be applied (the hairy skin known to be innervated by CT afferents rather than the glabrous skin on the palms, surely), and what brain regions and age groups we should be looking at.

The kinds of affective tactile stimuli considered so far have been studied in rather passive contexts: Infants are presented with painful or pleasant stimuli and their behavioral and brain responses are measured. In many ways this makes intuitive sense as these perceptual phenomena are more passive by nature. For instance, active exploration is probably the exceptional case for how most of us, including infants, experience pain. But with interpersonal touch, there is certainly a case to be made for considering the development of its more active, sensorimotor aspects. When do infants learn to actively seek out tactile contact with other individuals, engaging in reciprocal tactile interactions?

In fact some have even argued that such interactions are present before birth. Amazingly, one study using 4-D ultrasound has documented the occurrence of hand movements that the authors argued were intentionally aimed at touching the co-twin starting from the 14th week of gestation (Castiello et al., 2010). Their conclusions are based on a rather rich interpretation of their data, but are nonetheless provocative and exciting. However, I have not been able to find any other research documenting the development of "haptic" interpersonal tactile perception postnatally. Hopefully more research into this fascinating research area will be forthcoming.

9.4 The Developing Role of Touch in the Bodily Self

I have already stated that I consider it important to capture the development of both active and passive tactile perceptual experiences. Active tactile experiences are perhaps best captured by the haptic perceptual abilities already discussed. And yet these are almost certainly the exception in our rich array of tactile experiences. While reading this sentence for instance, all of us are receiving tactile inputs regarding the contact our bodies are making with the surfaces around us (I won't go into detail). If you doubt the importance of this, imagine for a second what it might be like to exist without such sensory inputs. Deafferent patients, as well as having considerable difficulties in controlling movement, sometimes report the sensation of not having a body, or that their body seems to be "floating" (Cole & Paillard, 1995). Given that touch is our first sense, there is much to be said for the idea that the full range of passive tactile inputs that we receive serve as the preeminent sensory scaffold on which our perceptions of ourselves and our relation to the world around us are constructed. So, what do we know about the development of tactile body representations?

9.4.1 The Origins of Tactile Body Maps in Brain and Behavior

We still know relatively little about how the human brain develops spatial maps of the body such as the somatosensory homunculus (Marshall & Meltzoff, 2015), but researchers have begun to probe this frontier. Some characterization of infants' early tactile body maps can be gained from early behavioral responses to touches. A number of "neonatal reflexes" are triggered by spatially specific tactile stimuli. One example is the crossed-extension reflex: If a newborn infant is touched close to the inguinal canal at the top of the leg they will flex and extend their other leg (Zappella & Simopoulos, 1966). Furthermore, Moreau, Helfgott, Weinstein, and Milner (1978) have observed the habituation of neonatal head turning to tactile stimulation, and Kisilevsky and Muir (1984) have demonstrated that sleeping neonates will habituate to a brush stroke on either the lips or ear and then dishabituate to brushing at the novel one of these two locations. Whether or not neonatal reflexes and habituation of this kind are mediated by cortical somatosensory maps of the body, such tactile spatial responses to touch seem likely to play an important role in the pre- and postnatal development of (or the developmental refinement of preexisting) tactile body maps, by providing a spatial structure to early sensorimotor experiences.

A number of recent studies now reveal some of the cortical topography of touch, "somatotopy." Meltzoff, Saby, and Marshall (2019) reported that somatosensory evoked potentials (SEPs) in 2-month-olds occupy distinct scalp sites depending on whether their feet, hands, or central upper lip receive the tactile stimulus, with hand stimulation eliciting stronger responses more laterally, foot stimulation more medially (see also Saby, Meltzoff, & Marshall, 2015), and midline lip stimulation producing a large bilateral response. We might question whether the differentiated response to lip stimulation is due more to the high sensitivity of that area of the skin rather than its distinct cortical topography, but the topographical differentiation of the more comparable hand and foot areas is clearer, and corresponding somatotopy in cortical tissue has now been confirmed in 7-month-olds via magnetoencephalography (MEG; Meltzoff et al., 2018). In fact, Milh et al. (2007) have reported a similar spatial differentiation of "delta-brush" electroencephalographic (EEG) oscillatory signals in response to tactile foot and hand stimulation in premature neonates (~30 weeks gestational age). These signals were apparent both when the hands and feet were stimulated by touch, and following spontaneous fetal movements that resulted in somatosensory feedback. On this basis, Milh et al. (2007) proposed that spontaneous fetal motor activity may lead to the differentiation of somatosensory body maps in the infant brain (see also Nevalainen et al., 2014; Tiriac, Sokoloff, & Blumberg, 2015). Given this proposal, it seems unsurprising that we might find some degree of somatotopic organization in the newborn (and preterm) brain given the extended period of gestation in which tactile sensory inputs have been available to structure that organization. It does also seem wise however, to consider whether this somatotopic organization might be experience independent. Under those circumstances, we might consider whether the development of differentiated movements of hands and feet arises due to the experience-independent differentiated somatosensory feedback that results from those movements.

Somatotopic organization in somatosensory cortex is certainly just one (admittedly fundamental) component of the kinds of representational maps that make up human bodily experience. There are a number of indications that the kind of somatotopy that newborn infants show is not sufficient alone to support a fully-fledged ability to represent one's body. For instance, studies of tactile localization in infancy (Begum Ali, Spence, & Bremner, 2015; Bremner, Mareschal, Lloyd-Fox, & Spence, 2008; Somogyi et al., 2018) indicate a contrasting protracted picture of the development of tactile spatial body representations. Furthermore, Brownell, Nichols, Svetlova, Zerwas, and Ramani

(2010) find that, even up to 30 months of age, infants are less than perfect in identifying body parts through naming and imitation of an experimenter's body part gestures. I shall come onto studies of tactile localization shortly. But, for the moment, let's consider one emerging research question: when and to what extent do infants come to perceive their body parts as distinct entities? Studies in adults and young children demonstrate that tactile spatial perception is structured around a topology of body parts. Pairs of tactile stimuli that cross the boundary between arm and hand (the wrist) are perceived as more distant than if those same tactile distances are presented within either the hand or the forearm (de Vignemont, Majid, Jola, & Haggard, 2009; Le Cornu Knight, Cowie, & Bremner, 2016; Le Cornu Knight, Longo, & Bremner, 2014). Researchers have recently begun to develop techniques that might measure this effect in infants (Shen, Weiss, Meltzoff, & Marshall, 2018), and it will be fascinating to probe developmental relationships between the acquisition of various behaviors that might lead children to differentiate body parts and categorical representations of body parts. The acquisition of body part names (which, interestingly, varies among cultures; Majid, 2010), and differentiated articulation of body parts are two such candidates for investigation (Le Cornu Knight, Bremner, & Cowie, 2020).

9.4.2 The Early Development of Proprioception and the Postural Schema

Tactile inputs, especially from proprioceptive receptors in the muscles and joints, play an important role in providing us with an accurate picture of the current layout of our body and limbs, what is typically referred to as the postural schema. That a newborn's mouth will open in anticipation of the arrival of the hand at the mouth or the perioral region (Butterworth & Hopkins, 1988; de Vries, Visser, & Prechtl, 1984) has been cited as evidence of an innate ability to represent the posture of the limbs for this particular behavior (Gallagher, 2005; Rochat, 2010). In this behavior, touch provides both proprioceptive information about limb position (relative to the mouth), and also what we might presume is the motivation for the action, tactile cutaneous contact between the hand and oral area.

One immediate query concerning hand–mouth coordination in newborns is whether the tactile representations underlying this behavior are underpinned by a more general ability to perceive the posture of the limbs across a wider range of contexts (Gallagher, 2005, does not think so). It is also important to consider whether hand–mouth behaviors could be learned rather than pre-programmed, as many authors have argued (Gallagher, 2005). The newborn has already had significant experience of hand to mouth movements prenatally. De Vries et al. (1984) report that hand–face contact occurs in the fetus 50–100 times an hour from as early as 12 weeks gestation. In the restricted environment of the uterus, this may be due, at least in part, to the proximity of the hands to the face and may also be encouraged by the rich somatosensory innervation of the hands and face/mouth. Thus claims about innate proprio-ceptive schemas for hand–mouth coordination should be balanced against the possibility that such seemingly complex and functionally relevant behaviors may result from the complex interaction of a range of factors during the ample opportunities for learning *in utero*.

Rochat and Hespos (1997) took another approach to identifying the pos-tural schema in young infants. They examined whether infants would perceive self-touch in a distinct manner to other kinds of touch. They compared new-borns' and 1-month-old infants' rooting responses to touches delivered to their cheeks, specifically examining whether there was any difference in response when that touch was self-applied versus applied by the experimenter. Rochat and Hespos (1997) found greater rooting to self-touch in the 1-month-olds, but no statistically reliable difference in rooting for newborns. This is an ingenious test of an ability to differentiate self versus other touch, but the study has a number of limitations (Bremner, 2018). Rochat and Hespos (1997) infer from their findings that newborn infants possess a spatial representation of the posi-tion of their limbs relative to one another that coordinates proprioception and cutaneous touch. However, simpler interpretations are that the infants root differently depending on the position of their limbs, or the kind of tactile input received. These simpler interpretations are also better aligned with more recent studies showing that infants do not perceive touches in external space until 6 months of age (Begum Ali et al., 2015; Bremner et al., 2008).

As adults we perceive touches not just on the body surface, but we also refer them to a place in external space. Recently, Jannath Begum Ali, Charles Spence, and I (Begum Ali et al., 2015) investigated the development of external spatial coding of touch in early infancy. To do this we compared infants' orient-ing responses to touches on their feet across conditions where their legs were in a familiar uncrossed posture or a less familiar crossed-legs posture. Sighted adults tend to find tactile localization more difficult in the crossed-feet posture likely because they automatically refer touches to a place in external space where their limb would normally rest (Schicke & Röder, 2006). In a series of trials, we measured which foot infants moved first when a touch was presented to one of their feet. An older group of 6-month-olds demonstrated the usual crossed-limb deficit with ~70% accuracy in the uncrossed posture, and chance (50%) performance in the crossed posture. In striking contrast, 4-month-olds showed no crossed-feet deficit, matching the performance of the 6-month-olds in the uncrossed-feet posture and outperforming them in the crossed-feet pos-ture. We concluded that, up until 5 to 6 months of age, infants perceive touches purely on the body and do not refer them to places in external space.

How do infants learn to locate touches in external space? Considering the role of action in the external environment seems important here. The onset of successful externally targeted reaching at around 4 to 5 months of age brings with it experiences of the location of touch in external spatial coordinates (in conjunction with bodily coordinates). Probably the richest information about external space that guides the targeting of these active tactile experiences comes from vision. In the next section we will see that multisensory interactions between vision and touch may be part of the developmental mechanism by which infants come to represent the relation between their body and external space.

9.4.3 The Development of Multisensory and Sensorimotor Body Representations

As adults, our representations of limb and body position result from the combination and integration of information from somatosensory receptors with the visual (and also auditory) information that is more suited to providing information about the external world (Holmes & Spence, 2004). There is very clear evidence that body representations are shaped by the developing interactions between the senses. It has been established for some time that congenitally blind adults show less interference of external spatial coordinates when locating touches on the body (Röder, Rösler, & Spence, 2004). However, one particular study with congenitally blind children who had had cataracts removed in the first months of life, indicates that visual experience plays a particular role only after 4 months of age: If cataracts were removed before 5 months of age, tactile localization developed typically (Azañón, Camacho, Morales, & Longo, 2018; see also Ley, Bottari, Shenoy, Kekunnaya, & Röder, 2013). And so, given that, in typically developing infants, successful visually targeted reaching emerges at around this time (5 months; just before the crossed-limbs effects indicating external spatial coding have been observed; Begum Ali et al., 2015; Bremner et al., 2008), it seems reasonable to conclude that visual experience has its effect on tactile spatial perception via the multisensory visual–tactile experience gained in the context of successful visually targeted reaching.

Let's look more closely at how infants learn about the multisensory links that underpin body representations. Several studies using infants' looking preferences have investigated an early ability to make cross-modal links between cues about the body coming from touch (both proprioception and cutaneous touch) and vision. These studies typically examine infants' preferences for visual movements of limbs projected on a screen that are either congruent or incongruent with their own limb movements perceived proprioceptively (Bahrick & Watson, 1985; Rochat, 1998). From as early as 3 months of age, infants' looking behavior demonstrates that they are able to differentiate multisensory bodily events on the basis of visual–proprioceptive (temporal and spatial) congruency. More recently, researchers have examined whether infants can detect whether a visually observed stroke to the skin occurs at the same time as a felt (tactile) stroke (Filippetti, Lloyd-Fox, Longo, Farroni, & Johnson, 2014; Zmyj, Jank, Schütz-Bosbach, & Daum, 2011). Even newborn infants are able to do this (Filippetti, Johnson, Lloyd-Fox, Dragovic, & Farroni, 2013), and more recent data also indicates an ability to code spatial congruence between touches felt on the skin and seen on a video screen in newborns (Filippetti, Orioli, Johnson, & Farroni, 2015). Early cross-modal competencies of this kind provide some reason to speculate that an ability to perceive the multisensory bodily self is well specified from birth (e.g., Rochat, 2010).

And so we have at present a rather confused picture of visual–tactile development in early life, with studies investigating tactile localization in visual/external space demonstrating protracted development across the first year (Begum Ali et al., 2015; Bremner et al., 2008; Rigato, Begum Ali, van Velzen, & Bremner, 2014), while studies probing infants' sensitivity to visual–tactile spatiotemporal congruency indicate much earlier competence (e.g., Bahrick & Watson, 1985; Filippetti et al., 2015; Rochat, 1998). However, the earliest demonstrations of infants' (newborns') sensitivity to visual–tactile congruency have involved visual–tactile pairings presented on the face (Filippetti et al., 2015), rather than the hands or feet, and also in situations where the visual cue is displayed on a video screen of the limbs or face, and well beyond the bounds of their own bodies, in external space. Reasoning that these might be special cases, researchers in my lab have investigated infants' sensitivity to visual–tactile and auditory–tactile spatiotemporal congruency.

Freier, Mason, and Bremner (2016) presented 6- and 10-month-old infants with visual (flashes) and tactile (vibrotactile) stimuli on their hands that were either colocated on one hand or spread across two hands (a touch on one hand and a light on the other). In contrast to the studies described earlier, in the congruent condition the bimodal stimuli only occupied one single place in both external and anatomical (bodily) space. Both 6- and 10-month-olds preferred to look at the incongruent displays. Given the changes in tactile spatial reference observed between 4 and 6 months of age (Begum Ali et al., 2015), we have also gone on to adapt this task for application to younger infants (Begum Ali, Thomas, Mullen, & Bremner, under review; Thomas et al., 2018). These latest studies indicate that 4-month-olds are also sensitive to visual–tactile and auditory–tactile colocation. The overall picture then appears to indicate that infants are sensitive to spatiotemporal congruency between touch and vision/audition from early in infancy, prior to skilled reaching, and prior to the developmental visual remapping of touch to an external spatial frame of reference.

The pattern of findings in the literature hint at how the multisensory interactions underlying body representations might develop. In demonstrations of tactile–visual colocation ability (e.g., Begum Ali et al., under review; Filippetti et al., 2015; Zmyj et al., 2011), tactile stimuli are presented concurrently with visual stimuli. It is possible that in this scenario, which probably is relatively ecological in nature, visual stimuli provide enough of a spatial cue for 4-month-old infants to colocate visual and tactile stimuli in the same external reference frame, but that without that visual cue the tactile stimuli would have remained unreferred. Indeed, an ability at 4 months of age to use visual spatial events as an external spatial anchor for concurrent tactile stimuli may be a precursor to the development of an ability to locate a touch in external space in the absence of concurrent visual and/or auditory stimuli. It may be that an exposure to multisensory information about the body might lead to a later ability to interpret bodily sensations under unisensory conditions (e.g., as proposed by Bahrick & Lickliter, 2012, in their account of multisensory development).

So far, I have characterized the early development of tactile body representations as the tuning and integration of touch and its cross-modal links for the purpose of sensory information about the body presented in a rather passive context (e.g., the interpretation of tactile information in the light of proprioceptive positions of limbs, or the localization of touches presented to the skin surface). This contrasts quite dramatically with the kinds of active tactile skills infants have to develop in more haptic contexts. But it is also possible to actively sense one's body through tactile inputs, and such sensing may be more directly relevant to the use of body representations to control the body in purposeful action.

A number of recent studies have traced the development of an ability to explore tactile sensations on the body. Chinn, Noonan, Hoffmann, and Lockman (2019) have shown that reaches with the hand to locate touches on the face improve substantially over the first year of life. An even more protracted developmental progression has been observed when infants use one hand to reach a tactile stimulus on the contralateral forelimb (Chinn, Hoffmann, Leed, & Lockman, 2019), possibly because there are more degrees of freedom to control in intermanual sensorimotor coordination than hand–face coordination. In a fascinating development in this area, researchers are now developing robotic simulations that examine how regimes of active somatosensory exploration (a constrained form of motor babbling) can constitute a developmental process whereby a sensorimotor representation of the body might be formed (see Hoffmann et al., 2017).

9.5 Summary: The Frontier of Infant Touch Research

Touch is the first of our senses to develop, providing us with the sensory scaffold on which multisensory perception is built (Gottlieb, 1971; Turkewitz, 1994). We have seen in this chapter that, despite a traditional neglect of this developmentally crucial sense (Bremner & Spence, 2017), research on tactile development is on the increase. There is a long tradition of research now into the development of haptic perception in early life. However, touch also provides us with crucial information about our own bodies, and plays a central role in affective aspects of perception. It is these previously neglected aspects of tactile development that are receiving renewed attention. Nonetheless, there is clearly a great deal more to be done, particularly in understanding the development of interpersonal affective touch, where quite some confusion remains, partly due to methodological inconsistency.

9.5.1 Policy Implications of Touch Development Research

Beyond understanding the sensory origins of our perceptions of ourselves and the world (a goal that we might consider particularly valuable in and of itself!), how might research into tactile development have more specific implications for society and help shape policy? There is already some substantial impact of touch research into enhancing the well-being and developmental outcomes of infants. Since Harlow and Zimmerman's (1959) harrowing observations of the motivational importance of comforting tactile contact to maternally deprived newborn macaques, many researchers have championed the value of early tactile input in optimizing infant outcomes, particularly interpersonal tactile input.

It is now clear that pain-related responses in infants can be decreased by parental touch. Pain during medical procedures (specifically, the heel lance procedure) is significantly reduced if the baby is held in skin-to-skin contact (sometimes known as "kangaroo care"), both for preterm and full-term neonates (e.g., Gray, Watt, & Blass, 2000). In Gray et al.'s (2000) study of full-term babies, crying and grimacing were reduced by skin-to-skin contact by 82% and 65%, respectively.

Despite some cautionary notes (e.g., Norris, Campbell, & Brenkert, 1981), evidence seems to indicate that physical handling of preterm babies is important for more long term developmental outcomes (e.g., Ang et al., 2012; Diego, Field, & Hernandez-Reif, 2005; Lee, 2005; Lipsitt, 2002). Field and colleagues also argue that touch can have more long-term benefits in full-term typically developing children. Field and Hernandez-Reif (2001) show that parents' evaluations of the quality of their infants' sleep improves more when they are receiving routine massage than when read to in a control group. Benefits of massage on cognitive performance are also thought to be present beyond infancy. Hart, Field, Hernandez-Reif, and Lundy (1998) have demonstrated that a session of massage led to improved cognitive performance and increased alertness and attentiveness in 4-year-olds relative to a control group who had a story read to them.

A critical area for further study in this area is to attempt to determine precisely what aspects of tactile experience (or the experiences that accompany tactile stimuli) are influencing development, and how. For instance, some of the most recent evidence in this area comes from Maitre et al. (2017), who showed that the degree to which somatosensory event-related potential (ERP) responses in preterm newborns are atypically attenuated is predicted positively by prior noxious somatosensory experiences and negatively by prior supportive tactile experiences. However, it is difficult to disentangle supportive versus noxious tactile experiences from other aspects of experience or an internal state that is correlated with those experiences. And so, it is unclear whether it is specifically touch that leads to positive/negative developmental outcomes.

9.5.2 Sociocultural Questions in Touch Development Research

One particularly ripe area for further research on tactile development concerns the role of sociocultural factors. Here I consider how the development of tactile perception itself might be influenced by sociocultural factors, but also how different tactile experiences might be mediated by sociocultural factors and impact on development more widely.

Starting with the latter of these considerations, it is important to mention the ideas of Tiffany Field, who is perhaps the best known for her research, just mentioned, on the effects of interpersonal touch (e.g., massage) in human development. One of Field's key arguments over the years has been that as adults and even as infants and children we are not provided with as much interpersonal touch as we require, and that modern (Western) society prevents or prohibits touch to such an extent that many of us may be "touch hungry" (Field, 2001). This is clearly a highly theoretical argument, but certainly one to take seriously given that the research covered above suggests potentially important impacts on early development.

There are numerous ways in which touch and tactile behavior is considered to vary according to social and cultural norms, and also between individuals (Classen, 2005). Such variations seem extremely likely to affect early experience via differences in caregiver handling, potentially propagating such variations across generations. Let's look at some examples. It is now well established that cultural differences in the physical aspects of child rearing can have notable impacts upon the trajectories of sensorimotor development (see Adolph, Karasik, & Tamis-LeMonda, 2010). Particularly relevant to this chapter, formal infant childcare routines involving massage as well as physical exercises vary between cultures, with a greater prevalence of practice in Africa, India, and the Caribbean. These care routines are known to speed the onset of certain sensorimotor abilities, such as head control and upright sitting posture even when considered as dose-response relationships within cultures (Hopkins & Westra, 1988). Consideration of these effects has focussed on the role of physical exercise (and the corresponding sensorimotor experience) in these caring routines, rather than the tactile inputs (e.g., Adolph et al., 2010; note that sensorimotor practice and tactile perceptual input probably both result from both massage as well as physical exercise). However, given the positive effects of massage already discussed, tactile inputs may have an important role. Although, given that some cultures severely restrict both physical exercise and tactile experience in early life, we can question whether such rich early experiences are critical to development (Karasik, Tamis-LeMonda, Ossmy, & Adolph, 2018).

Variations in caregiver handling also occur within cultures of course. A recent study by Crucianelli et al. (2019) has examined the relationship between higher-order social cognitive processes in mothers (mind-mindedness, a sensitivity to their infant's mental state that is known to be important in attachment and learning; Meins, Fernyhough, Fradley, & Tuckey, 2001) and their tactile interactions with their infants. Although the authors found no relationship between mind-mindedness and the degree to which the mother's tactile interactions were contingent on their infant's emotional behaviors, more emotionally noncontingent touch behaviors (rough, restrictive, or awkward tactile interactions) were more likely when the mother also made more non-attuned mind-related comments concerning their infant. Examining the role of such differences in handling on development seems a fascinating prospect.

Lastly, we can also ask how the development of touch perception itself might vary according to sociocultural factors. Very little research has been conducted in this area. However, there are a number of interesting possibilities to follow up. I mentioned earlier the possibility that segmentation of tactile perception according to body parts may be mediated by differences in the ways in which cultures segment the body into parts in the noun terms used in language. While the initial evidence from adults suggests that such categorical segmentation of touch may be universal in adults (Le Cornu Knight et al., 2020), further research with infants and children is necessary to determine whether such factors might not play a role earlier in development. As another example, Ma-Kellams, Blascovitch, and McCall (2012) found that East Asian adults perform more poorly on tests of interoceptive awareness (e.g., heartbeat counting) than do Western adults. This has been interpreted in the light of greater contextual processing in more collectivist (less individualistic) societies (e.g., Markus & Kitayama, 1991). Research on the developmental origins of such cultural differences would help verify this kind of account.

References

Ackerley, R., Backlund Wasling, H., Liljencrantz, J., Olausson, H., Johnson, R. D., & Wessberg, J. (2014). Human C-tactile afferents are tuned to the temperature of a skin-stroking caress. *Journal of Neuroscience, 34*, 2879–2883.

Adolph, K. E., Karasik, L. B., & Tamis-LeMonda, C. S. (2010). Motor skill. In M. Bornstein (Ed.), *Handbook of cultural developmental science* (pp. 61–89). New York, NY: Psychology Press.

Ang, J. Y., Lua, J. L., Mathur, A., Thomas, R., Asmar, B. I., Savasan, S., … Shankaran, S. (2012). A randomized placebo-controlled trial of massage therapy on the immune system of preterm infants. *Pediatrics, 130*, e1549–e1558.

Azañón, E., Camacho, K., Morales, M., & Longo, M. R. (2018). The sensitive period for tactile remapping does not include early infancy. *Child Development, 89*, 1394–1404.

Bahrick, L. E., & Lickliter, R. (2012). The role of intersensory redundancy in early perceptual, cognitive, and social development. In A. J. Bremner, D. J. Lewkowicz, & C. Spence (Eds.), *Multisensory development* (pp. 183–205). Oxford: Oxford University Press.

Bahrick, L. E., & Watson, J. S. (1985). Detection of intermodal proprioceptive-visual contingency as a potential basis of self-perception in infancy. *Developmental Psychology*, *21*, 963–973.

Bartocci, M., Bergqvist, L. L., Lagercrantz, H., & Anand, K. J. S. (2006). Pain activates cortical areas in the preterm newborn brain. *Pain*, *122*, 109–117.

Begum Ali, J., Spence, C., & Bremner, A. J. (2015). Human infants' ability to perceive touch in external space develops postnatally. *Current Biology*, *25*, R978–R979.

Begum Ali, J., Thomas, R. L., Mullen, S., & Bremner, A. J. (under review). Sensitivity to visual–tactile colocation on the body prior to skilled reaching in early infancy.

Botvinick, M., & Cohen, J. (1998). Rubber hands "feel" touch that eyes see. *Nature*, *391*, 756.

Bremner, A. J. (2018). The origins of body representations in early life. In A. J. T. Alsmith & F. de Vignemont (Eds.), *The subject's matter: Self-consciousness and the body* (pp. 3–32). Cambridge, MA: MIT Press.

Bremner, A. J., Lewkowicz, D. J., & Spence, C. (Eds.). (2012). *Multisensory development*. Oxford: Oxford University Press.

Bremner, A. J., Mareschal, D., Lloyd-Fox, S., & Spence, C. (2008). Spatial localization of touch in the first year of life: Early influence of a visual code, and the development of remapping across changes in limb position. *Journal of Experimental Psychology: General*, *137*, 149–162.

Bremner, A. J., & Spence, C. (2017). The development of tactile perception. In J. Benson (Ed.), *Advances in child development and behavior* (Vol. 52, pp. 227–268). Oxford: Elsevier.

Brownell, C. A., Nichols, S. R., Svetlova, M., Zerwas, S., & Ramani, G. (2010). The head bone's connected to the neck bone: When do toddlers represent their own body topography? *Child Development*, *81*, 797–810.

Bushnell, E. W., & Boudreau, J. P. (1993). Motor development and the mind: The potential role of motor abilities as a determinant of aspects of perceptual development. *Child Development*, *64*, 1005–1021.

Butterworth, G., & Hopkins, B. (1988). Hand–mouth coordination in the new-born baby. *British Journal of Developmental Psychology*, *6*, 303–314.

Castiello, U., Becchio, C., Zoia, S., Nelini, C., Sartori, L., Blason, L., … Gallese, V. (2010). Wired to be social: The ontogeny of human interaction. *PLoS ONE*, *5*, e13199.

Chinn, L. K., Hoffmann, M., Leed, J. E., & Lockman, J. J. (2019). Reaching with one arm to the other: Coordinating touch, proprioception, and action during infancy. *Journal of Experimental Child Psychology*, *183*, 19–32.

Chinn, L. K., Noonan, C. F., Hoffmann, M., & Lockman, J. J. (2019). Development of infant reaching strategies to tactile targets on the face. *Frontiers in Psychology*, *10*(9). https://doi.org/10.3389/fpsyg.2019.00009

Classen, C. (Ed.). (2005). *The book of touch*. Oxford: Berg.

Cole, J., & Paillard, J. (1995). Living without touch and peripheral information about body position and movement: Studies with deafferented subjects. In J. L. Bermudez, A. Marcel, & N. Eilan (Eds.), *The body and the self* (pp. 245–266). Cambridge, MA: MIT Press.

Craig, A. D. (2009). How do you feel – now? The anterior insula and human awareness. *Nature Reviews Neuroscience*, *10*, 59–70.

Crucianelli, L., Wheatley, L., Filippetti, M. L., Jenkinson, P. M., Kirk, E., & Fotopoulou, A. K. (2019). The mindedness of maternal touch: An investigation of maternal mind-mindedness and mother–infant touch interactions. *Developmental Cognitive Neuroscience*, *35*, 47–56.

Dematté, M. L., Sanabria, D., Sugarman, R., & Spence, C. (2006). Cross-modal interactions between olfaction and touch. *Chemical Senses*, *31*, 291–300.

de Vignemont, F., Majid, A., Jola, C., & Haggard, P. (2009). Segmenting the body into parts: evidence from biases in tactile perception. *Quarterly Journal of Experimental Psychology*, *62*, 500–512.

de Vries, J. I. P., Visser, G. H. A., & Prechtl, H. F. R. (1984). Fetal motility in the first half of pregnancy. *Clinics in Developmental Medicine*, *94*, 46–64.

Diego, M. A., Field, T., & Hernandez-Reif, M. (2005). Vagal activity, gastric motility, and weight gain in massaged preterm neonates. *Journal of Pediatrics*, *147*, 50–55.

Ernst, M. O., & Banks, M. S. (2002). Humans integrate visual and haptic information in a statistically optimal fashion. *Nature*, *415*, 429–433.

Fabrizi, L., Slater, R., Worley, A., Meek, J., Boyd, S., Olhede, S., & Fitzgerald, M. (2011). A shift in sensory processing that enables the developing human brain to discriminate touch from pain. *Current Biology*, *21*, 1552–1558.

Fairhurst, M. T., Löken, L., & Grossmann, T. (2014). Physiological and behavioral responses reveal 9-month-old infants' sensitivity to pleasant touch. *Psychological Science*, *25*, 1124–1131.

Field, T. (2001). *Touch*. Cambridge, MA: MIT Press.

Field, T., & Hernandez-Reif, M. (2001). Sleep problems in infants decrease following massage therapy. *Early Child Development & Care*, *168*, 95–104.

Filippetti, M. L., Johnson, M. H., Lloyd-Fox, S., Dragovic, D., & Farroni, T. (2013). Body perception in newborns. *Current Biology*, *23*, 2413–2416.

Filippetti, M. L., Lloyd-Fox, S., Longo, M. R., Farroni, T., & Johnson, M. H., (2014). Neural mechanisms of body awareness in infants. *Cerebral Cortex*, *25*(1), 1–9.

Filippetti, M. L., Orioli, G., Johnson, M. H., & Farroni, T. (2015). Newborn body perception: Sensitivity to spatial congruency. *Infancy*, *20*, 455–465.

Freier, L., Mason, L., & Bremner, A. J. (2016). Perception of visual-tactile colocation in the first year of life. *Developmental Psychology*, *52*, 2184–2190.

Gallace, A., & Spence, C. (2014). *In touch with the future: The sense of touch from cognitive neuroscience to virtual reality*. Oxford: Oxford University Press.

Gallagher, S. (2005). *How the body shapes the mind*. Oxford: Oxford University Press.

Gibson, J. J. (1966). *The senses considered as perceptual systems*. Oxford: Houghton-Mifflin.

Goksan, S., Hartley, C., Emery, F., Cockrill, N., Poorun, R., Moultrie, F., … Clare, S. (2015). fMRI reveals neural activity overlap between adult and infant pain. *ELIFE*, *4*, e06356.

Gori, M., Del Viva, M. M., Sandini, G., & Burr, D. C. (2008). Young children do not integrate visual and haptic form information. *Current Biology*, *18*, 694–698.

Gori, M., Sandini, G., Martinoli, C., & Burr, D. (2010). Poor haptic orientation discrimination in nonsighted children may reflect disruption of cross-sensory calibration. *Current Biology*, *20*, 223–225.

Gottlieb, G. (1971). Ontogenesis of sensory function in birds and mammals. In E. Tobach, L. R. Aronson, & E. Shaw (Eds.), *The biopsychology of development* (pp. 67–128). New York, NY: Academic Press.

Gray, L., Watt, L., & Blass, E. M. (2000). Skin-to-skin contact is analgesic in healthy newborns. *Pediatrics, 105*, e14.

Harlow, H. F., & Zimmerman, R. R. (1959). Affectional response in the infant monkey. *Science, 130*, 421–431.

Hart, S., Field, T., Hernandez-Reif, M., & Lundy, B. (1998). Preschoolers' cognitive performance improves following massage. *Early Child Development & Care, 143*, 59–64.

Held, R., Ostrovsky, Y., de Gelder, B., Gandhi, T., Ganesh, S., Mathur, U., & Sinha, P. (2011). The newly sighted fail to match seen with felt. *Nature Neuroscience, 14*, 551–553.

Hoffmann, M., Chinn, L. K., Somogyi, E., Heed, T., Fagard, J., Lockman, J. J., & O'Regan, J. K. (2017). *Development of reaching to the body in early infancy: From experiments to robotic models.* Paper presented at the 2017 Joint IEEE International Conference on Development and Learning and Epigenetic Robotics (ICDL-EpiRob), Lisbon, Portugal.

Holmes, N. P., & Spence, C. (2004). The body schema and multisensory representation(s) of peripersonal space. *Cognitive Processing, 5*, 94–105.

Hooker, D. (1952). *The prenatal origin of behavior.* Lawrence: University of Kansas Press.

Hopkins, B., & Westra, T. (1988). Maternal handling and motor development: An intracultural study. *Genetic, Social, and General Psychology Monographs, 114*, 377–408.

Humphrey, T. (1964). Some correlations between the appearance of human fetal reflexes and the development of the nervous system. *Progress in Brain Research, 4*, 93–135.

Jönsson, E. H., Kotilahti, K., Heiskala, J., Backlund Wasling, H., Olausson, H., Croy, I., ... Karlsson, L. (2018). Affective and non-affective touch evoke differential brain responses in 2-month-old infants. *NeuroImage, 169*, 162–171.

Jouen, F., & Molina, M. (2005). Exploration of the newborn's manual activity: A window onto early cognitive processes. *Infant Behavior & Development, 28*, 227–239.

Jousmäki, V., & Hari, R. (1998). Parchment-skin illusion: Sound-biased touch. *Current Biology, 8*, R190-R191.

Kahrimanovic, M., Bergmann Tiest, W. M., & Kappers, A. M. (2010). Haptic perception of volume and surface area of 3-D objects. *Attention, Perception, & Psychophysics, 72*, 517–527.

Kalagher, H., & Jones, S. S. (2011a). Developmental change in young children's use of haptic information in a visual task: The role of hand movements. *Journal of Experimental Child Psychology, 108*, 293–307.

    (2011b). Young children's haptic exploratory procedures. *Journal of Experimental Child Psychology, 110*, 592–602.

Karasik, L. B., Tamis-LeMonda, C. S., Ossmy, O., & Adolph, K. E. (2018). The ties that bind: Cradling in Tajikistan. *PLoS ONE, 13*, e0204428.

Kida, T., & Shinohara, K. (2013). Gentle touch activates the prefrontal cortex in infancy: A NIRS study. *Neuroscience Letters*, *541*, 63–66.

Kisilevsky, B. S., & Muir, D. W. (1984). Neonatal habituation and dishabituation to tactile stimulation during sleep. *Developmental Psychology*, *20*, 367–373.

Krsnik, Ž., Majić, V., Vasung, L., Huang, H., & Kostović, I. (2017). Growth of thalamocortical fibers to the somatosensory cortex in the human fetal brain. *Frontiers in Neuroscience*, *11*, 233.

Le Cornu Knight, F., Bremner, A. J., & Cowie, D. (2020). Does the language we use to segment the body, shape the way we perceive it? A study of tactile perceptual distortions. *Cognition*, 197, 104127. doi:10.1016/j.cognition.2019.104127

Le Cornu Knight, F., Cowie, D., & Bremner, A. J. (2016). Part-based representations of the body in early childhood: Evidence from perceived distortions of tactile space across limb boundaries. *Developmental Science*, *20*(6), e12439.

Le Cornu Knight, F., Longo, M., & Bremner, A. J. (2014). Categorical perception of tactile distance. *Cognition*, *131*, 254–262.

Lederman, S. J., & Klatzky, R. L. (2009). Haptic perception: A tutorial. *Attention, Perception, & Psychophysics*, *71*, 1439–1459.

Lee, H. K. (2005). The effect of infant massage on weight gain: Physiological and behavioral responses in premature infants. *Taehan Kanho Hakhoe Chi*, *35*, 1451–1460.

Ley, P., Bottari, D., Shenoy, B. H., Kekunnaya, R., & Röder, B. (2013). Partial recovery of visual–spatial remapping of touch after restoring vision in a congenitally blind man. *Neuropsychologia*, *51*, 1119–1123.

Lipsitt, L. P. (2002). The newborn as informant. In J. W. Fagan & H. Hayne (Eds.), *Progress in infancy research, vol. 2* (pp. 27–50). Mahwah, NJ: Lawrence Erlbaum Associates.

Löken, L. S., Wessberg, J., Morrison, I., McGlone, F., & Olausson, H. (2009). Coding of pleasant touch by unmyelinated afferents in humans. *Nature Neuroscience*, *12*, 547–548.

Maister, L., Tang, T., & Tsakiris, M. (2017). Neurobehavioral evidence of interoceptive sensitivity in early infancy. *ELIFE*, *6*, e25318.

Maitre, N. L., Key, A. P., Chorna, O. D., Slaughter, J. C., Matusz, P. J., Wallace, M. T., & Murray, M. M. (2017). The dual nature of early-life experience on somatosensory processing in the human infant brain. *Current Biology*, *27*, 1048–1054.

Majid, A. (2010). Words for parts of the body. In B. Malt, & P. Wolff (Eds.), *Words and the mind: How words capture human experience* (pp. 58–71). Oxford: Oxford University Press.

Ma-Kellams, C., Blascovich, J., & McCall, C. (2012). Culture and the body: East–West differences in visceral perception. *Journal of Personality and Social Psychology*, *102*, 718–28.

Marcus, L., Lejeune, F., Berne-Audéoud, F., Gentaz, E., & Debillon, T. (2012). Tactile sensory capacity of the preterm infant: Manual perception of shape from 28 gestational weeks. *Pediatrics*, *130*, e88–e94.

Markus, H. R., & Kitayama, S. (1991). Culture and the self: Implications for cognition, emotion, and motivation. *Psychological Review*, *98*, 224–253.

Marshall, P. J., & Meltzoff, A. N. (2015). Body maps in the infant brain. *Trends in Cognitive Sciences, 19*, 499–505.

Maurer, D., Stager, C. L., & Mondloch, C. J. (1999). Cross-modal transfer of shape is difficult to demonstrate in one-month-olds. *Child Development, 70*, 1047–1057.

Meins, E., Fernyhough, C., Fradley, E., & Tuckey, M. (2001). Rethinking maternal sensitivity: Mothers' comments on infants' mental processes predict security of attachment at 12 months. *Journal of Child Psychology and Psychiatry and Allied Disciplines, 42*, 637–648.

Meltzoff, A. N., & Borton, R. W. (1979). Intermodal matching by human neonates. *Nature, 282*, 403–404.

Meltzoff, A. N., Ramírez, R. R., Saby, J. N., Larson, E., Taulu, S., & Marshall, P. J. (2018). Infant brain responses to felt and observed touch of hands and feet: An MEG study. *Developmental Science, 21*, e12651.

Meltzoff, A. N., Saby, J. N., & Marshall, P. J. (2019). Neural representations of the body in 60-day-old human infants. *Developmental Science, 22*, e12698.

Miguel, H. O., Lisboa, I. C., Gonçalves, Ó. F., & Sampaio, A. (2019). Brain mechanisms for processing discriminative and affective touch in 7-month-old infants. *Developmental Cognitive Neuroscience, 35*, 20–27.

Milh, M., Kaminska, A., Huon, C., Lapillonne, A., Ben-Ari, Y., & Khazipov, R. (2007). Rapid cortical oscillations and early motor activity in premature human neonate. *Cerebral Cortex, 17*, 1582–1594.

Montagu, A. (1978). *Touching: The human significance of the skin*. New York, NY: Harper & Row.

Moreau, T., Helfgott, E., Weinstein, P., & Milner, P. (1978). Lateral differences in habituation of ipsilateral head-turning to repeated tactile stimulation in the human newborn. *Perceptual & Motor Skills, 46*, 427–436.

Murphy, J., Brewer, R., Catmur, C., & Bird, G. (2017). Interoception and psychopathology: A developmental neuroscience perspective. *Developmental Cognitive Neuroscience, 23*, 45–56.

Nevalainen, P., Lauronen, L., & Pihko, E. (2014). Development of human somatosensory cortical functions – what have we learned from magnetoencephalography: A review. *Frontiers in Human Neuroscience, 8*, 158.

Norris, S., Campbell, L. A., & Brenkert, S. (1981). Nursing procedures and alterations in transcutaneous oxygen tension in premature infants. *Nursing Research, 31*, 330–336.

Penfield, W., & Rasmussen, T. (1950). *The cerebral cortex of man: A clinical study of localization*. Oxford: Macmillan.

Pirazzoli, L., Lloyd-Fox, S., Braukmann, R., Johnson, M. H., & Gliga, T. (2019). Hand or spoon? Exploring the neural basis of affective touch in 5-month-old infants. *Developmental Cognitive Neuroscience, 35*, 28–35.

Quattrocki, E., & Friston, K. (2014). Autism, oxytocin and interoception. *Neuroscience & Biobehavioral Reviews, 47*, 410–430.

Radman, Z. (2013). *The hand, an organ of the mind: What the manual tells the mental*. Cambridge, MA: MIT Press.

Rigato, S., Begum Ali, J., van Velzen, J., & Bremner, A. J. (2014). The neural basis of somatosensory remapping develops in human infancy. *Current Biology, 24*, 1222–1226.

Rochat, P. (1998). Self-perception and action in infancy. *Experimental Brain Research*, *123*, 102–109.

(2010). The innate sense of the body develops to become a public affair by 2–3 years. *Neuropsychologia*, *48*, 738–745.

Rochat, P., & Hespos, S. J. (1997). Differential rooting response by neonates: Evidence for an early sense of self. *Early Development & Parenting*, *64*, 153–188.

Rochat, P., & Senders, S. J. (1991). Active touch in infancy: Action systems in development. In M. J. S. Weiss & P. R. Zelazo (Eds.), *Newborn attention: Biological constraints and the influence of experience* (pp. 412–442). Westport, CT: Ablex.

Röder, B., Rösler, F., & Spence, C. (2004). Early vision impairs tactile perception in the blind. *Current Biology*, *14*, 121–124.

Rose, S. A. (1994). From hand to eye: Findings and issues in infant cross-modal transfer. In D.J. Lewkowicz, & R. Lickliter (Eds.), *The development of intersensory perception: Comparative perspectives* (pp. 265–284). Hillsdale, NJ: Lawrence Erlbaum Associates.

Rose, S. A., Gottfried, A. W., & Bridger, W. H. (1981). Cross-modal transfer in 6-month-old infants. *Developmental Psychology*, *17*, 661–669.

Saby, J. N., Meltzoff, A. N., & Marshall, P. J. (2015). Neural body maps in human infants: Somatotopic responses to tactile stimulation in 7-month-olds. *NeuroImage*, *118*, 74–78.

Schicke, T., & Röder, B. (2006). Spatial remapping of touch: Confusion of perceived stimulus order across hand and foot. *Proceedings of the National Academy of Sciences of the United States of America*, *103*, 11808–11813.

Shen, G., Weiss, S. M., Meltzoff, A. N., & Marshall, P. J. (2018). The somatosensory mismatch negativity as a window into body representations in infancy. *International Journal of Psychophysiology*, *134*, 144–150.

Somogyi, E., Jacquey, L., Heed, T., Hoffmann, M., Lockman, J. J., Granjon, L., … O'Regan, J. K. (2018). Which limb is it? Responses to vibrotactile stimulation in early infancy. *British Journal of Developmental Psychology*, *36*, 384–401.

Stein, B. E. (Ed.) (2012). *The new handbook of multisensory processes*. Cambridge, MA: MIT Press.

Streri, A. (2012). Crossmodal interactions in the human newborn: New answers to Molyneux's question. In A. J. Bremner, D. J. Lewkowicz, & C. Spence (Eds.), *Multisensory development* (pp. 88–112). Oxford: Oxford University Press.

Streri, A., Lhote, M., & Dutilleul, S. (2000). Haptic perception in newborns. *Developmental Science*, *3*, 319–327.

Thomas, R. L., Misra, R., Akkunt, E., Ho, C., Spence, C., & Bremner, A. J. (2018). Sensitivity to auditory-tactile colocation in early infancy. *Developmental Science*, *21*, e12597.

Tiriac, A., Sokoloff, G., & Blumberg, M. S. (2015). Myoclonic twitching and sleep-dependent plasticity in the developing sensorimotor system. *Current Sleep Medicine Reports*, *1*, 74–79.

Turkewitz, G. (1994). Sources of order for intersensory functioning. In D. J. Lewkowicz, & R. Lickliter (Eds.), *The development of intersensory perception: Comparative perspectives* (pp. 3–18). Hillsdale, NJ: Lawrence Erlbaum Associates.

Tuulari, J. J., Scheinin, N. M., Lehtola, S., Merisaari, H., Saunavaara, J., Parkkola, R., ... Björnsdotter, M. (2019). Neural correlates of gentle skin stroking in early infancy. *Developmental Cognitive Neuroscience*, *35*, 36–41.

Zappella, M., & Simopoulos, A. (1966). The crossed-extension reflex in the newborn. *Annales Paediatriae Fenniae*, *12*, 30–33.

Zmyj, N., Jank, J., Schütz-Bosbach, S., & Daum, M. M. (2011). Detection of visual-tactile contingency in the first year after birth. *Cognition*, *120*, 82–89.

10 The Development of Infant Feeding

Julie A. Mennella, Catherine A. Forestell,
Alison K. Ventura, and Jennifer Orlet Fisher*

In this chapter, we review the scientific evidence, primarily from experimental research, that reveals important aspects of the ontogeny of feeding and the development of food preferences and food choice in the context of the mother. We focus on the first 2 years of life, when children make the drastic transition from eating an all-liquid diet to one containing solid foods. We focus on feeding in the context of the mother, exploring the contribution of each member of the dyad: the infant (who is being fed) and the mother (who is selecting the foods and feeding the child).

This scientific review highlights the biology of flavor perception and what children like to eat, how they learn to like new foods and flavors, and how and when they acquire the skills needed for eating – one of the most complex physical tasks that humans engage in. This biology that favors sweet and salty tastes may make children especially vulnerable in a food environment abundant in many highly palatable, nutrient-poor, easily accessible, and relatively inexpensive foods and beverages. Such changes in the food environment interact with the biology of the child's sensory systems that, although highly tuned to taste and pleasure, are plastic and open to learning about what foods are safe, and eaten and preferred by the mother and other family members and, in turn, drive eating behaviors and food choice (Mennella, Reiter, & Daniels, 2016). Although we acknowledge the importance of other caregivers, we refer to mothers herein when referring to caregivers.

10.1 Culture of Feeding

Habits and beliefs surrounding food – including what constitutes a food, who can eat the food and when, and how it is prepared and flavored – provide insight into a cultural group's pursuit of pleasure and health (Montanari, 2006; E. Rozin, 1973). Depending on availability in the environment and sustained by traditions passed down from generation to generation, food habits ensure that preferences for cultural foods are formed and that cultural identity is preserved (Wahlqvist & Lee, 2007). Sustainability of cultural identity

* The writing of this chapter was supported in part by NIH grant DC016616 (JAM, JOF).

through foods is perhaps most evident during immigration to a new country. Food traditions, which bridge the old with the new by adapting to foods available in the new environment, are often preserved long past the loss of the native language (P. Rozin, 1984) and are adapted to foods available in the new environment.

The transmission to the next generation of information about food, an important biological commodity, begins with the mother. While many maternal food choices during pregnancy are driven by internal factors, such as cravings and aversions, others are influenced by environmental factors, such as cultural food practices and beliefs (Forestell & Mennella, 2008). Beginning at weaning and continuing as the child develops the motor and cognitive skills needed to feed independently, the gradual and repeated familiarization with complementary foods in a positive family context guides the formation of flavor preferences and an understanding of the meaning a food has to the child's family and culture. With globalization of the food supply in many parts of the world, manufactured foods rich in added sugar and salt (Wahlqvist & Lee, 2007) are more available and affordable and, in turn, compete with or come to be defined as cultural foods. Cultural differences in children's consumption of sweets are seen as early as infancy. In China, for example, sweets and sugar-sweetened beverages (SSBs) are rarely consumed by infants and toddlers, whereas in the United States and Mexico SSB consumption increases with age (Afeiche, Koyratty, Wang, Jacquier, & Le, 2018), with Mexican infants and toddlers consuming two to three times more SSBs than do American children (Denney, Reidy, & Eldridge, 2016).

10.2 Early Feeding Patterns and Practices

During the past half century, how we feed infants when they transition to solid foods has changed. Instead of feeding mashed or pureed versions of the family diet, infants are fed specially prepared, prepackaged, manufactured foods, typically fruits and vegetables (Reidy et al., 2018), although sales of these types of baby foods declined in recent years. The food market has recently expanded to include a wide array of foods for toddlers (Moding et al., 2018). After several months of feeding a liquid diet of breast milk and/or formula, 75% of infants transition to solid foods in the form of a commercial cereal or puréed foods by 4 to 6 months of age (Roess et al., 2018). Although most foods geared for newly weaned infants now contain little to no added sugar and sodium, meals geared for toddlers contain relatively higher levels of sodium and added sugar (Maalouf et al., 2017).

During toddlerhood, diet patterns and quality begin to show some of the same problems as seen in adulthood and snacking becomes the focal context for dietary excesses (Deming et al., 2017). By 24 months, intakes of potassium, fiber, and vitamin D and vitamin E are low, reflecting declines in the consumption of healthful foods (Bailey et al., 2018). For instance, among US toddlers, >20% consumed no fruits or vegetables on a given day (Roess et al., 2018). Alternatively, approximately three-fourths of toddlers consumed a dessert or SSB on any given day, and close to 1 in 5 toddlers consumed a savory snack (Roess et al., 2018). These trends continue into preschool, where fried potatoes are the most commonly consumed vegetable, nearly all children consume sweets daily, and almost half consume SSBs on any day (Welker, Jacquier, Catellier, Anater, & Story, 2016).

By 1 year, the contribution of snacking to daily energy intake increases such that 95% of children snack daily. Snacks tend to be higher in carbohydrates, with cookies, crackers, and 100% juice among the top five snack foods (Deming et al., 2017), a feeding pattern that is troubling because low intakes of whole fruits and vegetables and high intakes of energy-dense processed foods, especially those with added sugars, are positively associated with increased risks for cardiovascular disease and obesity risk among children (Flynn et al., 2006; Swinburn, Caterson, Seidell, & James, 2004; Welsh & Cunningham, 2011; Welsh, Sharma, Cunningham, & Vos, 2011; Yang et al., 2014).

10.3 Ontogeny of Feeding Behaviors and Skills: Birth to 24 Months

Although it was once believed that the infant enters the world as a *tabula rasa* (i.e., blank slate) and is fully shaped by postnatal experiences, we now know that inborn characteristics also interact with prenatal experiences and that children are active agents during feeding and interactions with their mothers (Bronfenbrenner & Morris, 1998). During the first 2 years, the infant makes a drastic transition from passively feeding amniotic fluid *in utero* to interacting with the mother during the feeding of breast milk or artificial milk (i.e., infant formulas) and then to independent feeding of a mixed diet of liquids and solids of varying textures. In this section, we review the ontogeny of the senses that relay the flavor of foods and the motor and cognitive skills needed to progress to independent feeding, as well as the available, albeit limited, research on two key ways infants contribute to feeding interactions. While infants are dependent on mothers for the provision of food and comfort, they play an active role through their developing capacities to regulate intake, effectively signal hunger and satiation, and to modify behaviors during feeding in response to maternal cues.

10.3.1 The Neurobiology of Flavor Senses

Because we are what we eat and we eat what we like, one often overlooked driver of early feeding is the flavor of foods. The flavor of a food or beverage

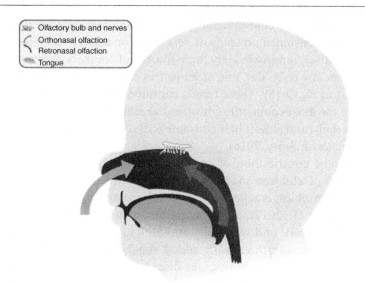

Figure 10.1. *Orthonasal (light gray arrow) and retronasal (dark gray arrow) routes of olfaction.*
Source: Designed by A. K. Ventura and B. Rubenstein. Adapted with permission from Lipchock, Reed, and Mennella (2011).

is a complex perception mediated by the three chemical senses of *taste* (sweet, sour, salty, bitter, umami), *volatile odors* that travels via the retronasal pathway to the olfactory receptors when foods or liquids are in the mouth (P. Rozin, 1982), and *chemesthesis*, the chemically initiated sensation that occurs via the touch system (e.g., coolness of mint, burn of chili peppers, tingle of carbonation). Most people associate the sense of smell only with inhaling odors through the nose (orthonasal perception) but retronasally perceived odor volatiles, which are often confused with tastes (P. Rozin, 1982), contribute most to the overall characteristics of the flavor of a food or beverage. Figure 10.1 illustrates the difference between orthonasal and retronasal perception of volatiles in the foods and beverages. Because of the lack of basic research on chemesthesis, our focus herein is on the ontogeny of the senses of taste and olfaction, particularly that which is retronasal and experienced during feeding.

Like other senses, taste and smell perception begins in the peripheral nervous system, where taste or olfactory ligands bind to known receptors or activate channels, and those signals are sent to the brain. While the senses of taste and smell are functioning *in utero*, they continue to develop throughout infancy and childhood. Thus, the child is not a miniature adult in terms of flavor perception. By the 12th week of gestation, the fetus begins to swallow and inhale large amounts of amniotic fluid (Pritchard, 1965), and by the last trimester the receptors that detect and bind to tastants and volatiles begin to communicate with the central nervous system and modulate behaviors (for a review see). Amniotic fluid and mother's milk, the first food of infants, contain a wide range of nutrients, as well as flavors (e.g., odor volatiles) and potential tastants (e.g., fatty acids [Ballard & Morrow, 2013]; nonnutritive sweeteners [NNS; Rother, Sylvetsky, Walter, Garraffo, & Fields, 2018]) that originate from the maternal diet. Whether the tastants are perceived remain unknown; hence we refer to them as *potential tastants*. However, the evidence suggests that the fetus and infant can detect the volatiles and that these experiences bias their behavioral responses during subsequent exposures.

10.3.1.1 *Taste*

Within hours of being born, newborns react as would be expected to pleasurable and aversive taste stimuli (Forestell & Mennella, 2015). The provision of sweet or umami (meaty) solutions to neonates elicits rhythmic tongue protrusions, lip smacks, lip and finger sucking, and elevation of the corners of the mouth, all of which have been interpreted as positive or hedonic responses (Rosenstein & Oster, 1988; Steiner, 1987). The detection of and preference for sweet taste presumably evolved to attract children to the sweet taste of mother's milk and then to energy-rich foods (e.g., fruits) during periods of maximal growth (Coldwell, Oswald, & Reed, 2009; Mennella, Finkbeiner, Lipchock, Hwang, & Reed, 2014). In contrast, neonates gape, wrinkle their noses, shake their heads, flail their arms, and frown in response to a bitter-tasting solution (Desor, Maller, & Andrews, 1975; Rosenstein & Oster, 1988), and purse their lips and, to a certain extent, gape, wrinkle their nose, flail arms, protrude their tongues and lip smack when tasting concentrated sour solutions (Rosenstein & Oster, 1988). However, unlike their responses to other basic tastes, neonates do not differentially respond to salt taste – the ability to detect and prefer salty taste does not emerge until later in infancy (Beauchamp, Cowart, & Moran, 1986).

Taste preferences are also dependent on what the infant is fed. Compared to infants fed cow milk formulas, which taste less bitter, sour, and more savory than extensively hydrolyzed protein formulas (EHF), infants fed EHF prefer savory-, sour-, and bitter-tasting foods and infants fed breast milk, which is rich in savory free amino acids (e.g., glutamate), prefer savory-tasting foods at weaning (Mennella, Forestell, Morgan, & Beauchamp, 2009). As infants grow, their taste preferences reflect the types of solid foods in their diet. An early diet rich in salt (e.g., grain products) is associated with greater acceptance of salty tastes after weaning from milk or formula (Mennella et al., 2009), which persists to childhood (Stein, Cowart, & Beauchamp, 2012). The effect of early experiences with different tastes in formula is long lasting; several years after the last formula exposure, children fed EHF during infancy exhibited higher preferences for sour-tasting juices and bitter vegetables (Mennella & Beauchamp, 2002). Taken together, these findings suggest that early experiences can modulate these inborn taste responses.

But perhaps the biggest change in taste preferences happens with the cessation of growth. By developing methods that are sensitive to cognitive development, researchers are able to directly compare taste preferences in children and adults, revealing that responses to some of the basic tastes are intensified during childhood. As a group, children prefer higher levels of sweet and salt than do adults (Mennella & Bobowski, 2015; Mennella et al., 2014), with preferences declining to adult levels during adolescence (Beauchamp & Cowart, 1990; Desor & Beauchamp, 1987), which coincides with the cessation of physical growth (Mennella et al., 2014). Although less studied, bitter taste sensitivity also changes during development. From an early age, children can detect lower levels of some bitter tastes compared to adults, with the adult pattern emerging during adolescence (Mennella, Pepino, Duke, & Reed, 2010); such bitter sensitivity makes evolutionary sense because of the risk of accidental poisoning while foraging for plant foods, some of which may be poisonous.

10.3.1.2 *Olfaction*

Psychophysical research on the ontogeny of another flavor sense – olfaction – has focused on odor volatiles perceived both orthonasally and retronasally (Figure 10.1). The olfactory sense is functioning prior to birth such that newborns can identify and prefer the olfactory signature of their mothers, and vice versa, with very little postnatal contact (Schaal & Marlier, 1998), indicating learning about each other's unique odor type is occurring during pregnancy (Beauchamp et al., 1995). Maternal odors serve to foster the transition from fetal to extrauterine life by helping infants identify and attach to their mothers (Sullivan, Perry, Sloan, Kleinhaus, & Burtchen, 2011), while the odors emanating from infants affect maternal brain processing (Nishitani, Kuwamoto, Takahira, Miyamura, & Shinohara, 2014), hormonal responsivity, and bonding with their child (Nagasawa, Okabe, Mogi, & Kikusui, 2012).

The scientific evidence regarding the infants' retronasal perception of food volatiles is discussed below in the context of children learning about foods via the transfer of volatiles from the maternal diet to amniotic fluid and breast milk. Nevertheless, what a mother eats contributes to her olfactory signature by changing her body odor; when infants experience odors in the presence of their mothers; these odors come to be identified as the mother's personal odor and can bias the child's subsequent response to the odor (Al Ain et al., 2017; Delaunay-El Allam, Soussignan, Patris, Marlier, & Schaal, 2010; Forestell & Mennella, 2005). Associative learning in the context of emotionally salient conditions is a powerful mechanism by which odors acquire personal significance, and when such learning occurs is important (Debiec & Sullivan, 2014).

The unique processing of olfactory information, and the olfactory system's immediate access to the neurological substrates underlying nonverbal aspects of emotion and memory, help explain why memories evoked by odors are more emotionally charged than those evoked by the other senses and, in turn, the large emotional component of food aromas. This, coupled with the finding that the most salient memories formed during the first decade of life will likely be olfactory in nature (Willander & Larsson, 2006), explains how food aromas can trigger memories of childhood (e.g., the smell of madeleines by Proust [Bartolomei, Lagarde, Medina Villalon, McGonigal, & Benar, 2017]) and why flavors and food aromas experienced during childhood remain preferred and, to some extent, can provide comfort.

10.3.2 Feeding Skills and Patterns

Over the first 2 years of life, children undergo dramatic development of oral, fine, and gross motor skills related to feeding (Carruth & Skinner, 2002), as well as the capacity to communicate interest and disinterest in eating (Hodges et al., 2013; McNally et al., 2016). These developmental gains are accompanied by significant shifts in feeding behavior and dietary intake. Infants start life relying on a single food (i.e., mother's milk or formula) as the sole source of nutrition and are completely dependent on their caregivers to provide nutrition. Suckling at the nipple is the primary feeding milestone of early infancy and is elegantly coordinated by the central nervous system with swallowing and breathing during breastfeeding in a way that allows the infant to continuously feed without breathing interruptions. The importance of this feeding skill is underscored by the fact that human milk and formula provide the majority of energy until late infancy; between 6 and 9 months of age, close to three-quarters of daily energy intake comes from eating occasions involving primarily breast milk or formula (Deming et al., 2017). Around this time, however, anatomical growth and maturation of sucking patterns occur, along with rapid gains in fine and gross motor control that facilitate the transition from a milk-based diet to the consumption of complementary foods of varying texture, flavor complexity, and nutritional profiles (Naylor & Morrow, 2001). For instance, at 4–5 months, infants are able to sit without help, open their mouth as a spoon approaches, and use their tongue to draw food back in the mouth to swallow (Carruth & Skinner, 2002). By 6–9 months, children can chew lumpy and soft foods, pick up finger foods, and drink from a cup (Carruth & Skinner, 2002).

Eating from a spoon requires using the upper lip to remove food from the spoon and bringing the bolus of food back into the mouth to swallow (Carruth & Skinner, 2002). Infants at 4 to 8 months old require approximately 6 weeks to master the skill of eating food from a spoon presented by the caregiver (van den Engel-Hoek, van Hulst, van Gerven, van Haaften, & de Groot, 2014). While current US guidelines recommend exclusive breastfeeding to 6 months, complementary foods are often introduced before 6 months (Grummer-Strawn, Scanlon, & Fein, 2008).

The progression to independent feeding milestones can be quite variable, reflecting individual differences in the acquisition of skills as well as maternal feeding practices and beliefs. To progress to independent feeding, the child needs to acquire skills that include the ability to pick up food, remove food from the spoon with the lips, and drink from a cup without assistance (Carruth & Skinner, 2002; Carruth, Ziegler, Gordon, & Hendricks, 2004). Normative data indicate that children acquire these self-feeding skills between the ages of 7 and 14 months (Carruth et al., 2004). Observational research has documented that around 10 months of age infants begin to reject being fed by caregivers, demonstrating a preference for self-feeding (Negayama, 1993). However, the transition to self-feeding may occur much earlier based on feeding practices and beliefs of the mother. Interestingly, for example, the movement toward "baby-led weaning" promotes infant self-feeding (i.e., picked up with fingers) from the onset of the introduction to solid or complementary foods at 6 months of age (Cameron, Heath, & Taylor, 2012). Proponents argue that baby-led approach to weaning mirrors the dynamics of breastfeeding during which the infant determines the pace and duration of the feed (Cameron et al., 2012). The extent to which the timing of the transition to self-feeding may influence the regulation of appetite or growth, however, remains largely unknown.

10.3.3 Communication Skills

Infants communicate when they are hungry and full using a broad array of behaviors that, from the perspective of the mother, range from subtle to overt. Signaling varies based on the individual and changes with age. For example, at a given age, infants are consistent in the number and types of behaviors displayed, suggesting each has his or her own behavioral repertoire of cues to communicate hunger and feelings of fullness (Ventura, Inamdar, & Mennella, 2015; Ventura & Mennella, 2017).

During infancy, common hunger cues include sucking on hands or feet, smacking lips, rooting, waking, and increased motor activity and crying; common satiation cues include decreasing or stopping sucking, not accepting the breast, bottle, or food when offered, turning the head, leaning away, exhibiting negative facial expressions, spitting out the nipple, and falling asleep (Hodges et al., 2013; Ventura et al., 2015; Ventura & Mennella, 2017). As infants develop greater motor, cognitive, and social skills and learn based on past interactions with their mothers, the type and extent to which these cues are displayed change over time (Hodges, Hughes, Hopkinson, & Fisher, 2008; Skinner et al., 1998). In general, infants exhibit more cues during breastfeeding than during formula feeding (Shloim, Vereijken, Blundell, & Hetherington, 2017), and they are more consistent in the types of behaviors used to signal satiation if their mothers are more responsive to such cues (Ventura & Mennella, 2017). Because the latter findings come from cross-sectional, observational research studies, it remains unknown whether breastfeeding or responsive feeding styles promote more consistent communication by infants or whether more consistent infant communication facilitates successful breastfeeding and the feeding styles of the mothers.

Given that many of the behaviors used to signal hunger and satiation are used to signal other needs, including desire for comfort, engagement, or disengagement, mothers are challenged to understand the meaning of infant behaviors within both feeding and nonfeeding contexts. For example, crying can occur in the absence of hunger and feeding (Hodges et al., 2008) but may be interpreted by some mothers as a signal that the infant needs to be fed (Gross et al., 2010). While hunger cues are more salient to mothers than are satiation cues (Hodges et al., 2008; Shloim et al., 2017; Ventura et al., 2015), and mothers indeed vary in their feeding styles and how responsive they are to their infant's signals (Thompson et al., 2009), the dyadic interaction is not unidirectional. Rather, this intimate interaction that takes place during feeding is bidirectional and reciprocal, and needed for infants to sustain the ability to self-regulate intake as they grow (Black & Aboud, 2011; Mennella, Papas, Reiter, Stallings, & Trabulsi, 2019).

10.3.4 Self-Regulation

In the late 1920s, pediatrician Dr. Clara Davis was concerned with the pediatric community's trend toward creating strict, prescribed diets that dictated when, what, and how much the child should eat (Strauss, 2006). Convinced that infants and children were more capable than their pediatricians and parents realized, Davis conducted an intensive, longitudinal study of a small sample of newly weaned infants wherein at every meal for 6 months infants were offered a wide array of healthy and developmentally appropriate foods that they were allowed to eat *ad libitum*, with no intervention from their caregivers (Davis, 1928). Assessments of energy intakes, growth, and health status revealed variation among infants in how much and what they ate from meal to meal, but "there were no failures of infants to manage their own diets; all had hearty appetites, all throve" (Davis, 1939, p. 258). This study was one of the first to document that, when offered a wide array of healthy foods, infants can self-regulate intake in a way that is supportive of healthy growth and development.

Since this landmark study, researchers have continued to investigate whether infants are capable of regulating intake in the short and long term (Fomon, Filmer, Thomas, Anderson, & Nelson, 1975; Fox, Devaney, Reidy, Razafindrakoto, & Ziegler, 2006; Ventura, Beauchamp, & Mennella, 2012), especially given that breast milk – the initial food infants evolved to feed – is complex and dynamic, with its composition changing during the course of lactation, as well as within and between breastfeeds. Given the importance of adequate calorie and nutrient intakes for supporting growth and development of the brain and body, it would be adaptive for infants to have the capacity to adjust how much they ingest in response to the energy or nutrient content of the diet. Experimental research has studied whether infants were able to self-regulate by modifying the caloric content and composition of what was fed to them. However, the methods, study design, and duration vary greatly across studies.

In the majority of studies, within- or between-study designs were used to understand whether infants responded, in terms of changes in intake or growth over the course of several weeks (Fomon, Filer, Thomas, Rogers, & Proksch, 1969; Fomon et al., 1975), to changes in formula composition (e.g., calories [Fomon et al., 1975], carbohydrate [Brown, Tuholski, Sauer, Minsk, & Rosenstern, 1960; Fomon, 1980], form of protein [Mennella, Ventura, & Beauchamp, 2011; Ventura et al., 2012], or sweetness [Fomon, Ziegler, Nelson, & Edwards, 1983]). The convergence of findings suggests that, by 4 months, infants have the capacity to regulate intake in response to certain characteristics of the milk fed, with evidence being strongest for regulation in response to changes in its caloric content (Fomon et al., 1969; Fomon et al., 1975) and levels of certain amino acids known to promote satiation when sensed in the gut (San Gabriel & Uneyama, 2013). For example, infants ingest smaller volumes of formula when given more energy-dense formulas, but such intake adjustments take approximately 6 weeks to emerge (Fomon et al., 1975; Fomon, Thomas, Filer, Anderson, & Nelson, 1976). Additionally, infants will begin signaling satiation sooner and will consume less formula to satiation when the formula contains high levels of free amino acids (Ventura et al., 2012; Ventura et al., 2015), which may be explained by findings that free amino acids are known modulators of gut activity (Uneyama, Niijima, San Gabriel, & Torii, 2006). Over the longer term, infants randomized to feed formulas high in free amino acids exhibited more normative weight gain during the first year compared with infants randomized to be fed cow milk formula (Mennella et al., 2018; Mennella et al., 2011).

In the short term, intake does not appear to be influenced by the fat content of breast milk (Cannon et al., 2017; Kent et al., 2006) or by changes in the fat content of breast milk (Woolridge, Baum, & Drewett, 1980) or formula (Chan, Pollitt, & Leibel, 1979) within a feed. However, in the longer term, the higher the fat content of breast milk, the more normative the weight gain patterns (Prentice et al., 2016). Consistent with aforementioned findings that infants exhibit a preference for sweet tastes, infants will ingest larger volumes of sweeter-tasting formula (and other foods), and this response to sweetness is immediate and sustained for at least 1 month (Fomon et al., 1983).

Limited observational data with infants, aged 6 to 11 months, suggest that the ability to regulate intake in response to caloric concentration is preserved during early solid food feeding (Fox et al., 2006). However, as discussed herein, feeding is reciprocal, and infants do not feed in isolation but, rather, are dependent on others for the provision of food and initiation of feeding. The mother can override the child's ability to self-regulate, especially if she perceives the child as being too small or too big (Derks et al., 2017) or misinterprets her infant's cues (Gross et al., 2010).Thus, the abilities of the mothers to effectively read the hunger and satiation cues of their infants and understand what constitutes appropriate eating and healthy weight gain patterns are key to supporting the infants' abilities to communicate their needs and getting them off to a healthy start.

10.4 The Dyad: Learning About Foods

Learning about flavors of foods begins before the child has a first taste of solid food, since sensory information regarding the foods and beverages the mother ingests and enjoys is transmitted to her infant via amniotic fluid and breast milk (see Table 10.1). This type of learning is not unique to humans but appears to be a fundamental feature of vertebrate learning (Provenza, 2018). Building on scientific findings in other animals (Mennella, 2007), including how volatiles from both the lung (what the cow breathes) and rumen (what the cow eats) transmit and flavor cow milk (Shipe et al., 1962), and on the sensory taste panel work of Barker and McDaniel that revealed the milk of one mother often tasted different from that of another (Barker, 1980; McDaniel, 1980), Mennella and Beauchamp began to systematically study the transfer of volatiles from the maternal diet to amniotic fluid and human milk and the effects on the behavior and preferences of the recipient infant (Mennella, 2007). In their early studies, collection of milk samples and evaluation of infant behaviors were done on two days, with testing occurring at the same time of day since both infant feeding and intake can be affected by daily rhythms (Butte, Wills, Jean, Smith, & Garza, 1985; Woolridge, Baum, & Drewett, 1982). After avoiding the test food and flavors for several days to ensure the baseline milk sample was devoid of its volatiles, in counterbalanced order mothers ingested a flavor on one day and a placebo or control beverage on another, and milk samples were collected before and at fixed intervals after ingestion (see Mennella, 2007 for a review). In subsequent research studies listed in Table 10.1, the effects after flavor ingestion were compared to before flavor ingestion.

10.4.1 Amniotic Fluid and Breast Milk: The First Foods

A variety of approaches were used to determine whether flavor volatiles (and their metabolites) and other chemicals (e.g., NNS) originating in the foods and beverages ingested by the mother were transmitted to and/or flavored

Table 10.1 *Summary of the evidence of transfer of volatiles from maternal diet to amniotic fluid (AF) and breast milk (BM) and the short- and long-term effects on the recipient child*

Maternal diet		Type of study, conditions, or groups	Effects on flavor of AF or BM		Effects on recipient child[c]		Reference, country
Flavor[a]	Stage		Analytic methods[b]	Sensory methods	During exposure/ when AF or BM is flavored	After exposure to flavor in AF or BM (days to years later)	
Alcohol	Pregnancy	Between-subject cohort (frequent vs. infrequent drinkers)				Newborns of frequent drinkers displayed more appetitive facial responses and more head and facial movements when smelling ethanol	Faas, March, Moya, & Molina, 2015; Faas, Sponton, Moya, & Molina, 2000 Argentina
Alcohol	Lactation	Within-subject study (alcohol vs. control beverage)	Ethanol in BM peaked 0.5–1 hr after alcohol ingestion and decreased thereafter	Sensory panel detected time-dependent change in BM after drinking alcohol that paralleled changes in ethanol content	Infants sucked more frequently and ingested less BM when flavored with alcohol[d]		Mennella & Beauchamp, 1991b; Mennella & Beauchamp, 1993a United States
Alcohol	Lactation	Within-subject study (alcohol vs. control)			Infants detected flavor in BM, as evidenced by changes in intake and sucking rhythm	Frequency of maternal drinking during lactation was related to the infants' suckling pattern while feeding alcohol-flavored BM	Mennella, 1997 United States

Table 10.1 (cont.)

Maternal diet		Type of study, conditions, or groups	Effects on flavor of AF or BM		Effects on recipient child[c]		Reference, country
Flavor[a]	Stage		Analytic methods[b]	Sensory methods	During exposure/ when AF or BM is flavored	After exposure to flavor in AF or BM (days to years later)	
Alcohol	Lactation	Within- and between-subject study (alcohol-scented vs. unscented toy; groups based on parental drinking)				Infants whose mothers (and fathers) were alcoholics spent more time mouthing alcohol-scented toy	Mennella & Beauchamp, 1998a United States
Garlic	Pregnancy	Between-subject study (mothers ingested garlic vs. placebo before amniocentesis)		Sensory panel detected odor differences in AF of women who ingested garlic			Mennella et al., 1995 United States
Garlic	Pregnancy	Between-subject study (garlic consumers vs. garlic avoiders)				Newborns whose mothers reported they ate garlic during last month of pregnancy spent more time orienting to garlic odor	Hepper, 1995 Northern Ireland
Garlic	Pregnancy	RCT (garlic eaters vs. garlic avoiders)				Children (8–9 years) whose mothers ate garlic when pregnant consumed more garlic-flavored potatoes	Hepper, Wells, Dornan, & Lynch, 2013 Northern Ireland

(continued)

Table 10.1 (*cont.*)

Maternal diet		Type of study, conditions, or groups	Effects on flavor of AF or BM		Effects on recipient child[c]		Reference, country
Flavor[a]	Stage		Analytic methods[b]	Sensory methods	During exposure/ when AF or BM is flavored	After exposure to flavor in AF or BM (days to years later)	
Garlic	Lactation	Within-subject study (garlic vs. placebo capsules)		Sensory panel detected time-dependent change in odor of BM after garlic ingestion	Infants breastfed longer and sucked more when BM was flavored with garlic		Mennella & Beauchamp, 1991a United States
Garlic	Lactation	RCT study (mothers ingested garlic for 1 or 3 days prior to testing or not at all)				More recent exposure to garlic flavor in BM modified duration of breastfeed	Mennella & Beauchamp, 1993b United States
Garlic	Lactation	Within-subject, raw garlic	Garlic-derived metabolites detected in BM 2–3 hours after ingestion	Sensory panel detected time-dependent changes in odor of BM after garlic ingestion that paralleled metabolite content of BM			Scheffler et al., 2016 Germany
Carrot	Lactation	Study 1: Within-subject (carrot juice vs. water) Study 2: Between-subject (1 week of carrot juice or water ingestion)		Study 1: Sensory panel detected time-dependent changes in odor of BM, and mothers detected taste change in their BM 2 hrs after carrot ingestion		Study 2: Recency of maternal carrot ingestion modified infant's response to carrot flavor in cereal	Mennella & Beauchamp, 1999 United States

Table 10.1 *(cont.)*

Maternal diet		Type of study, conditions, or groups	Effects on flavor of AF or BM		Effects on recipient child[c]		Reference, country
Flavor[a]	Stage		Analytic methods[b]	Sensory methods	During exposure/ when AF or BM is flavored	After exposure to flavor in AF or BM (days to years later)	
Carrot	Pregnancy or Lactation	RCT: Groups ingested carrot juice or water for 3 months during pregnancy and/or lactation				Infants exposed to carrot flavor in AF or BM were more accepting (fewer faces of distaste, more maternal perception of infant enjoyment) of carrot-flavored cereal after weaning	Mennella, Jagnow, & Beauchamp, 2001 United States
Carrot, beet, celery, vegetable	Lactation	RCT: Groups ingested vegetable juices or water for 1 or 3 months, with ingestion beginning 0.5, 1.5, or 2.5 months postpartum				Infants exposed to vegetable flavors during first month of lactation ate more and displayed fewer negative faces while eating carrot-flavored cereal after weaning	Mennella, Daniels, & Reiter, 2017 United States
Vanilla	Lactation	Within-subject study (vanilla or placebo capsules)		Sensory panel detected time-dependent changes in odor of BM after vanilla ingestion	Infants consumed more BM and spent longer time feeding when BM flavored with vanilla		Mennella & Beauchamp, 1994; Mennella & Beauchamp, 1996 United States

(continued)

Table 10.1 (*cont.*)

Maternal diet		Type of study, conditions, or groups	Effects on flavor of AF or BM		Effects on recipient child[c]		Reference, country
Flavor[a]	Stage		Analytic methods[b]	Sensory methods	During exposure/ when AF or BM is flavored	After exposure to flavor in AF or BM (days to years later)	
Vanilla	Lactation	Within- and between-subject study (vanilla vs. control scented toy); groups based on maternal reports of frequent vs. not frequent use of vanilla products				Infants whose mothers frequently used vanilla-scented products spent more time looking at the vanilla-scented toy	Mennella & Beauchamp, 1998a United States
Anise	Pregnancy	Between-subjects study (anise consumers vs. anise avoiders)				Newborns of mothers who ate anise made fewer negative faces and more mouthing movements and oriented head toward anise odor	Schaal, et al., 2000 France
Anise	Lactation	Within-subject study (anise and caraway tea)	No detection of volatiles	Sensory panel did not detect odor changes in BM			Denzer et al., 2015 Germany
Mint, caraway, anise, fruit	Lactation	Within-subject study (mint, caraway, anise, and fruit capsules)	Time-dependent detection of carvone (spearmint), anethole (anise), menthol (mint) in BM post ingestion; no detection of fruit (3-methylbutyl acetate) volatiles				Hausner, Bredie, Molgaard, Petersen, & Moller, 2008 Denmark

Table 10.1 (*cont.*)

Maternal diet		Effects on flavor of AF or BM		Effects on recipient child[c]		Reference, country
Flavor[a]	Stage	Analytic methods[b]	Sensory methods	During exposure/ when AF or BM is flavored	After exposure to flavor in AF or BM (days to years later)	
				Type of study, conditions, or groups		
Eucalyptus (1,8-cineole)	Lactation	Cineole detected in BM post ingestion	Sensory panel detected eucalyptus odor in BM at time of odor change in mothers' breath	Within-subject study (eucalyptus)		Kirsch, Beauchamp, & Buettner, 2012 Germany
Tobacco	Lactation	Nicotine peaked in BM 0.5–1 hr after smoking and decreased thereafter	Sensory panel detected time-dependent change in BM after smoking that paralleled changes in nicotine content	Within-subject study (smoked 1–2 nicotine- or non-nicotine-containing cigarettes)		Mennella & Beauchamp, 1998b United States
NNS in diet soda	Lactation	Sucralose and Ace K detected in BM after ingestion		Within-subject study (sucralose and Ace K diet soda beverage)		Rother et al., 2018 United States

Note: RCT = randomized controlled trial; AF = amniotic fluid; BM = breast milk; NNS = nonnutritive sweetener; Ace K = acesulfame K.

a The predominant flavor ingested by mothers during reproductive stages of pregnancy and lactation and then tested for acceptance by their children; each flavor contains many volatiles.

b Analytic methods included gas chromatography–mass spectrometry for all studies except for measurement of ethanol by nicotinamide adenine dinucleotide–alcohol dehydrogenase enzymatic assay and sucralose and acesulfame K by liquid chromatography–mass spectrometry.

c Depending on study design, findings relative to baseline values or control group.

d Subsequent research showed that differential response following maternal alcohol ingestion was also due to impact of alcohol ingestion on lactation performance (Mennella, 2012; and see 2010 Dietary Guidelines Advisory Committee [USDA, 2010] for a review).

amniotic fluid and breast milk, including analytic methods (e.g., enzymatic assay, gas or liquid chromatography/mass spectrometry) and psychophysical methods (e.g., sensory panel). The sensory analytic approaches included sensory panelists evaluating the odor of amniotic fluid or breast milk (orthonasal perception of volatiles), and mothers blindly tasting their own milk samples (Mennella & Beauchamp, 1999) and/or evaluating the recipient infant's (or child's) response to the odor or flavor previously ingested by the mother, in a variety of contexts, including orthonasal perception of volatiles, during breastfeeding, while exploring scented toys, or when eating similarly flavored foods.

The first study to systematically examine whether what a mother ingests gets transmitted to and flavors amniotic fluid and breast milk in a time-dependent manner focused on garlic (Mennella & Beauchamp, 1991a; Mennella, Johnson, & Beauchamp, 1995), a flavor that defines many cultural cuisines and has been shown in research in dairy cows to transmit many of its sulfur-containing volatiles to cow milk (Bassette, Fung, & Mantha, 1986; Shipe et al., 1978). As summarized in Table 10.1, a wide variety of flavors found in the beverages, foods, and flavor ingredients ingested or inhaled (e.g., tobacco) by the mother are transmitted to and flavor amniotic fluid and/or breast milk. In general, the flavor is not stored in breast milk. Rather, the flavor intensity increases significantly within hours after ingestion and decreases thereafter. While there is evidence that NNS sucralose and acesulfame K transmit to breast milk after lactating mothers ingest a beverage containing these NNSs (Rother et al., 2018), whether its transfer changes the taste of breast milk is an important area for future research.

Table 10.1 also shows that, for each of these flavors, there is evidence of a differential response by the recipient infant or child. While anise volatiles were not detected in breast milk after lactating women drank an anise- and caraway-flavored tea (Denzer, Kirsch, & Buettner, 2015), there is experimental evidence of differential response by newborns whose mothers routinely ingested an anise-containing beverage common in France (Schaal, Marlier, & Soussignan, 2000). This suggests that the methods used, timing of collection or low levels of volatiles in tea differentially contributed to the discrepancies between the analytic and sensory findings.

When focusing on the effects of prior experience with flavors in these first foods (amniotic fluid, breast milk), how the infant responds depends on when the mother ingested the beverage or food relative to when the infant was tested and/or when the infant was tested relative to when the flavor was experienced. In the short term, if mothers ate a bland diet and avoided the flavor for several days before testing, their infants displayed appetitive response (e.g., increased suckling) to the flavor in the short term (Mennella & Beauchamp, 1993b). However, if their mothers repeatedly ingested prior to testing, there was no increased suckling when breastfeeding garlic in their mothers' breast milk.

When aroused, mammalian infants will suck more and exhibit a variety of other oral behaviors (Bridger, 1961; Korner, Chuck, & Dontchos, 1968).

Evidence from randomized trials suggest that these flavor memories are retained. Infants whose mothers were randomized to drink carrot and/or other vegetable juices during either late pregnancy or early lactation were more accepting of the flavor in solid food that tested several months later (Mennella et al., 2017; Mennella et al., 2001). Exposure to flavors in mother's milk during the first month postpartum appears to have the strongest effect on intake, perhaps reflecting more frequent exposure due to more frequent breastfeeding (Mennella et al., 2017).That these sensory experiences are long-lasting is suggested by a randomized controlled trial conducted in Northern Ireland in which 8- to 9-year-old children whose mothers were randomized to feed garlic during their pregnancy ate more garlic-flavor potatoes than did the group whose mothers avoided garlic (Hepper et al., 2013). Taken together, these data suggest that prenatal flavor exposure may have long-term effects on flavor preferences and food choice.

10.4.2 Complementary Feeding

Opportunities to get children off to a healthy start do not end with gestation and breastfeeding. Continued exposure to flavors of healthy foods such as fruit and vegetables throughout complementary feeding promotes familiarization with their sensory properties and in turn enhances acceptance of these foods. Such functional plasticity, one of the main characteristics of the brain, highlights the ability to change behavior based on experience (Kolb & Gibb, 2011; Wilson, Best, & Sullivan, 2004).

Building on research in other animals (Capretta, Petersik, & Steward, 1975; Domjan & Gillan, 1976; Galef & Sherry, 1973), Birch and colleagues investigated the effects of repeated exposures (i.e., 5, 10, 15, or 20 times) to the taste of several fruits on acceptance by children aged 2 years and older (Birch & Marlin, 1982). The more frequent the exposure to a food, the more children learned to like its taste. This research then expanded to study infants during the time they transition from an all-milk diet to one containing solid foods. As summarized in Table 10.2, repeated exposure to a single food or a variety of foods, most often a fruit or vegetable, impacted infants' acceptance of the exposed food, as well as a novel food.

One of the biggest challenges in research on preverbal children is how to ask the question (e.g., design the experiment) and how to evaluate whether the experimental manipulation altered their acceptance of food. As such, the research typically used within- and between-subject designs such that acceptance was assessed before and then after an exposure period that lasted several days. Depending on the study, what was fed to infants repeatedly over the course of several days (within-subjects factor) differed between groups of infants (between-subjects factor); in the majority of studies, the foods were commercially prepared. The experimental manipulation involved providing infants with repeated opportunities to taste the target food, because merely looking at the foods had been shown not to modify acceptance among older children between the ages of 2 and 5 years (Birch, McPhee, Shoba, Pirok, & Steinberg, 1987). In some experiments, groups of infants were fed a single type of pureed fruit or vegetable, while others included groups of infants fed a variety of fruits and/or vegetables. The exposure to the target food typically occurred during a single meal of the day, which was then repeated for several days, but in some studies infants were fed pairs of foods within or between meals (Forestell & Mennella, 2007; Mennella et al., 2008). Acceptance was defined by a variety of outcome measures, including how much the infant ate (intake), the length or rate of feeding, the type of facial expressions made during feeding, and the mother's perception of whether her child enjoyed eating the food after versus before the exposure period.

10.4.2.1 *Repeated Exposure*

Regardless of whether infants are breast or formula fed, they learn to like foods through repeated exposure to a single food or a variety of foods. In Table 10.2, we summarize this body of research from the perspective of what infants were repeatedly fed – the type of food (i.e., fruit and/or vegetable), whether it was a single or variety of foods, and the duration of exposure period (i.e., number of days) – and then report on the subsequent effects on the infants' acceptance of the exposed food and in some cases a novel food.

The convergence of findings from this body of experimental research reveals that, similar to children aged 2 to 5 years (Birch & Marlin, 1982), infants are more accepting of a particular fruit or vegetable after repeatedly tasting it for 6–10 days or longer (Table 10.2). Repeated exposure to salted peas was as effective as repeated exposure to plain peas in increasing acceptance of both versions of the vegetable (S. A. Sullivan & Birch, 1994). In general, repeated exposure to one food generalizes to a novel food as long as it is within the same food category (i.e., fruit, vegetable) as the exposed food (Birch et al., 1998; Caton et al., 2013; Paul et al., 2011; S. A. Sullivan & Birch, 1994). Another effective strategy to increase infants' acceptance is to provide them with experience tasting a variety of fruits, vegetables, or both (Gerrish & Mennella, 2001; Mennella et al., 2008). After tasting a variety of puréed fruits (i.e., peaches, prunes, apples) presented once a day over the course of 8 days, infants were more accepting of a novel fruit (e.g., pears) compared to before the exposure (Mennella et al., 2008). Although these infants had not tasted pears, their acceptance after the exposure period was similar to that observed by infants who received 8 days of repeated exposure to only pears (Mennella et al., 2008). Similar effects have been observed for vegetables (Gerrish & Mennella, 2001; Mennella et al., 2008), as well as when infants were exposed to different foods both within and between meals (Mennella et al., 2008).

Table 10.2 *Summary of experimental studies on effects of repeated exposure to single or a variety of foods on infants' acceptance of target and novel fruits and vegetables*

Characteristics of repeated exposure paradigm[a]				Infants' acceptance of exposed and novel foods[b]		Reference, country
Food group	Single food or variety	Name and type of food(s)	Number of exposure days	Exposed food(s)	Novel food(s)	
Fruit	Single	Banana (puréed)	10	• Increased acceptance of commercial bananas (puréed) • No effect on acceptance of homemade bananas (mashed)	• No effect on acceptance of commercial peas (puréed) • Increased acceptance of commercial peaches, pears (puréed)	Birch, Gunder, Grimm-Thomas, & Laing, 1998 United States
Fruit	Single	Pear (puréed)	8	• Increased acceptance of pears (puréed)	• No effect on acceptance of green beans (puréed)	Mennella, Nicklaus, Jagolino, & Yourshaw, 2008 United States
Fruit	Variety	Apple (puréed, lumpy)	20		• Increased acceptance of novel texture of apple • Increased acceptance of diced texture among those exposed to lumpy texture	Lundy et al., 1998 United States
Fruit	Variety	Peach, prune, apple (puréed)	8		• Increased acceptance of pears (puréed) • No effect on acceptance of green beans (puréed)	Mennella et al., 2008 United States

Table 10.2 (*cont.*)

Characteristics of repeated exposure paradigm[a]				Infants' acceptance of exposed and novel foods[b]		Reference, country
Food group	Single food or variety	Name and type of food(s)	Number of exposure days	Exposed food(s)	Novel food(s)	
Fruit	Variety	Plum, apple banana, pear (puréed)	14	• Increased acceptance of plums, apples (puréed)	• No effect on acceptance of green beans (puréed)	Barends, de Vries, Mojet, & de Graaf, 2013 Netherlands
Vegetable, Fruit	Variety	Green bean meal followed by peach meal (puréed)	8	• Increased acceptance of green beans (puréed) • No effect on acceptance of peaches (puréed)		Forestell & Mennella, 2007 United States
Vegetable	Single	Green beans (puréed, plain, or salted)	10	• Increased acceptance of exposed flavor (puréed, plain, or salted) • Increased acceptance of differently flavored green beans (puréed, plain, or salted)	• Increased acceptance of peas (puréed, plain, or salted)	S. A. Sullivan & Birch, 1994 United States
Vegetable	Single	Green bean (puréed)	6–8	• Increased acceptance of green beans (puréed)	• No effect on acceptance of peaches (puréed)	Forestell & Mennella, 2007; Mennella et al., 2008; ; Paul et al., 2011 United States

Table 10.2 (cont.)

	Characteristics of repeated exposure paradigm[a]			Infants' acceptance of exposed and novel foods[b]		
Food group	Single food or variety	Name and type of food(s)	Number of exposure days	Exposed food(s)	Novel food(s)	Reference, country
Vegetable	Single	Peas (puréed, plain, or salted)	10	• Increased acceptance of exposed flavored peas (puréed, plain, or salted) • Increased acceptance of differently flavored peas (puréed, plain, or salted)	• Increased acceptance of green beans (puréed, plain, or salted)	S. A. Sullivan & Birch, 1994 United States
Vegetable	Single	(puréed)	6–10	• Increased acceptance of commercial peas (puréed) • No effect on acceptance of homemade peas (mashed)	• No effect on acceptance of commercial bananas (puréed) • Increased acceptance of commercial green beans, corn, carrots (puréed)	Birch et al., 1998; Paul et al., 2011 United States
Vegetable	Single	Carrot (puréed)	6–9	• Increased acceptance of carrot (puréed) after 9 days, but not after 6 days		Gerrish & Mennella, 2001; Paul et al., 2011 United States
Vegetable	Single	Potato (puréed)	9		• No effect on acceptance of carrots (puréed)	Gerrish & Mennella, 2001 United States
Vegetable	Single	Squash (puréed)	6	• Increased acceptance of squash (puréed)		Paul et al., 2011 United States

(continued)

Table 10.2 (cont.)

	Characteristics of repeated exposure paradigm[a]			Infants' acceptance of exposed and novel foods[b]		Reference, country
Food group	Single food or variety	Name and type of food(s)	Number of exposure days	Exposed food(s)	Novel food(s)	
Vegetable	Single	Artichoke (puréed: plain, with sugar, or with oil)	10	• Increased acceptance of the artichoke (puréed) regardless of flavor exposed	• Increased acceptance of carrots (puréed)	Caton et al., 2013 United Kingdom
Vegetable	Single	Artichoke (puréed plain, with sugar, or with oil)	10	• Increased acceptance of the artichoke (puréed) only among those exposed to plain or sweetened		Remy, Issanchou, Chabanet, & Nicklaus, 2013 France
Vegetable	Variety	Peas, potato, squash (puréed)	9		• Increased acceptance of carrots (puréed)	Gerrish & Mennella, 2001 United States
Vegetable	Variety	Squash, spinach, carrot (puréed)	8	• No increase in acceptance of carrots or spinach (puréed)	• No effect on acceptance of green beans (puréed)	Mennella et al., 2008 United States
Vegetable	Variety	Squash/pea, carrot/pea, squash/ spinach (puréed, within and between meals)	8	• Increased acceptance of carrots and spinach (puréed)	• Increased acceptance of green beans (puréed)	Mennella et al., 2008 United States

Table 10.2 (cont.)

	Characteristics of repeated exposure paradigm[a]				Infants' acceptance of exposed and novel foods[b]		Reference, country
Food group	Single food or variety	Name and type of food(s)	Number of exposure days		Exposed food(s)	Novel food(s)	
Vegetable	Variety	Artichoke, green beans, broccoli, cauliflower (puréed)	14		• Increased acceptance of green beans and artichokes (puréed)	• No effect on acceptance of apple (puréed)	Barends et al., 2013 Netherlands
Vegetable	Variety	Celeriac/swede (rutabaga), celeriac/turnip, or swede/turnip (one plain purée and other mixed with apple purée)	12–16		• Increased acceptance of exposed vegetables (puréed, plain) regardless of flavor exposed	• Increased acceptance of the novel vegetable (puréed, plain)	Ahern, Caton, Blundell, & Hetherington, 2014 United Kingdom
Vegetable	Variety	Carrot, green beans, spinach, broccoli[c]	24		• Increased acceptance of carrots, green beans (puréed)	• No increase in acceptance of parsnips (puréed)	Hetherington et al., 2015 United Kingdom

[a] Single foods were typically fed to the infants once per day and were often *commercially prepared*. In some studies, the type of flavor experience by the infants differed between groups (e.g., salted, plain). For studies that exposed infants to a variety of foods, each food was presented on separate days, the same day but separate meals, or within a meal and foods changed each day.

[b] Acceptance was defined as greater intake, fewer facial expressions of distaste during feeding, and/or mothers perceiving that their infant enjoyed the taste of the food after the exposure period.

[c] During exposure period, infants were fed vegetable purees added to formula once a day for 12 days and then added to rice cereal twice a day for 12 days.

The mechanisms underlying the effects of repeated exposure remain unknown. Perhaps over time the initially bitter (vegetable) or sour (fruit) taste attenuates, increasing the hedonic valence of the taste, as evidenced by a decrease in the facial expressions of distaste. Among adults, repeated tastings of a bittersweet beverage significantly increased the hedonic ratings of the taste of the beverage (Stein, Nagai, Nakagawa, & Beauchamp, 2003). Based on an extensive literature with rat models (Myers & Sclafani, 2006), the mechanisms most likely involve classical conditioning wherein the sensory characteristics of the exposed food become associated with its post-ingestive consequences (Garcia, Hankins, & Rusiniak, 1974; Sclafani & Ackroff, 1994). We propose that, after repeated exposures to a food, infants may associate its taste and volatile profile with feelings of satiation and enjoyment, which over time increase the liking and hedonic value of the particular food and may generalize to other foods that share similar volatiles or taste qualities. For those exposed to flavor variety, the experience of contrast across many sensory domains such as color, texture, and flavor may enhance acceptance of exposed foods and the unanticipated but similarly flavored novel foods.

Insights into the mechanisms of learning can be gained by comparing studies that focused on comparisons of differentially exposing groups of infants to the same vegetable that differed in how it was flavored (e.g., flavor–flavor conditioning, where volatiles and tastes associate with rewarding sweet taste) and its additional source of energy (flavor–nutrient conditioning). After 10–16 days of repeated exposure to either a plain puréed vegetable or the same puréed vegetable sweetened with fruit purée (Ahern et al., 2014) or sugar (Caton et al., 2013; Remy et al., 2013) or flavored with an oil (Caton et al., 2013; Remy et al., 2013), all groups ate more of the plain vegetable after the exposure period. We suggest that the failure to detect preferences conditioned by sweet taste or nutrients may be due to the limited measures of acceptance; that is, intake alone may be insufficient to detect shifts in infants' liking of a food.

As a case in point, in one study, infants received 8 days of repeated tastings of either puréed green beans alone or green beans followed by a sweet-tasting fruit (peaches). While intake of green beans increased in both exposure groups (Forestell & Mennella, 2007), those fed green beans and then peaches displayed significantly fewer facial expressions of distaste during the green bean feed compared to the other group. This shift in facial expressions suggests that only those who experienced peaches after green beans appeared to *like* the taste of the green beans more after exposure, despite the increased intake in both groups. Although measures of liking are related to intake (Berridge, 1996), they are governed by separate neural substrates and do not always change in tandem (Berridge, 1996; Forestell & LoLordo, 2003). This finding demonstrates that an important mechanism involved in shifts in conditioned acceptance involves a change in liking, or hedonic response, to the food.

The experimental manipulations in which repeated exposure to fruits or vegetables did not affect infants' acceptance of a novel food are equally informative (see Table 10.2). Generally, this occurs when the novel fruit or vegetable is from a different food category from the exposure food(s). For example, infants who were exposed to vegetables (peas or green beans, or a variety of vegetables) were not more accepting of a fruit; nor were those exposed to fruit more accepting of a green vegetable (Birch et al., 1998; Mennella et al., 2008).

While most experimental research reviewed herein used commercial baby food or lab-based foods, only one study investigated whether repeated exposure to commercial baby foods generalized acceptance to homemade versions of the foods. There was no such generalization. That is, repeated exposure to commercially prepared bananas or pea purées did not modify the acceptance of fresh, homemade versions of either food (Birch et al., 1998). Although the foods were both from the same food group, fresh fruit and vegetables vary in taste, volatiles, color, and texture, based on cultivar, season, and geography (Kyureghian, Stratton, Bianchini, & Albrecht, 2010; Spjut, 1994). This suggests that commercial jarred foods "don't taste like the real foods" (Birch et al., 1998) to which the child needs to be exposed to transition to the foods of the table. Nor does the flavor of the commercially prepared foods resemble the complex and varying flavors and textures of the whole (noncommercial) fruits and vegetables children eat once they are exposed to table foods (Birch et al., 1998). Since infants stop being fed commercial baby foods during the second year (Siega-Riz, Kinlaw, Deming, & Reidy, 2011), the lack of generalization suggests that infants fed commercial baby foods may have problems transitioning to the taste of whole vegetables and fruits (Birch et al., 1998; Laing et al., 1999). Indeed, feeding commercial baby foods is associated with lower intakes of fruits and vegetables later in life (Foterek, Hilbig, & Alexy, 2015).

10.4.3 Social Modeling

As children move into their second year of life, the development of feeding skills takes on a highly social nature, where eating behaviors are socialized to reflect the family and cultural norms (Montanari, 2006; E. Rozin, 1973). Increases in oral communication facilitates this type of learning where children can communicate hunger and fullness cues with increasing sophistication, as well as food likes and dislikes (Hodges et al., 2013). By this time, feeding has moved from an on-demand or scheduled pattern to include a varied diet organized into distinct meals and snacks (Deming, Briefel, & Reidy, 2014; Grimes, Szymlek-Gay, Campbell, & Nicklas, 2015).

From an early age, children learn through imitation and modeling (Couch, Glanz, Zhou, Sallis, & Saelens, 2014; Draxten, Fulkerson, Friend, Flattum, & Schow, 2014) and the contingencies between their action and its consequence; what infants observe influences what they do, and what they can do changes behaviors (Meltzoff, 2007). Children are quicker to try a new food, and they like and eat more healthy foods like fruits and vegetables, when the eating of those foods is modeled by an important other, such as a parent (Draxten et al., 2014; Fisher, Mitchell, Smiciklas-Wright, & Birch, 2002; Holley, Haycraft, & Farrow, 2015; Larsen et al., 2015; Sumonja & Novakovic, 2013). Children whose mothers were instructed to eat more fruits and vegetables tried more of these foods themselves (Fisher et al., 2002); the more fruits and vegetables eaten by the mother, the more likely her preschooler followed her lead (Worobey, Ostapkovich, Yudin, & Worobey, 2010); and the more fruits and vegetables in the home, the more fruits and vegetables the child ate at school (Taber, Chriqui, & Chaloupka, 2013). Further, repeated tastings of vegetables in a positive context with a parent (Remington, Anez, Croker, Wardle, & Cooke, 2012; Wardle, Carnell, & Cooke, 2005) increased its acceptance, which persisted over time (Remington et al., 2012).

10.5 Conclusions and Implications for Policy

From an early age, children learn the rules of their cultural cuisine – how to eat, what to eat, when to eat, and what foods are supposed to taste like (Mennella et al., 2016). This learning first begins in the context of the dynamic interplay between mother and child (Neville et al., 2012) and the food environment and culture in which they live, and is dependent on functioning and coordination of the sensory systems and motor and cognitive skills. In the beginning, the types and intensity of flavors experienced in amniotic fluid and if breastfed, then breast milk, are unique for each infant and characteristic of the culinary traditions of the family. Rapid increases in food acceptance by infants after a few days of repeated exposure contrast with slower changes seen in toddlers (Birch & Marlin, 1982), highlighting the importance of providing repeated exposures early in life. As the child grows, the social importance of early feeding highlights both the context of the experiences and the modeling from parents and other family members. The multiple routes of learning about food, a basic biological commodity, provide complementary and often redundant routes for children to learn about the types of safe and preferred foods available in the environment before they themselves begin to eat independently.

While the infant is dependent on the mother for the provision of early nutrition and comfort, the infant plays an active role in feeding, signaling when hungry and satiated. As a consequence of feeding interactions and the environment, both members of the dyad learn and modify their behaviors accordingly. A case in point, the current food environment rich in added sugars and salt – preferred human tastes – provides challenges for both young and old. While the biological attraction to sweet and salty tastes may have served children well in a feast-or-famine setting, today it makes them vulnerable to a food environment abundant in processed foods rich in added sugars and poor in healthy sweet foods like fruit.

Fortunately, our biology is not necessarily our destiny. The plasticity of the chemical senses interacts with experience with foods to modify our preferences, producing an interface between our biology and our culture, our past and our present. Because of the importance of early nutrition for healthy growth and the development of long-term dietary behaviors and preferences, the United States Department of Agriculture and Department of Health and Human Services initiated the "Pregnancy and Birth to 24 Months Project" to examine topics of public health importance for women who are pregnant and children from birth to 24 months (Obbagy, Blum-Kemelor, Essery, Lyon, & Spahn, 2014; Raiten, Raghavan, Porter, Obbagy, & Spahn, 2014). The topics reviewed herein provide some of the evidence-based strategies that may maximize acceptance of food during this sensitive period when children are transitioning to making their own food choices. The societal and clinical impact of promoting sustainable food habits is significant, since what a child eats determines in part what the child becomes.

References

Afeiche, M. C., Koyratty, B. N. S., Wang, D., Jacquier, E. F., & Le, K. A. (2018). Intakes and sources of total and added sugars among 4- to 13-year-old children in China, Mexico and the United States. *Pediatric Obesity, 13*(4), 204–212. doi:10.1111/ijpo.12234

Ahern, S. M., Caton, S. J., Blundell, P., & Hetherington, M. M. (2014). The root of the problem: Increasing root vegetable intake in preschool children by repeated exposure and flavour learning. *Appetite, 80*, 154–160. doi:10.1016/j.appet.2014.04.016

Al Ain, S., Perry, R. E., Nunez, B., Kayser, K., Hochman, C., Brehman, E., ... Sullivan, R. M. (2017). Neurobehavioral assessment of maternal odor in developing rat pups: Implications for social buffering. *Social Neuroscience, 12*(1), 32–49. doi:10.1080/17470919.2016.1159605

Bailey, R. L., Catellier, D. J., Jun, S., Dwyer, J. T., Jacquier, E. F., Anater, A. S., & Eldridge, A. L. (2018). Total usual nutrient intakes of US children (under 48 months): Findings from the Feeding Infants and Toddlers Study (FITS) 2016. *Journal of Nutrition, 148*(Suppl. 9), 1557S–1566S. doi:10.1093/jn/nxy042

Ballard, O., & Morrow, A. L. (2013). Human milk composition: Nutrients and bioactive factors. *Pediatric Clinics of North America, 60*(1), 49–74. doi:10.1016/j.pcl.2012.10.002

Barends, C., de Vries, J., Mojet, J., & de Graaf, C. E. (2013). Effects of repeated exposure to either vegetables or fruits on infant's vegetable and fruit acceptance at the beginning of weaning. *Food Quality and Preference, 29*, 157–165.

Barker, E. (1980). *Sensory evaluation of human milk*. Manitoba, Canada: University of Manitoba.

Bartolomei, F., Lagarde, S., Medina Villalon, S., McGonigal, A., & Benar, C. G. (2017). The "Proust phenomenon": Odor-evoked autobiographical memories triggered by direct amygdala stimulation in human. *Cortex, 90*, 173–175. doi:10.1016/j.cortex.2016.12.005

Bassette, R., Fung, D. Y. C., & Mantha, V. R. (1986). Off-flavors in milk. *CRC Critical Reviews in Food Science and Nutrition, 24*, 1–52.

Beauchamp, G. K., & Cowart, B. J. (1990). Preference for high salt concentrations among children. *Developmental Psychology, 26*(4), 539–545.

Beauchamp, G. K., Cowart, B. J., & Moran, M. (1986). Developmental changes in salt acceptability in human infants. *Developmental Psychobiology, 19*, 17–25.

Beauchamp, G. K., Katahira, K., Yamazaki, K., Mennella, J. A., Bard, J., & Boyse, E. A. (1995). Evidence suggesting that the odortypes of pregnant women are a compound of maternal and fetal odortypes. *Proceedings of the National Academy of the Sciences of the United States of America, 92*(7), 2617–2621.

Berridge, K. C. (1996). Food reward: Brain substrates of wanting and liking. *Neuroscience & Biobehavioral Reviews, 20*, 1–25. doi:0149-7634(95)00033-B [pii]

Birch, L. L., Gunder, L., Grimm-Thomas, K., & Laing, D. G. (1998). Infants' consumption of a new food enhances acceptance of similar foods. *Appetite, 30*, 283–295.

Birch, L. L., & Marlin, D. W. (1982). I don't like it; I never tried it: Effects of exposure on two-year-old children's food preferences. *Appetite, 3*, 353–360.

Birch, L. L., McPhee, L., Shoba, B. C., Pirok, E., & Steinberg, L. (1987). What kind of exposure reduces children's food neophobia? Looking vs. tasting. *Appetite, 9*, 171–178.

Black, M. M., & Aboud, F. E. (2011). Responsive feeding is embedded in a theoretical framework of responsive parenting. *Journal of Nutrition, 141*(3), 490–494. doi:10.3945/jn.110.129973

Bridger, W. H. (1961). Ethological concepts and human development. *Recent Advances in Biological Psychiatry, 4*, 95–107.

Bronfenbrenner, U., & Morris, P. (1998). The ecology of human developmental processes. In W. Damon & N. Eisenberg (Eds.), *Theoretical models of human development* (pp. 993–1028). New York, NY: John Wiley & Sons.

Brown, G. W., Tuholski, J. M., Sauer, L. W., Minsk, L. D., & Rosenstern, I. (1960). Evaluation of prepared milks for infant nutrition: Use of the Latin square technique. *Journal of Pediatrics, 56*, 391–398.

Butte, N. F., Wills, C., Jean, C. A., Smith, E. O., & Garza, C. (1985). Feeding patterns of exclusively breast-fed infants during the first four months of life. *Early Human Development, 12*(3), 291–300.

Cameron, S. L., Heath, A. L., & Taylor, R. W. (2012). How feasible is baby-led weaning as an approach to infant feeding? A review of the evidence. *Nutrients, 4*(11), 1575–1609. doi:10.3390/nu4111575

Cannon, A. M., Gridneva, Z., Hepworth, A. R., Lai, C. T., Tie, W. J., Khan, S., … Geddes, D. T. (2017). The relationship of human milk leptin and macronutrients with gastric emptying in term breastfed infants. *Pediatric Research, 82*(1), 72–78. doi:10.1038/pr.2017.79

Capretta, P. J., Petersik, J. T., & Steward, D. J. (1975). Acceptance of novel flavours is increased after early experience of diverse taste. *Nature, 254,* 689–691.

Carruth, B. R., & Skinner, J. D. (2002). Feeding behaviors and other motor development in healthy children (2–24 months). *Journal of the American College of Nutrition, 21*(2), 88–96.

Carruth, B. R., Ziegler, P. J., Gordon, A., & Hendricks, K. (2004). Developmental milestones and self-feeding behaviors in infants and toddlers. *Journal of the American Dietetic Association, 104*(Suppl. 1), s51–s56. doi:10.1016/j.jada.2003.10.019

Caton, S. J., Ahern, S. M., Remy, E., Nicklaus, S., Blundell, P., & Hetherington, M. M. (2013). Repetition counts: Repeated exposure increases intake of a novel vegetable in UK pre-school children compared to flavour–flavour and flavour–nutrient learning. *British Journal of Nutrition, 109,* 2089–2097. doi:S0007114512004126 [pii] 10.1017/S0007114512004126

Chan, S., Pollitt, E., & Leibel, R. (1979). Effect of nutrient cues on formula intake in 5-week-old infants. *Infant Behaviour and Development, 2,* 201–208.

Coldwell, S. E., Oswald, T. K., & Reed, D. R. (2009). A marker of growth differs between adolescents with high vs. low sugar preference. *Physiolology and Behavior, 96,* 574–580. doi:S0031-9384(08)00394-6 [pii] 10.1016/j.physbeh.2008.12.010

Couch, S. C., Glanz, K., Zhou, C., Sallis, J. F., & Saelens, B. E. (2014). Home food environment in relation to children's diet quality and weight status. *Journal of the Academy of Nutrition and Dietetics, 114,* 1569–1579. doi:10.1016/j.jand.2014.05.015 S2212-2672(14)00600-5 [pii]

Davis, C. M. (1928). Self-selection of diet by newly weaned infants: An experimental study. *American Journal of Diseases of Childhood, 36,* 361–659.

(1939). Results of the self-selection of diets by young children. *Canadian Medical Association Journal, 41*(3), 257–261.

Debiec, J., & Sullivan, R. M. (2014). Intergenerational transmission of emotional trauma through amygdala-dependent mother-to-infant transfer of specific fear. *Proceedings of the National Academy of the Sciences of the United States of America, 111*(33), 12222–12227. doi:10.1073/pnas.1316740111

Delaunay-El Allam, M., Soussignan, R., Patris, B., Marlier, L., & Schaal, B. (2010). Long-lasting memory for an odor acquired at the mother's breast. *Developmental Science, 13*(6), 849–863. doi:10.1111/j.1467-7687.2009.00941.x

Deming, D. M., Briefel, R. R., & Reidy, K. C. (2014). Infant feeding practices and food consumption patterns of children participating in WIC. *Journal of Nutrition Education and Behavior, 46,* S29–37. doi:10.1016/j.jneb.2014.02.020

Deming, D. M., Reidy, K. C., Fox, M. K., Briefel, R. R., Jacquier, E., & Eldridge, A. L. (2017). Cross-sectional analysis of eating patterns and snacking in the US Feeding Infants and Toddlers Study 2008. *Public Health Nutrition, 20*(9), 1584–1592. doi:10.1017/S136898001700043X

Denney, L., Reidy, K. C., & Eldridge, A. L. (2016). Differences in complementary feeding of 6 to 23 month olds in China, US and Mexico. *Journal of Nutritional Health and Food Science, 4*(3), 1–8. doi: http://dx.doi.org/10.15226/jnhfs.2016.00181

Denzer, M. Y., Kirsch, F., & Buettner, A. (2015). Are odorant constituents of herbal tea transferred into human milk? *Journal of Agriculture and Food Chemistry, 63*(1), 104–111. doi:10.1021/jf504073d

Derks, I. P., Tiemeier, H., Sijbrands, E. J., Nicholson, J. M., Voortman, T., Verhulst, F. C., ... Jansen, P. W. (2017). Testing the direction of effects between child body composition and restrictive feeding practices: Results from a population-based cohort. *American Journal of Clinical Nutrition, 106*(3), 783–790. doi:10.3945/ajcn.117.156448

Desor, J. A., & Beauchamp, G. K. (1987). Longitudinal changes in sweet preferences in humans. *Physiology and Behavior, 39*(5), 639–641.

Desor, J. A., Maller, O., & Andrews, K. (1975). Ingestive responses of human newborns to salty, sour, and bitter stimuli. *Journal of Comparative and Physiological Psychology, 89*, 966–970.

Domjan, M., & Gillan, D. (1976). Role of novelty in the aversion for increasingly concentrated saccharin solutions. *Physiology and Behavior, 16*(5), 537–542.

Draxten, M., Fulkerson, J. A., Friend, S., Flattum, C. F., & Schow, R. (2014). Parental role modeling of fruits and vegetables at meals and snacks is associated with children's adequate consumption. *Appetite, 78*, 1–7. doi:10.1016/j.appet.2014.02.017

Faas, A. E., March, S. M., Moya, P. R., & Molina, J. C. (2015). Alcohol odor elicits appetitive facial expressions in human neonates prenatally exposed to the drug. *Physiology and Behavior, 148*, 78–86. doi:10.1016/j.physbeh.2015.02.031

Faas, A. E., Sponton, E. D., Moya, P. R., & Molina, J. C. (2000). Differential responsiveness to alcohol odor in human neonates: Effects of maternal consumption during gestation. *Alcohol, 22*(1), 7–17.

Fisher, J. O., Mitchell, D. C., Smiciklas-Wright, H., & Birch, L. L. (2002). Parental influences on young girls' fruit and vegetable, micronutrient, and fat intakes. *Journal of the American Dietetic Association, 102*, 58–64.

Flynn, M. A., McNeil, D. A., Maloff, B., Mutasingwa, D., Wu, M., Ford, C., & Tough, S. C. (2006). Reducing obesity and related chronic disease risk in children and youth: A synthesis of evidence with "best practice" recommendations. *Obesity Review, 7*(Suppl. 1), 7–66. doi:10.1111/j.1467-789X.2006.00242.x

Fomon, S. J. (1980). Factors influencing food consumption in the human infant. *International Journal of Obesity, 4*(4), 348–350.

Fomon, S. J., Filmer, L. J., Jr., Thomas, L. N., Anderson, T. A., & Nelson, S. E. (1975). Influence of formula concentration on caloric intake and growth of normal infants. *Acta Paediatrica, 64*(2), 172–181.

Fomon, S. J., Filer, L. J., Jr., Thomas, L. N., Rogers, R. R., & Proksch, A. M. (1969). Relationship between formula concentration and rate of growth of normal infants. *Journal of Nutrition, 98*(2), 241–254. doi:10.1093/jn/98.2.241

Fomon, S. J., Thomas, L. N., Filer, L. J., Jr., Anderson, T. A., & Nelson, S. E. (1976). Influence of fat and carbohydrate content of diet on food intake and growth of male infants. *Acta Paediatrica, 65*(2), 136–144.

Fomon, S. J., Ziegler, E. E., Nelson, S. E., & Edwards, B. B. (1983). Sweetness of diet and food consumption by infants. *Proceedings of the Society for Experimental Biology and Medicine, 173*(2), 190–193.

Forestell, C. A., & LoLordo, V. M. (2003). Palatability shifts in taste and flavour preference conditioning. *Quarterly Journal of Experimental Psychology B, 56*, 140–160. doi:10.1080/02724990244000232

Forestell, C. A., & Mennella, J. A. (2005). Children's hedonic judgments of cigarette smoke odor: effects of parental smoking and maternal mood. *Psychology of Addictive Behaviors, 19*(4), 423–432.

(2007). Early determinants of fruit and vegetable acceptance. *Pediatrics, 120*(6), 1247–1254.

(2008). Food, folklore and flavor preference development. In C. Lammi-Keefe (Ed.), *Handbook of nutrition and pregnancy* (pp. 55–64). Totowa, NJ.: Humana Press.

(2015). The ontogeny of taste perception and preference throughout childhood. In R. L. Doty (Ed.), *Handbook of olfaction and gustation* (3rd ed., pp. 797–830). New York, NY: Wiley-Liss.

Foterek, K., Hilbig, A., & Alexy, U. (2015). Associations between commercial complementary food consumption and fruit and vegetable intake in children. Results of the DONALD study. *Appetite, 85,* 84–90. doi:10.1016/j.appet.2014.11.015

Fox, M. K., Devaney, B., Reidy, K., Razafindrakoto, C., & Ziegler, P. (2006). Relationship between portion size and energy intake among infants and toddlers: Evidence of self-regulation. *Journal of the American Dietetic Association, 106*(Suppl. 1), S77–83.

Galef, B. G. J., & Sherry, D. F. (1973). Mother's milk: A medium for transmission of cues reflecting the flavor of mother's diet. *Journal of Comparative and Physiological Psychology, 83*(3), 374–378.

Garcia, J., Hankins, W. G., & Rusiniak, K. W. (1974). Behavioral regulation of the milieu interne in man and rat. *Science, 185*(4154), 824–831.

Gerrish, C. J., & Mennella, J. A. (2001). Flavor variety enhances food acceptance in formula-fed infants. *American Journal of Clinical Nutrition, 73,* 1080–1085.

Grimes, C. A., Szymlek-Gay, E. A., Campbell, K. J., & Nicklas, T. A. (2015). Food sources of total energy and nutrients among U.S. infants and toddlers: National Health and Nutrition Examination Survey 2005–2012. *Nutrients, 7*(8), 6797–6836. doi:10.3390/nu7085310

Gross, R. S., Fierman, A. H., Mendelsohn, A. L., Chiasson, M. A., Rosenberg, T. J., Scheinmann, R., & Messito, M. J. (2010). Maternal perceptions of infant hunger, satiety, and pressuring feeding styles in an urban Latina WIC population. *Academic Pediatrics, 10*(1), 29–35. doi:10.1016/j.acap.2009.08.001

Grummer-Strawn, L. M., Scanlon, K. S., & Fein, S. B. (2008). Infant feeding and feeding transitions during the first year of life. *Pediatrics, 122*(Suppl. 2), S36–S42. doi:10.1542/peds.2008-1315d

Hausner, H., Bredie, W. L., Molgaard, C., Petersen, M. A., & Moller, P. (2008). Differential transfer of dietary flavour compounds into human breast milk. *Physiology and Behavior, 95*(1–2), 118–124.

Hepper, P. G. (1995). Human fetal "olfactory" learning *International Journal of Prenatal and Perinatal Psychology and Medicine, 7,* 147–151.

Hepper, P. G., Wells, D. L., Dornan, J. C., & Lynch, C. (2013). Long-term flavor recognition in humans with prenatal garlic experience. *Developmental Psychobiology, 55*(5), 568–574 doi:10.1002/dev.21059

Hetherington, M. M., Schwartz, C., Madrelle, J., Croden, F., Nekitsing, C., Vereijken, C. M., & Weenen, H. (2015). A step-by-step introduction to vegetables at the beginning of complementary feeding. The effects of early and repeated exposure. *Appetite, 84,* 280–290. doi:10.1016/j.appet.2014.10.014 S0195-6663(14)00494-2

Hodges, E. A., Hughes, S. O., Hopkinson, J., & Fisher, J. O. (2008). Maternal decisions about the initiation and termination of infant feeding. *Appetite, 50*(2–3), 333–339.

Hodges, E. A., Johnson, S. L., Hughes, S. O., Hopkinson, J. M., Butte, N. F., & Fisher, J. O. (2013). Development of the responsiveness to child feeding cues scale. *Appetite, 65,* 210–219. doi:10.1016/j.appet.2013.02.010

Holley, C. E., Haycraft, E., & Farrow, C. (2015). "Why don't you try it again?" A comparison of parent led, home based interventions aimed at increasing children's consumption of a disliked vegetable. *Appetite, 87,* 215–222. doi:10.1016/j.appet.2014.12.216

Kent, J. C., Mitoulas, L. R., Cregan, M. D., Ramsay, D. T., Doherty, D. A., & Hartmann, P. E. (2006). Volume and frequency of breastfeedings and fat content of breast milk throughout the day. *Pediatrics, 117*(3), e387–395. doi:10.1542/peds.2005-1417

Kirsch, F., Beauchamp, J., & Buettner, A. (2012). Time-dependent aroma changes in breast milk after oral intake of a pharmacological preparation containing 1, 8-cineole. *Clinical Nutrition, 31*(5), 682–692. doi:10.1016/j.clnu.2012.02.002

Kolb, B., & Gibb, R. (2011). Brain plasticity and behaviour in the developing brain. *Journal of the Canadian Academy of Child and Adolescent Psychiatry, 20,* 265–276.

Korner, A. K., Chuck, B., & Dontchos, S. (1968). Organismic determinants of spontaneous oral behavior in neonates. *Child Development, 39,* 1147–1157.

Kyureghian, G., Stratton, J., Bianchini, A., & Albrecht, J. (2010). *Nutritional comparison of frozen and non-frozen fruits and vegetables: Literature review.* Retrieved from https://pdfs.semanticscholar.org/fd90/0931812081bff85f304a557906852b9add90.pdf.

Laing, D. G., Oram, N., Burgess, J., Ram, P. R., Moore, G., Rose, G., ... Skurray, G. R. (1999). The development of meat-eating habits during childhood in Australia. *International Journal of Food Sciences and Nutrition, 50,* 29–37.

Larsen, J. K., Hermans, R. C., Sleddens, E. F., Engels, R. C., Fisher, J. O., & Kremers, S. P. (2015). How parental dietary behavior and food parenting practices affect children's dietary behavior. Interacting sources of influence? *Appetite, 89,* 246–257. doi: 10.1016/j.appet.2015.02.012

Lipchock, S. V., Reed, D. R., & Mennella, J. A. (2011). The gustatory and olfactory systems during infancy: Implications for development of feeding behaviors in the high-risk neonate. *Clinics in Perinatology,* 38(4), 627–641

Lundy, B., Field, T., Carraway, K., Hart, S., Malphurs, J., Rosenstein, M., ... Hernandez-Reif, M. (1998). Food texture preferences in infants versus toddlers. *Early Child Development and Care, 146,* 69–85.

Maalouf, J., Cogswell, M. E., Bates, M., Yuan, K., Scanlon, K. S., Pehrsson, P., ... Merritt, R. K. (2017). Sodium, sugar, and fat content of complementary infant and toddler foods sold in the United States, 2015. *American Journal of Clinical Nutrition, 105*(6), 1443–1452. doi:10.3945/ajcn.116.142653

McDaniel, M. R. (1980). Off-flavors in human milk. In G. Charalambous (Ed.), *The analysis and control of less desirable flavors in foods and beverages* (pp. 267–291). New York, NY: Academic Press.

McNally, J., Hugh-Jones, S., Caton, S., Vereijken, C., Weenen, H., & Hetherington, M. (2016). Communicating hunger and satiation in the first 2 years of life: A systematic review. *Maternal Child Nutrition, 12*(2), 205–228. doi:10.1111/mcn.12230

Meltzoff, A. N. (2007). Infants' causal learning: Intervention, observation, imitation. In A. Gopnik & L. Schulz (Eds.), *Causal learning: Psychology, philosophy, and computation* (pp. 37–41). Oxford: Oxford University Press

Mennella, J. A. (1997). Infants' suckling responses to the flavor of alcohol in mothers' milk. *Alcohol: Clinical and Experimental Research, 21*(4), 581–585.

(2007). The chemical senses and the development of flavor preferences in humans. In T. W. Hale & P. E. Hartmann (Eds.), *Textbook on human lactation* (pp. 403–414). Amarillo, TX: Hale.

(2012). Alcohol use during lactation: Effects on the mother–infant dyad. In R. R. Watson & V. R. Preedy (Eds.), *Nutrition and alcohol: Linking nutrient interactions and dietary intake* (pp. 63–82). New York, NY: Springer.

Mennella, J. A., & Beauchamp, G. K. (1991a). Maternal diet alters the sensory qualities of human milk and the nursling's behavior. *Pediatrics, 88*(4), 737–744.

(1991b). The transfer of alcohol to human milk. Effects on flavor and the infant's behavior. *New England Journal of Medicine, 325*(14), 981–985.

(1993a). Beer, breast feeding, and folklore. *Developmental Psychobiology, 26*(8), 459–466.

(1993b). The effects of repeated exposure to garlic-flavored milk on the nursling's behavior. *Pediatric Research, 34*, 805–808.

(1994). The infant's response to flavored milk. *Infant Behavior and Development, 19*(1), 1–19.

(1996). The human infants' responses to vanilla flavors in mother's milk and formula. *Infant Behavior and Development, 19*, 13–19.

(1998a). The infant's response to scented toys: Effects of exposure. *Chemical Senses, 23*, 11–17.

(1998b). Smoking and the flavor of breast milk. *New England Journal of Medicine, 339*, 1559–1560.

(1999). Experience with a flavor in mother's milk modifies the infant's acceptance of flavored cereal. *Developmental Psychobiology, 35*(3), 197–203.

(2002). Flavor experiences during formula feeding are related to preferences during childhood. *Early Human Development, 68*(2), 71–82.

(2015). The sweetness and bitterness of childhood: Insights from basic research on taste preferences. *Physiology and Behavior, 152*(Pt. B), 502–507. doi:10.1016/j.physbeh.2015.05.015

Mennella, J. A., Daniels, L. M., & Reiter, A. R. (2017). Learning to like vegetables during breastfeeding: A randomized clinical trial of lactating mothers and infants. *American Journal of Clinical Nutrition, 106*, 67–76. doi:10.3945/ajcn.116.143982

Mennella, J. A., Finkbeiner, S., Lipchock, S. V., Hwang, L. D., & Reed, D. R. (2014). Preferences for salty and sweet tastes are elevated and related to each other during childhood. *PLoS One, 9*(3), e92201. doi:10.1371/journal.pone.0092201

Mennella, J. A., Forestell, C. A., Morgan, L. K., & Beauchamp, G. K. (2009). Early milk feeding influences taste acceptance and liking during infancy. *American Journal of Clinical Nutrition, 90*(3), 780–788S. doi:10.3945/ajcn.2009.27462O

Mennella, J. A., Inamdar, L., Pressman, N., Schall, J., Papas, M. A., Schoeller, D., … Trabulsi, J. C. (2018). Type of infant formula increases early weight gain and impacts energy balance: A randomized controlled trial. *American Journal of Clinical Nutrition, 108*, 1–11. doi:doi: 10.1093/ajcn/nqy188

Mennella, J. A., Jagnow, C. P., & Beauchamp, G. K. (2001). Prenatal and postnatal flavor learning by human infants. *Pediatrics, 107*, E88.

Mennella, J. A., Johnson, A., & Beauchamp, G. K. (1995). Garlic ingestion by pregnant women alters the odor of amniotic fluid. *Chemical Senses, 20*(2), 207–209.

Mennella, J. A., Nicklaus, S., Jagolino, A. L., & Yourshaw, L. M. (2008). Variety is the spice of life: Strategies for promoting fruit and vegetable acceptance during infancy. *Physiology and Behavior, 94*(1), 29–38.

Mennella, J. A., Papas, M. A., Reiter, A. R., Stallings, V. A., & Trabulsi, J. C. (2019). Early rapid weight gain among formula-fed infants: Impact of formula type and maternal feeding styles. *Pediatric Obesity*, e12503. doi:10.1111/ijpo.12503

Mennella, J. A., Pepino, M. Y., Duke, F. F., & Reed, D. R. (2010). Age modifies the genotype–phenotype relationship for the bitter receptor TAS2R38. *BMC Genetics, 11*, 60. doi:10.1186/1471-2156-11-60

Mennella, J. A., Reiter, A. R., & Daniels, L. M. (2016). Vegetable and fruit acceptance during infancy: Impact of ontogeny, genetics, and early experiences. *Advances in Nutrition, 7*, 211S-219S. doi:10.3945/an.115.008649

Mennella, J. A., Ventura, A. K., & Beauchamp, G. K. (2011). Differential growth patterns among healthy infants fed protein hydrolysate or cow-milk formulas. *Pediatrics, 127*, 110–118. doi:10.1542/peds.2010-1675

Moding, K. J., Ferrante, M. J., Bellows, L. L., Bakke, A. J., Hayes, J. E., & Johnson, S. L. (2018). Variety and content of commercial infant and toddler vegetable products manufactured and sold in the United States. *American Journal of Clinical Nutrition, 107*(4), 576–583. doi:10.1093/ajcn/nqx079

Montanari, M. (2006). *Food is culture* (A. Sonnenfeld, Trans.). New York, NY: Columbia University Press.

Myers, K. P., & Sclafani, A. (2006). Development of learned flavor preferences. *Developmental Psychobiology, 48*(5), 380–388.

Nagasawa, M., Okabe, S., Mogi, K., & Kikusui, T. (2012). Oxytocin and mutual communication in mother–infant bonding. *Frontiers in Human Neuroscience, 6*, 31. doi:10.3389/fnhum.2012.00031

Naylor, A. J., & Morrow, A. L. (2001). Developmental readiness of normal full-term infants to progress from exclusive breastfeeding to the introduction of complementary foods *Reviews of the Relevant Literature Concerning Infantimmunologic, Gastrointestinal, Oral Motor and Maternal Reproductive and Lactational Development*. Retrieved from www.pronutrition.org/files/Developmental%20Readiness.pdf

Negayama, K. (1993). Weaning in Japan: A longitudinal study of mother and child behaviours during milk- and solid-feeding. *Infant Child Development, 2*, 29–37.

Neville, M. C., Anderson, S. M., McManaman, J. L., Badger, T. M., Bunik, M., Contractor, N., ... Williamson, P. (2012). Lactation and neonatal nutrition: Defining and refining the critical questions. *Journal of Mammary Gland Biology and Neoplasia, 17*, 167–188. doi:10.1007/s10911-012-9261-5

Nishitani, S., Kuwamoto, S., Takahira, A., Miyamura, T., & Shinohara, K. (2014). Maternal prefrontal cortex activation by newborn infant odors. *Chemical Senses, 39*(3), 195–202. doi:10.1093/chemse/bjt068

Obbagy, J. E., Blum-Kemelor, D. M., Essery, E. V., Lyon, J. M., & Spahn, J. M. (2014). USDA Nutrition Evidence Library: Methodology used to identify topics and develop systematic review questions for the birth-to-24-mo population. *American Journal of Clinical Nutrition, 99*(3), 692S-696S. doi:10.3945/ajcn.113.071670

Paul, I. M., Savage, J. S., Anzman, S. L., Beiler, J. S., Marini, M. E., Stokes, J. L., & Birch, L. L. (2011). Preventing obesity during infancy: A pilot study. *Obesity (Silver Spring), 19*(2), 353–361. doi:10.1038/oby.2010.182

Prentice, P., Ong, K. K., Schoemaker, M. H., van Tol, E. A., Vervoort, J., Hughes, I. A., ... Dunger, D. B. (2016). Breast milk nutrient content and infancy growth. *Acta Paediatrica, 105*(6), 641–647. doi:10.1111/apa.13362

Pritchard, J. A. (1965). Deglutition by normal and anencephalic fetuses. *Obstetrics and Gynecology, 25*, 289–297.

Provenza, F. (2018). *Nourishment: What animals can teach us about rediscovering our nutritional wisdom.* White River Junction, VT: Chelsea Green Publishing.

Raiten, D. J., Raghavan, R., Porter, A., Obbagy, J. E., & Spahn, J. M. (2014). Executive summary: Evaluating the evidence base to support the inclusion of infants and children from birth to 24 mo of age in the Dietary Guidelines for Americans – "the B-24 Project." *American Journal of Clinical Nutrition, 99*(3), 663S-691S. doi:10.3945/ajcn.113.072140

Reidy, K. C., Bailey, R. L., Deming, D. M., O'Neill, L., Carr, B. T., Lesniauskas, R., & Johnson, W. (2018). Food consumption patterns and micronutrient density of complementary foods consumed by infants fed commercially prepared baby foods. *Nutrition Today, 53*(2), 68–78. doi:10.1097/NT.0000000000000265

Remington, A., Anez, E., Croker, H., Wardle, J., & Cooke, L. (2012). Increasing food acceptance in the home setting: A randomized controlled trial of parent-administered taste exposure with incentives. *American Journal of Clinical Nutrition, 95*, 72–77. doi:10.3945/ajcn.111.024596

Remy, E., Issanchou, S., Chabanet, C., & Nicklaus, S. (2013). Repeated exposure of infants at complementary feeding to a vegetable puree increases acceptance as effectively as flavor–flavor learning and more effectively than flavor–nutrient learning. *Journal of Nutrition, 143*(7), 1194–1200. doi:10.3945/jn.113.175646

Roess, A. A., Jacquier, E. F., Catellier, D. J., Carvalho, R., Lutes, A. C., Anater, A. S., & Dietz, W. H. (2018). Food consumption patterns of infants and toddlers: Findings from the Feeding Infants and Toddlers Study (FITS) 2016. *Journal of Nutrition, 148*(Suppl. 3), 1525S–1535S. doi:10.1093/jn/nxy171

Rosenstein, D., & Oster, H. (1988). Differential facial responses to four basic tastes in newborns. *Child Development, 59*, 1555–1568.

Rother, K. I., Sylvetsky, A. C., Walter, P. J., Garraffo, H. M., & Fields, D. A. (2018). Pharmacokinetics of sucralose and acesulfame-potassium in breast milk following ingestion of diet soda. *Journal of Pediatric Gastroenterology and Nutrition, 66*(3), 466–470. doi:10.1097/MPG.0000000000001817

Rozin, E. (1973). *The flavor-principle cookbook.* New York, NY: Hawthorn Books.

Rozin, P. (1982). "Taste-smell confusions" and the duality of the olfactory sense. *Perception and Psychophysics*, *31*(4), 397–401.

———— (1984). The acquisition of food habits and preferences. In J. D. Mattarazzo, S. M. Weiss, J. A. Herd, N. E. Miller, & S. M. Weiss (Eds.), *Behavioral health: A handbook of health enhancement and disease prevention* (pp. 590–607). New York, NY: John Wiley & Sons.

San Gabriel, A., & Uneyama, H. (2013). Amino acid sensing in the gastrointestinal tract. *Amino Acids*, *45*, 451–461. doi:10.1007/s00726-012-1371-2

Schaal, B., & Marlier, L. (1998). Maternal and paternal perception of individual odor signatures in human amniotic fluid – potential role in early bonding? *Biology of the Neonate*, *74*(4), 266–273.

Schaal, B., Marlier, L., & Soussignan, R. (2000). Human foetuses learn odours from their pregnant mother's diet. *Chemical Senses*, *25*(6), 729–737.

Scheffler, L., Sauermann, Y., Zeh, G., Hauf, K., Heinlein, A., Sharapa, C., & Buettner, A. (2016). Detection of volatile metabolites of garlic in human breast milk. *Metabolites*, *6*(2). doi:10.3390/metabo6020018

Sclafani, A., & Ackroff, K. (1994). Glucose- and fructose-conditioned flavor preferences in rats: Taste versus postingestive conditioning. *Physiology and Behavior*, *56*(2), 399–405.

Shipe, W. F., Bassette, R., Deane, D. D., Dunkley, W. L., Hammond, E. G., Harper, W. J., … Scanlan, R. A. (1978). Off-flavors of milk: Nomenclature, standards and bibliography. *Journal of Dairy Science*, *61*, 855–868.

Shipe, W. F., Ledford, R. A., Peterson, R. D., Scanlan, R. A., Geerken, H. F., Dougherty, R. W., & Morgan, M. E. (1962). Physiological mechanisms involved in transmitting flavors and odors to milk. II: Transmission of some flavor components of silage. *Journal of Dairy Science*, *45*, 477–480.

Shloim, N., Vereijken, C., Blundell, P., & Hetherington, M. M. (2017). Looking for cues: Infant communication of hunger and satiation during milk feeding. *Appetite*, *108*, 74–82. doi:10.1016/j.appet.2016.09.020

Siega-Riz, A. M., Kinlaw, A., Deming, D. M., & Reidy, K. C. (2011). New findings from the Feeding Infants and Toddlers Study 2008. *Nestle Nutrition Workshop Series Pediatric Program*, *68*, 83–100. doi:10.1159/000325667

Skinner, J. D., Carruth, B. R., Houck, K., Moran, J., III, Reed, A., Coletta, F., & Ott, D. (1998). Mealtime communication patterns of infants from 2 to 24 months of age. *JNE*, *30*, 8–16.

Spjut, R. W. (1994). *A systematic treatment of fruit types*. New York, NY: New York Botanical Garden.

Stein, L. J., Cowart, B. J., & Beauchamp, G. K. (2012). The development of salty taste acceptance is related to dietary experience in human infants: A prospective study. *American Journal of Clinical Nutrition*, *95*(1), 123–129. doi:10.3945/ajcn.111.014282

Stein, L. J., Nagai, H., Nakagawa, M., & Beauchamp, G. K. (2003). Effects of repeated exposure and health-related information on hedonic evaluation and acceptance of a bitter beverage. *Appetite*, *40*(2), 119–129.

Steiner, J. E. (1987). What the neonate can tell us about umami. In Y. Kawamura & M. R. Kare (Eds.), *Umami: A basic taste* (pp. 97–103). New York, NY: Marcel Dekker.

Strauss, S. (2006). Clara M. Davis and the wisdom of letting children choose their own diets. *Canadian Medical Association Journal, 175*(10), 1199. doi:10.1503/cmaj.060990

Sullivan, R., Perry, R., Sloan, A., Kleinhaus, K., & Burtchen, N. (2011). Infant bonding and attachment to the caregiver: Insights from basic and clinical science. *Clinics in Perinatology, 38*(4), 643–655. doi:10.1016/j.clp.2011.08.011

Sullivan, S. A., & Birch, L. L. (1994). Infant dietary experience and acceptance of solid foods. *Pediatrics, 93*(2), 271–277.

Sumonja, S., & Novakovic, B. (2013). Determinants of fruit, vegetable, and dairy consumption in a sample of schoolchildren, northern Serbia, 2012. *Preventing Chronic Disease, 10*, E178. doi:10.5888/pcd10.130072

Swinburn, B. A., Caterson, I., Seidell, J. C., & James, W. P. (2004). Diet, nutrition and the prevention of excess weight gain and obesity. *Public Health Nutrition, 7*, 123–146.

Taber, D. R., Chriqui, J. F., & Chaloupka, F. J. (2013). State laws governing school meals and disparities in fruit/vegetable intake. *American Journal of Preventative Medicine, 44*, 365–372. doi:10.1016/j.amepre.2012.11.038

Thompson, A. L., Mendez, M. A., Borja, J. B., Adair, L. S., Zimmer, C. R., & Bentley, M. E. (2009). Development and validation of the Infant Feeding Style Questionnaire. *Appetite, 53*(2), 210–221. doi:10.1016/j.appet.2009.06.010

Uneyama, H., Niijima, A., San Gabriel, A., & Torii, K. (2006). Luminal amino acid sensing in the rat gastric mucosa. *American Journal of Physiology: Gastrointestinal and Liver Physiology, 291*(6), G1163–1170. doi:10.1152/ajpgi.00587.2005

USDA (2010). *Report of the Dietary Guidelines Advisory Committee on the dietary guidelines for Americans.* Retrieved from www.nutriwatch.org/05Guidelines/dga_advisory_2010.pdf.

van den Engel-Hoek, L., van Hulst, K. C., van Gerven, M. H., van Haaften, L., & de Groot, S. A. (2014). Development of oral motor behavior related to the skill assisted spoon feeding. *Infant Behaviour and Development, 37*(2), 187–191. doi:10.1016/j.infbeh.2014.01.008

Ventura, A. K., Beauchamp, G. K., & Mennella, J. A. (2012). Infant regulation of intake: The effect of free glutamate content in infant formulas. *American Journal of Clinical Nutrition, 95*(4), 875–881. doi:10.3945/ajcn.111.024919

Ventura, A. K., Inamdar, L. B., & Mennella, J. A. (2015). Consistency in infants' behavioural signalling of satiation during bottle-feeding. *Pediatric Obesity, 10*, 180–187. doi:10.1111/ijpo.250

Ventura, A. K., & Mennella, J. A. (2017). An experimental approach to study individual differences in infants' intake and satiation behaviors during bottle-feeding. *Child Obesity, 13*(1), 44–52. doi:10.1089/chi.2016.0122

Wahlqvist, M. L., & Lee, M. S. (2007). Regional food culture and development. *Asia Pacific Journal of Clinical Nutrition, 16* (Suppl. 1), 2–7.

Wardle, J., Carnell, S., & Cooke, L. (2005). Parental control over feeding and children's fruit and vegetable intake: How are they related? *Journal of the American Dietetic Association, 105*(2), 227–232.

Welker, E., Jacquier, E. F., Catellier, D. J., Anater, A. S., & Story, M. T. (2016). Room for improvement remains in food consumption patterns of young children aged 2–4 years. *Journal of Nutrition, 148*, 1–11.

Welsh, J. A., & Cunningham, S. A. (2011). The role of added sugars in pediatric obesity. *Pediatric Clinics of North America, 58*(6), 1455–1466. doi:10.1016/j.pcl.2011.09.009

Welsh, J. A., Sharma, A., Cunningham, S. A., & Vos, M. B. (2011). Consumption of added sugars and indicators of cardiovascular disease risk among US adolescents. *Circulation, 123*, 249–257. doi:10.1161/CIRCULATIONAHA.110.972166

Willander, J., & Larsson, M. (2006). Smell your way back to childhood: Autobiographical odor memory. *Psychosomatic Bulletin and Review, 13*(2), 240–244.

Wilson, D., Best, A., & Sullivan, R. (2004). Plasticity in the olfactory system: Lessons for the neurobiology of memory. *Neuroscientist, 10*, 513–524.

Woolridge, M. W., Baum, J. D., & Drewett, R. F. (1980). Does a change in the composition of human milk affect sucking patterns and milk intake? *Lancet, 2*(8207), 1292–1293.

(1982). Individual patterns of milk intake during breast-feeding. *Early Human Development, 7*(3), 265–272.

Worobey, H., Ostapkovich, K., Yudin, K., & Worobey, J. (2010). Trying versus liking fruits and vegetables: Correspondence between mothers and preschoolers. *Ecology of Food and Nutrition, 49*, 87–97. doi:10.1080/03670240903433261

Yang, Q., Zhang, Z., Gregg, E. W., Flanders, W. D., Merritt, R., & Hu, F. B. (2014). Added sugar intake and cardiovascular diseases mortality among US adults. *JAMA Internal Medicine, 174*(4), 516–524. doi:10.1001/jamainternmed.2013.13563

11 The Development of Multisensory Attention Skills

Individual Differences, Developmental Outcomes, and Applications

Lorraine E. Bahrick, Robert Lickliter, and James T. Torrence Todd

The world presents an array of constantly changing sights and sounds, tactile and vestibular experiences, far too much to be attended and processed at any one time. Perceivers must make sense of this dynamically changing flux of stimulation by selecting events and properties of events that provide information that is meaningful and relevant to their needs, goals, and actions as they change across time. Adults are highly skilled at selectively attending to this multisensory stimulation in a way that optimizes perception and learning and supports their actions and goals. However, this selective attention presents a remarkable challenge for young infants – how to learn to attend to the dimensions of stimulation that optimize meaningful perception and action and to filter out stimulation that is less relevant.

Social events are particularly demanding of attentional resources. Social interactions, including the faces and voices of persons speaking, provide a rich source of stimulation for infants. Social partners and caregivers offer a wealth of information about the world, scaffolding the development of language, emotion, object exploration, and social interaction. Infants must quickly learn to detect which sights and sounds belong together and constitute unitary events (e.g., the face and voice of a person speaking) and which are separate and unrelated, in order to accurately parse the stream of available stimulation and make use of the rich information provided by the social environment.

One way young infants get this process off the ground is by detecting "amodal information," dimensions of time, space, and intensity that can be specified across multiple senses. For example, rate, rhythm, duration, and temporal synchrony are common to the movements of the face and sounds of the voice during speech. By detecting the rhythm and synchrony common to a face and voice during speech (intersensory matching), infants can pick out a speaker in a crowd. Typically developing infants are adept perceivers of amodal information (see Section 11.3 Intersensory Redundancy as a Cornerstone for Perceptual Development). In the social world, infants must also learn to sustain attention to faces and voices during speech in the face of competing stimulation from concurrent events and to quickly disengage from less relevant stimulation to attend to the source of a sound. We call these "multisensory attention skills" – accuracy of matching sights and sounds from unitary events, speed of disengaging or switching away from concurrent events, and duration of sustained attention to multisensory events – in the context of competing stimulation to the various senses. These multisensory attention skills provide a foundation for infants to quickly assimilate the social and linguistic information provided by caregivers. Typically developing infants show a rapid improvement in these fundamental skills across the first year of life (Bahrick, Lickliter, & Castellanos, 2013; Bahrick, Todd, Castellanos, & Sorondo, 2016; Lewkowicz, 1992; Walker-Andrews, 1997). Although, in this chapter, we focus on the development of audiovisual multisensory attention, other modalities, particularly tactile, vestibular, and proprioception, also play an integral role in the development of multisensory attention and in turn language, cognitive, and social outcomes.

In contrast to the typical development of attention and perception, the past decade has witnessed an alarming increase in the prevalence of neurodevelopmental and attention impairments in childhood, including autism spectrum disorder (ASD), attention-deficit hyperactivity disorder (ADHD), and reading disorders. These impairments are also coupled with deficits in multisensory attention and intersensory processing skills (for reviews, see Bahrick & Todd, 2012; Hill, Crane, & Bremner, 2012). Thus, it is critical that scientists learn more about (1) how multisensory attention skills (e.g., matching, shifting, and sustaining attention to audible and visible events) typically develop across infancy and childhood; and (2) how they serve as building blocks for typical language, cognitive, and social development. In particular, we need to specify the pathways through which multisensory attention skills cascade to more complex skills at a level of detail that is appropriate for identifying risk for atypical development and guiding interventions.

A primary obstacle to this effort has, until recently, been the lack of fine-grained individual difference measures of multisensory attention skills appropriate for infants and young children. The field of multisensory processing has been dominated by a group-level approach in which groups of children are tested and data are averaged to characterize skills at specific ages. Unlike domains of language and social development, there have been no tests designed to assess the skill of one child relative to another, or to characterize developmental trajectories. To address this gap, we recently developed the first two individual difference measures of multisensory processing. The availability of measures that can characterize the competence of individual children opens the door to assessing developmental change and pathways from multisensory attention skills to more complex skills that rely on this foundation. This level of analysis can provide a basis for revealing pathways to optimal developmental outcomes, and inform theory, policy, and interventions. In this chapter, we briefly review the history, theory, and research on multisensory development, and then focus on new directions afforded by this shift to a science of the study of individual differences in these capabilities, developmental outcomes, identification of children at risk for atypical development, implications for sociocultural issues, education, policy, interventions, and the importance of fostering optimal development in children.

11.1 History and Conceptual Issues

Two prevailing theoretical views, known respectively as the integration view and the differentiation view, dominated the field of intersensory development during the last half of the twentieth century (see Bahrick & Pickens, 1994; Lewkowicz, 1994, for brief reviews). The "integration view" held that the different sensory modalities function as separate sensory systems in early development and become integrated across time through the infant's activity and experience with concurrent stimulation from different sensory modalities (Birch & Lefford, 1963; Piaget, 1952). In contrast, the "differentiation view" held that the senses form a primitive unity in early development; with experience, the modalities, and the sensory information arising from them become increasingly differentiated. From this view, infants are thought to differentiate finer and more complex multimodal relations across development (Bower, 1974; E. J. Gibson, 1969; J. J. Gibson, 1966). As a result of these opposing views, the most prominent questions guiding research on early intersensory development for several decades focused on whether intersensory development (a) proceeds from integration of information across initially separate senses to coordinated multimodal experience (integration view), or (b) is a process of differentiation and increasing specificity (differentiation view; Lewkowicz & Lickliter, 1994; Rose & Ruff, 1987).

Consistent with the differentiation view, there is now compelling neuro-anatomical, neurophysiological, and behavioral evidence of significant inter-action among the senses in newborns and young infants from a variety of species (Lewkowicz & Turkewitz, 1980; Lickliter, 1993; Mellon, Kraemer, & Spear, 1991). For example, infant animals are more likely to show intersensory integration than older animals, and in infants (both human and animal) the sensory modality through which an event is processed is not treated as an important attribute of the event for encoding and memory (i.e., amodal encoding; see Spear & McKinzie, 1994). Similarly, work with human infants indicates that newborns (but not adults) typically equate auditory and visual stimuli on the basis of the amodal property of intensity (Lewkowicz & Turkewitz, 1980). Newborns also coordinate audio/visual space, moving their eyes in the direction of a sound (Mendelson & Haith, 1976; Muir & Field, 1979) and infants detect temporal synchrony uniting sights and sounds of speech (e.g., Kuhl & Meltzoff, 1982).

This more "integrated" view of sensory organization can be traced to the ground-breaking work of the perceptual psychologists James J. Gibson and Eleanor Gibson. In a sharp break from the traditional association views of perceptual development described above, the Gibsons recognized that the existence of different forms of sensory stimulation was not a problem for the perception of unitary events, but instead provided an important foundation for it. They argued that all senses should be considered as a single "perceptual system" that interact and work together to pick up invariant aspects of stimulation. One important type of invariant information is *amodal* information, dimensions of time, space, and intensity that can be specified across multiple senses. For example, the rhythm or tempo of a ball bouncing can be conveyed visually or acoustically and is completely redundant across the two senses. One can detect the same rhythm and tempo by watching the ball's motion or by listening to its impact sounds. The sight and sound of hands clapping likewise share temporal synchrony, a common tempo of action, and a common rhythm.

We know from developmental research conducted over the past three decades, inspired in large part by the Gibsons' innovative approach to perception, that young infants are adept perceivers of amodal information (Bahrick & Lickliter, 2002; Bahrick & Pickens, 1994; Lewkowicz, 2000). Infants readily detect the temporal aspects of stimulation such as synchrony, rhythm, tempo, and prosody that unite visual and acoustic stimulation from objects and events, as well as spatial colocation of objects and their sound sources and changes in intensity across the senses during the first 6 months following birth (Bahrick, 1988; Lewkowicz, Leo, & Simion, 2010; Slater, Quinn, Brown, & Hayes, 1999; for a review, see Bahrick & Lickliter, 2012). Such demonstrations of infants' detection of amodal information seriously question the notion that young perceivers slowly learn to coordinate and somehow put together separate and distinct sources of information. By detecting higher-order amodal information common to more than one sense modality, even naive perceivers can explore a unitary multimodal event in a coordinated manner. The major task of perceptual development then becomes to differentiate increasingly more specific information through detecting invariant patterns of stimulation. Importantly, during early development selective attention appears to be biased toward stimulus properties that are common or redundant across sensory modalities (Bahrick & Lickliter, 2002, 2014). By attending to such amodal information, there is no need to learn to integrate stimulation across the senses in order to perceive unified objects and events, as proposed by integrationist accounts of early perceptual and cognitive development.

11.2 Neural and Physiological Evidence of Intersensory Processing

In keeping with available behavioral evidence, research findings obtained from neurophysiological research over the last several decades indicates that the brain is remarkably skilled at integrating input from the different sensory systems to maximize the information available for perception and action, even during infancy (Lewis & Noppeney, 2010; Werchan, Baumgartner, Lewkowicz, & Amso, 2018). Further, the ability to integrate information from different senses is not limited to any particular brain structure. Multisensory integration has been found in neurons at multiple locations in the nervous system, including subcortical areas like the superior colliculus, early cortical areas like the primary visual and auditory cortices, and higher cortical levels like the superior temporal sulcus and intraparietal areas (Ghazanfar & Schroeder, 2006). Available evidence from human brain imaging studies also indicate that cortical pathways once thought to be sensory specific can be modulated by signals from other sensory modalities (Feng, Stormer, Martinez, McDonald, & Hillyard, 2014; Macaluso, 2006; Schroeder & Foxe, 2005). It is now clear that multisensory processes are more broadly distributed throughout the nervous system than traditional views of sensation and perception allowed (see Stein, 2012).

Further, it is well documented that multisensory neurons are highly responsive to the spatial and temporal properties of multisensory stimulation. Stimuli that are spatially and temporally redundant give rise to enhanced neural responsiveness, and stimuli that are separated in space or time result in reduced levels of neural responsiveness (Stein & Meredith, 1993). Neurons are sensitive to timing information, responding strongest to inputs from different modalities arriving simultaneously.

We now know that the senses function in concert even in infancy. Brains are organized to use the information they derive from the various sensory systems to enhance the likelihood that objects and events will be detected rapidly, identified correctly, and responded to appropriately, even during very early development (Calvert, Spence, & Stein, 2004). For example, the role of multisensory processing in selective attention has recently been demonstrated in infants at the neural level using measures of event-related potentials. Five-month-old infants show heightened attentional salience (greater amplitude Nc) and longer and deeper processing (reduction in late slow wave) for synchronous audiovisual speech than asynchronous or unimodal visual speech (Reynolds, Bahrick, Lickliter, & Guy, 2014). This reveals that intersensory redundancy (the same information simultaneously available and temporally synchronized across two or more sensory systems) not only promotes selective attention to certain event properties, but also promotes longer engagement and deeper processing. A physiological index of infant attention, heart rate, has also shown similar results. Curtindale, Bahrick, Lickliter, and Colombo (2019) found that intersensory redundancy (provided by dynamic videos of a woman speaking with a temporally matching soundtrack) attracted and held 4- and 8-month-old infants' attention as measured by greater heart-rate decelerations when compared to infants in a similar condition that provided no intersensory redundancy (the soundtrack was delayed with respect to the video). This suggests that auditory and visual events presented in synchrony and out of synchrony elicit physiological changes that are associated with differing levels of attention and processing in infants (see also Pizur-Barnekow,

Kraemer, & Winters, 2008). Taken together these neurophysiological findings point to the effectiveness of intersensory redundancy in capturing attention and promoting perceptual processing in early development.

11.3 Intersensory Redundancy as a Cornerstone for Perceptual Development

Intersensory redundancy (the same information simultaneously available and temporally synchronized across two or more sensory systems) is provided by most naturalistic events. For example, when the rhythm and tempo of speech can be perceived by looking and listening, the rhythm and tempo are redundantly specified. By definition, only *amodal properties* (information not specific to a particular sensory system, e.g., tempo, rhythm, duration, intensity) can be redundantly specified across the senses. Consistent with the view advanced by the Gibsons (E. J. Gibson, 1969; J. J. Gibson, 1966), this is not a problem for perception, but instead is a central foundation for accurate perception. It is also important to note that *all* multimodal events not only provide redundant, amodal information, but they also provide nonredundant, modality-specific information (attributes available to only a specific sensory system) such as color, pattern, pitch, or timbre. Selective attention to amodal information in early development can thus guide and constrain perceptual learning such that more global properties are differentiated first, and later more specific details are detected (Bahrick, 2001; Bahrick & Lickliter, 2002). This promotes veridical perceptual processing in order of increasing specificity, and fosters appropriate generalization of learning, allowing details (which vary across events) to be perceived in the context of more global properties that show less variability (Bahrick, 2001, 2010; E. J. Gibson, 1969).

We have known for over three decades that young infants are adept perceivers of intersensory redundancy across auditory and visual stimulation. Behavioral studies using traditional group-level methods such as the intermodal preference method (Bahrick, 1988; Lewkowicz, 1992) and the infant-controlled habituation procedure (methods that typically provide a single measure designed for statistical approaches that average across a group of participants; Bahrick, 1992; Gogate & Bahrick, 1998) have revealed a great deal about capabilities of infants at different ages. They demonstrate that early detection of intersensory redundancy provides a foundation for important achievements such as detection of object composition and substance (Bahrick, 1987, 1988), word mapping (Gogate & Bahrick, 1998; Gogate & Hollich, 2010), emotion perception (Flom & Bahrick, 2007; Walker-Andrews, 1997), communicative intent (approval and prohibition; Bahrick, McNew, Pruden, & Castellanos, 2019), and social referencing (Vaillant-Molina & Bahrick, 2012). For example, 7-month-old infants learn to relate speech sounds with objects when adults provide synchronous (but not asynchronous) object movements and labeling (Gogate & Bahrick, 1998, 2001). Five-month-old infants learn to preferentially approach a toy an adult responds to with positive emotion (but not negative emotion) early in development if they receive synchronous audio-visual information rather than visual information alone (Vaillant-Molina & Bahrick, 2012). In sum, a rich body of data from studies such as these has revealed that infants possess a wide range of intersensory processing skills in early development and that these skills provide a foundation for more complex language, cognitive, and social competencies. However, without the availability of fine-grained individual difference measures, the specific pathways and processes involved have remained unclear.

Given that events provide both amodal and modality-specific information, and infants are adept perceivers of amodal information, how and under what conditions do infants learn to detect modality-specific information? How is detection of different levels of information inter-coordinated? For example, infants perceive the emotion and communicative intent in audiovisual speech, but under what conditions do they attend to the appearance of the face or the sound of the voice? Infants detect the substance (rigid vs. elastic) and composition (single vs. compound object) of objects striking a surface, but under what conditions do they detect their color and shape, or the pitch of their impact sound? These are modality-specific properties (e.g., facial features and their spatial arrangement; color and shape of an object; or the pitch and timbre of a particular voice or impact sound). In line with Gibson's principle of increasing specificity, early research (Bahrick, 1992, 2001) demonstrated that detection of properties of stimulation develops in order of increasing specificity across development, from amodal, global properties (e.g., amodal temporal information for object substance and composition) to later detection of modality-specific information (e.g., object color/shape and pitch of impact sound). Consistent with this perspective, a more recent conceptual framework, the Intersensory Redundancy Hypothesis (IRH), was proposed to explore and reveal specific developmental principles guiding the inter-coordination of amodal and modality-specific information (Bahrick & Lickliter, 2000, 2012, 2014).

11.3.1 The Intersensory Redundancy Hypothesis (IRH)

The IRH is a theory of selective attention that describes how attention is allocated to various properties of objects and events – amodal and modality specific – in multimodal and unimodal stimulation. The IRH was derived from a convergent-operations approach (Lickliter & Bahrick, 2000) in which parallel research questions are explored across human and nonhuman animal subjects to identify common developmental principles of early intersensory perception. Research consistently demonstrates that intersensory redundancy available in multimodal stimulation is highly salient to young infants (see Bahrick & Lickliter, 2012, for a review). This creates attentional salience hierarchies favoring detection of amodal information at the expense of modality-specific information in early development when attentional resources are most limited. Thus, the IRH describes how the detection of *amodal information* can guide selective attention and learning during early infancy and how this process is coordinated with perception of *modality-specific information*. During multimodal (but not unimodal) exploration of events, amodal properties such as synchrony, tempo, and rhythm are most salient and are processed first. This is referred to as *intersensory facilitation*, the principle that amodal properties are detected more readily and earlier in development when they are redundantly specified in multimodal stimulation than when the same amodal properties are detected in unimodal stimulation (Bahrick & Lickliter, 2000, 2012). In contrast, in unimodal exploration of events (e.g., viewing a silent person; talking on the phone), attention is not captured by salient intersensory redundancy and is thus free to focus on modality-specific properties. This makes the pitch and timbre of a voice, or the appearance and features of a face most salient and processed first. This is referred to as *unimodal facilitation*, the principle that modality-specific properties (e.g., color, pattern, pitch, timbre) are detected more readily and earlier in development when they are explored through only one sense, than when the same information is detected in multimodal, synchronous stimulation (Bahrick, 2010; Bahrick & Lickliter, 2012).

The principal of *intersensory facilitation* was originally demonstrated for the amodal property of rhythm. At 5 months, infants detect the rhythm of a toy hammer tapping in audiovisual synchronous, but not unimodal visual, auditory, or asynchronous stimulation (Bahrick & Lickliter, 2000). This principle was subsequently extended to social events. For example, by 4 months, infants discriminate affect (specified by a combination of amodal properties) in synchronous audiovisual speech but not in unimodal auditory, visual, or asynchronous audiovisual speech (Flom & Bahrick, 2007). Similarly, quail embryos learn and remember the rhythm and tempo of a maternal call following synchronous prenatal audiovisual exposure, but not following the equivalent amount of unimodal auditory or asynchronous audiovisual exposure (Lickliter, Bahrick, & Honeycutt, 2002).

The principle of *unimodal facilitation* was first documented for infant perception of spatial orientation for nonsocial events (Bahrick, Lickliter, & Flom, 2006) and more recently has provided new information about early face perception. Bahrick et al. (2013) demonstrated that 2-month-old infants are best at discriminating between the faces of two women speaking when their speech is silent as compared with when it is audible and synchronous with their voices. Even more striking, face discrimination is enhanced during asynchronous as compared with synchronous audiovisual speech, highlighting the interfering role of intersensory redundancy for detecting modality-specific information such as facial configuration. During audiovisual speech, intersensory redundancy captures attention, directing it to amodal properties of speech. In contrast, in the asynchronous control (in which intersensory redundancy was eliminated but the amount and type of stimulation were preserved), infants discriminated between the two faces. This *dual role* of intersensory redundancy (both facilitating and interfering) is often overlooked and instead it is assumed that intersensory redundancy enhances attention to *all* aspects of an event. Alternative hypotheses, including that the greater amount or complexity of stimulation from multimodal than unimodal events can account for findings can be discounted, as they do not explain both the facilitating and interfering roles of multimodal stimulation. Such arguments are also discounted by data from asynchronous control groups, which show no facilitating effects.

Although principles of the IRH are most apparent in early development because attentional resources are limited, and task difficulty is high in relation to skills of the perceiver, these principles also apply across the life span, particularly when attentional resources are challenged and task difficulty is high. As attention becomes more efficient and flexible across development, it can progress along the attentional salience hierarchy more quickly, and infants can then detect both amodal and modality-specific properties of stimulation in both multimodal and unimodal contexts within a single bout of exploration. Thus, infants of 2 months show unimodal facilitation of face discrimination (discriminating faces only when presented visually but not audiovisually), but by 3 months of age they no longer show unimodal facilitation. Instead, they discriminate the faces when presented visually as well as audiovisually (in the context of highly salient intersensory redundancy; Bahrick et al., 2013). Further, when task difficulty is high, the effects of salience hierarchies become evident in later development. Thus, although 5-month-olds show no intersensory facilitation for discriminating tempo contrasts of low difficulty, they do show intersensory facilitation when discriminating tempo contrasts of moderate and high difficulty (Bahrick, Lickliter, Castellanos, & Vaillant-Molina, 2010).

Taken together, studies generated by the IRH reveal a bidirectional or dual role (both facilitating and interfering effects) of the salience of intersensory redundancy on attention and perceptual processing of event properties (Bahrick & Lickliter, 2014). Specifically, multimodal and unimodal stimulation have opposite effects: Multimodal events facilitate detection of amodal properties at the expense of modality-specific properties, whereas unimodal stimulation facilitates detection of modality-specific properties at the expense of amodal properties. Because competition for processing resources underlies these effects, they are most evident in early development, but are also at play in later development for difficult tasks or conditions of high cognitive load. The convergence of data across species, developmental periods, event types, and methods provides strong evidence for these conclusions.

11.3.2 Educating Attention

Intersensory redundancy has also been shown to "educate attention" to amodal properties of events, much like transfer of training effects. Specifically, once intersensory redundancy directs attention to amodal properties in multimodal

stimulation, infants can detect the same amodal properties in subsequent unimodal stimulation, at younger ages and under exposure conditions that would
otherwise not support detection of amodal properties in unimodal stimulation.
Studies of bobwhite quail embryos and chicks illustrate this effect. Lickliter,
Bahrick, and Markham (2006) found that quail chicks showed no preference
for a familiarized maternal call when they had received relatively brief prenatal
unimodal auditory familiarization. In contrast, by first exposing embryos to
a redundant audiovisual presentation of the maternal call (call synchronized
with flashing light) followed by a unimodal auditory presentation (bimodal
→ unimodal), chicks showed a significant preference for the familiar auditory
maternal call 2 days after hatching. Embryos who received the reverse sequence
of exposure to the maternal call (unimodal → bimodal) showed no preference
for the familiarized maternal call in postnatal testing. Intersensory redundancy (in bimodal stimulation) apparently highlighted the temporal features
of the call and educated attention to these features in subsequent unimodal
stimulation. This education of attention to redundant temporal properties was
effective even after delays of 2 or 4 hours between initial bimodal stimulation
and subsequent unimodal stimulation (Lickliter et al., 2006).

Recent work with human infants has likewise shown the education of attention to specific properties of events. Bahrick, Lickliter, and Castellanos (2020)
assessed if 2-month-old human infants could detect the amodal property of
tempo in dynamic unimodal visual presentations of a toy hammer tapping (a
task typically too difficult for 2-month-olds) if infants had first been exposed
to audiovisual stimulation from the same toy hammer tapping, providing
intersensory redundancy, thereby educating attention to tempo. Infants were
all habituated to a visual-only display of the toy hammer tapping at a given
tempo and tested for detection of a change in tempo. There were three "pre-
exposure" conditions in which infants received a short exposure to the toy
hammer before the unimodal visual habituation session. Intersensory redundancy was either provided (audiovisual synchronous presentation of the hammer tapping) or not provided (unimodal visual presentation of the hammer
tapping; asynchronous audio and visual presentation of the hammer). Results
paralleled those of the study with quail embryos and chicks (Lickliter et al.,
2006) and indicated that only infants who received the synchronous audiovisual pre-exposure (and not those who received the unimodal visual or asynchronous audiovisual pre-exposure) showed evidence of detecting the change
in tempo in the unimodal visual habituation test. These findings suggest that
intersensory redundancy available in the audiovisual pre-exposure educated
infant attention to the amodal property of tempo. This attentional bias was
then extended to the subsequent unimodal visual habituation session and
promoted discrimination of tempo under conditions that would otherwise be
too difficult for 2-month-old infants. Taken together, our convergent results
suggest that education of attention can foster flexible perceptual processing
and promote developmental change in attentional selectivity, from detection

of amodal properties in multimodal stimulation to the detection of amodal properties in unimodal stimulation. As we discuss next, this insight remains unexplored in applications to educational settings.

11.3.3 Intersensory Redundancy, Educational Applications, and Implications for Policy

The IRH has advanced our understanding of the emergence and maintenance of a range of perceptual and cognitive skills observed during infancy, including the development of affect and prosody discrimination (Bahrick, McNew et al., 2019; Flom & Bahrick, 2007), rhythm and tempo discrimination (Bahrick, Flom, & Lickliter, 2002; Bahrick & Lickliter, 2000), numerical discrimination (Jordan, Suanda, & Brannon, 2008), sequence detection (Lewkowicz, 2004), abstract rule learning (Frank, Vul, & Johnson, 2009), and word mapping and segmentation (Gogate & Hollich, 2010; Hollich, Newman, & Jusczyk, 2005).

Facilitating effects of intersensory redundancy should also be apparent during early phases of learning for a variety of tasks across the life span. In other words, intersensory facilitation would be expected for learning in domains that are novel, for tasks that require effort, executive function, or discrimination of fine detail, for speeded responses, and for problems of relatively high cognitive load. Children and adults continue to develop expertise across the life span, acquiring new information and learning to perceive finer distinctions such as learning a new language or playing a new musical instrument. In early stages of learning, expertise is low in relation to task difficulty, and consequently task demands are high. Under these conditions, attention progresses more slowly along the processing salience hierarchy, and like infants, children and adults should experience intersensory facilitation. Similarly, unimodal facilitation (the interfering effects of intersensory redundancy) should also be evident across the life span when modality-specific tasks are difficult and cognitive load is high.

In educational settings, we propose that teachers carefully match learning strategies to the amodal and modality-specific properties of the information to be learned. For example, when learning material that is best conveyed visually (e.g., colors, numbers, the alphabet; discriminating between faces or complex objects), processing this modality-specific information will be enhanced in the absence of intersensory redundancy (i.e., without accompanying sounds that create salient audiovisual redundancy). Intersensory redundancy would interfere with learning by directing attention away from distinctive visual properties and toward properties common across sights, sounds, and tactile impressions (rhythm tempo, intensity patterns). If learning of visual material is accompanied by sound, the sound should not be coordinated with object movement (thereby not creating intersensory redundancy). For example, an unrelated sound (bell; utterance, look!) could engage attention without directing it away from the information to be learned. Similarly, when learning material best conveyed acoustically (e.g., letter sounds, verbal content, melody, language accent) learning about the nature of the sound (e.g., pitch, timbre) and speech content will also be enhanced in the absence of salient intersensory redundancy that directs attention away from modality-specific acoustic information.

In contrast, when learning material that relies on detecting amodal information (e.g., rhythm, tempo, intensity; prosody or affect in audiovisual speech), learning will be enhanced by presenting temporally coordinated multisensory information. For example, detecting communicative intent in utterances of prohibition will be facilitated by providing the natural, dynamic, temporally coordinated face and voice. This fosters unitized perception of the emotional expression and directs attention to salient properties of rhythm, tempo, and intensity changes across the face and voice that convey prohibition. Some material, including that supporting detecting emotion and communicative intent, provides both distinctive amodal as well as modality-specific properties. Thus, directing attention to a particular facial expression (e.g., a furrowed brow or frown) when conveying prohibition, would be facilitated in the absence of intersensory redundancy.

Finally, educating attention to amodal properties of events may also enhance learning. Teaching children to first perceive the target information in multimodal stimulation (e.g., emotion or prosody in the synchronous face and voice) and once it is detected, then presenting it in unimodal stimulation (face or voice alone; a more difficult learning context) may facilitate faster and more flexible learning about amodal properties that also extends beyond initial learning contexts. Recall, however, that across development, children become better at detecting both modality-specific and amodal properties in either multisensory or unimodal stimulation. Thus, the above principles are most applicable when tasks are difficult, attentional resources are challenged, or in teaching new skills. In typical exploration, perceivers seamlessly shift between detecting amodal and modality-specific properties as events become visible and audible or audible and visible together, and in accordance with their goals and intentions.

11.4 Intersensory Processing as a Foundation for Cognitive, Social, and Language Development

Intersensory processing serves as a critical foundation upon which more complex social, cognitive, and language skills can develop (Bahrick & Lickliter, 2012; Bahrick, Todd, & Soska, 2018; Barutchu et al., 2010; Pons, Bosch, & Lewkowicz, 2019). Rapidly shifting attention to locate the source of a sound allows children to unitize the sights and sounds of speech or object events, to pick out the speaker in a crowd, or attend to the object that is labeled. This selective attention, in turn, provides a basis for meaningful processing of these multimodal events. However, without reliable individual difference measures, researchers can only explore the capabilities of the average infant (derived from mean performance of a group) at a particular age, with no attention to individual variability. Variability across individuals in foundational skills, however, is a cornerstone for predicting developmental outcomes in individual children. Individual difference measures make use of this variability.

11.4.1 The Importance of Individual Difference Measures in Developmental Science

Developmental science has been undergoing an important shift in theory and methodology toward an individual difference approach, critical to addressing key questions about developmental change and pathways to outcomes (Lerner, Agans, DeSouza, & Hershberg, 2014; Overton, 2014). There have been significant advances in both theory and application from the creation of individual difference measures in many areas (e.g., language, cognition, clinical science) with assessments ranging from working memory to symptoms of autism and externalizing behaviors (Eyberg, Nelson, Duke, & Boggs, 2004; Fernald, Pinto, Swingley, Weinberg, & McRoberts, 1998; Lord, Rutter, DiLavore, & Risi, 2002; Rose, Feldman, & Jankowski, 2011). This has allowed researchers to link individual differences in these skills with later outcomes and to discover important developmental cascades. For example, greater language processing efficiency (speed/accuracy of looking to a labeled object) in toddlers has been found to predict accelerated vocabulary growth across early childhood and in turn, greater language proficiency and academic performance, even years later (Fernald & Marchman, 2012; Fernald, Perfors, & Marchman, 2006; Marchman & Fernald, 2008). We propose that the development of multisensory attention skills underlies developmental cascades leading to optimal language and social functioning. By creating and refining novel individual difference measures, we can dramatically enhance research, theory, and application of multisensory development to these critical domains. They will provide tools necessary for characterizing developmental trajectories and pathways from early developing skills to later outcomes.

11.4.2 Individual Difference Measures of Intersensory Processing

In particular, we have proposed that individual differences in the speed and accuracy of attention to intersensory redundancy should predict social, cognitive, and language competence (Bahrick, 2010; Bahrick & Lickliter, 2002; Bahrick & Todd, 2012). For example, intersensory processing is thought to underlie word mapping (Gogate & Hollich, 2010). Research using traditional approaches has shown that synchronous, but not asynchronous, object movement and verbal labeling promotes object–label mapping (Gogate & Bahrick, 1998; Jesse & Johnson, 2016), and this provides a gateway for further processing of object–label relations (Gogate, 2010; Gogate & Maganti, 2016). Moreover, children show improved word learning if parents more often spontaneously synchronize object movement and labeling (Nomikou, Koke, & Rohlfing, 2017; Suarez-Rivera, Smith, & Yu, 2018). These findings suggest that intersensory processing skills may promote a variety of downstream developmental improvements. Individual differences in the accuracy and speed of intersensory skills, such as face–voice or object–sound matching, as well as quickly shifting to and sustaining attention to these audiovisual events should predict individual performance in domains that rely on this foundation – from vocabulary growth and literacy skills, to social competence and school readiness.

However, until recently there were no commonly accepted measures of intersensory processing that were sufficiently fine-grained nor designed for assessing individual differences in infants or children. Without fine-grained individual differences measures, it has not been possible to determine if one child shows better intersensory processing skills than another, how these skills change across development, nor identify the pathways from these skills to later developmental outcomes. Consequently, we do not yet have a database documenting the typical development of these skills from infancy to childhood (the period across which identifying delays and disorders is most needed for intervention). An individual differences approach can reveal typical developmental trajectories of intersensory processing skills in infants and children, pathways between these basic skills and later developmental outcomes, and in turn, help identify performance that is atypical and outside the normal range of variability. The lack of fine-grained individual difference measures has thus limited advancement of developmental theory and application to education and to identifying developmental delays in these foundational skills. If multisensory attention skills (i.e., intersensory matching, shifting, maintaining attention to unitary multimodal events) are not well established in infancy, there may be far-reaching consequences for later language, social, and cognitive development (Bahrick, 2010; Bahrick & Lickliter, 2012; Bahrick & Todd, 2012; Bremner, Lewkowicz, & Spence, 2012; Falck-Ytter, Nyström, Gredebäck, Gliga, & Bölte, 2018).

We have therefore developed two new protocols for assessing individual differences in multisensory attention skills appropriate for preverbal participants. Both measures assess attention to audiovisual social and nonsocial events. The Multisensory Attention Assessment Protocol (MAAP; Bahrick, Todd et al., 2018) indexes intersensory processing (accuracy) as well as attention maintenance (duration), and shifting/disengaging (speed) for audiovisual events. The Intersensory Processing Efficiency Protocol (IPEP; Bahrick, Soska, & Todd, 2018) is more difficult and provides more fine-grained measures of just intersensory processing (accuracy and speed). In each of these protocols, both infants and children can be assessed using the same methods. These protocols now open the door to exploring the foundational role of intersensory processing and basic attention skills in ways not previously possible with traditional group-level approaches. Combining several measures within a protocol can reveal how basic attention skills (shifting, disengaging, maintaining attention) typically studied individually using primarily static or silent stimuli interact in individual children in overlapping, multisensory events. Because stimulation most salient to infants in multisensory events differs markedly from that of silent dynamic or static stimuli (Bahrick, Gogate, & Ruiz, 2002; Bahrick & Lickliter, 2014; Bahrick et al., 2013, 2016; Otsuka et al., 2009), the use of these protocols should yield new knowledge, generalizable to real-world, multisensory learning environments.

11.4.2.1 *The Multisensory Attention Assessment Protocol (MAAP)*

The Multisensory Attention Assessment Protocol (MAAP; Bahrick, Todd et al., 2018) assesses three multisensory attention skills, and the impact of competing visual stimulation on each, in a single protocol: duration of looking, accuracy of matching audio and visual stimulation, and speed of shifting, to social and nonsocial events (for a sample video, visit https://nyu.databrary .org/volume/326). It is designed to characterize fine-grained individual differences in attention to audiovisual events for infants and children. It is the only protocol to assess intersensory processing (matching sights and sounds) in the context of two other basic attention skills (shifting and maintaining attention to audiovisual events). Although attention is typically viewed as multifaceted (Colombo, 2001; Posner & Petersen, 1990; Ruff & Rothbart, 1996), attention and its development have typically been studied piecemeal, with various measures assessed in separate studies using different methods and stimuli, making comparisons across age and studies challenging. The MAAP provides a basis for assessing interrelations among all three attention skills and fosters comparisons across studies and ages. The MAAP adapts traditional looking-time measures and thus requires no verbal instructions or responses and is suitable for both nonverbal and verbal participants. Typically, nonverbal methods are used with infants (e.g., Colombo, Shaddy, Richman, Maikranz, & Blaga, 2004; Fagan, Holland, & Wheeler, 2007), whereas methods for children have required verbal responses or following instructions. The MAAP provides a single, common protocol for assessing development across infancy and early childhood, the period during which symptoms of developmental disorders (e.g., ASD, ADHD) emerge and are most responsive to intervention.

In the MAAP protocol (see Figure 11.1), each trial begins with a 3-second dynamic central visual stimulus (silent, colorful moving shapes) followed by two 10-second side-by-side lateral events. Social (two women speaking) and nonsocial events (two objects striking a surface) are played in different trial blocks with a natural soundtrack synchronous with one of the two events. On half of the trials, the central competing stimulus remains on during the lateral events, serving as the visual distractor (high-competition trials), and on the other half, it is turned off when the lateral events appear (low-competition trials). *Duration* of looking to the two events, *accuracy* of matching the audible and visual stimulation, and *speed* of shifting to the

Social: Low Competition Trials

Social: High Competition Trials

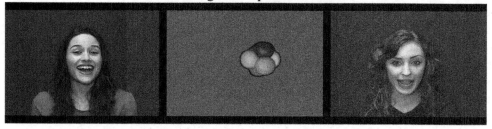

Nonsocial: Low Competition Trials

Nonsocial: High Competition Trials

Figure 11.1. *Static images of the dynamic audiovisual events from the MAAP. On all trials, a 3-second central stimulus (computerized geometric shape) was followed by two side-by-side lateral events (social, nonsocial), one of which was synchronous with its appropriate soundtrack. On low-competition trials, the central stimulus was turned off during the lateral events, whereas on high-competition trials, the central stimulus remained on during the lateral events.*

visual events is assessed under conditions of high and low competition. This design allows assessing relations among multisensory attention skills (duration, accuracy, speed) and the effects of concurrent, distracting events on these skills.

11.4.2.2 *The Intersensory Processing Efficiency Protocol (IPEP)*

The Intersensory Processing Efficiency Protocol (IPEP; Bahrick, Soska et al., 2018) focuses exclusively on intersensory processing (for a sample video, visit https://nyu.databrary.org/volume/326). It leverages traditional looking-time measures to derive indices of speed and accuracy (using remote eye tracking) in a context of multiple, concurrent events, both social and nonsocial. In the IPEP, participants attempt to locate an acoustically synchronized target event amid five competing visual distractors. The IPEP thus indexes intersensory processing in the context of multiple competing, naturalistic events, providing a meaningful basis for generalizing intersensory skills to natural, multimodal learning contexts. In traditional methods only one or two events are shown together, often with simple repetitive sounds, limiting their relevance to complex, real-world learning settings. In the IPEP (see Figure 11.2), participants see six concurrent events, while hearing the synchronous and appropriate soundtrack to one of them, simulating the "noisiness" of the natural world of overlapping events. The audiovisual events are rich and varied, depicting women speaking fluid, child-directed speech (social events) and objects of various shapes and compositions striking a surface in varied temporal patterns (nonsocial events). The events provide both macro-synchrony (onset and offset of head and large lip movements or object impacts against a surface) and micro-synchrony (specific speech sounds and fine-grained lip movements, or fine-grained temporal structure of object impacts). The protocol resembles the task of picking out a speaker in a crowd. The IPEP does not require verbal responses or understanding language, and thus can be administered at any age across the life span.

11.4.2.3 *Developmental Change in Multisensory Attention Skills (MAAP and IPEP Measures)*

Ongoing research in our lab is focusing on establishing developmental trajectories for multisensory attention skills in typically developing infants and young children to characterize the emergence of these skills and their refinement across early childhood. Thus far, findings reveal significant developmental improvements across 6 to 24 months in intersensory processing accuracy as assessed by the IPEP (McNew, Todd, Edgar, & Bahrick, 2018). Also, between 3 and 12 months, infants show improvements in multisensory attention skills assessed by the MAAP (maintaining attention, speed of attention shifting) in the presence of competing stimulation. Findings demonstrate a significant

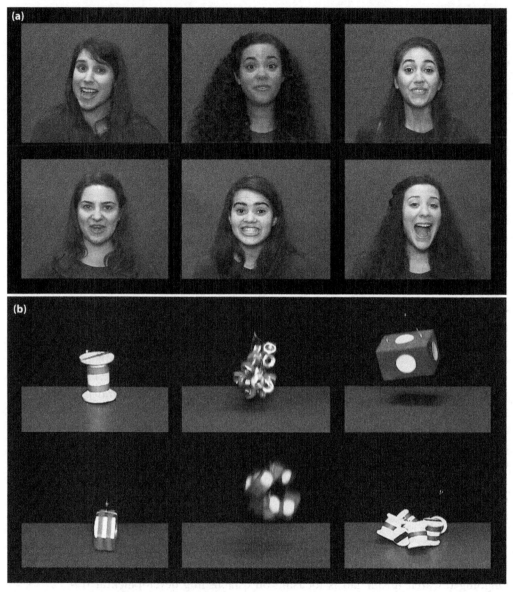

Figure 11.2. *Static images of the dynamic social (A) and nonsocial (B) events from the IPEP. On all trials, all six events (women, objects) were shown moving, but on each trial the movements of a different woman or object were synchronized with the accompanying, natural soundtrack.*

cost of competing stimulation on attention that decreases across age as infants become better at filtering out irrelevant stimulation (e.g., visual distractors; Todd, McNew, Soska, & Bahrick, 2016). Further studies indicate that multi-sensory attention skills continue to improve across age in older children, particularly for social events (Bahrick, Todd et al., 2018).

11.5 Links Between Multisensory Attention Skills and Language and Social Outcomes

The development of individual difference measures that show meaningful changes across age in multisensory attention skills opens the door to studies that can assess relations among these skills and language and social outcomes. We and others have argued that multisensory attention skills – matching sights and sounds from unitary events (e.g., a person speaking) and shifting and sustaining attention to these events in the presence of distractors – are foundational for both language and social development (Bahrick & Lickliter, 2012; Gogate & Hollich, 2010; Lewkowicz, 2014; Mundy & Burnette, 2005). For instance, intersensory processing (e.g., detecting synchrony between naming and gesturing to an object) helps infants link speech sounds with objects, serving as a basis for "word mapping" (Gogate & Hollich, 2010; Gogate, Walker-Andrews, & Bahrick, 2001). Multisensory attention skills also promote social development during face-to-face interactions between infants and caregivers. Fine-grained intersensory processing skills are required to coordinate the timing and intensity patterns across visual vocal, tactile, and affective communication (Beebe et al., 2016; Feldman, 2007). Caregivers are highly responsive to these infant behaviors, and the temporally coordinated and contingent responses provided by caregivers predict infant language learning (Tamis-LeMonda, Kuchirko, & Song, 2014).

Our working model (see Figure 11.3) illustrates the important role of basic attention skills (speed of shifting/disengaging, attention maintenance) and the mediational role of intersensory processing in language, social, and cognitive development during infancy. Basic attention skills (speed of shifting/disengaging, attention maintenance) predict accuracy of intersensory processing (selective attention to a sound synchronous event in the context of distracting events), which in turn predicts language, social, and cognitive outcomes. The relation between intersensory processing and language, social, and cognitive outcomes is moderated by the quality and quantity of infant–caregiver social interaction.

Recent findings are consistent with our model and provide support for the proposal that individual differences in multisensory attention skills are associated with individual differences in language and social functioning in both typically and atypically developing children. In one study, 2- to 5-year-old typically developing children received the MAAP along with the Mullen Scales of Early Learning (MSEL; Mullen, 1995), a standardized measure of cognitive and language functioning (Bahrick, Todd et al., 2018). Interrelations among MAAP measures and MSEL scores were evident. A structural equation model (SEM) revealed that children who showed longer maintenance of attention (duration) to social events showed greater intersensory matching (accuracy) of audiovisual speech events, and in turn higher scores on the receptive and expressive language scales of the MSEL, even after controlling for chronological age. Thus, consistent with our working model, accuracy of matching

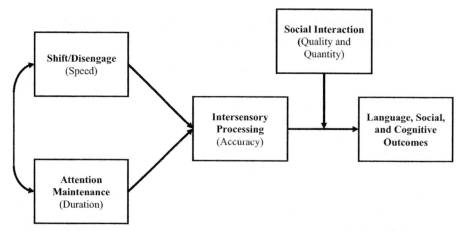

Figure 11.3. *Working model illustrates the mediational role of intersensory processing in language, social, and cognitive development during infancy. Basic attention skills (speed of shifting/disengaging, attention maintenance) predict accuracy of intersensory processing (selective attention to a sound synchronous event in the context of distracting events), which in turn predicts language, social, and cognitive outcomes. The relation between intersensory processing and language, social, and cognitive outcomes is moderated by the quality and quantity of multimodal social interaction.*

auditory and visual stimulation across faces and voices mediates the relation between sustained attention to speech events and receptive and expressive language functioning.

Individual differences in multisensory attention skills to social events assessed by the MAAP also predict social competence in typically developing children. At 6 months of age, longer attention maintenance to faces, greater intersensory matching of faces and voices, and faster speed of attentional shifting predict 18-month social competence scores on the Infant–Toddler Social Emotional Assessment (Carter & Briggs-Gowan, 2000). These preliminary findings are also consistent with our working model that multisensory attention skills are foundational for social functioning (Todd et al., 2018). These exciting findings illustrate the important new directions afforded by the availability of individual difference measures of multisensory attention skills and the inclusion of multiple measures within a single protocol. Models such as those described above can inform application and guide interventions to enhance language and social development.

Relations among multisensory attention skills and social-communicative functioning are also evident in atypically developing children. In one study, 2- to 5-year-old children with a diagnosis of autism on the Autism Diagnostic Observation Schedule (ADOS) (Lord et al., 2002) received the MAAP along with multiple outcomes measures (Bahrick & Todd, 2012; Todd & Bahrick, in preparation). MAAP measures including attention maintenance, speed of disengagement, and intersensory matching predicted symptom severity (ADOS standard scores). These MAAP measures also predicted social functioning on several standard scales including the Social Responsiveness Scale (Constantino & Gruber, Charles, 2005), the Social Communication Questionnaire (Rutter, Bailey, & Lord, 2003), and ESCS (a measure of joint attention; Mundy et al., 2003). Analyses revealed that attention maintenance to social events mediates relations among other multisensory attention skills (accuracy of matching, speed of shifting) and language and social outcomes (Todd & Bahrick, in preparation). Greater accuracy and faster speed may cascade into enhanced social attention, which in turn leads to better language and social functioning. These novel findings demonstrate the viability of the MAAP as a potential predictor of ASD symptomology and social functioning in children at risk for atypical development.

Finally, in kindergarten children at risk for reading delays, individual differences in multisensory attention skills predict school readiness skills (preliteracy, self-regulation) that are central for academic success. Intersensory processing is a foundation for word mapping (Gogate & Bahrick, 1998; Gogate & Hollich, 2010), which in turn promotes preliteracy skills (letter name and sound mapping), and in turn, reading abilities (Whitehurst & Lonigan, 1998). Intersensory processing also requires attention control and filtering out irrelevant stimulation (e.g., asynchronous visual movement), skills that are also critical for behavioral self-regulation. We tested a sample of 66 Latino children from predominately low-income families (rising K and first graders) with a touchscreen tablet version of the IPEP along with tests of letter names and letter sounds (Oral Reading Fluency, ORF; Fuchs, Fuchs, & Hosp, 2001) and a measure of behavioral self-regulation (the Head, Toes, Knees, and Shoulders Task, HTKS; Ponitz, McClelland, Matthews, & Morrison, 2009). Accuracy of target selection predicted performance on tests of letter names and sounds on the ORF, even after controlling for chronological age (Bahrick et al., 2017) and greater performance predicted better self-regulation on the HTKS (McNew, Todd, Zambrana, Hart, & Bahrick, 2019). These exciting findings suggest that intersensory processing provides an important foundation for a developmental cascade leading to preliteracy skills, behavioral self-regulation, and potentially to academic success.

11.6 Atypical Development

11.6.1 Intersensory Processing in Autism and Implications for Policy

Children with ASD show early disturbances in intersensory processing (Bahrick & Todd, 2012; Falck-Ytter et al., 2018; Stevenson et al., 2014), but links between intersensory processing impairments and ASD are not yet well understood. Bahrick and Todd (2012) proposed that an intersensory processing disturbance was one critical basis for this worsening cascade of social and communicative impairments across development. Given that social events are highly demanding of multisensory attention skills (with rapidly changing, temporally coordinated faces, voices, and gestures), impairments in intersensory processing may lead to selective impairments in social attention, including reduced attentional salience of audiovisual speech (social orienting impairment; Dawson, Meltzoff, Osterling, Rinaldi, & Brown, 1998; also see Bahrick, 2010; Bahrick & Todd, 2012; Mundy & Burnette, 2005). These selective impairments in social attention would then lead to language and social functioning impairments. In our view, symptoms of autism worsen in part because small deficits in basic "building blocks" of attention and intersensory processing amplify across development, reduce attention maintenance to social events, and impact social and communication skills that rely on these foundations (Bahrick, 2010; Bahrick & Todd, 2012; Mundy & Burnette, 2005).

Consistent with this proposal, children with ASD, who show impairments in social and language functioning, also show impairments in intersensory processing (for reviews, see Bahrick & Todd, 2012; Hill et al., 2012; Stevenson et al., 2014). Compared to typically developing children, children with ASD show impairments in matching visual and auditory stimulation from speech, have an enlarged audiovisual temporal binding window for audiovisual speech, and perform poorly on speech-in-noise tasks (Bebko, Weiss, Demark, & Gomez, 2006; Foxe et al., 2013; Stevenson et al., 2014). Finally, findings from our lab demonstrate that accuracy of intersensory matching and speed of attention shifting predict attention to social events, which in turn predicts language and social impairments in children with ASD (Todd & Bahrick, in preparation). These findings are consistent with an early intersensory processing disturbance in children with ASD.

Impairments in intersensory processing have also been identified in other developmental disorders of attention. For example, children with dyslexia show impaired intersensory processing skills (Hairston, Burdette, Flowers, Wood, & Wallace, 2005; Wallace, 2009). Similarly, research from our lab described above demonstrates intersensory processing predicts knowledge of letter names and letter sounds in children who are at risk for reading delays.

Early disturbances of intersensory processing – especially of social events, which provide extraordinary amounts of intersensory redundancy across faces and voices – could induce a cascade leading to poor integration of faces and voices, piecemeal processing of multimodal events, and delayed social, cognitive, and language development (Bahrick, 2010; Bahrick & Todd, 2012; Stevenson et al., 2018). Identifying the potential cascades stemming from poor early intersensory processing requires fine-grained measures of individual differences in intersensory processing. Such measures are key to early detection of risk for delays and for guiding interventions.

Given the importance of multisensory attention skills for the typical development of higher-level skills, we propose that infants routinely be screened for multisensory processing and basic attention impairments, along with basic tests of unisensory auditory and visual functioning. It is also important to determine if delayed intersensory processing skills stem from impairments in unimodal sensory functioning (auditory or visual) or in the integration of auditory and visual information, or both. Once the typical developmental trajectories for measures indexed by the MAAP and IPEP are established (data collection in progress in our lab), the MAAP and IPEP can serve as a basis for screening for intersensory processing impairments. However, this will also require developing screener tests assessing the same auditory and visual information separately (e.g., dynamic faces, speaking voices) to rule out impairments in unisensory skills as a source of an intersensory impairment.

11.6.2 Preterm Birth and Implications for Policy

The significant modifications of sensory experience that come with preterm birth are likely to have a range of effects on the normal course of sensory and perceptual development (Lickliter, 2000, 2011). That being said, investigators are a long way from understanding the particulars. Given that auditory experience is typically available prenatally and that patterned visual experience is not normally available until after birth, is there some necessary period or level of auditory experience without competing visual experience needed in the period before birth to ensure the emergence of normal patterns of postnatal perception? Does the unusually early visual experience associated with preterm birth and the resulting dramatic increase in the intensity and amount of auditory and visual stimulation present in the neonatal intensive care unit (NICU) interfere with normal auditory or visual development? What kinds of sensory stimulation is the fetus, preterm infant, and full-term infant particularly sensitive to? These important questions remain mostly unanswered at present.

We do know that the full-term fetus experiences intersensory stimulation across the auditory, vestibular, and tactile senses during the third trimester of gestation. For example, when the mother walks, the sounds of her footsteps can be coordinated with tactile feedback as the fetus experiences changing pressure corresponding with the temporal patterning and shifting intensity of her movements, as well as the accompanying and coordinated vestibular changes. In addition, the mother's speech sounds, her laughter, heartbeat, or sounds of breathing may create tactile stimulation that shares the temporal patterning of her sounds as a result of changes in the musculature involved in producing the sounds. Interestingly, this may provide a foundation for fetal learning – in the third trimester of gestation, fetuses can discriminate auditory stimulation on the basis of temporal patterning such as prosody (e.g., DeCasper & Spence, 1991).

The conditions in the NICU, coupled with the limited motor skills of the preterm infant, minimize the preterm's exposure to temporally coordinated stimulation in two or more sensory modalities. In the full-term newborn, auditory stimulation typically elicits an orienting response; infants turn their eyes in the direction of the sound source. This allows the infant to unitize the audiovisual stimulation and perceive the visual characteristics of the audible event. In the NICU, however, sound sources are often not visible to the infant, even if the infant is able to turn toward them. Sounds (such as respiratory and monitoring equipment) typically occur independent of stimulation to other sensory modalities and provide little if any opportunity for the infant to match a particular sound with its visual and tactile referents. Similarly, the dramatically reduced tactile and vestibular stimulation available to the preterm infant limits the opportunities for synchronous tactile and auditory stimulation. The short-term and possible long-term consequences of these reduced opportunities for intersensory redundancy on the preterm infant's emerging patterns of selective attention, perceptual processing, and learning are presently unknown and merit further research attention.

We propose that a shift in research focus from the effects of modifications to individual sensory modalities in the NICU (e.g., reducing visual stimulation, increasing tactile stimulation) to a focus on how redundant multisensory experiences at particular times and stages of development influence the course of intersensory development is needed. Such a timeline could provide a road map to promoting optimal development in this high-risk population by contributing to progress in the design of care *and* intervention programs for infants born at different levels of prematurity.

11.7 Social Context, Culture, and Implications for Policy

As described above, early experiences, starting *in utero*, shape and promote the development of infant multisensory attention skills. Opportunities for further developing and enhancing multisensory attention skills abound through reciprocal, bidirectional interactions as the infant interacts with objects, events, and people. Active exploration of objects provides coordinated visual, auditory, and tactile feedback and promotes an understanding of object affordances (E. J. Gibson, 1988; Lockman & Kahrs, 2017) and the development of multisensory attention skills. And social interactions with responsive caregivers provide infants one of the richest sources of input for developing multisensory attention skills (Bahrick & Lickliter, 2012; Tamis-LeMonda et al., 2014). Caregivers engage in face-to-face communication with infants, generating multisensory and temporally coordinated speech, gesture, eye gaze, facial movement, and touch (Beebe et al., 2016; Feldman, 2007). They scaffold the development of selective attention and attention control and promote language development by creating infant–caregiver social feedback loops. Caregivers provide feedback contingent on infant vocalizations and gestures and coordinate verbal labels with synchronous showing and naming objects. In response, infant vocalizations increase in frequency and become more adult-like (Gogate & Hollich, 2010; Goldstein & Schwade, 2008; Tamis-LeMonda et al., 2014; Tamis-LeMonda, Kuchirko, & Tafuro, 2013; Warlaumont, Richards, Gilkerson, & Oller, 2014). Through contingent responsiveness, engaging in affective communication, and establishing emotional attunement, caregivers also promote a sense of competence in infants and foster the development of self-regulation skills. These interactions with significant caregivers provide the foundation for developmental cascades leading to language and social outcomes.

However, there are large differences across families in the quality and quantity of interactions. Research indicates that parents with greater education and income, in general, are more responsive (by providing prompt feedback contingent on infant actions), interact more, and provide higher-quality speech input (richness, complexity) than parents with lower education and income (Hart & Risley, 1995; Hirsh-Pasek et al., 2015; Rowe, 2018; Tamis-LeMonda et al., 2014). In fact, the powerful role of "parent language input" for promoting speech and vocabulary growth in infants and young children has recently been highlighted by automated measures of child-directed speech using language environment analysis (LENA) (e.g., Warlaumont et al., 2014; Weisleder & Fernald, 2013). This has catalyzed nationwide efforts for parents (particularly of low socioeconomic status, SES) to increase language to infants to offset the "30-million word gap" (Hart & Risley, 1995) and in turn, to enhance language, school readiness, literacy, and academic achievement (Leffel & Suskind, 2013; National Early Literacy Panel, 2008; Whitehurst & Lonigan, 1998).

We propose that along with "language input" (the quantity and quality of words spoken to the child), more emphasis should be placed on the amount and richness of *multisensory face-to-face interaction* in promoting optimal social, cognitive, and language outcomes (see Figure 11.3). Language in the context of face-to-face interaction with responsive caregivers should promote the development of multisensory attention skills, and in turn language growth and self-regulation skills across childhood (Tamis-LeMonda et al., 2014). Further, promoting object exploration, especially in the context of interaction with responsive caregivers, should likewise enhance multisensory attention skills and language growth. For example, scaffolding infant object exploration with coordinated gaze and contingent naming facilitates word mapping (Gogate & Hollich, 2010; Gogate et al., 2001). Thus, we suggest that optimal growth of multisensory attention skills will be fostered by (1) providing opportunities for infants to explore objects in their environment in the context of responsive caregiver interactions that support their natural curiosity; and (2) engaging in face-to-face interactions with responsive caregivers, which include bidirectional, coregulated interactions involving contingent responsiveness and affective communication. In line with developmental systems perspectives (e.g., Gogate et al., 2001; Goldstein & Schwade, 2008; Suanda, Smith, & Yu, 2016; Tamis-LeMonda et al., 2014), by actively engaging in these interactions involving coordinating attention to people and objects in multimodal, interactive settings, caregivers in effect train infant attention, and scaffold social feedback loops whereby infant responses generate the input needed (from both caregivers and the environment) for supporting language, social, and cognitive development.

11.8 Future Directions

The use of individual difference measures of multisensory attention skills promises to enhance our understanding of developmental processes and how they lead to optimal language, cognitive, and social outcomes. This will make research on multisensory processing and the resulting knowledge base more relevant to application for education and intervention. Several future research directions are needed to effect this change.

11.8.1 Developmental Cascades to Outcomes

We must clarify the developmental pathways through which these basic multisensory skills cascade to more complex language, cognitive, and social skills by assessing relations between individual differences in these skills, the role of multimodal social interaction with caregivers (quality and quantity of language input, contingent responsiveness, coordinated gaze and object exploration, etc.), and later outcomes. This will allow researchers to derive models depicting developmental cascades and establish which specific skills lead to specific developmental outcomes, and how these relations are moderated by the multimodal social environment. This can eventually provide a basis for appropriately targeting interventions to foundational skills.

11.8.2 Developmental Trajectories for Multisensory Attention Skills

The developmental trajectories of multisensory attention skills in typically developing children also need to be established. By characterizing the typical development of multisensory attention skills – matching synchronous sights and sounds of social or nonsocial events, quickly shifting to these events, and sustaining attention to these events in the face of distracting events – researchers will be able to identify infants and children whose skills fall outside the range of typical variability and are at risk for delays. The availability of the MAAP and IPEP allow testing of young infants as well older children using the same protocols, making it feasible to establish developmental trajectories using the same measures across ages.

11.8.3 Detecting Early Risk

In conjunction with models of developmental cascades, knowledge of typical developmental trajectories will allow researchers to determine which children are in need of intervention and which skills would be most effective for accelerating development for different outcomes. Assessing multisensory attention skills in early development will open the door to much earlier identification of risk for delays in attention skills and in the outcomes that rely on these skills than currently possible. Thus, early identification can provide opportunities for early intervention to optimize development.

11.8.4 Training Multisensory Attention Skills

Another future direction that will be needed to lay the groundwork for effective interventions is to establish successful protocols for training multisensory attention skills, including intersensory processing (synchrony detection), attention maintenance, and rapid shifting to audiovisual events. This will require exploring the effectiveness of training studies, monitoring progress on the skills in question, assessing generalization to events and contexts not trained, and assessing long-term effects of training.

11.8.5 Promoting Optimal Development

Finally, the availability of individual difference measures also makes possible a shift in the focus of developmental science from normative development versus atypical development – to one conceptualizing development along a continuum, from suboptimal to optimal (e.g., Karmiloff-Smith, 1998). This not only characterizes atypical development along a continuum with typical development, but also opens the door to a new focus on the study of optimal developmental outcomes. Given the importance of intersensory processing and attention regulation for school readiness, social competence, and academic success (Blair & Raver, 2012, 2015), it is imperative that developmental science focus research effort on how to maximize outcomes for typically developing children (alongside the focus on atypically developing children). Consistent with the recent emergence of the field of positive psychology and the discovery of its enormous benefits for health and well-being (e.g., Fredrickson, 2000; Seligman & Csikszentmihalyi, 2000; Slavich & Cole, 2012), the use of individual difference measures provides tools for developmental scientists to study factors and processes that support children – not just performing at level – but thriving. This calls for developmental scientists to focus on factors that support optimal language, social, and cognitive outcomes – outcomes that will promote overall well-being and a sense of competence in children.

References

Bahrick, L. E. (1987). Infants' intermodal perception of two levels of temporal structure in natural events. *Infant Behavior and Development, 10,* 387–416. doi:10.1016/0163-6383(87)90039-7

(1988). Intermodal learning in infancy: Learning on the basis of two kinds of invariant relations in audible and visible events. *Child Development, 59,* 197–209. doi:10.2307/1130402

(1992). Infants' perceptual differentiation of amodal and modality-specific audiovisual relations. *Journal of Experimental Child Psychology, 53,* 180–199. doi:10.1016/0022-0965(92)90048-B

(2001). Increasing specificity in perceptual development: Infants' detection of nested levels of multimodal stimulation. *Journal of Experimental Child Psychology, 79,* 253–270. doi:10.1006/jecp.2000.2588

(2010). Intermodal perception and selective attention to intersensory redundancy: Implications for typical social development and autism. In J. G. Bremner & T. D. Wachs (Eds.), *The Wiley-Blackwell handbook of infant development* (Vol. 1, 2nd ed., pp. 120–165). Malden, MA: Wiley-Blackwell. doi:10.1002/9781444327564.ch4

Bahrick, L. E., Flom, R., & Lickliter, R. (2002). Intersensory redundancy facilitates discrimination of tempo in 3-month-old infants. *Developmental Psychobiology, 41,* 352–363. doi:10.1002/dev.10049

Bahrick, L. E., Gogate, L. J., & Ruiz, I. (2002). Attention and memory for faces and actions in infancy: The salience of actions over faces in dynamic events. *Child Development, 73,* 1629–1643. doi:10.1111/1467–8624.00495

Bahrick, L. E., & Lickliter, R. (2000). Intersensory redundancy guides attentional selectivity and perceptual learning in infancy. *Developmental Psychology, 36,* 190–201. doi:10.1037//0012-1649.36.2.190

(2002). Intersensory redundancy guides early perceptual and cognitive development. In R. V. Kail (Ed.), *Advances in child development and behavior* (Vol. 30, pp. 153–187). San Diego, CA: Academic Press.

(2012). The role of intersensory redundancy in early perceptual, cognitive, and social development. In A. J. Bremner, D. J. Lewkowicz, & C. Spence (Eds.), *Multisensory development* (pp. 183–206). New York, NY: Oxford University Press.

(2014). Learning to attend selectively: The dual role of intersensory redundancy. *Current Directions in Psychological Science, 23,* 414–420. doi:10.1177/0963721414549187

Bahrick, L. E., Lickliter, R., & Castellanos, I. (2013). The development of face perception in infancy: Intersensory interference and unimodal visual facilitation. *Developmental Psychology, 49,* 1919–1930. doi:10.1037/a0031238

(2020). *Educating infant attention to the amodal property of tempo: The role of intersensory redundancy.* Manuscript submitted for publication.

Bahrick, L. E., Lickliter, R., Castellanos, I., & Vaillant-Molina, M. (2010). Increasing task difficulty enhances effects of intersensory redundancy: Testing a new prediction of the Intersensory Redundancy Hypothesis. *Developmental Science, 13,* 731–737. doi:10.1111/j.1467-7687.2009.00928.x

Bahrick, L. E., Lickliter, R., & Flom, R. (2006). Up versus down: The role of intersensory redundancy in the development of infants' sensitivity to the orientation of moving objects. *Infancy, 9,* 73–96. doi:10.1207/s15327078in0901_4

Bahrick, L. E., McNew, M. E., Pruden, S. M., & Castellanos, I. (2019). Intersensory redundancy promotes infant detection of prosody in infant-directed speech. *Journal of Experimental Child Psychology, 183,* 295–309. doi:10.1016/j.jecp.2019.02.008

Bahrick, L. E., McNew, M. E., Todd, J. T., Martinez, J., Mira, S., Cheatham-Johnson, R., & Hart, K. C. (2017). *Individual differences in intersensory processing predict pre-literacy skills in young children.* Poster presented at the meeting of the Society for Research in Child Development, Austin, TX.

Bahrick, L. E., & Pickens, J. N. (1994). Amodal relations: The basis for intermodal perception and learning. In D. J. Lewkowicz & R. Lickliter (Eds.), *The development of intersensory perception: Comparative perspectives* (pp. 204–233). Hillsdale, NJ: Lawrence Erlbaum Associates.

Bahrick, L. E., Soska, K. C., & Todd, J. T. (2018). Assessing individual differences in the speed and accuracy of intersensory processing in young children: The Intersensory Processing Efficiency Protocol. *Developmental Psychology, 54,* 2226–2239. doi:10.1037/dev0000575

Bahrick, L. E., & Todd, J. T. (2012). Multisensory processing in autism spectrum disorders: Intersensory processing disturbance as a basis for atypical development. In B. E. Stein (Ed.), *The new handbook of multisensory processes* (pp. 1453–1508). Cambridge, MA: MIT Press.

Bahrick, L. E., Todd, J. T., Castellanos, I., & Sorondo, B. M. (2016). Enhanced attention to speaking faces versus other event types emerges gradually across infancy. *Developmental Psychology, 52,* 1705–1720. doi:10.1037/dev0000157

Bahrick, L. E., Todd, J. T., & Soska, K. C. (2018). The Multisensory Attention Assessment Protocol (MAAP): Characterizing individual differences in multisensory attention skills in infants and children and relations with language and cognition. *Developmental Psychology, 54,* 2207–2225. doi:10.1037/dev0000594

Barutchu, A., Crewther, S. G., Fifer, J., Shivdasani, M. N., Innes-Brown, H., Toohey, S., … Paolini, A. G. (2010). The relationship between multisensory integration and IQ in children. *Developmental Psychology, 47,* 877–885. doi:10.1037/a0021903

Bebko, J. M., Weiss, J. A., Demark, J. L., & Gomez, P. (2006). Discrimination of temporal synchrony in intermodal events by children with autism and children with developmental disabilities without autism. *Journal of Child Psychology and Psychiatry, 47,* 88–98. doi:10.1111/j.1469-7610.2005.01443.x

Beebe, B., Messinger, D., Bahrick, L. E., Margolis, A., Buck, K. A., & Chen, H. (2016). A systems view of mother–infant face-to-face communication. *Developmental Psychology, 52,* 556–571. doi:10.1037/a0040085

Birch, H. G., & Lefford, A. (1963). Intersensory development in children. *Monographs of the Society for Research in Child Development, 28,* 1–48. doi:10.2307/1165681

Blair, C., & Raver, C. C. (2012). Child development in the context of adversity: Experiential canalization of brain and behavior. *American Psychologist, 67*(4), 309–318. doi:10.1037/a0027493

(2015). School readiness and self-regulation: A developmental psychobiological approach. *Annual Review of Psychology, 66,* 711–731. doi:10.1146/annurev-psych-010814-015221

Bower, T. G. R. (1974). *Development in infancy.* Oxford: W. H. Freeman.

Bremner, A. J., Lewkowicz, D. J., & Spence, C. (2012). *Multisensory development.* Oxford: Oxford University Press.

Calvert, G. A., Spence, C., & Stein, B. E. (2004). *The handbook of multisensory processes.* Cambridge, MA: MIT Press.

Carter, A. S., & Briggs-Gowan, M. (2000). *Infant toddler social and emotional assessment*. New Haven, CT: Yale University, Connecticut Early Development Project.

Colombo, J. (2001). The development of visual attention in infancy. *Annual Review of Psychology, 51*, 337–367. doi:10.1146/annurev.psych.52.1.337

Colombo, J., Shaddy, D. J., Richman, W. A., Maikranz, J. M., & Blaga, O. M. (2004). The developmental course of habituation in infancy and preschool outcome. *Infancy, 5*, 1–38. doi:10.1207/s15327078in0501_1

Constantino, J. N., & Gruber, Charles, P. (2005). *The social responsiveness scale*. Los Angeles. CA: Western Psychological Services.

Curtindale, L. M., Bahrick, L. E., Lickliter, R., & Colombo, J. (2019). Effects of multimodal synchrony on infant attention and heart rate during events with social and nonsocial stimuli. *Journal of Experimental Child Psychology, 178*, 283–294. doi:10.1016/j.jecp.2018.10.006

Dawson, G., Meltzoff, A. N., Osterling, J., Rinaldi, J., & Brown, E. (1998). Children with autism fail to orient to naturally occurring social stimuli. *Journal of Autism and Developmental Disorders, 28*, 479–485. doi:10.1023/A:1026043926488

DeCasper, A. J., & Spence, M. J. (1991). Auditorily mediated behavior during the perinatal period: A cognitive view. In M. J. Salomon Weiss & P. R. Zelazo (Eds.), *Newborn attention: Biological constraints and the influence of experience* (pp. 142–176). Westport, CT: Ablex.

Eyberg, S. M., Nelson, M. M., Duke, M., & Boggs, S. R. (2004). *Manual for the dyadic parent–child interaction coding system* (3rd ed.). Retrieved from http://citeseerx.ist.psu.edu/viewdoc/download?doi=10.1.1.627.4254&rep=rep1&type=pdf

Fagan, J. F., Holland, C. R., & Wheeler, K. (2007). The prediction, from infancy, of adult IQ and achievement. *Intelligence, 35*, 225–231. doi:10.1016/j.intell.2006.07.007

Falck-Ytter, T., Nyström, P., Gredebäck, G., Gliga, T., & Bölte, S. (2018). Reduced orienting to audiovisual synchrony in infancy predicts autism diagnosis at 3 years of age. *Journal of Child Psychology and Psychiatry, 59*, 872–880. doi:10.1111/jcpp.12863

Feldman, R. (2007). Parent–infant synchrony: Biological foundations and developmental outcomes. *Current Directions in Psychological Science, 16*, 340–345. doi:10.1111/j.1467-8721.2007.00532.x

Feng, W., Stormer, V. S., Martinez, A., McDonald, J. J., & Hillyard, S. A. (2014). Sounds activate visual cortex and improve visual discrimination. *Journal of Neuroscience, 34*, 9817–9824. doi:10.1523/JNEUROSCI.4869-13.2014

Fernald, A., & Marchman, V. A. (2012). Individual differences in lexical processing at 18 months predict vocabulary growth in typically developing and late-talking toddlers. *Child Development, 83*, 203–222. doi:10.1111/j.1467-8624.2011.01692.x

Fernald, A., Perfors, A., & Marchman, V. A. (2006). Picking up speed in understanding: Speech processing efficiency and vocabulary growth across the 2nd year. *Developmental Psychology, 42*, 98–116. doi:10.1037/0012-1649.42.1.98

Fernald, A., Pinto, J. P., Swingley, D., Weinberg, A., & McRoberts, G. W. (1998). Rapid gains in speed of verbal processing by infants in the 2nd year. *Psychological Science, 9*, 228–231. doi:10.1111/1467–9280.00044

Flom, R., & Bahrick, L. E. (2007). The development of infant discrimination of affect in multimodal and unimodal stimulation: The role of intersensory redundancy. *Developmental Psychology*, *43*, 238–252. doi:10.1037/0012-1649.43.1.238

Foxe, J. J., Molholm, S., Del Bene, V. A., Frey, H. -P. P., Russo, N. N., Blanco, D., ... Ross, L. A. (2013). Severe multisensory speech integration deficits in high-functioning school-aged children with autism spectrum disorder (ASD) and their resolution during early adolescence. *Cerebral Cortex*, *25*, 298–312. doi:10.1093/cercor/bht213

Frank, M. C., Vul, E., & Johnson, S. P. (2009). Development of infants' attention to faces during the first year. *Cognition*, *110*, 160–170.

Fredrickson, B. L. (2000). Cultivating positive emotions to optimize health and well-being. *Prevention & Treatment*, *3*, Article 0001a. doi:10.1037/1522-3736.3.1.31a

Fuchs, L. S., Fuchs, D., & Hosp, M. K. (2001). Oral reading fluency as an indicator of reading competence: A theoretical, empirical, and historical analysis. *Scientific Studies of Reading*, *5*, 257–288. doi:10.1207/S1532799XSSR0503

Ghazanfar, A. A., & Schroeder, C. E. (2006). Is neocortex essentially multisensory? *Trends in Cognitive Sciences*, *10*, 278–285.

Gibson, E. J. (1969). *Principles of perceptual learning and development*. East Norwalk, CT: Appleton-Century-Crofts.

(1988). Exploratory behavior in the development of perceiving, acting, and the acquiring of knowledge. *Annual Review of Psychology*, *39*, 1–41. doi:10.1146/annurev.psych.39.1.1

Gibson, J. J. (1966). *The senses considered as perceptual systems*. Boston, MA: Houghton Mifflin.

Gogate, L. J. (2010). Learning of syllable–object relations by preverbal infants: The role of temporal synchrony and syllable distinctiveness. *Journal of Experimental Child Psychology*, *105*, 178–197. doi:10.1016/j.jecp.2009.10.007

Gogate, L. J., & Bahrick, L. E. (1998). Intersensory redundancy facilitates learning of arbitrary relations between vowel sounds and objects in seven-month-old infants. *Journal of Experimental Child Psychology*, *69*, 133–149. doi:10.1006/jecp.1998.2438

(2001). Intersensory redundancy and 7-month-old infants' memory for arbitrary syllable-object relations. *Infancy*, *2*, 219–231. doi:10.1207/S15327078IN0202_7

Gogate, L. J., & Hollich, G. (2010). Invariance detection within an interactive system: A perceptual gateway to language development. *Psychological Review*, *117*, 496–516. doi:10.1037/a0019049

Gogate, L. J., & Maganti, M. (2016). The dynamics of infant attention: Implications for crossmodal perception and word-mapping research. *Child Development*, *87*, 345–364. doi:10.1111/cdev.12509

Gogate, L. J., Walker-Andrews, A. S., & Bahrick, L. E. (2001). The intersensory origins of word comprehension: An ecological–dynamic systems view. *Developmental Science*, *4*, 1–37. doi:10.1111/1467–7687.00143

Goldstein, M. H., & Schwade, J. A. (2008). Social feedback to infants' babbling facilitates rapid phonological learning. *Psychological Science*, *19*, 515–523. doi:10.1111/j.1467-9280.2008.02117.x

Hairston, W. D., Burdette, J. H., Flowers, D. L., Wood, F. B., & Wallace, M. T. (2005). Altered temporal profile of visual-auditory multisensory interactions in dyslexia. *Experimental Brain Research, 166*, 474–480. doi:10.1007/s00221-005-2387-6

Hart, B., & Risley, T. R. (1995). *Meaningful differences in the everyday experience of young American children.* Baltimore, MD: Brookes.

Hill, E. L., Crane, L., & Bremner, A. J. (2012). Developmental disorders and multisensory perception. In A. J. Bremner, D. J. Lewkowicz, & C. Spence (Eds.), *Multisensory development* (pp. 273–300). Oxford: Oxford University Press.

Hirsh-Pasek, K., Adamson, L. B., Bakeman, R., Owen, M. T., Golinkoff, R. M., Pace, A., … Suma, K. (2015). The contribution of early communication quality to low-income children's language success. *Psychological Science, 26*, 1071–1083. doi:10.1177/0956797615581493

Hollich, G., Newman, R. S., & Jusczyk, P. W. (2005). Infants' use of synchronized visual information to separate streams of speech. *Child Development, 76*, 598–613. doi:10.1111/j.1467-8624.2005.00866.x

Jesse, A., & Johnson, E. K. (2016). Audiovisual alignment of co-speech gestures to speech supports word learning in 2-year-olds. *Journal of Experimental Child Psychology, 145*, 1–10. doi:10.1016/j.jecp.2015.12.002

Jordan, K. E., Suanda, S. H., & Brannon, E. M. (2008). Intersensory redundancy accelerates preverbal numerical competence. *Cognition, 108*, 210–221. doi:10.1016/j.cognition.2007.12.001

Karmiloff-Smith, A. (1998). Development itself is the key to understanding developmental disorders. *Trends in Cognitive Sciences, 2*, 389–398. doi:10.1016/S1364-6613(98)01230-3

Kuhl, P. K., & Meltzoff, A. N. (1982). The bimodal perception of speech in infancy. *Science, 218*, 1138–1141. doi:10.1126/science.7146899

Leffel, K., & Suskind, D. (2013). Parent-directed approaches to enrich the early language environments of children living in poverty. *Seminars in Speech and Language, 34*, 267–277. doi:10.1055/s-0033-1353443

Lerner, R. M., Agans, J. P., DeSouza, L. M., & Hershberg, R. M. (2014). Developmental science in 2025: A predictive review. *Research in Human Development, 11*, 255–272. doi:10.1080/15427609.2014.967046

Lewis, R., & Noppeney, U. (2010). Audiovisual synchrony improves motion discrimination via enhanced connectivity between early visual and auditory areas. *Journal of Neuroscience, 30*, 12329–12339. doi:10.1523/JNEUROSCI.5745-09.2010

Lewkowicz, D. J. (1992). Infants' response to temporally based intersensory equivalence: The effect of synchronous sounds on visual preferences for moving stimuli. *Infant Behavior & Development, 15*, 297–324.

(1994). Development of intersensory perception in human infants. In D. J. Lewkowicz & R. Lickliter (Eds.), *The development of intersensory perception: Comparative perspectives* (pp. 165–204). Hillsdale, NJ: Lawrence Erlbaum Associates.

(2000). The development of intersensory temporal perception: An epigenetic systems/limitations view. *Psychological Bulletin, 126*, 281–308. doi:10.1037//0033-2909.126.2.281

(2004). Perception of serial order in infants. *Developmental Science, 7*, 175–184. doi:10.1111/j.1467-7687.2004.00336.x

(2014). Early experience and multisensory perceptual narrowing. *Developmental Psychobiology, 56,* 292–315. doi:10.1002/dev.21197

Lewkowicz, D. J., Leo, I., & Simion, F. (2010). Intersensory perception at birth: Newborns match nonhuman primate faces and voices. *Infancy, 15,* 46–60. doi:10.1111/j.1532-7078.2009.00005.x

Lewkowicz, D. J., & Lickliter, R. (1994). *The development of intersensory perception: Comparative perspectives.* Hillsdale, NJ: Lawrence Erlbaum Associates.

Lewkowicz, D. J., & Turkewitz, G. (1980). Cross-modal equivalence in early infancy: Auditory-visual intensity matching. *Developmental Psychology, 16,* 597–607. doi:10.1037/0012-1649.16.6.597

Lickliter, R. (1993). Timing and the development of perinatal perceptual organization. In G. Turkewitz & D. A. Devenny (Eds.), *Developmental time and timing* (pp. 105–124). Hillsdale, NJ: Lawrence Erlbaum Associates.

(2000). Atypical perinatal sensory stimulation and early perceptual development: Insights from developmental psychobiology. *Journal of Perinatology, 20,* S45–S54. doi:10.1016/B978-1-4557-7566-8.00096-X

(2011). The integrated development of sensory organization. *Clinics in Perinatology, 38,* 591–603. doi:10.1016/j.clp.2011.08.007

Lickliter, R., & Bahrick, L. E. (2000). The development of infant intersensory perception: Advantages of a comparative convergent-operations approach. *Psychological Bulletin, 126,* 260–280. doi:10.1037/0033-2909.126.2.260

Lickliter, R., Bahrick, L. E., & Honeycutt, H. (2002). Intersensory redundancy facilitates prenatal perceptual learning in bobwhite quail (*Colinus virginianus*) embryos. *Developmental Psychology, 38,* 15–23. doi:10.1037/0012-1649.38.1.15

Lickliter, R., Bahrick, L. E., & Markham, R. G. (2006). Intersensory redundancy educates selective attention in bobwhite quail embryos. *Developmental Science, 9,* 604–615. doi:10.1111/j.1467-7687.2006.00539.x

Lockman, J. J., & Kahrs, B. A. (2017). New insights into the development of human tool use. *Current Directions in Psychological Science, 26,* 330–334. doi:10.1177/0963721417692035

Lord, C., Rutter, M., DiLavore, P., & Risi, S. (2002). *Autism diagnostic observation schedule: Manual.* Los Angeles, CA: Western Psychological Services.

Macaluso, E. (2006). Multisensory processing in sensory-specific cortical areas. *Neuroscientist, 12,* 327–338. doi:10.1177/1073858406287908

Marchman, V. A., & Fernald, A. (2008). Speed of word recognition and vocabulary knowledge in infancy predict cognitive and language outcomes in later childhood. *Developmental Science, 11,* F9–F16. doi:10.1111/j.1467-7687.2008.00671.x

McNew, M. E., Todd, J. T., Edgar, E. V, & Bahrick, L. E. (2018). *Development of intersensory perception of social events: Longitudinal trajectories across 6–24 months of age.* Poster presented at the meeting of the International Society for Developmental Psychobiology, San Diego, CA.

McNew, M. E., Todd, J. T., Zambrana, K., Hart, K. C., & Bahrick, L. E. (2019). Individual differences in intersensory processing predicts executive functioning and preliteracy skills. Poster presented at the meeting of the Society for Research in Child Development, Baltimore, MD.

Mellon, R. C., Kraemer, P. J., & Spear, N. E. (1991). Development of intersensory function: Age-related differences in stimulus selection of multimodal compounds in rats as revealed by Pavlovian conditioning. *Journal of Experimental Psychology: Animal Behavior Processes, 17,* 448–464. doi:10.1037/0097-7403.17.4.448

Mendelson, M. J., & Haith, M. M. (1976). The relation between audition and vision in the human newborn. *Monographs of the Society for Research and Child Development, 41,* 1–72. doi:10.2307/1165922

Muir, D., & Field, J. (1979). Newborn infants orient to sounds. *Child Development, 50,* 431–436. doi:10.2307/1129419

Mullen, E. M. (1995). *Mullen scales of early learning* (AGS ed.). Circle Pines, MN: American Guidance Service.

Mundy, P., & Burnette, C. (2005). Joint attention and neurodevelopmental models of autism. In F. R. Volkmar, R. Paul, A. Klin, & D. Cohen (Eds.), *Handbook of autism and pervasive developmental disorders. Vol. 1: Diagnosis, development, neurobiology, and behavior* (3rd ed., pp. 650–681). Hoboken, NJ: John Wiley & Sons.

Mundy, P., Delgado, C., Block, J., Venezia, M., Hogan, A., & Seibert, J. (2003). A manual for the abridged Early Social Communication Scales (ESCS). Retrieved from www.ucdmc.ucdavis.edu/mindinstitute/ourteam/faculty_staff/ESCS.pdf.

National Early Literacy Panel (2008). *Developing early literacy: Report of the National Early Literacy Panel.* Washington, DC: National Institute for Early Literacy.

Nomikou, I., Koke, M., & Rohlfing, K. J. (2017). Verbs in mothers' input to six-month-olds: Synchrony between presentation, meaning, and actions is related to later verb acquisition. *Brain Sciences, 7,* 1–19. doi:10.3390/brainsci7050052

Otsuka, Y., Konishi, Y., Kanazawa, S., Yamaguchi, M. K., Abdi, H., & O'Toole, A. J. (2009). Recognition of moving and static faces by young infants. *Child Development, 80,* 1259–1271. doi:10.1111/j.1467-8624.2009.01330.x

Overton, W. F. (2014). Relational developmental systems and developmental science: A focus on methodology. In P. C. M. Molenaar, R. M. Lerner, & K. M. Newell (Eds.), *Handbook of developmental systems: Theory and methodology* (7th ed, pp. 19–65). New York, NY: Guilford Press.

Piaget, J. (1952). *The origins of intelligence in children.* New York, NY: International Universities Press.

Pizur-Barnekow, K., Kraemer, G. W., & Winters, J. M. (2008). Pilot study investigating infant vagal reactivity and visual behavior during object perception. *American Journal of Occupational Therapy, 62*(2), 198–205. doi:10.5014/ajot.62.2.198

Ponitz, C. C., McClelland, M. M., Matthews, J. S., & Morrison, F. J. (2009). A structured observation of behavioral self-regulation and its contribution to kindergarten outcomes. *Developmental Psychology, 45,* 605–619. doi:10.1037/a0015365

Pons, F., Bosch, L., & Lewkowicz, D. J. (2019). Twelve-month-old infants' attention to the eyes of a talking face is associated with communication and social skills. *Infant Behavior and Development, 54,* 80–84. doi:10.1016/j.infbeh.2018.12.003

Posner, M. I., & Petersen, S. E. (1990). The attention system of the human brain. *Annual Review of Neuroscience, 13,* 25–42. doi:10.1146/annurev.neuro.13.1.25

Reynolds, G. D., Bahrick, L. E., Lickliter, R., & Guy, M. W. (2014). Neural correlates of intersensory processing in five-month-old infants. *Developmental Psychobiology, 56,* 355–372. doi:10.1002/dev.21104

Rose, S. A., Feldman, J. F., & Jankowski, J. J. (2011). Modeling a cascade of effects: The role of speed and executive functioning in preterm/full-term differences in academic achievement. *Developmental Science, 14,* 1161–1175. doi:10.1111/ j.1467-7687.2011.01068.x

Rose, S. A., & Ruff, H. A. (1987). Cross-modal abilities in human infants. In J. D. Osofsky (Ed.), *The Handbook of infant development* (2nd ed., pp. 318–362). Oxford: John Wiley & Sons.

Rowe, M. L. (2018). Understanding socioeconomic differences in parents' speech to children. *Child Development Perspectives, 12,* 122–127. doi:10.1111/ cdep.12271

Ruff, H. A., & Rothbart, M. K. (1996). *Attention in early development: Themes and variations.* New York, NY: Oxford University Press.

Rutter, M., Bailey, A., & Lord, C. (2003). *The social communication questionnaire.* Los Angeles, CA: Western Psychological Services.

Schroeder, C. E., & Foxe, J. (2005). Multisensory contributions to low-level, "unisensory" processing. *Current Opinion in Neurobiology, 15,* 454–458. doi:10.1016/ j.conb.2005.06.008

Seligman, M. E. P., & Csikszentmihalyi, M. (2000). Positive psychology: An introduction. *American Psychologist, 55,* 5–14. doi:10.1007/978-94-017-9088-8_18

Slater, A., Quinn, P. C., Brown, E., & Hayes, R. (1999). Intermodal perception at birth: Intersensory redundancy guides newborn infants' learning of arbitrary auditory-visual pairings. *Developmental Science, 2,* 333–338. doi:10.1111/ 1467–7687.00079

Slavich, G. M., & Cole, S. W. (2012). The emerging field of human social genomics. *Clinical Psychological Science, 1,* 233–245. doi:10.1016/j.dcn.2011.01.002.

Spear, N. E., & McKinzie, D. L. (1994). Intersensory integration in the infant rat. In D. J. Lewkowicz & R. Lickliter (Eds.), *The development of intersensory perception: Comparative perspectives* (pp. 133–161). Hillsdale, NJ: Lawrence Erlbaum Associates.

Stein, B. E. (2012). *The new handbook of multisensory processing.* Cambridge, MA: MIT Press.

Stein, B. E., & Meredith, M. A. (1993). *The merging of the senses.* Cambridge, MA: MIT Press.

Stevenson, R. A., Segers, M., Ncube, B. L., Black, K. R., Bebko, J. M., Ferber, S., & Barense, M. D. (2018). The cascading influence of multisensory processing on speech perception in autism. *Autism, 22,* 609–624. doi:10.1177/ 1362361317704413

Stevenson, R. A., Siemann, J. K., Schneider, B. C., Eberly, H. E., Woynaroski, T. G., Camarata, S. M., & Wallace, M. T. (2014). Multisensory temporal integration in autism spectrum disorders. *Journal of Neuroscience, 34,* 691–697. doi:10.1523/JNEUROSCI.3615-13.2014

Suanda, S. H., Smith, L. B., & Yu, C. (2016). The multisensory nature of verbal discourse in parent-toddler interactions. *Developmental Neuropsychology, 41,* 324–341. doi:10.1080/87565641.2016.1256403

Suarez-Rivera, C., Smith, L. B., & Yu, C. (2018). Multimodal parent behaviors within joint attention support sustained attention in infants. *Developmental Psychology, 55,* 96–109. doi:10.1037/dev0000628

Tamis-LeMonda, C. S., Kuchirko, Y., & Song, L. (2014). Why is infant language learning facilitated by parental responsiveness? *Current Directions in Psychological Science, 23,* 121–126. doi:10.1177/0963721414522813

Tamis-LeMonda, C. S., Kuchirko, Y., & Tafuro, L. (2013). From action to interaction: Infant object exploration and mothers' contingent responsiveness. *IEEE Transactions on Autonomous Mental Development, 5*, 202–209. doi:10.1109/TAMD.2013.2269905

Todd, J. T., & Bahrick, L. E. (in preparation). *Individual differences in multisensory attention skills in children with autism spectrum disorder predict language functioning and symptom severity: Evidence from the Multisensory Attention Assessment Protocol.* Manuscript in preparation.

Todd, J. T., McNew, M. E., Edgar, E. V., Miller, J., Barroso, N. E., Bahrick, L. E., & Bagner, D. M. (2018). *Speed, accuracy, and duration of multisensory attention to social events at 6 months predicts social competence at 18 months.* Poster presented at the meeting of the International Congress on Infant Studies, Philadelphia, PA.

Todd, J. T., McNew, M. E., Soska, K. C., & Bahrick, L. E. (2016). *Assessing the cost of competing stimulation on attention to multimodal events: Longitudinal findings from 3 to 12 months.* Poster presented at the meeting of the Society for Research in Child Development, Austin, TX.

Vaillant-Molina, M., & Bahrick, L. E. (2012). The role of intersensory redundancy in the emergence of social referencing in 5½-month-old infants. *Developmental Psychology, 48*, 1–9. doi:10.1037/a0025263

Walker-Andrews, A. S. (1997). Infants' perception of expressive behaviors: Differentiation of multimodal information. *Psychological Bulletin, 121*, 437–456. doi:10.1037//0033-2909.121.3.437

Wallace, M. T. (2009). Dyslexia: Bridging the gap between hearing and reading. *Current Biology, 19*, R260–R262. doi:10.1016/j.cub.2009.01.025

Warlaumont, A. S., Richards, J. A., Gilkerson, J., & Oller, D. K. (2014). A social feedback loop for speech development and its reduction in autism. *Psychological Science, 25*, 1314–1324. doi:10.1177/0956797614531023

Weisleder, A., & Fernald, A. (2013). Talking to children matters: Early language experience strengthens processing and builds vocabulary. *Psychological Science, 24*, 2143–2152. doi:10.1177/0956797613488145

Werchan, D. M., Baumgartner, H. A., Lewkowicz, D. J., & Amso, D. (2018). The origins of cortical multisensory dynamics: Evidence from human infants. *Developmental Cognitive Neuroscience, 34*, 75–81. doi:10.1016/j.dcn.2018.07.002

Whitehurst, G. J., & Lonigan, C. J. (1998). Child development and emergent literacy. *Child Development, 69*, 848–872. doi:10.1111/j.1467–8624.1998.tb06247.x

PART III

Cognitive Development

12 Infant Memory

Harlene Hayne and Jane S. Herbert

12.1 Introduction

Researchers and parents alike have long assumed that experiences that occur during infancy are fundamental to both behavioral and cognitive development. Paradoxically, not only do adults typically fail to recall events that occurred prior to the age of 3, but until the middle part of the twentieth century, there was limited evidence of long-term retention during the infancy period itself. By way of example, although acquiring our first words or taking our first steps was undoubtedly monumental at the time it occurred, we have no conscious recollection of achieving these milestones. In contrast, our memories of other important achievements that took place slightly later in development, like our first day of school or the first time we rode a bike without training wheels, often survive the test of time and eventually form part of our autobiography.

The lack of memory for our infancy and early childhood is often referred to as childhood amnesia. Although the boundary of childhood amnesia is lower in children and adolescents than it is in adults (Jack, MacDonald, Reese, & Hayne, 2009; Peterson, Grant, & Boland, 2005; Peterson, Warren, & Short, 2011; Reese, Jack, & White, 2010; Tustin & Hayne, 2010), the fact remains that most of our early experiences eventually become veiled from recollection. Freud was the first to coin the term childhood amnesia. He referred to childhood amnesia as "the peculiar amnesia which, in the case of most people, though by no means all, hides the earliest beginnings of their childhood up to their sixth or eight year" (Freud, [1905] 1953, p. 174). The phenomenon of childhood amnesia raises important questions about memory development in particular and cognitive development in general. Given the limited recollection of our early experiences, researchers have often wondered how these experiences help to build a child's knowledge base and help to shape subsequent behavior (Barr, Walker, Gross, & Hayne, 2014; Hayne, 2006; Rovee-Collier & Hayne, 1987). In short, the phenomenon of childhood amnesia raises important questions about if and how infants and young children use their prior experiences to guide their future behavior during the period of early development and beyond.

Freud's views of childhood amnesia were guided by his clinical practice and were retrospective in nature; he drew conclusions about the source and timing of childhood amnesia by asking adults to recall their early experiences in the context of therapy. In contrast to Freud, our approach, and that of many of our colleagues, has been prospective in nature, tracing changes in memory that unfold as a function of age and experience during the period of infancy and early childhood. Although this prospective approach has shown that Freud potentially overestimated the period of childhood amnesia, studying memory as it develops has also highlighted some fundamental changes in memory processing that undoubtedly contribute to our inability to recall much about our early life experiences. It has also highlighted how infants and young children begin to take their memories with them, using their prior experience to build a fledgling knowledge base. In this chapter, we will describe memory development in infants and young children and outline how these changes are linked to brain maturation, prior experience, and cultural context. We will also pose new directions for research, policy, and practice.

12.2 Empirical Methods to Study Infant Memory

The period of infancy extends from birth to a child's second or third birthday. The word infancy is derived from the Latin *infantem* and it literally means, "not able to speak." Although most children say their first words prior to their first birthday, their language skills remain limited, and between 18–30 months most toddlers have a productive vocabulary of around only 200–300 words (Otto, 2018). Given this limited language skill, the key challenge for researchers who study infant memory has been to develop nonverbal tasks in which both the researcher's instructions and the infant's memory response do not require language. Over the last several decades, researchers have developed a number of experimental procedures that meet this requirement including the visual recognition memory (VRM) paradigm, the mobile conjugate reinforcement and operant train paradigms, and the deferred imitation paradigm.

12.2.1 Visual Recognition Memory (VRM) Paradigm

The underlying theoretical assumption of the standard VRM paradigm is that infants form internal representations of stimuli that they attend to; with repeated exposure to a particular stimulus, the internal representation becomes more complete and the infant then turns his or her attention to novel stimuli in the environment (Sokolov, 1963). This theoretical assumption has been borne out through decades of research showing that infants typically exhibit a robust preference for novelty, looking longer at novel stimuli than at familiar ones. In the VRM paradigm, infants are given the opportunity to view a stimulus and, following a delay, they are presented with that original stimulus and a novel one.

The infant's visual behavior (looking time) toward the novel stimulus relative to the familiar stimulus is then compared. Researchers typically infer that the infant remembers the familiar stimulus if he or she looks significantly longer at the novel one during the test (i.e., the infant exhibits a novelty preference). Longer looking toward the familiar stimulus has also been used as an index of memory particularly if the participants are extremely young (Pascalis, de Schonen, Morton, Deruelle, & Fabre-Grenet, 1995) or if they are tested after a very long delay (Bahrick & Pickens, 1995). Across the infancy period, longer looking times are also associated with incomplete or partial encoding of the stimulus in the first place (Rose, Gottfried, Melloy-Carminar, & Bridger, 1982). The VRM paradigm was originally developed to study memory during infancy, but it has also been modified to study memory in young children (Hayne, Jaeger, Sonne, & Gross, 2016; Imuta, Scarf, & Hayne, 2013; Morgan & Hayne, 2006a, 2006b, 2007, 2011) and adults (Gross, Gardiner, & Hayne 2016; McKee & Squire, 1993; Richmond, Colombo, & Hayne, 2007; Richmond, Sowerby, Colombo, & Hayne, 2004), making it a particularly powerful developmental tool.

12.2.2 Mobile Conjugate Reinforcement and Operant Train Paradigms

In the mobile conjugate reinforcement paradigm, 2- to 6-month-old infants learn to kick their feet to produce movement in an overhead crib mobile. In a procedurally identical task, 6- to 18-month old infants learn to push a lever to make a toy train move around a track. In both the mobile and the train task, researchers measure the infant's baseline response rate during a period of nonreinforcement at the outset of the first session and they measure retention during a period of nonreinforcement at the outset of a test session conducted days, weeks, or months after the conclusion of training. Because the learning and memory performance of 6-month-old infants is identical in the mobile and the train task, combining the findings from both have provided the opportunity to trace age-related changes in memory processing across the first 18 months of life (Hartshorn, Rovee-Collier, Gerhardstein, Bhatt, Klein et al. 1998; Hartshorn, Rovee-Collier, Gerhardstein, Bhatt, Wondoloski et al., 1998).

12.2.3 Deferred Imitation Paradigm

In the deferred imitation paradigm, an experimenter models a series of actions with objects and then tests the infant's ability to reproduce those actions either immediately or after a delay of days, weeks, or months (Bauer, Wenner, Dropik, & Wewerka, 2000; Hayne, 2004; Meltzoff, 1995). Researchers infer that the infant has remembered the demonstration by comparing the performance of infants in the demonstration condition to that of infants who have not seen the target actions or the objects prior to the test. In some versions of this task, infants in the demonstration condition are given the opportunity to practice the target actions prior to the retention interval (i.e., elicited imitation), but in other versions of this task, the infant's memory is based on observation alone (i.e., deferred imitation). Given that the elicited imitation paradigm and deferred imitation paradigms yield different estimates of infant retention (Barr & Hayne, 2000; Hayne, Barr, & Herbert, 2003; Hayne, Boniface, & Barr, 2000; see also Hayne, 2004 for a review), we will focus our attention here on studies of deferred imitation. By varying the complexity of the experimental objects and the target actions, the deferred imitation paradigm can be used with participants who range from 6 to 30 months of age.

12.3 Age-Related Changes in Basic Memory Processing

Despite the procedural differences in the VRM, mobile conjugate reinforcement, operant train, and deferred imitation paradigms, the data they yield are remarkably similar. Research with all of these paradigms has provided a consistent picture of age-related changes in memory between 2 and 30 months of age. Using these paradigms, researchers have identified three general principles of memory development: (1) older infants encode information faster than younger infants, (2) older infants remember information longer than younger infants, and (3) older infants exploit a wider range of retrieval cues than do younger infants (for a review, see Hayne, 2004). A selection of studies supporting these principles are shown in Table 12.1.

The data summarized in Table 12.1 illustrate that as infants mature and gain more experience, their ability to encode and retain information increases. These basic age-related changes in encoding and retention have been documented using each of the three major infant memory paradigms and reflect highly replicable developmental processes. Age-related changes in basic encoding and retention provide some explanation for the phenomenon of childhood amnesia (see also, Bauer, 2015; Hayne & Jack, 2011). That is, our ability to recall our earliest experiences is undoubtedly hindered by slower and less complete encoding and by more rapid forgetting. In addition, however, age-related changes in representational flexibility, or the ability to retrieve and use memories in novel situations, also increases the probability that a given memory will be retrieved, used, strengthened, and retained. For example, as highlighted in Table 12.1, research conducted using the VRM, mobile conjugate reinforcement, operant train, and deferred imitation paradigms all demonstrate that memory retrieval by younger infants is highly restricted to the conditions of original encoding; changes in either context or stimulus materials disrupts retrieval of the original memory representation. In essence, infants are an example of Tulving's encoding specificity principle (Tulving & Thomson, 1973), *in extremis*. Only when the conditions of retrieval match the conditions of encoding almost exactly, can young infants retrieve and use their memories of prior experiences after a delay. Although this high degree of specificity reflects the encoding of

Table 12.1 *Sample experimental evidence supporting three general principles of infant memory development*

Principle of infant memory development	Visual recognition memory (VRM) paradigm	Mobile conjugate reinforcement and operant train paradigms	Deferred imitation paradigm
Older infants encode information faster than younger infants	Hunter & Ames, 1988; Morgan & Hayne, 2006	cf. Davis & Rovee-Collier, 1983; Greco, Rovee-Collier, Hayne, Griesler, & Earley, 1986; Hill, Borovsky, & Rovee-Collier, 1988 Hartshorn, Rovee-Collier, Gerhardstein, Bhatt, Wondoloski et al., 1998	Barr, Dowden, & Hayne, 1996; Hayne, Boniface et al., 2000
Older infants remember longer than younger infants[a]	Morgan & Hayne, 2011	Hartshorn, Rovee-Collier, Gerhardstein, Bhatt, Wondoloski et al., 1998	Barr & Hayne, 2000; Herbert & Hayne, 2000b
Older infants exploit a wider range of retrieval cues than do younger infants	Robinson & Pascalis, 2004	Hartshorn, Rovee-Collier, Gerhadstein, Bhatt, Klein et al., 1998	Barnat, Klein, & Meltzoff, 1996; Barr & Hayne, 2000; Hanna & Meltzoff, 1993; Hayne et al., 1997; Hayne, Boniface et al., 2000; Herbert & Hayne, 2000a; Klein & Meltzoff, 1999

[a] It is often difficult to disentangle age-related changes in retention that are independent of age-related changes in encoding; for that reason, only studies in which infants' performance was identical after a zero delay are included here.

detailed memory representations, it also severely hampers the opportunity for retrieval to occur over time as the nature of the original encoding environment changes.

Despite the highly specific nature of memory retrieval by younger infants, older infants and young children gradually escape the shackles of encoding specificity, retrieving their memories in new contexts or when confronted with new stimuli. For example, when tested in the mobile conjugate reinforcement, operant train, or deferred imitation paradigms, changes in the environmental context preclude memory retrieval by 3- and 6-month-olds, but these same changes have no effect on memory retrieval by infants aged 12 months and older (Butler & Rovee-Collier, 1989; Hartshorn, Rovee-Collier, Gerhardstein, Bhatt, Klein et al., 1998; Hartshorn, Rovee-Collier, Gerhardstein, Bhatt, Wondoloski et al., 1998; Hayne, MacDonald, & Barr, 1997). When tested in the VRM paradigm, changes in the context disrupt memory retrieval by 6- and 12-month-olds, but they have no effect on memory retrieval by 18- or 24-month-olds (Hanna & Meltzoff, 1993; Robinson & Pascalis, 2004). Similarly, even minor changes in the experimental stimuli disrupt memory retrieval by 2-, 3-, 6-, and 12-month-olds (Hayne, Greco, Earley, Griesler, & Rovee-Collier, 1986; Hayne et al., 1997; Rovee-Collier, Patterson, & Hayne, 1985), but these same changes have no effect on the performance of infants aged 18 months and older (Hayne, Boniface et al., 2000; Hayne et al., 1997; Herbert & Hayne, 2000a). These age-related decreases in the requisite specificity of effective retrieval cues increases the probability that older infants will retrieve and express their memories in a wider range of situations. This age-related increase in representational flexibility allows older infants and young children to take their memories with them, using them to solve new problems in new contexts; it also increases the probability that a given memory will be retrieved and strengthened, further enhancing its longevity.

12.4 Memory Reactivation

Although forgetting occurs rapidly during the infancy period, researchers have also shown that apparently forgotten memories can be retrieved and expressed given the appropriate circumstances. In the seminal demonstration of the reactivation of forgotten memories in human infants, Rovee-Collier, Sullivan, Enright, Lucas, and Fagen (1980) modified a procedure originally developed for infant rats (Spear & Parsons, 1976) and used it with 3-month-old infants who had been trained and tested in the mobile conjugate reinforcement paradigm. In their study, 3-month-olds learned to kick their feet to produce movement in an overhead mobile; these infants were then tested either 2 or 4 weeks later. Some of the infants in each group were briefly exposed to the moving mobile as a reminder 24 hours prior to the retention test. Rovee-Collier et al. (1980) found that, in the absence of the reminder treatment, infants exhibited no retention whatsoever after either delay. Infants who received the brief reminder, on the other hand, performed at a level that was equivalent to that seen at the conclusion of training 2 or 4 weeks earlier. In addition, the rate of forgetting of the reactivated memory was equivalent to the rate of forgetting of the original memory.

Following this landmark study, Rovee-Collier, her students, and other investigators have replicated and extended the reactivation phenomenon in studies with infants who range in age from 2 to 24 months and who have been tested in the VRM (Cornell, 1979; Morgan & Hayne, 2006a), operant train (Hill et al., 1988), and deferred imitation (Hayne, Barr et al., 2003) paradigms. In these studies, brief exposure to the context (Hayne & Findlay, 1995; Rovee-Collier, Griesler, & Earley, 1985) or to stimuli that were part of the original event (Fagen & Rovee-Collier, 1983; Hayne, Barr et al., 2003; Hill et al., 1988) alleviates forgetting after delays ranging from days to weeks. Furthermore, repeated reminding increases the speed of memory retrieval (Hayne, Gross, Hildreth, & Rovee-Collier, 2000) and flattens the forgetting function (Hartshorn, 2003; Hayne, 1990), extending the duration of retention. Finally, effective reminders must be virtually identical to stimuli or contexts that were part of the original learning episode (Hayne, Rovee-Collier, & Borza, 1991; Rovee-Collier, Patterson et al., 1985) unless infants encountered multiple stimuli or multiple contexts at the time of original learning (Greco, Hayne, & Rovee-Collier, 1990).

12.5 The Role of Language

In additional to physical cues, verbal cues also play a pervasive role in memory retrieval by human adults. For example, relatively nonspecific verbal information (e.g., "Remember the last time we ate at that restaurant?") can often cue vivid recollections of a past event, bringing to mind information that we may have not pondered for weeks, years, or even decades. Furthermore, once we can store and retrieve information through language we are no longer bound by the conditions under which the information was originally learned; instead, we can take our memories with us, augmenting them with new information that we encounter along the way. For this reason, many experts agree that the ability to exploit linguistic retrieval cues represents a major hallmark in human evolution and development.

In order to chart age-related changes in the effectiveness of verbal retrieval cues during early childhood, Imuta et al. (2013) familiarized 2-, 3-, and 4-year-olds with a novel cartoon face in the VRM paradigm and tested them 1 to 2 weeks later. For participants in the experimental condition, the experimenter asked the following questions prior to the test: "Can you remember coming here a little while ago?" "Can you remember what face you saw the last time you came here?" Participants in the control condition received the same initial exposure to the cartoon face and the test, but they were not given a verbal reminder prior to the test. At all three ages, participants in the control condition exhibited no retention, looking equally at the novel and the familiar cartoon face during the test. In contrast, participants who received the verbal reminder exhibited excellent retention, looking longer at the novel cartoon face during the test (see also Morgan & Hayne, 2007). Thus, despite the high level of specificity of memory retrieval exhibited by young infants, by the end of the infancy period, another person's language can be used as a key to unlock an otherwise forgotten memory.

The ability to use language (both our own and that of others) is a major developmental milestone, increasing the probability that a memory will be retrieved and expressed after a delay. In fact, several lines of evidence now suggest that the early dense amnesia that we experience for events that we experienced prior to the age of 2 or 3 is due, at least in part, to a difficulty in gaining verbal access to memories that were encoded largely without language. For example, if we plot the number of early childhood memories recalled by adults as a function of their age at the time of the event, the slope of that function is identical to that of the function that is obtained by plotting the number of new words that are incorporated into children's vocabularies as a function of age (Waldfogel, 1948). In addition, the most rapid increase in vocabulary words during childhood occurs between 2½ and 4½ years of age – a period that coincides with the average age of adults' earliest memories (Morrison & Conway, 2009). Finally, as children acquire language, the words they learn are not easily superimposed on their preverbal representations. For example, when tested after a delay, children find it difficult (Jack, Simcock, & Hayne, 2011; Morris & Baker-Ward, 2007) if not impossible (Simcock & Hayne, 2002) to describe aspects of an event using words that were not part of their productive vocabulary at the time the event originally took place; this finding is obtained even though these same children exhibit nonverbal recall of the event and have acquired the language skills necessary to describe it.

Taken together, both retrospective studies with adults and prospective studies with children suggest that language acquisition plays an important role in the decline of the dense amnesia we experience for events that occurred during infancy and early childhood. In many ways, however, the ability to use language in the service of memory is just one example of the other forms of representational flexibility that characterize memory development during late infancy and early childhood. As a function of both age and experience, infants and young children become increasingly facile in exploiting cues that were not part of their original experience (see Table 12.1), increasing the probability that a particular memory will survive.

12.6 The Role of Brain Maturation in Memory Development

The first years of life mark a time of rapid growth in the overall size, structure, and complexity of the human brain (for a review see Dehaene-Lambertz & Spelke, 2015) and brain maturation undoubtedly contributes to the age-related changes in infant memory performance that are outlined in Table 12.1. Surprisingly, perhaps, a direct link between brain maturation and memory development has yet to be established. Brain maturation is not a linear process and different areas of the brain mature at different rates, with motor and sensory areas maturing early, and higher-order association areas continuing to mature well into early adulthood (for a review, see Casey, Tottenham,

Liston & Durston, 2005). Recent evidence from MRI studies reveals that increases in cortical thickness and overall cortical surface area are greatest in the first year of life compared to the second year (for a review, see Haartsen, Jones, & Johnson, 2016). Even within a single area of the brain, structural and functional maturity occurs at different rates. Research with nonhuman primates suggests that although the major structures of the hippocampus are present early, considerable changes occur to structure and function of the hippocampus in the first 2 years of life (Gilmore et al., 2012; Lavenex & Lavenex, 2013).

If memory development is due exclusively to brain maturation, we might predict dramatic shifts in memory processing would coincide with the time at which functional changes in the brain occur. In contrast to this prediction, behavioral research indicates that age-related changes in memory performance during infancy and early childhood are gradual in nature. Furthermore, attempts to link specific age-related changes in brain function to age-related changes in memory development have consistently failed (for a review, see Rovee-Collier & Cuevas, 2009). By way of example, two different systems are widely assumed to be responsible for processing different types of learning experiences, often referred to as declarative and nondeclarative memory (Squire, 1992). Declarative memory is available to conscious recall, and can be assessed by verbal recall in adults, for example by asking someone to name a specific country's capital city. Because the formation of new declarative memories in adults is dependent on the hippocampus and surrounding cortices, and that the hippocampus is thought to develop late in ontogeny, it has been argued that declarative memory should also develop late and should coincide with the maturation of the hippocampus. In contrast, nondeclarative memory is difficult to access verbally, is distributed more widely across the brain, and is thought to be responsible for lower forms of memory such as habit formation and skill acquisition. Because the neural structures that support nondeclarative memory in adults emerge early during ontogeny, it has been argued that nondeclarative memory should be present early in life. Both the declarative and nondeclarative memory systems are thought to consist of several component processes, each responsible for encoding, storage, and retrieval of specific types of information (Squire, 1992).

Although the existence of these memory systems is well established in adults, the existence and ontogeny of different memory systems in infancy remains controversial (cf. Hayne, 2004; Richmond & Nelson, 2007; Rovee-Collier & Cuevas, 2009). Given that infants cannot verbally declare whether they experience conscious recollection, it is difficult to directly investigate the emergence of two, separate memory systems during the infancy period. Given this, an alternative approach has been to test human adults with hippocampal damage on tasks that are commonly used with typically developing human infants. Research of this kind has shown that human adults who suffer from amnesia fail on tests of deferred imitation and visual recognition memory (e.g., McDonough, Mandler, McKee, & Squire, 1995; McKee & Squire, 1993) – tests that human infants pass as early as 6 months of age. Thus, despite the potential to map age-related changes in memory processing to the maturation of specific brain structures that support memory processing in adults, research with infants has shown that there is not a sudden shift from one memory system to another, and that infants have at least rudimentary access to both systems at 6 months.

Richmond and Nelson (2007) have speculated that age-related changes in the rate of encoding might be attributed to the maturation of brain connections (myelination), while age-related changes in retention and memory flexibility reflect the prolonged development of the hippocampus and surrounding cortex. However, consistent with previous attempts to link brain maturation to memory development, direct evaluations of the link in human infants have yet to be fully investigated. Establishing a direct link between brain maturation and memory development will undoubtedly remain complex because measurement of brain function usually requires the participant to be still or resting, and to undergo long periods of assessment. These requirements are not well suited to working with typically developing infants. Furthermore, despite claims to the contrary, assumptions regarding a one-to-one mapping between a specific brain area and particular tests of memory processing are undoubtedly misguided. As Rovee-Collier and Cuevas (2009) remind us, no task is process pure. Given this, our ultimate understanding of the relation between brain maturation and memory function will depend not only on new ways to measure brain maturation during infancy and early childhood, but also on new ways to study memory.

12.7 Individual Differences

Although a large body of normative data allows us to predict approximately how an age group might perform on a memory task, there are individual differences in memory performance. The ability to remember and flexibly apply memory in new situations reflects, at least in part, the richness of the encoding situation that the infant experiences. Events that are well understood, linked to previous knowledge, and supported by a wide range of cues during encoding, result in memory representations that are longer lasting and more flexible. For example, simple verbal cues that explain the goals (e.g., "We can use these things to make a rattle") and actions (e.g., "Push the ball into the cup") in a deferred imitation task double the duration of retention for 18-month-olds (Hayne & Herbert, 2004). Memory performance is further facilitated when the learning occurs in multiple contexts (Robinson & Pascalis, 2004), when there are opportunities to practice the target actions during encoding (Hayne, Barr et al., 2003), or when experiences build upon each other (Barr et al., 2014). Thus, the way in which a learning opportunity is supported by adults or by the environment plays an important role in determining whether a unique learning event will be available for the infant to retrieve and use over the long term.

In addition to the type and quality of the information provided at encoding, there are also individual differences in the efficiency with which infants process information. In studies using the VRM paradigm, infants who attend to new objects with shorter rather than longer looks, exhibit better performance in later tests of recognition memory, as well as on measures of language, representational play, and intelligence. "Short-looking" infants process information faster, but also attend to different features of the event, focusing initially on global properties of stimuli before tuning in to the local elements. In contrast, "long lookers" do not show this global-precedence effect (for a review see Reynolds, 2015). Thus there are differences in the speed at which individual infants process information, but also where and how they direct their attention that will influence what information is later available for retrieval.

With the development of independent locomotion (e.g., crawling) at around 8–9 months of age, infants become able to actively explore and make decisions, traverse greater distances, and control their proximity to objects and people. These developments are transformative, providing experiences and learning opportunities, which may be critical for cognitive development. Experience seeing familiar people and objects in new locations and from new perspectives potentially encourages the infant to attend to new aspects of their environment, to learn and retrieve information in new settings, to perform more goal-directed activities, and to consider concepts like constancy and change. Such experiences may explain why representational flexibility has been shown to vary as a function of motor status. For example, although both crawling and noncrawling 9-month-olds exhibit retention after a 24-hour delay in a deferred imitation task, only crawlers apply that knowledge flexibly when tested in a new context with a functionally similar, but perceptually different, object (Herbert Gross, & Hayne, 2007). Crawlers also outperform noncrawlers on a range of other cognitive tasks, including spatial search tasks, object permanence, and mental rotation (for a review, see Anderson et al., 2013). Thus, motor development may interact in a dynamic way with cognitive development such that individual differences in one domain contribute to individual differences in the other, including memory.

Individual differences in the experiences that infants encounter in their broader daily lives, such as the opportunity to sleep, also impact memory performance. A growing body of research shows that the opportunity for a well-timed nap plays a role in memory consolidation, supporting both retention and the generalization of memory (Seehagen, Konrad, Herbert, & Schneider, 2015; Seehagen, Zymj, & Herbert, 2019). For example, in a test of deferred imitation, only 6- and 12-month-old infants who had a nap in the 4 hours after learning showed the ability to reproduce the demonstrated actions 4 or 24 hours later. Furthermore, only 12-month-old infants who took a nap after learning were able to reproduce the target actions when tested with a functionally similar, but perceptually different, stimulus 4 hours later.

12.8 Culture and Memory

Infants who are growing up in a bilingual home also exhibit an advantage on tests of representational flexibility, which may reflect enhanced attentional skills or the richer networks of knowledge that may come from exposure to two languages. For example, when tested in a deferred imitation task, 9 of 15 bilingual 18-month-old infants generalized their knowledge across a stimulus change when they were tested 30 minutes after the demonstration; in contrast, only 1 out of 15 monolingual infants exhibited the same kind of representational flexibility (Brito & Barr, 2012). Although the underlying mechanisms for these differences in memory performance are the focus of ongoing study, the extant body of research indicates that infants who experience an environment rich in learning experiences, integrated with opportunities for consolidation, appear better positioned to exhibit more mature memory abilities, including enhanced representational flexibility.

Despite decades of research on early memories, researchers cannot predict the exact age or content of any one individual's first autobiographical memory. The chances of an event becoming part of our verbally accessible personal history increases if the original experience is better understood (e.g., knowing that an evacuation was caused by a fire alarm; Pillemer, Picarielle, & Pruett, 1994), easier to date (e.g., moving house, parental separation, starting school; Artioli & Reese, 2013; Mullen, 1994), or supported through social and language cues (e.g., past-event conversations and shared-life stories; Jack et al., 2009; Reese, Haden, & Fivush, 1993).

Cultural differences in the value placed on engaging with the past and in the richness of the narrative input that children receive has also been linked to individual differences in the age and content of early personal memories (for a review see Fivush, Haden, & Reese, 2006). For example, Maori New Zealand mothers engage in different kinds of reminiscing with their preschoolers relative to European New Zealand mothers, which, in turn, affects the reminiscing style of those preschoolers and the age and content of their earliest autobiographical memories as adolescents and adults (e.g., MacDonald, Uesiliana, & Hayne, 2000; Reese, Hayne, & MacDonald, 2008). Earlier first memories are also observed in participants who have grown up in families that had a multigenerational (parents plus additional adults living in the house) or nonnuclear structure (e.g., Artioli, Reese & Hayne, 2015). Thus, individual differences in cultural and social experiences influence the rehearsal and retrieval of early experiences, leading to systematic differences in the age and content of participants' earliest autobiographical memories.

12.9 Implications for Policy

The majority of studies examining early memory development assess infants in an ideal learning environment. Testing is typically scheduled at a time of day that the parent has identified as an alert/awake period, and the to-be-remembered information is presented with minimal distractions at encoding and test. Measuring performance in these ideal conditions provides the foundations for understanding the ways in which learning and memory occurs, or fails to occur, in more complex environments. For example, symbolic artefacts like storybooks, videos, computers, and tablets are prevalent in many children's lives and can provide a diverse range of learning opportunities. Despite their prevalence, young children find it surprisingly difficult to learn and remember information from these sources. Although infants imitate some actions after observing them performed on television (e.g., Barr & Hayne, 1999; Hayne, Herbert, & Simcock, 2003) or in a storybook (e.g., Simcock & DeLoache, 2008), they learn less and remember for a shorter period of time than when the same information is encountered through a live demonstration (e.g., Brito, Barr, McIntyre, & Simcock, 2012).

A number of attentional, memory, language, and social factors undoubtedly contribute to this transfer deficit (for a review, see Barr, 2013). From a memory perspective, one of the key constraints on transferring knowledge from these information sources is the lack of representational flexibility during infancy and early childhood. The mismatch between a two dimensional information source at encoding and a three-dimensional object at test, or vice versa, constrains learning from media sources during the first years of life (e.g., Zack, Barr, Gerhardstein, Dickerson, & Meltzoff, 2009). By utilizing techniques shown to enhance learning from live demonstrations by young infants, such as doubling exposure to the imitation demonstration (Barr, Dowden, & Hayne, 1996), it becomes possible to improve infants' learning from other complex information sources such as books, television, and tablets (Barr, Muentener, Garcia, Fujimoto, & Chavez, 2007; Simcock & DeLoache, 2008). Thus, if we apply the basic principles of memory development from Table 12.1 to situations when knowledge acquisition or retrieval appears to fail, we can scaffold children's experiences so that they benefit from a wider range of learning resources. In the absence of this kind of scaffolding, exposure to these devices is likely to lead to little additional learning and memory. Similarly, understanding the relation between sleep and memory can help us to schedule infants' naps in a way that maximizes the opportunity for consolidation, memory, and representational flexibility.

As researchers continue to document infants' ability to form and retrieve memories and to develop complex associative networks, it becomes increasingly possible to translate research into early educational and health policy and practice. For children over the age of 3 years there is a considerable body of knowledge about the long-term benefits of the provision of high-quality education (Sylva, Melhuish, Sammons, Siraj-Blatchford, & Taggart, 2010). Prior to 3 years of age, however, a child's cognitive needs are inconsistently recognized; the primary focus of early education is typically on supporting early social and emotional development. A lack of emphasis on cognitive development is somewhat concerning, particularly in light of the fact that socioeconomic disparities in language and memory development are apparent by 21 months of age (Noble et al., 2015) and that memory performance at this same age predicts memory ability in school-age children (Riggins, Cheatham, Stark, & Bauer, 2013). These data highlight not only the negative impact of early deprivation, but also raise hope for the value of additional, early educational experiences in reversing the impact. What we do know is that in the absence of intervention through education and other means, the cognitive gap between the haves and the have-nots continues to increase (Reardon, 2011).

In the past, the evidence base required for developing effective early educational policy has been limited because assessing cognitive skill through changes in behavior alone is complex. Despite this complexity, the research reviewed here consistently shows that even very young infants encode information about people, objects, and contexts, and are capable of detailed discrimination between a stored memory representation and a new experience. When an infant receives the opportunity to interact physically with objects and hears appropriate language cues during a focused experience, his or her ability to remember and apply information encoded from that event increases. As that memory is retrieved, other memories that were associated with it, even briefly, are activated and strengthened (Barr et al., 2014). These early experiences sculpt the infant's brain and set them up for learning across the life span (Nelson, 2000).

The World Health Organization's Global Strategy (2016–30; WHO, n.d.) has made a significant commitment to ensuring newborns and children "not just survive, but thrive," through access to high-quality early childhood education. We argue here that access to age-appropriate, rich, and varied educational experiences is crucial for knowledge acquisition and for supporting the healthy cognitive development of the child. Given the breadth and depth of basic research on infant memory, we are now in an excellent position to provide governments, policy agencies, and education providers with the information they need to design experiences for infants that will maximize their outcomes.

12.10 Conclusions and Future Directions

The principles of memory development that we have discussed in this chapter have been established based on findings obtained across a range of procedures that rely on simple action–object associations, eye movements, and the copying of actions. Despite the highly consistent pattern of results outlined in Table 12.1, it is important to acknowledge that much of the research on infant memory development has been derived from WEIRD (Western, educated, industrialized, rich, and democratic) participants (Nielsen, Haun, Kärtner, & Legare, 2017). In contrast to our emerging understanding of the role of social and cultural practices in motor development (for a review, see Adolph & Hoch, 2019) and autobiographical memory (MacDonald et al., 2000; Reese et al., 2008; Wang, 2003, 2006a, 2006b, Wang, Conway, & Hou, 2004), we know little or nothing about the role of culture in memory development during the infancy period. Given that there are cultural differences in the way in which parents talk to children about the past, and that these differences translate into differences in adults' earliest memories, it is highly likely that cultural practices also play an important role in memory development beginning in infancy. The role of culture in infant memory development is a fruitful area for future research.

As we begin to investigate cross-cultural differences in infant memory, we should be mindful that a cross-cultural approach to research could trip us up if we are not careful. For example, deferred imitation typically involves an element of joint attention between an infant and an unfamiliar adult; this kind of joint attention may be deemed inappropriate or disrespectful for some cultural groups. The onus will remain on researchers to determine whether their means of measurement are culturally appropriate, in the same way that they are age appropriate. For example, it will be important to ensure that the stimuli (e.g., faces, puppets, unfamiliar objects) and the environment (e.g., home, unfamiliar lab) are designed with culture in mind, allowing us to capture an infant's skills and interests irrespective of the experiences that he or she brings to the session.

Although international research is clearly a focus for the future, we question the value of simply replicating extant studies with new participants drawn from different cultural groups. Although such an approach might confirm (or refute) the universality of the basic principles of memory development outlined in Table 12.1, in our view, this approach also runs the risk of creating deficit models by highlighting how well or how poorly one cultural group performs on a specific memory task relative to another without consideration for the specific mechanisms involved. Instead, we would encourage a slightly different approach, whereby diversifying to other cultural groups can continue to advance knowledge on how experience, in addition to age, establishes strong and complex memory networks across the infancy period. For example, as described earlier, there is now a body of research showing that participants growing up in bilingual environments show more mature representational flexibility in their early memory abilities (Brito & Barr, 2012, 2014). By conducting memory research with children who have daily experience in selecting and inhibiting between two (or more) languages, researchers have the opportunity to develop a better understanding of the processes by which memories are made accessible for future problem solving. Further advances will likely come as memory researchers begin to work more closely with families who experience greater connections to their physical environment, or who provide children with extended and multigenerational social networks early in development. In our work, we have personally benefitted from the supervision of graduate students who have come to us from around the world. These bright young people have cast their own cultural lens on our work, raising new and important questions about the role of experience, including cultural context, in memory development during infancy, early childhood, and beyond. In our view, this more global approach will continue to make important contributions to our understanding of memory development.

References

Adolph, K. E., & Hoch, J. E. (2019). Motor development: Embodied, embedded, enculturated, and enabling. *Annual Review of Psychology, 70,* 26.1–26.24.

Anderson, D. I., Campos, J. J., Witherington, D. C., Dahl, A., Rivera, M., He, M., ... Barbu-Roth, M. (2013). The role of locomotion in psychological development. *Frontiers in Psychology, 4,* 440.

Artioli, F., & Reese, E. (2013). Early memories in young adults from separated and non-separated families, *Memory, 22,* 1082–1102

Artioli, F., Reese, E., & Hayne, H. (2015). Benchmarking the past: Children's early memories and maternal reminiscing as a function of family structure. *Journal of Applied Research in Memory and Cognition, 4,* 136–143.

Bahrick, L., & Pickens, J. (1995). Infant memory for object motion across a period of three months: Implications for a four-phase attention function. *Journal of Experimental Child Psychology, 59,* 343–371.

Barnat, S. A., Klein, P. J., & Meltzoff, A. N. (1996). Deferred imitation across changes in context and object: Memory and generalization in 14-month-old infants. *Infant Behavior and Development, 19,* 241–251.

Barr, R. (2013). Memory constraints on infant learning from picture books, television, and touchscreens. *Child Development Perspectives, 7,* 205–210.

Barr, R., Dowden, A., & Hayne, H. (1996). Developmental changes in deferred imitation by 6- to 24-month-old infants. *Infant Behavior and Development, 19,* 159–170.

Barr, R., & Hayne, H. (1999). Developmental changes in imitation from television during infancy. *Child Development, 70,* 1067–1081.

(2000). Age-related changes in imitation: Implications for memory development. In C. Rovee-Collier, L. P. Lipsitt, & H. Hayne (Eds.), *Progress in infancy research* (Vol. 1, pp. 21–67). Hillsdale, NJ: Lawrence Erlbaum Associates.

Barr, R., Muentener, R., Garcia, A., Fujimoto, M., & Chavez, V. (2007). The effect of repetition on imitation from television during infancy. *Developmental Psychobiology, 49,* 196–207.

Barr, R., Walker, J., Gross, J., & Hayne, H. (2014). Age-related changes in spreading activation during infancy. *Child Development, 85,* 549–563.

Bauer, P. (2015). A complementary processes account of the development of childhood amnesia and a personal past. *Psychological Review, 122,* 204–231.

Bauer, P. J., Wenner, J. A., Dropik, P. L., & Wewerka, S. S. (2000). Parameters of remembering and forgetting in the transition from infancy to early childhood. *Monographs of the Society for Research in Child Development, 65,* 1–204.

Brito, N., & Barr, R. (2012). Influence of bilingualism on memory generalisation during infancy. *Developmental Science, 15,* 812–816.

(2014). Flexible memory retrieval in bilingual 6-month-old infants. *Developmental Psychobiobiology*, *56*, 1156–1163.

Brito, N., Barr, R., McIntyre, P., & Simcock, G. (2012). Long-term transfer of learning from books and video during infanthood. *Journal of Experimental Child Psychology*, *111*, 108–119.

Butler, J., & Rovee-Collier, C. (1989). Contextual gating of memory retrieval. *Developmental Psychobiology*, *22*, 533–552.

Casey, B. J., Tottenham, N., Liston, C., & Durston, S. (2005) Imaging the developing brain: what have we learned about cognitive development? *Trends in Cognitive Science*, *9*, 104–110.

Cornell, E. (1979). Infants' recognition memory, forgetting, and savings. *Journal of Experimental Child Psychology*, *28*, 359–374.

Davis , J., & Rovee-Collier, C. (1983). Alleviated forgetting of a learned contingency in 8-week-old infants. *Developmental Psychology*, *19*, 353–365.

Dehaene-Lambertz, G., & Spelke, E. S. (2015). The infancy of the human brain. *Neuron*, *88*, 93–109.

Fagen, J. W., & Rovee-Collier, C. (1983). Memory retrieval: A time-locked process in infancy. *Science*, *222*, 1349–1352.

Fivush, R., Haden, C., & Reese, E. (2006). Elaborating on elaborations: Role of maternal reminiscing style in cognitive and socioemotional development. *Child Development*, *77*, 1568–1588.

Freud, S. [1905] (1953). Three essays on the theory of sexuality. In J. Strachey (Ed.), *The standard edition of the complete psychological works of Sigmund Freud* (Vol. 7, pp. 125–248). London: Hogarth Press.

Gilmore, J. H., Shi, F., Woolson, S. L., Knickmeyer, R. C., Short, S. J., Lin, W., … Shen, D. (2012). Longitudinal development of cortical and subcortical gray matter from birth to 2 years. *Cerebral Cortex*, *22*, 2478–2485.

Greco, C., Hayne, H., & Rovee-Collier, C. (1990). Roles of function, reminding, and variability in categorization by 3-month-old infants. *Journal of Experimental Psychology: Learning, Memory, and Cognition*, *16*, 617–633.

Greco, C., Rovee-Collier, C., Hayne, H., Griesler, P., & Earley, L. (1986). Ontogeny of early event memory I: Forgetting and retrieval by 2- and 3-month-olds. *Infant Behavior and Development*, *9*, 441–460.

Gross, J., Gardiner, B., & Hayne, H. (2016). Developmental reversals in recognition memory in children and adults. *Developmental Psychobiology*, *58*, 52–59.

Haartsen, R., Jones, E. J. H., & Johnson, M. H. (2016). Human brain development over the early years. *Current Opinion in Behavioral Science*, *10*, 149–54.

Hanna, E., & Meltzoff, A. N. (1993). Peer imitation by toddlers in laboratory, home, and day-care contexts: Implications for social learning and memory. *Developmental Psychology*, *29*, 701–710.

Hartshorn, K. (2003). Reinstatement maintains a memory in human infants for 1½ years. *Developmental Psychobiology*, *42*, 269–282.

Hartshorn, K., Rovee-Collier, C., Gerhardstein, P. C., Bhatt, R. S., Klein, P. J., Aaron, F., … Wurtzel, N. (1998). Developmental changes in the specificity of memory over the first year of life. *Developmental Psychobiology*, *33*, 61–78.

Hartshorn, K., Rovee-Collier, C., Gerhardstein, P. C, Bhatt, R. S., Wondoloski, T. L., Klein, P., … Campos-de-Carvalho, M. (1998). Ontogeny of long-term memory over the first year and a half of life. *Developmental Psychobiology*, *32*, 69–89.

Hayne, H. (1990). The effect of multiple reminders on long-term retention in human infants. *Developmental Psychobiology*, *23*, 453–477.

(2004). Infant memory development: Implications for childhood amnesia. *Developmental Review*, *24*, 33–73.

(2006). Age-related changes in infant memory retrieval: Implications for knowledge acquisition. In Y. Munakata & M. H. Johnson (Eds.), *Processes of change in brain and cognitive development: Attention and performance XXI* (pp. 209–231). New York, NY: Oxford University Press.

Hayne, H., Barr, R., & Herbert, J. (2003). The effect of prior practice on memory reactivation and generalization. *Child Development*, *74*, 1615–1627.

Hayne, H., Boniface, J., & Barr, R. (2000). The development of declarative memory in human infants: Age-related changes in deferred imitation. *Behavioral Neuroscience*, *114*, 77–83.

Hayne, H., & Findlay, N. (1995). Contextual control of memory retrieval in infancy: Evidence for associative priming. *Infant Behavior and Development*, *18*, 195–207.

Hayne, H., Greco, C., Earley, L. A., Griesler, P. C., & Rovee-Collier, C. (1986). Ontogeny of early event memory II: Encoding and retrieval by 2- and 3-month-olds. *Infant Behavior and Development*, *9*, 461–472.

Hayne, H., Gross, J., Hildreth, K., & Rovee-Collier, C. (2000). Repeated reminders increase the speed of memory retrieval by 3-month-old infants. *Developmental Science*, *3*, 312–318.

Hayne, H., & Herbert, H. (2004). Verbal cues facilitate memory retrieval during infancy. *Journal of Experimental Child Psychology*, *89*, 127–139.

Hayne, H., Herbert, J., & Simcock, G. (2003). Imitation from television by 24- and 30-month-olds. *Developmental Science*, *6*, 254–261.

Hayne, H., & Jack, F. (2011). Childhood amnesia. *Wiley Interdisciplinary Reviews in Cognitive Science*, *2*, 136–145.

Hayne, H., Jaeger, K., Sonne, T., & Gross, J. (2016). Visual attention to meaningful stimuli by 1- to 3-year-olds: Implications for the measurement of memory. *Developmental Psychobiology*, *58*, 808–816.

Hayne, H., MacDonald, S., & Barr, R. (1997). Developmental changes in the specificity of memory over the second year of life. *Infant Behavior and Development*, *20*, 237–249.

Hayne, H., Rovee-Collier, C., & Borza, M. A. (1991). Infant memory for place information. *Memory and Cognition*, *19*, 378–386.

Herbert, J., Gross, J., & Hayne, H. (2007). Crawling is associated with more flexible memory retrieval by 9-month-old infants. *Developmental Science*, *10*, 183–189.

Herbert, J., & Hayne, H. (2000a). Memory retrieval by 18–30-month-olds: Age-related changes in representational flexibility. *Developmental Psychology*, *36*, 473–484.

(2000b). The ontogeny of long-term retention during the second year of life. *Developmental Science*, *3*, 50–56.

Hill, W. H., Borovsky, D., & Rovee-Collier, C. (1988). Continuities in infant memory development over the first half-year. *Developmental Psychobiology*, *21*, 43–62.

Hunter, M., & Ames, E. (1988). A multifactor model of infant preferences for novel and familiar stimuli. In C. Rovee-Collier & L. P. Lipsitt (Eds.), *Advances in infancy research* (Vol. 5, pp. 69–95). Norwood, NJ: Ablex.

Imuta, K., Scarf, D., & Hayne, H. (2013). The effect of verbal reminders on memory reactivation in 2-, 3-, and 4-year-old children. *Developmental Psychology, 49,* 1056–1065.

Jack, F., MacDonald, S., Reese, E., & Hayne, H. (2009). Maternal reminiscing style during early childhood predicts the age of adolescents' earliest memories. *Child Development, 80,* 496–505.

Jack, F., Simcock, G., & Hayne, H. (2011). Magic memories: Young children's verbal recall after a 6-year delay. *Child Development, 83,* 159–172.

Klein, P. J., & Meltzoff, A. N. (1999). Long-term memory, forgetting, and deferred imitation in 12-month-old infants. *Developmental Science, 2,* 102–113.

Lavenex, P., & Lavenex, P. B. (2013). Building hippocampal circuits to learn and remember: insights into the development of human memory. *Behavioral Brain Research, 254,* 8–21.

MacDonald, S., Uesiliana, K., & Hayne, H. (2000). Cross-cultural and gender differences in childhood amnesia. *Memory, 8,* 365–376.

McDonough, L., Mandler, J. M., McKee, R. D., & Squire, L. R. (1995). The deferred imitation task as a nonverbal measure of declarative memory. *Proceedings of the National Academy of Science, 92,* 7580–7584.

McKee, R. D., & Squire, L. R. (1993). On the development of declarative memory. *Journal of Experimental Psychology: Learning, Memory, and Cognition, 19,* 397–404.

Meltzoff, A. N. (1995). What infant memory tells us about infantile amnesia: Long-term recall and deferred imitation. *Journal of Experimental Child Psychology, 59,* 497–515.

Morgan, K., & Hayne, H. (2006a). Age-related changes in memory reactivation by 1- and 2-year-old human infants. *Developmental Psychobiology, 48,* 48–57.

  (2006b). The effect of encoding time on retention by infants and young children. *Infant Behavior & Development, 29,* 599–602.

  (2007). Nonspecific verbal cues alleviate forgetting by young children. *Developmental Science, 10,* 727–733.

  (2011). Age-related changes in visual recognition memory during infancy and early childhood. *Developmental Psychobiology, 53,* 157–165.

Morris, G., & Baker-Ward, L. (2007). Fragile but real: Children's capacity to use newly acquired words to convey preverbal memories. *Child Development, 78,* 448–458.

Morrison, C. M., & Conway, M. A. (2009, July). *First words and first memories.* Paper presented at the 8th Biennial Meeting of the Society for Applied Research in Memory and Cognition, Kyoto, Japan.

Mullen, M. K. (1994). Earliest recollections of childhood: A demographic analysis. *Cognition, 52,* 55–79.

Nelson, C. A. (2000). Neural plasticity and human development: The role of early experience sculpting memory systems. *Developmental Science, 3,* 115–130.

Nielsen, M., Haun D., Kärtner, J., & Legare, C. H. (2017). The persistent sampling bias in developmental psychology: a call to action. *Journal of Experimental Child Psychology, 162,* 31–38.

Noble, K. G., Engelhardt, L. E., Brito, N. H., Mack, L. J., Nail, E. J., Angal, J., ... Elliott, A. J. (2015). Socioeconomic disparities in neurocognitive development in the first two years of life. *Developmental Psychobiology*, *57*, 535–551.

Otto, B. (2018). Language development of infants and toddlers. In B. Otto, *Language development in early childhood education* (5th ed., pp. 111–113). New York, NY: Pearson.

Pascalis, O., de Schonen, S., Morton, J., Deruelle, C., & Fabre-Grenet, M. (1995). Mother's face recognition by neonates: A replication and an extension. *Infant Behavior and Development*, *18*, 79–85.

Peterson, C., Grant, V., & Boland, L. (2005). Childhood amnesia in children and adolescents: Their earliest memories. *Memory*, *13*, 622–637.

Peterson, C., Warren, K. L., & Short, M. M. (2011). Infantile amnesia across the years: A 2-year follow-up of children's earliest memories. *Child Development*, *82*, 1092–1105.

Pillemer, D. B., Picariello, M. L., & Pruett, J. C. (1994). Very long-term memories of a salient preschool event. *Applied Cognitive Psychology*, *8*, 95–106.

Reardon, S. F. (2011). The widening academic-achievement gap between the rich and the poor: New evidence and possible explanations. In G. J Duncan & R. J. Murnane (Eds.), *Whither opportunity?: Rising inequality, schools, and children's life chances* (pp. 91–116). New York, NY: Russell Sage Foundation.

Reese, E., Haden, C. A., & Fivush, R. (1993). Mother–child conversations about the past: Relationships of style and memory over time. *Cognitive Development*, *8*, 403–430.

Reese, E., Hayne, H., & MacDonald, S. (2008). Looking back to the future: Māori and Pakeha mother–child birth stories. *Child Development*, *79*, 114–125.

Reese, E., Jack, F., & White, N. (2010). Origins of adolescents' autobiographical memories. *Child Development*, *25*, 352–367.

Reynolds, G. (2015). Infant visual attention and object recognition. *Behavioral Brain Research*, *285*, 34–43.

Richmond, J., Colombo, M., & Hayne, H. (2007). Interpreting visual preferences in the visual paired-comparison task. *Journal of Experimental Psychology: Learning, Memory, and Cognition*, *33*, 823–831.

Richmond, J., & Nelson, C. A. (2007). Accounting for change in declarative memory: A cognitive neuroscience perspective. *Developmental Review*, *27*, 349–373.

Richmond, J., Sowerby, P., Colombo, M., & Hayne, H. (2004). The effect of familiarization time, retention interval, and context change on adult's performance in the visual paired-comparison task. *Developmental Psychobiology*, *44*, 146–155.

Riggins, T., Cheatham, C. L., Stark, E., & Bauer, P. J. (2013). Elicited imitation performance at 20 months predicts memory abilities in school-aged children. *Journal of Cognition and Development*, *14*, 593–606.

Robinson, A. J., & Pascalis, O. (2004). Development of flexible visual recognition memory in human infants. *Developmental Science*, *7*, 527–533.

Rose, S. A., Gottfried, A. W., Melloy-Carminar, P., & Bridger, W. H. (1982). Familiarity and novelty preferences in infant recognition memory: Implications for information processing. *Developmental Psychology*, *18*, 704–713.

Rovee-Collier, C., & Cuevas, K. (2009). Multiple memory systems are unnecessary to account for infant memory development: An ecological model. *Developmental Psychology, 45*, 160–174.

Rovee-Collier, C., Griesler, P., & Earley, L. (1985). Contextual determinants of retrieval in three-month-old infants. *Learning and Motivation, 16*, 139–157.

Rovee-Collier, C., & Hayne, H. (1987). Reactivation of infant memory: Implications for cognitive development. In H. W. Reese (Ed.), *Advances in child development and behavior* (Vol. 20, pp. 185–238). New York, NY: Academic Press.

Rovee-Collier, C., Patterson, J., & Hayne, H. (1985). Specificity in the reactivation of infant memory. *Developmental Psychobiology, 18*, 559–574.

Rovee-Collier, C., Sullivan, M., Enright, M., Lucas, D., & Fagen, J. W. (1980). Reactivation of infant memory. *Science, 208*, 1159–1161.

Seehagen, S., Konrad, C., Herbert, J. S., & Schneider, S. (2015). Timely sleep facilitates declarative memory consolidation in infants. *PNAS, 112*, 1625–1629.

Seehagen, S., Zmyj, N., & Herbert, J. S. (2019). Remembering in the context of internal states: The role of sleep for infant memory. *Child Development Perspectives, 13*, 110–115.

Simcock, G., & DeLoache, J. S. (2008). The effect of repetition on infants' imitation from picture books. *Infancy, 13*, 687–697.

Simcock, G., & Hayne, H. (2002). Breaking the barrier: Children do not translate their preverbal memories into language. *Psychological Science, 13*, 225–231.

Sokolov, E. N. (1963). *Perception and the conditioned reflex.* New York, NY: Macmillan.

Spear, N. E., & Parsons, P. J. (1976). Analysis of a reactivation treatment: Ontogenetic determinants of alleviated forgetting. In D. L. Medin, W. A. Roberts, & R. T. Davis, (Eds.), *Process of animal memory* (pp. 135–165). Hillsdale, NJ: Lawrence Erlbaum Associates.

Squire, L. R. (1992). Memory and the hippocampus: A synthesis from findings with rats, monkeys, and humans. *Psychological Review, 99*(2), 195–231.

Sylva, K., Melhuish, E., Sammons, P., Siraj-Blatchford, I., & Taggart, B. (2010). *Early childhood matters: Evidence from the effective pre-school and primary education project.* London: Routledge

Tulving, E., & Thomson, D. M. (1973). Encoding specificity and retrieval processes in episodic memory. *Psychological Review, 80*, 352–373.

Tustin, K., & Hayne, H. (2010). Defining the boundary: Age-related changes in childhood amnesia. *Developmental Psychology, 46*, 1049–1061.

Waldfogel, S. (1948). The frequency and affective character of childhood memories. *Psychological Monographs, 62*, 1–39.

Wang, Q. (2003). Infantile amnesia reconsidered: A cross-cultural analysis. *Memory, 11*, 65–80.

(2006a). Earliest recollections of self and others in European American and Taiwanese young adults. *Psychological Science, 17*, 708–714.

(2006b). Relations of maternal style and child self-concept to autobiographical memories in Chinese, Chinese immigrant, and European American 3-year-olds. *Child Development, 77*, 1794–1809.

Wang, Q., Conway, M., & Hou, Y. (2004). Infantile amnesia: A cross-cultural investigation. *Cognitive Sciences, 1*, 123–135.

World Health Organization (n.d.). *The global strategy for women's, children's and adolescents' health (2016–2030)*. Geneva. Retrieved from www.who.int/life-course/partners/global-strategy/en.

Zack, E., Barr, R., Gerhardstein, P., Dickerson, K., & Meltzoff, A. N. (2009). Infant imitation from television using novel touch-screen technology. *British Journal of Developmental Psychology, 27*, 13–26.

13 Infant Physical Knowledge

Susan J. Hespos and Erin M. Anderson*

Physical reasoning is the ability to go beyond the information in the immediate perceptual array. For example, if I were to dangle my keys in front of me with the intention of letting go of them, everyone would predict that the moment I let go of the keys, they will fall towards the ground. Similarly, if I hide my keys behind my back, everyone has the expectation that the keys continue to exist and that the shape and size of the keys remain the same as they were before they were hidden from view. These two examples demonstrate that people share the same basic ideas about how objects behave and interact. These expectations may be universal across all humans, and they may even be shared by some other species. However, researchers are still puzzled by some aspects of these fundamental abilities. For instance, even though most people can effortlessly draw similar predictions about these events, we have yet to build a computer that can rival the physical reasoning abilities of a typically developing 1-year-old infant. In this chapter, we argue that one way to resolve some of the mysteries about physical reasoning is to look at the origins of the abilities and how they change over time. We start by reviewing the literature on the physical reasoning abilities of human infants. First, we present two case studies: knowledge about objects and knowledge about substances (e.g., liquid, sand, etc.). Each case begins by offering key distinctions that define physical reasoning abilities and then reviews the evidence that support these claims and how these findings provide information about the nature of the representation abilities. The final sections review how these findings relate to neuroscience, sociocultural, and policy perspectives.

The psychological theory of core knowledge has motivated a great deal of research on physical reasoning in infants. The key tenet of this approach is that underneath all the things that vary across humans, there exist a set of perceptual and conceptual capacities common to everyone. The research motivated by the core knowledge approach strives to characterize the nature of these abilities and how they develop. In particular, core knowledge abilities are evident early in development and they are used continuously throughout life.

* This chapter is based upon work supported by the National Science Foundation under Grant Nos. BCS-1423917 and BCS-1729720 and a Department of Education, Institute of Education Sciences, Multidisciplinary Program in Education Sciences, Grant Award #R305B140042.

The abilities are universal across human cultures and shared among a variety of other species. A well-studied example of a core knowledge system is the ability to discriminate quantities. This system is called the approximate number system. We use the approximate number system to discriminate between a crowd with 200 people versus a crowd of 100 people and which pile of food is larger. The ability does not require counting; it is dependent on the ratio between the compared amounts. It does not require formal schooling: In fact, newborn infants can discriminate a 1:3 ratio (Izard, Sann, Spelke, & Streri, 2009). There is improvement in the precision of the ratio over development, in that 9-month-old infants can discriminate a 2:3 ratio and adults can do a 7:8 ratio (Lipton & Spelke, 2003). These findings provide evidence that quantity discrimination is continuous across ages and becomes refined through experience. The approximate number system is not unique to humans: A variety of foraging species have the same ratio-dependent discrimination ability (Jordan, Brannon, Logothetis, & Ghazanfar, 2005). Because of its focus on the aspects of development that are continuous, the core knowledge theoretical view is often portrayed as a contrast to Piaget's (1952, 1954) stage-like progression. The interesting questions moving forward are to use the comparisons between humans' core cognitive capacities and those of other animals to see where these paths diverge. The uniquely human cognitive abilities may be grounded in the core knowledge systems as a foundation for building new cognitive skills. Perhaps the reason humans seem so smart is that we can combine the core knowledge domains to create entirely new representation systems such as language and the natural numbers.

13.1 Case Study 1: Objects

We all have the expectation that an unsupported object should fall down and that an object that is under a cloth still continues to exist even if we can no longer see it. But, when did we acquire this information? There is no explicit training in terms of how to represent objects. The study of infants' expectations about objects provides evidence that the way a 3-month-old and an adult perceive the world is fundamentally similar. In infancy, early object concepts are primitive, but through experience in the environment, infants elaborate these initial concepts and identify increasingly refined variables that allow them to predict the outcomes of events with more accuracy (Baillargeon et al., 2012). Early research on this topic focused on mapping out the nature of these representations and detailing what infants know at different ages. More recently, this foundation has allowed us to focus on the process through which infants acquire this knowledge. Situations where knowledge develops through experience, but without instruction, tend to involve a process of continuity and elaboration. Therefore, studies of the origins and early development of physical reasoning abilities can lend insights to the mature ability (Spelke, 1990).

The first challenge to understanding the development of physical reasoning is to figure out a way to ask preverbal infants what they know. One method that has been developed over the past 30 years is looking-time tasks (Baillargeon et al., 2012; Oakes, 2017). From an early age, infants have good control over their eyes. In addition, infants tend to look at things that they find novel and to look away from things when they get bored. In a typical experiment, an infant is seated on their parent's lap in front of a puppet stage. A curtain on the stage is raised and the experimenter manipulates objects on the stage. The dependent measure is the duration of an infant's looks at the events on stage across trials. To capture the looking duration there is a small video camera beneath the stage floor videotaping the infant's face when the curtain is up. The video image is viewed by two research assistants in a separate room. Their job is to press a button when the infant is attending to the events on the stage and to let go of the button when the infant looks away. If the infant looks away from the stage for two consecutive seconds, this is interpreted as the infant losing interest and the trial ends.

Using this method, Spelke, Breinlinger, Macomber, and Jacobson (1992) demonstrated that at 2 months, infants know that two objects should not pass through one another. In the experiment, the infants were shown an empty stage with a barrier wall on the right side (see Figure 13.1). A screen was put on stage covering the right side of the stage and the lower portion of the barrier. The experimenter brought out a ball and waved it to draw the infant's attention, then rolled the ball so that it went behind the screen and came to rest next to the barrier wall. The screen was then removed and looking time to the outcome was recorded. This trial type was repeated until infants showed a decline in looking. The decline in looking over repeated trials is called *habituation*. Habituation trials are designed to teach infants the contingency between their looking away and the trial ending, as well as to familiarize them to the objects in the events. After the habituation trials, infants were shown two types of test trials that alternated. In the *expected* test trials, a second barrier wall was introduced to the middle of the display. The same screen was placed on the stage, covering the lower portion of the barriers. The experimenter brought out a ball, waved it to call the infant's attention, then rolled the ball so that it went behind the screen and came to rest on the near side of the new barrier wall. The screen was removed and looking time to the outcome was recorded. The *unexpected* test trial was identical except that, when the screen was removed, the ball was against the far barrier wall (as if it had passed through the barrier). Looking time at the *expected* test trials was compared to looking time at an *unexpected* test trial. The results showed that infants looked significantly longer at the unexpected outcome revealing that infants expected the ball to be stopped by the barrier and looked longer at events that violated this expectation. More broadly, research using looking-time paradigms has revealed that infants have sophisticated expectations about how objects behave and interact. These findings provide evidence that Piaget may have underestimated infants' abilities because his methodology required complex motoric and cognitive abilities.

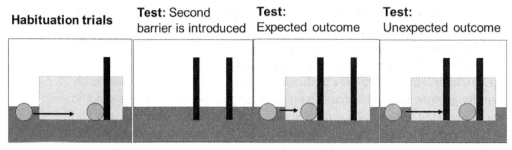

Figure 13.1. *Schematic of the events used in Spelke et al. (1992).*

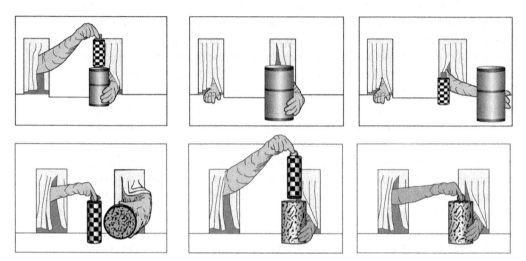

Figure 13.2. *Schematic of the events used in the unexpected outcome trials for Hespos and Baillargeon (2001b).*

The findings from looking-time experiments are interpreted as evidence that infants have core knowledge about objects. More specifically, infants expect objects to be *continuous* (e.g., they do not blink in and out of existence) and *solid* (e.g., two objects cannot occupy the same space at the same time). This initial finding has been replicated and extended in two ways. A study by Hespos and Baillargeon (2001b) found converging evidence for continuity and solidity using different events. In this study, 2-month-old infants expected that an object placed inside a container should travel with the container when the container was moved to a new location and looked significantly longer at an event that violated this expectation (see Figure 13.2, top row). In a different experiment, 2-month-old infants expected that two objects cannot pass through one another and they looked significantly longer at an event that violated this expectation (see Figure 13.2, bottom row). It is particularly striking that this knowledge is evident before infants have the manual dexterity to construct these expectations through interacting with the environment.

 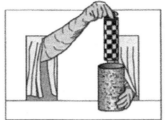 

  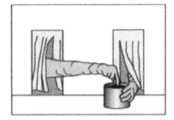

Figure 13.3. *The expected (tall container event) and unexpected (short container event) from Hespos and Baillargeon (2001a).*

These initial concepts of continuity and solidity are primitive and leave many aspects of object knowledge undefined. What changes over the course of development is that, through an infant's experience interacting with the environment, these initial concepts are elaborated and refined. Over the course of several months, infants learn to identify variables that let them predict the outcomes of events more precisely. For example, 2-month-old infants have not yet identified how the height of an object determines how much of it will be hidden inside a container. Experiments with 5-month-old infants show that infants do not detect the violation if a very tall object is completely hidden in a short container because they look for equal durations at the events depicted in Figure 13.3 (Hespos & Baillargeon, 2001a). However, by 8 months of age, infants looked significantly longer at the short event compared to the tall event. These findings suggest that the infants gained more experience manipulating objects in their environment and now expect that a tall object would be only partially hidden if lowered into a short container. More broadly, these findings indicate that the change in physical reasoning is one of elaboration and refinement.

One may think that developmental changes such as the ability to detect a violation in the variable of height in a containment event at 8 months, but not at 5 months of age could be due to maturation alone. However, this interpretation is unlikely because expectations about the variable of height emerge at different times depending on the physical event. Infants have expectations about the variable of height in occlusion events as early as 3.5 months of age (Baillargeon & DeVos, 1991; Hespos & Baillargeon, 2001b), height in containment events emerges at 8 months of age (Hespos & Baillargeon, 2001a; Wang, Baillargeon, & Paterson, 2005), and height in covering events emerges at 12 months (Wang et al., 2005). This progression aligns with the prevalence of these events in everyday environments in that occlusion is more common than containment and containment is more common than covering. We speculate that this developmental change may instead be based on experience. Recent evidence demonstrated a way to test these ideas. Casasola, Bhagwat, Doan, and Love (2017) provided parent–child dyads with nesting toys and recorded spontaneous interactions. They found that 18-month-old infants demonstrated more containment events than support events. Similarly their caretakers labeled containment more than support. However, in dyadic play, where parents had the opportunity to lead the interactions, support was more frequent than containment. Future studies could extend this paradigms to interactions with occluders, containers, and covers to better understand the roles of self-guided play and language in developing knowledge about objects.

Another factor that interacts with the development of object knowledge is individual differences in postural milestones like sitting, crawling, and walking. Various studies have shown that object manipulation and experience is rate limited by postural constraints (Higgins, Campos, & Kermoian, 1996; Rochat, 1992; Soska & Adolph, 2014). For example, self-sitting allows an infant to hold an object with one hand and probe its contours with the other hand and this has implications for their expectations about how objects behave and interact. A full account of physical knowledge will need to consider the interaction between cognitive, cultural, and motoric influences.

Infants' understanding of physical reasoning with regard to support events provides another example of initial knowledge that gets elaborated through identifying increasingly refined variables (see Figure 13.4). As early as 3 months of age, infants have the initial concept that unsupported objects should fall and they look significantly longer at an event that violates this expectation (Needham & Baillargeon, 1993). By 5 months of age, this initial concept becomes elaborated to discriminate the difference between the type of support, in that a box supported by being placed on top of a horizontal surface should provide support but a box placed against a vertical surface should not provide support. By 7 months infants identify a new variable, namely the amount of contact. Infants expect that 70% contact with the horizontal surface should provide support but only 15% contact with the horizontal surface (where the majority of the box is dangling over the edge) would not provide support (Baillargeon, Needham, & DeVos, 1993). Just after a year of age infants identify yet another variable about the shape of the supported object. Infants expect that an asymmetric object that is placed with the larger portion of the object on a box will be supported by the box. However, if the smaller portion of an asymmetric object is placed on the box so that that larger portion of the box is extended without support, then infants expect the box to fall. Together, these studies provide converging evidence for a developmental

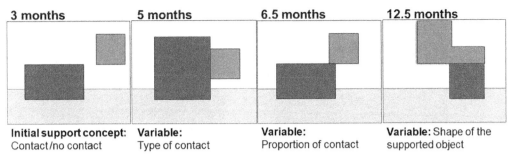

| 3 months | 5 months | 6.5 months | 12.5 months |

Initial support concept: Contact/no contact

Variable: Type of contact

Variable: Proportion of contact

Variable: Shape of the supported object

Figure 13.4. *Schematic of the support violations that infants detect at increasing ages.*

progression of initial knowledge that is elaborated through experience in the environment. Future studies could determine whether these developmental patterns exist across different exposure rates and cultures. Additionally, work from Needham and colleagues has shown that increasing 3- and 4-month-olds' active reaching experience by giving them sticky mittens (so they can pick up objects before they have the manual dexterity to grasp them with their own fingers) leads to improvements in parsing goal-directed actions with objects and mental rotation (Slone, Moore, & Johnson, 2018; Sommerville, Woodward, & Needham, 2005). Paradigms using interventions like the sticky mittens could be used to disentangle the roles of experience and maturation in the development of physical reasoning.

All of the physical reasoning evidence described thus far has relied on looking-time tasks to measure infants' knowledge. This raises the question: would infants demonstrate the same knowledge with action tasks? The answer seems to be yes. Infants in the first months of life do not have fine motor skills, but paradigms designed for infants to perform gross motor movements allow infants to execute choices based on their actions, like a swipe at one or another object. For example, infants were presented with a plush toy frog that was very tall. After playing with the frog for a little while, the experimenter took the frog from the infant and hid it behind a screen, then removed the screen revealing two containers that had frog feet sticking out of them (Figure 13.5). One of the containers was taller than the frog and it was feasible that the entire frog could be hidden inside the container. The other container was one-third the size of the toy frog and it was not feasible that the entire frog would fit inside the short container. The experimenter drew the infant's attention to each container and then pushed both containers to the edge of the infant's reaching space and recorded which container the infants reached toward. The rationale was that the infant wanted to recapture the toy that was taken away and if the infant remembered the height of the frog then they would reach for the tall instead of the short container. This is exactly what happened when we tested 8-month-old infants (Figure 13.5; Hespos & Baillargeon, 2006). In contrast, 5-month-old infants showed no preference

Pre-trial   Main trial

 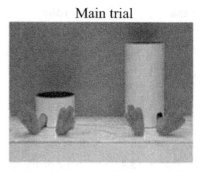

Figure 13.5. *Pictures of the stimuli from Hespos and Baillargeon (2006).*

between the tall and short containers. These findings align with the developmental changes in the looking-time tasks. Further studies that did action tasks testing the support variables of type of contact and amount of contact also revealed the same developmental changes at the same time providing converging evidence across looking and reaching paradigms for the development of physical reasoning abilities (Hespos & Baillargeon, 2008).

Together, these findings are important because they capture the interplay between two developmental trajectories. One is the core knowledge of continuity and solidity that is evident early and does not rely on experience. The other is a more protracted, experience-based trajectory that is characterized by identifying variables that allow infants to elaborate the initial concepts and become more precise. Together, looking-time paradigms provide considerable evidence that a 2-month-old and an adult perceive objects in fundamentally similar ways. The idea that infants have sophisticated expectations about how objects behave and interact is at odds with Piaget's notion of qualitative shifts in their object concept (Piaget, 1952).

This early work documented *what* infants understand about objects at certain ages. This sets the stage for investigating *how* infants' physical knowledge interacts with other cognitive abilities. One cognitive ability that comes into play is language. Human languages vary in meanings and children must learn which distinctions their languages use. For example, tight/loose fit is a spatial distinction that is marked linguistically in Korean but not English. Adult Korean speakers – but not adult English speakers – are sensitive to the conceptual distinction of tight and loose fit when they categorize spatial relations (Bowerman, 1996). As a matter of fact, language-specific differences in spatial categories are evident early in language acquisition. Korean children differ from English-speaking children on spatial category tasks in accord with their ambient languages (Choi & Bowerman, 1991). Is it possible that language specifies the spatial category boundaries, or do infants have expectations about spatial categories prior to language?

Casasola and Cohen (2002) revealed that 10-month-old infants have expectations about containment and support prior to language production. Similarly, we found that 5-month-old infants in an English-speaking environment were sensitive to the Korean-marked tight–loose spatial category even though it was not marked in their ambient language (Hespos & Spelke, 2004). These findings indicate that the process that governs learning word meanings has a developmental trajectory where preverbal infants are sensitive to nonnative distinctions. Spatial language learning seems to develop by linking linguistic forms to universal, preexisting concepts. In these respects, the early development of spatial categories parallels the development of phonological perception. The infant's native language capitalizes on preexisting conceptual or acoustic distinctions and experience with a language influences the prominence of distinctions that are marked in the ambient language(s).

A second example of *how* physical knowledge interacts with other cognitive systems comes from studies on how infants allocate their attention to specific aspects of their environment. For example, infants who saw a solidity or no-contact support violation (similar to those described earlier) attend to that object more closely in subsequent interactions and learned to associate a novel sound with the object. In contrast, when the same teaching event was coupled with expected solidity or support events, infants failed to learn this new sound property (Stahl & Feigenson, 2015). Additionally, Stahl and Feigenson (2015) found that infants are active participants in their own knowledge acquisition. That is, infants who saw violations spent more time interacting with the object involved, compared to a distractor object. These infants also tested the objects in ways that suggested they were trying to replicate the unexpected behavior: Infants who saw a ball appear on the other side of a wall spent more time banging the ball against a high-chair tray, while infants who saw the ball float unsupported spent more time dropping the ball off the high-chair tray. This paradigm represents an exciting new approach to understanding how infants select what to learn.

To summarize the lessons from the first case study on objects, research using looking and reaching paradigms demonstrates that infants have expectations about how objects behave and interact. There is one early developing set of expectations about continuity and solidity that appear before infants have the opportunity to construct this knowledge through interacting with their environment. There is a second, experience-based trajectory characterized by identifying variables that allow infants to elaborate the initial concepts over the course of the first year. Together, these examples reveal that our knowledge about objects goes beyond the information available in the immediate environment. The expectations about how objects behave and interact is remarkably similar across humans in that these expectations require little experience and there may too be little variation across species.

13.2 Case Study 2: Substances

When a cup containing pencils is tipped over, not much happens. However, when a cup containing coffee is tipped over, panic can ensue as one tries to catch the cup before too much coffee spills. These reactions to spills are the result of understanding that objects and liquids have different physical properties and therefore behave differently. These reactions may seem obvious, but when do we develop the expectation that liquids deform to fill the space? This ontological categorical distinction has captivated linguists who trace cross-linguistic differences in count/mass nouns (Imai & Mazuka, 2007). In the philosophical domain of metaphysics, there are distinctions between entities that are separable or nonseparable (Rips & Hespos, 2015). In the field of psychology, there is a growing interest in looking at the origins and development of knowledge about substances and how it compares to the representations that guide expectations about objects (Hespos & vanMarle, 2012). For example, unlike objects, liquids deform to fit a container and a solid object can pass through them. Yet, like objects, liquids are common and some expectations about how they behave are probably universal across cultures and species. Given that there is evidence of sophisticated knowledge about objects early in development, the question we tackle in case study 2 is whether there is sophisticated knowledge about substances early in development.

Early evidence suggested that the answer was no: infants did not have principled expectations for substances (Cheries, Mitroff, Wynn, & Scholl, 2008; Chiang & Wynn, 2000; Huntley-Fenner, Carey, & Solimando, 2002; Rosenberg & Carey, 2009). In one study, Huntley-Fenner et al. (2002) showed 8-month-old infants a pile of sand, then concealed the pile behind a screen and poured a second pile of sand behind a nearby but spatially separated screen. The test trials alternated between expected and unexpected outcomes, and looking time was the dependent measure. The expected outcome was to reveal two piles of sand – one behind each screen when the screens were removed. The unexpected outcome was to reveal only a single pile behind one of the screens and nothing behind the other screen. The infants' looking times did not differ between the expected and unexpected events, providing evidence that they did not detect the violation when one sand pile disappeared. In contrast, when the sand substance was replaced with solid objects that were shaped like sand piles, then the infants looked significantly longer at the unexpected test trials. Infants' difficulties in tracking sand extended to collections of objects, like a pile of Legos (Chiang & Wynn, 2000). Together, these findings were interpreted as evidence that infants have principled expectations for objects but not for substances (Spelke & Kinzler, 2007).

Bourgeois, Khawar, Neal, and Lockman (2005) introduced a different approach to ask whether infants had any expectations about substances. They presented infants with stimuli that varied in qualities of hard versus soft versus liquid versus netting and found that 6- to 10-month-old infants adjust their

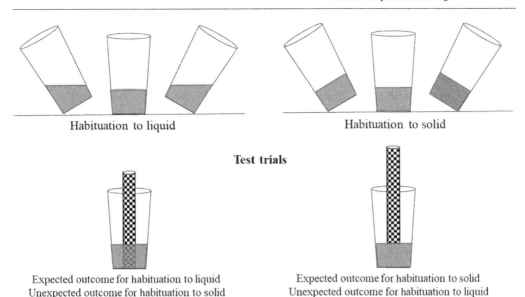

Habituation to liquid

Habituation to solid

Test trials

Expected outcome for habituation to liquid
Unexpected outcome for habituation to solid

Expected outcome for habituation to solid
Unexpected outcome for habituation to liquid

Figure 13.6. *A schematic of the habituation and test trials used in Hespos et al. (2009).*

actions towards objects based on the material-specific qualities of the stimuli. This finding was important because it demonstrated that infants approach objects and liquids with different behaviors. In turn, the starting point for our research was to focus on the different ways that objects and substances behave. For example, objects tend to be solid such that two objects cannot pass through one another, but liquids are loosely bonded so a straw can penetrate the surface of the liquid and come to rest on the bottom of the glass. Using a looking paradigm, 5-month-old infants were habituated to either a glass that contained liquid or a perceptually similar looking solid (see Figure 13.6). The glass was tipped back and forth and the motion cues specified whether the contents were liquid or solid. Next, in test trials, all infants saw trials of a straw being lowered into a glass. On half the trials, the contents of the glass were liquid and the straw penetrated the surface of the liquid and came to rest on the bottom of the glass. On the other half of the trials, the contents of the glass were solid and the straw stopped when it came in contact with the surface of the solid. Infants dishabituated (i.e., showed a significant increase in looking time compared to their last habituation trials) when there was a state change from liquid to solid or from solid to liquid. This suggests that infants have different expectations for the ways that solids and liquids behave (Hespos, Ferry, & Rips, 2009). These findings begin to clarify how 5-month-old infants comprehend the physical properties of substances.

We started with a solid object and a water-like liquid because they are the clearest examples of their kinds. However, this initial finding raises questions about how far infants' knowledge extends. Do infants develop expectations about liquids because they have extensive experience drinking and bathing or would they generalize such expectations to any event that shared the same physical attributes? More specifically, would an infant who has never been to a beach have expectations that a cup containing sand should pour out and not tumble? Our next study provided evidence that the answer to this question is yes (Hespos, Ferry, Anderson, Hollenbeck, & Rips, 2016). The events were similar to those depicted in Figure 13.6, but we replaced the liquid with sand and found similar results. Together, these findings provide evidence that expectations about substances emerge early and these inferences are based on little or no experience. A remaining question is whether violations of substance properties would lead to increased exploration and learning, such as Stahl and Feigenson (2015) found with violations of object knowledge. Answering this question would help reveal whether expectations for substances are treated as having consistent principles, despite the less constrained nature of nonsolid substances.

The results we have presented suggest that infants can grasp simple physical properties that apply to nonsolid substances. However, the previous research showing success with objects and failure with substances in otherwise identical paradigms raises questions about the extent of their knowledge (Chiang & Wynn, 2000; Huntley-Fenner et al., 2002; Rosenberg & Carey, 2009). Infants are apparently unable to predict the number of piles that result from pouring sand behind adjacent screens. But it is possible that this is due more to the working memory demands of the pouring event than a lack of expectations for substances. In a recent study, we tested infants' expectations about the mechanical properties of sand in a simplified pouring event. Although nonsolid substances can sometimes spread to fit the space allotted, constraints particular to sand limit its ability to do so. If infants see two cups of sand poured at opposite ends of a tray behind a screen, would it violate their expectations to reveal a single pile? What if just one cup was poured behind the screen? Would it be surprising if a single pour resulted in two separate piles? Our findings show that the answers are yes (see Figure 13.7). We found that 5-month-old infants look longer at events in which pours from two separate cups result in a single pile. In a separate condition, we found infants look longer if a single pour of sand results in two sand piles. The picture that is emerging is that infants have core principles for substances that are distinct from their expectations about objects.

To summarize the lessons from the second case study on substances, research using looking paradigms demonstrates that infants have expectations about how substances behave and interact. More specifically, the motion cues that specify that the contents of a glass are a substance lead infants to have expectations about how substances can divide and accumulate. In contrast to the vast literature on object knowledge, the study of substance knowledge in infants is new and there are only a handful of studies. Future research will need to test the youngest age groups to find out whether 2-month-olds have expectations about how liquids and sand divide and accumulate. In addition, mapping out

Habituation to one pour   ## Habituation to two pours

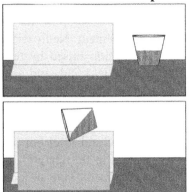
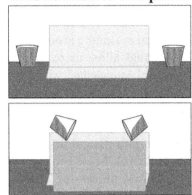

Two-pile outcome   ## One-pile outcome

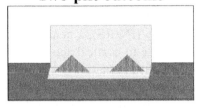
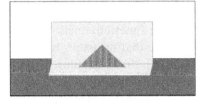

Unexpected for one-pour condition
Expected for two-pour condition

Expected for one-pour condition
Unexpected for two-pour condition

Figure 13.7. *A schematic of the habituation and test trials used in Anderson, Hespos, and Rips (2018).*

the developmental trajectory of this knowledge will be important. Do infants have expectations about the viscosity of liquids like the difference between water versus honey? If so, is this elaboration of knowledge about substances experience-based and when does it come into play?

To consider object and substance case studies together could shed new light on the nature of our representational systems. Object and substance knowledge may develop in parallel and it is an empirical question about whether there are two distinct domains of core knowledge that become connected through other cognitive systems, or whether there is one physical reasoning domain where distinctions between object and substances are situation-specific variables that are identified through experience. For example, as adults we can simultaneously construe a single entity as an object and a substance (Rips & Hespos, 2015). That is, I am seated at an object that I consider a table because it supports my computer while I write. However, if I were cold and in need of warmth I might also consider that the table is made of wood and I could burn it for warmth. A question for future research is: when does this flexibility between object and substance construal develop?

13.3 Implications for Neuroscience/Psychophysiology

The behavioral studies suggest that the developmental change in physical reasoning is one of elaboration and refinement. Neuroscience methods could allow us to approach a central question raised by research on physical knowledge: when a young infant, an older child, and an adult all exhibit a behavioral discrimination, how can we tell if the same underlying mechanism leads to behavioral discrimination across ages? If true continuity exists in physical knowledge, then we may expect to see convergent findings in infants and adults not only at the behavioral level but also at the neural level. More broadly, the majority of data in this chapter relies on a behavioral process of habituation – a decrease in looking time as stimuli become familiar. It would be fascinating to know whether there is converging evidence for infants' habituation at the neural level indicated by changes in blood flow due to functional activation or changes in electrophysiological response over time. Initial evidence for exactly this pattern has been reported using functional near-infrared spectroscopy (fNIRS), a neuroimaging technique that measures blood flow changes due to cortical activity (Lloyd-Fox et al., 2019). Similar to the habituation–dishabituation response found in looking time, neuroimaging revealed a significant decline in activity over the course of familiarization trials and a significant increase in activity during novel trials.

We have divided this chapter into reasoning about objects and reasoning about substances, but neuroscience could offer clues into how distinct these processes are and whether they diverge over the course of development. Evidence from adults suggests that representations of objects are associated with activation in the lateral occipital complex (Kourtzi & Kanwisher, 2001). It would be interesting to learn whether, in infancy, these areas are activated by looking-time displays featuring only objects or by those featuring substances as well. This could tell us whether object and substance representations are linked in infants' physical reasoning or whether these are separate domains.

13.4 Implications for Sociocultural Perspectives

The lack of variance in physical reasoning abilities across ontogeny and phylogeny suggests that there may be little variance across culture in these abilities as well. However, languages vary in how they describe space. While English differentiates containment (in) and support (on), and Korean distinguishes between a tight fit and a loose fit, languages like Dutch make even further distinctions for different types of contact (Bowerman, 1996; Gentner & Bowerman, 2009). As described above, Hespos and Spelke (2004) provides evidence that we start with a universal set of concepts about how entities in our world interact, and then language enhances or diminishes specific spatial relations. Though Hespos and Spelke (2004) showed that 5-month-old infants have nonnative concepts where adults' perceptions tend to mirror their ambient linguistic distinctions, it is clear from the research of Choi and Bowerman that as soon as children start using language, these linguistic distinctions are in place (Bowerman & Choi, 2003; Choi & Bowerman, 1991; Choi, McDonough, Bowerman & Mander, 1999). It would be interesting to map out these developmental changes for a variety of languages and spatial categories.

13.5 Conclusions and Policy Implications

Together, this chapter has argued that core concepts critical to early physical reasoning – such as object and substance knowledge – are likely a part of our evolutionary endowment. In addition, we have also described how these concepts become elaborated and refined as infants become increasingly able to explore the world. Because this process of elaboration is so closely linked to experience in the environment, it has clear policy implications. The research described above touches on the ways in which core knowledge interacts with other systems. These insights can provide valuable guidelines to practitioners and educators about the flexibility in our learning systems. There is evidence that language may capitalize on preexisting spatial concepts and change the way that adults perceive spatial events, so understanding whether a person speaks multiple languages and how these languages align or contrast in spatial terms could aid acquisition of a second language. There is also evidence that postural milestones like the onset of sitting, crawling, and walking can influence how infants interact with objects in their environment. This, in turn, influences when infants identify variables that allow them to predict the outcome of events with more accuracy. For children with developmental delays in reaching postural milestones, it may facilitate cognitive development to provide artificial postural support so that infants can manipulate objects and gain experience that might be rate limited by delayed postural milestones. Previously mentioned work from Casasola et al. (2017) shows how infant play tends to focus on containment while dyadic play with parents leads to a greater mix of support and containment. This example highlights how parents or older peers can scaffold infants' interaction with objects, giving them the opportunity to consider new variables sooner. As our field begins to incorporate large datasets, such as videos over the first year of life, we can use these data to better understand the role of play in constructing this knowledge and how the trajectory varies across cultures. This in turn will allow us to pinpoint the most fruitful times and methods for intervention.

References

Anderson, E., Hespos, S. J., & Rips, L. (2018). Five-month-old infants have expectations for the accumulation of nonsolid substances. *Cognition, 175,* 1–10. https://doi.org/10.1016/j.cognition.2018.02.009

Baillargeon, R., & DeVos, J. (1991). Object permanence in young infants: Further evidence. *Child Development, 62*(6), 1227–1246.

Baillargeon, R., Needham, A., & DeVos, J. (1993). The development of young infants' intuitions about support. *Infant and Child Development, 1*(2), 69–78.

Baillargeon, R., Stavans, M., Wu, D., Gertner, R., Setoh, P., Kittredge, A. K., & Bernard, A. (2012). Object individuation and physical reasoning in infancy: An integrative account. *Language Learning and Development, 8,* 4–46.

Bourgeois, K. S., Khawar, A. W., Neal, A., & Lockman J. (2005). Infant manual exploration of objects, surfaces, and their interrelations, *Infancy, 8,* 233–252,

Bowerman, M. (1996). Learning how to structure space for language: A crosslinguistic perspective. In P. Bloom, M. A. Peterson, L. Nadel, & M. F. Garrett (Eds.), *Language and space* (pp. 385–436). Cambridge, MA: MIT Press.

Bowerman, M., & Choi, S. (2003). Space under construction: Language-specific spatial categorization in first language acquisition. In D. Gentner & S. Goldin-Meadow (Eds.), *Language in mind* (pp. 387–428). Cambridge, MA: MIT Press.

Casasola, M. Bhagwat, J., Doan, S. N., & Love, H. (2017). Getting some space: Infants' and caregivers' containment and support spatial constructions during play. *Journal of Experimental Child Psychology, 159,* 110–128.

Casasola, M., & Cohen, L. (2002). Infant categorization of containment, support, and tight-fit spatial relationships. *Developmental Science, 5*(2), 247–264.

Cheries, E. W., Mitroff, S. R., Wynn, K., & Scholl, B. J. (2008). Cohesion as a constraint on object persistence in infancy. *Developmental Science, 11,* 427–432.

Chiang, W. C., & Wynn, K. (2000). Infants' tracking of objects and collections. *Cognition, 77,* 169–195.

Choi, S., & Bowerman, M. (1991). Learning to express motion events in English and Korean: The influence of language-specific lexicalization patterns. *Cognition, 41*(1–3), 83–121.

Choi, S., McDonough, L., Bowerman, M., & Mandler, J. M. (1999). Early sensitivity to language-specific spatial categories in English and Korean. *Cognitive Development, 14*(2), 241–268.

Gentner, D., & Bowerman, M. (2009). Why some spatial semantic categories are harder to learn than others: The typological prevalence hypothesis. In J. Guo, E. Lieven, S. Ervin-Tripp, N. Budwig, S. Özçaliskan, & K. Nakamura (Eds.). *Crosslinguistic approaches to the psychology of language: Research in the tradition of Dan Isaac Slobin* (pp. 465–480). New York, NY: Lawrence Erlbaum Associates.

Hespos, S. J., & Baillargeon, R. (2001a). Infants' knowledge about occlusion and containment: A surprising discrepancy. *Psychological Science, 12*(2), 141–147.

(2001b). Reasoning about containment events in very young infants. *Cognition, 78,* 207–245.

(2006). Decalage in infants' reasoning about occlusion and containment events: Converging evidence from action tasks. *Cognition, 99,* B31–B41.

(2008). Young infants' actions reveal their developing knowledge of support variables: Converging evidence for violation-of-expectation findings. *Cognition*, *107*(1), 304–316.

Hespos, S. J., Ferry, A., Anderson, E., Hollenbeck, E., & Rips, L. (2016). Five-month-old infants have expectations about how substances behave and interact. *Psychological Science*, *27*(2), 244–256. https://doi.org/10.1177/0956797615617897

Hespos, S. J., Ferry, A., & Rips, L. (2009). Five-month-old infants have different expectations for solids and liquids. *Psychological Science*, *20*(5), 603–611.

Hespos, S. J., & Spelke, E. S. (2004). Conceptual precursors to spatial language. *Nature*, 430, 453–456.

Hespos, S. J., & vanMarle, K. (2012). Physics for infants: Characterizing the origins of knowledge about objects, substances, and number. *Wiley Interdisciplinary Reviews: Cognitive Science*, *3*(1), 19–27.

Higgins, C., Campos, J., & Kermoian, R. (1996). Effects of self-produced locomotion on infant postural compensation to optic flow. *Developmental Psychology*, *32*, 836–841.

Huntley-Fenner, G., Carey, S., & Solimando, A. (2002). Objects are individuals but stuff doesn't count: Perceived rigidity and cohesiveness influence infants' representations of small groups of discrete entities. *Cognition*, *85*, 203–221.

Imai, M., & Mazuka, R. (2007). Language-relative construal of individuation constrained by universal ontology: Revisiting language universals and linguistic relativity. *Cognitive Science: A Multidisciplinary Journal*, *31*(3), 385–413.

Izard, V., Sann, C., Spelke, E. S., & Streri, A. (2009). Newborn infants perceive abstract numbers. *Proceedings of the National Academy of Sciences of the United States of America*, *106*(25), 10382–10385.

Jordan, K. E., Brannon, E. M., Logothetis, N. K., & Ghazanfar, A. A. (2005). Monkeys match the number of voices they hear to the number of faces they see. *Current Biology*, *15*(11), 1034–1038.

Kourtzi, Z., & Kanwisher, N. (2001). Representation of the perceived object shape by the human lateral occipital complex. *Science*, *293*(5534), 1506–1509.

Lipton, J. S., & Spelke, E. S. (2003). Origins of number sense. Large-number discrimination in human infants. *Psychological Science*, *14*, 396–401.

Lloyd-Fox, S., Blasi, A., McCann, S., Rozhiko, M., Katus, L., Mason, L., ... Elwell, C. E. (2019). Habituation and novelty detection fNIRS brain responses in 5- and 8-month-old infants: The Gambia and UK. *Developmental Science*, *22*(5), e12817. doi: 10.1111/desc.12817

Needham, A., & Baillargeon, R. (1993). Intuitions about support in 4.5-month-old infants. *Cognition*, *47*, 121–148.

Oakes, L. M., (2017). Sample size, statistical power, and false conclusions in infant looking-time research. *Infancy*, *22*, 436–469.

Piaget, J. (1952). *The origins of intelligence in children*. New York, NY: W. W Norton & Co. (1954). *The construction of reality in the child*. New York, NY: Basic Books.

Rips, L. J., & Hespos, S. J. (2015). Mental divisions of the physical world: Objects and substances. *Psychological Bulletin*, *141*(4), 786–811.

Rochat, P. (1992). Self-sitting and reaching in 5- to 8-month-old infants: The impact of posture and its development on early eye–hand coordination. *Journal of Motor Behavior*, *24*(2), 210–220.

Rosenberg, R. D., & Carey, S. (2009). Infants' representations of material entities. In B. M. Hood & L. R. Santos (Eds.), *The origins of object knowledge* (pp. 165–188). Oxford: Oxford University Press.

Slone, L. K., Moore D. S., & Johnson S. P. (2018) Object exploration facilitates 4-month-olds' mental rotation performance. *PLoS ONE 13*(8), e0200468.

Sommerville, J. A., Woodward, A. L., & Needham, A. (2005). Action experience alters 3-month-old infants' perception of others' actions. *Cognition, 96*(1), B1–B11.

Soska, K. C., & Adolph, K. E. (2014). Postural position constrains multimodal object exploration in infants. *Infancy, 19*(2), 138–161.

Spelke, E. S. (1990). Principles of object perception. *Cognitive Science, 14*(1), 29–56.

Spelke, E. S., Breinlinger, K., Macomber, J., & Jacobson, K. (1992). Origins of knowledge. *Psychological Review, 99*(4), 605–632.

Spelke, E. S., & Kinzler, K. D. (2007). Core knowledge. *Developmental Science, 10*(1), 89–96. doi: 10.1111/j.1467-7687.2007.00569.x

Stahl, A. E., & Feigenson, L. (2015). Observing the unexpected enhances infants' learning and exploration. *Science, 348*(6230), 91–94.

Wang, S., Baillargeon, B., & Paterson, S. (2005). Detecting continuity violations in infancy: a new account and new evidence from covering and tube events. *Cognition, 95*(2), 129–173.

14 Infant Categorization

Lisa M. Oakes

This chapter is about *categorization* in infancy. In general, *categories* refer to groups of objects in the world, and *concepts* refers to our mental representations of those categories. Whereas categories can refer to groups of objects based on any kind of similarity (e.g., shape, such as round things, function, such as things you throw), concepts often are thought to include information that goes beyond the perceptual, for example understanding that dogs and birds are both living things, and that airplanes and birds are different things despite similarity in shape and function. Categories and concepts have been described as "the glue that holds our mental world together" (Murphy, 2002, p. 1) and that without them "mental life would be chaotic" (E. E. Smith & Medin, 1981, p. 1). Therefore, categories, and the processes we use to form them, are central to cognition. As pointed out by Bruner, Goodnow, and Austin (1956), by forming categories we can efficiently and effectively store information about collections of items, rather than treating each individual object we encounter as unique and storing it independently. Categories and concepts allow us to make inferences about unseen properties of new items, such as whether a new object will eat or bite or make a sound when pushed. And categories are critical for language acquisition, as many words refer to labels for categories. It is therefore not surprising that for decades researchers have been interested in the developmental origins of categorization and the processes that allow categorization.

One challenge for the study of the developmental origins of categorization is that categories and concepts are not stable and unchanging, but rather are flexible, dynamic, and change over development, with experience, and in different contexts. Consider the object depicted in Figure 14.1. Perhaps you immediately categorize this object as a "coffee mug." You can label it this way; you consider the similarity between this coffee mug and other coffee mugs you have encountered; you believe you could use it to drink coffee, and so on. Although this may be your initial categorization of this item, you could actually include it in many other categories, and you likely would under other circumstances. It might belong to the category of things that are dirty and need to be put in the dishwasher, items that need to be packed in boxes labeled "kitchen" when planning a move, drinking vessels, or things that could be given as a joke gift exchange at the holidays. In fact, all of these are legitimate categories that

Figure 14.1. *A common item that can be categorized.*

might include the item depicted in Figure 14.1. And, your category of "coffee mug" might change over time and context as well. Initially, it may include only the mugs that came with a set of dishes, only later to include mugs like that shown here. Your child may make you a coffee mug in art class that bears no resemblance to this coffee mug, but nevertheless can be used to drink coffee and your child intended it for that purpose. The situation becomes even more complex when considering cultural differences in categories. What may be a legitimate category in one cultural context is nonsensical in another cultural context. The point is that categories and the processes of categorization are flexible, dynamic, and change over time.

The study of categorization in infancy is further complicated by a lack of agreement about how prelinguistic categories (and the processes used to form them) are related to superficially similar categories (and processes) used by older, linguistic individuals, and whether early categories can possibly be related to the rich, abstract concepts used by older children and adults thousands of times each day. Perhaps because it has been so difficult to resolve these issues, research on categorization in infancy has tended to focus on how infants form or respond to specific kinds of categories, such as animals (Mandler, Bauer, & McDonough, 1991; Oakes, Coppage, & Dingel, 1997; Quinn, Eimas, & Rosenkrantz, 1993), faces (Ramsey, Langlois, & Marti, 2005), and spatial relations (Casasola & Cohen, 2002). Other work has examined how language and categorization interact in infancy (Balaban & Waxman, 1997; Plunkett, Hu, & Cohen, 2008; Waxman & Braun, 2005).

The goal of this chapter is to provide an overview of what is known about categorization in infancy, with an eye to where the field is going into the future.

The first section describes what categorization *is*. The next section describes methods for studying infants' categorization and how we measure infants' categorization; in other words, how we know that infants are categorizing. The third section is about what develops in categorization, and factors that influence categorization. Throughout these sections, the discussion will focus on how advances in neuroscience have added to our understanding of infants' categorization, and how categorization in infancy is influenced by culture and context. Finally, the last section discusses future directions and policy implications.

14.1 What Is Categorization?

When we categorize, we group together items that are discriminable but share some commonality. That commonality may be perceptual (e.g., shades of red, four-legged animals) or nonperceptual (e.g., luxury items, vegetarians). The individual items within a category must be *discriminable* – if it is impossible to tell the items apart, we cannot know whether they are similar but different items versus different encounters with the same item. Thus, when items are not discriminable, or when encountering the same item in different contexts, the resulting representation is of a single object. When the items are discriminable, the resulting representation is of a collection of objects that share commonalities.

Categorization, therefore, is a process by which people (and other animals) group into a single mental representation multiple different items that share some commonality or set of commonalities. Concepts, in contrast, are the mental representations that result from the process of categorization (and perhaps other processes). This distinction is not always clear, and because of this lack of clarity there have been many heated debates about the nature of categories and concepts, and how the categories infants form are related (or unrelated) to the concepts prevalent in thought and representation by older individuals. For example, historically theorists debated whether representations of categories and concepts are abstract summaries or linked exemplars or individual instances (E. E. Smith & Medin, 1981). Contemporary research with adults has focused on how different brain structures support representation of category exemplars and abstractions (Mack, Love, & Preston, 2016; Weber, Thompson-Schill, Osherson, Haxby, & Parsons, 2009). Regardless of the nature of the representation, by categorizing and forming representations for groups of items such as *dog*, *fruit*, and *city*, we can more efficiently and effectively represent the world around us. When you hear a term such as "dog," you know the range of things that are included in that category (e.g., Poodles and Great Danes are both dogs, whereas Tabby cats and bunny rabbits are not); know what a *typical* item is (e.g., a Labrador is a more typical dog than a Chihuahua); and can make inferences about a new member of a category (e.g., you have expectations for what dogs eat, that they bark, and that they like to go on walks). Clearly categories help us organize a significant amount of information.

Despite the utility of categorization, it is not easy to find a single definition of *categorization* or *category* that is used across the literature. For example, some researchers, such as Murphy (2002, 2010), have argued that *categories* and *concepts* overlap to such an extent that it is not useful to treat them separately. Sloutsky and Deng (2017), in contrast, argue that *concepts*, but not *categories*, are *lexicalized*. This raises the possibility that adults, who are the primary subjects of Murphy's work, may have categories and concepts that are difficult to distinguish, but that at some points in development categories and concepts are distinct, especially during the period of language acquisition. Indeed, there are varying views about how infants' categories relate to later concepts. Often, this is discussed in terms of a perceptual-to-conceptual shift, with young infants possessing or forming categories primarily based on perceptual similarities (for example treating balls, round candles, and oranges as similar), and older children possessing conceptual categories based on other types of knowledge (for example, recognizing that dogs and birds are both living things, despite differences in appearance, and airplanes and birds are different kinds of things, despite similarities in form and function).

But, there is no single unified account for how such a shift might occur. According to Deng and Sloutsky's view, an individual without language – such as a prelinguistic infant – presumably can have categories but not concepts. In her seminal book, Mandler (2004) argues that concepts, but not categories, go beyond perceptual input. But unlike Deng and Sloutsky, Mandler did not believe that forming concepts requires language, and she and her colleagues provide data they interpret as prelinguistic infants having both concepts and perceptual categories. Quinn and his colleagues have argued for a mechanism by which perceptual categories gradually become enriched to form conceptual representations (Quinn & Eimas, 1997), a process that may involve but does not require language. Despite lively discussion of this issue, the field has not converged on common definitions of category and concept, or how they are related across development and/or the acquisition of language.

14.2 How Do We Know That Infants Are Categorizing?

How do we know that infants have formed a category or are capable of forming categories? As described earlier, one feature of categories is that people treat nonidentical items in the same way – e.g., call them by the same label, perform the same action on them, sort them into a group. Thus, we might argue that when infants treat objects in the same way they are responding to those objects as members of a category. However, infants have a limited repertoire of behaviors, and they exhibit those behaviors on a wide range of objects. For example, infants will stick their feet, blocks, the corner of a blanket, and a pacifier in their mouths. Although according to Piaget (1952) these may be examples of assimilating all these objects into the infants' *sucking scheme* (which might be considered a type of category), this indiscriminate sucking of *any* object does not seem to fit with the general notion that items within a category are treated similarly.

In addition, as mentioned earlier, we can only be certain that an individual is *categorizing* if they can discriminate the items. Clearly, we expect that the infant can discriminate between her own toes, a block, the corner of a blanket, and a pacifier. However, if an infant responds to any *ball* he sees by pushing it across the floor, how can we be certain that he actually can tell the difference between those balls? If he is unable to discriminate between the balls, then the fact that he performs the same action on the balls does not indicate that he has categorized them, but rather may reflect him performing the same action on what he perceives as a single object. Even if the infant selectively rolls balls and not other items (such as oranges), it is difficult to know whether performing the same action on all balls reflects the infant categorizing different balls in a single group (that excludes oranges), or whether the infant is performing this action on what he perceives to be different encounters with the same object (recognizing that oranges are different objects).

The point of these examples is that it is very difficult to determine whether infants recognize and form categories from their overt behavior. It is therefore not surprising that psychologists long thought infants incapable of categorizing (Gelman, 1978; Mervis & Rosch, 1981), a belief consistent with Piagetian views that classification was a concrete operational skill (Gelman, 1978). But, it also persisted because there was a lack of techniques that allowed researchers to assess infants' categorization abilities. Significant gains in our understanding of infants' categorization were made beginning in the late 1970s by adapting other methods to assess categorization abilities. The following sections discuss different kinds of evidence of categorization derived from different procedures.

14.2.1 Conditioning

Rovee-Collier and her colleagues (Greco, Hayne, & Rovee-Collier, 1990; Hayne, Rovee-Collier, & Perris, 1987) studied infant categorization using tasks that involved training infants to exhibit a behavioral response (kicking) through reinforcement (the movement of a mobile), and assessing their generalization of the learned behavior to new instances. Following her pioneering work using this task to study infant memory, Rovee-Collier asked whether infants who were trained on several different mobiles that conformed to a category (e.g., the mobile seen on each day was decorated with different colored As – red As on day 1, blue As on day 2, etc.) would show the same kind of learning and memory as would infants who were trained on a single mobile (e.g., red As on each training day). In fact, infants in both groups learned, but whereas infants trained with variable mobiles generalized their learned behavior (kicking) to a novel mobile from the same category (e.g., kicked when they saw a mobile decorated with a new color As), infants trained with only one mobile did not (Hayne et al., 1987). This was taken as evidence of categorization: Infants learned to respond in the same way to a collection of different mobiles that were similar in some way (e.g., decorated with different colored As), and they generalized their behavior to a new mobile from the same category. Although this task was useful for establishing that infants categorize, it was not widely used because infants have a small repertoire of behaviors that can be conditioned, and conditioning takes several sessions across several days.

14.2.2 Familiarization Test

The most common procedures to study infant categorization are variations of familiarization-test procedures. The first version was developed in the late 1970s and early 1980s, by adapting the habituation of looking-time procedure to assess infants' categorization. This technique had been used extensively to study aspects of infants' visual attention, perception, and memory (Cohen & Gelber, 1975), and was based on the observation that when infants were presented with the same stimulus on several successive trials, their looking time gradually decreased, or habituated. When subsequently shown a novel stimulus, infants' looking time increased, or they dishabituated. Initially researchers presented during the habituation phase only a single stimulus and then tested infants on a novel stimulus (see Figure 14.2A). For example, infants were habituated to one checkerboard and then tested with a new checkerboard (e.g., Cohen, DeLoache, & Rissman, 1975).

The study of infants' categorization was facilitated by the development of the "multiple habituation" procedure (Figure 14.2B), in which during habituation infants were shown several different items – for example several views of the same object, several faces showing the same facial expression, or several items from the same category. The logic was that if infants recognized the commonalities or similarities among the items, they would learn over trials those commonalities or similarities. The characteristic decrease in looking would indicate that infants had habituated to the common object, facial expression, or category rather than to an individual item. Infants' generalization to new exemplars was tested by assessing their looking to both new items from the familiar set (e.g., a new view of the object, a new face with the familiar facial expression, or a new member of the category) and new items from a completely different set (e.g., a different object, a different facial expression, or an item from a different category). If infants remember only the individual items (and not the category), then both novel items will be familiar. But, if they learned the category, the novel out-of-category item will be novel, but the novel item from within the familiar category will be familiar. Using this procedure, researchers established that before the onset of language infants are

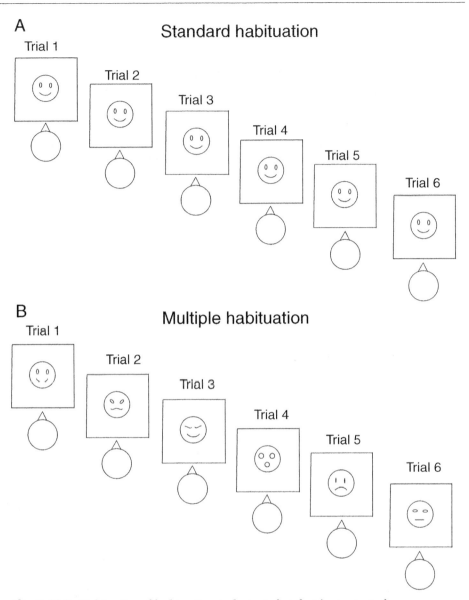

Figure 14.2. *Habituation of looking-time tasks to study infants' memory and discrimination (standard habituation) and categorization (multiple habituation). Source: From Oakes (2008). Copyright © 2008 Elsevier Inc. Reprinted with permission.*

sensitive to superordinate categories (e.g., "food" vs. "furniture"; G. S. Ross, 1980), basic-level categories (eg., "bird"; Roberts, 1988), and social categories (e.g., emotional expressions; Kestenbaum & Nelson, 1990).

Variations of this procedure have successfully shown that infants categorize. For example, Quinn and Eimas (Eimas & Quinn, 1994; Quinn et al., 1993) assessed categorization by presenting during familiarization a series of pairs of items from within a category (e.g., pairs of dogs, pairs of horses), and then presenting during a subsequent novelty preference test trial a new item from the familiar category paired with a new item from a novel category. With this procedure, 3- to 4-month-old infants have shown a "novelty" preference for the novel *category* (not the novel *object*) when familiarized with animal categories such as dog, cat, and horse (Eimas & Quinn, 1994; Quinn et al., 1993), as well as furniture categories such as bed and couch (Behl-Chadha, 1996). Oakes, Madole, and Cohen (1991) developed a familiarization-test task in which infants are given 3-D items to manipulate, look at, mouth, etc. As in any familiarization task, in this *object-examining* procedure, infants first are presented with a collection of items from within a category and then their exploration of, manipulation of, and attention to novel items within the familiar category and novel categories is assessed. This procedure has been used to demonstrate categorization in infants in the second half of the first year (K. T. Ferguson & Casasola, 2015; Kovack-Lesh & Oakes, 2007; Mandler & McDonough, 1998a; Oakes et al., 1997), and to ask how infants use information other than what objects look like, such as object *function* (Madole, Oakes, & Cohen, 1993).

14.2.3 Infants' Manipulation of Objects

The familiarization tasks differ in many ways from how categorization is assessed in older children and adults. Thus, researchers have developed other tasks that appear to be more active and intentional. For example, in an effort to approximate sorting tasks, Mandler and colleagues (Mandler et al., 1991; Mandler, Fivush, & Reznick, 1987) used the *sequential-touching task*, in which older infants and toddlers (typically 12- to 36-month-old children) are presented with two sets of items simultaneously (e.g., four animals and four vehicles) and their touching of the items is measured. Although they do not sort, the logic is that if infants recognize the categories presented, they will systematically touch items from within a category in sequence. Indeed, infants and toddlers in the second year sequentially touch categories such as animals versus vehicles (Mandler et al., 1991), kitchen things versus bathroom things (Mandler et al., 1987), and telephones versus hairbrushes (Arterberry & Bornstein, 2012).

Another more active task comes from adaptations of imitation procedures. In these tasks, which have been used with infants as young as 9 months, a model (experimenter) performs an action using props (e.g., giving a dog a drink from a cup), and then the child is given props to imitate the action. Importantly, the "actor" in the sequence of events (e.g., the dog) is different in the props given to the child than that used by the model. For example, if the model imitates a German Shepherd drinking from a cup, the question is whether infants will imitate that action with a novel dog, a cat, or even a car. Generally, by 12 months infants and toddlers generalize actions within categories of animates, including animals and people, but not across the distinction between animates and vehicles – for example, infants would imitate drinking when modeled a dog drinking and then given a cat as a prop, but would not imitate drinking when given a vehicle as a prop (Mandler & McDonough, 1998b; McDonough & Mandler, 1998; Poulin-Dubois, Frenkiel-Fishman, Samantha, & Johnson, 2006).

14.3 Evidence of Infant Categorization from Neuroscience Methods

Of course, one problem with each of the procedures described in the previous section is that they depend on infants' emitting an observable (voluntary) behavior. Advances in neuroscience have allowed researchers to probe for infants' categorization using brain responses. Specifically, scalp electroencephalography (EEG), in which electrical signals generated by brain activity are recorded via electrodes affixed to the scalp, can be used to assess infants' sensitivity to categories. Researchers time lock these signals to the onset of specific stimuli and the resulting averaged and filtered signal is called the event-related potential, or ERP (for a description of these methods in general see Luck, 2014). In adults, specific patterns of EEG activity or specific ERP waveforms have been associated with processes such as visual or auditory processing, semantic recognition, memory consolidation, and so on (Luck & Kappenman, 2011). The signals in infants are less clear and do not map directly onto the signals observed in adults, which can sometimes make it difficult to draw definitive conclusions from these procedures about infants' cognitive processes. Nevertheless, several researchers have shown systematic ERP responses that indicate sensitivity to categorical groupings. For example, ERPs are recorded as infants view items from a frequently presented category (80% of the time) and an infrequently presented category (20% of the time) – the *oddball*. In studies with 7-month-old infants, waveforms for the oddball and frequent categories differ when the two categories are different colors (Clifford, Franklin, Davies, & Holmes, 2009) or different object categories, such as animals versus people (Marinović, Hoehl, & Pauen, 2014). In rapid repetition procedures, in which two items are presented in succession, 7-month-old infants' ERPs to the second item varies when the two items are from two different categories (e.g., a dog and boat) but not when they are categorically related (e.g., two pieces of furniture) (Peykarjou, Wissner, & Pauen, 2017).

It is important to consider what these procedures reveal beyond what is uncovered with more traditional behavioral methods. One advantage of ERP methods in adults is that responses can be understood in terms of specific cognitive processing. By examining the timing of a response, the shape of the waveform, and approximately where the response was generated in the brain, researchers can determine whether the response is primarily sensory, related to language, or a function of attention, and so on. ERP responses in infants are not as easily classified. Because each ERP component reflects a number of cognitive processes, as well as activity by neurons in many different brain regions, infant ERP waveforms do not map directly onto adult ERP waveforms. In addition, although ERPs have been assessed in infants for decades, it has been difficult to identify the processes reflected by particular ERP components in infants except in very broad terms. Nevertheless, some conclusions based on variations in ERP waveforms have been drawn. In studies with 6-month-old infants, the negative central (Nc) component, which occurs within 500 ms of the stimulus onset and is thought to reflect attention, differs in response to categorical contrasts (Grossmann, Gliga, Johnson, & Mareschal, 2009; Quinn, Westerlund, & Nelson, 2006). ERP activity observed 1,000 ms after the stimulus onset, thought to reflect memory processes, varies as a function of category familiarity (Grossmann et al., 2009; Quinn et al., 2006). Thus, some aspects of categorization appear to involve early attentional processes and other aspects of categorization appear to involve later occurring memory processes. However, much work needs to be done in this area, and methods and analyses need to be carefully considered before drawing strong conclusions (see Luck & Gaspelin, 2017, for a discussion of how ERP results can be misleading).

14.4 What Develops in Infants' Categorization?

The previous section demonstrates categorical responding in infancy, confirming that infants do categorize and are sensitive to many adult-defined categorical distinctions. This work provides a foundation for understanding the origins and early development of categorization. Next, it is important to consider how categorization develops in infancy and early childhood.

14.4.1 The Origins of Categorization

There is robust evidence that by 3 to 4 months infants are sensitive to object categories such as cats, dogs, and horses (Eimas & Quinn, 1994; Oakes & Ribar, 2005; Quinn et al., 1993), and even some evidence of sensitivity to object categories at 2 months (Quinn & Johnson, 2000). However, there is little evidence that newborn infants are sensitive to such categories. Quinn, Slater, Brown, and Hayes (2001) tested newborn infants' sensitivity to *form* categories (triangles, squares, circles, and crosses) and found that although 3-month-old infants responded to these categories, newborn infants did not. Turati, Simion, and Zanon (2003) did find that infants less than 3 days old showed a novelty preference for the new item from the new category following familiarization with either open shapes (cross, X) or closed shapes (circle, square). For example, infants preferred a new open shape if they had been familiarized with a collection of closed shapes. Importantly, Turati et al. (2003) also showed that newborn infants can discriminate between the items within the class.

Does the lack of strong evidence of categorization in newborns mean that categorization does not emerge until later? The fact that there are few published studies on categorization in newborns does not necessarily mean that newborns do not have the capacity to categorize. Newborn infants are notoriously difficult to study, and there are few research teams who undertake studies of infants in the first postnatal weeks. Thus, the lack of a large literature may simply reflect the fact that there have been few attempts to demonstrate categorization in newborn infants. We may have better evidence of categorization abilities present at birth by examining other literatures. For example, although there are few studies of newborn infants' categorization of *visual* stimuli, there is a larger literature demonstrating newborn infants' categorization of speech sounds (Aldridge, Stillman, & Bower, 2001; Bertoncini, Bijeljac-Babic, Jusczyk, Kennedy, & Mehler, 1988; Eimas, Siqueland, Jusczyk, & Vigorito, 1971). These studies often do not include evidence that infants can actually discriminate the individual exemplars, however, making it difficult to know if infants respond categorically simply because they are unable to hear the differences between the sounds within categories. Given that even adults have difficulty discriminating exemplars within a speech category, it is not clear how categorical perception of speech sounds relates to other aspects of categorization, but this work does show that from birth infants are sensitive to features that map onto categories for older individuals. Newborn infants also treat as similar different viewpoints of the same object, for example recognizing commonalities in views of an object that vary in retinal size (Slater, Mattock, & Brown, 1990) or slant (Slater & Morison, 1985). Although not clearly the same process as recognizing commonalities across a collection of dogs that differ in color, markings, and other features, the ability to recognize commonalities across different views of an object may reflect the rudiments of categorization ability.

Even if researchers attempted to examine newborn infants' object categories, they may often observe failure. That is, despite evidence that newborn infants have many of the basic abilities that would allow them to form categories, it may be very difficult for newborn infants to recognize categories such as dog versus cat or even animals versus vehicles. At birth, infants' categorization of speech sounds may be more advanced than their categorization of visual object categories simply because their auditory system is more developed than their visual system. At birth, infants' visual acuity is extremely poor (Johnson, 2011), making it unlikely that they can accurately make out details of objects that helps them to differentiate them. Given the poor state of their color vision (Brown, 1990), they are not likely to be able to use color cues to differentiate natural objects either. In addition, infants have extensive prenatal experience with human speech (DeCasper & Spence, 1986; Gervain, 2015), whereas they have no exposure to visual object categories. The point is that infants may have the cognitive abilities required to detect commonalities among visual items, and to form perceptual representations that reflect those commonalities, but their visual abilities do not allow them to perceive the similarities and differences among items that support that categorization.

Indeed, French, Mermillod, Quinn, Chauvin, and Mareschal (2002) suggested that young infants' poor visual abilities may actually bootstrap categorization. That is, using a computational model, French and colleagues found they could replicate infants' categorization performance by reducing the model's visual acuity. Much like the "less-is-more" idea in language development (Elman, 1993; Newport, 1990), the idea is that poor visual acuity reduces the amount of information to be processed actually supporting infants' ability to detect commonalities in the visual information available. In addition, French et al. (2002) suggest that the information that remained when visual acuity was reduced supported categorization at a global level, which appears to be the first level categorized by young infants. Despite this promising start, little research has attempted to understand newborns' abilities and limitations with respect to categorization. However, there is little doubt that the basic components of categorization – detecting commonalities, forming associations, representing information – are present from birth.

14.4.2 Perceptual Versus Conceptual Categorization

Using visual familiarization techniques, researchers have shown that infants between 2 and 7 months of age respond to a wide variety of adult-defined categories including cats versus dogs (Oakes & Ribar, 2005; Quinn et al., 1993) and furniture versus mammals (Behl-Chadha, 1996; Quinn & Johnson, 2000), male versus female faces (Quinn, Yahr, Kuhn, Slater, & Pascalis, 2002; Rennels & Kayl, 2017; Rennels, Kayl, Langlois, Davis, & Orlewicz, 2016), and emotional expressions (Kestenbaum & Nelson, 1990). There is broad agreement that these early categories are *perceptual*, and that such categories reflect infants' detection of the visible features of the items.

Indeed, infants' perceptual categories vary as a function of stimulus features. Quinn et al. (1993) found that 3- to 4-month-old infants differentiated images of *cats* from *dogs* if they were familiarized with cats, but not if they were familiarized with dogs. On close inspection, Quinn and colleagues discovered that their dog stimuli were more variable than the cat stimuli. In a follow-up study, infants familiarized with a less variable collection of dogs did differentiate dogs from cats when familiarized with dogs. Oakes et al. (1997) found a similar effect in 10-month-old infants' categorization of *land animals* versus *sea animals* in an object-examining task. Ribar, Oakes, and Spalding (2004) found that infants could form a very narrow category, one that included only black and white land animals, if the familiarization set supported that category. Similar effects of the range of variability and distribution of items during familiarization have been reported by Plunkett and colleagues for infants' categorization of schematic drawings of animals (Gliozzi, Mayor, Hu, & Plunkett, 2009).

Infants' perceptual categories have many of the same properties of categories formed by adults. Infants form average prototypes when learning novel categories of unfamiliar animal-like stimuli or human faces (Cohen & Strauss, 1979; Younger, 1985). They treat as most familiar an average prototype, even when that item had never before been seen (de Haan, Johnson, Maurer, & Perrett, 2001), just as has been observed in adult participants (Homa & Vosburgh, 1976; Posner & Keele, 1968; J. D. Smith & Minda, 1998). Infants also remember individual exemplars of categories (Oakes & Kovack-Lesh, 2013; Younger, 1990), suggesting that they not only form an average prototype, but like adults both remember individual items and form a prototype (Goldstone, Kersten, & Carvalho, 2018; J. D. Smith & Minda, 1998). The point is that many of the processes used to form novel perceptual categories are similar to the processes used by adults when learning artificial categories in the lab.

Despite the evidence that infants form perceptual categories, and that those perceptual categories are similar in many ways to adults' categories, the question remains how these perceptual categories provide a developmental foundation for *concepts*. As described earlier, many have argued that concepts are fundamentally different from the perceptual categories formed early in infancy. Mandler (2004), for example, argues that *concepts* are more closely linked to *declarative memory* or knowledge, whereas perceptual categories are more like *procedural knowledge*. She argues that through a process of *perceptual meaning analysis*, infants translate perceptual information into accessible, conceptual knowledge. Thus, for Mandler there are two separate systems of knowledge, with distinct developmental trajectories. Others have argued for a developmental continuum from early developing perceptual categories to more conceptual representations (Quinn & Eimas, 1997; Rakison & Lupyan, 2008; Westermann & Mareschal, 2012). According to these approaches, early categories formed by detecting perceptual commonalities are enriched through associations with nonobvious features, object labels, and other information. This enrichment allows infants to go beyond visible perceptual commonalities to link nonobvious features to categories without engaging a separate process or set of representations.

Regardless of which perspective one adopts, it is useful to consider what evidence we have that infants have *conceptual representations* – that is, whether their categories reflect more than (visual) perceptual similarities among the items, and include richer, higher-level information. Mandler and her colleagues have argued that the presence of global, superordinate-like, or contextual categories early in infancy suggests that these categories are conceptual rather than perceptual. That is, infants' categories such as "things found in the kitchen" (Mandler et al., 1987) or "vehicles" (including a car, motorcycle, and boat) (Mandler et al., 1991; Mandler & McDonough, 1993) must be based on information other than perceptual similarities. Of course, it is possible that some of these categories are formed through associations (e.g., associations between high chairs, bibs, and bananas may be formed through repeated experience with those items together). But, because Mandler and McDonough (1993) reported that 7- to 11-month-old infants responded to the perceptually diverse categories of *animals* and *vehicles* as separate, they concluded that at least by 9 months infants make a "conceptual differentiation of animals and vehicles as different kinds of things" (p. 312).

This claim has been the source of controversy. Several studies using sequential touching tasks raise questions about the foundation of toddlers' attention to diverse, superordinate categories. For example, Rakison and Butterworth (1998) demonstrated that toddlers' attention to the animal–vehicle distinction is influenced by the presence of functional *parts* (e.g., legs and wheels). Mareschal and Tan (2007) reported that 18-month-old infants' categorization of items that fell in the animal–vehicle distinction was predicted by perceptual similarity. Clearly, infants' attention to superordinate categories may reflect conceptual understanding, but given findings about infants' use of perceptual similarity when making those judgments, it is impossible to know for certain when infants are engaged in *conceptual* categorization, grouping based on perceptual similarity, or some combination.

A second way of examining whether infants' categorization is conceptual is to probe their recognition of nonobvious features. The logic is that if infants' categorization goes beyond the perceptual features, they will include in their categories nonperceptual features (e.g., what actions can be performed on a category of objects) and generalize nonperceptual features (e.g., which objects drink from cups) to new category members. For example, researchers have asked whether infants use object *function*, which is presumably a nonperceptual feature, in their categorization. Horst, Oakes, and Madole (2005) observed that 10-month-old infants habituated to a series of events in which a variety of different objects appeared to have the same function (e.g., a hand reached in and performed the same action on each object), apparently forming a category of diverse items based on their shared function. Similarly, Booth, Schuler, and Zajicek (2010) found that 16-month-old toddlers detected commonality in function in a familiarization task. Träuble and Pauen (2007) used an object-examining task and found that demonstrating the function of to-be-categorized items influence 11- to 12-month-old infants' categorization. Thus, at least in familiarization tasks, infants and toddlers use common functions to categorize items.

Other work has shown the conditions under which infants *infer* that items have the same function or nonobvious property. That is, showing that infants *can* form categories based on function does not provide insight into whether they are drawn to more "perceptual" or "conceptual" features. The studies examining the effect of object function on infants' categorization do hint to the power of function (relative to perceptual features) on infants' categorization, but drawing such conclusions is difficult. Stronger conclusions have been drawn from the inductive generalization task by Mandler and McDonough (Mandler & McDonough, 1998b; McDonough & Mandler, 1998). In these studies, infants between 7 and 12 months would imitate a model making animals drink from cups, but would not generalize to vehicles. That is, their imitation generalized only within conceptual boundaries, leading Mandler and McDonough to conclude that infants' understanding of distinctions such as animal versus vehicle did not solely reflect perceptual features or similarities (e.g., has legs vs. has wheels), but also reflects their conceptual understanding of this distinction. For Mandler and McDonough, the imitation pattern infants exhibited reflected the "knowledge base that year-old infants have built up about animals and vehicles" (Mandler & McDonough, 1998b, p. 89).

However, others have shown how perceptual similarity or specific features influence infants' generalization in this task. Rakison (2007), for example, found that infants only generalized appropriate actions when items shared the same parts (e.g., legs or wheels), even though the actions did not require those parts. Graham and her colleagues found that infants' and toddlers' generalization of actions performed on novel objects (i.e., objects created by the experimenters for the purpose of the study) is highly influenced by perceptual similarity (Graham, Kilbreath, & Welder, 2004; Welder & Graham, 2001). Thus, although some of the findings with this task may reflect conceptual knowledge that infants have acquired before coming to the lab, this task can certainly be used to examine infants' use of perceptual similarity to construct knowledge in the moment.

14.4.3 Language and Infants' Categorization

The early work on infants' categorization was motivated, in part, on determining whether prelinguistic infants form categories (see Mervis, 1985). It is therefore not surprising that a number of studies have examined the interaction between language and categorization in infancy. Infants' early vocabulary seems to reflect categorization, as a large proportion of children's first words are object categories such as *car*, *doll*, and *shoe* (Fenson et al., 1994). Moreover, L. B. Smith and colleagues have argued that children's learning of labels for categories defined by shape (such as *car*, *doll*, and *shoe*) contributes to their future language learning (L. B. Smith, Jones, Landau, Gershkoff-Stowe, & Samuelson, 2002).

A number of studies have shown that infants' categorization both of familiar items (e.g., rabbits, animals) and novel categories can be enhanced by the use of a common label. Typically, in these studies infants are shown a series of familiarization or habituation trials with items from one category (e.g., a series of rabbits), and for some children the category is labeled (e.g., "look, it's a rabbit") and for other children the items are presented in silence or with a non-labeling utterance ("look at that"). Following familiarization, infants' looking on trials with novel items from within the category (e.g., a novel rabbit) and novel items from a contrasting category (e.g., a pig) is measured. Using variations of this procedure, researchers have found that infants who hear a consistent label across familiarization show a greater preference for (i.e., look longer at) the novel out-of-category items than novel items within the familiar category (Balaban & Waxman, 1997; Waxman & Braun, 2005). Using several different labels does not have the same effect (Waxman & Braun, 2005). Other work suggests that for young infants any linguistic sound can have this effect, although nonlinguistic tones do not (Ferry, Hespos, & Waxman, 2010).

Clearly, therefore, hearing and learning object labels affects children's categorization. The question is *why*. For some, labels are category markers or invitations to form categories (B. Ferguson & Waxman, 2017). In this view, linguistic input has a special status that *induces* or *invites* categorization specifically. Using a common word to label items highlights similarities and promotes the formation of a category of those items. Others have argued that labels act as a *feature* of categories (Deng & Sloutsky, 2015; Gliozzi et al., 2009), at least early in development. According to this view, labels are not category markers, but rather are another common feature of the items. This is a subtle difference, but it is based on the idea that common labels *are* a common feature of within-category items, rather than a specific cue that induces the process of categorization. For example, Plunkett et al. (2008) observed that when familiarized with a collection of schematic animals that could either be included in a single category or divided into two categories, 10-month-old infants who heard the same consistent label on each familiarization trial formed a single category that included all the schematic animals, and infants who heard two labels during familiarization (one when presented with items from one subcategory and the other when presented with items from the other subcategory) formed two categories. Thus, whether or not infants responded to the single global category or the two subcategories was determined by how the items were labeled during familiarization. Althaus and Westermann (2016) found similar results with a very different stimulus set. Furthermore, category labels or auditory signals can actually interfere with infants' learning of visual categories (Robinson & Sloutsky, 2007), and in at least one experiment infants learned categories defined by *motion* better than categories defined by a common *label* (Deng & Sloutsky, 2015).

This issue is not yet resolved. It is clear that labels facilitate infants' category formation, and that infants form different categories in the presence of consistent labels. One way to answer these questions is to understand how infants use words or labels versus other kinds of cues to categorization. Some studies examining the effect of nonlinguistic sounds, such as tones, have shown no benefit for infants' categorization (Ferry et al., 2010; Fulkerson & Waxman, 2007; Goldwater, Brunt, & Echols, 2018; Waxman & Markow, 1995). It is important to point out that this work has been limited to a small set of nonlinguistic auditory cues, and has been conducted primarily by one research group. Although this work has provided valuable insight into this process, additional work with a variety of acoustic signals is needed. For example, some work suggests that other signals, such as nonhuman vocalizations, are effective at influencing categorization in infants under 6 months, but not in infants older than 6 months (Ferry, Hespos, & Waxman, 2013). A resolution to this issue will require a systematic study of a variety of cues to categorization.

14.5 Social and Cultural Influences on Infants' Categorization

Infants' categorization does not occur in isolation. Categories are formed as infants interact with parents, caregivers, siblings, and others. Indeed, many aspects of categorization in infancy reflect this effect of social factors. A very salient example is how the language spoken to infants and young children influences the categories they form. L. B. Smith and colleagues found that children acquiring English as their first language learned to focus on shape-based categories as they learned labels for categories of objects with similar shapes (L. B. Smith et al., 2002). And, children learning different languages (that emphasize different kinds of nouns) have different categorization knowledge and structures (Yoshida & Smith, 2001).

But the effect of context and culture go beyond the language spoken around the child. Kovack-Lesh, Horst, and Oakes (2008), for example, observed that 4-month-old infants' categorization of cat and dog images was related to whether or not they had a pet dog or cat at home. Apparently, living with a dog or cat gave young infants daily experience viewing that animal, and that experience shaped how they formed categories and represented images presented in a laboratory context. Similar effects of experience have been observed for infants' representation of faces. Although little work has been done with infants' categorization of faces based on race, research has examined infants' developing sensitivity to the differences between individual faces from own- (familiar) race faces and other- (novel) race faces. At 3 months, infants can differentiate between individual faces from familiar and unfamiliar races, but by 9 months infants can only differentiate between faces from familiar races; they seem to be insensitive to the differences between individual faces from unfamiliar racial categories (Kelly et al., 2007). This is not precisely evidence of experience on categorization, but it suggests that experience with faces of one race influence how infants process faces as a function of racial category. Similar effects have been observed for infants' differentiation of human versus monkey faces; young infants are sensitive to between-individual differences in both human and monkey faces, and older infants are sensitive between-individual differences only in human faces (Pascalis, de Haan, & Nelson, 2002). Moreover, experimentally manipulating infants' everyday experience with monkey faces helps infants maintain their ability to discriminate between individual monkey faces (Pascalis et al., 2005; Scott & Monesson, 2009). These types of effects have also been observed for infants' perception of speech sounds, which are shaped by the language they hear (for a comparison of the effects of experience on speech and face perception see Maurer & Werker, 2014).

The effect of experience is also evident in asymmetries in infants' categorization, particularly in their categorization of human faces. Specifically, infants' categorization of female faces is advanced relative to their categorization of male faces (Quinn et al., 2002; Ramsey et al., 2005). Presumably such effects

reflect the fact that more infants have female primary caregivers, and these differences reflect their increased exposure to and experience with female faces
(Rennels & Kayl, 2017). Indeed, when examined in the lab, infants who have
more exposure to and experience with male caregivers show different patterns
of responding to male and female faces (Quinn et al., 2002; Rennels et al., 2017).

Although not well understood, it is likely that parents and caregivers interact with infants in ways that shape their categorization. Bornstein, Arterberry,
Mash, and Manian (2010) found that they could induce differences in infants'
categorization by providing objects to parents and having them play with those
objects at home for a period of time before infants' categorization was tested
in the lab. Manipulations like this demonstrate that home experience can shape
infants' responses in laboratory tasks. Other work has shown that instructing
parents to provide infants with specific experience reaching for and manipulating objects at home induces differences in how infants explore and investigate
objects in the lab (Libertus & Needham, 2010; Wiesen, Watkins, & Needham,
2016). Moreover, the social interaction in these experiences seems to be an
important component for inducing these differences (Libertus & Needham,
2014). This work has not yet been extended to the study of categorization per
se, but given that infants' categorization is likely influenced by their manipulation and exploration of objects, it seems likely that such interactions also influence the ways in which infants categorize the objects they encounter.

This potential is seen most clearly from work with toddlers demonstrating
that the kinds of words used with young children can determine how they generalize new labels to categories of items. When children hear and learn more
labels for shape-based categories, they develop an expectation that words refer
to categories based on shape (L. B. Smith, Jones, & Landau, 1996). In this case,
as children learn language – through social interactions – they detect statistical
regularities that influence their expectations for forming categories. Indeed,
L. B. Smith and colleagues found that they could actually induce these strategies in children by giving them experience in the lab that emphasized labeling shape-based categories (L. B. Smith et al., 2002). Moreover, as described
above, cultural differences in how adults speak to children seem to be responsible, at least in part, for cultural differences in categorization. For example,
Yoshida and Smith (2001) found that not only did Japanese- and English-
speaking mothers use different types of nouns with their young children, but
that Japanese-learning and English-learning children had different concepts
for *animates* that seemed to reflect those language differences.

It should be clear that little work has directly examined social and cultural
influences on infant categorization, despite the recognition that there are significant cultural influences on categorization by adults and older children
(Medin, Lynch, Coley, & Atran, 1997; N. Ross, Medin, Coley, & Atran, 2003).
Nevertheless, infants' categorization must be influenced by social interactions
and social influences. Future work can make use of the methods described
in the preceding paragraphs to examine asymmetries in categorization as a

function of social influences, examining the effect of experimentally manipulating social interactions, or evaluating statistical regularities infants may learn as a function of their social interactions. The point is that conclusions about the role of social influences on infants' categorization requires more systematic study aimed at addressing these specific questions.

14.6 Neural Underpinnings of Infants' Categorization

Clearly, infants' developing categorization abilities are related to their developing neural structures. However, the neural underpinnings of *categorization* per se are not well understood. Despite the increase in the use of methods such as EEG to study infants' neural responses during categorization, the studies have primarily focused on providing additional information *that* infants categorize, not on providing understanding into the neural underpinnings of infants' categorization.

To be clear, there is a large literature aimed at understanding the neural underpinnings of adults' categorization and concept representation. This work suggests that concept representation is distributed across multiple systems. For example, Martin (2016) argued that object concepts, such as *pencil*, are represented in the perception, action, and emotion systems. Thus, the locations of object concept representations can be predicted from our knowledge of the spatial layout of the perceptual, action, and emotion processing systems. Huth, Nishimoto, Vu, and Gallant (2012) argued that semantic information is represented widely over the cortex, with semantic space reflecting dimensions such as *animate* versus *nonanimate*.

Clearly, if the neural underpinnings of conceptual representations are based on understanding connectivity between or patterns of distributed activity across different brain regions during concept formation and recognition (Huth et al., 2012; Mahon, 2015), it will be difficult to identify the origins of such neural underpinnings in early childhood. We currently do not have the tools to ask how these networks and connections operate during the formation, recognition, and representation of categories in young infants.

Rather, as described earlier, researchers can use EEG and ERP methods to examine differences in infants' responses to categories. These methods allow us to determine that infants are sensitive to categorical distinctions, as well as to establish some of the neural signatures of the category response. For example, Marinović et al. (2014) found that when tested with an oddball procedure contrasting humans and animals, 7-month-old infants showed a systematic ERP response to the infrequently occurring category whereas 4-month-old infants did not. This is despite behavioral evidence showing sensitivity to the human–animal distinction at 4 months (Quinn, Lee, Pascalis, & Slater, 2007).

Researchers also ask whether infants' differential ERP responses to novel and familiar category items occur relatively early or relatively late, suggesting *perceptual* (early ERP) or *memory* (late ERP) processes. For example, Grossmann et al. (2009) found that when tested with categories such as *birds* versus *fish*, 6-month-old infants had relatively later responses localized over anterior cortical regions when discriminating *between* categories, but had relatively early responses localized over posterior regions when processing individual items. Similarly, Dixon et al. (2017) observed stronger early (P1) responses when 9-month-old infants were engaged in learning individual monkey faces as compared to when they were learning a category of monkey faces. In this study, 9-month-old infants showed stronger responses later in Nc and P400 components during categorization. Quinn and colleagues (Quinn, Doran, Reiss, & Hoffman, 2010; Quinn et al., 2006), in contrast, reported that 6-month-old infants' response to items within a category occurred later than did their response to items from a new category. These studies used different experimental designs, examined different aspects of the ERP waveform, and focused on different scalp placements of the electrodes. Any of these differences may contribute to varying results, but it is clear that it is difficult to evaluate the neural underpinnings of infants' categorization from this literature. To be clear, such studies are important for demonstrating that we can examine aspects of infants' categorization using ERPs, but the field requires agreement about the methods to use, electrode sites to evaluate, and aspects of the waveforms to focus on to generate a more consistent body of work.

14.7 Future Directions and Policy Implications

The preceding sections support a biopsychosocial view of the development of categorization. Variations in infants' categorization across time and context reflect their cognitive capacities to make comparisons, to detect commonalities, and form memories, as well as their social interactions, cultural context, and the development of their neurological processes.

This makes considering the *early* development of categorization challenging. As described here, from early in infancy the basic abilities to form categories likely are present. Newborn infants can form visual memories, they habituate and dishabituate (suggesting the capacity to make comparisons and detect similarities and differences), and they demonstrate aspects of object recognition closely related to categorization. However, does this mean that newborn infants categorize? And how are those categories related to the categories later in development?

Future research on infants' categorization should consider multiple factors. For example, one approach is to understand how categorization is related to infants' developing memory processes. Research with adults suggests that the neural structures that subserve memory representations are also involved in representations of categories and concepts. For example, Mack et al. (2016; Mack, Love, & Preston, 2017) have argued that hippocampal activity is responsible not only for forming memories of individual objects (and experiences or episodes with those objects), but also for conceptual representations. Some researchers have connected memory and categorization processes in infants. Oakes and Kovack-Lesh (2007), for example, point out that the procedures used to assess infants' categorization actually evaluate their *memory* for categories, and that infants must form the relevant category in these tasks by encoding and representing individual items before detecting and encoding commonalities among the items. Westermann and Mareschal (2012) proposed that infant categorization reflects both a hippocampally based fast learning system for representing within-category information and cortically based slow learning system that allows infants to incorporate background knowledge and experience.

Models like those described by Westermann and Mareschal (2012) are likely to advance an understanding into the development of categorization. Such models can also address critical questions about the neural underpinnings of categorization, and provide direction to guide future research as advances in technology and methods allow us better ways of evaluating the development of brain responses during memory formation and categorization.

In addition, research should focus on how social interactions shape categorization. A number of studies suggest that infants' categorization incorporates their previous experience – for example, categorization of animals reflects infants' pet experience (Kovack-Lesh et al., 2008). *Language* may be one type of social interaction that has a particularly powerful influence on infants' categorization. For example, toddlers' attention to shape-based categories is related to the words they learn that refer to shape-based categories (L. B. Smith et al., 2002), and using a consistent label for category exemplars can facilitate infants' attention to the category (Waxman & Braun, 2005). These findings suggest that categorization and language are inextricably linked, although there is significant disagreement about the nature of that link. However, it is clear that future research should consider the ways in which infants' and young children's social interactions, and language in particular, may shape their categorization processes.

Finally, future research should continue to examine the neural underpinnings of infants' categorization. The existing literature has revealed clever experimental procedures and some results that demonstrate the potential of this approach to add to our understanding of infants' categorization. However, a full understanding of the role of changes in the neural structures that support categorization will require agreed-upon standards on how to record and evaluate brain responses in infancy.

Categorization in early childhood has not been the focus of social policy. Indeed, it is not immediately apparent how social policy could influence categorization, or what the goal of such policy would be. However, understanding contextual and cultural influences on categorization may reveal social policy implications. For example, a large number of children being raised in poverty are exposed to multiple languages; however, there is not always support for raising bilingual children (e.g., immersion school programs, supporting parents who speak multiple languages or who are not fluent in the dominant language). Recently, Kroll and Dussias (2017) suggested that developmental advantages for bilingual infants may overcome the disadvantages of being raised in poverty.

Indeed, research does suggest that bilingual infants' developing cognitive skills differ from that of monolingual infants, and that they may have some advantages with respect to conceptual development. In infants as young as 6 months, bilingual and monolingual experience seems to have differential influences on visual attention (Comishen, Bialystok, & Adler, 2019), supporting the idea that from an early age the input for categorization differs as a function of language experience. A more direct example is that the effect of language on categorization also differs as a function of language experience. For example, in contrast to the work showing that monolingual infants have different expectations when hearing one versus two labels, bilingual infants as young at 9 months seem insensitive to this difference (Byers-Heinlein, 2017). It is not immediately clear how this difference in how infants interpret the use of one versus two words in references to objects, but it is a difference that may translate to differences in categorization. Work with older children suggests that monolingual and bilingual children differently understand the mutual exclusivity constraint when learning novel names for objects (Groba et al., 2019), and even by 17 months toddlers already differently interpret object labels as a function of language experience (Kandhadai, Hall, & Werker, 2017). Clearly further work needs to be done, but from a social policy perspective, it may be that the best support for the development of categorization in low-income families will be in encouraging and facilitating bilingualism.

In conclusion, the field has made great strides in our understanding of infants' categorization, demonstrating that categorization abilities are evident during the first postnatal months. In addition, the literature as a whole shows how infants' developing categorization abilities are multiply determined by their cognitive structures, social interactions, and maturation of neural systems. Our understanding of the development of categorization in infancy will be advanced in future research that examines how these forces work together.

References

Aldridge, M. A., Stillman, R. D., & Bower, T. G. R. (2001). Newborn categorization of vowel-like sounds. *Developmental Science, 4*, 220–232.

Althaus, N., & Westermann, G. (2016). Labels constructively shape object categories in 10-month-old infants. *Journal of Experimental Child Psychology, 151*, 5–17.

Arterberry, M. E., & Bornstein, M. H. (2012). Categorization of real and replica objects by 14- and 18-month-old infants. *Infant Behavior and Development, 35*, 606–612.

Balaban, M. T., & Waxman, S. R. (1997). Do words facilitate object categorization in 9-month-old infants? *Journal of Experimental Child Psychology, 64*, 3–26.

Behl-Chadha, G. (1996). Basic-level and superordinate-like categorical representations in early infancy. *Cognition*, *60*, 105–141.

Bertoncini, J., Bijeljac-Babic, R., Jusczyk, P. W., Kennedy, L. J., & Mehler, J. (1988). An investigation of young infants' perceptual representations of speech sounds. *Journal of Experimental Psychology: General*, *117*, 21–33.

Booth, A. E., Schuler, K., & Zajicek, R. (2010). Specifying the role of function in infant categorization. *Infant Behavior and Development*, *33*, 672–684.

Bornstein, M. H., Arterberry, M. E., Mash, C., & Manian, N. (2010). Discrimination of facial expression by 5-month-old infants of nondepressed and clinically depressed mothers. *Infant Behavior and Development*, *34*, 100–106.

Brown, A. M. (1990). Development of visual sensitivity to light and color vision in human infants: A critical review. *Vision Research*, *30*, 1159–1188.

Bruner, J., Goodnow, J., & Austin, G. (1956). *A study of thinking*. New York, NY: Wiley.

Byers-Heinlein, K. (2017). Bilingualism affects 9-month-old infants' expectations about how words refer to kinds. *Developmental Science*, *20*, e12486.

Casasola, M., & Cohen, L. B. (2002). Infant categorization of containment, support and tight-fit spatial relationships. *Developmental Science*, *5*, 247–264.

Clifford, A., Franklin, A., Davies, I. R. L., & Holmes, A. (2009). Electrophysiological markers of categorical perception of color in 7-month-old infants. *Brain and Cognition*, *71*, 165–172.

Cohen, L. B., DeLoache, J. S., & Rissman, M. W. (1975). The effect of stimulus complexity on infant visual attention and habituation. *Child Development*, *46*, 611–617.

Cohen, L. B., & Gelber, E. R. (1975). Infant visual memory. In L. B. Cohen & P. Salapatek (Eds.), *Infant perception: From sensation to cognition. Volume I: Basic visual Processes* (pp. 347–404). New York, NY: Academic Press.

Cohen, L. B., & Strauss, M. S. (1979). Concept acquisition in the human infant. *Child Development*, *50*, 419–424.

Comishen, K. J., Bialystok, E., & Adler, S. A. (2019). The impact of bilingual environments on selective attention in infancy. *Developmental Science*, *22*(4), e12797.

de Haan, M., Johnson, M. H., Maurer, D., & Perrett, D. I. (2001). Recognition of individual faces and average face prototypes by 1- and 3-month-old infants. *Cognitive Development*, *16*, 659–678.

DeCasper, A. J., & Spence, M. J. (1986). Prenatal maternal speech influences newborns' perception of speech sounds. *Infant Behavior and Development*, *9*, 133–150.

Deng, W. S., & Sloutsky, V. M. (2015). Linguistic labels, dynamic visual features, and attention in infant category learning. *Journal of Experimental Child Psychology*, *134*, 62–77.

Dixon, K. C., Reynolds, G. D., Romano, A. C., Roth, K. C., Stumpe, A. L., Guy, M. W., & Mosteller, S. M. (2017). Neural correlates of individuation and categorization of other-species faces in infancy. *Neuropsychologia*, *18*, 126–127.

Eimas, P. D., & Quinn, P. C. (1994). Studies on the formation of perceptually based basic-level categories in young infants. *Child Development*, *65*, 903–917.

Eimas, P. D., Siqueland, E. R., Jusczyk, P., & Vigorito, J. (1971). Speech perception in infants. *Science*, *171*, 303–306.

Elman, J. L. (1993). Learning and development in neural networks: The importance of starting small. *Cognitive Psychology*, *48*, 71–99.

Fenson, L., Dale, P. S., Reznick, J. S., Bates, E., Thal, D. J., Pethick, S. J., ... Stiles, J. (1994). Variability in early communicative development. *Monographs of the Society for Research in Child Development, 59*, i.

Ferguson, B., & Waxman, S. R. (2017). Linking language & categorization in infancy. *Journal of Child Language, 44*(3), 527–552.

Ferguson, K. T., & Casasola, M. (2015). Are you an animal too? US and Malawian infants' categorization of plastic and wooden animal replicas. *Infancy, 20*, 189–207.

Ferry, A. L., Hespos, S. J., & Waxman, S. R. (2010). Categorization in 3- and 4-month-old infants: An advantage of words over tones. *Child Development, 81*, 472–479.

(2013). Nonhuman primate vocalizations support categorization in very young human infants. *Proceedings of the National Academy of Sciences of the United States of America, 110*, 15231–15235.

French, R. M., Mermillod, M., Quinn, P. C., Chauvin, A., & Mareschal, D. (2002). The importance of starting blurry: Simulating improved basic-level category learning in infants due to weak visual acuity. In *Proceedings of the 24th Annual Conference of the Cognitive Science Society* (pp. 322–327). Mahwah, NJ: Lawrence Erlbaum Associates.

Fulkerson, A. L., & Waxman, S. R. (2007). Words (but not tones) facilitate object categorization: Evidence from 6- and 12-month-olds. *Cognition, 105*, 218–228.

Gelman, R. (1978). Cognitive development. *Annual Review of Psychology, 29*, 297–332.

Gervain, J. (2015). Plasticity in early language acquisition: The effects of prenatal and early childhood experience. *Current Opinion in Neurobiology, 35*, 13–20.

Gliozzi, V., Mayor, J., Hu, J. F., & Plunkett, K. (2009). Labels as features (not names) for infant categorization: A neurocomputational approach. *Cognitive Science: A Multidisciplinary Journal, 33*, 709–738.

Goldstone, R. L., Kersten, A., & Carvalho, P. F. (2018). Concepts and categorization. In J. T. Wixted & S. Thompson-Schill (Eds.), *Steven's handbook of experimental psychology, Language and thought* (4th ed., pp. 607–630). New York, NY: Wiley & Sons.

Goldwater, M. B., Brunt, R. J., & Echols, C. H. (2018). Speech facilitates the categorization of motions in 9-month-old infants. *Frontiers in Psychology, 9*, 1–13.

Graham, S. A., Kilbreath, C. S., & Welder, A. N. (2004). Thirteen-month-olds rely on shared labels and shape similarity for inductive inferences. *Child Development, 75*, 409–427.

Greco, C., Hayne, H., & Rovee-Collier, C. (1990). Roles of function, reminding, and variability in categorization by 3-month-old infants. *Journal of Experimental Psychology: Learning Memory and Cognition, 16*, 617–633.

Groba, A., de Houwer, A., Obrig, H., Rossi, S., Groba, A., de Houwer, A., ... Rossi, S. (2019). Bilingual and monolingual first language acquisition experience differentially shapes children's property term learning: Evidence from behavioral and neurophysiological measures. *Brain Sciences, 9*, 40.

Grossmann, T., Gliga, T., Johnson, M. H., & Mareschal, D. (2009). The neural basis of perceptual category learning in human infants. *Journal of Cognitive Neuroscience, 21*, 2276–86.

Hayne, H., Rovee-Collier, C., & Perris, E. E. (1987). Categorization and memory retrieval by three-month-olds. *Memory, 58*, 750–767.

Homa, D., & Vosburgh, R. (1976). Category breadth and the abstraction of prototypical information. *Journal of Experimental Psychology: Human Perception and Performance, 2*, 322–330.

Horst, J. S., Oakes, L. M., & Madole, K. L. (2005). What does it look like and what can it do? Category structure influences how infants categorize. *Child Development, 76*, 614–631.

Huth, A. G., Nishimoto, S., Vu, A. T., & Gallant, J. L. (2012). A continuous semantic space describes the representation of thousands of object and action categories across the human brain. *Neuron, 76*, 1210–1224.

Johnson, S. P. (2011). Development of visual perception. *Wiley Interdisciplinary Reviews: Cognitive Science, 2*, 515–528.

Kandhadai, P., Hall, D. G., & Werker, J. F. (2017). Second label learning in bilingual and monolingual infants. *Developmental Science, 20*, e12429.

Kelly, D. J., Quinn, P. C., Slater, A. M., Lee, K., Ge, L., & Pascalis, O. (2007). The other-race effect develops during infancy. *Psychological Science, 18*, 1084.

Kestenbaum, R., & Nelson, C. A. (1990). The recognition and categorization of upright and inverted emotional expressions by 7-month-old infants. *Infant Behavior and Development, 13*, 497–511.

Kovack-Lesh, K. A., Horst, J. S., & Oakes, L. M. (2008). The cat is out of the bag: The joint influence of previous experience and looking behavior on infant categorization. *Infancy, 13*, 285–307.

Kovack-Lesh, K. A., & Oakes, L. M. (2007). Hold your horses: How exposure to different items influences infant categorization. *Journal of Experimental Child Psychology, 98*, 69–93.

Kroll, J. F., & Dussias, P. E. (2017). The benefits of multilingualism to the personal and professional development of residents of the US. *Foreign Language Annals, 50*, 248–259.

Libertus, K., & Needham, A. W. (2010). Teach to reach: The effects of active vs. passive reaching experiences on action and perception. *Vision Research, 50*, 2750–2757.

   (2014). Encouragement is nothing without control: Factors influencing the development of reaching and face preference. *Journal of Motor Learning and Development, 2*, 16–27.

Luck, S. J. (2014). *An introduction to the event-related potential technique* (2nd ed.). Cambridge, MA: MIT Press.

Luck, S. J., & Gaspelin, N. (2017). How to get statistically significant effects in any ERP experiment (and why you shouldn't). *Psychophysiology, 54*(1), 146–157.

Luck, S. J., & Kappenman, E. S. (Eds.). (2011). *The Oxford handbook of event-related potential components*. New York, NY: Oxford University Press.

Mack, M. L., Love, B. C., & Preston, A. R. (2016). Dynamic updating of hippocampal object representations reflects new conceptual knowledge. *Proceedings of the National Academy of Sciences, 113*, 13203–13208.

   (2017). Building concepts one episode at a time: The hippocampus and concept formation. *Neuroscience Letters, 680*, 31–38.

Madole, K. L., Oakes, L. M., & Cohen, L. B. (1993). Developmental changes in infants' attention to function and form-function correlations. *Cognitive Development, 8*, 189–209.

Mahon, B. Z. (2015). Missed connections: A connectivity-constrained account of the representation and organization of object concepts. In E. Margolis & S. Laurence (Eds.), *The conceptual mind: New directions in the study of concepts* (pp. 79–115). Cambridge, MA: MIT Press.

Mandler, J. M. (2004). *The foundations of mind: Origins of conceptual thought.* New York, NY: Oxford University Press.

Mandler, J. M., Bauer, P. J., & McDonough, L. (1991). Separating the sheep from the goats: Differentiating global categories. *Cognitive Psychology, 23,* 263–298.

Mandler, J. M., Fivush, R., & Reznick, J. S. (1987). The development of contextual categories. *Cognitive Development, 2,* 339–354.

Mandler, J. M., & McDonough, L. (1993). Concept formation in infancy. *Cognitive Development, 8,* 281–318.

  (1998a). On developing a knowledge base in infancy. *Developmental Psychology, 34,* 1274–1288.

  (1998b). Studies in inductive inference in infancy. *Cognitive Psychology, 37,* 60–96.

Mareschal, D., & Tan, S. H. (2007). Flexible and context-dependent categorization by eighteen-month-olds. *Child Development, 78,* 19–37.

Marinović, V., Hoehl, S., & Pauen, S. (2014). Neural correlates of human–animal distinction: An ERP-study on early categorical differentiation with 4- and 7-month-old infants and adults. *Neuropsychologia, 60,* 60–76.

Martin, A. (2016). GRAPES – grounding representations in action, perception, and emotion systems: How object properties and categories are represented in the human brain. *Psychonomic Bulletin and Review, 23,* 979–990.

Maurer, D., & Werker, J. F. (2014). Perceptual narrowing during infancy: A comparison of language and faces. *Developmental Psychobiology, 56,* 154–178.

McDonough, L., & Mandler, J. M. (1998). Inductive generalization in 9- and 11-month-olds. *Developmental Science, 1,* 227–232.

Medin, D. L., Lynch, E. B., Coley, J. D., & Atran, S. (1997). Categorization and reasoning among tree experts: do all roads lead to Rome? *Cognitive Psychology, 32,* 49–96.

Mervis, C. B. (1985). On the existence of prelinguistic categories: A case study. *Infant Behavior and Development, 8,* 293–300.

Mervis, C. B., & Rosch, E. (1981). Categorization of natural objects. *Annual Review of Psychology, 32,* 89–115.

Murphy, G. L. (2002). *The big book of concepts.* Cambridge, MA: MIT Press.

  (2010). What are categories and concepts. In D. Mareschal, P. C. Quinn, & S. Lea (Eds.), *The making of human concepts* (pp. 11–28). Oxford: Oxford University Press.

Newport, E. L. (1990). Maturational constraints on language learning. *Cognitive Science: A Multidisciplinary Journal, 14,* 11–28.

Oakes, L. M. (2008). Categorization skills and concepts. In M. M. Haith & J. B. Benson (Eds.), *Encyclopedia of infant and early childhood development* (pp. 249–259). San Diego, CA: Academic Press.

Oakes, L. M., Coppage, D. J., & Dingel, A. (1997). By land or by sea: The role of perceptual similarity in infants' categorization of animals. *Developmental Psychology, 33,* 396–407.

Oakes, L. M., & Kovack-Lesh, K. A. (2007). Memory processes and categorization in infancy. *Special Issue: The Development of Categorization, 11,* 661–677.

  (2013). Infants' visual recognition memory for a series of categorically related items. *Journal of Cognition and Development, 14,* 63–86.

Oakes, L. M., Madole, K. L., & Cohen, L. B. (1991). Infants' object examining: Habituation and categorization. *Cognitive Development, 6,* 377–392.

Oakes, L. M., & Ribar, R. J. (2005). A comparison of infants' categorization in paired and successive presentation familiarization tasks. *Infancy, 7,* 85–98.

Pascalis, O., de Haan, M., & Nelson, C. A. (2002). Is face processing species-specific during the first year of life? *Science, 296,* 1321–1323.

Pascalis, O., Scott, L. S., Kelly, D. J., Shannon, R. W., Nicholson, E., Coleman, M., & Nelson, C. A. (2005). Plasticity of face processing in infancy. *PNAS Proceedings of the National Academy of Sciences of the United States of America, 102,* 5297–5300.

Peykarjou, S., Wissner, J., & Pauen, S. (2017). Categorical ERP repetition effects for human and furniture items in 7-month-old infants. *Infant and Child Development, 26,* e2016.

Piaget, J. (1952). *Origins of intelligence in children* (M. Cook, Ed.). New York, NY: International Universities Press.

Plunkett, K., Hu, J. -F., & Cohen, L. B. (2008). Labels can override perceptual categories in early infancy. *Cognitive Psychology, 106,* 665–681.

Posner, M. I., & Keele, S. W. (1968). On the genesis of abstract ideas. *Journal of Experimental Psychology, 77,* 353–363.

Poulin-Dubois, D., Frenkiel-Fishman, S., Samantha, N., & Johnson, S. (2006). Infants' inductive generalization of bodily, motion, and sensory properties to animals and people. *Journal of Cognition and Development, 7,* 431–453.

Quinn, P. C., Doran, M. M., Reiss, J. E., & Hoffman, J. E. (2010). Neural markers of subordinate-level categorization in 6- to 7-month-old infants. *Developmental Science, 13,* 499–507.

Quinn, P. C., & Eimas, P. D. (1997). A reexamination of the perceptual-to-conceptual shift in mental representations. *Review of General Psychology, 1,* 171–187.

Quinn, P. C., Eimas, P. D., & Rosenkrantz, S. L. (1993). Evidence for representations of perceptually similar natural categories by 3- and 4-month-old infants. *Perception, 22,* 463–475.

Quinn, P. C., & Johnson, M. H. (2000). Global-before-basic object categorization in connectionist networks and 2-month-old infants. *Infancy, 1,* 31–46.

Quinn, P. C., Lee, K., Pascalis, O., & Slater, A. M. (2007). In support of an expert-novice difference in the representation of humans versus non-human animals by infants: Generalization from persons to cats occurs only with upright whole images. *Cognitie Creier Comportament. Special Issue: The Development of Categorization, 11,* 679–694.

Quinn, P. C., Slater, A. M., Brown, E., & Hayes, R. A. (2001). Developmental change in form categorization in early infancy. *British Journal of Developmental Psychology, 19,* 207–218.

Quinn, P. C., Westerlund, A. J., & Nelson, C. A. (2006). Neural markers of categorization in 6-month-old infants. *Psychological Science, 17,* 59–66.

Quinn, P. C., Yahr, J., Kuhn, A., Slater, A. M., & Pascalis, O. (2002). Representation of the gender of human faces by infants: A preference for female. *Perception, 31*, 1109–1121.

Rakison, D. H. (2007). Inductive categorization: A methodology to examine the basis for categorization and induction in infancy. *Cognitie Creier Comportament. Special Issue: The Development of Categorization, 11*, 773–790.

Rakison, D. H., & Butterworth, G. E. (1998). Infants' use of object parts in early categorization. *Developmental Psychology, 34*, 49–62.

Rakison, D. H., & Lupyan, G. (2008). Developing object concepts in infancy: An associative learning perspective. *Monographs of the Society for Research in Child Development, 73*(7), 1–110.

Ramsey, J. L., Langlois, J. H., & Marti, N. C. (2005). Infant categorization of faces: Ladies first. *Developmental Review, 25*, 212–246.

Rennels, J. L., Juvrud, J., Kayl, A. J., Asperholm, M., Gredeback, G., & Herlitz, A. (2017). Caregiving experience and its relation to perceptual narrowing of face gender. *Developmental Psychology, 53*, 1437–1446.

Rennels, J. L., & Kayl, A. J. (2017). How experience affects infants' facial categorization. In H. Cohen & C. Lefebvre (Eds.), *Handbook of categorization in cognitive science* (Vol. 331, pp. 637–652). San Diego, CA: Elsevier.

Rennels, J. L., Kayl, A. J., Langlois, J. H., Davis, R. E., & Orlewicz, M. (2016). Asymmetries in infants' attention toward and categorization of male faces: The potential role of experience. *Journal of Experimental Child Psychology, 142*, 137–157.

Ribar, R. J., Oakes, L. M., & Spalding, T. L. (2004). Infants can rapidly form new categorical representations. *Psychonomic Bulletin and Review, 11*, 536–541.

Roberts, K. (1988). Retrieval of a basic-level category in prelinguistic infants. *Developmental Psychology, 24*, 21–27.

Robinson, C. W., & Sloutsky, V. M. (2007). Linguistic label and categorization in infancy: Do labels facilitate or hinder? *Infancy, 11*, 233–253.

Ross, G. S. (1980). Categorization in 1- to 2-year-olds. *Developmental Psychology, 16*, 391–396.

Ross, N., Medin, D., Coley, J. D., & Atran, S. (2003). Cultural and experiential differences in the development of folkbiological induction. *Cognitive Development, 18*, 25–47.

Scott, L. S., & Monesson, A. (2009). The origin of biases in face perception. *Psychological Science, 20*, 676–680.

Slater, A. M., Mattock, A., & Brown, E. (1990). Size constancy at birth: Newborn infants' responses to retinal and real size. *Journal of Experimental Child Psychology, 322*, 314–322.

Slater, A. M., & Morison, V. (1985). Shape constancy and slant perception at birth. *Perception, 14*, 337–344.

Sloutsky, V. M., & Deng, W. S. (2017). Categories, concepts, and conceptual development. *Language, Cognition and Neuroscience, 34*(10), 1284–1297.

Smith, E. E., & Medin, D. L. (1981). *Categories and concepts*. Cambridge, MA: Harvard University Press.

Smith, J. D., & Minda, J. P. (1998). Prototypes in the mist: The early epochs of category learning. *Journal of Experimental Psychology: Learning Memory and Cognition, 24*, 1411–1436.

Smith, L. B., Jones, S. S., & Landau, B. (1996). Naming in young children: A dumb attentional mechanism? *Cognitive Psychology*, *60*, 143–171.

Smith, L. B., Jones, S. S., Landau, B., Gershkoff-Stowe, L., & Samuelson, L. K. (2002). Object name learning provides on-the-job training for attention. *Psychological Science*, *13*, 13–19.

Träuble, B., & Pauen, S. (2007). The role of functional information for infant categorization. *Cognition*, *105*, 362–379.

Turati, C., Simion, F., & Zanon, L. (2003). Newborns' perceptual categorization for closed and open geometric forms. *Infancy*, *4*, 309–325.

Waxman, S. R., & Braun, I. (2005). Consistent (but not variable) names as invitations to form object categories: New evidence from 12-month-old infants. *Cognitive Psychology*, *95*, B59–B68.

Waxman, S. R., & Markow, D. B. (1995). Words as invitations to form categories: Evidence from 12- to 13-month-old infants. *Cognitive Psychology*, *29*, 257–302.

Weber, M., Thompson-Schill, S. L., Osherson, D., Haxby, J., & Parsons, L. (2009). Predicting judged similarity of natural categories from their neural representations. *Neuropsychologia*, *47*, 859–868.

Welder, A. N., & Graham, S. A. (2001). The influences of shape similarity and shared labels on infants' inductive inferences about nonobvious object properties. *Child Development*, *72*, 1653–1673.

Westermann, G., & Mareschal, D. (2012). Mechanisms of developmental change in infant categorization. *Cognitive Development*, *27*, 367–382.

Wiesen, S. E., Watkins, R. M., & Needham, A. W. (2016). Active motor training has long-term effects on infants' object exploration. *Frontiers in Psychology*, *7*, 599.

Yoshida, H., & Smith, L. B. (2001). Early noun lexicons in English and Japanese. *Cognitive Psychology*, *82*, B63–B74.

Younger, B. A. (1985). The segregation of items into categories by ten-month-old infants. *Child Development*, *56*, 1574–1583.

(1990). Infant categorization: Memory for category-level and specific item information. *Journal of Experimental Child Psychology*, *50*, 131–155.

15 Early Knowledge About Space and Quantity

Nora S. Newcombe

Over the past decades, we have learned a great deal about what infants bring to the task of mastering space and quantity, and what they subsequently add to these starting points. The accumulating findings are richly descriptive, and they are beginning to illuminate long-standing questions concerning the origins of knowledge in these domains. Broadly speaking, there have been two contending theoretical approaches. The core knowledge view claims that infants are born with representationally specific processing modules tuned to picking up the geometry of *space* (the geometric module), forming representations of *objects* (continuity, cohesion, contact, tracking small sets), and assessing the *number* of objects (the approximate number system) (Feigenson, Dehaene, & Spelke, 2004; Spelke & Kinzler, 2007). In this way of thinking, subsequent developmental change comes mainly from augmentation of the power and scope of these innate modules, as children acquire language and other forms of symbolic processing. By contrast, a neoconstructivist view proposes that the newborn human mind is broadly prepared to acquire knowledge from interaction with the structure of the expectable environment (e.g., for quantity, Cantrell & Smith, 2013; for space, Newcombe & Huttenlocher, 2006). Representational preprogramming is not essential, because infants inevitably encounter crucial information in a world constrained by the laws of physics. The developmental unfolding of sensory, motor, and brain maturation creates a sequence of relevant experiences that lead to typical development. Sensory or physical limitations, or variations in brain structure, may set spatial and quantitative development on a different path (Ansari & Karmiloff-Smith, 2002; Landau & Ferrara, 2013).

There are many points at issue in this modern version of the nativist–empiricist debate. One key methodological question regards the interpretation of infant looking-time data. Although the correlation between theory and methodology is not perfect, core knowledge theorists (and some others) typically see such data as revealing the basic design of the human mind, what babies would tell us if only they could speak. In contrast, neoconstructivist investigators mostly regard looking time as reflecting weak and inchoate tendencies or perceptual biases, rather than knowledge that can support actions, judgments, and decisions (Karmiloff-Smith, 1992; Munakata, McClelland, Johnson, & Siegler, 1997; Thelen & Smith, 1994). In line with this position, success on search tasks generally appears later than success on looking-time paradigms, sometimes substantially later (Keen, 2003). Taking the neoconstructivist view, this chapter stresses tasks in which babies act on the world in some way– such as search for hidden objects, or insertion of an object in an aperture – or make active choices or judgments. It considers evidence from looking-time studies as providing information regarding possible early starting points (rather than full-blown competencies).

Another key issue in the modern nativist–empiricist debate is the place of infancy in an overall story of development that includes childhood and adolescence. The core-knowledge and the neoconstructivist views agree that spatial and mathematical development are far from complete by the end of infancy. The acquisition of spatial and mathematical language ("in/on/under," the list of count words, modifiers such as "many") only gets under way around 2 years of age (e.g., Barner, Brooks, & Bale, 2011; Pruden, Levine, & Huttenlocher, 2011), and 2 years also sees the dawning of understanding of nonlinguistic symbol systems, such as models and maps (e.g., DeLoache, 1987). However, as we have noted, the importance of symbol acquisition varies for the two accounts. For the core knowledge approach, language and other symbols play a pivotal role (as they also do, interestingly, in Vygotskyan accounts). For neoconstructivist theories, language and other symbols are important, but they are only one among several forces propelling development. Other factors are also vital, such as increasing integration of cue systems (adaptive combination; Newcombe & Huttenlocher, 2006) and environmental input, nonlinguistic as well as linguistic.

This chapter contains three sections, covering navigation, object manipulation, and quantitative estimation. Many investigators discuss only two domains, the spatial and the quantitative, although note that the core knowledge position postulates three relevant modules. Indeed, it is now clear that there is not a single domain of "space." There are two psychologically and neurally separable ways of acting in space: navigation and object manipulation. They have different adaptive functions and evolutionary histories, and they operate across different spatial scales (Newcombe, 2017). All mobile animals navigate, and hence our species shares a long evolutionary heritage in how we accomplish this function, especially with mammalian species, but also with birds, insects, and so forth, who have developed various ways to solve the computational challenge of wayfinding. Navigation typically occurs across environmental scale, i.e., spaces in which movement creates distinctively different views of each local area, and not all objects and landmarks are intervisible. Object manipulation contrasts with navigation in species specificity and in scale of operation. Although there seems to be some tool use in nonhuman species including chimpanzees, dolphins, and corvids (Seed & Byrne, 2010), our species uses objects as tools extensively, in part because we have opposable thumbs, freed by upright locomotion, that allow for the flexible manipulation of objects. Furthermore, our symbolic capacity allows us to leverage this talent further, to invent new tools. In terms of scale, object manipulation operates over a small scale, ideally of objects within reaching distance. We can also approach and reach for and handle objects that are visible within vista space – the space that we can see from a single location.

15.1 Navigation System

There are several models of the mature navigational system, and how we characterize that system frames the way we see the problem of development. This section reviews research on infants that stems from three different conceptualizations, each associated with a distinctive approach to the nativist–empiricist debate. The dominant model in the navigation literature involves a balance of inertial and allocentric systems, supported by both neural and behavioral evidence. The development of this combined system as a function of environmental experience fits a neoconstructivist position. We will also review the proposal of a geometric module, which fits the core knowledge position, and Piaget's conceptualization of spatial representation, which was part of his stage approach to development.

15.1.1 Computational and Neural Model of Navigation

The most widely used computational and neural model of navigation in the contemporary literature delineates two kinds of information used for way-finding, inertial and allocentric information, and posits that they adaptively interact and combine (e.g., Barry & Burgess, 2014). Inertial information, also called path integration, refers to information derived from kinesthetic, vestibular, and visual flow information regarding direction and distance of motion. It supports representation of the shape of a path and the location of points along it from the current position, e.g., pointing back to a starting point. Allocentric information refers to information derived from encoding direction and distance of objects in the environment from stable environmental features, including boundaries and landmarks. Encoding of inertial and allocentric information is the product of the work of a dizzying array of specialized cells, including place cells, head direction cells, grid cells, boundary cells, object vector cells and more (see Poulter, Hartley, & Lever, 2018 for an overview). Various structures in the brain house these cells, including the hippocampus, the parahippocampal place area, entorhinal cortex, retrosplenial cortex, and parts of parietal cortex.

In studying human babies, we cannot view cells directly, nor can we image the relevant neural systems, given the limits of current technology. Instead, we must rely on behavioral paradigms that tap the use of inertial and allocentric information, as well as their integration, together with information gleaned from work with nonhuman animals, including infant rodents. Paradigms that work across species are especially valuable. There are various maze tasks suitable for both humans and rodents, most famously the Morris Water Maze, which depends on the functioning of the neural navigation system (Morris, Garrud, Rawlins, & O'Keefe, 1982). Maze tasks require that babies be able to crawl or walk to search for a goal, such as a hidden object, in a vista space. Thus, we cannot test babies under 9 months.

As young as 12 months, babies show some knowledge of location in such tasks, for example, by looking in the general areas where they saw an object hidden under one of a collection of small identical pillows in a circular enclosure (Bushnell, McKenzie, Lawrence, & Connell, 1995). However, representations are likely limited. Bushnell et al. (1995) only tested search from a fixed vantage point, so it is unclear if the babies were remembering a fixed path, or encoding objects in an allocentric framework, i.e., showed place learning. In any case, searches were not very precise. With a simple version of a maze task and high motivation, Clearfield (2004) found that babies could search successfully towards the end of the first year and the beginning of the second, with success depending on weeks of experience with locomotion.

By the end of the second year, representation is much more mature. At 18 months, toddlers can encode location metrically, even when shifted laterally between observation of hiding and search (Huttenlocher, Newcombe, & Sandberg, 1994). There is then a marked transition, between 18 and 24 months, to greater capacity and durability (Sluzenski, Newcombe, & Satlow, 2004). Place learning in child-friendly versions of the Morris Water Maze (i.e., tasks without water that require the use of distal cues) is first evident around 21 months (Balcomb, Newcombe, & Ferrara, 2011; Newcombe, Huttenlocher, Drummey, & Wiley, 1998). The development of place learning is not complete at that point, however. Only children well above 2 years succeed when there are more demands on the system, e.g., to code several locations at once (Ribordy, Jabès, Lavenex, & Lavenex, 2013), to navigate in virtual environments (Laurance, Learmonth, Nadel, & Jacobs, 2003), to use substantial distances in large-scale space (Overman, Pate, Moore, & Peuster, 1996) or to use different strategies concurrently (Bullens et al., 2010).

Rodent studies also show that place learning takes time to appear, although of course the time course is much more compressed as infants develop quickly. In rats, successful search in the Morris Water Maze appears at 21 days after birth, about the same time as weaning and fully independent exploration (Tan, Wills, & Cacucci, 2017). This success is the end point of development that begins around postnatal day 12 and unfolds over the next 10 days. At the cellular level, the earliest cells to mature are the head direction cells, followed by the place cells, the boundary cells, and lastly the grid cells. Figure 15.1, taken from the review by Tan et al. (2017), summarizes this sequence. Head direction cells predate movement and even eye opening in baby rats, but they seem to require input from vision and motion to stabilize (Tan, Bassett, O'Keefe, Cacucci, & Wills, 2015). Place-cell networks show basic properties as soon as baby rats

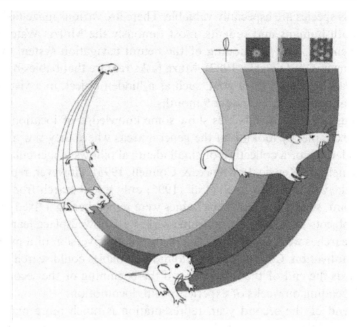

Figure 15.1. *Sequence of development of spatially relevant cell systems in the infant rat. Head direction cells appear first, followed by place, boundary, and grid cells. Each system matures after its first appearance.*
Source: Adapted from Tan et al. (2017).

start to explore (Muessig, Hauser, Wills, & Cacucci, 2015) but take close to 2 months to exhibit mature stability and accuracy (Wills, Cacucci, Burgess, & O'Keefe, 2010). Even in adult animals, input is required to maintain basic elements of the system. Grid cells exhibit some basic firing properties in the dark but require visual input to exhibit hexagonal symmetry (Chen, Manson, Cacucci, & Wills, 2016). Thus, in rats, we see an interplay between the innate capacities of the navigation system present in neural architecture at birth, and the environmental interaction required to bring them to an adult form.

Like rats, human babies also likely require sensory and motor experience for spatial development, although there are obvious differences in the sequence and pacing of development. Vision is present from birth in humans, with good acuity and accommodation by 3 months. Motion takes longer to get under way. Stable independent sitting with rotational trunk movement may allow for initial development of spatial location coding (McKenzie, Day, & Ihsen, 1984). More important milestones are crawling at around 8 months and walking at 12 to 14 months. Crawling and (even more) walking are crucial transitions, because we know that infants who are passively transported experience very different statistics of optic flow and motion (Raudies, Gilmore, Kretch, Franchak, & Adolph, 2012) that challenge an inertial navigation system. The onset of crawling (or placement in a walker, i.e., a seat that allows an infant to sit upright and self-propel using the wheels of the walker) gives experience that leads to more focus on distant landmarks. Upright walking brings with it the ability to see distal landmarks even better as motion through the world occurs at will; the view of the world obtained by the crawling infant is limited (Adolph & Tamis-LeMonda, 2014). Seeing distal landmarks and realizing that can aid in navigation is a vital part of constructing an allocentric spatial framework. There is empirical evidence for the influence of these motor milestones on spatial behavior (see review by Campos et al., 2000). However, regrettably, most studies to date have involved search in reaching space or a small vista space, except for Clearfield (2004), who linked a simple form of place learning to the onset of both crawling and walking.

15.1.2 The Geometric Module Debate

There is an alternative view of the navigation system (Wang & Spelke, 2002; see Burgess, 2006 for a critique). As in the standard model, inertial information is important, but the only kind of allocentric information comes from the shape of enclosing spaces, i.e., "geometry." This model of mature functioning is linked to the postulation of an innate geometric module, a central plank in the core knowledge position. The hypothesis has been studied using an experimental paradigm that began with research on rats (Cheng, 1986), called the reorientation paradigm. Rats searched for food hidden in one corner of a rectangular box in which one wall had a distinctive color or design and the other walls were different but the same as each other. Surprisingly, they used the geometry but failed to use the features in search, i.e., they went equally often to the target and to the diagonally opposite corner. This pattern led to the idea of an encapsulated geometric module (Cheng, 1986; Gallistel, 1990). Gallistel (1990) argued further that the modularity model fits with evolution, because geometric properties are more likely to remain stable than featural properties.

Adapting this paradigm for human children in several ways, e.g., using toys instead of food, Hermer and Spelke (1996) found that children between the ages of 18 months and 6 years of age looked pretty much like Cheng's rats. They ignored a colored wall in a rectangular room, and instead searched for the hidden toy in the two geometrically equivalent corners. However, adults did use features. Hermer-Vazquez, Moffett, and Munkholm (2001) found that the shift occurred between the ages of 5 and 6 years, and argued that it was due to spatial language, based on a correlation between children's accurate production of the words "left" and "right" and success in using features to search.

The failure of toddlers to use features is not always observed, however. Children as young as 18 months succeed in using a colored wall to find the correct corner when the room is larger than the very small room used in the initial studies (Learmonth, Nadel, & Newcombe, 2002; Learmonth, Newcombe, & Huttenlocher, 2001). This room-size effect has now been found in human adults

(Ratliff & Newcombe, 2008), as well as in a variety of nonhuman and nonlinguistic species (see Cheng & Newcombe, 2005). The room-size effect is important, given that navigation and reorientation evolved to support way finding in very large spaces. Indeed, the larger enclosure used by Learmonth et al. is a rather small enclosure by real-world standards, an instance of vista space (i.e., the area we can see from a stationary position) rather than environmental space (i.e., the various areas that we can see as we move in the world, many of which are not intervisible; Montello, 1993). The size of the space is widely recognized to have crucial implications for research on navigation and reorientation (Jacobs & Menzel, 2014; Lew, 2011; Wolbers & Wiener, 2014). In addition, the natural environment includes very few regular and fully enclosed spaces.

A complete explanation of the overall data pattern does require a mechanism to account for the sharp age transition in the small room. A Bayesian model of data from several of the key reorientation experiments has been proposed (Y. Xu, Regier, & Newcombe, 2017), but it is agnostic about the candidate factors. Language could certainly be relevant, either spatial language (*at the red wall*) or task-relevant nonspatial language (*red can help you*); both phrases help children reorient in a small room (Shusterman, Lee, & Spelke, 2011). Two other possibilities are hippocampal development that allows for increasingly effective binding of spatial cues (Sutton & Newcombe, 2014; Vieites, Nazareth, Reeb-Sutherland, & Pruden, 2015), or the cumulative impact of experience with cue validity (Learmonth, Newcombe, Sheridan, & Jones, 2008; Twyman, Friedman, & Spetch 2007). Rearing environment changes weighting of geometry and features, at least for convict fish (Brown, Spetch, & Hurd, 2007) and mice (Twyman, Newcombe, & Gould, 2013), although not for chicks (Chiandetti & Vallortigara, 2008, 2010). In sum, language is one of several candidate factors for explaining the developmental transition in a very particular environment, namely the very small room.

15.1.3 Piaget's View

An older proposal regarding the mature spatial system came from Piaget, who wrote about it as "projective" and "Euclidean" and characterized infants as "topological" and "egocentric," with a shift from egocentric to allocentric and from topological to projective Euclidean. Research based on this model used techniques such as the A-not-B search error that Piaget originally used to investigate the development of the object concept, and studies in which investigators rotate babies by 180 degrees (e.g., Acredolo, 1978; Bremner & Bryant, 1977). Both techniques seemed to look at an egocentric to allocentric shift. Searching in the A location, after observing hiding at the B location, seems egocentric, i.e., defining a location in relation to a body in a fixed position; looking or reaching to the same side after 180-degree rotation also seems egocentric.

There are hundreds of papers on these paradigms. In the rotation paradigm, it turned out that even babies of 6 months or so succeeded when there were very salient visual landmarks (e.g., flashing stars around a window), or if tested in their own home, where they may be more emotionally secure (see review by Newcombe & Huttenlocher, 2000). For example, at 6 months they can use indirect as well as direct landmarks to locate an interesting event (Lew, Foster, Crowther, & Green, 2004). Even 4-month-olds expect that objects will occur at allocentrically defined locations following rotation when given prior experience with passive motion (Kaufman & Needham, 2011). These data suggest reweighting of two coexisting systems with experience rather than a stage-like shift. It is also possible that a reweighting account explains the A-not-B error (Newcombe & Huttenlocher, 2000). Contending theories of the A-not-B error all involve the roles of memory, strength of representation, motor habit, and inhibition, to varying degrees and in different ways (Diamond, 1998; Munakata et al., 1997; Smith, Thelen, Titzer, & McLin, 1999), but resolving conflict among coexisting spatial coding systems may be key to all of them. In sum, research stemming from the Piagetian tradition largely supports the emerging view, using the inertial-allocentric integration framework, that infants are moving towards a mature system in which various coexisting systems are both used, in a fashion paced by growth and experience.

15.1.4 Cultural Context and Policy Implications

If the initial development of navigation skills depends on the maturation of sensory and motor systems, combined with environmental feedback and emerging adaptive combination, then relatively little variation in typical development is expected. Although cultures differ in whether they swaddle infants, encourage early sitting and walking, or allow toddlers to roam widely, these differences likely affect the pace but not the outcome of development. The requisite experience is inevitably encountered sooner or later, probably with no need for special enrichment. However, there may be limits to this conclusion. Adults show considerable individual variation in cognitive map formation (Weisberg & Newcombe, 2016), and the roots of this variation are unknown. By the age of 12 years, children show adult levels of performance in terms of means and ranges (Nazareth, Weisberg, Margulis, & Newcombe, 2018), but we do not know how early individual differences arise and become stable. It is certainly possible they arise before the end of infancy, although perhaps unlikely because even preschool children are rarely allowed to roam widely or find their own way. Probably the main policy implications of the navigation literature that are relevant to infancy occur in cases where infants have sensory or motor limitations, as when they have low vision or cerebral palsy. In these cases, babies will likely benefit from adaptations that allow them as much freedom to explore as possible (e.g., Galloway, Ryu, & Agrawal, 2008).

15.2 Object Manipulation System

Navigation is a crucial challenge that humans face along with all mobile species. Thus, our functioning has much in common with other mammals, albeit different in some ways (e.g., less use of smell gradients, more use of symbolic communication). By contrast, a distinctive skill of the human species is an ability to represent and transform the shapes of objects. We can grasp objects physically and manipulate them based on their shape, modifying that shape to our purposes. In planning for tool use, we may generate mental images of two-dimensional shapes or three-dimensional objects, and transform them in various ways, e.g., rotating, bending, or folding them. Such flexible representations allow for anticipating the effects of actions when manipulating objects, as well as for inventing new tools. This section first reviews the development of physical interactions with objects and associated cognitive effects, and then examines the development of mental representations and transformations of shape and location.

There is less clash between theoretical points of view in this domain than in the other two topics covered in this chapter, although there are differences in emphasis. The core knowledge approach focuses on understanding of principles of cohesion, continuity, and contact (Spelke, 1990), and argues that basic appreciation of these characteristics, as assessed by looking time, is in place when grasping begins. However, the expression of this knowledge in judgment tasks is not apparent until the third year of life (Keen, 2003). Furthermore, early visual experience may be vital to the looking-time effects found at 3 or 4 months. Although very young infants track cohesion, continuity, and contact in optimal situations, there seem to be changes over the first few months as visual experience accumulates (Johnson & Aslin, 1995). This review takes a neoconstructivist approach in stressing the unfolding of abilities rather than the starting points in infancy.

15.2.1 Neural Substrates

Manual interactions with objects are built on a neural substrate involved with allowing effective actions in the world, which consists of two separate but related processing streams. There is a ventral *what* stream responsible for object identification, including processing the shape and size of objects, and a dorsal *where–how* stream responsible for locating these objects in egocentric coordinates that allow for reaching (see Figure 15.2). We have a good amount of information on the two systems in infancy, summarized by Wilcox and Biondi (2015). Briefly, behavioral data and glimpses of neural functioning derived from fNIRS suggest that the two streams are present in some form early in the first year of life, but that they are also dynamically changing, influenced by motor maturation and environmental experience, just as we saw with navigation.

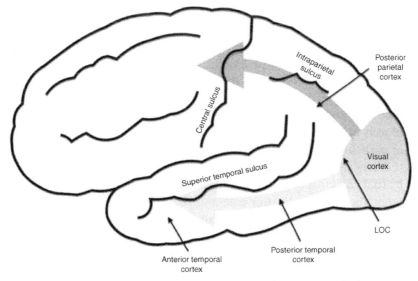

Figure 15.2. *Lateral view of an adult brain. Dorsal stream is in dark gray and ventral stream is in light gray.*
Note: LOC – lateral occipital cortex.
Source: Adapted from Wilcox and Biondi (2015).

We also mentally imagine the movements of objects in space, as in mental rotation of shapes in two- or three-dimensional space. Neurally, mental rotation (MR) depends on the intraparietal sulcus, which is a part of the dorsal stream. This fact suggests a close linkage between actual and imagined movement, as does the fact that we also see activation in the medial superior precentral cortex when tasks favor motor simulation.

15.2.2 Grasping and Manipulating Real Objects

Processing shape is a key output of the ventral *what* stream. The pivotal milestone in motor maturation for this line of development is the onset of grasping at around 4 months of age and subsequent refinement in skill and speed. Grasping is important to learning about objects, their shapes, and their names, as shown most clearly by studies with "sticky mittens." Accelerated grasping experience through the provision of sticky mittens leads to more mature object processing and exploration (Libertus, Joh, & Needham, 2016; Needham, Barrett, & Peterman, 2002; Soska, Adolph, & Johnson, 2010) and to increments in sensitivity to the goal-directed actions of others (Gerson & Woodward, 2014). In the second year, the shape of objects is a key attribute underlying vocabulary acquisition, as toddlers focus on clean one-object-at-a-time views during which labeling has maximum effect (Smith, Yu, & Pereira, 2011) and as the shape bias is formed (i.e., the focus on shape as determining the extension of novel vocabulary items for objects; Landau, Smith, & Jones, 1998). Although other attributes of objects, notably color, take longer than shape to be recognized as important attributes of objects, the ventral system probably operates in a mature fashion at the end of the first year (Wilcox & Biondi, 2015).

To study the dorsal *where–how* stream, studies of infants and toddlers have used the classic "posting" tasks developed for use in studies of adults, where objects of a certain shape fit through slots of a certain shape only when held in particular ways. The data show a gradual evolution in the degree to which toddlers can smoothly complete shape-insertion tasks. Initially they proceed by trial and error but later they anticipate how to hold the object in the correct orientation early in the movement of the hand and arm to "post." Age-related change in these posting tasks occurs between 18 and 24 months, with refinements continuing to 3 years of age (Jung, Kahrs, & Lockman, 2015, 2018; Örnkloo & von Hofsten, 2007; Street, James, Jones, & Smith, 2011). Thus, in contrast to the ventral stream, which calibrates over the first 12 months, the dorsal stream may take 2 to 3 years to operate smoothly. Alternatively, although along similar lines, it may be that posting tasks require integration of the ventral and dorsal streams, in which case, the behavioral data may be reflecting the development of integration as well as (or instead of) development of the dorsal stream per se.

15.2.3 Mental Representations of Objects

The data just reviewed concern the processing and handling of physically present objects. Importantly, however, humans can manipulate objects mentally as well as physically. We can imagine many transformations of objects, such as bending them, folding them, or cutting them. Although there are paradigms and tests to assess bending, folding, and cutting, by far the best-studied type of mental transformation is MR. There are many reasons to surmise that MR would not be evident in infancy, including the relatively late maturation of the dorsal stream and the fact that preschoolers often show low sensitivity to mirror images in judgment tasks (e.g., Fisher, 1979). Indeed, multiple studies of children's performance in child-friendly versions of classic MR tasks suggest that age of onset of MR is not until 4 or 5 years, or even later (Dean & Harvey, 1979; Estes, 1998; Frick, Ferrara, & Newcombe, 2013; Frick, Hansen, & Newcombe, 2013; Hawes, LeFevre, Xu, & Bruce, 2015).

Infant looking-time studies to explore the early roots of MR are beginning to suggest that manual experience with objects that can be rotated lays the groundwork for mature MR as it appears in traditional judgment tasks. There is a pattern in which babies can succeed on supportive MR tasks using simple stimuli over short delays with manual experience with the stimuli, followed by success at older ages without manual experience, but difficulty with more demanding paradigms. One such sequence emerged in a paradigm used in the first year (Frick & Mohring, 2013; Mohring & Frick, 2013). Babies either held or manually explored an asymmetrical object whose two sides differed markedly in color and design or watched as the experimenter turned it from side to side. The object then moved straight down behind a screen with only one side showing. When the screen was lowered, the babies saw either the same object or its mirror image in one of five different orientations. At 6 months, babies with manual exploration experience looked longer at the impossible than at the possible outcomes, suggesting that they discriminated mirror images. Visual displays alone were not enough to create sensitivity to the impossible outcome until 10 months of age, and success was correlated with parents' report of motor development. A similar sequence emerged in the second year of life, using a paradigm with a more complex object placed on a rotating tray. Frick and Wang (2014) found that 14-month-olds looked longer at incongruent than at congruent outcome orientations of the object if they had hands-on experience, whereas 16-month-olds succeeded even without it. In short, MR seems to leverage the systems involved in motor planning and execution, more strongly in children well into elementary school than in adults (Frick, Daum, Walser, & Mast, 2009). An unexplored area is the transition from performance on these tasks to success on judgment tasks with complex stimuli, i.e., what happens between 2 and 4 years. Children of these ages play a great deal with shapes and such experience may support the transition to true mental processes.

Some investigators have claimed, however, that infants show MR abilities before the age of manual grasping (Moore & Johnson, 2008, 2011; Quinn & Liben, 2008, 2014). How can we reconcile these studies with the embodied account of development just offered? One factor leading to apparent MR may be that infants in these studies saw objects in actual physical rotation before the test, or in multiple static orientations. Such presentation may allow infants to extrapolate motion or to interpolate between familiar views, rather than represent and rotate object shape. That is, infants' reasoning may be limited to recognizing incongruities *retrospectively*, and they may simply react to violations of basic principles such as object solidity and continuity. It is an open question whether such sensitivities lay the foundation for the sequence of development that follows the onset of grasping and manipulation. Furthermore, it is notable that, even using this paradigm, crawling seems to affect the likelihood of recognizing the unpredicted view (Schwarzer, Freitag, Buckel, & Lofruthe, 2013).

15.2.4 Cultural Context and Policy Implications

Like navigation skills, grasping skills and the mental manipulations that grow out of them seem to depend on the maturation of sensory and motor systems, combined with months of exploration and environmental feedback. Such experiences are ubiquitous, and the eventual outcome may hence be assured. Cultures obviously differ in the extent to which adults provide infants with purpose-built shape sorters, however, and interaction with such play materials differs across caretakers in infancy (Casasola, Bhagwat, Doan, & Love, 2017). Although any handy objects may ultimately provide the requisite experience, we really do not know the trajectory of the individual differences ultimately seen in adults in spatial transformation skills, including substantial sex differences in MR (Voyer, Voyer, & Bryden, 1995), and lack evidence regarding whether the roots of these differences lie in infancy, although one recent study suggests that both hormonal differences and parental expectations may have some effect (Constantinescu, Moore, Johnson, & Hines, 2018). However, a limitation of the Constantinescu et al. (2018) study is its use of the Moore–Johnson paradigm that we have argued may or may not be in a continuous line of development with adult MR. Of course, as with navigation, if infants have sensory or motor limitations, or atypical genetic endowments, the situation may be different. For example, Williams syndrome is a congenital disorder associated with problems in the dorsal system (e.g., Dilks, Hoffman, & Landau, 2008).

15.3 Magnitude System

As the queen of the sciences, in Gauss' memorable phrase, mathematics would seem to involve supremely human symbolic and abstract processes. However, there is now a great deal of evidence that nonhuman animals have impressive abilities to estimate the quantity of both small and large numbers of objects, as well as of other quantitative dimensions such as volume or area (Cantlon & Brannon, 2006; Meck & Church, 1983). Infants do too, at least as indicated by various looking-time paradigms. The first reports of infant sensitivity to number (e.g., Starkey, Spelke, & Gelman, 1983) involved small numbers from 1 to 4 that are likely tracked by an object tracking system and are part of the object system discussed in the prior section. However, subsequent work indicated that infants were also sensitive to larger numbers that cannot be based on object tracking, and that must tap a separate system, called the approximate number system (ANS) by core knowledge theorists (F. Xu & Spelke, 2000; F. Xu, Spelke, & Goddard, 2005). Interestingly, however, manual search paradigms usable by about the end of the first year have shown discrimination of smaller but not larger numbers (Feigenson & Carey, 2003), suggesting that babies of that age may have active understanding only of numbers in the object tracking range.

The interpretation of these findings is hotly disputed. The core knowledge view is that the object tracking system and the ANS jointly constitute the two innate modules that underlie the subsequent acquisition of formal mathematics, with the ANS influencing mathematical achievement in children, adolescents, and adults (Halberda, Mazzocco, & Feigenson, 2008; but see Schneider et al., 2017 for a critical meta-analysis). However, the alternative neoconstructivist view is that the findings reflect the operation of an approximate magnitude system (AMS) in infancy. In this way of thinking, infants' early sensitivity is to magnitude of various kinds, including not only the number of discrete objects (i.e., the integer system), but also continuous quantitative dimensions such as size, area, contour length, volume, time, and speed. Importantly, number and the various quantitative dimensions are typically correlated with each other in the real world. For example, having more cookies generally implies having more volume of cookie, as well as more area, more perimeter, more weight, more calories, and so forth, although the correlation is not perfect, as when 10 tiny cookies provide less to eat than 2 gigantic ones. Infants seem to encode all the various quantitative dimensions tested to date, although again the evidence comes from looking-time studies (Addyman, Rocha, & Mareschal, 2014; Brannon, Lutz, & Cordes, 2006; Brannon, Suanda, & Libertus, 2007; Hespos, Dora, Rips, & Christie, 2012; Möhring, Libertus, & Bertin, 2012).

There is a great deal of data and debate on all aspects of this controversy (for reviews see Cantrell & Smith, 2013; Hamamouche & Cordes, 2019; Leibovich, Katzin, Harel, & Henik, 2017 and associated commentary; Mix, Levine, & Newcombe, 2016). One key issue initially seemed to be methodological but has turned out to have further-reaching ramifications. Clearfield and Mix (1999) and Mix, Huttenlocher, and Levine (2002) made the point that infant number studies had not been well controlled for quantitative dimensions other than number. Subsequently, proponents of an ANS worked to control their studies better (e.g., Feigenson, Carey, & Spelke, 2002). However, these attempts run into trouble for at least two reasons. First, it is very difficult, arguably impossible, to control for all continuous dimensions at once. Ten tiny cookies may have more perimeter than two gigantic ones, even when they have less area. Second, in attempting to control for quantitative dimensions other than number, experimenters may be providing an ideal opportunity for infant learning, teaching babies to focus on number, as argued by Thelen and Smith (1994) as a general point about infant looking-time studies. Third, attempts at control typically assume experiment-wide averaging by infants, an assumption that has not been tested.

Another aspect of the debate concerns the fact that infants show cross-dimension transfer in looking-time studies. They form expectations about number based on length and based on temporal duration, as well as vice versa (de Hevia & Spelke, 2010; Lourenco & Longo, 2010; Srinivasan & Carey, 2010), even as neonates (de Hevia, Izard, Coubart, Spelke, & Streri, 2014). Infants may even show cross-modal transfer to the auditory dimension, at least for pitch (Dolscheid, Hunnius, Casasanto, & Majid, 2014), although Srinivasan and Carey (2010) found no transfer between length and loudness. Cross-dimension and cross-modal transfer is very consistent with an AMS, although proponents of an ANS may simply counter that there is innate mapping between systems as well as innate number competence.

Because adults do appreciate the integer system as a distinct measurement system, postulating an initial AMS requires specifying a developmental process in which various form of magnitude are differentiated from each other. As Cantrell and Smith (2013) argued, the correlated quantitative dimensions need to proceed from an integral to a separable state, a process already studied at later ages and for different kinds of stimuli (Smith & Kemler, 1978). There is some support for the idea of a differentiation process (Cantrell, Boyer, Cordes, & Smith, 2015; Odic, Hock, & Halberda, 2014), although much more research needs to be done. Dramatic cases of inverse correlation might be especially helpful for children learning to differentiate different dimensions of quantity, e.g., when 100 ants take up much less space than 1 elephant. It would be helpful to know how often such cases of inverse correlation occur in the daily lives of babies, and whether caretakers draw attention to them. Untangling correlated quantitative dimensions seems to be a special case of statistical learning, as studied in other domains (Aslin & Newport, 2012), but knowing the input statistics would be helpful for experimentation and modeling.

15.3.1 Neural Bases of Magnitude and Number

Behavior is not the only source of data on how we represent and process magnitude and number. Research on the neural bases of quantity and number reveals that adults show substantial overlap in the brain areas engaged in processing nonsymbolic magnitude, nonsymbolic number, and symbolic number, suggesting commonality between magnitude and number at maturity, although there are also some brain areas specific to nonsymbolic and symbolic number (Sokolowski, Fias, Ononye, & Ansari, 2017). Very intriguingly, this pattern of overlapping activation extends to mental rotation (Hawes, Sokolowski, Ononye, & Ansari, 2019). Magnitude is important for gauging whether and how we can hold, shape, and turn objects. In fact, the intraparietal sulcus (IPS) may be a "spatial hub," helping the navigation system to encode spatial direction and relate egocentric to allocentric coordinates (Byrne, Becker, & Burgess, 2007; Weisberg, Marchette, & Chatterjee, 2018).

The existence of common neural areas does not imply that identical ensembles of neurons are necessarily involved at a fine-grained level, and in fact there is recent evidence suggesting neural specialization in adults (Castaldi, Piazza, Dehaene, Vignaud, & Eger, 2019). Nevertheless, the proximity of function is very suggestive of common roots, and we do not yet have data on the development of fine-grained specialization within the IPS. One way to conceptualize the overlap of processes in the IPS is in terms of a Venn diagram (see Figure 15.3), which shows the hypothesized centrality of magnitude processing and space–number mappings. Indeed, behavioral studies show the spatial roots of mathematic thinking at a variety of ages and levels of expertise (Amalric & Dehaene, 2016; Frick, 2019; Gunderson, Ramirez, Beilock. & Levine, 2012; Hawes, Moss, Caswell, Seo, & Ansari, 2019; Verdine, Golinkoff, Hirsh-Pasek, & Newcombe, 2017).

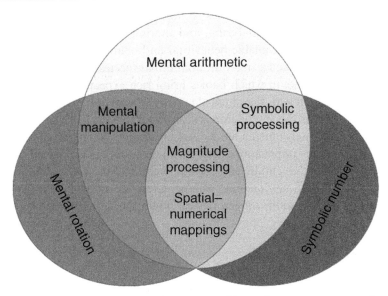

Figure 15.3. *Venn diagram showing possible overlap among aspects of spatial and numerical processing.*
Source: Adapted from Hawes et al. (2019).

15.3.2 Cultural Context and Policy Implications

Cultures differ dramatically in their number systems, with some languages providing only a rudimentary list of count words and no formal mathematical instruction, other cultures offering more complex but still cumbersome systems, and complex societies offering well-developed and culturally valued ways to calculate (e.g., Pica, Lemer, Izard, & Dehaene, 2004; Saxe, 2015). In Western industrialized countries, and especially in middle- and high-socioeconomic status groups, adults may use number words and engage in number activities with infants, at least starting in the second year (Mix, 2009). There is evidence that number-relevant input affects children's mathematical development in the preschool years, and even after formal schooling starts, given both correlational and experimental evidence (Berkowitz et al., 2015; Gunderson & Levine, 2011; Klibanoff, Levine, Huttenlocher, Vasilyeva, & Hedges, 2006). We need much more evidence, however, regarding what matters in the first 3 years of life, and about how much of what kind of input to provide when and how.

15.4 Conclusion

This review of spatial and quantitative development shows how much we have learned over the past decades. While theoretical interpretations differ, there are increasingly sharp issues to adjudicate, better methods with which to proceed in gathering, analyzing, and sharing larger data sets across varied cultural settings, and available behavioral and neural models of mature functioning in adults, as well as relevant nonhuman species. Most investigators now subscribe to a model in which babies bring rich expectations and predispositions to interaction with the physical and social world. In all three domains we examined, most of this interaction is along lines that are likely universal, except in cases where environments are severely restricted or biological endowments are atypical. Policy implications are thus unclear for typically developing babies at present. Given that children and adults eventually show important individual differences in all three domains, whether there are environments or types of interaction that could lift trajectories early needs a more careful look.

References

Acredolo, L. P. (1978). Development of spatial orientation in infancy. *Developmental Psychology*, *14*(3), 224–234.

Addyman, C., Rocha, S., & Mareschal, D. (2014). Mapping the origins of time: Scalar errors in infant time estimation. *Developmental Psychology*, *50*(8), 2030–2035

Adolph, K. E., & Tamis-LeMonda, C. S. (2014). The costs and benefits of development: The transition from crawling to walking. *Child Development Perspectives*, *8*(4), 187–192.

Amalric, M., & Dehaene, S. (2016). Origins of the brain networks for advanced mathematics in expert mathematicians. *Proceedings of the National Academy of Sciences*, *113*(18), 4909–4917.

Ansari, D., & Karmiloff-Smith, A. (2002). Atypical trajectories of number development: A neuroconstructivist perspective. *Trends in Cognitive Sciences 6*, 511–516.

Aslin, R. N., & Newport, E. L. (2012). Statistical learning: From acquiring specific items to forming general rules. *Current Directions in Psychological Science*, *21*, 170–176.

Balcomb, F., Newcombe, N. S., & Ferrara, K. (2011). Finding where and saying where: Developmental relationships between place learning and language in the first year. *Journal of Cognition and Development*, *12*(3), 315–331.

Barner, D., Brooks, N., & Bale, A. (2011). Accessing the unsaid: The role of scalar alternatives in children's pragmatic inference. *Cognition*, *118*(1), 84–93.

Barry, C., & Burgess, N. (2014). Neural mechanisms of self-location. *Current Biology*, *24*(8), R330–R339.

Berkowitz, T., Schaeffer, M. W., Maloney, E. A., Peterson, L., Gregor, C., Levine, S. C., & Beilock, S. L. (2015). Math at home adds up to achievement in school. *Science*, *350*(6257), 196–198.

Brannon, E. M., Lutz, D., & Cordes, S. (2006). The development of area discrimination and its implications for numerical abilities in infancy. *Development Science*, *9*(6), F59–F64.

Brannon, E. M., Suanda, S., & Libertus, K., (2007). Temporal discrimination increases in precision over development and parallels the development of numerosity discrimination. *Developmental Science*, *10*(6), 770–777.

Bremner, J. G., & Bryant, P. E. (1977). Place versus response as the basis of spatial errors made by young infants. *Journal of Experimental Child Psychology*, *23*(1), 162–171.

Brown, A. A., Spetch, M. L., & Hurd, P. L. (2007). Growing in circles: Rearing environment alters spatial navigation in fish. *Psychological Science*, *18*(7), 569–573.

Bullens, J., Nardini, M., Doeller, C. F., Braddick, O., Postma, A., & Burgess, N. (2010). The role of landmarks and boundaries in the development of spatial memory. *Developmental Science*, *13*(1), 170–180.

Burgess, N. (2006). Spatial memory: How egocentric and allocentric combine. *Trends in Cognitive Sciences*, *10*(12), 551–557.

Bushnell, E. W., McKenzie, B. E., Lawrence, D. A., & Connell, S. (1995). The spatial coding strategies of one-year-old infants in a locomotor search task. *Child Development*, *66*(4), 937–958.

Byrne, P., Becker, S., & Burgess, N. (2007). Remembering the past and imagining the future: A neural model of spatial memory and imagery. *Psychological Review*, *114*(2), 340–375.

Campos, J. J., Anderson, D. I., Barbu-Roth, M. A., Hubbard, E. M., Hertenstein, M. J., & Witherington, D. (2000). Travel broadens the mind. *Infancy*, *1*(2), 149–219.

Cantlon, J. F., & Brannon, E. M. (2006). Shared system for ordering small and large numbers in monkeys and humans. *Psychological Science*, *17*(5), 401–406.

Cantrell, L., Boyer, T. W., Cordes, S., & Smith, L. B. (2015). Signal clarity. An account of the variability in infant quantity discrimination tasks. *Developmental Science*, *18*(6), 877–893.

Cantrell, L., & Smith, L. B. (2013). Open questions and a proposal: A critical review of the evidence on infant numerical abilities. *Cognition*, *128*(3), 331–352.

Casasola, M., Bhagwat, J., Doan, S. N., & Love, H. (2017). Getting some space: Infants' and caregivers' containment and support spatial constructions during play. *Journal of Experimental Child Psychology*, *159*, 110–128.

Castaldi, E., Piazza, M., Dehaene, S., Vignaud, A., & Eger, E. (2019). Attentional amplification of neural codes for number independent of other quantities along the dorsal visual stream. *bioRxiv*, 527119. http://dx.doi.org/10.7554/eLife.45160

Chen, G., Manson, D., Cacucci, F., & Wills, T. J. (2016). Absence of visual input results in the disruption of grid cell firing in the mouse. *Current Biology*, *26*(17), 2335–2342.

Cheng, K. (1986). A purely geometric module in the rat's spatial representation. *Cognition*, *23*(2), 149–178.

Cheng, K., & Newcombe, N. S. (2005). Is there a geometric module for spatial orientation? Squaring theory and evidence. *Psychonomic Bulletin and Review*, *12*, 1–23.

Chiandetti, C., & Vallortigara, G. (2008). Is there an innate geometric module? Effects of experience with angular geometric cues on spatial re-orientation based on the shape of the environment. *Animal Cognition*, *11*(1), 139–146.

(2010). Experience and geometry: Controlled-rearing studies with chicks. *Animal Cognition, 13*(3), 463–470.

Clearfield, M. W. (2004). The role of crawling and walking experience in infant spatial memory. *Journal of Experimental Child Psychology, 89*(3), 214–241.

Clearfield, M. W., & Mix, K. S. (1999). Number versus contour length in infants' discrimination of small visual sets. *Psychological Science, 10*(5), 408–411.

Constantinescu, M., Moore, D. S., Johnson, S. P., & Hines, M. (2018). Early contributions to infants' mental rotation abilities. *Developmental Science, 21*(4), e12613.

Dean, A. L., & Harvey, W. O. (1979). An information-processing analysis of a Piagetian imagery task. *Developmental Psychology, 15*(4), 474–475.

de Hevia, M. D., Izard, V., Coubart, A., Spelke, E. S., & Streri, A. (2014). Representations of space, time, and number in neonates. *Proceedings of the National Academy of Sciences, 111*(13), 4809–4813.

de Hevia, M. D., & Spelke, E. S. (2010). Number-space mapping in human infants. *Psychological Science, 21*(5), 653–660.

DeLoache, J. S. (1987). Rapid change in the symbolic functioning of very young children. *Science, 238*(4833), 1556–1557.

Diamond, A. (1998). Understanding the A-not-B error: Working memory vs. reinforced response, or active trace vs. latent trace. *Developmental Science, 1*(2), 185–189.

Dilks, D. D., Hoffman, J. E., & Landau, B. (2008). Vision for perception and vision for action: Normal and unusual development. *Developmental Science, 11*(4), 474–486.

Dolscheid, S., Hunnius, S., Casasanto, D., & Majid, A. (2014). Prelinguistic infants are sensitive to space–pitch associations found across cultures. *Psychological Science, 25*(6), 1256–1261.

Estes, D. (1998). Young children's awareness of their mental activity: The case of mental rotation. *Child Development, 69*(5), 1345–1360.

Feigenson, L., & Carey, S. (2003). Tracking individuals via object-files: Evidence from infants' manual search. *Developmental Science, 6*(5), 568–584.

Feigenson, L., Carey, S., & Spelke, E. (2002). Infants' discrimination of number vs. continuous extent. *Cognitive Psychology, 44*(1), 33–66.

Feigenson, L., Dehaene, S., & Spelke, E. (2004). Core systems of number. *Trends in Cognitive Sciences, 8*(7), 307–314.

Fisher, C. B. (1979). Children's memory for orientation in the absence of external cues. *Child Development, 50*(4), 1088–1092.

Frick, A. (2019). Spatial transformation abilities and their relation to later mathematics performance. *Psychological Research, 83*, 1465–1484.

Frick, A., Daum, M. M., Walser, S., & Mast, F. W. (2009). Motor processes in children's mental rotation. *Journal of Cognition and Development, 10*(1–2), 18–40.

Frick, A., Ferrara, K., & Newcombe, N. S. (2013). Using a touch-screen paradigm to assess the development of mental rotation between 3½ and 5½ years of age. *Cognitive Processing, 14*(2), 117–127.

Frick, A., Hansen, M. A., & Newcombe, N. S. (2013). Development of mental rotation in 3- to 5-year-old children. *Cognitive Development, 28*(4), 386–399.

Frick, A., & Möhring, W. (2013). Mental object rotation and motor development in 8- and 10-month-old infants. *Journal of Experimental Child Psychology, 115*(4), 708–720.

Frick, A., & Wang, S. H. (2014). Mental spatial transformations in 14- and 16-month-old infants: Effects of action and observational experience. *Child Development*, *85*(1), 278–293.

Gallistel, C. R. (1990). *The organization of learning* (Vol. 336). Cambridge, MA: MIT Press.

Galloway, J. C. C., Ryu, J. C., & Agrawal, S. K. (2008). Babies driving robots: Self-generated mobility in very young infants. *Intelligent Service Robotics*, *1*(2), 123–134.

Gerson, S. A., & Woodward, A. L. (2014). Learning from their own actions: The unique effect of producing actions on infants' action understanding. *Child Development*, *85*(1), 264–277.

Gunderson, E. A., & Levine, S. C. (2011). Some types of parent number talk count more than others: Relations between parents' input and children's cardinal-number knowledge. *Developmental Science*, *14*(5), 1021–1032.

Gunderson, E. A., Ramirez, G., Beilock, S. L., & Levine, S. C. (2012). The relation between spatial skill and early number knowledge: The role of the linear number line. *Developmental Psychology*, *48*(5), 1229–1241.

Halberda, J., Mazzocco, M. M., & Feigenson, L. (2008). Individual differences in non-verbal number acuity correlate with maths achievement. *Nature*, *455*(7213), 665–668.

Hamamouche, K., & Cordes, S. (2019). Number, time, and space are not singularly represented: Evidence against a common magnitude system beyond early childhood. *Psychonomic Bulletin & Review*, *26*, 1–22.

Hawes, Z., LeFevre, J. A., Xu, C., & Bruce, C. D. (2015). Mental rotation with tangible three-dimensional objects: A new measure sensitive to developmental differences in 4- to 8-year-old children. *Mind, Brain, and Education*, *9*(1), 10–18.

Hawes, Z., Moss, J., Caswell, B., Seo, J., & Ansari, D. (2019). Relations between numerical, spatial, and executive function skills and mathematics achievement: A latent-variable approach. *Cognitive Psychology*, *109*, 68–90.

Hawes, Z., Sokolowski, H. M., Ononye, C. B., & Ansari, D. (2019). Neural underpinnings of numerical and spatial cognition: An fMRI meta-analysis of brain regions associated with symbolic number, arithmetic, and mental rotation. *Neuroscience & Biobehavioral Reviews*, *103*, 316–336.

Hermer, L., & Spelke, E. (1996). Modularity and development: The case of spatial reorientation. *Cognition*, *61*(3), 195–232.

Hermer-Vazquez, L., Moffet, A., & Munkholm, P. (2001). Language, space, and the development of cognitive flexibility in humans: The case of two spatial memory tasks. *Cognition*, *79*(3), 263–299.

Hespos, S. J., Dora, B., Rips, L. J., & Christie, S. (2012). Infants make quantity discriminations for substances. *Child Development*, *83*(2), 554–567.

Huttenlocher, J., Newcombe, N., & Sandberg, E. (1994). The coding of spatial location in young children. *Cognitive Psychology*, *27*, 115–147.

Jacobs, L. F., & Menzel, R. (2014). Navigation outside of the box: what the lab can learn from the field and what the field can learn from the lab. *Movement Ecology*, *2*(1), 1–22.

Johnson, S. P., & Aslin, R. N. (1995). Perception of object unity in 2-month-old infants. *Developmental Psychology*, *31*(5), 739–745.

Jung, W. P., Kahrs, B. A., & Lockman, J. J. (2015). Manual action, fitting, and spatial planning: Relating objects by young children. *Cognition, 134,* 128–139.

   (2018). Fitting handled objects into apertures by 17- to 36-month-old children: The dynamics of spatial coordination. *Developmental Psychology, 54*(2), 228–239.

Karmiloff-Smith, A. (1992). *Beyond modularity: A developmental perspective on cognitive science.* Cambridge, MA: MIT Press.

Kaufman, J., & Needham, A. (2011). Spatial expectations of young human infants, following passive movement. *Developmental Psychobiology, 53*(1), 23–36.

Keen, R. (2003). Representation of objects and events: Why do infants look so smart and toddlers look so dumb? *Current Directions in Psychological Science, 12*(3), 79–83.

Klibanoff, R. S., Levine, S. C., Huttenlocher, J., Vasilyeva, M., & Hedges, L. V. (2006). Preschool children's mathematical knowledge: The effect of teacher "math talk." *Developmental Psychology, 42*(1), 59–69.

Landau, B., & Ferrara, K. (2013). Space and language in Williams syndrome: Insights from typical development. *Wiley Interdisciplinary Reviews: Cognitive Science, 4*(6), 693–706.

Landau, B., Smith, L., & Jones, S. (1998). Object perception and object naming in early development. *Trends in Cognitive Sciences, 2*(1), 19–24.

Laurance, H. E., Learmonth, A. E., Nadel, L., & Jacobs, W. J. (2003). Maturation of spatial navigation strategies: Convergent findings from computerized spatial environments and self-report. *Journal of Cognition and Development, 4*(2), 211–238.

Learmonth, A. E., Nadel, L., & Newcombe, N. S. (2002). Children's use of landmarks: Implications for modularity theory. *Psychological Science, 13*(4), 337–341.

Learmonth, A. E., Newcombe, N. S., & Huttenlocher, J. (2001). Toddlers' use of metric information and landmarks to reorient. *Journal of Experimental Child Psychology, 80*(3), 225–244.

Learmonth, A. E., Newcombe, N. S., Sheridan, N., & Jones, M. (2008). Why size counts: Children's spatial reorientation in large and small enclosures. *Developmental Science, 11*(3), 414–426.

Leibovich, T., Katzin, N., Harel, M., & Henik, A. (2017). From "sense of number" to "sense of magnitude": The role of continuous magnitudes in numerical cognition. *Behavioral and Brain Sciences, 40,* 1–62.

Lew, A. R. (2011). Looking beyond the boundaries: Time to put landmarks back on the cognitive map? *Psychological Bulletin, 137*(3), 484–507.

Lew, A. R., Foster, K. A., Crowther, H. L., & Green, M. (2004). Indirect landmark use at 6 months of age in a spatial orientation task. *Infant Behavior and Development, 27*(1), 81–90.

Libertus, K., Joh, A. S., & Needham, A. W. (2016). Motor training at 3 months affects object exploration 12 months later. *Developmental Science, 19*(6), 1058–1066.

Lourenco, S. F., & Longo, M. R. (2010). General magnitude representation in human infants. *Psychological Science, 21*(6), 873–881.

McKenzie, B. E., Day, R. H., & Ihsen, E. (1984). Localization of events in space: Young infants are not always egocentric. *British Journal of Developmental Psychology, 2*(1), 1–9.

Meck, W. H., & Church, R. M. (1983). A mode control model of counting and timing processes. *Journal of Experimental Psychology: Animal Behavior Processes, 9*(3), 320–334.

Mix, K. S. (2009). How Spencer made number: First uses of the number words. *Journal of Experimental Child Psychology, 102*(4), 427–444.

Mix, K. S., Huttenlocher, J., & Levine, S. C. (2002). Multiple cues for quantification in infancy: Is number one of them? *Psychological Bulletin, 128*(2), 278–294.

Mix, K. S., Levine, S. C., & Newcombe, N. S. (2016). Development of quantitative thinking across correlated dimensions. In A. Henik & W. Fias (Eds.), *Continuous issues in numerical cognition* (pp. 1–33). London: Academic Press.

Möhring, W., & Frick, A. (2013). Touching up mental rotation: Effects of manual experience on 6-month-old infants' mental object rotation. *Child Development, 84*(5), 1554–1565.

Möhring, W., Libertus, M., & Bertin, E. (2012). Speed discrimination in 6- and 10-month-old infants follows Weber's law. *Journal of Experimental Child Psychology, 111*, 405–418.

Montello, D. R. (1993). Scale and multiple psychologies of space. In A. U. Frank & I. Campari (Eds.), *Spatial information theory: A theoretical basis for GIS* (pp. 312–321). European Conference on Spatial Information Theory, Berlin: Springer.

Moore, D. S., & Johnson, S. P. (2008). Mental rotation in human infants: A sex difference. *Psychological Science, 19*(11), 1063–1066.

Moore, D. S., & Johnson, S. P. (2011). Mental rotation of dynamic, three-dimensional stimuli by 3-month-old infants. *Infancy, 16*(4), 435–445.

Morris, R. G. M., Garrud, P., Rawlins, J. A., & O'Keefe, J. (1982). Place navigation impaired in rats with hippocampal lesions. *Nature, 297*(5868), 681–683.

Muessig, L., Hauser, J., Wills, T. J., & Cacucci, F. (2015). A developmental switch in place cell accuracy coincides with grid cell maturation. *Neuron, 86*(5), 1167–1173.

Munakata, Y., McClelland, J. L., Johnson, M. H., & Siegler, R. S. (1997). Rethinking infant knowledge: Toward an adaptive process account of successes and failures in object permanence tasks. *Psychological Review, 104*(4), 686–713.

Nazareth, A., Weisberg, S. M., Margulis, K., & Newcombe, N. S. (2018). Charting the development of cognitive mapping. *Journal of Experimental Child Psychology, 170*, 86–106.

Needham, A., Barrett, T., & Peterman, K. (2002). A pick-me-up for infants' exploratory skills: Early simulated experiences reaching for objects using "sticky mittens" enhances young infants' object exploration skills. *Infant Behavior and Development, 25*(3), 279–295.

Newcombe, N. S. (2017). *Harnessing spatial thinking to support STEM learning*. OECD Education Working Papers, No. 161. Paris: OECD Publishing.

Newcombe, N. S., & Huttenlocher, J. (2000). *Making space: The development of spatial representation and reasoning*. Cambridge, MA: MIT Press.

(2006). Development of spatial cognition. In D. Kuhn & R. S. Siegler (Eds.), *Handbook of child psychology* (6th ed., pp. 734–776). Hoboken, NJ: John Wiley & Sons.

Newcombe, N. S., Huttenlocher, J., Drummey, A. B., & Wiley, J. (1998). The development of spatial location coding: Place learning and dead reckoning in the second and third years. *Cognitive Development, 13*, 185–201.

Odic, D., Hock, H., & Halberda, J. (2014). Hysteresis affects approximate number discrimination in young children. *Journal of Experimental Psychology: General*, *143*(1), 255–265.

Örnkloo, H., & von Hofsten, C. (2007). Fitting objects into holes: On the development of spatial cognition skills. *Developmental Psychology*, *43*(2), 404–416.

Overman, W. H., Pate, B. J., Moore, K., & Peuster, A. (1996). Ontogeny of place learning in children as measured in the radial arm maze, Morris search task, and open field task. *Behavioral Neuroscience*, *110*(6), 1205–1228.

Pica, P., Lemer, C., Izard, V., & Dehaene, S. (2004). Exact and approximate arithmetic in an Amazonian indigene group. *Science*, *306*(5695), 499–503.

Poulter, S., Hartley, T., & Lever, C. (2018). The neurobiology of mammalian navigation. *Current Biology*, *28*(17), R1023–R1042.

Pruden, S. M., Levine, S. C., & Huttenlocher, J. (2011). Children's spatial thinking: Does talk about the spatial world matter? *Developmental Science*, *14*(6), 1417–1430.

Quinn, P. C., & Liben, L. S. (2008). A sex difference in mental rotation in young infants. *Psychological Science*, *19*(11), 1067–1070.

(2014). A sex difference in mental rotation in infants: Convergent evidence. *Infancy*, *19*(1), 103–116.

Ratliff, K. R., & Newcombe, N. S. (2008). Reorienting when cues conflict: Evidence for an adaptive-combination view. *Psychological Science*, *19*(12), 1301–1307.

Raudies, F., Gilmore, R. O., Kretch, K. S., Franchak, J. M., & Adolph, K. E. (2012, November). *Understanding the development of motion processing by characterizing optic flow experienced by infants and their mothers*. Paper presented at the Development and Learning and Epigenetic Robotics (ICDL), 2012 IEEE International Conference, San Diego, CA.

Ribordy, F., Jabès, A., Lavenex, P. B., & Lavenex, P. (2013). Development of allocentric spatial memory abilities in children from 18 months to 5 years of age. *Cognitive Psychology*, *66*(1), 1–29.

Saxe, G. B. (2015). *Culture and cognitive development: Studies in mathematical understanding*. New York, NY: Psychology Press.

Schneider, M., Beeres, K., Coban, L., Merz, S., Schmidt, S., Stricker, J., & de Smedt, B. (2017). Associations of non-symbolic and symbolic numerical magnitude processing with mathematical competence: A meta-analysis. *Developmental Science*, *20*(3), e12372.

Schwarzer, G., Freitag, C., Buckel, R., & Lofruthe, A. (2013). Crawling is associated with mental rotation ability by 9-month-old infants. *Infancy*, *18*(3), 432–441.

Seed, A., & Byrne, R. (2010). Animal tool use. *Current Biology*, 20(23), R1032–R1039.

Shusterman, A., Lee, S. A., & Spelke, E. S. (2011). Cognitive effects of language on human navigation. *Cognition*, *120*(2), 186–201.

Sluzenski, J., Newcombe, N. S., & Satlow, E. (2004). Knowing where things are in the second year of life: Implications for hippocampal development. *Journal of Cognitive Neuroscience*, *16*, 1443–1451.

Smith, L. B., & Kemler, D. G. (1978). Levels of experienced dimensionality in children and adults. *Cognitive Psychology*, *10*(4), 502–532.

Smith, L. B., Thelen, E., Titzer, R., & McLin, D. (1999). Knowing in the context of acting: The task dynamics of the A-not-B error. *Psychological Review*, *106*(2), 235–260.

Smith, L. B., Yu, C., & Pereira, A. F. (2011). Not your mother's view: The dynamics of toddler visual experience. *Developmental Science, 14*(1), 9–17.

Sokolowski, H. M., Fias, W., Ononye, C. B., & Ansari, D. (2017). Are numbers grounded in a general magnitude processing system? A functional neuroimaging meta-analysis. *Neuropsychologia, 105,* 50 69.

Soska, K. C., Adolph, K. E., & Johnson, S. P. (2010). Systems in development: motor skill acquisition facilitates three-dimensional object completion. *Developmental Psychology, 46*(1), 129–138.

Spelke, E. S. (1990). Principles of object perception. *Cognitive Science, 14*(1), 29–56.

Spelke, E. S., & Kinzler, K. D. (2007). Core knowledge. *Developmental Science, 10*(1), 89–96.

Srinivasan, M., & Carey, S. (2010). The long and the short of it: On the nature and origin of functional overlap between representations of space and time. *Cognition, 116*(2), 217–241.

Starkey, P., Spelke, E. S., & Gelman, R. (1983). Detection of intermodal numerical correspondences by human infants. *Science, 222*(4620), 179–181.

Street, S. Y., James, K. H., Jones, S. S., & Smith, L. B. (2011). Vision for action in toddlers: The posting task. *Child Development, 82*(6), 2083–2094.

Sutton, J. E., & Newcombe, N. S. (2014). The hippocampus is not a geometric module: Processing environment geometry during reorientation. *Frontiers in Human Neuroscience, 8,* 1–6.

Tan, H. M., Bassett, J. P., O'Keefe, J., Cacucci, F., & Wills, T. J. (2015). The development of the head direction system before eye opening in the rat. *Current Biology, 25*(4), 479–483.

Tan, H. M., Wills, T. J., & Cacucci, F. (2017). The development of spatial and memory circuits in the rat. *Wiley Interdisciplinary Reviews: Cognitive Science, 8*(3). doi: 10.1002/wcs.1424.

Thelen, E., & Smith, L. B. (1994). *A dynamic systems approach to the development of perception and action.* Cambridge, MA: MIT Press.

Twyman, A. D., Friedman, A., & Spetch, M. L. (2007). Penetrating the geometric module: Catalyzing children's use of landmarks. *Developmental Psychology, 43*(6), 1523–1530.

Twyman, A. D., Newcombe, N. S., & Gould, T. J. (2013). Malleability in the development of spatial reorientation. *Developmental Psychobiology, 55*(3), 243–255.

Verdine, B. N., Golinkoff, R. M., Hirsh-Pasek, K., & Newcombe, N. S. (2017). I. Spatial skills, their development, and their links to mathematics. *Monographs of the Society for Research in Child Development, 82*(1), 7–30.

Vieites, V., Nazareth, A., Reeb-Sutherland, B. C., & Pruden, S. M. (2015). A new biomarker to examine the role of hippocampal function in the development of spatial reorientation in children: A review. *Frontiers in Psychology, 6,* 490.

Voyer, D., Voyer, S., & Bryden, M. P. (1995). Magnitude of sex differences in spatial abilities: A meta-analysis and consideration of critical variables. *Psychological Bulletin, 117*(2), 250–270.

Wang, R. F., & Spelke, E. S. (2002). Human spatial representation: Insights from animals. *Trends in Cognitive Sciences, 6*(9), 376–382.

Weisberg, S. M., Marchette, S. A., & Chatterjee, A. (2018). Behavioral and neural representations of spatial directions across words, schemas, and images. *Journal of Neuroscience, 38(*21), 4996–5007.

Weisberg, S. M., & Newcombe, N.S. (2016). How do (some) people make a cognitive map? Routes, places and working memory. *Journal of Experimental Psychology: Learning, Memory, and Cognition, 42*, 768–785.

Wilcox, T., & Biondi, M. (2015). Object processing in the infant: Lessons from neuroscience. *Trends in Cognitive Sciences, 19*(7), 406–413. doi:10.1016/j.tics.2015.04.009

Wills, T. J., Cacucci, F., Burgess, N., & O'Keefe, J. (2010). Development of the hippocampal cognitive map in preweanling rats. *Science, 328*(5985), 1573–1576.

Wolbers, T., & Wiener, J. M. (2014). Challenges for identifying the neural mechanisms that support spatial navigation: the impact of spatial scale. *Frontiers in Human Neuroscience, 8*(571), 1–12.

Xu, F., & Spelke, E. S. (2000). Large number discrimination in 6-month-old infants. *Cognition, 74*(1), B1–B11.

Xu, F., Spelke, E. S., & Goddard, S. (2005). Number sense in human infants. *Developmental Science, 8*(1), 88–101.

Xu, Y., Regier, T., & Newcombe, N. S. (2017). An adaptive cue combination model of human spatial reorientation. *Cognition, 163*, 56–66.

16 Infant Learning in the Digital Age

Sylvia N. Rusnak and Rachel Barr

Media is so embedded in the lives of infants and toddlers that it should no longer be considered a nuisance variable that could affect development but rather a fundamental part of the context in which development occurs. Parents, educators, and policy makers often remain polarized in the adoption of digital devices, either acting with extreme concern or overly optimistic enthusiasm (Lauricella, Blackwell, & Wartella, 2017). Researchers have recognized that it is not only the amount of time with which children were interacting with these technologies but also how and what they were engaging with that predicted learning and other outcomes (Lauricella et al., 2017). However, accurately assessing the content and context of media use during early childhood has been problematic, with some methods leading to overestimation and others to underreporting of media exposure (Vandewater & Lee, 2009). Obtaining a clear picture of the overall family media ecology and the infant's cumulative exposure to media is integral to understanding how media exposure relates to later outcomes. Therefore, children's individual history with media requires a more comprehensive assessment of family media exposure than has been conducted in past research (Barr & Linebarger, 2017).

In this chapter, we take a multilevel approach, describing how the infant's media environment is associated with social and perceptual factors that influence learning from media. As with other contextual factors, it is essential to accurately measure past and present media use. It is also crucial to measure learning at multiple levels. Although there are currently few developmental cognitive neuroscience theories of media learning during infancy, we describe how neuroimaging measures have and could be applied to understanding how the brain processes media content. Taken together, this multilevel approach will be critical for policy and practice that aims to harness the potential benefit and limit the potential harm of media use during infancy.

16.1 The Digital Landscape in Infancy

16.1.1 Current Media Environment

The introduction of the iPhone in 2007 and the iPad in 2010 heralded a rapid shift in the availability of mobile technology in the homes of infants. Nearly all

US homes with young children (95%) have a smartphone, and three-quarters have a tablet (Rideout, 2017). Research and policy will need to adapt to the rapidly changing media landscape for very young audiences. The American Academy of Pediatrics (AAP) discourages screen time for children under 18 months of age other than video chat, which is seen as an exception to traditional screen time rules in both policy makers' and parents' eyes (AAP, 2016; McClure, Chentsova-Dutton, Barr, Holochwost, & Parrott, 2015). For children 18 months to 5 years of age, the AAP recommends that parents limit screen time use to 1 hour of high-quality programming that is supported with a co-viewing parent (AAP, 2016).

Parents are not closely following these recommendations. For infants and toddlers, video content is the most common form of screen use. US parents report that 35% of children under 2 years of age view television (TV) each day, for ~29 minutes per day, which comprises 72% of their overall screen time (Rideout, 2017). Although the amount of time that infants and toddlers spend with media overall has not changed significantly over the past decade, the way in which media is consumed has changed: Almost half (46%) of children under 2 years of age have viewed content on a mobile device (Rideout, 2017). More frequent mobile usage begins during toddlerhood; 2- to 4-year-olds interact with mobile devices for nearly an hour daily, viewing streaming video content and playing games on applications (apps). This may stem from a majority of parents (61%) identifying the ages of 2 to 2.5 years as being acceptable ages for their children to use technology (Wood et al., 2016). In addition to video content, infants and toddlers use mobile apps, such as games marketed specifically for a young audience. However, the actual quality of these apps, whether they can promote early learning, and the context in which their use does and should occur has not been well investigated (Hirsh-Pasek et al., 2015). Finally, some families are using video chat to stay in contact with distant parents and relatives. Some research suggests that as many as one-third of children under the age of 6 years use video chat at least once per week (e.g., McClure et al., 2015) but nationally representative reports are lower (Rideout, 2017). Many parents report video chat as an exception to their screen-time or media rules, perhaps because it is often used as a tool to maintain and strengthen valued familial relationships, such as those with remote grandparents (McClure et al., 2015).

Digital media pervades daily activities – from driving in the car to eating a meal with family at a restaurant (e.g., Radesky, Kistin et al., 2014) – and is no longer limited to the family TV set. Most assessments of media exposure have focused on parental reports of intentional direct exposure to TV, but other assessments have considered the overall family media ecology (Linebarger, Barr, Ribner, & Coyne, 2016). Media-exposure measures often account for the amount of time but do not delineate what children are doing with mobile devices (e.g., watching a program, video chatting with a relative) or whether the TV or other media is playing in the background of other activities (Barr & Linebarger, 2017).

16.1.2 Sociocultural Context of Media Use

Within the United States, media access and use is associated with socioeconomic factors, particularly household income and parental education. In 2017, the gap had closed in terms of access to smartphones; however, there was still a digital divide between children in lower- and higher-income households. Namely, children in lower-income homes were less likely to have a home computer (25% gap), a tablet (24% gap), or access to high-speed stable internet (22% gap). Media-usage patterns also differ across cultural groups. Kabali et al. (2015) surveyed largely African American parents in a low-resourced community. Consistent with prior research showing that African American families have traditionally been early adopters of new technology (Calvert, Rideout, Woolard, Barr, & Strouse, 2005), 83% of households had a tablet device and 77% had smartphones. Parents reported that half or more of the apps downloaded on their phones had been specifically downloaded for their child's use.

There are also significant differences in usage as a function of parental education and income. Although these data are not broken down by age, Rideout (2017) reported significant differences in the amount of time spent on devices between children aged 8 years and younger from lower- and higher-income homes (3 hours, 29 minutes vs. 1 hour, 50 minutes, respectively). Equivalent numbers of low-income and higher-income parents have downloaded apps for their child to use. Additionally, parents with less formal education reported that their children consumed 2 hours and 50 minutes of screen media a day compared to the 1 hour and 37 minutes in homes reported by parents with higher levels of formal education.

The overall home environment moderates media choices and learning outcomes. Choi et al. (2018) found that when mothers provided a more cognitively stimulating home environment, this predicted whether they would later choose educational media for their children. The reverse, however, was not true: Greater early use of educational programming did not predict increased cognitive stimulation in the home. Under conditions of higher parental stress, perhaps counterintuitively, parents reported using more educational content. Parents may have used educational media to provide cognitive stimulation when they were unable to do so themselves or when their infants were more irritable (Bank et al., 2012; Lauricella, Wartella, & Rideout, 2015; Pempek & McDaniel, 2016; Radesky, Silverstein, Zuckerman, & Christakis, 2014). Interpretation of media-usage patterns should consider both the instrumental and psychological function of parental media usage.

Media resources, when they are used in a supportive context, provide an opportunity for otherwise low-resources families. Latin American parents were more likely to co-engage with tablets compared to European American parents, even when controlling for parent age and education, child age and gender, and parent's time with the device and time with the child (Connell, Lauricella, & Wartella, 2015). Such joint media engagement (JME; see the next section) can support early learning. For example, in one study of low-income, immigrant mothers and their infants, JME during TV viewing at 6 months predicted language development at 14 months (Mendelsohn et al., 2010).

Unfortunately, there is only a limited international perspective regarding the range of media use in infancy. Very few studies have measured household media use during infancy outside of the United States, but patterns of media exposure appear to be similar in international contexts. One study found that in Bangladesh, nearly half of a national sample of preschool-aged children watched TV daily in 2007 (Khan, Chakraborty, Rahman, & Nasrin, 2007). Furthermore, in a survey of French parents with children aged 5 to 40 months, 75% of families used touchscreen technology such as tablets to view videos or photos, and 50% reported using tablet apps advertised to be used with infants (Cristia & Seidl, 2015).

The next two sections will explain how the content and context of early media exposure are associated with more positive outcomes via joint media engagement (Section 16.1.3) and more negative outcomes via technoference (Section 16.1.4).

16.1.3 Joint Media Engagement

Two factors contribute significantly to whether or not an infant can learn from media: the content and design of the program and the context of JME in which it is used (Barr & Linebarger, 2017). The types of strategies that parents typically use when reading picture books to their children are the same strategies, such as pointing and labeling, that are effective for JME with TV and tablets (Bus, Takacs, & Kegel, 2015).

A number of factors predict whether parents will engage in JME or not (Connell et al., 2015). In research examining families with children aged 8 years and younger, fathers were more likely to co-engage with video games and mobile technology, perhaps because these devices offer more opportunities for playful interactions than other types of media. Overall, more parents co-engaged with TV and books compared to smartphones and tablets. Parents may have the misconception that because they can process audiovisual content so easily themselves, they may not need to scaffold media use for their children, especially when an app is interactive and responsive to the child (Barr & Linebarger, 2017; Guernsey, 2012).

16.1.3.1 *TV and JME*

Joint media engagement with TV may be particularly important because studies of looking time have shown that the content developed for preschoolers was difficult for infants and toddlers to process and that they have to learn how to selectively view content. Early in development, infants are unable to distinguish between comprehensible and incomprehensible content. For example, it was not until 18 months that infants looked longer at content that was cor-rectly sequenced compared to incorrectly sequenced (Pempek et al., 2010; J. E. Richards 2010). Kirkorian, Anderson, and Keen (2012) used eye tracking to show that when 12- to 15-month-olds were shown a clip from *Sesame Street*, their gaze pattern was more scattered around the screen than that of 4-year-olds. Furthermore, it is likely that fantastical content is incomprehensible to infants because it is not grounded in their understanding of everyday life. In fact, studies with preschoolers show that viewing fantastical programs, fea-turing unrealistic characters and settings, had a more negative effect on their executive functioning (Lillard, Drell, Richey, Boguszewski, & Smith, 2015). However, the same effect did not hold for preschoolers when they played an interactive game on a tablet (Li, Subrahmanyam, Bai, Xie, & Liu, 2018).

During the 1990s, the availability of commercial infant-directed DVDs advertised for language learning proliferated. Unfortunately, while infant-directed videos made strong education claims, they were largely poorly designed (Fenstermacher, Barr, Salerno et al., 2010). These videos lacked good language strategies (Vaala et al., 2010) or many examples of par-ent–child interactions (Fenstermacher, Barr, Brey et al., 2010). Perhaps for this reason, findings were mixed about whether infants could learn any new language from these programs. Linebarger and Walker (2005) found that greater exposure to children's TV programming that included interactive characters, such as those in *Blue's Clues* and *Dora the Explorer*, during infancy was associated with greater vocabulary at 30 months. Some stud-ies of familiar content demonstrated no learning from video presentations (DeLoache et al., 2010). Other studies showed some evidence of learning novel words (Richert, Robb, Fender, & Wartella, 2010) and novel American Sign Language (ASL) gestures (Dayanim & Namy, 2015), but only when supported by JME. Interactions that occur over the screen, such as a video-chat interaction, can also support learning (see Section 16.2.1.2 Testing Explanations of the Transfer Deficit).

Researchers have closely examined parent–child interactions during TV viewing and app use. Barr, Zack, Garcia, and Muentener (2008) found that 12- to 18-month-olds who viewed infant-directed videos with their parents looked longer at the videos and were more responsive (e.g., vocalizing, point-ing) to them when their parents provided high degrees of JME during view-ing. Looking behavior also becomes synchronized when parents and infants co-view. Even with parents' verbal scaffolding controlled, Demers, Hanson, Kirkorian, Pempek, and Anderson (2013) reported that immediately after their parent looked at an infant-directed video, 18- and 21-month-olds also looked at it and looked for longer than if a parent did not look toward the video. In an experimental study, Strouse and Troseth (2014) randomly assigned 2-year-olds to a word-learning task with or without parental support. When 2-year-olds watched a 5-minute video in which a novel object was labeled four times, they were able to label the object in a video test but were unable to transfer the label to a 3-D context (Strouse & Troseth, 2014). However, when the parent reinforced the similarity between the object on the screen and the 3-D object, toddlers could transfer the novel label from the screen to the 3-D object. Thus, parents can facilitate transfer learning by drawing connections across the dimensional divide.

16.1.3.2 *New Media and JME*

Parents may believe that they do not need to be involved when their young children use tablets. In fact, only 25% of parents report JME with their children during tablet use (Rideout, 2017). This is despite the fact that JME can enhance learning. Zack and Barr (2016) found that when parents engaged in high-quality JME with their 15-month-olds, their infants were significantly more likely to transfer learning from the touchscreen to an object in the physical world. In other words, strategies such as simple explanations and labeling of key features, attempts to organize the task for the infant, praise, and encouragement enhanced transfer of learning among very young children who typically do not transfer.

Research has begun to examine JME during video chat. An observational study with 6- to 24-month-olds found that it was cognitively demanding for younger infants to jointly attend to objects across the dimensional divide (McClure, Chentsova-Dutton, Holochwost, Parrott, & Barr, 2017). As such, many parents engaged in quite elaborate JME strategies to facilitate video chat between grandparents and their grandchildren (McClure et al., 2017). An experimental study by Myers, Crawford, Murphy, Aka-Ezoua, and Felix (2018) found that JME around video chat was important for 24- to 30-month-olds' novel word learning. Toddlers were taught novel information by an on-screen (video-chat) partner who either had aligned or misaligned gaze. A co-viewing adult who was either responsive or nonresponsive to the video-chat partner also sat next to the toddler. The responsive co-viewer modeled appropriate responses, drew attention to the screen, and demonstrated contingent responses to the on-screen partner; on the other hand, the nonresponsive co-viewer only paid attention to the screen. Toddlers who had a responsive co-viewer looked more frequently and for longer toward the on-screen partner than toddlers who had a nonresponsive co-viewer. These toddlers also learned more novel words. Taken together, these results show that during the infancy and toddlerhood period, JME can potentiate learning from TV, tablets, and video chat.

16.1.4 Technoference

"Technoference" is defined as everyday interruptions to interpersonal interactions or time spent together that occur due to digital media (McDaniel & Radesky, 2018). The introduction of technology may disrupt the infant's ability to self- or co-regulate attention and emotions during typical routines and play. Early childhood may be a particularly vulnerable time for technoference, because media usage is entirely governed by family household media patterns.

16.1.4.1 *Technoference via Background TV*

The most common and pervasive form of technoference occurs with background TV exposure; 42% of US parents reported that the TV is on most of the time even if no one is watching it (Rideout, 2017). Background TV typically includes adult-directed shows such as sitcoms or game shows, which are mostly on while young children play. It is estimated that US children under 3 years of age are exposed to an average of 5.5 hours of background TV per day, which represents approximately 40% of a child's waking life (Lapierre, Piotrowski, & Linebarger, 2012). Using in-home language environment analysis (LENA) audio recording devices, Christakis et al. (2009) reported a 7% decrease in adult speech per hour, decreased child vocalizations, and decreased conversational turn-taking when the TV was on. Even if toddlers were only exposed to half as much background TV, it is estimated that children would hear approximately 13,400 fewer child-directed words per week (Anderson & Hanson, 2017).

Such background TV decreases parent–child interactional quality as well as child play quality and disrupts attention and language processing (Kirkorian, Pempek, Murphy, Schmidt, & Anderson, 2009; Schmidt, Pempek, Kirkorian, Lund, & Anderson, 2008; Setliff & Courage, 2011). Setliff and Courage (2011) measured looking time directed towards toys while TV was on in the background. They found that 6-, 12-, and 24-month-olds spent less time attending to the toys when the TV was on. Even though they glanced frequently at the TV, half of these looks were <2s, suggesting that they were not processing the content but rather being repeatedly interrupted during play. Schmidt et al. (2008) examined 12-, 24-, and 36-month-olds' looking time and play behavior while an adult-directed game show played in the background. Although children only attended to the game show 5% of the time, their play episodes were shorter, less complex, and included less focused attention when the TV was on than when it was off. Parents may believe that because their infants are not "watching" background TV, their infants are not being affected by it (Anderson & Pempek, 2005).

Furthermore, adult-directed TV reduced the quality and quantity of parent–child interactions. Kirkorian et al. (2009) compared parent engagement with their 12- to 36-month-olds in an hour-long free play session during which background TV was on for half of the session. Parents actively engaged with their children significantly less when the TV was on than when the TV was off. Parents also were slower to respond to bids for attention and responded in a more passive manner (Kirkorian et al., 2009). Child-directed speech decreased when an adult-selected program was playing than when it was not (Pempek, Kirkorian, & Anderson, 2014). Additionally, regardless of program content (child- or adult-directed), when the TV was on, parents interacted less with their children than when the TV was off (Courage, Murphy, Goulding, & Setliff, 2010; Kirkorian et al., 2009).

Background TV exposure may tax cognitive functioning. Several longitudinal studies have shown that exposure to background TV is negatively associated with children's language development, cognitive development, and executive functioning (EF) skills (Barr, Lauricella, Zack, & Calvert, 2010; Linebarger, Barr, Lapierre, & Piotrowski, 2014; Nathanson, Aladé, Sharp, Rasmussen, & Christy, 2014). Linebarger et al. (2014) examined parent reports from a large, nationally representative sample and found that exposure to higher levels of noneducational foreground TV and background TV by preschoolers was associated with poorer EF but that certain parenting practices and parent socio-economic status (SES) moderated the relation. Barr, Lauricella et al. (2010) found that higher background TV exposure during infancy predicted poorer EF at 4 years. Nathanson et al. (2014) similarly reported that greater cumulative exposure to higher overall amounts of TV throughout the infancy and toddler period was associated with poorer EF in preschoolers. Parents may be unaware of the impact of background TV on their children's play and learning. Assessing media exposure as it occurs across contexts is an important future direction for researchers (see Section 16.1.5 Future Directions).

16.1.4.2 *Technoference via Background Cell-Phone Use*

Technoference can also occur with mobile devices and presents other challenges for parent–child interactions. An observational study of 55 parents and their young children eating at fast-food restaurants found that the more time that parents interacted with mobile devices, the more likely their children were to increase their negative bids for their parents' attention, which sometimes led to negative responses from parents (Radesky, Kistin et al., 2014). This may be due to the fact that when checking cell phones, parents' faces typically have no expression, which may be perceived by young children as a "still face," to which children respond aversively (Adamson & Frick, 2003). A still face occurs when the adult stops interacting with the child and assumes a neutral facial expression. Goldstein, Schwade, and Bornstein (2009) found that when 5-month-olds were exposed to a still face by an unfamiliar adult in a face-to-face interaction, infants initially attempted to reengage the adult but then gave up. In a modified version of the still-face procedure, researchers asked mothers of 50 7- to 23-month-olds to participate in a mobile device version of the still face. In an initial free play session, mothers were instructed to play freely with their infants. Then in the still-face phase, they were asked to view their cell phone. Finally, there was a second free play phase, called the reunion phase. Infants explored the room more during the first free play session than they did during the still-face or reunion phases. When parents viewed their mobile device during the still-face phase, infants exhibited the typical protest and distress response exhibited in other versions of the still-face paradigm (Myruski et al., 2018).

Cell-phone use also disrupts language learning in toddlers. In an experimental study, Reed, Hirsh-Pasek, and Golinkoff (2017) asked mothers to teach their 2-year-olds two novel words. Mothers received a call that interrupted them while teaching one of the words, but not the other word. Children were significantly more likely to learn the uninterrupted word than the interrupted word. This finding remained despite the children hearing the novel word the same number of times in both conditions. Because mobile-device use occurs in brief, intermittent bursts (Oulasvirta, Tamminen, Roto, & Kuorelahti, 2005), parents' self-report or recall of mobile-device use is often inaccurate (Goedhart, Kromhout, Wiart, & Vermeulen, 2015). Like lack of awareness of the impact of background TV, parents are unlikely to be aware of how their own mobile media usage is affecting parent–infant interactions.

Technoference occurs at other times when parents use their phones for instrumental functions. Frequent use of these strategies may interfere with typical opportunities for face-to-face interactions or with the infant's own ability to learn self-regulatory skills. For example, parents frequently report using mobile devices so that they can do chores such as making dinner, run errands, traveling, eat out at a restaurant, calm a child during transitions, or help a child fall asleep (Kabali et al., 2015; Wartella, Rideout, Lauricella, & Connell, 2014). This pass-back behavior indicates that parents may be using mobile devices as "digital pacifiers" to manage children's behavior, whether to calm them or distract them in order to accomplish other tasks (Kabali et al., 2015). This is despite the fact that parents report concern that their children's media usage is replacing opportunities for important social skills to develop or influencing children's attentional capacities. For example, parents of 15- to 36-month-olds at the Women, Infants, and Children (WIC) nutrition clinics were asked about their children's socioemotional development and their use of mobile devices: specifically, whether mobile devices were used during family routines, such as at bedtime or while doing chores, and if they used devices to calm their infants (Radesky, Peacock-Chambers, Zuckerman, & Silverstein, 2016). Parental report of socioemotional difficulties was associated with parental use of mobile devices as a calming tool but not with other uses. It is unknown whether parents with more difficult infants use mobile devices more for calming, whether parents who felt more overwhelmed used mobile devices, or if mobile devices were likely to result in more socioemotional difficulties. The authors speculated that frequent use of mobile devices for self-regulation may result in the development of fewer other regulatory strategies by parents and children (Radesky et al., 2016).

16.1.5 Future Directions

In the digital age, media provides a context in which children develop. Future research, therefore, must comprehensively measure not only the quantity of media exposure but the content and the context in which it occurs. While global quantity estimates of child and parent media use have been previously collected, these measures were biased, resulting in over- or under-reporting of media use

(Vandewater & Lee, 2009). They failed to focus on the context in which media was used or the content with which children engaged. Mixed methods across studies limit cross-study comparison, and the rapidly changing digital landscape calls for a method (or methods) that allows for an assessment of media use that can be flexibly applied to many types of media and contexts, including inside and outside the home. A clearer picture of children's individual history with media is necessary in order to understand their ability to learn from it (Barr & Linebarger, 2017). New platforms and apps, background media, as well as media quantity and quality should be measured (Eunice Kennedy Shriver National Institute on Child Health and Human Development; NICHD, 2018). Future research will need to be conducted globally and more carefully consider children's media exposure across SES and health and learning outcomes.

Measuring media usage has become increasingly complicated as the number of devices and different media options have exponentially increased. The most effective approach to studying media exposure will be to use multiple methods in conjunction with one another (NICHD, 2018; Vandewater & Lee, 2009) to gather a holistic picture of media exposure during infancy. Features, such as Screen Time on Apple devices, can passively record how many times a user picks up their mobile device and for how long they use it. Passive sensing may be particularly useful for briefer instances of media use, such as with mobile devices. Shorter bursts of attention to TV are less likely to be remembered than longer looks are, and this retrospective recall difficulty may also translate to mobile devices (Barr & Linebarger, 2017).

To investigate the family media ecology, an international consortium of researchers has developed the Comprehensive Assessment of Family Media Exposure (CAFE) tool to assess media usage in children under 5 years of age. The CAFE tool includes a detailed survey, a 24-hour time-use diary, and a passive sensing app for mobile devices (Barr et al., in revision). This synergistic data collection approach will address two prior limitations to our understanding of early media exposure: a limited international perspective and poor understanding of media use across the SES spectrum.

16.2 What Can Infants Learn from Media?

In this section, we focus on content developed for infants both commercially and in the laboratory. Understanding the factors that facilitate or detract from learning from media shifts attention from the sheer amount of time to the content and the context of media use (Barr & Linebarger, 2017).

16.2.1 Transfer Learning

Broadly speaking, learning from media involves a transfer of learning, applying knowledge from media to the real world. This transfer involves shifts in the physical context (and thus, the cues provided by the environment), the temporal context (with a delay of a few seconds to longer), and the modality – as children may handle 3-D objects but need to transfer learning to 2-D objects that are physically manipulated in different ways. Generalizing across 3-D and 2-D modalities may seem trivial to adults but can actually be cognitively demanding for young children who have fewer cognitive resources available (Barnett & Ceci, 2002; Barr, 2010, 2013; Zack, Barr, Gerhardstein, Dickerson, & Meltzoff, 2009).

Despite this difficulty, children do learn from 2-D media. Five-month-olds can discriminate between two pictures of faces that are perceptually different (Dirks & Gibson, 1977). They can recognize line drawings, though differentiation is stronger when stimuli are more realistic (DeLoache, Strauss, & Maynard, 1979). Infants also learn social information. Mumme and Fernald (2003) reported that after viewing an experimenter show negative affect toward a toy on TV, 12-month-olds immediately avoided the real toy when it was presented to them. Infants as young as 6 months can imitate simple actions they see on TV, both immediately afterward and up to 24 hours later (Barr, Muentener, & Garcia, 2007); by 18 months, toddlers can remember brief sequences that they saw on TV or in a book for 2 weeks, and by 2 years of age, they can remember these sequences for 1 month (Simcock, Garrity, & Barr, 2011).

However, there is a cost associated with transfer. Young children show a transfer deficit when they are tasked with learning information in a media context, such as from TV or a tablet, and transferring that knowledge to a real-world context. For example, for 12-, 15-, and 18-month-olds, the ability to imitate a multistep sequence from TV lags behind their ability to learn from a live demonstration of the same action (Barr & Hayne, 1999). Similarly, when 2-year-olds are told via a prerecorded video where to find an attractive toy hidden in a room, they are typically unable to locate the toy, even though they are perfectly capable of doing so when given the same information in person (Troseth, Saylor, & Archer, 2006). This finding has been replicated across many types of tasks, demonstrating the broad impact of this transfer deficit. The size or type of screen (TV, phone, or tablet) does not alter this finding. The transfer deficit emerges during infancy and persists into early childhood, depending on task complexity (Hipp et al., 2017).

16.2.1.1 *Explanations of the Transfer Deficit*

Constraints on the developing memory system during early childhood contribute to the transfer deficit and offer explanations for its bidirectional nature (i.e., children demonstrate difficulty learning from 2-D and applying to 3-D and vice versa; see the next section). The ability to retrieve cues in a context that is different than the one present during encoding is known as memory flexibility, which allows young children to generalize beyond the specific details of a memory (Barr, 2013). Successful transfer requires memory flexibility (Barnett & Ceci, 2002).

Poor memory flexibility likely contributes to the difficulty in transferring learning in the face of cue or context changes. Young children may encode characteristics of 2-D sources that may not match characteristics that are present during subsequent retrieval in a 3-D context (or vice versa; Barr, 2013). For example, 2-D images are perceptually impoverished; that is, perceptual cues on 2-D images are often smaller and lack cues that are features of 3-D objects, such as depth (Barr & Hayne, 1999; McCall et al., 1977). The context surrounding encoding may not match the retrieval context. For example, a child may encode irrelevant features of a 2-D context, such as a button at the base of a tablet.

Poor memory flexibility may also contribute to poor symbolic representation, another potential mechanism underlying the transfer deficit (Troseth, 2010). Symbolic artifacts are informational tools; they stand for their referents. For example, an image on a TV can represent a real-life person or object. For symbolic artifacts to be effective informational tools, children must have some understanding of the relation between the image or symbol and the real object (DeLoache, 1995). Immaturity in symbolic understanding limits children's ability to understand that objects and people on the screen represent objects and people in real life. It is possible that children may learn that televised content does not stand for information in the real world from repeated experience with noncontingent video (Troseth, 2010). However, the development of symbolic understanding and memory flexibility may not be mutually exclusive. Memory flexibility itself may be necessary for the emergence of symbolic understanding.

The lack of social contingency from a prerecorded video or a touchscreen has also been proposed as another mechanism underlying the transfer deficit. Infants are born into an environment in which human interactions are predicated on social contingency, or the appropriate and timely back-and-forth manner of response (Bornstein & Tamis-LeMonda, 2008). Responsive parent–child interactions are the bedrock for healthy social attachment formation, language development, and cognitive development (Bornstein & Tamis-LeMonda, 2008). Infants are sensitive to fluctuations in the timing (Henning & Striano, 2011) and frequency of contingent responses by caregivers (Goldstein et al., 2009). Infants are similarly sensitive to the contingency between their own behavior and that of their caregivers (Murray & Trevarthen, 1985). The detection of social contingency is a bidirectional process. When caregivers respond contingently, infants do so as well (Kuchirko, Tafuro, & Tamis-LeMonda, 2018). Noncontingent video may violate infants' expectations of contingency, such that infants and toddlers discount noncontingent media as a viable source of information.

16.2.1.2 *Testing Explanations of the Transfer Deficit*

Poor memory flexibility and the lack of social contingency both impact the trajectory of the transfer deficit. Prior studies may have confounded these two factors. Televised demonstrations in these prior investigations either did not include social cues, or the social cues presented in the video were not truly relevant. Consequently, researchers have tested transfer learning on touchscreen-enabled devices, which can keep the social nature of the task (e.g., there is a live demonstrator) constant and manipulate perceptual features (e.g., the 2-D perceptual image). Even under these conditions, the transfer deficit persists. Zack et al. (2009) tested 15-month-olds using a one-step imitation task. Children observed a demonstration of how to press a button box, either in 3-D or on a touchscreen. They were then asked to imitate in the same or opposite dimension. Those who were tested in a transfer condition (2-D–3-D or 3-D–2-D) performed significantly worse than those tested under conditions of no transfer, that is, when there was a high degree of perceptual similarity between the learning and testing contexts (3-D–3-D or 2-D–2-D).

In a series of follow-up studies with older children, Dickerson, Gerhardstein, Zack, and Barr (2013) developed the puzzle task to more precisely manipulate social and perceptual factors. Using this task, an experimenter demonstrated how to construct a puzzle either on a touchscreen or on a magnet board with 3-D pieces. The magnet board could be easily transformed into the touchscreen or video screen and vice versa, which allowed manipulation of the transfer conditions (e.g., 2-D to 3-D). With this task, it was not until 3.5 years of age that children showed the same level of imitation after both the live and video conditions (Dickerson et al., 2013). Furthermore, Moser et al. (2015) reported that the bidirectional transfer deficit persisted in older children. 2.5- and 3-year-olds who viewed a demonstration of a puzzle being assembled on a 3-D magnet board also performed poorly when asked to recall this information on a 2-D touchscreen. Taken together, these studies demonstrate that the transfer deficit is bidirectional, such that children not only have difficulty transferring learning from 2-D to 3-D sources, but also from 3-D to 2-D contexts (Moser et al., 2015; Zack et al., 2009). Although the transfer deficit is not initially observed in 6-month-olds, from 12 months onwards it is consistently observed through the third year of life (Barr, 2013). The difficulty of transferring is attributable to changes between demonstration and test and not solely to the perceptual impoverishment of the 2-D learning experience (Hipp et al., 2017).

A number of factors can reduce the transfer deficit, such as judicious addition of visual and auditory cues. With 6-, 12-, and 18-month-olds, adding background music to a video demonstration disrupted transfer learning but addition of sound effects restored transfer learning (Barr, Shuck, Salerno, Atkinson, & Linebarger, 2010). In another study, 2-year-olds who engaged with interactive videos on touchscreen tablets demonstrated increased word learning as compared to toddlers who viewed noninteractive videos on tablets (Kirkorian, Choi, & Pempek, 2016). However, there were age related differences in the effectiveness of different cues: 2-year-olds benefited most when they were directed by the app to interact with specific information on the screen, whereas 2.5-year-olds did better when they could choose for themselves where to interact on the screen. Researchers determined in another study an optimal level of prompting from a prerecorded video (Nussenbaum & Amso, 2016). In this study, the experimenter on the screen taught 36-month-olds a novel word, followed by a prompt of high, medium, or low level of interactivity. In the low-interactivity condition, the experimenter on the screen asked if the child knew how to say the novel word but did not wait for the child's response. In the medium-interactivity condition, the experimenter paused for a few seconds, apparently waiting for the response. In the high-interactivity condition, the experimenter added, after the pause, "You're right!" Children in the medium-interactivity condition performed best.

Removal of distracting cues also increases performance. In one study, 2-year-olds were unable to find the object when they viewed the hiding event or heard the description over video (Troseth & DeLoache, 1998). If 2-year-olds watched a TV but were told that they were looking through a window, their performance improved compared to the video condition but was still poorer than actually watching through a window (Troseth & DeLoache, 1998). This is perhaps because toddlers were not distracted by irrelevant cues, such as the TV frame, during encoding and retrieval. The addition of cues might explain why the transfer deficit is reduced after repeated exposure to content (Barr, Muentener, Garcia, Fujimoto, & Chávez, 2007; Krcmar, 2010). Repetition of content presumably allows for the encoding of a more complete representation of the memory attributes (Carver, Meltzoff, & Dawson, 2006; Zack et al., 2009), leading to an increase in the cues that later can be retrieved at test (Barnett & Ceci, 2002). Prior experience with certain interactive media may also be an important mediator of transfer success (Kirkorian & Choi, 2017). Future research should continue to assess whether the child's typical media usage is associated with transfer of learning.

Socially contingent video interactions also enhance infants' and toddlers' transfer learning. When 2-year-olds first engaged in a social interaction with an experimenter over video chat and then were tasked with finding a hidden object, they could reliably do so (Troseth et al., 2006). In other tasks, toddlers are taught novel labels or verbs over video. Roseberry, Hirsh-Pasek, and Golinkoff (2014) taught 24- to 30-month-olds novel verbs in one of three conditions: live interaction, socially contingent video chat, or noncontingent video. Toddlers demonstrated a transfer deficit, learning less from the noncontingent video than the live interaction. However, performance was comparable in the live interaction and socially contingent video-chat conditions, indicating that the transfer deficit can be ameliorated with a socially contingent interaction, even one that occurs over video. In another study, 9-month-olds were unable to learn a phonetic discrimination when it was presented repeatedly on TV but could learn to distinguish between phonemes from face-to-face interactions (Kuhl, Tsao, & Liu, 2003). When 9-month-old infants were paired together and were able to interact with a tablet to stop and start the videos themselves, however, they did learn the phonetic discrimination from a video demonstration but failed to do so when they interacted with the tablet alone (Roseberry, Garcia-Sierra, & Kuhl, 2018).

Similarly, 12- to 25-month-olds were randomly assigned to either a video chat or prerecorded video condition (Myers, LeWitt, Gallo, & Maselli, 2017). Most notably, these prerecorded videos were not yoked videos from previous experimenter–child interactions, so they lacked inaccurate personal information. After a week of daily training and interaction on novel words and actions, children were tested on preference and recognition of the person they saw on the video chat or prerecorded video (compared to an unfamiliar experimenter), as well as the novel words and actions. Children in the video-chat condition, but not the video condition, preferred the person they saw on the video chat to the unfamiliar experimenter. The oldest children (22- to 24-month-olds) in the video-chat condition learned more novel words than the oldest children in the video condition did. One explanation for the effects of social contingency that can be ruled out is enhanced overall looking time or engagement with content. There are no differences between overall looking time or responsiveness to contingent and noncontingent video (Lauricella, Pempek, Barr, & Calvert, 2010; Myers et al., 2017; Troseth et al., 2006).

One important caveat is that some studies have yoked other children's video-chat sessions for their noncontingent conditions. Infants and toddlers are able to detect inaccuracy, which could reduce their learning from such yoked videos (Koenig & Woodward, 2010). Consequently, children in the yoked video conditions may have heard the incorrect name, as well as other irrelevant information (e.g., information about another child's pet; Roseberry et al., 2014; Troseth et al., 2006). Children recognize their own name by 4.5 months of age (Mandel, Jusczyk, & Pisoni, 1995), so they may have been confused by this misinformation and subsequently discounted any other information provided by the adult in the video. Future research should test learning from prerecorded videos in ways that do not lead infants and toddlers to discount on-screen information.

16.2.2 Summary and Future Directions

Learning from media during early childhood is characterized by a transfer deficit that can be explained by the child's poor memory flexibility and the lack of social contingency available in most media (Barr, 2010, 2013; Kirkorian, 2018). However, individual factors (e.g., children's personal history of interactive and noninteractive media use), the addition of social contingency, the addition of visual and auditory cues, and the repetition of content have been shown to increase transfer success (Barr, 2013; Kirkorian, 2018). These information-processing challenges are due to more general mechanisms of perceptual and social development. In Figure 16.1, we present a summary of the data with social factors along one axis and perceptual factors along the other axis.

There are a number of potential social and perceptual mechanisms that influence learning from media. Due to the slow development of memory flexibility during early childhood, media often places high demands that can

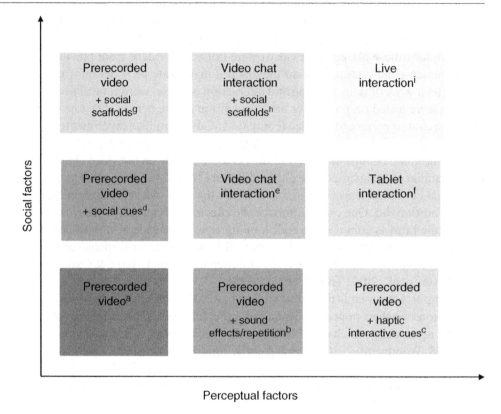

Figure 16.1. *Factors that ameliorate the transfer deficit.*

[a] Barr and Hayne, 1999; Barr, Muentener, and Garcia, 2007; Dickerson et al., 2013; Roseberry et al., 2014; Simcock et al., 2011; Troseth et al., 2006.
[b] Barr, Muentener, Garcia, Fujimoto et al., 2007.
[c] Kirkorian et al., 2016; Roseberry et al., 2018.
[d] Nussenbaum and Amso, 2016.
[e] Myers et al., 2017; Roseberry et al., 2014.
[f] Kirkorian et al., 2016; Roseberry et al., 2018.
[g] Demers et al., 2013.
[h] Myers et al., 2018.
[i] Barr and Hayne, 1999; Dickerson et al., 2013; Kuhl et al., 2003; Moser et al., 2015; Roseberry et al., 2014; Troseth et al., 2006; Zack et al., 2009.

easily overwhelm cognitive capacity, leading to a transfer deficit. Infants and toddlers are able to detect appropriateness of contingency in noncontingent media content (Myers et al., 2017; Nussenbaum & Amso, 2016; Roseberry et al., 2014) and disruptions to video-chat connectivity may reduce learning from video chat as well. Drawing attention to relevant information on the screen, and thus what is important to encode, can therefore enhance learning. Media content can be enhanced both perceptually (e.g., Kirkorian et al., 2016) and socially (Roseberry et al., 2014). Experiencing contingency may change children's concepts about what video can do and help the child to draw a connection between the video and reality. This connection between video and the real world may allow children to focus on the informational value of the video content (Krcmar, 2010; Nielsen, Simcock, & Jenkins, 2008). Future research should test infants' and toddlers' sensitivity to varied levels of contingency over different types of media.

16.3 How Does the Brain Process Media During Early Childhood?

Learning from media relies upon a number of perceptual, social, and demographic factors as illustrated in Sections 16.1 and 16.2. Although a number of behavioral studies have investigated the contexts in which successful transfer learning can occur (JME, repetition, social contingency), fewer studies involving neuroimaging techniques have examined how the brain processes information during encoding from media or transfer of learning. Behavioral studies alone may be insufficient to isolate the mechanisms that underlie the transfer deficit, but neuroimaging techniques appropriate for young children (e.g., functional near-infrared spectroscopy, fNIRS) have the potential to increase our understanding of this process. In this section, we will review existing neuroimaging and media studies and integrate these findings with theoretical models of information processing in the media context.

16.3.1 Existing Findings

To examine basic processing of media, two neuroimaging techniques are suitable for studying young children: electroencephalography (EEG) and functional near-infrared spectroscopy (fNIRS). EEG and fNIRS each hold certain benefits: FNIRS has superior spatial resolution compared to EEG, but EEG has superior temporal resolution (Aslin, 2012; Gervain et al., 2011; Wilcox & Biondi, 2015). FNIRS is an indirect measure of neural activity, whereas EEG is a more direct electrophysiological measure (Gervain et al., 2011).

FNIRS uses light to detect changes in blood oxygenation evoked by neural activity, due to differential absorption of light by oxygenated and deoxygenated blood (Aslin, 2012). The probes on the fNIRS cap act as sources or detectors. Sources shine light of two different wavelengths, which optimally differentiate between changes in oxygenated and deoxygenated blood (Gervain et al., 2011). As with many other types of infant studies, screens were the easiest way of presenting information to infants while wearing an fNIRS cap, and early studies demonstrated such feasibility. Meek et al. (1998) confirmed that the occipital cortex in 3-day to 14-week-olds is activated when viewing a flickering checkerboard pattern on a screen. Other studies examined auditory processing in infants using fNIRS. Peña et al. (2003) found left temporal cortex activation in 2- to 5-day-old sleeping infants when recordings of infant-directed speech played normally, compared to when they played backwards. Bortfeld, Wruck, and Boas (2007) showed 6- to 9-month-olds visual images alone or an audio-visual presentation. Not surprisingly, occipital areas were activated during visual stimuli, and both occipital and temporal areas were activated during audiovisual presentations. In other studies, researchers examined activation as infants viewed 3-D objects. Converging with adult neuroimaging studies, 3- to 12-month-olds show occipital cortical activation while viewing objects as well as anterior temporal and posterior parietal cortex activation during object individuation (Wilcox & Biondi, 2015).

Other studies have directly compared live versus televised demonstrations. In one study, neural activation was measured via fNIRS channels placed over the sensorimotor cortex while 6- to 7-month-olds watched a live experimenter or a televised experimenter move an object or watched the object move by itself either live or on TV. Shimada and Hiraki (2006) found that activation patterns differed as a function of whether the infants viewed the action live or on TV. Although sensorimotor activation was measurable in both live and televised conditions, the difference between the experimenter-demonstrated and object-only presentations was significant only in the live condition. That is, when infants observed the experimenter acting on an object in the live condition, there was greater sensorimotor activation than when the object moved by itself. However, in the TV condition, there was no difference in activation patterns when the object was moved by the experimenter compared to when the object moved by itself. This finding suggests that actions may be processed differently by infants when they are presented in a live context versus over video.

Similarly, an EEG study measured mu rhythm over the sensorimotor cortex while 18- to 36-month-olds observed an action performed either live or on TV and then were given the opportunity to imitate the action with real objects (Ruysschaert, Warreyn, Wiersema, Metin, & Roeyers, 2013). Mu rhythm suppression is generated when an infant performs an action and when an infant observes another person perform the same action. It is thought to index the firing of mirror neurons (Cuevas, Cannon, Yoo, & Fox, 2013). Such firing patterns are suggested to allow the mapping of behaviors from self to other and to be related to imitation and theory of mind (Cuevas et al., 2013). During demonstration, mu suppression was observed only for the live condition and not the video condition. During imitation, mu suppression was stronger during the live condition than it was during the video condition. Consistent with other studies, imitation was poorer following the video demonstration but the difference was not significant. Unfortunately, behavioral performance and its association with neural activation was not reported. Dickerson, Gerhardstein, and Moser (2017) have argued that poor learning from digital media may be due in part to the inability of digital media to activate the mirror neuron system early in development.

EEG studies often take advantage of excellent temporal resolution and measure event-related potentials (ERPs), which require specifically timed presentation of stimuli and measurement of electrical activity in response to the presentation. ERPs allow researchers to index speed of processing and item recognition. These studies often use 2-D presentations because the timing is easier to control. In a clever variation, Carver et al. (2006) developed a method to compare timed presentations of real objects and photos. They measured infants' recognition of familiar and unfamiliar objects presented to them either live or in a still photo as indexed via ERPs. Eighteen-month-olds differentiated familiar and unfamiliar objects in both live and video settings but more quickly differentiated the objects when they saw the real object compared to the photo. Carver and colleagues suggested that the later ERP response to the photo indicated that more processing time was required to make the familiarity judgment when viewing photos than real objects. Taken together, these studies highlight that 2-D media are processed differently than real objects. Developmental cognitive neuroscientists have begun to titrate age- and task-related differences in cognitive processing in preschoolers using fNIRS (see Buss, Fox, Boas, & Spencer, 2014; Perlman, Huppert, & Luna, 2015). This approach will be necessary to increase the precision of measurement in media studies during infancy.

16.3.2 Potential Cognitive Developmental Neuroscience Mechanisms

Theories that integrate brain and behavior with respect to media learning during early childhood are limited. It is likely that behavioral and neural processes rely upon more general attentional, perceptual, and social factors to support processing of and learning from media. Markant and Scott (2018) outline the interaction of attentional, perceptual, and social factors that leads to changes in the specificity of neural representations for faces. Initial, bottom-up attentional biases for faces and face-like stimuli lead to the efficient neural representation of familiar faces. Infants not only have bottom-up biases, but also top-down selective-attention biases towards familiar faces and subsequently an enhancement in the ability to differentiate between similar familiar stimuli. This model may also apply to the media context. Salient features that occur within media (e.g., congruent audiovisual effects; Barr, Shuck et al., 2010) engage bottom-up attentional mechanisms; attending to media may in turn add to infants' repertoire of knowledge about the perceptual properties of media. In fact, Heron-Delaney et al. (2011) assigned parents of 6- to 9-month-old Caucasian infants to read picture books that included Chinese faces. Exposure to Chinese faces allowed infants to maintain their ability to discriminate between Chinese faces at 9 months. Consequently, exposure to media may support more efficient neural processing of a diverse range of 2-D images. Individual differences in exposure to different types of media may impact attention and perceptual learning from media as well. This may have implications when investigating neural responses to 2-D images in children from a range of social and cultural backgrounds. Again, it is important for researchers to assess a child's history of media exposure and particularly the content of their media intake as it may have downstream effects on neural processing of this media.

Studies with infants and adults demonstrate that multiple neural systems are recruited during media processing. Learning from narrative and interactive media may rely on the default mode network (DMN) and the dorsal attention network (DAN), respectively (Anderson & Davidson, 2019). Trajectories associated with the development of these networks may support different types of learning and comprehension during infancy. The DMN includes the posterior cingulate cortex (PCC), the inferior parietal lobule (IPL), and the ventral (medial) prefrontal cortex and has been characterized as the most connected neural network in the brain (Anderson & Davidson, 2019). Anderson, Fite, Petrovich, and Hirsch (2006) reported that significant nodes of the DMN were active while adults viewed coherent, but not incoherent, film (see also Nakano, Kato, Morito, Itoi, & Kitazawa, 2013). Because the DMN is also involved in processing auditory and written narrative (e.g., Regev, Honey, Simony, & Hasson, 2013), DMN activation has been interpreted as necessary for more general narrative comprehension, integrating contextual information across time, and is associated with better memory for that content, regardless of presentation (Hasson, Yang, Vallines, Heeger, & Rubin, 2008). The DMN undergoes rapid development during childhood, with weaker connections (Fair et al., 2008) that are first seen in imaging studies of 2-year-olds (Gao et al., 2009). Consistent with this neural developmental trajectory, sustained visual attention indexed via heart rate and looking time to coherently sequenced video increases across early childhood (Pempek et al., 2010; J. E. Richards, 2010). Furthermore, children with attention-deficit hyperactivity disorder (ADHD) have weaker connections between the DMN and attention control nodes (Sudre, Szekely, Sharp, Kasparek, & Shaw, 2017) and also fewer sustained looks towards TV (Landau, Lorch, & Milich, 1992).

In tasks that require focused attention, the DMN tends to be deactivated while the DAN is activated (Lin et al., 2016). Furthermore, West, Konishi, and Bohbot (2017) suggest that focused, fast, and frequent responses characteristic of video games leads to activation of the caudate nucleus of the striatum (and associative learning) and reduced hippocampal activation. Thus, the DAN might promote learning that is tightly bound to specific moments that are not sensitive to the context or to an ongoing integrated narrative, such as during interactive screen media including video chat. The engagement of DAN during interactive screen media versus DMN during narrative media has not yet been directly tested. Future research could directly manipulate different types of media to interrogate the development of these neural networks.

Neither of these models consider the role of social contingency. The integration of perceptual and social factors are clearly important in processing and learning from media especially during early childhood (see Figure 16.1).

Dickerson et al. (2017) propose that neural detection of temporal, spatial, and social disruptions present in digital media lead to a less efficient transfer across the dimensional divide. Specifically, a lack of social contingency may contribute to less neural activation across multiple sensorimotor and memory systems (Dickerson et al., 2017). Other changes in social cues, such as eye gaze, may also dampen typical neural activation associated with social cues during media presentations. Overall, several neural systems are likely necessary to meet the social, perceptual, and memory demands inherent in learning from media.

16.4 Policy and Recommendations

Beginning in 1999, the AAP (1999) published policy guidelines about media exposure. Over the next decade, a small but growing body of literature emerged, examining early media exposure and learning (Barr & Linebarger, 2017). The most recent AAP recommendations (AAP, 2016) reflect the growing empirical database, and there has been a shift in focus that includes recommendations not only about exposure, but also about the content and context of media (AAP, 2016). Specifically, the AAP (2016) recommends exposure only to high-quality educational content that is accompanied by parental support whenever possible beginning around 18 months. The policy differentiates between video chat and other screen media, with no age limit applied to video chat. Parents report little knowledge of the AAP recommendations, with only 20% citing the AAP as guiding their media choices for their young children, most of whom were educated and wealthy parents (Rideout, 2017). The amount of exposure per day is unlikely to be the best predictor of outcomes. In a large population-based study of almost 20,000 parents, Przybylski and Weinstein (2017) reported that the amount of time (1 or 2 hours per day or above the recommendation) of exposure in 2- to 5-year-olds was not associated with child well-being measures.

As highlighted throughout this chapter, a shift to focus parents' attention on the importance of the content and context of media exposure is paramount. Joint media engagement by caregivers plus high-quality content and technology provide the best opportunities for maximizing the promise of digital media during early childhood. Basic cognitive and social information-processing mechanisms apply to learning from media. Taking this approach, Zosh, Lytle, Golinkoff, and Hirsh-Pasek (2017) applied science of learning principles to the media context. They provided evidence that children learn best when they are active, engaged, and focused, when they are learning material that is meaningful to them, and when learning occurs within a supportive social context. These pillars can be used by parents, teachers, and other adults to help identify high-quality children's media.

Zero to Three (ZTT) released a set of guidelines called Screen Sense (Barr, McClure, & Palarkain, 2018; Lerner & Barr, 2015) specifically developed for parents of children under 3 years of age. These guidelines considered the highly saturated parental media environment and the likely greater negative impact of forms of background media via background TV or interruptions from constant access to mobile devices. ZTT recommended mindful media use, encouraging parents to: (1) develop healthy media habits and avoid background TV and media exposure during the bedtime routine, (2) carefully choose educational media content that includes a clear learning goal or storyline, (3) share the experience with the child, (4) be mindful of the impact that parents' own media use might have on their children, and (5) engage in activities to facilitate transfer learning from the screen to the real world with their children. The guidelines provided parents with the acronym "E-AIMS" (engaging, actively involved, meaningful, and social) to remember the four pillars of science that had been described by Zosh et al. (2017). "Engaging" material should focus the child's learning on a consistent learning goal and limit distracting or irrelevant details. "Actively involved" refers to cognitive activity or mental effort. The content and any interactive component should be age appropriate and neither too easy nor too difficult. The content should be "meaningful" to the child, increasing the likelihood that the material can be connected and transferred to a real-world context and integrated into the child's existing knowledge base. Finally, the content should take place within a "social" context.

The National Association for the Education of Young Children (NAEYC) and the Fred Rogers Center (2012) released a similar position statement supporting developmentally appropriate and intentional use of technology in early childhood education. Media policy statements continue to be updated as new research is released and as new forms of media evolve, such as virtual reality (e.g., Oculus) and intelligent agent systems on phones (e.g., Siri) or home speakers (e.g., Alexa or Google), which access the Internet more easily and are increasingly embedded into real toys to guide child play (M. N. Richards & Calvert, 2017).

16.5 Conclusion

Growing up in the digital age provides a number of unique opportunities and challenges during infancy. Infants are exposed to media from an early age but experience a transfer deficit in applying knowledge to the real world. General socio-cognitive developmental principles apply to learning from media. Joint media engagement is essential during infancy, because infants need support to learn the affordances of media that often do not apply in the 3-D world. Media is, however, a double-edged sword, providing opportunities to extend learning within the parent–child context but also to interfere with that relationship. Future research should focus on two main areas: a better assessment of the family media ecology and examination of neural activity while learning from media. Given our knowledge of both the pros and cons of parenting in the digital age, this is, however, a time of promise for access to resources for many infants around the globe.

References

Adamson, L. B., & Frick, J. E. (2003). The still face: A history of a shared experimental paradigm. *Infancy*, 4, 451–473.

American Academy of Pediatrics (AAP) Committee on Public Education (1999). Media education. *Pediatrics*, *104*, 341–343. doi: 10.1542/peds.104.2.341

American Academy of Pediatrics (AAP) Council on Communications and Media (2016). Children and adolescents and digital media. *Pediatrics*, *138*. doi: 10.1542/peds.2016-2593

Anderson, D. R., & Davidson, M. C. (2019). Receptive versus interactive video screens: A role for the brain's default mode network in learning from media. *Computers in Human Behavior*, 99, 168–180. https://doi.org/10.1016/j.chb.2019.05.008

Anderson, D. R., Fite, K. V., Petrovich, N., & Hirsch, J. (2006). Cortical activation while watching video montage: An fMRI study. *Media Psychology*, *8*, 7–24.

Anderson, D. R., & Hanson, K. G. (2017). Screen media and parent–child interactions. In R. Barr & D. N. Linebarger (Eds.), *Media exposure during infancy and early childhood. The effects of content and context on learning and development* (pp 173–194). Cham, Switzerland: Springer.

Anderson, D. R., & Pempek, T. A. (2005). Television and very young children. *American Behavioral Scientist*, *48*, 505–522.

Aslin, R. N. (2012). Questioning the questions that have been asked about the infant brain using near-infrared spectroscopy. *Cognitive Neuropsychology*, *29*, 7–33.

Bank, A. M., Barr, R., Calvert, S. L., Parrott, W. G., McDonough, S. C., & Rosenblum, K. (2012). Maternal depression and family media use: A questionnaire and diary analysis. *Journal of Child and Family Studies*, *21*, 208–216. doi: 10.1007/s10826-011-9464-1.

Barnett, S. M., & Ceci, S. J. (2002). When and where do we apply what we learn? A taxonomy for far transfer. *Psychological Bulletin*, *128*, 612–637. doi:10.1037/0033-2909.128.4.612.

Barr, R. (2010). Transfer of learning between 2D and 3D sources during infancy: Informing theory and practice. *Developmental Review*, *30*, 128–154. doi:10.1016/j.dr.2010.03.001.

(2013). Memory constraints on infant learning from picture books, television, and touch-screens. *Child Development Perspectives*, *7*, 205–210. doi:10.1111/cdep.12041.

Barr, R., & Hayne, H. (1999). Developmental changes in imitation from television during infancy. *Child Development*, *70*, 1067–1081.

Barr, R., Kirkorian, H., Radesky, J., Coyne, S., Nichols, D., Blanchfield, O., Rusnak, S., Stockdale, L., Ribner, A., Durnez, J., Epstein, M., Heimann, M., Koch, F.-S., Sundqvist, A., Birberg-Thornberg, U., Konrad, C., Slussareff, M., Bus, A.,

Bellagamba, F., Fitzpatrick, C. and CAFE Consortium Key Investigators (in revision). Beyond Screen Time: A synergistic approach to a more comprehensive assessment of family media exposure during early childhood.

Barr, R., Lauricella, A., Zack, E., & Calvert, S. L. (2010). The relation between infant exposure to television and executive functioning, cognitive skills, and school readiness at age four. *Merrill Palmer Quarterly*, *56*, 21–48.

Barr, R., & Linebarger, D. N. (Eds.) (2017). *Media exposure during infancy and early childhood: The effects of content and context on learning and development.* Cham, Switzerland: Springer.

Barr, R., McClure, E., & Palarkain, R. (2018). What the research says about the impact of media on children aged 0–3 years old. Retrieved from www.zerotothree .org/resources/series/screen-sense.

Barr, R., Muentener, P., & Garcia, A. (2007). Age-related changes in deferred imitation from television by 6- to 18-month-olds. *Developmental Science*, *10*, 910–921.

Barr, R., Muentener, P., Garcia, A., Fujimoto, M., & Chávez, V. (2007). The effect of repetition on imitation from television during infancy. *Developmental Psychobiology*, *49*, 196–207.

Barr, R., Shuck, L., Salerno, K., Atkinson, E., & Linebarger, D. L. (2010). Music interferes with learning from television during infancy. *Infant and Child Development: An International Journal of Research and Practice*, *19*, 313–331.

Barr, R., Zack, E., Garcia, A., & Muentener, P. (2008). Infants' attention and responsiveness to television increases with prior exposure and parental interaction. *Infancy*, *13*, 30–56.

Bornstein, M. H., & Tamis-LeMonda, C. S. (2008). Mother–infant interaction. In J. G. Bremner & T. D. Wachs (Eds.), *The Wiley-Blackwell handbook of infant development* (pp. 269–295). Malden, MA: Wiley-Blackwell.

Bortfeld, H., Wruck, E., & Boas, D. A. (2007). Assessing infants' cortical response to speech using near-infrared spectroscopy. *Neuroimage*, *34*, 407–415.

Bus, A. G., Takacs, Z. K., & Kegel, C. A. T. (2015). Affordances and limitations of electronic storybooks for young children's emergent literacy. *Developmental Review*, *35*, 79–97.

Buss, A. T., Fox, N., Boas, D. A., & Spencer, J. P. (2014). Probing the early development of visual working memory capacity with functional near-infrared spectroscopy. *Neuroimage*, *85*, 314–325, doi: 10.1016/j.neuroimage.2013.05.034

Calvert, S. L., Rideout, V. J., Woolard, J. L., Barr, R. F., & Strouse, G. A. (2005). Age, ethnicity, and socioeconomic patterns in early computer use: A national survey. *American Behavioral Scientist*, *48*, 590–607.

Carver, L. J., Meltzoff, A. N., & Dawson, G. (2006). Event-related potential (ERP) indices of infants' recognition of familiar and unfamiliar objects in two and three dimensions. *Developmental Science*, *9*, 51–62.

Choi, J. H., Mendelsohn, A. L, Weisleder, A., Brockmeyer Cates, C., Canfield, C., Seery, A., … Tomopoulos, S. (2018). Real-world usage of educational media does not promote parent–child cognitive stimulation activities. *Academic Pediatrics*, *18*, 172–178. doi: 10.1016/j.acap.2017.04.020.

Christakis, D. A., Gilkerson, J., Richards, J. A., Zimmerman, F. J., Garrison, M. M., Xu, D., … Yapanel, U. (2009). Audible television and decreased adult words, infant vocalizations, and conversational turns: A population-based study. *Archives of Pediatric & Adolescent Medicine*, *163*, 554–558.

Connell, S. L., Lauricella, A. R., & Wartella, E. (2015). Parental co-use of media technology with their parents in the U.S.A. *Journal of Children and Media*, *9*, 5–21.

Courage, M. L., Murphy, A. N., Goulding, S., & Setliff, A. E. (2010). When the television is on: The impact of infant-directed video on 6- and 18-month-olds' attention during toy play and on parent–infant interaction. *Infant Behavior and Development*, *33*, 176–188.

Cristia, A., & Seidl, A. (2015) Parental reports on touch screen use in early childhood. *PLoS ONE*, *10*. https://doi.org/10.1371/journal.pone.0128338

Cuevas, K., Cannon, E. N., Yoo, K., & Fox, N. A. (2013). The infant EEG Mu rhythm: Methodological considerations and best practices. *Developmental Review*, *34*, 26–43.

Dayanim, S., & Namy, L. L. (2015). Infants learn baby signs from video. *Child Development*, *86*, 800–811.

DeLoache, J. S. (1995). Early symbol understanding and use. *Psychology of Learning and Motivation*, *33*, 65–116.

DeLoache, J. S., Chiong, C., Sherman, K., Islam, N., Vanderborght, M., Troseth, G. L., … O'Doherty, K. (2010). Do babies learn from baby media?. *Psychological Science*, *21*, 1570–1574.

DeLoache, J. S., Strauss, M. S., & Maynard, J. (1979). Picture perception in infancy. *Infant Behavior and Development*, *2*, 77–89.

Demers, L. B., Hanson, K. G., Kirkorian, H. L., Pempek, T. A., & Anderson, D. R. (2013). Infant gaze following during parent–infant coviewing of baby videos. *Child Development*, *84*, 591–603. doi: 10.1111/j.1467-8624.2012.01868.x

Dickerson, K., Gerhardstein, P., & Moser, A. (2017). The role of the human mirror neuron system in supporting communication in a digital world. *Frontiers in Psychology*, *8*, 698.

Dickerson, K., Gerhardstein, P., Zack, E., & Barr, R. (2013). Age-related changes in learning across early childhood: A new imitation task. *Developmental Psychobiology*, *55*, 719–732. doi:10.1002/dev.21068.

Dirks, J., & Gibson, E. (1977). Infants' perception of similarity between live people and their photographs. *Child Development*, *48*(1), 124–130.

Eunice Kennedy Shriver National Institute of Child Health and Human Development (NICHD) (2018). Media exposure and early child development workshop. Retrieved from www.nichd.nih.gov/about/meetings/2018/012518.

Fair, D. A., Cohen, A. L., Dosenbach, N. U. F., Church, J. A., Miezin F. M., Barch, D. M., … Schlaggar, B. L. (2008). The maturing architecture of the brain's default network. *Proceedings of the National Academy of Sciences*, *105*, 4028–4032.

Fenstermacher, S. K., Barr, R., Brey, E., Pempek, T. A, Ryan, M., Calvert, S., … Linebarger, D. (2010). Interactional quality depicted in infant-directed videos: Where are the interactions? *Infant and Child Development*, *19*, 594–612. doi: 10.1002/icd.714

Fenstermacher, S. K., Barr, R., Salerno, K., Garcia, A., Shwery, C. E., Calvert, S. L., & Linebarger, D. L. (2010). Infant-directed media: An analysis of product information and claims. *Infant & Child Development*, *19*, 557–576.

Gao, W., Zhu, H., Giovanello, K. S., Smith, J. K., Dinggang, S., Gilmore, J. H., & Lin, W. (2009). Evidence on the emergence of the brain's default network from 2-week-old to 2-year-old healthy pediatric subjects. *Proceedings of the National Academy of Sciences*, *106*, 6790–6795.

Gervain, J., Mehler, J., Werker, J. F., Nelson, C. A., Csibra, G., Lloyd-Fox, S., ... Aslin, R. N. (2011). Near-infrared spectroscopy: A report from the McDonnell infant methodology consortium. *Developmental Cognitive Neuroscience, 1*, 22–46.

Goedhart, G., Kromhout, H., Wiart, J., & Vermeulen, R. (2015). Validating self-reported mobile phone use in adults using a newly developed smartphone application. *Occupational & Environmental Medicine, 72*(1), 812–818.

Goldstein, M. H., Schwade, J. A., & Bornstein, M. H. (2009). The value of vocalizing: Five-month-old infants associate their own noncry vocalizations with responses from caregivers. *Child Development, 80*, 636–644.

Guernsey, L. (2012). *Screen time: How electronic media – from baby videos to educational software – affects your young child.* Philadelphia, PA: Basic Books.

Hasson, U., Yang, E., Vallines, I., Heeger, D.J., & Rubin, N. (2008). A hierarchy of temporal receptive windows in human cortex. *Journal of Neuroscience, 28*, 2539–2550.

Henning, A., & Striano, T. (2011). Infant and maternal sensitivity to interpersonal timing. *Child Development, 82*, 916–931.

Heron-Delaney, M., Anzures, G., Herbert, J. S., Quinn, P. C., Slater, A. M., Tanaka, J. W., ... Pascalis, O. (2011). Perceptual training prevents the emergence of the other race effect during infancy. *PLoS ONE, 6.* http://doi.org/10.1371/journal.pone.0019858

Hipp, D., Gerhardstein, P., Zimmermann, L., Moser, A., Taylor, G., & Barr, R. (2017). The dimensional divide: Learning from TV and touchscreens during early childhood. In R. Barr & D. N. Linebarger (Eds.), *Media exposure during infancy and early childhood: The effects of content and context on learning and development* (pp. 33–54). Cham, Switzerland: Springer.

Hirsh-Pasek, K., Zosh, J. M., Golinkoff, R. M., Gray, J. H., Robb, M. B., & Kaufman, J. (2015). Putting education in "educational" apps: Lessons from the science of learning. *Psychological Science in the Public Interest, 16*, 3–34.

Kabali, H. K., Irigoyen, M. M., Nunez-Davis, R., Budacki, J. G., Mohanty, S. H., Leister, K. P., & Bonner Jr, R. L. (2015). Exposure and use of mobile media devices by young children. *Pediatrics, 136*, 1044–1050.

Khan, M., Chakraborty, N., Rahman, A., & Nasrin, T. (2007). *2007 follow-up (wave II) evaluation of the reach and impact of Sisimpur: A technical report.* Dhaka, Bangladesh: Associates for Community and Population Research.

Kirkorian, H. L. (2018). When and how do interactive digital media help children connect what they see on and off the screen? *Child Development Perspectives, 12*, 210–214. doi.org/10.1111/cdep.12290.

Kirkorian, H. L., Anderson, D. R., & Keen, R. (2012). Age differences in online processing of video: An eye movement study. *Child Development, 83*, 497–507.

Kirkorian, H. L., & Choi, K. (2017). Associations between toddlers' naturalistic media experience and observed learning from screens. *Infancy, 22*, 271–277.

Kirkorian, H. L., Choi, K., & Pempek, T. A. (2016). Toddlers' word learning from contingent and noncontingent video on touchscreens. *Child Development, 87*, 405–413. doi: 10.1111/cdev.12508

Kirkorian, H. L., Pempek, T. A., Murphy, L. A., Schmidt, M. E., & Anderson, D. R. (2009). The impact of background television on parent–child interaction. *Child Development, 80*, 1350–1359.

Koenig, M. A., & Woodward, A. L. (2010). Sensitivity of 24-month-olds to the prior inaccuracy of the source: Possible mechanisms. *Developmental Psychology*, *46*, 815.

Krcmar, M. (2010). Can social meaningfulness and repeat exposure help infants and toddlers overcome the video deficit?. *Media Psychology*, *13*, 31–53.

Kuchirko, Y., Tafuro, L., & Tamis-LeMonda, C.S. (2018). Becoming a communicative partner: Infant contingent responsiveness to maternal language and gestures. *Infancy*, *23*, 558–576. doi: 10.1111/infa.12222

Kuhl, P. K., Tsao, F. M., & Liu, H. M. (2003). Foreign-language experience in infancy: Effects of short-term exposure and social interaction on phonetic learning. *Proceedings of the National Academy of Sciences*, *100*, 9096–9101.

Landau, S., Lorch, E.P., & Milich, R. (1992). Visual attention to and comprehension of television in attention-deficit hyperactivity disordered and normal boys. *Child Development*, *63*, 928–937.

Lapierre, M. A., Piotrowski, J. T., & Linebarger, D. L. (2012). Background television in the homes of US children. *Pediatrics*, *130*, 839–846.

Lauricella, A. R., Blackwell, C. K., & Wartella, E. (2017). The "new" technology environment: The role of content and context on learning and development from mobile media. In R. Barr & D. N. Linebarger (Eds.), *Media exposure during infancy and early childhood: The effects of content and context on learning and development* (pp. 1–24). Cham, Switzerland: Springer.

Lauricella, A. R., Pempek, T. A., Barr, R., & Calvert, S. L. (2010). Contingent computer interactions for young children's object retrieval success. *Journal of Applied Developmental Psychology*, *31*, 362–369.

Lauricella, A. R., Wartella, E., & Rideout, V. (2015). Young children's screen time: The complex role of parent and child factors. *Journal of Applied Developmental Psychology*, *36*, 11–17. doi.org/10.1016/j.appdev.2014.12.001

Lerner, C., & Barr, R. (2015). Screen sense: Setting the record straight – research-based guidelines for screen use for children under 3 years old. *Zero to Three*, *35*, 1–10.

Li, H., Subrahmanyam, K., Bai, X., Xie, X., & Liu, T. (2018). Viewing fantastical events versus touching fantastical events: Short-term effects on children's inhibitory control. *Child Development*, *89*, 48–57. https://doi.org/10.1111/cdev.12820

Lillard, A. S., Drell, M. B., Richey, E. M., Boguszewski, K., & Smith, E. D. (2015). Further examination of the immediate impact of television on children's executive function. *Developmental Psychology*, *51*, 792–805. doi: 10.1037/a0039097

Lin, P., Yang, Y., Jovicich, J., de Pisapia, N., Wang, X., Zuo, C. S., & Levitt, J. J. (2016). Static and dynamic posterior cingulate cortex nodal topology of default mode network predicts attention task performance. *Brain Imaging and Behavior*, *10*, 212–225.

Linebarger, D. L., Barr, R., Lapierre, M. A., & Piotrowski, J. T. (2014). Associations between parenting, media use, cumulative risk, and children's executive functioning. *Journal of Developmental & Behavioral Pediatrics*, *35*, 367–377.

Linebarger, D. L., & Walker, D. (2005). Infants' and toddlers' television viewing and language outcomes. *American Behavioral Scientist*, *48*, 624–645.

Mandel, D. R., Jusczyk, P. W., & Pisoni, D. B. (1995). Infants' recognition of the sound patterns of their own names. *Psychological Science*, *6*, 314–317.

Markant, J., & Scott, L. S. (2018). Attention and perceptual learning interact in the development of the other-race effect. *Current Directions in Psychological Science*, *27*(3), 163–169.

Mendelsohn, A. L., Brockmeyer, C. A., Dreyer, B. P., Fierman, A. H., Berkule-Silberman, S. B., & Tomopoulos, S. (2010). Do verbal interactions with infants during electronic media exposure mitigate adverse impacts on their language development as toddlers? *Infant and Child Development*, *19*, 577–593. http://doi.org/10.1002/icd.711.

McCall, R. B., Parke, R. D., Kavanaugh, R. D., Engstrom, R., Russell, J., & Wycoff, E. (1977). Imitation of live and televised models by children one to three years of age. *Monographs of the Society for Research in Child Development*, 1–94.

McClure, E. R., Chentsova-Dutton, Y. E., Barr, R. F., Holochwost, S., & Parrott, W. G. (2015). "FaceTime doesn't count": Video chat as an exception to media restrictions for infants and toddlers. *International Journal of Child-Computer Interaction*, *6*, 1–6. doi: x10.1016/j.ijcci.2016.02.002

McClure, E. R., Chentsova-Dutton, Y. E., Holochwost, S. J., Parrott, W. G., & Barr, R. (2017). Look at that! Video chat and joint visual attention development among babies and toddlers. *Child Development*, *89*(1), 27–36. doi:10.1111/cdev.12833

McDaniel, B. T., & Radesky, J. S. (2018). Technoference: Parent distraction with technology and associations with child behavior problems. *Child Development*, *89*, 100–109. doi:10.1111/cdev.12822

Meek, J. H., Firbank, M., Elwell, C. E., Atkinson, J., Braddick, O., & Wyatt, J. S. (1998). Regional hemodynamic responses to visual stimulation in awake infants. *Pediatric Research*, *43*(6), 840.

Moser, A., Zimmermann, L., Dickerson, K., Grenell, A., Barr, R., & Gerhardstein, P. (2015). They can interact, but can they learn? Toddlers' transfer learning from touchscreens and television. *Journal of Experimental Child Psychology*, *137*, 137–155. doi:10.1016/j.jecp.2015.04.002.

Mumme, D. L., & Fernald, A. (2003). The infant as onlooker: Learning from emotional reactions observed in a television scenario. *Child Development*, *74*, 221–237.

Murray, L., & Trevarthen, C. (1985). Emotional regulation of interactions between two-month-olds and their mothers. In T. Field & N. Fox (Eds.), *Social perception in infants* (pp. 177–197). Norwood, NJ: Ablex.

Myers, L. J., Crawford, E., Murphy, C., Aka-Ezoua, E., & Felix, C. (2018). Eyes in the room trump eyes on the screen: Effects of a responsive co-viewer on toddlers' responses to and learning from video chat. *Journal of Children and Media*, *12*(3), 275–294.

Myers, L. J., LeWitt, R. B., Gallo, R. E., & Maselli, N. M. (2017). Baby FaceTime: Can toddlers learn from online video chat?. *Developmental Science*, 20(4), 1–15.

Myruski, S., Gulyayeva, O., Birk, S., Pérez-Edgar, K., Buss, K. A., & Dennis-Tiwary, T. A. (2018) Digital disruption? Maternal mobile device use is related to infant social-emotional functioning. *Developmental Science*, *21*, e12610. https://doi.org/10.1111/desc.12610

Nakano, T., Kato, M., Morito, Y., Itoi, S., & Kitazawa, S. (2013). Blink-related momentary activation of the default mode network while viewing videos. *Proceedings of the National Academy of Sciences*, *110*, 702–706.

Nathanson, A. I., Aladé, F., Sharp, M. L., Rasmussen, E. E., & Christy, K. (2014). The relation between television exposure and executive function among preschoolers. *Developmental Psychology, 50*, 1497.

National Association for the Education of Young Children & the Fred Rogers Center for Early Learning and Children's Media at Saint Vincent College. (2012, January). Technology and interactive media as tools in early childhood programs serving children from birth through age 8. Joint position statement. Reston, VA.

Nielsen, M., Simcock, G., & Jenkins, L. (2008). The effect of social engagement on 24 month olds' imitation from live and televised models. *Developmental Science, 11*, 722–731. doi:10.1111/j.1467-7687.2008.00722.x.

Nussenbaum, K., & Amso, D. (2016). An attentional Goldilocks effect: An optimal amount of social interactivity promotes word learning from video. *Journal of Cognition and Development, 17*, 30–40.

Oulasvirta, A., Tamminen, S., Roto, V., & Kuorelahti, J. (2005, April). Interaction in 4-second bursts: The fragmented nature of attentional resources in mobile HCI. In *Proceedings of the SIGCHI conference on Human factors in computing systems* (pp. 919–928). New York, NY: ACM. https://doi.org/10.1145/1054972.1055101

Pempek, T. A., Kirkorian, H. L., & Anderson, D. R. (2014). The effects of background television on the quantity and quality of child-directed speech by parents. *Journal of Children and Media, 8*, 211–222.

Pempek, T. A., Kirkorian, H. L., Richards, J. E., Anderson, D. R., Lund, A. F., & Stevens, M. (2010). Video comprehensibility and attention in very young children. *Developmental Psychology, 46*, 1283–1293.

Pempek, T. A., & McDaniel, B. T. (2016). Young children's tablet use and associations with maternal well-being. *Journal of Child and Family Studies, 25*, 2636–2647.

Peña, M., Maki, A., Kovacic, D., Dehaene-Lambertz, G., Koizumi, H., Bouquet, F., & Mehler, J. (2003). Sounds and silence: An optical topography study of language recognition at birth. *Proceedings of the National Academy of Sciences, 100*, 11702–11705.

Perlman, S. B., Huppert, T. J., & Luna, B. (2015). Functional near-infrared spectroscopy evidence for development of prefrontal engagement in working memory in early through middle childhood. *Cerebral Cortex, 26*, 2790–2799.

Przybylski, A. K., & Weinstein, N. (2017). Digital screen time limits and young children's psychological well-being: Evidence from a population-based study. *Child Development, 90*(1), e56–e65. doi.org/10.1111/cdev.13007

Radesky, J. S., Kistin, C. J., Zuckerman, B., Nitzberg, K., Gross, J., Kaplan-Sanoff, M., … Silverstein, M. (2014). Patterns of mobile device use by caregivers and children during meals in fast-food restaurants. *Pediatrics, 133*, 843–849.

Radesky, J. S., Peacock-Chambers, E., Zuckerman, B., & Silverstein, M. (2016). Use of mobile technology to calm upset children: Associations with social-emotional development. *JAMA Pediatrics, 170*, 397–399.

Radesky, J. S., Silverstein, M., Zuckerman, B., & Christakis, D. A. (2014). Infant self-regulation and early childhood media exposure. *Pediatrics, 133*(5), e1172–e1178. doi: 10.1542/peds.2013-2367

Reed, J., Hirsh-Pasek, K., & Golinkoff, R. M. (2017). Learning on hold: Cell phones sidetrack parent–child interactions. *Developmental Psychology, 53,* 1428.

Regev, M., Honey, C. J., Simony, E., & Hasson, U. (2013). Selective and invariant neural responses to spoken and written narratives. *Journal of Neuroscience, 33,* 15978–15988.

Richards, J. E. (2010). The development of attention to simple and complex visual stimuli in infants: Behavioral and psychophysiological measures. *Developmental Review, 30,* 203–219.

Richards, M. N., & Calvert, S. L. (2017). Media characters, parasocial relationships, and the social aspects of children's learning across media platforms. In R. Barr & D. N. Linebarger (Eds.), *Media exposure during infancy and early childhood: The effects of content and context on learning and development* (pp. 141–163). Cham, Switzerland: Springer.

Richert, R. A., Robb, M. B., Fender, J. G., & Wartella, E. (2010). Word learning from baby videos. *Archives of Pediatrics & Adolescent Medicine, 164,* 432–437.

Rideout, V. (2017). *Zero to eight: Children's media use in America 2017.* San Francisco, CA: Common Sense Media. Retrieved from www.commonsensemedia.org/research/zero-to-eight-childrens-media-use-in-america-2017.

Roseberry, S. L., Garcia-Sierra, A., & Kuhl, P. K. (2018). Two are better than one: Infant language learning from video improves in the presence of peers. *Proceedings of the National Academy of Sciences of the United States of America,* 115(40), 9859–9866.

Roseberry, S. L., Hirsh-Pasek, K., & Golinkoff, R. M. (2014). Skype me! Socially contingent interactions help toddlers learn language. *Child Development, 85,* 956–970. doi:10.1111/ cdev.12166.

Ruysschaert, L., Warreyn, P., Wiersema, J. R., Metin, B., & Roeyers, H. (2013). Neural mirroring during the observation of live and video actions in infants. *Clinical Neurophysiology, 124,* 1765–1770. doi: 10.1016/j.clinph.2013.04.007

Schmidt, M. E., Pempek, T. A., Kirkorian, H. L., Lund, A. F., & Anderson, D. R. (2008). The effects of background television on the toy play behavior of very young children. *Child Development, 79,* 1137–1151.

Setliff, A. E., & Courage, M. L. (2011). Background television and infants' allocation of their attention during toy play. *Infancy, 16,* 611–639.

Shimada, S., & Hiraki, K. (2006). Infant's brain responses to live and televised action. *Neuroimage, 32,* 930–939. doi: 10.1016/j.neuroimage.2006.03.044

Simcock, G., Garrity, K., & Barr, R. (2011). The effect of narrative cues on infants' imitation from television and picture books. *Child Development, 82,* 1607–1619. doi: 10.1111/j.1467-8624.2011.01636.x

Strouse, G. A., & Troseth, G. L. (2014). Supporting toddlers' transfer of word learning from video. *Cognitive Development, 30,* 47–64.

Sudre, G., Szekely, E., Sharp, W., Kasparek, S., & Shaw, P. (2017). Multimodal mapping of the brain's functional connectivity and the adult outcome of attention deficit hyperactivity disorder. *Proceedings of the National Academy of Sciences, 114,* 11787–11792.

Troseth, G. L. (2010). Is it life or is it Memorex? Video as a representation of reality. *Developmental Review, 30,* 155–175. doi:10.1016/j.dr.2010.03.007.

Troseth, G. L., & DeLoache, J. S. (1998). The medium can obscure the message: Young children's understanding of video. *Child Development*, *69*, 950–965.

Troseth, G. L., Saylor, M. M., & Archer, A. H. (2006). Young children's use of video as a source of socially relevant information. *Child Development*, *77*, 786–799.

Vaala, S. E., Linebarger, D. L., Fenstermacher, S. K., Tedone, A., Brey, E., Barr, R., ... Calvert, S. L. (2010). Content analysis of language-promoting teaching strategies used in infant-directed media. *Infant and Child Development*, *19*, 628–648.

Vandewater, E. A., & Lee, S. -J. (2009). Measuring children's media use in the digital age: Issues and challenges. *American Behavioral Scientist*, *52*, 1152–1176.

Wartella, E., Rideout, V., Lauricella, A., & Connell, S. (2014). *Revised parenting in the age of digital technology: A national survey*. Evanston, IL: Northwestern University. Retrieved from http://web5.soc.northwestern.edu/cmhd/wp-content/uploads/2014/08/NWU.MediaTechReading.Hispanic.FINAL2014.pdf.

West, G. L., Konishi, K., & Bohbot, V. D. (2017). Video games and hippocampus-dependent learning. *Current Directions in Psychological Science*, *26*, 152–158.

Wilcox, T., & Biondi, M. (2015). fNIRS in the developmental sciences. *Wiley Interdisciplinary Reviews: Cognitive Science*, *6*, 263–283.

Wood, F., Petkovski, M., de Pasquale, D., Gottardo, A., Evans, M. A., & Savage, R. S. (2016). Parent scaffolding of young children when engaged with mobile technology. *Frontiers in Psychology*, *7*, 690. http://doi.org/10.3389/fpsyg.2016.00690

Zack, E., & Barr, R. (2016). The role of interactional quality in learning from touch screens during infancy: Context matters. *Frontiers in Psychology*, *7*, 1264.

Zack, E., Barr, R., Gerhardstein, P., Dickerson, K., & Meltzoff, A. N. (2009). Infant imitation from television using novel touch screen technology. *British Journal of Developmental Psychology*, *27*, 13–26.

Zosh, J. M., Lytle, S. R., Golinkoff, R. M., & Hirsh-Pasek, K. (2017). Putting the education back in educational apps: How content and context interact to promote learning. In R. Barr & D. N. Linebarger (Eds.), *Media exposure during infancy and early childhood: The effects of content and context on learning and development* (pp. 259–282). Cham, Switzerland: Springer.

PART IV

Action

17 Action in Development

Plasticity, Variability, and Flexibility

Jaya Rachwani, Justine Hoch, and Karen E. Adolph*

17.1 Introduction: Infant Motor Development

Infant motor skill acquisition is so rapid and dramatic that a century of researchers – and eons of parents – have marveled at the scope of developmental change. At birth, infants are essentially prisoners of gravity, unable to lift their heads from their caregivers' chest. But by 2 years of age, infants can "pluck a pellet with fine pincer prehension" (Gesell, 1929, p. 132) and race on two feet across the living room floor. This remarkable transformation in action characterizes the development of basic motor skills – posture for supporting the body against gravitational and inertial forces, manual skills for interacting with objects and surfaces, and locomotion for moving the body through the environment (Adolph & Berger, 2015)

17.1.1 Transformations in Posture, Manual Actions, and Locomotion

Before birth, posture is supported by the buoyancy of the mother's womb. After birth, gravity poses a continual challenge as infants acquire increasingly erect postures over an increasingly small base of support. Generally, posture develops top down, from head to toe (Assaiante & Amblard, 1995; Saavedra, van Donkelaar, & Woollacott, 2012). Newborns struggle to hold their heads upright, new sitters work to control the segments of the spine, and new walkers cope with balance at the hip, knee, and ankle joints.

Keeping balance, however, is rarely an end unto itself. Rather, postural control provides the foundation for other actions (Adolph & Berger, 2006, 2015; Adolph & Franchak, 2016). While sitting or standing, turning to look around or lifting an arm to reach displaces the body's center of mass and pulls the body off balance. Thus, posture must be sufficiently developed to anticipate and control for the potential loss of equilibrium. Postural control must precede the development of other motor actions and the opportunities they provide (Adolph & Hoch, 2019; Adolph & Robinson, 2015). For example, before infants have sufficient postural control to sit up, their visual and social world

* This chapter was supported by grants from the National Institute of Child Health and Human Development (NICHD; grants R01-HD033486 and R01-HD086043) to KEA. We thank Minxin Cheng for her wonderful line drawings and figure design.

is small. Their experiences are limited to the objects and faces that appear overhead while lying supine in a crib or the scenes revealed while held in a caregiver's arms (Jayaraman, Fausey, & Smith, 2017; Kretch & Adolph, 2015). After infants can sit independently, their visual and social world expands.

Manual actions appear long before birth. Fetuses flex and extend their arms, wiggle their fingers, and clench their fists; they grasp the umbilical cord, rub the wall of the uterus, and bring hand to mouth to suck their thumb (Reissland, Francis, Aydin, Mason, & Schaal, 2014; Sparling, van Tol, & Chescheir, 1999). Spontaneous arm and hand movements continue after birth (Piek & Carman, 1994; Thelen, 1979). Intentional manual actions generally follow a proximal to distal progression, from control of the shoulder to fine movements of the hands and fingers. Infants' arm flaps transform into goal-directed swats at a target (Bhat & Galloway, 2006), which in turn become successful reaching and grasping (Berthier & Keen, 2006; Clifton, Muir, Ashmead, & Clarkson, 1993; Witherington, 2005). Manual exploration progresses from holding and dropping objects to rubbing, squeezing, and fingering them (Rochat, 1989; Soska & Adolph, 2014). Simple hand-to-mouth actions become manual actions directed to other parts of the face and body (Chinn, Noonan, Hoffman, & Lockman, 2019). Exploring surfaces with hands (Fontenelle, Kahrs, Neal, Newton, & Lockman, 2007) precedes banging and swiping objects on surfaces (Bourgeois, Khawar, Neal, & Lockman, 2005), which in turn precedes relating objects to each other by stacking them and putting them into and out of containers (Keen, 2011) and using spoons and hammers as tools (Connolly & Dalgleish, 1989; Lockman & Kahrs, 2017; McCarty, Clifton, & Collard, 2001).

Locomotor movements also begin before birth with fetal leg kicks (de Vries, Visser, & Prechtl, 1982). Leg movements continue after birth, but newborns' kicking and stepping doesn't take them anywhere because they cannot keep balance or support their body weight. With increased postural control and strength, true mobility generally progresses from more to fewer body parts on the ground – first pivoting and belly crawling with the abdomen on the ground, then crawling on hands and knees or bum shuffling in a sitting position, then cruising while holding furniture for support, and finally walking independently.

Whereas postural and manual actions facilitate visual and manual exploration of the surrounding environment and objects, locomotor actions involve whole-body exploration of surfaces and places (Gibson, 1988; Gibson & Schmuckler, 1989). Locomotion – moving the whole body from one location to another – allows infants to move away from their caregivers or to move closer to them. They can engage with distant objects, visit familiar or new places, and interact with the structural layout of the environment (e.g., crawl up stairs or under chairs).

17.1.2 Motor Milestones

The best-known representation of the dramatic transformations in motor development is the normative infant milestone chart (Figure 17.1). The typical chart depicts an age-related sequence of postural and locomotor skills, illustrated with line drawings and/or averages and percentiles. Most readers assume that the items on the chart are infants' most important achievements, that the averages represent healthy development, that the criteria for each skill are meaningful, and that each line drawing portrays something essential about the target skill. However, these assumptions are misguided. The milestone chart is more historical relic than developmental fact (Adolph, Hoch, & Cole, 2018; Adolph & Robinson, 2013, 2015).

Milestones are the legacy of the early pioneers in infant motor development (Bayley, 1936; Gesell, 1946; McGraw, 1945; Shirley, 1931). The skills on the chart in Figure 17.1 (sitting, standing, crawling, walking, and so on) derived from original cinematic recordings by Gesell, McGraw, and others of homogeneous samples of US infants, as did the notion of accompanying age norms. The line drawings and freeze-frame photographs originated in their frame-by-frame analyses of film recordings; but it was the series of frames that captured the behavior, not any single image. Their selection of skills was largely arbitrary (Adolph, Karasik, & Tamis-LeMonda, 2010a). Gesell and McGraw, for example, documented a wide assortment of prone movements and sitting positions. But most milestone charts include only crawling on hands and knees and sitting with legs outstretched on the floor. The criteria for achieving a milestone (number of crawling steps, duration of sitting, etc.) were also arbitrary and differ from one chart to another. And despite studying infants in a variety of tasks (climbing stairs, descending slopes and pedestals, etc.), in the effort to distill the essence of motor development, the early pioneers depicted infants isolated from the surrounding context (as in the milestone chart in Figure 17.1 and the classical depiction of postural, manual, and locomotor skills in Figure 17.2A–C).

The milestone charts in modern-day developmental textbooks, parenting guides, and the pediatrician's office perpetuate the distorted legacy of the early pioneers. Although their intention was to study the shape of behavior in real time and over development (Figure 17.2A–C), the surviving charts emphasize age-related stages over developmental process. In McGraw's (1932) words (with her italics for emphasis), too much "attention has been centered on determining *when* particular characteristics appear without proper analysis as to the process or the means whereby they are acquired" (p. 291). Moreover, data from most cultures are missing from the milestone charts. Babies from around the world are commonly compared to Western age-norms for items selected by Western researchers nearly a century ago (Adolph et al., 2010a). Even the milestone chart produced by the World Health Organization only includes data from infants in five countries. Worse still, the WHO presents this chart as a prescriptive standard that all infants should meet – a universal age-related sequence of infant development – rather than descriptive norms of particular populations (Martorell et al., 2006).

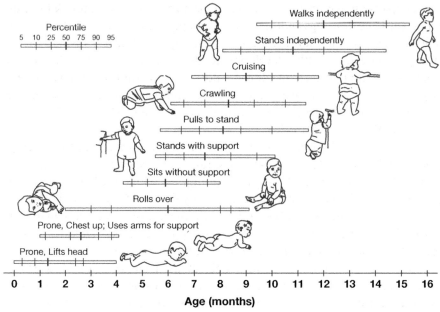

Figure 17.1. *Infant motor milestone chart. The line drawings and normative age bands show an age-related progression of postural and locomotor skills. As is typical, age increases from left to right, and skills improve from bottom to top. The length of the horizontal bars represents the 5th to 95th percentiles, and ticks denote the 10th, 25th, 50th, 75th, and 90th percentiles. Source: Normative data for lifting the head while prone, propping the chest up while prone, rolling over, and pulling to stand are from the Alberta, Infant Motor Scale (AIMS), based on a cross-sectional sample of 2,200 infants in Alberta, Canada (Piper & Darrah, 1994). Data for sitting without support, crawling on hands and knees, cruising upright along furniture, standing while holding furniture, standing independently, and walking independently are from the World Health Organization (WHO) standards based on a prospective longitudinal sample of 816 infants from Ghana, India, Norway, Oman, and the United States (Martorell et al., 2006; Wijnhoven et al., 2004). Figure adapted from Santrock (2006), reprinted with permission.*

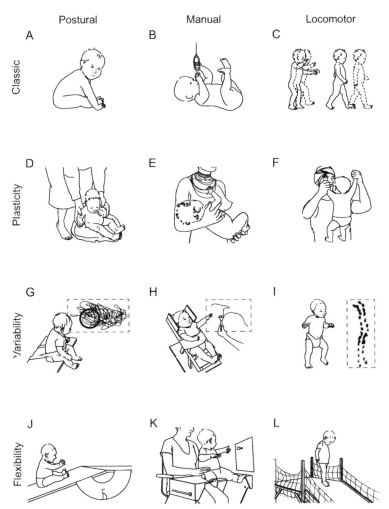

Figure 17.2. *Grid illustrating conceptions of infant motor development based on the classic approach and examples of plasticity, variability, and flexibility in basic postural, manual, and locomotor skills. Row 1: Line drawings from classic texts by the early pioneers in motor development portraying an infant: (A) sitting; (B) reaching for a toy at midline; and (C) walking. Row 2: Childrearing practices that demonstrate plasticity in motor development: (D) infant practicing sitting with caregiver's help; (E) infant grasping and exploring the beads around her mother's neck while held in caregiver's arms; and (F) infant practicing upright stepping with caregiver's support. Row 3: Examples of intraindividual variability: (G) variability in postural sway of a novice sitter, plot shows overhead view of head position relative to the base of support as represented by drawn circle; (H) variable reaching path of a 19-week-old infant with infant's posture supported by a specialized chair; and (I) variable steps of a novice walker on a pressure-sensitive mat that records the timing and placement of each step. Row 4: Paradigms for testing behavioral flexibility: (J) infant sitting on an adjustable backward slope; (K) infant reaching for a toy while sitting on a rotating chair; and (L) walking infant at the top of an adjustable slope.*

Figure 17.2. Caption (*Cont.*)

Source: (A) Adapted from McGraw (1941b), reprinted with permission from Taylor & Francis; (B) adapted from Gesell and Armatruda (1945), reprinted with permission; (C) adapted from McGraw (1940), reprinted with permission; (D) as described by Super (1976); (E) as described by Konner (1972); (F) adapted from Hopkins and Westra (1988), reprinted with permission from Taylor & Francis; (G) data from Saavedra et al., (2012); (H) data from von Hofsten (1991), reprinted with permission from Taylor & Francis; (I) data from Lee, Cole, Golenia, and Adolph, (2018); (J) Rachwani, Soska, & Adolph (2017); (K) Rachwani, Golenia, Herzberg, & Adolph (2019); and (L) Adolph (1997).

17.1.3 Chapter Overview

This chapter argues that the representation of motor development in the typical infant milestone chart is deceptively universal, consistent, and rigid (Adolph & Hoch, 2019; Adolph et al., 2018). Rather than a universal, obligatory series of ages and stages, *plasticity* is intrinsic to motor skill acquisition. The skills infants acquire, the ages they first appear, and their subsequent developmental trajectories are highly responsive to cultural and historical differences in childrearing practices and infants' everyday experiences. In contrast to the consistent and orderly progression implied by the milestone chart, both intra- and interindividual *variability* are hallmarks of infant motor development. At first, infants cannot perform skills in the same way repeatedly, and later they choose not to. Moreover, each infant finds unique solutions to solve the problem of moving. Rather than being rigid and fixed, *flexibility* is fundamental for motor behavior. Variety in motor actions is often a choice, not a by-product of poor motor control. Motor actions must be flexible because infants' bodies and environments are continually changing. Thus, infants modify ongoing actions, select different actions from their repertoire, and create new actions on the fly to adapt to changes in local conditions. Finally, we discuss the implications of plasticity, variability, and flexibility in infant motor development for developmental neuroscience and clinical intervention.

17.2 Plasticity

Experience shapes motor skill acquisition, and infants' everyday experiences differ widely depending on the childrearing practices of their caregivers, which in turn depend on the larger cultural and historical context (Adolph & Hoch, 2019; Adolph et al., 2010a; Adolph & Robinson, 2013, 2015). As a consequence, motor development is extremely plastic (Figure 17.2D–F). Indeed, seemingly mundane activities such as how caregivers hold, carry, bathe, dress, and position their infants for sleeping affect the form and timing of motor development. Deliberate exercise, restraint, and habitual practice do likewise, but the items and age bands on normative milestone charts such as the WHO standards do not reflect the global diversity of infants' experiences.

17.2.1 Effects of Cultural-Historical Differences in Childrearing Practices

Across cultures, caregivers have different expectations about the necessary input for healthy motor development. In many cultures, caregivers handle young infants like a fragile carton of eggs by supporting infants' heads and torsos against gravity. But in some African and Caribbean cultures, caregivers expect infants to withstand gravity on their own. Caregivers pick up infants by an arm, suspend them by their ankles or head, and toss them in the air and catch them (Hopkins & Westra, 1988, 1990; Super, 1976). Moving infants slowly and gently is the norm in some cultures, but in others, intense vestibular stimulation is common. Mali caregivers carry infants in slings while engaging in vigorous activities like pounding grain (Bril & Sabatier, 1986). Tajik caregivers rock infants' cradles so forcefully that the cradle bed is nearly perpendicular to the floor (Karasik, Tamis-LeMonda, Ossmy, & Adolph, 2018). Many caregivers around the world create or purchase toys to encourage infants' manual actions. But !Kung infants grasp and explore the beads around their mother's neck (Figure 17.2E) and play with sticks, leaves, and adult artifacts (Konner, 1972).

Childrearing practices can accelerate motor development relative to the WHO standards. Caregivers in some parts of Africa and the Caribbean deliberately exercise infants to teach them to sit and to walk (Adolph et al., 2010a; Adolph & Robinson, 2013, 2015). Starting from the newborn period, caregivers prop infants on their laps or in a basin (Figure 17.2D) and provide minimal support for sitting balance. Caregivers stand young infants on their laps and bounce them (Figure 17.2F), and "walk" infants up their chests (Super, 1976). They hold infants' hands and encourage them to make stepping movements. The result of all the shaking, jouncing, tossing, and exercise is that infants hold their heads up, sit, walk, and run at earlier ages than expected by the WHO standards (Geber, 1961; Hopkins & Westra, 1990). Crawling is discouraged in these cultures, so many infants skip crawling altogether, or crawl at the same age that they begin walking.

Childrearing practices can also delay infants' motor development by restricting infants' movements. Caregivers in Central Asia bind infants, neck to toe, in a "gahvora" cradle to keep them clean, warm, and safe (Karasik et al., 2018). In rural China where water is scarce, caregivers lay infants supine in sandbags to toilet them and keep them safe (Mei, 1994). The restrictive bindings and heavy sand constrain infants' movements for long periods resulting in weeks and months of delays in motor development relative to the WHO standards. Similarly, heavy clothing restricts infants' movements and results in later onset ages for postural and locomotor skills and less proficient walking (Benson, 1993; Theveniau, Boisgontier, Verieras, & Olivier, 2014). Merely wearing a diaper causes less mature gait patterns compared to walking naked (Cole, Lingeman, & Adolph, 2012).

Within a culture, historical changes in childrearing practices can affect motor development. In the late 1800s when US infants commonly wore long gowns, most infants log-rolled and hitched instead of crawling to avoid getting tangled in their garments (Trettien, 1900). In 1992, the American Academy of Pediatrics instituted the "back to sleep" program, which recommended care-givers to place infants on their backs to sleep instead of their stomachs to avoid sudden infant death syndrome (Kattwinkel, Hauck, Keenan, Malloy, & Moon, 2005). As an inadvertent consequence, less time in a prone position caused delays in crawling and other prone skills relative to earlier generations of infants who were put to sleep on their stomachs (Davis, Moon, Sachs, & Ottolini, 1998; Pin, Eldridge, & Galea, 2007). Pediatricians now recommend awake "tummy time" to counteract the delay of prone skills (Dudek-Shriber & Zelazy, 2007). Similarly, seasonal changes in childrearing practices (e.g., more clothing and less floor time in colder months) affect the ages when children begin crawling (Atun-Einy, Cohen, Samuel, & Scher, 2013; Benson, 1993).

Cultural practices can affect the form and developmental trajectory of motor skills long after the infancy period (Adolph et al., 2010a; Adolph & Robinson, 2013, 2015). Various adult sitting postures, for example, depend on years of habitual practice in childhood – the deep squat (used in many cultures to rest or defecate), deep kneel (prayer position), cross-legged sit, and so on (Hewes, 1955). Sitting with legs outstretched on the floor, as depicted on infant milestone charts, is typically lost in Western adults due to disuse. Tarahumara children and adults (both men and women) run the distance of several marathons (150–300 km) in 24–48 hours at speeds from 6–11 minutes per mile during everyday activity and for sport (Devine, 1985). Persistence hunters in the Kalahari Desert run during the hottest time of the day and chase antelope until the animals drop from exhaustion (Liebenberg, 2006). Children and adults in Nepal and in some African cultures carry loads 70–200% greater than their body weight for long distances over rugged mountain terrain (Bastien, Willems, Schepens, & Heglund, 2016; Minetti, Formenti, & Ardigo, 2006). Centuries of women in China learned to walk as infants and then again as young girls after their feet had been broken and bound (Fang & Yu, 1960). Ballerinas leap and twirl balanced solely on their toes. And millions of Western women work, walk, run, and dance in high-heeled shoes.

17.2.2 Experimental Manipulations of Developmental Timing and Form

Although useful, cultural comparisons – so-called "natural experiments" – are beset with biological and environmental confounds. However, true experiments with random assignment to training and control groups confirm the facilitative effects of augmented experience. For example, 3 weeks of daily postural training at 2 months of age leads to immediate and long-term advances in head control, prone skills, reaching, sitting, crawling, and walking compared with infants in a control group who receive only enhanced social interactions (Lobo & Galloway, 2012). Three weeks of practice with crawling movements results in more advanced crawling skills compared to infants who do not receive specific training (Lagerspetz, Nygard, & Strandvik, 1971). In neonates, 8 weeks of practice with upright stepping results in earlier onset of walking compared to infants who receive passive exercise or no exercise at all (Zelazo, Zelazo, & Kolb, 1972). Twelve weeks of practice with standing (on an experimenter's hand!) facilitates standing for 15 seconds in 4-month-olds (Sigmundsson, Loras, & Haga, 2017).

Experience may facilitate motor skill acquisition through enhanced motivation and attention. At 3 months of age, infants' reaches are jerky and slow, and they cannot grasp objects on their own. Three days of training leads 3-month-olds to increase their attempts to reach and to display straighter arm movements compared with infants who receive only social interactions (Cunha, Lobo, Kokkoni, Galloway, & Tudella, 2015). With the help of sticky Velcro mittens, 3-month-olds can "pick up" Velcro-covered toys (Needham, Barrett, & Peterman, 2002). Two weeks of sticky mitten training facilitates more sophisticated object exploration and more reaches to toys when tested bare-handed (Libertus & Needham, 2010). Moreover, sticky-mitten experience at 3 months of age facilitates more coordinated visual–manual object exploration with bare hands 12 months later (Libertus, Joh, & Needham, 2016).

17.3 Variability

Movements depend on biomechanics – muscle activations, body position, and the environment. Such intrinsic and extrinsic factors vary from moment to moment, so movements, like snowflakes, are never exactly the same (Bernstein, 1996). Moreover, infants' neuromuscular system is highly variable. As a consequence of variable biomechanical factors and a noisy control system, intraindividual variability is endemic in infant motor behavior (Figure 17.2G–I). Although the normative milestone chart implies an orderly lock-step progression of skills, interindividual variability is also characteristic of motor development. Each baby's body and motivations are different, so infants find their own unique solutions for learning to move. Infants differ widely in the ages when they acquire a particular skill (see age bands in Figure 17.1), and the rate of developmental improvement.

17.3.1 Intraindividual Variability

Intraindividual variability is apparent at every timescale – the milliseconds of a single step, the seconds spanning a series of steps, and the weeks and months of developmental improvements in walking skill. In situations where consistency is paramount, intraindividual variability typically decreases over development (Adolph, Cole, & Vereijken, 2015; Adolph & Robinson, 2015). For example, when the task is to sit quietly on a flat surface, posture in new sitters is erratic, and infants lose balance in every direction (Saavedra et al., 2012). After a few weeks, infants pull themselves upright, flop forward or backward, then pull upright again (see trace of infant's head position in Figure 17.2G). Eventually, swaying motions become more regular and constrained to the area within the base of support. Similarly, when the task is to reach repeatedly to a target at midline, intraindividual variability decreases and infants' reaches become more predictable, accurate, and efficient. At first, infants' hands move in a jerky, zig-zag path (see trace of infant's hand path in Figure 17.2H), more than double the distance of a straight-line path to the target (Konczak, Borutta, Topka, & Dichgans, 1995; von Hofsten, 1991). Over the ensuing months, infants' reaches become straighter, smoother, and more consistent (Berthier & Keen, 2006; von Hofsten, 1991). Likewise, when the task is to walk in a straight path over uniform ground, intraindividual variability decreases. When infants first begin walking, almost every aspect of their gait is variable – the placement of their feet on the ground (see trace of infant's footsteps in Figure 17.2I), the duration of their leg movement in the air, the coordination between joints, the muscle activations that produce forces for propulsion, and the consequent forces (Adolph, Vereijken, & Shrout, 2003; Chang, Kubo, Buzzi, & Ulrich, 2006; Hallemans, de Clercq, Otten, & Aerts, 2005; Ivanenko et al., 2004). Variability decreases with experience so that each footstep becomes smoother and more similar to the last.

However, when the situation does not require consistency, intraindividual variability typically does not decrease over development (Adolph et al., 2015; Adolph & Robinson, 2015). In everyday life, infants do not walk continuously with forward steps in a straight path over uniform ground. Instead, infants' natural locomotion is highly variable – with frequent starts and stops, steps in every direction, along curving and twisting paths (Adolph et al., 2012; Lee et al., 2018). Discontinuous, omnidirectional, curving paths persist unabated from infants' first week of walking until at least 10 months later. Variability is not merely a function of a cluttered environment. Infants produce variable walking paths even in an empty room with no obstacles to navigate, no toys to go to, and no caregiver to play with (Hoch, O'Grady, & Adolph, 2018). Indeed, intraindividual variability is a valuable feature of infants' natural locomotion, not a bug. When simulated robots are trained to walk on variable infant paths, they outperform robots trained on straight paths or other geometrically shaped paths. And the more variability the better. Training on more variable infant paths leads to better outcomes than training on less variable infant paths (Ossmy et al., 2018).

17.3.2 Individual Differences and Unique Solutions

Researchers commonly describe development in terms of group averages, but motor development is characterized by large individual differences in onset ages, the sequence of skills, starting points, and rate of improvement – even within the same culture and historical cohort (Adolph et al., 2015). For example, healthy infants begin sitting anywhere between 4.3 and 8.0 months (5th to 95th percentiles on the WHO standards) and begin walking between 9.4 and 15.3 months (Martorell et al., 2006); see age bands in Figure 17.1. Some infants crawl on their bellies before crawling on hands and knees; others skip belly crawling and proceed straight to hands and knees; and still others skip crawling altogether and instead hitch, bum shuffle, or just get up and walk (Adolph, 1997; Adolph, Vereijken, & Denny, 1998; Patrick, Noah, & Yang, 2012; Robson, 1984). The general pattern is from less to more upright postures, but sitting, hands–knees crawling, pulling to stand, standing, and cruising sideways along furniture appear in a variety of orders across infants (Adolph, Berger, & Leo, 2011; Atun-Einy, Berger, & Scher, 2012; Martorell et al., 2006). Motivation may play a role in the wide age bands and varied sequences. Indeed, infants with more motivation to move (as indexed by higher spontaneous activity levels, more persistence, and fewer requirements for social encouragement) achieve their milestones at earlier ages than less motivated infants (Atun-Einy, Berger, & Scher, 2013).

Within each skill, developmental improvements are generally fastest in the first few months after onset and slower thereafter. When viewed from a wide-angle lens, all infants show straighter more consistent reaching and walking paths over development. But when analyzed up close and in detail, each infant's developmental trajectory improves at its own rate, with its own messy progressions and regressions. Each begins at a different starting point and forges a unique developmental path. For example, infants show large individual differences in hand speed when they first begin to reach, and fluctuations between periods of faster, jerkier reaches and slower, more controlled reaches occur at different points in development before hand speed becomes stable (Thelen, Corbetta, & Spencer, 1996). Similarly, the duration of each step differs among infants at walk onset, fluctuates across weeks of walking, and decreases at different rates (McGraw & Breeze, 1941).

Moreover, because bodies, brains, and motivations differ among infants, each infant has a different movement problem to solve. All first reaches are not the same. More active infants learn to guide their hands to the target by dampening down the inertial forces from their spontaneous arm flaps; more sedentary infants learn to power up their stationary arms (Thelen et al., 1993). Likewise, all first steps are not the same. "Twisters" create angular momentum by twisting their trunk to swing each leg around; "fallers" launch forward while their feet hurry to catch up; and "steppers" minimize disruptions to balance by lifting their knee to initiate each short step (Bisi & Stagni, 2015; Snapp-Childs & Corbetta, 2009). All infants learn to modulate forces for reaching and walking, of course, but each finds a unique solution to the problem. Eventually, reaching and walking converge to similar adult-like templates in standard laboratory tasks. Put another way, multiple developmental pathways can lead to similar outcomes.

17.4 Flexibility

Infants acquire new postural, manual, and locomotor skills in a body and environment that are constantly in flux. Infants can grow nearly 2 cm in a single day (Lampl, Veldhuis, & Johnson, 1992). Their clothing and footwear can change from one hour to the next. The people, objects, and places in the environment can change from moment to moment. Variations in infants' bodies and environments require behavioral flexibility – the ability to tailor motor actions to changing body–environment relations (Figure 17.2J–L). Infants must generate and use perceptual information to modify ongoing actions, select appropriate actions from their repertoire, or construct new actions to fit the current situation and accomplish their goals. Moreover, multiple solutions are often possible and infants (like older children and adults) use different solutions to solve the same motor problems. Variety of means is an important aspect of behavioral flexibility.

17.4.1 Functional Action in a Changing Environment

The typical milestone chart depicts infants' various postural achievements stripped from context and isolated from everyday tasks. The pictured skills are only demonstrations, not functional actions for getting things done. For example, the typical chart shows an infant sitting erect on a flat surface with hands free (as in Figure 17.1). However, infants learn to sit on a variety of surfaces (caregiver's lap, hard floor, soft mattress) while performing a variety of tasks (looking at and interacting with objects and people). Functional sitting requires infants to modify their posture to cope with changes in local conditions (Rachwani et al., 2017).

By the time infants can sit independently, they show impressive behavioral flexibility. Sitting infants modify their postural sway to keep balance on varied ground surfaces such as foam surfaces varying in compliance (Kokkoni, Haworth, Harbourne, Stergiou, & Kyvelidou, 2017). Infants anticipate destabilizing forces due to their own movements by activating trunk muscles before stretching their arm out to reach (Rachwani, Santamaria, Saavedra, & Woollacott, 2015). They respond to external perturbations by showing directionally specific postural responses when the floor moves unexpectedly forward or backward (Hedberg, Carlberg, Forssberg, & Hadders-Algra, 2005) or when visual flow information simulates forward or backward movement of the body (Bertenthal & Bai, 1989). Moreover, independent sitters flexibly modify posture to cope with multiple threats to balance at once. They stay upright by quickly adjusting their sitting posture when the floor unexpectedly increases in slant and they maintain balance on the altered surface by leaning farther backward on increasingly steep forward slopes and leaning farther forward on increasingly steep backward slopes (Rachwani et al., 2017; see Figure 17.2J).

Researchers typically study reaching with infants sitting on a caregiver's lap or strapped into a semi-reclined seat (as in Figure 17.2H) with the object presented in full view at midline (Clifton et al., 1993; von Hofsten, 1991), but real-life reaches are rarely so restricted. Alluring objects can appear at any location and while the object or the body is in motion. Thus, functional reaching requires infants to select and modify their manual actions depending on the location of the object relative to the body. Infants select the nearest hand to reach for objects presented at various locations around their bodies (Jacquet, Esseily, Rider, & Fagard, 2012). They chase slow moving objects with their near hand but use their far hand to anticipate the location of fast-moving objects (von Hofsten, Vishton, Spelke, Feng, & Rosander, 1998). When seated on a chair that pivots their bodies 360° past a toy in varying vertical locations (see Figure 17.2K), experienced sitting infants can coordinate their postural, visual, and manual actions to quickly prehend the target – first with their eyes and then with their hands (Rachwani et al., 2019).

Because objects differ in orientation, shape, and size, infants must use visual information to prospectively modify their grip. Infants use visual information about object properties to appropriately orient their hands to grasp horizontal and vertical rods (Lockman, Ashmead, & Bushnell, 1984; Witherington, 2005) and to adjust their grip location for asymmetrical objects (Barrett & Needham, 2008). For small objects, infants use a precision grip and adjust the space between their index finger and thumb as their hand approaches the object (Fagard, 2000; Schum, Jovanovic, & Schwarzer, 2011). For large objects, infants select one or two hands depending on the object's size and scale the space between their hands accordingly (van Wermeskerken, van der Kamp, & Savelsbergh, 2011). Eventually children perceive the requirements for reaching so precisely that they switch from a one- to a two-handed grasp when the object exceeds the size of their grip aperture (Huang, Ellis, Wagenaar, & Fetters, 2013).

Infants' locomotor skill is usually tested on a motorized treadmill or while infants crawl or walk along straight paths over open, uniform ground (as in Figure 17.2I). But functional locomotion occurs in a cluttered environment with variations in the terrain. Infants learn to walk amid a maze of obstacles – furniture, stairs, toys, and people – and over ground that can be slippery, squishy, sloping, or rough. When first confronted with impossibly high drop-offs, steep slopes, narrow bridges, or wide gaps in the surface of support, novice crawlers and walkers plunge straight over the brink (Adolph, 1997, 2000; Kretch & Adolph, 2013a, 2013b). But over weeks of crawling and walking experience, infants' judgments become increasingly accurate until they can discern safe from risky ground within 1–2 cm on adjustable drop-offs and bridges and 2° on adjustable slopes (Adolph, 1997; Kretch & Adolph, 2013a, 2013b). As obstacles become more challenging, infants slow down and shorten their step length as they approach; they explore at the edge of the precipice before deciding whether to go (Figure 17.2L); and when walking is possible, they alter their steps to navigate the obstacle (Gill, Adolph, & Vereijken, 2009). Experienced infant walkers can even update their judgments to take into account experimentally induced changes in their bodies due to lead-weighted shoulder packs or slippery Teflon-soled shoes (Adolph & Avolio, 2000; Adolph, Karasik, & Tamis-LeMonda, 2010b).

17.4.2 Variety of Means

Behavioral flexibility enables infants to achieve the same functional outcome using a variety of means. When there is more than one way to solve a problem, infants use a range of strategies. New solutions can arise through repurposing existing actions for a new situation or by inventing a new solution to suit the current constraints. For example, crawlers transport objects by pushing them along the floor, holding them in their hand or holding them in their mouth while they crawl, or by scooting in a sitting position with the object in hand or under an arm (Karasik, Adolph, Tamis-LeMonda, & Zuckerman, 2012). Cruising infants keep balance using a low handrail for support by hunching over on some trials and walking on their knees on other trials (Berger, Chan, & Adolph, 2014).

Similarly, walking infants display a variety of effective strategies from trial to trial while using a wobbly foam handrail to augment balance on narrow bridges. They crouch over while pressing the stretchy handrail below their knees, slide their arm along the handrail to prevent it from depressing too deeply, or use it as a rope to pull themselves forward like a mountain climber, or walk sideways holding the handrail as if windsurfing (Berger, Adolph, & Lobo, 2005). When faced with impossibly steep slopes or large drop-offs, experienced walking infants typically do not avoid descent. Instead, they vary descent strategies from trial to trial by scooting down in a sitting position, descending backward feet first, crawling on hands and knees, or on slopes sliding down headfirst with arms outstretched in a Superman position (Adolph, 1997; Kretch & Adolph, 2013a). In many cases, infants discover alternative solutions in the midst of the task despite having previously displayed successful solutions already in their repertoires.

17.5 Implications for Neuroscience and Clinical Intervention

The early pioneers, led by Gesell and McGraw, viewed motor development as the embodied manifestation of behavioral growth (Adolph & Berger, 2006). Images such as those in Figure 17.2A–C were literally drawn from their cinematic recordings, and thus are a direct readout of movements evolving in real time and over development. Figure 17.2C shows critical differences in real-time movements between infants' first walking steps and a more mature developmental phase when infants evidence a heel strike and swing their arms reciprocally.

Gesell and McGraw also viewed motor development as a window into neural function. But the neural underpinnings of movement cannot be directly observed. Like modern-day researchers, the early pioneers lacked direct access to the gold standard – neural control of motor behavior in a living, moving, human infant. Even today, access to developmental changes in neural physiology and structure is limited to stationary infants or cadavers and provides only correlational evidence at best. In McGraw's hands, the real-time and developmental sequences of behaviors were a strong foundation for inference about the underlying neural mechanisms. Her papers boast titles like "Neuromuscular Development of the Human Infant as Exemplified in the Achievement of Erect Locomotion" (McGraw, 1940), "Development of Neuromuscular Mechanisms as Reflected in the Crawling and Creeping Behavior of the Human Infant" (McGraw, 1941a), "Neuromotor Maturation of Anti-Gravity Functions as Reflected in the Development of a Sitting Posture" (McGraw, 1941b), and so on, culminating in her book, *The Neuromuscular Maturation of the Human Infant* (McGraw, 1945).

Gesell tied sequences of infant and child behaviors to particular age norms His famous developmental schedules, including the infant motor milestone chart, broadly popularized the notion of age-linked developmental stages, and led to a century of developmental screening tests. Like Gesell's original schedules, modern-day researchers and clinicians continue to use developmental screening tests to diagnose developmental delay and disability (e.g., Bayley, 2006).

Here, we suggest that viewing motor development in terms of plasticity, variability, and flexibility, provides new insights into neuromuscular development. These insights, in turn, have important implications for clinical practice and intervention.

17.5.1 Plasticity

Cultural, historical, and experimental data show that motor development is remarkably plastic and dependent on childrearing practices. The everyday experiences that lead to plasticity in motor development surely reflect and promote changes in both the body and the brain. Self-generated motor experience requires a sufficiently mature body (muscle strength, balance, body mass, and size, etc.) to allow particular movements and a sufficiently mature brain to control them. Motor experience, in turn, strengthens infants' muscles and bones and provides input to the developing brain (Ulrich, 2010) Behavior, body, and brain are linked in every direction.

One important consideration concerns the amount of self-generated experience. The natural input for basic postural, manual, and locomotor skills is immense. Researchers and parents may have the sense that infants move a lot, but documentation of the actual input is a recent advance. No one would have imagined the tremendous amounts of input generated by a typical infant. Across a variety of cultures (the United States, Italy, Argentina, Korea, Kenya, and Cameroon), 5-month-olds spend 30% of each waking hour in a sitting posture, and the average increases to 50% of each hour for infants who can sit independently (Karasik, Tamis-LeMonda, Adolph, & Bornstein, 2015). By 24 months of age, infants spend about 80% of each hour actively sitting or standing (Logan et al., 2015). In just 1 minute of object interaction, 4- to 7-month-olds generate an impressive array of sophisticated manual actions – averaging 3 bouts of transferring the object from hand to hand, 7 bouts of putting the object into the mouth and taking it out to look at it, 14 bouts of rotating the object while looking at it, and 25 bouts of fingering the object (Soska & Adolph, 2014). For 11- to 24-month-olds, half of each hour is spent spontaneously interacting with objects (Karasik, Tamis-LeMonda, & Adolph, 2011; Logan et al., 2015). And in each hour of free play, the average toddler takes 2,400–4,000 steps, travels the length of 9 US football fields, and falls 17 times (Adolph et al., 2012; Hoch et al., 2018).

A second important finding concerns the distribution of infants' movement experience across the waking day. Albeit immense, infants practice their motor skills in short bouts interspersed with rest periods when they do something else (e.g., Adolph et al., 2012). A third insight concerns the developmental timing of experience. Infants who begin practicing basic motor skills earlier in development acquire their skills at younger ages. Neonatal exercise of leg movements, for example, leads to earlier onset of walking (Zelazo et al., 1972).

What are the implications for clinical intervention of early, time-distributed, and immense quantities of movement input to and from the developing body and brain? Most clinical interventions for children with disabilities or delays provide only a tiny fraction of the enormous amount of practice documented in typically developing infants. Referral for intervention – and hence the developmental timing of therapy – typically occurs late in the game, long after typically developing infants acquire basic motor skills (Bailey, Hebbeler, Scarborough, Spiker, & Mallik, 2004). And therapy is commonly distributed in brief periods separated by several days. In the United States, early intervention programs normally schedule 2 hours of services per week or less (Hebbeler et al., 2007). Optimally, diagnosis and referral would begin at birth, therapy sessions would increase in frequency and duration, and caregivers would be trained and encouraged to facilitate practice throughout the day (Ulrich, 2010).

17.5.2 Variability

Since the days of the early pioneers, researchers have recognized that intraindividual variability is endemic in infant motor-skill acquisition. In tasks requiring consistency (e.g., guiding the hand straight to a target, taking forward steps along a straight path), intraindividual variability is likely a symptom of poor neuromuscular control (Adolph et al., 2015). Nonetheless, each jerky, inefficient reach provides feedback to the developing nervous system. Each tottering postural sway and each clumsy step is a tiny exploration of the possible state space. Even "catastrophic" failures – such as missing the target or falling over – are opportunities for learning. Moreover, errors are relatively inconsequential, and many attempts at goal-directed actions will eventually end in success. A brain–body system that does not try to move cannot learn to move. And a system that is too rigidly consistent in early stages of motor-skill acquisition cannot adapt to new situations (Vereijken, 2010).

In situations where variability is welcome (such as locomotor free play), intraindividual variability likely promotes neuromuscular control. Learning to walk by taking continuous forward steps on a treadmill or along a straight path can build leg strength (Ulrich, 2010), but learning to walk along a curving, irregular locomotor path requires the brain to control the two sides of the body differently and to execute a variety of motor commands. Put another way, anencephalic infants can make alternating leg movements, but only babies with an intact cortex can wind their way along a sinuous path. Omnidirectional steps and frequent short bouts require the brain to control balance in every direction and to initiate disequilibrium and recapture equilibrium for every bout. During natural locomotion, the brain has lots to do.

Interindividual variability is also a hallmark of infant motor development – when and how infants first solve the problems of postural, manual, and locomotor actions. Each motor skill depends on a suite of underlying factors (neuromuscular, biomechanical, perceptual, motivational, etc.), each developing at its own rate (Thelen & Smith, 1994). Individual differences reflect different growth rates in these underlying factors. For example, high motivation to go combined with a low level of balance control may induce some infants to belly crawl as their first solution for mobility, whereas lower motivation to move may cause some infants to skip belly crawling and await sufficient balance to crawl on hands and knees.

What are the clinical implications of such notions about intra- and interindividual variability? Some prevalent approaches to pediatric physical therapy encourage consistent, repetitive "normal" movements and discourage "abnormal patterns" in children with disabilities (Bobath & Bobath, 1984). Treadmill training is common (Mutlu, Krosschell, & Gaebler-Spira, 2009; Ulrich, 2010). Many therapists assume that earlier stages are prerequisites for later stages and thus encourage crawling prior to walking or reaching prior to grasping. Instead, what is needed are therapeutic approaches that emphasize function over form. For basic postural, manual, and locomotor skills, therapists should aim for the "Goldilocks" amount of intraindividual variability – the "just-right" amount that allows infants to explore the problem space while allowing for functional outcomes (Vereijken, 2010). The therapist's role is to create the optimal environmental context to constrain variability when the child's movements are too inconsistent or to increase variability when the child's movements are too rigid to be functional (Fetters, 2010). Put another way, the therapist's job is to figure out whether intraindividual variability is part of the problem or part of the solution (Vereijken, 2010). If the task is accomplished, intraindividual variability is acceptable and often desirable in early periods of skill acquisition.

17.5.3 Flexibility

The development of behavioral flexibility may provide the largest window into the developing brain because higher mental functions – perception and cognition – are intimately involved in motor planning. Functional motor behavior must take moment-to-moment variations in the body and environment into account. Thus, infants must learn to use perceptual information about the current status of their body and the environment to plan their next action. Planning is required to modify ongoing actions, select different actions, and create new actions. For multistep actions (e.g., grasp the handle of a rake, turn it to orient the tines, and use it to rake in a distant target), infants must plan two or more movements into the future (Keen, 2011). Because perceptual information about the later steps in the plan may not yet exist, cognition is involved. Although the inklings of perceptually guided action are evident in neonates, prospective control improves for each motor skill in infant development, and for multistep actions, it continues to develop long into childhood (Adolph & Robinson, 2015).

Learning plays a central role in the acquisition of behavioral flexibility. For example, infants require about 20 weeks of everyday locomotor experience before they can distinguish safe from risky slopes and drop-offs (Adolph, 1997). Presumably, the neural mechanisms underlying the acquisition of behavioral flexibility involve changes in patterns of connectivity within and between perceptual and motor brain regions. Generally, neurons that fire together wire together (Hebb, 1949), but changes in connectivity can involve adding new connections, or remodeling or removing existing connections. The rate of change is likely greatest in early development.

The bidirectional processes between behavioral flexibility and neural connectivity have important implications for clinical practice. Generally, the goal of therapy is to promote skilled movements, but therapy should not end there. Rather than mastering particular movements, children must learn to adapt to changes in the body and the environment. Current interventions should seek to replicate the varied experiences generated by healthy infants in real-world settings. Therapists and caregivers can intervene by strategically adjusting the environment to target the perceptual-motor systems that support behavioral flexibility. Indeed, the most effective interventions for children with disabilities incorporate child-initiated movement and environmental modification (Morgan et al., 2016).

17.6 Conclusions

The best-known characterization of the rapid and dramatic transformations in infant motor development is the normative motor milestone chart. However, the acquisition of basic postural, manual, and locomotor actions is better characterized by experience-induced *plasticity*, *variability* in and among infants, and *flexibility* in an ever-changing body and world. The central nervous system both contributes to and is responsive to these fundamental features of motor development. This framing suggests several implications for clinical intervention: Start early. More is better. Function over form. Adapt to change. And learn by doing.

References

Adolph, K. E. (1997). Learning in the development of infant locomotion. *Monographs of the Society for Research in Child Development*, *62*(3, Serial No. 251), 1–140.

(2000). Specificity of learning: Why infants fall over a veritable cliff. *Psychological Science*, *11*, 290–295.

Adolph, K. E., & Avolio, A. M. (2000). Walking infants adapt locomotion to changing body dimensions. *Journal of Experimental Psychology: Human Perception and Performance*, *26*, 1148–1166.

Adolph, K. E., & Berger, S. E. (2006). Motor development. In D. Kuhn & R. S. Siegler (Eds.), *Handbook of child psychology. Vol. 2: Cognition, perception, and language* (6th ed., pp. 161–213). New York, NY: Wiley.

(2015). Physical and motor development. In M. H. Bornstein & M. E. Lamb (Eds.), *Development science: An advanced textbook* (7th ed., pp. 261–333). New York, NY: Psychology Press.

Adolph, K. E., Berger, S. E., & Leo, A. J. (2011). Developmental continuity? Crawling, cruising, and walking. *Developmental Science*, *14*, 306–318.

Adolph, K. E., Cole, W. G., Komati, M., Garciaguirre, J. S., Badaly, D., Lingeman, J. M., … Sotsky, R. B. (2012). How do you learn to walk? Thousands of steps and dozens of falls per day. *Psychological Science, 23*, 1387–1394.

Adolph, K. E., Cole, W. G., & Vereijken, B. (2015). Intraindividual variability in the development of motor skills in childhood. In M. Diehl, K. Hooker, & M. Sliwinski (Eds.), *Handbook of intraindividual variability across the lifespan* (pp. 59–83). New York, NY: Routledge.

Adolph, K. E., & Franchak, J. M. (2016). The development of motor behavior. *Wiley Interdisciplinary Reviews: Cognitive Science (WIREs)*, *8*(1–2).

Adolph, K. E., & Hoch, J. E. (2019). Motor development: Embodied, embedded, enculturated, and enabling. *Annual Review of Psychology*, *70*, 141–164.

Adolph, K. E., Hoch, J. E., & Cole, W. G. (2018). Development (of walking): 15 suggestions. *Trends in Cognitive Sciences*, *22*(699–711).

Adolph, K. E., Karasik, L. B., & Tamis-LeMonda, C. S. (2010a). Motor skills. In M. H. Bornstein (Ed.), *Handbook of cultural development science. Vol. 1. Domains of development across cultures* (pp. 61–88). New York, NY: Taylor & Francis.

(2010b). Using social information to guide action: Infants' locomotion over slippery slopes. *Neural Networks*, *23*, 1033–1042.

Adolph, K. E., & Robinson, S. R. (2013). The road to walking: What learning to walk tells us about development. In P. Zelazo (Ed.), *Oxford handbook of developmental psychology* (pp. 403–443). New York, NY: Oxford University Press.

(2015). Motor development. In L. Liben & U. Muller (Eds.), *Handbook of child psychology and developmental science. Vol. 2: Cognitive processes* (7th ed., pp. 113–157). New York, NY: Wiley.

Adolph, K. E., Vereijken, B., & Denny, M. A. (1998). Learning to crawl. *Child Development*, *69*, 1299–1312.

Adolph, K. E., Vereijken, B., & Shrout, P. E. (2003). What changes in infant walking and why. *Child Development*, *74*, 474–497.

Assaiante, C., & Amblard, B. (1995). An ontogenetic model for the sensorimotor organization of balance control in humans. *Human Movement Science*, *14*, 13–43.

Atun-Einy, O., Berger, S. E., & Scher, A. (2012). Pulling to stand: Common trajectories and individual differences. *Developmental Psychobiology*, *54*, 187–198.

(2013). Assessing motivation to move and its relationship to motor development in infancy. *Infant Behavior and Development*, *36*, 457–469.

Atun-Einy, O., Cohen, D., Samuel, M., & Scher, A. (2013). Season of birth, crawling onset, and motor development in 7-month-old infants. *Journal of Reproductive and Infant Psychology*, *31*(4), 342–351.

Bailey, D. B., Hebbeler, K., Scarborough, A., Spiker, D., & Mallik, S. (2004). First experiences with early intervention: A national perspective. *Pediatrics*, *113*, 887–896.

Barrett, T. M., & Needham, A. W. (2008). Developmental differences in infants' use of an object's shape to grasp it securely. *Developmental Psychobiology*, *50*(1), 97–106.

Bastien, G. J., Willems, P. A., Schepens, B., & Heglund, N. C. (2016). The mechanics of head-supported load carriage by Nepalese porters. *Journal of Experimental Biology*, *219*, 3626–3634.

Bayley, N. (1936). The development of motor abilities during the first three years: A study of 61 infants tested repeatedly. *Monographs of the Society for Research in Child Development*, *1*, 1–26.

(2006). *Bayley scales of infant and toddler development: Bayley-III* (3rd ed. Vol. 7). San Antonio, TX: Harcourt Assessment, Psychological Corporation.

Benson, J. B. (1993). Season of birth and onset of locomotion: Theoretical and methodological implications. *Infant Behavior and Development*, *16*, 69–81.

Berger, S. E., Adolph, K. E., & Lobo, S. A. (2005). Out of the toolbox: Toddlers differentiate wobbly and wooden handrails. *Child Development*, *76*, 1294–1307.

Berger, S. E., Chan, G., & Adolph, K. E. (2014). What cruising infants understand about support for locomotion. *Infancy*, *19*, 117–137.

Bernstein, N. A. (1996). On dexterity and its development. In M. L. Latash & M. T. Turvey (Eds.), *Dexterity and its development* (pp. 3–244). Mahwah, NJ: Lawrence Erlbaum Associates.

Bertenthal, B. I., & Bai, D. L. (1989). Infants' sensitivity to optical flow for controlling posture. *Developmental Psychology*, *25*, 936–945.

Berthier, N. E., & Keen, R. E. (2006). Development of reaching in infancy. *Experimental Brain Research, 169,* 507–518.

Bhat, A. N., & Galloway, J. C. (2006). Toy-oriented changes during early arm movements: Hand kinematics. *Infant Behavior and Development, 29,* 358–372.

Bisi, M. C., & Stagni, R. (2015). Evaluation of toddler different strategies during the first six-months of independent walking: A longitudinal study. *Gait and Posture, 41,* 574–579.

Bobath, K., & Bobath, B. (1984). The neuro-developmental treatment. In D. Scrutton (Ed.), *Management of the motor disorders of children with cerebral palsy* (pp. 6–18). London: Spastics International Medical Publications.

Bourgeois, K. S., Khawar, A. W., Neal, S. A., & Lockman, J. J. (2005). Infant manual exploration of objects, surfaces, and their interrelations. *Infancy, 8,* 233–252.

Bril, B., & Sabatier, C. (1986). The cultural context of motor development: Postural manipulations in the daily life of Bambara babies (Mali). *International Journal of Behavioral Development, 9,* 439–453.

Chang, C. L., Kubo, M., Buzzi, U., & Ulrich, B. (2006). Early changes in muscle activation patterns of toddlers during walking. *Infant Behavior and Development, 29,* 175–188.

Chinn, L. K., Noonan, C. F., Hoffman, M., & Lockman, J. J. (2019). Development of infant reaching strategies to tactile targets on the face. *Frontiers in Psychology, 10,* 9.

Clifton, R. K., Muir, D. W., Ashmead, D. H., & Clarkson, M. G. (1993). Is visually guided reaching in early infancy a myth? *Child Development, 64,* 1099–1110.

Cole, W. G., Lingeman, J. M., & Adolph, K. E. (2012). Go naked: Diapers affect infant walking. *Developmental Science, 15,* 783–790.

Connolly, K. J., & Dalgleish, M. (1989). The emergence of a tool-using skill in infancy. *Developmental Psychology, 25,* 894–912.

Cunha, A. B., Lobo, M. A., Kokkoni, E., Galloway, J. C., & Tudella, E. (2015). Effect of short-term training on reaching behavior in infants: A randomized controlled clinical trial. *Journal of Motor Behavior, 48,* 132–142.

Davis, B. E., Moon, R. Y., Sachs, H. C., & Ottolini, M. C. (1998). Effects of sleep position on infant motor development. *Pediatrics, 102,* 1135–1140.

de Vries, J. I. P., Visser, G. H. A., & Prechtl, H. F. R. (1982). The emergence of fetal behaviour. I: Qualitative aspects. *Early Human Development, 7,* 301–322.

Devine, J. (1985). The versatility of human locomotion. *American Anthropologist, 87,* 550–570.

Dudek-Shriber, L., & Zelazy, S. (2007). The effects of prone positioning on the quality and acquisition of developmental milestones in four-month-old infants. *Pediatric Physical Therapy, 19,* 48–55.

Fagard, J. (2000). Linked proximal and distal changes in the reaching behavior of 5- to 12-month-old human infants grasping objects of different sizes. *Infant Behavior and Development, 23,* 317–329.

Fang, H. S. Y., & Yu, F. Y. K. (1960). Foot binding in Chinese women. *Canadian Journal of Surgery, 293,* 195–202.

Fetters, L. (2010). Perspective on variability in the development of human action. *Physical Therapy, 90,* 1860–1867.

Fontenelle, S. A., Kahrs, B. A., Neal, S. A., Newton, A. T., & Lockman, J. J. (2007). Infant manual exploration of composite substrates. *Journal of Experimental Child Psychology, 98,* 153–167.

Geber, M. (1961). Longitudinal study and psycho-motor development among Baganda children. In G. Nielson (Ed.), *Proceedings of the XIV International Congress of Applied Psychology* (Vol. 3, pp. 50–60). Oxford: Munksgaard.

Gesell, A. (1929). *Infancy and human growth.* New York, NY: Macmillan.

(1946). The ontogenesis of infant behavior. In L. Carmichael (Ed.), *Manual of child psychology* (pp. 295–331). New York, NY: John Wiley.

Gesell, A., & Armatruda, C. S. (1945). *The embryology of behavior: The beginnings of the human mind.* New York, NY: Harper & Brothers.

Gibson, E. J. (1988). Exploratory behavior in the development of perceiving, acting, and the acquiring of knowledge. *Annual Review of Psychology, 39,* 1–41.

Gibson, E. J., & Schmuckler, M. A. (1989). Going somewhere: An ecological and experimental approach to development of mobility. *Ecological Psychology, 1,* 3–25.

Gill, S. V., Adolph, K. E., & Vereijken, B. (2009). Change in action: How infants learn to walk down slopes. *Developmental Science, 12,* 888–902.

Hallemans, A., de Clercq, D., Otten, B., & Aerts, P. (2005). 3D joint dynamics of walking in toddlers: A cross-sectional study spanning the first rapid development phase of walking. *Gait and Posture, 22,* 107–118.

Hebb, D. O. (1949). *The organization of behavior.* New York, NY: Wiley.

Hebbeler, K., Spiker, D., Bailey, D. B., Scarborough, A., Mallik, S., Simeonsson, R., … Nelson, L. (2007). *Early intervention for infants and toddlers with disabilities and their families: participants, services, and outcomes: Final report of the National Early Intervention Longitudinal Study (NEILS).* Retrieved from www.sri.com/publication/national-early-intervention-longitudinal-study-neils-final-report.

Hedberg, A., Carlberg, E. B., Forssberg, H., & Hadders-Algra, M. (2005). Development of postural adjustments in sitting position during the first half year of life. *Developmental Medicine and Child Neurology, 47,* 312–320.

Hewes, G. W. (1955). World distribution of certain postural habits. *American Anthropologist, 57,* 234–244.

Hoch, J. E., O'Grady, S. M., & Adolph, K. E. (2018). It's the journey, not the destination: Locomotor exploration in infants. *Developmental Science, 22*(2), e12740.

Hopkins, B., & Westra, T. (1988). Maternal handling and motor development: An intracultural study. *Genetic, Social and General Psychology Monographs, 114,* 379–408.

(1990). Motor development, maternal expectations, and the role of handling. *Infant Behavior and Development, 13,* 117–122.

Huang, H., Ellis, T. D., Wagenaar, R. C., & Fetters, L. (2013). The impact of body-scaled information on reaching. *Physical Therapy, 93,* 41–49.

Ivanenko, Y. P., Dominici, N., Cappellini, G., Dan, B., Cheron, G., & Lacquaniti, F. (2004). Development of pendulum mechanism and kinematic coordination from the first unsupported steps in toddlers. *Journal of Experimental Biology, 207,* 3797–3810.

Jacquet, A. Y., Esseily, R., Rider, D., & Fagard, J. (2012). Handedness for grasping objects and declarative pointing: A longitudinal study. *Developmental Psychobiology, 54,* 36–46.

Jayaraman, S., Fausey, C. M., & Smith, L. B. (2017). Why are faces denser in the visual experiences of younger than older infants? *Developmental Psychology*, *53*, 38–49.

Karasik, L. B., Adolph, K. E., Tamis-LeMonda, C. S., & Zuckerman, A. (2012). Carry on: Spontaneous object carrying in 13-month-old crawling and walking infants. *Developmental Psychology*, *48*, 389–397.

Karasik, L. B., Tamis-LeMonda, C. S., & Adolph, K. E. (2011). Transition from crawling to walking and infants' actions with objects and people. *Child Development*, *82*, 1199–1209.

Karasik, L. B., Tamis-LeMonda, C. S., Adolph, K. E., & Bornstein, M. H. (2015). Places and postures: A cross-cultural comparison of sitting in 5-month-olds. *Journal of Cross-Cultural Psychology*, *46*, 1023–1038.

Karasik, L. B., Tamis-LeMonda, C. S., Ossmy, O., & Adolph, K. E. (2018). The ties that bind: Cradling in Tajikistan. *PLoS ONE*, *13*, e0204428.

Kattwinkel, J., Hauck, F. R., Keenan, M. E., Malloy, M., & Moon, R. Y. (2005). The changing concept of sudden infant death syndrome: Diagnostic coding shifts, controversies regarding the sleeping environment, and new variables to consider in reducing risk. *Pediatrics*, *116*, 1245–1255.

Keen, R. (2011). The development of problem solving in young children: A critical cognitive skill. *Annual Review of Psychology*, *62*, 1–21.

Kokkoni, E., Haworth, J. L., Harbourne, R. T., Stergiou, N., & Kyvelidou, A. (2017). Infant sitting postural control appears robust across changes in surface context. *Somatosensory and Motor Research*, *34*, 265–272.

Konczak, J., Borutta, M., Topka, H., & Dichgans, J. (1995). The development of goal-directed reaching in infants: Hand trajectory formation and joint torque control. *Experimental Brain Research*, *106*, 156–168.

Konner, M. J. (1972). Aspects of the developmental ethology of a foraging people. In N. Blurton-Jones (Ed.), *Ethological studies of child behavior* (pp. 285–304). Cambridge, UK: Cambridge University Press.

Kretch, K. S., & Adolph, K. E. (2013a). Cliff or step? Posture-specific learning at the edge of a drop-off. *Child Development*, *84*, 226–240.

(2013b). No bridge too high: Infants decide whether to cross based on the probability of falling not the severity of the potential fall. *Developmental Science*, *16*, 336–351.

(2015). Active vision in passive locomotion: Real-world free viewing in infants and adults. *Developmental Science*, *18*, 736–750.

Lagerspetz, K., Nygard, M., & Strandvik, C. (1971). The effects of training in crawling on the motor and mental development of infants. *Scandinavian Journal of Psychology*, *12*, 192–197.

Lampl, M., Veldhuis, J. D., & Johnson, M. L. (1992). Saltation and stasis: A model of human growth. *Science*, *258*, 801–803.

Lee, D. K., Cole, W. G., Golenia, L., & Adolph, K. E. (2018). The cost of simplifying complex developmental phenomena: A new perspective on learning to walk. *Developmental Science*, *21*, e12615.

Libertus, K., Joh, A. S., & Needham, A. W. (2016). Motor training at 3 months affects object exploration 12 months later. *Developmental Science*, *19*, 1058–1066.

Libertus, K., & Needham, A. W. (2010). Teach to reach: The effects of active vs. passive reaching experiences on action and perception. *Vision Research*, *50*, 2750–2757.

Liebenberg, L. (2006). Persistence hunting by modern hunter-gatherers. *Current Anthropology*, *47*, 1017–1025.

Lobo, M. A., & Galloway, J. C. (2012). Enhanced handling and positioning in early infancy advances development throughout the first year. *Child Development*, *83*, 1290–1302.

Lockman, J. J., Ashmead, D. H., & Bushnell, E. W. (1984). The development of anticipatory hand orientation during infancy. *Journal of Experimental Child Psychology*, *37*, 176–186.

Lockman, J. J., & Kahrs, B. A. (2017). New insights into the development of human tool use. *Current Directions in Psychological Science*, *26*, 330–334.

Logan, S. W., Schreiber, M. A., Lobo, M. A., Pritchard, B., George, L., & Galloway, J. C. (2015). Real-world performance: Physical activity, play, and object-related behaviors of toddlers with and without disabilities. *Pediatric Physical Therapy*, *27*, 433–441.

Martorell, R., Onis, M., Martines, J., Black, M., Onyango, A., & Dewey, K. G. (2006). WHO motor development study: Windows of achievement for six gross motor development milestones. *Acta Paediatrica*, *95* (S450), 86–95.

McCarty, M. E., Clifton, R. K., & Collard, R. R. (2001). The beginnings of tool use by infants and toddlers. *Infancy*, *2*, 233–256.

McGraw, M. B. (1932). From reflex to muscular control in the assumption of an erect posture and ambulation in the human infant. *Child Development*, *3*, 291–297.

(1940). Neuromuscular development of the human infant as exemplified in the achievement of erect locomotion. *Journal of Pediatrics*, *17*, 747–771.

(1941a). Development of neuro-muscular mechanisms as reflected in the crawling and creeping behavior of the human infant. *Journal of Genetic Psychology*, *58*, 83–111.

(1941b). Neuro-motor maturation of anti-gravity functions as reflected in the development of a sitting posture. *Journal of Genetic Psychology*, *59*, 155–175.

(1945). *The neuromuscular maturation of the human infant*. New York, NY: Columbia University Press.

McGraw, M. B., & Breeze, K. W. (1941). Quantitative studies in the development of erect locomotion. *Child Development*, *12*, 267–303.

Mei, J. (1994). The Northern Chinese custom of rearing babies in sandbags: Implications for motor and intellectual development. In J. H. A. van Rossum & J. I. Laszlo (Eds.), *Motor development: Aspects of normal and delayed development* (pp. 41–48). Amsterdam, the Netherlands: VU Uitgeverij.

Minetti, A. E., Formenti, F., & Ardigo, L. P. (2006). Himalayan porter's specialization: Metabolic power, economy, efficiency, and skill. *Proceedings of the Royal Society of London B: Biological Sciences*, *273*, 2791–2797.

Morgan, C., Darrah, J., Gordon, A. M., Harbourne, R. T., Spittle, A., Johnson, R., & Fetters, L. (2016). Effectiveness of motor interventions in infants with cerebral palsy: A systematic review. *Developmental Medicine and Child Neurology*, *58*, 900–909.

Mutlu, A., Krosschell, K., & Gaebler-Spira, D. (2009). Treadmill training with partial body-weight support in children with cerebral palsy. *Developmental Medicine and Child Neurology, 51*, 268–275.

Needham, A. W., Barrett, T., & Peterman, K. (2002). A pick-me-up for infants' exploratory skills: Early simulated experiences reaching for objects using "sticky" mittens enhances young infants' object exploration skills. *Infant Behavior and Development, 25*, 279–295.

Ossmy, O., Hoch, J. E., MacAlpine, P., Hasan, S., Stone, P., & Adolph, K. E. (2018). Variety wins: Soccer-playing robots and infant walking. *Frontiers in Neurorobotics, 12*, 19.

Patrick, S. K., Noah, J. A., & Yang, J. F. (2012). Developmental constraints of quadrupedal coordination across crawling styles in human infants. *Journal of Neurophysiology, 107*, 3050–3061.

Piek, J. P., & Carman, R. (1994). Developmental profiles of spontaneous movements in infants. *Early Human Development, 39*, 109–126.

Pin, T., Eldridge, B., & Galea, M. P. (2007). A review of the effects of sleep position, play position, and equipment use on motor development in infants. *Developmental Medicine and Child Neurology, 49*, 858–867.

Piper, M. C., & Darrah, J. (1994). *Motor assessment of the developing infant.* Philadelphia, PA: WB Saunders.

Rachwani, J., Golenia, L., Herzberg, O., & Adolph, K. E. (2019). Postural, visual, and manual coordination in the development of prehension. *Child Development, 90*, 1559–1568.

Rachwani, J., Santamaria, V., Saavedra, S., & Woollacott, M. H. (2015). The development of trunk control and its relation to reaching in infancy: A longitudinal study. *Frontiers in Human Neuroscience, 9*, 1–12.

Rachwani, J., Soska, K. C., & Adolph, K. E. (2017). Behavioral flexibility in learning to sit. *Developmental Psychobiology, 59*, 937–948.

Reissland, N., Francis, B., Aydin, E., Mason, J., & Schaal, B. (2014). The development of anticipation in the fetus: A longitudinal account of human fetal mouth movements in reaction to and anticipation of touch. *Developmental Psychobiology, 56*, 955–963.

Robson, P. (1984). Prewalking locomotor movements and their use in predicting standing and walking. *Child Care, Health, and Development, 10*, 317–330.

Rochat, P. (1989). Object manipulation and exploration in 2- to 5-month-old infants. *Developmental Psychology, 25*, 871–884.

Saavedra, S. L., van Donkelaar, P., & Woollacott, M. H. (2012). Learning about gravity: Segmental assessment of upright control as infants develop independent sitting. *Journal of Neurophysiology, 108*, 2215–2229.

Santrock , J. (2006). *Life-span development* (10th ed.). New York, NY: McGraw Hill.

Schum, N., Jovanovic, B., & Schwarzer, G. (2011). Ten- and twelve-month-olds' visual anticipation of orientation and size during grasping. *Journal of Experimental Child Psychology, 109*, 218–231.

Shirley, M. M. (1931). *The first two years: A study of twenty-five babies. Postural and locomotor development (Vol. 1).* Minneapolis: University of Minnesota Press.

Siegler, R., Deloache, J., Eisenberg, N. (2006). *How children develop* (2nd ed.). New York, NY: Worth.

Sigmundsson, H., Loras, H. W., & Haga, M. (2017). Exploring task-specific independent standing in 3- to 5-month-old infants. *Frontiers in Psychology, 8*, 657.

Snapp-Childs, W., & Corbetta, D. (2009). Evidence of early strategies in learning to walk. *Infancy, 14*, 101–116.

Soska, K. C., & Adolph, K. E. (2014). Postural position constrains multimodal object exploration in infants. *Infancy, 19*, 138–161.

Sparling, J. W., van Tol, J., & Chescheir, N. C. (1999). Fetal and neonatal hand movement. *Physical Therapy, 79*, 24–39.

Super, C. M. (1976). Environmental effects on motor development: The case of "African infant precocity". *Developmental Medicine and Child Neurology, 18*, 561–567.

Thelen, E. (1979). Rhythmical stereotypies in normal human infants. *Animal Behavior, 27*, 699–715.

Thelen, E., Corbetta, D., Kamm, K., Spencer, J. P., Schneider, K., & Zernicke, R. F. (1993). The transition to reaching: Mapping intention and intrinsic dynamics. *Child Development, 64*, 1058–1098.

Thelen, E., Corbetta, D., & Spencer, J. P. (1996). Development of reaching during the first year: Role of movement speed. *Journal of Experimental Psychology: Human Perception and Performance, 22*, 1059–1076. doi:10.1037/0096-1523.22.5.1059

Thelen, E., & Smith, L. B. (1994). *A dynamic systems approach to the development of cognition and action*. Cambridge, MA: MIT Press.

Theveniau, N., Boisgontier, M. P., Verieras, S., & Olivier, I. (2014). The effects of clothes on independent walking in toddlers. *Gait and Posture, 39*, 659–661.

Trettien, A. W. (1900). Creeping and walking. *American Journal of Psychology, 12*, 1–57.

Ulrich, B. D. (2010). Opportunities for early intervention based on theory, basic neuroscience, and clinical science. *Physical Therapy, 90*, 1868–1880.

van Wermeskerken, M., van der Kamp, J., & Savelsbergh, G. J. P. (2011). On the relation between action selection and movement control in 5- to 8-month-old infants. *Experimental Brain Research, 211*, 51–62.

Vereijken, B. (2010). The complexity of childhood development: Variability in perspective. *Physical Therapy, 90*, 1850–1859.

von Hofsten, C. (1991). Structuring of early reaching movements: A longitudinal study. *Journal of Motor Behavior, 23*, 280–292.

von Hofsten, C., Vishton, P. M., Spelke, E. S., Feng, Q., & Rosander, K. (1998). Predictive action in infancy: Tracking and reaching for moving objects. *Cognition, 67*, 255–285.

Wijnhoven, T. M. A., de Onis, M., Onyango, A. W., Wang, T., Bjoerneboe, G. A., Bhandari, N., … Rashidi, B. (2004). Assessment of gross motor development in the WHO Multicentre Growth Reference Study. *Food and Nutrition Bulletin, 25*, S37–S45.

Witherington, D. C. (2005). The development of prospective grasping control between 5 and 7 months: A longitudinal study. *Infancy, 7*, 143–161.

Zelazo, P. R., Zelazo, N. A., & Kolb, S. (1972). "Walking" in the newborn. *Science, 176*, 314–315.

18 The Mirror Neuron System and Social Cognition

Nathan A. Fox, Virginia C. Salo, Ranjan Debnath, Santiago Morales, and Elizabeth G. Smith

The ability to understand others' actions and intentions is at the core of human social competence. Action understanding, what it means and how it develops, has received much attention in developmental research because it is viewed as one of the most fundamental abilities in early social-cognitive development. For example, there is a growing body of evidence linking early action understanding with later theory of mind (Brooks & Meltzoff, 2015; Charman et al., 2000; Wellman, Phillips, Dunphy-Lelii, & LaLonde, 2004), and to the development of communicative skills (e.g., Brooks & Meltzoff, 2008). Increasing evidence suggests that the mirror neuron system (MNS) is a key neural correlate of action understanding. In this chapter, we discuss the role the MNS is thought to play in the development of social cognitive skills in infancy. We also discuss the current challenges of measuring the MNS that are unique to work with infants, what such studies have found in both typical and atypical populations, and how this work can impact our understanding of development.

18.1 The Mirror Neuron System

The MNS is a network of brain regions that are active when performing an action as well as when observing others perform the same or similar actions. Originally described as single neurons in nonhuman primates in area F5 of the ventral premotor cortex (di Pellegrino, Fadiga, Fogassi, Gallese, & Rizzolatti, 1992), the MNS is now considered to be a more extensive network involving parietal and premotor areas (Rizzolatti & Craighero, 2004) and more recently, limbic structures involved in communication and emotion (Ferrari, Gerbella, Coudé, & Rozzi, 2017). Convergent evidence from several neuroimaging techniques, including functional magnetic resonance imaging (fMRI; Caspers, Zilles, Laird, & Eickhoff, 2010; Molenberghs, Cunnington, & Mattingley, 2012), functional near-infrared spectroscopy (fNIRS; Sun et al., 2018), electroencephalogram (EEG; Fox et al., 2016), transcranial magnetic stimulation (TMS; Cattaneo, Sandrini, & Schwarzbach, 2010; Stadler et al., 2012), transcranial direct current stimulation (tDCS: Avenanti, Paracampo, Annella, Tidoni, & Aglioti, 2018), and single-cell recordings (Mukamel, Ekstrom, Kaplan, Iacoboni, & Fried, 2010) support presence of an analogous

MNS in humans. The human MNS is considered to be a broad network of brain regions that show a mirror-like pattern of activation involving the superior parietal lobe, the inferior parietal lobe/intraparietal sulcus (IPL), superior temporal sulcus (STS), posterior middle temporal gyrus, dorsal premotor, and ventral premotor/inferior frontal gyrus (IFG) (Caspers et al., 2010; Molenberghs et al., 2012). Because most studies investigating the MNS in humans involve noninvasive neuroimaging techniques and cannot examine the mirroring properties of specific neurons, we use the term MNS to describe the broad network of regions that display similar "mirroring" activity during both action execution and action observation.

Since its discovery, the MNS has been thought to support social cognition (di Pellegrino et al., 1992; Gallese, Fadiga, Fogassi, & Rizzolatti, 1996; Rizzolatti, Fadiga, Gallese, & Fogassi, 1996). For example, it has been proposed that the MNS underlies a variety of social and cognitive processes including the ability to understand others' actions and intentions, imitation, language, theory of mind, and empathy (Gallese & Goldman, 1998; Gallese, Keysers, & Rizzolatti, 2004; Iacoboni, 2009). This has led to widespread interest in both the scientific literature as well as the popular media, implicating the MNS in several neurological disorders (Arbib & Mundhenk, 2005; Dapretto et al., 2006; Oberman et al., 2005). However, some have questioned the significance and involvement of the MNS in higher-order cognitive processes as well as neurological disorders (Hickok, 2009; Southgate & Hamilton, 2008; van Overwalle & Baetens, 2009). Given that the abilities to understand and execute actions emerge early in development and change considerably during infancy and early childhood, examining the early development of the MNS may provide important insight into the function and significance of this system (Ferrari, Tramacere, Simpson, & Iriki, 2013; Woodward & Gerson, 2014).

In this chapter, we highlight the utility of a developmental perspective in understanding this system and its purported functions. We begin by providing an overview of the theoretical perspectives about the development of the MNS, followed by a description and discussion of how the MNS is measured during infancy. We then review recent findings regarding the role of the MNS in action understanding in infancy and discuss applications to neuro-atypical populations and implications for policy. Finally, we conclude with recommendations for future research.

18.2 Theories of How the MNS Develops

There are several theories for how a mechanism for matching self and other actions might develop and how it may support action understanding. According to the direct matching hypothesis, perceptions of others' actions are mapped onto internal representations of one's own actions in a one-to-one overlapping system (Rizzolatti & Craighero, 2004; Rizzolatti, Fogassi, &

Gallese, 2001). For example, the activation in an infant's sensorimotor cortex while they perform an action directly matches the activation that occurs while the infant observes that same action. More specifically, a simulation process occurs in which the visual information received during observation of another's action is mapped onto the corresponding motor representation within the observer. This resonant activation of the motor system enables one to understand the observed actions and intentions behind those actions (Blakemore & Decety, 2001). This bottom-up hypothesis fits well with many cognitive theories of action understanding including Tomasello's emphasis on intention understanding in social cognitive development (Tomasello, Carpenter, Call, Behne, & Moll, 2005; Tomasello, Carpenter, & Liszkowski, 2007; the theory of embodied cognition (Shapiro, 2011), and the "like me" theory (Marshall & Meltzoff, 2014; Meltzoff, 2007; Meltzoff & Gopnik, 1993). These will be briefly reviewed here.

According to Tomasello, when an infant perceives another's action, the infant understands that action in terms of the outcomes it is designed to achieve, that is, an understanding of the actor's intentions (Tomasello, 1995; Tomasello et al., 2005; Tomasello, Kruger, & Ratner, 1993). An important aspect of this theory is that the infant first comes to understand herself as an intentional agent, and then recognizes that others are intentional agents as well. Several researchers have noted the coinciding development of infants' action understanding and the cognitive skills acquired in accordance with Piaget's sensorimotor stages (Piaget, 1952). Achievement of these cognitive milestones may therefore change the way the infant perceives her own and others' behavior, as well as her understanding of the physical world. With an understanding of one's agency and the effect that one can have on the environment, actions are perceived as being not necessarily performed in and of themselves, but as a means toward a particular end. This supports the interpretation of actions in terms of the intended goals or "ends."

The theory of embodied cognition (Shapiro, 2011) also emphasizes the importance of sensorimotor experiences in development (Overton, 2006). According to the theory of embodied cognition, learning and development are supported by, and in some cases impossible without, direct sensorimotor interaction with the environment (Engel, Maye, Kurthen, & König, 2013; Foglia & Wilson, 2013). Acting on and interacting with the environment (e.g., through grasping an object), provides the sensorimotor information necessary to learn not only about the affordances of an object but also the affordances of one's own actions. Further, the sensorimotor experience of observing others act becomes linked to the sensorimotor experience of an infant's own actions and in this way, others' actions become interpretable. Meltzoff has developed a similar theory in the developmental realm, the "like me" theory of social cognition (Meltzoff, 2007; Meltzoff & Gopnik, 1993). According to Meltzoff: "The recognition of self–other equivalences is the foundation ... of social cognition. The acts of the self and other are represented within a supramodal code, transcending and integrating sensory modalities. This provides infants with an interpretive framework for understanding the behavior they see" (Meltzoff, 2007, p. 126). Infants are able to recognize others' behavior as "commensurate" with their own actions, and this you-to-me matching allows infants to use their own behavior and experiences as a basis for interpreting the behavior of others.

Combining these separate but related cognitive theories of action understanding leads to an ontogenetic developmental picture in which the infant learns about her own agency and ability to act via intentional sensorimotor exploration. Once an infant understands that she is able to act intentionally on the environment to achieve certain outcomes, she then applies this interpretation of intention to the actions she observes others perform. According to the direct-matching theory, the MNS provides the neural substrate for a connection between self and other that supports this bottom-up process of action understanding.

The direct-matching theory put forth by Rizzolatti and colleagues (Rizzolatti & Craighero, 2004; Rizzolatti et al., 2001) contends that the MNS and its capability of mapping observed actions onto our own motor repertoire is a specific adaptation for action understanding and is present and active at birth. This theory has been challenged by several researchers, who contend that the MNS is not directly involved in the complex processes of goal and intention understanding (e.g., Hickok, 2009). Through the associative learning theory Heyes (2010, 2013) contends that the MNS is in fact a product of domain-general associative learning processes, not a unique social-cognitive adaptation, and is not directly involved in action understanding per se. Specifically, Heyes argues that the link between action and perception develops through repeated co-occurrence of the internal experience of performing an action and the perceptual experience of watching one's own or others' actions. Alternatively, Paulus (2012) has proposed applying the ideomotor theory of actions to an understanding of the MNS, according to which actions are represented in terms of their perceivable outcomes or effects (Shin, Proctor, & Capaldi, 2010). Within this framework, the representation of an action's effect is distinct from that of the action itself, but a bidirectional link develops over time between the perception of the performed action and that action's effect due to their temporal and spatial co-occurrence. When an observed action activates one's own motor program, this subsequently activates the representation of the associated effect, which in turn facilitates behaviors that indicate an understanding of the goal or intention of the action such as an anticipatory look toward the expected target or outcome (Paulus, 2012). This theory strikes a sort of middle ground by proposing that the motor resonance that occurs while watching another person act produces an associative learning process wherein the sensorimotor activity representing either the observed or performed action becomes linked with the representation of its outcome. The MNS is therefore indirectly involved in understanding an observed action, according to this theory. These sets of theories thus differ in their prediction of both when and how the ability to map one's own and others' actions develops. Importantly, however, these different theories share the assumption that activity of the motor system is in some way, either directly or indirectly, related to our understanding of others' actions.

Perhaps as a way of acknowledging the complex relation between the MNS and development of action understanding, the MNS has recently been conceptualized as a system or network that extends beyond the motor cortex and involves interactions with other brain regions, particularly those known to be involved in higher-order social cognitive processes. This perspective of the MNS as part of a network responsible for social cognitive processes, which has been investigated largely in adult populations, is supported by evidence for connectivity between typical mirroring areas of the brain and those involved in inferring mental states and planning (Bridgeman, 2005; Cavallo et al., 2015; Yang, Andric, & Mathew, 2015). Our own work with infants (Debnath, Salo, Buzzell, Yoo, & Fox, 2019) supports functional connectivity between distinct regions in both sensorimotor cortex and occipital cortex during observation of actions, supporting a role for integration of the MNS and visual systems early in development. Indeed, Pineda (2005) suggested that during observation of an action, a common underlying mechanism for both motor and other sensory/cognitive processes can act together to support communication across brain regions.

18.3 Measuring the MNS in Infancy

What we know about how the MNS develops, how it interacts with other neural systems, and the functional role it plays in higher-order social cognitive skills is in part determined by available neuroimaging techniques. Although researchers have employed several different noninvasive brain imaging methods such as fMRI, EEG, MEG, and TMS to the study of the MNS, these techniques are particularly limited in their flexibility when considering work with infants and children. However, in recent years, mu rhythm, as measured via EEG, has been extensively used as a potential index of mirroring system activity in humans (Fox et al., 2016). This is due in large part to the following advantages of EEG over other neuroimaging techniques such as fMRI: (1) EEG is easy to use and relatively inexpensive, (2) EEG offers better temporal resolution to examine the timing of the activation related to the execution and observation of an action, and critically (3) EEG is easier to use with infants and children as they do not have to be separated from their caregiver and the signal is more tolerant of motion-induced artifacts. These features make EEG particularly suitable for examining the development of the MNS.

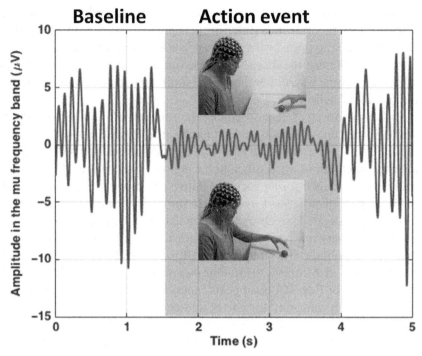

Figure 18.1. *Simulation of mu rhythm desynchronization in the 8–13 Hz frequency band. There is a decrease in EEG amplitude from baseline during action observation or execution (action event; highlighted in gray). Source: Reprinted with permission from APA.*

18.3.1 The EEG Mu Rhythm as a Measure of the MNS

The mu rhythm is an EEG oscillation in the alpha frequency range recorded over scalp areas overlying the sensorimotor cortex. Mu rhythm is typically measured within ~8–13 Hz in adults and ~6–9 Hz in infants and young children (Marshall, Bar-Haim, & Fox, 2002). When a person is at rest, neurons in the sensorimotor cortex fire in synchrony, which produces rhythmic oscillatory activities in the mu frequency band. However, when a person performs an action, the firing of neurons becomes desynchronized (see Figure 18.1). The desynchronized neural activity leads to attenuation or reduction of the amplitude of the signal, which is commonly known as mu desynchronization or mu suppression (Pfurtscheller, Neuper, Andrew, & Edlinger, 1997). Mu desynchronization is thus measured as changes of activity relative to a resting baseline time period, and is characteristic of an active brain state and considered as an electrophysiological correlate of sensorimotor cortex activation (Hari, 2006; Pfurtscheller et al., 1997). Mu desynchronization during execution and observation of an action has been reported in several studies with adults (Cochin, Barthelemy, Roux, & Martineau, 1999; Muthukumaraswamy, Johnson, &

McNair, 2004), infants (Cannon et al., 2016), and children (Rayson, Bonaiuto, Ferrari, & Murray, 2016), which has led researchers to argue that mu desynchronization reflects activity of the MNS in humans.

Especially in developmental neuroscience, researchers have begun to widely utilize mu rhythm desynchronization as a measure of MNS activity and to investigate the role of the MNS in a wide range of social-cognitive skills in infants (Fox et al., 2016). However, no measure is perfect, and some concerns have been raised regarding its viability. EEG is recorded by electrodes placed over the scalp, which roughly correspond to different areas of cerebral cortex (e.g., frontal, central, parietal, temporal, occipital), and mu rhythm is measured from electrodes overlying sensorimotor cortex. However, EEG signal recorded at a particular electrode does not exclusively reflect neural activity of cortical area below that electrode, as neural activity from one brain region can be spread to another physically distinct brain region via volume conduction. This reduces spatial precision of EEG, which has led to concern about the specific functional relation between mu rhythm and the MNS. Further, because mu and alpha rhythms occur in the same frequency band, the mu rhythm may be contaminated with concurrent alpha activity from the occipital cortex (Hobson & Bishop, 2016). Occipital alpha activity occurs in response to the presentation of visual stimuli and is associated with visual attention. It has thus been argued that mu desynchronization might reflect changes in visual attention rather than MNS activity during observation of another person's action (Hobson & Bishop, 2016). However, there is strong evidence that mu rhythm is not merely a reflection of alpha activity in the occipital cortex spreading to the central region (Pineda, 2005). Several source localization studies have identified the origin of mu rhythm around the central sulcus in sensorimotor areas (Salmelin, Hámáaláinen, Kajola, & Hari, 1995; Salmelin & Hari, 1994). Other studies using MEG (Manshanden, de Munck, Simon, & Lopes da Silva, 2002) as well as EEG (Thorpe, Cannon, & Fox, 2016) have also confirmed the source of mu rhythm concentrated primarily in the central-parietal region. Critically, a simultaneous measurement of fMRI and EEG located the source of mu rhythm recorded on the central electrode sites in the sensorimotor cortex (Mizuhara & Inui, 2011). These findings provide strong support that mu rhythm desynchronization is a valid means for examining mirror system activity in humans.

Although there has been a rapid increase in developmental research utilizing mu rhythm, methodological issues hinder integration of these findings into a comprehensive theory of mu rhythm development and MNS activity in humans (see Table 18.1 for a summary). The methods for eliciting and quantifying mu rhythm desynchronization vary considerably across studies (Cuevas, Cannon, Yoo, & Fox, 2014). Studies across laboratories have used various baseline measures, including the absence of a stimulus, static images, moving objects, and moving body parts to quantify mu rhythm attenuation. Many studies do not include an execution condition, which is critical to identify the

Table 18.1 *Areas of design and processing in infant studies utilizing mu rhythm as a measure of mirroring in which considerable methodological variations exist*

Areas of methodological variation	Recommendations and considerations
Study design	
Baseline periods	Researchers should carefully consider how different baseline comparisons may impact the interpretation of results
Inclusion of execution condition	There should be a direct comparison between execution and observation conditions, to fully consider an effect as mirroring
Stimuli used for observation	As with baseline differences, the interpretation of findings and generalizability are influenced by the type of stimuli (live vs. video, whole body vs. limb, interactive vs. noninteractive) presented
Processing and analysis	
Consideration of volume conduction	To account for the co-occurrence of occipital and central alpha/mu activity, consider applying surface Laplacian transformations to the EEG data. Also, activity from electrodes overlying all scalp regions should be analyzed, beyond just those over the central region
Artifact rejection	In addition to removing noise in the EEG data, it is important to remove trials with movement during action observation condition

frequency band of mu rhythm at different points in development (Marshall & Meltzoff, 2011). In studies that include only a passive observation condition and do not include an execution condition, it is difficult to identify the infant mu frequency band and to demonstrate mirroring activity during observation of an action. Across studies, participants observe different types of actions – live action (Cannon et al., 2016), videos (Rayson et al., 2016), single-hand grasping (Muthukumaraswamy et al., 2004), and whole-body movement (Orgs, Dombrowski, Heil, & Jansen-Osmann, 2008), which might affect mu activity (Ruysschaert, Warreyn, Wiersema, Metin, & Roeyers, 2013; Stapel, Hunnius, van Elk, & Bekkering, 2010). There is also variation in the use of offline re-referencing montages (e.g., average reference of all electrodes, averaged mastoid sites) to calculate mu desynchronization. Lastly, because the mu rhythm is generated in the sensorimotor cortex and is particularly strong when an individual performs an action, it is imperative to take account of and remove any

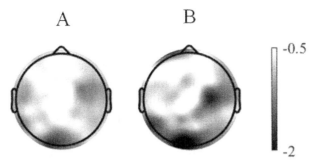

Figure 18.2. *Topographic plots of activity in the 6–9 Hz band during observation of a grasp in 9-month-old infants. (A) All activity, no trials excluded. (B) Activity after excluding trials in which the infant was moving.*

instances of movement when the participant is supposed to be observing an action. This is a particularly important point in research with infants. In our own experience, we take great care to remove any observation trials in which the infant is performing an action or making gross motor movements. We recently compared mu desynchronization values in a sample of 9-month-olds (1) across the average of all trials and (2) after excluding trials including infant motion. Specifically, we excluded trials in which the infant grasped, reached, performed a gross movement of the upper body, kicked or moved their legs, or if the parent interfered in anyway. As can be seen in Figure 18.2, removing these trials was associated with higher mu desynchronization values compared to including all trials.

These methodological discrepancies can potentially influence the observed characteristics of mu rhythm and limit the generalization of findings across domains, age groups, and disciplines. To minimize the effects of these methodological variations, specific guidelines have been laid down for future research aiming to examine mu rhythm and mirror system activity in developmental populations (Cuevas et al., 2014; Fox et al., 2016). If care is taken to address these methodological issues, research utilizing mu rhythm in infancy and throughout the life span has the potential to extend the current understanding of a wide range of social and cognitive functions, such as imitation, empathy, motor skill development, language development, understanding others' actions, and specifically the role of the MNS in the development of these skills.

18.3.2 Other Measures of Mirroring in Infants

While EEG mu suppression has been the most frequently used method for investigation of neural mirroring in human infants, other neuroimaging techniques have demonstrated potential in clarifying underlying structural and functional properties of the developing system. For example, fNIRS, which relies on differential absorption of infrared light by oxygenated and deoxygenated hemoglobin to probe neural activation, has been used with increasing frequency to investigate action, action observation, and imitation across development. One advantage to fNIRS, particularly in comparison to EEG, is increased spatial resolution, which allows for measuring functional activity across distinct brain regions associated with the neural mirroring network. Another advantage is that the fNIRS signal is less susceptible to motion artifacts compared to other neuroimaging methods. Because signal quality is relatively unaffected by motion, fNIRS is an ideal measure both for use with infants generally and in naturalistic studies involving infant action more specifically (McDonald & Perdue, 2018). Using fNIRS in 4- to 6-month-old infants, Lloyd-Fox and colleagues have shown that hemodynamic change during action observation within right-hemisphere STS is positively correlated with an infant's motor skills (Lloyd-Fox, Wu, Richards, Elwell, & Johnson, 2015). Other studies using fNIRS in infants have detected hemodynamic change during perception of human action across frontal and temporal regions (Biondi, Boas, & Wilcox, 2016; Grossmann et al., 2008; Ichikawa, Kanazawa, Yamaguchi, & Kakigi, 2010; Lloyd-Fox et al., 2009; Shimada & Hiraki, 2006). While these studies focus on action perception, fNIRS is well suited for measuring brain activation in infants during action execution.

While much of the adult literature on neural mirroring has used fMRI (see Caspers et al., 2010), fMRI studies in infants are generally restricted to presentation of auditory stimuli during an infant's natural sleep. To date, no studies of action perception in infants or toddlers are reported, and there is only one fMRI study in children that compares action production to observation (Morales, Bowman, Velnoskey, Fox, & Redcay, 2019). However, structural MRI has been used to characterize anatomical changes in the brain over the first years of life, including changes in thickness and surface area of the cortex across regions associated with neural mirroring (Li, Lin, Gilmore, & Shen, 2015; Li et al., 2013). In and of themselves, longitudinal structural brain changes can contribute to our understanding of anatomical changes underlying emergence of neural mirroring in infants and can also be used to aid in source localization of infant EEG mu suppression (Thorpe et al., 2016).

18.4 Studies and Findings Using Mu Rhythm in Infants

As mentioned above, the EEG mu rhythm is the measure most commonly utilized in studies of the MNS in infants. In this section we review this body of work and examine how various findings support or refute the different MNS theories outlined previously.

In a study with 9-month-olds, Southgate and colleagues compared infants' mu rhythm activity while executing or observing grasping actions and found evidence that the infant MNS is recruited in action prediction (Southgate, Johnson, Osborne, & Csibra, 2009). The inclusion of both an execution and observation condition and the fact that results show overlap in activity across the conditions provides strong support for them having captured the mirroring mechanism. Interestingly, during the observation condition infants exhibited two periods of mu rhythm desynchronization: during the action and just prior to the onset of the action. This earlier activity specifically occurred during the latter half of the task, suggesting that once the infants learned to expect an action, the motor system came on board to facilitate prediction of that action.

Several studies have examined the kind of actions that the infant MNS is sensitive to. For example, in a study with infants ranging from 4 to 11 months old, Virji-Babul, Rose, Moiseeva, and Makan (2012) measured infants' mu rhythm activity while infants observed videos of a human walking, a hand reaching for objects, and nonhuman object motion (e.g., a ball rolling). On average, infants exhibited significant mu rhythm desynchronization in response to all three types of stimuli, which the authors interpreted as evidence that infants' MNS exists prior to specific experience and is initially sensitive to all coherent motion. Additionally, researchers have examined whether the infant MNS is sensitive to the goal directedness of an action. Nystrom and colleagues (Nyström, 2008; Nyström, Ljunghammar, Rosander, & von Hofsten, 2011) have observed a developmental trend in which the MNS becomes more sensitive to the goal directedness of action with age. Six-month-olds do not exhibit differential sensitivity based on the goal directedness of an observed action (Nyström, 2008), whereas 8- to 9-month-olds exhibit greater mu desynchronization during observation of a goal-directed action as compared to during observation of a nongoal-directed action (Nyström et al., 2011). Older children (Lepage & Théoret, 2006) and adults (e.g., Muthukumaraswamy et al., 2004; Nyström, 2008) also show greater mu rhythm desynchronization to goal- versus nongoal-directed actions. Integration of these findings suggests that while mirroring mechanisms are indeed present early in development, experience plays a role in refining the system, as the direct-matching hypothesis theory might suggest, rather than in shaping it from the beginning, as the associative theory would suggest. In line with this, Southgate, Johnson, Karoui, and Csibra (2010) found evidence for greater MNS activity during observation of actions that can be interpreted as goal directed versus those that cannot. They showed infants videos of a hand reaching as if to grasp or in a flipped position so that the back of the hand faced down, and for each of these hand positions the action either ended behind an occluder or not. The authors contended that if the infant MNS reflects processes of goal interpretation or prediction, the only condition in which they would see MNS activity would be when the typical grasping hand reached behind an occluder, that is, when a goal could be inferred. Indeed, they found significant mu rhythm desynchronization in that condition, but not in the other three, suggesting that MNS activity is involved in the inference of goals.

More recently, researchers have begun examining how MNS activity in infants during observation of actions might relate to individual differences in behavioral measures of their action understanding abilities. For example, Filippi et al. (2016) found that mu rhythm desynchronization during observation of grasping actions in 7-month-olds predicted infants' propensity to imitate the same action. To our knowledge, this is the only infant study that has examined individual differences in motor system activity during action observation in relation to a subsequent behavioral manifestation of action understanding. However, an unpublished study provides further evidence. Yoo, Thorpe, and Fox (2016) found that mu rhythm desynchronization during observation of grasping actions predicted infants' ability to learn a novel means–end motor task (retrieving a toy with a cane) whereas it did not predict their learning in a visual pattern task. Combined, these findings suggest that motor system activity is related not only to concurrent processes but also to general abilities across action processing and goal interpretation.

Other studies have examined the potential role of the mirroring system in social interactions and in developing higher-order social skills such as cooperation and theory of mind. Reid, Striano, and Iacoboni (2011) found that 14-month-olds exhibit greater mu rhythm desynchronization during dyadic, back-and-forth interactions with an experimenter as compared to nondyadic interactions.

Taken as a whole, these studies provide evidence for the direct-matching hypothesis of the MNS. Specifically, mirroring activity is seen early in development, in response to motor activity and actions that are sometimes outside of the infant's own repertoire, and seems to be related to understanding the goals and intentions of others' observed behaviors. In the following section, we will review a body of literature that has examined how experience with specific sets of actions may influence or shape the MNS.

18.5 The Role of Experiences, Context, and Culture

There is also evidence for a relation between action experience and motor system activity. Examining this within adults, several studies have compared mu rhythm desynchronization during observation of actions in "experts" versus "novices" for a variety of tasks or activities. In a study with dancers, Orgs et al. (2008) found that professional dancers exhibited greater mu rhythm desynchronization than nondancers while observing dance movements. Importantly, there was no difference between the groups when observing everyday actions familiar to both groups. Cannon et al. (2014) experimentally manipulated experience by randomly assigning adult participants into three groups who either received physical experience using a novel claw tool to grasp objects, visual experience watching an experimenter use the tool, or no experience. They found that participants who had physical experience with the tool exhibited greater mu desynchronization during observation of tool use when compared to both participants in the visual experience group and the novices.

Studies relating motor experience and mu suppression with infants show similar findings. Crawling experience (i.e., how long they had been crawling) in 14- to 16-month-old infants was related to the strength of mu rhythm desynchronization while observing videos of other infants crawling (van Elk, van Schie, Hunnius, Vesper, & Bekkering, 2008). In a 2016 study, Cannon et al. (2016) found that infants' reaching and grasping skill, measured as a composite of latency to reach, reaching errors (misjudgments of distance or position), preshaping of the hand, and whether the grasp was made with one hand or two, was related to the strength of mu desynchronization while observing reach/grasp actions. Yoo, Cannon, Thorpe, and Fox (2015) found a relation between grasping skill and mu rhythm desynchronization during observation of grasping within 12-month-olds, but not within 9-month-olds, suggesting that the strength of the coupling of action and perception also increases with experience. One study interestingly contrasts the finding in adults that first-hand experience is necessary to alter one's understanding or neural representation of an action. De Klerk, Southgate, and Csibra (2016) observed predictive eye movements and mu rhythm activity in prewalking 8-month-olds while they watched videos of infants walking. Their findings of mu desynchronization in prewalkers suggests that first-hand experience is not necessary, but that observational experience may also be related to the strength of motor system activity during observation of actions.

The idea that observational experience may influence the strength of the MNS has potentially important implications when thinking about the environment in which an infant is raised and the experiences he or she is exposed to. One of our more recent studies suggests that increasing the amount of communicative gestures a parent used with their child could have a positive impact on the strength of infants' MNS activity while observing gestures, and this increase in MNS activity may in turn predict a positive increase in infants' language skills (Salo, 2018). The hypothesis has been forwarded that the MNS may be fundamental for the acquisition of language and, relatedly, to the transmission of human culture (Rizzolatti & Arbib, 1998). This recent finding supports this view. Further, based on the link between experience and strength of MNS activity, one might expect to see cultural differences in MNS specific to actions that are more or less prevalent in different cultures. That is, infants in one culture may show greater activation of the MNS when observing actions often seen or experienced in their culture relative to infants from another culture where those actions are rarely observed or performed. Green, Li, Lockman, and Gredebäck (2016), for example, found that Chinese infants showed anticipatory looking to the mouth when a model was eating with chopsticks, but Swedish infants did not. While this study did not directly test MNS activation, the findings suggest that the Chinese infants, but not the Swedish infants, understood the goal associated with using the chopsticks, thus one might expect to see similar cultural differences in the infants' MNS activity. However, such a hypothesis has yet to be examined directly.

From this body of work, we can conclude that the MNS is malleable not only in infancy but in adulthood as well. This characteristic has been taken as evidence in favor of the associative accounts for the MNS (Heyes, 2013). However, others contend that as one's own motor repertoire expands the pre-existing MNS adapts to the individual's changing perception of the world. In the following section, we examine how studies of individuals with autism and other developmental disabilities might lend more insight into the development and function of the MNS.

18.6 Application to Neuro-Atypical Populations

Because of its documented and putative role in typical social development, the MNS has been investigated in individuals with developmental disabilities including autism spectrum disorders (ASDs). While characterized by impairments in social communication combined with restrictive/repetitive behaviors and preferences, ASDs are also associated with impairments in imitation (Cossu et al., 2012) that emerge early (Charman et al., 1997), and are correlated with both concurrent symptom severity (Rogers, Hepburn, Stackhouse, & Wehner, 2003) and outcome (Toth, Munson, Meltzoff, & Dawson, 2006). However, thus far results from studies of the MNS in ASD using a variety of neuroimaging techniques and with populations across the life span have been mixed (Hamilton, 2013). For example, some studies show a lack of neural mirroring during action observation in ASD alongside typical activation during action execution (Dumas, Soussignan, Hugueville, Martinerie, & Nadel, 2014; Martineau, Cochin, Magne, & Barthelemy, 2008; Oberman et al., 2005) suggesting impairment in the MNS, whereas other studies show subtle or no differences from controls (Fan, Decety, Yang, Liu, & Cheng, 2010; Oberman, Ramachandran, & Pineda, 2008; Raymaekers, Wiersema, & Roeyers, 2009; Ruysschaert, Warreyn, Wiersema, Oostra, & Roeyers, 2014). Other studies focus on demonstrating a relation between neural activity during action observation and imitation skills within ASDs rather than group differences (Bernier, Aaronson, & McPartland, 2013; Bernier, Dawson, Webb, & Murias, 2007). In the search for a biomarker or neurocognitive mechanism for the social communicative impairments for ASDs, enthusiasm for the MNS has therefore waned. However, most studies of neural mirroring, in addition to requiring participants to hold still for certain types of imaging, have used paradigms designed for use in typical development and dependent on completion of nonsalient actions. For example, action execution (e.g., opening and closing your hand) in these paradigms is traditionally motivated by either spontaneous imitation or verbal prompts, creating task demands that would affect ASD and control groups differently. Additionally, investigations of the MNS in ASD have focused on older, higher-functioning participants with average IQs, making it difficult to generalize findings across either the spectrum of impairment or across the life span (i.e., in infants who go on to develop ASD). In the only study of children with

ASD under the age of 3, no differences in mu suppression patterns were seen between the ASD and control groups (Ruysschaert et al., 2014).

The relation between motor experiences, development of the MNS, and motor impairments in ASDs and other developmental disorders further complicates this literature. Infants at risk for autism show differences in motor development compared to infants with typical development within the first year of life, including impaired gross and fine motor development (Bhat, Galloway, & Landa, 2012; Libertus, Sheperd, Ross, & Landa, 2014), postural instability (Iverson & Wozniak, 2007), and oral motor difficulties (Gernsbacher, Sauer, Geye, Schweigert, & Goldsmith, 2008). Motor delays in ASD persist into toddlerhood, predict symptom severity in children with ASD and those with global developmental delay, and predict diagnostic outcome in toddlers at risk for ASD (Brian et al., 2008; MacDonald, Lord, & Ulrich, 2013; Sutera et al., 2007). Given that infants' own motor experiences/competencies influence the degree of mu suppression when watching others' actions (Cannon et al., 2016; de Klerk, Johnson, Heyes, & Southgate, 2015; van Elk et al., 2008), it is possible that any group differences in the MNS in infants with ASD could be driven by differences in motor experiences alone. Further, motor delays in infants and young children with ASD could in and of themselves contribute to delayed or deviant development of the MNS.

In sum, there are several important methodological considerations to be mindful of when investigating the potential link between the MNS and ASDs. Going forward, the onus is on researchers to design studies with the appropriate controls and task demands in order to clarify any potential role of the MNS in ASDs. Additionally, while studies of mu suppression during action execution and observation in infants at risk for ASDs will be an important next step towards understanding the role that neural mirroring plays in imitation and other social cognitive impairments, careful measurement of and attention to motor skill development will be an essential feature for future study designs.

The MNS has also been investigated in children and adults diagnosed with other developmental disorders, including developmental coordination disorder (Reynolds et al., 2017), Down syndrome (Virji-Babul et al., 2008), and Williams syndrome (Ng et al., 2016). More research in neural mirroring, and infant mu suppression specifically, across multiple developmental disorders and idiopathic developmental delays will help to clarify the relation between early motor delays, general developmental delays, and development of the MNS.

18.7 Policy Implications

Understanding the neural bases of the emergence of social cognition may have important implications for understanding, preventing, and treating a number of disorders and problems in social communication. This is particularly the case given accumulating evidence for the role of early intervention in altering trajectories for infants and young children with and at risk for social communication disorders (Zwaigenbaum et al., 2015). Emerging evidence suggests that in typically developing infants, acquiring skills (e.g., motor and action representation skills) may alter how those infants interact with the world, potentially providing scaffolding for earlier acquisition of developmental milestones (Libertus, Joh, & Needham, 2016). Therefore, in theory, enhancing motor experience and learning in infants may be a window into interventions for deficits in social communication. At this time, however, basic research on the mechanisms linking motor experience, motor training, and emerging social skills in infants and young children is too limited to have practical policy implications. Key research areas to address in order to facilitate development of interventions include the mechanistic links between motor experience/motor delays and emerging social cognition, the role and timing of sensitive and critical periods in early development of the neural mirroring system, and characterizations of early MNS development as either delayed or deviant in social communication disorders (Rogers et al., 2003; Young et al., 2011).

18.8 Conclusions

The MNS is purported to play an important role in key social cognitive functions in infancy and throughout the life span, including action understanding, imitation, cooperation, language, and theory of mind. Research exploring the development and function of the MNS is still very much in its infancy, and as such the body of work reviewed here is somewhat equivocal in terms of which theories are best supported. In fact, much of the research that is focused on these questions and theories has been completed in older children and adults, whose age places them outside of the actual developmental period in which these social-cognitive skills are emerging. Further work is thus needed, particularly within the infant age range. This work will benefit from agreement on methodological guidelines within the scientific community, particularly as they relate to study design and data processing, including those special methodological considerations necessary for working with the unique population of infants and children. In this chapter, we argue that examining the MNS during infancy, the developmental period when the abilities to understand and execute actions are emerging, may provide unique understanding into the function and significance of the MNS system.

References

Arbib, M. A., & Mundhenk, T. N. (2005). Schizophrenia and the mirror system: An essay. *Neuropsychologia*, *43*(2), 268–280. https://doi.org/10.1016/J.NEUROPS YCHOLOGIA.2004.11.013

Avenanti, A., Paracampo, R., Annella, L., Tidoni, E., & Aglioti, S. M. (2018). Boosting and decreasing action prediction abilities through excitatory and inhibitory tDCS of inferior frontal cortex. *Cerebral Cortex*, *28*(4), 1282–1296. https://doi.org/10.1093/cercor/bhx041

Bernier, R., Aaronson, B., & McPartland, J. (2013). The role of imitation in the observed heterogeneity in EEG mu rhythm in autism and typical development. *Brain and Cognition*, *82*(1), 69–75. https://doi.org/10.1016/J.BANDC.2013.02.008

Bernier, R., Dawson, G., Webb, S., & Murias, M. (2007). EEG mu rhythm and imitation impairments in individuals with autism spectrum disorder. *Brain and Cognition*, *64*(3), 228–237. https://doi.org/10.1016/J.BANDC.2007.03.004

Bhat, A. N., Galloway, J. C., & Landa, R. J. (2012). Relation between early motor delay and later communication delay in infants at risk for Autism. *Infant Behavior and Development*, *35*(4), 838–846. https://doi.org/10.1016/J.INFBEH.2012.07.019

Biondi, M., Boas, D. A., & Wilcox, T. (2016). On the other hand: Increased cortical activation to human versus mechanical hands in infants. *NeuroImage*, *141*, 143–153. https://doi.org/10.1016/J.NEUROIMAGE.2016.07.021

Blakemore, S., & Decety, J. (2001). From the perception of action to the understanding of intention. *Nature Reviews Neuroscience*, *2*(8), 561–567. https://doi.org/10.1038/35086023

Brian, J., Bryson, S. E., Garon, N., Roberts, W., Smith, I. M., Szatmari, P., & Zwaigenbaum, L. (2008). Clinical assessment of autism in high-risk 18-month-olds. *Autism*, *12*(5), 433–456. https://doi.org/10.1177/1362361308094500

Bridgeman, B. (2005). Action planning supplements mirror systems in language evolution. *Behavioral and Brain Sciences*, *28*(2), 129–130. https://doi.org/10.1017/S0140525X0526003X

Brooks, R., & Meltzoff, A. N. (2008). Infant gaze following and pointing predict accelerated vocabulary growth through two years of age: A longitudinal, growth curve modeling study. *Journal of Child Language*, *35*, 207–220. https://doi.org/10.1017/S030500090700829X

(2015). Connecting the dots from infancy to childhood: A longitudinal study connecting gaze following, language, and explicit theory of mind. *Journal of Experimental Child Psychology*, *130*, 67–78. https://doi.org/10.1016/j.jecp.2014.09.010

Cannon, E. N., Simpson, E. A., Fox, N. A., Vanderwert, R. E., Woodward, A. L., & Ferrari, P. F. (2016). Relations between infants' emerging reach-grasp competence and event-related desynchronization in EEG. *Developmental Science*, *19*(1), 50–62. https://doi.org/10.1111/desc.12295

Cannon, E. N., Yoo, K. H., Vanderwert, R. E., Ferrari, P. F., Woodward, A. L., & Fox, N. A. (2014). Action experience, more than observation, influences mu rhythm desynchronization. *PloS ONE*, *9*(3), e92002. https://doi.org/10.1371/journal.pone.0092002

Caspers, S., Zilles, K., Laird, A. R., & Eickhoff, S. B. (2010). ALE meta-analysis of action observation and imitation in the human brain. *NeuroImage*, *50*(3), 1148–1167. https://doi.org/10.1016/j.neuroimage.2009.12.112

Cattaneo, L., Sandrini, M., & Schwarzbach, J. (2010). State-dependent TMS reveals a hierarchical representation of observed acts in the temporal, parietal, and premotor cortices. *Cerebral Cortex*, *20*(9), 2252–2258. https://doi.org/10.1093/cercor/bhp291

Cavallo, A., Lungu, O., Becchio, C., Ansuini, C., Rustichini, A., & Fadiga, L. (2015). When gaze opens the channel for communication: Integrative role of IFG and MPFC. *NeuroImage*, *119*, 63–69. https://doi.org/10.1016/j.neuroimage.2015.06.025

Charman, T., Baron-Cohen, S., Swettenham, J., Baird, G., Cox, A., & Drew, A. (2000). Testing joint attention, imitation, and play as infancy precursors to language and theory of mind. *Cognitive Development*, *15*(4), 481–498. https://doi.org/10.1016/S0885-2014(01)00037-5

Charman, T., Swettenham, J., Baron-Cohen, S., Cox, A., Baird, G., & Drew, A. (1997). Infants with autism: An investigation of empathy, pretend play, joint attention, and imitation. *Developmental Psychology*, *33*(5), 781–789. https://doi.org/10.1037/0012-1649.33.5.781

Cochin, S., Barthelemy, C., Roux, S., & Martineau, J. (1999). Observation and execution of movement: Similarities demonstrated by quantified electroencephalography. *European Journal of Neuroscience*, *11*(5), 1839–1842. https://doi.org/10.1046/j.1460-9568.1999.00598.x

Cossu, G., Boria, S., Copioli, C., Bracceschi, R., Giuberti, V., Santelli, E., & Gallese, V. (2012). Motor representation of actions in children with autism. *PLoS ONE*, *7*(9), e44779. https://doi.org/10.1371/journal.pone.0044779

Cuevas, K., Cannon, E. N., Yoo, K. H., & Fox, N. A. (2014). The infant EEG mu rhythm: Methodological considerations and best practices. *Developmental Review*, *34*(1), 26–43. https://doi.org/10.1016/j.dr.2013.12.001

Dapretto, M., Davies, M. S., Pfeifer, J. H., Scott, A. A., Sigman, M., Bookheimer, S. Y., & Iacoboni, M. (2006). Understanding emotions in others: Mirror neuron dysfunction in children with autism spectrum disorders. *Nature Neuroscience*, *9*(1), 28–30. https://doi.org/10.1038/nn1611

de Klerk, C. C. J. M., Johnson, M. H., Heyes, C. M., & Southgate, V. (2015). Baby steps: Investigating the development of perceptual-motor couplings in infancy. *Developmental Science*, *18*(2), 270–280. https://doi.org/10.1111/desc.12226

de Klerk, C. C. J. M., Southgate, V., & Csibra, G. (2016). Predictive action tracking without motor experience in 8-month-old infants. *Brain and Cognition*, *109*, 131–139. https://doi.org/10.1016/j.bandc.2016.09.010

Debnath, R., Salo, V. C., Buzzell, G. A., Yoo, K. H., & Fox, N. A. (2019). Mu rhythm desynchronization is specific to action execution and observation: Evidence from time-frequency and connectivity analysis. *NeuroImage*, *184*, 496–507. https://doi.org/10.1016/j.neuroimage.2018.09.053

di Pellegrino, G., Fadiga, L., Fogassi, L., Gallese, V., & Rizzolatti, G. (1992). Understanding motor events: A neurophysiological study. *Experimental Brain Research*, *91*(1), 176–180. https://doi.org/10.1007/BF00230027

Dumas, G., Soussignan, R., Hugueville, L., Martinerie, J., & Nadel, J. (2014). Revisiting mu suppression in autism spectrum disorder. *Brain Research*, *1585*, 108–119. https://doi.org/10.1016/J.BRAINRES.2014.08.035

Engel, A. K., Maye, A., Kurthen, M., & König, P. (2013). Where's the action? The pragmatic turn in cognitive science. *Trends in Cognitive Sciences*, *17*(5), 202–209. https://doi.org/10.1016/j.tics.2013.03.006

Fan, Y. -T., Decety, J., Yang, C. -Y., Liu, J. -L., & Cheng, Y. (2010). Unbroken mirror neurons in autism spectrum disorders. *Journal of Child Psychology and Psychiatry*, *51*(9), 981–988. https://doi.org/10.1111/j.1469-7610.2010.02269.x

Ferrari, P. F., Gerbella, M., Coudé, G., & Rozzi, S. (2017). Two different mirror neuron networks: The sensorimotor (hand) and limbic (face) pathways. *Neuroscience*, *358*(45), 300–315. https://doi.org/10.1016/j.neuroscience.2017.06.052

Ferrari, P. F., Tramacere, A., Simpson, E. A., & Iriki, A. (2013). Mirror neurons through the lens of epigenetics. *Trends in Cognitive Sciences*, *17*(9), 450–457. https://doi.org/10.1016/j.tics.2013.07.003

Filippi, C. A., Cannon, E. N., Fox, N. A., Thorpe, S. G., Ferrari, P. F., & Woodward, A. L. (2016). Motor system activation predicts goal imitation in 7-month-old infants. *Psychological Science*, *27*(5), 675–684. https://doi.org/10.1177/0956797616632231

Foglia, L., & Wilson, R. A. (2013). Embodied cognition. *WIREs Cognitive Science*, *4*(3), 319–325. https://doi.org/10.1002/wcs.1226

Fox, N. A., Bakermans-Kranenburg, M. J., Yoo, K. H., Bowman, L. C., Cannon, E. N., Vanderwert, R. E., … van IJzendoorn, M. H. (2016). Assessing human mirror activity with EEG mu rhythm: A meta-analysis. *Psychological Bulletin*, *142*(3), 291–313. https://doi.org/10.1037/bul0000031

Gallese, V., Fadiga, L., Fogassi, L., & Rizzolatti, G. (1996). Action recognition in the premotor cortex. *Brain*, *119*(2), 593–609. https://doi.org/10.1093/brain/119.2.593

Gallese, V., & Goldman, A. (1998). Mirror neurons and the simulation theory of mind-reading. *Trends in Cognitive Sciences*, *2*(12), 493–501. https://doi.org/10.1016/S1364-6613(98)01262-5

Gallese, V., Keysers, C., & Rizzolatti, G. (2004). A unifying view of the basis of social cognition. *Trends in Cognitive Sciences*, *8*(9), 396–403. https://doi.org/10.1016/j.tics.2004.07.002

Gernsbacher, M. A., Sauer, E. A., Geye, H. M., Schweigert, E. K., & Goldsmith, H. H. (2008). Infant and toddler oral- and manual-motor skills predict later speech fluency in Autism. *Journal of Child Psychology and Psychiatry*, *49*(1), 43–50. https://doi.org/10.1111/j.1469-7610.2007.01820.x

Green, D., Li, Q., Lockman, J. J., & Gredebäck, G. (2016). Culture influences action understanding in infancy: Prediction of actions performed with chopsticks and spoons in Chinese and Swedish infants. *Child Development*, *87*(3), 736–746. https://doi.org/10.1111/cdev.12500

Grossmann, T., Johnson, M. H., Lloyd-Fox, S., Blasi, A., Deligianni, F., Elwell, C., & Csibra, G. (2008). Early cortical specialization for face-to-face communication in human infants. *Proceedings. Biological Sciences*, *275*(1653), 2803–2811. https://doi.org/10.1098/rspb.2008.0986

Hamilton, A. F. (2013). Reflecting on the mirror neuron system in autism: A systematic review of current theories. *Developmental Cognitive Neuroscience*, *3*, 91–105. https://doi.org/10.1016/J.DCN.2012.09.008

Hari, R. (2006). Action–perception connection and the cortical mu rhythm. *Progress in Brain Research*, *159*, 253–260. https://doi.org/10.1016/S0079-6123(06)59017-X

Heyes, C. (2010). Where do mirror neurons come from? *Neuroscience & Biobehavioral Reviews*, *34*(4), 575–583. https://doi.org/10.1016/j.neubiorev.2009.11.007

(2013). A new approach to mirror neurons: Developmental history, system-level theory and intervention experiments. *Cortex*, *49*(10), 2946–2948. https://doi.org/10.1016/j.cortex.2013.07.002

Hickok, G. (2009). Eight problems for the mirror neuron theory of action understanding in monkeys and humans. *Journal of Cognitive Neuroscience*, *21*(7), 1229–1243. https://doi.org/10.1162/jocn.2009.21189

Hobson, H. M., & Bishop, D. V. M. (2016). Mu suppression: A good measure of the human mirror neuron system? *Cortex*, *82*, 290–310. https://doi.org/10.1016/j.cortex.2016.03.019

Iacoboni, M. (2009). Imitation, empathy, and mirror neurons. *Annual Review of Psychology*, *60*(1), 653–670. https://doi.org/10.1146/annurev.psych.60.110707.163604

Ichikawa, H., Kanazawa, S., Yamaguchi, M. K., & Kakigi, R. (2010). Infant brain activity while viewing facial movement of point-light displays as measured by near-infrared spectroscopy (NIRS). *Neuroscience Letters*, *482*(2), 90–94. https://doi.org/10.1016/J.NEULET.2010.06.086

Iverson, J. M., & Wozniak, R. H. (2007). Variation in vocal-motor development in infant siblings of children with Autism. *Journal of Autism and Developmental Disorders*, *37*(1), 158–170. https://doi.org/10.1007/s10803-006-0339-z

Lepage, J. -F., & Théoret, H. (2006). EEG evidence for the presence of an action observation-execution matching system in children. *European Journal of Neuroscience*, *23*(9), 2505–2510. https://doi.org/10.1111/j.1460-9568.2006.04769.x

Li, G., Lin, W., Gilmore, J. H., & Shen, D. (2015). Spatial patterns, longitudinal development, and hemispheric asymmetries of cortical thickness in infants from birth to 2 years of age. *Journal of Neuroscience*, *35*(24), 9150–9162. https://doi.org/10.1523/JNEUROSCI.4107–14.2015

Li, G., Nie, J., Wang, L., Shi, F., Lin, W., Gilmore, J. H., & Shen, D. (2013). Mapping region-specific longitudinal cortical surface expansion from birth to 2 years of age. *Cerebral Cortex*, *23*(11), 2724–2733. https://doi.org/10.1093/cercor/bhs265

Libertus, K., Joh, A. S., & Needham, A. W. (2016). Motor training at 3 months affects object exploration 12 months later. *Developmental Science*, *19*(6), 1058–1066. https://doi.org/10.1111/desc.12370

Libertus, K., Sheperd, K. A., Ross, S. W., & Landa, R. J. (2014). Limited fine motor and grasping skills in 6-month-old infants at high risk for Autism. *Child Development*, *85*(6), 2218–2231. https://doi.org/10.1111/cdev.12262

Lloyd-Fox, S., Blasi, A., Volein, A., Everdell, N., Elwell, C. E., & Johnson, M. H. (2009). Social perception in infancy: A near infrared spectroscopy study. *Child Development*, *80*(4), 986–999. https://doi.org/10.1111/j.1467-8624.2009.01312.x

Lloyd-Fox, S., Wu, R., Richards, J. E., Elwell, C. E., & Johnson, M. H. (2015). Cortical activation to action perception is associated with action production abilities in young infants. *Cerebral Cortex*, *25*(2), 289–297. https://doi.org/10.1093/cercor/bht207

MacDonald, M., Lord, C., & Ulrich, D. (2013). The relationship of motor skills and adaptive behavior skills in young children with autism spectrum disorders. *Research in Autism Spectrum Disorders*, *7*(11), 1383–1390. https://doi.org/10.1016/J.RASD.2013.07.020

Manshanden, I., de Munck, J. C., Simon, N. R., & Lopes da Silva, F. H. (2002). Source localization of MEG sleep spindles and the relation to sources of alpha band rhythms. *Clinical Neurophysiology, 113*(12), 1937–1947. https://doi.org/10.1016/S1388-2457(02)00304-8

Marshall, P. J., Bar-Haim, Y., & Fox, N. A. (2002). Development of the EEG from 5 months to 4 years of age. *Clinical Neurophysiology, 113*(8), 1199–1208. https://doi.org/10.1016/j.cogpsych.2012.08.001

Marshall, P. J., & Meltzoff, A. N. (2011). Neural mirroring systems: Exploring the EEG mu rhythm in human infancy. *Developmental Cognitive Neuroscience, 1*(2), 110–123. https://doi.org/10.1016/j.dcn.2010.09.001

(2014). Neural mirroring mechanisms and imitation in human infants. *Philosophical Transactions of the Royal Society B: Biological Sciences, 369*(1644), 20130620–20130620. https://doi.org/10.1098/rstb.2013.0620

Martineau, J., Cochin, S., Magne, R., & Barthelemy, C. (2008). Impaired cortical activation in autistic children: Is the mirror neuron system involved? *International Journal of Psychophysiology, 68*(1), 35–40. https://doi.org/10.1016/J.IJPSYCHO.2008.01.002

McDonald, N. M., & Perdue, K. L. (2018, April 1). The infant brain in the social world: Moving toward interactive social neuroscience with functional near-infrared spectroscopy. *Neuroscience and Biobehavioral Reviews, 87*, 38–49. https://doi.org/10.1016/j.neubiorev.2018.01.007

Meltzoff, A. N. (2007). "Like me": A foundation for social cognition. *Developmental Science, 10*(1), 126–134. https://doi.org/10.1111/j.1467-7687.2007.00574.x

Meltzoff, A. N., & Gopnik, A. (1993). The role of imitation in understanding persons and developing a theory of mind. In S. Baron-Cohen, H. Tager-Flusberg, & D. J. Cohen (Eds.), *Understanding other minds: Perspectives from Autism* (pp. 335–366). New York, NY: Oxford University Press.

Mizuhara, H., & Inui, T. (2011). Is mu rhythm an index of the human mirror neuron system? A study of simultaneous fMRI and EEG. In R. Wang & F. Gu (Eds.), *Advances in cognitive neurodynamics (II): Proceedings of the Second International Conference on Cognitive Neurodynamics* (pp. 123–127). Dordrecht: Springer Science & Business Media. https://doi.org/10.1007/978-90-481-9695-1_19

Molenberghs, P., Cunnington, R., & Mattingley, J. B. (2012). Brain regions with mirror properties: A meta-analysis of 125 human fMRI studies. *Neuroscience & Biobehavioral Reviews, 36*(1), 341–349. https://doi.org/10.1016/J.NEUBIOREV.2011.07.004

Morales, S., Bowman, L. C., Velnoskey, K. R., Fox, N. A., & Redcay, E. (2019). An fMRI study of action observation and action execution in childhood. *Developmental Cognitive Neuroscience, 37*. https://doi.org/10.1016/j.dcn.2019.100655

Mukamel, R., Ekstrom, A. D., Kaplan, J., Iacoboni, M., & Fried, I. (2010). Single-neuron responses in humans during execution and observation of actions. *Current Biology, 20*(8), 750–756. https://doi.org/10.1016/j.cub.2010.02.045

Muthukumaraswamy, S. D., Johnson, B. W., & McNair, N. A. (2004). Mu rhythm modulation during observation of an object-directed grasp. *Cognitive Brain Research, 19*(2), 195–201. https://doi.org/10.1016/j.cogbrainres.2003.12.001

Ng, R., Brown, T. T., Erhart, M., Järvinen, A. M., Korenberg, J. R., Bellugi, U., & Halgren, E. (2016). Morphological differences in the mirror neuron system in Williams syndrome. *Social Neuroscience, 11*(3), 277–288. https://doi.org/10.1080/17470919.2015.1070746

Nyström, P. (2008). The infant mirror neuron system studied with high density EEG. *Social Neuroscience, 3*(3–4), 334–347. https://doi.org/10.1080/17470910701563665

Nyström, P., Ljunghammar, T., Rosander, K., & von Hofsten, C. (2011). Using mu rhythm desynchronization to measure mirror neuron activity in infants. *Developmental Science, 14*(2), 327–335. https://doi.org/10.1111/j.1467-7687.2010.00979.x

Oberman, L. M., Hubbard, E. M., McCleery, J. P., Altschuler, E. L., Ramachandran, V. S., & Pineda, J. A. (2005). EEG evidence for mirror neuron dysfunction in autism spectrum disorders. *Cognitive Brain Research, 24*(2), 190–198. https://doi.org/10.1016/J.COGBRAINRES.2005.01.014

Oberman, L. M., Ramachandran, V. S., & Pineda, J. A. (2008). Modulation of mu suppression in children with autism spectrum disorders in response to familiar or unfamiliar stimuli: The mirror neuron hypothesis. *Neuropsychologia, 46*(5), 1558–1565. https://doi.org/10.1016/J.NEUROPSYCHOLOGIA.2008.01.010

Orgs, G., Dombrowski, J. -H., Heil, M., & Jansen-Osmann, P. (2008). Expertise in dance modulates alphabeta event-related desynchronization during action observation. *European Journal of Neuroscience, 27*(12), 3380–3384. https://doi.org/10.1111/j.1460-9568.2008.06271.x

Overton, W. F. (2006). Developmental psychology: Philosophy, concepts, methodology. In W. I. Damon & R. M. Lerner (Eds.), *Handbook of child psychology. Vol. 1: Theoretical models of human development* (6th ed., pp. 18–88). Hoboken, NJ: John Wiley & Sons. https://doi.org/10.1002/9780470147658.chpsy0102

Paulus, M. (2012). Action mirroring and action understanding: An ideomotor and attentional account. *Psychological Research, 76*(6), 760–767. https://doi.org/10.1007/s00426-011-0385-9

Pfurtscheller, G., Neuper, C., Andrew, C., & Edlinger, G. (1997). Foot and hand area mu rhythms. *International Journal of Psychophysiology, 26*(1–3), 121–135. https://doi.org/10.1016/S0167-8760(97)00760-5

Piaget, J. (1952). *The origins of intelligence in children.* New York, NY: Norton.

Pineda, J. A. (2005). The functional significance of mu rhythms: Translating "seeing" and "hearing" into "doing." *Brain Research Reviews, 50*(1), 57–68. https://doi.org/10.1016/j.brainresrev.2005.04.005

Raymaekers, R., Wiersema, J. R., & Roeyers, H. (2009). EEG study of the mirror neuron system in children with high functioning autism. *Brain Research, 1304*, 113–121. https://doi.org/10.1016/J.BRAINRES.2009.09.068

Rayson, H., Bonaiuto, J. J., Ferrari, P. F., & Murray, L. (2016). Mu desynchronization during observation and execution of facial expressions in 30-month-old children. *Developmental Cognitive Neuroscience, 19*, 279–287. https://doi.org/10.1016/j.dcn.2016.05.003

Reid, V. M., Striano, T., & Iacoboni, M. (2011). Neural correlates of dyadic interaction during infancy. *Developmental Cognitive Neuroscience, 1*(2), 124–130. https://doi.org/10.1016/j.dcn.2011.01.001

Reynolds, J. E., Billington, J., Kerrigan, S., Williams, J., Elliott, C., Winsor, A. M., … Licari, M. K. (2017). Mirror neuron system activation in children with developmental coordination disorder: A replication functional MRI study. *Research in Developmental Disabilities, 84*, 16–27. https://doi.org/10.1016/J.RIDD.2017.11.012

Rizzolatti, G., & Arbib, M. A. (1998). Language within our grasp. *Trends in Neurosciences, 21*(5), 188–194.

Rizzolatti, G., & Craighero, L. (2004). The mirror-neuron system. *Annual Review of Neuroscience, 27*, 169–192. https://doi.org/10.1146/annurev.neuro.27.070203 .144230

Rizzolatti, G., Fadiga, L., Gallese, V., & Fogassi, L. (1996). Premotor cortex and the recognition of motor actions. *Cognitive Brain Research, 3*(2), 131–141. https://doi.org/10.1016/0926-6410(95)00038-0

Rizzolatti, G., Fogassi, L., & Gallese, V. (2001). Neurophysiological mechanisms underlying the understanding and imitation of action. *Nature Reviews Neuroscience, 2*(9), 661–670. https://doi.org/10.1038/35090060

Rogers, S. J., Hepburn, S. L., Stackhouse, T., & Wehner, E. (2003). Imitation performance in toddlers with Autism and those with other developmental disorders. *Journal of Child Psychology and Psychiatry, 44*(5), 763–781. https://doi.org/10.1111/1469-7610.00162

Ruysschaert, L., Warreyn, P., Wiersema, J. R., Metin, B., & Roeyers, H. (2013). Neural mirroring during the observation of live and video actions in infants. *Clinical Neurophysiology, 124*(9), 1765–1770. https://doi.org/10.1016/j.clinph .2013.04.007

Ruysschaert, L., Warreyn, P., Wiersema, J. R., Oostra, A., & Roeyers, H. (2014). Exploring the role of neural mirroring in children with autism spectrum disorder. *Autism Research, 7*(2), 197–206. https://doi.org/10.1002/aur.1339

Salmelin, R., Hämäaläinen, M., Kajola, M., & Hari, R. (1995). Functional segregation of movement-related rhythmic activity in the human brain. *NeuroImage, 2*(4), 237–243. https://doi.org/10.1006/NIMG.1995.1031

Salmelin, R., & Hari, R. (1994). Spatiotemporal characteristics of sensorimotor neuromagnetic rhythms related to thumb movement. *Neuroscience, 60*(2), 537–550. https://doi.org/10.1016/0306-4522(94)90263-1

Salo, V. C. (2018). Examining the role of the motor system in early communicative development (Unpublished doctoral dissertation). University of Maryland, College Park.

Shapiro, I. (2011). *Embodied cognition*. New York, NY: Routledge.

Shimada, S., & Hiraki, K. (2006). Infant's brain responses to live and televised action. *NeuroImage, 32*(2), 930–939. https://doi.org/10.1016/J.NEUROIMAGE.2006.03.044

Shin, Y. K., Proctor, R. W., & Capaldi, E. J. (2010). A review of contemporary ideomotor theory. *Psychological Bulletin, 136*(6), 943–974. https://doi.org/10.1037/a0020541

Southgate, V., & Hamilton, A. F. (2008). Unbroken mirrors: Challenging a theory of Autism. *Trends in Cognitive Sciences, 12*(6), 225–229. https://doi.org/10.1016/j.tics.2008.03.005

Southgate, V., Johnson, M. H., Karoui, I. E., & Csibra, G. (2010). Motor system activation reveals infants' on-line prediction of others' goals. *Psychological Science, 21*(3), 355–359. https://doi.org/10.1177/0956797610362058

Southgate, V., Johnson, M. H., Osborne, T., & Csibra, G. (2009). Predictive motor activation during action observation in human infants. *Biology Letters, 5*(6), 769–772. https://doi.org/10.1098/rsbl.2009.0474

Stadler, W., Ott, D. V. M., Springer, A., Schubotz, R. I., Schütz-Bosbach, S., & Prinz, W. (2012). Repetitive TMS suggests a role of the human dorsal premotor cortex in action prediction. *Frontiers in Human Neuroscience*, *6*, 20. https://doi.org/10.3389/fnhum.2012.00020

Stapel, J. C., Hunnius, S., van Elk, M., & Bekkering, H. (2010). Motor activation during observation of unusual versus ordinary actions in infancy. *Social Neuroscience*, *5*(5–6), 451–460. https://doi.org/10.1080/17470919.2010.490667

Sun, P. -P., Tan, F. -L., Zhang, Z., Jiang, Y. -H., Zhao, Y., & Zhu, C. -Z. (2018). Feasibility of functional near-infrared spectroscopy (fNIRS) to investigate the mirror neuron system: An experimental study in a real-life situation. *Frontiers in Human Neuroscience*, *12*, 86. https://doi.org/10.3389/fnhum.2018.00086

Sutera, S., Pandey, J., Esser, E. L., Rosenthal, M. A., Wilson, L. B., Barton, M., ... Fein, D. (2007). Predictors of optimal outcome in toddlers diagnosed with autism spectrum disorders. *Journal of Autism and Developmental Disorders*, *37*(1), 98–107. https://doi.org/10.1007/s10803-006-0340-6

Thorpe, S. G., Cannon, E. N., & Fox, N. A. (2016). Spectral and source structural development of mu and alpha rhythms from infancy through adulthood. *Clinical Neurophysiology*, *127*(1), 254–269. https://doi.org/10.1016/j.clinph.2015.03.004

Tomasello, M. (1995). Joint attention and social cognition. In C. Moore & P. J. Dunham (Eds.), *Joint attention: Its origins and role in development* (pp. 103–130). Hillsdale, NJ: Lawrence Erlbaum Associates.

Tomasello, M., Carpenter, M., Call, J., Behne, T., & Moll, H. (2005). Understanding and sharing intentions: The origins of cultural cognition. *Behavioral and Brain Sciences*, *28*(5), 675–691. https://doi.org/10.1017/S0140525X05000129

Tomasello, M., Carpenter, M., & Liszkowski, U. (2007). A new look at infant pointing. *Child Development*, *78*(3), 705–722. https://doi.org/10.1111/j.1467-8624.2007.01025.x

Tomasello, M., Kruger, A. C., & Ratner, H. H. (1993). Cultural learning. *Behavioral and Brain Sciences*, *16*(3), 495. https://doi.org/10.1017/S0140525X0003123X

Toth, K., Munson, J., Meltzoff, A. N., & Dawson, G. (2006). Early predictors of communication development in young children with autism spectrum disorder: Joint attention, imitation, and toy play. *Journal of Autism and Developmental Disorders*, *36*(8), 993–1005. https://doi.org/10.1007/s10803-006-0137-7

van Elk, M., van Schie, H. T., Hunnius, S., Vesper, C., & Bekkering, H. (2008). You'll never crawl alone: Neurophysiological evidence for experience-dependent motor resonance in infancy. *NeuroImage*, *43*(4), 808–814. https://doi.org/10.1016/j.neuroimage.2008.07.057

van Overwalle, F., & Baetens, K. (2009). Understanding others' actions and goals by mirror and mentalizing systems: A meta-analysis. *NeuroImage*, *48*(3), 564–584. https://doi.org/10.1016/j.neuroimage.2009.06.009

Virji-Babul, N., Moiseev, A., Cheung, T., Weeks, D., Cheyne, D., & Ribary, U. (2008). Changes in mu rhythm during action observation and execution in adults with Down syndrome: Implications for action representation. *Neuroscience Letters*, *436*(2), 177–180. https://doi.org/10.1016/J.NEULET.2008.03.022

Virji-Babul, N., Rose, A., Moiseeva, N., & Makan, N. (2012). Neural correlates of action understanding in infants: Influence of motor experience. *Brain and Behavior*, *2*(3), 237–242. https://doi.org/10.1002/brb3.50

Wellman, H. M., Phillips, A. T., Dunphy-Lelii, S., & LaLonde, N. (2004). Infant social attention predicts preschool social cognition. *Developmental Science, 7*(3), 283–288. https://doi.org/10.1111/j.1467-7687.2004.00347.x

Woodward, A. L., & Gerson, S. A. (2014). Mirroring and the development of action understanding. *Philosophical Transactions of the Royal Society of London. Series B, Biological Sciences, 369*(1644), 20130181. https://doi.org/10.1098/rstb.2013.0181

Yang, J., Andric, M., & Mathew, M. M. (2015). The neural basis of hand gesture comprehension: A meta-analysis of functional magnetic resonance imaging studies. *Neuroscience & Biobehavioral Reviews, 57*, 88–104. https://doi.org/10.1016/j.neubiorev.2015.08.006

Yoo, K. H., Cannon, E. N., Thorpe, S. G., & Fox, N. A. (2015). Desynchronization in EEG during perception of means–end actions and relations with infants' grasping skill. *British Journal of Developmental Psychology, 34*(1), 24–37. https://doi.org/10.1111/bjdp.12115

Yoo, K. H., Thorpe, S. G., & Fox, N. A. (2016). *Neural correlates of motor learning in infants*. Paper presented at the Biennial International Conference on Infant Studies, New Orleans, LA.

Young, G. S., Rogers, S. J., Hutman, T., Rozga, A., Sigman, M., & Ozonoff, S. (2011). Imitation from 12 to 24 months in autism and typical development: A longitudinal Rasch analysis. *Developmental Psychology, 47*(6), 1565–1578. https://doi.org/10.1037/a0025418

Zwaigenbaum, L., Bauman, M. L., Choueiri, R., Kasari, C., Carter, A., Granpeesheh, D., … Natowicz, M. R. (2015). Early intervention for children with autism spectrum disorder under 3 years of age: Recommendations for practice and research. *Pediatrics, 136*(Suppl. 1), S60–S81. https://doi.org/10.1542/peds.2014-3667E

19 Infant Object Manipulation and Play

Catherine S. Tamis-LeMonda and Jeffrey J. Lockman*

Natural and manufactured objects saturate human culture. Infants need not do much or go far to find objects of different shapes, textures, sizes, and functions throughout their environments. And, as they manipulate and play with objects, they learn quite a lot along the way. From the time they can swipe and grab, infants spend most of their awake hours exploring objects – moving seamlessly from object to object in short bursts of activity distributed over time. These bouts of object interaction allow infants to practice and refine manual skills, learn about object features and functions, and test the fit between body and environment. Object interactions also allow infants to extend the limits of reality. Infants can pretend that objects exist when they do not, use objects to stand for other objects, and generate unique ways to use objects beyond their intended design. Indeed, to fully engage human artifact culture, infants must become proficient at using objects in twin planes of action – the real and the imagined.

Here, we describe how infants develop in their real and imagined use of objects. We draw from literature on object manipulation and infant play, which remains largely separate theoretically and empirically. Researchers of object manipulation primarily investigate infants' development of manual skills, emphasizing perception–action feedback loops and object affordances, with less attention to how infants embark on the imagined "as if" world of symbolic or pretend play. By contrast, researchers of object play primarily focus on the development of pretense and view object manipulation as undifferentiated actions that are later supplanted by more "cognitively sophisticated behaviors" indicative of representational thought (Belsky & Most, 1981; Piaget, 1952).

Our goal is to dismantle this artificial divide by showing that object manipulation and play are more intertwined than traditionally thought. Object manipulation and play follow similar developmental paths, reciprocally influence one another throughout development, involve related neural pathways, and are embedded in sociocultural practice. We consider theoretical perspectives on the development of object manipulation and play, and examine how

* The preparation of this chapter was supported by R01-HD086034 from the National Institute of Child Health and Human Development (NICHD) and the LEGO Foundation. We thank the children and families who have participated in our studies.

different approaches have cast unique lenses onto infants' object interactions. Finally, we consider implications of our synthesis for practice and policy.

19.1 Theoretical Foundations

19.1.1 Piaget's Theory

Research on infant object manipulation and play share a theoretical basis in the writings of Piaget, who studied object manipulation to characterize infants' nascent knowledge about the physical world, and symbolic play to characterize infants' abilities to mentally represent their worlds (Piaget, 1952, 1954). The two lines of research, however, have since diverged toward perception–action and cognitive-representational approaches.

For Piaget, object manipulation was of interest less as a topic in its own right than as a means to discover what infants understand about the physical environment. The particular actions that infants use to manipulate and explore objects or how those actions develop were beyond the scope of Piaget's focus. Instead, he looked to the heterogeneity and quality of infants' actions on objects to reveal whether infants understood that objects exist independently of the self, and more generally, whether infants had developed a capacity for representational thinking.

According to Piaget, up until sensorimotor stage 4 (roughly beginning at 8 months), infants typically deploy similar routines to manipulate objects, regardless of objects' features or properties. They may bang, shake, rotate, or mouth an object in hand. Occasionally, infants discover an interesting consequence of their actions and then try to repeat the action – what Piaget termed circular reactions – but this consequence was largely unanticipated, reflecting a gap in infants' representational thinking. Even during stage 4, infants do not immediately foresee what manual routine is appropriate for an object. Rather, infants engage their repertoire of manual actions as if to discover which behaviors evoke interesting effects. Thus, Piaget characterized object manipulation during most of the first year as involving largely undifferentiated and nondiscriminating manual activity.

In the second year – stages 5 and 6 of the sensorimotor period – Piaget noted a qualitative shift in infants' interactions with objects. Infants could now reason fully about objects and appreciate that objects exist independently of the self. Most centrally, Piaget contended that by the end of the sensorimotor period, infants' understanding of objects reflected their general capacity to represent the world symbolically. According to Piaget, pretend play was a key manifestation of infants' underlying symbolic understanding, along with language, object permanence, and deferred imitation.

Researchers from a play tradition have since put Piaget's ideas to the test. If changes to play reflect developments in infants' mental representational skills, then play should follow a progression similar to language and relate to the language skills of children at an individual level. This is indeed the case. Developments in infant play closely correspond to developments in language, and associations between children's play and language skills are modest to strong (Orr & Geva, 2015; Quinn, Donnelly, & Kidd, 2018). Across the first 2 years, play progresses from exploration, to concrete actions on objects, to extended bouts of symbolic play that contain elaborate storylines (Bornstein & Tamis-LeMonda, 1995, 2006; Lillard, 2015; McCune, 1995; Tamis-LeMonda & Bornstein, 1991). Across the same developmental period, language progresses from babbles, to single-word utterances about the "here and now," to simple sentences and decontextualized talk about the "there and then" (Gillespie & Zittoun, 2010; Hoff, 2013; McCune, 1995; McCune-Nicolich, 1981). Later, in early childhood, symbolic play develops into complex role play, in line with children's gains in narrative skills (Uccelli, Hempill, Pan, & Snow, 2006).

The cognitive perspective on infant play has led researchers to leverage the play context to test infant cognitive development across a range of areas. Play has become a principal way to assess other things, as has also been the case with object manipulation. Because infants quickly become immersed in play, researchers often observe infant and child play or act out pretend stories to test causal reasoning, perspective taking, theory of mind, generic knowledge about object categories, and understanding of others' goals and intentions (e.g., Leslie, 1987; Lillard, 2015; Sutherland & Friedman, 2013). Furthermore, cognitive approaches to play have sparked the study of infants and children with specific developmental disorders. For example, the connection between pretend play and social-cognitive understanding helps explain why infants at risk for autism spectrum disorder show delays in pretend play (Campbell et al., 2018).

19.1.2 Gibson and Perception–Action Theory

Eleanor Gibson offered an alternative view to Piaget's theory of infant object manipulation and play, focusing primarily on how infants use action to explore and gain information from the environment (E. J. Gibson & Pick, 2000). In the Gibsonian account, perception and action are integrally intertwined. Humans and animals perceive opportunities for action or "affordances" in the environment that are scaled to their own physical characteristics and capabilities (E.J. Gibson, 1982; J. J. Gibson, 1979). Like other features of the environment, the Gibsons considered objects to be rich in information about affordances. And, infants already possess a suite of action systems, including looking, mouthing, and manipulating, which allow them to explore, register, and use this information (E. J. Gibson & Pick, 2000; J. J. Gibson, 1979). The developmental task for young perceivers then is not to supplement or construct information about objects from impoverished stimulation as Piaget suggested, but to recruit and integrate existing action systems to differentiate the relevant affordance information.

In this regard, consider the human object manipulation system. Human hands are exquisitely designed to pick up information about an object's affordances. Humans possess an opposable thumb, which facilitates exploratory actions such as grasping, holding, and pressing. These actions may occur either against the surface of the palm, where a power grip might be involved, or against a surface in the environment, when the object is held with a precision grip extending from the hand (Napier, 1962). Additionally, relative to other primate species, humans possess a more flexible wrist, which can undergo a relatively broad range and arc of motion (Marzke, 1997). When applied to hand-held objects, these types of movements permit considerable rotation, thereby facilitating information pickup, oftentimes jointly with other action systems, such as looking. And relative to other primate species, human fingers have evolved to become proportionately shorter, permitting greater control and more effective instrumental action with objects (Wolfe, Crisco, Orr, & Marzke, 2006). Collectively, these morphological and associated functional adaptations of the hand enable a wide range of exploratory and performative actions with objects, and are consistent with J. J. Gibson's characterization of the manual system as one that sustains "active touch" (J. J. Gibson, 1966). Thus, from a developmental perspective, the Gibsons perception–action approach directed researchers to consider how infants begin to harness these unique adaptations of the hand, in concert with other perception–action systems, to explore and register information about object affordances.

For the most part, however, the Gibsons' contributions have not been integrated into the study of play, likely because play researchers viewed the functions and morphology of the hand, for example, as secondary to the primary driver of infant object play – mental representational capacities. We challenge this theoretical dichotomy later in the chapter by showing that object manipulation and play are two sides of the same coin.

19.2 Neural Underpinnings

Researchers have long recognized that advances in object manipulation and play are linked to the development of the nervous system. Arnold Gesell, in his pioneering work on normative development, tied the achievement of various milestones in manual and adaptive behavior, some of which also involved play with objects, to the maturation of the central nervous system (Gesell & Thompson, 1934). Although Gesell had neither identified the specific brain areas underlying motor achievements, nor considered the role of experience in central nervous system maturation, he is nevertheless recognized as drawing connections between changes in brain and behavioral development.

Since Gesell's writings, advances in theory and methods – particularly with respect to the role and timing of experience in brain development – have led to a deeper understanding of how changes in manual behavior are tied to developments in specific areas and networks within and across brain regions. At the same time, relating developmental changes in object manipulation and play to brain development poses challenges for infancy researchers. Currently, the most popular methods (electroencephalography, EEG; functional magnetic resonance imaging, fMRI) require infants to remain relatively stationary to guard against motion artifacts in the data. Object manipulation and play, however, are inherently about movement, and certain behaviors in particular, such as object banging, can be quite vigorous. Newer techniques, such as functional near-infrared spectroscopy (fNIRS), may be more forgiving of infant movement than EEG and fMRI, but whether fNIRS can adequately capture functional changes in brain activity as infants manipulate and play with objects remains an open question.

A further challenge to understanding the neural bases of object manipulation and play development centers on theory. Although considerable gains have been made in understanding sensitive periods and experience expectant effects in the perceptual and language domains (see reviews by Maurer, Chapter 6 this volume; and Reh & Werker, Chapter 21 this volume), much less is known about whether such corresponding phenomena occur for domains involving eye–hand coordination and associated experiences during human infancy. Nevertheless, this is a fundamental question for the pediatric rehabilitation sciences, where issues about timing, dosage and delivery of experience are critical for outcome (Heathcock & Lockman, 2019). We return to this issue when we consider policy implications.

With these caveats in mind, knowledge about brain and central nervous system development can enhance an understanding of developments in infant object manipulation and object play. Here, we consider two sets of relevant neural pathways: the pyramidal/extrapyramidal tracts and the ventral and dorsal streams.

The pyramidal tract runs from the motor cortices (primary, pre-, and supplementary) to the brainstem and spinal cord. Among other roles, it is responsible for the highly skilled and flexible motor movements of the hands and individual fingers, and receives and integrates inputs from different sensory modalities for this purpose (Martin, 2005). In contrast, the extrapyramidal tract comprises a diffuse collection of connections from different parts of the brain to the spinal cord. The extrapyramidal tract is largely associated with involuntary forms of movement, and does not play much if any role in regulating the fine movements of the hand and fingers.

Comparative work offers clues about the development of the neural substrates of manual function in humans. Studies with rhesus monkeys indicate that the extrapyramidal tract develops before the pyramidal tract (Kuypers, 1962; Lawrence & Hopkins, 1972). Likewise, in humans, the pyramidal tract is relatively immature at birth and undergoes a protracted period of development, with myelination of this tract proceeding gradually in the first 2 years (Martin, 2005). Some have suggested that the relatively protracted development of the pyramidal tract is reflected in the gradual development of functionality of the human hand: from clenched fist, to open hand, to gradual control of the fingers individually and relative to one another (Martin 2005; Welniarz, Delsart, & Roze, 2017). This idea is consistent with perception–action approaches reviewed in previous sections, which suggest that motor development may developmentally pace specificity of action during object manipulation (Bushnell & Boudreau, 1993; Lockman & Ashmead, 1983).

Another organizing framework for understanding the neural bases of some forms of object manipulation and play can be found in work on visual processing by the ventral and dorsal streams (Milner & Goodale, 1995, 2008; Ungerleider & Mishkin, 1982). In broad strokes, the ventral and dorsal streams can be distinguished both structurally and functionally. Both ventral and dorsal streams arise in the primary visual cortex. The ventral stream, however, then continues along the ventral surface into the temporal cortex. In contrast, the dorsal stream continues along the dorsal surface into the parietal cortex. The two streams have also been associated with different functions. Whereas the ventral stream is considered the vision for perception or the "what" stream (e.g., visual recognition of shapes and objects), the dorsal stream is considered the vision for action or the "how" stream (e.g., moment-to-moment visual guidance of reaching with respect to an object's location, shape, orientation). Although it is tempting to suggest that object manipulation and some forms of object play primarily engage the dorsal pathway given the involvement of action, it is more likely that ventral and dorsal streams serve object behaviors jointly and in complementary ways (Street, James, Jones, & Smith, 2011). The latter idea thus suggests that advances in object manipulation and some forms of object play may be associated with growth in functional connectivity between the ventral and dorsal pathways.

19.3 The Development of Object Manipulation

As noted, for many years, object manipulation was not studied as a skill in its own right, but as a means to investigate some other cognitive capacity. Furthermore, studies that rely on object manipulation as a proxy to investigate some other ability, including play, typically include objects that vary simultaneously across many physical dimensions, precluding clear conclusions about whether infants are relating their manual behaviors to the physical properties of the objects that they are holding. Other work on object manipulation, however, in part inspired by Gibsonian theory, has directly considered object manipulation as a skill in which manipulation is broken down into its component actions. Additionally, researchers often systematically control the physical properties of objects to examine how and to what extent infants appropriately relate hand to object. In some of this work, researchers distinguish between adjustments of the hand that occur prior to and subsequent to contact of the object, with adjustments prior to contact considered as evidence for planning or prospective visuomotor control (von Hofsten, 2007).

When researchers systematically vary the material and/or spatial characteristics of objects that they present to infants a consistent picture emerges. During the second half year, as infants gain more and more control of their finger, hand, and arm movements, they increasingly tailor their manual actions to the properties of the object that they are handling (for reviews see Bushnell & Boudreau, 1993, 1998; Lockman & Ashmead, 1983; Lockman & McHale, 1989). Contrary to accounts that suggest that object manipulation and play are undifferentiated during most of the first year (Belsky & Most; 1981; Piaget, 1952, 1954), infants manipulate objects in a targeted manner, closely gearing their actions to an object's physical characteristics.

To illustrate, when 6-month-old infants are presented with objects that vary in *texture* (smooth or rough), they display more scratching of rough than smooth objects (Bushnell & Boudreau, 1993, 1998; Lockman & McHale, 1989; Ruff, 1984). When presented with objects that vary in *pliability*, 6-month-old infants show more squeezing of soft than rigid objects (Palmer, 1989; Ruff 1984). By the same token, when 6-month-olds are presented objects that vary in *color*, they show more rotation of objects when the sides are differently rather than uniformly colored (Lockman & McHale, 1989). And when infants in the first half of the second half year are presented objects that vary in terms of their *sound potential*, they are more likely to bang a rigid than a soft object, and shake a noise-producing object than one that remains silent when shaken (Bushnell & Boudreau, 1993, 1998; Lockman & McHale, 1989; Palmer, 1989). Even newborn infants (Molina & Jouen, 1998) and infants in the first couple of months (Rochat, 1989) may tailor their manual behaviors to an object's pliability by pressing these objects differentially, although the interpretation of this variation in manual activity as purposeful exploration versus a cyclical grasp–release pattern evoked by a yielding surface is a matter of some debate (Striano & Bushnell, 2005).

What underlies infants' increased specificity of object manipulation in the second half year? Some researchers have suggested that changes in targeted manipulation stem less from advances in cognitive growth (Piaget, 1952, 1954) than motor control (Bushnell & Boudreau, 1993; 1998; Lockman & Ashmead, 1983). In the latter view, the motor system acts as a rate-limiting factor vis-à-vis object exploration. As new manual capabilities (e.g., the ability to fractionate movement of the fingers, to control of the wrist, to produce a pincer grip) come online during the first year, new opportunities arise to apply previously unavailable types of action to objects. In one version of this account, progress in motor development enables infants to engage in new haptic exploratory procedures to register information about objects (Bushnell & Boudreau, 1993, 1998; Lederman & Klatzky, 1987). On this account, developmental changes in the manual skills that underlie haptic exploration would largely predict when sensitivity to different kinds of material properties (e.g., substance, weight, texture) emerges during the first year. This approach is consistent with a Gibsonian theory, which as noted, highlights a reciprocal relation between perception and action in real and developmental time.

19.3.1 Object Manipulation: Prospective Adjustments

Individuals typically adjust the hand to match an object's properties even before they physically contact the object (Jeannerod, 1988; von Hofsten, 2007). Prospective adjustments like these help ensure that once an object is contacted, subsequent manipulation will be efficient and effective. Prospective adjustments of the hand are typically evoked by visual information about an object and thus involve a form of visuomotor coordination. Even infants show prospective adjustments for object features while reaching, and for some object features before others. Although infants extend their arms in the radial direction of an object soon after birth (von Hofsten, 1983), infants generally only begin to show prospective adjustments of the hand to other spatial features of objects (e.g., orientation, size, shape) during the second half year. Specifically, when reaching, infants increasingly make appropriate anticipatory adjustments of the hand based on an object's *orientation* before the middle part of the second half year (Lockman, Ashmead, & Bushnell, 1984; von Hofsten & Fazel-Zandy, 1984; Witherington, 2005). Likewise, they systematically vary reaching strategies (uni- vs. bi-manual reaches) and hand-opening width based on the visually perceived *size* of an object by the middle or latter part of the second half year (Berthier & Carrico, 2010; Corbetta, Thelen, & Johnson, 2000; Fagard & Jacquet, 1996; von Hofsten & Rönnqvist, 1988). And they begin to prospectively vary their grips according to an object's shape during the second half year, and to other aspects of an object's spatial structure (e.g., symmetry) by the end or even after the first year (Barrett & Needham, 2008; Smith, Street, Jones, & James, 2014). Finally, when multiple spatial features (e.g., size and orientation) of an object change across trials, 10-month-old infants experience difficulty in prospectively adjusting their grips, even though they prospectively adjust their grips when only one such feature changes (Schum, Jovanovic, & Schwarzer, 2011). Here, then, the role of cognitive load or complexity in constraining early forms of skilled action becomes apparent, an issue we return to when considering the early development of play.

19.3.2 Objects and Surfaces: Putting It Together

When infants manipulate objects, they not only palpate them in their hands, but also combine them with surfaces. Such combinatorial acts generate information about object composition and the effects produced by particular object–surface interactions. As in research on object manipulation and play, it was long assumed that infants combine objects and surfaces indiscriminately during much of the first year (Belsky & Most, 1981; Piaget, 1952, 1954). Infants, for instance, were thought to relate objects to surfaces indiscriminately, independent of the material composition of each and without regard to the object's conventional use (e.g., banging a spoon against a tabletop surface).

When researchers, however, began to systematically control the material composition of the objects and surfaces presented to infants, a new picture began to emerge about the specificity of infants' object–surface combinations (Bourgeois, Khawar, Neal, & Lockman, 2005; Palmer, 1989; Rips & Hespos, 2015). In many instances, infants in the first half of the second half year are already selective in how they combine objects and surfaces, taking into account the material properties of each. For instance, infants display more striking of hard than soft objects on rigid surfaces, and more striking of hard objects on rigid than flexible foam surfaces (Bourgeois et al., 2005; Palmer, 1989). Likewise, they show similar patterns when playing with objects on hardwood versus carpeted floors (Morgante & Keen, 2008). Moreover, even when transitions in the material composition of surfaces are abrupt (e.g., a tabletop surface that is half rigid, half flexible), infants adjust their manual behaviors with an object appropriately, based on the particular substrate that infants contact with the object (Fontenelle, Kahrs, Neal, Newton, & Lockman, 2007). Together, these findings highlight the specificity of infants' manual actions: Infants combine objects with surfaces selectively, taking into account the material properties of each.

19.3.3 Object Manipulation as a Gateway to Tool Use

The fact that infants relate objects to surfaces in systematic ways has led some researchers to suggest that object manipulation in the first year paves the way for the emergence of tool use in the second year (Lockman 2000; Lockman & Kahrs, 2017). On this account, objects change the affordances or functional capabilities of the hand. As infants during the first year explore and relate objects to surfaces, they learn how objects cause different effects on surfaces – a key requirement of tool use. As they do so, infants also gain practice in performing certain actions that they subsequently incorporate into tool use. For instance, object banging in the first year, transitions into controlled hammering in the second and third years (Kahrs, Jung, & Lockman, 2013, 2014). Likewise, infants may adapt object scooting into scribbling, as they begin moving graphic tools across surfaces in the second year. More generally, such developmental patterns suggest a synergy between affordance and motor learning. As infants combine objects and surfaces in real time, they gain expertise in the action patterns that they later will adapt for tool use (Lockman & Kahrs, 2017).

19.4 The Development of Object Play

Although the study of infant object manipulation is systematically grounded in how infants interact with objects of different shapes, textures, sizes, and so forth – whether a spoon or block or sponge – research on infant object play traditionally focused on infants' interactions with *toys*. Thus, a key aim of play research is to document how infants progress from actions based on the functions of specific toys – such as pushing buttons on a busy box – to using toys to reenact experiences in pretend stories. Typically, researchers describe the ways that object play changes in form and content across development as infants acquire new skills. And, just as is the case for object manipulation, motor, cognitive, social, and language abilities govern what infants can and will do at any moment in time with the objects available to them. A young infant might bang a spoon in play; a 1-year-old might pretend to eat imagined food; and a 2-year-old might place a bowl on her head as though it were a hat. Although developmental changes in infant play have been described at different levels of granularity, three broad types can be distinguished: exploration, nonsymbolic play, and symbolic play, with symbolic play being the most advanced in terms of representational demands.

19.4.1 Exploration

Infants' entry into play begins with exploration. Yet, unlike the rich characterization of object manipulation described by perception–action researchers, play researchers have largely ignored the nuanced behaviors that comprise infants' exploratory actions, such as how infants modify their actions as they explore different objects. The general lack of attention to exploratory play reflects the favoring of symbolic play as most cognitively advanced. In fact, because exploration is an early emerging, basic form of object interaction, some researchers consider it to fall outside the scope of play entirely (Lillard, 2015).

19.4.2 Nonsymbolic Play

Toward the end of the first year, infants shift from primarily exploring objects visually, orally, and manually to engaging in nonsymbolic or functional play (Ruff, 1984). Infants begin to discover the designed features of objects, as when they press buttons on phones or turn dials on busy boxes. At first, infants primarily direct nonsymbolic play actions to single objects, but soon relate objects to one another, for example placing objects onto or into other objects. Despite the exquisite specificity seen in infant object manipulation, as described previously, researchers of play sometimes consider infants' initial object combinations to be random: An infant might put a plate on top of a cup, or a cup inside a toy truck. With experience and motor skill, infants gradually combine objects in the ways that objects were intentionally designed. Thus, infants transition from what has (inappropriately) been referred to as "inappropriate object combinations" toward combinations based on perceptual similarities and functional relations – fitting lids on teapots and blocks into shape sorters (Belsky & Most, 1981; Bornstein & Tamis-LeMonda, 2006; Damast, Tamis-LeMonda, & Bornstein, 1996). As infants combine and fit objects, they acquire critical knowledge about spatial relations, including concepts around object support (a block can rest on a larger block) and containment (a cup can nest in a larger cup) (Casasola, 2017).

Again, a solely cognitive focus on play development, to the exclusion of considering motor skill, has led to shortfalls in how researchers assess nonsymbolic play behaviors. Typically, the infant's presumed intention rather than success at implementation reigns most central. So, for example, an infant who attempts to fit blocks into a shape sorter would be coded as playing nonsymbolically, whether or not the infant succeeded at inserting the shapes. Even something as seemingly straightforward as creating 3-D designs with blocks such as Duplo requires much more than spatial-cognitive know-how about where to place the bricks in replicating simple designs. Infants must twist their hands and hold a Duplo brick just so, align the studs of one brick with the holes of another, and press down with sufficient force to ensure interlocking (Kaplan et al., 2018). The perceptual and biomechanic requirements involved in implementing the designed actions of many toys explains why it takes months and even years for children to transition from simply interlocking bricks to creating complex designs (Kaplan et al., 2018).

19.4.3 Symbolic Play

Around the start of the second year, object play grows in abstractness as infants move from sensorimotor exploration and functional, nonsymbolic actions to displaying their first acts of symbolic or pretend play. Infants shift from seemingly asking, "What can this object do?" to "projecting an imagined situation onto an actual one" (Lillard, 1993, p. 349; Lillard, 2015). As toddlers imbue objects with imagined characteristics and functions, play grows in complexity and symbolic demand. For example, infants who pretend to feed teddy transform their prior experiences at mealtime into an "as if" scenario (Fein, 1981; Garvey, 1990), reenacting the past in a nonliteral present context. In reality, there is no food, and teddy is an inanimate object. An infant who cups her hand to her ear, pretending to talk on a phone, has transformed her hand into an imagined object and created a scenario in which someone is speaking on the other end. In both instances, infants have entered the imagined plane of object use. Pretend play, therefore, is quite special. It reflects the child's understanding that actions with objects can be based on made-up situations that are separate from reality (Vygotsky, 1967).

Like all forms of play, symbolic play grows in complexity across development. The simple, fleeting bouts of early pretend play at the start of the second year evolve into lengthier, elaborated play scenes from the second through third years, as infants increasingly string actions together to create play scripts, extend their play from self-directed actions to other-directed actions – such as when a toddler feeds then burps a doll, lays a doll on a pillow, and pats a doll to sleep – and begin to use objects to stand in for other objects.

Again, however, studies on symbolic play emphasize intention, rather than outcome or process, in line with the dominant cognitive foundation. Thus, unsuccessful attempts remain undistinguished from successful outcomes, overlooking how motor skills might contribute to implementation. For example, pretending to have a tea party requires fitting a lid squarely on top of a teapot, tipping the pot over at a specific angle without knocking the cup over, and stirring with a spoon without banging the cup's sides. Infants might be credited with "symbolic play" whether or not the teacup falls over during the pour or the stir.

19.5 Bridging the Divide: The Distancing of Object Interactions

There remains a curious disconnect between studies of infant object manipulation, guided by a perception–action framework, and studies of infant play, guided by a cognitive-developmental framework. The artificial divide lacks ecological validity and falls short of capturing changes in what infants do with objects on a regular basis. Infants explore objects, discover how to use objects in the ways they were designed, and then flexibly extend objects to novel uses in planful ways, whether playing with toys or tools. Thus, "object manipulation" and "toy play" offer complementary perspectives to identifying the mechanisms that underlie how infants engage with their physical environments. As infants move from real to imagined planes in their interactions with objects, they display increased *distancing* – from the concrete properties of objects, from the self, and in time and space.

19.5.1 Distancing from the Self

Infants initially direct actions to the self, and then extend actions to other people and inanimate objects such as stuffed animals. Distancing from the self extends to everyday object manipulation, tool use, and pretend play. Changes in motor and cognitive skills enable these developments. Specifically, the perception–action demands involved in directing an action toward oneself differ from those required when acting toward others. For example, tying your own shoelaces is a lot easier than tying the laces of someone else. Likewise, it is easier for infants to feed themselves than to feed someone else. That's because although infants learn to correctly orient a spoon to feed themselves, it takes several months for them to successfully modify their grip to orient the spoon to feed others. Similar advantages for self-directed relative to other-directed actions are evident when infants use other common tools (McCarty, Clifton, & Collard, 2001). Cognitive development, however, also contributes, as evidenced in the ability to anticipate which grips will be most comfortable given the goals of a task and as expressed vividly in the extension of pretend acts beyond the self.

Indeed, play's progression from self-to-other directed pretense exemplifies theories of cognitive decentering or distancing (Piaget, 1945; Werner & Kaplan, 1963). Infants direct their first pretend acts toward the self, often simulating their own activities, such as eating, drinking, and sleeping (Fenson & Ramsey, 1980). But several months later, infants pretend toward others, whether a caregiver, pet, or doll, with play becoming increasingly abstract and distanced from the child's own sensorimotor actions (McCune-Nicolich, 1981). For example, infants pretend to eat from a spoon or drink from a cup before they pretend to feed dad or teddy (Tamis-LeMonda & Bornstein, 1993, 1996). Still later, toddlers engage in vicarious forms of play, in which the "other" is not simply a passive recipient of actions, but instead is actively involved, such as when a toddler pretends a puppet is combing its own hair or talking on a phone (Fenson & Ramsay, 1980).

19.5.2 Distancing from the Functions of Objects

Manufactured objects are designed to serve specific purposes. Infants must learn the functions of objects and how to successfully implement them if they are to navigate a world brimming with cultural artifacts. After a prolonged period of exploration, as infants gain the perceptual and manual skills and know-how required to exploit the unique functions of objects, they increasingly use objects as manufacturers intended (Rachwani, Tamis-LeMonda, Lockman, Karasik, & Adolph, 2020). Infants use spoons to scoop up food, toothbrushes to clean teeth, and blocks to create towers. In some instances, however, the actions required to use the object as intended by manufacturers or by the everyday larger artifact culture that infants inhabit may not be transparent or immediately detectable. Consider containers with twist-off or pull-off lids. Infants may need to engage in exploration over an extended period of developmental time spanning the first few years until they routinely and effectively implement the required actions of stabilizing the base while twisting to the left (Rachwani et al., 2020).

Likewise, infants must also learn that objects can be used in novel ways to solve new problems. In essence, infants' actions with objects must flexibly move beyond the conventional uses of objects to identify alternative possibilities. This takes time. At first, infants rigidly adhere to the common functions of objects, in tool use and pretend play. In tool use, once infants discover how to use specific implements, they have difficulties considering alternative uses of the object, a phenomenon related to the concept of functional fixedness (Duncker, 1945). For example, when an experimenter encourages infants near a year of age to light up a box by inserting the long handle of a spoon into a hole, infants insist on grasping the spoon's handle as they would to eat, which prevents them from inserting the handle into the hole to illuminate the box. By 18 months of age, however, infants will flip the spoon around and insert the slim handle into the hole to accomplish the novel goal (Barrett, Davis, & Needham, 2007).

Pretend play likewise shifts from the use of objects as designed to using objects flexibly and imaginatively. For example, around the start of the second year, infants might pretend to drink tea from empty teacups, stir hot food in empty bowls, and put tired animals to sleep on miniature blankets. But, midway through the second year and into the third year, infants gain the representational insight that objects can stand for other things (DeLoache, 2004). Representational insight allows toddlers to creatively substitute objects for other objects – sticks and pencils can function as spoons to stir in empty cups, blocks can substitute as cars to be driven around the floor, and boxes can serve as cradles for dolls. That is, although pretending is initially tied to knowledge about what is typically done with specific objects, with age and cognitive advance, children distance themselves from concrete object functions to imagined ones (McCune-Nicolich, 1981). Later in development, around 3.5 years of age, children substitute objects that are highly dissimilar in shape and form for the objects that they are meant to replace, such as by using a shoe as a hammer or a softball as a pencil to write (Hopkins, Smith, Weisberg, & Lillard, 2016). Children's novel application of objects to purposes beyond the objects' intended design lies at the core of creativity and divergent thinking (Bruner, 1978).

19.5.3 Distancing in Time and Space

With development, infants grow in planning and prospective control, thereby distancing their actions in time and space. As reviewed previously, infants' growing abilities at visual and manual integration allow them to prospectively control their actions, as seen when infants alter the speed of arm approach and the shape of their hands before a grasp when reaching for objects of specific sizes and shapes, or when infants effectively change the orientation of their hands and objects as they relate objects to other objects. By the middle of the second year, infants begin to anticipate which grip will prove most effective for accomplishing a subsequent goal with a handheld object, even if that means initially grasping the object in a physically awkward manner (McCarty et al., 2001). And by 24 months, when presented with an object fitting task, children will pre-align the object even before it contacts the aperture, suggesting that they anticipate how the object must be oriented in order to solve the task (Jung, Kahrs, & Lockman, 2015, 2018). In short, during the first 2 years, infants become increasingly better at planning manual actions with objects that extend beyond the here and now, and beyond immediately available information.

In play, planning develops as well. During nonsymbolic play, infants visually search for the next block once they have fitted a prior block, seemingly planning the next step in ways that extend their bouts of play. In symbolic play, sequenced actions that follow a logical order indicate that toddlers are laying out a pretend story not yet evident in the context-dependent, single acts of pretense seen at the start of the second year. That is, 1-year-olds will act on whatever objects are available, often serendipitously stumbling upon objects for play, perhaps pretending to pour from a toy teapot, or drink from an empty toy cup, or stir in a toy bowl in front of them. Notably, however, each pretend action occurs largely in isolation of the next. There is no evidence that the infant has a plan in mind about how the story will go.

Several months later, between 18 months and 2 years of age, infants logically combine actions in sequence, indicating their planning verbally and through search behaviors. For example, a child might pretend to eat from a bowl, and then remark "mommy spoon" while searching for another spoon to feed mommy, or even without speaking a word, the infant will persist in trying to find another spoon to permit the story's continuity. The child's verbal and search behaviors suggest that the child has mentally constructed a pretend story *before* acting, rather than simply acting on whatever object happens to be nearby (McCune-Nicolich, 1981).

Notably, prospective control and planning likely work together to support increasingly longer bouts of play across early development. Improvements in prospective control allow infants to more effectively manipulate and interact with objects, making it unlikely that the infant will tip a teapot while placing a lid on top. Successful implementation, then, might support sustained pretend play. A cup that falls over during stirring might interrupt the play flow in ways that limit the episode to a single action rather a string of smoothly executed actions – stirring, pouring, drinking, pouring again, and so forth. Whether and how developments in motor skill work in concert with developments in symbolic understanding to facilitate the length and complexity of play remains an open question.

19.6 Social Influences on Object Manipulation and Play

Developments in brain and body, together with infants' experiences interacting with hundreds of objects over the course of a day, contribute to changes in infant object manipulation and play over the first years of life. But, infants' experiences with objects largely depend on social input and opportunities. That is, caregivers guide what infants do with objects, when, where, and with whom. And, adults serve as models who interact with hundreds of objects over the course of a day, offering infants opportunities to watch what can be done with specific objects. Thus, developments in object manipulation and play cannot be divorced from social life or the home environment in which children develop. In fact, Vygotsky observed that in the context of joint activity with a caregiver, young children begin to master skills that they would be unable to perform independently. And, decades of research on object manipulation and play confirm that experienced members of the culture bridge or scaffold young children's skills. Over time, children internalize what they've learned through their interactions with caregivers until they are able to perform a particular action on their own.

19.6.1 Scaffolding of Infant Object Manipulation

The theoretical accounts of Piaget and the Gibsons largely neglected the contribution of caregivers to the development of infants' sensorimotor or perception–action skills. Indeed, caregivers' contributions to the development of object manipulation have been sorely underestimated (Lockman & McHale, 1989). In Western cultures at least, caregivers often demonstrate to infants how to handle and explore objects and they manipulate objects with their infants in targeted ways. In essence, caregivers act like a coach. To illustrate, when properties such as color, texture, and sound potential are systematically varied across objects, allowing clear conclusions about the appropriateness of action, mothers not only demonstrate actions that are tailored to those object properties, but jointly perform the relevant actions with their 6- to 10-month-old infants (Lockman & McHale, 1989). Other investigators have likewise observed that caregivers often exaggerate their actions – such as through greater amplitude and more frequent repetitions of actions – when showing an object to their infants as compared to familiar adults (Brand, Baldwin, & Ashburn, 2002). Such infant-directed action, often referred to as "motionese," enhances attention and exploration of objects by 8- to 10-month-old infants (Koterba & Iverson, 2009). Thus, infants have opportunities to hone their object manipulation skills by watching and jointly interacting with others.

19.6.2 Scaffolding of Infant Play

Although parents and other caregivers have often been neglected in the study of object manipulation, parents' role in infant play has been the focus of study for several decades. Parents introduce objects for play and model play for children (Bornstein & Tamis-LeMonda, 1995); contingently respond to infants' object play by naming, describing, and talking about actions and object functions (Bornstein, Tamis-LeMonda, Hahn, & Haynes, 2008; Tamis-LeMonda, Kuchirko, & Tafuro, 2013); and verbally elaborate on and encourage exploration, nonsymbolic and symbolic actions in their infants (Bretherton, 1984; Damast et al., 1996; Quinn et al., 2018). Furthermore, the mere presence of an adult during play allows infants to embellish storylines in new ways, such as by extending actions with objects from self to other when pretending to feed mommy after feeding teddy.

Parents' keen attunement to the play skills of their infants makes them especially effective play partners. When mothers and infants play with toys, mothers' play actions closely correspond to those of their infants. Mothers' nonsymbolic play acts relate to toddlers' nonsymbolic acts, and mothers' symbolic play acts relate to infants' symbolic play acts, with associations seen at the transition to symbolic play (13 months) and midway through the second year when symbolic play is frequent (20 months) (Tamis-LeMonda & Bornstein, 1991). Furthermore, analysis of the real-time unfolding of dyadic play shows that mothers respond within 3 seconds of infant behaviors, recommending play at levels that match or are slightly more advanced than infants' play actions. But, mothers rarely suggest lower levels of play to their infants, such as prompting exploration to a child who is pretending (Damast et al., 1996). The temporal attunement of mother–infant play in real time cuts across age. Over the course of infants' second year of life, mothers shift to more advanced forms of symbolic play in line with their infants' growing skills (Haight & Miller, 1993; Tamis-LeMonda and Bornstein, 1991).

As infant–mother dyads participate in symbolic play in particular, they engage in frequent joint engagement and verbal and nonverbal forms of communication (Quinn & Kidd, 2018). Compared to nonsymbolic play, infants and mothers display high rates of iconic/representational gestures, like cupping the hand to represent a cup, and similarly low levels of deictic gestures such as pointing during symbolic play (Quinn & Kidd, 2018).

Additionally, mothers deploy a variety of behaviors to scaffold infants' understanding that they are merely "pretending." For example, when researchers instructed mothers to interact with their 18-month-old infants in real and pretend activities such as grooming and eating, mothers displayed distinct behaviors during pretend activities versus actual activities, even though the content of the activities was identical: they looked at infants more, used more words, sound effects, prolonged actions such as holding a hand to the mouth for an exaggerated period while eating, and engaged in more frequent and longer "social referencing smiles," likely to communicate that the infant should not take the activity seriously (Lillard, 2007, 2011; Lillard et al., 2007).

Infants, in turn, benefit from the responsive attunement and social inputs that mothers provide during play. Infants look at objects longer during bouts when their mothers touch and talk about objects than during bouts when mothers do not get involved (Yu & Smith, 2016). Mothers also scaffold infants to higher levels of play, with infants engaging in more frequent and sophisticated forms of symbolic play, including more object substitutions and longer bouts of symbolic play in the presence of their mothers than when playing alone (e.g., Belsky and Most 1981; Bretherton, O'Connell, Shore, & Bates, 1984; Campbell et al., 2018; Fein, 1981; Fiese, 1990; Haight & Miller, 1992; Lillard, 2007; O'Connell & Bretherton, 1984; Slade, 1987).

19.7 Cultural Variation

Most of what is known about infant object manipulation and play is based on families from WEIRD cultures (Western, educated, industrialized, rich, democracies). However, the process by which skills are socially transmitted from more to less experienced individuals may vary from culture to culture and even within a culture. Cultural norms or beliefs about infant development shape how often, for example, parents jointly manipulate objects or participate in play with their infants, thereby establishing different social contexts for learning. In some cultures, caregivers engage in overt pedagogy, whereas in others, caregivers expect infants and young children to learn through observation (Rogoff et al., 1993). In some cultures, manufactured toys are rare, and in others, it can be challenging to get around without stumbling across an object for play. Yet, the narrow, convenience sampling of developmental research leaves relatively unexamined the characteristics of infant object manipulation and play across cultural communities that differ in beliefs and practices.

19.7.1 Cultural Differences in Caregiver Play Participation

Parents vary considerably in their perceptions of play, the value they place on play, and how often they play with their infants (Fogle & Mendez, 2006; LaForett & Mendez, 2017), with much variation explained by cultural norms and expectations. In US Caucasian families, many parents consider themselves to be play partners to infants, until siblings and peers take over when children are around 3 to 4 years of age (Lillard, 2015). Parents' belief in the educational benefits of play and their ability to impact children's learning helps account for their frequent encouragement and modeling of play.

However, parents in many communities – as observed in certain regions in Mexico, Guatemala, Indonesia, and in hunter-gatherer and agricultural villages – view play as solely for a child's amusement, rather than a vehicle for learning, and do not think that it is appropriate for adults to engage in play with their children (Edwards & Whiting, 1993; Farver & Howes, 1993; Farver & Wimbarti, 1995; Power, 2000; Rogoff, Mistry, Göncü, Mistry, & Mosier, 1991; Rogoff et al., 1993). As a result, sibling caregiving is common, even at very young ages (Hrdy, 2009; Weisner, 1987).

19.7.2 Cultural Differences in Object Interactions

Cultural communities also differ in *how* parents play with their infants in the context of object play. For example, when researchers compared mother–toddler play in US middle-income families to a non-Western indigenous community of Ni-Van caregivers from Vanuatu, they found that Ni-Van caregivers displayed less visual attention to their infants' faces than did US mothers, but greater physical touch. During play, Ni-Van caregivers coordinated their touching of objects with touching of their toddlers and did so without looking to one another's faces (Little, Carver, & Legare, 2016).

19.7.3 Cultural Differences in Materials for Play

Finally, cultures differ in the physical materials available for infant play. Infants from different cultural communities encounter and interact with different types of objects, which then affects their learning and expectations about object functions. For example, 8-month-old Chinese but not Swedish infants visually anticipate the goal of feeding actions with chopsticks (Green, Li, Lockman, & Gredebak, 2016), suggesting that object-goal knowledge is already becoming culturally specific early in the second half year. Presumably, such differences would also be evident during object manipulation, although cultural studies on this issue remain scarce.

Materials for everyday play differ across cultural communities as well. Most infants in the United States have access to many toys, and parents commonly play with their infants using replica objects, such as miniature cups, trucks, furniture, and so forth (Lillard, 2011). Toys cover the floors or walls of even common spaces like living rooms, dens, kitchens, and dining rooms. Toys are likewise pervasive in other countries, such as Taiwan (Gaskins, Haight, & Lancy, 2007).

However, infants often play with objects other than toys. As infants navigate their environments, they encounter dozens of objects along the way, pausing to play for a few seconds, and sometimes several minutes with whatever is available – small and large household objects, food, clothes, and so forth (Orit et al., 2018). In communities where toys are largely absent, rocks, sticks, flowers, pots, and empty water bottles serve as play objects (Karasik, Schneider, Kurchirko, & Tamis-LeMonda, 2018). Cultural differences in the availability of objects for play affect the types of play infants display and even the complexity of play (Gaskins et al., 2007; Lillard, 2015). However, cultural descriptions of infant play in the natural home environments are rare, and questions on how play partners and materials intersect with object manipulation and play development remain largely unanswered.

As a cautionary note, cultural differences are often conflated with differences in family socioeconomic status (SES), which might also influence the materials available to infants, caregivers' time for play and views around play, and thus the frequency and quality of infant object manipulation and play. When high- and low-SES infants in the United States are compared on their object manipulation and exploration skills, infants in the second half year from high- relative to low-SES households in the United States show more complex forms of object manipulation, including more transferring and rotating of objects and more selective forms of object-surface exploration (Clearfield, Bailey, Jenne, Stanger & Tacke, 2014; Tacke, Bailey, & Clearfield, 2015). These studies help to illuminate the processes that underlie the effects of poverty on early perception and cognition and suggest avenues for intervention, as discussed next.

19.8 Practice and Policy Directions

Interactions with objects provide opportunities for infants to learn about themselves and the world – how objects work, what can be done with objects, how to create pretend stories, and even the words that map onto objects and actions. Still, parents, educators, and policy makers may be unaware of the benefits of object manipulation and play for learning. Furthermore, adults often wonder about how much they should involve themselves in play, and which types of toys they should purchase to maximize their infants' interest and learning. In particular, messages about the importance of play sometimes fail to reach families who are most in need of support. In this final section, we suggest directions for programming and policy that should be incorporated into public campaigns, parenting workshops, parenting programs, early interventions, and federally funded curricula for infants and toddlers, such as Early Head Start.

19.8.1 Working with Parents

Parent–infant play promotes learning. Yet, infants also learn a lot through independent exploration and play, including how to control their body and actions and the types of actions that objects afford. So, how much should parents involve themselves in infant object manipulation and play, and when should they get involved? Balance is key. Parents cannot always stop what they are doing to interact with their infants around objects, and so messages to parents should include when infants might need assistance and guidance and when they should be left to explore independently. In many situations, parents should do no more than allow infants to navigate their environments safely. Yet, parents can also scaffold infant object engagement and play, including guiding infants around how to use objects and co-constructing pretend and elaborated stories through prompts, demonstrations, turn-taking, and hands-on participation.

Indeed, interventions around object manipulation and play have long been shown to foster motor, language, and cognitive development in infants. Historically, federal programs such as Head Start and home-based interventions recognized interactive object exploration and play as a primary source of support for infant learning in both typically developing and high-risk infants (e.g., Field, 1983; Scarr-Salapatek and Williams, 1973). And, a 2-week intervention aimed at helping parents from lower SES households explore objects in targeted ways with their infants led to sustained improvements in infant object manipulation weeks after the intervention ended (Clearfield, 2019). Additionally, interventions aimed at promoting playful interactions between parents and toddlers during block play resulted in greater vocabulary growth in children in a treatment compared to control group of toddlers (Christakis, Zimmerman, & Garrison, 2007).

However, it is insufficient to merely educate parents on the importance of infant object manipulation and play. Rather, parents must be aware of the ingredients to productive interactions, including the value of hands-on learning and the types of objects that facilitate discovery and learning. Unfortunately, the current toy market contains many popular toys with unnecessary bells and whistles. These enticing toys can be deceiving: Infants' initial attraction does little to scaffold learning and may in fact interfere with the imaginative plane of play. Moreover, adult guidance decreases in the context of electronic toy play.

Adults display fewer bouts of pretense and elaboration (Bergen, Hutchinson, Nolan, & Weber, 2009), lower responsiveness to children's bids (Wooldridge & Shapka, 2012), fewer references to spatial concepts (Zosh et al., 2015), and less parent–child discussion during play with electronic toys than with non-electronic counterparts (Parish-Morris, Mahajan, Hirsh-Pasek, Golinkoff, & Collins, 2013). Because the digital media and electronic landscape will continue to expand over the future years, parents should be educated on ways to use such toys responsibly (Dore, Zosh, Hirsh-Pasek, & Golinkoff, 2017). Furthermore, parents should be aware of how much infants learn through interactions with everyday objects. Indeed, the imaginative potential of object play can expand when toddlers are allowed to create new affordances out of regular materials. Cross-cultural studies serve as a reminder that infants find ways to play with whatever is available – boxes, empty containers, and keys.

19.8.2 Working with Educators

Play is disappearing from preschool and kindergarten classrooms. Play in infant/toddler daycare and programs might soon diminish as well. A comparison of two nationally representative data sets, one from 1998 and another from 2010, found that Kindergarten classrooms increasingly resembled older elementary classrooms: Standardized assessments grew as activities around arts, music, and play declined (Bassok, Latham, & Rorem, 2016). Often, teachers choose "learning" over play due to performance pressures, an orientation that is erroneously grounded in the idea that play and learning are incompatible (Tamis-LeMonda & Schatz, 2019).

Although educational play curricula are rarely studied in infancy and toddlerhood, research with young children shows that "guided play" offers a promising approach for teaching children foundational school-relevant skills (Weisberg, Hirsh-Pasek, Golinkoff, Kittredge, & Klahr, 2016). Guided play curricula encourage children to express their autonomy and curiosity by initiating play, as teachers or parents follow, lead, offer structured feedback, and introduce materials in a game-like fashion (e.g., Alfieri, Brooks, Aldrich, & Tenenbaum, 2011; Fisher, Hirsh-Pasek, Newcombe, & Golinkoff, 2013; Morris, Croker, Zimmerman, Gill, & Romig, 2013). Play-based curricula include *Tools of the Mind* (Bodrova & Leong, 2015), Montessori (Lillard, 2013), and guided play (Weisberg et al., 2016), which commonly recognize that children learn *through* play, not outside play.

19.8.3 Working with Practitioners

Finally, research on interventions to promote early object manipulation and play in children with typical development holds promise for improving outcomes in infants and young children who face motor challenges. Research on pre-reaching infants with typical development suggests that the use of "sticky mittens" (mittens covered with Velcro) for 10 minutes a day over a 2-week period at 3 months of age facilitates immediate grasping and exploration of objects (Needham, Barrett, & Peeterman, 2002) and leads to more advanced forms of object exploration and play 1 year later at 15 months (Libertus, Joh, & Needham, 2016). The sticky-mitten manipulation mirrors a growing trend in the pediatric rehabilitation sciences involving the use of wearables – clothing or devices that can be worn for an extended period of time – to deliver experience and/or increase the likelihood that young children will obtain needed experience to promote development (Lobo et al., 2019). At the same time, the use of wearables can enable researchers to address fundamental questions about how the dosing, timing, and delivery of experience affects the development of action-based skills, including object manipulation and play (Heathcock & Lockman, 2019).

19.9 Conclusions

Infant object manipulation and infant play have remained siloed domains of inquiry, despite being two sides of the same coin. Object manipulation and play reflect common developments in perception–action, cognitive, and neural domains that allow infants to display increased *distancing* – from the self, from the conventional use of objects, and in time and space. Moreover, object manipulation and play unfold in sociocultural contexts that determine which objects are available to infants, how caregivers interact with infants around objects, and what object-specific actions infants acquire. Theoretical and empirical integration of the object manipulation and play literatures can generate new knowledge about how infants act on objects in real and imagined planes, while informing translational efforts to benefit children and families.

References

Alfieri, L., Brooks, P. J., Aldrich, N. J., & Tenenbaum, H. R. (2011). Does discovery-based instruction enhance learning? *Journal of Educational Psychology, 103*(1), 1–18.

Barrett, T. M., Davis, E. F., & Needham, A. (2007). Learning about tools in infancy. *Developmental Psychology, 43*(2), 352–368.

Barrett, T. M., & Needham, A. (2008). Developmental differences in infants' use of an object's shape to grasp it securely. *Developmental Psychobiology, 50*(1), 97–106.

Bassok, D., Latham, S., & Rorem, A. (2016). Is kindergarten the new first grade? *AERA Open, 1*(4), 1–31.

Belsky, J., & Most, R. K. (1981). From exploration to play: A cross-sectional study of infant free play behavior. *Developmental Psychology, 17*(5), 630–639.

Bergen, D., Hutchinson, K., Nolan, J. T., & Weber, D. (2009). Effects of infant–parent play with a technology-enhanced toy: Affordance-related actions and communicative interactions. *Journal of Research in Childhood Education, 24*(1), 1–17.

Berthier, N. E., & Carrico, R. L. (2010). Visual information and object size in infant reaching. *Infant Behavior and Development, 33*(4), 555–566.

Bodrova, E., & Leong, D. J. (2015). Vygotskian and post-Vygotskian views on children's play. *American Journal of Play, 7*(3), 371–388.

Bornstein, M. H., & Tamis-LeMonda, C. S. (1995). Parent–child symbolic play: Three theories in search of an effect. *Developmental Review, 15*(4), 382–400.

Bornstein, M. H., & Tamis-LeMonda, C. S. (2006). Infants at play: Development, partners and functions. In A. Slater & M. Lewis (Eds.), *Introduction to Infant Development*. New York, NY: Oxford University Press.

Bornstein, M. H., Tamis-LeMonda, C. S., Hahn, C. S., & Haynes, O. M. (2008). Maternal responsiveness to young children at three ages: Longitudinal analysis of a multidimensional, modular, and specific parenting construct. *Developmental Psychology, 44*(3), 867–874.

Bourgeois, K. S., Khawar, A. W., Neal, S. A., & Lockman, J. J. (2005). Infant manual exploration of objects, surfaces, and their interrelations. *Infancy, 8*(3), 233–252.

Brand, R. J., Baldwin, D. A., & Ashburn, L. A. (2002). Evidence for "motionese": Modifications in mothers' infant-directed action. *Developmental Science, 5*(1), 72–83.

Bretherton, I. (1984). Representing the social world in symbolic play: Reality and fantasy. In I. Bretherton (Ed.), *Symbolic play: The development of social understanding* (pp. 3–41). Orlando, FL: Academic Press.

Bretherton, I., O'Connell, B., Shore, C., & Bates, E. (1984). The effect of contextual variation on symbolic play development from 20 to 28 months. In I. Bretherton (Ed.), *Symbolic play: The development of social understanding* (pp. 271–298). Orlando, FL: Academic Press.

Bruner, J. (1978). The role of dialogue in language acquisition. In A. Sinclair, R. J. Jarville, & W. J. M. Levelt (Eds.), *The child's conception of language* (pp. 241–256). New York, NY: Springer.

Bushnell, E. W., & Boudreau, J. P. (1993). Motor development and the mind: The potential role of motor abilities as a determinant of aspects of perceptual development. *Child Development, 64*(4), 1005–1021.

(1998). Exploring and exploiting objects with the hands during infancy. In K. Connolly (Ed.), *The psychobiology of the hand* (pp. 144–161). Cambridge, UK: Mac Keith Press.

Campbell, S. B., Mahoney, A. S., Northrup, J., Moore, E. L., Leezenbaum, N. B., & Brownell, C. A. (2018). Developmental changes in pretend play from 22 to 34months in younger siblings of children with autism spectrum disorder. *Journal of Abnormal Child Psychology, 46*(3), 639–654.

Casasola, M. (2017). Above and beyond objects: The development of infants' spatial concepts. In J. B. Benson (Ed.), *Advances in child development and behavior* (Vol. 54, pp. 87–121). San Diego, CA: Elsevier Academic.

Christakis, D. A., Zimmerman, F. J., & Garrison, M. M. (2007). Effect of block play on language acquisition and attention in toddlers: A pilot randomized controlled trial. *Archives of Pediatrics & Adolescent Medicine, 161*(10), 967–971.

Clearfield, M. W. (2019). Play for success: An intervention to boost object exploration in infants from low-income households. *Infant Behavior and Development*, 55, 112–122.

Clearfield, M. W., Bailey, L. S., Jenne, H. K., Stanger, S. B., & Tacke, N. (2014). Socioeconomic status affects oral and manual exploration across the first year. *Infant Mental Health Journal*, 35(1), 63–69.

Corbetta, D., Thelen, E., & Johnson, K. (2000). Motor constraints on the development of perception–action matching in infant reaching. *Infant Behavior and Development*, 23(3–4), 351–374.

Damast, A. M., Tamis-LeMonda, C. S., & Bornstein, M. H. (1996). Mother–child play: Sequential interactions and the relation between maternal beliefs and behaviors. *Child Development*, 67(4), 1752–1766.

DeLoache, J. S. (2004). Becoming symbol-minded. *Trends in Cognitive Sciences*, 8(2), 66–70.

Dore, R. A., Zosh, J. M., Hirsh-Pasek, K., & Golinkoff, R. M. (2017). Plugging into word learning: the role of electronic toys and digital media in language development. In F. C. Blumberg & P. J. Brooks (Eds.), *Cognitive development in digital contexts* (pp. 75–91). Orlando, FL: Academic Press.

Duncker, K. (1945). On problem-solving. *Psychological Monographs*, 58(5), i–113.

Edwards, C. P., & Whiting, B. B. (1993). Mother, older sibling, and me": The overlapping roles of caregivers and companions in the social world of two- to three-year-olds in Ngeca, Kenya. In K. MacDonald (Ed.), *Parent–child play: Descriptions and implications* (pp. 305–329). Albany: State University of New York Press.

Fagard, J., & Jacquet, A. Y. (1996). Changes in reaching and grasping objects of different sizes between 7 and 13 months of age. *British Journal of Developmental Psychology*, 14(1), 65–78.

Farver, J. M., & Howes, C. (1993). Cultural differences in American and Mexican mother–child pretend play. *Merrill-Palmer Quarterly (1982–)*, 39(3), 344–358.

Farver, J. A., & Wimbarti, S. (1995). Indonesian children's play with their mothers and older siblings. *Child Development*, 66(5), 1493–1503.

Fein, G. G. (1981). Pretend play in childhood: An integrative review. *Child Development*, 52(4), 1095–1118.

Fenson, L., & Ramsay, D. S. (1980). Decentration and integration of the child's play in the second year. *Child Development*, 51(1), 171–178.

Field, T. (1983). High-risk infants "have less fun" during early interactions. *Topics in Early Childhood Special Education*, 3(1), 77–87.

Fiese, B. H. (1990). Playful relationships: A contextual analysis of mother–toddler interaction and symbolic play. *Child Development*, 61(5), 1648–1656.

Fisher, K. R., Hirsh-Pasek, K., Newcombe, N., & Golinkoff, R. M. (2013). Taking shape: Supporting preschoolers' acquisition of geometric knowledge through guided play. *Child Development*, 84(6), 1872–1878.

Fogle, L. M., & Mendez, J. L. (2006). Assessing the play beliefs of African American mothers with preschool children. *Early Childhood Research Quarterly*, 21(4), 507–518.

Fontenelle, S. A., Kahrs, B. A., Neal, S. A., Newton, A. T., & Lockman, J. J. (2007). Infant manual exploration of composite substrates. *Journal of Experimental Child Psychology*, 98(3), 153–167.

Garvey, C. (1990). *Play* (Vol. 27). Cambridge, MA: Harvard University Press.

Gaskins, S., Haight, W., & Lancy, D. F. (2007). The cultural construction of play. In A. Göncü & S. Gaskins (Eds.), *Play and development: Evolutionary, sociocultural, and functional perspectives* (pp. 179–202). Mahwah, NJ: Lawrence Erlbaum Associates.

Gesell, A., & Thompson, H.(1934). *Infant behavior: Its genesis and growth.* New York, NY: Greenwood Press.

Gibson, E. J. (1982). The concept of affordances in development: The renascence of functionalism. In W. A. Collins (Ed.), *The concept of development: The Minnesota symposia on child psychology* (Vol. 15, pp. 55–81). Mahwah, NJ: Lawrence Erlbaum Associates.

Gibson, E. J., & Pick, A. D. (2000). *An ecological approach to perceptual learning and development.* New York, NY: Oxford University Press.

Gibson, J. J. (1966). *The senses considered as perceptual systems.* Boston, MA: Houghton Mifflin.

(1979). *The ecological approach to visual perception.* Boston, MA: Houghton Mifflin.

Gillespie, A., & Zittoun, T. (2010). Using resources: Conceptualizing the mediation and reflective use of tools and signs. *Culture & Psychology, 16*(1), 37–62.

Green, D., Li, Q., Lockman, J. J., & Gredebäck, G. (2016). Culture influences action understanding in infancy: Prediction of actions performed with chopsticks and spoons in Chinese and Swedish infants. *Child Development, 87*(3), 736–746.

Haight, W. L., & Miller, P. J. (1992). The development of everyday pretend play: A longitudinal study of mothers' participation. *Merrill-Palmer Quarterly (1982–), 38*, 331–349.

(1993). *Pretending at home: Early development in a sociocultural context.* Albany, NY: State University of New York Press.

Heathcock, J. C., & Lockman, J. J. (2019). Infant and child development: Innovations and foundations for rehabilitation. *Physical Therapy, 99*, 643–646. https://doi .org/10.1093/ptj/pzz067

Hoff, E. (2013). *Language development.* Belmont, CA: Wadsworth Cengage Learning.

Hopkins, E. J., Smith, E. D., Weisberg, D. S., & Lillard, A. S. (2016). The development of substitute object pretense: The differential importance of form and function. *Journal of Cognition and Development, 17*(2), 197–220.

Hrdy, S. B. (2009). *The woman that never evolved.* Cambridge, MA: Harvard University Press.

Jeannerod, M. (1988). *The neural and behavioural organization of goal-directed movements.* New York, NY: Clarendon Press/Oxford University Press.

Jung, W. P., Kahrs, B. A., & Lockman, J. J. (2015). Manual action, fitting, and spatial planning: Relating objects by young children. *Cognition, 134*, 128–139.

(2018). Fitting handled objects into apertures by 17-to 36-month-old children: The dynamics of spatial coordination. *Developmental Psychology, 54*(2), 228–239.

Kahrs, B. A., Jung, W. P., & Lockman, J. J. (2013). Motor origins of tool use. *Child Development, 84*(3), 810–816.

(2014). When does tool use become distinctively human? Hammering in young children. *Child Development, 85*(3), 1050–1061.

Kaplan, B., Rachwani, J., Sida, A., Vasa, A., Tamis-LeMonda, C. S., & Adolph, K. E. (2018, June). *Perceptual-motor exploration and problem solving: Learning to implement the designed action of Duplo bricks.* Paper presented at the International Congress on Infant Studies, Philadelphia, PA.

Karasik, L. B., Schneider, J. L., Kuchirko, Y. A. & Tamis-LeMonda, C. S. (2018, June). *Not so WEIRD object play in Tajikistan.* Paper presented at the International Congress on Infant Studies, Philadelphia, PA.

Koterba, E. A., & Iverson, J. M. (2009). Investigating motionese: The effect of infant-directed action on infants' attention and object exploration. *Infant Behavior and Development, 32*(4), 437–444.

Kuypers, H. G. (1962). Corticospinal connections: postnatal development in the rhesus monkey. *Science, 138*(3541), 678–680.

LaForett, D. R., & Mendez, J. L. (2017). Children's engagement in play at home: A parent's role in supporting play opportunities during early childhood. *Early Child Development and Care, 187*(5–6), 910–923.

Lawrence, D. G., & Hopkins, D. A. (1972). Developmental aspects of pyramidal motor control in the rhesus monkey. *Brain Research, 40*, 117–118.

Lederman, S. J., & Klatzky, R. L. (1987). Hand movements: A window into haptic object recognition. *Cognitive Psychology, 19*(3), 342–368.

Leslie, A. M. (1987). Pretense and representation: The origins of "theory of mind." *Psychological Review, 94*(4), 412–426.

Libertus, K., Joh, A. S., & Needham, A. W. (2016). Motor training at 3 months affects object exploration 12 months later. *Developmental Science, 19*(6), 1058–1066.

Lillard, A. S. (1993). Pretend play skills and the child's theory of mind. *Child Development, 64*(2), 348–371.

(2007). Pretend play in toddlers. In C. Brownell & C. Kopp (Eds.), *Socioemotional development in the toddler years: Transitions and transformations* (pp. 149–176). New York, NY: Guilford Press.

(2011). Mother–child fantasy play. In P. Nathan & A. D. Pelligrini (Eds.), *The Oxford handbook of the development of play* (pp. 284–295). New York, NY: Oxford University Press.

(2013). Playful learning and Montessori education. *NAMTA Journal, 38*(2), 137–174.

(2015). The development of play volume. In R. M. Lerner (Ed.), *Handbook of child psychology and developmental science* (7th ed., Vol. 2, pp. 425–468). Hoboken, NJ: Wiley-Blackwell.

Lillard, A., Nishida, T., Massaro, D., Vaish, A., Ma, L., & McRoberts, G. (2007). Signs of pretense across age and scenario. *Infancy, 11*(1), 1–30.

Little, E. E., Carver, L. J., & Legare, C. H. (2016). Cultural variation in triadic infant–caregiver object exploration. *Child Development, 87*(4), 1130–1145.

Lobo, M., Hall, M. L., Greenspan, B., Rohloff, P., Prosser, L. A., & Smith, B. A. (2019). Wearables for pediatric rehabilitation: How to optimally design and use products to meet the needs of users. *Physical Therapy, 99*, 647–657. https://doi.org/10.1093/ptj/pzz024

Lockman, J. J. (2000). A perception–action perspective on tool use development. *Child development, 71*(1), 137–144.

Lockman, J. J., & Ashmead, D. H. (1983). Asynchronies in the development of manual behavior. *Advances in Infancy Research, 2*, 113–136.

Lockman, J. J., Ashmead, D. H., & Bushnell, E. W. (1984). The development of anticipatory hand orientation during infancy. *Journal of Experimental Child Psychology, 37*(1), 176–186.

Lockman, J. J., & Kahrs, B. A. (2017). New insights into the development of human tool use. *Current Directions in Psychological Science, 26*(4), 330–334.

Lockman, J. J., & McHale, J. P. (1989). Object manipulation in infancy. In J. J. Lockman & J. P. McHale (Eds.), *Action in social context* (pp. 129–167). New York, NY: Plenum.

Martin, J. C. (2005). The corticospinal system: From development to motor control. *Neuroscientist, 11*, 161–173.

Marzke, M. W. (1997). Precision grips, hand morphology, and tools. *American Journal of Physical Anthropology, 102*(1), 91–110.

McCarty, M. E., Clifton, R. K., & Collard, R. R. (2001). The beginnings of tool use by infants and toddlers. *Infancy, 2*(2), 233–256.

McCune, L. (1995). A normative study of representational play in the transition to language. *Developmental Psychology, 31*(2), 198–206. doi:10.1037/0012-1649.31.2.198

McCune-Nicolich, L. (1981). Toward symbolic functioning: Structure of early pretend games and potential parallels with language. *Child Development, 52*, 785–797. doi:10.2307/1129078

Milner, A. D., & Goodale, M. A. (1995). *The visual brain in action.* Oxford: Oxford University Press.

(2008). Two visual systems re-viewed. *Neuropsychologia, 46*(3), 774–785.

Molina, M., & Jouen, F. (1998). Modulation of the palmar grasp behavior in neonates according to texture property. *Infant Behavior and Development, 21*(4), 659–666.

Morgante, J. D., & Keen, R. (2008). Vision and action: The effect of visual feedback on infants' exploratory behaviors. *Infant Behavior and Development, 31*(4), 729–733.

Morris, B., Croker, S., Zimmerman, C., Gill, D., & Romig, C. (2013). Gaming science: The "Gamification" of scientific thinking. *Frontiers in Psychology, 4*, 1–16.

Napier, J. (1962). The evolution of the hand. *Scientific American, 207*(6), 56–65.

Needham, A., Barrett, T., & Peterman, K. (2002). A pick-me-up for infants' exploratory skills: Early simulated experiences reaching for objects using "sticky mittens" enhances young infants' object exploration skills. *Infant Behavior and Development, 25*(3), 279–295.

O'Connell, B., & Bretherton, I. (1984). Toddler's play, alone and with mother: The role of maternal guidance. In I. Bretherton (Ed.), *Symbolic play: The development of social understanding* (pp. 337–368). Orlando, FL: Academic Press.

Orr, E., & Geva, R. (2015). Symbolic play and language development. *Infant Behavior and Development, 38*, 147–161.

Palmer, C. F. (1989). The discriminating nature of infants' exploratory actions. *Developmental Psychology, 25*(6), 885–893.

Parish-Morris, J., Mahajan, N., Hirsh-Pasek, K., Golinkoff, R. M., & Collins, M. F. (2013). Once upon a time: Parent–child dialogue and storybook reading in the electronic era. *Mind, Brain, and Education, 7*(3), 200–211.

Piaget, J. (1945). *Play, dreams, and imitation in childhood.* New York, NY: Norton.

(1952). *The origins of intelligence in children.* New York, NY: W.W. Norton & Co.

(1954). *The construction of reality in the child* (M. Cook, Trans.). New York, NY: Basic Books.

Power, T. G. (2000). *Play and exploration in children and animals*. Mahwah NJ: Lawrence Erlbaum Associates.

Quinn, S., Donnelly, S., & Kidd, E. (2018). The relationship between symbolic play and language acquisition: A meta-analytic review. *Developmental Review, 49*, 121–135.

Quinn, S., & Kidd, E. (2018). Symbolic play promotes non-verbal communicative exchanges in infant–caregiver dyads. *British Journal of Developmental Psychology, 37*(1), 33–50.

Rachwani, J., Tamis-LeMonda, C. S., Lockman, J. J., Karasik, L. B., & Adolph, K. E. (2020). Learning the designed actions of everyday objects. *Journal of Experimental Psychology: General,* 149(1), 67–78. https://doi.org/10.1037/xge0000631

Rips, L. J., & Hespos, S. J. (2015). Divisions of the physical world: Concepts of objects and substances. *Psychological Bulletin, 141*(4), 786–811.

Rochat, P. (1989). Object manipulation and exploration in 2- to 5-month-old infants. *Developmental Psychology, 25*(6), 871–884.

Rogoff, B., Mistry, J., Göncü, A., & Mosier, C. (1991). Cultural variation in the role relations of toddlers and their families. In M. Bornstein (Ed.), *Cultural approaches to parenting* (pp. 173–183). Hillsdale, NJ: Lawrence Erlbaum Associates.

Rogoff, B., Mistry, J., Göncü, A., Mosier, C., Chavajay, P., & Heath, S. B. (1993). Guided participation in cultural activity by toddlers and caregivers. *Monographs of the Society for Research in Child Development*, i–179.

Ruff, H. A. (1984). Infants' manipulative exploration of objects: Effects of age and object characteristics. *Developmental Psychology, 20*(1), 9–20.

Scarr-Salapatek, S., & Williams, M. L. (1973). The effects of early stimulation on low-birth-weight infants. *Child Development*, 94–101.

Schum, N., Jovanovic, B., & Schwarzer, G. (2011). Ten- and twelve-month-olds' visual anticipation of orientation and size during grasping. *Journal of Experimental Child Psychology, 109*(2), 218–231.

Slade, A. (1987). Quality of attachment and early symbolic play. *Developmental Psychology, 23*(1), 78–85.

Smith, L. B., Street, S., Jones, S. S., & James, K. H. (2014). Using the axis of elongation to align shapes: Developmental changes between 18 and 24 months of age. *Journal of Experimental Child Psychology, 123*, 15–35.

Street, S. Y., James, K. H, Jones, S. S., & Smith, L. B. (2011). Vision for action in toddlers: The posting task. *Child Development, 82*, 2083–2094.

Striano, T., & Bushnell, E. W. (2005). Haptic perception of material properties by 3-month-old infants. *Infant Behavior and Development, 28*(3), 266–289.

Sutherland, S. L., & Friedman, O. (2013). Just pretending can be really learning: Children use pretend play as a source for acquiring generic knowledge. *Developmental Psychology, 49*(9), 1660–1668.

Tacke, N. F., Bailey, L. S., & Clearfield, M. W. (2015). Socio-economic status (SES) affects infants' selective exploration. *Infant and Child Development, 24*(6), 571–586.

Tamis-LeMonda, C. S., & Bornstein, M. H. (1991). Individual variation, correspondence, stability, and change in mother and toddler play. *Infant Behavior and Development, 14*(2), 143–162.

(1993). Play and its relations to other mental functions in the child. *New Directions for Child and Adolescent Development, 1993*(59), 17–28.

(1996). Variation in children's exploratory, nonsymbolic, and symbolic play: An explanatory multidimensional framework. In C. Rovee-Collier & L. P. Lipsitt (Ed.), *Advances in infancy research* (pp. 37–78). Westport, CT: Ablex.

Tamis-LeMonda, C. S., Kuchirko, Y., & Tafuro, L. (2013). From action to interaction: Infant object exploration and mothers' contingent responsiveness. *IEEE Transactions on Autonomous Mental Development, 5*(3), 202–209.

Tamis-LeMonda, C. S., & Schatz, J. (2019). Learning language in the context of play. In J. Horst, J. von Koss, & K. Torkildsen (Eds.) *International handbook of language development* (pp. 442–461). New York, NY: Routledge.

Uccelli, P., Hemphill, L., Pan, B. A., & Snow, C. (2006). Conversing with toddlers about the nonpresent: Precursors to narrative development in two genres. In L. Balter & C. S. Tamis-LeMonda (Eds.), *Child psychology: A handbook of contemporary issues* (pp. 215–237). New York, NY: Psychology Press.

Ungerleider, L. G., & Mishkin, M. (1982). Two cortical visual systems. Analysis of visual behavior. In D. J. Ingle, M. A. Goodale, & R. J. W. Mansfield (Eds.), *Analysis of visual behavior* (pp. 549–586). Cambridge, MA: MIT Press.

von Hofsten, C. (1983). Catching skills in infancy. *Journal of Experimental Psychology: Human Perception and Performance, 9*(1), 75–85.

(2007). Action in development. *Developmental Science, 10*(1), 54–60.

von Hofsten, C., & Fazel-Zandy, S. (1984). Development of visually guided hand orientation in reaching. *Journal of Experimental Child Psychology, 38*(2), 208–219.

von Hofsten, C., & Rönnqvist, L. (1988). Preparation for grasping an object: A developmental study. *Journal of Experimental Psychology: Human Perception and Performance, 14*(4), 610–621.

Vygotsky, L. S. (1967). Play and its role in the mental development of the child. *Soviet Psychology, 5*(3), 6–18.

Weisberg, D. S., Hirsh-Pasek, K., Golinkoff, R. M., Kittredge, A. K., & Klahr, D. (2016). Guided play: Principles and practices. *Current Directions in Psychological Science, 25*(3), 177–182.

Weisner, T. S. (1987). Socialization for parenthood in sibling caretaking societies. In J. Altmann (Ed.), *Parenting across the life span: Biosocial dimensions* (pp. 237–270). New York, NY: Routledge.

Welniarz, Q., Delsart, I., & Roze, E. (2017). The corticospinal tract: Evolution, development, and human disorders. *Developmental Neurobiology, 77*, 810–829.

Werner, H., & Kaplan, B. (1963). *Symbol formation.* Oxford: Wiley.

Witherington, D. (2005). The development of prospective grasping control between 5 and 7 months. *Infancy, 7*, 143–161.

Wolfe, S. W., Crisco, J. J., Orr, C. M., & Marzke, M. W. (2006). The dart-throwing motion of the wrist: is it unique to humans? *Journal of Hand Surgery, 31*(9), 1429–1437.

Wooldridge, M. B., & Shapka, J. (2012). Playing with technology: Mother–toddler interaction scores lower during play with electronic toys. *Journal of Applied Developmental Psychology, 33*(5), 211–218.

Yu, C., & Smith, L. (2016). The social origins of sustained attention in 1-year-old human infants. *Current Biology, 26*(9), R357–R359.

Zosh, J. M., Verdine, B. N., Filipowicz, A., Golinkoff, R. M., Hirsh-Pasek, K., & Newcombe, N. S. (2015). Talking shape: Parental language with electronic versus traditional shape sorters. *Mind, Brain, and Education, 9*(3), 136–144.

20 The Infant's Visual World

The Everyday Statistics for Visual Learning

Swapnaa Jayaraman and Linda B. Smith

The prowess of human vision is central to many domains of human intelligence (DiCarlo & Cox, 2007). We discriminate thousands of individual faces, recognize thousands of object categories, and excel under challenging visual conditions. We can become visual experts in recognizing birds, mathematical equations, art, and more. The developmental path to these achievements is protracted with mature levels of competence not fully reached until adolescence (Hadad, Maurer, & Lewis, 2011; Nishimura, Scherf, & Behrmann, 2009). The evidence also shows marked changes in infancy in the domains of face processing and object recognition. The evidence makes clear that visual experience itself is a significant driver of these changes (Maurer, Mondloch, & Lewis, 2007; Smith, 2009). A complete theory of learning in any domain requires an understanding of both the learning mechanisms and the experiences – the data – on which those mechanisms operate. Although much research is directed to determining the developing mechanisms, little has been directed to visual experience itself. Seminal research indicates that the changes in sensory-motor abilities in the first 2 years of postnatal life define a curriculum of changing visual tasks that spur developments in perception and cognition (Bertenthal, Campos, & Barrett, 1984; E. W. Bushnell & Boudreau, 1993; Iverson, 2010; Soska, Adolph, & Johnson, 2010). Accordingly, this chapter focuses on an emerging research that attempts to measure the natural statistics of infants' everyday visual environments and how they change with sensory-motor development.

20.1 Egocentric Vision

Considerable progress in understanding adult vision has been made by studying the visual properties of scenes represented by photographs of the natural (Geisler, 2008; Simoncelli, 2003) and artifact-filled (Brockmole & Henderson, 2006; Castelhano & Witherspoon, 2016; Im, Park, & Chong, 2015; Wolfe, Võ, Evans, & Greene, 2011) worlds. These studies analyze the statistical regularities in lower-level visual features such as spatial frequency, contrast, orientations, mid-level ensemble statistics, and higher-level contents such as object categories. The findings yield two general conclusions about mature visual prowess. First, the precision and sensitivity of adult visual processing from lower to higher levels in the visual system aligns closely to the regularities in these scenes (e.g., Geisler, 2008; Simoncelli, 2003). Second, adult visual attention, discrimination, and categorization exploit these predictive regularities to yield contextually nuanced visual intelligence that homes in on the relevant visual properties for specific tasks and context (Brockmole & Henderson, 2006; Wolfe et al., 2011). The photographs that are the bases for these analyses, however, are biased (Braddick & Atkinson, 2011; Smith, Yu, Yoshida, & Fausey, 2015) by a mature body and visual system that purposely holds the camera and selects the content and frames of the scene. What is needed to understand the visual statistics of everyday infant environments, given their bodies and sensory-motor abilities, are scenes captured from the developing infant's point of view (Franchak & Adolph, 2010; Smith, Yu, & Pereira, 2011; Yoshida & Smith, 2008; Yurovsky, Smith, & Yu, 2013).

Egocentric vision uses head cameras and head-mounted eye trackers to study vision from the perspective of freely moving individuals. Analyses of these first-person scenes show that the way people look at the world when they are moving and performing everyday tasks differs fundamentally from the way they take photographs and how they look at still images (Fathi, Ren, & Rehg, 2011; Foulsham, Walker, & Kingstone, 2011; Tatler, Hayhoe, Land, & Ballard, 2011). The rationale for an egocentric vision approach to studying infant visual environments is threefold (see Figure 20.1).

First, relevant visual information is not framed by a purposely held and still camera but is the image projected to the retina. This *proximal* image is determined by (1) the *intrinsic* properties of the to-be-perceived or *distal* object; and (2) *extrinsic* factors including the spatial relation of the object to the sensors, the nature of the illumination, and the journey taken by photons to reach the sensors. The most fundamental unsolved problem in all of human vision is how we perceive the intrinsic properties of the distal object as constant – a round cup is round – given the transformational effects of extrinsic factors on the retinal image. Developmental research on visual cognition has often skipped over this core problem to the higher-order tasks of discrimination and classification, and has used clean adult canonical images (an upright cup on a white background). But all vision begins with the image projected to the retina. Head-camera images capture a reasonable approximation (Yoshida & Smith, 2008) and force visual analyses to reckon with the extrinsic variability (Figure 20.1A). Second, an individual perceiver's view is highly selective. The bottle, the ball, and parts of the blocks and the car in Figure 20.1B are in the infant's view and are captured by the head camera. Many things in the room that are spatially near the infant – the dog, the train, her mother's face – are not in view unless the infant turns her head and looks. The perceiver's location, posture, and ability or motivation to change their posture systematically bias egocentric visual information. Third, if bodies, posture, and interests change with development, which they do, then the statistical regularities in

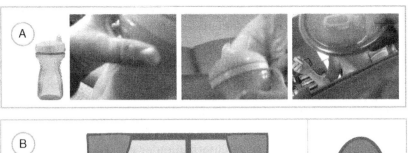

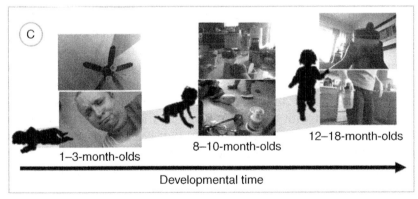

Figure 20.1. *An egocentric approach to the study of visual environments. (A) Canonical views of objects look different from egocentric views that more closely approximate the proximal images that fall on visual sensors. (B) Views of the environment are determined by the perceiver's location, posture, and motorical abilities. (C) Perceivers' views change systematically with development.*

the visual environment will also change. Each new sensory-motor achievement milestone – rolling over, reaching, crawling, walking, manipulating objects – opens and closes gates to specific visual experiences (Figure 20.1C). Newborns have limited vision and locomotion. Much of what they see depends on what caregivers put in front of and close to the infant's face, which is often their own face (Jayaraman, Fausey, & Smith, 2015, 2017; Sugden, Mohamed-Ali, & Moulson, 2014). An older crawling baby can see much further and can move to a distant object for a closer view. When moving, the crawler creates new patterns of dynamic visual information or optic flow (Gilmore, Baker, & Grobman, 2004; Higgins, Campos, & Kermoian, 1996) and sees only the floor. She actually has to stop crawling and sit up to see social partners (Franchak, Kretch, & Adolph, 2018). How do these egocentric experiences change and how do those changes inform visual development?

20.2 Biased Early Experiences

Human face perception is remarkable for its precision and for its relevance to species-important tasks (Haxby, Hoffman, & Gobbini, 2000). Although the exact mechanisms behind the development of face perception are still debated, it is understood that it develops over an extended period and is tuned by experience (Carey & Diamond, 1994; Gauthier & Tarr, 1997; Johnson & Morton, 1991; Kanwisher, 2000). The first 3 months of postnatal life appear especially important. At birth, infants show a bias towards high-contrast, low-spatial-frequency face-like patterns (Fantz, 1963; Johnson, Dziurawiec, Ellis, & Morton, 1991; Macchi, Turati, & Simion, 2004), which may be related to their nascent ocular structure that limits abilities to bring objects into focus (Dobson, Teller, & Belgum, 1978; Maurer & Lewis, 2001a, 2001b; Oruç & Barton, 2010). Despite these limitations, or perhaps partly because of them, infants during these first 3 months preferentially look at frontal views of faces close to their own and recognize and discriminate faces that are similar (in race, gender, age) to those of their caregivers (W. Bushnell, 2003; Pascalis et al., 2014; Scott, Pascalis, & Nelson, 2007; Scherf & Scott, 2012). Consistent with these early biases and learning, head-camera studies (Scherf & Scott, 2012; Sugden et al., 2014) of face experiences in everyday life indicate that infants primarily encounter faces that are frontal views, close, female, and of the same race as the infants themselves (Jayaraman et al., 2015; Sugden et al., 2014).

One series of studies is based on a large corpus of head-camera recordings of 51 infants (25 females) between the ages of 1 and 15 months (Fausey, Jayaraman, & Smith, 2016; Jayaraman et al., 2015, 2017; Jayaraman & Smith, 2018). Recordings of everyday scenes were collected as infants went about their daily activities with no experimenters present and in multiple locations (home, playground, store, church; see Jayaraman et al., 2015 for details of data collection). The average length of recordings from each infant was over 4 hours, resulting in a corpus of over 25 million frames.

Figure 20.2A shows the proportion of images in which a face was present as a function of the age of individual infants. For infants 3 months and younger, faces were present in over 15 minutes per recorded hour; for infants between 12 and 15 months, faces were present in only about 6 minutes per recorded hour. The face views for all infants were mostly frontal but views of younger infants featured more up-close faces (Jayaraman et al., 2015; see Figure 20.2B) that were also temporally more enduring (Jayaraman & Smith, 2018; see Figure 20.2C). In brief, the data for learning about faces appears to have unique properties – frequency, proximity, and duration – for infants 3 months of age and younger.

Studies of infants whose everyday visual experiences were disrupted by institutionalization or early visual problems suggest that observed natural statistics of early face experiences may be crucial to mature face processing (Maurer, 2017; Maurer et al., 2007; Moulson, Westerlund, Fox, Zeanah, & Nelson, 2009). Institutionalized infants who lacked typical exposure to caretakers show measurable oddities when tested for their neural responses to face stimuli (Moulson et al., 2009). Individuals with congenital cataracts that were removed between 4 to 6 months of age also lack typical early visual experiences and show permanent deficits in configural face processing (Maurer, 2017; Maurer et al., 2007). Configural face processing – the sensitivity to second-order relations that adults can use effectively only with upright faces, and only when low spatial frequencies are present – is a late-developing property of the human visual system, one that only emerges in childhood and is not fully mature until adolescence (Scherf & Scott, 2012). Thus, these deficits in early visual experience are characterized as "sleeper effects," a late-emerging consequence of much earlier sensory deprivation (Maurer et al., 2007).

Infants' early and apparently crucial experiences of faces are substantial *but not massive*. By the end of the first 3 months, using the estimates of 15 minutes of face time per hour and 12 waking hours a day, an infant would have experienced 270 hours of predominantly close frontal views of faces (Jayaraman et al., 2015). The consequences of missing these 270 hours of experience appear to be permanent deficits not counteracted by a lifetime of seeing faces. Thus, the first 3 months of postnatal life may be characterized as a sensitive period of development in which specific experiences have an outsized effect on long-term outcome. While sensitive periods may reflect fundamental changes in neural plasticity (Oakes, 2017), developmentally changing visual environments may also play a role. Infants with cataracts removed at 4 months may not "catch up" in face processing not solely because of limited neural plasticity but because they do not encounter the same structured data set: dense close frontal views of faces enduring in time, experiences dependent on the infant's own sensory-motor, cognitive, and emotional abilities and the caregiver behaviors they elicit.

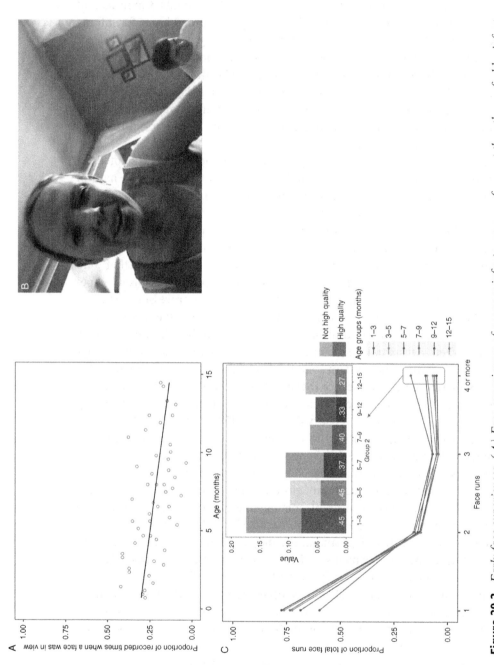

Figure 20.2. *Early face experiences. (A) Face experiences of younger infants are more frequent than those of older infants. (B) Younger infants predominantly experienced faces within 2 feet of the head camera. (C) Faces are temporally more enduring in the visual environments of younger infants.*

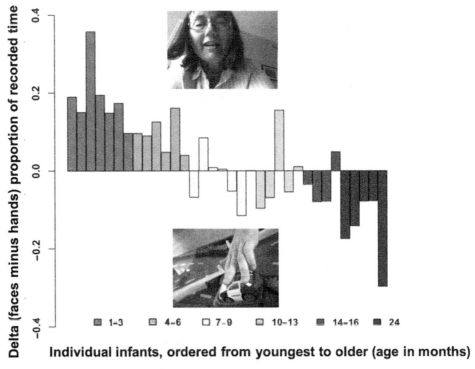

Figure 20.3. *Developmental transition from visual experiences dense in faces to those dense in hands.*

20.3 Developmentally Changing Content

The frequency of faces in infant egocentric images decreases with age, but the frequency of people does not. Other people's bodies are present in about 40% of head-camera images for all infants from birth to 24 months (Jayaraman et al., 2017). As shown in Figure 20.3, the developmental transition is from egocentric images with many faces to egocentric images with hands (Fausey et al., 2016). In 85% of all infant head cameras with hands in view, those hands are acting on objects – showing, giving, attaching, moving. The transition in scene content is thus from faces to hands acting on objects.

Before they are 6 months of age, infants show clear expectations about possible/typical versus impossible/atypical hand actions (Sommerville, Woodward, & Needham, 2005; Woodward, 1998). Older infants are highly sensitive to the causal and semantic structure of manual actions (Sommerville, Upshaw, & Loucks, 2012) and to how points, gestures, and manual actions guide visual attention to objects (e.g., Gogate, Bahrick, & Watson, 2000; Goldin-Meadow & Wagner, 2005; Yu & Smith, 2013). A growing body of findings indicates that infants' own hand actions play a key role in their understanding of others' actions (Brandone, 2015; Krogh-Jesperson & Woodward, 2018). This link is often viewed as interconnected neural representations for interpreting and performing actions and/or for building an understanding of intentions and goals (e.g., Falck-Ytter, Gredebäck, & von Hofsten, 2006; Flanagan & Johansson, 2003; Gerson, Meyer, Hunius, & Bekkering, 2017; Krogh-Jesperson & Woodward, 2018). But how could this work *visually*? From the egocentric view, images of one's own hand actions are very different from others (Bambach, Crandall, & Yu, 2015). One plausible hypothesis is that an infant's ability to perform a particular action invites others to jointly engage with objects (Striano & Reid, 2006) providing visual data from learning to match one's own hand actions to others. As infants' manual abilities become more sophisticated and their own hands appear more densely in view, so may the hands of others performing similar actions. This would provide direct visual evidence with regard to the common intrinsic properties of own versus other hand actions with the same purpose, and the visual basis for systematic expectations about others that are linked to one's own actions. The field's current understanding of these phenomena could benefit from the systematic study of visual experiences of hand actions "in the wild" of everyday life.

The developmental shift from a visual world dense in faces to one dense in hands seems highly relevant to social development. Very young infants follow another's gaze in highly restricted viewing contexts (e.g., Farroni, Johnson, Brockbank, & Simion, 2000; Farroni, Pividori, Simion, Massaccesi, & Johnson, 2004), but the spatial resolution of gaze following is often not sufficient for navigating real-time social interactions in more spatially complex social settings (e.g., Doherty, Anderson, & Howieson, 2009; Loomis, Kelly, Pusch, Bailenson, & Beall, 2008; Vida & Maurer, 2012; Yu & Smith, 2013). The *spatial* complexity explodes as infants become more physically active and transition from interactions dominated by face-to-face play to interactions dominated by shared engagement with objects (see Striano & Reid, 2006). One study using simultaneous head-mounted eye trackers worn by toddlers and parents (Yu & Smith, 2013) found that 1-year-old infants coordinated their own gaze with that of the parent, not by following parent eye gaze, but by fixating on parent hand movements to objects (to which parent eye gaze was also dynamically coordinated), perhaps reflecting a shift from faces to hands in social interactions and social competency.

All of this is the tip of a very large and likely important factor in development. Because of the marked changes in infant sensory-motor abilities, cognitive abilities, and behavior, there are likely major changes from low-level to high-level properties of visual experiences. Moreover, the hierarchical structure of the neural visual pathways (Figure 20.4) suggest that it is highly unlikely that a domain-specific experience will have strictly domain-specific consequences (e.g., Hochstein & Ahissar, 2002; Yamins & DiCarlo, 2016). Instead, early experiences of all kinds will tune processes at early layers that underlie all visual judgments. In this way, learning about faces and about *nonface object categories* will both depend on the precision, tuning, and activation patterns

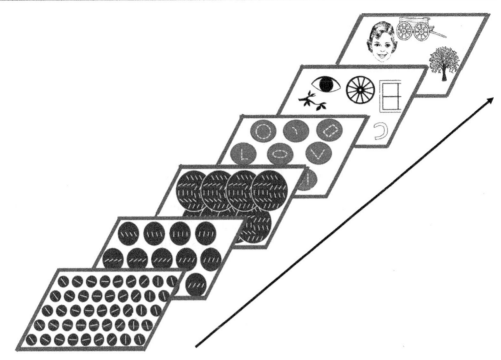

Figure 20.4. *A schematic of the cascade of feature abstraction in the human visual cortex, beginning with the spatially localized extraction of simple features in the lower layers and category-specific features and object categories in the upper layers.*

of the same lower layers. Simple visual discriminations at lower layers can have far-reaching generality across higher-level visual processes, and top-down connections between layers also drive lower changes that can affect processing across multiple domains (e.g., Ahissar & Hochstein, 1997; Cadieu et al., 2014).

Although Maurer et al. (2007) used the term "sleeper effects" to refer to *deficits* in experience, the role of early visual experience on later emerging achievements may be conceptualized both negatively and positively. Regularities in an individual's early experiences may set up potentially hidden competencies that are critical to and play out in later learning. For example, the precision of visual discrimination of dot arrays predicts later mathematics achievement (Halberda, Mazzocco, & Feigenson, 2008) and the shape bias in toddlers predicts the ability to learn letters (Augustine, Jones, Smith, & Longfield, 2015) and objects that comprise a category (Smith, 2005, 2009). The early layer representations formed in one task will be reused and in principle can influence – both negatively and positively – the solutions that are found in learning other tasks. The computational value of ordered training sets for such hierarchically layered learning systems is not yet well understood but is critical to a complete understanding of visual development.

20.4 Everyday Visual Tasks

Experiments, computational models, and machine learning see the problem of learning as one of classification and discrimination: Is this the face of person A or person B? Is this a cup, or a bowl, or a vase? Both models and experimental data suggest that the best training for this kind of learning consists of a uniform frequency distribution of many examples from many categories (e.g., Foody, McCulloch, & Yates, 1995; Perry, Samuelson Malloy, & Schiffer, 2010). However, an extensive literature (Clerkin, Hart, Rehg, Yu, & Smith, 2017; Montag, Jones, & Smith, 2018; Salakhutinov, Torralba, & Tenenbaum, 2011) shows that everyday learning environments are characterized by *skewed* frequency distributions in which a very few types (the mother's face, the sippy cups) are very frequent, but most types (all the different faces encountered at a grocery store, other cups in the cupboard) are encountered quite rarely. For example, in the visual world of infants dense with faces, just three individual faces account for over 95% of all face images (Jayaraman et al., 2015). This number declines only slightly to 80% for 1-year-old infants. From this highly selective and nonuniform sampling of faces, infants learn to recognize and discriminate faces in general. How does this work?

Distributions shaped like the one illustrated in Figure 20.5 emerge because our experiences – tied to our physical bodies and physical locations – are constrained by space and time: We do not discretely jump between contexts like randomized slides in an experiment but transition continuously between visual moments in a smoothly changing physical location. Given these physical constraints of space and time, the faces of family members and caregivers will account for most face experiences, the infant's favorite sippy cup will account for most cup experiences; the family dog will account for most dog experiences. Training expertise with a single object may well be the optimal start for human category learning. In an elegant series of experiments, Oakes and colleagues (Hurley & Oakes, 2015; Kovach-Lesh, Horst & Oakes, 2008; Kovack-Lesh, Oakes & McMurray, 2012) tested the ability of infants raised with and without a dog (or other pets) to recognize and discriminate different animal categories. The extensive visual experiences of infants with their own family dog was associated with advanced recognition of dogs in particular and advanced discrimination and categorization of *other* animals in general. The extensive experience with the proximal images of the dog under various conditions – up close, profile, in clutter, while running, in poor light, from seeing a shadow of the tail – has enabled recognition of the distal object (dog). Extremely skewed distributions with many different visual experiences of one or a very few instances may be optimal for solving this core problem.

Infants learn object names and object categories before they can actually say those names, before their first birthday (Bergelson & Swingley, 2012). How they do so is not clear as the everyday world is visually cluttered and viewing conditions are often far from optimal. The statistics of egocentric images

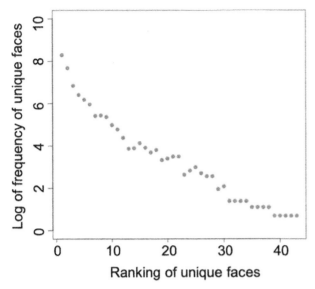

Figure 20.5. *The (log) frequency distribution of individual people's faces in infant head-camera images, ranked by appearance.*

of 8- to 10-month-old infants may hold the solution. Infants this age can sit steadily, even crawl, and play with objects, but their manual skills are quite limited compared to older infants. Neither faces nor hands acting on objects are statistically dominant in their images; instead, images contain a mixture of the various body parts of nearby people (Fausey et al., 2016; Jayaraman et al., 2017). Overall, these scenes are highly cluttered (Figure 20.6), containing many objects (Clerkin et al., 2017). However, a small number of object categories are pervasively present, with most object types being quite rare. Across similar contexts, such as mealtimes, very few objects (spoons, bottles) are repetitively present and many more objects (jugs, salad tongs, ketchup bottles) were present in only a very few scenes (Clerkin et al., 2017). The pervasive repetition of instances from a select set of categories could help infants to find and attend to those objects – even in clutter – and provide a foundation for linking those objects to their names.

20.5 Relevance to Developmental Neuroscience

Human perception, behavior, and cognition is the product of dynamic neural activity; that activity changes the microarchitecture at the local neural level and changes the changing brain connectivity as "both" cause and consequence of developmental changes in the brain and in behavior (Edelman, 1987; James, 2010; Lloyd-Fox, Wu, Richards, Elwell, & Johnson, 2013; Menon, 2013; Power, Fair, Schlaggar, & Petersen, 2010; Sporns & Edelman, 1993). An

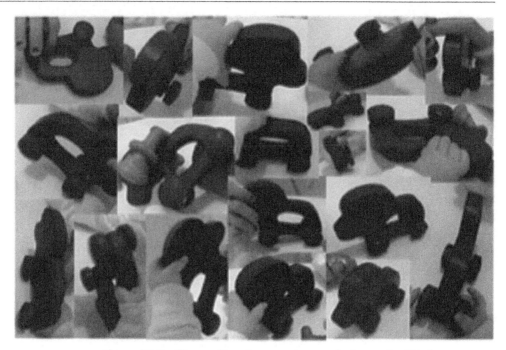

Figure 20.6. *Cluttered head-camera image of a 9-month-old infant, containing many different objects and body parts.*

expansion of studies examining age-related changes in these networks (James, 2010; Menon, 2013; Power et al., 2010) and their consequences for local change has set the stage for new research approaches directed to understanding the processes through which one dynamic system, that is the brain at one age, turns into the dynamic system that is the brain at a later age. Because the neural activity at any moment in the brain is a product of its intrinsic properties (themselves a product of a developmental history), the bodily behavior generated by the brain, and the sensory input, studying brain development cannot be separated from the study of behavior and experience. For example, when 4- and 5-year-old children are first learning to write the letters of the alphabet, they connect in new ways the neural processes underlying motor behavior, motor planning, and the visual system. The manual act of writing letters – which recruits this functional neural network – appears essential not just to forming this network but also to tuning the specialized regions for letter recognition within the ventral pathway in the visual cortex (James, 2010; James & Atwood, 2009). The path to specialized and localized visual processing of letters involves the functional connectivity of that system to motor planning and to behavior (James, 2010; James & Atwood, 2009). These advances should move us beyond timeworn debates about innate versus experience-dependent (and experience malleable) processes. This debate has, for example, been a core driving issue in the development of face perception. Are the specialized visual processes for human face perception evident in adults principally determined by genetic processes or are they the product of massive visual experience? The argument on the innate side points to the biological importance of faces and the existence of specialized circuitry for face processing (Bentin, Allison, Puce, Perez, & McCarthy, 1996; Goren, Sarty, & Wu, 1975; Johnson et al., 1991; Kanwisher, 2000; McKone, Crookes, Jeffery, & Dilks, 2012). A specific distributed network of brain areas is preferentially involved in face processing, including the "fusiform face area" within the inferotemporal cortex (Adolphs, 2002; Haxby, Hoffman, & Gobbini, 2002; Iidaka et al., 2001; Kanwisher, McDermott, & Chun, 1997). The development of this specialized region has multiple intrinsic biases supporting it, including the optics of newborn infant eyes that strongly favor inputs with low-level visual properties of up-close frontal views of faces as well as the neediness of young babies and the emotional attachment of parents that make up-close frontal views plentiful. But experience of faces is nonetheless essential. Recent studies of nonhuman primates show that without face experiences, infant monkeys do not develop their species-specific and specialized regions for face processing (Arcaro, Schade, Vincent, Ponce, & Livingstone, 2017), a finding that has similarities to the results of infants born with cataracts. Moreover, the existence of specialized areas for face processing, although perhaps more strongly biased by infant optics and parent behaviors, may emerge nonetheless from the same general principles as specialized visual regions for unnatural object categories such as letters of the alphabet and buildings (Aguirre, Zarahn, & D'esposito, 1998; Cohen & Dehaene, 2004).

Disruptions in early sensory-motor coordination have been implicated as early diagnostic markers along several atypical developmental pathways (D'Souza, D'Souza, & Karmiloff-Smith, 2017; Hinton, et. al., 2013; Iverson, 2010) and may be perturbations in the developmental trajectory with far-reaching consequences, including language learning (D'Souza et al., 2017; Iverson, 2010), social interactions (Leonard & Hill, 2014), attention (Ravizza, Solomon, Ivry, & Carter, 2013), behavioral control, and school achievement (Cameron, Cottone, Murrah, & Grissmer, 2016). Focused behavioral training with respect to these early perturbations provides a principled means for optimizing developmental outcomes of individuals with different developmental disorders. However, doing so requires an understanding of the role of behavior, not just as a phenotype but also as part of the causal pathway in brain development. Considerable and growing research suggests that disparities in children's developmental environments have serious consequences for brain development and for social, emotional, and cognitive behaviors. If we are to fully understand human visual development, and human brain development more generally, we need to situate the developing brain within the developing organism and the extended brain–behavior–experience network (Byrge, Sporns, & Smith, 2014). Human variation emerges as each individual organism travels along its unique developmental path, a path surely started – and influenced throughout the lifetime – by genetic components, but pushed forward by the developing child's own interactions with the world.

20.6 Social and Cultural Contexts

Infants do not develop alone but do so in the company of adults. Infants' egocentric views – and the data on which visual learning depends is strongly influenced by those adults. Long before infants hold objects on their own, as early as when infants are 3 months of age, parents hold, bring, and show objects to their infants (Clark & Estigarribia, 2011; Libertus & Needham, 2011; Zukow, 1990). One recent study (Burling & Yoshida, 2018) used head-mounted eye trackers to directly measure visual object information as infants aged 5 to 24 months played with objects with a parent. The parent's hand actions created the views for younger infants, with the views created by the infant's own hand actions increasing with the age of the infant. The analyses showed similarities between parent-generated views for younger infants and the views that were self-generated by the older infants. Held objects – and the targets of infant gaze regardless of who was holding – were large in the image, close to the perceiver, and segregated from the background. Other studies show that parent behavior linked to the infant's own behavior. For example, parents are more likely to jointly attend to and talk about objects when infants hold objects or carry the object while walking (Karasik, Tamis-LeMonda, & Adolph, 2011; Yu & Smith, 2017).

What parents do in social contexts with their infants, however, depends on their own history, culture, and geography. There are marked cultural differences in the physical and visual properties of environments (e.g., Dolgin, 2015), in parenting practices (e.g., Lansford et al., 2018; Prevoo & Tamis-LeMonda, 2017), and in motor development (e.g., Karasik, Tamis-LeMonda, Adolph, & Bornstein, 2015). These differences could, in principle, affect visual development. One relevant line of research concerns scene processing in Western adults (residing in North America and Europe) and Eastern adults (residing in China, Japan, and Korea), cultures that in wealth, education, the character of work and family have many similarities. Nonetheless, a large number of studies have documented fundamental differences in visual scene processing by a variety of measures, including recognition measures (Ishii, Tsukasaki, & Kitayama, 2009; Masuda & Nisbett, 2001, 2006), eye tracking (Chua, Boland, & Nisbett, 2005; Kelly, Miellet, & Caldara, 2010; Masuda et al., 2008), and brain imaging (Goh et al., 2013; Han & Northoff, 2008; Hedden, Ketay, Aron, Markus, & Gabrieli, 2008; Masuda, Russell, Chen, Hioki, & Caplan, 2014). In aggregate, the findings suggest that Western perceivers are more selective, more focused on local elements in scenes, and less affected by visual context than Eastern perceivers. In contrast, Eastern perceivers are more holistic and more sensitive to the relational structure among elements in a scene (e.g., Chua et al., 2005; Hedden et al., 2008; Kitayama, Duffy, Kawamura, & Larsen, 2003; Masuda et al., 2008; Masuda & Nisbett, 2001, 2006; Miyamoto, Yoshikawa, & Kitayama, 2011; Nisbett & Masuda, 2003; Nisbett & Miyamoto, 2005; Nisbett, Peng, Choi, & Norenzayan, 2001). These cultural differences in visual processing have also been reported in children (Duffy, Toriyama, Itakura, & Kitayama, 2009; Imada, Carlson, & Itakura, 2013; Moriguchi, Evans, Hiraki, Itakura, & Lee, 2012; Senzaki, Masuda, & Nand, 2014), including those as young as 3 years of age (Kuwabara & Smith, 2012, 2016; Kuwabara, Son, & Smith, 2011). Much like object processing, adults from Eastern societies tend to process faces more holistically by centrally fixating around the nose when learning and recognizing faces, while their Western counterparts are more analytical and fixate around salient parts of the face like the eyes and mouth (Blais, Jack, Scheepers, Fiset, & Caldara, 2008; Kelly, et al., 2011). Understanding the nature and origins of these cultural differences – and thus the adaptive nature of human visual prowess – requires the direct study of *visual* environments across different cultural contexts.

To fully understand human vision, we need to understand the full variety of infant experiences, not just those in typical Western societies that make up for only an eighth of the world population (Henrich, Heine, & Norenzayan, 2010a, 2010b).

20.7 Policy Implications

Descartes in 1628 gave us the basic approach to science. In studying any phenomenon, reduce it to its essential components and dissect away everything else. This analytic approach is motivated by the belief that complicated systems are most fruitfully investigated, and causes most precisely determined, at the lowest possible level. The goal is to find components that are simple enough to fully analyze, explain, and control. The spectacular success of this methodology in modern biology is undeniable. It has led to unprecedented knowledge of the molecular components of life. It has not led to a corresponding understanding of how large collections of such components operate *as systems* (Bechtel & Richardson, 1993; Keller, 2007; Kitson et al., 2018). This failure is evident in the challenge of effective translation of basic science. Mechanisms clearly and cleanly specified in laboratories often fail to work in real life (Collins, 2011; Lenfant, 2003; Norman, 2010). For developmental psychologists, Descartes' tenet has meant moving the phenomena out of everyday life and into the laboratory, using logically clean and well-controlled experiments that manipulate hypothesized variables to determine individual causes. But as in other biological sciences, our ability to take those findings into the world in all its complexity and variability is limited (Henrich et al., 2010a, 2010b).

The study of "egocentric vision," capturing the visual structure of the learning environment, like the sister efforts in language trying to capture the language input with day-long recordings (Bergelson, Amatuni, Dailey, Koorathota, & Tor, 2019), is a start to trying to understand real-world environments. These studies are relatively new, and there is much we do not know, we still have a long way to go and still lack the right analytic tools for understanding the properties of the environment at scale. Consider the case of current research on the disparities in children's language learning environments. Researchers are now using wearable audio recorders that can capture all the words a child hears in a day. They use algorithmic analyses that operate on the raw recorded sounds to estimate the number of words in child-directed speech. These studies (as well as earlier ones using more traditional speech sampling and transcription) reveal that the average preschool child hears about 20,000–38,000 total words a day (Fernald & Weisleder, 2015; Hart & Risley, 1995; Shneidman, Arroyo, Levine, & Goldin-Meadow, 2013; Weisleder & Fernald, 2013). But there is extreme variability, some children hear as few as 2,000 child-directed words a day and some as many as 50,000 words a day (Fernald & Weisleder, 2015; Hart & Risley, 1995; Weisleder & Fernald, 2013). These differences in amount of talk to individual children are strongly predictive of the child's vocabulary size and early school achievement (Dickinson, Golinkoff, & Hirsh-Pasek, 2010; Hart & Risley, 1995; Hoff, 2003; Huttenlocher, Waterfall, Vasilyeva, Vevea, & Hedges, 2010; Rowe, 2012; Walker, Greenwood, Hart, & Carta, 1994) and are also highly associated with the socioeconomic standing of the families (Hoff, 2003; Hurtado, Marchman, & Fernald, 2008; Huttenlocher et al., 2010; Weisleder & Fernald, 2013). By some estimates (Hart & Risley 1995) there is a 30-million-word gap in the cumulative number of words directed to children from poorer versus richer families. As a result, there is now a considerable public health effort directed to increasing parent talk to young children (Leffel & Suskind, 2013; Reese, Sparks, & Leyva, 2010; Roberts & Kaiser, 2011; and public health initiatives such as Providence Talks, First 5 California, and Too Small to Fail, among many others). Talking to children seems a likely positive factor in child development but doubts about the basic idea have been raised (Sperry, Sperry, & Miller, 2018), contested (Golinkoff, Hoff, Rowe, Tamis-LeMonda, & Hirsh-Pasek, 2018), and there many open questions (Montag et al., 2018; Romeo et al., 2018). What exactly is the pathway to learning? Is it really just more words? Does the context of talk matter? Or, perhaps, is the amount of parent talk correlated with some other environmental factor that is more critical? To answer these questions, we need to know how to measure and compare developmental environments beyond just counting words. This is a much more complex problem than it might seem because the scale of everyday experience is huge; for example, the average child who hears 20,000 child-directed words a day hears over 7 million words in a year (Bergelson et al., 2019; Hart & Risley, 1995; Shneidman et al., 2013). The problem is also complicated by the fact that the frequency distribution of words in produced language (like the frequency distribution of objects in the world) is not normal and thus the usual assumptions about sampling from normal distributions and statistical inference do not apply (Clerkin et al., 2017; Montag et al., 2018; Salakhutinov et al., 2011). Usual assumptions about attention, memory, and learning pathways may also not apply because what we know about these processes is based on small-scale experiments and uniform distributions of learning items (Clerkin et al., 2017). These issues – in the study of language, of visual environments, of social environments – are becoming urgent as both the data indicating consequential disparities in environments advances and as new methods emerge to capture environmental regularities at scale advance (Gilkerson & Richards, 2008; Roy et al., 2006; VanDam et al., 2016) as do large data sets of many children in common contexts like Many Babies (Frank et al., 2017), Homeview (Jayaraman & Smith, 2017), and Play & Learning Across a Year (Adolph, Tamis-LeMonda, Gilmore, & Soska, 2018).

20.8 Conclusion

Development is a personal journey, albeit one that is taken in the supportive company of others. But it is the personal vantage point of the learner, selective and localized, and their own path that constitute the tasks, behaviors, and experiences that determine and build the competencies of the individual. Although we most definitely need fine grained laboratory experiments of the development of behavior, cognition, and neural processes, we also need to study the developmental structure of environments and ideally do so at the level of the individual. Here we considered visual environments and visual cognition. But more generally, the developmental study of the environments may also yield a deeper understanding of individual differences in early cognitive development. The source of differences – and interventions to support healthy development in all children – may emerge in part from the developmental structure of the data for learning, data that are determined by the immediate surroundings of the learner and their developing behaviors in those surroundings.

References

Adolph, K., Tamis-LeMonda, C., Gilmore, R. O., & Soska, K. (2018). Play & learning across a year (PLAY) project summit (2018-06-29 Philadelphia). *Databrary*. Retrieved from http://doi.org/10.17910/B7.724.

Adolphs, R. (2002). Recognizing emotion from facial expressions: Psychological and neurological mechanisms. *Behavioral and Cognitive Neuroscience Reviews*, *1*(1), 21–62.

Aguirre, G. K., Zarahn, E., & D'Esposito, M. (1998). An area within human ventral cortex sensitive to "building" stimuli: Evidence and implications. *Neuron, 21*, 373–383.

Ahissar, M., & Hochstein, S. (1997). Task difficulty and the specificity of perceptual learning. *Nature*, *387*(6631), 401.

Arcaro, M. J., Schade, P. F., Vincent, J. L., Ponce, C. R., & Livingstone, M. S. (2017). Seeing faces is necessary for face-domain formation. *Nature Neuroscience*, *20*(10), 1404.

Augustine, E., Jones, S. S., Smith, L. B., & Longfield, E. (2015). Relations among early object recognition skills: Objects and letters. *Journal of Cognition and Development*, *16*(2), 221–235.

Bambach, S., Crandall, D. J., & Yu, C. (2015). Viewpoint integration for hand-based recognition of social interactions from a first-person view. *Proceedings of the 2015 ACM on International Conference on Multimodal Interaction*, November, 351–354.

Bechtel, W., & Richardson, R. (1993). *Discovering complexity: Decomposition and localization as strategies in scientific research*. Princeton, NJ: Princeton University Press.

Bentin, S., Allison, T., Puce, A., Perez, E., & McCarthy, G. (1996). Electrophysiological studies of face perception in humans. *Journal of Cognitive Neuroscience*, *8*(6), 551–565.

Bergelson, E., Amatuni, A., Dailey, S., Koorathota, S., & Tor, S. (2019). Day by day, hour by hour: Naturalistic language input to infants. *Developmental Science*, *22*(1), e12715.

Bergelson, E., & Swingley, D. (2012). At 6–9 months, human infants know the meanings of many common nouns. *Proceedings of the National Academy of Sciences*, *109*(9), 3253–3258.

Bertenthal, B. I., Campos, J. J., & Barrett, K. C. (1984). Self-produced locomotion. In B. I. Bertenthal, J. J. Campos, & K. C. Barrett (Eds.), *Continuities and discontinuities in development* (pp. 175–210). New York, NY: Springer.

Blais, C., Jack, R. E., Scheepers, C., Fiset, D., & Caldara, R. (2008). Culture shapes how we look at faces. *PloS One*, *3*(8), e3022.

Braddick, O., & Atkinson, J. (2011). Development of human visual function. *Vision Research*, *51*(13), 1588–1609.

Brandone, A. C. (2015). Infants' social and motor experience and the emerging understanding of intentional actions. *Developmental Psychology*, *51*(4), 512.

Brockmole, J. R., & Henderson, J. M. (2006). Using real-world scenes as contextual cues for search. *Visual Cognition*, *13*(1), 99–108.

Burling, J. M., & Yoshida, H. (2018). Visual constancies amidst changes in handled objects for 5- to 24-month-old infants. *Child Development*, *90*(2), 452–461.

Bushnell, E. W., & Boudreau, J. P. (1993). Motor development and the mind: The potential role of motor abilities as a determinant of aspects of perceptual development. *Child Development*, *64*(4), 1005–1021.

Bushnell, W. (2003). Newborn face recognition. In O. Pascalis & A. Slater (Eds.), *The development of face processing in infancy and early childhood* (pp. 41–53) New York, NY: Nova Science.

Byrge, L., Sporns, O., & Smith, L. B. (2014). Developmental process emerges from extended brain–body–behavior networks. *Trends in Cognitive Sciences*, *18*(8), 395–403.

Cadieu, C. F., Hong, H., Yamins, D. L., Pinto, N., Ardila, D., Solomon, E. A., & DiCarlo, J. J. (2014). Deep neural networks rival the representation of primate

IT cortex for core visual object recognition. *PLoS Computational Biology*, *10*(12), e1003963.

Cameron, C. E., Cottone, E. A., Murrah, W. M., & Grissmer, D. W. (2016). How are motor skills linked to children's school performance and academic achievement? *Child Development Perspectives*, *10*(2), 93–98.

Carey, S., & Diamond, R. (1994). Are faces perceived as configurations more by adults than by children? *Visual Cognition*, *1*(2–3), 253–274.

Castelhano, M. S., & Witherspoon, R. L. (2016). How you use it matters: Object function guides attention during visual search in scenes. *Psychological Science*, *27*(5), 606–621.

Chua, H. F., Boland, J. E., & Nisbett, R. E. (2005). Cultural variation in eye movements during scene perception. *Proceedings of the National Academy of Sciences*, *102*(35), 12629–12633.

Clark, E. V., & Estigarribia, B. (2011). Using speech and gesture to introduce new objects to young children. *Gesture*, *11*(1), 1–23.

Clerkin, E. M., Hart, E., Rehg, J. M., Yu, C., & Smith, L. B. (2017). Real-world visual statistics and infants' first-learned object names. *Philosophical Transactions of the Royal Society B*, *372*(1711), 20160055.

Cohen, L., & Dehaene, S. (2004). Specialization within the ventral stream: The case for the visual word form area. *Neuroimage*, 22(1), 466–476.

Collins, F. S. (2011). Reengineering translational science: The time is right. *Science Translational Medicine*, *3*(90). doi: 10.1126/scitranslmed.3002747.

D'Souza, D. E., D'Souza, H., & Karmiloff-Smith, A. (2017). Precursors to language development in typically and atypically developing infants and toddlers: The importance of embracing complexity. *Journal of Child Language*, *44*(3), 591–627.

DiCarlo, J. J., & Cox, D. D. J. (2007). Untangling invariant object recognition. *Trends in Cognitive Science*, *11*(8), 333–341.

Dickinson, D. K., Golinkoff, R. M., & Hirsh-Pasek, K. (2010). Speaking out for language: Why language is central to reading development. *Educational Researcher*, *39*(4), 305–310.

Dobson, V., Teller, D. Y., & Belgum, J. J. (1978). Visual acuity in human infants assessed with stationary stripes and phase-alternated checkerboards. *Vision Research*, *18*(9), 1233–1238.

Doherty, M. J., Anderson, J. R., & Howieson, L. (2009). The rapid development of explicit gaze judgment ability at 3 years. *Journal of Experimental Child Psychology*, *104*(3), 296–312.

Dolgin, E. (2015). The myopia boom. *Nature*, *519*(7543), 276.

Duffy, S., Toriyama, R., Itakura, S., & Kitayama, S. (2009). Development of cultural strategies of attention in North American and Japanese children. *Journal of Experimental Child Psychology*, *102*, 351–359.

Edelman, G. M. (1987). *Neural Darwinism: The theory of neuronal group selection*. New York, NY: Basic Books.

Falck-Ytter, T., Gredebäck, G., & von Hofsten, C. (2006). Infants predict other people's action goals. *Nature Neuroscience*, *9*(7), 878.

Fantz, R. L. (1963). Pattern vision in newborn infants. *Science*, *140*(3564), 296–297.

Farroni, T., Johnson, M. H., Brockbank, M., & Simion, F. (2000). Infants' use of gaze direction to cue attention: The importance of perceived motion. *Visual Cognition*, *7*(6), 705–718.

Farroni, T., Pividori, D., Simion, F., Massaccesi, S., & Johnson, M. H. (2004). Eye gaze cueing of attention in newborns. *Infancy, 5*(1), 39–60.

Fathi, A., Ren, X., & Rehg, J. M. (2011). *Learning to recognize objects in egocentric activities*. Paper presented at the 2011 IEEE Conference on Computer Vision and Pattern Recognition (CVPR), Colorado Springs, CO.

Fausey, C. M., Jayaraman, S., & Smith, L. B. (2016). From faces to hands: Changing visual input in the first two years. *Cognition, 152*, 101–107.

Fernald, A., & Weisleder, A. (2015). Twenty years after "meaningful differences," it's time to reframe the "deficit" debate about the importance of children's early language experience. *Human Development, 58*(1), 1.

Flanagan, J. R., & Johansson, R. S. (2003). Action plans used in action observation. *Nature, 424*(6950), 769.

Foody, G. M., McCulloch, M. B., & Yates, W. B. (1995). The effect of training set size and composition on artificial neural network classification. *International Journal of Remote Sensing, 16*, 1707–1723

Foulsham, T., Walker, E., & Kingstone, A. (2011). The where, what and when of gaze allocation in the lab and the natural environment. *Vision Research, 51*(17), 1920–1931.

Franchak, J. M., & Adolph, K. E. J. (2010). Visually guided navigation: Head-mounted eye-tracking of natural locomotion in children and adults. *Vision Research, 50*(24), 2766–2774.

Franchak, J. M., Kretch, K. S., & Adolph, K. E. (2018). See and be seen: Infant–caregiver social looking during locomotor free play. *Developmental Science, 21*(4), e12626.

Frank, M. C., Bergelson, E., Bergmann, C., Cristia, A., Floccia, C., Gervain, J., ... Lew-Williams, C. (2017). A collaborative approach to infant research: Promoting reproducibility, best practices, and theory-building. *Infancy, 22*(4), 421–435.

Gauthier, I., & Tarr, M. J. (1997). Becoming a "Greeble" expert: Exploring the face recognition mechanisms. *Vision Research, 37*(12), 1673–1682.

Geisler, W. S. (2008). Visual perception and the statistical properties of natural scenes. *Annual Review of Psychology, 59*, 167–192.

Gerson, S. A., Meyer, M., Hunnius, S., & Bekkering, H. (2017). Unravelling the contributions of motor experience and conceptual knowledge in action perception: A training study. *Scientific Reports, 7*, 46761.

Gilkerson, J., & Richards, J. A. (2008). *The LENA natural language study*. Boulder, CO: LENA Foundation.

Gilmore, R. O., Baker, T. J., & Grobman, K. (2004). Stability in young infants' discrimination of optic flow. *Developmental Psychology, 40*(2), 259.

Gogate, L. J., Bahrick, L. E., & Watson, J. D. (2000). A study of multimodal motherese: The role of temporal synchrony between verbal labels and gestures. *Child Development, 71*(4), 878–894.

Goh, J. O. S., Hebrank, A. C., Sutton, B. P., Chee, M. W. L., Sim, S. K. Y., & Park, D. C. (2013). Culture-related differences in default network during visuo-spatial judgments. *Social Cognitive and Affective Neuroscience, 8*, 134–142.

Goldin-Meadow, S., & Wagner, S. M. (2005). How our hands help us learn. *Trends in Cognitive Sciences, 9*(5), 234–241.

Golinkoff, R. M., Hoff, E., Rowe, M. L., Tamis-LeMonda, C. S., & Hirsh-Pasek, K. (2018). Language matters: Denying the existence of the 30-million-word gap has serious consequences. *Child Development*, *90*(3), 985–992.

Goren, C. C., Sarty, M., & Wu, P. Y. (1975). Visual following and pattern discrimination of face-like stimuli by newborn infants. *Pediatrics*, *56*(4), 544–549.

Hadad, B. S., Maurer, D., & Lewis, T. L. (2011). Long trajectory for the development of sensitivity to global and biological motion. *Developmental Science*, *14*(6), 1330–1339.

Halberda, J., Mazzocco, M. M., & Feigenson, L. (2008). Individual differences in non-verbal number acuity correlate with maths achievement. *Nature*, *455*(7213), 665.

Han, S., & Northoff, G. (2008). Reading direction and culture. *Nature Reviews Neuroscience*, *9*(12), 965.

Hart, B., & Risley, T. R. (1995). *Meaningful differences in the everyday experience of young American children*. Baltimore, MD: Paul H. Brookes.

Haxby, J. V., Hoffman, E. A., & Gobbini, M. I. (2000). The distributed human neural system for face perception. *Trends in Cognitive Science*, *4*(6), 223–233.

(2002). Human neural systems for face recognition and social communication. *Biological Psychiatry*, *51*(1), 59–67.

Hedden, T., Ketay, S., Aron, A., Markus, H. R., & Gabrieli, J. D. E. (2008). Cultural influences on neural substrates of attentional control. *Psychological Science*, *19*, 12–17.

Henrich, J., Heine, S. J., & Norenzayan, A. (2010a). Beyond WEIRD: Towards a broad-based behavioral science. *Behavioral and Brain Sciences*, *33*(2–3), 111–135.

(2010b). The weirdest people in the world? *Behavioral and Brain Sciences*, *33*(2–3), 61–83.

Higgins, C. I., Campos, J. J., & Kermoian, R. (1996). Effect of self-produced locomotion on infant postural compensation to optic flow. *Developmental Psychology*, *32*(5), 836.

Hinton, R., Budimirovic, D. B., Marschik, P. B., Talisa, V. B., Einspieler, C., Gipson, T., & Johnston, M. V. (2013). Parental reports on early language and motor milestones in fragile X syndrome with and without autism spectrum disorders. *Developmental Neurorehabilitation*, *16*(1), 58–66.

Hochstein, S., & Ahissar, M. (2002). View from the top: Hierarchies and reverse hierarchies in the visual system. *Neuron*, *36*(5), 791–804.

Hoff, E. (2003). The specificity of environmental influence: Socioeconomic status affects early vocabulary development via maternal speech. *Child Development*, *74*(5), 1368–1378.

Hurley, K. B., & Oakes, L. M. (2015). Experience and distribution of attention: Pet exposure and infants' scanning of animal images. *Journal of Cognition and Development*, *16*(1), 11–30.

Hurtado, N., Marchman, V. A., & Fernald, A. (2008). Does input influence uptake? Links between maternal talk, processing speed and vocabulary size in Spanish-learning children. *Developmental Science*, *11*(6), F31–F39.

Huttenlocher, J., Waterfall, H., Vasilyeva, M., Vevea, J., & Hedges, L. V. (2010). Sources of variability in children's language growth. *Cognitive Psychology*, *61*(4), 343–365.

Iidaka, T., Omori, M., Murata, T., Kosaka, H., Yonekura, Y., Okada, T., & Sadato, N. (2001). Neural interaction of the amygdala with the prefrontal and temporal cortices in the processing of facial expressions as revealed by fMRI. *Journal of Cognitive Neuroscience, 13*(8), 1035–1047.

Im, H. Y., Park, W. J., & Chong, S. C. (2015). Ensemble statistics as units of selection. *Journal of Cognitive Psychology, 27*(1), 114–127.

Imada, T., Carlson, S. M., & Itakura, S. (2013). East–West cultural differences in context sensitivity are evident in early childhood. *Developmental Science, 16*, 198–208.

Ishii, K., Tsukasaki, T., & Kitayama, S. (2009). Culture and visual perception: Does perceptual inference depend on culture? *Japanese Psychological Research, 51*(2), 103–109.

Iverson, J. M. (2010). Developing language in a developing body: The relationship between motor development and language development. *Journal of Child Language, 37*(2), 229–261.

James, K. H. (2010). Sensori-motor experience leads to changes in visual processing in the developing brain. *Developmental Science, 13*(2), 279–288.

James, K. H., & Atwood, T. P. (2009). The role of sensorimotor learning in the perception of letter-like forms: Tracking the causes of neural specialization for letters. *Cognitive Neuropsychology, 26*(1), 91–110.

Jayaraman, S., Fausey, C. M., & Smith, L. B. (2015). The faces in infant-perspective scenes change over the first year of life. *PloS one, 10*(5), e0123780.

(2017). Why are faces denser in the visual experiences of younger than older infants? *Developmental Psychology, 53*(1), 38.

Jayaraman, S., & Smith, L. B. (2017). *The homeview project*. Retrieved from www.iub .edu/~cogdev/homeview.html.

(2018). Faces in early visual environments are persistent not just frequent. *Vision Research, 157*, 213–221.

Johnson, M. H., Dziurawiec, S., Ellis, H., & Morton, J. (1991). Newborns' preferential tracking of face-like stimuli and its subsequent decline. *Cognition, 40*(1–2), 1–19.

Johnson, M. H., & Morton J. (1991) *Biology and cognitive development: The case of face recognition*. Oxford: Blackwell.

Kanwisher, N. J. (2000). Domain specificity in face perception. *Nature Neuroscience, 3*(8), 759.

Kanwisher, N. J., McDermott, J., & Chun, M. M. (1997). The fusiform face area: A module in human extrastriate cortex specialized for face perception. *Journal of Neuroscience, 17*(11), 4302–4311.

Karasik, L. B., Tamis-LeMonda, C. S., & Adolph, K. E. (2011). Transition from crawling to walking and infants' actions with objects and people. *Child Development, 82*(4), 1199–1209.

Karasik, L. B., Tamis-LeMonda, C. S., Adolph, K. E., & Bornstein, M. H. (2015). Places and postures: A cross-cultural comparison of sitting in 5-month-olds. *Journal of Cross-Cultural Psychology, 46*(8), 1023–1038.

Keller, E. F. (2007). The disappearance of function from "self-organizing systems." In F. Boogerd, F. Bruggeman, J. H. Hofmeyre, & H. V. Westerhoff (Eds.), *Systems biology* (pp. 303–317). Amsterdam: Elsevier.

Kelly, D. J., Liu, S., Rodger, H., Miellet, S., Ge, L., & Caldara, R. (2011). Developing cultural differences in face processing. *Developmental Science*, *14*(5), 1176–1184.

Kelly, D. J., Miellet, S., & Caldara, R. (2010). Culture shapes eye movements for visually homogeneous objects. *Frontiers in Psychology*, *1*, 6.

Kitayama, S., Duffy, S., Kawamura, T., & Larsen, J. T. (2003). Perceiving an object and its context in different cultures: A cultural look at new look. *Psychological Science, 14*, 201–206.

Kitson, A., Brook, A., Harvey, G., Jordan, Z., Marshall, R., O'Shea, R., & Wilson, D. (2018). Using complexity and network concepts to inform healthcare knowledge translation. *International Journal of Health Policy and Management*, *7*(3), 231.

Kovack-Lesh, K. A., Horst, J. S., & Oakes, L. M. (2008). The cat is out of the bag. The joint influence of previous experience and looking behavior on infant categorization. *Infancy*, *13*(4), 285–307.

Kovack-Lesh, K. A., Oakes, L. M., & McMurray, B. (2012). Contributions of attentional style and previous experience to 4-month-old infants' categorization. *Infancy*, *17*(3), 324–338.

Krogh-Jespersen, S., & Woodward, A. L. (2018). Reaching the goal: Active experience facilitates 8-month-old infants' prospective analysis of goal-based actions. *Journal of Experimental Child Psychology*, *171*, 31–45.

Kuwabara, M., & Smith, L. B. (2016) Cultural differences in visual object recognition in 3-year-old children. *Journal of Experimental Child Psychology*, *147*, 22–38.

Kuwabara, M., & Smith, L. B. (2012). Cross-cultural differences in cognitive development: Attention to relations and objects. *Journal of Experimental Child Psychology*, *113*, 20–35.

Kuwabara, M., Son, J. Y., & Smith, L. B. (2011). Attention to context: U.S. and Japanese children's emotional judgments. *Journal of Cognition and Development*, *12*, 502–517.

Lansford, J. E., Godwin, J., Al-Hassan, S. M., Bacchini, D., Bornstein, M. H., Chang, L., & Malone, P. S. (2018). Longitudinal associations between parenting and youth adjustment in twelve cultural groups: Cultural normativeness of parenting as a moderator. *Developmental Psychology*, *54*(2), 362.

Leffel, K., & Suskind, D. (2013, November). Parent-directed approaches to enrich the early language environments of children living in poverty. *Seminars in Speech and Language*, *34*(4), 267–278

Lenfant, C. (2003). Clinical research to clinical practice: Lost in translation? *New England Journal of Medicine*, *349*(9), 868–874.

Leonard, H. C., & Hill, E. L. (2014). The impact of motor development on typical and atypical social cognition and language: A systematic review. *Child and Adolescent Mental Health*, *19*(3), 163–170.

Libertus, K., & Needham, A. (2011). Reaching experience increases face preference in 3-month-old infants. *Developmental Science*, *14*, 1355–1364.

Lloyd-Fox, S., Wu, R , Richards, J. E., Elwell, C. E., & Johnson, M. H. (2013). Cortical activation to action perception is associated with action production abilities in young infants. *Cerebral Cortex*, *25*(2), 289–297.

Loomis, J. M., Kelly, J. W., Pusch, M., Bailenson, J. N., & Beall, A. C. (2008). Psychophysics of perceiving eye-gaze and head direction with peripheral vision: Implications for the dynamics of eye-gaze behavior. *Perception, 37*(9), 1443–1457.

Macchi, C. V., Turati, C., & Simion, F. (2004). Can a nonspecific bias toward top-heavy patterns explain newborns' face preference? *Psychological Science, 15*(6), 379–383.

Masuda, T., Ellsworth, P. C., Mesquita, B., Leu, J., Tanida, S., & van de Veerdonk, E. (2008). Placing the face in context: cultural differences in the perception of facial emotion. *Journal of Personality and Social Psychology, 94*(3), 365.

Masuda, T., & Nisbett, R. E. (2001). Attending holistically versus analytically: Comparing the context sensitivity of Japanese and Americans. *Journal of Personality and Social Psychology, 81*(5), 922.

(2006). Culture and change blindness. *Cognitive Science, 30*(2), 381–399.

Masuda, T., Russell, M. J., Chen, Y. Y., Hioki, K., & Caplan, J. B. (2014). N400 incongruity effect in an episodic memory task reveals different strategies for handling irrelevant contextual information for Japanese than European Canadian. *Cognitive Neuroscience, 5*, 17–25.

Maurer, D. J. (2017). Critical periods re-examined: Evidence from children treated for dense cataracts. *Cognitive Development, 42*, 27–36.

Maurer, D. J., & Lewis, T. L. (2001a). Visual acuity: The role of visual input in inducing postnatal change. *Clinical Neuroscience Research, 1*(4), 239–247.

Maurer, D., & Lewis, T. (2001b). Visual acuity and spatial contrast sensitivity: Normal development and underlying mechanisms. In C. A. Nelson & M. Luciana (Eds.), *Handbook of developmental cognitive neuroscience* (pp. 237–250). Cambridge, MA: MIT Press.

Maurer, D., Mondloch, C. J., & Lewis, T. L. (2007). Sleeper effects. *Developmental Science, 10*(1), 40–47.

McKone, E., Crookes, K., Jeffery, L., & Dilks, D. D. (2012). A critical review of the development of face recognition: Experience is less important than previously believed. *Cognitive Neuropsychology, 29*(1–2), 174–212.

Menon, V. (2013). Developmental pathways to functional brain networks: Emerging principles. *Trends in Cognitive Sciences, 17*(12), 627–640.

Miyamoto, Y., Yoshikawa, S., & Kitayama, S. (2011). Feature and configuration in face processing: Japanese are more configural than Americans. *Cognitive Science, 35*, 563–574.

Montag, J. L., Jones, M. N., & Smith, L. B. (2018). Quantity and diversity: Simulating early word learning environments. *Cognitive Science, 42*, 375–412.

Moriguchi, Y., Evans, A. D., Hiraki, K., Itakura, S., & Lee, K. (2012). Cultural differences in the development of cognitive shifting: East–West comparison. *Journal of Experimental Child Psychology, 111*, 156–163.

Moulson, M. C., Westerlund, A., Fox, N. A., Zeanah, C. H., & Nelson, C. A. (2009). The effects of early experience on face recognition: An event-related potential study of institutionalized children in Romania. *Child Development, 80*(4), 1039–1056.

Nisbett, R. E., & Masuda, T. (2003). Culture and point of view. *Proceedings of the National Academy of Sciences, 100*(19), 11163–11170.

Nisbett, R. E., & Miyamoto, Y. (2005). The influence of culture: Holistic versus analytic perception. *Trends in Cognitive Sciences, 9*, 467–473.

Nisbett, R. E., Peng, K. P., Choi, I., & Norenzayan, A. (2001). Culture and systems of thought: Holistic versus analytic cognition. *Psychological Review, 108*, 291–310.

Nishimura, M., Scherf, S., & Behrmann, M. (2009). Development of object recognition in humans. *F1000 Biology Reports, 1*, 56.

Norman, D. A. (2010). The research-practice gap: The need for translational developers. *Interactions, 17*(4), 9–12.

Oakes, L. M. (2017). Plasticity may change inputs as well as processes, structures, and responses. *Cognitive Development, 42*, 4–14.

Oruç, İ., & Barton, J. (2010). Critical frequencies in the perception of letters, faces, and novel shapes: Evidence for limited scale invariance for faces. *Journal of Vision, 10*(12), 20-20.

Pascalis, O., Loevenbruck, H., Quinn, P. C., Kandel, S., Tanaka, J. W., & Lee, K. (2014). On the links among face processing, language processing, and narrowing during development. *Child Development Perspectives, 8*(2), 65–70.

Perry, L. K., Samuelson, L. K., Malloy, L. M., & Schiffer, R. N. (2010). Learn locally, think globally: Exemplar variability supports higher-order generalization and word learning. *Psychological Science, 21*(12), 1894–1902.

Power, J. D., Fair, D. A., Schlaggar, B. L., & Petersen, S. E. (2010). The development of human functional brain networks. *Neuron, 67*(5), 735–748.

Prevoo, M. J., & Tamis-LeMonda, C. S. (2017). Parenting and globalization in Western countries: Explaining differences in parent–child interactions. *Current Opinion in Psychology, 15*, 33–39.

Ravizza, S. M., Solomon, M., Ivry, R. B., & Carter, C. S. (2013). Restricted and repetitive behaviors in autism spectrum disorders: The relationship of attention and motor deficits. *Development and Psychopathology, 25*(3), 773–784.

Reese, E., Sparks, A., & Leyva, D. (2010). A review of parent interventions for preschool children's language and emergent literacy. *Journal of Early Childhood Literacy, 10*(1), 97–117.

Roberts, M. Y., & Kaiser, A. P. (2011). The effectiveness of parent-implemented language interventions: A meta-analysis. *American Journal of Speech-Language Pathology, 20*(3), 180–199.

Romeo, R. R., Leonard, J. A., Robinson, S. T., West, M. R., Mackey, A. P., Rowe, M. L., & Gabrieli, J. D. (2018). Beyond the 30-million-word gap: Children's conversational exposure is associated with language-related brain function. *Psychological Science, 29*(5), 700–710.

Rowe, M. L. (2012). A longitudinal investigation of the role of quantity and quality of child-directed speech in vocabulary development. *Child Development, 83*(5), 1762–1774.

Roy, D., Patel, R., DeCamp, P., Kubat, R., Fleischman, M., Roy, B., … Levit, M. (2006, September). The human speechome project. In C. Nehaniv, P. Vogt, Y. Sugita, & E. Tuci (Eds.), *Symbol grounding and beyond: Third International Workshop on Emergence and Evolution of Linguistic Communication* (pp. 192–196). Berlin: Springer.

Salakhutdinov, R., Torralba, A., & Tenenbaum, J. (2011). Learning to share visual appearance for multiclass object detection. *Proceedings of the 2011 IEEE Conference on Computer Vision and Pattern Recognition,* 1481–1488. https://doi.org/10.1109/CVPR.2011.5995720

Scherf, K. S., & Scott, L. S. (2012). Connecting developmental trajectories: Biases in face processing from infancy to adulthood. *Developmental Psycholobiology*, *54*(6), 643–663.

Scott, L. S., Pascalis, O., & Nelson, C. A. (2007). A domain-general theory of the development of perceptual discrimination. *Current Directions in Psychological Science*, *16*(4), 197–201.

Senzaki, S., Masuda, T., & Nand, K. (2014). Holistic versus analytic expressions in artworks: Cross-cultural differences and similarities in drawings and collages by Canadian and Japanese school-aged children. *Journal of Cross-Cultural Psychology*, *45*, 1297–1316.

Shneidman, L. A., Arroyo, M. E., Levine, S. C., & Goldin-Meadow, S. (2013). What counts as effective input for word learning? *Journal of Child Language*, *40*, 672–686.

Simoncelli, E. P. (2003). Vision and the statistics of the visual environment. *Current Opinion in Neurobiology*, *13*(2), 144–149.

Smith, L. B. (2005). Action alters shape categories. *Cognitive Science*, *29*(4), 665–679.
    (2009). From fragments to geometric shape: Changes in visual object recognition between 18 and 24 months. *Current Directions in Psychological Science*, *18*(5), 290–294.

Smith, L. B., Yu, C., & Pereira, A. F. J. D. S. (2011). Not your mother's view: The dynamics of toddler visual experience. *Developmental Science*, *14*(1), 9–17.

Smith, L. B., Yu, C., Yoshida, H., & Fausey, C. M. (2015). Contributions of head-mounted cameras to studying the visual environments of infants and young children. *Journal of Cognition and Development*, *16*(3), 407–419.

Sommerville, J. A., Upshaw, M. B., & Loucks, J. (2012). The nature of goal-directed action representations in infancy. *Advances in Child Development and Behavior*, *43*, 351–387.

Sommerville, J. A., Woodward, A. L., & Needham, A. (2005). Action experience alters 3-month-old infants' perception of others' actions. *Cognition*, *96*, B1–B11.

Soska, K. C., Adolph, K. E., & Johnson, S. P. (2010). Systems in development: Motor skill acquisition facilitates three-dimensional object completion. *Developmental Psychology*, *46*(1), 129.

Sperry, D. E., Sperry, L. L., & Miller, P. J. (2018). Reexamining the verbal environments of children from different socioeconomic backgrounds. *Child Development*, *90*(4), 1303–1318.

Sporns, O., & Edelman, G. M. (1993). Solving Bernstein's problem: A proposal for the development of coordinated movement by selection. *Child Development*, *64*(4), 960–981.

Striano, T., & Reid, V. M. (2006). Social cognition in the first year. *Trends in Cognitive Sciences*, *10*(10), 471–476.

Sugden, N. A., Mohamed-Ali, M. I., & Moulson, M. C. (2014). I spy with my little eye: Typical, daily exposure to faces documented from a first-person infant perspective. *Developmental Psychobiology*, *56*(2), 249–261.

Tatler, B. W., Hayhoe, M. M., Land, M. F., & Ballard, D. H. (2011). Eye guidance in natural vision: Reinterpreting salience. *Journal of Vision*, *11*(5), 5.

VanDam, M., Warlaumont, A. S., Bergelson, E., Cristia, A., Soderstrom, M., de Palma, P., & MacWhinney, B. (2016). HomeBank: An online repository of daylong child-centered audio recordings. *Seminars in Speech and Language*, *37*(2), 128–142.

Vida, M. D., & Maurer, D. (2012). Gradual improvement in fine-grained sensitivity to triadic gaze after 6 years of age. *Journal of Experimental Child Psychology*, *111*(2), 299–318.

Walker, D., Greenwood, C., Hart, B., & Carta, J. (1994). Prediction of school outcomes based on early language production and socioeconomic factors. *Child Development*, *65*(2), 606–621.

Weisleder, A., & Fernald, A. (2013). Talking to children matters: Early language experience strengthens processing and builds vocabulary. *Psychological Science*, *24*(11), 2143–2152.

Wolfe, J. M., Võ, M. L. H., Evans, K. K., & Greene, M. R. (2011). Visual search in scenes involves selective and nonselective pathways. *Trends in Cognitive Sciences*, *15*(2), 77–84.

Woodward, A. L. (1998). Infants selectively encode the goal object of an actor's reach. *Cognition*, *69*, 1–34.

Yamins, D. L., & DiCarlo, J. J. (2016). Using goal-driven deep learning models to understand sensory cortex. *Nature Neuroscience*, *19*(3), 356.

Yoshida, H., & Smith, L. B. (2008). What's in view for toddlers? Using a head camera to study visual experience. *Infancy*, *13*(3), 229–248.

Yu, C., & Smith, L. B. (2013). Joint attention without gaze following: Human infants and their parents coordinate visual attention to objects through eye–hand coordination. *PloS One*, *8*(11), e79659.

(2017). From infant hands to parent eyes: Hand–eye coordination predicts joint attention. *Child Development*, *88*(6), 2060–2078.

Yurovsky, D., Smith, L. B., & Yu, C. (2013). Statistical word learning at scale: The baby's view is better. *Developmental Science*, *16*(6), 959–966.

Zukow, P. G. (1990). Socio-perceptual bases for the emergence of language: An alternative to innatist approaches. *Developmental Psychobiology*, *23*, 705–726. https://doi.org/10.1002/dev.420230711

PART V

Language

21 Infant Speech Perception

Rebecca K. Reh and Janet F. Werker*

Human infants are born well prepared to acquire language, with impressive speech perception abilities well before the onset of productive language. Over the first years of life, these perceptual capacities are tuned to the native language. Rich social experience interacts with intrinsic neurobiological systems to scaffold perceptual abilities that support language acquisition. At birth – indeed, as early as 26 weeks gestation, prior to input from developing auditory pathways – the basic neural architecture is in place for processing language. Experience and further development lead to an elaboration and refinement of this architecture. At birth, perceptual biases are in place that predispose infants to listen more attentively when they hear speech and to look toward human faces – two core communicative sensitivities that lay the foundation for acquiring the native language. A variety of learning mechanisms are operative that enable infants to become experts at perceiving and ultimately producing their native language(s). Moreover, the kinds of information to which the infant is attracted and from which she is able to learn change across the first weeks and months of life as different capabilities develop, and as cascading sensitivities to different aspects of language emerge. In this chapter we focus on how intrinsic biases and circuit capabilities interact with and are modified by language experience to shape early speech perceptual abilities, optimally positioning the infant to acquire their native language(s).

We begin by laying out the language perceptual abilities of infants at birth. We then review evidence that brain maturation and language experience interact to shape perception of language features over the first year of life. Following this, we consider how the multimodal nature of infants' communicative interaction supports attunement to the native language. Next, we discuss how growing familiarity with native-language prosody, phonetics, and phonotactics scaffolds word segmentation and learning, the impact of social cues, and the interactive nature of this process, whereby word learning facilitates phoneme category formation. Importantly, we consider how these processes

* The authors gratefully acknowledge support from the Canadian Institute for Advanced Research (RKR and JFW), the Alva Foundation (RKR), the Natural Sciences and Engineering Research Council of Canada (RGPIN-2015–03967 to JFW), and the Social Sciences and Humanities Research Council of Canada (435-2014-0917 to JFW). Special thanks to both Savannah Nijeboer and Jacqueline Hart Smith for their editorial assistance and to Savannah for creating the figure.

are impacted in cases where the social environment leads to differences in language experience, as seen in the case of infants growing up bilingual.

We then shift our focus to the neurobiological underpinnings of this process, including how early neural specialization for language processing interacts with environmental input to shape perceptual processes. We consider the importance of critical periods for language development and evidence that these periods can be shifted by environmental exposures. Finally, we consider the policy implications of the importance of early, rich language experience to support later language development.

21.1 Attunement to the Native Language Begins Before Birth

Both biological preparedness and auditory experience *in utero* act to direct acoustic preferences. Newborn infants listen longer to speech over matched nonspeech sounds (Vouloumanos & Werker, 2007); while this preference requires experience to be fully refined to the human voice (given that monkey calls are also preferred over sine wave analogues; Vouloumanos, Hauser, Werker, & Martin, 2010), the neonatal preference for the unfiltered speech heard outside the womb is equal to presentations of the filtered speech mimicking that heard in the womb, suggesting that this preference is not entirely dependent on experience (Vouloumanos & Werker, 2007). Yet, the imprint of experience is also evident at birth. Newborn infants prefer their mother's voice over that of an unfamiliar female (DeCasper & Fifer, 1980), and also prefer stories read by their mother during gestation (DeCasper & Spence, 1986). These early preferences suggest that experience *in utero* shapes infants' expectations of the auditory environment, guiding early auditory attention.

Due to the low-pass filtering properties of the womb, the pitch and rhythm of the speech signal are more preserved than other aspects of language. Developmentally, the rhythmical information in speech is one of the first aspects of language to which infants show sensitivity and may set the stage for subsequent learning about the native language (see Wanner & Gleitman, 1982, for the first suggestion of "prosodic bootstrapping"). Newborns discriminate between languages of different rhythmical classes regardless of experience, however, they prefer to listen to their native language (Mehler et al., 1988). Neuronal imaging work with newborns confirms that while language in general is processed differently than nonlinguistic stimuli, there is an even greater response for the language heard *in utero* over an unfamiliar language (May, Gervain, Carreiras, & Werker, 2017).

21.2 Language Rhythmicity

While newborn infants can discriminate languages from different rhythmical classes, the ability to discriminate the mother tongue from an unfamiliar language with a similar stress pattern is typically not seen until 4–5 months of age (Nazzi, Jusczyk, & Johnson, 2000; but see Molnar, Gervain, & Carreiras, 2014 for within-class discrimination at 3.5 months). This ability appears to derive from increased familiarity with the native language, as infants of 4–5 months remain unable to discriminate two unfamiliar languages that share the native stress pattern (Nazzi et al., 2000). Interestingly, this experience-driven increase in native-language discrimination is maturationally constrained; infants born prematurely – who have thus had 6 months of post-natal listening experience, but whose brains are maturationally comparable to full-term 3-month-old infants – do not show distinct neural activation patterns to the native language when compared to a language from the same rhythmical class (Peña, Pittaluga, & Mehler, 2010).

Nazzi and colleagues have suggested that the rhythmic structure of a language may provide the foundation for the divergence in segmentation strategies observed in infants learning different languages (Nazzi & Ramus, 2003). The rhythmical structure is associated with word order, providing a gateway to bootstrap grammatical knowledge (Nespor et al., 2008; Wanner & Gleitman, 1982). Speech rhythmicity is cued by several distinct acoustic properties, including pitch, duration, and intensity. Infants are able to use these cues to group nonspeech tones by 8 months of age (Trainor & Adams, 2000), and this grouping is influenced by language background (Molnar et al., 2014; Yoshida et al., 2010). By 8 months of age, infants clearly track rhythmicity using pitch and duration cues, and this information influences their segmentation strategies.

21.3 Forming Phoneme Categories

Young infants show broad-based phonetic discrimination. Early in life, this performance is independent of specific linguistic experience, enabling infants to discriminate many minimal pair phonetic distinctions, including some not found in their native language (Werker & Tees, 1984). Listening experience over the first year of life attunes phonetic perception such that infants become experts at discriminating the speech sound distinctions used in their native language, with sharpened discrimination of native distinctions (Kuhl et al., 2006; Sundara, Polka, & Genesee, 2006) and declines in discrimination of nonnative distinctions (Kuhl, Williams, Lacerda, Stevens, & Lindblom, 1992; Werker & Tees, 1984). This is the dominant pattern reported for many speech sound distinctions including consonants (Werker & Tees, 1984), vowels (Kuhl et al., 1992), tones (Mattock & Burnham, 2006), and linguistic signs (Palmer, Fais, Golinkoff, & Werker, 2012).

Still unknown is exactly what are the learning mechanisms that underlie perceptual attunement to native phonetic categories. In speech, babies hear noncontinuous variation in the acoustic-phonetic properties of the sounds and syllables used in their native language. For example, we expect that an infant growing up in English will hear variations in the production of a voiced "d" sound that are distributed around a central mean, and that an infant growing up in Hindi will hear two distinct distributions of "d" sounds, one centered around a more frontal, dental /da/ and the other centered around a more anterior, retroflex /d/. We and others have investigated whether babies can learn from distributional variation. After familiarization to syllables taken from an eight-step continuum spanning two phonetic categories (e.g., ba and pa), wherein there are more instances of the end points than the center points of the continuum, infants will bifurcate the distinction and do a better job of discriminating the two endpoints than infants who have been familiarized to a set of syllables wherein there are more instances of the two center points along the continuum (Maye, Weiss, & Aslin, 2008; Maye, Werker, & Gerken, 2002). Of interest to our later discussion of critical periods, distributional learning is most effective during the age period when infants are actively attuning to the speech sound categories of the native language (Liu & Kager, 2017).

Distributional learning is not the only proposed mechanism for phonetic category learning. Indeed, computational models suggest that the distributional statistics alone may be insufficient in naturally heard language to support phonetic category development (McMurray, Aslin, & Toscano, 2009 but see Schatz, Feldman, Goldwater, Cao & Dupoux, 2019). Some research has suggested that familiar word forms – even devoid of meaning – provide anchors that support phonetic category learning (Feldman, Griffiths, Goldwater, & Morgan, 2013). We examined whether the co-occurrence of phonetically distinct words with distinct objects facilitates phonetic category learning. Yeung and Werker (2009) tested this experimentally by pairing two minimally contrastive words with two different objects. Importantly, the words differed in a non-English phonetic difference. Following experience with these pairings, 9-month-olds were better at discriminating the phonetic contrast than they were if the two words were paired interchangeably with the objects (Yeung & Werker, 2009). Infants benefit most from these consistent pairings if there are also referential or communicative cues that signal the task is one of word learning (Yeung & Nazzi, 2014). Thus, infants likely use multiple sources of information to attune to the phonetic distinctions utilized in their native language – including distributional regularities, but also the co-occurrence, or labeling, of objects with words – to establish the phoneme repertoire of their native language.

21.4 The Development of Multimodal Speech Perception

Arguably, the most engaging speech for infants comes from *en face* interaction, providing information not just about acoustics, but also visual speech. This visual information can help infants disambiguate an otherwise ambiguous auditory distinction (Teinonen, Aslin, Alku, & Csibra, 2008), and change an auditory percept if the visual information is mismatching (Rosenblum, Schmuckler, & Johnson, 1997). The earliest and most robust evidence of audiovisual (AV) speech perception comes from studies of matching. When shown two side-by-side faces of the same person silently articulating either one sound (e.g., the vowel /u/) or another (e.g., the vowel /a/), and played one or the other sound in synchrony with the moving faces, infants look longer to the side that matches what they are hearing (Kuhl & Meltzoff, 1982). Infants also show AV matching of nonnative speech (Pons, Lewkowicz, Soto-Faraco, & Sebastián-Gallés, 2009) and show that they detect the mismatch by looking longer at the mouth when nonnative heard and seen speech do not match (Danielson, Bruderer, Kandhadai, Vatikiotis-Bateson, & Werker, 2017), suggesting that experience with specific speech syllables is not required to learn the association between seen and heard speech.

Just as auditory phonetic speech discrimination attunes to the repertoire of the native language, so too does AV detection of the match/mismatch. By 10–11 months of age, Spanish-learning infants no longer detect the match of an English-specific (non-Spanish) distinction (Pons et al., 2009). And, although English-learning infants can detect the difference between matching and mismatching non-English phones at 7 months, they no longer do so at 11 months (Danielson et al., 2017). This attunement is also seen in visual-only language discrimination (Weikum et al., 2007). Thus, perceptual attunement appears to be "bisensory," involving both auditory and visual perception of spoken language.

Oral-motor movements also influence speech perception in young infants. Correlational studies find babies with better-developed babbling show more precise phonetic discrimination (DePaolis, Vihman, & Keren-Portnoy, 2011). To test whether oral-motor feedback alters infant perception, we designed a task in which the caregiver held a finger or small object (pacifier or teething toy) in the infant's mouth, and found that the presence of a toy in the mouth did change AV matching (Yeung & Werker, 2013). The same effect occurs during auditory-only speech perception. When 6-month-old infants were tested on their ability to discriminate the nonnative retroflex versus dental distinction /da/-/Da/, interfering with the articulators necessary for producing the distinction via depression of the tongue tip with a flat teether disrupted discrimination (Bruderer, Danielson, Kandhadai, & Werker, 2015). This oral-motor influence on discrimination of a nonnative contrast suggests that – as observed with infants' detection of AV phonetic congruence – this cross-model representation does not require specific learning. Still unknown is whether there is perceptual attunement to oral-motor influences on speech perception. Here, we might expect a different kind of effect wherein the feedback from oral-motor movements is less important once a more abstract representation of the phonological category is established. And indeed, this might be why the motor influences are found, but less consistently so, among adults.

21.5 Word Segmentation

One of the challenges of language perception is segmenting the speech stream into individual words. Contrary to our perception as fluent adult speakers of a language, pauses in the auditory speech stream do not reliably signal word boundaries. Instead, the rapidity of speech leads to coarticulation, such that the articulation of one phoneme directly affects the articulation of the following. This occurs both within and between words, leading to a continuous auditory signal without clear breaks to demarcate word boundaries.

Infants face an even more challenging situation, given their lack of a priori knowledge that the speech stream contains words for them to find. Instead, discovering words and parsing the speech stream occur in tandem during development. The auditory speech stream contains a number of cues demarcating word boundaries, including statistical regularities, prosodic stress patterns, phonotactic regularities, and allophonic variations. Infants are sensitive to a number of these cues, and by the second half of their first year of life, are able to exploit these regularities to segment words from the continuous stream of speech (see Mattys & Bortfeld, 2016, for a comprehensive review of speech segmentation work).

Prosody is one cue to word boundaries. Infants show sensitivity to the prosody of their native language by 6 months (Jusczyk, Cutler, & Redanz, 1993; Höhle, Bijeljac-Babic, Herold, Weissenborn, & Nazzi, 2009) and by 9 months, infants are able to group clusters of syllables based on their prosody (Morgan & Saffran, 1995). English-learning infants correctly isolate from fluent speech words that follow the trochaic stress pattern, but not words that violate it (Johnson & Jusczyk, 2001); at this same age French-learning infants segment words that follow the iambic pattern more common in French (Nazzi, Mersad, Sundara, Iakimova, & Polka, 2013).

Another cue to word boundaries is phonotactics, which constrain the possible ordering of sound segments in a word. For example, clusters of stop consonants at the beginning of a word are allowable in Polish (as in the Polish word "kto"), but not English. Infants show sensitivity to the phonotactic regularities of their native language by 9 months of age (Jusczyk, Friederici, Wessels, Svenkerud, & Jusczyk, 1993) and listen longer to lists of nonwords containing commonly occurring phonotactic sequences (e.g., "chun") over rare phonotactic sequences (e.g., "cherg") (Jusczyk, Luce and Charles-Luce, 1994), suggesting that infants may learn phonotactic rules by tracking the statistical frequency with which two sounds co-occur. Infants use these cues to segment speech (Mattys & Jusczyk, 2001), however this ability is constrained by infants' previous experience with speech sound combinations; 9-month-olds are able to identify word boundaries when they are delineated by commonly occurring phonotactic sequences (e.g., pl or tr), but not those delineated by illegal or uncommonly occurring sequences (e.g., tl or dr) (Archer & Curtin, 2016).

For infants to learn the stress patterns and phonotactics that signal word boundaries in their language, some initial speech segmentation must take place. It is possible infants are able to learn these regularities through encounters with single words. Indeed, Bortfeld and colleagues have shown that infants can use highly familiar words such as their own names or the word "Mommy" to segment words on either side (Bortfeld, Morgan, Golinkoff, & Rathbun, 2005). Given that we now know that by 6 months of age infants recognize, and even show basic associative understanding of, other highly common words (see Bergelson & Swingley, 2012; Tincoff & Jusczyk, 1999), reliance on known words might play a bigger role in word segmentation than previously thought.

Statistical properties – in particular, transitional probabilities between syllables – also help infants pull out words. For example, while "pretty baby" may occur, "pretty" and "baby" also occur in other contexts. Thus the sounds "pretty" and "bab-by" are more likely to occur than are "ty-ba." Infants are sensitive to this statistical information in artificial language learning tasks (Saffran, Aslin, & Newport, 1996) as well as natural speech (Hay, Pelucchi, Graf-Estes, & Saffran, 2011).

The richness of natural language – where the acoustic signal contains multiple patterns that signal word boundaries – supports word segmentation, providing candidates for lexical learning. Indeed, Curtin, Mintz, and Christiansen (2005) found that not only did 7-month-olds use stress to pull out words, the infants stored stress information along with the word form. And, in work with older infants, Graf-Estes and colleagues have found that the word forms detected by statistical learning are better candidates for learning word-to-world mappings (Graf Estes, Evans, Alibali, & Saffran, 2007; see also Hay et al., 2011).

21.6 Mapping Meaning: Acoustic Foundations and Social Influences

A growing body of research has addressed the relationship between attunement to the native phonetic repertoire and the establishment of native phonological categories that can guide word recognition and word learning. Three levels of word understanding can be distinguished. First, whether infants use native phonetic categories to distinguish previously heard word forms versus mispronunciations, independent of tying them to meaning. Second, meaningful word recognition: recognizing the match between known words and known objects, wherein the words can be either correctly pronounced or have a (native or nonnative) phonetic feature change. And finally, studies of meaningful word learning: do infants use native phonetic/phonological categories to guide the learning of new words.

The word-form recognition studies overlap considerably with the word segmentation studies. In addition to asking what cues enable infants to pull out words from continuous speech, word-form recognition studies ask what the detail is in such remembered words. Infants of even the youngest ages tested can discriminate familiarized word forms from single-feature mispronunciations (Jusczyk & Aslin, 1995). Thus, there is no difficulty in discriminating native phonetic differences. However, when infants are tested without a prefamiliarization period, infants will, in some tasks, treat a single phonetic feature mispronunciation as an acceptable variant of the familiar word form (Mills et al., 2004).

When tested in word-learning tasks, infants have more difficulty using single-feature phonetic differences to guide their mapping. In a word–object associative learning task, 14-month-olds learn to pair two phonetically dissimilar words with two different objects, but they fail to do so if the words differ in only a single phonetic feature – even though they discriminate this difference in a nonsense syllable discrimination task. However, this is not an "all or nothing" phenomenon. If infants are first given clear cues that the task is one of word learning, they can then succeed when tested on the novel word–object pairs (Fennell & Waxman, 2010).

By 17–20 months, infants more reliably learn to map two words that differ in a native phonological distinction onto two different objects (Thiessen, 2007; Werker, Fennell, Corcoran, & Stager, 2002) but not if the distinction is nonnative (Dietrich, Swingley, & Werker, 2007), demonstrating that native phonological categories guide word learning by this age. A number of studies show that by this age, there is improvement in the use of native contrasts to guide word learning, and a concomitant decline in the success of using nonnative distinctions (see Hay, Graf Estes, Wang, & Saffran, 2015 for data and a review). Due to the specificity of the representation, infants struggle to accommodate accented speech; even 24-month-olds fail to recognize newly learned words presented in a novel accent at test (Schmale, Cristià, Seidl, & Johnson, 2010).

Early language and social experience interact to guide toddlers' word-learning strategies. Toddlers who grow up hearing more variation are able, at an earlier age, to recognize accented words (van Heugten & Johnson, 2017). This ability is influenced by social context – toddlers are more willing to accept a mispronunciation of a word from a speaker of a different race (Weatherhead & White, 2018). Thus, while the phonological system plays a bigger role in guiding children's word processing across age, the phenomenon is not "all or none."

The studies cited above show a relation – at increasingly more abstract levels of word processing – between the establishment of native phonological categories and word processing, with native categories first guiding segmentation, then retention and recognition, and then word learning. Recently, however, researchers have begun to explore whether this might be a bidirectional process. Just as infants start using native-language phonological categories to guide word recognition and word learning, they also use their understanding of which words go with which objects to help them attune to their native phonetic categories (Figure 21.1). With multiple studies now affirming that infants begin to recognize not just word forms, but actual word–object pairings by as early as 6 months of age, many in the field have begun to speculate that this early word learning might simultaneously support native phonetic category learning. The attunement to native phonetic categories and the beginning of

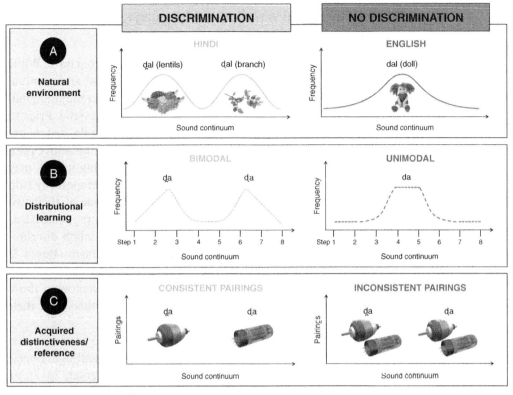

Figure 21.1. *Schematics of speech contrast discrimination in infancy within the context of different learning environments. (A) The variability in the pronunciation of "da" an infant might hear in a natural language environment, depending on whether the infant is growing up learning Hindi or English. (B) How the variability present in natural learning environments is modeled in studies of distributional learning, using relative frequencies of sounds that are created along a continuum from / ḍa/ to / ḍa/. (C) How the same variability is modeled in studies of acquired distinctiveness, in which two consistent sound–object pairings are presented to highlight the distinction between / ḍa/ and /ḍa/ in comparison to inconsistent pairings. Source: Adapted from Werker, Yeung, and Yoshida (2012), and reprinted from Werker (2018).*

phonemic use to distinguish lexical items might begin much earlier in development than we once thought, and, at the same time, last longer. Thus, while attunement to the native phonetic repertoire is involved in, and sets the limits on, establishing a lexicon, the dynamics of perceptual attunement do not adhere to the conceptual use of phonological distinctions in lexical recognition and understanding.

21.7 Sociocultural Variations on Language Experience: The Bilingual Baby

Many babies grow up learning two or more languages from birth. While there are differences in the trajectory of perceptual attunement and eventual language learning, the course of acquisition is similar between monolingual-learning and bilingual-learning infants (see Hoff, 2015, for a review). Prior to perceptual attunement, young bilingual-learning infants are able, just as are monolingual-learning infants, to discriminate both native and nonnative phonetic distinctions. While some studies suggest bilingual-learning infants may go through a period, around 8–10 months of age, where they temporarily stop discriminating an infrequent phonetic contrast used in only one of their two native languages (Bosch & Sebastián-Gallés, 2003), the literature is consistent in suggesting that by the end of the first year of life, they maintain discrimination of the distinctions used in both of their native languages (Bosch & Sebastián-Gallés, 2003; Sundara, Polka, & Molnar, 2008). Some research suggests bilingual infants maintain sensitivity to nonnative distinctions – those not used in either native language – for a longer period of time than their monolingual-learning peers.

Debates continue as to whether the prolonged attunement to nonnative distinctions observed in bilingual-learning infants comes from attentional boosting (see Sebastián-Gallés, Albareda-Castellot, Weikum, & Werker, 2012), or from reduced exposure to the properties of each language and thus a delay (see Anderson, Morgan, & White, 2003, for evidence that frequency of exposure influences the timing of perceptual attunement). In either case, prolonged discrimination could result from higher-level, general cognitive processes that boost attention and/or executive function – two effects that have been reported in bilingual populations (Bialystok & Viswanathan, 2009). Another possibility is that the differential experience of being a bilingual gates plasticity in the actual critical period circuits under consideration in this chapter. Further research is needed to tease apart these explanations, and to search for the underlying mechanism.

Like monolingual-learning infants, bilingual-learning infants use the phonological categories established in each of their native languages to guide word learning. Early data indicated this might emerge at a later age (Fennell, Byers-Heinlein, & Werker, 2007), however subsequent work showed that if bilingual infants were first given information about which language they were hearing, they could succeed at the same age as monolinguals (Byers-Heinlein & Fennell, 2014; Mattock, Polka, Rvachew, & Krehm, 2010). These results suggest it is not an age difference in establishment of native phonological categories, but rather the appropriateness of the stimuli that accounts for differences observed in bilingual and monolingual infants' learning of word–object pairs.

21.8 The Development of Neural Specialization for Language

Brain networks that support language processing in the adult are already present in the infant brain. Speech activates a language network that includes primary and associative auditory regions, as well as frontal and premotor areas including the superior temporal gyrus (Wernicke's area), the planum temporale, and the inferior frontal gyrus (Broca's area; Dehaene-Lambertz, Dehaene, & Hertz-Pannier, 2002; Perani et al., 2011). Key regions in this network are already activated by speech stimuli in premature infants, suggesting that the foundations of the language network are driven by intrinsic rather than experiential factors (Mahmoudzadeh et al., 2013).

While there are clear asymmetries in speech processing in adults, speech processing in newborns is more bilateral, although conflicting results have been found in the field that complicate the interpretation. Studies in neonates using functional near-infrared spectroscopy (fNIRS) and functional magnetic resonance imaging (fMRI) reveal evidence for bilateral (e.g., May et al., 2017), left-lateralized (e.g., Sato et al., 2012), and right-lateralized processing of speech (e.g., Perani et al., 2011). Differences in results may lie in the techniques used for analysis or with the characteristics of the language stimuli used. Lateralization of language processing in the adult brain has been hypothesized to arise from differences in how auditory association regions process the temporal features of the acoustic signal (Poeppel, 2003). Sensitivity to both the rapidly changing acoustic features that distinguish distinct phonemes as well as the subtle differences in frequency used to distinguish speaker intonation require processing the acoustic signal with both high-temporal and high-spectral resolution. The asymmetrical timing model (Poeppel, 2003) hypothesizes that the left and right hemispheres sample the incoming auditory signal at different rates – the left with a time window optimized to capture phonetic information, and the right with a time window optimized to capture syllabic information. These differences are driven by intrinsic differences in the neuronal properties and connectivity in different cortical regions. Consistent with this model, speech stimuli that have been altered to highlight prosodic information are more likely to activate language areas in infants' right hemisphere, as is music (Perani et al., 2010; Perani et al., 2011). Telkemeyer et al. (2009) directly investigated the sensitivity of the newborn brain to sounds with varying temporal structure. Acoustic stimuli varying with a temporal rate matching the rate of change of formants that support phonetic discrimination elicited a strong bilateral hemodynamic response in inferior temporal regions. Stimuli with slower fluctuations elicited slightly smaller responses in the same regions, as well as right-lateralized responses in the superior temporoparietal region, consistent with an early right-processing bias for slower acoustic signals. Thus, at birth, the most consistent evidence for specialization is that of the right hemisphere showing early specialization for the processing of slowly changing acoustic features.

By 3 months of age, speech also engages prefrontal cortical areas that have been implicated in word recall, and may reflect a growing familiarity with speech input (Dehaene-Lambertz et al., 2002). Left lateralization in response to normal speech is more consistently observed, and may reflect increases in the specialization of left auditory regions for the processing of more rapidly changing acoustic signals (Dehaene-Lambertz et al., 2002; Dehaene-Lambertz et al., 2006). Connectivity analyses in infants reveal rapid changes in the temporo-frontal connectivity that support language networks – ventral pathways are initially more mature than dorsal pathways, however, the rapid maturation of dorsal pathways over the first 5 months of life closes this gap (Dubois et al., 2016). Connectivity analysis finds an increase in interhemispheric connectivity from birth until 11.5 months of age, at which point intrahemispheric connectivity increases (Emerson, Gao, & Lin, 2016). These structural results suggest that language processing should become more asymmetric after 1 year.

Whether lateralization is driven by maturational changes inherent in a biological program or by environmental experience is an active area of research. The presence of some level of asymmetrical processing in the newborn brain suggests these processes may be the result of a maturational program. However, the slightly earlier right bias for rhythmical processing may reflect experience accumulated *in utero*, where infants have more access to the slowly changing acoustic features in their environment. When considering this question, it is interesting to address whether nonspeech sounds activate the language network in infants and how this early processing is shaped by experience.

Neonates show a preference for speech over nonspeech auditory stimuli (Vouloumanos & Werker, 2007). However, at this age, they also show a preference for rhesus monkey vocalizations; over the first 3 months of life, infants' perceptual preferences narrow, and they prefer speech over other species' vocalizations (Vouloumanos et al., 2010). Neuroimaging work supports the view that while the newborn brain is tuned to the speech signal, it is less selective for speech than that of older infants (Cristia, Minagawa, & Dupoux, 2014). By about 1 month of age, magnetic resonance imaging (MRI) activity reveals selectivity for speech sounds over noncommunicative human signals, monkey vocalizations, and other auditory stimuli, with activation in response to speech specifically seen in the left temporal cortex (Shultz, Vouloumanos, Bennett, & Pelphrey, 2014).

In summation, neuroimaging studies reveal that at birth, speech engages early language networks. However, this early brain response is not specific, and is also observed in response to communicative vocalizations from other species. Over the first year of life, innate developmental programs and environmental input interact to drive increased specificity for native speech processing in these networks. A similar process is observed for the formation of native phonological categories over the first year of life.

Neurons in the posterior superior temporal gyrus integrate spectro-temporal acoustic features to facilitate phonetic categorization in adults (Mesgarani,

Cheung, Johnson, & Chang, 2014). As discussed, infants' phonetic boundaries shift to accommodate language experience. Neuroimaging data has revealed changes in processing that reflect perceptual narrowing as infants' native phoneme categories take shape. Even before birth, initial perceptual boundaries between different phones are observed, presumably driven by intrinsic biases in auditory processing. Premature infants between 28 and 33 weeks gestation show a larger hemodynamic response when deviant phones are embedded in the presentation of a sequence of standard phones (i.e., the syllable "ga" following a string of "ba"), suggesting that even at this age infants are able to detect the difference (Mahmoudzadeh et al., 2013). The ability of other species to perceive acoustic changes that signal phonetic boundaries, such as changes in voice onset time, suggest innate perceptual biases in the auditory cortex may support phonetic category formation (Kuhl & Miller, 1975).

On the other hand, even in young infants, evidence suggests that phones are processed at a linguistic level, and that the perception of phoneme categories is not simply based on low-level acoustic features. Using an event-related-potential (ERP) mismatch response paradigm, Cheour-Luhtanen et al. (1995) demonstrated that newborn infants can detect a change in vowel. Interestingly, newborns are more sensitive to a change in phoneme as opposed to a change in the pitch contour of a given phoneme, suggesting that the newborn brain is already tuned to detect acoustic changes that signal a change in phoneme (Kujala et al., 2004). By 3–4 months, presentation of a deviant speech sound that crosses a phonetic boundary generates a larger mismatch response than a deviant with similar acoustic distance but that lies within the same phonetic category as the standard (Dehaene-Lambertz & Baillet, 1998). A mismatch response is also seen when the same phoneme produced by multiple speakers is used as the standard, suggesting a level of robustness to these acoustic features (Dehaene-Lambertz & Peña, 2001). Perceptual narrowing and native-language attunement lead to changes in the neuronal response to native and nonnative phonetic contrasts over the first year of life. While 6-month-old Finnish infants showed a comparable mismatch response to a native and nonnative (Estonian) vowel change, 12-month-old Finnish infants showed a much larger mismatch response to the native than nonnative vowel change. This pattern is reversed in Estonian 12-month-olds (Cheour et al. 1998).

21.9 The Opening and Closing of Critical Period Windows During Development

While it is clear that the developing cortex is sensitive to auditory experience before birth, the extent to which cortical circuits are rewired in response to environmental input is controlled by critical periods. The classic definition of a critical period (CP) is a window of time during which experience is able to rewire neuronal circuitry – experience outside of this window has limited ability to alter the cortical circuit. Multiple, cascading critical periods tune neuronal responses in different systems, supporting the acquisition of higher-order cognitive capacities such as language. These windows are gated by molecular cues that regulate the timing at which these periods occur over development, aligning circuit plasticity with appropriate environmental experience.

The opening of critical periods is regulated by the maturation of inhibitory circuits (Takesian & Hensch, 2013). The integration of inhibitory interneurons into the cortical circuit lags behind that of excitatory cells (Petanjek, Kostovic, & Esclapez, 2009), with inhibitory cell migration continuing to frontal cortical regions up to 7 months postnatally (Paredes et al., 2016). Inhibitory cell maturation is staggered across different cortical regions (Honig, Herrmann, & Shatz, 1996), which may mediate the cascading nature of CP opening across different systems (see Werker & Hensch, 2015, for a discussion of cascading CPs in speech perception). Interestingly, CP closure is mediated not by a reduction in the factors that first permitted plasticity, but instead by an accumulation of brake-like factors that actively limit it. These include developmental changes in the regulation of inhibitory cell activity and neuromodulatory systems, as well as increases in structural barriers to plasticity (for a complete review of the molecular mechanisms involved, see Takesian & Hensch, 2013).

Changes in oscillatory brain activity over development may provide a window into the maturational state of cortical inhibition. Oscillatory activity in the low gamma frequency range (30–60 Hz) is of particular interest, as inhibitory cells play a pivotal role in the generation of rhythmic activity in this frequency range (for a review, see Hu, Gan, & Jonas, 2014). As the inhibitory circuit matures, cell responses become faster and more precisely timed – these properties are reflected in the gamma oscillation, which becomes stronger and more coherent with age (Uhlhaas et al., 2009). Oscillatory activity in response to language changes across development, perhaps reflecting changes in the inhibitory circuit that mediate the opening and closing of sensitive periods across domains. At 6 months, when environmental input is actively shaping phoneme categories, the presentation of a native phonemic contrast leads to a rise in low gamma power (Ortiz-Mantilla, Hämäläinen, Realpe-Bonilla, & Benasich, 2016). By 1 year of age, the critical window for phoneme attunement has passed, and the rise in low gamma power is no longer observed. Activity in this frequency range is maturationally constrained – premature infants do not show an elevation in gamma power in response to the rhythmical structure of their native language when compared to their age-matched peers, despite equal environmental exposure (Peña et al., 2010). Interestingly, the time course of premature infants' formation of native phonological categories is also aligned with their conceptual age as opposed to their overall speech experience, suggesting this process occurs during a CP in brain development that is regulated by intrinsic brain maturation (Peña, Werker, Dehaene-Lambertz, 2012).

21.10 How Experience Can Change Critical Period Timing: Diet, Drug Exposure

Critical period windows for different domains are staggered across development. The time when these windows of plasticity open and close is determined by the maturation of the underlying neuronal circuitry, thus, experiences and exposures that alter the development of this circuitry shift the timing of CP windows. This phenomenon has been extensively documented in animal models. Delays in the maturation of inhibitory cell development lead to either a delay or failure of the opening of the CP, while early maturation of inhibition can trigger a precocious CP (Takesian & Hensch, 2013). Several studies in humans, described below, suggest that similar shifts in the CP for native phoneme mapping occur.

Innis, Gilley, and Werker (2001) examined the effect of nutrition during the first 3 months of life on later sensitivity to nonnative sound contrasts. The level of the long-chain polyunsaturated fatty acid DHA present in the blood at 2 months of age was positively correlated with an infant's ability to discriminate nonnative contrast at 9 months of age. Thus, alterations in the mother's diet – leading to a change in breastfeeding infants' DHA intake – alter either the duration or timing of perceptual narrowing during the first year of life.

Drug exposure *in utero* also alters the timing of the CP for phoneme perception. Weikum, Oberlander, Hensch, and Werker (2012) compared the speech discrimination abilities of infants born to mothers diagnosed with depression and who were either being treated with serotonin reuptake inhibitors (SRIs) during pregnancy (SRI-exposure group) or who were not (depression-only group). At 6 months of age, infants in a control group (whose mothers were not diagnosed with depression) showed the expected ability to discriminate nonnative phonetic contrasts in both an auditory-only and a visual-only speech discrimination paradigm. Neither the SRI-exposure group nor the depression-only group were able to discriminate nonnative contrasts. When the infants were tested again at 10 months, the control group showed the expected decline in nonnative speech discrimination. However, the depression-only group were now able to discriminate the nonnative contrasts. Intriguingly, the SRI-exposure group were able to discriminate consonant contrasts when tested *in utero*, before infants in the depression only or control group were able to. This suggests that the critical window for phoneme attunement may be precocious in infants exposed to SRIs *in utero*, and delayed in infants born to mothers diagnosed with depression.

21.11 Policy Perspectives

Early language experience is critical for speech acquisition. The evidence presented in this chapter highlights that the acquisition of a language from birth is an active process; rich language experience and genetically driven developmental programs interact over the first years of life to wire up the language systems in the brain during a number of early, cascading critical periods that support later language development.

While we do not offer specific policy prescriptions in this chapter, we believe that policy should strive to support access to a rich early language environment for infants. This includes parental leave policies that allow parents to be with their children during the first year of life, and provide support for mothers suffering from depression. Successful language acquisition requires more than just exposure to auditory streams of speech, it requires interaction with the caregiver. Social interactions provide visual and tactile information that support the formation of multimodal representations, enable contingent interactions that support language learning, and afford numerous opportunities for the caregiver to direct the infant's attention (Hoff, 2006). Infants born to mothers who have been diagnosed with depression show delayed tuning to native-language contrasts, which may be due to reduced interactive language input and maternal sensitivity (Weikum et al., 2012).

The research presented in this chapter has important implications for pediatricians and early child educators. There are a number of cases where differences in early environmental exposure affect language acquisition, including infants born prematurely. Speech perception is tuned to the native language through a complex interaction between the brain and the environment. For infants born prematurely, there is a mismatch between environmental input and biological preparedness – exposure to broadcast speech begins at a point when the brain maturation is in a state where it normally receives sounds attenuated and filtered in the uterine environment. Many infants born prematurely suffer from language delays (van Noort-van der Spek, Franken, & Weisglas-Kuperus, 2012). As discussed previously in this chapter, several aspects of speech perceptual development, including sensitivity to the native-language rhythm and phoneme category formation, are gated by critical periods, and do not show precocious development in response to this early exposure to broadcast speech (Peña et al., 2010; Peña et al., 2012). However, other aspects of language development, such as sensitivity to native phonotactic rules, seem to be reliant on the accumulation of experience (Gonzalez-Gomez & Nazzi, 2012). This results in not only a mismatch between brain maturation and environmental input, but also a misalignment between the development of different speech perceptual abilities. Our growing understanding of how early perceptual attunement to different aspects of the speech signal work together to support word learning in an interactive process, as well as the biological mechanisms regulating this attunement, will better position us to support language acquisition in premature infants, as well as other clinical populations where language critical periods may be altered or shifted.

References

Anderson, J. L., Morgan, J. L., & White, K. S. (2003). A statistical basis for speech sound discrimination. *Language and Speech, 46*, 155–182.

Archer, S. L., & Curtin, S. (2016). Nine-month-olds use frequency of onset clusters to segment novel words. *Journal of Experimental Child Psychology, 148*, 131–141.

Bergelson, E., & Swingley, D. (2012). At 6–9 months, human infants know the meanings of many common nouns. *Proceedings of the National Academy of Sciences of the United States of America, 109*(9), 3253–3258.

Bialystok, E., & Viswanathan, M. (2009). Components of executive control with advantages for bilingual children in two cultures. *Cognition, 112*(3), 494–500.

Bortfeld, H., Morgan, J., Golinkoff, R., & Rathbun, K. (2005). Mommy and me: Familiar names help launch babies into speech stream segmentation. *Psychological Science, 16*, 298–304.

Bosch, L., & Sebastián-Gallés, N. (2003). Simultaneous bilingualism and the perception of a language-specific vowel contrast in the first year of life. *Language and Speech, 46*, 217–243.

Bruderer, A. G., Danielson, D. K., Kandhadai, P., & Werker, J. F. (2015). Sensorimotor influences on speech perception in infancy. *Proceedings of the National Academy of Sciences, 112*(44), 13531–13536.

Byers-Heinlein, K., & Fennell, C. T. (2014). Perceptual narrowing in the context of increased variation: Insights from bilingual infants. *Developmental Psychobiology, 56*(2), 274–291.

Cheour, M., Ceponiene, R., Lehtokoski, A., Luuk, A., Allik, J., Alho, K., & Näätänen, R. (1998). Development of language-specific phoneme representations in the infant brain. *Nature Neuroscience, 1*, 351–353.

Cheour-Luhtanen, M., Alho, K., Kujala, T., Sainio, K., Reinikainen, K., Renlund, M., … Näätänen, R. (1995). Mismatch negativity indicates vowel discrimination in newborns. *Hearing Research, 82*(1), 53–58.

Cristia, A., Minagawa, Y., & Dupoux, E. (2014). Responses to vocalizations and auditory controls in the human newborn brain. *PLOS ONE, 9*(12), e115162.

Curtin, S., Mintz, T. H., & Christiansen, M. H. (2005). Stress changes the representational landscape: Evidence from word segmentation. *Cognition, 96*, 233–262.

Danielson, D. K., Bruderer, A. G., Kandhadai, P., Vatikiotis-Bateson, E., & Werker, J. F. (2017) The organization and reorganization of audiovisual speech perception in the first year of life. *Cognitive Development, 42*, 37–48.

DeCasper, A. J., & Fifer, W. P. (1980). Of human bonding: Newborns prefer their mothers' voices. *Science, 208*(4448), 1174–1176.

DeCasper, A. J., & Spence, M. J. (1986). Prenatal maternal speech influences newborns' perception of speech sounds. *Infant Behavior & Development, 9*(2), 133–150.

Dehaene-Lambertz, G., & Baillet, S. (1998). A phonological representation in the infant brain. *NeuroReport, 9*(8), 1885–1888.

Dehaene-Lambertz, G., Dehaene, S., & Hertz-Pannier, L. (2002). Functional neuroimaging of speech perception in infants. *Science, 298*(5600), 2013–2015.

Dehaene-Lambertz, G., Hertz-Pannier, L., Dubois, J., Mériaux, S., Roche, A., Sigman, M., & Dehaene, S. (2006). Functional organization of perisylvian activation during presentation of sentences in preverbal infants. *Proceedings of the National Academy of Sciences of the United States of America, 103*(38), 14240–14245.

Dehaene-Lambertz, G., & Peña, M. (2001). Electrophysiological evidence for automatic phonetic processing in neonates. *NeuroReport, 12*(14), 3155–3158.

DePaolis, R. A., Vihman, M. M., & Keren-Portnoy, T. (2011). Do production patterns influence the processing of speech in prelinguistic infants? *Infant Behavior & Development, 34*(4), 590–601.

Dietrich, C., Swingley, D., & Werker, J. F. (2007). Native language governs interpretation of salient speech sound differences at 18 months. *Proceedings of the National Academy of Sciences of the United States of America, 104*(41), 16027–16031.

Dubois, J., Poupon, C., Thirion, B., Simonnet, H., Kulikova, S., Leroy, F., ... Dehaene-Lambertz, G. (2016). Exploring the early organization and maturation of linguistic pathways in the human infant brain. *Cerebral Cortex, 26*(5), 2283–2298.

Emerson, R. W., Gao, W., & Lin, W. (2016). Longitudinal study of the emerging functional connectivity asymmetry of primary language regions during infancy. *Journal of Neuroscience, 36*(42), 10883–10892.

Feldman, N. H., Griffiths, T. L., Goldwater, S., & Morgan, J. L. (2013). A role for the developing lexicon in phonetic category acquisition. *Psychological Review, 120*(4), 751–778.

Fennell, C. T., Byers-Heinlein, K., & Werker, J. F. (2007). Using speech sounds to guide word learning: The case of bilingual infants. *Child Development, 78*(5), 1510–1525.

Fennell, C. T., & Waxman, S. R. (2010). What paradox? Referential cues allow for infant use of phonetic detail in word learning. *Child Development, 81*(5), 1376–1383.

Gonzalez-Gomez, N., & Nazzi, T. (2012). Phonotactic acquisition in healthy preterm infants. *Developmental Science, 15*(6), 885–894.

Graf Estes, K., Evans, J. L., Alibali, M. W., & Saffran, J. R. (2007). Can infants map meaning to newly segmented words? Statistical segmentation and word learning. *Psychological Science, 18*(3), 254–260.

Hay, J. F., Graf Estes, K., Wang, T., & Saffran, J. R. (2015). From flexibility to constraint: The contrastive use of lexical tone in early word learning. *Child Development, 86*(1), 10–22.

Hay, J. F., Pelucchi, B., Graf Estes, K., & Saffran, J. R. (2011). Linking sounds to meanings: Infant statistical learning in a natural language. *Cognitive Psychology, 63*(2), 93–106.

Hoff, E. (2006). How social contexts support and shape language development. *Developmental Review, 26*(1), 55–88.

(2015). Language development in bilingual children. In E. Bavin & L. Naigles (Eds.), *The Cambridge handbook of child language* (2nd ed., pp. 483–503). Cambridge, UK: Cambridge University Press.

Höhle, B., Bijeljac-Babic, R., Herold, B., Weissenborn, J., & Nazzi, T. (2009). Language specific prosodic preferences during the first half year of life: Evidence from German and French infants. *Infant Behavior & Development, 32*(3), 262–274.

Honig, L, S., Herrmann K., & Shatz, C, J. (1996). Developmental changes revealed by immunohistochemical markers in human cerebral cortex. *Cerebral Cortex*, 6(6), 794–806.

Hu, H., Gan, J, & Jonas, P. (2014). Fast-spiking, parvalbumin⁺ GABAergic interneurons: From cellular design to microcircuit function. *Science*, 345(6196), 1255263.

Innis, S. M., Gilley, J., & Werker, J. F. (2001). Are human milk long-chain polyunsaturated fatty acids related to visual and neural development in breast-fed term infants? *Journal of Pediatrics*, 139, 532–538.

Johnson, E. K., & Jusczyk, P. W. (2001). Word segmentation by 8-month-olds: When speech cues count more than statistics. *Journal of Memory and Language*, 44(4), 548–567.

Jusczyk, P. W., & Aslin, R. N. (1995). Infants' detection of the sound patterns of words in fluent speech. *Cognitive Psychology*, 29(1), 1–23.

Jusczyk, P. W., Cutler, A., & Redanz, N. J. (1993). Infants' preference for the predominant stress patterns of English words. *Child Development*, 64, 675–687.

Jusczyk, P. W., Friederici, A. D., Wessels, J. M., Svenkerud, V. Y., & Jusczyk, A. M. (1993). Infants' sensitivity to the sound patterns of native language words. *Journal of Memory and Language*, 32(3), 402–420.

Jusczyk, P. W., Luce, P. A., & Charles-Luce, J. (1994). Infants' sensitivity to phonotactic patterns in the native language. *Journal of Memory and Language*, 33(5), 630–645.

Kuhl, P. K., & Meltzoff, A. N. (1982). The bimodal perception of speech in infancy. *Science*, 218(4577), 1138–1141.

Kuhl, P. K., & Miller, J. D. (1975). Speech perception by the chinchilla: Voiced-voiceless distinction in alveolar plosive consonants. *Science*, 190(4209), 69–72.

Kuhl, P. K., Stevens, E., Hayashi, A., Deguchi, T., Kiritani, S., & Iverson, P. (2006). Infants show a facilitation effect for native language phonetic perception between 6 and 12 months. *Developmental Science*, 9(2), F13–F21.

Kuhl, P. K., Williams, K. A., Lacerda, F., Stevens, K. N., & Lindblom, B. (1992). Linguistic experience alters phonetic perception in infants by 6 months of age. *Science*, 255(5044), 606–608.

Kujala, A., Huotilainen, M., Hotakainen, M., Lennes, M., Parkkonen, L., Fellman, V., & Näätänen, R. (2004). Speech-sound discrimination in neonates as measured with MEG. *NeuroReport*, 15(13), 2089–2092.

Liu, L., & Kager, R. (2017). Statistical learning of speech sounds is most robust during the period of perceptual attunement. *Journal of Experimental Child Psychology*, 164, 192–208

Mahmoudzadeh, M., Dehaene-Lambertz, G., Fournier, M., Kongolo, G., Goudjil, S., Dubois, J., … Wallois, F. (2013). Syllabic discrimination in premature human infants. *Proceedings of the National Academy of Sciences of the United States of America*, 110(12), 4846–4851.

Mattock, K., & Burnham, D. (2006). Chinese and English infants' tone perception: Evidence for perceptual reorganization. *Infancy*, 10, 241–265.

Mattock, K., Polka, L., Rvachew, S., & Krehm, M. (2010). The first steps in word learning are easier when the shoes fit: Comparing monolingual and bilingual infants. *Developmental Science*, 13(1), 229–243.

Mattys, S. L., & Bortfeld, H. (2016). *Speech segmentation*. In G. Gaskell, & J. Mirkovic (Eds.), *Speech perception and spoken word recognition* (pp. 55–75). London: Psychology Press.

Mattys, S. L., & Jusczyk, P. W. (2001). Phonotactic cues for segmentation of fluent speech by infants. *Cognition, 78*(2), 91–121.

May, L., Gervain, J., Carreiras, M., & Werker, J. F. (2017). The specificity of the neural response to speech at birth. *Developmental Science,* 21(3), e12564.

Maye, J., Weiss, D. J., & Aslin, R. N. (2008). Statistical phonetic learning in infants: Facilitation and feature generalization. *Developmental Science, 11*(1), 122–134.

Maye, J., Werker, J. F., & Gerken, L. A. (2002). Infant sensitivity to distributional information can affect phonetic discrimination. *Cognition, 82*(3), B101–B111.

McMurray, B., Aslin, R. N., & Toscano, J. C. (2009). Statistical learning of phonetic categories: Insights from a computational approach. *Developmental Science, 12*(3), 369–378.

Mehler, J., Jusczyk, P., Lambertz, G., Halsted, N., Bertoncini, J., & Amiel-Tison, C. (1988). A precursor of language acquisition in young infants. *Cognition, 29*(2), 143–178.

Mesgarani, N., Cheung, C., Johnson, K., & Chang, E. F. (2014). Phonetic feature encoding in human superior temporal gyrus. *Science, 343*(6174), 1006–1010.

Mills, D. L., Prat, C., Zangl, R., Stager, C. L., Neville, H. J., & Werker, J. F. (2004). Language experience and the organization of brain activity to phonetically similar words: ERP evidence from 14- and 20-month-olds. *Journal of Cognitive Neuroscience,* 16(8), 1–13.

Molnar, M., Gervain, J., & Carreiras, M. (2014). Within-rhythm class native language discrimination abilities of Basque-Spanish monolingual and bilingual infants at 3.5 months of age. *Infancy, 19*, 326–337.

Morgan, J. L., & Saffran, J. R. (1995). Emerging integration of sequential and suprasegmental information in preverbal speech segmentation. *Child Development, 66*(4), 911–936.

Nazzi, T., Jusczyk, P. W., & Johnson, E. K. (2000). Language discrimination by English-learning 5-month-olds: Effects of rhythm and familiarity. *Journal of Memory and Language, 43*(1), 1–19.

Nazzi, T., Mersad, K., Sundara, M., Iakimova, G., & Polka, L. (2013). Early word segmentation in infants acquiring Parisian French: Task-dependent and dialect-specific aspects. *Journal of Child Language, 41*(3), 600–633.

Nazzi, T., & Ramus, F. (2003). Perception and acquisition of linguistic rhythm by infants. *Speech Communication, 41*(1), 233–243.

Nespor, M., Shukla, M., van de Vijver, R., Avesani, C., Schraudolf, H., & Donati, C. (2008). Different phrasal prominence realizations in VO and OV languages. *Lingue e Linguaggio, 2*, 1–29.

Ortiz-Mantilla, S., Hämäläinen, J. A., Realpe-Bonilla, T., & Benasich, A. A. (2016). Oscillatory dynamics underlying perceptual narrowing of native phoneme mapping from 6 to 12 months of age. *Journal of Neuroscience, 36*(48), 12095–12105.

Palmer, S. B., Fais, L., Golinkoff, R. M., & Werker, J. F. (2012). Perceptual narrowing of linguistic sign occurs in the first year of life. *Child Development, 83*(2), 543–53.

Paredes, M. F., James, D., Gil-Perotin, S., Kim, H., Cotter, J. A., Ng, C., ... Alvarez-Buylla, A. (2016). Extensive migration of young neurons into the infant human frontal lobe. *Science*, *354*(6308), aaf7073.

Peña, M., Pittaluga, E., & Mehler, J. (2010). Language acquisition in premature and full-term infants. *Proceedings of the National Academy of Sciences of the United States of America*, *107*(8), 3823–3828.

Peña, M., Werker, J. F., & Dehaene-Lambertz, G. (2012). Earlier speech exposure does not accelerate speech acquisition. *Journal of Neuroscience*, *32*(33), 11159–11163.

Perani, D., Saccuman, M. C., Scifo, P., Anwander, A., Spada, D., Baldoli, C., ... Friederici, A. D. (2011). Neural language networks at birth. *Proceedings of the National Academy of Sciences of the United States of America*, *108*(38), 16056–16061.

Perani, D., Saccuman, M. C., Scifo, P., Spada, D., Andreolli, G., Roveli, R., ... Koelsch, S. (2010). Functional specializations for music processing in the human newborn brain. *Proceedings of the National Academy of Sciences of the United States of America*, *107*(10), 4758–4763.

Petanjek, Z., Kostovic, I., & Esclapez, M. (2009). Primate-specific origins and migration of cortical GABAergic neurons. *Frontiers in Neuroanatomy*, *3*, 26

Poeppel, D. (2003). The analysis of speech in different temporal integration windows: cerebral lateralization as "asymmetric sampling in time." *Speech Communication*, *41*, 245–2555.

Pons, F., Lewkowicz, D. J., Soto-Faraco, S., & Sebastián-Gallés, N. (2009). Narrowing of intersensory speech perception in infancy. *Proceedings of the National Academy of Sciences of the United States of America*, *106*(26), 10598–10602.

Rosenblum, L. D., Schmuckler, M. A., & Johnson, J. A. (1997). The McGurk effect in infants. *Perception & Psychophysics*, *59*(3), 347–357.

Saffran, J. R., Aslin, R. N., & Newport, E. L. (1996). Statistical learning by 8-month-old infants. *Science*, *274*(5294), 1926–1928.

Sato, H., Hirabayashi, Y., Tsubokura, H., Kanai, M., Ashida, T., Konishi, I., ... Maki, A. (2012). Cerebral hemodynamics in newborn infants exposed to speech sounds: A whole-head optical topography study. *Human Brain Mapping*, *33*, 2092–2103.

Schmale, R., Cristià, A., Seidl, A., & Johnson E. K. (2010) Developmental changes in infants' ability to cope with dialect variation in word recognition. *Infancy*, *15*(6), 650–662.

Sebastián-Gallés, N., Albareda-Castellot, B., Weikum, W. M., & Werker, J. F. (2012). A bilingual advantage in visual language discrimination in infancy. *Psychological Science*, *23*(9), 994–999.

Schatz, T., Feldman, N., Goldwater, S., Cao, X., & Dupoux, E. (2019). Early phonetic learning without phonetic categories: Insights from large-scale simulations on realistic input. https://doi.org/10.31234/osf.io/fc4wh

Shultz, S., Vouloumanos, A., Bennett, R. H., & Pelphrey, K. (2014). Neural specialization for speech in the first months of life. *Developmental Science*, *17*(5), 766–774.

Sundara, M., Polka, L., & Genesee, F. (2006). Language-experience facilitates discrimination of /d-th/ in monolingual and bilingual acquisition of English. *Cognition*, *100*(2), 369–388.

Sundara, M., Polka, L., & Molnar, M. (2008). Development of coronal stop perception: bilingual infants keep pace with their monolingual peers. *Cognition*, *108*(1), 232–242.

Takesian, A. E., & Hensch, T. K. (2013). Balancing plasticity/stability across brain development. *Progress in Brain Research*, *207*, 3–34.

Teinonen, T., Aslin, R. N., Alku, P., & Csibra, G. (2008). Visual speech contributes to phonetic learning in 6-month-old infants. *Cognition*, *108*(3), 850–855.

Telkemeyer, S., Rossi, S., Koch, S. P., Nierhaus, T., Steinbrink, J., Poeppel, D., ... Wartenburger, I. (2009). Sensitivity of newborn auditory cortex to the temporal structure of sounds. *Journal of Neuroscience*, *29*(47), 14726–14733.

Thiessen, E. D. (2007). The effect of distributional information on children's use of phonemic contrasts. *Journal of Memory and Language*, *56*(1), 16–34.

Tincoff, R., & Jusczyk, P. W. (1999). Some beginnings of word comprehension in 6-month-olds. *Psychological Science*, *10*(2), 172–175.

Trainor, L. J., & Adams, B. (2000). Infants' and adults' use of duration and intensity cues in the segmentation of tone patterns. *Perception & Psychophysics*, *62*, 333–340.

Uhlhaas, P. J., Roux, F., Singer, W., Haenschel, C., Sireteanu, R., & Rodriguez, E. (2009). The development of neural synchrony reflects late maturation and restructuring of functional networks in humans. *Proceedings of the National Academy of Sciences of the United States of America*, *106*(24), 9866–9871.

van Heugten, M., & Johnson, E. K. (2017) Input matters: Multi-accent language exposure affects word recognition from infancy. *Journal of the Acoustical Society of America*, *142*(2), EL196–200.

van Noort-van der Spek, I. L., Franken, M. C., & Weisglas-Kuperus, N. (2012). Language functions in preterm-born children: A systematic review and meta-analysis. *Pediatrics*, *129*, 745–754.

Vouloumanos, A., Hauser, M. D., Werker, J. F., & Martin, A. (2010). The tuning of human neonates' preference for speech. *Child Development*, *81*(2), 517–527.

Vouloumanos, A., & Werker, J. F. (2007). Listening to language at birth: Evidence for a bias for speech in neonates. *Developmental Science*, *10*(2), 159–164.

Wanner, E., & Gleitman, L. R. (Eds.) (1982). *Language acquisition: The state of the art*. Cambridge, UK: Cambridge University Press.

Weatherhead, D., & White, K. S. (2018) And then I saw her race: Race-based expectations affect infants' word processing. *Cognition*, *177*, 87–97.

Weikum, W. M., Oberlander, T. F., Hensch, T. K., & Werker, J. F. (2012). Prenatal exposure to antidepressants and depressed maternal mood alter trajectory of infant speech perception. *Proceedings of the National Academy of Sciences of the United States of America*, *109*(2), 17221–17227.

Weikum, W., Vouloumanos, A., Navarra, J., Soto-Faraco, S., Sebastián-Gallés, N., & Werker, J. F. (2007). Visual language discrimination in infancy. *Science*, *316*(5828), 1159.

Werker, J. F. (2018). Perceptual beginnings to language acquisition. *Applied Psycholinguistics, 39*(4), 703–728.

Werker, J. F., Fennell, C. T., Corcoran, K., & Stager, C. L. (2002). Infants' ability to learn phonetically similar words: Effects of age and vocabulary size. *Infancy*, *3*(1), 1–30.

Werker, J. F., & Hensch, T. K. (2015). Critical periods in speech perception: New directions. *Annual Review of Psychology*, *66*, 173–96.

Werker, J. F., & Tees, R. C. (1984). Cross-language speech perception: Evidence for perceptual reorganization during the first year of life. *Infant Behavior and Development*, *7*(1), 49–63.

Werker, J. F., Yeung, H. H., & Yoshida, K. A. (2012). How do infants become experts at native speech perception? *Current Directions in Psychological Science*, *21*(4), 224–226.

Yeung, H. H., & Nazzi, T. (2014). Object labeling influences infant phonetic learning and generalization. *Cognition*, *132*(2), 151–163.

Yeung, H. H., & Werker, J. F. (2009). Learning words' sounds before learning how words sound: 9-month-olds use distinct objects as cues to categorize speech information. *Cognition*, *113*, 234–243.

(2013). Lip movements affect infant audiovisual speech perception. *Psychological Science*, *24*(5), 603–612.

Yoshida, K. A., Iversen, J. R., Patel A. D., Mazuka R., Nito H., Gervain J., & Werker, J. F. (2010). The development of perceptual grouping biases in infancy: A Japanese-English cross-linguistic study. *Cognition*, *115*(2), 356–361.

22 Infant Vocal Learning and Speech Production

Anne S. Warlaumont*

During the first year of life, human infants undergo an extraordinary process of vocal learning, unmatched by other primates. This lays a key foundation for meaningful speech production. The first sections of this chapter describe major milestones and other features of the development of prelinguistic and early speech sounds, including the acquisition of new sound types and of conversational turn-taking skills. The chapter then discusses what we know about the roles of exploratory play, social input, and neural systems in human vocal learning. A section on computational modeling reviews theoretical work that informs our understanding of how these mechanisms interact. Effects of sociocultural and clinical differences on infant vocal development are then discussed. The final section of the chapter discusses policy perspectives on research and interventions in this domain.

22.1 Prelinguistic Vocalization Types

At birth, most infant vocalizations are limited to cries, vegetative sounds (such as burps and sucking sounds, produced as byproducts of other processes), and short, quiet sounds where there is vibration of the vocal folds but the upper vocal tract (throat, tongue, mouth, and nasal cavity) is in a neutral position (Oller, 2000). These short, quiet sounds are considered to be the earliest precursors to speech and are considered a type of "protophone." Protophones can be defined as sounds that are clearly communicative or playful (in contrast with vegetative sounds, which if they serve communicative functions do so only incidentally) and yet do not have a set communicative function (in contrast with cries and laughs, which communicate similar things across all cultures) (Oller et al., 2013).

* Thanks to Kim Oller for many helpful discussions on this topic. The writing of this chapter was facilitated by a James S. McDonnell Foundation Scholar Award in Understanding Human Cognition and by National Science Foundation grants SMA-1539129/1827744 and BCS-1529127 funding related work. Any opinions, findings, and conclusions or recommendations expressed in this chapter are those of the author and do not necessarily reflect the views of the National Science Foundation or the James S. McDonnell Foundation.

Within the next 2 to 3 months of life, infants begin to produce a much wider variety of vocalization types. These vary more substantially in duration, amplitude, pitch, and vocal quality, to include growls, squeals, yells, and whispers. Infants also begin to posture the tongue and lips. This enables them to produce fully resonant vowels of different types. It also enables the production of primitive consonant-like elements, formed either by a brief pause in phonation (vibration of the vocal folds within the larynx) or by movement of the tongue or lips that closes off the vocal tract (Buder, Warlaumont, & Oller, 2013; Oller, 1986, 2000). Interestingly, "raspberries," where the lips are set into vibration against each other or against the teeth, are also very common in infancy but are extremely uncommon in adult language. Clicks are also produced at this stage. Not all of these new vocalization types emerge at the same time. Some can take months longer than others to appear, and there seem to be considerable individual differences in which of these early protophones are produced most frequently at any particular age (Stark, 1980).

By about 7 months of age, infants begin to consistently (if not very frequently at first) produce canonical syllables. A canonical syllable is a vocalization in which there is at least one full vowel sound following or preceding a consonant, where the transition between consonant and vowel is not overly long (sounding slurred). By some definitions the consonant must be a true consonant, made by movement of the tongue or lips, and not only involving a change in vocal fold vibration (Buder et al., 2013; Oller, 1986, 2000). When canonical syllables are produced without having a clear meaning, the term canonical babble applies. Canonical syllables can be produced alone or in sequence, either repeating the same consonant and vowel elements (reduplicated babbling), or varying them (variegated babbling) (Smith, Brown-Sweeney, & Stoel-Gammon, 1989). The onset of canonical babbling tends to be a salient transition for caregivers (Oller, Eilers, & Basinger, 2001). Over the next year or more of life (through 18 months of age), canonical syllables become more frequent elements in infants' vocal productions. The types of consonants and vowels included also become more varied (both overall and within utterances) and rising and falling pitch and amplitude changes are combined with the babbling to create a sense of prosodic structure (this type of babbling has sometimes been referred to as "jargon") (Oller, 2000). Infant vocal productions thus begin to sound more and more like adult speech. It is important to note that as new sound types are added to the infant's repertoire, previous sound types do not disappear but typically continue to be produced, if at decreasing rates in some cases. Similarly, once infants begin producing meaningful speech (see the next section), nonword babble continues to be produced at high rates, decreasing only gradually (Robb, Bauer, & Tyler, 1994). See Figure 22.1 for examples of three different infant vocalization types and for an example of infant-directed adult speech.

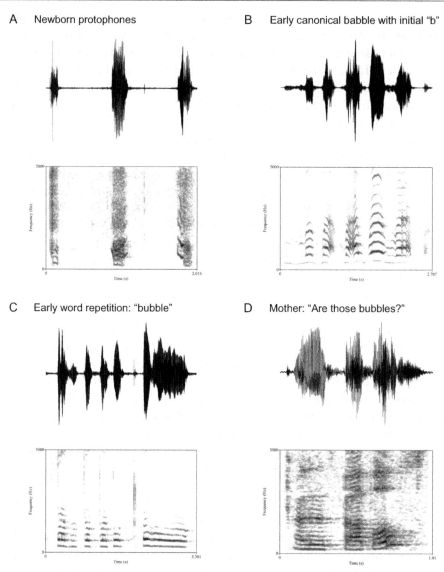

Figure 22.1. *(A) Waveform and spectrogram illustrating a protophone sequence produced by a 19-day-old infant. The sounds are short, quiet, and do not contain consonant margins. The first sound could be coded as vowel like and the second and third as growls. (B) A sequence of syllable vocalizations produced by the same infant at 4 months and 20 days. This is one of the first canonical babble sequences produced by the infant. (C) Early word production by the same infant at 1 year, 2 months, and 20 days. The sequence could be transcribed as "bubble buh buh buh bubble." (D) The maternal utterance, "Are those bubbles?" that preceded the infant vocalization shown in (C).*

Note: The sound files corresponding to the images are available at https://doi.org/10.6084/m9.figshare.7119578.

22.2 Early Meaningful Speech

Often before the first birthday, but sometimes many months later, parents report that infants begin to produce their first words (Schneider, Yurovsky, & Frank, 2015). From a motor production standpoint, infants at this point typically have the capability to produce canonical syllables incorporating at least a few different consonant and vowel types, which puts them in a position to produce approximations of words, such as "mama" and "baba" (McCune & Vihman, 2001; Oller, 2000; Vihman, Macken, Miller, Simmons, & Miller, 1985). When infants begin to produce a sound sequence reliably correlated with the presence or desire for a particular object, event, or other referent, i.e., when there is a "conventionalized sound-meaning correspondence" (Vihman et al., 1985), these can be considered the infant's first words. Nouns tend to be more prominent in infants' early productions than in their caregivers' speech to them in the same contexts, compared to verbs (Tardif, Gelman, & Xu, 1999). At first, words are typically produced in isolation, and in instances where an infant appears to produce multiple words, e.g., "what's this?" the combination acts more like a single lexical unit, with the component words not yet being used independently or being recombined with other words (Lieven, Pine, & Barnes, 1992). During the second year of life, many children show a quickening rate of expressive vocabulary growth and begin combining multiple lexical items flexibly into primitive sentences (Clark, 2003).

Children's early speech is typically much more intelligible to their primary caregiver(s) than it is to strangers (Baudonck, Buekers, Gillebert, & van Lierde, 2009; Weist & Kruppe, 1977). The sounds that are present in canonical babbling tend to be the same sounds that are used to produce meaningful speech (Locke, 1989; Vihman et al., 1985), with sounds often being deleted, substituted, or sometimes even added in comparison to the adult word form (Oller, Wieman, Doyle, & Ross, 1976). Even when particular consonants and vowels are present in the infant's repertoire, some sequences of those sounds may be difficult for the infant to produce, leading the child to omit or substitute even some sounds that they can create in other contexts. Consonant clusters can be particularly difficult for young children.

22.3 Development of Conversational Turn-Taking

Well before word production or even canonical babbling occur, infants begin to exhibit conversational turn-taking skills. From as early as 2 months, infant–adult vocal interactions tend to occur in distinct turns (Gratier et al., 2015). At early ages, caregivers appear to drive more of the turn-taking than infants, but over the course of the first year of life, infants are increasingly able to contribute to minimizing overlap between their own and their conversation partner's vocalizations (Harder, Lange, Foget Hansen, Vaever, & Køppe, 2015).

The ability of an infant and an adult to exhibit such coordination in vocalization timing, particularly matching the timing of pauses between the other speaker's vocalization offset and one's own vocalization onset, at 4 months has been shown to be correlated with later infant attachment security and cognitive skills at 12 months (Jaffe, Beebe, Feldstein, Crown, & Jasnow, 2001). Interestingly, at least one study has found that infants have increased lags in their vocal responses to caregiver vocalizations at around 9 months, when infants are on the cusp of producing first words; this may be because of the increased cognitive and motor demands incurred by the process of formulating verbal responses (Hilbrink, Gattis, & Levinson, 2015). Kuchirko, Tafuro, and Tamis-LeMonda (2018) have shown increases from 14 to 24 months of age in the likelihood of infant vocal responses to maternal referential language, indicating that development of conversational turn-taking continues after the first year of life.

22.4 Mechanisms of Vocal Learning and Speech Production Development

Having provided some description of the types of changes we see in vocalization, speech, and language production over the course of the first 2 years of life, we turn our attention to some of the factors and mechanisms that underlie these changes.

22.4.1 Intrinsically Motivated Play

A major contributor to infant vocal motor learning may be intrinsically motivated processes that combine random exploration around an existing skill base with a desire to expand that skill base. Infants often produce vocalizations when they are not actively engaged in social interaction with others (S. J. Jones & Moss, 1971). Moreover, infants tend to repeat particular sound types in bouts (Gratier & Devouche, 2011; Oller et al., 2013). Anecdotally, this repetition can appear to some observers to suggest goal-directed behavior, although it is unclear whether a goal-oriented process is actually in place or there just exists momentum in the infant vocalization system. The potential advantage of goal-directed exploration for prelinguistic vocal learning has been demonstrated in computational modeling studies (more on this below). Although intrinsically motivated exploration and learning can in principle take place without any social input, social influences are certainly also involved.

22.4.2 Social Input

The input infants receive from adult caregivers is clearly related to infants' language development. In terms of promoting the vocalization and early speech milestones described above, two roles that social input seem to play are (1) to provide positive reinforcement (reward) to infants when they produce relatively advanced behaviors, and (2) to provide targets that infants may try to imitate.

22.4.2.1 *Adult Responses as Positive Reinforcers*

We know that even young infants can detect sequential contingencies between external stimuli and between their own behaviors and the consequences of those behaviors (Tarabulsy, Tessier, & Kappas, 1996). Converging evidence from naturalistic observation of infant–parent interactions and from experimental studies supports the idea that this contingency learning plays a role in infants' prelinguistic vocal learning.

Parent speech to infants differs acoustically, semantically, and syntactically from speech directed to other adults. For example, infant-directed utterances tend to be higher in pitch, have more exaggerated prosodic contours, be shorter, have longer pause durations, include more repetition, and be semantically and syntactically simpler (Fernald et al., 1989; Soderstrom, 2007). Infant-directed speech is also salient and appealing to infants, being preferred both to adult-directed speech and to nonspeech stimuli (Fernald, 1985; Fernald & Kuhl, 1987; Vouloumanos & Werker, 2004). Infants may therefore be motivated to produce behavior that increases the quantity of infant-directed speech they hear. Since infant-directed adult vocalizations also tend to follow infant speech-related vocalization productions (Gros-Louis, West, Goldstein, & King, 2006; Warlaumont, Richards, Gilkerson, & Oller, 2014) adult vocalizations likely serve to reinforce infants' increased production of speech-related sounds.

Indeed, experimental work by Nathani and Stark (1996) has found that a few minutes' interaction with a researcher who provides consistent positive vocal responses whenever the infant produces a speech-related (protophone) vocalization leads to the infant producing increased numbers of these vocalizations during an immediately following recording session. Increased frequency of infant vocalization can in turn be expected to increase the opportunities for adults to provide high-quality responses to infant vocal behavior that facilitate infant communication development (Leezenbaum, Campbell, Butler, & Iverson, 2013; Tamis-LeMonda, Bornstein, & Baumwell, 2001; Tamis-LeMonda, Kuchirko, & Suh, 2018; Warlaumont et al., 2014).

Supporting the idea that contingent adult responses selectively increase infants' rates of protophones as opposed to cries, Warlaumont et al. (2014) studied children ranging in age from 10 to 48 months and found that when speech-related infant vocalizations were followed by adult responses, this was associated with an increased likelihood of the following child vocalization being speech-related as opposed to a cry. Moreover, rates of adult responses to the children's vocalizations predicted faster growth, over the 3-year period, in the increase of speech-related vocalizations relative to cries and other reflexive and vegetative sounds. Looking more closely at different infant protophone types, Gros-Louis and Miller (2018) found that 10-month-old infant vocalizations were more likely to be vowel only (as opposed to consonant–vowel combinations) when the previous infant vowel-only vocalization received an adult response than when it received no response; they found a similar pattern for 12-month-old infant consonant–vowel vocalizations, and an opposite tendency for 12-month-old vowel vocalizations. Taken together, these studies suggest that when adult responses are contingent on infant vocalizations of a certain type (whether that's a broad category such as speech-related vocalization or a somewhat narrower subcategory of speech-related vocalizations), this can promote subsequent infant vocalizations of that type. On the other hand, the studies also suggest that this may not be true for all vocalization types at all points in development – there must be other factors involved besides just positive reinforcement selectively shaping infant vocalization frequency and type.

Many studies have found a positive relationship between the quantity and diversity of child-directed language a child hears and the child's expressive vocabulary (Golinkoff, Can, Soderstrom, & Hirsh-Pasek, 2015; Hart & Risley, 1995; Ramírez-Esparza, García-Sierra, & Kuhl, 2014). This positive association may in part reflect the fact that child-directed speech is both contingent on (i.e., responsive to) infant vocalizations and salient to infants, so that quantity of child-directed speech may be a good proxy for quantity of positive reinforcement for infants' productions. However, adult vocalizations themselves also have acoustic and linguistic content, and this content provides a rich source of additional information.

22.4.2.2 *Adult Input as Targets for Imitation*
Another way that the content of adult vocalizations may influence infant productions is by creating targets for infant vocal play. As an infant learns that there is some correspondence between the sets of sounds she herself can produce and those that the adults around her produce, this may encourage her to consider any sound types that adults produce as potential additions to her own repertoire. Along these lines, computational modeling work has shown how a single intrinsically motivated algorithm for choosing acoustic targets can account for an increased interest as an infant gets older in imitating adult vocalizations (Moulin-Frier, Nguyen, & Oudeyer, 2014). This is consistent with work finding that during the first year of life true vocal imitation in response to input in an experimental context is rare (S. S. Jones, 2009), but that during the second year children start to actively imitate arbitrary sounds directed to them by adults (S. S. Jones, 2007).

Experimental work has shown that learning from the content of adult vocalizations is especially powerful when those adult vocalizations have been produced in response to an infant's own vocalizations. In a study of 9.5-month-olds by Goldstein and Schwade (2008), mothers were told when and how to interact with their infant by a researcher who was observing the interaction from a control room. In one condition the parent was instructed to approach and vocalize to the infant immediately following every speech-related (protophone) vocalization produced by the infant and was also told what kind of sound to make. In this condition, infants' vocalizations shortly after the controlled interaction period came to take on the broad phonetic properties of the sounds produced by the parent. Moreover, when the parent vocalizations were canonical consonant–vowel syllables, infants tended to produce more canonical syllables; when they were fully resonant vowels without consonant sounds, the infants came to produce more fully resonant vowel sounds. The adaptation did not take place in a yoked-control condition in which the same quantity and type of parental vocalizations occurred but were not timed to immediately follow the infant's vocalizations. Along similar lines, Bloom (1988) found that when adults engaged in verbal turn-taking with 3-month-old infants, subsequent infant vocalizations had a greater tendency to incorporate primitive syllabic elements, compared to nonverbal turn-taking. (Interestingly, Goldstein, King, & West [2003] found that even nonverbal contingent responses to 8-month-olds' vocalizations led to a subsequent increase in canonical babbling rates.)

22.4.3 Neural Underpinnings

How does an infant's neurophysiology support these exploratory and socially guided vocal learning processes? One possibility is that speech and prespeech vocal motor control relies heavily on the recruitment of neural circuitry that previously evolved for the production of reflexive vocal signals such as cries and laughs or other reflexive vocal tract movements, such as those involved in feeding. MacNeilage (1998) has argued that the production of syllabically structured vocalizations relies on existing mechanisms for producing rhythmic feeding movements, particularly the rhythmic jaw movement involved in chewing. Presumably, according to this theory, the fact that the onset of rhythmic babbling does not occur until about 7 months of age would be related to delay in maturation of the chewing jaw movement circuitry, and possibly could be related to the time it takes for children to learn to combine phonation with jaw movement. On the other hand, the timing of syllabic vocalizations, and the increase in rate of jaw movement with increasing age, indicate that human syllabic vocalization development has more in common with nonhuman primate lip-smacks than to chewing vocalizations (lip-smacks are a communicative signal produced by alternating mouth closure and opening without concomitant phonation) (Morrill, Paukner, Ferrari, & Ghazanfar, 2012). However, even if lip-smacking and syllabic vocalization are homologous this still leaves many open questions about the neural bases of their development, including whether (gradual or delayed) recruitment of brain-stem circuitry for reflexive vocalization or other oral behavior is involved.

A contrasting perspective is that prespeech vocal motor control is driven primarily by cortical learning that more directly controls vocal motor effectors, in a circuit that bypasses those involved in production of reflexive signals. Key evidence supporting this view comes from anatomical studies comparing the direct pathway tracts between laryngeal regions of primary motor cortex and laryngeal motor neurons of the brain stem between humans and non-human primates (Jürgens, 2002): It appears that in humans there are more robust direct (pyramidal) connections as well as indirect connections from the primary motor cortex to circuits in the hindbrain and spinal cord that more immediately control the vocal tract muscles (see Figure 22.2). In contrast, at least some nonhuman primates show far less connectivity of this sort and must therefore rely more on the midbrain structures, in particular a region called the periaqueductal gray, which control involuntary vocalizations in both human and nonhuman primates. Having robust direct motor cortex connections to the neurons that immediately affect vocal tract muscles suggests a greater role of motor cortex in the generation of vocalizations in humans. This is consistent with studies that have electrically stimulated frontal cortex regions and found that while such stimulation can generate vocalizations, including syllabic vocalizations, in adult humans (Penfield & Welch, 1951), it does not reliably elicit vocalization in squirrel monkeys (Jürgens, 1974). More recently, electrocorticography of the lateral sensorimotor cortex has revealed that when adult humans produce tongue and lip movements to make specific speech sounds, such as /b/, /d/, or /g/, there is a corresponding rise in activation of the primary motor cortex regions associated with the body part (lips, anterior tongue, posterior tongue) most involved in the speech sound (Bouchard, Mesgarani, Johnson, & Chang, 2013). This indicates that vocal tract activity for the production of speech sounds may be driven directly by activation of the motor cortex.

These neuroanatomical and neurophysiological findings implicating direct pathways from the motor cortex to brain stem fit well with findings that while some nonhuman primates do exhibit substantial vocal learning (e.g., Ghazanfar & Zhang, 2016; Gultekin & Hage, 2018; Perlman & Clark, 2015; Russell, McIntyre, Hopkins, & Taglialatela, 2013), humans demonstrate vocal learning and voluntary control of vocalization to an extreme extent (this has to be the case for the oral language of modern humans to exist at all and may account for some of the difficulties in teaching nonhuman primates oral language). The neuroanatomical and neurophysiological findings are also consistent with acoustic analyses of adult human laughter. Real and fake laughs have distinctly different acoustic properties, suggesting separate neural mechanisms (Bryant & Aktipis, 2014). In learning to produce fake laughter, humans may learn to produce movement patterns that resemble real laughter rather than simply activating real laughter circuitry. Finally, recent computational modeling studies (see the next section) have demonstrated how cortical learning mechanisms can readily account for some of the changes we see in vocal productions across the first year of life in typically developing infants, including the transition to producing syllabically structured vocalizations (Warlaumont

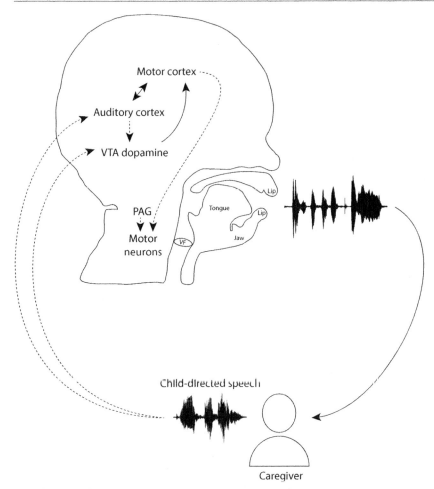

Figure 22.2. *Schematic illustration of some of the major anatomical structures and neural and social pathways involved in infant vocalization and vocal learning. Dashed lines illustrate pathways where various subcortical regions make up part of the pathway but are not shown.*
Note: VTA = ventral tegmental area; PAG = periaqueductal gray; VF = vocal folds.

& Finnegan, 2016). It seems likely therefore that there is a route for cortical motor learning that does not rely on additional circuitry for generating patterns of vocal tract muscle activation for mastication or for reflexive vocalization.

Regarding the debate about whether or not adult speech involves the (possibly learned) reuse of existing circuitry for reflexive behavior involving the vocal tract or learning new motor behaviors essentially "from scratch," it is worth noting that the two possibilities are not mutually exclusive. It is possible that some combination of the two takes place during development. It is also possible that the two pathways represent redundant pathways to mature communicative vocal signals in humans. It is also worth noting that none of the studies mentioned above involved human infant participants. So far, methodological challenges to recording and eliciting neural activity from human infants have forced us to extrapolate from data with adult human participants, nonhuman animal subjects, and computational modeling to infer what the results might mean for the neurophysiological underpinnings of human infant vocal learning.

Although functional brain imaging has so far been impractical to study infant vocalization production directly, it can be used to study infant auditory perception, and this has yielded some interesting data on the activity of motor regions during speech perception. In particular, Kuhl, Ramírez, Bosseler, Lin, and Imada (2014) found that infant perception of native and nonnative speech sounds stimulated not only the auditory cortex but also the motor cortex, and that the relative activity of the motor cortex compared to that of the auditory cortex was higher for native-language sounds for 7-month-olds but for nonnative sounds for 11- to 12-month-olds. Of course, there are many additional open questions about the neurophysiological basis of speech production development in infancy beyond those discussed here.

22.5 Computational Models

Computational modeling is used to formulate and test theories about how infants learn to produce both more mature-sounding vocalizations and meaningful speech. The earliest computational models in this domain were connectionist models (neurally inspired but not anatomically or neurophysiologically detailed) consisting simply of a set of perceptual nodes and a set of motor nodes with weighted connections between the two (e.g., Kröger, Kannampuzha, & Neuschaefer-Rube, 2009; Westermann & Miranda, 2004; Yoshikawa, Asada, Hosada, & Koga, 2003). The models learned by producing random movements, sometimes referred to as "motor babbling" in the developmental computational modeling literature. The random movements led to a specific pattern of activation of motor nodes and each motor pattern served as input to a vocal tract simulation that would synthesize a sound based on that motor pattern. Acoustic features of that sound known to be important in human speech perception, most notably formant frequencies, were then measured and input to the perceptual neurons in the model. The coactivation of perceptual neurons and motor neurons allows for self-organized learning of the correspondences between motor commands and perceptual consequences. After experiencing many rounds of this process, a model can build up sufficient knowledge about motor-perceptual mappings to be able to reliably produce a target sound, for example in imitation of a sound input by another individual (Heintz, Beckman, Fosler-Lussier, & Ménard, 2009).

One challenge for models of this type is that different individuals have differently shaped vocal tracts and therefore differences in the range of acoustic features they can produce. Adult humans naturally account for this, for example when categorizing a particular combination of formant frequencies as an instantiation of a particular vowel type. However, the procedure just described does not lead to a model that performs this normalization across vocal tracts (Heintz et al., 2009). An approach that has proved successful is to assume that adult caregivers frequently imitate infants, and that this imitation can serve as a cue to the correspondences between one speaker's vocal tract and another's; selective imitation only of sounds that fit into categories in the adult interaction partner's language can also be used to decide which vocal categories and perceptual-motor mappings to retain (Howard & Messum, 2014; Miura, Yoshikawa, & Asada, 2007).

When dealing with the large number of motor degrees of freedom present in a full vocal tract model and the additional complexity introduced when trying to model the production of dynamically changing vocal tract movements (for example in order to produce the movements of the vocal tract needed to produce consonant sounds), it has proved important to move beyond a completely random motor babbling approach. This is in part because many combinations of vocal tract movements are not very useful for generating speech-like sounds (Warlaumont, Westermann, Buder, & Oller, 2013). It is better if the model, and by extension the human infant, can first discover which kinds of motor activities are worth the most focused exploration at a given point in the learning process. An approach that has demonstrated both the severity of this problem for vocal learning and a possible solution has been an intrinsically motivated goal-babbling approach (Moulin-Frier et al., 2014).

In Moulin-Frier et al.'s (2014) model, vocal exploration at any point in time is guided by a desire to achieve a particular acoustic goal. The model identifies and then executes the combination of motor actions that it believes are most likely to achieve the acoustic outcome. At first the selection is based on completely random exploration of motor space to get a rough idea of some of the acoustic consequences associated with movements. After trying the action and observing the actual outcome, the model adjusts its stored knowledge of the relationships between motor patterns and acoustic patterns. Thus, as learning progresses the model's knowledge of motor-acoustic mappings becomes more accurate. The model also learns how likely various acoustic goals are to lead to a high rate of learning. At a given point in the learning process, some goals may be too difficult for the agent to achieve and therefore be unlikely to lead to much helpful refinement of the agent's motor-acoustics knowledge; at that same time point some other goals may already be so easy for the agent to achieve that not much learning is likely to result from pursuing them either. For example, in Moulin-Frier et al.'s model, early on the model attempts to produce silence, a goal it quickly masters. It then moves on to primarily choosing goals that consist of a single combination of formant frequencies, somewhat akin to producing a single vowel in isolation. After improving performance on these goals, it has an increased likelihood of choosing goals that have a combination of two specific sounds in a specific sequence. This model also includes two modes, one in which goals are chosen purely through this endogenous intrinsically motivated process and another in which an external input is supplied as a potential target for imitation. As the model advances in its capabilities, it becomes more interested in using imitation as a means for selecting goals and driving learning.

Thus, the intrinsically motivated goal-oriented learning model captures the transition from unphonated to phonated to complex sounds and from primarily endogenously driven exploration to imitation-oriented learning. In other words, the model provides an explanation for why infants' spontaneous vocal productions will initially tend to be simpler sounds with vowel sequences, syllabic consonant–vowel transitions, and variegated babbling only becoming more frequent later in development. It is also important to note that although the model demonstrates the power that goal babbling has for vocal learning, it does not necessarily imply that infant vocalizations are always goal directed. The model itself undergoes an initial brief phase of completely random (not goal-driven) exploration in order to initialize its motor-acoustic map. It is conceivable that goal-oriented babbling plays a crucial role despite only operating some of the time.

Such an algorithmic approach is helpful for understanding the possible strategies that might characterize infants' active vocal learning. More detailed models would be needed to link such strategies to possible neural implementations. More biologically detailed computational modeling has not yet achieved this, but has demonstrated some possible neural bases for the dynamic generation of muscle activity patterns and for the shaping of spontaneously generated actions through selective reinforcement (either intrinsic or social). Recently, a spiking neural network model has demonstrated how electrical activity in a small population of cortical neurons can be summed and low-pass filtered to generate fluctuating activity in muscles that control the opening and closing of the vocal tract (Warlaumont & Finnegan, 2016). As a result of random input as well as random interconnections among neurons in the local cortical network, the model generates spontaneous activity. At first, overall muscle activity and fluctuation in activity levels are too low to consistently generate sounds that alternate opening and closing of the vocal tract, so instead of producing syllabically structured vocalizations, the model produces primarily simple vowel sounds. However, with selective reinforcement for the rare production of a consonant-like sound, the model receives surges of dopamine (see Figure 22.2). These increase the learning rate between neurons in the cortical network, leading to increased likelihood of those patterns of neural activity that generate consonant–vowel sequences. The selective reinforcement could come either from caregivers' positive contingent responses or from an infant's intrinsic excitement about the sound it just produced. The model thus increases its rate of canonical babbling over the course of learning, using a biologically, psychologically, and socially plausible learning mechanism. While the model lacks many of the neural systems that are known to play a role in motor learning in humans (such as basal ganglia and cerebellum) and even lacks most of the degrees of freedom present in an actual vocal tract, it nevertheless represents an important step toward linking infant vocal learning to neural mechanisms and informs current debates about the origins of syllabic sounds in human evolution and development.

All the models just described have focused exclusively on prelinguistic vocal learning, without addressing infants' development of productive vocabulary. To address meaningful speech production requires that models incorporate some representation of the things in the world that first words tend to refer to. A number of computational models (e.g., Li, Zhao, & MacWhinney, 2007) have taken a more abstract approach to representing the sound production processes in order to focus on the development of mappings between sounds and world knowledge. They demonstrate how infants can form word-meaning mappings not only for purposes of word recognition but also to generate appropriate speech sound sequences in the presence of particular referents.

Recently, a model by Forestier and Oudeyer (2017) has integrated vocal learning and learning to obtain objects (by reaching with the arm, reaching with a tool, or asking a caregiver) within the same system. The model includes a three-degree-of-freedom arm placed in a two-dimensional simulated environment. Also in the environment are three objects and a caregiver. The agent also has a seven-degree-of-freedom vocal tract that produces output trajectories in a two-dimensional acoustic space (acoustic dimensions are the first two formant frequencies, i.e., the lowest two resonant frequencies of the vocal tract, which change as vocal tract shape changes). The caregiver can also produce sounds in this vocal space and knows the labels for all three objects. The infant can learn to produce the names of objects, and uttering an object name has the effect of getting the caregiver to place the object within the infant's reach. Likewise, when the infant grasps an object, the caregiver utters the object's name. On some learning trials, the infant's goal is to imitate caregiver vocalizations, on some trials it is to generate a random sound sequence, and on other trials the goals are to move the hand, the tool, or the objects along a randomly set goal trajectory. An interesting result is that after training, the model is more successful at imitating the sounds that correspond to the three objects' words than it is at imitating the sounds of nonwords, despite having experienced equal numbers of imitation trials for the two sound categories. The implication is that infant vocal learning ought to be enhanced by having experience in a physical and social environment in which vocalization can be used as a social tool to manipulate the physical environment. This implies that research on human infant vocal learning should consider not only the social but also the physical (visual and tactile) environments in which infants vocalize.

22.6 Sociocultural Perspectives

Since input from caregivers has been shown to affect both infant vocal learning and early speech production, we would expect differences in infants' social environments to be associated with differences in infant vocalizations and in the pace or trajectory of infant vocal learning. The following sections discuss three dimensions of difference in infants' social environments, socioeconomic, linguistic, and cultural, and what is known about how each affects infant vocal development.

22.6.1 Socioeconomic Status

A number of studies have demonstrated that, in North America and Europe, higher socioeconomic status (SES), usually measured through parental, especially maternal, educational attainment and sometimes including income, is associated with faster language acquisition by infants (Golinkoff et al., 2015). There is more evidence that this matters for early word production than for prelinguistic vocal development. One study that tested for a relationship between SES and infant protophone vocalizations during the first year of life found that higher SES was associated with increased infant volubility (i.e., infants vocalized more often) but did not detect any relationship between SES and the age of onset of canonical babbling (Eilers et al., 1993). This is perhaps surprising, considering that higher SES is associated with higher rates of sensitive caregiver responding to infant vocal behavior and sensitive responding promotes vocal learning. It is possible that more sensitive measures or larger sample sizes would reveal an association between SES and prelinguistic vocalization milestones. Melvin et al. (2017) found that phonetic perceptual tuning (measured by an infant's insensitivity to phonetic contrasts that don't exist in their native language) at 9 months was related to features of the home environment that promote language and literacy but was not related to SES. Canonical babbling age of onset might similarly turn out to also be associated fairly strongly with specific features of the home environment but only weakly or not at all with SES more generally. Another possibility is that because intrinsically motivated play drives much of prelinguistic vocal development during the first year, like other motor milestones, achievement of prelinguistic vocal milestones is relatively robust to differences in the social environment that correlate with SES (Eilers et al., 1993; Oller, 2000).

Early productive vocabulary development, on the other hand, is clearly positively correlated with SES. A seminal study by Hart and Risley (1995) found that children of higher SES typically heard a greater number and variety of words, and also received more expansive responses to their own productions. This was reflected in how the children's linguistic productions evolved over the first few years of life. The number of different words the child spoke, both overall and relative to the total number of word tokens spoken, was greater for children of professors than from children receiving welfare. Differences were apparent even at the earliest stages of word production, before infants were 18 months old, and the gap widened as children grew older. More recent research has replicated this SES effect on vocabulary development, has highlighted the importance of interactive child-directed speech and lexical diversity, and has also indicated that additional factors, such as exposure to rich gestural input, may be involved (Golinkoff, Hoff, Rowe, Tamis-LeMonda, & Hirsh-Pasek, 2018; Hoff, 2003; Huttenlocher, Waterfall, Vasilyeva, Vevea, & Hedges, 2010; Rowe, Raudenbush, & Goldin-Meadow, 2012).

22.6.2 Linguistic Differences

The question of at what age infants' vocal productions reflect the phonology of the infant's home language(s) has received a fair amount of attention. On the one hand, it has been reported that newborn infant cry acoustics differ for children exposed to French versus German, two languages with distinctly different stress patterns (Mampe, Friederici, Christophe, & Wermke, 2009). Follow-up studies comparing Swedish to German (Prochnow, Hesse, & Wermke, 2017), and Mandarin to German (Wermke et al., 2017) have found similar results. There is some question though whether these results should be trusted since statistical analyses were at the cry utterance level rather than at the child level, which could mean that the results are primarily driven by individual differences in children's cry acoustics rather than being driven by language-related differences (Gustafson, Sanborn, Lin, & Green, 2017).

   If there are indeed language-related differences in newborn cry, this could be due to infants' subconsciously processing the acoustic patterns to which they have been exposed and modifying their reflexive vocalization acoustics to match. An alternative explanation could be that differences in caregiving practices across cultures lead to different intensities of cry and subsequently different average cry acoustics. One reason to doubt the first explanation is that detectable differences in protophone vocalizations have not been reported until 10 months of age, and even at that point, the reported differences are controversial.

   The evidence for differences in babbling at 10 months comes from phonetic transcription of infant vocalizations, showing differing distributions of phones in the babble of infants exposed to four different languages (de Boysson Bardies & Vihman, 1991). The controversy stems from the fact that the transcribers were knowledgeable about the infant's home language, had access to the ambient language the infants heard during the naturalistic recordings, and spoke the same language as the home language of the infant whose babble they transcribed, making it possible that the results could be due primarily to transcriber bias. Subsequent studies with tighter controls for transcriber bias have not identified differences in the distribution of sound types across babble from infants exposed primarily to English versus Spanish (Thevenin, Eilers, Oller, &

Lavoie, 1985). On the other hand, there are good reasons to believe that infants at 10 months should be capable of incorporating the sounds produced by conversation partners into their own productions (Goldstein & Schwade, 2008), so the null results in the latter study could very well be due to small sample size, insufficient phonological differences across the two languages, or a focus on the wrong phonological measures.

As first words begin to be produced we can expect to see differences between infants learning different languages since word recognition by caregivers is by definition language specific. That said, in early word production, there do appear to be some consistencies that may be driven in part by language-universal constraints on motor control and cognition. For example, stop consonants (such as /b/, /p/, /d/, /t/, /g/), which are common in both infant babble and in early word production, are also common to all adult languages, whereas liquids (such as /l/ and /r/) and consonant clusters (such as /st/ and /sp/) are less common in babble, early words, and in adult speech across languages (Vihman, Ferguson, & Elbert, 1986).

22.6.3 Cross-Cultural Perspectives

In addition to SES and linguistic differences in infants' social environments, cultural differences appear to affect early language production and may also have effects on prespeech vocalization. Numerous differences have been found across cultures in the degree to which parents engage in protoconversations and conversations with their infants, the contexts and routines in which these conversations take place, the linguistic and semantic features of adults' speech to children, and the diversity and ages of people a child frequently interacts with (Tamis-LeMonda & Song, 2012). These differences are associated with differences in children's verbal productions and various other aspects of their behavior. For example, children whose parents frequently engage them in book-reading activities tend to have larger vocabularies (Tamis-LeMonda & Song, 2012). However, it has not yet been determined whether there are substantial cultural effects on infants' prelinguistic vocalization frequency, types, and developmental timelines.

Of particular relevance to the infant vocal learning milestones and mechanisms discussed above, there are some cultures in which there is an expectation that adults talk frequently even to preverbal infants and other cultures in which adults talk much less to their infants (Cristia, Dupoux, Gurven, & Siteglitz, 2017; Richman, Miller, & LeVine, 1992; Tamis-LeMonda & Song, 2012). Infant-directed talk is sometimes even actively avoided due to beliefs about negative effects it could have on the infant and about the infant's mental abilities (Weber, Fenald, & Diop, 2017). On the one hand, we know that contingent adult responses shape infant vocalization rates and maturity, at least at short timescales. Based on this, we would expect infants to have lower vocalization rates and somewhat later achievement of prespeech vocalization milestones in cultures in which contingent adult responses to infant proto-phone vocalizations are less highly valued, and therefore presumably both less frequent and less dependent on infant vocalization type. On the other hand, the fact that differences in canonical babbling age of acquisition have not been found for children from lower SES households suggests that the major pre-linguistic infant vocalization type milestones may be relatively unaffected by cultural differences and may be more biologically driven or at least endoge-nously driven (Oller, 2000). And even when adult vocalizations to infants are less frequent, if they are equally contingent on infant vocal maturity (i.e., more likely following more advanced infant sound types than others), the effects on infant vocal development may be minor. It might also be expected that when infants are exposed to less adult speech that has been acoustically modi-fied to accommodate infant perceptual preferences (Tamis-LeMonda & Song, 2012), infants' vocalizations might tend to have proportionally more adult-like as opposed to exaggerated vocalization acoustics. On the other hand, endoge-nous exploration may play a greater role in prelinguistic vocal development for such infants and this might drive those infants toward less adult-speech-like and more idiosyncratic vocal productions.

These questions can only be answered by actually studying the frequencies with which different vocalization types are produced by infants at a range of ages across cultures with different behaviors and beliefs concerning infants' prelinguistic vocalizations. And the concern that absence of documented dif-ferences in vocalization milestones with SES may be due to insufficiently sensi-tive methodology will likely also be relevant for studies of cultural differences in prelinguistic vocal milestones.

22.7 Clinical Perspectives

We now turn to the question of how clinical differences among infants affect early vocal development. The focus is on the two disorders for which there is the most evidence of effects on prelinguistic vocal development, con-genital hearing loss and autism spectrum disorder.

22.7.1 Congenital Hearing Loss

In cases of severe or profound hearing loss without amplification, infants show both delays and differences in their prelinguistic vocal development. In partic-ular, while they do eventually transition from noncanonical to canonical bab-bling, they typically do so at 10 months or older, which is a considerable delay compared to typically developing infants (Oller & Eilers, 1988). They also may show different distributions of various consonant types within their babble, with more glottal stops (where there is alternation between vibration and no vibration at the larynx but no closure due to tongue, jaw, or lip movement) and glides (such as /j/, the consonant in "yeah," and /w/) (Stoel-Gammon & Otomo, 1986). Less severe hearing loss is associated with lower rates of canonical babbling and with delays in consonant inventory growth (Ertmer & Nathani Iyer, 2010). It is possible that these differences emerge from the fact that much early vocal learning is driven by an intrinsic interest in learning about the sensory consequences of motor actions. For infants with severe or profound hearing loss, the sensory consequences of vocalization would primarily take the form of tactile and proprioceptive sensations in the neck and head, and the act of phonating (creating sound through vibration of the vocal folds) might generate particularly salient stimuli for these children (Ertmer & Nathani Iyer, 2010). The effects on sound of creating contact between the tongue and the roof of the mouth while phonating might be less salient for these children than for hearing children. This could account for both the delay in canonical babbling onset and for the differences in consonant type frequencies after the onset of canonical babbling. Another possible factor could be that children with hearing loss have different social environments, characterized by fewer adult responses to children's vocalizations (Nittrouer, 2009). Of course, when sign language is used by a fluent caregiver to interact with an infant, this provides an alternate path for language production development that is unimpaired by the hearing loss. Interestingly, infants who receive sign language input exhibit a manual babbling behavior analogous to vocal babbling (Petitto & Marentette, 1991).

22.7.2 Autism Spectrum Disorder (ASD)

Lately there has been strong interest in identifying earlier risk factors for ASD, so the prelinguistic babble of infants with ASD or at high familial risk for ASD has received attention. Patten et al. (2014) retrospectively analyzed home videos of infants later diagnosed with ASD and found that most of the infants produced less canonical babbling than typically developing infants. Interestingly, two of the infants with ASD produced more canonical babble than typically developing infants; the researchers suspected that for these children, canonical babbling was a type of motor stereotypy. Similarly, Swanson et al. (2018) found increased vocalization rates among a subgroup of infants who had older siblings with ASD, with that subgroup not showing the high rates of conversational turns with adults that would be expected for typically developing infants with high vocalization rates. Paul, Fuerst, Ramsay, Chawarska, and Klin (2011) also found differences in the vocalizations of high-risk infants, namely reduced rates of speech-like vocalizations, reduced inventories of consonant types produced, and reduced numbers of different syllable shapes, compared to low-risk infants. Paul et al. (2011) also found that differences in early productions were associated with differences in ASD symptoms during the second year of life for the high-risk infants. It thus seems that differences in preverbal infants' speech-related vocalizations may be potential early indicators of autism risk. Moreover, given the relationship between pre-linguistic noncry vocalizations and later meaningful language production, for infants identified as high risk, early intervention around vocal communication may be justified.

22.8 Policy Perspectives

The final section of this chapter discusses some of the currently rec-ommended approaches to encouraging timely speech production development in infants, particularly those with clinical disorders or from socioeconomically disadvantaged communities. The section then discusses how issues of cultural sensitivity affect both researchers and interventionists.

22.8.1 Interventions to Promote Infant Vocal Learning and Speech Production

Beginning at birth, and even for premature infants (Caskey, Stephens, Tucker, & Vohr, 2011), clinicians and scientists encourage caregivers to provide lots of verbal input to infants and to be attentive and responsive to their infants' vocalizations, facial expressions, and gestures. In most of the clinical cases mentioned above the primary treatments are behavioral interventions that include educating the infant's primary caregivers on methods for creating a physical and social environment that promotes language development. Even in cases of hearing loss, while amplification and/or cochlear implants are also provided, behavioral interventions to create environments especially rich in input and sensitive responding are a key component of treatment (Moeller, Carr, Seaver, Stredler-Brown, & Holzinger, 2013).

In cases where infants are typically developing but are members of (usually lower-SES) communities where children's language development is slower com-pared to other groups, behavioral interventions are often provided. The goal is to create an environment that provides ample high-quality child-directed lan-guage input, not too much background noise, and frequent sensitive, positive responses to infants' communication acts (Hirsh-Pasek et al., 2015; Yazejian et al., 2017). A randomized controlled study with low-SES American partici-pants found that such interventions can, at least in the short term, be effective in increasing child vocalization rates, adult speech heard by children, and con-versational turns between children and adults (Suskind et al., 2016). A simi-lar approach has been shown to be effective in increasing maternal speech to infants and infant volubility and expressive language skills in a culture that traditionally discourages infant-directed speech and gaze (Weber et al., 2017). The larger purpose is to even the playing field for infants, regardless of back-ground, to have the skills that help prepare them for formal schooling, and to promote cognitive development and economic success.

Relatedly, there has been a push for all families, regardless of clinical or socioeconomic status, to limit infants' screen time, such as television viewing and smartphone or tablet usage, experienced by infants. For example, the American Academy of Pediatrics recommended no screen time before the age of 2 years and only a very limited (1 hour or less) daily upper limit of screen time after that (Council on Communications and Media, 2013). There are other reasons for such recommendations, such as promoting physical activity, but a large part of the motivation comes from evidence that increased screen time is associated with both reduced adult–infant conversations and slower rates of language development (Christakis et al., 2009; Zimmerman et al., 2009). Experimental work supports this recommendation, finding that 9-month-old infants cannot learn phonetic properties of a nonnative language, at least not as well, from television or prerecorded audio-only input, while they can learn from an equivalent duration of live exposure to lessons by a speaker of that language (Kuhl, Taso, & Liu, 2003). There is every reason to expect that this effect would also hold for infant vocal production. We know that contingent responses affect infant vocal productions and recorded input and even more interactive games and toys (at least at this point in history) are not contingent on infant vocalization and infant vocalization type. Moreover, even the presence of interactive toys (those that make an electronic sound or automatic movement in response to manipulation) as opposed to more traditional toys (such as nesting cups and balls) has been shown to be associated with reduced infant vocalizations and parent responses to infant vocalizations (Miller, Lossia, Suarez-Rivera, & Gros-Louis, 2017). Relatedly, caregivers' own use of electronic devices can also be cause for concern when it distracts adults from attending to their infants. For older children, maternal use of mobile devices is associated with decreased mother–child interactions (Radesky et al., 2015) and interruptions to word learning (Reed, Hirsh-Pasek, & Golinkoff, 2017).

22.8.2 Culturally Sensitive Policies

Despite the ubiquity of interventions designed to encourage certain types of adult interactions with infants, such as frequent, positive responses to infants' speech-related vocalizations that reinforce the infants' emerging communication skills by incorporating imitation, expansion, object labeling, and so on, these recommendations are not without controversy (Weber et al., 2017). Often the controversies center around the perspective that members of groups considered "at risk" should not be pressured to conform to a pattern of development that is typical with reference to some particular cultural standpoint. For example, the neurodiversity movement has argued that being on the autism spectrum should not be considered a disorder but rather a difference, and that individuals on the spectrum should be valued for the diversity they bring to society, culture, and the workplace (Kapp, Gillespie-Lynch, Sherman, & Hutman, 2013). Perspectives and policies that imply or seem to imply that parents of children with or at risk for autism are not interacting optimally with their children from some mainstream cultural perspective might harm families. They may interfere with parents' more natural, intuitive styles of interaction, which may already be essentially optimized from the perspective of that child's and family's happiness as well as from the perspective of a society that values diversity (Akhtar, Jaswal, Dinishak, & Stephan, 2016). This being acknowledged, some families may appreciate having information about what helps promote oral language development in infancy. Parents may be eager to modify their caregiving practices and/or their infant's physical and social environment accordingly (Warlaumont, Richards, Gilkerson, Messinger, & Oller, 2016), and such interventions may prove important for maximizing individuals' and communities' economic success (Weber et al., 2017). The challenges are to conduct research that is culturally sensitive and appreciates the multidimensionality of infant development and the trade-offs of risks and benefits of various perspectives and practices, and to present research findings in a way that is descriptive and informative but not prescriptive or judgmental. Likewise, interventions that target the natural caregiving practices of parents, whether they are members of subgroups of a larger society, such as is often the case for families of lower SES in the United States for example, or whether members of a nonindustrial society, can and should be questioned as to whether they are truly in the best interests of an infant and her family and community or whether they are instead impositions of cultural values of a more dominant culture or subculture.

A methodological challenge to achieving this goal has been the difficulty in obtaining data from diverse populations, so that our understanding of typical development can be more comprehensive and less biased (Henrich, Heine, & Norenzayan, 2010). Fortunately, data-sharing initiatives, such as the well-established CHILDES (CHIld Language Data Exchange System) (MacWhinney, 2000) and newer initiatives such as the Databrary system for sharing video data of research studies with children (Gilmore & Adolph, 2017) and the HomeBank resource for sharing long-form audio recordings from child-worn recorders (VanDam et al., 2016) provide a range of resources for researchers to contribute to and access repositories of raw data that are larger and more diverse.

22.9 Conclusion

Infant vocal behavior changes dramatically over the course of the first year of life, and this is considered by many to be one of the defining features of our species. At birth, human infants produce only cries, vegetative sounds, and short, quiet initial precursors to speech. By the end of the first year most children can produce long sequences that include a variety of speech sounds, can coordinate their vocalizations in turn-taking patterns with other humans, and in many cases are beginning to use their vocal sound-making apparatus to produce meaningful, recognizable (if not completely correctly pronounced) words. It appears that this process of vocal learning is the product of endogenous exploration influenced by social input from responsive caregivers. We are beginning to gain an understanding, aided by computational modeling studies and by neuroscientific research on humans and other animals, of some of the neurophysiological mechanisms underlying infant vocal learning. In particular, there is some evidence that spontaneous activity and reinforcement-driven learning in cortical regions play a major role. It also appears that while there are some sociocultural and clinical differences in vocal learning and early speech production (particularly evident for individuals with severe congenital hearing loss and increasingly documented for individuals at risk of later autism diagnosis), many aspects of the prelinguistic vocal learning process are fairly robust. Interventions to increase infant vocalization rates and language learning more generally tend to focus on increasing adult caregivers' verbal input, particularly in the form of sensitive responding to infant vocalization and other behaviors.

There are a number of areas that future research should especially target. Intrinsic motivation appears to play a large role in infant vocal development, yet has not received as much attention as social input has. This may be due in part to methodological challenges. For example, as a researcher, it is easier to track moments when a positive social response is received than it is to track moments when a child is intrinsically rewarded for producing a particular sound. Of course, social input and intrinsic motivations likely mutually influence each other, and these mutual influences are an interesting and important topic for future research. Neurophysiological bases of human infant vocal learning are also difficult to study given the methodological limitations to studying neural activity in awake, healthy infants. Improvements in imaging technology and in computational models may help overcome some of these challenges in the future. Studies of sociocultural differences may also benefit from future advances in methods for characterizing and classifying infant vocalizations of different types, and from increases in sample size and diversity thanks to data sharing. Data sharing also has the advantages of promoting replicable science, reducing research costs, and facilitating interdisciplinary collaboration for example with audio-processing and speech-recognition experts who can advance methods to study infant vocal communication development. Finally, besides informing our understanding of how typically developing infants acquire vocal communication skills, future research on these and other topics covered in this chapter can be expected to facilitate the development of culturally appropriate interventions to reduce gaps in school readiness and better enable children with communication disorders.

References

Akhtar, N., Jaswal, V. K., Dinishak, J., & Stephan, C. (2016). On social feedback loops and cascading effects in autism: A commentary on Warlaumont, Richards, Gilkerson, and Oller (2014). *Psychological Science*, 27, 1528–1530.

Baudonck, N. L. H., Buekers, R., Gillebert, S., & van Lierde, K. M. (2009). Speech intelligibility of Flemish children as judged by their parents. *Folia Phoniatrica et Logopaedica, 61*, 288–295.

Bloom, K. (1988). Quality of adult vocalizations affects the quality of infant vocalizations. *Journal of Child Language, 15*, 469–480.

Bouchard, K. E., Mesgarani, N., Johnson, K., & Chang, E. F. (2013). Functional organization of human sensorimotor cortex for speech articulation. *Nature, 495*, 327–332.

Bryant, G. A., & Aktipis, C. A. (2014). The animal nature of spontaneous human laughter. *Evolution and Human Behavior, 35*, 327–335.

Buder, E. H., Warlaumont, A. S., & Oller, D. K. (2013). An acoustic phonetic catalog of prespeech infant vocalizations from a developmental perspective. In B. Peter & A. N. MacLeod (Eds.), *Comprehensive perspectives on child speech development and disorders: Pathways from linguistic theory to clinical practice*. New York, NY: Nova Science Publishers.

Caskey, M., Stephens, B., Tucker, R., & Vohr, B. (2011). Importance of parent talk on the development of preterm infant vocalizations. *Pediatrics, 128*, 910–916.

Christakis, D. A., Gilkerson, J., Richards, J. A., Garrison, M. M., Xu, D., Gray, S., & Yapanel, U. (2009). Audible television and decreased adult words, infant vocalizations, and conversational turns: A population-based study. *Archives of Pediatrics & Adolescent Medicine, 163*, 554–558.

Clarke, E. V. (2003). *First language acquisition*. Cambridge, UK: Cambridge University Press

Council on Communications and Media (2013). Children, adolescents, and the media. *Pediatrics, 132*, 958–961.

Cristia, A., Dupoux, E., Gurven, M., & Stieglitz, J. (2017). Child-directed speech is infrequent in a forager-farmer population: A time allocation study. *Child Development, 90*(3), 759–773. doi: 10.1111/cdev.12974

de Boysson Bardies, B., & Vihman, M. (1991). Adaptation to language: Evidence from babbling and first words in four languages. *Language, 67*, 297–319.

Eilers, R. E., Oller, D. K., Levine, S., Basinger, D., Lynch, M. P., & Urbano, R. (1993). The role of prematurity and socioeconomic status in the onset of canonical babbling in infants. *Infant Behavior and Development, 16*, 297–315.

Ertmer, D. J., & Nathani Iyer, S. (2010). Prelinguistic vocalizations in infants and toddlers with hearing loss: Identifying and stimulating auditory-guided speech development. In M. Marschark & P. E. Spencer (Eds.), *The Oxford handbook of deaf studies, language, and education* (pp. 360–375). Oxford: Oxford University Press.

Fernald, A. (1985). Four-month-old infants prefer to listen to motherese. *Infant Behavior and Development, 8*, 181–195.

Fernald, A., & Kuhl, P. (1987). Acoustic determinants of infant preference for motherese speech. *Infant Behavior and Development, 10*, 279–293.

Fernald, A., Taeschner, T., Dunn, J., Papousek, M., de Boysson-Bardies, B., & Fukui, I. (1989). A cross language study of prosodic modifications in mothers' and fathers' speech to preverbal infants. *Journal of Child Language, 16*, 477–501.

Forestier, S., & Oudeyer, P.-Y. (2017). A unified model of speech and tool use early development. In G. Gunzelmann, A. Howes, T. Tenbrink, & E. Davelaar (Eds.), *Proceedings of the 39th Annual Meeting of the Cognitive Science Society* (pp. 1459–1460). Austin, TX: Cognitive Science Society.

Ghazanfar, A. A., & Zhang, Y. S. (2016). The autonomic nervous system is the engine for vocal development through social feedback. *Current Opinion in Neurobiology*, *40*, 155–160.

Gilmore, R. O., & Adolph, K. E. (2017). Video can make behavioural science more reproducible. *Nature Human Behaviour*, *1*, 0128.

Goldstein, M. H., King, A. P., & West, M. J. (2003). Social interaction shapes babbling: Testing parallels between birdsong and speech. *Proceedings of the National Academy of Sciences of the United States of America*, *100*, 8030–8035.

Goldstein, M. H., & Schwade, J. A. (2008). Social feedback to infants' babbling facilitates rapid phonological learning. *Psychological Science*, *19*, 515–523.

Golinkoff, R. M., Can, D. D., Soderstrom, M., & Hirsh-Pasek, K. (2015). (Baby) talk to me: The social context of infant-directed speech and its effects on early language acquisition. *Current Directions in Psychological Science*, *24*, 339–344.

Golinkoff, R. M., Hoff, E., Rowe, M. L., Tamis-LeMonda, C. S., & Hirsh-Pasek, K. (2018). Language matters: Denying the existence of the 30-million-word gap has serious consequences. *Child Development*, *90*(3), 985–992. doi: 10.1111/cdev.13128

Gratier, M., & Devouche, E. (2011). Imitation and repetition of prosodic contour in vocal interaction at 3 months. *Developmental Psychology*, *47*, 67–76.

Gratier, M., Devouche, E., Guellai, B., Infanti, R., Yilmaz, E., & Parlato-Oliveira, E. (2015). Early development of turn-taking in vocal interaction between mothers and infants. *Frontiers in Psychology*, *6*, 1167.

Gros-Louis, J., & Miller, J. L. (2018). From "ah" to "bah": Social feedback loops for speech sounds at key points of developmental transition. *Journal of Child Language*, *45*, 807–825.

Gros-Louis, J., West, M. J., Goldstein, M. H., & King, A. P. (2006). Mothers provide differential feedback to infants' prelinguistic sounds. *International Journal of Behavioral Development*, *30*, 509–516.

Gultekin, Y. B., & Hage, S. R. (2018). Limiting parental interaction during vocal development affects acoustic call structure in marmoset monkeys. *Science Advances*, *4*(4), eear4012. doi: 10.1126/sciadv.aar4012.

Gustafson, G. E., Sanborn, S. M., Lin, H. -C., & Green, J. A. (2017). Newborns' cries are unique to individuals (but not to language environment). *Infancy*, *22*(6), 736–747. doi: 10.1111/infa.12192

Harder, S., Lange, T., Foget Hansen, G., Væver, M., & Køppe, S. (2015). A longitudinal study of coordination in mother–infant vocal interaction from age 4 to 10 months. *Developmental Psychology*, *51*, 1778–1790.

Hart, B., & Risley, T. R. (1995). *Meaningful differences in the everyday experience of young American children*. Baltimore, MD: Paul H. Brookes.

Heintz, I., Beckman, M., Fosler-Lussier, E., & Ménard, L. (2009). Evaluating parameters for mapping adult vowels to imitative babbling. In *Proceedings of the 10th Annual Conference of the International Speech Communication Association (INTERSPEECH)* (pp. 688–691). Baixas, France: International Speech Communication Association.

Henrich, J., Heine, S. J., & Norenzayan, A. (2010). Most people are not WEIRD. *Nature*, *466*, 29.

Hilbrink, E. E., Gattis, M., & Levinson, S. C. (2015). Early developmental changes in the timing of turn-taking: A longitudinal study of mother–infant interaction. *Frontiers in Psychology*, *6*, 1492.

Hirsh-Pasek, K., Adamson, L. B., Bakeman, R., Owen, M. T., Golinkoff, R. M., Pace, A., ... Suma, K. (2015). The contribution of early communication quality to low-income children's language success. *Psychological Science*, *26*, 1071–1083.

Hoff, E. (2003). The specificity of environmental influence: Socioeconomic status affects early vocabulary development via maternal speech. *Child Development*, *74*, 1368–1378.

Howard, I. S., & Messum, P. (2014). Learning to pronounce first words in three languages: An investigation of caregiver and infant behavior using a computational model of an infant. *PLoS ONE*, *9*, e110334.

Huttenlocher, J., Waterfall, H., Vasilyeva, M., Vevea, J., & Hedges, L. V. (2010). Sources of variability in children's language growth. *Cognitive Psychology*, *61*, 343–365.

Jaffe, J., Beebe, B., Feldstein, S., Crown, C. L., & Jasnow, M. D. (2001). Rhythms of dialogue in infancy: Coordinated timing in development. *Monographs of the Society for Research in Child Development*, *66*, 1–32.

Jones, S. J., & Moss, H. A. (1971). Age, state, and maternal behavior associated with infant vocalizations. *Child Development*, *42*, 1039–1051.

Jones, S. S. (2007). Imitation in infancy: The development of mimicry. *Psychological Science*, *18*, 593–599.

(2009). The development of imitation in infancy. *Philosophical Transactions of the Royal Society B: Biological Sciences*, 364(1528), 2325–2335. doi: 10.1098/rstb.2009.0045

Jürgens, U. (1974). On the elicitability of vocalization from the cortical larynx area. *Brain Research*, *81*, 564–566.

(2002). Neural pathways underlying vocal control. *Neuroscience and Biobehavioral Reviews*, *26*, 235–258.

Kapp, S. K., Gillespie-Lynch, K., Sherman, L. E., & Hutman, T. (2013). Deficit, difference, or both? Autism and neurodiversity. *Developmental Psychology*, *49*, 59–71.

Kröger, B. J., Kannampuzha, J., & Neuschaefer-Rube, C. (2009). Towards a neurocomputational model of speech production and perception. *Speech Communication*, *51*, 793–809.

Kuchirko, Y., Tafuro, L., & Tamis-LeMonda, C. S. (2018). Becoming a communicative partner: Infant contingent responsiveness to maternal language and gestures. *Infancy*, 23(4), 558–576. doi: 10.1111/infa.12222

Kuhl, P. K., Ramírez, R. R., Bosseler, A., Lin, J. -F. L., & Imada, T. (2014). Infants' brain responses to speech suggest analysis by synthesis. *Proceedings of the National Academy of Sciences, 2014*, *111*, 11238–11245.

Kuhl, P. K., Tsao, F.-M., & Liu, H. -M. (2003). Foreign-language experience in infancy: Effects of short-term exposure and social interaction on phonetic learning. *Proceedings of the National Academy of Sciences of the United States of America*, *100*, 9096–9101.

Leezenbaum, N. B., Campbell, S. B., Butler, D., & Iverson, J. M. (2013). Maternal verbal responses to communication of infants at low and heightened risk of autism. *Autism*, *18*, 694–703.

Li, P., Zhao, X., & MacWhinney, B. (2007). Dynamic self-organization and early lexical development in children. *Cognitive Science*, *31*, 581–612.

Lieven, E. V. M., Pine, J. M., & Barnes, H. D. (1992). Individual differences in early vocabulary development: Redefining the referential-expressive distinction. *Journal of Child Language*, *19*, 287–310.

Locke, J. L. (1989). Babbling and early speech: Continuity and individual differences. *First Language, 9*, 191–206.

MacNeilage, P. F. (1998). The frame/content theory of evolution of speech production. *Behavioral and Brain Sciences, 21*, 499–511.

MacWhinney, B. (2000). *The CHILDES Project: Tools for analyzing talk* (3rd ed.). Mahwah, NJ: Lawrence Erlbaum Associates.

Mampe, B., Friederici, A., Christophe, A., & Wermke, K. (2009). Newborns' cry melody is shaped by their native language. *Current Biology*, 1994–1997.

McCune, L., & Vihman, M. M. (2001). Early phonetic and lexical development: A productivity approach. *Journal of Speech, Language, and Hearing Research, 44*, 670–684.

Melvin, S. A., Brito, N. H., Mack, L. J., Engelhardt, L. E., Fifer, W. P., Elliott, A. J., & Noble, K. G. (2017). Home environment, but not socioeconomic status, is linked to differences in early phonetic perception ability. *Infancy, 22*, 42–55.

Miller, J. L., Lossia, A., Suarez-Rivera, C., & Gros-Louis, J. (2017). Toys that squeak: Toy type impacts quality and quantity of parent-child interactions. *First Language, 37*, 630–647.

Miura, K., Yoshikawa, Y., & Asada, M. (2007). Unconscious anchoring in maternal imitation that helps find the correspondence of a caregiver's vowel categories. *Advanced Robotics, 21*, 1583–1600.

Moeller, M. P., Carr, G., Seaver, L., Stredler-Brown, A., & Holzinger, D. (2013). Best practices in family-centered early intervention for children who are deaf or hard of hearing: An international consensus statement. *Journal of Deaf Studies and Deaf Education, 18*, 429–445.

Morrill, R. J., Paukner, A., Ferrari, P., & Ghazanfar, A. A. (2012). Monkey lipsmacking develops like the human speech rhythm. *Developmental Science, 15*, 557–568.

Moulin-Frier, C., Nguyen, S. M., & Oudeyer, P.-Y. (2014). Self-organization of early vocal development in infants and machines: The role of intrinsic motivation. *Frontiers in Psychology, 4*, 1006.

Nathani, S., & Stark, R. E. (1996). Can conditioning procedures yield representative infant vocalizations in the laboratory? *First Language, 16*, 365–387.

Nittrouer, S. (2009). *Early development of children with hearing loss*. San Diego, CA: Plural Publishing.

Oller, D. K. (1986). Metaphonology and infant vocalizations. In B. Lindblom & R. Zetterström (Eds.), *Precursors of early speech* (pp. 21–36). New York, NY: Stockton Press.

  (2000). *The emergence of the speech capacity*. Mahwah, NJ: Lawrence Erlbaum Associates.

Oller, D. K., Buder, E. H., Ramsdell, H. L., Warlaumont, A. S., Chorna, L., & Bakeman, R. (2013). Functional flexibility of infant vocalization and the emergence of language. *Proceedings of the National Academy of Sciences of the United States of America, 110*, 6318–6323.

Oller, D. K., & Eilers, R. E. (1988). The role of audition in infant babbling. *Child Development, 59*, 441–449.

Oller, D. K., Eilers, R., & Basinger, D. (2001). Intuitive identification of infant vocal sounds by parents. *Developmental Science, 4*, 49–60.

Oller, D. K., Wieman, L. A., Doyle, W. J., & Ross, C. (1976). Infant babbling and speech. *Journal of Child Language, 3*, 1–11.

Patten, E., Belardi, K., Baranek, G. T., Watson, L. R., Labban, J. D., & Oller, D. K. (2014). Vocal patterns in infants with autism spectrum disorder: Canonical babbling status and vocalization frequency. *Journal of Autism and Developmental Disorders*, *44*, 2413–2428.

Paul, R., Fuerst, Y., Ramsay, G., Chawarska, K., & Klin, A. (2011). Out of the mouths of babes: Vocal production in infant siblings of children with ASD. *Journal of Child Psychology and Psychiatry*, *52*, 588–598.

Penfield, W., & Welch, K. (1951). The supplementary motor area of the cerebral cortex: A clinical and experimental study. *A.M.A. Archives of Neurology and Psychiatry*, *66*, 289–317.

Perlman, M., & Clark, N. (2015). Learned vocal and breathing behavior in an enculturated gorilla. *Animal Cognition*, *2015*, 1–15.

Petitto, L. A., & Marentette, P. F. (1991). Babbling in the manual mode: Evidence for the ontogeny of language. *Science*, *251*, 1493–1496.

Prochnow, S., Hesse, V., & Wermke, K. (2017). Does a "musical" mother tongue influence cry melodies? A comparative study of Swedish and German newborns. *Musicae Scientiae*, *23*(2), 143–156. doi: 10.1177/1029864917733035

Radesky, J., Miller, A. L., Rosenblum, K. L., Appugliese, D., Kaciroti, N., & Lumeng, J. C. (2015). Maternal mobile device use during a structured parent–child interaction task. *Academic Pediatrics*, *15*, 238–244.

Ramírez-Esparza, N., García-Sierra, A., & Kuhl, P. K. (2014). Look who's talking: Speech style and social context in language input to infants are linked to concurrent and future speech development. *Developmental Science*, *17*, 880–891.

Reed, J., Hirsh-Pasek, K., & Golinkoff, R. M. (2017). Learning on hold: Cell phones sidetrack parent–child interactions. *Developmental Psychology*, *53*, 1428–1436.

Richman, A. L., Miller, P. M., & LeVine, R. A. (1992). Cultural and educational variations in maternal responsiveness. *Developmental Psychology*, *28*, 614–621.

Robb, M. P., Bauer, H. R., & Tyler, A. A. (1994). A quantitative analysis of the single-word stage. *First Language*, *14*, 37–48.

Rowe, M. L., Raudenbush, S. W., & Goldin-Meadow, S. (2012). The pace of vocabulary growth helps predict later vocabulary skill. *Child Development*, *83*, 508–525.

Russell, J. L., McIntyre, J. M., Hopkins, W. D., & Taglialatela, J. P. (2013). Vocal learning of a communicative signal in captive chimpanzees, Pan troglodytes. *Brain and Language*, *127*, 520–525.

Schneider, R. M., Yurovsky, D., & Frank, M. C. (2015). Large-scale investigations of variability in children's first words. In D. C. Noelle, R. Dale, A. S. Warlaumont, J. Yoshimi, T. Matlock, C. D. Jennings, & P. P. Maglio (Eds.), *Proceedings of the 37th Annual Meeting of the Cognitive Science Society* (pp. 2110–2115). Austin, TX: Cognitive Science Society.

Smith, B., Brown-Sweeney, S., & Stoel-Gammon, C. (1989). A quantitative analysis of reduplicated and variegated babbling. *First Language*, *9*, 175–189.

Soderstrom, M. (2007). Beyond babytalk: Re-evaluating the nature and content of speech input to preverbal infants. *Developmental Review*, *27*, 501–532.

Stark, R. E. (1980). Stages of speech development in the first year of life. *Child Phonology, Vol. 1: Production*. New York, NY: Academic Press.

Stoel-Gammon, C., & Otomo, K. (1986). Babbling development of hearing-impaired and normally hearing subjects. *Journal of Speech and Hearing Disorders*, *51*, 33–41.

Suskind, D. L., Leffel, K. R., Graf, E., Hernandez, M. W., Gunderson, E. A., Sapolich, S. G., ... Levine, S. C. (2016). A parent-directed language intervention for children of low socioeconomic status: A randomized controlled pilot study. *Journal of Child Language*, *43*, 366–406.

Swanson, M. R., Shen, M. D., Wolff, J. J., Boyd, B., Clements, M., Rehg, J., ... the IBIS Network. (2018). Naturalistic language recordings reveal "hypervocal" infants at high familial risk for autism. *Child Development*, *89*, e60–e73.

Tamis-LeMonda, C. S., Bornstein, M. H., & Baumwell, L. (2001). Maternal responsiveness and children's achievement of language milestones. *Child Development*, *72*, 748–767.

Tamis-LeMonda, C. S., Kuchirko, Y., & Suh, D. D. (2018). Taking center stage: Infants' active role in language learning. In M. Saylor & P. Ganea (Eds.), *Active learning from infancy to childhood*. New York, NY: Springer.

Tamis-LeMonda, C. S., & Song, L. (2012). Parent–infant communicative interactions in cultural context. In R. M. Lerner, E. Easterbrooks, & J. Mistry (Eds.), *Handbook of psychology* (2nd ed., Vol. 6, pp. 143–170). Hoboken, NJ: John Wiley & Sons.

Tarabulsy, G. M., Tessier, R., & Kappas, A. (1996). Contingency detection and the contingent organization of behavior in interactions: Implications for socio-emotional development in infancy. *Psychological Bulletin*, *120*, 25–41.

Tardif, T., Gelman, S., & Xu, F. (1999). Putting the noun bias in context: A comparison of English and Mandarin. *Child Development*, *70*, 620–635.

Thevenin, D. M., Eilers, R. E., Oller, D. K., & Lavoie, L. (1985). Where's the drift in babbling drift? A cross-linguistic study. *Applied Psycholinguistics*, *6*, 3–15.

VanDam, M., Warlaumont, A. S., Bergelson, E., Cristia, A., Soderstrom, M., de Palma, P., & MacWhinney, B. (2016). HomeBank: An online repository of daylong child-centered audio recordings. *Seminars in Speech and Language*, *37*, 128–142.

Vihman, M. M., Ferguson, C. A., & Elbert, M. (1986). Phonological development from babbling to speech: Common tendencies and individual differences. *Applied Psycholinguistics*, *7*, 3–40.

Vihman, M. M., Macken, M. A., Miller, R., Simmons, H., & Miller, J. (1985). From babbling to speech: A re-assessment of the continuity issue. *Language*, *61*, 397–445.

Vouloumanos, A, & Werker, J. F. (2004). Tuned to the signal: The privileged status of speech for young infants. *Developmental Science*, *7*, 270–276.

Warlaumont, A. S., & Finnegan, M. K. (2016). Learning to produce syllabic speech sounds via reward-modulated neural plasticity. *PLOS ONE*, *11*, e0145096.

Warlaumont, A. S., Richards, J. A., Gilkerson, J., Messinger, D. S., & Oller, D. K. (2016). The social feedback hypothesis and communicative development in autism spectrum disorder: A response to Akhtar, Jaswal, Dinishak, and Stephan (2016). *Psychological Science*, *27*, 1531–1533.

Warlaumont, A. S., Richards, J. A., Gilkerson, J., & Oller, D. K. (2014). A social feedback loop for speech development and its reduction in autism. *Psychological Science*, *25*, 1314–1324.

Warlaumont, A. S., Westermann, G., Buder, E. H., & Oller, D. K. (2013). Prespeech motor learning in a neural network using reinforcement. *Neural Networks*, *38*, 64–75.

Weber, A., Fernald, A., & Diop, Y. (2017). When cultural norms discourage talking to babies: Effectiveness of a parenting program in rural Senegal. *Child Development, 88*, 1513–1526.

Weist, R. M., & Kruppe, B. (1977). Parent and sibling comprehension of children's speech. *Journal of Psycholinguistic Research, 6*, 49–58.

Wermke, K., Ruan, Y., Feng, Y., Dobnig, D., Stephan, S., Wermke, P., … Shu, H. (2017). Fundamental frequency variation in crying of Mandarin and German neonates. *Journal of Voice, 31*, 255.e25–255.e30.

Westermann, G., & Miranda, E. R. (2004). A new model of sensorimotor coupling in the development of speech. *Brain and Language, 89*, 393–400.

Yazejian, N., Bryant, D. M., Hans, S., Horm, D., St. Clair, L., File, N., & Burchinal, M. (2017). Child and parenting outcomes after 1 year of educare. *Child Development, 88*, 1651–1688.

Yoshikawa, Y., Asada, M., Hosoda, K., & Koga, J. (2003). A constructivist approach to infants' vowel acquisition through mother–infant interaction. *Connection Science, 15*, 245–258.

Zimmerman, F. J., Gilkerson, J., Richards, J. A., Christakis, D. A., Xu, D., Gray, S., & Yapanel, U. (2009). Teaching by listening: The importance of adult–child conversations to language development. *Pediatrics, 124*, 342–349.

23 Infant Word Learning and Emerging Syntax

Dani Levine, Kathy Hirsh-Pasek,
and Roberta Michnick Golinkoff

> Language is the blood of the soul into which thoughts run and out of which they grow.
>
> Oliver Wendell Holmes

For centuries philosophers and scientists have puzzled over the meaning of words and the intricacies of grammar. How did the human species develop such a complex system that allowed us to work collaboratively and to share experiences – be it about the past or future? How did the species derive a system that allowed for optimal representation of the world in a way that also optimized quick communication among members of the species? Our language can mend conflicts, share grand ideas, and allow us to express and grow our everyday thoughts.

The past half century has witnessed a boom in our understanding of language and of the ways in which it develops in virtually every child and in every culture throughout history. Children master much of this complex and intricate system before they can even tie their shoes. The story we tell in these pages moves from mastery of first words to the ways children learn to combine those words into coherent thoughts and sentences. It is told through research on how children navigate what has been called the *problem of reference* – how words map to world, and the problem of syntax or how little minds come to recognize that words are connected to reveal propositions about the world they live in. This chapter outlines the latest thinking on these issues and highlights how the field has changed in the past decade to reveal that language development is an interactive and integrated system that is like a rope with many strands (Scarborough, 2001).

One of the driving forces behind word-learning studies was born from the Quinean conundrum (Quine, 1960). A linguist in a foreign land sees a rabbit hopping by while uttering "gavagai." The reference for gavagai is far from obvious – possibly referring to the rabbit's hopping, the fur, or even the thump on the ground rather than the whole rabbit. How is a child to solve this seemingly intractable problem? We came to realize that word learning is socially mediated (L. Bloom, 2000; Hollich et al., 2000; Tomasello, 1992).

At the same time, the young learner must learn grammatical rules characterizing infinite linguistic strings from finite input (Chomsky, 1965; Pinker, 1987).

Chomsky (1965) proposed a language acquisition device uniquely constituted for language learning, but ultimately we came to recognize that language is a dynamic and adaptive system of numerous developmental processes working together (Beckner et al., 2009; D'Souza, D'Souza, & Karmiloff-Smith, 2017; Elman, 2003; Hirsh-Pasek & Golinkoff, 1996; Hollich et al., 2000; Tucker & Hirsh-Pasek, 1993). Further, the learning of words and grammar are not divorced from one another but are mutually dependent (Bates & Goodman, 1997; Harris, Golinkoff, & Hirsh-Pasek, 2011; Marchman & Bates, 1994).

While reviewing each of these areas and how they intersect, we make the case that language development initially proceeds through domain-general processes that are seeded by a few language-specific attentional givens. We hold that the infants' language system develops in the context of a larger developing system, the caregiver–child dyad, which dynamically shapes both word learning (Tamis-LeMonda, Kuchirko, & Song, 2014) and the emergence of syntax (Cameron-Faulkner, Lieven, & Tomasello, 2003). We further hold that the same processes operate across languages and, to the extent we have data, are supported by neurological signatures. With this growing consensus in mind, we then explore the sociocultural variation and ask what policy implications flow from our knowledge base. Several themes dominate our policy conclusions. First, key processes that enable language growth are available early so if we want to intervene, 0 to 3 years of age is the period where our policies will have the greatest impact. Second, having two languages is a good thing, and should be supported rather than discouraged. Third and finally, strong language skills, in terms of both vocabulary and syntax, are key to sustaining social and cognitive growth. So, it is important to heighten attention to language learning outside of the laboratory to create language-rich communities.

23.1 Word Learning

Learning words is a remarkably challenging task. Infants must prune their discrimination of phonemes to those contained in their native language (Kuhl et al., 2008), and infants who are better at phonological segmentation have better word-learning skills later (Newman, Ratner, Jusczyk, Jusczyk, & Dow, 2006; Tsao, Liu, & Kuhl, 2004; Werker & Yeung, 2005). Moreover, garnering even a basic understanding of word meaning is far from a simple challenge that has been termed the mapping problem. Were this not enough, many researchers argue that mere sounds (or gestures for signers) do not reach the status of a word until infants generalize the word to other members of the same category (P. Bloom, 2002; Golinkoff, Mervis, & Hirsh-Pasek, 1994; Werker, Cohen, Lloyd, Casasola, & Stager, 1998). That is, just saying the word "fleur" (French for flower) to a particular dandelion does not count as a word, until it can be generalized to the rose in the kitchen vase. Even by this strict definition, infants demonstrate comprehension of words referring to object *categories* by 6 months (Bergelson & Swingley, 2012; Tincoff & Jusczyk, 2012).

23.1.1 Leveraging Domain-General Processes for Word Learning

23.1.1.1 *Finding Word-to-World Mappings: Associations, Hypothesis Testing, and Bayesian Inference*

Models of word learning once focused on single mechanisms, but it is now widely accepted that it is a product of several processes working interdependently (Booth & Waxman, 2008; Hollich et al., 2000). Infants increasingly use social cues such as eye gaze and grammatical cues for word learning as they gain language experience, but the mechanism by which word-to-world mappings are formed independently of these additional cues has been debated. Competing theoretical models of word learning propose associative mechanisms, hypothesis testing mechanisms, and Bayesian mechanisms.

Associative word-learning theories (i.e., cross-situational models) posit that infants store associations between each word and multiple possible meanings of the word, tracking the statistical regularity with which each word is heard in the presence of all possible referents over time (Yu & Smith, 2012b). Statistical learning is a domain-general process of tracking associations in input without relying on prior knowledge (see Aslin, 2017; Saffran & Thiessen, 2007, for reviews), and the argument is that infants may gain a toehold in word learning by noting statistical regularities within and across language-relevant strands like sounds and events. Infants may capitalize on statistical learning not only to find phonological units that reliably cohere in the speech stream (see Saffran & Kirkham, 2018, for a review) and nonlinguistic units of events that cohere in the visual stream of experience (Roseberry, Richie, Hirsh-Pasek, Golinkoff, & Shipley, 2011; Stahl, Romberg, Roseberry, Golinkoff, & Hirsh-Pasek, 2014), but also to learn mappings of word to world (see Yu & Smith, 2012b, for a review). A simple example of this would be if an infant heard "banana" and "apple" while viewing a banana and an apple, and at a later time heard "banana" and "orange" while viewing a banana and an orange. There is some experimental evidence that infants can track multiple word-referent pairings across these types of ambiguous trials (Scott & Fisher, 2012; L. Smith & Yu, 2008). However, other researchers argue that the storage of *all* possible referents from *all* ambiguous word-learning situations for *all* words is unlikely (Medina, Snedeker, Trueswell, & Gleitman, 2011).

Hypothesis-testing accounts offer an alternative word-learning strategy, in which infants form a single hypothesis about a word's meaning in any given ambiguous word-learning situation and track this hypothesized meaning across experiences involving that word (Aravind et al., 2018; Medina et al., 2011); then, if a subsequent experience leads children to hypothesize a different meaning, they may shift to tracking both hypothesized meanings until further information is obtained (Stevens, Gleitman, Trueswell, & Yang,

2017). Hypothesis-testing accounts are bolstered by children's one-trial learning: children are often successful at fast mapping a novel word onto a novel item among distractor items in a single trial and then extending this word to a different exemplar from the same category (Aravind et al., 2018; Golinkoff, Hirsh-Pasek, Bailey, & Wenger, 1992). However, research using a measure of fast mapping from the Quick Interactive Language Screener (QUILS) with hundreds of preschoolers revealed that when children's initial guess on a fast mapping trial is incorrect, children perform at chance on the extension trial (Aravind et al., 2018). Thus, children seem to retain only their hypothesized mapping of a word, to the exclusion of other statistically possible meanings.

Bayesian inference models of word learning incorporate aspects of both associative and hypothesis-testing models. Bayesian models posit that word learners entertain multiple word-meaning hypotheses, and, given experience with particular word-learning situations and the use of principled inference procedures, the likelihood of a particular hypothesis is probabilistically increased or decreased (Xu & Tenenbaum, 2007). For example, the likelihood that the word "fruit" refers to a group of sweet-tasting foods would be increased by hearing this word in the presence of a banana, an apple, and an orange as opposed to just a banana, and this combines with all of infants' principled assumptions about word learning (e.g., assumption that words refer to taxonomic categories, whole objects) to lead to word learning (Liu, Golinkoff, & Sak, 2001). The psychological reality of these ideal learner models is uncertain (Yu & Smith, 2012b), though they have much success in uncovering word-referent mappings from real-world co-occurrences.

In sum, infants may use a variety of methods to find and track word-meaning mappings over time. With more language experience, infants may shift their reliance from perceptual mechanisms of word learning to mechanisms that rely increasingly on social and grammatical cues (Hollich et al., 2000).

23.1.1.2 Attentional Control: Sustaining and Shifting Attention to Word Referents

To successfully map a word onto its referent in a given situation, infants must attend to the correct referent of the word rather than attending to incorrect alternatives. In part, this capacity can be attributed to exogenous attractors of attention in the caregiver–child dyadic context, which will be discussed in the next section. However, infants' endogenous control over their attention plays a significant role as well, in two primary ways.

First, infants' selective and sustained attention toward objects that are of interest to them provides opportunities for adults to engage in joint attention with the infant – which in turn extends infants' selective attention (Yu & Smith, 2016) – and for adults to name objects at these opportune, referentially transparent learning moments (Pereira, Smith, & Yu, 2014; Tamis-LeMonda, Kuchirko, & Tafuro, 2013; Trueswell et al., 2016; Yu & Smith, 2012a; see also Hollich et al., 2000). As P. Bloom (2000) argued, the new words children hear are like Fauconnier's brick: Just as there is only one missing place for the brick to go during the building process, so too there is only one focus of the child's attention for a word to map onto at a given moment. Infants' sustained attention to objects is derived in part from their ability to physically select objects, bring the objects close to their face, and inhibit movement of their head – these behaviors reduce the distraction of other objects in their visual field (Yu & Smith, 2012a). Individual differences in infants' sustained attention to objects at 9 months predict vocabulary size months later (Yu, Suanda, & Smith, 2019). Thus, sustained attention, supported by motor development, contributes to infants' word learning (Pereira et al., 2014; Yu & Smith, 2012a).

Second, word learning demands that infants learn to *shift* their attention when adults point out objects to them (Hollich et al., 2000; Morales et al., 2000; Mundy et al., 2007; Yurovsky & Frank, 2017). Infants must disengage from what is initially salient to them, whether it is an interesting object (Hollich et al., 2000) or the caregiver's face (Yurovsky & Frank, 2017). Individual differences in this attention-shifting ability at 6 months predict vocabulary size up to 18 months later (Morales, Mundy, & Rojas, 1998). Moreover, improvement in attention-shifting skill during the first years of life is accompanied by improvements in word learning (Mundy et al., 2007; Yurovsky & Frank, 2017).

23.1.2 Infants' Word Learning Is Social: Making the Most of Dyadic Interaction

Infants as young as 6 months understand that human speech is a unique acoustic signal that serves to communicate information from one person to another (Ferry, Hespos, & Waxman, 2013; Vouloumanos, Martin, & Onishi, 2014), and successful word learning typically occurs in an interactive context (Carpenter, Nagell, Tomasello, Butterworth, Moore, 1998). Dyadic interactions throughout infancy with nurturing adults create a communication foundation ripe for word learning (Adamson, Bakeman, Deckner, & Nelson, 2014; Hirsh-Pasek et al., 2015).

23.1.2.1 *Infant-Directed Speech: Exaggerated Articulations Support Word Learning*

Infant-directed speech (IDS) is spontaneously used by adults and children when interacting with infants (Fernald et al., 1989; Shatz & Gelman, 1973). Compared to adult-directed speech (ADS), the prosody (i.e., acoustic, rhythmic aspects of speech) of IDS is characterized by higher and more variable pitches, slower rates of speech, elongated vowels and pauses, phrase-final lengthening, shorter utterances, and greater positive affect (e.g., Fernald et al., 1989; Martin, Igarashi, Jincho, & Mazuka, 2016). IDS also has more nested clustering, from the level of the stressed syllable to the level of the word to the level of the syntactic phrase (Falk & Kello, 2017); in other words, IDS seems to emphasize the hierarchical organization of language and provides more reliable information than ADS about lexical and syntactic boundaries in speech (Falk & Kello, 2017; Martin et al., 2016). Indeed, infants are better able to statistically segment a novel stream of speech into lexical units when the speech is in the form of IDS (Thiessen, Hill, & Saffran, 2005; Kemler Nelson, Hirsh-Pasek, Jusczyk, & Cassidy, 1989). Further, infants succeed at mapping novel words to novel objects when the words are presented in IDS, but not ADS (Graf Estes & Hurley, 2013; Ma, Golinkoff, Houston, & Hirsh-Pasek, 2011). Caregiver speech directed to infants predicts language outcomes, while speech that is only overheard by infants does not (Golinkoff, Hoff, Rowe, Tamis-LeMonda, & Hirsh-Pasek, 2019; Kuhl, Tsao, & Liu, 2003; Shneidman & Goldin-Meadow, 2012; Weisleder & Fernald, 2013; but see Ferguson, Graf, & Waxman, 2018; Sperry, Sperry, & Miller, 2018).

How might IDS facilitate word learning? While some aspects of IDS, such as exaggerated pitch and emotional expression elicit infants' attention and may therefore support adult–infant communication broadly (Fernald et al., 1989; Singh, Morgan, & Best, 2002), there is one feature of IDS that predicts infants' vocabulary acquisition specifically: vowel hyperarticulation (Hartman, Ratner, & Newman, 2017). Adults' exaggeration of vowels in their speech may support infants' word learning by increasing the distinction between different vowel categories, thereby making it easier for infants to phonologically distinguish new words and recognize repetitions of familiar words (Hartman et al., 2017; Kuhl et al., 1997). Importantly, IDS is not determined by the adult alone (Golinkoff, Can, Soderstrom, & Hirsh-Pasek, 2015). Adults modulate their IDS in real time in response to infant feedback (N. A. Smith & Trainor, 2008), and their use of vowel hyperarticulation is specifically responsive to infants' language abilities (Kalashnikova, Goswami, & Burnham, 2018).

Furthermore, cross-linguistic differences in the content of IDS have implications for word learning. American English-speaking mothers tend to focus more on objects and eliciting object labels from infants (Bornstein et al., 1992; Fernald & Morikawa, 1993), whereas Chinese-speaking caregivers use relatively more verbs with their children (Tardif, Shatz, & Naigles, 1997) because Chinese permits "prodrop" or the dropping of noun arguments. These linguistic differences in IDS input are reflected in the proportion of nouns and verbs in children's developing vocabularies (Tardif et al., 1997). Yet, the noun bias is a cross-linguistic phenomenon (Waxman et al., 2013), and the higher ratio of nouns to other word classes in American English IDS likely just exaggerates this more general developmental pattern.

23.1.2.2 *Communicative Context: Co-Construction of the Communication Foundation*

The social context of the dyad contributes to word learning not only through the use of IDS, but, perhaps even more fundamentally, through the dyad's ongoing co-construction of a communication foundation (Adamson et al.,

2014; Bruner, 1983; Hirsh-Pasek et al., 2015; Tamis-LeMonda et al., 2014). The quality of caregiver–child communication is a more potent predictor of children's language outcomes than the quantity of input (Cartmill et al., 2013; Hirsh-Pasek et al., 2015; Rowe, 2012), and three features of the communication foundation that may be most critical for developing infants' word-learning skills are the dyad's joint attentional engagement, routines and rituals, and the fluency and connectedness of dyadic interactions.

Joint engagement of the infant–caregiver dyad with objects creates opportune word-learning situations, because the attention of the dyad has a shared focus that can be marked with symbols (Baldwin, 1995). Indeed, the more infants and their caregivers jointly engage with objects, and the more caregivers follow their infants' focus of attention with relevant language (i.e., providing object labels), the larger infants' vocabularies are months later (Adamson, Bakeman, & Deckner, 2004; Carpenter et al., 1998; but see Akhtar & Gernsbacher, 2007, for a discussion of word learning absent joint attention in atypically developing children). The extent of this symbol infusion is influenced by adults' implicit judgments of infants' word knowledge (Adamson et al., 2004), suggesting that advancements in joint engagement – which are critical for word learning – are co-constructed by the caregiver and infant.

Also co-constructed by the dyad are routines and rituals such as familiar games (e.g., peek-a-boo) and cultural activities (e.g., book reading) that provide rich pragmatic frames for word learning (Bruner, 1983; Hirsh-Pasek et al., 2015; Rohlfing, Wrede, Vollmer, & Oudeyer, 2016). These interactional structures involve a sequence of actions, coordinated by the dyad, that are oriented toward particular goals and that recur and emerge over time (Bruner, 1983; Rohlfing et al., 2016). The quantity and quality of maternal language varies systematically by the activity in which the dyad is engaged (Tamis-LeMonda, Custode, Kuchirko, Escobar, & Lo, 2019), and individual differences in the use of structured routines during infancy predict children's later vocabulary knowledge (Hirsh-Pasek et al., 2015). Thus, these emerging frames may complement interactional joint engagement in contributing to word learning.

Fluency and connectedness describes the balance within dyadic interaction, or the extent to which the caregiver and infant contribute equally to back-and-forth exchanges. Even before infants utter their first word, they engage actively in conversations with caregivers through nonverbal behaviors and pre-linguistic vocalizations (Wu & Gros-Louis, 2014). The responsiveness of caregivers (providing responses that build on infant interests and are close in time to infant behaviours) is critical for constructing a communication foundation characterized by fluency and connectedness (Reed, Hirsh-Pasek, & Golinkoff, 2016; Tamis-LeMonda et al., 2014). This is why children generally fail to learn words from televised displays lacking contingent conversations (Roseberry, Hirsh-Pasek, & Golinkoff, 2014; see also Kuhl et al., 2003), and also why word learning is disrupted when contingent conversations are interrupted (Reed, Hirsh-Pasek, & Golinkoff, 2017). Not only does the fluency and connectedness of caregiver–child interaction predict children's vocabulary a year later, but the contributions of both joint engagement *and* routines and rituals to later vocabulary are statistically nonsignificant once fluency and connectedness is controlled (Hirsh-Pasek et al., 2015).

23.1.3 Word Learning Gets Specific: Bootstrapping via Familiar Vocabulary and Syntax

23.1.3.1 *Acquiring Phonological and Semantic Biases Constrains Word Learning*

As infants become familiar with more and more words, they notice consistent patterns in the phonology and semantics of their native language that constrain word learning. Among the earliest consistencies infants focus on are phonological regularities, including the predominant prosodic stress pattern (e.g., in English, stressed syllables mark word onsets as in *ba*by or *mom*my; Jusczyk, Houston, & Newsome, 1999) and phonotactic patterns (e.g., in English, phoneme orderings such as *-iss*, or *-ate*; Jusczyk, Luce, and Charles-Luce, 1994). Infants' early word learning prioritizes mapping words whose prosodic stress and phonotactic patterns are most common in their native language (Graf Estes & Bowen, 2013). Infants growing up in bilingual environments simultaneously learn the phonological regularities of two languages (Burns, Yoshida, Hill, & Werker, 2007), and bilingual infants are as successful as monolingual infants at learning similar-sounding novel words (Mattock, Polka, Rvachew, & Krehm, 2010), with some evidence for a bilingual advantage (Singh, Fu, Tay, & Golinkoff, 2018).

Learning semantics also helps constrain possible word meanings, through the acquisition of word-learning biases. For example, infants with sufficient experience mapping words onto object categories defined by shape (e.g., *ball*, *cup*) acquire a *shape bias*, a helpful heuristic for quickly learning new object labels (Landau, Smith, & Jones, 1988). Additionally, children's experience with word learning leads them to the assumption that a novel word they hear likely does not map onto an object for which they already have a label (Golinkoff et al., 1994; Markman & Wachtel, 1988; Merriman, Bowman, & MacWhinney, 1989). Rather, children infer that the novel word maps onto a novel, nameless object (Golinkoff et al., 1992) or a subpart or feature of a familiar object (Markman & Wachtel, 1988). This heuristic for fast mapping, called the *mutual exclusivity bias*, is used by monolingual infants as early as 17 months to constrain word learning (Halberda, 2003); it is used less consistently by bilingual/multilingual infants, likely because they expect to learn multiple labels for the same objects (Byers-Heinlein & Werker, 2009).

Importantly, the specific vocabulary items that infants have acquired determine the development of these semantic biases (Borovsky, Ellis, Evans, & Elman, 2016; Perry & Samuelson, 2011). For example, infants who have acquired more words for solid objects whose labels are defined by material (e.g., *chalk*, *ice*) rather than shape (e.g., *ball*, *cup*) are less likely to utilize a shape bias when learning new words (Perry & Samuelson, 2011). Similarly, when 2-year-olds' vocabularies contain many words in a particular domain (e.g., animals), they are better able to learn new words in that domain relative to a domain in which they have less semantic knowledge (Borovsky et al., 2016). In short, infants' word learning leads to the development of word-learning biases, which in turn facilitate word learning.

23.1.3.2 *Using Emerging Syntax to Bootstrap Word Learning*

Emerging syntactic knowledge can be leveraged for word learning as when infants harbor expectations about grammatical categories (Gerken, Landau, & Remez, 1990; Shi & Werker, 2001; Shipley, Smith, & Gleitman, 1969; Yuan, Fisher, & Snedeker, 2012). By 12 months, infants successfully map novel words that phonologically resemble nouns (e.g., *wug*) onto novel objects, but fail to form word-to-world mappings when the novel words are phonologically similar to function words (e.g., *iv*) (MacKenzie, Curtin, & Graham, 2012). That is, infants use their knowledge of syntactic categories to selectively map content but not function words onto novel objects.

Infants' emerging syntax plays a particularly vital role in verb learning. Verbs are conceptually more difficult than nouns (Gentner & Boroditsky, 2001; Gleitman, Cassidy, Nappa, Papafragou, & Trueswell, 2005; Maguire, Hirsh-Pasek, & Golinkoff, 2006), and depend on the speaker's perspective (e.g., *give* and *receive* label the same event). Through a process called *syntactic bootstrapping*, children use familiar syntactic structures to disambiguate verb referents (Gleitman, 1990; Naigles, 1990). For example, 2-year-olds hearing a novel verb in a transitive frame ("The duck is gorping the bunny!") mapped the verb *gorping* onto a scene of a duck performing a novel action on a bunny, rather than mapping the verb onto a scene of the duck and bunny performing novel actions independently, which would be described in an intransitive frame ("The duck and the bunny are gorping!"; Naigles, 1990). Even before children's sophisticated use of syntactic bootstrapping, infants use simple structural cues (i.e., one-to-one mapping between number of nouns and number of event participants) to guide interpretation of novel verbs (Yuan et al., 2012). For example, 19-month-olds interpreted a transitive sentence involving two nouns ("He's gorping him!") as referring to a novel event involving two participants, and rejected the possibility that this sentence referred to a novel event involving a single participant, even if there was a second, nonparticipating bystander in the scene (Yuan et al., 2012). Furthermore, young children are more likely to learn new words when they are presented in the typical syntactic frames their language uses (Imai et al., 2008). Thus, Japanese- and Chinese-speaking children learn new verbs best when subject and object arguments are omitted (e.g., "Look! Twilling!"), while English-speaking children learn new verbs best when argument structure is available (e.g., "Look! She is twilling it!"). As syntax knowledge in children's native language emerges, so too does children's skill at leveraging syntax to bootstrap novel word meanings.

23.2 Emerging Syntax

Word learning in the absence of syntax would fail to capture the power of using fuller propositions for expression. For example, the words *see*, *the*, *do*, *pretty*, *you*, *flowers* take on a unique communicative meaning when combined into the sentence: "Do you see the pretty flowers"? Thus, paralleling the mapping problem of word learning is the challenge of learning the copious set of syntactic rules that are unique to each language. Yet here too, learning begins early. By 2 months, infants detect patterns in how words are ordered (Mandel, Kemler Nelson, & Jusczyk, 1996) and organized into syntactic units (e.g., clauses; Mandel, Jusczyk, & Kemler Nelson, 1994). By 14 months, infants demonstrate an understanding of the syntactic relations between words; for example, infants hearing "She's kissing the keys!" looked toward a video of a woman kissing keys and holding a ball rather than a video of a woman kissing a ball and holding keys (Golinkoff, Hirsh-Pasek, Gordon, & Cauley, 1987). Further, some key aspects of grammatical structure are universally emergent, manifest even in the homesign systems created by isolated deaf children (Goldin-Meadow, 2003) and in the newly emerging Nicaraguan Sign Language developed by cohorts of Nicaraguan deaf children (Senghas, Kita, & Özyürek, 2004).

23.2.1 Leveraging Domain-General Processes for Emerging Syntax

23.2.1.1 *Tracking Structure in the Input to Uncover Syntactic Rules*
Syntax uses a system of rules that allow us to communicate verifiable propositions in the world with clarity and brevity. It is an "evolutionary innovation" for aggregating and exchanging information (Miller, 1990) as we move deftly from sound to meaning and meaning to sound. Chomsky (1965) first posited that syntax was so complex that it could not be learned if there was not an innate system in which children discovered parameters like word order and classifiers that distinguished one language from another. Languages like English with more fixed word orders have weaker classifier systems, and languages like Turkish with richer classifier systems have more flexible word orders – thus, children could use the structure of the input as a guide to uncover the parameters of their native language.

Statistical learning alone would be insufficient for learning syntax without predispositions or constraints that guide distributional learning (Hirsh-Pasek & Golinkoff, 1996). However, building on these constraints, the domain-general approach of tracking regularities in the input does play a role in syntax acquisition (Bates & MacWhinney, 1982). One way that statistical learning may initially bootstrap syntax acquisition is by clueing infants into which word orderings are grammatical and which are not. Saffran and Wilson (2003) tested this idea by presenting 12-month-olds with a fluent speech stream in which multisyllabic words, defined only by transitional probabilities between syllables, were organized into multiword sentences according to a novel, simple grammar. Following exposure, infants successfully distinguished new sentences with grammatical word orderings from new sentences with ungrammatical orderings. Thus, infants use statistical learning to track multiple layers of structure, from syllable-level combinations to word-level combinations.

Infants' use of statistical learning goes beyond tracking regularities in the ordering of particular words, to tracking abstract relations in linguistic structure. Marcus and colleagues showed that 7-month-olds could extract "algebraic-like" rules such as ABA or ABB from sequences of speech (e.g., *ga ti ga, li na li*) and generalize these rules to new sets of syllables (Marcus, Fernandes, & Johnson, 2007; Marcus, Vijayan, Rao, & Vishton, 1999; see also Seidenberg & Elman, 1999, for computational modeling of statistically driven syntactic learning). Follow-up work revealed even more nuance in infants' distributional learning of grammar. Gerken (2006) attempted to teach 9-month-olds the grammatical pattern ABA by either presenting infants with exemplars that kept B constant (e.g., *le di le, wi di wi*) or exemplars that varied B (e.g., *le di le, wi je wi*). Only the infants exposed to exemplars with varied B made the generalization to an ABA grammar. Keeping B constant led infants to a narrower generalization (i.e., A*di*A) (Gerken, 2006), suggesting that infants are sensitive to the Bayesian principle of "suspicious coincidences": It would be surprising to only hear structures of the form A*di*A if in fact the more general ABA was the linguistic structure and if the exemplars were a random sample of that structure (Xu & Tenenbaum, 2007). Additionally, after extensive exposure to the grammatical pattern A*di*A, providing infants with just three counter-examples of ABA with varied B shifted infants to the broader generalization (Gerken, 2010). Thus, infants' grammatical rule learning may follow a Bayesian framework (Gerken, 2010), with infants considering multiple hypotheses about the appropriate generalization of a linguistic structure and selecting the hypothesis that is most probable based on the distribution of the input. It is crucial to note, however, that none of this is conscious on the infant's part.

Beyond this evidence that infants *can* learn abstract grammatical patterns in a constrained experimental setting, there is evidence that infants actually do learn grammatical patterns based on input distribution in their native language over time (Mintz, 2003; van Heugten & Johnson, 2010). For example, by 24 months (but not 17 months), Dutch-learning infants have learned the dependency between the definite article *het* and the diminutive suffix *-je*, but not the dependency between the definite article *de* and the plural suffix *-en*, paralleling the input children heard (van Heugten & Johnson, 2010).

23.2.1.2 *Temporal Attention: Learning Dependencies Between Nonadjacent Grammatical Elements*

Acquiring syntax demands that infants learn to attend not only to adjacent grammatical relations, as in "the girl is playing" (number agreement), but also to nonadjacent relations, which have some level of temporal distance separating the dependency, as in "the girl is playing" (relation between auxiliary and inflectional morpheme) (de Diego-Balaguer, Martinez-Alvarez, & Pons, 2016). In many cases the intervening elements are lengthier, as in "the girl is always playing." Infants' attention must be retained across sizeable temporal windows. While neonates learn only adjacent dependencies in speech (Gervain, Macagno, Cogoi, Peña, & Mehler, 2008), 7-month-olds learn adjacent and nonadjacent dependencies (Gervain & Werker, 2013; Marcus et al., 1999; Marcus et al., 2007). Processing limitations, specifically limitations in attention, likely prevent newborns from tracking nonadjacent dependencies.

Even older infants have difficulty learning nonadjacent relations when too many syllables intervene (Santelmann & Jusczyk, 1998). For example, 18-month-old English-learning infants recognize the dependent relation between the auxiliary verb *is* and a verb with the ending -*ing*, but only over a distance of one- to three-syllables (e.g., *is baking*); when four or five syllables intervene (e.g., *is cheerfully baking*), infants at this age do not detect the relation, likely due to a "limited processing window" (Santelmann & Jusczyk, 1998).

23.2.2 Infants' Syntax Is Socially Dependent: Prosodic Bootstrapping and Communicative Signals

23.2.2.1 *Infant-Directed Speech: Prosodic Bootstrapping of Syntactic Units*

The prosodic bootstrapping hypothesis proposes that infants take advantage of prosody in speech to identify syntactic boundaries and learn about syntactic structure (Gleitman & Wanner, 1982). Indeed, when prosody is the only cue to the syntactic structure of a novel stream of speech, 19-month-olds distinguish grammatical from ungrammatical movement of syntactic constituents (Hawthorne & Gerken, 2014). IDS prosody facilitates detection of clausal units, the largest syntactic units of structure and meaning (Hirsh-Pasek et al., 1987; Seidl, 2007) in infants as young as 2 months (Mandel et al., 1994). Additionally, IDS prosody is used by infants as early as 6 months to detect syntactic units smaller than clauses, specifically phrasal units, such as noun phrases (e.g., *the small dog*) and verb phrases (e.g., *pets her dog*) (Soderstrom, Seidl, Kemler Nelson, & Jusczyk, 2003). This is important, because much of conversational speech, particularly IDS, involves back-and-forth communication (Golinkoff et al., 2015), in which sentence fragments rather than complete clauses are exchanged (Cameron-Faulkner et al., 2003). However, as with many cues to grammar, prosodic bootstrapping cannot be the whole story for the extraction of syntactic units (Gerken, Jusczyk, & Mandel, 1994). When a sentence starts with a pronoun, for example, infants cannot use stress on the first syllable to find syntactic constituents.

23.2.2.2 *Syntax Learning Is Specific to Communicative Contexts*

As with infants' word learning, infants' learning of syntax appears to rely on infants' recognition of a communicative signal. Marcus et al. (2007) showed that by 7.5 months, infants learn rules for speech but not nonspeech sounds, unless the rule was first learned in speech. Ferguson and Lew-Williams (2016) demonstrated that the likely reason for this finding is that unlike speech, which infants have learned is a communicative signal (see also Ferguson & Waxman, 2016), the nonspeech sounds were not placed in a communicative context. Infants were presented with a video of two individuals communicating in a back-and-forth social exchange, with one person using speech and the other using sine-wave tones, and both seeming to understand the other. Following this experience, infants succeeded at learning grammatical patterns in sine-wave tones (Ferguson & Lew-Williams, 2016), suggesting it is infants' interest in socially communicative signals that leads them to seek grammatical structure in language input.

23.2.3 Bootstrapping Emerging Syntax via Familiar Syntax and Vocabulary

23.2.3.1 *Rudimentary Syntactic Representations Bolster Further Syntactic Acquisition*

Infants' knowledge of the syntactic rules of their native language develops gradually. For example, by 15 months, English-learning infants have learned to segment the *-ing* suffix from words, and not to segment word endings that are not bound morphemes in English such as *-ot* (Mintz, 2013; see also Hirsh-Pasek, 2000; Shipley et al., 1969). In contrast, 8-month-olds with less language experience do not segment *-ing* differently than other word endings that are not bound morphemes (Mintz, 2013). However, although 15-month-olds have learned to segment the ending *-ing*, they still fail to recognize the non-adjacent dependency between the auxiliary verb *is* and verbs with the ending *-ing* (Santelmann & Jusczyk, 1998). Together, these studies suggest that infants gradually acquire grammar in their native language, with later learning (e.g., nonadjacent dependencies) building on earlier learning (e.g., learning to segment bound morphemes).

More broadly, researchers acknowledge a discrepancy between infants' precocious grammatical knowledge and the ways in which older children struggle with grammatical understanding (Soderstrom, 2008). Understanding the semantic implications of grammar, such as the ability to determine whether one or multiple actors is implied by a verb (e.g., *swims* vs. *swim*) in the absence of other cues, has a more protracted development (Johnson, de Villiers, & Seymour, 2005; see also Gleitman et al., 2005).

23.2.3.2 *Using Word Knowledge to Bootstrap Emerging Syntax*

Word knowledge may be particularly useful for supporting infants' learning of syntax when syntactic understanding is emergent and fragile. For example, when 2- and 3-year-olds hear a highly familiar verb used in an ungrammatical word order, they invariably correct it to the grammatical order (i.e., in English, subject–verb–object), but when they hear less familiar or novel verbs used in an ungrammatical word order, their responses are more variable: sometimes they correct the word order, and sometimes they go along with the ungrammatical order. In contrast, by age 4, children consistently make grammatical word-order corrections even for novel verbs (Akhtar, 1999; Matthews, Lieven, Theakston, & Tomasello, 2005). These studies suggest that prior lexical knowledge and usage experience matter for progression to increasingly abstract grammatical knowledge.

23.2.4 Neuroscience Perspectives: Neural Mechanisms Underlying Language Emergence

At birth, the infant brain is equipped to learn language. The precursors of the left-localized adult language system are present at birth, with newborns' processing of linguistic stimuli – but not nonlinguistic auditory stimuli – lateralized primarily to the left hemisphere of the brain (Molfese & Molfese, 1979; Peña et al., 2003). However, regions of both hemispheres activate in response to language at birth, and connectivities within this neural network are initially immature (Perani et al., 2011). Moreover, research is beginning to reveal the remarkable plasticity of this system. Children who experienced left-hemispheric strokes within days of birth had normal language skills, with neuroimaging revealing complete reorganization of the language system to right-hemisphere brain areas homologous to the areas on the left that typically subserve language functions (Newport et al., 2017). Language drives development of the brain by adaptively capitalizing on particular brain density regions that are primed and available for language input.

Beyond demonstrating preparedness for learning language, studies of the infant brain bolster specific claims regarding word learning and emerging syntax (i.e., derived from behavioral research) by revealing neural mechanisms underlying these processes. First, the domain-general mechanisms with which infants are equipped for finding structure in language are reflected in neural mechanisms present at birth. Neonates' brains are sensitive to the statistical structure of language, as evidenced by their event-related brain responses to a statistical word segmentation task (Teinonen, Fellman, Näätänen, Alku, & Huotilainen, 2009). A study of neonates' brains using near-infrared spectroscopy (NIRS) further revealed that newborns could differentiate simple repetition-based grammars (e.g., *ba-ba-mu* vs. *mu-ba-ba*); the differential response to these grammars involved neural activity localized in the inferior frontal region (possibly Broca's area; Gervain, Berent, & Werker, 2012). The neonate brain is prepared to discover structural regularities in the input, setting infants up for learning words and acquiring syntax.

Second, language learning is "gated by the social brain" – that is, neural computations of input are largely restricted to signals from humans (Kuhl, 2007). Lytle, Garcia-Sierra, and Kuhl (2018) showed that 9-month-olds' learning of phonemes from foreign language speech, as indicated by neural phonetic discrimination, was enhanced by the mere presence of a similarly aged peer, suggesting effects of social arousal on language learning. Neurophysiological evidence also supports the particular importance of caregiver–infant interactions over time for learning language. Parise and Csibra (2012) found that 9-month-olds exhibited an N400 event-related potential component, indicating they detected a mismatch between a familiar label and a subsequently presented object only when the person producing the labels was their mother, and not when the interacting partner was an experimenter. The researchers had instructed mothers to interact with their infants as they would typically, and it is likely that the familiar communication context helped infants to "recognize the situation as a naming game" and succeed at this task (Parise & Csibra, 2012). Further, Romeo et al. (2018) found that children's neural activations in Broca's area during language processing mediated the relation between adult–child conversational turns at home and children's language skills, revealing a neural mechanism for how language skills develop in response to social language experience.

Finally, neuroscientific research also provides insights into how language learning builds on earlier language knowledge. In a longitudinal study, Kuhl et al. (2008) found that better neural discrimination of *native* phonetic contrasts at 7.5 months predicted greater advancement in vocabulary and syntax 2 years later, while better neural discrimination of *nonnative* phonetic contrasts predicted poorer language outcomes. For bilingual infants, proficiency in each language is predicted by earlier neural discrimination of language-specific phonetic contrasts (Garcia-Sierra et al., 2011), though the neural commitment to native phonetic contrasts occurs, on average, more slowly for infants learning two languages, likely as an "adaptive and advantageous response to increased variability in language input" (Ferjan Ramírez, Ramírez, Clarke, Taulu, & Kuhl, 2017, p. 13). Thus, there is a bidirectional process whereby later language skills are built on the foundation of neural processes already in place during the first year of life, and language learning further drives development of the brain.

23.2.5 Communicative Contexts Vary Across Sociocultural Settings

Across sociocultural settings, words and syntax are learned through collaborative interactions with members of the infant's community, especially their parents (Tamis-LeMonda et al., 2014). Yet, sociocultural differences exist in the communicative contexts inherent in those interactions. For example, in the United States, Mexican and Dominican immigrant mothers use more nonverbal strategies (i.e., gestures) when engaging infants with toys and books relative to African American mothers, who tend to use more verbal modes of communication (Tamis-LeMonda, Song, Leavell, Kahana-Kalman, & Yoshikawa, 2012; see also Luo & Tamis-LeMonda, 2016). This sociocultural difference in the relative use of verbal and nonverbal communication is reflected in infants' developing verbal and nonverbal skills (Tamis-LeMonda et al., 2012).

More globally, research from non-Western, nonurban sociocultural settings reveals greater diversity in communicative contexts that calls into question the universality of developmental patterns of language growth. Schieffelin and Ochs (1983) point out that in non-Western cultures such as the Kaluli in Papua New Guinea, parents do not talk to their infants until they can talk back, and infants do not receive input in the form of IDS. In Samoa, parents often offload caregiving responsibilities onto a range of individuals including the infants' older siblings (Schieffelin & Ochs, 1983), so the idea of constructing a foundation of communication within a specific caregiver–infant dyad may not be applicable in these sociocultural contexts. And in Bolivia, those from the Tsimane village direct many fewer utterances to their children (Scaff, Stieglitz, Casillas, & Cristia, 2019).

As a result of the more limited availability or frequency of caregiver–child interactions in many communities in the non-Western world (Richman, Miller, & LeVine, 1992), much of what children experience is overheard speech rather than speech directed toward the child (Shneidman & Goldin-Meadow, 2012). The effects of these input differences are reflected in language outcomes, which are influenced by infant-directed, but not overheard speech (Shneidman & Goldin-Meadow, 2012; but see Sperry et al., 2018). Interestingly, Mastin and Vogt (2016) found that correlations between children's vocabulary size and aspects of dyadic interaction differed for urban and rural Mozambican infants: while joint attention positively correlated with vocabulary in the urban community (as it does in Western countries; Adamson et al., 2004; Carpenter et al., 1998), joint attention negatively correlated with vocabulary in the rural community (Little, Carver, & Legare, 2016). Nevertheless, throughout infancy, rural children spent significantly more overall time unengaged (i.e., with a partner or object) than urban children, and their vocabularies were smaller (Mastin & Vogt, 2016). In some cultural climates, as in rural Senegal, talking directly to children is even considered taboo, though an intervention by Weber, Fernald, and Diop (2017) suggests that language-learning techniques can be introduced in culturally sensitive ways, helping caregivers scaffold early language skills to improve their children's school readiness.

23.3 Policy Perspectives: Addressing Socioeconomic Status Gaps in Language Skills

There are sociocultural differences in caregiver–child interactions and emergent language skills across diverse societies that span the globe. However, there are also differences *within* societies that have particular consequences given the ways societies choose to label success. For example, within the United States, socioeconomic status (SES) disparities in infants' language skills are well documented by the second year of life and persist across development (Fernald, Marchman, & Weisleder, 2013; Hart & Risley, 1995; Vasilyeva,

Waterfall, & Huttenlocher, 2008). Moreover, although there are strong predictive relations between infant language measures and school-age outcomes, including IQ, working memory, language skills, and literacy (Marchman & Fernald, 2008; Pace, Luo, Hirsh-Pasek, & Golinkoff, 2017; Pace, Alper, Burchinal, Golinkoff, & Hirsh-Pasek, 2019), there is some controversy about the extent of a word gap. Sperry et al. (2018) have argued that by excluding the contributions of multiple caregivers and speech that is overheard by (rather than directed to) the child, research has underestimated the language environment of children from low-income families. However, Golinkoff et al. (2019) have noted that overheard speech is not as effective as child-directed speech for word learning, and that differences in the quality and quantity of child-directed language, both across and within SES groups, are linked with differences in children's language skills.

Key processes that foster language growth are available early, *making the period from 0 to 3 years of age an opportune window of time for high-impact policies*. Researchers have taken the vast literature of how caregivers support infants' language development (reviewed in this chapter) and have applied this literature to design interventions aimed at building a strong language foundation in all children. Interventions that equip caregivers with language-learning techniques are effective at improving infants' language environment and language skills (McGillion, Pine, Herbert, & Matthews, 2017; Pae et al., 2016; Suskind et al., 2016; Weber et al., 2017, but see Wake et al., 2011). Interventions seem to be most effective when they start early, have high dosage (Weber et al., 2017), are sensitive to the home environment (Suskind et al., 2016), and are continued over time rather than being delivered for just a brief period (McGillion et al., 2017; Suskind et al., 2016).

In addition to moving towards policies that recognize that the language system develops early, policies should also move towards recognizing that for many children, the language system is comprised of two languages rather than just one, and *successful outcomes for bilingual children rely on high-quality and high-quantity experiences with both languages*. Bilingualism is common worldwide, but in the United States bilingualism is confounded with poverty, so that children from low-SES backgrounds have lower quality and lower quantity of experiences in both languages (McCabe et al., 2013). What matters for outcomes is becoming language proficient – whether in one language or two – and to become proficient, what is needed is exposure to quality input from multiple native speakers (Place & Hoff, 2016). Evidence suggests that children do not benefit from exposure to nonproficient, *nonnative* language speakers, as when immigrants to an English-speaking country use English at home with children (Paradis, 2011; Place & Hoff, 2016). Thus, contrary to advice often given to immigrant parents, it is best for them *not* to avoid speaking their native language with their children in favor of the nonnative majority language (Hoff & Ribot, 2017). Rather, bilingual children would benefit from additional exposure to native speakers of the majority language and of their home language to bolster school readiness. Teaching children two languages in early childhood programs and schools serving children who are English-language learners (ELL) could support the development of language, and ultimately could serve to mitigate the SES gap in academic achievement – if and only if children's experiences with each language are high in quality and quantity.

Finally, there is a need for policies that open the door to *more language-rich or "languagized" experiences throughout communities*. Research has found that something as simple and inexpensive as signage in supermarkets, with prompts for adult–child conversation can significantly boost the quality and quantity of talk among low-SES families (Ridge, Weisberg, Ilgaz, Hirsh-Pasek, & Golinkoff, 2015). Research is also beginning to explore how public spaces like bus stops can be redesigned to incorporate games and architecture that stimulate language-rich interactions (Hassinger-Das, Bustamante, Hirsh-Pasek, & Golinkoff, 2018). There is much untapped potential for transforming communal spaces into hubs that promote language-rich playful interaction.

23.4 Conclusion

Remarkably, in spite of the diversity of infants' language experiences across the globe, all children learn language. They do so using a panoply of intersecting processes, including attention and statistical learning, together with principled assumptions such as the whole object bias, all within the context of socially communicative interactions. Many additional biases including the shape bias are learned via experience, building on these existing processes. Infants' brains are prepared for language input, and their language experiences continually transform the structure and function of the brain. Although there are sociocultural differences in infants' language environments worldwide as well as socioeconomic differences within societies, language development is universally benefitted by speech that is directed toward the infant and that is of high quantity and quality.

References

Adamson, L. B., Bakeman, R., & Deckner, D. F. (2004). The development of symbol-infused joint engagement. *Child Development*, *75*(4), 1171–1187.

Adamson, L. B., Bakeman, R., Deckner, D. F., & Nelson, P. B. (2014). From interactions to conversations: The development of joint engagement during early childhood. *Child Development*, *85*(3), 941–955.

Akhtar, N. (1999). Acquiring basic word order: Evidence for data-driven learning of syntactic structure. *Journal of Child Language*, *26*(2), 339–356.

Akhtar, N., & Gernsbacher, M. A. (2007). Joint attention and vocabulary development: A critical look. *Language and Linguistics Compass*, *1*(3), 195–207.

Aravind, A., de Villiers, J., Pace, A., Valentine, H., Golinkoff, R., Hirsh-Pasek, K., … Wilson, M. S. (2018). Fast mapping word meanings across trials: Young children forget all but their first guess. *Cognition, 177*, 177–188.

Aslin, R. N. (2017). Statistical learning: A powerful mechanism that operates by mere exposure. *Wiley Interdisciplinary Reviews: Cognitive Science, 8*, 1–7.

Baldwin, D. A. (1995). Understanding the link between joint attention and language. In C. Moore C & P. J. Dunham (Eds.), *Joint attention: Its origins and role in development* (pp. 131–158). Hillsdale, NJ: Lawrence Erlbaum Associates.

Bates, E., & Goodman, J. C. (1997). On the inseparability of grammar and the lexicon: Evidence from acquisition, aphasia and real-time processing. *Language and Cognitive Processes, 12*, 507–584.

Bates, E., & MacWhinney, B. (1982). Functionalist approaches to grammar. In E. Wanner & L. Gleitman (Eds.), *Language acquisition: The state of the art* (pp. 173–218). New York, NY: Cambridge University Press.

Beckner, C., Blythe, R., Bybee, J., Christiansen, M. H., Croft, W., Ellis, N. C., … Schoenemann, T. (2009). Language is a complex adaptive system: Position paper. *Language Learning, 59*, 1–26.

Bergelson, E., & Swingley, D. (2012). At 6–9 months, human infants know the meanings of many common nouns. *Proceedings of the National Academy of Sciences, 109*(9), 3253–3258.

Bloom, L. (2000). The intentionality model of word learning: How to learn a word, any word. In R. M. Golinkoff & K. Hirsh-Pasek (Eds.), *Becoming a word learner: A debate on lexical acquisition* (pp. 19–50). Oxford.: Oxford University Press.

Bloom, P. (2002). Mindreading, communication and the learning of names for things. *Mind & Language, 17*(1–2), 37–54.

Booth, A. E., & Waxman, S. R. (2008). Taking stock as theories of word learning take shape. *Developmental Science, 11*(2), 185–194.

Bornstein, M. H., Tal, J., Rahn, C., Galperin, C. Z., Pecheux, M. G., Lamour, M., … Tamis-LeMonda, C. S. (1992). Functional analysis of the contents of maternal speech to infants of 5 and 13 months in four cultures: Argentina, France, Japan, and the United States. *Developmental Psychology, 28*(4), 593–603.

Borovsky, A., Ellis, E. M., Evans, J. L., & Elman, J. L. (2016). Lexical leverage: Category knowledge boosts real-time novel word recognition in 2-year-olds. *Developmental Science, 19*(6), 918–932.

Bruner, J. (1983). *Child's talk: Learning to use language*. New York, NY: W. W. Norton.

Burns, T. C., Yoshida, K. A., Hill, K., & Werker, J. F. (2007). The development of phonetic representation in bilingual and monolingual infants. *Applied Psycholinguistics, 28*(3), 455–474.

Byers-Heinlein, K., & Werker, J. F. (2009). Monolingual, bilingual, trilingual: Infants' language experience influences the development of a word-learning heuristic. *Developmental Science, 12*(5), 815–823.

Cameron-Faulkner, T., Lieven, E., & Tomasello, M. (2003). A construction-based analysis of child directed speech. *Cognitive Science, 27*(6), 843–873.

Carpenter, M., Nagell, K., Tomasello, M., Butterworth, G., & Moore, C. (1998). Social cognition, joint attention, and communicative competence from 9 to 15 months of age. *Monographs of the Society for Research in Child Development*, i–174.

Cartmill, E. A., Armstrong, B. F., Gleitman, L. R., Goldin-Meadow, S., Medina, T. N., & Trueswell, J. C. (2013). Quality of early parent input predicts child vocabulary 3 years later. *Proceedings of the National Academy of Sciences, 110,* 11278–11283.

Chomsky, N. (1965). *Aspects of the theory of syntax.* Cambridge, MA: MIT Press.

de Diego-Balaguer, R., Martinez-Alvarez, A., & Pons, F. (2016). Temporal attention as a scaffold for language development. *Frontiers in Psychology, 7,* 44.

D'souza, D., D'souza, H., & Karmiloff-Smith, A. (2017). Precursors to language development in typically and atypically developing infants and toddlers: The importance of embracing complexity. *Journal of Child Language, 44*(3), 591–627.

Elman, J. (2003). Development: It's about time. *Developmental Science, 6*(4), 430–433.

Falk, S., & Kello, C. T. (2017). Hierarchical organization in the temporal structure of infant-direct speech and song. *Cognition, 163,* 80–86.

Ferguson, B., Graf, E., & Waxman, S. R. (2018). When veps cry: Two-year-olds efficiently learn novel words from linguistic contexts alone. *Language Learning and Development, 14*(1), 1–12.

Ferguson, B., & Lew-Williams, C. (2016). Communicative signals support abstract rule learning by 7-month-old infants. *Scientific Reports, 6,* 25434.

Ferguson, B., & Waxman, S. R. (2016). What the [beep]? Six-month-olds link novel communicative signals to meaning. *Cognition, 146,* 185–189.

Ferjan Ramírez, N., Ramírez, R. R., Clarke, M., Taulu, S., & Kuhl, P. K. (2017). Speech discrimination in 11-month-old bilingual and monolingual infants: A magnetoencephalography study. *Developmental Science, 20,* e12427.

Fernald, A., Marchman, V. A., & Weisleder, A. (2013). SES differences in language processing skill and vocabulary are evident at 18 months. *Developmental Science, 16*(2), 234–248.

Fernald, A., & Morikawa, H. (1993). Common themes and cultural variations in Japanese and American mothers' speech to infants. *Child Development, 64*(3), 637–656.

Fernald, A., Taeschner, T., Dunn, J., Papousek, M., de Boysson-Bardies, B., & Fukui, I. (1989). A cross-language study of prosodic modifications in mothers' and fathers' speech to preverbal infants. *Journal of Child Language, 16*(3), 477–501.

Ferry, A. L., Hespos, S. J., & Waxman, S. R. (2013). Nonhuman primate vocalizations support categorization in very young human infants. *Proceedings of the National Academy of Sciences, 110*(38), 15231–15235.

Garcia-Sierra, A., Rivera-Gaxiola, M., Percaccio, C. R., Conboy, B. T., Romo, H., Klarman, L., … Kuhl, P. K. (2011). Bilingual language learning: An ERP study relating early brain responses to speech, language input, and later word production. *Journal of Phonetics, 39*(4), 546–557.

Gentner, D., & Boroditsky, L. (2001). Individuation, relativity, and early word learning. *Language Acquisition and Conceptual Development, 3,* 215–256.

Gerken, L. (2006). Decisions, decisions: Infant language learning when multiple generalizations are possible. *Cognition, 98*(3), B67–B74.

  (2010). Infants use rational decision criteria for choosing among models of their input. *Cognition, 115*(2), 362–366.

Gerken, L., Jusczyk, P. W., & Mandel, D. R. (1994). When prosody fails to cue syntactic structure: 9-month-olds' sensitivity to phonological versus syntactic phrases. *Cognition*, *51*(3), 237–265.

Gerken, L., Landau, B., & Remez, R. E. (1990). Function morphemes in young children's speech perception and production. *Developmental Psychology*, *26*(2), 204–216.

Gervain, J., Berent, I., & Werker, J. F. (2012). Binding at birth: The newborn brain detects identity relations and sequential position in speech. *Journal of Cognitive Neuroscience*, *24*(3), 564–574.

Gervain, J., Macagno, F., Cogoi, S., Peña, M., & Mehler, J. (2008). The neonate brain detects speech structure. *Proceedings of the National Academy of Sciences*, *105*(37), 14222–14227.

Gervain, J., & Werker, J. F. (2013). Learning non-adjacent regularities at age 0;7. *Journal of Child Language*, *40*(4), 860–872.

Gleitman, L. R. (1990). The structural sources of verb meanings. *Language Acquisition*, *1*, 3–55.

Gleitman, L. R., Cassidy, K., Nappa, R., Papafragou, A., & Trueswell, J. C. (2005). Hard words. *Language Learning and Development*, *1*(1), 23–64.

Gleitman, L. R., & Wanner, E. (1982). Language acquisition: The state of the art. In E. Wanner & L. R. Gleitman (Eds.), *Language acquisition: The state of the art* (pp. 3–48). Cambridge, UK: Cambridge University Press.

Goldin-Meadow, S. (2003). *The resilience of language: What gesture creation in deaf children can tell us about how all children learn language*. New York, NY: Psychology Press.

Golinkoff, R. M., Can, D. D., Soderstrom, M., & Hirsh-Pasek, K. (2015). (Baby) talk to me: The social context of infant-directed speech and its effects on early language acquisition. *Current Directions in Psychological Science*, *24*(5), 339–344.

Golinkoff, R. M., Hirsh-Pasek, K., Bailey, L. M., & Wenger, N. R. (1992). Young children and adults use lexical principles to learn new nouns. *Developmental Psychology*, *28*(1), 99–108.

Golinkoff, R. M. & Hirsh-Pasek, K. Gordon, L. & Cauley, K. (1987). The eyes have it: Lexical and word order comprehension in a new context. *Journal of Child Language*, *14*, 23–45.

Golinkoff, R. M., Hoff, E., Rowe, M., Tamis-LeMonda, C., & Hirsh-Pasek, K. (2019). Language matters: Denying the existence of the 30-million-word gap has serious consequences. *Child Development,* *90*(3), 985–992.

Golinkoff, R. M., Mervis, C. B., & Hirsh-Pasek, K. (1994). Early object labels: The case for a developmental lexical principles framework. *Journal of Child Language*, *21*(1), 125–155.

Graf Estes, K., & Bowen, S. (2013). Learning about sounds contributes to learning about words: Effects of prosody and phonotactics on infant word learning. *Journal of Experimental Child Psychology*, *114*(3), 405–417.

Graf Estes, K., & Hurley, K. (2013). Infant-directed prosody helps infants map sounds to meanings. *Infancy*, *18*(5), 797–824.

Halberda, J. (2003). The development of a word-learning strategy. *Cognition*, *87*(1), B23–B34.

Harris, J., Golinkoff, R. M., & Hirsh-Pasek, K. (2011). Lessons from the crib for the classroom: How children really learn vocabulary. *Handbook of Early Literacy Research*, *3*, 49–65.

Hart, B., & Risley, T. R. (1995). *Meaningful differences in the everyday experience of young American children*. Baltimore, MD: Paul H. Brookes.

Hartman, K. M., Ratner, N. B., & Newman, R. S. (2017). Infant-directed speech (IDS) vowel clarity and child language outcomes. *Journal of Child Language*, *44*(5), 1140–1162.

Hassinger-Das, B., Bustamante, A. S., Hirsh-Pasek, K., & Golinkoff, R. M. (2018). Learning landscapes: Playing the way to learning and engagement in public spaces. *Education Sciences*, *8*(2), 74.

Hawthorne, K., & Gerken, L. (2014). From pauses to clauses: Prosody facilitates learning of syntactic constituency. *Cognition*, *133*(2), 420–428.

Hirsh-Pasek, K. (2000). Beyond Shipley, Smith, and Gleitman: Young children's comprehension of bound morphemes. In B. Landau, J. Sabini, J. Jonides & E. L. Newport (Eds.), *Perception, cognition and language: Essays in honor of Henry and Lila Gleitman* (pp. 191–201). Cambridge, MA: MIT Press.

Hirsh-Pasek, K., Adamson, L. B., Bakeman, R., Owen, M. T., Golinkoff, R. M., Pace, A., … Suma, K. (2015). The contribution of early communication quality to low-income children's language success. *Psychological Science*, *26*(7), 1071–1083.

Hirsh-Pasek, K., & Golinkoff, R. M. (1996). *The origins of grammar: Evidence from comprehension*. Cambridge, MA: MIT Press.

Hirsh-Pasek, K., Kemler Nelson, D. G., Jusczyk, P. W., Cassidy, K. W., Druss, B., & Kennedy, L. (1987). Clauses are perceptual units for young infants. *Cognition*, *26*(3), 269–286.

Hoff, E., & Ribot, K. M. (2017). Language growth in English monolingual and Spanish-English bilingual children from 2.5 to 5 years. *Journal of Pediatrics*, *190*, 241–245.

Hollich, G. J., Hirsh-Pasek, K., Golinkoff, R. M., Brand, R. J., Brown, E., Chung, H. L., … Bloom, L. (2000). Breaking the language barrier: An emergentist coalition model for the origins of word learning. *Monographs of the Society for Research in Child Development*, i–135.

Imai, M., Li, L., Haryu, E., Okada, H., Hirsh-Pasek, K., Golinkoff, R. M., & Shigematsu, J. (2008). Novel noun and verb learning in Chinese-, English-, and Japanese-speaking children. *Child Development*, *79*(4), 979–1000.

Johnson, V. E., de Villiers, J. G., & Seymour, H. N. (2005). Agreement without understanding? The case of third person singular/s. *First Language*, *25*(3), 317–330.

Jusczyk, P. W., Houston, D. M., & Newsome, M. (1999). The beginnings of word segmentation in English-learning infants. *Cognitive Psychology*, *39*(3–4), 159–207.

Jusczyk, P. W., Luce, P. A., & Charles-Luce, J. (1994). Infants' sensitivity to phonotactic patterns in the native language. *Journal of Memory and Language*, *33*(5), 630–645.

Kalashnikova, M., Goswami, U., & Burnham, D. (2018) Mothers speak differently to infants at-risk for dyslexia. *Developmental Science*, *21*(1), e12487.

Kemler Nelson, D., Hirsh-Pasek, K., Jusczyk, P., & Cassidy, K. W. (1989). How the prosodic cues in motherese might assist language learning. *Journal of Child Language*, *16*, 55–68.

Kuhl, P. K. (2007). Is speech learning "gated" by the social brain? *Developmental Science, 10*(1), 110–120.

Kuhl, P. K., Andruski, J. E., Chistovich, I. A., Chistovich, L. A., Kozhevnikova, E. V., Ryskina, V. L., … Lacerda, F. (1997). Cross-language analysis of phonetic units in language addressed to infants. *Science, 277*(5326), 684–686.

Kuhl, P. K., Conboy, B. T., Coffey-Corina, S., Padden, D., Rivera-Gaxiola, M., & Nelson, T. (2008). Phonetic learning as a pathway to language: new data and native language magnet theory expanded (NLM-e). *Philosophical Transactions of the Royal Society B: Biological Sciences, 363*(1493), 979–1000.

Kuhl, P. K., Tsao, F. M., & Liu, H. M. (2003). Foreign-language experience in infancy: Effects of short-term exposure and social interaction on phonetic learning. *Proceedings of the National Academy of Sciences, 100*(15), 9096–9101.

Landau, B., Smith, L. B., & Jones, S. S. (1988). The importance of shape in early lexical learning. *Cognitive Development, 3*(3), 299–321.

Little, E. E., Carver, L. J., & Legare, C. H. (2016). Cultural variation in triadic infant–caregiver object exploration. *Child Development, 87*(4), 1130–1145.

Liu, J., Golinkoff, R. M., & Sak, K. (2001). One cow does not an animal make: Young children can extend novel words at the superordinate level. *Child Development, 72*(6), 1674–1694.

Luo, R., & Tamis-LeMonda, C. S. (2016). Mothers' verbal and nonverbal strategies in relation to infants' object-directed actions in real time and across the first three years in ethnically diverse families. *Infancy, 21*(1), 65–89.

Lytle, S. R., Garcia-Sierra, A., & Kuhl, P. K. (2018). Two are better than one: Infant language learning from video improves in the presence of peers. *Proceedings of the National Academy of Sciences, 115*(40), 9859–9866.

Ma, W., Golinkoff, R. M., Houston, D. M., & Hirsh-Pasek, K. (2011). Word learning in infant-and adult-directed speech. *Language Learning and Development, 7*(3), 185–201.

MacKenzie, H., Curtin, S., & Graham, S. A. (2012). Class matters: 12-month-olds' word–object associations privilege content over function words. *Developmental Science, 15*(6), 753–761.

Maguire, M. J., Hirsh-Pasek, K., & Golinkoff, R. M. (2006). A unified theory of word learning: Putting verb acquisition in context. In K. Hirsh-Pasek & R. M. Golinkoff (Eds.), *Action meets word: How children learn verbs*. New York, NY: Oxford University Press.

Mandel, D. R., Jusczyk, P. W., & Kemler Nelson, D. G. (1994). Does sentential prosody help infants organize and remember speech information? *Cognition, 53*(2), 155–180.

Mandel, D. R., Kemler Nelson, D. G., & Jusczyk, P. W. (1996). Infants remember the order of words in a spoken sentence. *Cognitive Development, 11*(2), 181–196.

Marcus, G. F., Fernandes, K. J., & Johnson, S. P. (2007). Infant rule learning facilitated by speech. *Psychological Science, 18*(5), 387–391.

Marcus, G. F., Vijayan, S., Rao, S. B., & Vishton, P. M. (1999). Rule learning by seven-month-old infants. *Science, 283*, 77–80.

Marchman, V. A., & Bates, E. (1994). Continuity in lexical and morphological development: A test of the critical mass hypothesis. *Journal of Child Language, 21*(2), 339–366.

Marchman, V. A., & Fernald, A. (2008). Speed of word recognition and vocabulary knowledge in infancy predict cognitive and language outcomes in later childhood. *Developmental Science*, *11*(3), F9–F16.

Markman, E. M., & Wachtel, G. F. (1988). Children's use of mutual exclusivity to constrain the meanings of words. *Cognitive Psychology*, *20*(2), 121–157.

Martin, A., Igarashi, Y., Jincho, N., & Mazuka, R. (2016). Utterances in infant-directed speech are shorter, not slower. *Cognition*, *156*, 52–59.

Mastin, J. D., & Vogt, P. (2016). Infant engagement and early vocabulary development: a naturalistic observation study of Mozambican infants from 1; 1 to 2; 1. *Journal of Child Language*, *43*(2), 235–264.

Matthews, D., Lieven, E., Theakston, A., & Tomasello, M. (2005). The role of frequency in the acquisition of English word order. *Cognitive Development*, *20*(1), 121–136.

Mattock, K., Polka, L., Rvachew, S., & Krehm, M. (2010). The first steps in word learning are easier when the shoes fit: Comparing monolingual and bilingual infants. *Developmental Science*, *13*(1), 229–243.

McCabe, A., Tamis-LeMonda, C. S., Bornstein, M. H., Cates, C. B., Golinkoff, R., Guerra, A. W., ... Mendelsohn, A. (2013). Multilingual children. *Social Policy Report*, *27*(4), 2014–2451.

McGillion, M., Pine, J. M., Herbert, J. S., & Matthews, D. (2017). A randomised controlled trial to test the effect of promoting caregiver contingent talk on language development in infants from diverse socioeconomic status backgrounds. *Journal of Child Psychology and Psychiatry*, *58*(10), 1122–1131.

Medina, T. N., Snedeker, J., Trueswell, J. C., & Gleitman, L. R. (2011). How words can and cannot be learned by observation. *Proceedings of the National Academy of Sciences*, *108*(22), 9014–9019.

Merriman, W. E., Bowman, L. L., & MacWhinney, B. (1989). The mutual exclusivity bias in children's word learning. *Monographs of the Society for Research in Child Development*, i–129.

Miller, G. A. (1990). The place of language in a scientific psychology. *Psychological Science*, *1*(1), 7–14.

Mintz, T. H. (2003). Frequent frames as a cue for grammatical categories in child directed speech. *Cognition*, *90*(1), 91–117.

(2013). The segmentation of sub-lexical morphemes in English-learning 15-month-olds. *Frontiers in Psychology*, *4*, 24.

Molfese, D. L., & Molfese, V. J. (1979). Hemisphere and stimulus differences as reflected in the cortical responses of newborn infants to speech stimuli. *Developmental Psychology*, *15*(5), 505–511.

Morales, M., Mundy, P., Delgado, C. E., Yale, M., Messinger, D., Neal, R., & Schwartz, H. K. (2000). Responding to joint attention across the 6- through 24-month age period and early language acquisition. *Journal of Applied Developmental Psychology*, *21*(3), 283–298.

Morales, M., Mundy, P., & Rojas, J. (1998). Following the direction of gaze and language development in 6-month-olds. *Infant Behavior and Development*, *21*(2), 373–377.

Mundy, P., Block, J., Delgado, C., Pomares, Y., van Hecke, A. V., & Parlade, M. V. (2007). Individual differences and the development of joint attention in infancy. *Child Development*, *78*(3), 938–954.

Naigles, L. (1990). Children use syntax to learn verb meanings. *Journal of Child Language, 17*(2), 357–374.

Newman, R., Ratner, N. B., Jusczyk, A. M., Jusczyk, P. W., & Dow, K. A. (2006). Infants' early ability to segment the conversational speech signal predicts later language development: A retrospective analysis. *Developmental Psychology, 42*(4), 643–655.

Newport, E. L., Landau, B., Seydell-Greenwald, A., Turkeltaub, P. E., Chambers, C. E., Dromerick, A. W., … Gaillard, W. D. (2017). Revisiting Lenneberg's hypotheses about early developmental plasticity: Language organization after left-hemisphere perinatal stroke. *Biolinguistics, 11*, 407–421.

Pace, A., Alper, R., Burchinal, M. R., Golinkoff, R. M., & Hirsh-Pasek, K. (2019). Measuring success: Within and cross-domain predictors of academic and social trajectories in elementary school. *Early Childhood Research Quarterly, 46*, 112–125.

Pace, A., Luo, R., Hirsh-Pasek, K., & Golinkoff, R. M. (2017). Identifying pathways between socioeconomic status and language development. *Annual Review of Linguistics, 3*, 285–308.

Pae, S., Yoon, H., Seol, A., Gilkerson, J., Richards, J. A., Ma, L., & Topping, K. (2016). Effects of feedback on parent–child language with infants and toddlers in Korea. *First Language, 36*(6), 549–569.

Paradis, J. (2011). Individual differences in child English second language acquisition: Comparing child-internal and child-external factors. *Linguistic Approaches to Bilingualism, 1*(3), 213–237.

Parise, E., & Csibra, G. (2012). Electrophysiological evidence for the understanding of maternal speech by 9-month-old infants. *Psychological Science, 23*(7), 728–733.

Peña, M., Maki, A., Kovačić, D., Dehaene-Lambertz, G., Koizumi, H., Bouquet, F., & Mehler, J. (2003). Sounds and silence: An optical topography study of language recognition at birth. *Proceedings of the National Academy of Sciences, 100*(20), 11702–11705.

Perani, D., Saccuman, M. C., Scifo, P., Awander, A., Spada, D., Baldoli, C., … Friederici, A. D. (2011). Neural language networks at birth. *Proceedings of the National Academy of Sciences, 108*, 16056–16061.

Pereira, A. F., Smith, L. B., & Yu, C. (2014). A bottom-up view of toddler word learning. *Psychonomic Bulletin & Review, 21*(1), 178–185.

Perry, L. K., & Samuelson, L. K. (2011). The shape of the vocabulary predicts the shape of the bias. *Frontiers in Psychology, 2*, 345.

Pinker, S. (1987). The bootstrapping problem in language acquisition. In B. MacWhinney (Ed.), *Mechanisms of language acquisition* (pp. 399–441). Hillsdale, NJ: Lawrence Erlbaum Associates.

Place, S., & Hoff, E. (2016). Effects and noneffects of input in bilingual environments on dual language skills in 2 ½-year-olds. *Bilingualism: Language and Cognition, 19*(5), 1023–1041.

Quine, W. V. (1960). *Word and object*. Cambridge, MA: MIT Press.

Reed, J., Hirsh-Pasek, K., & Golinkoff, R. M. (2016). Meeting children where they are: Adaptive contingency builds early communication skills. In P. L. Witt (Ed.) *Communication and learning* (Handbooks of Communication Science, pp. 601–628). Berlin: deGruyter Mouton.

Reed, J., Hirsh-Pasek, K. & Golinkoff, R.M. (2017). Learning on hold: Cell phones sidetrack parent–child interactions. *Developmental Psychology*, *53*(8), 1428–1436.

Richman, A. L., Miller, P. M., & LeVine, R. A. (1992). Cultural and educational variations in maternal responsiveness. *Developmental Psychology*, *28*(4), 614–621.

Ridge, K. E., Weisberg, D. S., Ilgaz, H., Hirsh-Pasek, K. A., & Golinkoff, R. M. (2015). Supermarket speak: Increasing talk among low-socioeconomic status families. *Mind, Brain, and Education*, *9*(3), 127–135.

Rohlfing, K. J., Wrede, B., Vollmer, A. L., & Oudeyer, P. Y. (2016). An alternative to mapping a word onto a concept in language acquisition: Pragmatic frames. *Frontiers in Psychology*, *7*, 470.

Romeo, R. R., Leonard, J. A., Robinson, S. T., West, M. R., Mackey, A. P., Rowe, M. L., & Gabrieli, J. D. (2018). Beyond the 30-million-word gap: Children's conversational exposure is associated with language-related brain function. *Psychological Science*, *29*(5), 700–710.

Roseberry, S., Hirsh-Pasek, K., & Golinkoff, R.M. (2014). Skype me! Socially contingent interactions help toddlers learn language. *Child Development, 85*(3), 956–970.

Roseberry, S., Richie, R., Hirsh-Pasek, K., Golinkoff, R. M., & Shipley, T. F. (2011). Babies catch a break: 7- to 9-month-olds track statistical probabilities in continuous dynamic events. *Psychological Science*, *22*(11), 1422–1424.

Rowe, M. L. (2012). A longitudinal investigation of the role of quantity and quality of child-directed speech in vocabulary development. *Child Development, 83*(5), 1762–1774.

Saffran, J. R., & Kirkham, N. Z. (2018). Infant statistical learning. *Annual Review of Psychology*, *69*, 181–208.

Saffran, J. R., & Thiessen, E. D. (2007). Domain-general learning capacities. In E. Hoff & M. Shatz (Eds.), *Handbook of language development* (pp. 68–86). Cambridge, UK: Blackwell.

Saffran, J. R., & Wilson, D. P. (2003). From syllables to syntax: Multilevel statistical learning by 12-month-old infants. *Infancy*, *4*(2), 273–284.

Santelmann, L. M., & Jusczyk, P. W. (1998). Sensitivity to discontinuous dependencies in language learners: Evidence for limitations in processing space. *Cognition*, *69*(2), 105–134.

Scaff, C., Stieglitz, J., Casillas, M., & Cristia, A. (2019, March). Language input in a small-scale society: Estimations from daylong recordings in a Tsimané village. Poster presented at the Interdisciplinary Study of Language Evolution Inaugural Workshop, Zurich, Switzerland.

Scarborough, H. S. (2001). Connecting early language and literacy to later reading (dis) abilities: Evidence, theory, and practice. In S. B. Neuman & D. K. Dickinson (Eds.), *Handbook of early literacy research* (pp. 97–110). New York, NY: Guilford Press.

Schieffelin, B. & Ochs, E. (1983). A cultural perspective on the transition from prelinguistic to linguistic communication. In R. M. Golinkoff (Ed.), *The transition from prelinguistic to linguistic communication* (pp. 115– 131). Hillsdale, NJ: Lawrence Erlbaum Associates.

Scott, R. M., & Fisher, C. (2012). 2.5-year-olds use cross-situational consistency to learn verbs under referential uncertainty. *Cognition*, *122*(2), 163–180.

Seidenberg, M. S., & Elman, J. L. (1999). Do infants learn grammar with algebra or statistics?. *Science, 284*(5413), 433–433.

Seidl, A. (2007). Infants' use and weighting of prosodic cues in clause segmentation. *Journal of Memory and Language, 57*(1), 24–48.

Senghas, A., Kita, S., & Özyürek, A. (2004). Children creating core properties of language: Evidence from an emerging sign language in Nicaragua. *Science, 305*(5691), 1779–1782.

Shatz, M., & Gelman, R. (1973). The development of communication skills: Modifications in the speech of young children as a function of listener. *Monographs of the Society for Research in Child Development*, 1–38.

Shi, R., & Werker, J. F. (2001). Six-month-old infants' preference for lexical words. *Psychological Science, 12*(1), 70–75.

Shipley, E. F., Smith, C. S., & Gleitman, L. R. (1969). A study in the acquisition of language: Free responses to commands. *Language, 45*, 322–342.

Shneidman, L. A., & Goldin-Meadow, S. (2012). Language input and acquisition in a Mayan village: How important is directed speech?. *Developmental Science, 15*(5), 659–673.

Singh, L., Fu, C. S., Tay, Z. W., & Golinkoff, R. M. (2018). Novel word learning in bilingual and monolingual infants: Evidence for a bilingual advantage. *Child Development, 89*(3), e183–e198.

Singh, L., Morgan, J. L., & Best, C. T. (2002). Infants' listening preferences: Baby talk or happy talk?. *Infancy, 3*(3), 365–394.

Smith, N. A., & Trainor, L. J. (2008). Infant-directed speech is modulated by infant feedback. *Infancy, 13*(4), 410–420.

Smith, L., & Yu, C. (2008). Infants rapidly learn word-referent mappings via cross-situational statistics. *Cognition, 106*(3), 1558–1568.

Soderstrom, M. (2008). Early perception–late comprehension of grammar? The case of verbal-s: a response to de Villiers & Johnson (2007). *Journal of Child Language, 35*(3), 671–676.

Soderstrom, M., Seidl, A., Kemler Nelson, D. G., & Jusczyk, P. W. (2003). The prosodic bootstrapping of phrases: Evidence from prelinguistic infants. *Journal of Memory and Language, 49*(2), 249–267.

Sperry, D. E., Sperry, L. L., & Miller, P. J. (2018). Reexamining the verbal environments of children from different socioeconomic backgrounds. *Child Development, 90*(4), 1303–1318.

Stahl, A. E., Romberg, A. R., Roseberry, S., Golinkoff, R. M., & Hirsh-Pasek, K. (2014). Infants segment continuous events using transitional probabilities. *Child Development, 85*(5), 1821–1826.

Stevens, J. S., Gleitman, L. R., Trueswell, J. C., & Yang, C. (2017). The pursuit of word meanings. *Cognitive Science, 41*(4), 638–676.

Suskind, D. L., Leffel, K. R., Graf, E., Hernandez, M. W., Gunderson, E. A., Sapolich, S. G., … & Levine, S. C. (2016). A parent-directed language intervention for children of low socioeconomic status: A randomized controlled pilot study. *Journal of Child Language, 43*(2), 366–406.

Tamis-LeMonda, C. S., Custode, S., Kuchirko, Y., Escobar, K., & Lo, T. (2019). Routine language: Speech directed to infants during home activities. *Child Development, 90*(6), 2135–2152.

Tamis-LeMonda, C. S., Kuchirko, Y., & Song, L. (2014). Why is infant language learn-ing facilitated by parental responsiveness?. *Current Directions in Psychological Science, 23*(2), 121–126.

Tamis-LeMonda, C. S., Kuchirko, Y., & Tafuro, L. (2013). From action to interac-tion: Infant object exploration and mothers' contingent responsiveness. *IEEE Transactions on Autonomous Mental Development, 5*(3), 202–209.

Tamis-LeMonda, C. S., Song, L., Leavell, A. S., Kahana-Kalman, R., & Yoshikawa, H. (2012). Ethnic differences in mother–infant language and gestural commu-nications are associated with specific skills in infants. *Developmental Science, 15*(3), 384–397.

Tardif, T., Shatz, M., & Naigles, L. (1997). Caregiver speech and children's use of nouns versus verbs: A comparison of English, Italian, and Mandarin. *Journal of Child Language, 24*(3), 535–565.

Teinonen, T., Fellman, V., Näätänen, R., Alku, P., & Huotilainen, M. (2009). Statistical language learning in neonates revealed by event-related brain potentials. *BMC Neuroscience, 10*(1), 21.

Thiessen, E. D., Hill, E. A., & Saffran, J. R. (2005). Infant-directed speech facilitates word segmentation. *Infancy, 7*(1), 53–71.

Tincoff, R., & Jusczyk, P. W. (2012). Six-month-olds comprehend words that refer to parts of the body. *Infancy, 17*(4), 432–444.

Tomasello, M. (1992). The social bases of language acquisition. *Social Development, 1*(1), 67–87.

Trueswell, J. C., Lin, Y., Armstrong, B., III, Cartmill, E. A., Goldin-Meadow, S., & Gleitman, L. R. (2016). Perceiving referential intent: Dynamics of reference in natural parent–child interactions. *Cognition, 148*, 117–135.

Tsao, F. M., Liu, H. M., & Kuhl, P. K. (2004). Speech perception in infancy predicts language development in the second year of life: A longitudinal study. *Child Development, 75*(4), 1067–1084.

Tucker, M., & Hirsh-Pasek, K. (1993). Systems and language: Implications for acquisi-tion. In L. Smith & E. Thelen (Eds.) *Dynamical systems approach to develop-ment* (pp. 359–384). Cambridge, MA: MIT Press.

van Heugten, M., & Johnson, E. K. (2010). Linking infants' distributional learning abilities to natural language acquisition. *Journal of Memory and Language, 63*(2), 197–209.

Vasilyeva, M., Waterfall, H., & Huttenlocher, J. (2008). Emergence of syntax: Commonalities and differences across children. *Developmental Science, 11*(1), 84–97.

Vouloumanos, A., Martin, A., & Onishi, K. H. (2014). Do 6-month-olds understand that speech can communicate?. *Developmental Science, 17*(6), 872–879.

Wake, M., Tobin, S., Girolametto, L., Ukoumunne, O. C., Gold, L., Levickis, P., … Reilly, S. (2011). Outcomes of population based language promotion for slow to talk toddlers at ages 2 and 3 years: Let's Learn Language cluster ran-domised controlled trial. *British Medical Journal, 343*, d4741.

Waxman, S., Fu, X., Arunachalam, S., Leddon, E., Geraghty, K., & Song, H. J. (2013). Are nouns learned before verbs? Infants provide insight into a long-standing debate. *Child Development Perspectives, 7*(3), 155–159.

Weber, A., Fernald, A., & Diop, Y. (2017). When cultural norms discourage talk-ing to babies: effectiveness of a parenting program in rural Senegal. *Child Development, 88*(5), 1513–1526.

Weisleder, A., & Fernald, A. (2013). Talking to children matters: Early language experience strengthens processing and builds vocabulary. *Psychological Science*, *24*(11), 2143–2152.

Werker, J. F., Cohen, L. B., Lloyd, V. L., Casasola, M., & Stager, C. L. (1998). Acquisition of word-object associations by 14-month-old infants. *Developmental Psychology*, *34*(6), 1289–1309.

Werker, J. F., & Yeung, H. H. (2005). Infant speech perception bootstraps word learning. *Trends in Cognitive Sciences*, *9*(11), 519–527.

Wu, Z., & Gros-Louis, J. (2014). Infants' prelinguistic communicative acts and maternal responses: Relations to linguistic development. *First Language*, *34*(1), 72–90.

Xu, F., & Tenenbaum, J. B. (2007). Word learning as Bayesian inference. *Psychological Review*, *114*(2), 245–272.

Yu, C., & Smith, L. B. (2012a). Embodied attention and word learning by toddlers. *Cognition, 125*(2), 244–262.

   (2012b). Modeling cross-situational word-referent learning: Prior questions. *Psychological Review*, *119*(1), 21–39.

   (2016). The social origins of sustained attention in one-year-old human infants. *Current Biology*, *26*(9), 1235–1240.

Yu, C., Suanda, S. H., & Smith, L. B. (2019) Infant sustained attention but not joint attention to objects at 9 months predicts vocabulary at 12 and 15 months. *Developmental Science*, *22*(1), e12735.

Yuan, S., Fisher, C., & Snedeker, J. (2012). Counting the nouns: Simple structural cues to verb meaning. *Child Development*, *83*(4), 1382–1399.

Yurovsky, D., & Frank, M. C. (2017). Beyond naïve cue combination: Salience and social cues in early word learning. *Developmental Science*, *20*(2), e12349.

24 Dual Language Exposure and Early Learning

Natalie H. Brito

24.1 Introduction

With close to 7,000 languages in use around the world today (Lewis, Simons, & Fennig, 2009) and only 195 countries (United Nations, 2018), being completely monolingual is quite rare as multilingualism is often the norm (Grin, 2004). Looking through the research literature, however, it would appear as though bilinguals are a unique population with distinct advantages or disadvantages from monolinguals. Spear (1984) proposed that what infants of all species learn and remember at any time in development is determined by the ecological challenges posed by their current environment and the survival value of responding successfully to them. Learning trajectories of monolingual and bilingual children are more similar than different, with differences reflecting the bilingual brain's adaptations to the surrounding linguistic conditions. The rate and ease at which children learn language is surprising, as language acquisition is a very complex task, with infants having to quickly learn how to identify patterns within a continuous string of speech sounds (Saffran, Aslin, & Newport, 1996). For children learning two or more languages, this is more complicated as multilingual infants must differentiate their languages, extract the correct patterns for each of their languages, and control two interacting language systems (Bialystok, 2007; Bosch & Sebastián-Gallés, 2001; Byers-Heinlein, Morin-Lessard, & Lew-Williams, 2017). But young children do acquire two, three, or even more languages/dialects at a time (de Angelis, 2007; Olshtain & Nissim-Amitai, 2004; Paradis, 2007) – indicating that the human brain is equipped to process this type of complex input.

This chapter will focus on dual language exposure and early learning as it relates to processing within the domains of language, memory, and social interactions. Each section will also incorporate perspectives highlighting brain–behavior associations on early learning. The chapter will conclude with issues surrounding dual-language learners and how these issues relate to culture and public policy. Studies presented will focus on unimodal dual-language learners, rather than bimodal (i.e., sign language and spoken language). The Office of Head Start defines dual language learners as "children who acquire two or more languages simultaneously and learn a second language while continuing to develop their first" (Office of Head Start, 2008). Categorizing children who are exposed to multiple languages is never precise. The endless variations in language exposure, use, age of acquisition, and context all contribute to the spectrum of multilingualism that children can classify into (Escobar & Tamis-LeMonda, 2017). As the focus of this handbook is on infants, the terms dual-language learner and bilingual will be used interchangeably and the current chapter will primarily focus on simultaneous bilinguals (children who learn both of their languages from birth) rather than sequential bilinguals (children who learn one language after they have sufficiently acquired their first).

24.1.1 Dual-Language Exposure and Attention: Looking Time and Neuroimaging Approaches

There has been an ongoing dispute whether there are clear cognitive advantages to learning more than one language, outside of the obvious benefit of being able to speak multiple languages. This debate has primarily focused on cognitive control and includes studies predominantly testing adolescents or adults (de Bruin, Treccani, & Della Sala, 2015; Paap & Greenberg, 2013). The early prevailing hypothesis on why bilingual cognitive advantages may arise posited that because bilinguals have two "active" languages, they must have to inhibit one language in order to produce another, and that this daily practice of inhibitory control produces boosts in cognitive control or executive function (Bialystok, 1999; Green, 1998). Preliminary results supporting this hypothesis led to a surge of studies examining executive function abilities of dual-language learners from early childhood to late adulthood (e.g., Bialystok, 1999; Bialystok & Martin, 2004; Carlson & Meltzoff, 2008; Hartanto, Toh, & Yang, 2018; Poulin-Dubois, Blaye, Coutya, & Bialystok, 2011).

Research examining the impact of dual-language exposure on early learning during the infancy period provided an important step in understanding cognitive trajectories for monolingual and bilingual infants. Kovács and Mehler (2009a) used eye trackers within an anticipatory cue cognitive control paradigm and presented infants with an auditory speech cue during training. Infants learned to look at one of two locations to see a toy and at test, a novel speech cue signaled the appearance of the toy in an alternate location. While past research had found that monolingual 7-month-olds fail to shift from one location to another (Diamond, 1990), in this study bilingual infants used the novel cue to switch their attention to the alternate location. Singh et al. (2015) also reported that bilingual 6-month-olds outperformed their monolingual peers on a visual habituation task – a paradigm that tests basic processing of nonlinguistic visual information. These studies with preverbal infants suggest that simply perceiving and processing sounds from multiple native languages early in life may differentially affect specific attention and learning mechanisms, most likely due to neurocognitive adaptations to the early linguistic environment (Antovich & Graf Estes, 2018; Bialystok, 2017; Brito, Grenell, & Barr, 2014; Costa & Sebastián-Gallés, 2014).

Infant studies using neuroimaging techniques may also provide support for the hypothesis that early exposure to multiple languages enhances early attentional processes. Kuipers and Thierry (2013) investigated if dual-language learners differ in attention allocation compared to their monolingual peers and how this difference in attention may relate to semantic processing efficiency. They recorded neural activity (event-related potentials, ERPs) and measured allocation of attention and cognitive effort (pupil dilation) while toddlers were presented with a spoken word and a picture that either matched or didn't match the meaning of the spoken word. There was no difference between groups when the word and picture matched, but when the word and picture were unrelated, bilingual infants showed greater pupil dilation (suggesting distributed attention) and a distinct pattern of neural activity reflective of diminished effort involved in semantic integration (decrease in N400 amplitude), whereas monolingual infants showed the exact opposite pattern. These results suggest that, although there was no evidence of a semantic processing delay or semantic processing advantage for bilingual infants, attention to unexpected stimuli seems to hamper semantic integration for monolinguals but boosts integration for bilinguals. It is possible that for bilingual infants, this integration enhancement from attention to unexpected stimuli may be a consequence of having to attend to and process multiple unpredictable language cues during everyday experiences.

What could be other underlying mechanisms for these early attentional differences? Thinking about the dual language environment, it is assumed that parents of bilingual children do not speak more to their children than parents of monolingual children. Therefore, bilingual children must acquire both languages while experiencing reduced input to each (Werker, 2012). Additionally, bilinguals must constantly discriminate between and minimize interference across their languages as they develop their linguistic skills. Growing up in this linguistically demanding environment may increase information-processing and attention capabilities (Brito et al., 2014; Singh et al., 2015). Thus, being raised in a multilingual environment has the potential to enhance and promote the development of a flexible attention system – possibly triggering a cascade of ramifications for later language, cognitive, and social development.

24.2 Language

Bilingual children experience language divided between two complex linguistic systems, but do not demonstrate significant delays or impairments in language acquisition (Hoff et al., 2012). Like monolinguals, language trajectories of bilingual children are dependent on the quantity and quality of the input they hear in each of their languages (Place & Hoff, 2011; Ramírez-Esparza, García-Sierra, & Kuhl, 2017). Longitudinal studies show that monolingual and bilingual children reach many milestones (e.g., first words) at similar time points during infancy and have comparable conceptual vocabularies (de Houwer, Bornstein, & Putnick, 2014; Hoff et al., 2012; Pearson, Fernández, & Oller, 1993; Werker, 2012). Although there is a myriad of potential linguistic properties to review, here the focus will be on early phonetic perception, speech-pattern detection, and word-learning efficiency as these abilities have been highly predictive of later language skills (Fernald, Marchman, & Weisleder, 2013: Kuhl, Conboy, Padden, Nelson, & Pruitt, 2005; Kuhl, Tsao, & Liu, 2003; Newman, Ratner, Jusczyk, Jusczyk, & Dow, 2006; Rivera-Gaxiola, Silva-Pereyra, & Kuhl, 2005).

24.2.1 Phonetic Perception

Early and repeated exposure to language is necessary for the development of language processing skills (Kuhl, 1994; Newport, Bavelier, & Neville, 2001; Oyama, 1976). The ability to identify spoken language from other sounds starts prenatally, as newborns demonstrate a preference for their mother's speech over an unfamiliar voice (DeCasper & Fifer, 1980). Byers-Heinlein, Burns, and Werker (2010) examined language preferences for bilingual neonates and found that monolingual neonates whose caregivers only spoke English during pregnancy showed a robust preference for English, whereas bilingual neonates whose caregivers spoke both English and Tagalog regularly during pregnancy showed equal preference to both languages. To ensure that these preferences were not due to the inability to discriminate between the two languages, a follow-up study found that both English monolingual and Tagalog-English bilingual neonates could indeed discriminate English from Tagalog. These results suggest that the underlying mechanisms that support early language acquisition for monolinguals are also at play for the bilingual environment (Byers-Heinlein et al., 2010).

In the first 6 months of life, infants have a capacity to discriminate phonemic contrasts (native and nonnative) from most, if not all, of the world's languages. By 10–12 months, infants are more highly sensitive to the phonetic contrasts found in their native language – indicating that early linguistic experience shapes concurrent and future language development. This pattern of "perceptual narrowing" also occurs for bilinguals in both of their native languages (Eimas, Siqueland, Jusczyk, & Vigorito, 1971; Kuhl, 2007; Newport & Aslin, 2004; Saffran et al., 1996; Weikum et al., 2007; Werker & Tees, 1984). Behavioral studies have reported that phonetic processing and discrimination is somewhat similar for both bilingual and monolingual infants, with some distinctions in timing (Bosch & Sebastián-Gallés, 2003; Burns, Yoshida, Hill, & Werker, 2007; Sundara, Polka, & Molnar, 2008; Sundara & Scutellaro, 2011). Using a functional near-infrared spectroscopy (fNIRS) paradigm to examine brain activation during a phonetic processing task, Petitto et al. (2012) found that both monolinguals and bilinguals demonstrated activation in language-specific areas of the brain (left superior temporal gyrus and left inferior frontal cortex), with interesting developmental patterns. Activation in the left superior temporal gyrus was observed early in life (4–6 months) and remained consistent over time, whereas the left inferior cortex showed greater activation in older infants (10–12 months), right around the time when infants reach their first-word milestone. One difference between language groups was that older bilingual infants remained sensitive to nonnative phonetic contrasts and the monolinguals did not (Petitto et al., 2012). In a recent study, Ferjan Ramírez, Ramírez, Clarke, Taulu, and Kuhl (2017) replicated this result using magnetoencephalography (MEG) technology, similarly finding that, compared to a single language, neural encoding of two languages may take more time and infants with exposure to multiple languages show neural sensitivity to both languages at 11 months of age. The same researchers also found evidence that bilingual neural activity extended into the prefrontal and orbitofrontal cortex (regions of the brain commonly associated with executive functions) – suggesting domain-general activation during language tasks for these early dual language learners (Ferjan Ramírez et al., 2017).

24.2.2 Speech-Pattern Detection

Another challenge dual language learners must overcome involves detecting individual words in continuous speech from two language systems. Segmentation is difficult as words are usually heard surrounded by other words, with few pauses or obvious cues to indicate to the infant where word boundaries occur (Aslin, Woodward, LaMendola, & Bever, 1996). Studies have demonstrated that infants can use statistical regularities, or probabilities of syllables that are likely or not likely to occur together, to segment words from a continuous speech stream (Aslin, Saffran, & Newport, 1998; Saffran et al., 1996). Antovich and Graf Estes (2018) tested monolingual and bilingual 14-month-olds' abilities to segment speech using transitional probability cues within two artificial languages. When the languages were presented separately, monolinguals had no problems segmenting speech streams but when the languages were interleaved together, increasing the cognitive load, monolinguals failed. In contrast, infants growing up in multiple language households were able to learn from the interleaved languages. The authors suggest that despite discrepancies in language environments, monolinguals and bilinguals can use comparable learning strategies to process speech (Antovich & Graf Estes, 2018). Furthermore, tracking syllable probabilities in multiple languages requires the bilingual infant to segment syllables from two different linguistic codes, possibly requiring increased or distinct engagement of working memory, inhibitory control, and attentional flexibility.

24.2.3 Word Learning

The ability to acquire vocabulary is crucial to communication, first for comprehension and then later for production. Words must first be identified from their distinct sound patterns before meanings can be attached to them. Past studies with monolinguals have demonstrated that even 7.5-month-olds are capable of segmenting and recognizing familiar word forms within speech passages and can discriminate these words from similar-sounding passages (Jusczyk & Aslin, 1995). The skill of matching a word to its referent develops at a slower rate. Werker, Cohen, Lloyd, Casasola, and Stager (1998) used the switch paradigm to test word learning at 14 months. In this paradigm, infants were first habituated to two novel objects with labels. Then, the infants were presented with a switch trial (a familiar word and familiar object were paired in a novel combination) and a same trial (a familiar word–object pairing). If infants successfully learn the word–object association, then they will look longer at the switch trials than the same trials. If they did not learn the associated link, then the infants should look for an equal duration at switch or same trials. Werker et al. (1998) found that infants as young as 14 months can detect the switch in object–word pairings if the two words sounded different but failed when the two words were similar sounding. It was not until 17 months of age that infants could learn the associated link for words that sounded similar (Werker, Fennell, Corcoran, & Stager, 2002), suggesting that learning word–object pairs for similar sounding words may be more challenging or require additional exposure to those words for infants to succeed.

Examining word-learning capacities with early dual-language learners, Fennell, Byers-Heinlein, and Werker (2007) tested English-French and English-Cantonese bilinguals and found that bilingual infants could not learn similar sounding words until 20 months of age. This result was puzzling as past studies reported bilingual advantages in children's metalinguistic awareness. Metalinguistic skills include explicit awareness of abstract linguistic representations. Bilingual children have been shown to be more likely to accept a novel or unusual name for an object than monolingual children, with the hypothesis that bilingual children may recognize that the connection between an object and its label is arbitrary (Ben-Zeev, 1977; Cummins, 1978). These findings indicate that bilingual infants may begin to use phonetic detail later than their monolingual peers and may rely on the use of relevant language sounds to direct word learning. As this delayed reliance on sounds does not seem to negatively impact overall word-learning capabilities, the authors speculated that bilingual infants may use this initial compensatory approach (allowing divergence of cognitive resources toward learning a word–object link quickly) to combat the additional demands of word learning in two languages (Fennell et al., 2007; Newport, 1990; Werker & Fennell, 2004).

A subsequent study by Mattock, Polka, Rvachew, and Krehm (2010) examined two competing hypotheses about early bilingual word learning. One side of the debate hypothesizes that delays in speech perception may be the underlying cause for delays in early word learning for bilinguals. On the other hand, bilingual differences in early word-learning abilities may be specifically tied to task demands. In the Fennell et al., (2007) task the crucial difference between the Switch and Same trials was the /b/ versus /d/ contrast (spoken by an English speaker), which contain differences in the phonetic realization of the /bih/ and /dih/ word forms across the two languages. To resolve this issue, Mattock et al. (2010) tested a group of English-French bilingual 17-month-olds on the same switch paradigm, but this time they only changed the initial consonant of the syllable. The researchers specifically chose a consonant pair that was unlikely to be perceived as perceptually difficult and also likely to be equally salient for the bilingual infant. Additionally, the researchers had a bilingual adult produce French and English pronunciations of each word. When the task demands changed, bilingual 17-month-olds were shown to have a processing advantage relative to monolingual infants, but decreased mono-lingual performance was attributed to the introduction of unfamiliar, other-language variants in the stimulus set. When stimuli matched the monolinguals' native language, monolinguals were once again able to make word–object associations (Mattock et al., 2010). When explicit cues to language identity prior to word presentation are given (Fennell & Byers-Heinlein, 2011) or stim-uli constraints are modified (Singh, Fu, Tay, & Golinkoff; 2018; Singh, Poh, & Fu, 2016) bilingual gains in word learning have been demonstrated. These results reveal that monolingual and bilingual task performance may be heavily determined by linguistic input as well as the similarities between task demands and their daily experiences.

The experience of learning words may impact the organization of brain systems devoted to language (Conboy & Mills, 2006; Mills, Plunkett, Prat, & Schafer, 2005). Using ERPs to examine neural responses to words, Conboy and Mills (2006) tested Spanish-English bilingual toddlers (19–22 months) and found different neural patterns for dominant versus nondominant languages, but not Spanish versus English. They also reported lateral asymmetry (i.e., impacting one side of the brain) of the P100 – a neural component that has been found to be indicative of faster rates of learning (Mills, Conboy, & Paton, 2005). Finally, results yielded neural differences to known and unknown words, but these differences were not due to phonetic differences between English and Spanish. The results indicate that linguistic differences in experience may drive underlying neural activity to words and that there are qualitative differences in brain activity for bilingual versus monolingual children.

24.3 Memory

To learn two languages successfully, it is possible that children who routinely hear complex linguistic input may recruit other cognitive resources for processing. For example, past research has demonstrated that 7-month-olds are able to generalize a repetition rule (i.e., AAB or ABB) to novel words (Marcus, Vijayan, Rao, & Vishton, 1990). Extending this research, Kovács and Mehler (2009b) found that 12-month-old bilingual infants could simultane-ously learn and flexibly apply two separate repetition-based patterns embedded in speech-like stimuli, whereas monolingual infants could only learn one pattern at a time. The researchers concluded that individual differences in linguistic input may lead to greater cognitive flexibility, even when infants are preverbal, and this flexibility could be related to different but converging cognitive processes (Kovács & Mehler, 2009b).

Another domain of cognition that requires both attention and flexibility is memory. Measures of attention and processing speed have been found to be correlated with visual recognition memory – infants with better attention and faster encoding on average have better memory (Rose, Feldman, & Jankowski, 2003). Memory flexibility is vital to the learning process as it allows past experiences to be applied to a range of future scenarios that are not likely to be perceptually the same as the original learning episode. Tulving and Thomson's (1973) encoding specificity hypothesis states that a memory of an event will only be retrieved if the cues at the time of retrieval match the same cues previously seen at the time of the original encoding. This hypothesis has been tested in infants using the deferred imitation paradigm (see Barr & Brito, 2013; Hayne, 2006, for a review). The deferred imitation paradigm requires the infant to encode, retain, and retrieve a memory – all without the production of language. Hayne, MacDonald, and Barr (1997) used the deferred imitation task to demonstrate that 6-month-old monolingual infants could imitate a previously seen demonstration (i.e., pull mitten, shake mitten, replace mitten on a puppet stuffed animal) after 24 hours if the infants were tested with the same stimuli (gray mouse to gray mouse), but failed the task when the stimuli changed in shape or color. Infants in the test condition are always compared to a baseline control group (group of infants shown the stimuli without a demonstration to test the spontaneous production of the target actions) to assess memory. Past studies demonstrate age-related changes in memory flexibility after a 24-hour delay: memory flexibility across color (gray mouse to pink mouse) emerging around 12 months, across color and shape (gray mouse to pink rabbit) around 18 months, and across more drastic changes in color and shape (black and white cow to yellow duck) around 21 months of age (Hayne, Boniface, & Barr, 2000).

Learning across different perceptual cues can be enhanced early in development by exposing young infants to different stimuli or to different learning contexts during the original encoding (Amabile & Rovee-Collier, 1991; Fagen, Morrongiello, Rovee-Collier, & Gekoski, 1984; Greco, Hayne, & Rovee-Collier, 1990; Learmonth, Lambert, & Rovee-Collier, 2004; Rovee-Collier & Dufault, 1991). For example, Herbert, Gross, and Hayne (2007) examined two groups of 9-month-old infants: crawlers and noncrawlers. The onset of crawling is highly variable among infants. It also affords infants the opportunity to explore their environment and encounter different objects and contexts (Campos et al., 2000). The researchers tested infants on a memory recall condition (when the stimuli matched from encoding to retrieval) and a memory flexibility condition (when the stimuli differed) and found that, although both groups were able to remember the demonstration when the stimuli and environmental context stayed the same, only the crawlers were able to remember the target actions during the memory flexibility conditions. The researchers suggested that as infants are presented with more opportunities to encode information in a variety of contexts, they are able to make more associations and take advantage of a wider range of retrieval cues to boost their memory. Thinking about the daily bilingual language environment, bilingual infants are exposed to more varied speech patterns than monolinguals and are also presented with more opportunities to encode information in a variety of language contexts. This variable linguistic experience may possibly contribute to the enhancement of memory flexibility.

24.3.1 Dual Language Exposure and Memory Flexibility: Experiential and Neural Mechanisms

To examine the influence of dual language exposure on memory flexibility, Brito and Barr (2012) replicated the Hayne et al. (1997) study with a group of monolingual and bilingual 18-month-olds. The researchers imposed a 30-minute delay between demonstration and test and counterbalanced stimuli (yellow duck and black and white cow) across participants. Results indicated that 18-month-old bilinguals outperformed both the monolingual and baseline control groups; only 1 out of 15 monolinguals completed any of the target actions compared to 9 out of 15 bilinguals. These results suggest that the bilingual infants were able to flexibly recall the visual cues across the different puppets after a 30-minute delay. In a subsequent study, Brito and Barr (2014) replicated this finding with 6-month-old infants. After a 30-minute delay, if the stimuli changes were quite minimal (gray mouse to pink mouse), both monolingual and bilingual groups were able to flexibly recall cues across the puppets. However, once task complexity increased (gray mouse to pink rabbit), only bilinguals were once again able to recall cues across stimuli. To examine if these differences in memory were specific to memory flexibility, Brito et al. (2014) tested groups of monolingual and bilingual 24-month-olds on memory recall, memory flexibility, and working memory. The delay between demonstration and test was increased from 30 minutes to 24 hours to increase difficulty for these older infants. Like previous studies, bilingual 24-month-olds outperformed both the monolingual and baseline control groups on the memory flexibility condition, but results indicated no significant differences between groups on the memory recall or working memory tasks. Finally, a third study replicated memory flexibility findings again at 18 months, but also found no differences in memory flexibility for bilingual infants with rhythmically similar (Spanish-Catalan) versus rhythmically dissimilar (Spanish-English) languages, suggesting that the type of language pair did not moderate this effect (Brito, Sebastián-Gallés, & Barr, 2015).

What are possible mechanisms that could account for the bilingual infants' success on the memory flexibility task? Although not exhaustive, there are three potential explanations for differences in memory flexibility performance by dual language status. First, changes in attentional processing and control may directly affect memory processing. As noted in the previous language section, bilingual infants are exposed to more varied speech input, and as a result of dual-context statistical learning, may be more attuned to detecting and recalling patterns in both auditory and visual stimuli (Antovich & Graf Estes, 2018). Second, researchers have theorized that age-dependent changes in memory flexibility could be due to an early inability to form relational representations. The daily exposure to variable language could impact a child's ability to make relational associations between stimuli – enabling the child to form hierarchical memories earlier in development. Declarative memories are encoded in networks of representations that allow new memories to be linked to previous information (see Eichenbaum, 2000 for a review). Therefore, in order to flexibly recall cues across stimuli, infants must be able to encode the cues in an ordered manner and form memories that are bonded by causal, logical, or temporal relations (Eichenbaum, 2000; Jones & Herbert, 2006). To be successful on the deferred imitation task, the infant must prioritize the most important features of the event over the peripheral details. The three target actions of the puppet task (remove mitten, shake mitten, then replace mitten) all necessitate attention to the mitten. So, it is possible that bilingual infants may organize their memories in a more hierarchical manner and selectively attend to the focal cue, whereas monolinguals attend to extraneous information such as the color or shape of the stimuli.

Finally, researchers have hypothesized that the capacity to flexibly recall cues across different visual elements reflects the transition to a higher-level hippocampus-dependent memory system (Bauer, 1997; Eichenbaum, 2000). But it seems highly unlikely that exposure to multiple languages would result in a rapid maturation of the hippocampus by 6 months of age. Like most cognitive tasks, performance on the deferred imitation paradigm is likely to be dependent on other brain structures in addition to the hippocampus. Howe (2011) has argued that experience-based changes in the acquisition and expression of memory during infancy may be due to development of the association cortices rather than changes to medial temporal lobe structures (i.e., the hippocampus). These differences in memory flexibility could also be mediated by activation of the prefrontal cortex. Specifically, to succeed on the memory flexibility task, infants must encode the elements of the target object and the sequence of ordered events to build a relational representation, before selecting the appropriate motor response to a new stimulus at test. The prefrontal cortex has been identified as a key brain structure needed for these behaviors (i.e., sequencing, planning, selecting) and perhaps the faster maturation of the slow-developing prefrontal cortex could account for these differences (Nelson & Webb, 2003). Furthermore, connectivity between brain regions could also potentially explain these discrepancies in findings. Richmond and Nelson (2007) argue that age-related changes in deferred imitation performance are related to hippocampal development but recognize that either maturation of the prefrontal cortex or connectivity between the medial temporal lobe and prefrontal cortex regions could also impact memory performance. Whether it may be differences in brain structure, modifications in attentional processing, earlier capacities to form relational representations, or a combination of several of these factors, the experience of processing multiple languages early in life seems to influence social learning and memory.

24.4 Social Interactions

The ability to initiate interactions, respond appropriately, and take turns during bouts of communication are important aspects of growing up in a social world. Social interaction is an important aspect of early language learning (Kuhl et al., 2003) and infants from monolingual or bilingual experiences may grow up in very different social environments, possibly leading bilingual children to distinct abilities needed in order to successfully facilitate communication. Past studies have found that bilingual children code switch, alternating between their languages depending on their communication partner, in order to avoid conversational breakdowns (Comeau, Genesee, & Mendelson, 2007; Tare & Gelman, 2010). Early exposure to more than one language may possibly enhance their social interaction or communication skills. Infants growing up in bilingual environments must track multiple linguistic systems while encoding linguistic and pragmatic cues from each of their languages – often encountering barriers in communication as they figure out which speakers understand which language.

Bilingual children may be able to learn a speaker's intention by efficiently making use of communicative cues (Yow & Markman 2011, 2015). For example, Liberman, Woodward, Keysar, and Kinzler (2017) examined social communication abilities in bilingual 16-month-olds by presenting the infants with visible and occluded toys. One toy was mutually visible to both the infant and speaker and the other toy was blocked from the speaker's view by an opaque barrier. This task required the infant to consider the speaker's perspective and reach for the toy that was mutually visible. Only infants from bilingual backgrounds were above chance in selecting the correct toy. The authors argued that growing up in linguistically different environments may impact attention to social interaction cues as a way to improve communication between speakers (Liberman et al., 2017).

A neurodevelopmental disorder that is linked with severe social impairments is autism spectrum disorder (ASD). Children with ASD often demonstrate deficits with social communication, including difficulty with eye contact, joint attention, and understanding another person's point of view (APA, 2016). Oftentimes, when children have language, cognitive, or socioemotional difficulties, parents are often given the misguided advice to not expose their child to a second language (de Houwer, 2009; Kay-Raining Bird, Lamond, & Holden, 2012; Paradis, 2007). Studies have investigated the influence of multiple-language exposure on communication skills for young children with ASD (Hambly & Fombonne, 2012; Ohashi et al., 2012). Results suggest that children (ages 24–52 months) with ASD who are exposed to more than one language do not experience additional delays in language development. With reference to timing of dual-language acquisition, whether the bilingual exposure was introduced during infancy versus post-infancy did not impact language outcomes in the child's dominant language (Hambly & Fombonne, 2012). So, although having ASD may result in impairments in key bilingual differences such as speech perception, joint attention, and social communication, the addition of a second language is not associated with additional vulnerabilities for bilingual ASD children compared to their single-language exposed ASD peers. There has been no evidence to suggest that caregivers of children with ASD should be discouraged from maintaining bilingual environments, as this may disrupt social communication abilities with family members or sever cultural ties.

24.5 Sociocultural Considerations

There is a developmental path for language regardless of culture, but as interactions with others always occur within cultural contexts, culture should always be taken into consideration as a robust moderator of behavior. Language is a pathway for the transmission of cultural values, beliefs, and ideas (Rogoff, 1990; Vygotsky, 1978). Maintaining dual-language status may help to promote cultural identity and sustain familial ties (Espinosa, 2006). A child learning multiple languages may need to navigate between two different sets of cultural expectations that may influence potential behavioral outcomes. Researchers have argued that various environmental factors such as cultural background or socioeconomic status (SES) may potentially explain any differences in learning between monolinguals and bilinguals (Morton & Harper, 2007).

24.5.1 Cultural Background

According to the US Census Bureau, 1 in 8 residents are foreign born and almost 30% of children aged 0–4 live in a household where English is not the primary language (Kominski, Shin, & Marotz, 2008). There is significant overlap between dual-language learners and children of immigrants (Castro-Vázquez, 2009) and as ethnic and racial minorities tend to experience more economic and social hardship, studies examining samples of dual-language learners often conflate findings with immigration-related characteristics or

SES. Researchers have claimed that this misconstrues the data and obscures potential assets in dual-language learners' development (Cabrera, Beeghly, & Eisenberg, 2012). Research has demonstrated that most children from immigrant families score in the typical ranges on behavioral and psychological assessments (Fuligni, 1998; Weiss, Goebel, Page, Wilson, Warda, 1999) and some studies have found that immigrant children have better social-emotional competence and fewer behavioral problems compared with nonimmigrants (Crosnoe, 2005, 2007). Few studies have teased apart contributions to early learning from dual-language status versus immigration, but Brito et al. (2015) did test memory flexibility in monolingual and bilingual 18-month-olds in the United States and Spain and found that both groups of bilinguals (Spanish-English and Spanish-Catalan) outperformed both monolingual groups. In this sample, 75% of Spanish-English bilinguals had at least one parent who immigrated, compared to just 7% of the Spanish-Catalan families. In relation to dual-language status, variation in immigration status or cultural practices do not appear to strongly predict outcomes for dual language learners.

24.5.2 Socioeconomic Background

Among the more economically developed countries, the United States has one of the highest levels of childhood poverty, with more than 1 in 5 children (approximately 15 million) living in poor households. Very young children are even more susceptible to poverty, with 1 in 4 infants and toddlers currently living in impoverished environments. Additionally, poverty rates for children of color (Black, Hispanic, and American Indian) are twice as high than their age-matched peers from White households (Proctor, Semega, & Kollar, 2016). By the time of school entry, children from higher-SES homes outperform their age-matched peers from lower-SES homes on standardized measures of language comprehension and production (Ginsborg, 2006). These SES disparities in language skills may already be present in infancy. Noble et al. (2015) tested a sample of 189 infants on measures of memory and language. Consistent with past studies demonstrating socioeconomic disparities in early language skills by the age of 2 (Fernald et al., 2013; Halle et al., 2009; Hoff, 2003; Rowe & Goldin-Meadow, 2009), SES disparities in language emerged between 15 and 21 months of age, with children of highly educated parents scoring approximately 4/5 of a standard deviation higher in both language and memory than children of less educated parents. Characteristics of the home environment, including literacy resources and parent–child interactions, partially accounted for disparities in language, but not memory (Noble et al., 2015).

SES-related differences in the quantity and quality of the home language environment have been shown to be associated with language outcomes for both monolingual and bilingual children (Place & Hoff, 2011; Ramirez-Esparaza et al., 2017). Hoff (2003) reported that the quality of maternal speech explained differences in expressive vocabulary growth between children from higher- versus lower-SES households. Past studies have found that children from lower-SES households experience less child-directed language and engage in fewer complex conversations relative to their higher-SES peers (Gilkerson et al., 2017; Hoff, 2003, 2006; Hoff-Ginsberg, 1998; Huttenlocher, Waterfall, Vasilyeva, Vevea, & Hedges, 2010; Rowe, 2008). Children from dual-language homes receive reduced linguistic input to each of their languages already, so in theory, bilingual children from lower-SES households may be at a greater risk as they may not receive enough input in either language. Investigating the interactive effects of SES and dual-language exposure, Brito, Leon-Santos, Fifer, and Noble (2017) found no impact of SES on bilingual differences in memory flexibility using the deferred imitation puppet task. Eighteen-month-olds from four different language and SES backgrounds (monolingual lower SES; monolingual higher SES; bilingual lower SES; bilingual higher SES) were tested on measures of cued recall, memory flexibility, and working memory. No significant differences were found between monolingual and bilingual infants on cued recall or working memory. Replicating past research (Brito & Barr, 2012), differences by language group were found for memory flexibility, with both low- and high-SES bilingual groups outperforming monolingual groups. This finding indicates that family SES alone may not explain robust differences in memory flexibility performance for dual-language learners, but other key factors such as language context and frequency of exposure still need to be investigated.

24.6 Conclusions

As early language ability is a robust predictor of school readiness and later academic achievement (Hoff, 2013; Burchinal, Pace, Alper, Hirsh-Pasek, Golinkoff, 2016), it is critical for infants growing up in bilingual or minority-language households to hear their caregivers speak in their native heritage language. Increasing both the amount and diversity of language interactions within the home can positively influence language development, regardless of SES. Repeated exposure to words and phrases increases the opportunity to learn and remember the word, although there are no set criteria for the number of exposures needed (McGregor, Sheng, & Ball, 2007). The diversity and complexity of grammar, the contingency of language to the child, and the use of questions have all been found to be critical for language development (Bornstein, Tamis-LeMonda, Hahn, & Haynes, 2008; Huttenlocher et al., 2010; Rowe, 2012). In addition to the frequency of language input, the activities through which caregivers communicate with their children also results in variations in children's language development (Tamis-LeMonda, Custode, Kuchirko, Escobar, & Lo, 2018).

Variations in lexical, grammatical, processing efficiency, and vocabulary development by bilinguals are mediated by the amount of exposure to each of their languages and the language context (Marchman, Martínez, Hurtado, Grüter, & Fernald, 2017; Oller & Eilers, 2002; Pearson, Fernández, Lewedge, & Oller, 1997; Place & Hoff, 2016). Likewise, degree of brain activity to each language within a bilingual child is also associated with the quantity and quality of speech they hear in each language (Garcia-Sierra, Ramírez-Esparza, & Kuhl, 2016; Garcia-Sierra et al., 2011). Past studies have shown that when children hear a language for less than 25% of the time, children tend to not fully acquire that language (Pearson et al., 1997). An important point should be made when comparing children from different linguistic backgrounds. Even though studies have reported that children who are learning two languages have lower levels of language ability in each of their languages compared to their monolingual peers (Marchman, Fernald, & Hurtado, 2010; Vagh, Pan, & Mancilla-Martinez, 2009) or peers from similar SES backgrounds (Hoff et al., 2012), this does not necessarily suggest that they are learning total language at a slower rate. Studies that have measured bilingual toddlers' language skills by combining across both of their languages illustrate that bilingual toddlers either equal or in some cases exceed monolingual toddlers in their rates of vocabulary and grammatical development (Hoff et al., 2012; Pearson et al., 1993). In addition, the tools used to measure language ability may be biased, as these measures have been developed using monolingual children as the normed sample. Children learning two languages may do so in different contexts (e.g., Spanish at home, English in the community) or with different language partners (e.g., Spanish with dad, English with mom) and these differences may lead to variations in language acquisition and linguistic knowledge.

24.6.1 Future Studies and Policy Implications

Longitudinal research with larger and more diverse samples of children are needed to truly understand how variability in dual language learners' environments contribute to language and cognitive development. In most multilingualism studies, the theoretical framework for bilingualism has been used to study trilinguals, and most studies do not distinguish between bilinguals, trilinguals, or multilinguals (Cenoz & Genesee, 1998). Within studies of multilingual adults, some studies have found differences between bilinguals and trilinguals (Kave, Eval, Shorek, & Cohen-Mansfield, 2008), whereas others have not (Poarch & van Hell, 2012). Two studies by Brito and colleagues (Brito et al., 2014; Brito et al., 2015) have found differences at 18 and 24 months between bilingual and trilingual infants, with bilinguals outperforming trilinguals and no differences between monolinguals and trilinguals on memory flexibility tasks. As monolingual frameworks for language acquisition and neurocognitive development should not necessarily be directly applied to the study of bilingual processes, bilingual frameworks may also be inappropriate for trilingual studies as well.

More research characterizing different children's language experiences, and how they vary across social contexts, will illuminate how to approach interventions and policies for infants from dual-language or minority-language families. Studies that describe the ways in which parents from different ethnolinguistic groups use language with their children and whether pedagogical interventions can significantly increase positive cross-linguistic influences are needed (National Academy of Sciences, 2017). Until then, policies and programs must focus on accommodating infants and young children from a wide range of cultural and linguistic backgrounds.

The studies reviewed in this chapter suggest, with some exceptions, similar learning mechanisms employed by monolinguals to attend to and process a single language are also used to prepare the bilingual infant to attend to and process their two languages. Deviations in neurocognitive trajectories between dual-language learners and their monolingual peers may be a by-product of adaptations to demanding learning conditions that infants in bilingual environments face. Ultimately, exposure to multiple languages should be encouraged, not for the consequential enhancements or deviations in select neurocognitive functions, but because being able to communicate in another language opens up new literatures, traditions, and ideas to children. This may, in turn, promote greater openness to other cultural groups (Cummins, 1989) and nurture the human connections necessary for optimal neurocognitive development.

References

Amabile, T. A., & Rovee-Collier, C. (1991). Contextual variation and memory retrieval at six months. *Child Development, 62*(5), 1155–1166

American Psychiatric Association (2016). *Diagnostic and statistical manual of mental disorders (DSM-V)* (5th ed.) Washington, DC: American Psychiatric Association.

Antovich, D. M., & Graf Estes, K. (2018). Learning across languages: Bilingual experience supports dual language statistical word segmentation. *Developmental Science, 21*(2), e12548.

Aslin, R. N., Saffran, J. R., & Newport, E. L. (1998). Computation of conditional probability statistics by 8-month-old infants. *Psychological Science, 9*(4), 321–324.

Aslin, R. N., Woodward, J. Z., LaMendola, N. P., & Bever, T. G. (1996). Models of word segmentation in fluent maternal speech to infants. In J. L. Morgan & K. Demuth (Eds.), *Signal to syntax: Bootstrapping from speech to grammar in early acquisition* (pp. 117–134). Hillsdale, NJ: Lawrence Erlbaum Associates.

Barr, R., & Brito, N. (2013). From specificity to flexibility: Developmental changes during infancy. In P. Bauer (Ed.), *The Blackwell handbook on the development of children's memory* (pp. 453–479). Hoboken, NJ: Wiley-Blackwell.

Bauer, P. J. (1997). *Development of memory in early childhood*. London: Psychology Press.

Ben-Zeev, S. (1977). The influence of bilingualism on cognitive strategy and cognitive development. *Child Development, 48*(3), 1009–1018.

Bialystok, E. (1999). Cognitive complexity and attentional control in the bilingual mind. *Child Development*, *70*(3), 636–644.

(2007). Acquisition of literacy in bilingual children: A framework for research. *Language Learning*, *57*, 45–77.

(2017). The bilingual adaptation: How minds accommodate experience. *Psychological Bulletin*, *143*(3), 233.

Bialystok, E., & Martin, M. M. (2004). Attention and inhibition in bilingual children: Evidence from the dimensional change card sort task. *Developmental Science*, *7*(3), 325–339.

Bornstein, M. H., Tamis-LeMonda, C. S., Hahn, C. S., & Haynes, O. M. (2008). Maternal responsiveness to young children at three ages: Longitudinal analysis of a multi-dimensional, modular, and specific parenting construct. *Developmental Psychology*, *44*(3), 867.

Bosch, L., & Sebastián-Gallés, N. (2001). Evidence of early language discrimination abilities in infants from bilingual environments. *Infancy*, *2*(1), 29–49.

(2003). Simultaneous bilingualism and the perception of a language-specific vowel contrast in the first year of life. *Language and Speech*, *46*(2–3), 217–243.

Brito, N., & Barr, R. (2012). Influence of bilingualism on memory generalization during infancy. *Developmental Science*, *15*(6), 812–816.

(2014). Flexible memory retrieval in bilingual 6-month-old infants. *Developmental Psychobiology*, *56*(5), 1156–1163.

Brito, N. H., Grenell, A., & Barr, R. (2014). Specificity of the bilingual advantage for memory: Examining cued recall, generalization, and working memory in monolingual, bilingual, and trilingual toddlers. *Frontiers in Psychology*, *5*, 1369.

Brito, N. H., Leon-Santos, A., Fifer, W. P., Noble, K. G. (2017). *Early linguistic environment and neurocognitive adaptations: Examining the bilingual experience.* Talk presented at Society for Research in Child Development (SRCD) Biennial Meeting, Austin, TX.

Brito, N. H., Sebastián-Gallés, N., & Barr, R. (2015). Differences in language exposure and its effects on memory flexibility in monolingual, bilingual, and trilingual infants. *Bilingualism: Language and Cognition*, *18*(4), 670–682.

Burchinal, M. R., Pace, A., Alper, R., Hirsh-Pasek, K., & Golinkoff, R. M. (2016). *Early language outshines other predictors of academic and social trajectories in elementary school.* Paper presented at the Administration for Children and Families Conference (ACF), Washington, DC, July.

Burns, T. C., Yoshida, K. A., Hill, K., & Werker, J. F. (2007). The development of phonetic representation in bilingual and monolingual infants. *Applied Psycholinguistics*, *28*(3), 455–474.

Byers-Heinlein, K., Burns, T. C., & Werker, J. F. (2010). The roots of bilingualism in newborns. *Psychological Science*, *21*(3), 343–348.

Byers-Heinlein, K., Morin-Lessard, E., & Lew-Williams, C. (2017). Bilingual infants control their languages as they listen. *PNAS*, *114*(34), 9032–9037.

Cabrera, N. J., Beeghly, M., & Eisenberg, N. (2012). Positive development of minority children: Introduction to the special issue. *Child Development Perspectives*, *6*(3), 207–209.

Campos, J. J., Anderson, D. I., Barbu-Roth, M. A., Hubbard, E. M., Hertenstein, M. J., & Witherington, D. (2000). Travel broadens the mind. *Infancy*, *1*(2), 149–219.

Carlson, S. M., & Meltzoff, A. N. (2008). Bilingual experience and executive functioning in young children. *Developmental Science, 11*(2), 282–298.

Castro-Vázquez, G. (2009). Immigrant children from Latin America at Japanese schools: Homogeneity, ethnicity, gender and language in education. *Journal of Research in International Education, 8*(1), 57–80.

Cenoz, J., & Genesee, F. (Eds.). (1998). *Beyond bilingualism: Multilingualism and multilingual education* (Vol. 110). Bristol, UK: Multilingual Matters.

Comeau, L., Genesee, F., & Mendelson, M. (2007). Bilingual children's repairs of breakdowns in communication. *Journal of Child Language, 34*(1), 159–174.

Conboy, B. T., & Mills, D. L. (2006). Two languages, one developing brain: Event-related potentials to words in bilingual toddlers. *Developmental Science, 9*(1), F1–F12.

Costa, A., & Sebastián-Gallés, N. (2014). How does the bilingual experience sculpt the brain? *Nature Reviews Neuroscience, 15*(5), 336.

Crosnoe, R. (2005). Double disadvantage or signs of resilience? The elementary school contexts of children from Mexican immigrant families. *American Educational Research Journal, 42*(2), 269–303.

(2007). Early child care and the school readiness of children from Mexican immigrant families. *International Migration Review, 41*(1), 152–181.

Cummins, J. (1978). Bilingualism and the development of metalinguistic awareness. *Journal of Cross-Cultural Psychology, 9*(2), 131–149.

(1989). A theoretical framework for bilingual special education. *Exceptional Children, 56*(2), 111–119.

de Angelis, G. (2007). *Third or additional language acquisition* (Vol. 24). Bristol, UK: Multilingual Matters.

de Bruin, A., Treccani, B., & Della Sala, S. (2015). Cognitive advantage in bilingualism: An example of publication bias? *Psychological Science, 26*(1), 99–107.

de Houwer, A. (2009). *Bilingual first language acquisition*. Bristol, UK: Multilingual Matters.

de Houwer, A., Bornstein, M. H., & Putnick, D. L. (2014). A bilingual–monolingual comparison of young children's vocabulary size: Evidence from comprehension and production. *Applied Psycholinguistics, 35*(6), 1189–1211.

DeCasper, A. J., & Fifer, W. P. (1980). Of human bonding: Newborns prefer their mothers' voices. *Science, 208*(4448), 1174–1176.

Diamond, A. (1990). The development and neural bases of memory functions as indexed by the AB and delayed response tasks in human infants and infant monkeys. *Annals of the New York Academy of Sciences, 608*(1), 267–317.

Eichenbaum, H. (2000). A cortical–hippocampal system for declarative memory. *Nature Reviews Neuroscience, 1*(1), 41.

Eimas, P. D., Siqueland, E. R., Jusczyk, P., & Vigorito, J. (1971). Speech perception in infants. *Science, 171*(3968), 303–306.

Escobar, K., & Tamis-LeMonda, C. S. (2017). Conceptualizing variability in US Latino children's dual-language development. In N. J. Cabrera & B. Leyendecker (Eds.), *Handbook on positive development of minority children and youth* (pp. 89–106). Cham, Switzerland: Springer.

Espinosa, L. M. (2006). Social, cultural, and linguistic features of school readiness in young Latino children. In B. Bowman & E. K. Moore (Eds.), *School readiness and social-emotional development: Perspectives on cultural diversity* . Silver Spring, MD: National Black Child Development Institute.

Fagen, J. W., Morrongiello, B. A., Rovee-Collier, C., & Gekoski, M. J. (1984). Expectancies and memory retrieval in three-month-old infants. *Child Development*, *55*(3), 936–943.

Fennell, C. T., & Byers-Heinlein, K. (2011). Sentential context improves bilingual infants' use of phonetic detail in novel words. *Conference on Language Development*, *178*, 189.

Fennell, C. T., Byers-Heinlein, K., & Werker, J. F. (2007). Using speech sounds to guide word learning: The case of bilingual infants. *Child Development*, *78*(5), 1510–1525.

Ferjan Ramírez, N., Ramírez, R. R., Clarke, M., Taulu, S., & Kuhl, P. K. (2017). Speech discrimination in 11-month-old bilingual and monolingual infants: A magnetoencephalography study. *Developmental Science*, *20*(1), e12427.

Fernald, A., Marchman, V. A., & Weisleder, A. (2013). SES differences in language processing skill and vocabulary are evident at 18 months. *Developmental Science*, *16*(2), 234–248.

Fuligni, A. J. (1998). The adjustment of children from immigrant families. *Current Directions in Psychological Science*, *7*(4), 99–103.

Garcia-Sierra, A., Ramírez-Esparza, N., & Kuhl, P. K. (2016). Relationships between quantity of language input and brain responses in bilingual and monolingual infants. *International Journal of Psychophysiology*, *110*, 1–17.

Garcia-Sierra, A., Rivera-Gaxiola, M., Percaccio, C. R., Conboy, B. T., Romo, H., Klarman, L., … Kuhl, P. K. (2011). Bilingual language learning: An ERP study relating early brain responses to speech, language input, and later word production. *Journal of Phonetics*, *39*(4), 546–557.

Gilkerson, J., Richards, J. A., Warren, S. F., Montgomery, J. K., Greenwood, C. R., Oller, D. K., … Paul, T. D. (2017). Mapping the early language environment using all-day recordings and automated analysis. *American Journal of Speech-Language Pathology*, *26*(2), 248–265.

Ginsborg, J. (2006). The effects of socio-economic status on children's language acquisition and use. In J. Clegg & J. Ginsborg (Eds.), *Language and social disadvantage: Theory into practice* (pp. 9–27). Chichester, UK: John Wiley & Sons.

Greco, C., Hayne, H., & Rovee-Collier, C. (1990). Roles of function, reminding, and variability in categorization by 3-month-old infants. *Journal of Experimental Psychology: Learning, Memory, and Cognition*, *16*(4), 617.

Green, D. W. (1998). Mental control of the bilingual lexico-semantic system. *Bilingualism: Language and Cognition*, *1*(2), 67–81.

Grin, F. (2004). Robert Phillipson. English-only Europe? Challenging language policy. *Language Policy*, *3*(1), 67–71.

Halle, T., Forry, N., Hair, E., Perper, K., Wandner, L., Wessel, J., & Vick, J. (2009). *Disparities in early learning and development: Lessons from the Early Childhood Longitudinal Study–Birth Cohort (ECLS-B)*. Washington, DC: Child Trends.

Hambly, C., & Fombonne, E. (2012). The impact of bilingual environments on language development in children with autism spectrum disorders. *Journal of Autism and Developmental Disorders*, *42*(7), 1342–1352.

Hartanto, A., Toh, W. X., & Yang, H. (2018). Bilingualism narrows socioeconomic disparities in executive functions and self-regulatory behaviors during early childhood: Evidence From the Early Childhood Longitudinal Study. *Child Development*, 90(4), 1215–1235.

Hayne, H. (2006). Age-related changes in infant memory retrieval: Implications for knowledge acquisition. Processes of brain and cognitive development. *Attention and performance, 21*, 209–231.

Hayne, H., Boniface, J., & Barr, R. (2000). The development of declarative memory in human infants: Age-related changes in deferred imitation. *Behavioral Neuroscience, 114*(1), 77.

Hayne, H., MacDonald, S., & Barr, R. (1997). Developmental changes in the specificity of memory over the second year of life. *Infant Behavior and Development*, 20(2), 233–245.

Herbert, J., Gross, J., & Hayne, H. (2007). Crawling is associated with more flexible memory retrieval by 9-month-old infants. *Developmental Science, 10*(2), 183–189.

Hoff, E. (2003). The specificity of environmental influence: Socioeconomic status affects early vocabulary development via maternal speech. *Child Development*, 74(5), 1368–1378.

(2006). How social contexts support and shape language development. *Developmental Review, 26*(1), 55–88.

(2013). *Language development*. Belmont, CA: Cengage Learning.

Hoff, E., Core, C., Place, S., Rumiche, R., Señor, M., & Parra, M. (2012). Dual language exposure and early bilingual development. *Journal of Child Language*, 39(1), 1–27.

Hoff-Ginsberg, E. (1998). The relation of birth order and SES to children's language experience and language development. *Applied Psycholinguistics, 19*(4), 603–629.

Howe, M. L. (2011). *The nature of early memory: An adaptive theory of the genesis and development of memory*. Oxford: Oxford University Press.

Huttenlocher, J., Waterfall, H., Vasilyeva, M., Vevea, J., & Hedges, L. V. (2010). Sources of variability in children's language growth. *Cognitive Psychology*, 61(4), 343–365.

Jones, E. J., & Herbert, J. S. (2006), Exploring memory in infancy: deferred imitation and the development of declarative memory. *Infant and Child Development, 15*, 195–205. doi:10.1002/icd.436

Jusczyk, P. W., & Aslin, R. N. (1995). Infants' detection of the sound patterns of words in fluent speech. *Cognitive Psychology*, 29(1), 1–23.

Kavé, G., Eyal, N., Shorek, A., & Cohen-Mansfield, J. (2008). Multilingualism and cognitive state in the oldest old. *Psychology and Aging*, 23(1), 70.

Kay-Raining Bird, E., Lamond, E., & Holden, J. (2012). Survey of bilingualism in autism spectrum disorders. *International Journal of Language & Communication Disorders, 47*(1), 52–64.

Kominski, R., Shin, H., & Marotz, K. (2008, April). *Language needs of school-age children*. Paper presented at the Annual Meeting of the Population Association of America, New Orleans, LA.

Kovács, Á. M., & Mehler, J. (2009a). Cognitive gains in 7-month-old bilingual infants. *Proceedings of the National Academy of Sciences, 106*(16), 6556–6560.

(2009b). Flexible learning of multiple speech structures in bilingual infants. *Science*, *325*(5940), 611–612.

Kuhl, P. K. (1994). Learning and representation in speech and language. *Current Opinion in Neurobiology*, *4*(6), 812–822.

(2007). Is speech learning "gated" by the social brain? *Developmental Science*, *10*(1), 110–120.

Kuhl, P. K., Conboy, B. T., Padden, D., Nelson, T., & Pruitt, J. (2005). Early speech perception and later language development: Implications for the "critical period." *Language Learning and Development*, *1*(3–4), 237–264.

Kuhl, P. K., Tsao, F. M., & Liu, H. M. (2003). Foreign-language experience in infancy: Effects of short-term exposure and social interaction on phonetic learning. *Proceedings of the National Academy of Sciences*, *100*(15), 9096–9101.

Kuipers, J. R., & Thierry, G. (2013). ERP-pupil size correlations reveal how bilingualism enhances cognitive flexibility. *Cortex*, *49*(10), 2853–2860.

Learmonth, A. E., Lamberth, R., & Rovee-Collier, C. (2004). Generalization of deferred imitation during the first year of life. *JECP*, *88*(4), 297–318.

Lewis, M. P., Simons, G. F., & Fennig, C. D. (2009). *Ethnologue: Languages of the world* (Vol. 16). Dallas, TX: SIL international.

Liberman, Z., Woodward, A. L., Keysar, B., & Kinzler, K. D. (2017). Exposure to multiple languages enhances communication skills in infancy. *Developmental Science*, *20*(1), e12420.

Marchman, V. A., Fernald, A., & Hurtado, N. (2010). How vocabulary size in two languages relates to efficiency in spoken word recognition by young Spanish–English bilinguals. *Journal of Child Language*, *37*(4), 817–840.

Marchman, V. A., Martínez, L. Z., Hurtado, N., Grüter, T., & Fernald, A. (2017). Caregiver talk to young Spanish-English bilinguals: Comparing direct observation and parent-report measures of dual-language exposure. *Developmental Science*, *20*(1), e12425.

Marcus, G. F., Vijayan, S., Rao, S. B., & Vishton, P. M. (1999). Rule learning by seven-month-old infants. *Science*, *283*(5398), 77–80.

Mattock, K., Polka, L., Rvachew, S., & Krehm, M. (2010). The first steps in word learning are easier when the shoes fit: Comparing monolingual and bilingual infants. *Developmental Science*, *13*(1), 229–243.

McGregor, K. K., Sheng, L., & Ball, T. (2007). Complexities of expressive word learning over time. *Language, Speech, and Hearing Services in Schools*, *38*(4), 353–364.

Mills, D., Conboy, B. T., & Paton, C. (2005). How learning new words shapes the organization of the infant brain. *Symbol Use and Symbolic Representation*, 123–153.

Mills, D. L., Plunkett, K., Prat, C., & Schafer, G. (2005). Watching the infant brain learn words: Effects of vocabulary size and experience. *Cognitive Development*, *20*(1), 19–31.

Morton, J. B., & Harper, S. N. (2007). What did Simon say? Revisiting the bilingual advantage. *Developmental Science*, *10*(6), 719–726.

National Academies of Sciences, Engineering, and Medicine (2017). *Promoting the educational success of children and youth learning English: Promising futures.* Washington, DC: National Academies Press.

Nelson, C. A., & Webb, S. J. (2003). A cognitive neuroscience perspective on early memory development. In M. de Haan & M. H. Johnson (Eds.), *The cognitive neuroscience of development* (pp. 99–125). London: Psychology Press.

Newman, R., Ratner, N. B., Jusczyk, A. M., Jusczyk, P. W., & Dow, K. A. (2006). Infants' early ability to segment the conversational speech signal predicts later language development: a retrospective analysis. *Developmental Psychology*, *42*(4), 643.

Newport, E. L. (1990). Maturational constraints on language learning. *Cognitive Science*, *14*(1), 11–28.

Newport, E. L., & Aslin, R. N. (2004). Learning at a distance I. Statistical learning of non-adjacent dependencies. *Cognitive Psychology*, *48*(2), 127–162.

Newport, E. L., Bavelier, D., & Neville, H. J. (2001). Critical thinking about critical periods: Perspectives on a critical period for language acquisition. In E. Dupoux (Ed.), *Language, brain and cognitive development: Essays in honor of Jacques Mehler* (pp. 481–502). Cambridge, MA: MIT Press.

Noble, K. G., Engelhardt, L. E., Brito, N. H., Mack, L. J., Nail, E. J., Angal, J., ... PASS Network. (2015). Socioeconomic disparities in neurocognitive development in the first two years of life. *Developmental Psychobiology*, *57*(5), 535–551.

Office of Head Start (2008). *Dual language learning: What does it take?* Head Start dual language report. Retrieved from http://eclkc.ohs.acf.hhs.gov/hslc/tta-.

Ohashi, J. K., Mirenda, P., Marinova-Todd, S., Hambly, C., Fombonne, E., Szatmari, P., ... Volden, J. (2012). Comparing early language development in monolingual- and bilingual-exposed young children with autism spectrum disorders. *Research in Autism Spectrum Disorders*, *6*(2), 890–897.

Oller, D. K., & Eilers, R. E. (Eds.). (2002). *Language and literacy in bilingual children* (Vol. 2). Bristol, UK: Multilingual Matters.

Olshtain, E., & Nissim-Amitai, F. (2004). Being trilingual or multilingual: Is there a price to pay. In C. Hoffman & J. Ytsma (Eds.), *Trilingualism in family, school and community* (pp. 30–50). Bristol, UK: Multilingual Matters.

Oyama, S. (1976). A sensitive period for the acquisition of a nonnative phonological system. *Journal of Psycholinguistic Research*, *5*(3), 261–283.

Paap, K. R., & Greenberg, Z. I. (2013). There is no coherent evidence for a bilingual advantage in executive processing. *Cognitive Psychology*, *66*(2), 232–258.

Paradis, J. (2007). Second language acquisition in childhood. In E. Hoff & M. Shatz (Eds.), *The Blackwell handbook of language development* (pp. 387–405). Malden, MA: Blackwell.

Pearson, B. Z., Fernandez, S. C., Lewedge, V & Oller, D. K. (1997). The relation of input factors to lexical learning by bilingual infants. *Applied Psycholinguistics*, *18*, 41–58

Pearson, B. Z., Fernández, S. C., & Oller, D. K. (1993). Lexical development in bilingual infants and toddlers: Comparison to monolingual norms. *Language Learning*, *43*(1), 93–120.

Petitto, L. A., Berens, M. S., Kovelman, I., Dubins, M. H., Jasinska, K., & Shalinsky, M. (2012). The "perceptual wedge hypothesis" as the basis for bilingual babies' phonetic processing advantage: New insights from fNIRS brain imaging. *Brain and Language*, *121*(2), 130–143.

Place, S., & Hoff, E. (2011). Properties of dual language exposure that influence 2-year-olds' bilingual proficiency. *Child Development*, *82*(6), 1834–1849.

(2016). Effects and noneffects of input in bilingual environments on dual language skills in 2 ½-year-olds. *Bilingualism: Language and Cognition, 19*(5), 1023–1041.

Poarch, G. J., & van Hell, J. G. (2012). Executive functions and inhibitory control in multilingual children: Evidence from second-language learners, bilinguals, and trilinguals. *Journal of Experimental Child Psychology, 113*(4), 535–551.

Poulin-Dubois, D., Blaye, A., Coutya, J., & Bialystok, E. (2011). The effects of bilingualism on toddlers' executive functioning. *Journal of Experimental Child Psychology, 108*(3), 567–579.

Proctor, B. D., J. L. Semega, & M. A. Kollar (2016). *U.S. Census Bureau, current population reports, P60-256(RV): Income and poverty in the United States: 2015.* Washington, DC: US Government Printing Office.

Ramírez-Esparza, N., García-Sierra, A., & Kuhl, P. K. (2017). The impact of early social interactions on later language development in Spanish–English bilingual infants. *Child Development, 88*(4), 1216–1234.

Richmond, J., & Nelson, C. A. (2007). Accounting for change in declarative memory: A cognitive neuroscience perspective. *Developmental Review, 27*(3), 349–373.

Rivera-Gaxiola, M., Silva-Pereyra, J., & Kuhl, P. K. (2005). Brain potentials to native and non-native speech contrasts in 7-and 11-month-old American infants. *Developmental Science, 8*(2), 162–172.

Rogoff, B. (1990). *Apprenticeship in thinking: Cognitive development in social context.* Oxford: Oxford University Press.

Rose, S. A., Feldman, J. F., & Jankowski, J. J. (2003). Infant visual recognition memory: independent contributions of speed and attention. *Developmental Psychology, 39*(3), 563.

Rovee-Collier, C., & Dufault, D. (1991). Multiple contexts and memory retrieval at three months. *Developmental Psychobiology, 24*(1), 39–49.

Rowe, M. L. (2008). Child-directed speech: Relation to socioeconomic status, knowledge of child development and child vocabulary skill. *Journal of Child Language, 35*(1), 185–205.

(2012). A longitudinal investigation of the role of quantity and quality of child-directed speech in vocabulary development. *Child Development, 83*(5), 1762–1774.

Rowe, M. L., & Goldin-Meadow, S. (2009). Differences in early gesture explain SES disparities in child vocabulary size at school entry. *Science, 323*(5916), 951–953.

Saffran, J. R., Aslin, R. N., & Newport, E. L. (1996). Statistical learning by 8-month-old infants. *Science, 274*(5294), 1926–1928.

Singh, L., Fu, C. S., Rahman, A. A., Hameed, W. B., Sanmugam, S., Agarwal, P., … GUSTO Research Team (2015). Back to basics: A bilingual advantage in infant visual habituation. *Child Development, 86*(1), 294–302.

Singh, L., Fu, C. S., Tay, Z. W., & Golinkoff, R. M. (2018). Novel word learning in bilingual and monolingual infants: evidence for a bilingual advantage. *Child Development, 89*(3), e183–e198.

Singh, L., Poh, F. L., & Fu, C. S. (2016). Limits on monolingualism? A comparison of monolingual and bilingual infants' abilities to integrate lexical tone in novel word learning. *Frontiers in Psychology, 7*, 667.

Spear, N. E. (1984). Ecologically Determined Dispositions Control the Ontogeny of Learning and. *Comparative perspectives on the development of memory*, 325.

Sundara, M., Polka, L., & Molnar, M. (2008). Development of coronal stop perception: Bilingual infants keep pace with their monolingual peers. *Cognition*, *108*(1), 232–242.

Sundara, M., & Scutellaro, A. (2011). Rhythmic distance between languages affects the development of speech perception in bilingual infants. *Journal of Phonetics*, *39*(4), 505–513.

Tamis-LeMonda, C. S., Custode, S., Kuchirko, Y., Escobar, K., & Lo, T. (2018). Routine language: Speech directed to infants during home activities. *Child Development*, 90(6), 2132–2152.

Tare, M., & Gelman, S. A. (2010). Can you say it another way? Cognitive factors in bilingual children's pragmatic language skills. *Journal of Cognition and Development*, *11*(2), 137–158.

Tulving, E., & Thomson, D. M. (1973). Encoding specificity and retrieval processes in episodic memory. *Psychological Review*, *80*(5), 352.

United Nations (2018). *United Nations General Assembly Member States*. Retrieved from www.un.org/en/member-states/index.html.

Vagh, S. B., Pan, B. A., & Mancilla-Martinez, J. (2009). Measuring growth in bilingual and monolingual children's English productive vocabulary development: The utility of combining parent and teacher report. *Child Development*, *80*(5), 1545–1563.

Vygotsky, L. (1978). Interaction between learning and development. *Readings on the Development of Children*, *23*(3), 34–41.

Weikum, W. M., Vouloumanos, A., Navarra, J., Soto-Faraco, S., Sebastián-Gallés, N., & Werker, J. F. (2007). Visual language discrimination in infancy. *Science*, *316*(5828), 1159–1159.

Weiss, S. J., Goebel, P., Page, A., Wilson, P., & Warda, M. (1999). The impact of cultural and familial context on behavioral and emotional problems of preschool Latino children. *Child Psychiatry and Human Development*, 29(4), 287–301.

Werker, J. (2012). Perceptual foundations of bilingual acquisition in infancy. *Annals of the New York Academy of Sciences*, *1251*(1), 50–61.

Werker, J. F., Cohen, L. B., Lloyd, V. L., Casasola, M., & Stager, C. L. (1998). Acquisition of word–object associations by 14-month-old infants. *Developmental Psychology*, *34*(6), 1289.

Werker, J. F., & Fennell, C. T. (2004). Listening to sounds versus listening to words: Early steps in word learning. In G. Hall & S. R. Waxman (Eds.), *Weaving a lexicon* (pp. 79–109). Cambridge, MA: MIT Press.

Werker, J. F., Fennell, C. T., Corcoran, K. M., & Stager, C. L. (2002). Infants' ability to learn phonetically similar words: Effects of age and vocabulary size. *Infancy*, *3*(1), 1–30.

Werker, J. F., & Tees, R. C. (1984). Cross-language speech perception: Evidence for perceptual reorganization during the first year of life. *Infant Behavior and Development*, *7*(1), 49–63.

Yow, W. Q., & Markman, E. M. (2011). Bilingualism and children's use of paralinguistic cues to interpret emotion in speech. *Bilingualism: Language and Cognition*, *14*(4), 562–569.

(2015). A bilingual advantage in how children integrate multiple cues to understand a speaker's referential intent. *Bilingualism: Language and Cognition*, *18*(3), 391–399.

PART VI

Emotional and Social Development

25 Infant Attachment (to Mother and Father) and Its Place in Human Development

Five Decades of Promising Research (and an Unsettled Issue)

Or Dagan and Abraham Sagi-Schwartz

"There are few blows to the human spirit so great as the loss of someone near and dear," wrote Bowlby in one of many groundbreaking papers.

> Traditional wisdom knows that we can be crushed by grief and die of a broken heart, and also that a jilted lover is apt to do things that are foolish or dangerous to himself and others. It knows, too, that neither love nor grief are felt for just any other human being but for one, or a few, particular and individual human beings. The core of what I am terming an affectional bond is the attraction that one individual has for another individual. (Bowlby, 1979, pp. 83–84)

This is one of the constitutive statements of Bowlby's attachment theory, one of the most widely researched and clinically applied theories in the field of human development. The present chapter cannot aspire to cover the breadth and depth of research and discussion surrounding attachment theory. The *Handbook of Attachment: Theory, Research, and Clinical Applications*, currently in its third edition, with more than 1,000 pages organized into 43 chapters, is now the most authoritative reference on the subject (Cassidy & Shaver, 2016).

This chapter contains a brief review of the main tenets of attachment theory and describes how infant attachment is commonly assessed both in the laboratory and in natural settings. The chapter is divided into three sections. The first section surveys five decades of theory and research focusing on the infant's emotional tie to a single caregiver, mostly the mother. It touches on the universality and specificity of infant–caregiver attachment across cultures, and cites empirical findings that bring to light the central role that the quality of infant attachment to a caregiver plays in socioemotional, psychophysiological, and neurodevelopmental outcomes. The second section brings to the fore a key unresolved issue in the field of attachment theory and research: that of the network of infant attachments to two primary caregivers, the mother and the father. Based on the little empirical evidence available to date, we propose a theoretical framework to better understand the joint effect of the infant's attachment to both parents on developmental outcomes. In the third section we conclude the chapter with final remarks on the important implications of attachment theory and research for practice and public policy.

25.1 One Infant, One Caregiver

25.1.1 Attachment Theory: The Centrality of the Infant–Caregiver Emotional Tie

The main tenet of attachment theory is that infants' tendency to form relationships with their primary caregivers is an *existential need*. In Bowlby's words, "mother love in infancy is as important for mental health as are vitamins and proteins for physical health" (Bowlby, 1953, p. 158). Attachment, according to Bowlby, is a strong disposition to seek proximity and contact with a specific caregiver, and to do so when one is distressed, i.e., in need of physical and psychological security (Ainsworth, Blehar, Waters, & Wall, 1978; Bowlby, 1969; Sroufe & Waters, 1977). Attachment theory thus assumes that all infants, regardless of their cultural niche, are innately biased to become attached to primary caregivers.

The second main tenet of attachment theory is that the quality of the infant–caregiver attachment relationship varies depending on the caregiving environment and specifically on the caregivers' sensitivity to the infants' proximity seeking cues and communications (Fearon & Roisman, 2017). Accumulating evidence from twin studies attests to a substantial shared environmental influence on the quality of infants' and children's attachment, and limited genetic influences (Bokhorst et al., 2003; Fearon et al., 2006; O'Connor & Croft, 2001; Roisman & Fraley, 2008). Two of these studies have found that the common environmental influences on attachment quality were correlated with the quality of maternal sensitivity, suggesting that the central environmental variable influencing attachment quality is the caregiving environment. Studies regarding the effect of single genes and their interaction with parental sensitivity produced mixed results (Fearon & Belsky, 2016; Luijk et al., 2012), bolstering the current notion that attachment quality is influenced mainly by environmental factors. Although more robust studies are still needed, findings to date provide relatively strong evidence for the proposition that variation in attachment is driven primarily by caregiving influences (Bakermans-Kranenburg & van IJzendoorn, 2016).

A third central tenet of attachment theory is that the quality of infant–caregiver attachment shapes one's future relational patterns in the form of expectations, attitudes, and beliefs regarding the self and others. These self–other schemas are also known as internal working models (Bowlby, 1969,

1973), and are thought to consist of a well-organized, yet dynamic representational structure that is hypothesized to operate primarily outside of conscious awareness (Bowlby, 1980; Bretherton, 1985; Main, Kaplan, & Cassidy, 1985). Consistent with the psychoanalytic and evolutionary roots of attachment theory, internal working models are thought to serve as defenses against threats to the psychological well-being of the individual (Bowlby, 1980; Cassidy & Kobak, 1988; Main, 1981), and as adaptation to early rearing environmental conditions ensures immediate survival and future reproduction (Belsky, 2002; Simpson & Belsky, 2016). Internal working models are assumed to influence the individual's attentional biases and to involve processes that affect memory and the interpretation of events (Pietromonaco & Barrett, 2000). As such, they tend to shape future relationships with peers and romantic partners (Bowlby, 1988; Feeney, 2008; Groh et al., 2014; Holland & Roisman, 2010), as well as with nonfamiliar others (Roisman, 2006). Later in this chapter we present in more detail some critical developmental outcomes associated with different qualities of infant attachment patterns.

25.1.2 Attachment Assessments in Infancy

In infancy, attachment strategies are assessed with a 20-minute laboratory procedure, which has become the gold standard for infant attachment assessment: the strange situation procedure (SSP; Ainsworth et al., 1978). The SSP is designed to assess infants' expectations of their parents' availability at times of need by observing their behavior when reunited with parents following brief separations. In the course of two separations and reunions with the caregiver, and having been in the room with a stranger while the parent is both present (before leaving) and absent, infants are assessed for their use of the caregiver as a secure base from which to explore their environment (Ainsworth et al., 1978). Despite the SSP being administered most widely in North America and Europe, it has been successfully used in Asia, Africa, and Central and South America; we elaborate on the SSP's cross-cultural capacity towards the end of this chapter.

The SSP is valid for assessment of infants aged 12–18 months, and is administered to both the infant and its caregiver in a setting of a room equipped with toys that encourage exploration of the environment. After introducing the room to the dyad, the caregiver is instructed to let the infant settle in and explore the room and assist the infant only if necessary. Then, a stranger is introduced and attempts to play with the infant, ensued by the parent exiting the room. The caregiver is then instructed to return to the room and reunite with the infant, while the stranger leaves quietly. A similar second round of separation and reunion is then set in motion; in this second phase, the infant is left alone in the room and the stranger enters the room after 3 minutes to stay and interact with the infant, if necessary, until reunited with its caregiver.

During episodes of separation, most infants stand in the vicinity of the door and cry. When the caregiver returns, most infants tend to seek proximity and contact with the caregiver. Infants are normally able to become soothed and comforted by their caregiver relatively quickly, and resume their exploration and play in the room. This attachment pattern has been termed *secure* attachment (type B).

Not all infants, however, show the same behavioral pattern. Some infants minimize displays of distress by avoiding the caregiver after she returns, looking away, or rejecting the caregiver's attempts at contact. These infants are classified as *insecure-avoidant* (type A) attachment. It has been argued that insecure-avoidant infants use strategies to minimize their distress so as to maintain proximity to the caregiver and not drive her away (Main & Weston, 1981), or to avoid proximity altogether (Mikulincer & Shaver, 2012). Insecure-avoidant infants are characterized by distant, self-reliant behavior when distressed in the presence of the caregiver (Ainsworth et al., 1978; Main, 2000). Infants in the third group tend to protest and show excessive distress when the caregiver leaves the room, and appear angry with the caregiver upon reunion. The caregiver then fails to soothe the infant, who often resists comforting. These infants are referred to as having *insecure-resistant* or *insecure-ambivalent* (type C) attachment. It has been suggested that these infants express anger or resistance toward the caregiver and at the same time seek her proximity to ensure more consistent attention and care (Cassidy & Berlin, 1994).

Both secure and insecure infants, the marked differences between them notwithstanding, develop what in the field of attachment is referred to as an *organized attachment* strategy; they adapt to the behavior of their attachment figures. Some infants, however, fail to develop an organized attachment pattern, and their regulatory strategy is altogether absent or compromised (Main & Solomon, 1990). These infants, referred to as *disorganized*, tend to behave oddly, display anomalous movements during the SSP, such as freezing or stilling for periods of time, or simultaneously display both avoidance and proximity-seeking (Hesse & Main, 2006). Attachment disorganization is thought to develop in the context of parental abuse or neglect, or parental behavior that is perceived as frightened or frightening. Disorganized attachment is believed to reflect an insoluble dilemma, where infants perceive their caregiver as a haven of safety and at the same time as a threat (Hesse & Main, 2006).

Although the SSP has produced massive amounts of meaningful findings, it has been criticized for its limited ecological validity. Criticism has focused mainly on the reliance of SSP on a laboratory environment, and for being restricted to the beginning of the second year of life, overlooking later developmental phases. In response, several other infant attachment evaluation methods were developed.

A common procedure that has been widely used alongside the SSP has been the Attachment Q-Set (AQS; Waters & Deane, 1985), which was designed to provide a natural-setting observation alternative to the SSP. In this procedure, administered to infants and children up to 5 years old, trained observers or parents are asked to sort 90 cards that portray various behavioral characteristics of the child. The items are sorted to evaluate the child's secure-base behaviors, reflecting such features of receiving support from an attachment figure at times of need and using the caregiver to freely explore the environment when the infant is not distressed (e.g., "[Infant] keeps track of mother's location when he plays around the house" and "[Infant] runs to mother with a shy smile when new people visit the home"). The results, collected in the course of up to three home observations of 2–6 hours each, are compared with the prototypical profile of a secure child provided by experts, leading to a security score with no specified cut-off point between secure and insecure children. The observer AQS security score (less so the parental reports) has shown convergent validity with the SSP secure versus insecure classifications, and similarly to the SSP, it displays strong predictive validity with parental sensitivity measures, a known antecedent of the quality of the child's attachment (van IJzendoorn, Vereijken, Bakermans-Kranenburg, & Riksen-Walraven, 2004).

25.1.3 The Quality of Early Infant–Caregiver Relationship Influences Developmental Outcomes

According to attachment theory, early experiences with one's caregivers are the foundations on which infants develop attachment relationships with their caregivers (Bowlby, 1988). The quality of these attachment relationships, in turn, have been hypothesized to influence short- and long-term socioemotional, psychophysiological, and neurodevelopmental outcomes.

25.1.3.1 *Socioemotional Outcomes*
Cumulative evidence from research over the past five decades has supported the association between the infant's quality of attachment and socioemotional outcomes in childhood. A recent programmatic synthesis of findings regarding the link between early attachment security and later developmental outcomes, assessing over 5,000 infants and children, has confirmed that children who were classified as securely attached as infants and in early childhood showed better socioemotional outcomes than did insecure children, as indicated by the quality of peer relationships, and by internalizing and externalizing behaviors (Fearon, Bakermans-Kranenburg, van IJzendoorn, Lapsley, & Roisman, 2010; Groh et al., 2014; Groh, Fearon, van IJzendoorn, Bakermans-Kranenburg, & Roisman, 2016; Groh, Roisman, van IJzendoorn, Bakermans-Kranenburg, & Fearon, 2012).

It is clear therefore that the early infant–caregiver relationship plays a crucial role in the socioemotional trajectory of the individual. Accordingly, research has moved forward to identify the explanatory physiological mechanisms that may give rise to the differential developmental trajectories that individuals follow as a result of their early attachment patterns, or at least under the influence of these patterns. Consistent with the notion that the caregiver provides a sense of safety and a secure base to which the child can retreat in times of need to alleviate negative affect and arousal (Bowlby, 1969, 1973), attachment theory conceptualized the attachment relationship as a modulator of stress, with the attachment figure serving as a co-regulator of the infant's physiological and corresponding behavioral responses to stress (Gunnar & Quevedo, 2007). Research on the mechanisms explaining the association between attachment patterns in early life and later maladaptive socioemotional outcomes has focused on children's stress responses at both the hormonal and neurodevelopmental levels. Below we briefly touch on two lines of research concerning the stress physiology of attachment: one involves the hypothalamic-pituitary-adrenal (HPA) axis, the other the neural brain circuitry.

25.1.3.2 *Psychophysiological Outcomes*

Of several stress physiology biological markers, the HPA axis has been most extensively researched. The HPA axis is a key physiological stress reactivity system, of which the hormonal product, cortisol, affects many aspects of neurobehavioral development in humans (Gunnar & Vazquez, 2006). Findings suggest that HPA axis activity in general, and levels of cortisol secretion in particular, are strongly influenced by early childhood attachment relationships (Gunnar & Hostinar, 2015; Gunnar & Quevedo, 2007). HPA axis function can be examined by assessing the diurnal rhythm of cortisol, which typically emerges at the age of several months and matures through the preschool years. The diurnal rhythm is characterized by a peak in cortisol levels in the morning, followed by a decline throughout the day (Larson, White, Cochran, Donzella, & Gunnar, 1998). Both diurnal cortisol and cortisol reactivity to stressors have been found to be affected by parental sensitivity and attachment quality (Bernard & Dozier, 2010; Pendry & Adam, 2007; Schieche & Spangler, 2005; Spangler & Grossmann, 1993; Spangler, & Schieche, 1998; van Bakel & Riksen-Walraven, 2004).

Furthermore, threats to early attachment relationships, such as early caregiving adversity in the form of neglect or placement in foster care, have been consistently linked with children's low levels of morning cortisol and blunted rhythms across the day (Bernard, Butzin-Dozier, Rittenhouse, & Dozier, 2010; Bruce, Fisher, Pears, & Levine, 2009; Carlson & Earls, 1997). Even in the absence of severe caregiving adversity, parent–child relationship quality has been associated with diurnal cortisol production. For example, in the National Institute of Child Health and Human Development Study of Early Childcare and Youth Development, insensitive maternal parenting in the first 3 years of life predicted lower morning cortisol levels at age 15 (Roisman et al., 2009).

Perhaps some of the most compelling evidence of the role of early attachment in HPA axis function and diurnal cortisol regulation comes from studies of attachment-based parenting interventions, which showed higher morning cortisol and steeper morning-to-evening rhythms in children who received attachment-based interventions compared with control children (Bernard, Dozier, Bick, & Gordon, 2015; Bernard, Hostinar, & Dozier, 2014; Slopen, McLaughlin, & Shonkoff, 2010). These findings suggest that the quality of early attachment relationship and its correlates, such as parental sensitivity, significantly affect stress regulation, as indicated by cortisol secretion patterns and reactivity in infants and children.

25.1.3.3 *Neurodevelopmental Outcomes*
In the past two decades, new evidence has emerged regarding the role of early attachment relationship quality in stress responses, as observed in the developing brain, drawing attention to the brain circuitry underlying the observed behaviors (Coan, 2016; Tang, Reeb-Sutherland, Romeo, & McEwen, 2014). Consistent with a fundamental assumption of developmental psychology, according to which early experiences with one's caregivers "get under the skin" to cause persistent alterations in the organization of the underlying neural circuitry (Gunnar & Quevedo, 2007; Kolb et al., 2012), studies have demonstrated the influence of persistent stressful caregiving environments, on the programming of circuitry underlying emotion processing (Perry, Blair, & Sullivan, 2017).

Specifically, early experiences of stress that occur in association with attachment insecurity influence neural development in sensitive brain regions responsible for emotion encoding and regulation, including the amygdala (Gunnar & Quevedo, 2007; Lupien, McEwen, Gunnar, & Heim, 2009). The amygdala is sensitive to signs of threat (Johansen, Cain, Ostroff, & LeDoux, 2011), and therefore particularly vulnerable to the effects of early caregiving quality. One measure of affective neurodevelopment in the context of attachment and its correlates has been amygdala volume. For example, youths with a history of early parental neglect or little parental caregiving, experiences attesting to insensitive caregiving and typically associated with insecure attachment (Bakermans-Kranenburg, van IJzendoorn, & Juffer, 2003), have exhibited enlarged amygdala volumes (Lupien et al., 2011; Mehta, Cowan, & Cowan, 2009; Tottenham et al., 2010).

Early attachment insecurity has been shown to also influence amygdala function and functional connectivity to the medial prefrontal cortex (mPFC), a brain region highly involved in emotion processing and regulation (Coan & Allen, 2004; Ray & Zald, 2012). For example, insecure infant attachment (as assessed with the SSP) was found to be associated with both greater amygdala volumes (Lyons-Ruth, Pechtel, Yoon, Anderson, & Teicher, 2016; Moutsiana et al., 2015) and emotion regulation processes (Moutsiana et al., 2014; Quevedo et al., 2017) in early adulthood. Taken together, these findings suggests that early experiences with one's caregivers have a lasting effect on brain circuitry long after childhood years, and consequently on psychological and socioemotional functioning later in life (Vantieghem et al., 2017).

25.1.4 Sociocultural Contexts: Universality and Specificity

Bowlby (1969, 1982) suggested that the attachment relationship infants form with their caregivers is the outcome of an innate evolutionary bias. The universality of the infants' bias to become attached, regardless of the cultural niche to which they happen to belong, is a core element of attachment theory. This assumption has been extensively tested and confirmed in North American and European samples, but much fewer studies exist in non-Anglo-Saxon and non-European cultures. Below we briefly present four main universal hypotheses derived from attachment theory, and some evidence of their cross-cultural validity. Of note, all of the studies we present employed standardized methods to assess infant attachment patterns (i.e., SSP and AQS), with the exception of one study (Kermoian & Leiderman, 1986); in this study, a modified SSP was implemented (i.e., one separation–reunion episode with the mother, a nonparental caretaker that is familiar with and responsible for the care of the infant, and a stranger) to better adjust to the multiple caregivers' rearing environment common in the Gusii culture.

Across cultures, attachment security also depends on childrearing antecedents, in particular sensitive and prompt responses to the infants' attachment signals, as the "sensitivity hypothesis" postulates (van IJzendoorn, 1990). In a large sample of 1,150 Asian families living in the United States, with 87% of participants born in Asia, maternal sensitivity showed a significant correlation with infant attachment security (Huang, Lewin, Mitchell, & Zhang, 2012). The sensitivity hypothesis is further confirmed by findings showing a strong correlation between maternal beliefs about the ideal sensitive mother and attachment theory's descriptions of such mothers in 26 cultural groups from 15 countries (Emmen, Malda, Mesman, Ekmekci, & van IJzendoorn, 2012; Mesman et al., 2016).

Furthermore, there is evidence that the rates of contingent responding are rather similar across cultures, but also that responsiveness is channeled through culture-dependent modalities (Kärtner, Keller, & Yovsi, 2010). In some cultures, for example, touching or stroking the infant is considered an appropriate response to vocalization; in others, imitating the sound that the infant made or smiling at the infant would be considered more appropriate (Kärtner et al., 2010; Keller et al., 2009). Similarly, the ways in which infant distress is attended to differ widely across cultures. Soothing by nursing or feeding, for example, is far more common in non-Western than in Western cultures (e.g., Ainsworth et al., 1978; True, Pisani, & Oumar, 2001).

According to the "universality hypothesis" (van IJzendoorn, 1990), all infants without severe neurophysiological impairment become attached to one or more caregivers. The universality hypothesis has received strong support from cross-cultural studies. The three organized attachment patterns – secure, avoidant, and resistant – have been observed in studies conducted in Africa, East Asia, and Latin America, in a variety of samples, including hunter-gatherer societies characterized by high levels of alloparental care, alongside urban environments, both affluent and deprived (Mesman, van IJzendoorn, & Sagi-Schwartz, 2016).

At the same time, when considering the caregiving arrangements, culture-specific patterns and local customs must be taken into account. For example, studies have found securely attached infants attach not only to their mother, but to nonmaternal caregivers as well (Goossens & van IJzendoorn, 1990; Kermoian & Leiderman, 1986; Sagi-Schwartz & Aviezer, 2005; Sagi-Schwartz et al., 1995; van IJzendoorn, Sagi, & Lambermon, 1992). Furthermore, infants' exploration behaviors and their ways of expressing attachment needs have been found to vary depending on cultural norms and customs. Hausa caregivers, for example, generally restrict infants physically in their locomotion. As result, the infants are less free to explore the environment by themselves (Marvin, VanDevender, Iwanaga, LeVine, & LeVine, 1977); instead, they do so in visual and manipulative ways, only when they are close to an attachment figure, and cease to do so as soon as the caregiver leaves. It is clear, however, that Hausa infants use adult caregivers as secure bases from which to explore, and they differentiate between attachment figures and strangers (Marvin et al., 1977).

Attachment theory also predicts that in environments that do not inherently threaten human health and survival, most infants are securely attached. This is known as the "normativity hypothesis" (van IJzendoorn, 1990). There is strong cross-cultural evidence for the normativity hypothesis, and nearly all cross-cultural studies have classified most infants as securely attached (Mesman et al., 2016). But although secure attachment appears to be the norm in most cultures, the rates of secure attachment reported in the studies outside the Anglo-Saxon world and Europe vary. For example, compared to the average secure attachment rates in Western cultures' samples (46%; Bakermans-Kranenburg & van IJzendoorn, 2009), the rates of secure attachments were particularly low in a poor rural Mexican sample (32%; Gojman et al., 2012) and in an undernourished Chilean sample (7%; Valenzuela, 1997). These findings attest to the important role that socioeconomic conditions play in shaping family life and parenting patterns; these findings are consistent with the Family Stress Model, which suggests that unfavorable economic circumstances can be an obstacle to optimal parenting because of parental stress, which has negative effects on child development.

Cross-cultural variations also appear in the distribution of attachment classifications within the insecure category, which may be due to differences in common insensitive parenting practices (Mesman et al., 2016). For example, the insecure-avoidant attachment pattern, which is generally associated with unresponsive parenting, is less prevalent in cultures where highly proximal and indulgent parenting is common. In these cultures, insensitive care is more likely to be intrusive than unavailable, which generally fosters resistant rather than avoidant attachment (Jin, Jacobvitz, Hazen, & Jung, 2012).

Last, according to the "competence hypothesis" (van IJzendoorn, 1990), infant secure attachment leads to positive child outcomes in a variety of developmental domains. A study conducted among the Gusii tribe (Kermoian & Leiderman, 1986) found that the nutritional status of the secure infants was better than that of the insecure ones, a result replicated in Chile with undernourished infants (Valenzuela, 1997). Despite the remarkable finding of an association between attachment and health status, the cause–effect relation between attachment security and nutritional status is not entirely conclusive. It is not unreasonable to assume that healthier infants induce more care in general, and in particular more sensitive care, especially if economic deprivation compels parents to be selective in their investment of time and energy (Finerman, 1995).

In sum, cross-cultural attachment research suggests that the attachment phenomenon is universal in nature, and at the same time that its universal characteristics may manifest in unique ways depending on the cultural norms. Universality and specificity of attachment patterns across cultures are both essential constituents of attachment theory, attesting to its cross-cultural validity. More research is needed in populous countries such as India, Islamic countries, and large parts of Africa, Asia, and Latin America to fully characterize the contextual components and universalist aspects of the attachment phenomenon.

25.2 One Infant, Two Caregivers

25.2.1 Infant Attachment Network to Mother *and* Father: An Unsettled Issue

Although researchers have long recognized the important role both parents play in their children's upbringing and development, most studies were based on the underlying assumption that there is a primary attachment figure, usually the mother. In recent decades, however, expectations concerning gender roles and parenting have changed the normative patterns of early childhood care, which nowadays often involves both parents to various degrees (Cabrera, Volling, & Barr, 2018). This has resulted in the inclusion of fathers in infant attachment theory and research (Bretherton, 2010), which in turn has stimulated research focusing on early attachment patterns to both parents. Because many children are raised by both mothers and fathers, assessing attachment patterns to both parents rather than examining the effects of a single attachment relationship can provide a more ecologically valid understanding of the individual's developmental trajectory (Belsky, 1981).

About a quarter of a century ago, van IJzendoorn et al. (1992) addressed the issue of infants' independent attachment relationships with mothers and fathers, and raised the following question: Given that infants form simultaneously independent attachments to mothers and fathers (Easterbrooks & Goldberg, 1984; Grossmann et al., 2002; Grossmann, Grossman, Huber, & Wartner, 1981; Main & Weston, 1981; Sagi-Schwartz & Aviezer, 2005), how can infant attachment *to only one caregiver*, usually the mother, predict developmental outcomes? Several studies have assessed the degree to which two early parental attachment relationships act *jointly* to influence developmental outcomes (known in the literature as "the integrative hypothesis;" van IJzendoorn et al., 1992). These studies sought to extend the scope of attachment theory to include cultures in which children are raised by more than one caregiver, and to enhance the predictive power of early attachment patterns on later outcomes, which was shown to be modest in size when assessed with only one caregiver.

To shed light on the role that infants' attachment to mothers and fathers jointly plays in predicting developmental outcomes, the authors (Dagan & Sagi-Schwartz, 2018) reviewed the published work in the field and assessed the four possible attachment configurations: infants who are insecure with both mother and father (I-I), secure with mother and insecure with father (S_M-I_F), insecure with mother and secure with father (I_M-S_F), and secure with both mother and father (S-S). They identified two main questions that call for further assessment, framed them as empirical questions, and based on this empirical evidence, offered two competing hypotheses presented as potential answers to each issue (Figure 25.1).

The first question is: *Does the number of secure attachments matter in predicting developmental outcomes, or is one secure attachment sufficient for optimal development?* Some studies suggest that the integration of the infant's parental attachment patterns is best described by what the authors term the *additive hypothesis.* According to this hypothesis, a linear correlation exists between the number of secure attachment patterns and developmental outcomes, so that a larger number of secure relationships formed by an infant results in better developmental outcomes. The additive hypothesis draws support from studies showing that infants who are securely attached to both parents have the best outcomes, followed by those who are securely attached to only one parent, and finally by those who are insecurely attached to both parents. For example, infants who were securely attached to both parents were more ready (or less inhibited) to engage positively with an unfamiliar person in a clown costume at age 12 months (Main & Weston, 1981), and to resolve conflicts more autonomously during play with peers at age 5 (Suess, Grossmann, & Sroufe, 1992), than were infants who were securely attached to only one parent. Infants who exhibited more secure patterns of parental attachment also scored higher on socioemotional (preschool peer play behavior) and cognitive (IQ index) outcomes (Sagi-Schwartz & Aviezer, 2005; van IJzendoorn et al., 1992).

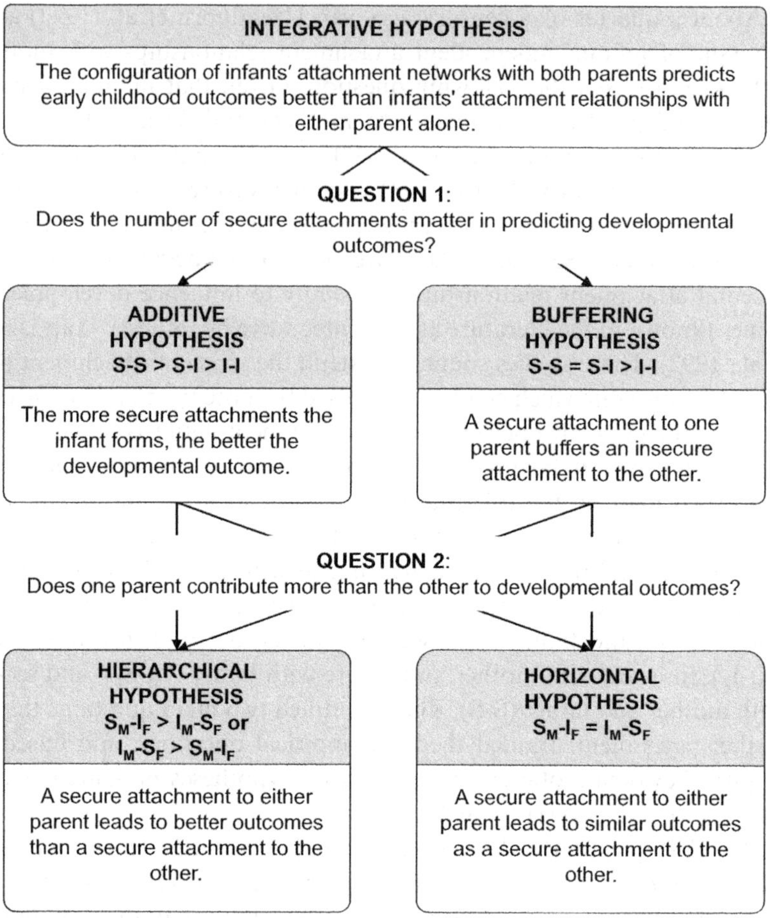

Figure 25.1. *Four competing hypotheses ordered according to the issue they address.*

Note: S-S = secure with mother and father; I-I = insecure with mother and father; S_M = secure with mother; S_F = secure with father; I_M = insecure with mother; I_F = insecure with father.

Source: Based on Dagan and Sagi-Schwartz (2018).

Other studies, however, support what the authors term the *buffering hypothesis*, according to which early secure attachment to one parent offsets the risks posed by insecure attachment to the other. Some studies have shown that the developmental outcomes of infants who are securely attached to only one parent are not worse than those of infants who are securely attached to both parents, and both types of infants have significantly better outcomes than those who are insecurely attached to both parents. For example, infants who were securely attached to only one parent showed as little internalizing and externalizing behaviors as those who were securely attached to both parents, and less than infants who were insecurely attached to both parents (Kochanska & Kim, 2013; Suess et al., 1992).

To reach a more nuanced description of the differences between infants who are securely attached only to their mothers and those who are securely attached only to their fathers the authors formulated a second question regarding the infant attachment network to mother and father: *Does one parent contribute more than the other to developmental outcomes, or do they matter equally?* This question gains expression in the *hierarchical hypothesis* (Bowlby, 1969; Bretherton, 1985; van IJzendoorn et al., 1992), according to which one parent influences the developmental outcomes of the child more than the other. Studies supporting this hypothesis (Main & Weston, 1981; Suess et al., 1992) found that infants who were securely attached only to their mothers were more ready (or less inhibited) to engage positively with a stranger in a clown costume at age 12 months than were infants who were securely attached only to their fathers, and resolved conflicts with other children more autonomously at age 5 than did children who as infants were securely attached only to their fathers.

By contrast, what the authors termed the *horizontal hypothesis* suggests that infants with secure attachment to either parent have developmental outcomes similar to those with secure attachment to the other parent. Some studies supporting this hypothesis reported that children who had only one secure attachment in infancy, to either their fathers or their mothers, exhibited a similar degree of externalizing behaviors at age 8 (Kochanska & Kim, 2013), and comparable severity of abnormal behaviors at age 5 (Suess et al., 1992).

For future research, the authors (Dagan & Sagi-Schwartz, 2018) proposed to combine the two pairs of dichotomized hypotheses (additive vs. buffering and hierarchical vs. horizontal) into four mutually exclusive models that capture the various relations between the attachment network configurations: *additive-hierarchical, additive-horizontal, buffering-hierarchical*, and *buffering-horizontal* (Table 25.1). Each model offers predictions that simultaneously answer the two questions raised earlier, and each model explains one or more outcomes, but no two models explain the same outcome.

To conclude, little attention has been paid to the integrative effect of attachment relationships to both mothers and fathers on developmental outcomes, and the question has remained unanswered for a long time (Thompson, 2000; Thompson & Raikes, 2003). The authors propose an organizational framework from which investigators can embark on research to inform and expand attachment theory and research, toward a better understanding of the role of early attachment relationships in individuals' development. Early infant network of attachment models may function as more complex, more thoroughly elaborated, and more ecologically valid predictors of developmental outcomes than the ones that have been conceptually and empirically formulated. In addition, understanding infant attachment as part of an attachment network may broaden the scope of attachment theory to include non-Westernized cultures in which a common rearing practice includes nonparental caregivers (e.g., grandparents, siblings, and other relatives).

25.3 Implications of Attachment Theory and Research on Practice and Public Policy

Attachment research continues to grow and develop in multiple and promising directions. But similar to other clinical scientific theories, it bears little significance if it does not seek to influence public policy; if attachment theory and research advance the understanding of the crucial role that early infant–parent interactions play in the individual's physiological and psychological well-being, one must consider the ways in which this knowledge may be disseminated through channels that are readily accessible to those in need.

Attachment research has clearly established the importance for child development of the early experiences of infants with their parents. Yet, many parents enter parenthood without sufficient understanding of the importance of sensitive and responsive caregiving for the development of a healthy child (Cassidy et al., 2013). It is important that researchers and practitioners work together to develop future parent curricula that can be implemented as part of high school and university education. Although there are several empirically supported parent training programs based on attachment research (Berlin, Zeanah, & Lieberman, 2016), they are yet to be made a part of general education.

In addition, many parents are struggling to balance work and family responsibilities, and to find quality care for their children while they are at work. There is a need, therefore, to develop policies that will ensure high standards of group care. It has been well established that the quality of early group care matters, and that low-quality settings produce negative developmental outcomes (Love et al., 2003; Sagi, Koren-Karie, Gini, Ziv, & Joels, 2002). There is also a need to formulate family policies that would enable more flexible work arrangements that recognize childcare as a prime societal concern. This includes reexamination of parental leave policies that often require parents to return to work too soon after childbirth, either because of company policy or because of financial necessity (for a review of family policies in various countries, see Robila, 2014).

In some extreme cases, such as child maltreatment, children are removed from their biological parents by the welfare system, and placed in out-of-home group care arrangements. In both small and large group settings, also known as institutionalized care settings, forming secure attachment with a caregiver is significantly less likely than in all other home-based settings (Ahnert, Pinquart, & Lamb, 2006; Dozier, Zeanah, Wallin, & Shauffer, 2012). A secure attachment with at least one parental figure during the first year of life is not only possible in nonparental, family-based arrangements such as foster care and adoption (Raby & Dozier, 2018; van den Dries, Juffer, van IJzendoorn, & Bakermans-Kranenburg, 2009), but is also crucial in reducing and even preventing problematic behaviors and interpersonal difficulties (Dobrova-Krol, Bakermans-Kranenburg, van IJzendoorn, & Juffer, 2010; McLaughlin, Zeanah, Fox, & Nelson, 2012).

In this regard, a consensus statement on group care for children and adolescents, which has been endorsed as a statement of policy by the American

Table 25.1 *Model-based outcome predictions*

Integrative model	Prediction[a]	Brief description
(a) Additive-hierarchical	$S\text{-}S > S_M\text{-}I_F > I_M\text{-}S_F > I\text{-}I$ OR $S\text{-}S > I_M\text{-}S_F > S_M\text{-}I_F > I\text{-}I$	Secure attachment to only one parent (but not the other) leads to better outcomes than insecure attachment to both parents, but poorer outcomes than secure attachment to both parents
(b) Additive-horizontal	$S\text{-}S > S_M\text{-}I_F = I_M\text{-}S_F > I\text{-}I$	Secure attachment to either parent (but not the other) leads to better outcomes than insecure attachment to both parents, but poorer outcomes than secure attachment to both parents
(c) Buffering-hierarchical	$S\text{-}S = S_M\text{-}I_F > I_M\text{-}S_F > I\text{-}I$ OR $S\text{-}S = I_M\text{-}S_F > S_M\text{-}I_F > I\text{-}I$	Secure attachment to only one parent (but not the other) leads to as good outcomes as secure attachment to both parents
(d) Buffering-horizontal	$S\text{-}S = S_M\text{-}I_F = I_M\text{-}S_F > I\text{-}I$	Secure attachment to either parent (but not the other) leads to as good outcomes as secure attachment to both parents, all better than insecure attachment to both parents

[a] All models assume that the I-I group has poorer outcomes than the other three configuration groups.

Note: Greater than symbols represent better developmental outcomes. S-S = secure with mother and father; I-I = insecure with mother and father; S_M = secure with mother; S_F = secure with father; I_M = insecure with mother; I_F = insecure with father.
Source: Adapted from Dagan and Sagi-Schwartz (2018).

Orthopsychiatric Association, declared that due to its inherent detrimental effects on the development of children, group care should be used only when therapeutic mental health services cannot be delivered in a less restrictive setting (Dozier, Kaufman et al., 2014). Supporting the consensus statement on group care for children is a large body of literature showing that group care has harmful effects on the development of young children (Dozier et al., 2012). Negative outcomes include structural and functional brain abnormalities (Nelson III, Bos, Gunnar, & Sonuga-Barke, 2011), vulnerability to attachment disturbances, and lasting clinical disorders of attachment (e.g., reactive attachment disorder and disinhibited social engagement disorder; Nelson, Fox, &

Zeanah, 2014; Rutter et al., 2007; Zeanah & Gleason, 2015; Zeanah, Smyke, & Dumitrescu, 2002). By contrast, placement in adoptive or foster families has been shown to be the optimal solution for children at risk of suffering from the harming effects of abusive caregiving or lack of parental availability. Such placement has been reported to lead to the formation of secure attachments (Smyke, Zeanah, Fox, Nelson, & Guthrie, 2010) and reduced likelihood to experience subsequent psychopathology or problematic peer relations (Dobrova-Krol et al., 2010; McLaughlin et al., 2012).

Another childcare policy matter of considerable importance pertains to the issue of an increasing number of children who grow up with divorced parents (McIntosh, 2011). Among a host of issues arising with regard to optimal post-divorce parental practices, one question that is strongly tied to attachment theory and research is whether young children should spend post-divorce time (including overnights) predominantly in the care of the same parent (usually the mother) or divided more evenly between the two parents. Given the evidence we present in the previous section of this chapter, according to which infants develop independent attachment relationship with both parents, it is reasonable to expect that post-divorce practices should include both parents, to the extent that this is possible (i.e., that both parents are deemed reasonably adept in child-rearing practicing). In the case of infants who may still be in the process of developing attachment relationships with their parents, continuing post-divorce relationships with two parents increases their chances of developing at least one secure attachment, known to lead to better developmental outcomes than having no secure attachment relationships with either parent. Furthermore, depriving young children of overnights with their fathers leads to dissatisfaction regarding the amount of post-divorce contact they have with their fathers (Hetherington & Kelly, 2002; Kelly, 2012; Warshak & Santrock, 1983), and may also compromise the quality of developing father–child relationship (Fabricius & Luecken, 2007; Warshak, 2014).

Based on the available albeit not robust research on the subject, a consensus statement endorsed by 110 international experts from various countries called for policy making that would enforce consistent day and night parental availability of both parents in the child's life after divorce (Warshak, 2014). To maintain high-quality, secure attachment relationships with their children, parents must have regular interaction with them (e.g., bedtime and waking rituals, transitions to and from school, and extracurricular and recreational activities; Lamb, Sternberg, & Thompson, 1997). The degree to which these child–parent interactions are accomplished, however, should be flexibly tailored to the various needs and circumstances of the child concerned, including implementing appropriate intervention in the case of an insecure child–parent attachment relationship (rather than restricting the development of this relationship).

Finally, attachment theory has also inspired the clinical arena and the field of intervention to aid children and families that are exposed to adversity (for a review of attachment-based interventions, see Steele & Steele, 2018). To date, various attachment-based interventions designed to target the quality of high-risk child–parent interactions, such as Attachment and Biobehavioral Catch-up (ABC; Dozier, Meade, & Bernard, 2014) and Circle of Security (Marvin, Cooper, Hoffman, & Powell, 2002), have shown to be effective in increasing parental sensitivity, leading to enhanced attachment security (Bakermans-Kranenburg et al., 2003; Facompré, Bernard, & Waters, 2017). In integrating such interventions into common clinical practice, especially with children who are exposed to high levels of environmental stress and are at risk of poor social, academic, and mental health outcomes, it is necessary to ensure that children receive the best parental caregiving possible, which would establish them early on a healthy developmental path.

The growing number of evidence-based interventions that have been shown to improve outcomes for children in the child welfare system (Fisher, Gunnar, Dozier, Bruce, & Pears, 2006; Steele & Steele, 2018) underscores the compelling need to expand child protection from its traditional narrowed concern with physical safety and custody, to include a broader focus on the emotional, social, and cognitive costs of maltreatment. Early implementation of such clinical interventions will substantially add to the current effort to change the health care system from an acute sick-care model to a preventative well-care model (Shonkoff et al., 2012). By following this approach, the origins of deleterious developmental outcomes, including insecure and disorganized infant–caregiver attachment relationships and their correlates, can be identified and addressed early in life rather than treated later, promoting the well-being of children and setting them on a healthy trajectory for adulthood.

References

Ahnert, L., Pinquart, M., & Lamb, M. E. (2006). Security of children's relationships with nonparental care providers: A meta-analysis. *Child Development, 74*(3), 664–679. https://doi.org/10.1111/j.1467-8624.2006.00896.x

Ainsworth, M. D. S., Blehar, S., Waters, E., & Wall, S. (1978). *Patterns of attachment: A psychological study of the strange situation.* Hillsdale, NJ: Lawrence Erlbaum Associates.

Aviezer, O., Sagi, A., Resnick, G., & Gini, M. (2002). School competence in young adolescence: Links to early attachment relationships beyond concurrent self-perceived competence and representations of relationships. *International Journal of Behavioral Development, 26*(5), 397–409. https://doi.org/10.1080/01650250143000328

Bakermans-Kranenburg, M. J., & van IJzendoorn, M. H. (2009). The first 10,000 adult attachment interviews: Distributions of adult attachment representations in clinical and non-clinical groups. *Attachment & Human Development, 11*(3), 223–263. https://doi.org/10.1080/14616730902814762

(2016). Attachment, parenting, and genetics. In P. Cassidy, J & Shaver (Ed.), *Handbook of attachment: Theory, research, and clinical applications* (3rd ed., pp. 155–179). New York, NY: Guilford Press.

Bakermans-Kranenburg, M. J., van IJzendoorn, M. H., & Juffer, F. (2003). Less is more: Meta-analyses of sensitivity and attachment interventions in early childhood. *Psychological Bulletin, 129*(2), 195–215. https://doi.org/10.1037/0033-2909.129.2.195

Belsky, J. (1981). Early human experience: A family perspective. *Developmental Psychology, 17*(1), 3–23. https://doi.org/10.1037/0012-1649.17.1.3

(2002). Developmental origins of attachment styles. *Attachment and Human Development, 4*(2), 166–170. https://doi.org/10.1080/1461673021015751

Berlin, L. J., Zeanah, C. H., & Lieberman, A. F. (2016). Prevention and intervention programs for supporting early attachment security: A move to the level of the community. In J. Cassidy & P. R. Shaver (Eds.), *Handbook of attachment: Theory, research, and clinical applications* (3rd ed., pp. 739–758). New York, NY: Guilford Press.

Bernard, K., Butzin-Dozier, Z., Rittenhouse, J., & Dozier, M. (2010). Cortisol production patterns in young children living with birth parents vs children placed in foster care following involvement of child protective services. *Archives of Pediatrics & Adolescent Medicine, 164*(5), 438–43. https://doi.org/10.1001/archpediatrics.2010.54

Bernard, K., & Dozier, M. (2010). Examining infants' cortisol responses to laboratory tasks among children varying in attachment disorganization: Stress reactivity or return to baseline? *Developmental Psychology, 46*(6), 1771–1778. https://doi.org/10.1037/a0020660

Bernard, K., Dozier, M., Bick, J., & Gordon, M. K. (2015). Intervening to enhance cortisol regulation among children at risk for neglect: Results of a randomized clinical trial. *Development and Psychopathology, 27*(3), 829–841. https://doi.org/10.1017/S095457941400073X

Bernard, K., Hostinar C. E., & Dozier M. (2014). Intervention effects on diurnal cortisol rhythms of child protective services-referred infants in early childhood: Preschool follow-up results of a randomized clinical trial. *JAMA Pediatrics, 169*(2), 112–119. https://doi.org/10.1001/jamapediatrics.2014.2369w

Bokhorst, C. L., Bakermans-Kranenburg, M. J., Fearon, R. M. P., van IJzendoorn, M. H., Fonagy, P., & Schuengel, C. (2003). The importance of shared environment in mother–infant attachment security: A behavioral genetic study. *Child Development, 74*(6), 1769–1782. https://doi.org/10.1046/j.1467-8624.2003.00637.x

Bowlby, J. (1953). *Child care and the growth of love.* Baltimore, MD: Pelican Books.

(1969). *Attachment and loss. Vol. 1: Attachment.* New York, NY: Basic Books.

(1973). *Attachment and loss. Vol. 2: Separation.* New York, NY: Basic Books.

(1979). *The making and breaking of affectional bonds.* London: Tavistock.

(1980). *Attachment and loss. Vol. 3: Loss, sadness and depression.* New York, NY: Basic Books.

(1982). Attachment and loss: Retrospect and prospect. *American Journal of Orthopsychiatry, 52*(4), 664–678. https://doi.org/10.1111/j.1939-0025.1982.tb01456.x

(1988). *A secure base: Parent–child attachment and healthy human development.* New York, NY: Basic Books.

Bretherton, I. (1985). Attachment theory: Retrospect and prospect. *Monographs of the Society for Research in Child Development, 50*(1–2), 3–35. https://doi.org/http://dx.doi.org.libproxy.newschool.edu/10.2307/3333824

(1991). Pouring new wine into old bottles: The social self as internal working model. In M. R. Gunnar & L. A. Sroufe (Eds.), *Minnesota symposia in child psychology: Self processes in development* (pp. 1–41). Hillsdale, NJ: Lawrence Erlbaum Associates.

(2010). Fathers in attachment theory and research: A review. *Early Child Development and Care, 180*(1/2), 9–23. https://doi.org/10.1080/03004430903414661

Bruce, J., Fisher, P. A., Pears, K. C., & Levine, S. (2009). Morning cortisol levels in preschool-aged foster children: Differential effects of maltreatment type. *Developmental Psychobiology, 51*(1), 14–23. https://doi.org/10.1002/dev.20333

Cabrera, N. J., Volling, B. L., & Barr, R. (2018). Fathers are parents, too! Widening the lens on parenting for children's development. *Child Development Perspectives, 12*(3), 152–157. https://doi.org/10.1111/cdep.12275

Callaghan, B. L., & Tottenham, N. (2016a). The neuro-environmental loop of plasticity: A cross-species analysis of parental effects on emotion circuitry development following typical and adverse caregiving. *Neuropsychopharmacology, 41*(1), 163–176. https://doi.org/10.1038/npp.2015.204

(2016b). The stress acceleration hypothesis: Effects of early-life adversity on emotion circuits and behavior. *Current Opinion in Behavioral Sciences, 7*, 76–81. https://doi.org/10.1016/j.cobeha.2015.11.018

Carlson, M., & Earls, F. (1997). Psychological and neuroendocrinological sequelae of early social deprivation in institutionalized children in Romania. *Annals of the New York Academy of Sciences, 807*, 419–28.

Casement, M. D., Guyer, A. E., Hipwell, A. E., McAloon, R. L., Hoffmann, A. M., Keenan, K. E., & Forbes, E. E. (2014). Girls' challenging social experiences in early adolescence predict neural response to rewards and depressive symptoms. *Developmental Cognitive Neuroscience, 8*, 18–27. https://doi.org/10.1016/j.dcn.2013.12.003

Cassidy, J., & Berlin, L. J. (1994). The insecure/ambivalent pattern of attachment: Theory and research. *Child Development, 65*(4), 971–991. https://doi.org/10.2307/1131298

Cassidy, J., Jones, J. D., & Shaver, P. R. (2013). Contributions of attachment theory and research: A framework for future research, translation, and policy. *Development and Psychopathology, 25*, 1415–1434. https://doi.org/10.1017/S0954579413000692

Cassidy, J., & Kobak, R. (1988). Avoidance and its relation to other defensive processes. In J. Belsky & T. Nezworski (Eds.), *Clinical implications of attachment theory* (pp. 300–323). Hillsdale, NJ: Lawrence Erlbaum Associates.

Cassidy, J., & Shaver, P. R. (Eds.). (2016). *Handbook of attachment: Theory, research, and clinical applications* (3rd ed.). New York, NY: Guilford Press.

Coan, J. A. (2016). Toward a neuroscience of attachment. In J. Cassidy & P. R. Shaver (Eds.), *Handbook of attachment: Theory, research and clinical applications* (pp. 242–269). New York, NY: Guilford Press.

Coan, J. A., & Allen, J. J. B. (2004). Frontal EEG asymmetry as a moderator and mediator of emotion. *Biological Psychology, 67*(1–2), 7–49. https://doi.org/10.1016/j.biopsycho.2004.03.002

Conger, R. D., & Donnellan, M. B. (2007). An interactionist perspective on the socioeconomic context of human development. *Annual Review of Psychology, 58*(1), 175–199. https://doi.org/10.1146/annurev.psych.58.110405.085551

Cyr, C., Euser, E. M., Bakermans-Kranenburg, M. J., & van IJzendoorn, M. H. (2010). Attachment security and disorganization in maltreating and high-risk families: A series of meta-analyses. *Development and Psychopathology*, *22*(1), 87–108. https://doi.org/10.1017/S0954579409990289

Dagan, O., & Sagi-Schwartz, A. (2018). Early attachment network with mother and father: An unsettled issue. *Child Development Perspectives*, *12*(2), 115–121. https://doi.org/10.1111/cdep.12272

Dobrova-Krol, N. A., Bakermans-Kranenburg, M. J., van IJzendoorn, M. H., & Juffer, F. (2010). The importance of quality of care: Effects of perinatal HIV infection and early institutional rearing on preschoolers' attachment and indiscriminate friendliness. *Journal of Child Psychology and Psychiatry and Allied Disciplines*, *51*(12), 1368–1376. https://doi.org/10.1111/j.1469-7610.2010.02243.x

Dozier, M., Kaufman, J., Kobak, R., O'Connor, T. G., Sagi-Schwartz, A., Scott, S., … Zeanah, C. H. (2014). Consensus statement on group care for children and adolescents: A statement of policy of the American Orthopsychiatric Association. *American Journal of Orthopsychiatry*, *84*(3), 219–225. https://doi.org/10.1037/ort0000005

Dozier, M., Meade, E. B., & Bernard, K. (2014). Attachment and biobehavioral catch-up: An intervention for parents at risk of maltreating their infants and toddlers. In S. Timmer & A. Urquiza (Eds.), *Evidence-based approaches for the treatment of child maltreatment* (pp. 43–59). New York, NY: Springer.

Dozier, M., Zeanah, C. H., Wallin, A. R., & Shauffer, C. (2012). Institutional care for young children: Review of literature and policy implications. *Social Issues and Policy Review*, *6*(1), 1–25. https://doi.org/10.1111/j.1751-2409.2011.01033.x.Institutional

Easterbrooks, M. A., & Goldberg, W. A. (1984). Toddler development in the family: Impact of father involvement and parenting characteristics. *Child Development*, *55*(3), 740–52. https://doi.org/10.2307/1130126

Emmen, R. A. G., Malda, M., Mesman, J., Ekmekci, H., & van IJzendoorn, M. H. (2012). Sensitive parenting as a cross-cultural ideal: Sensitivity beliefs of Dutch, Moroccan, and Turkish mothers in the Netherlands. *Attachment and Human Development*, *14*(6), 601–619. https://doi.org/10.1080/14616734.2012.727258

Fabricius, W. V., & Luecken, L. J. (2007). Post-divorce living arrangements, parent conflict, and long-term physical health correlates for children of divorce. *Journal of Family Psychology*, *21*(2), 195–205. https://doi.org/10.1007/s11837-018-3024-8

Facompré, C. R., Bernard, K., & Waters, T. E. A. (2017). Effectiveness of interventions in preventing disorganized attachment: A meta-analysis. *Development and Psychopathology*, *30*(1), 1–11. https://doi.org/10.1017/S0954579417000426

Fearon, R. M. P., Bakermans-Kranenburg, M. J., van IJzendoorn, M. H., Lapsley, A.-M., & Roisman, G. I. (2010). The significance of insecure attachment and disorganization in the development of children's externalizing behavior: A meta-analytic study. *Child Development*, *81*(2), 435–456. https://doi.org/10.1111/j.1467-8624.2009.01405.x

Fearon, R. M. P., & Belsky, J. (2016). Precursors of attachment security. In J. Cassidy & P. R. Shaver (Eds.), *Handbook of attachment: Theory, research and clinical applications* (3rd ed., pp. 291–313). New York, NY: Guilford.

Fearon, R. M. P., & Roisman, G. I. (2017). Attachment theory: Progress and future directions. *Current Opinion in Psychology*, *15*, 131–136. https://doi.org/10.1016/j.copsyc.2017.03.002

Fearon, R. M. P., van IJzendoorn, M. H., Fonagy, P., Bakermans-Kranenburg, M. J., Schuengel, C., & Bokhorst, C. L. (2006). In search of shared and nonshared environmental factors in security of attachment: A behavior-genetic study of the association between sensitivity and attachment security. *Developmental Psychology*, *42*(6), 1026–1040. https://doi.org/10.1037/0012-1649.42.6.1026

Feeney, J. A. (2008). Adult romantic attachment: Developments in the study of couple relationship. In J. Cassidy & P. R. Shaver (Eds.), *Handbook of attachment: Theory, research and clinical applications* (pp. 456–481). New York, NY: Guilford Press.

Finerman, R. (1995). "Parental incompetence" and "selective neglect": Blaming the victim in child survival. *Social Science and Medicine*, *40*(1), 5–13. https://doi.org/10.1016/0277-9536(94)00122-A

Fisher, P. A., Gunnar, M. R., Dozier, M., Bruce, J., & Pears, K. C. (2006). Effects of therapeutic interventions for foster children on behavioral problems, caregiver attachment, and stress regulatory neural systems. *Annals of the New York Academy of Sciences*, *1094*, 215–225. https://doi.org/10.1196/annals.1376.023

Gee, D. G., Gabard-Durnam, L. J., Flannery, J., Goff, B., Humphreys, K. L., Telzer, E. H., … Tottenham, N. (2013). Early developmental emergence of human amygdala-prefrontal connectivity after maternal deprivation. *Proceedings of the National Academy of Sciences of the United States of America*, *110*(39), 15638–15643. https://doi.org/10.1073/pnas.1307893110/-/DCSupplemental.www.pnas.org/cgi/doi/10.1073/pnas.1307893110

Gee, D. G., Gabard-Durnam, L., Telzer, E. H., Humphreys, K. L., Goff, B., Shapiro, M., … Caldera, C. (2014). Maternal buffering of human amygdala-prefrontal circuitry during childhood but not during adolescence. *Psychological Science*, *25*(11), 2067–2078. https://doi.org/10.1177/0956797614550878.Maternal

Gojman, S., Millán, S., Carlson, E., Sánchez, G., Rodarte, A., González, P., & Hernández, G. (2012). Intergenerational relations of attachment: A research synthesis of urban/rural Mexican samples. *Attachment & Human Development*, *14*(6), 553–566. https://doi.org/10.1080/14616734.2012.727255

Goossens, A., & van IJzendoorn, M. H. (1990). Quality of infants' attachments to professional caregivers: Relation to infant–parent attachment and day-care characteristics. *Child Development*, *61*(3), 832–837. https://doi.org/10.2307/1130967

Groh, A. M., Fearon, R. P., Bakermans-Kranenburg, M. J., van IJzendoorn, M. H., Steele, R. D., & Roisman, G. I. (2014). The significance of attachment security for children's social competence with peers: A meta-analytic study. *Attachment & Human Development*, *16*(2), 103–136. https://doi.org/10.1080/14616734.2014.883636

Groh, A. M., Fearon, R. M. P., van IJzendoorn, M. H., Bakermans-Kranenburg, M. J., & Roisman, G. I. (2016). Attachment in the early life course: Meta-analytic evidence for its role in socioemotional development. *Child Development Perspectives*, *11*(1), 70–76. https://doi.org/10.1111/cdep.12213

Groh, A. M., Roisman, G. I., van IJzendoorn, M. H., Bakermans-Kranenburg, M. J., & Fearon, R. P. (2012). The significance of insecure and disorganized attachment for children's internalizing symptoms: A meta-analytic study. *Child Development*, *83*(2), 591–610. https://doi.org/10.1111/j.1467-8624.2011.01711.x

Grossmann, K., Grossmann, K. E., Fremmer-Bombik, E., Kindler, H., Scheuerer-Englisch, H., & Zimmermann, P. (2002). The uniqueness of the child–father attachment relationship: Fathers' sensitive and challenging play as a pivotal variable in a 16-year longitudinal study. *Social Development, 11*(3), 307–331. https://doi.org/10.1111/1467–9507.00202

Grossmann, K. E., Grossmann, K., Huber, F., & Wartner, U. (1981). German children's behavior towards their mothers at 12 months and their fathers at 18 months in Ainsworth's Strange Situation. *International Journal of Behavioral Development, 4,* 157–181.

Gunnar, M. R., & Hostinar, C. E. (2015). The social buffering of the hypothalamic-pituitary-adrenocortical axis in humans: Developmental and experiential determinants. *Social Neuroscience, 10*(5), 479–488. https://doi.org/10.1080/17470919.2015.1070747

Gunnar, M. R., & Quevedo, K. (2007). The neurobiology of stress and development. *Annual Review of Psychology, 58,* 145–173. https://doi.org/10.1146/annurev.psych.58.110405.085605

Gunnar, M. R., & Vazquez, D. (2006). Stress neurobiology and developmental psychopathology. In D. Cicchetti & D. J. Cohen (Eds.), *Developmental psychopathology: Developmental neuroscience* (pp. 533–577). Hoboken, NJ: John Wiley & Sons.

Hesse, E., & Main, M. (2006). Frightened, threatening, and dissociative parental behavior: Theory and associations with parental adult attachment interview status and infant disorganization. *Development and Psychopathology, 18,* 309–343. https://doi.org/10.1017/S0954579406060172

Hetherington, E. M., & Kelly, J. (2002). *For better or for worse: Divorce reconsidered.* New York, NY: Norton.

Holland, A. S., & Roisman, G. I. (2010). Adult attachment security and young adults' dating relationships over time: Self-reported, observational, and physiological evidence. *Developmental Psychology, 46*(2), 552–557. https://doi.org/10.1037/a0018542

Huang, Z. J., Lewin, A., Mitchell, S. J., & Zhang, J. (2012). Variations in the relationship between maternal depression, maternal sensitivity, and child attachment by race/ethnicity and nativity: Findings from a nationally representative Cohort study. *Maternal and Child Health Journal, 16*(1), 40–50. https://doi.org/10.1007/s10995-010-0716-2

Jin, M. K., Jacobvitz, D., Hazen, N., & Jung, S. H. (2012). Maternal sensitivity and infant attachment security in Korea: Cross-cultural validation of the strange situation. *Attachment & Human Development, 14*(1), 33–44. https://doi.org/10.1080/14616734.2012.636656

Johansen, J. P., Cain, C. K., Ostroff, L. E., & LeDoux, J. E. (2011). Molecular mechanisms of fear learning and Mmemory. *Cell, 147*(3), 509–524. https://doi.org/10.1016/j.cell.2011.10.009

Kärtner, J., Keller, H., & Yovsi, R. D. (2010). Mother–infant interaction during the first 3 months: The emergence of culture-specific contingency patterns. *Child Development, 81*(2), 540–554. https://doi.org/10.1111/j.1467-8624.2009.01414.x

Keller, H., Borke, J., Staufenbiel, T., Yovsi, R. D., Abels, M., Papaligoura, Z., … Su, Y. (2009). Distal and proximal parenting as alternative parenting strategies during infants' early months of life: A cross-cultural study. *International*

Journal of Behavioral Development, 33(5), 412–420. https://doi.org/10.1177/0165025409338441

Kelly, J. B. (2012). Risk and protective factors associated with child and adolescent adjustment following separation and divorce: Social science applications. In K. Kuehnle & L. Drozd (Eds.), *Parenting plan evaluations: Applied research for the family courts* (pp. 49–84). New York, NY: Oxford University Press.

Kermoian, R., & Leiderman, P. H. (1986). Infant attachment to mother and child caretaker in an East African community. *International Journal of Behavioral Development, 9*(4), 455–469.

Kochanska, G., & Kim, S. (2013). Early attachment organization with both parents and future behavior problems: From infancy to middle childhood. *Child Development, 84*(1), 283–296. https://doi.org/10.1111/j.1467-8624.2012.01852.x

Kolb, B., Mychasiuk, R., Muhammad, A., Li, Y., Frost, D. O., & Gibb, R. (2012). Experience and the developing prefrontal cortex. *Proceedings of the National Academy of Sciences, 109*(Suppl. 2), 17186–17193. https://doi.org/10.1073/pnas.1121251109

Lamb, M. E., Sternberg, K. J., & Thompson, R. A. (1997). The effects of divorce and custody arrangements on children's behavior, development, and adjustment. *Family and Conciliation Courts Review, 35*(4), 393–404.

Larson, M. C., White, B. P., Cochran, A., Donzella, B., & Gunnar, M. (1998). Dampening of the cortisol response to handling at 3 months in human infants and its relation to sleep, circadian cortisol activity, and behavioral distress. *Developmental Psychobiology, 33*(4), 327–337. https://doi.org/10.1002/(SICI)1098-2302(199812)33:4<327::AID-DEV4>3.0.CO;2-S

Love, J., Harrison, L., Sagi-Schwartz, A., van IJzendoorn, M., Ross, C., Ungerer, J., … Chazan-Cohen, R. (2003). Child care quality matters: How conclusions may vary with context. *Child Development, 74*(4), 1021–1033. https://doi.org/10.1111/1467-8624.00584

Luijk, M. P. C., Roisman, G. I., Haltigan, J. D., Henning, T., Booth-LaForce, C., van IJzendoorn, M. H., … Bakermans-Kranenburg, M. J. (2012). Dopaminergic, serotonergic, and oxytonergic candidate genes associated with infant attachment security and disorganization? In search of main and interaction effects. *Journal of Child Psychology and Psychiatry, 52*(12), 1295–1307. https://doi.org/10.1111/j.1469-7610.2011.02440.x

Lupien, S. J., McEwen, B. S., Gunnar, M. R., & Heim, C. (2009). Effects of stress throughout the lifespan on the brain, behaviour and cognition. *Nature Reviews Neuroscience, 10*(6), 434–445. https://doi.org/10.1038/nrn2639

Lupien, S. J., Parent, S., Evans, A. C., Tremblay, R. E., David, P., & Corbo, V. (2011). Larger amygdala but no change in hippocampal volume in 10-year-old children exposed to maternal depressive symptomatology since birth. *Proceedings of the National Academy of Sciences, 108*(34), 14324–14329. https://doi.org/10.1073/pnas.1105371108/-/DCSupplemental.www.pnas.org/cgi/doi/10.1073/pnas.1105371108

Lyons-Ruth, K., Pechtel, P., Yoon, S. A., Anderson, C. M., & Teicher, M. H. (2016). Disorganized attachment in infancy predicts greater amygdala volume in adulthood. *Behavioural Brain Research, 308*, 83–93. https://doi.org/10.1016/j.bbr.2016.03.050

Main, M. (1981). Avoidance in the service of attachment: A working paper. In K. Immelman, G. Barlow, L. Petrinovich, & M. Main (Eds.), *Behavioral development: The Bielfeld interdisciplinary project* (pp. 651–693). New York, NY: Cambridge University Press.

(2000). The organized categories of infant, child, and adult attachment: Flexible vs. inflexible attention under attachment-related stress. *Journal of the American Psychoanalytic Association*, *48*(4), 1055–1096; discussion 1175–1187. https://doi.org/10.1177/00030651000480041801

Main, M., Kaplan, N., & Cassidy, J. (1985). Security in infancy, childhood, and adulthood: A move to the level of representation. *Monographs of the Society for Research in Child Development*, *50*(1–2), 66–104. https://doi.org/http://dx.doi.org.libproxy.newschool.edu/10.2307/3333827

Main, M., & Solomon, J. (1990). Procedures for identifying disorganized/disoriented infants during the Ainsworth strange situation. In M. Greenberg, D. Cicchetti, & M. Cummings (Eds.), *Attachment in the preschool years* (pp. 121–160). Chicago, IL: University of Chicago Press.

Main, M., & Weston, D. R. (1981). The quality of the toddler's relationship to mother and to father: Related to conflict behavior and the readiness to establish new relationships. *Child Development*, *52*(3), 932–940.

Marvin, R. S., Cooper, G., Hoffman, K., & Powell, B. (2002). The circle of security project: Attachment-based intervention with caregiver-pre-school child dyads. *Attachment & Human Development*, *4*(1), 107–124. https://doi.org/10.1080/14616730252982491

Marvin, R. S., VanDevender, T. L., Iwanaga, M. I., LeVine, S., & LeVine, R. A. (1977). Infant–caregiver attachment among the Hausa of Nigeria. In H. McGurk (Ed.), *Ecological factors in human development* (pp. 247–259). Amsterdam: North-Holland.

McIntosh, J. E. (2011). Guest editor's introduction to special issue on attachment theory, separation, and divorce: Forging coherent understandings for family law. *Family Court Review*, *49*(3), 418–846. https://doi.org/10.1111/j.1744-1617.2011.01382.x

McLaughlin, K. A., Zeanah, C. H., Fox, N. A., & Nelson, C. A. (2012). Attachment security as a mechanism linking foster care placement to improved mental health outcomes in previously institutionalized children. *Journal of Child Psychology & Psychiatry & Allied Disciplines*, *53*(1), 46–55. https://doi.org/10.1111/j.1469-7610.2011.02437.x.Attachment

Mehta, N., Cowan, P. A., & Cowan, C. P. (2009). Working models of attachment to parents and partners: Implications for emotional behavior between partners. *Journal of Family Psychology*, *23*(6), 895–899. https://doi.org/10.1037/a0016479

Mesman, J., van IJzendoorn, M., Behrens, K., Carbonell, O. A., Cárcamo, R., Cohen-Paraira, I., … Zreik, G. (2016). Is the ideal mother a sensitive mother? Beliefs about early childhood parenting in mothers across the globe. *International Journal of Behavioral Development*, *40*(5), 385–397. https://doi.org/10.1177/0165025415594030

Mesman, J., van IJzendoorn, M. H., & Sagi-Schwartz, A. (2016). Cross-cultural patterns of attachment: Universal and contextual dimensions. In J. Cassidy & P. R. Shaver (Eds.), *Handbook of attachment: Theory, research and clinical applications* (3rd ed., pp. 790–815). New York, NY: Guilford Press.

Mikulincer, M., & Shaver, P. R. (2012). An attachment perspective on psychopathology. *World Psychiatry*, *11*(1), 11–15. https://doi.org/10.1037/14498-005

Moutsiana, C., Fearon, P., Murray, L., Cooper, P., Goodyer, I., Johnstone, T., & Halligan, S. (2014). Making an effort to feel positive: Insecure attachment in infancy predicts the neural underpinnings of emotion regulation in adulthood. *Journal of Child Psychology and Psychiatry and Allied Disciplines*, *55*(9), 999–1008. https://doi.org/10.1111/jcpp.12198

Moutsiana, C., Johnstone, T., Murray, L., Fearon, P., Cooper, P. J., Pliatsikas, C., … Halligan, S. L. (2015). Insecure attachment during infancy predicts greater amygdala volumes in early adulthood. *Journal of Child Psychology and Psychiatry and Allied Disciplines*, *56*(5), 540–548. https://doi.org/10.1111/jcpp.12317

Nelson, C. A., Fox, N. A., & Zeanah, C. H. (2014). *Romania's abandoned children: Deprivation, brain development, and the struggle for recovery*. Cambridge, MA: Harvard University Press.

Nelson, C. A., III, Bos, K., Gunnar, M. R., & Sonuga-Barke, E. J. S. (2011). The neurobiological toll of early human deprivation. *Monographs of the Society for Research in Child Development*, *76*(4), 127–146. https://doi.org/10.1126/science.1249749.Ribosome

O'Connor, T. G., & Croft, C. M. (2001). A twin study of attachment in preschool children. *Child Development*, *72*(5), 1501–1511. https://doi.org/10.1111/1467-8624.00362

Pendry, P., & Adam, E. K. (2007). Associations between parents' marital functioning, maternal parenting quality, maternal emotion and child cortisol levels. *International Journal of Behavioral Development*, *31*(3), 218–231. https://doi.org/10.1177/0165025407074634

Perry, R. E., Blair, C., & Sullivan, R. M. (2017). Neurobiology of infant attachment: Attachment despite adversity and parental programming of emotionality. *Current Opinion in Psychology*, 17, 1–6. https://doi.org/https://doi.org/10.1016/j.copsyc.2017.04.022

Pietromonaco, P. R., & Barrett, L. F. (2000). The internal working models concept: What do we really know about the self in relation to others? *Review of General Psychology*, *4*(2), 155–175. https://doi.org/10.1037/1089-2680.4.2.155

Pietromonaco, P. R., & Power, S. I. (2015). Attachment and health-related physiological stress processes. *Current Opinion in Psychology*, *1*, 34–39. https://doi.org/10.1038/jid.2014.371

Quevedo, K., Waters, T. E. A., Scott, H., Roisman, G. I., Shaw, D. S., & Forbes, E. E. (2017). Brain activity and infant attachment history in young men during loss and reward processing. *Development and Psychopathology*, *29*(2), 465–476. https://doi.org/10.1017/S0954579417000116

Raby, K. L., & Dozier, M. (2018). Attachment across the lifespan: Insights from adoptive families. *Current Opinion in Psychology*, *25*, 81–85. https://doi.org/10.1016/j.copsyc.2018.03.011

Ray, R. D., & Zald, D. H. (2012). Anatomical insights into the interaction of emotion and cognition in the prefrontal cortex. *Neuroscience and Biobehavioral Reviews*, *36*(1), 479–501. https://doi.org/10.1016/j.neubiorev.2011.08.005

Robila, M. (Ed.). (2014). *Handbook of family policies across the globe*. New York, NY: Springer.

Roisman, G. I. (2006). The role of adult attachment security in non-romantic, non-attachment-related first interactions between same-sex strangers. *Attachment & Human Development*, 8(4), 341–352. https://doi.org/10.1080/ 14616730601048217

Roisman, G. I., & Fraley, R. C. (2008). A behavior-genetic study of parenting quality, infant attachment security, and their covariation in a nationally representative sample. *Developmental Psychology*, 44(3), 831–839. https://doi.org/10.1037/ 0012-1649.44.3.831

Roisman, G. I., Susman, E., Barnett-Walker, K., Booth-LaForce, C., Owen, M. T., Belsky, J., ... NICHD Early Child Care Research Network. (2009). Early family and child-care antecedents of awakening cortisol levels in adolescence. *Child Development*, 80(3), 907–20. https://doi.org/10.1111/j.1467-8624.2009.01305.x

Rutter, M., Beckett, C., Castle, J., Colvert, E., Kreppner, J., Mehta, M., ... Sonuga-Barke, E. (2007). Effects of profound early institutional deprivation: An overview of findings from a UK longitudinal study of Romanian adoptees. *European Journal of Developmental Psychology*, 4(3), 332–350. https://doi .org/10.1080/17405620701401846

Sagi-Schwartz, A., & Aviezer, O. (2005). Correlates of attachment to multiple caregivers in kibbutz children from birth to emerging adulthood: The Haifa longitudinal study. In K. E. Grossmann, K. Grossmann, & E. Waters (Eds.), *Attachment from infancy to adulthood* (pp. 165–197). New York, NY: Guilford Press.

Sagi-Schwartz, A., van IJzendoorn, M. H., Aviezer, O., Donnell, F., Koren-Karie, N., Joels, T., & Harel, Y. (1995). Attachments in a multiple-caregiver and multiple-infant environment: The case of the Israeli kibbutzim. *Monographs of the Society for Research in Child Development*, 60(2/3), 71–91.

Sagi, A., Koren-Karie, N., Gini, M., Ziv, Y., & Joels, T. (2002). Shedding further light on the effects of various types and quality of early child care on infant–mother attachment relationship: The Haifa study of early child care. *Child Development*, 73(4), 1166–1186. https://doi.org/10.1111/ 1467–8624.00465

Schieche, M., & Spangler, G. (2005). Individual differences in biobehavioral organization during problem-solving in toddlers: The influence of maternal behavior, infant-mother attachment, and behavioral inhibition on the attachment-exploration balance. *Developmental Psychobiology*, 46(4), 293–306. https:// doi.org/10.1002/dev.20065

Schuengel, C., Bakermans-Kranenburg, M. J., & van IJzendoorn, M. H. (1999). Frightening maternal behavior linking unresolved loss and disorganized infant attachment. *Journal of Consulting and Clinical Psychology*, 67(1), 54–63. https://doi.org/10.1080/02646839808404575

Shonkoff, J. P., Garner, A. S., Siegel, B. S., Dobbins, M. I., Earls, M. F., Garner, A. S., ... Wood, D. L. (2012). The lifelong effects of early childhood adversity and toxic stress. *Pediatrics*, 129(1), e232–e246. https://doi.org/10.1542/peds.2011–2663

Simpson, J. A., & Belsky, J. (2016). Attachment theory within a modern evolutionary framework. In J. Cassidy & P. R. Shaver (Eds.), *Handbook of attachment: Theory, research and clinical applications* (3rd ed., pp. 91–116). New York, NY: Guilford Press.

Slopen, N., McLaughlin, K. A., & Shonkoff, J. P. (2010). Interventions to improve cortisol regulation in children: A systematic review. *Pediatrics*, 133(2), 312–326. https://doi.org/10.1542/peds.2013-1632

Smyke, A. T., Zeanah, C. H., Fox, N. A., Nelson, C. A., & Guthrie, D. (2010). Placement in foster care enhances attachment among young children in institutions. *Child Development, 81*(1), 212–223. https://doi.org/10.1111/j.1467-8624.2009.01390.x

Spangler, G., & Grossmann, K. E. (1993). Biobehavioral organization in securely and insecurely attached infants. *Child Development, 64*(5), 1439–1450. https://doi.org/10.1111/j.1467–8624.1993.tb02962.x

Spangler, G., & Schieche, M. (1998). Emotional and adrenocortical responses of infants to the Strange Situation: The differential function of emotional expression. *International Journal of Behavioral Development, 22*, 681–706. https://doi.org/10.1080/016502598384126

Sroufe, L. A., & Waters, E. (1977). Attachment as an organizational construct. *Child Development, 48*(4), 1184. https://doi.org/10.2307/1128475

Steele, H., & Steele, M. (Eds.). (2018). *Handbook of attachment-based interventions*. New York, NY: Guilford Press.

Suess, G. J., Grossmann, K. E., & Sroufe, L. (1992). Effects of infant attachment to mother and father on quality of adaptation in preschool: From dyadic to individual organisation of self. *International Journal of Behavioral Development, 15*(1), 43–65.

Tang, A. C., Reeb-Sutherland, B. C., Romeo, R. D., & McEwen, B. S. (2014). On the causes of early life experience effects: Evaluating the role of mom. *Frontiers in Neuroendocrinology, 35*(2), 245–251. https://doi.org/10.1016/j.yfrne.2013.11.002

Thompson, R. A. (2000). The legacy of early attachments. *Child Development, 71*(1), 145–152. https://doi.org/10.1111/1467–8624.00128

Thompson, R. A., & Raikes, H. A. (2003). Toward the next quarter-century: Conceptual and methodological challenges for attachment theory. *Special Issue: Conceptual, Methodological, and Statistical Issues in Developmental Psychopathology: A Special Issue in Honor of Paul E. Meehl, 15*(3), 691–718. https://doi.org/10.1017/S0954579403000348

Tottenham, N. (2014). The importance of early experiences for neuro-affective development. *Current Topics in Behavioral Neurosciences, 16*, 109–129. https://doi.org/10.1007/7854_2013_254

Tottenham, N., Hare, T. A., Millner, A., Gilhooly, T., Zevin, J. D., & Casey, B. J. (2011). Elevated amygdala response to faces following early deprivation. *Developmental Science, 14*(2), 190–204. https://doi.org/10.1111/j.1467-7687.2010.00971.x

Tottenham, N., Hare, T. A., Quinn, B. T., McCarry, T. W., Nurse, M., Gilhooly, T., … Casey, B. J. (2010). Prolonged institutional rearing is associated with atypically large amygdala volume and difficulties in emotion regulation. *Developmental Science, 13*(1), 46–61. https://doi.org/10.1111/j.1467-7687.2009.00852.x

Tottenham, N., Shapiro, M., Telzer, E. H., & Humphreys, K. L. (2012). Amygdala response to mother. *Developmental Science, 15*(3), 307–319. https://doi.org/10.1111/j.1467-7687.2011.01128.x

True, M. M., Pisani, L., & Oumar, F. (2001). Infant-mother attachment among the Dogon of Mali. *Child Development, 72*(5), 1451–1466. https://doi.org/10.1111/1467–8624.00359

Valenzuela, M. (1997). Maternal sensitivity in a developing society: The context of urban poverty and infant chronic undernutrition. *Developmental Psychology, 33*(5), 845–855. https://doi.org/10.1037/0012-1649.33.5.845

van Bakel, H. J. A., & Riksen-Walraven, J. M. (2004). Stress reactivity in 15-month-old infants: Links with infant temperament, cognitive competence, and attachment security. *Developmental Psychobiology, 44*(3), 157–167. https://doi.org/10.1002/dev.20001

van den Dries, L., Juffer, F., van IJzendoorn, M. H., & Bakermans-Kranenburg, M. J. (2009). Fostering security? A meta-analysis of attachment in adopted children. *Children and Youth Services Review, 31*(3), 410–421. https://doi.org/10.1016/j.childyouth.2008.09.008

van IJzendoorn, M. H. (1990). Developments in cross-cultural research on attachment: Some methodological notes. *Human Development, 33*(1), 3–9. https://doi.org/http://dx.doi.org.libproxy.newschool.edu/10.1159/000276498

van IJzendoorn, M. H., Sagi, A., & Lambermon, M. W. E. (1992). The multiple caretaker paradox: Data from Holland and Israel. *New Directions for Child and Adolescent Development, 57*, 5–24. https://doi.org/10.1002/cd.23219925703

van IJzendoorn, M. H., Vereijken, C. M., Bakermans-Kranenburg, M. J., & Riksen-Walraven, J. M. (2004). Assessing attachment security with the Attachment Q-sort: Meta-analytic evidence for the validity of the observer AQS. *Child Development, 75*(4), 1188–1213.

Vantieghem, M. R., Gabard-Durnam, L., Goff, B., Flannery, J., Humphreys, K. L., Telzer, E. H., … Tottenham, N. (2017). Positive valence bias and parent–child relationship security moderate the association between early institutional caregiving and internalizing symptoms. *Development and Psychopathology, 29*(2), 519–533. https://doi.org/10.1017/S0954579417000153

Warshak, R. A. (2014). Social science and parenting plans for young children: A consensus report. *Psychology, Public Policy, and Law, 20*(1), 46–67. https://doi.org/10.1037/law0000005

Warshak, R. A., & Santrock, J. W. (1983). The impact of divorce in father-custody and mother-custody homes: The child's perspective. In L. A. Kurdek (Ed.), *Children and divorce* (pp. 29–46). San Francisco, CA: Jossey-Bass.

Waters, E., & Deane, K. E. (1985). Defining and assessing individual differences in attachment relationships: Q-methodology and the organization of behavior in infancy and early childhood. *Monographs of the Society for Research in Child Development, 50*(1–2), 41–65. https://doi.org/http://dx.doi.org.libproxy.newschool.edu/10.2307/3333826

Zeanah, C. H., & Gleason, M. M. (2015). Annual research review: Attachment disorders in early childhood – clinical presentation, causes, correlates, and treatment. *Journal of Child Psychology and Psychiatry and Allied Disciplines, 56*(3), 207–222. https://doi.org/10.1111/jcpp.12347

Zeanah, C. H., Smyke, A. T., & Dumitrescu, A. (2002). Attachment disturbances in young children. II: Indiscriminate behavior and institutional care. *Journal of the American Academy of Child and Adolescent Psychiatry, 41*(8), 983–989. https://doi.org/10.1097/00004583-200208000-00017

26 Infant Emotion Development and Temperament

Evin Aktar and Koraly Pérez-Edgar

Caregivers of young infants are often well practiced in detecting and interpreting the presence or absence of infant emotion. This is particularly true in the case of negative emotions, motivating caregivers to take on the mantel of detective. Why is the baby crying? Is he/she hungry? Cold? Too hot? Angry? Gassy? Tired? Bored? A caregiver's need to search for clues reflects infants' rather limited communicative repertoire, coupled with a restricted behavioral toolbox. Over the first 2 years of life, children's expression and experience of emotion becomes more expansive, providing greater insight into the cause of any one emotional experience and the needed response. However, even at this point, parents and caregivers play an important role in modulating infants' emotional experiences, since much of emotion regulation is first implemented externally until the child can internalize and develop effective stand-alone regulatory responses.

Constructs as complex as emotion and emotion regulation have multiple contributing factors that reside in the individual, among social relationships, and within cultures that are then expressed over time. The current chapter will focus on one relatively thin slice of this network. In particular, we review the relations between emotion and emotion regulation as a function of early temperamental differences. These three essential components of socioemotional development (i.e., emotion, emotion regulation, and temperament) share five core features. First, all three components reflect aspects of functioning that are related to social and psychological well-being in childhood, adolescence, and adulthood (e.g., Degnan, Almas, & Fox, 2010). Second, all three have a constitutional/reflexive basis that is likely genetic in nature, but quickly develops into relatively less automatic and more elaborate forms with the maturation of brain and physiological systems in the first 2 years of life (Rothbart & Derryberry, 1981; Silvers, Buhle, & Ochsner, 2013). Third, basic attention processes that allow the infants to select, orient to, disengage, or shift from relevant stimuli in the environment (Posner, Rothbart, Sheese, & Voelker, 2014) are fundamental for the expression and regulation of infant emotion, as well as infant temperament. Fourth, the development of emotion, emotion regulation, and temperament influences, and is influenced by, the infants' experience of the social environment (Campos, Campos, & Barrett, 1989). This includes the immediate caregiving environment as well as the broader cultural context.

Finally, emotion, emotion regulation, and infant temperament are multilayered complex phenomena involving physiological, neural, and cognitive components that may work in parallel or interact to give rise to observed behavioral reactions. Thus, capturing emotion, emotion regulation, and temperament in infancy requires simultaneously taking into consideration how these different components operate in tandem over time.

In this chapter our discussion first begins by outlining the foundational approaches often taken with emotion and emotion regulation, including thorny issues of operational definition. After outlining behavioral and neurophysiological underpinnings of normative developmental trends in emotion and emotion regulation, we introduce temperament, a core source of individual differences. Individual differences also emerge in tandem with variation in the infant environment, parental characteristics, and culturally bound expectations. In the remaining sections of the chapter, we focus on the sociocultural context and discuss the influence that socialization forces, such as culture and parents, can have on early emotional development to guide future policies that enhance infant development.

26.1 Approaching Emotion and Emotion Regulation in Infancy

Recent technological advances in infant-friendly research tools have allowed infant researchers to more systematically study the genetic and biological underpinnings of infants' development, helping capture the complexity of processes fueling the tremendous socioemotional changes observed in the first 2 years of life, through a better integrated interdisciplinary perspective. For example, a number of recent studies have begun to bridge biopsychosocial and developmental psychopathology perspectives to examine the early emergence of long-term socio-affective trajectories (Calkins, 2015). To tackle these interdisciplinary challenges, we must understand how early biological predispositions (including temperament) interact with the socioemotional environment during infancy to shape early patterns of adaptive and maladaptive behavior. These patterns, in turn, set the stage for later well-being or psychopathology.

26.2 Basic Constructs

Building on previous research (Cole, Martin, & Dennis, 2004; Fu & Pérez-Edgar, 2015), we have adopted the following working definitions of emotion, emotion regulation, and temperament. By emotion, we refer to an evolutionarily adapted set of physiological, neural, cognitive, behavioral, and subjective reactions, triggered by the detection of a personally significant event in the environment. The personal significance of a given event is determined by one's perception of the event and one's own goals (Scherer, Schorr, & Johnstone,

2001). Early in development, these goals are largely confined to short-term states driven by immediate needs and sensations. Thus, they are likely to be more biological than social or cultural in origin. Social and cultural processes insert their influence early in life, as caregivers bring socialization goals to their increasingly interactive encounters with infants (Denham, Bassett, & Wyatt, 2007). Despite a general lack of consensus on the exact definition of emotion, emotion theories converge on the notion that emotions act as a rapid detection and response system and were preserved in our evolutionary history because they helped our ancestors stay away from threats to survival while enhancing opportunities for well-being and mastery of the environment (Cole et al., 2004).

By emotion regulation, we specifically refer to the processes that lead to changes in the occurrence, valence, intensity, duration, and timing of the physiological, neural, cognitive, behavioral, and subjective components of infants' emotional reactions to the environment (Cole & Hollenstein, 2018). Regulation can encompass processes within the self or actions undertaken by caregivers. In addition, while much of the focus on emotion-regulation research has been on modulating negative emotion, the expression and regulation of positive emotions are importance forces in infant emotional development.

Marking the distinction between emotion and emotion regulation is not straightforward, since the processes that generate and regulate emotion involve overlapping brain and biological systems are closely intertwined in observed behavior, and dynamically unfold over time (Cole & Hollenstein, 2018). Further complications arise from the fact that emotional experiences, by definition, have inherent regulatory qualities as they modulate one's physiology, behavior, and subjective experience (Ekas, Braungart-Rieker, & Messinger, 2018).

By temperament, we refer to biologically rooted individual variations in children's emotional, attentional, and motor reactions to the environment as well as variation in their regulation of these reactions (Campos, Frankel, & Camras, 2004; Rothbart, 2011). The timing and intensity of infants' verbal, physical, and vocal emotional reactions reflect early temperamental dispo-sitions in their rawest form, before social and cognitive processes start to systematically exert their influence (Goldsmith & Campos, 1982). There is an inherent puzzle in trying to disentangle the interwoven relations between emotion, emotion regulation, and temperament. That is, we often risk a cir-cular argument in studying temperament in that we argue that variations in temperament fuel observed differences in expressed emotion and social behavior (Bowman & Fox, 2018) and we use expressed emotion and social behavior to assess temperament (Pérez-Edgar, 2019).

26.3 Thorny Questions of Operational Definitions

Although the utility of studying emotion regulation as a concept distinct from emotion is well acknowledged, the extent to which regulation processes can be mechanistically distinguished from the initial emotional experience seems to vary with the specific definition of emotion in play (Gross & Feldman Barrett, 2011). The distinction seems to be relatively clear in models operationalizing separate emotions like joy, fear, anger, and surprise as discrete, unique mental states with their own distinct cause, form, and function (e.g., Izard & Malatesta, 1987) versus perspectives that define emotions as a continuously emerging, dynamic stream of experiences (e.g., Camras, 2011).

Discrete emotions models have been highly influential in both adult-focused and developmental approaches to emotions, shaping working definitions of emotion in infancy (Gross & Feldman Barrett, 2011). These models, such as the differential emotions theory by Izard and colleagues (Izard & Malatesta, 1987), operationalize different emotions as discrete hard-wired systems consisting of a neural, an expressive, and an experiential component programmed to emerge at different stages of development. This theory assumes that infants' expressions of emotion mirror their experience of emotion. It further relies on the perception of discrete emotions by adult observers. This model also argues for a direct correspondence between infant and adult morphology of emotional facial expressions, a direct relation between infants' facial and non-facial emotional expressions, and a discrete, reliable, link between emotional expressions and the events that trigger these expressions.

In contrast to discrete emotions models, differentiation-oriented perspectives on emotion build on the idea that emotions emerge globally in infancy and become more differentiated over the course of development (Camras, 2011). Thus, according to this perspective, emotions initially emerge on a broader level as positive and negative affective states in infancy, and gradually develop into discrete positive and negative emotions over the first 2 years of life.

Other perspectives highlight the interpersonal and functional utility of emotion in their operationalization. The functionalist perspective by Campos and colleagues, for example, highlights the relational quality of emotion expressions, which are operationalized as the person's attempts to manage his or her connection to the environment (Barrett & Campos, 1987; Campos et al., 1989). Thus, according to this perspective, the communicative utility of a given expression determines the likelihood an infant will express an emotion in a specific situation. For example, early expression of frustration or anger are useful as they may call on caregivers to address (and hopefully remove) the component of the environment blocking the infant's current goal.

More contemporary perspectives adopting a dynamic systems approach (Camras, 2011; Cole, Bendezú, Ram, & Chow, 2017) operationalize emotion as a dynamically developing system consisting of nested components (such as emotion expressions and other emotional behaviors) that continually interact with each other and the environment over the course of development. This shift towards more dynamic and integrative perspectives centers the challenge on making a distinction between emotion generation and emotion regulation (Camras, 2011), often addressed through the use of novel dynamic statistical techniques (Morales, Ram et al., 2017). The focus, of course, inevitably turns to the type of empirical data that are (or can) be used to distinguish between emotion and emotion regulation.

26.4 Behavioral Markers of Emotion and Emotion Regulation

Although we see rapid changes in regulatory abilities in infancy, discrete emotion theory builds on the idea that infants are unable to voluntarily change or regulate their emotional expressions. Thus, an infants' *expressions* of emotion directly reflect their *experience* of emotion (Izard & Malatesta, 1987). As a result, much of the empirical evidence on behavioral indices of emotion generation in infants is focused almost entirely on infants' outwards expressions of emotion. These were systematically investigated in emotion-eliciting situations (such as visual cliff, or stranger approach; Hiatt, Campos, & Emde, 1979) and coded by human observers or using standardized protocols (MAX and AFFEX, Izard, 1979, Izard, Dougherty, & Hembree, 1983). In a parallel vein, the systematic observation of infant regulatory strategies relies highly on observing *changes* in a child's emotional reaction in situations that elicit an initial emotion. Because the field has historically been most interested in negative emotions such as fear, anger/frustration, and sadness, there are a wide range of paradigms eliciting negative emotions, such as stranger approach, parental separation, delay, and still-face situations.

To infer infants' self-regulatory strategy or intent, three broad categories of behaviors are most commonly used (Ekas, Lickenbrock, & Braungart-Rieker, 2013): Attentional strategies (e.g., shifting gaze away from the distress elicitor and towards the mother), self-comforting (e.g., touching the head, bringing hands to mouth, thumb-sucking), or active avoidance (e.g., arching the back or pushing away, withdrawing the hands, or retracting the arms). In this way, researchers attempt to decouple the emotion (operationalized as facial and bodily expressions) and regulation (operationalized as larger-order responses). However, studying the effectiveness of these strategies relies highly on simultaneous or subsequent measurement of infants' emotional expressions of affect using a shared operational definition of emotion and emotion regulation (Buss & Goldsmith, 1998). In this way, emotion and emotion-regulation processes are inferred from time-series data working to capture an overlapping variable of interest – emotional expression. One strategy for decoupling emotion from emotion regulation has been to introduce multiple levels of analysis that encompass behavioral, neural, and physiological components (Morris, Robinson, & Eisenberg, 2006; Pérez-Edgar & Bar-Haim, 2010).

26.5 Neural and Physiological Underpinnings of Emotion and Emotion Regulation

The most rapid and radical developmental changes in the structure and functions of brain systems occur in the first 2 years of life (Herschkowitz, 2000). Neuroscientific approaches to adult emotion and emotion regulation typically make a broad distinction between two interconnected brain systems underlying the arousal/reactivity component of an emotional state and the regulation of the emotion state (Dennis, O'Toole, & de Cicco, 2013). A ventral system consisting of amygdala, the insula, the striatum, and the medial orbitofrontal cortex is involved in relatively nonvoluntary and rapid responses to motivational goals. In comparison, a dorsal system consisting of the lateral and medial prefrontal cortex, the lateral orbitofrontal cortex, and the anterior cingulate cortex is implicated in the more effortful processes underlying the regulation of emotional experiences. The ventral system, which is ontogenetically older in human evolution and development, is functional and preeminent in the early years of life, while the dorsal system is thought to only have limited functionality and follow a more protracted developmental course (Casey, Getz, & Galvan, 2008). Note, however, that the experience (and regulation) of emotion triggers largely distributed neural networks that include the ventral and dorsal system, with the relative "weight" varying with the individual's state and task at hand. Thus, over the course of development, the key structures in the ventral and the dorsal systems are interconnected, mutually influence one another, and operate together to give rise to observed emotion (Ochsner et al., 2009). Taken together, it seems that our measures of brain activity reflect the cooperation and interaction of emotional arousal as well as regulatory processes, just like our measures of infants' observable behavioral responses.

While there is a rich tradition of using neuroimaging in emotion research with adults and older children, parallel studies with infants are only now emerging (Graham, Fisher, & Pfeifer, 2013; Sylvester et al., 2017). In the infant literature, a greater emphasis has been placed on (electro-)physiological indices of emotion functions. Similar to behavioral indices, electroencephalogram (EEG) measures of infant brain activity in response to negative elicitors such as maternal separation and stranger approach (Hane, Fox, Henderson, & Marshall, 2008) were used to assess both emotion generation/arousal and regulation processes.

For example, asymmetry in frontal EEG activity (particularly in alpha power) has been used both as an index of emotional arousal and regulation beginning in the first months of life (Hane et al., 2008; Reznik & Allen, 2018). Right frontal EEG activity is thought to reflect withdrawal tendencies and is often associated with more negative arousal and less regulation. In contrast, left frontal EEG activity reflects approach tendencies, evident typically in more positive arousal and presumed to reflect better regulation (Fox, Henderson, Rubin, Calkins, & Schmidt, 2001). Right frontal EEG asymmetry is associated with more negative affect (stress and crying) during maternal separation and greater activity in the left (vs. right) frontal area is shown to predict infants' responses to positive stimuli (Hane et al., 2008).

One benefit of EEG is the ability to capture processes at baseline and in response to socially challenging situations (such as adults giving a speech about one's most embarrassing moment; Pérez-Edgar, Kujawa, Nelson, Cole, & Zapp, 2013). Observing changes in EEG activity can provide insight into trait-level proclivities and the individual's active response to challenge or reward. Similarly, overall frontal EEG activity during a frustration task (vs. baseline) can capture levels of regulation. For example, 5-month-old infants who process a novel stimulus quicker (shorter looking times to novelty) are more likely to use regulatory strategies during a frustration task and respond with higher EEG activity during the task, which is considered an index of effective effortful regulatory strategies (Diaz & Bell, 2011).

Similar to behavioral indices of emotion and emotion regulation, researchers have used "state" measures of time-sensitive physiological responses such as event-related potentials (ERPs), electromyography (EMG), and heart rate as an index of emotional arousal. In part, change in these physiological responses over time has been used to capture emotion regulation processes. Here we highlight cardiac measures, namely heart rate and vagal tone, as an example of state measures that have been incorporated into the study of both emotional arousal and regulation. Higher respiratory sinus arrhythmia (RSA) during baseline and more RSA suppression during emotionally arousing situations reflect more positive and responsive emotional states (Stifter & Corey, 2001), as well as better regulatory abilities (longer attention span, better soothability, and better dyadic synchrony; Calkins & Hill, 2007; Moore & Calkins, 2004). Changes in heart rate seem to go hand in hand with changes in the expression of negative affect, thus its regulation (Haley & Stansbury, 2003). For example, an acceleration in heart rate was found to precede crying in an aversive situation in 8- to 18-month-old children (Vaughn & Sroufe, 1979).

26.6 Using Time to Distinguish Emotion and Emotion Regulation

Temporal dynamics have been at the center of empirical efforts to delineate emotion generation from emotion-regulation processes (Cole & Hollenstein, 2018). Establishing the construct validity for emotion-regulation strategies (for example based on behavioral and/or physiological correlates) relies on the assessment of consecutive changes in emotion-linked biological markers, behaviors, and expressions over time. This two-factor approach assumes that regulation starts to operate only after the emotion is activated, and that it is possible to capture the transition from an early phase of emotional experience, in which "pure" arousal processes are observed, to a later phase in which cooperation between arousal and regulation can be observed. Here, the focus is on temporally sensitive measures and repeated assessment of infants' emotional experiences. One critique of this approach argues that we lack an ontological or neurobiological distinction between arousal and regulation, rejecting the idea of an early phase in which emotional arousal would be observable in the absence of regulatory processes (Campos et al., 2004). These models suggest instead that regulation can take place at all phases of the emotional reaction, even before the arousal becomes observable.

Note however that regulation processes embedded within the individual may apply to more mature and effortful forms of regulation that only develop at later stages of development, when reactive and regulation processes become increasingly better integrated (Fox & Calkins, 2003). This sequence implies that it may be possible to observe in early infancy an early phase of emotional reactivity, before regulation processes start to come into play.

26.7 Normative Developmental Trends in Emotion and Emotion Regulation

Recent advances in technology have revealed that infants express a variety of positive and negative facial emotion even before birth (Reissland, Francis, & Mason, 2011; 2013) and an array of expressions are evident in the early months of life (Galati & Lavelli, 1997). Recent work challenges several assumptions of the discrete emotion perspectives. First, there is little empirical support for a direct correspondence between infants' emotional expressions and emotion-eliciting situations. For example, 2- to 6-month-old infants may express negative emotions like anger and disgust during putatively pleasant face-to-face interactions with their mother (Matias & Cohn, 1993).

Second, adults often perceive infants' negative emotional expressions as an ongoing blend of multiple "discrete" negative emotions, rather than a specific category of emotion (e.g., Oster, Hegley, & Nagel, 1992). Specific discrete negative emotions seem to be relatively more differentiable at 12 months compared to 4 months, suggesting an increase in the specificity of infants' negative emotional expressions in this period (Bennett, Bendersky, & Lewis, 2005). (A more thorough review of these developmental processes can be found in Mitsven, Messinger, Moffitt, & Ahn, Chapter 27 this volume.)

On the flip side, evidence on infants' processing of others' emotional expressions suggests that infants categorically perceive and can discriminate between several discrete adult emotional expressions (see Grossmann, 2010, for a review). Making use of habituation–dishabituation paradigms researchers have shown that newborns can discriminate between surprised, sad, or happy facial expressions despite poor visual acuity (T. M. Field, Cohen, Garcia, & Collins, 1983). Moreover, studies reveal that infants show a general interest for positive emotional expressions from the neonatal period onwards in the first 5 months of life (i.e., longer preferential looking to happy then neutral or fearful faces; Bayet et al., 2015; Farroni, Menon, Rigato, & Johnson, 2007), followed by a shift to biases in infants' attention in favor of negative, especially fearful expressions between 5 and 7 months of age (see Vaish, Grossmann, & Woodward 2008).

An accumulating body of evidence has consistently revealed that 7-month-old infants look longer at fearful than neutral or happy faces, and are slower to disengage from fearful, as compared to happy and neutral faces (e.g., Peltola, Hietanen, Forssman & Leppänen, 2013). This biased processing of fear is also evident in neural (e.g., ERPs; Yrttiaho, Forssman, Kaatiala & Leppänen, 2014) and physiological (e.g., heart-rate variability; Peltola et al., 2013) indices of emotion and attention. Importantly, infants do not seem to display fearful reactions while processing fearful expressions, illustrating that a bias to attend to a specific emotional state is not equivalent to the *experience* of an emotional state (Morales, Fu & Pérez-Edgar, 2016).

Affect-biased attention (particularly to fear) may be evolutionarily programmed to emerge at around the time of locomotion in typical development, as infants start to gradually move away from the caregiver with the onset of crawling and walking. A bias, in this developmental context, may increase infants' chances of survival during their exploration of the distal environment (Campos et al., 2000; Vaish et al., 2008). We know relatively less regarding the developmental course of the fear bias in the period between infancy and childhood (A. P. Field & Lester, 2010). Preservation of this fear bias beyond this specific period in infancy may be an early marker of later maladaptive developmental pathways and psychopathology (A. P. Field & Lester, 2010; Morales et al., 2016), as it no longer serves the acute protective role.

26.8 Rudimentary Regulation Emerges in Infancy

Although infants show some rudimentary ability to regulate their own emotional experiences in emotionally arousing situations, these initial capabilities are limited to more reflexive strategies such as sucking or visual reorienting (Kopp, 1982), and have a limited effectiveness in regulating infants' emotional experiences (Cole et al., 2017). Although still primitive, the first forms of voluntary regulation start to emerge at around 3 months of age. Infants' emotion self-regulation abilities in the early months of life are highly social in nature and rely on parents' assistance as external sources of regulation (Denham et al., 2007). Infants will display an emotion and caregivers will proceed to interpret the emotion, identify the putative cause, and seek to remediate (or sustain, if the emotion is positive). Thus, early emotion regulation is an inherently social process, embedded in dyadic interactions. While internal regulatory processes will soon emerge, it is important to note that these early socially embedded regulatory relations shape long-term socioemotional profiles, carrying the effects of parental socialization and cultural expectations of emotion.

A shift from more reflexive and primitive to relatively more elaborate and active forms of emotion self-regulation emerges in infants between 3 and 7 months thanks to maturational changes in attentional, motor, and cognitive systems (Kopp, 1989). For example, they use gaze aversion in more sophisticated ways, more actively search the environment, and exert control over (sustain or redirect) attention at the end of the first year (Ekas et al., 2013). Developmental trajectories for different emotion-regulation strategies suggest that primitive strategies (such as mouthing or thumb-sucking) get replaced by more effective regulation (seeking stimulation, active engagement, shifting attention towards or away from the caregiver) strategies with further maturation of cognitive and motor skills (Rothbart, 2011).

Moreover, there is some support for long-term impacts on regulatory ability based on the presence of these early strategies. For example, infants who disengage attention from the nonresponsive parent during the still face, and engage in self-soothing behaviors, show a decrease in negative affect from 3 to 7 months of age (Ekas et al., 2013). Similarly, infants who at 6 months engage in self-soothing and look away when confronted with a novel toy show subsequent reductions in stress (Crockenberg & Leerkes, 2004). Although also present by 12 months, self-soothing behaviors and problem-focused regulation strategies become more common around 18 months of age (Parritz, 1996). Between 12 and 24 months active regulatory strategies such as self-distraction and help seeking were also more frequently observed, along with enhanced ability to delay gratification (Bridges & Grolnick, 1995).

Although the overall consistency or uniformity in the regulatory strategies adopted by infants starts to increase by the age of 12 months, adopted strategies show some context specificity (Parritz, 1996). Moreover, the effectiveness of a given regulatory strategy depends on the intensity of stress that the infants experience, illustrating the fragility of these newly emerging skills. For example, infants are more likely to use approach as a regulation strategy when they experience low levels of fear, but avoidant strategies such as withdrawal or shifting attention to mother when experiencing higher levels of fear (Buss & Goldsmith, 1998). Finally, the effectiveness of a given regulatory strategy also seems to differ as a function of the type of stress elicited in the situation. For example, strategies like looking away, looking at mother, or looking to the experimenter seem to be effective in reducing anger, but not fear, in 6- to 18-month-old children. Thus, the specific negative emotions experienced by the infant may require different regulatory strategies.

26.9 Temperamental Variations on Emotion and Emotion Regulation

Up to this point, much of the current discussion has focused on broad, generally applicable patterns of emotion and emotion regulation in infancy, in line with our often nomothetic view of development (Pérez-Edgar & Hastings, 2018). However, there are systematic and well-documented variations in the pattern and intensity of emotion, and subsequent regulation, that are long-lasting, evident across contexts, and emergent in the first months of life (Pérez-Edgar, 2019). Some of these differences reflect variation in the infant environment, parental characteristics and behavior, and culturally bound expectations. Each of these will be discussed in turn below. First, however, we look to an individual difference variable, temperament, which is biologically based, early-appearing, relatively stable, and often bound, by definition, to variations in the experience, expression, and regulation of emotion (Goldsmith & Rothbart, 1996). Much of the temperament literature in infancy begins by examining variations in infants' responses to discrete sensory stimuli and novel people and objects. Often, the measures used center on the display, perception, and processing of emotion. This can place the field in a bit of an ontological conundrum.

On the one hand, there is the belief that temperament traits are conceptually separable from emotion (Bates, Goodnight, & Fite, 2008). Indeed, Bowman and Fox (2018, p. 54) make the clear declaration that "emotion is not a core feature of temperament." Instead, they argue that temperament encompasses individual differences in the response to specific stimuli, particularly those that convey threat, novelty, and reward. There is no inherent need to invoke emotion under this formulation. Rather, one can focus on motor activity, attention, biological markers, and broad approach–withdrawal behaviors. The Bowman and Fox (2018) approach argues that temperament is centered on a child's reactivity and subsequent regulation in response to the environment, but it need not center on the child's reactivity to and subsequent regulation of *emotion*.

This approach contrasts with other lines of work that center the experience and expression of emotion in the approach to temperament. Indeed, temperament is often conceptualized as the probability of showing a specific emotion within specific contexts (Goldsmith & Campos, 1982). For example, the laboratory temperament assessment battery (LAB Tab; Goldsmith & Rothbart, 1996) is designed to assess patterns of expressed emotion and behavior by manipulating events putatively linked to anger (arm restraint), joy (peek-a-boo), and fear (stranger approach), among others. Here, emotion is the marker of temperament, while at the same time temperament is seen to be the driver of emotion reactivity and subsequent emotion regulation. Thus, although researchers take different conceptual approaches, the data generated are often circular in practice, if not in theory.

One way to move beyond this problem is to place a temperamental trait within a constellation of emotions, cognitions, and behaviors, in the context of a specific trigger. Across the multiple approaches to temperament (Fu & Pérez-Edgar, 2015), there are a set of temperamental traits most often represented in the literature. For example, infants marked by high temperamental negative affect will respond to novel or threatening stimuli with negative vocalizations or utterances (depending on age), withdrawal, and clear outwards signs of distress, including facial sadness, fear, and crying. In contrast, temperamental positive affect is marked by joyful vocalizations, approach, and happy facial expressions. In addition, profiles of temperament couple valence with additional markers characterizing the expanse of the emotion. This includes the stimulus threshold needed to trigger the emotion, the speed, and intensity of the emotion, and the time course until the return to baseline.

Temperamental approaches to emotion incorporate the tight convergence between initial emotional reactivity and subsequent emotion regulation. Rothbart (2011), in particular, put forth the model that both reactivity and regulation are themselves separate, though interacting, temperamental traits. Thus, individual children with mellow or intense emotional responses to the world could also deploy inefficient or effective emotion regulation strategies. Although some argue that emotion and emotion regulation are functionally inseparable (Campos, Frankel, & Camras, 2004), temperament researchers typically have worked under the goal of disentangling each component from the other.

Another methodological strategy has been to examine variation in emotional and behavioral responses as early as possible. Indeed, Kagan and Snidman (1991) and Fox et al. (2001) first looked for differences in temperamental reactivity at 4 months of age. The argument is that this time window follows the definitional axiom that temperamental variation is early appearing, while allowing for individual differences to emerge above and beyond the brain-stem functional cycles (eat, sleep) that dominate the first months of life. Among many temperament researchers, 4 to 6 months of age is a critical window into "pure" temperamental reactivity before variation in temperamental regulation can systematically take hold. As the overall expression and intensity of emotion decreases with age, it can become more difficult to capture distinct markers of temperament.

Thus, the second methodological strategy has been to incorporate biological and cognitive markers of temperamental variation. In initially describing the temperamental trait of behavioral inhibition, Garciá-Coll, Kagan, and Reznick (1984) suggested that the observed phenotype reflected a hyper-responsive amygdala response to novelty. This neural signature was then expanded to include neural regions associated with reward and regulation, as well as peripheral markers such as EEG, RSA, and EMG (Fox, Hane & Pérez-Edgar, 2006). Other temperamental traits, such as exuberance, also have distinct neural and biological profiles centered on reward and decision-making regions (Degnan et al., 2011). In addition, cognitive measures, such as attention biases, are also evident early in life (Morales et al., 2016). While a normative marker in infancy, variation in affect-biased attention can predict long-term variations in socioemotional functioning when coupled with specific emotional profiles or parental contexts.

One benefit of a multi-method approach is that it allows researchers to examine measures across a wider age range, making it easier to examine rank-order stability in the individual response to the environment, even in the face of developmentally expected changes in the phenotypic expression of temperament-linked emotional reactivity (Morris et al., 2006). Thus, we can better assess how socioemotional profiles in later childhood and adulthood are outgrowths of early variations in temperament.

Lamb (2015) suggests that in examining temperament we should remember that these traits are not immutable, evident, and unchanging from the first days of life. Rather, they are "biogenic propensities shaped by sociogenic experiences." To this mix, we would also add that they are constrained by cognitive mechanisms. Thus, the initial patterns of emotion and emotion regulation rooted in temperament are open to being shaped by the environment, aided by the child's own assessment of his or her place in the larger social context. Although temperament is not the same as emotion, its strongest expression is often in the open display of emotion.

26.10 Placing Temperament and Emotion in a Developmental Context

The experience-expectant and experience-dependent nature of emotion development suggests that child temperament may modulate both how emotion generation and regulation processes emerge and the extent to which extrinsic contextual/environmental influences shape their emergence. Thus, in addition to their unique and independent contributions to emotional development, temperament and contextual forces may interact to determine emerging trajectories of emotional development. The dynamic interactions between infants' temperament and contextual influences are at the center of diathesis-stress/dual-risk (Ingram & Luxton, 2005) and differential susceptibility (Belsky, Bakermans-Kranenburg, & van IJzendoorn, 2007; Ellis, Boyce, Belsky, Bakermans-Kranenburg, & van IJzendoorn, 2011) models. Both of these theoretical perspectives suggest that temperamentally negative children display an increased receptivity to environmental influences. Diathesis-stress/dual-risk models primarily focus on the increased vulnerability of temperamentally negative children in the face of environmental or contextual adversity, whereas differential susceptibility models extend the idea of a greater sensitivity/receptivity of temperamentally negative children to supportive/positive contextual influences. These theories propose that temperamentally negative infants are not only affected more by adverse environments, but they also benefit more from supportive environments. Thus, they are open to environmental influences both "for better and for worse" (Belsky et al., 2007).

26.11 Parenting as a Moderator of Temperamental Expression

Parenting is among the most extensively studied contextual factors in early development and its links to children's later socioemotional development and well-being are well established (Kiff, Lengua, & Zalewski, 2011). Note, however, that the moderating role of child temperament on parental influences has only recently been incorporated in infant emotion research (Hinshaw, 2008). This may reflect underlying presumptions regarding the maturational progress of the earliest emotions, relative to the clear evidence of emotional variability in older children. As it is, studies investigating infant outcomes in the context of temperament–parenting interactions have had a broader focus on social behavior and psychological functioning, rather than a tight focus on specific measures of emotion and emotion regulation (Kiff et al., 2011).

26.11.1 Parenting Behaviors Impacting Emotion and Emotion Regulation

Theoretical accounts of early emotional development converge on the view that parents' positive emotional expressions, and their accompanying synchronous and sensitive responding to infants' emotional expressions, provide the main framework for both the early experience and regulation of emotion (Tronick, 1989). In line with this idea, observational studies consistently find that young infants seem to instantly tune in to changes in their parents' expressions of emotion and their emotional expressions seem to mirror those of their parents during these interactions (Aktar & Bögels, 2017). Thus, infants are more positive when parents express more positive affect. Additionally, infants express less positive and more negative affect when parents stop responding in these dyadic interactions, such as in the still-face paradigm (Mesman, van IJzendoorn, & Bakermans-Kranenburg, 2009).

Infants' self-regulatory capacity develops within early relationships with caregivers. Parents who are positive, sensitive, and responsive towards their infants in early interactions are thought to provide the optimal environment for supporting self-regulation. Therefore, the infancy literature typically focuses on parenting dimensions that relate to the early parent–child relationship, such as mutual responsivity, synchrony, attachment security, or to parents' interactive quality such as emotional synchrony, availability, and sensitivity (e.g., Kiel & Kalomiris, 2015; Kim, Stifter, Philbrook, & Teti, 2014). Synchrony between parent and infant emotion in early face-to-face interactions, captured in both behavior and physiology, is suggested to be the key co-regulation process providing the foundation for infants' self-regulatory skills (Feldman, 2003).

Earlier evidence has shown that positive aspects of parenting and mutual responsivity in early parent–child relationships seem to be especially beneficial for emotion regulation in children with temperamental difficulties. For example, children who experience more affective synchrony in their emotional expressions during face-to-face interactions with their mother at 3 months and 9 months were found to show better self-regulation at 2 years of age, especially if they have high levels of difficult temperament (Feldman, Greenbaum, & Yirmiya, 1999). In a parallel vein, high levels of mother–child mutually responsive orientation at 15 months seems to be related to better self-regulation at 25 months, only for children with high levels of temperamental negative affect (Kim & Kochanska, 2012).

On the flip side, lower levels of maternal emotional availability and sensitivity, as well the lack of secure attachment, seem to have stronger links to emotion regulation in children with high levels of temperamental negative affect. For example, Kim et al. (2014) showed that children high (vs. low) in temperamental negative affect were more likely to employ a maladaptive regulatory strategy at 12 and 18 months when the mother is emotionally less available. Moreover, infants with an insecure/avoidant attachment type, coupled with high levels of temperamental negative affect, were more likely to engage in a less effective regulatory strategy than securely attached infants with high temperamental negative affect. Likewise, evidence suggests that infants with negative temperament show more dysregulated behavior and less adaptive regulation in frustrating situations when mothers have low levels of sensitivity (at 3 and 6 months; Gunning, Halligan, & Murray, 2013; Thomas, Letourneau, Campbell, Tomfohr-Madsen, & Giesbrecht, 2017). Taken together, the evidence supports the differential susceptibility hypothesis, showing that temperamentally negative infants' emotion regulation skills are more susceptible to parenting influences both "for better and for worse" (Belsky et al., 2007).

26.11.2 Parental Characteristics

Parents play an active and outsized role in scaffolding infants' expression and regulation of emotions as they are the most prominent source and target of emotional expressions in an infant's environment. As such, there is no doubt that individual variation in parents' reactivity and regulation is likely to have a direct influence on infants' developing emotion and emotion regulation skills. The effects of parents' emotional reactivity have most often been investigated in the context of parents' emotionality, depression, and anxiety, which is the main focus in the following sections.

26.11.3 Parental Characteristics in the Context of Emotion and Emotion Regulation

The effect of parental affective style on parents' emotional expressions, parenting, and relationship quality have been predominantly investigated in the context of parental depression and anxiety. Observational studies find that both parents with depression and their infants are more affectively "flat," expressing less positive and more negative emotion during early face-to-face interactions (Aktar, Colonnesi, de Vente, Majdandžić, & Bögels, 2017; Feldman et al., 2009). Behaviorally, the interactive style of depressed parents is described as intrusive, overcontrolling, and overstimulating on the one end of the continuum, and as passive, withdrawn, and understimulating on the other (Malphurs, Raag, Field, Pickens & Peláez-Nogueras, 1996).

Moreover, depression seems to interfere with a mother's ability to sensitively respond to, and synchronize with, their infants' emotional expression (Feldman, 2003; Granat, Gadassi, Gilboa-Schechtman & Feldman, 2017) and to provide an optimum level of stimulation for infants' emotional development (Paulson, Dauber, & Leiferman, 2006). For example, depressed parents are less likely to read, tell stories, sing, or play with their infants. Mothers with depression are additionally more negative and less positive during parent–infant interactions involving emotionally ambiguous stimuli (Hart, Field, Del Valle, & Peláez-Nogueras, 1998) and may be less available to provide appropriate emotional reactions for the coregulation of infants' emotional responses to these situations (Gewirtz & Peláez-Nogueras, 1992).

Moreover, there is some evidence for indirect links between anxiety and depression diagnosis in mothers' and infants' processing of facial expressions. For example, infants of mothers with, versus without, depression show less interest to sad facial expressions at 3 and 6 months (Diego et al. 2004; T. M. Field, Pickens, Fox, Gonzalez, & Nawrocki, 1998), and take longer to disengage from happy facial expressions at 3 months (Hernandez-Reif, Field, Diego, Vera, & Pickens, 2006). These differences are thought to reflect the enhanced novelty of positive expressions for infants of depressed parents. Moreover, 3- to 6-month-old infants of parents with depression are less positive and more negative in their interactions with mothers and strangers, they show greater right frontal EEG asymmetry to happy and sad facial expressions during and elevated salivary cortisol levels following these interactions (Diego et al., 2004).

The described effects of parental depression on the expression of emotion and sensitivity seem to be especially pronounced in cases of comorbid high-trait parental anxiety in the first (e.g., in 3- to 6-month-olds; Weinberg & Tronick, 1998) and second (10- to 14-month-olds; Nicol-Harper, Harvey, & Stein, 2007) half of the first year. In contrast, parental anxiety without comorbid depression does not seem to affect parents' expressions or synchrony of emotion in everyday face-to-face interactions with their 4-month-old infants (Aktar et al., 2017).

Strikingly, none of the studies mentioned so far in this section have considered the modulating role of infant temperament on early emotional exchanges between infants and their parents in face-to-face interactions. The only exception is the study by Aktar et al. (2017), which did not find a significant moderation by temperament on the link between parents' depression or anxiety and 4-month-old infants' facial expressions.

In comparison to studies focused on early parent–infant interactions, the role of infant temperamental negative affect is relatively better integrated into studies investigating the role of parental anxiety on the child's anxious reactions to ambiguous stimuli at the end of first year. To highlight, Murray et al. (2008) reported a longitudinal change in infants' observed avoidant reactions to strangers: Behaviorally inhibited infants (measured at 14 months) showed a larger increase in their avoidant responses to strangers from 10 to 14 months when mothers had a diagnosis of social anxiety disorder. This effect was linked to heightened parental anxiety expressions in the stranger situation. A later study (Aktar, Majdandžić, de Vente, & Bögels, 2013) reported a similar interplay as behaviorally inhibited 12-month-olds were more avoidant of strangers if the parents expressed higher levels of anxiety towards the stranger in the situation. To summarize, both studies point to an enhanced vulnerability of temperamentally inhibited children to parents' nonverbal expressions of anxiety during confrontations with a stranger.

The link between parents' anxiety and infants' emotion processing has also been investigated as a function of infant temperament. Although only now emerging, it appears that maternal characteristics may "set the stage" for temperament-linked variation in emotion and emotion processing. For example, recent work by Morales, Brown et al. (2017) suggests that greater maternal anxiety is associated with difficulty in disengaging from angry faces in infants ages 4 to 24 months. This link was not significantly moderated by infants' temperamental negative affect.

As with most traits of interest, the initial relations with emotional expression and experience are also then associated with individual variation in emotion regulation. As an example, Feldman et al. (2009) targeted mothers low and high in anxiety and depression and observed that mothers with depression and anxiety showed less sensitivity and had less socially engaged infants. Another study by Granat et al. (2017) noted that infants of depressed parents were more likely to use the maladaptive regulation strategy of avoidance, and were less likely to engage in social gaze, during play interactions.

26.12 Emotion Development in a Cultural Context

The previous sections outline the impact parental behaviors, and parental characteristics, may have on variation in infant emotion and emotion regulation. In particular, parents can potentiate infant patterns among children temperamentally open to environmental input (Ellis et al., 2011). Shifting slightly our view of this relation, we can also see that specific temperamental traits can elicit targeted parental socialization attempts (Denham et al., 2007). Consciously, or unconsciously, parents will try to mitigate emotional profiles they view as maladaptive or problematic while reinforcing and potentiating valued traits. These behaviors, in turn, are shaped by cultural expectations of adaptive and "ideal" profiles of emotion and emotion regulation (Chen, Rubin, & Li, 1995). Within Western cultures, this often means that parents try to increase the display of positive emotions while minimizing the displays of negative emotions (Chen et al., 1995; Holodynski & Friedlmeier, 2006).

Early in infancy, regulation is often embedded in social relationships. Parents will shape and mirror acceptable emotions and reinforce preferred emotion-regulation strategies (Holodynski & Friedlmeier, 2006). For example, Western mothers tend to minimize signs of shyness in children, particularly in boys, but are unlikely to discourage boisterous exuberance (Degnan et al., 2011). In the United States, we often note decreases in the phenotypic expression of behavioral inhibition in children over time as parents and teachers try to draw out the withdrawn child (Fox et al., 2001). In contrast, up until recently, one often saw increases in behavioral inhibition over time in mainland China. This reflects the traditional values of demure or reserved demeanor. Indeed, inhibited children were often held up as leaders in their school community (Chen et al., 1995; Chen, Rubin, Li, & Li, 1999). This pattern is still evident in rural, more traditional, areas of the country. In contrast, behaviorally inhibited children in rapidly urbanizing cities now show the same negative outcomes – shyness, withdrawal, loneliness – seen in the West (Chen, 2010). This shift in pattern suggests that socialization agents, namely parents and teachers, are now evaluating patterns of emotion and emotion regulation in a more Westernized manner and are responding accordingly.

Cultural norms and ideals also shape how we come to assess maternal sensitivity. As noted above, noncontingent, dismissing, and overly intrusive behaviors are linked to maladaptive socioemotional profiles, marked by increased negative affect and poor self-regulation skills (Kiel & Kalomiris, 2015). Cross-cultural work suggests that infant outcomes are not necessarily tied to specific emotional profiles. Rather, maternal sensitivity is evident in the match to cultural expectations (Friedlmeier & Trommsdorff, 1999). For example, German mothers focus on the cause of an emotion to scaffold independent and instrumental responses, while Japanese mothers often target the child's emotional display in order to mold emotion expressions that support harmony within the social group.

Although infants typically express a fairly standard array of emotional signals early in life, variation is initially introduced with the emergence of temperament-linked profiles of emotion and emotion regulation (Rothbart, 2011). Quickly, however, we see culture-specific transformations of these expressions into socially embedded communicative signs (Holodynski & Friedlmeier, 2006). For children whose initial temperament does not match the cultural ideal, there is an additional pull on emerging regulatory mechanisms to align the individual with social partners. Thus, an open question in the developmental literature centers on the extent to which parents mirror the emotions of their children and then engage in culturally informed regulation of their emotions. Important, as well, is to ask how early in development cultural differences in emotion shaping emerge.

26.13 Policy Implications and Conclusions

Decades of research has puzzled with how to best define the emergence and evolution of emotion in infancy. In tandem, the literature has strived to find the best way to capture variation in emotion and the growing influence of personally directed emotion-regulation strategies. Much of this work has focused on outlining theoretical and empirical operations of emotion and emotion regulation, striving to describe universal axioms (Pérez-Edgar & Hastings, 2018). However, temperament-linked variation is patently evident in the first months of life. Adding another layer of complexity is the fact that outside forces, often parents, act as external regulators of the child, shaping emotion and behavior to reflect both individual characteristics and cultural norms. Hence, it is not surprising that we are only now scratching the surface of these complex networks of constructs, contexts, and mechanisms.

Puzzling through these complexities is important, as maladaptive emotion and emotion-regulation processes are implicated in long-term profiles of socioemotional and cognitive functioning, influencing social, academic, and mental health outcomes. Given the pervasiveness of emotional processes in everyday life, we need to better understand and identify points of risk. With this knowledge, early interventions can target mechanisms that shape the individual, the context, and the *interactive* relation between the individual and the environment. To roughly organize research and intervention, there are four factors that should be examined together in order to generate a three-dimensional view of emotional development in infancy: person, timing, experience, and context (Pérez-Edgar, 2019).

With respect to person, we need to assess individual variation across multiple levels of functioning. This involves the expression of emotion, the contextual forces that trigger emotion, biological correlates, and cognitive profiles. Each source of information is unique and is likely not wholly overlapping with any other source of information. As such, bringing together these channels of emotion will provide additional information.

Within and beyond the person, new analytic approaches can capture the timing of emotion over time, helping extract regulatory mechanisms and eventual socioemotional outcomes. As such, we can now speak to micro-longitudinal methods that examine shifts in emotion markers within the course of a single episode (Cole & Hollenstein, 2018). These micro-trajectories are then embedded within longer-scale trajectories typically examined in developmental research. This work may help capture the mechanisms that underlie our largely descriptive representations of emotional development over time.

The next broad goal is to couple the timing of personal responses with specific experiences. At a small-scale level, this can encompass exposure to constrained triggers that are designed to elicit variation in emotional displays – the LAB Tab, for example, is designed for this purpose. At a larger scale, variation in sociocultural, sociohistorical, and socioeconomic forces will determine the rhythm of exposure to events that can support or hinder adaptive functioning. For example, children exposed to traumatic events, such as family separation, will not have the typical scaffolding experiences provided by parents.

This brings us to the question of context. Oddly enough, although this is the most overarching component of interest in our work, we often ignore or overlook its influence. That is, we constrain experimental studies, or narrowly define more descriptive studies, in order to boost our ability to detect a core construct and its associated mechanisms. Yet outcomes are often discussed using language with an implicit nod to universality. Qualifying language outlining restrictions to specific persons, reacting to experiences across time, in a defined context is often thought to diminish the importance of a finding. However, in striving to remove context from the equation, we have effectively limited our understanding of the breadth of variation in emotion that can emerge over the course of development. As an example, some cultures value exposing children to emotion-eliciting events in order to shape the child's response (Holodynski & Friedlmeier, 2006). In contrast, other cultures will preemptively remove potential emotional elicitors in order to engender a more even-keeled emotional state. One can imagine that the pattern of emotions to the environment, the strategies employed for emotion regulation, and the broader relation between emotion and functioning, may look quite different across cultures.

Complexity is not a limitation. Rather it is a conduit to identifying active mechanisms that shape observed emotional profiles – the very profiles that motivate us to engage in research. A broad literature base has noted individual differences in the presentation and regulation of emotion, often linked to individual differences in temperament. These presentations are then acted upon by socialization agents, typically in the form of parents, who scaffold regulation and modulate emotion in light of both their own traits and the broader sociocultural ideals. Better understanding the intersection of the individual and the context they are embedded in is crucial for building effective policies that enhance infant development, help parents scaffold and support children, and build environments that enhance both individual and community development.

References

Aktar, E., & Bögels, S. M. (2017). Exposure to parents' negative emotions as a developmental pathway to the family aggregation of depression and anxiety in the first year of life. *Clinical Child and Family Psychology Review, 20*, 369–390.

Aktar, E., Colonnesi, C., de Vente, W., Majdandžić, M., & Bögels, S. M. (2017). How do parents' depression and anxiety, and infants' negative temperament relate to parent–infant face-to-face interactions? *Development and Psychopathology, 29*, 697–710.

Aktar, E., Majdandžić, M., de Vente, W., & Bögels, S. M. (2013). The interplay between expressed parental anxiety and infant behavioural inhibition predicts infant avoidance in a social referencing paradigm. *Journal of Child Psychology and Psychiatry, 54*, 144–156.

Barrett, K. C., & Campos, J. J. (1987). Perspectives on emotional development II: A functionalist approach to emotions. In J. D. Osofsky (Ed.), *Handbook of infant development* (pp. 555–578). Oxford: John Wiley & Sons.

Bates, J. E., Goodnight, J. A., & Fite, J. E. (2008). Temperament and emotion. In M. Lewis, J. J. Haviland-Jones, & L. F. Barrett (Eds.), *Handbook of emotions* (pp. 485–496). New York, NY: Guilford Press.

Bayet, L., Quinn, P. C., Tanaka, J. W., Lee, K., Gentaz, É., & Pascalis, O. (2015). Face gender influences the looking preference for smiling expressions in 3.5-month-old human infants. *PLOS ONE, 10*, e0129812. http://doi.org/10.1371/journal.pone.0129812

Belsky, J., Bakermans-Kranenburg, M. J., & van IJzendoorn, M. H. (2007). For better and for worse: Differential susceptibility to environmental influences. *Current Directions in Psychological Science, 16*, 300–304.

Bennett, D. S., Bendersky, M., & Lewis, M. (2005). Does the organization of emotional expression change over time? Facial expressivity from 4 to 12 months. *Infancy, 8*(2), 167–187.

Bowman, L. C., & Fox, N. A. (2018). Distinctions between temperament and emotion: Examining reactivity, regulation, and social understanding. In A. S. Fox, R. C. Lapate, A. J. Shackman, & R. J. Davidson (Eds.). *The nature of emotion: Fundamental questions.* (pp. 54–58). Oxford: Oxford University Press.

Bridges, L. J., & Grolnick, W. S. (1995). The development of emotional self-regulation in infancy and early childhood. In N. Eisenberg (Ed.), *Social development* (pp. 185–211). Thousand Oaks, CA: Sage.

Buss, K. A., & Goldsmith, H. H. (1998). Fear and anger regulation in infancy: Effects on the temporal dynamics of affective expression. *Child Development, 69*, 359–374.

Calkins, S. D. (Ed.). (2015). *Handbook of infant biopsychosocial development.* New York, NY: Guilford.

Calkins, S. D., & Hill, A. (2007). Caregiver influences on emerging emotion regulation: Biological and environmental transactions in early development. In J. J. Gross (Ed.), *The handbook of emotion regulation* (pp. 229–248). New York, NY: Guilford.

Campos, J. J., Anderson, D. I., Barbu-Roth, M. A., Hubbard, E. M., Hertenstein, M. J., & Witherington, D. (2000). Travel broadens the mind. *Infancy, 1*, 149–219.

Campos, J. J., Campos, R. G., & Barrett, K. C. (1989). Emergent themes in the study of emotional development and emotion regulation. *Developmental Psychology, 25*, 394–402. http://dx.doi.org/10.1037/0012-1649.25.3.394

Campos, J. J., Frankel, C. B., & Camras, L. (2004). On the nature of emotion regulation. *Child Development, 7*(5), 317–333. https://doi.org/10.1111/j.1467-8624.2004.00681.x

Camras, L. A. (2011). Differentiation, dynamical integration, and functional emotional development. *Emotion Review, 3*, 138–146.

Casey, B. J., Getz, S., & Galvan, A. (2008). The adolescent brain. *Developmental Review, 28*(1), 62–77. https://doi.org/10.1016/j.dr.2007.08.003

Chen, X. (2010). Shyness-inhibition in childhood and adolescence: A cross-cultural perspective. In K. H. Rubin & R. J. Coplan (Eds.), *The development of shyness and social withdrawal* (pp. 213–235). New York, NY: Guilford Press.

Chen, X., Rubin, K. H., & Li, Z. Y. (1995). Social functioning and adjustment in Chinese children: A longitudinal study. *Developmental Psychology, 31*(4), 531.

Chen, X., Rubin, K. H., Li, B. S., & Li, D. (1999). Adolescent outcomes of social functioning in Chinese children. *International Journal of Behavioral Development, 23*(1), 199–223.

Cole, P. M., Bendezú, J. J., Ram, N., & Chow, S. M. (2017). Dynamical systems modeling of early childhood self-regulation. *Emotion, 17*, 684–699.

Cole, P. M., & Hollenstein, T. (Eds.). (2018). *Emotion regulation: A matter of time.* New York, NY: Routledge.

Cole, P. M., Martin, S. E., & Dennis, T. A. (2004). Emotion regulation as a scientific construct: Methodological challenges and directions for child development research. *Child Development, 75*, 317–333.

Crockenberg, S. C., & Leerkes, E. M. (2004). Infant and maternal behaviors regulate infant reactivity to novelty at 6 months. *Developmental Psychology, 40*, 1123.

Degnan, K. A., Almas, A. N., & Fox, N. A. (2010). Temperament and the environment in the etiology of childhood anxiety. *Journal of Child Psychology and Psychiatry, 51*, 497–517.

Degnan, K. A., Hane, A. A., Henderson, H. A., Moas, O. L., Reeb-Sutherland, B. C., & Fox, N. A. (2011). Longitudinal stability of temperamental exuberance and social–emotional outcomes in early childhood. *Developmental Psychology, 47*(3), 765.

Denham, S. A., Bassett, H. H., & Wyatt, T. (2007). The socialization of emotional competence. In J. E. Grusec & P. D. Hastings (Eds.), *Handbook of socialization: Theory and research* (pp. 614–637). New York, NY: Guilford Press.

Dennis, T. A., O'Toole, L. J., & DeCicco, J. M. (2013). Emotion regulation from the perspective of developmental neuroscience: What, where, when, and why. In K. C. Barrett, N. A. Fox, G. A. Morgan, D. J. Fidler, & L. A. Daunhauer (Eds.), *Handbook of self-regulatory processes in development: New directions and international perspectives* (pp. 135–172). New York, NY: Psychology Press.

Diaz, A., & Bell, M. A. (2011). Information processing efficiency and regulation at five months. *Infant Behavior and Development, 34*, 239–247.

Diego, M. A., Field, T., Jones, N. A., Hernandez-Reif, M., Cullen, C., Schanberg, S., & Kuhn, C. (2004). EEG responses to mock facial expressions by infants of depressed mothers. *Infant Behavior and Development, 27*, 150–162.

Ekas, N. V., Braungart-Rieker, J. M., & Messinger, D. S. (2018). The development of infant emotion regulation: Time is of the essence. In P. M. Cole & T. Hollenstein (Eds.), *Emotion regulation: A matter of time* (pp. 49–69). New York, NY: Routledge.

Ekas, N. V., Lickenbrock, D. M., & Braungart-Rieker, J. M. (2013). Developmental trajectories of emotion regulation across infancy: Do age and the social partner influence temporal patterns. *Infancy, 18*, 729–754.

Ellis, B. J., Boyce, W. T., Belsky, J., Bakermans-Kranenburg, M. J., & van IJzendoorn, M. H. (2011). Differential susceptibility to the environment: An evolutionary–neurodevelopmental theory. *Development and Psychopathology, 23,* 7–28.

Farroni, T., Menon, E., Rigato, S., & Johnson, M. H. (2007). The perception of facial expressions in newborns. *European Journal of Developmental Psychology, 4,* 2–13. http://doi.org/10.1080/17405620601046832

Feldman, R. (2003). Infant–mother and infant–father synchrony: The coregulation of positive arousal. *Infant Mental Health Journal, 24,* 1–23.

Feldman, R., Granat, A., Pariente, C., Kanety, H., Kuint, J., & Gilboa-Schechtman, E. (2009). Maternal depression and anxiety across the postpartum year and infant social engagement, fear regulation, and stress reactivity. *Journal of the American Academy of Child & Adolescent Psychiatry, 48,* 919–927.

Feldman, R., Greenbaum, C. W., & Yirmiya, N. (1999). Mother–infant affect synchrony as an antecedent of the emergence of self-control. *Developmental Psychology, 35,* 2230231.

Field, A. P., & Lester, K. J. (2010). Is there room for "development" in developmental models of information processing biases to threat in children and adolescents? *Clinical Child and Family Psychology Review, 13,* 315–332.

Field, T. M., Cohen, D., Garcia, R. & Collins, R. (1983). Discrimination and imitation of facial expressions by term and preterm neonates. *Infant Behavior and Development, 6,* 485–489.

Field, T. M., Pickens, J., Fox, N. A., Gonzalez, J., & Nawrocki, T. (1998). Facial expression and EEG responses to happy and sad faces/voices by 3-month-old infants of depressed mothers. *British Journal of Developmental Psychology, 16,* 485–494.

Fox, N. A., & Calkins, S. D. (2003). The development of self-control of emotion: Intrinsic and extrinsic influences. *Motivation and Emotion, 27,* 7–26.

Fox, N. A., Hane, A. A., & Pérez-Edgar, K. (2006). Psychophysiological methods for the study of developmental psychopathology. In D. Cicchetti & D. Cohen (Eds.), *Developmental psychopathology* (Vol. 2, 2nd ed., 381–426. New York, NY: Wiley.

Fox, N. A., Henderson, H. A., Rubin, K. H., Calkins, S. D., & Schmidt, L. A. (2001). Continuity and discontinuity of behavioral inhibition and exuberance: Psychophysiological and behavioral influences across the first four years of life. *Child Development, 72,* 1–21.

Friedlmeier, W., & Trommsdorff, G. (1999). Emotion regulation in early childhood: A cross-cultural comparison between German and Japanese toddlers. *Journal of Cross-Cultural Psychology, 30*(6), 684–711.

Fu, X., & Pérez-Edgar, K. (2015). Theories of temperament development. In J. D. Wright (Ed.), *International encyclopedia of social & behavioral sciences* (2nd ed., pp. 191–198. Oxford: Elsevier.

Galati, D., & Lavelli, M. (1997). Neonate and infant emotion expression perceived by adults. *Journal of Nonverbal Behavior, 21*(1), 57–83.

García-Coll, C., Kagan, J., & Reznick, J. S. (1984). Behavioral inhibition in young children. *Child Development, 55*(3), 1005–1019.

Gewirtz, J. L., & Peláez-Nogueras, M. (1992). Social referencing as a learned process. In Feinman, S. (Ed.), *Social referencing and the social construction of reality in infancy* (pp. 151–173). New York, NY: Plenum Press.

Goldsmith, H. H., & Campos, J. J. (1982). Toward a theory of infant temperament. In R. N. Emde & R. J. Harmon (Eds.), *The development of attachment and affiliative systems* (pp. 161–193). New York, NY: Plenum.

Goldsmith, H. H., & Rothbart, M. K. (1996). *The laboratory temperament assessment battery (LAB-TAB): Locomotor version. Technical manual.* Madison, WI: Department of Psychology, University of Wisconsin.

Graham, A. M., Fisher, P. A., & Pfeifer, J. H. (2013). What sleeping babies hear: A functional MRI Study of interparental conflict and infants' emotion processing. *Psychological Science, 24*, 782–789.

Granat, A., Gadassi, R., Gilboa-Schechtman, E., & Feldman, R. (2017). Maternal depression and anxiety, social synchrony, and infant regulation of negative and positive emotions. *Emotion, 17*, 11–27.

Gross, J. J., & Feldman Barrett, L. (2011). Emotion generation and emotion regulation: One or two depends on your point of view. *Emotion Review, 3*, 8–16.

Grossmann, T. (2010). The development of emotion perception in face and voice during infancy. *Restorative Neurology and Neuroscience, 28*, 219–236.

Gunning, M., Halligan, S. L., & Murray, L. (2013). Contributions of maternal and infant factors to infant responding to the still face paradigm: A longitudinal study. *Infant Behavior and Development, 36*, 319–328.

Haley, D. W., & Stansbury, K. (2003). Infant stress and parent responsiveness: Regulation of physiology and behavior during still-face and reunion. *Child Development, 74*(5), 1534–1546.

Hane, A. A., Fox, N. A., Henderson, H. A., & Marshall, P. J. (2008). Behavioral reactivity and approach–withdrawal bias in infancy. *Developmental Psychology, 44*(5), 1491.

Hart, S., Field, T., Del Valle, C., & Peláez-Nogueras, M. (1998). Depressed mothers' interactions with their one-year-old infants. *Infant Behavior and Development, 21*, 519–525.

Herschkowitz, N. (2000). Neurological bases of behavioral development in infancy. *Brain and Development, 22*, 411–416.

Hernandez-Reif, M., Field, T., Diego, M., Vera, Y., & Pickens, J. (2006). Happy faces are habituated more slowly by infants of depressed mothers. *Infant Behavior and Development, 29*, 131–135.

Hiatt, S. W., Campos, J. J., & Emde, R. N. (1979). Facial patterning and infant emotional expression: Happiness, surprise, and fear. *Child Development*, 50(4), 1020–1035.

Hinshaw, S. P. (2008). Developmental psychopathology as a scientific discipline. In T. P. Beauchaine, & S. P. Hinshaw, (Eds.), *Child and adolescent psychopathology* (pp. 3–28). Hoboken, NJ: Wiley.

Holodynski, M., & Friedlmeier, W. (2006). *Development of emotions and emotion regulation* (Vol. 8). New York, NY: Springer Science & Business Media.

Ingram, R. E., & Luxton, D. (2005). Vulnerability-stress models. In B. L. Hankin & J. R. Z. Abela (Eds.), *Development of psychopathology: A vulnerability-stress perspective.* (pp. 32–46). New York, NY: Sage.

Izard, C. E. (1979). *The maximally discriminative facial movement coding system (MAX).* Newark: Instructional Resources Center, University of Delaware.

Izard, C. E., Dougherty, L., & Hembree, E. (1983). *A system for identifying affect expressions by holistic judgments (AFFEX).* Newark: Instructional Resources Center, University of Delaware.

Izard, C. E., & Malatesta, C. (1987). Perspectives on emotional development I: Differential emotions theory of early emotional development. In J. Osofsky (Ed.), *Handbook of infant development* (2nd ed., pp. 494–554). New York, NY: Wiley.

Kagan, J., & Snidman, N. (1991). Infant predictors of inhibited and uninhibited profiles. *Psychological Science*, *2*(1), 40–44.

Kiel, E. J., & Kalomiris, A. E. (2015). Current themes in understanding children's emotion regulation as developing from within the parent–child relationship. *Current Opinion in Psychology*, *3*, 11–16.

Kiff, C. J., Lengua, L. J., & Zalewski, M. (2011). Nature and nurturing: Parenting in the context of child temperament. *Clinical Child and Family Psychology Review*, *14*, 251–301.

Kim, S., & Kochanska, G. (2012). Child temperament moderates effects of parent–child mutuality on self-regulation: A relationship-based path for emotionally negative infants. *Child Development*, *83*, 1275–1289.

Kim, B. R., Stifter, C. A., Philbrook, L. E., & Teti, D. M. (2014). Infant emotion regulation: Relations to bedtime emotional availability, attachment security, and temperament. *Infant Behavior and Development*, *37*, 480–490.

Kopp, C. B. (1982). Antecedents of self-regulation: A developmental perspective. *Developmental Psychology*, *18*, 199–214.

(1989). Regulation of distress and negative emotions: A developmental view. *Developmental Psychology*, *25*, 343–354.

(2002). Commentary: The codevelopments of attention and emotion regulation. *Infancy*, *3*, 199–208.

Lamb, M. E. (2015). Processes underlying social, emotional, and personality development. In M. E. Lamb & R. M. Lerner (Eds.), *Handbook of child psychology and developmental science, socioemotional processes* (Vol. 3, pp. 1–10). Hoboken, NJ: John Wiley & Sons.

Malphurs, J. E., Raag, T., Field, T., Pickens, J., & Pelaez-Nogueras, M. (1996). Touch by intrusive and withdrawn mothers with depressive symptoms. *Early Development and Parenting: An International Journal of Research and Practice*, *5*, 111–115.

Matias, R., & Cohn, J. (1993). Are MAX-specified infant facial expressions during face-to-face interaction consistent with differential emotions theory? *Developmental Psychology*, *29*, 524–531.

Mesman, J., van IJzendoorn, M. H., & Bakermans-Kranenburg, M. J. (2009). The many faces of the still-face paradigm: A review and meta-analysis. *Developmental Review*, *29*, 120–162.

Morales, S., Brown, K. M., Taber-Thomas, B. C., LoBue, V., Buss, K. A., & Pérez-Edgar, K. E. (2017). Maternal anxiety predicts attentional bias towards threat in infancy. *Emotion*, *17*, 874–883.

Morales, S., Fu, X., & Pérez-Edgar, K. E. (2016). A developmental neuroscience perspective on affect-biased attention. *Developmental Cognitive Neuroscience*, *21*, 26–41.

Morales, S., Ram, N., Buss, K. A., Cole, P. M., Helm, J. L., & Chow, S. M. (2017). Age-related changes in the dynamics of fear-related regulation in early childhood. *Developmental Science*, *21*, e12633.

Moore, G. A., & Calkins, S. D. (2004). Infants' vagal regulation in the still-face paradigm is related to dyadic coordination of mother–infant interaction. *Developmental Psychology*, *40*, 1068–1080.

Morris, A. S., Robinson, L. R., & Eisenberg, N. (2006). Applying a multimethod perspective to the study of developmental psychology. In M. Eid & E. Diener (Eds.), *Handbook of multimethod measurement in psychology* (pp. 371–384). Washington, DC: American Psychological Association.

Murray, L., de Rosnay, M., Pearson, J., Bergeron, C., Schofield, E., Royal-Lawson, M., & Cooper, P. J. (2008). Intergenerational transmission of social anxiety: The role of social referencing processes in infancy. *Child Development, 79*, 1049–1064.

Nicol-Harper, R., Harvey, A. G., & Stein, A. (2007). Interactions between mothers and infants: Impact of maternal anxiety. *Infant Behavior and Development, 30*, 161–167.

Ochsner, K. N., Ray, R. R., Hughes, B., McCrae, K., Cooper, J. C., Weber, J., ... Gross, J. J. (2009). Bottom-up and top-down processes in emotion generation: Common and distinct neural mechanisms. *Psychological Science, 20*, 1322–1331. https://doi.org/10.1111/j.1467-9280.2009.02459.x

Oster, H., Hegley, D., & Nagel, L. (1992). Adult judgments and fine-grained analysis of infant facial expressions. *Developmental Psychology, 28*, 1115–1131

Parritz, R. H. (1996). A descriptive analysis of toddler coping in challenging circumstances. *Infant Behavior and Development, 19*, 171–180.

Paulson, J. F., Dauber, S., & Leiferman, J. A. (2006). Individual and combined effects of postpartum depression in mothers and fathers on parenting behavior. *Pediatrics, 118*, 659–668.

Peltola, M. J., Hietanen, J. K., Forssman, L., & Leppänen, J. M. (2013). The emergence and stability of the attentional bias to fearful faces in infancy. *Infancy, 18*, 905–926.

Pérez-Edgar, K. (2019). Through the looking glass: Temperament and emotion as separate and interwoven constructs. In V. LoBue, K. Pérez-Edgar, & K. Buss (Eds.), *Handbook of emotional development* (pp. 139–168). Cham, Switzerland: Springer.

Pérez-Edgar, K., & Bar-Haim, Y. (2010). Application of cognitive-neuroscience techniques to the study of anxiety-related processing biases in children. In J. Hadwin & A. Field (Eds.), *Information processing biases in child and adolescent anxiety* (pp. 183–206). Chichester, UK: John Wiley & Sons.

Pérez-Edgar, K., & Hastings, P. D. (2018). Emotion development from an experimental and individual differences lens. In J. T. Wixted (Ed.), *The Stevens' handbook of experimental psychology and cognitive neuroscience* (Vol. 4, 4th ed., pp. 289–321. New York, NY: Wiley.

Pérez-Edgar, K., Kujawa, A., Nelson, S. K., Cole, C., & Zapp, D. J. (2013). The relation between electroencephalogram asymmetry and attention biases to threat at baseline and under stress. *Brain and Cognition, 82*(3), 337–343.

Posner, M. I., Rothbart, M. K., Sheese, B. E., & Voelker, P. (2014). Developing attention: behavioral and brain mechanisms. *Advances in Neuroscience, 1*, 405094. https://doi.org/10.1155/2014/405094

Reissland, N., Francis, B., & Mason, J. (2011). Do facial expressions develop before birth? *PloS One, 6*, e24081.

     (2013). Can healthy fetuses show facial expressions of "pain" or "distress"? *PloS One, 8*, e65530.

Reznik, S. J., & Allen, J. J. (2018). Frontal asymmetry as a mediator and moderator of emotion: An updated review. *Psychophysiology, 55*(1), e12965.

Rothbart, M. K. (2011). *Becoming who we are: Temperament and personality in development*. New York, NY: Guilford Press.

Rothbart, M. K., & Derryberry, D. (1981). Development of individual differences in temperament. In M. E. Lamb & A. L. Brown (Eds.), *Advances in developmental psychology* (Vol. 1, pp. 37–86). Hillsdale, NJ: Lawrence Erlbaum Associates.

Scherer, K. R., Schorr, A., & Johnstone, T. (Eds.). (2001). *Appraisal processes in emotion: Theory, methods, research*. Oxford: Oxford University Press.

Silvers, J. A., Buhle, J. T., & Ochsner, K. N. (2013). The neuroscience of emotion regulation: Basic mechanisms and their role in development, aging and psychopathology. In K. N. Ochsner and S. M. Kosslyn (Eds.). *The handbook of cognitive neuroscience* (Vol. 1, pp. 52–78). New York, NY: Oxford University Press.

Stifter, C. A., & Corey, J. M. (2001). Vagal regulation and observed social behavior in infancy. *Social Development, 10*, 189–201.

Sylvester, C. M., Smyser, C. D., Smyser, T., Kenley, J., Ackerman Jr, J. J., Shimony, J. S., … Rogers, C. E. (2017). Cortical functional connectivity evident after birth and behavioral inhibition at age 2. *American Journal of Psychiatry, 175*(2), 180–187.

Thomas, J. C., Letourneau, N., Campbell, T. S., Tomfohr-Madsen, L., & Giesbrecht, G. F. (2017). Developmental origins of infant emotion regulation: Mediation by temperamental negativity and moderation by maternal sensitivity. *Developmental Psychology, 53*, 611–628.

Tronick, E. Z. (1989). Emotions and emotional communication in infants. *American Psychologist, 44*, 112–119.

Vaish, A., Grossmann, T., & Woodward, A. (2008). Not all emotions are created equal: The negativity bias in social-emotional development. *Psychological Bulletin, 134*, 383–403.

Vaughn, B., & Sroufe, L. A. (1979). The temporal relationship between infant heart rate acceleration and crying in an aversive situation. *Child Development, 50*, 565–567.

Weinberg, M. K., & Tronick, E. Z. (1998). The impact of maternal psychiatric illness on infant development. *Journal of Clinical Psychiatry, 59*, 53–61.

Yrttiaho, S., Forssman, L., Kaatiala, J., & Leppänen, J. M. (2014). Developmental precursors of social brain networks: The emergence of attentional and cortical sensitivity to facial expressions in 5 to 7 months old infants. *PloS One, 9*(6), e100811.

27 Infant Emotional Development

Samantha Mitsven, Daniel S. Messinger,
Jacquelyn Moffitt, and Yeojin Amy Ahn*

Infants are emotional. From peals of laughter to disconsolate crying, infants are notorious for both the intensity and lability of their emotional displays. From the 1-year-old's distress in pursuing a retreating parent to the 2-year-old's joyful pursuit of a favorite pet, emotion appears to be a central motivator of infant action. Infancy is also characterized by rapid emotional development. Neonates exhibit high rates of crying, but by 6 months broad-mouthed smiles are a common feature of social play. Infants develop sadness expressions in the first year, demonstrate empathy by 2 years, and pride by 3.

Despite the clarity of some features of infant emotional life, multiple theories of emotional development exist and the chapter begins by summarizing competing and complementary theoretical perspectives. In light of unresolved theoretical questions, we review what is known about the development of negative and positive emotions in the first years of life, and report similarities in the expression of positive and negative emotion. This is followed by a discussion of the neural underpinnings of emotion perception where we note the relative lack of research on the neural concomitants of emotion expression. We next illustrate the complexities of emotional development by reviewing behavioral, cognitive, and caregiving dimensions involved in the emergence of empathy. The penultimate section of the chapter provides perspective by investigating cross-cultural differences in emotional development. Finally, we discuss policies that may support optimal emotional functioning, and conclude with suggestions for future research.

27.1 Theoretical Orientations

Theories of emotional development differ as to the defining features of infant emotion and how emotions develop (Camras, Fatani, Fraumeni, & Shuster, 2018). They offer competing perspectives on how behaviors such as crying are associated with emotional states such as distress. Most important,

* Work on this chapter was supported, in part, by grants to the second author from the National Science Foundation (1620294) and the Institute of Education Sciences (R324A180203).

however, is the degree to which these theories have generated productive research on infant emotional development.

27.1.1 Cognitive Differentiation

Developmentalists have long posited that emotional development involves the emergence of more differentiated emotional states from more diffuse states (Bridges, 1932). More undifferentiated distress expressions manifested in crying and accompanying facial expressions, for example, are characteristic of the first months of life while facial expressions of anger, sadness, and fear emerge over the first year (Sroufe, 1979; Sroufe & Waters, 1976; Tomkins, 1962). This differentiation perspective is typically aligned with a theoretical emphasis on the role of cognitive understanding as a defining characteristic of emotion (L. F. Barrett, 2006; Bridges, 1932; Sroufe, 1996).

A cognitive differentiation perspective holds that infants must be aware of their own affective reaction for emotion to be present (Lewis, 2018). In the first 2 to 3 months of life, for example, smiles are thought to be a pre-emotional signal of sensory pleasure – and to index a relaxation in cognitive tension related to recognition of a visual stimulus. Only when the infant, sometime after 6 months, is at least implicitly aware of their own emotional response – seeking and finding the parent's face during peek-a-boo, for example – is joy said to be present (Sroufe, 1996). Likewise, toward the end of the second year of life, the cognitive ability to recognize another's pain heralds the emergence of emotions such as empathy (Lewis, 2018). The emphasis on cognitive awareness of feelings as a defining characteristic of emotion contrasts with discrete emotion perspectives.

27.1.2 Discrete Emotion Theory

Discrete emotion theories regard core affective feelings as the defining feature of infant emotions (Ackerman, Abe, & Izard, 1998; Bridges, 1932; Izard & Ackerman, 2000; Sroufe, 1996; Tomkins, 1962). The elation of joy or the dejection of sadness are thought to be developmentally invariant characteristics of emotion states. These feeling states are hypothesized to be the product of discrete affect programs that also output specific patterns of expressive action such as facial expressions (Ackerman et al., 1998; Izard & Ackerman, 2000). As neurophysiologically based affect programs give rise to both expressive actions and feelings, the expressive actions are thought to typically index feeling states during infancy (though exceptions are allowed in early infancy; (Izard & Abe, 2004). Through its emphasis on facial expressions as markers of feeling states, discrete emotion theory can be thought of as the implicit theoretical basis for the vast quantities of research that use facial expressions as dependent variables to examine individual and group differences in expressivity. Discrete emotion theory, however, has also motivated a body of research that challenges its own account of the correspondence between expression and emotion in infancy.

27.1.3 Functionalist Theory

While discrete theories hold that emotion exists within the individual, functionalist theory holds that emotions are defined by maintaining and altering relationships with the social environment (K. C. Barrett, 1993; Campos, Mumme, Kermoian, & Campos, 1994; Witherington, Campos, & Hertenstein, 2001). Emotion, then, resides in the infant's relationships. Sadness, for example, functions to elicit succor and tenderness from caregivers. Oster (2005) proposes an ontogenetic variant of functionalist theory, which asks what expressive behaviors are available to the infant at a given age and how they allow the infant to function in his or her environment. More broadly, the functionalist perspective has served to direct attention to vocal, gestural, and whole-body expressions of emotion in context.

27.1.4 Sociocultural Theory

Sociocultural theory considers the proximal cultural rules and scripts that guide interactions as the rubric in which emotional development occurs (Holodynski, 2009; Holodynski & Friedlmeier, 2006). Holodynski and colleagues argue that in educated Western families, when infants make initial signals of an emotional experience such as pleasure and distress, parents respond with more discrete models of the initial signal such as smiles or an exaggerated sadness display, and frequently label the infant's presumed emotional experience. In this way, preverbal expressions of infant emotions develop more culturally meaningful forms. Depending on cultural values, expressions of infant emotions are differentially imitated and imbued with linguistic meaning.

27.1.5 Dynamic Systems

A dynamic systems approach focuses on emotional process as the transaction of multiple interfacing constituents including expressive actions, physiological arousal, and the social surround (Camras et al., 2018; Messinger, Fogel, & Dickson, 1997; Thelen & Smith, 1994). Emotion is thought to be the emergent outcome of the bottom-up inter-relationship of neural, expressive, social, and physiological constituents. In this chapter, we employ a dynamic systems approach as a meta-theoretical orientation with which to integrate insights from other perspectives in part to emphasize their areas of overlap and agreement. The differentiation perspective, for example, highlights the development of self-referential cognition as critical to the emergence of emotions such as empathy. This perspective is consonant with a dynamic systems emphasis on the bottom-up interplay of nonobvious constituents in emotional development.

27.2 Negative Emotional Development

Below we review the development of negative emotions, noting the overwhelming evidence for the prevalence of the cry-face expression from before birth through at least 6 months of postnatal age. In that context, we discuss the appearance of facial expressions of negative emotion including distress, anger, sadness, and fear in the first year of life. The evidence suggests that expressions of these discrete emotions are rare, difficult to recognize, and do not consistently occur in the contexts hypothesized to elicit the emotions in question. However, we also note that facial expressions of anger and sadness are associated with different patterns of physiological responsivity and patterns of motor (in)activity, which suggest different functional roles for these emotions.

27.2.1 Early Cry-Face Expressions

27.2.1.1 *Distress Expressions in Fetuses*
Recent advances in the use of three- and four-dimensional ultrasonography have allowed researchers to explore the fetal origins of emotional expression. Fetuses were observed displaying cry-face pain/distress expressions in which brow knotting was combined with stretching of the lower lip and/or mouth opening as early as 20 weeks of gestational age (Dondi et al., 2012). To chart this prenatal development, Reissland, Francis, and Mason (2013) reliably coded components of the cry-face configuration including brow lowering, upper-lip raising, and mouth opening. Between 24 and 36 weeks gestation, there was an increase in the likelihood of such facial components co-occurring to produce increasingly complex cry-face configurations. In sum, facial movements involved in cry faces appear to be part of an early developing muscular synergy such as those proposed by dynamic systems theorists (Messinger et al., 1997).

27.2.1.2 *Postnatal Cry Faces*
Undifferentiated distress manifested in cry faces and accompanying cry/fuss vocal expressions are the most salient and common expressions of negative emotions in the first months of life. Although postnatal cry faces may occur (as in the fetuses) without known cause, they frequently reflect a continuum of negative response from discomfort to pain. Infant pain accompanying immunization, for example, is signaled by a cry-face expression involving deepening of the nasolabial furrow, raising of the upper lip, tightening of the lower eyelids, cheek raising, jaw dropping, and horizontal mouth stretching (Kohut, Riddell, Flora, & Oster, 2012). Different combinations of these core facial actions, including the presence or absence of eye constriction and the intensity

of mouth stretching, reflect the intensity of the pain as well as infants' ability to regulate their own distress (Kohut et al., 2012).

27.2.2 The Development of Discrete Negative Emotions

Given the predominance of distress, a preeminent question in the first years of life is when (and if) discrete negative emotional states of anger, fear, and sadness emerge. Four overlapping areas of evidence are relevant here: (1) Do the expressions of negative emotion specified by differential emotions theory tend to occur as discrete entities? (2) Do adults perceive the target facial expressions as presentations of the emotion in question (face validity)? (3) Are the emotion displays reliably elicited by contexts and situations designed to elicit them (situational specificity)? (4) Do these displays co-occur with behaviors or physiological patterns consonant with the emotional meaning represented by the facial expression (withdrawal with sadness, for example)?

27.2.2.1 The Occurrence of Discrete Negative Expressions

The first question is whether the full-face expressions specified by discrete emotion theory (e.g., anger) occur more frequently than blended expressions. Matias and Cohn (1993) compared the longitudinal occurrence of full-face expressions of discrete emotion and blended expressions (e.g., an anger brow together with a mouth configured in pouting sadness configuration) at 2, 4, and 6 months. Proportions of full-face and blended expressions did not differ or change with age, indicating that discrete expressions of negative emotion are not more common than blends.

The morphology of the discrete emotion anger expression itself overlaps with the distress/pain cry-face expression. In the discrete emotion description of the early anger expression, the brow is lowered, the upper lip is lifted, the corners of the mouth are drawn to the side, and the mouth is opened to produce a squarish configuration (Izard, Dougherty, & Hembree, 1983; Izard, Hembree, Dougherty, & Spizzirri, 1983). If the muscle surrounding the eyes (orbicularis oculi) now contracts, raising the cheeks (pars lateralis) and squinting the eyes (pars palpebralis), the anger configuration becomes a cry-face or distress-pain expression. It is possible, then, that anger expressions may occur as infants move in and out of cry-face expressions. More radically, the anger constellation may be an attenuated version, and perhaps the developmental outgrowth, of the cry-face (distress) expression (Camras et al., 2018).

27.2.2.2 Adult Perception of Infants' Discrete Negative Expressions

When young infants do exhibit expressions of discrete emotion, it is reasonable to expect that adults can accurately identify these facial expressions. When viewing prototypical exemplars of discrete joy, interest, and surprise (Izard, 1979; Izard, Dougherty et al., 1983), adults were accurate (83%) in identifying the exemplar emotions (Oster, Hegley, & Nagel, 1992). However, adults identified infant facial expressions reflecting discrete negative emotions of disgust, fear, anger, and sadness with very low (6%) accuracy. Camras, Sullivan, and Michel (1993) also found low levels of adult recognition using dynamic (video) displays where infant facial expressions of negative emotion were accompanied by corresponding body movements and vocalizations. Adults rated each negative emotion higher on distress than on the discrete emotion being depicted. In sum, adult judgment studies suggest that through 2 years of age infants display a generalized distress-linked emotion expression rather than discrete facial expressions of anger, fear, and sadness (Oster et al., 1992).

27.2.2.3 Negative Emotion Expression in Emotion-Eliciting Situations

Research on infants' facial expressions in response to situations hypothesized to differentially elicit discrete emotion expressions has failed to find evidence of specificity for negative emotion expressions of anger, disgust, sadness, and fear. Bennett, Bendersky, and Lewis (2002) found that, contrary to hypotheses, surprise and joy expressions were 4-month-olds' most common response to both arm restraint and being approached by a masked stranger, and that sadness expressions were the most common reaction to a sour taste. Camras et al. (2007) reported a similar lack of differentiation of facial expressions. Anger expressions were the most common reaction to both anger- and fear-eliciting conditions. Likewise, Bennett, Bendersky, and Lewis (2005) reported increases in full-face anger expressions in response to arm restraint (9% to 22%) from 4 to 12 months of age, but also observed that anger expressions were elevated at both ages in response to the fear-eliciting condition. These results suggest increasing specificity of discrete facial expressions to targeted emotion elicitors in the first year of life, although few infants produced the target expressions overall.

27.2.2.4 Actions and Vocalizations Distinguishing Anger and Sadness Expression

Although concordance between emotion-eliciting contexts and specific facial expressions is rare, early anger and sadness may be linked to specific action patterns. Four-month-olds who are suddenly unable to make a display appear, display anger expressions and persistent arm pulling. When the display was removed from same-age infants who never learned to control it, sadness and decreased arm pulling was observed. Likewise, Weinberg and Tronick (1994) found moderate evidence for the behavioral specificity of anger and sadness behavioral configurations in the face-to-face/still-face (FFSF) protocol at 6 months. Sad facial expressions were associated with fussy vocalizations and spitting up. Angry expressions were associated not only with fussy vocalizations but also with crying, pick-me-up gestures, and avoidance (turning away from the partner) movements. There was no evidence of situational specificity as both anger and sadness behavior constellations increased during the maternal still-face and remained high when mother reinitiated play. These results suggest overlapping but distinguishable anger and sadness states as early as 4 months of age.

27.2.2.5 *Physiological Specificity of Negative Emotion Expressions*

In conjunction with reports of distinguishable motor activity patterns, differential associations between physiological and emotional responses to a blocked goal have been observed. At 4 months, increases in sadness following the extinction of a learned arm-pulling response were associated with higher cortisol levels (Lewis & Ramsay, 2005) as were 6-month-olds' increases in sadness in the still-face episode of the FFSF protocol (Lewis & Ramsay, 2005; Lewis, Ramsay, & Sullivan, 2006). These results suggest that, at least in response to loss of control, infant sadness and anger facial expressions coincide with specific physiologically mediated responses. However, infants who exhibited higher increases in anger also exhibited higher increases in sadness, suggesting these were not entirely disparate emotional reactions.

27.2.2.6 *Body Movement and Negative Emotion Expressions*

Toward 1 year of age, there is evidence that infant body movements reflect different emotional states (Camras et al., 2007). Eleven-month-old infants withdrew, struggled, and turned toward their caregiver more frequently in response to arm restraint but tended to increase respiration and stilling in response to a growling gorilla (Camras et al., 2007). Likewise, adults tended to rate infant discomfort and anger expressions as being accompanied by flexed, jerky, and active body movements while sadness displays were described by depressed body activity (Camras et al., 1993). These results seem consistent with a motivational model where anger and sadness/fear are differentially related to approach and withdrawal tendencies. (Buss & Kiel, 2004).

27.2.3 Negative Emotion Conclusions

In summary, cry faces develop *in utero* as increasing numbers of facial components of the expression co-occur in the apparent absence of negative emotion elicitors. After birth, the cry-face expression is a prepotent response to pain and is used to index distress. In fact, an attenuated version of the cry face in which the eyes are constricted but not squeezed shut is the basis of discrete anger expressions, which suggests variations of distress are infants' most common negative emotion expression through 1 year of life. Relatedly, discrete expressions of negative emotion including anger, fear, and sadness occur in the first 6 months of life but not more frequently than blends of these expressions. Moreover, they tend to be perceived by adults as expressions of distress more so than that of the specific target emotion. There is evidence that facial expressions of anger and disgust (but not fear) become more likely in contexts designed to elicit these emotions over the first year of life, but the overall number of infants who display the expressions is low. When anger and sadness expressions do occur after 4 months of age, they appear to reflect different developing emotional orientations to the environment. Anger is associated with increased heart rate and instrumental bodily movements while sadness expressions are associated with bodily stilling and cortisol reactivity, suggesting that distinct functions for these two emotions emerge over the first years of life.

Oster argues that infant emotions should be understood not in terms of adult emotion categories but from a functionalist ontogenetic perspective (Camras et al., 2018; Oster, 2005). From this perspective, one might suggest that through the first year of life, cry-face expressions and associated crying and fussing are reliable tools for soliciting caregiving from parents and others (Bell & Mary, 1972). The emergence of anger expressions from distress expressions involves a decoupling of intense eye squinting from the squared mouth of the anger configuration in the service of active visual engagement with the object of the emotion. As infant motor coordination improves, instrumental actions such as arm batting and body twisting (supported by increased heart rate) are incorporated into angry responses. Distress, which is perhaps prototypically *about* the self (I am overwhelmed by negative affect), yields anger, which is *about* the environment (that situation must change). Meanwhile, beginning in the first year and becoming more evident in the second year, a more passive withdrawal associated with sadness becomes an increasingly effective medium for indicating that a situation is displeasing to the infant.

27.3 Positive Emotional Development

Infants express happiness and joy most clearly through facial expressions and laugher and, with less specificity, through vocalizations, touch, and physical movement. Adults perceive infant smiles to be direct expressions of joyful feelings (Abe, Beetham, & Izard, 2002; Darwin, [1872] 1998). Infant laughter is a rhythmic vocalization that indexes especially intense joy (Sroufe & Waters, 1976) and is frequently elicited by tickling and other physically stimulating games (Cohn & Tronick, 1987; Davila-Ross, Jesus, Osborne, & Barad, 2015; Lewis & Granic, 2000; Owren & Amoss, 2014). Scientific observers posit that children clap their hands and jump with joy (Darwin, [1872] 1998). However, like nonlaughter vocalizations, these actions appear to accentuate smiles and laughter but may not be independently associated with positive affect (Hsu, Fogel, & Messinger, 2001; Weinberg & Tronick, 1994; Yale, Messinger, & Cobo-Lewis, 2003).

Taken as a whole, infant facial expressions of happiness and joy are differentially elicited by situations posited to elicit positive emotion, and are easily discernible as such to adult observers. Next, we review behavioral expressions of happiness and joy and their heterogeneity, discuss the emergence of positive emotional interaction in the first 6 months of life, and describe how smiles are embedded in referential communicative gesturing between 8 and 18 months. We conclude by asking whether different types of infant smiling reflect different types of positive affect, and suggest that infant positive affect expression is inherently social.

27.3.1 Varieties of Positive Emotion Expression

Although levels of infant smiling as a whole rise between 2 and 6 months, infants exhibit different types of smiling with different developmental trajectories.

27.3.1.1 *Strong Smiles*
Infant smiles vary continuously. Degree of zygomaticus major contraction (the muscle controlling lip-corner retraction) determines a smile's strength. Parent tickling produces stronger smiling than not tickling (Fogel, Hsu, Shapiro, Nelson-Goens, & Secrist, 2006), and stronger smiles are perceived as more positive than weaker smiles. As infant smiles become stronger and weaker, the strength of co-occurring eye constriction and the extent of co-occurring mouth opening increase as well (Messinger, Mattson, Mahoor, & Cohon, 2012). All of these features index the intensity of early joy (see Figure 27.1).

27.3.1.2 *Duchenne Smiles and Open-Mouth Smiles*
Duchenne smiles are a well-known signal of joy, which may index reciprocated positive affect in infants. Duchenne smiles involve eye constriction produced by orbicularis oculi (pars lateralis), the Duchenne marker (Duchenne, [1862] 1990). Through 6 months, Duchenne smiles are most common when gazing at mother, and, at 12 months, when infants are approached by their smiling mothers (Fox & Davidson, 1988). Heart rate, however, does not appear to vary between smiles with and without the Duchenne marker (Mattson, Ekas et al., 2013). Frequently elicited by excited social engagement, infant smiles involving mouth opening (jaw dropping) are most likely to occur while infants look at their mothers' faces (Messinger et al., 2012) and are a frequent context for laughter (Davila-Ross et al., 2015; Nwokah, Hsu, Davies, & Fogel, 1999; Sroufe & Waters, 1976).

27.3.1.3 *Combined Open-Mouth Duchenne Smiles*
Infant smiles that involve the Duchenne marker also tend to involve mouth opening (see Figure 27.1) (Messinger, Fogel, & Dickson, 1999), and tend to occur during particularly positive epochs of interaction such as when infants gaze at their smiling mothers (Messinger, Fogel, & Dickson, 2001). Moreover, open-mouth Duchenne smiles exhibit developmental specificity (Mendes & Seidl-de-Moura, 2014). Through the first 6 months, these smiles became relatively more likely than other smiles when infants were gazing at their smiling mothers (the most positive eliciting context) but showed relative declines when mothers were not smiling and infants were gazing away from mother (Messinger et al., 2001). By 1 year, open-mouth Duchenne smiles are most likely to occur in contexts that elicit intense joy such as tickling (Fogel et al.,

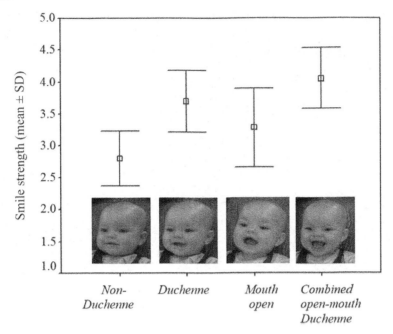

Figure 27.1. *Mean smile strength from 1–5 of different smile types. Source: Fogel et al. (2006).*

2006) and physical play with parents (Dickson, Walker, & Fogel, 1997). Overall, stronger smiles and smiles that involve both mouth opening and the Duchenne marker (eye constriction) are the most joyful, while smiles without these features are more likely to index less intense happiness (Messinger et al., 2012).

27.3.1.4 *Laughter*

Laughter emerges developmentally between 2 and 5 months (Nwokah, Hsu Dobrowolska, & Fogel, 1994; Washburn, 1929), and between 6 and 12 months of age, infants become more likely to laugh during active social games such as peek-a-boo (Sroufe & Waters, 1976). Between 1 and 2 years, infant and mother laugh onsets and offsets come to follow one another more closely in time, indicating increasing interactive coordination of joyful expressions (Nwokah et al., 1994). The form of laughter also appears to change developmentally (Sauter, Evans, Venneker, & Kret, 2018). At 3 months, infants tend to laugh both while inhaling and exhaling, a pattern shared with chimpanzees; older infants, however, tend to laugh only while exhaling, a pattern seen in older children and adults.

27.3.2 The Development of Happiness and Joy

27.3.2.1 *Prenatal and Neonatal Smiling*

Reissland, Francis, Mason, and Lincoln (2011) observed smiling, eye constriction (the Duchenne marker), and lip parting at 32.5 weeks gestation, and found that these smiling configurations become increasingly complex between

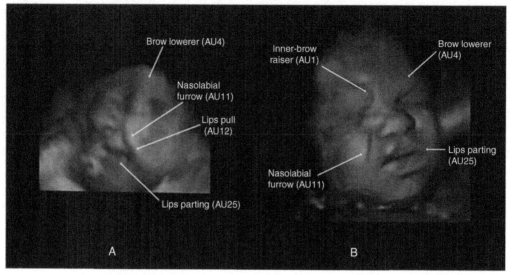

Figure 27.2. *In utero smile and cry-face configurations at 32 weeks gestation. Action units (AUs) are defined by the Facial Action Coding System (Ekman & Friesen, 1992). (A) Facial AUs associated with a prenatal smile configuration. (B) Facial AUs associated with cry-face configurations.*
Source: Reprinted from Reissland et al. (2011).

24 and 34 weeks gestation (see Figure 27.2). An intriguing feature of these prenatal results was the occurrence of brow lowering that, postnatally, does not overlap with smiling (Oster, 1978). Smiling is present from birth in both full-term and preterm neonates (Emde & Koenig, 1969; Emde, McCartney, & Harmon, 1971) but occurs predominantly in sleeping/drowsy states involving rapid eye movement (Dondi et al., 2007). In full-term neonates, smiles with strong zygomaticus major contraction and the Duchenne marker occur in roughly equal proportion to weaker smiles without eye constriction (Dondi et al., 2007; Messinger et al., 2002). Although stronger Duchenne smiles in the neonate suggest positive emotion, these smiles rarely occur outside of sleep and are not integrated into social interaction.

27.3.2.2 The Transition to Social Smiling Between 1 and 2 Months

Smiles during sleep states decrease in frequency and stronger smiles increase during alert states toward 1 month of age (Harmon & Emde, 1972; Mizuno, Takeshita, & Matsuzawa, 2006; Wolff, 1987). In the second month, infants spend more time in alert states, which facilitates gazing at caregivers' faces and interaction (Lavelli & Fogel, 2005). This sets the stage for the emergence of social smiles. A 3–20-second epoch of brow knitting and gazing at the mother's face, is typically followed by relaxation of the brows and smiling

(Anisfeld, 1982; Lavelli & Fogel, 2005; Oster, 1978). Thus, a period of effort, perhaps linked to recognition of the parent's face, appears to precede the first social expressions of happiness. Physiological arousal is hypothesized to drive neonatal smiles, while a relaxation of cognitive tension occurring when infants recognize the parental face as meaningful, is hypothesized to drive social smiles (Sroufe, 1996).

27.3.3 Developments in Interactive Smiling Between 2 and 6 Months

As infant social smiles become more frequent in interaction around 2 months of age, maternal positive expressions also increase (Lavelli & Fogel, 2002). Turn-taking in which mothers and infants alternate initiating and terminating smiles increases (Messinger, Ruvolo, Ekas, & Fogel, 2010) and smiling interactions become faster paced between 2 and 6 months (Malatesta, Culver, Tesman, & Shepard, 1989). At the same time, individual infants' smiling levels from 1 week to the next become more similar to each other over successive weeks of interaction – and the same pattern is evident for mother smiling (Messinger et al., 2010). That is, infants (and mothers) develop increasingly stable levels of positive affect expression. Infants also become accustomed to specific levels of partner responsivity. Two-month-olds smile less to an interactive partner who is either more or less responsive to the infant's smiles than the infant's mother (Biglow & Rochat, 2006). Thus, infant expressions of positive affect become increasingly tied to their partner's levels of smiling and responsivity.

27.3.3.1 *Temporal Patterning of Smiles*
Infant expressions of joy develop in tandem with changes in the patterning of infant attention to the partner's face. Between 2 and 6 months, infants devote less time to gazing at their mothers' faces, but become more likely to smile when they are doing so (Kaye & Fogel, 1980). The temporal patterning of smiling and attending to the parent's face also changes (Yale et al., 2003). Three-month-olds' smiles occur within a gaze at the parent's face. By 6 months, infants continue to initiate smiles while gazing at the parent's face but then gaze away from the parent before they end the smile. In fact, when 5-month-olds play peek-a-boo, they are more likely to gaze away from the mother's face for longer periods of time during stronger, longer-lasting smiles (Stifter & Moyer, 1991). This suggests that as infants increasingly participate in arousing social exchanges with intensely joyful smiles, they become more likely to regulate their own involvement in interchanges by gazing away from their interactive partners.

27.3.3.2 *Infant and Mother Responsivity to Smiling*
The FFSF protocol is well suited to examining dynamic changes in infant positive and negative affect. In the FFSF, an episode of face-to-face play is followed by the still-face episode (in which the parent maintains a still face and does not respond to the infant's bids) and then a reunion episode in which the

parent resumes playing with the infant (Adamson & Frick, 2003; Mesman, van IJzendoorn, & Bakermans-Kranenburg, 2009). As a whole, smiling declines precipitously over the course of the still face (Ekas, Haltigan, & Messinger, 2013) and rises again when the parent reengages with the infant, although not quite to initial face-to-face play levels.

27.3.3.3 Contingent Responsiveness

Parents' expressive responses to infant smiling during face-to-face interactions allow infants to experience themselves as instigators of positive interactions with others. Infants aged 2 to 3 months, for example, whose mothers exhibit higher vocal contingent responsiveness display more smiles when their mother adopts a still face (as a way to reengage their mothers) than do infants of less responsive mothers (Bigelow & Power, 2016). Descriptive data suggest that infant and mother continuously affect one another's joyful expressions such that stronger infant smiling is mirrored by stronger mother smiling (Messinger, Mahoor, Chow, & Cohen, 2009).

Although infants and parents respond to one another in play, this responsiveness is asymmetric. Infant smiles reliably elicit mother smiles, typically within a 2-second window (Malatesta & Haviland, 1982; van Egeren, Barratt, & Roach, 2001). However, mother smiles are less reliable elicitors of infant smiles than the reverse (Cohn & Tronick, 1987; Kaye & Fogel, 1980) and mothers frequently smile when infants are not smiling (Messinger et al., 2010). Parent smiles in the absence of infant smiles reduce the degree to which the parent smiles and are contingent on those of the infant (Symons & Moran, 1994). In fact, infant smiles are most likely in response to multimodal parental displays involving some combination of smiling, laughter, touching the infant, and high-pitched infant-directed speech (Cohn & Tronick, 1987; Feldman, 2003; Feldman, Greenbaum, & Yirmiya, 1999; Fogel, 1988).

27.3.3.4 Increases in Smiling Intensity During Interaction

When caregivers respond to their infants' smiles with increasingly intense smiles, infants are likely to perceive the increase in the parental positive emotion and simultaneously perceive an increase in their own joy. Processes implicated in infants' positive responses to their parent's positive expressivity may include a hypothesized mirror neuron system (Marshall & Meltzoff, 2014) or automatic facial mimicry (de Klerk, Lamy-Yang, & Southgate, 2018; Isomura & Nakano, 2016). Interactions in which infants simultaneously experience their own positive emotions, and the role of their own joyful expression in augmenting the expressions of others, suggest that one path to the development of joy involves interactively experiencing another's joy (Holodynski, 2009).

27.3.3.5 Why Infants Smile

Inverse optimal reinforcement modeling allows one to infer infant and mother probable goals during interactions (Ruvolo, Messinger, & Movellan, 2015). Goals are inferred from the likely consequences of beginning and ending smiles on the durations of ensuing dyadic states such as mutual smiling. This modeling indicates that mothers act to increase time in mutual smiling. Infants, on the other hand, act to increase time in states when mother is smiling but the infant is not smiling. Infants enact this goal, for example, by smiling briefly until the mother smiles and then ending their own smile. These findings are challenging because they suggest that infants do not act to increase the time they are expressing happiness. Instead, infant smiles may be part of a dyadic process that involves creating and then disengaging from moments of mutual positive emotion expression (Stifter & Moyer, 1991).

27.3.4 Smiling Between 6 and 18 Months

In the first 6 months of life, smiles and laughter appear to represent nonreflective expressions of ongoing emotional experience (Kaye & Fogel, 1980). Between 6 and 12 months, infants become increasingly intentional communicators, and are more likely to coordinate smiling with gestures and gazes that reference objects and events (Striano & Bertin, 2005). The coordination of positive affect expressions with referential communication represents the type of cognitive awareness that differentiation theorists argue heralds the emergence of joy and other emotions (Adamson & Bakeman, 1985; Messinger & Fogel, 1998).

27.3.4.1 Anticipatory Smiling
Anticipatory smiling is a pattern of referential communication, which emerges around 8 months of age and increases in frequency through 12 months. Anticipatory smiling occurs when infants gaze at an object or event, smile, and then continue to smile as they shift their attention to a social partner who is also attending to the object or event (Venezia, Messinger, Thorp, & Mundy, 2004). Anticipatory smiles often appear to communicate something like, "That was funny, wasn't it?" (Mundy, Thorpe, Hogan, & Doehring, 1996; Seibert, Hogan, & Mundy, 1982). Anticipatory smiling is associated with the comprehension of means–end relationships (Jones & Hong, 2001), suggesting that anticipatory smiling indexes infants' emerging understanding that positive affect can be shared with another (Venezia et al., 2004).

27.3.4.2 Happiness and Pretense
Incongruous (unexpected and unthreatening) events such as placing a ball on one's head elicit joyful reactions early in development. Five-month-old infants are more likely to smile and laugh in response to a confederate engaging in absurd actions (e.g., poking a clown nose and saying "beep") than ordinary actions (Mireault et al., 2018). Between 5 and 7 months, infants are faster to initiate smiles and laughs when their parents provide positive affective cues following an absurd event (Mireault et al., 2015), a pattern also observed in 18-month-olds (Lillard et al., 2007; Nishida & Lillard, 2007). Incongruous events appear to elicit happiness and joy between 5 and 18 months, although the importance of smiles displayed by those around the infant requires continued investigation.

27.3.5 Positive Emotion Conclusions

27.3.5.1 *Positive Affect Multiplicity?*

Overall, smiling develops from an endogenous neonatal expression to a signal of intense positive social engagement at 6 months, which becomes embedded in referential communications by 12 months. The discrete perspective holds that there is a single happiness/joy emotion in infancy, which is accompanied by specific feeling states. However, the infancy literature suggests that Duchenne smiles involve reciprocated positive affect, smiles involving mouth opening are associated with arousing sociality, and strong smiles with both features mark the climax of mutually positive states. The possibility that different types of smiling (and laughter) index different types of positive emotion is antithetical to a discrete perspective, which holds that there is one form of positive emotion. An alternate (and parsimonious) possibility holds that different types of smiling and laughter reflect a continuum of positive emotion. Relatedly, Duchenne smiles are often regarded as unique signals of joy (Ekman, Davidson, & Friesen, 1990). In early infancy, however, non-Duchenne and Duchenne smiles appear to reflect a range of positive emotion and frequently follow one another in time (Messinger et al., 1999).

27.3.5.2 *Is Early Positive Affect Expression Exclusively Social?*

Smiling faces – typically the smiles of playful social partners – are a potent elicitor of smiling and laughter in the first year of life. In fact, with the decline of smiling to audio stimuli during the first 2 months of life, it is unclear whether smiles and laughter can be reliably elicited by nonsocial stimuli. There is some evidence that infants between 9 and 11 months are more likely to smile and laugh when engaging in difficult motor actions (e.g., pulling to stand) than less difficult actions (e.g., pulling to sit) (Mayes & Zigler, 2006; but see Yarrow, Morgan, Jennings, Harmon, & Gaiter, 1982). However, these actions were observed in naturalistic settings where social contact was uncontrolled. Likewise, Watson (1972) found that after 3–5 days of daily exposure to a contingently controlled visual mobile, 8-week-old infants were reported by their mothers to engage in vigorous smiling and cooing. However, the sociality of the conditions in which mothers reported smiling could not be determined. It remains unknown, then, whether early positive affect expression – by far the most reliable index of happiness and joy – are linked to positive social interaction. If so, this would suggest that infants' prototypical expression of positive affect has an inherently social function.

27.4 Positive *and* Negative Emotion

Having discussed the development of negative and positive emotion separately, we now discuss the generalized Duchenne intensification hypothesis,

Figure 27.3. *Dynamic expressions of infant emotions showing increasing intensity of both smiling (top) and cry face (bottom). This 6-month-old infant's Duchenne marker (eye constriction) and mouth opening provide a parsimonious means for indexing the intensity of both positive (top) and negative (bottom) infant emotions. Notably, the Duchenne marker intensifies from left to right in both smiles and cry faces, accompanied by stronger pulling of the lip corners and mouth opening in smiles and horizontal mouth stretching in cry faces.*
Source: Messinger et al. (2012).

which posits similarities between smile and cry-face expressions. A dynamic systems perspective suggests that specific facial actions may have similar functions across positive and negative expressive configurations. Both smiles and cry face can involve the Duchenne marker – eye constriction produced by the muscle orbiting the eyes (orbicularis oculi, pars lateralis). As indexed by neurophysiological activity, eliciting situations, and signal value, the Duchenne marker appears to index both greater positive valence in smile expressions and greater negative valence of cry-face expressions (see Figure 27.3).

Electrophysiological evidence suggests greater left than right cerebral activation during Duchenne smiles than non-Duchenne smiles in 10-month-olds (Fox & Davidson, 1988), a pattern associated with approach motivation in adults (L. F. Barrett & Wager, 2006; Murphy, Nimmo-Smith, & Lawrence, 2003). The opposite pattern of electroencephalograph (EEG) asymmetries was observed during sadness and anger expressions with strong eye constriction

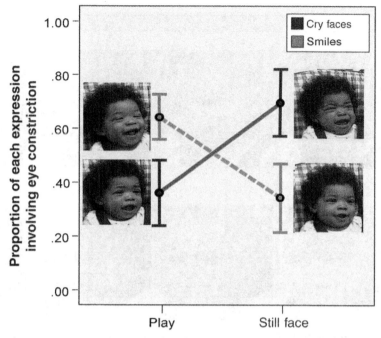

Figure 27.4. *Eye constriction (the Duchenne marker) indexes positive and negative affective intensity in the face-to-face/ still face (FFSF). Smiling during the face-to-face play with the parent involved a higher proportion of smiling with eye constriction than smiling during the still face. The still face involved a higher proportion of cry faces with eye constriction than face-to-face play.*
Source: Mattson, Cohn et al. (2013).

(as indexed by crying) (Fox & Davidson, 1988). The results support the general Duchenne intensification hypothesis, which was recently tested using the FFSF protocol (Mattson, Cohn, Mahoor, Gangi, & Messinger, 2013; but see Mattson, Ekas et al., 2013). Smiles during the positive-emotion-eliciting face-to-face play episode were more likely to involve eye constriction than smiles occurring during the negative-emotion-eliciting still face. In a cross-over effect, the proportion of cry faces involving eye constriction was higher during the still face than during face-to-face play (see Figure 27.4).

The general Duchenne intensification hypothesis was also tested using objective measurements (computer vision) of the intensity of facial actions (Messinger et al., 2012). Just as smiling actions were stronger in Duchenne smiles, the lateral mouth pulling of the cry face was stronger in the presence of the Duchenne marker. Even when controlling for the strength of smiling and mouth-pulling cry-face actions, eye constriction was a unique predictor of continuous ratings of positive emotional valence during smiles and negative emotional valence during cry faces. The results suggest that specific facial actions such as eye constriction can have a generalized intensifying effect. The possibility that specific facial actions have general functional roles in multiple types of facial expressions is an exciting area of future investigation (Susskind et al., 2008).

27.4.1 The Heritability of Positive and Negative Expressivity

Behavioral genetic analyses have shed light on the sources of early positive and negative emotional variability. Parent reports of infant smiling and laughter (temperament-linked indices of happiness and joy) typically reveal roughly similar levels of genetic and environmental influence (Goldsmith, Buss, & Lemery, 1997; Goldsmith, Lemery, Buss, & Campos, 1999). By contrast, parent reports of infant negative emotion expression yield higher genetic and lower environmental effects. However, a recent investigation of observed and parent-reported affect in a large sample of mono- and dizygotic twins produced striking results (Planalp, van Hulle, Lemery-Chalfant, & Goldsmith, 2017). Genetic (inherited) variability in negative emotion was not detectable, while shared environmental variance was evident in both observed and reported positive affect at both 6 and 12 months. These findings underscore the role of familial processes in the socialization of happiness and joy, and raise questions about the role of genetic variance in observed negative expressivity.

27.5 The Neural Context of Infant Emotional Development

Caregivers' facial expressions provide infants with information regarding the caregiver's emotional state and – in the case of fear expressions, for example – threats in the surrounding environment. Research on the neural underpinnings of emotional processing uses both event-related potentials (ERPs) – time-locked EEG – and near-infrared spectroscopy (NIRS) to examine the infant's processing of positive and negative emotional stimuli. In the ERP domain, infant N290 and P400 ERP components – negative and positive deviations of the EEG signal at 290 and 400 ms – show specificity to upright human faces (de Haan & Nelson, 1999; de Haan, Pascalis, & Johnson, 2002). Affective cues modulate activation in the negative central (Nc) component, which reflects attentional allocation to salient stimuli (Nelson & Monk, 2001).

The responsivity of infant face-sensitive (N290 and P400) and attention-associated Nc components suggest that a neural network for facial emotion processing emerges in the first year of life. The amplitude of the N290 and P400 response tends to distinguish between different combinations of happy, fearful, and angry expressions, although the direction of effects associated with the contrast between expressions is not consistent (Hoehl & Striano, 2008; Jessen & Grossmann, 2015; Kobiella, Grossman, Reid, & Striano, 2008; Leppänen, Moulson, Vogel-Farley, & Nelson, 2007; van den Boomen, Munsters, &

Kemner, 2019; Xie, McCormick, Westerlund, Bowman, & Nelson, 2018). As with the N290 and P400, investigations of the Nc component have yielded variable results. In 7-month-old infants, heightened Nc component amplitudes have been observed in response to fearful faces relative to happy expressions (Leppänen et al., 2007; Nelson & de Haan, 1996), angry relative to fearful faces (Kobiella et al., 2008), angry faces relative to happy and fearful faces (Xie et al., 2018), and happy relative to angry faces (Grossmann, Striano, & Friederici, 2005). Differences in results may be due to differences in the psychophysics of stimulus presentation and the intensity of the emotion displayed (Sprengelmeyer & Jentzsch, 2006). The use of source analysis and increased attention to developmental changes within the first year of life may ultimately contribute to greater understanding of the functional meaning of cortical responses to facial expressions (Xie et al., 2018). Finally, as discussed above, infants do not reliably produce fear faces in response to relevant experimental stimuli. Increased attention to individual differences in infant fearfulness would help integrate research on infants' perception of emotional stimuli and their production of emotional behavior.

27.5.1 Neural Bases of Affective Prosody Processing

At the same age at which infants exhibit differential responses to emotional facial expressions, they also exhibit differential responses to affective prosody. Words spoken with angry prosody are more attention-capturing – as indexed by the heightened amplitude of the Nc component in frontal and central scalp regions – to 7-month-old infants than those spoken with happy or neutral prosody (Grossmann et al., 2005). Likewise, sad vocalizations elicit significantly greater neural activation in brain regions that support processing of affective stimuli, including the insula and orbitofrontal cortex, than happy (i.e., laughing) and neutral vocalizations (i.e., coughing, sneezing; Blasi et al., 2011). Infants' amplified response to negative stimuli such as a fearful face or an angry tone of voice suggests increased allocation of attentional resources to negative affective information that may be associated with negative consequences for the infant.

27.5.2 Perception of Smiles

Research using NIRS suggests that brain regions involved in encoding reward value become functional toward 1 year of age (Mingawa-Kawai et al., 2009). Between 9 and 13 months of age, infants exhibited increased activation in the anterior orbitofrontal cortex, a region implicated in processing rewarding social information, in response to video clips of their mother's smile relative to mother's neutral expression. The infants exhibited more attenuated activation of the orbitofrontal cortex in response to an unfamiliar mother's smile. These findings suggest that orbitofrontal activation is especially responsive to positive emotional expressions from known and, arguably, rewarding individuals.

27.5.3 Neural Bases and Correlates of Emotional Expressivity

Spontaneous facial expressions involve an extrapyramidal pathway involving subcortical structures, such as the basal ganglia, and deep cortical structures, such as the amygdala, which communicate with the facial motor nucleus (Elliot, 1969; Williams, Warwick, Dyson, & Bannister, 1989). Relative to the substantial body of work examining the neural correlates of emotion processing, however, the literature examining the neural correlates of emotional expressivity is limited. Following Fox and Davidson's seminal research (1988), there have been few EEG-based studies of the neural correlates of infants' *production* of emotional expressions and, to our knowledge, no relevant neuroimaging studies. Portable methods for the acquisition of cortical hemodynamics through NIRS represent one method for addressing the urgent need to investigate the neural basis of infant emotional functioning *in situ* (Perlman, Luna, Hein, & Huppert, 2014). An understanding of the neural correlates of emotion expression, and the association between neural responsivity to emotional stimuli and the infant's production of emotional behavior, will require a new generation of research activity.

27.6 Empathy Development

Empathy, sharing another's emotional experience, is not a discrete emotion such as happiness, sadness, or fear. Instead, the development of empathy reflects the confluence of behavioral, cognitive, and expressive factors that characterize the emergence of emotional functioning more broadly. We review the development of empathy to illustrate emotional development as an evolving interface of perception, motoric responses, and actions that are influenced both by inherited and relational factors.

27.6.1 Responses to Other Infants' Cries

Precursors of empathy appear to be present in neonates (Sagi & Hoffman, 1976; Simner, 1971). Within 3 to 4 days of birth, infants produce more intense distress reactions when exposed to a newborn cry than when exposed to a computer-generated synthetic cry, white noise, silence (Sagi & Hoffman, 1976; Simner, 1971), or their own cry (Dondi, Simion, & Caltran, 1999). This contagious cry phenomenon continues without evident developmental change between 1 and 9 months of age (Geangu, Benga, Stahl, & Striano, 2010), although evidence of increased autonomic emotional arousal in the form of pupil dilation in response to another infant's cry has not been documented before 6 months (Geangu, Hauf, Bhardwaj, & Bentz, 2011). With respect to individual differences, however, it is not clear whether distress or autonomic arousal in response to another infant's crying in the first year of life is related to later responsiveness to adult distress.

27.6.2 Responsiveness to Adult Distress

The development of empathic concern is typically assessed by recording infants' responses to a caregiver or stranger who feigns a distressing event such as stubbing a toe (Zahn-Waxler, Radke-Yarrow, Wagner, & Chapman, 1992). Infants' potential empathy-related behaviors include attempts to alleviate distress or prosocial behavior (e.g., kisses), empathic concern for the distressed victim (e.g., "I'm sorry"), attempts to understand the cause of distress or hypothesis testing (e.g., "What happened?"), and attempts to replicate another's experience or self-referential behaviors (e.g., rubbing one own toe). Exploratory work indicates that empathic concern and hypothesis testing are observable by 8 months of age (Roth-Hanania, Davidov, & Zahn-Waxler, 2011). More generally, the frequency of prosocial behaviors, empathic concern, and hypothesis testing increases significantly from 13 to 25 months, and the entire repertoire of prosocial behaviors is observable by 2 years (Zahn-Waxler, Radke-Yarrow et al., 1992).

27.6.3 Genetic Influence on Empathy Development

By 14 months, there is a higher concordance of prosocial behavior, empathic concern, and hypothesis-testing behaviors among monozygotic (MZ) than dizygotic (DZ) twins, suggesting these empathy-related behaviors are influenced by genetic factors (Zahn-Waxler, Robinson, & Emde, 1992). Moreover, genetic concordance for individual differences in empathy emerged at 20 months and increased through 36 months in a separate study, while shared environmental effects that were evident at 14 months gradually declined with age (Knafo, Zahn-Waxler, van Hulle, Robinson, & Rhee, 2008). These findings highlight increases in hereditary influence on emerging empathy-related behaviors.

27.6.4 Contributions of Early Interactions to Empathy Development

In addition to the genetic influences indicated by twin studies, maternal responsiveness during mother–infant interactions is associated with individual differences in empathy development. Infants whose mothers were more responsive at 9 months – which encompassed the quality of mothers' responses to infants' bids, distress, need for help, or physiological signals – were more empathic when their mothers feigned distress at 22 months of age (Kochanska, Forman, & Coy, 1999). Along with maternal responsiveness, infants whose mothers were rated as exhibiting greater warmth were more empathic at 14 and 20 months than those whose mothers were rated lower on maternal warmth (Robinson, Zahn-Waxler, & Emde, 1994). These findings point to the importance of early warmth and responsivity in fostering empathic responding.

27.6.5 Empathy Conclusions

The development of empathy illustrates the importance of longitudinal studies integrating early potential behavioral substrates – negative affect and pupil dilation in response to a conspecific's cry – with later empathic action. Finally, understanding the intersecting roles of hereditary and caregiver responsiveness on empathy development will require increased attention to genetic correlates of parental behavior, parental warmth, and gene by environment interactions in the first years of life.

27.7 Cultural Differences in Infant Emotional Development

The majority of research on infant emotional development has been conducted in Western societies with highly educated samples (Henrich, Heine, & Norenzayan, 2010). There are, however, multiple pathways to infant emotional development. Of particular note are cultural emphases on collectivism versus individualism, and the valuing of emotional experience and expression (Halberstadt & Lozada, 2011). Here we explore cultural differences and similarities in parental expectations of infant emotion, parent responses to emotion, and differences in infant emotion expressions (Kärtner, Holodynski, & Wörman, 2013).

27.7.1 Culturally Divergent Parental Emotional Expectations

In broad strokes, Western and more educated mothers value expressions of positive emotion in their infants, and tend to try to elicit these expressions during dyadic interactions (Kärtner et al., 2013). Mothers from subsistence cultures, on the other hand, tend to value quiet contentment in their infants, and focus on soothing them. Keller and Otto (2009), for example, investigated infant emotional development in urban, independent German families, and rural, interdependent Nso (Cameroonian) families. While Nso mothers report expecting and valuing calm behavior in their children, and frequently use corrective language to suppress negative emotional displays in their infants, German mothers report valuing expressivity in their infants and expect their infants to display both positive and negative emotions earlier than Nso mothers. Likewise, German mothers expect expressions of joy in their infants starting around 2 months, while Nso mothers expect these expressions around 7 months of age. A notable exception involved self-referential emotions (shame and guilt), which Nso mothers expect to see about 10 months earlier than German mothers, reflecting a cultural valuing of group cohesion (Keller & Otto, 2009). Such differences in parent expectations appear to be associated with differences in behavioral responses to infant emotional displays.

27.7.2 Cultural Differences in Emotional Displays and Parental Responses

Wörmann, Holodynski, Kärtner, and Keller (2012) found that levels of infant smiling and maternal imitative smiles did not differ between Nso and German groups at 6 weeks. By 12 weeks, however, German mothers and their infants engaged in more social smiles and imitation than Nso mother–infant dyads. A developmental divergence was also evident in the infant's behavior responses to maternal imitation (Wörmann, Holodynski, Kärtner, & Keller, 2014). Maternal imitation of infant smiles was associated with increases in the duration of infant smiles in the German sample at 8 weeks, but was not evident in the Nso sample until 12 weeks. This careful documentation of developmental differences in parental (and infant) responsivity suggests how culturally mediated differences in emotional expressions arise.

Differences between the more interdependent (Nso) and more independent (German) cultures were also evident at a molar behavioral level. Over the first 3 months of life, Nso mothers engaged in more body contact and fewer face-to-face interactions. By contrast, German mothers increasingly engaged in face-to-face interactions and exhibited increases in vocal contingent responsiveness (Kärtner, Heller, & Yovsi, 2010; Keller, Borke, Lamm, Lohaus, & Dzeaye Yovsi, 2011). Nso mothers report breastfeeding to help their infants regulate negative emotions, while German mothers report breastfeeding primarily to satisfy hunger (Keller & Otto, 2009). Likewise, Richman, Miller, and LeVine (1992) found that Gusii mothers in an interdependent Kenyan culture focused on soothing and calming responses to 4- and 10-month-old infant emotional displays, while American mothers attempted to engage the infants in emotionally arousing conversation-style interaction. Moreover, an early investigation found that !Kung San infants in Botswana initiated more frequent cries of briefer duration than Dutch or American infants (Barr, Konner, Bakeman, & Adamson, 1991). However, the differences apparent in targeted contrasts of more and less developed societies are not always apparent in multinational studies. Specifically, a large (N = 684) observational study in Argentina, Belgium, Brazil, Cameroon, France, Kenya, Israel, Italy, Japan, South Korea, and the United States did not reveal differences in the likelihood a mother would pick up and hold her distressed infant (Bornstein et al., 2008). This suggests the need for in-depth observational research of infant–parent emotional interaction across multiple cultural contexts.

27.8 Policy Implications

Cross-cultural comparisons suggest a diversity of normative caregiving styles and trajectories of infant emotional development. Moreover, beliefs, practices, and infant emotionality are part of larger cultural and societal systems. They reflect implicit and explicit beliefs about what is necessary and ideal in a developing child (are toddler temper tantrums, for example, mortifying or unavoidable?).

Cultural diversity has policy implications because of the multi-ethnic nature of most Western societies, and the degree to which American society is host to diverse parenting cultures associated with differences in ethnicity and income

(Sperry, Sperry, & Miller, 2018). Overall, however, the importance of direct social interaction with parents, other caregivers, and peers to infant emotional development cannot be overstated. Thus, generous parental leave policies are imperative in allowing both mothers and fathers adequate time to build relationships with their infants. Moreover, infant care, preschool, and prekindergarten programs – including Head Start – are important contexts for emotional development (Santos, Daniel, Fernandes, & Vaughn, 2015). Adequate funding of such programs has both immediate and long-term consequences for positive social development and sound fiscal policy (van Huizen, Dumhs, & Plantenga, 2017).

27.8.1 Specific Policy Issues

The recognition of expressions of pain in the young infant remains an important policy issue in neonatal medicine (Cruz, Fernandes, & Oliveira, 2016). In this vein, it is important to recognize the importance of both the cry face and cry vocalizations as prima facie indices of distress. Cry faces and crying are robustly elicited by pain (Izard, Hembree et al., 1983) – and neonatal pain appears to be associated with long-term pain sensitivity (Valeri et al., 2016). With respect to positive emotion, it is noteworthy that modern, educated cultures place a larger emphasis on visually mediated positive engagement than do many more traditional cultures. Thus, we suggest that for parents, the development and occurrence of positive emotion (e.g., social smiling) should be seen as an opportunity for relaxed positive engagement rather than a goal to be achieved (Beebe et al., 2016).

Finally, the increase in electronic media exposure and active digital use by infants is concerning (Chang, Park, Yoo, Lee, & Shin, 2018). Parents of infants with reported social-emotional difficulties indicate greater use of mobile technology to regulate their children' negative affect (Radesky, Peacock-Chambers, Zuckerman, & Silverstein, 2016), and greater use of such technologies is associated with parental ratings of risk for social-emotional delay (Raman et al., 2017). Limitations on infant exposure to electronics (with the exception of video chatting with family) has been recommended by the American Academy of Pediatrics (McClure, Chentsova-Dutto, Barr, Holochwost, & Parrott, 2015). Nevertheless, not only are infants increasingly engaged with digital interfaces, but parents increasingly monitor their infants using digital equipment (Messinger et al., 2015). High-quality research exploring the impact of these factors on infant social and emotional development is necessary to better understand their long-term consequences.

27.9 Future Directions

This chapter's review of infant emotional development suggests three salient directions for future research: (1) integration of multiple indices of emotional process, (2) increased attention to the temporality of emotional processes and emotional regulation, and (3) use of naturally occurring elicitors of strong emotion.

First, reports on infant facial expressions would be enhanced by documenting their correspondence with related expressive vocal and bodily actions. Pointedly, research on infant facial expressions rarely employs a thorough analysis of infant vocalization (and vice versa). There is a clear need for careful multimodal analysis of facial, bodily, and vocal behavior – ideally integrated with measures of heart rate and skin conductance – to identify emerging infant emotional states such as sadness and anger. Such research would be further strengthened by the integration of neurophysiological measures of cerebral activity provided by EEG and functional near-infrared spectroscopy (fNIRS) into studies of emotion production. Inclusion of neural and physiological measures of emotion would provide the opportunity to address unanswered questions such as the extent to which positive emotional expressions reflect a decrease in cognitive tension and physiological arousal, a supposition that has been posited for decades but for which evidence is limited (Sroufe & Waters, 1976).

Second, by incorporating potential behavioral attenuators of expressive actions, research on temporal associations would, in turn, elucidate the development of infant mechanisms for regulating emotion (Ekas, Braungart-Rieker, & Messinger, 2018). Here, we have suggested that anger expressions are an attenuated version of the cry face. In a similar vein, observations by both Camras and Oster suggest that the raised chin and pouting (protruding) lower lip characteristic of the sadness expression may occur prior to cry-face expressions and help regulate negative affect – but these temporal patterns require rigorous study. Research on the degree to which these different expressive configurations in fact co-occur and follow one another in time would shed new light on the behavioral and developmental emergence of anger and sadness expressions and their components. However, fine-grained coding of facial and vocal expression is frequently a rate-limiting factor in research on infant emotional production and emotion regulation. Future research in emotion regulation and emotional development more broadly is likely to involve increased integration of advances in the use of computer vision and signal processing to reliably measure infant and caregiver emotional expressions, vocalizations, and body movements (Hammal et al., 2019; Messinger et al., 2009; Rao et al., 2017).

Third, low levels of concordance between emotion-eliciting contexts and facial expressions of discrete negative emotion might lead investigators to pursue such investigations at later ages in the hopes of detecting clear evidence for expressions of discrete emotion states. These expressions would have to be interpreted as such by adult raters. A difficulty with this strategy, however, is a lack of clear evidence for the consistency with which even adults display discrete negative emotions (Aviezer, Trope, & Todorov, 2012; Yik & Russell, 1999). An alternate possibility is that ethical, appropriate constraints on research limit understanding of infants' reactions to especially potent negative stimuli. In this regard, researchers may consider the use of publicly posted videos on sites such as YouTube.com as well as initiatives to have citizen scientist parents record and submit emotional behaviors such as temper tantrums for analysis (Camras et al., 2018). These resources – as well as recording of events such as vaccinations – may provide access to potent emotion-eliciting situations that will expand our understanding of infant emotion (Backer, Quigley, & Stifter, 2018).

References

Abe, J., Beetham, M., & Izard, C. E. (2002). What do smiles mean? An analysis in terms of differential emotions theory. In M. H. Abel (Ed.), *Mellen studies in psychology* (Vol. 4, pp. 83–109). Lewiston, NY: Edwin Mellen Press.

Ackerman, B. P., Abe, J. A. A., & Izard, C. E. (1998). Differential emotions theory and emotional development: Mindful of modularity. In M. F. Mascolo & S. Griffin (Eds.), *What develops in emotional development?* (pp. 85–106). New York, NY: Plenum Press.

Adamson, L. B., & Bakeman, R. (1985). Affect and attention: Infants observed with mothers and peers. *Child Development*, 56, 582–593.

Adamson, L. B., & Frick, J. E. (2003). The still face: A history of a shared experimental paradigm. *Infancy*, 4, 451–473.

Anisfeld, E. (1982). The onset of social smiling in preterm and full-term infants from two ethnic backgrounds. *Infant Behavior and Development*, 5, 387–395.

Aviezer, H., Trope, Y., & Todorov, A. (2012). Body cues, not facial expressions, discriminate between intense positive and negative emotions. *Science*, 338(6111), 1225–1229.

Backer, P. M., Quigley, K. M., & Stifter, C. A. (2018). Typologies of dyadic mother–infant emotion regulation following immunization. *Infant Behavior and Development*, 53, 5–17.

Barr, R. G., Konner, M., Bakeman, R., & Adamson, L. (1991). Crying in !Kung San infants: A test of the cultural specificity hypothesis. *Developmental Medicine and Child Neurology*, 33, 601–610.

Barrett, K. C. (1993). The development of nonverbal communication of emotion: A functionalist perspective. *Journal of Nonverbal Behavior*, 17(3), 145–169.

Barrett, L. F. (2006). Solving the emotion paradox: Categorization and the experience of emotion. *Personality and Social Psychology Review*, 10, 20–46.

Barrett, L. F., & Wager, T. D. (2006). The structure of emotion: Evidence from neuroimaging studies. *Current Directions in Psychological Science*, 15(2), 79–83.

Beebe, B., Messinger, D., Bahrick, L. E., Margolis, A., Buck, K. A., & Chen, H. (2016). A systems view of mother–infant face-to-face communication. *Developmental Psychology*, 52(4), 556–571.

Bell, S. M., & Mary, D. S. A. (1972). Infant crying and maternal responsiveness. *Child Development*, 43(4), 1171–1190.

Bennett, D. S., Bendersky, M., & Lewis, M. (2002). Facial expressivity at 4 months: A context by expression analysis. *Infancy*, 3(1), 97–113.

Bennett, D. S., Bendersky, M., & Lewis, M. (2005). Does the organization of emotional expression change over time? Facial expressivity from 4 to 12 months. *Infancy*, *8*(2), 167–187.

Bigelow, A. E., & Power, M. (2016). Effect of maternal responsiveness on young infants' social bidding-like behavior during the still face task. *Infant Child Development*, *25*(3), 256–276.

Bigelow, A. E., & Rochat, P. (2006). Two-month-old infants' sensitivity to social contingency in mother–infant and stranger–infant interaction. *Infancy*, *9*, 313–325.

Blasi, A., Mercure, E., Lloyd-Fox, S., Thomson, A., Brammer, M., Sauter, D., ... Murphy , G. M. (2011). Early specialization for voice and emotion processing in the infant brain. *Current Biology*, *21*(14), 1220–1224.

Bornstein, M. H., Putnick, D. L., Rigo, P., Esposito, G., Swain, J. E., Suwalsky, J. T. D., ... Venuti, P. (2008). Neurobiology of culturally common maternal responses to infant cry. *Proceedings of the National Academy of Sciences of the United States of America*, *114*(45), E9465–E9473.

Bridges, K. M. B. (1932). Emotional development in early infancy. *Child Development*, *3*, 324–341.

Buss, K. A., & Kiel, E. J. (2004). Comparison of sadness, anger, and fear facial expressions when toddlers look at their mothers. *Child Development*, *75*(6), 1761–1773.

Campos, J. J., Mumme, D. L., Kermoian, R., & Campos, R. G. (1994). A functionalist perspective on the nature of emotion. In N. A. Fox (Ed.), *Monographs of the Society for Research in Child Development* (Vol. 59, pp. 282–303, Serial No. 240). Chicago, IL: University of Chicago Press.

Camras, L. A., Fatani, S. S., Fraumeni, B. R., & Shuster, M. M. (2018). The development of facial expressions: Current perspectives on infant emotions. In L. F. Barrett, M. Lewis, & J. M. Haviland-Jones (Eds.), *Handbook of emotions* (4th ed., pp. 255–271). New York, NY: Guilford Press.

Camras, L. A., Oster, H., Bakeman, R., Meng, Z., Ujiie, T., & Campos, J. J. (2007). Do infants show distinct negative facial expressions for fear and anger? Emotional expression in 11-month-old European American, Chinese, and Japanese infants. *Infancy*, *11*(2), 131–155.

Camras, L. A., Sullivan, J., & Michel, G. (1993). Do infants express discrete emotions? Adult judgments of facial, vocal, and body actions. *Journal of Nonverbal Behavior*, *17*(3), 171–186.

Chang, H. Y., Park, E. -J., Yoo, H. -J., Lee, J. W., & Shin, Y. (2018). Electronic media exposure and use among toddlers. *Psychiatry Investigation*, *15*(6), 568–573.

Cohn, J., & Tronick, E. (1987). Mother–infant face-to-face interaction: The sequence of dyadic states at 3, 6, and 9 months. *Developmental Psychology*, *23*(1), 68–77.

Cruz, M. D., Fernandes, A. M., & Oliveira, C. R. (2016). Epidemiology of painful procedures performed in neonates: A systematic review of observational studies. *European Journal of Pain*, *20*(4), 489–498.

Darwin, C. [1872] (1998). *The expression of the emotions in man and animals* (3rd ed.). New York, NY: Oxford University.

Davila-Ross, M., Jesus, G., Osborne, J., & Bard, K. A. (2015). Chimpanzees (pan troglodytes) produce the same types of "laugh faces" when they emit laughter and when they are silent. *PLoS One*, *10*(6), e0127337.

de Haan, M., & Nelson, C. A. (1999). Brain activity differentiates face and object processing in 6-month-old infants. *Developmental Psychology, 35*(4), 1113.

de Haan, M., Pascalis, O., & Johnson, M. H. (2002). Specialization of neural mechanisms underlying face recognition in human infants. *Journal of Cognitive Neuroscience, 14*(2), 199–209.

de Klerk, C. C. J. M., Lamy-Yang, I., & Southgate, V. (2018). The role of sensorimotor experience in the development of mimicry in infancy. *Developmental Science, 22*(3), e12771.

Dickson, K. L., Walker, H., & Fogel, A. (1997). The relationship between smile-type and play-type during parent–infant play. *Developmental Psychology, 33*(6), 925–933.

Dondi, M., Gervasi, M. T., Valente, A., Vacca, T., Bogana, G., de Bellis, I., ... Oster, H. (2012). Spontaneous facial expressions of distress in fetuses. Paper presented at the 14th European Conference on Facial Expression, Lisboa-Almada, Portugal.

Dondi, M., Messinger, D., Colle, M., Tabasso, A., Simion, F., Barba, B. D., & Fogel, A. (2007). A new perspective on neonatal smiling: differences between the judgments of expert coders and naive observers. *Infancy, 12*(3), 235–255.

Dondi, M., Simion, F., & Caltran, G. (1999). Can newborns discriminate between their own cry and the cry of another newborn infant? *Developmental Psychology, 35*(2), 418–426.

Duchenne, G. B. [1862] (1990). *The mechanism of human facial expression* (R. A. Cuthbertson, Trans.). New York, NY: Cambridge University Press.

Ekas, N. V., Braungart-Rieker, J. M., & Messinger, D. S. (2018). The development of infant emotion regulation: Time is of the essence. In P. M. Cole & T. Hollenstein (Eds.), *Emotion regulation: A matter of time* (pp. 49–69). New York, NY: Routledge.

Ekas, N. V., Haltigan, J. D., & Messinger, D. S. (2013). The dynamic still-face effect: do infants decrease bidding over time when parents are not responsive? *Developmental Psychology, 49*(6), 1027–1035.

Ekman, P., Davidson, R.J., Friesen, W. (1990). The Duchenne smile: Emotional expression and brain physiology: II. *Journal of Personality and Social Psychology, 58*(2), 343–353.

Ekman, P., & Friesen, W. (1992). *Changes in FACS scoring (instruction manual)*. San Francisco, CA: Human Interaction Lab.

Elliot, H. C. (1969). *Textbook of neuroanatomy* (2nd ed.). Philadelphia: J. B. Lippincott.

Emde, R. N., & Koenig, K. (1969). Neonatal smiling and rapid eye movement states. *Journal of the American Academy of Child Psychiatry, 8*, 57–67.

Emde, R. N., McCartney, R. D., & Harmon, R. J. (1971). Neonatal smiling in REM states, IV: Premature study. *Child Development, 42*, 1657–1661.

Feldman, R. (2003). Infant–mother and infant–father synchrony: The coregulation of positive arousal. *Infant Mental Health Journal, 24*(1), 1–23.

Feldman, R., Greenbaum, C. W., & Yirmiya, N. (1999). Mother–infant affect synchrony as an antecedent of the emergence of self-control. *Developmental Psychology, 35*(1), 223–231.

Fogel, A. (1988). Cyclicity and stability in mother–infant face-to-face interaction: A comment on Cohn and Tronick. *Developmental Psychology, 24*(3), 393–395.

Fogel, A., Hsu, H. -C., Shapiro, A. F., Nelson-Goens, G. C., & Secrist, C. (2006). Effects of normal and perturbed social play on the duration and amplitude of different types of infant smiles. *Developmental Psychology, 42*, 459–473.

Fox, N., & Davidson, R. J. (1988). Patterns of brain electrical activity during facial signs of emotion in 10 month old infants. *Developmental Psychology, 24*(2), 230–236.

Geangu, E., Benga, O., Stahl, D., & Striano, T. (2010). Contagious crying beyond the first days of life. *Infant Behavior and Development, 33*(3), 279–288.

Geangu, E., Hauf, P., Bhardwaj, R., & Bentz, W. (2011). Infant pupil diameter changes in response to others' positive and negative emotions. *PLoS ONE, 6*(11), e27132.

Goldsmith, H. H., Buss, K. A., & Lemery, K. S. (1997). Toddler and childhood temperament: Expanded content, stronger genetic evidence, new evidence for the importance of environment. *Developmental Psychology, 33*(6), 891–905.

Goldsmith, H. H., Lemery, K. S., Buss, K. A., & Campos, J. J. (1999). Genetic analyses of focal aspects of infant temperament. *Developmental Psychology, 35*(4), 972–985.

Grossmann, T., Striano, T., & Friederici, A. D. (2005). Infants' electric brain responses to emotional prosody. *NeuroReport, 16*(16), 1825–1828.

Halberstadt, A. G., & Lozada, F. T. (2011). Emotion development in infancy through the lens of culture. *Emotion Review, 3*(2), 158–168.

Hammal, Z., Wallace, E. R., Speltz, M. L., Heike, C. L., Birgfeld, C. B., & Cohn, J. F. (2019). Dynamics of face and head movement in infants with and without craniofacial microsomia: An automatic approach. *Plastic and Reconstructive Surgery – Global Open, 7*(1), e2081.

Harmon, R. J., & Emde, R. N. (1972). Endogenous and exogenous smiling systems in early infancy. *Journal of the American Academy of Child Psychiatry, 11*, 77–100.

Henrich, J., Heine, S. J., Norenzayan, A. (2010). The weirdest people in the world? *Behavioral and Brain Sciences, 33*, 61–135.

Hoehl, S., & Striano, T. (2008). Neural processing of eye gaze and threat-related emotional facial expressions in infancy. *Child Development, 79*(6), 1752–1760.

Holodynski, M. (2009). Milestones and mechanisms of emotional development. In H. J. Markowitsch & B. Röttger-Rössler (Eds.), *Emotions as bio-cultural processes* (pp. 1–25). New York, NY: Springer.

Holodynski, M., & Friedlmeier, W. (2006). *Development of emotions and emotion regulation*. New York, NY: Springer.

Hsu, H. -C., Fogel, A., & Messinger, D. S. (2001). Infant non-distress vocalization during mother–infant face-to-face interaction: Factors associated with quantitative and qualitative differences. *Infant Behavior & Development, 24*(1), 107–128.

Isomura, T., & Nakano, T. (2016). Automatic facial mimicry in response to dynamic emotional stimuli in five-month-old infants. *Proceedings of the Royal Society B: Biological Sciences, 283*(1844). https://doi.org/10.1098/rspb.2016.1948

Izard, C. E. (1979). *The maximally discriminative facial coding system*. Newark: University of Delaware.

Izard, C. E., & Abe, J. A. A. (2004). Developmental changes in facial expressions of emotions in the strange situation during the second year of life. *Emotion, 4*(3), 251–265.

Izard, C. E., & Ackerman, B. P. (2000). Motivational, organizational, and regulatory functions of discrete emotions. In M. Lewis & J. M. Haviland-Jones (Eds.), *Handbook of emotions* (2nd ed., pp. 253–264). New York, NY: Guilford Press.

Izard, C. E., Dougherty, L. M., & Hembree, E. A. (1983). *A system for identifying affect expressions by holistic judgements*. Newark: Instructional Resource Center, University of Deleware.

Izard, C. E., Hembree, E. A., Dougherty, L. M., & Spizzirri, C. L. (1983). Changes in facial expressions of 2- to 19-month-old infants following acute pain. *Developmental Psychology, 19*, 418–426.

Jessen, S., & Grossmann, T. (2015). Neural signatures of conscious and unconscious emotional face processing in human infants. *Cortex, 64*, 260–270.

Jones, S. S., & Hong, H.-W. (2001). Onset of voluntary communication: Smiling looks to mother. *Infancy, 2*(3), 353–370.

Kärtner, J., Holodynski, M., & Wörmann, V. (2013). Parental ethnotheories, social practice and the culture-specific development of social smiling in infants. *Mind, Culture, and Activity, 20*(1), 79–95.

Kärtner, J., Keller, H., & Yovsi, R. D. (2010). Mother–infant interaction during the first 3 months: The emergence of culture-specific contingency patterns. *Child Development, 81*(2), 540–554.

Kaye, K., & Fogel, A. (1980). The temporal structure of face-to-face communication between mothers and infants. *Developmental Psychology, 16*(5), 454–464.

Keller, H., Borke, J., Lamm, B., Lohaus, A., & Dzeaye Yovsi, R. (2011). Developing patterns of parenting in two cultural communities. *International Journal of Behavioral Development, 35*(3), 233–245.

Keller, H., & Otto, H. (2009). The cultural socialization of emotion regulation during infancy. *Journal of Cross-Cultural Psychology, 40*(6), 996–1011.

Knafo, A., Zahn-Waxler, C., van Hulle, C., Robinson, J. L., & Rhee, S. H. (2008). The developmental origins of a disposition toward empathy: Genetic and environmental contributions. *Emotion, 8*(6), 737–752.

Kobiella, A., Grossmann, T., Reid, V. M., & Striano, T. (2008). The discrimination of angry and fearful facial expressions in 7-month-old infants: An event-related potential study. *Cognition and Emotion, 22*(1), 134–146.

Kochanska, G., Forman, D. R., & Coy, K. C. (1999). Implications of the mother–child relationship in infancy socialization in the second year of life. *Infant Behavior & Development, 22*(2), 249–265.

Kohut, A. S., Riddell, P., Flora, D., & Oster, H. (2012). A longitudinal analysis of the development of infant facial expressions in response to acute pain: immediate and regulatory expressions. *Pain, 153*(12), 2458–2465.

Lavelli, M., & Fogel, A. (2002). Developmental changes in mother–infant face-to-face communication: Birth to 3 months. *Developmental Psychology, 38*(2), 288–305.

(2005). Developmental changes in the relationship between the infant's attention and emotion during early face-to-face communication: The 2-month transition. *Developmental Psychology, 41*(1), 265–280.

Leppänen, J. M., Moulson, M. C., Vogel-Farley, V. K., & Nelson, C. A. (2007). An ERP study of emotional face processing in the adult and infant brain. *Child Development, 78*(1), 232–245.

Lewis, M. D. (2018). The emergence of human emotions. In L. F. Barrett, M. Lewis, & J. M. Haviland-Jones (Eds.), *Handbook of emotions* (4th ed., pp. 272–292). New York, NY: Guilford Press.

Lewis, M. D., & Granic, I. (2000). *Emotion, development, and self-organization: Dynamic systems approaches to emotional development* (Vol. 8). Cambridge, UK: Cambridge University Press.

Lewis, M. D., & Ramsay, D. S. (2005). Infant emotional and cortisol responses to goal blockage. *Child Development, 76*(2), 518–530.

Lewis, M. D., Ramsay, D. S., & Sullivan, M. (2006). The relation of ANS and HPA activation to infant anger and sadness response to goal blockage. *Developmental Psychobiology, 48*(5), 397–405.

Lillard, A., Nishida, T., Massaro, D., Vaish, A., Ma, L., & McRoberts, G. (2007). Signs of pretense across age and scenario. *Infancy, 11*(1), 1–30.

Malatesta, C. Z., Culver, C., Tesman, J. R., & Shepard, B. (1989). Engaging the commentaries: When is an infant affective expression an emotion? *Monographs of the Society for Research in Child Development, 54*(1–2, Serial No. 219), 125–136.

Malatesta, C. Z., & Haviland, J. M. (1982). Learning display rules: The socialization of emotion expression in infancy. *Child Development, 53*(4), 991–1003.

Marshall, P. J., & Meltzoff, A. N. (2014). Neural mirroring mechanisms and imitation in human infants. *Philosophical Transactions of the Royal Society B Biological Sciences, 369*(1644), 20130620.

Matias, R., & Cohn, J. F. (1993). Are MAX-specified infant facial expressions during face-to-face interaction consistent with differential emotions theory? *Developmental Psychology, 29*(3), 524–531.

Mattson, W. I., Cohn, J. F., Mahoor, M. H., Gangi, D. N., & Messinger, D. S. (2013). Darwin's Duchenne: Eye constriction during infant joy and distress. *PLoS ONE, 8*(11), e80161.

Mattson, W. I., Ekas, N. V., Lambert, B., Tronick, E., Lester, B. M., & Messinger, D. S. (2013). Emotional expression and heart rate in high-risk infants during the face-to-face/still-face. *Infant Behavior & Development, 36*(4), 776–785.

Mayes, L., C., & Zigler, E. (2006). An observational study of the affective concomitants of mastery in infants. *Journal of Child Psychology and Psychiatry, 33*(4), 659–667.

McClure, E. R., Chentsova-Dutton, Y. E., Barr, R. F., Holochwost, S. J., & Parrott, W. G. (2015). "Facetime doesn't count": Video chat as an exception to media restrictions for infants and toddlers. *International Journal of Child–Computer Interaction, 6*, 1–6.

Mendes, D. M. L. F., & Seidl-de-Moura, M. L. (2014). Different kinds of infants' smiles in the first six months and contingency to maternal affective behavior. *Spanish Journal of Psychology, 17*, e80. https://doi.org/10.1017/sjp.2014.86

Mesman, J., van IJzendoorn, M. H., & Bakermans-Kranenburg, M. J. (2009). The many faces of the still-face paradigm: A review and meta-analysis. *Developmental Review, 29*(2), 120–162.

Messinger, D., Dondi, M., Nelson-Goens, G. C., Beghi, A., Fogel, A., & Simion, F. (2002). How sleeping neonates smile. *Developmental Science, 5*(1), 48–54.

Messinger, D. S., Duvivier, L. L., Warren, Z. E., Mahoor, M., Baker, J., Warlaumont, A., & Ruvolo, P. (2015). *Affective computing, emotional development, and autism* New York, NY: Oxford University Press.

Messinger, D. S., & Fogel, A. (1998). Give and take: The development of conventional infant gestures. *Merrill-Palmer Quarterly*, *44*(4), 566–590.

Messinger, D. S., Fogel, A., & Dickson, K. L. (1997). A dynamic systems approach to infant facial action. In J. A. Russell & F. M. Dols (Eds.), *The psychology of facial expression* (pp. 205–226). New York, NY: Cambridge University Press.

Messinger, D. S., Fogel, A., & Dickson, K. (1999). What's in a smile? *Developmental Psychology*, *35*(3), 701–708.

   (2001). All smiles are positive, but some smiles are more positive than others. *Developmental Psychology*, *37*(5), 642–653.

Messinger, D. S., Mahoor, M. H., Chow, S.-M., & Cohn, J. F. (2009). Automated measurement of facial expression in infant–mother interaction: A pilot study. *Infancy*, *14*(3), 285–305.

Messinger, D. S., Mattson, W. I., Mahoor, M. H., & Cohn, J. F. (2012). The eyes have it: Making positive expressions more positive and negative expressions more negative. *Emotion*, *12*(3), 430–436.

Messinger, D. S., Ruvolo, P., Ekas, N., & Fogel, A. (2010). Applying machine learning to infant interaction: The development is in the details. *Neural Networks*, *23*(10), 1004–1016.

Mingawa-Kawai, Y., Matsuoka, S., Dan, I., Naoi, N., Nakamura, K., & Kojima, S. (2009). Prefrontal activation associated with social attachment: Facial-emotion recognition in mothers and infants. *Cerebral Cortex*, *19*(2), 284–292.

Mireault, G. C., Crockenberg, S. C., Heilman, K., Sparrow, J. E., Cousineau, K., & Rainville, B. (2018). Social, cognitive, and physiological aspects of humour perception from 4 to 8 months: Two longitudinal studies. *British Journal of Developmental Psychology*, *36*(1), 98–109.

Mireault, G. C., Crockenberg, S. C., Sparrow, J. E., Cousineau, K., Pettinato, C., & Woodard, K. (2015). Laughing matters: Infant humor in the context of parental affect. *Journal of Experimental Child Psychology*, *136*, 30–41.

Mizuno, Y., Takeshita, H., & Matsuzawa, T. (2006). Behavior of infant chimpanzees during the night in the first 4 months of life: Smiling and suckling in relation to behavioral state. *Infancy*, *9*(2), 221–240.

Mundy, P., Hogan, A., & Doehring, P. (1996). *A preliminary manual for the abridged Early Social-Communication Scales*. Retrieved from www.psy.miami.edu/faculty/pmundy.

Murphy, F. C., Nimmo-Smith, I., & Lawrence, A. D. (2003). Functional neuroanatomy of emotions: A meta-analysis. *Cognitive, Affective & Behavioral Neuroscience*, *3*(3), 207–233.

Nelson, C. A., & de Haan, M. (1996). Neural correlates of infants' visual responsiveness to facial expressions of emotion. *Developmental Psychobiology*, *29*(7), 577–595.

Nelson, C. A., & Monk, C. S. (2001). The use of event-related potentials in the study of cognitive development. In C. A. Nelson & M. Luciana (Eds.), *Handbook of developmental cognitive neuroscience* (pp. 125–136). Cambridge, MA: MIT Press.

Nishida, T. K., & Lillard, A. S. (2007). The informative value of emotional expressions: "social referencing" in mother–child pretense. *Developmental Science*, *10*(2), 205–212.

Nwokah, E. E., Hsu, H.-C., Davies, P., & Fogel, A. (1999). The integration of laughter and speech in vocal communication: A dynamic systems perspective. *Journal of Speech, Language, and Hearing Research, 42*(4), 880–894.

Nwokah, E. E., Hsu, H.-C., Dobrowolska, O., & Fogel, A. (1994). The development of laughter in mother–infant communication: Timing parameters and temporal sequences. *Infant Behavior & Development, 17*(1), 23–35.

Oster, H. (1978). Facial expression and affect development. In M. Lewis & L. A. Rosenblum (Eds.), *The development of affect* (pp. 43–74). New York, NY: Plenum Press.

   (2005). The repertoire of infant facial expressions: An ontogenetic perspective. In J. Nadel & D. Muir (Eds.), *Emotional development* (pp. 261–292). New York, NY: Oxford University Press.

Oster, H., Hegley, D., & Nagel, L. (1992). Adult judgments and fine-grained analysis of infant facial expressions: Testing the validity of a priori coding formulas. *Developmental Psychology, 28*(6), 1115–1131.

Owren, M., & Amoss, R. (2014). Spontaneous human laughter. In M. M. Tugdale, M. N. Shiota, & L. D. Kirby (Eds.), *Handbook of positive emotions* (pp. 159–178). New York, NY: Guilford Press.

Perlman, S. B., Luna, B., Hein, T. C., & Huppert, T. J. (2014). fNIRS evidence of prefrontal regulation of frustration in early childhood. *Neuroimage, 85*(Pt. 1), 326–334.

Planalp, E. M., van Hulle, C., Lemery-Chalfant, K., & Goldsmith, H. H. (2017). Genetic and environmental contributions to the development of positive affect in infancy. *Emotion, 17*(3), 412–420.

Radesky, J. S., Peacock-Chambers, E., Zuckerman, B., & Silverstein, M. (2016). Use of mobile technology to calm upset children: Associations with social-emotional development. *JAMA Pediatrics, 170*(4), 397–399.

Raman, S., Guerrero-Duby, S., McCullough, J. L., Brown, M., Ostrowski-Delehanty, S., Langkamp, D., & Duby, J. C. (2017). Screen exposure during daily routines and a young child's risk for having social-emotional delay. *Clinical Pediatrics, 56*(13), 1244–1253.

Rao, H., Clements, M. A., Li, Y., Swanson, M. R., Piven, J., & Messinger, D. S. (2017). Paralinguistic analysis of children's speech in natural environments. In J. M. Rehg, S. A. Murphy, & S. Kumar (Eds.), *Mobile health: Sensors, analytic methods, and applications* (pp. 219–238). Cham, Switzerland: Springer International Publishing.

Reissland, N., Francis, B., & Mason, J. (2013). Can healthy fetuses show facial expressions of "pain" or "distress"? *PLOS ONE, 8*(6), e65530.

Reissland, N., Francis, B., Mason, J., & Lincoln, K. (2011). Do facial expressions develop before birth? *PLOS ONE, 6*(8), e24081.

Richman, A. L., Miller, P. M., & LeVine, R. A. (1992). Cultural and educational variations in maternal responsiveness. *Developmental Psychology, 28*(4), 614–621. doi:610.1037/0012-1649.1028.1034.1614.

Robinson, J. L., Zahn-Waxler, C., & Emde, R. N. (1994). Patterns of development in early empathic behavior: Environmental and child constitutional influences. *Social Development, 3*(2), 125–145.

Roth-Hanania, R., Davidov, M., & Zahn-Waxler, C. (2011). Empathy development from 8 to 16 months: Early signs of concern for others. *Infant Behavior and Development, 34*(3), 447–458.

Ruvolo, P., Messinger, D., & Movellan, J. (2015). Infants time their smiles to make their moms smile. *PLoS ONE, 10*(9), e0136492.

Sagi, A., & Hoffman, M. L. (1976). Empathic distress in the newborn. *Developmental Psychology, 12*(2), 175–176.

Santos, A. J., Daniel, J. R., Fernandes, C., & Vaughn, B. E. (2015). Affiliative subgroups in preschool classrooms: Integrating constructs and methods from social ethology and sociometric traditions. *PLOS ONE, 10*(7), e0130932.

Sauter, D., Evans, B., Venneker, D., & Kret, M. (2018). How do babies laugh? *Journal of the Acoustical Society of America, 144*(3), 1840–1840.

Seibert, J. M., Hogan, A. E., & Mundy, P. C. (1982). Assessing interactional competencies: The Early Social-Communication Scales. *Infant Mental Health Journal, 3*(4), 244–258.

Simner, M. L. (1971). Newborns' response to the cry of another infant. *Developmental Psychology, 5*(1), 136–150.

Sperry, D. E., Sperry, L. L., & Miller, P. (2018). Reexamining the verbal environments of children from different socioeconomic backgrounds. *Child Development, 90*(1). doi: 10.1111/cdev.13072

Sprengelmeyer, R., & Jentzsch, I. (2006). Event related potentials and the perception of intensity in facial expressions. *Neuropsychologia, 44*(14), 2899–2906.

Sroufe, L. A. (1979). Socioemotional development. In J. Osofsky (Ed.), *Handbook of infant development* (pp. 462–516). New York, NY: Wiley.

(1996). *Emotional development: The organization of emotional life in the early years.* New York, NY: Cambridge University Press.

Sroufe, L. A., & Waters, E. (1976). The ontogenesis of smiling and laughter: A perspective on the organization of development in infancy. *Psychological Review, 83*(3), 173–189.

Stifter, C. A., & Moyer, D. (1991). The regulation of positive affect: Gaze aversion activity during mother–infant interaction. *Infant Behavior and Development, 14*, 111–123.

Striano, T., & Bertin, E. (2005). Coordinated affect with mothers and strangers: A longitudinal analysis of joint engagement between 5 and 9 months of age. *Cognition & Emotion, 19*(5), 781–790.

Susskind, J. M., Lee, D. H., Cusi, A., Feiman, R., Grabski, W., & Anderson, A. K. (2008). Expressing fear enhances sensory acquisition. *Nature Neuroscience, 11*, 843–850.

Symons, D., & Moran, G. (1994). Responsiveness and dependency are different aspects of social contingencies: An example from mother and infant smiles. *Infant Behavior and Development, 17*(2), 209–214.

Thelen, E., & Smith, L. B. (1994). *A dynamic systems approach to the development of cognition and action.* Cambridge, MA: MIT Press.

Tomkins, S. S. (1962). *Affect, imagery, consciousness: The positive affects* (Vol. 1). New York, NY: Springer-Verlag.

Valeri, B. O., Ranger, M., Chau, C. M. Y., Cepeda, I. L., Synnes, A., Linhares, M. B. M., & Grunau, R. E. (2016). Neonatal invasive procedures predict pain intensity at school age in children born very preterm. *Clinical Journal of Pain, 32*(12), 1086–1093.

van den Boomen, C., Munsters, N. M., & Kemner, C. (2019). Emotion processing in the infant brain: The importance of local information. *Neuropsychologia, 126*, 62–68.

van Egeren, L. A., Barratt, M. S., & Roach, M. A. (2001). Mother–infant responsiveness: Timing, mutual regulation, and interactional context. *Developmental Psychology*, *37*(5), 684–697.

van Huizen, T., Dumhs, L., & Plantenga, J. (2017). The costs and benefits of investing in universal preschool: Evidence from a Spanish reform. *Child Development*, *90*(3), e386–e406.

Venezia, M., Messinger, D. S., Thorp, D., & Mundy, P. (2004). The development of anticipatory smiling. *Infancy*, *6*(3), 397–406.

Washburn, R. W. (1929). A study of the smiling and laughing of infants in the first year of life. *Genetic Psychology Monographs*, *5*(5–6), 397–537.

Watson, J. S. (1972). Smiling, cooing, and "the game." *Merrill-Palmer Quarterly, 18*(4), 323–339.

Weinberg, M. K., & Tronick, E. Z. (1994). Beyond the face: An empirical study of infant affective configurations of facial, vocal, gestural, and regulatory behaviors. *Child Development*, *65*(5), 1503–1515.

Williams, P. L., Warick, R., Dyson, M., & Bannister, L. H. (1989). *Gray's anatomy*. Edinburgh: Churchill Livingstone.

Witherington, D. C., Campos, J. J., & Hertenstein, M. J. (2001). Principles of emotion and its development in infancy. In G. Bremner & A. Fogel (Eds.), *Blackwell handbook of infant development* (pp. 427–464). Malden, MA: Blackwell.

Wolff, P. H. (1987). *The development of behavioral states and the expression of emotions in early infancy: New proposals for investigation*. Chicago, IL: University of Chicago Press.

Wörmann, V., Holodynski, M., Kärtner, J., & Keller, H. (2012). A cross-cultural comparison of the development of the social smile: A longitudinal study of maternal and infant imitation in 6- and 12-week-old infants. *Infant Behavior and Development*, *35*(3), 335–347.

(2014). The emergence of social smiling: The interplay of maternal and infant imitation during the first three months in cross-cultural comparison. *Journal of Cross-Cultural Psychology*, *45*(3), 339–361.

Xie, W., McCormick, S. A., Westerlund, A., Bowman, L. C., & Nelson, C. A. (2018). Neural correlates of facial emotion processing in infancy. *Developmental Science*, *22*(3), e12758.

Yale, M. E., Messinger, D. S., & Cobo-Lewis, A. B. (2003). The temporal coordination of early infant communication. *Developmental Psychology*, *39*(5), 815–824.

Yarrow, L. J., Morgan, G. A., Jennings, K. D., Harmon, R. J., & Gaiter, J. L. (1982). Infants' persistence at tasks: Relationships to cognitive functioning and early experience. *Infant Behavior and Development*, *5*(2), 131–141.

Yik, M. S. M., & Russell, J. A. (1999). Interpretation of faces: A cross-cultural study of a prediction from Fridlund's theory. *Cognition and Emotion*, *13*(1), 93–104.

Zahn-Waxler, C., Radke-Yarrow, M., Wagner, E., & Chapman, M. (1992). Development of concern for others. *Developmental Psychology*, *28*(1), 126–136.

Zahn-Waxler, C., Robinson, J. L., & Emde, R. N. (1992). The development of empathy in twins. *Developmental Psychology*, *28*(6), 1038–1047.

28 Understanding and Evaluating the Moral World in Infancy

J. Kiley Hamlin and Miranda Sitch

28.1 Introduction: Origins of Morality

A capacity for moral judgment, whereby certain actions and individuals are deemed good or bad and worthy of praise or punishment, is one of the defining characteristics of human social life. Although exactly which acts and individuals are considered worthy of moral consideration varies across cultures, it appears that all humans nevertheless share an overall tendency to see some things, commonly within the broad domains of harm and fairness, as morally right, good, permissible, or obligatory, and others as wrong, bad, impermissible, or forbidden (Brown, 1991). Perhaps most notably, humans do not merely evaluate the acts and individuals that directly influence themselves and their loved ones, but also readily evaluate those whose positive and negative acts solely influence unknown others. That is, the human moral sense does not appear to be characterized by concerns for what is right or wrong *for me*, but instead what is right or wrong *in general*.

Given these features, philosophers and scientists alike have long debated where morality comes from. These questions have taken many forms, including considerations of why humans are unique in the animal kingdom (as in, why do humans make moral judgments while other animals do not?) as well as what accounts for moral judgment within the life of an individual human (as in, how is it that humans come to develop moral capacities within their lifetimes?). Answers to these questions are also diverse. Some fields argue that the moral sense emerged over humans' evolutionary history, stressing its role in cooperation and successful group living (e.g., Alexander, 1987; Cosmides & Tooby, 1992; de Waal, 2009; Henrich & Henrich, 2007; Joyce, 2007; Katz, 2000). Other fields have tended to focus on moral development within individual lifetimes, stressing the importance of both morally relevant experience as well as how children actively construct their own sense of right and wrong (for in-depth reviews, see Killen & Smetana, 2014).

Notably, the evolutionary and developmental perspectives need not be mutually exclusive: Like anything else, the moral sense is likely the result of an interplay between built-in and acquired features occurring throughout the lifetime. Ancient Chinese philosopher Mencius argued that humans are born with moral "sprouts," consisting of innate capacities to sympathize with others, recognize the difference between right and wrong, respect rules, and feel shameful for failing to behave in a righteous manner (cited in Chan, 1963, 2A6). Mencius believed that these capacities exist from birth, and that they provide humans with a head start in the development of a moral sense. Critically, however, Mencius did not view his moral sprouts as equivalent to full-fledged morality. Instead, he argued that full-fledged morality emerges over the lifetime, via fostering from the right environmental inputs (and presumably advances in various other social and cognitive capacities as well).

Although Mencius did not invoke evolutionary explanations for his moral sprouts, they are nevertheless consistent with theories claiming morality is a by-product of the evolution of cooperation (see reviews in Henrich & Henrich, 2007; Joyce, 2007; Katz, 2000; Nowak, 2006). These theories note that all human societies can be characterized as cooperative systems, in which individuals regularly take costs to themselves for the benefit of unrelated others. These cooperative systems allow groups of individuals to achieve much more than any single individual could on her own; however, they are placed at significant risk by individuals who cheat or "free ride" by accepting the benefits of others' costly cooperative acts while performing no costly acts of their own. That cooperative systems have flourished despite this risk strongly suggests that humans evolved various risk-mitigating tendencies alongside their cooperative ones. These tendencies have been theorized to include adopting norms specifying which actions are ok to do (cooperating, helping, reciprocating, etc.) and which are not (cheating, lying, harming, etc.), noticing and negatively evaluating individuals who fail to perform cooperative acts, and responding to failures of cooperation in kind (e.g., punishment). In sum, these theories argue that tendencies to adopt, abide by, and police the norms of one's group may have been selected for over human history.

Both evolutionary theories and Mencius' sprouts point to the possibility that human moral judgment and action are not solely based on cultural learning during the life span, and are facilitated by some sort of natural moral endowment. But how can we determine whether such an endowment exists? One way, which has grown increasingly popular in recent years, is to study whether human infants possess any morally relevant capacities. Because preverbal infants have much less experience in the moral world than do older children and adults, and are not typically seen as possessing the cognitive abilities thought to be required to make moral judgments, it has been argued that evidence for tendencies related to adults' moral capacities during infancy suggest that some foundational features of morality are built in (e.g., Bloom, 2013; Hamlin, 2013b; Premack & Premack, 1994; Wynn & Bloom, 2014).

The purpose of this chapter is to review recent research suggestive that infants and toddlers *understand* various morally relevant actions, *differentially evaluate* individuals who perform positive versus negative acts, and *respond to* prosocial and antisocial actors in kind. Although our examination of responses to others' prosocial and antisocial acts will include some discussion of infants' and toddlers' own valenced behaviors, due to space limitations a more comprehensive discussion of the emergence of morally relevant actions is outside the scope of this review (but see recent in-depth reviews by, e.g., Davidov, Vaish, Knafo-Noam, & Hastings, 2016; Kana, Henry, Slaughter, Selcuk, & Ruffman, 2016; Warneken, 2015). Throughout the chapter we focus specifically on the domains of help/harm and fairness/unfairness, as these are consistently considered morally relevant across cultures (Haidt & Graham, 2007; Haidt, Koller, & Dias, 1993), and because prominent theories of moral development have defined moral judgments as encompassing these two domains (e.g., Kohlberg, 1969; Turiel, 1983); they have also most frequently been studied to date. Our concluding sections discuss what is known about how neural mechanisms and the sociocultural context support infants' emerging capacities, as well as potential implications of these findings for policy.

28.2 Methods for Exploring Infants' Nascent Moral Sense

Prior to the last decade, research examining the development of the moral sense typically probed children's assessments of morally relevant acts and those who perform them via explicit verbal questioning, examining the nature of children's judgments at various points across childhood (e.g., Kohlberg, 1969; Piaget, 1932; see also reviews in Killen & Smetana, 2006, 2014). Though verbal methods have been incredibly fruitful in documenting changes in moral reasoning across childhood, they are nevertheless clearly poorly suited to examining whether preverbal infants and toddlers show any sensitivity to the moral world. Thus, recent studies have utilized methods that require neither understanding nor producing language. In these, infants are presented with depictions of simple morally relevant interactions taking place between two or more individuals (including people, but more commonly infant-friendly hand puppets or cartoon characters), and various spontaneous responses are measured. Infants' *understanding* of morally relevant actions are probed via their attentional patterns, based on the assumption that infants will attend longer to events they find inconsistent or surprising. Infants' *evaluations* of individuals who perform morally relevant actions are assessed via their patterns of preferential attention and reaching. Finally, older infants' and toddlers' evaluations are measured via their selective performance of simple prosocial and antisocial acts. In what follows, we first review evidence for infants' understanding of morally relevant actions, and then move to evidence for infants' and toddlers' evaluations.

28.3 Infants' Understanding of Morally Relevant Acts

28.3.1 Understanding Helpful Versus Harmful Acts

The first study to probe infants' understanding of morally relevant actions was by Premack and Premack (1997), who examined what infants understand about valenced social interactions. Twelve-month-olds were habituated to simple cartoons depicting interactions between two circles. Some infants were habituated to interactions with positive valence, e.g., helping to achieve a simple goal or positive physical contact (caressing); others were habituated to actions with negative valence, e.g., hindering a goal or negative physical contact (hitting). After habituation, infants were shown a new action, which was either consistent with the valence of the first (e.g., children who were habituated to hindering saw hitting) or inconsistent with the valence of the first (e.g., children who were habituated to caressing saw hitting). Looking-time analyses revealed that infants who saw valence-inconsistent acts looked longer than did those who saw valence-consistent acts, even when physical differences between the two consistent acts were greater than between the two inconsistent ones. These results suggested that by 12 months of age, infants extract valence from morally relevant social interactions including helping, hindering, and hitting, and utilize valence as a way of categorizing distinct interaction types.

28.3.2 Expectations for How Recipients of Help and Harm Will Behave

The next study to explore infants' understanding of morally relevant actions examined whether infants understand how individuals who receive helping and hindering from others are likely to behave toward their helpers and hinderers. That is, do infants understand that individuals are likely to prefer those who help versus hinder them? Here, Kuhlmeier, Wynn, and Bloom (2003) showed 12-month-olds cartoon animations in which a small circular object appeared to repeatedly try, but fail, to reach the top of a hill. During alternating events, infants saw the climber be pushed up the hill by a "helper" and down the hill by a "hinderer"; all characters were distinguishable by shape and color. Following habituation, infants were shown test events in which the climber alternately approached the helper (consistent with their previous positive interaction) and the hinderer (inconsistent with their previous negative interaction). Infants looked reliably longer at the consistent, approach-helper event, suggestive that they understood something about who the climber would interact with after having been helped and hindered.

Notably, this initial result was somewhat surprising: Although infants often, though not always, look longer at events that are inconsistent with their expectations (see, e.g., Kidd, Piantadosi, & Aslin, 2012), infants in Kuhlemeier et al.'s (2003) study looked longer at the consistent event. Despite this, subsequent studies utilizing the same paradigm have suggested that infants' longer looking to the consistent event may have had something to do with specific features of the stimuli Kuhlmeier et al. (2003) used. Specifically, although characters moved as though they were animate, they did not have eyes, and so their goals may have been difficult to understand. Thus, infants may have looked longer to the consistent, approach-helper event simply because it was the only one they could make any sense out of (see Kidd et al., 2012). Suggestive that this was the case, infants in subsequent studies have viewed the same interactions between characters with eyes, and have both looked reliably longer following approach-hinderer versus approach-helper events by 10 months (Hamlin, Wynn, & Bloom, 2007), and looked from the climber toward the helper in advance of the climber's approach by 12 months (Fawcett & Liszkowski, 2012). Together, these results suggest that by late in the first year infants expect recipients of helping and hindering to preferentially approach their helpers rather than their hinderers.

What drives infants' expectations in these studies? Infants could respond as they do because they expect recipients to approach those who help them, to avoid those who hinder them, or to do both. A recent iteration of the hill paradigm has attempted to distinguish these possibilities by showing infants hill events involving neutral characters. Depending on condition, both 6- and 10-month-old infants viewed *either* helper *or* hinderer hill events, but not both; these events alternated with unvalenced events involving a neutral character. During test events, the climber alternately approached the helper and the neutral character (helper condition) or the hinderer and the neutral character (hinderer condition), and their looking times were measured. Results showed that infants in the hinderer condition distinguished the approach events, looking longer following approach-hinderer than approach-neutral events. In contrast, infants in the helper conditions looked equally following approach-helper and approach-neutral events (Chae & Song, 2018; cf. Hamlin et al., 2007). These results suggest that an understanding that others tend to avoid and/or dislike those who hinder them emerges by 6 months of age, and may emerge earlier in development than an expectation that others tend to approach and/or like those who help them. This developmental difference is consistent with other studies suggestive that negative social information may be particularly salient early in development (see Vaish, Grossmann, & Woodward, 2008 for a review; see also Hamlin, Wynn, & Bloom, 2010).

Given the critical role that intentions play in adults' moral judgments (Cushman, 2008; Kant, [1789] 1959; Malle, 1999), additional studies using the hill paradigm have attempted to isolate the role of valenced intentions versus valenced outcomes in driving infants' expectations for the climber's approach behavior. For example, 12-month-olds have been shown to look longer at approach-hinderer than approach-helper events even when no outcomes were shown and so could not have driven infants' expectations (Lee, Yun, Kim, & Song, 2015). Furthermore, 16-month-olds (though not 12-month-olds) in the same paper looked longer at approach-hinderer events even when the helper *tried but failed* to help, so that both the helper and the hinderer were associated with the climber experiencing a negative outcome. Thus, between 12 and 16 months of age, infants appear to increasingly recognize that recipients of morally relevant acts will evaluate helpful and harmful agents based on their prosocial and antisocial intentions, rather than the outcomes they are associated with.

28.3.3 Expectations for How Observers of Help and Harm Will Behave

As noted in the introduction, humans readily evaluate individuals whose actions have no effect on us; for instance, those we merely observe helping and harming third parties. Do infants expect observers of helping and harming to differentially evaluate helpers versus harmers? To date, several studies suggest that they do. For instance, Kanakogi et al. (2017) examined how 6- and 10-month-olds expect observers of an aggressive interaction to subsequently treat both the aggressor and the victim. Infants first saw one cartoon agent (the aggressor) repeatedly hit another (the victim), while a third agent (the observer) watched the interaction. Subsequently, infants either saw the observer help both the victim and the aggressor (helping condition), or saw the observer hit both the victim and the aggressor (harming condition). Patterns of attention differed across conditions; specifically, whereas infants in the helping condition looked longer when the observer helped the aggressor versus the victim, infants in the harming condition looked longer when the observer hit the victim versus the aggressor. This pattern of results suggests that in addition to expecting recipients of hindering to subsequently avoid their hinderers, by 6 months of age infants expect mere observers of aggression to treat victims both more positively and less negatively than they treat aggressors. Critically, another study suggests that infants only expect certain individuals to treat aggressors negatively, that is, those who actually saw the aggressive act occur (Choi & Luo, 2015).

28.3.4 Expectations for How Individuals Tend to Treat Each Other

Other studies have explored whether infants recognize that certain valenced behaviors are more likely to emerge within particular relationships. For instance, it has recently been demonstrated that infants from 4 months of age look longer when an adult ignores, rather than approaches and tends to, an infant in distress (Jin, Houston, Baillargeon, Groh, & Roisman, 2018). Because infants in a different condition did not look longer when an adult approached an infant who laughed, these results suggest that 4-month-olds specifically expect adults to approach infants in need (this pattern was also observed in 8- and 12-month-olds). In a study examining infants' expectations for how individuals treat in-group and out-group members, 17-month-olds looked longer when an adult ignored, rather than helped, a group member in need, but looked equally at ignoring and helping when the interaction was between out-group members (Jin & Baillargeon, 2017). These results suggest that by the middle of the second year infants do expect group members to help each other, but hold no baseline expectations for how out-group members will interact. That said, a study by Rhodes, Hetherington, Brink, and Wellman (2015) suggests that infants in the second year do sometimes hold expectations for how individuals who are not identified as part of the same group will interact: 16-month-olds who initially saw two individuals conflict subsequently looked longer when friends of those individuals cooperated rather than conflicted.

Taken together, these studies suggest that infants expect agents to selectively approach and positively interact with certain third parties, such as those who have previously been helpful, kin in distress, and group members. The first two of these expectations have been demonstrated to emerge by just 6 months of age, and the latter approximately a year later. Although the reason for the later-demonstrated emergence of sensitivity to how group membership influences sociomoral behavior is not explicitly known (and indeed, future studies may demonstrate earlier sensitivity), it may be that infants in the first year simply fail to identify which individuals belong to the same group. On the other hand, perhaps younger infants can recognize which individuals are in the same group (see, e.g., Liberman, Woodward, Sullivan, & Kinzler, 2016; Powell & Spelke, 2013) but have yet to recognize that in-group and out-group members tend to treat each other differently. These possibilities should be teased apart in future work.

The work reviewed above also highlights that infants do not expect *all* third parties to positively interact. Indeed, infants do not expect positive interaction with individuals who have previously been antisocial, with nonneedy kin, or with out-group members, and in some cases they even appear to expect negative interactions. Together, these results suggest that infants have a fairly narrow sense of the circumstances under which help and harm are likely to occur. This narrowness is further suggested by results from studies measuring infants' attention following helping versus nonhelping events (e.g., hindering, ignoring) that occur between entirely unknown individuals. Critically, in these studies infants are given no a priori reason to expect the individuals to interact in any particular way: No past actions by any of the characters are shown, group membership is unspecified, etc. Infants in these studies have consistently looked equally following helping and nonhelping events regardless of the age tested, suggestive that although infants can utilize various forms of information to constrain their interpretations of how third parties will interact, they nevertheless hold no baseline expectation that individuals will help each other (e.g., Hamlin, 2013b, 2014; Jin & Baillargeon, 2017; Lee et al., 2015; Premack & Premack, 1997).

28.3.5 Fairness and Unfairness

In contrast to helping versus harming, studies suggest that infants *do* possess baseline expectations for how resources are likely to be distributed among third parties. These studies are based on the observation that morality incorporates principles of distributive justice, which hold that fair distribution of resources requires adhering to principles of equality and equity (Deutsch, 1975). The equality principle holds that at baseline, equal distributions are fair and unequal distributions are unfair. In contrast, the equity principle holds that cases exist in which unequal distributions are fairer, including when one recipient has greater need than the other, has worked harder than the other, etc.

Researchers have explored infants' sensitivity to principles of equality and equity by measuring their attention to third-party distribution events in which an agent divides goods among two recipients, resulting in either an equal or an unequal outcome. For instance, Schmidt and Sommerville (2011) showed 15-month-olds events in which a person distributed graham crackers among two unknown human recipients. Across alternating events, a distributor divided the crackers both equally (2:2) and unequally (3:1). Infants looked longer following unequal versus equal distributions, suggestive that they were surprised by the unequal distribution. Further, a new group of 15-month-olds did not distinguish events in which resources were distributed to inanimate objects rather than humans, suggestive that attention in the human recipient condition was not based solely on low-level aspects of the displays (see similar results/control conditions in Sloane, Baillargeon, & Premack, 2012; Sommerville, Schmidt, Yun & Burns, 2013). Other work suggests that an expectation for equal distributions within this paradigm emerges by 12 months of age, and is positively related to infants' own tendency to generously share goods with others as well as the presence of siblings in the home (Schmidt & Sommerville, 2011; Ziv & Sommerville, 2017).

Does infants' expectation for fairness emerge by 12 months of age as a result of sharing experience, or does sharing experience merely facilitate a sensitivity to fairness that already exists? Recent studies utilizing simpler distributions than the 2:2 versus 3:1 distributions described above suggest that experience facilitates an existing sensitivity. For example, in a recent study 4-month-olds watched a human experimenter divide two cookies either equally or unequally between two animated puppets (Buyukozer Dawkins, Sloane, & Baillargeon, 2019; see also Meristo, Strid, & Surian, 2016). Here, both 4- and 9-month-olds looked longer following the unequal distribution than the equal one, suggestive that a sensitivity to fairness emerges by 4 months of age, at least in this very simple context. Given that 4-month-olds are barely able to reach for objects themselves much less pass them to others, these results suggest that sharing experience cannot be responsible for the emergence of infants' sensitivity to fairness. Instead, experience likely facilitates the depth and scope of infants' fairness understanding; for example, by allowing infants to process more complex distributions.

28.3.5.1 *Fairness and Unfairness: Recipients*

Although sensitivity to the equality principle appears to be in place from early in the first year, evidence for sensitivity to the equity principle, or that distributions will be proportional to various considerations of what recipients deserve, currently exists only in infants later in the second year of life. For example, Sloane et al. (2012; see also Wang & Henderson, 2018) examined whether 21-month-olds' expectations for equal distributions are eliminated if, prior to the distribution event, one recipient put in less work to complete a task. Indeed, infants in an unequal work condition were surprised by an equal distribution, but only if they knew that the distributor had watched one of the recipients do less, and so knew they were unequally deserving.

Infants' equality expectations also appear to be sensitive to whether or not a distributor is in the same group as a recipient, but only when resources are limited (Bian, Sloane, & Baillargeon, 2018). Specifically, a set of studies examining the role of group membership on 19-month-olds' fairness expectations found that when there were enough resources for everyone, infants looked longer at all unequal distributions than at equal ones, suggestive that infants always expect equality when resources are plentiful. However, when there were not enough resources for all, infants looked least at an unequal distribution favoring the in-group, suggestive that infants may expect in-group-favoring when resources are scarce.

28.3.5.2 *Expectations for How Observers of Fair and Unfair Distributions Will Behave*

Other studies have explored infants' expectations for how observers of equal and unequal distributions will subsequently behave toward the distributors. To date, these studies have generally utilized interactions between cartoon agents, and have demonstrated that infants recognize that observers of fair and unfair distributions will be differentially likely to approach (Geraci & Surian, 2011), reward (Meristo & Surian, 2013), and punish (Meristo & Surian, 2014) fair versus unfair distributors from late in the first year/early in the second. It is important to note, however, that across studies the direction of the effects (e.g., longer looking to the expected versus the unexpected event) has been somewhat inconsistent, and so more work needs to be done to determine exactly how infants are interpreting actions that observers direct toward fair and unfair distributors.

28.4 Preference/Choice Paradigms

The studies described above suggest that infants in their first and second years possess a developing understanding of several of the behaviors that adults consider relevant to the moral domain, including helping, hindering, aggression, fairness, and unfairness. Indeed, infants appear to view fair distributions as generally more likely than unfair ones, to generate expectations about how actors are likely to be treated by those who both experience and observe their morally relevant acts, and to be sensitive to which kinds of valenced acts are likely to emerge within particular relationships. All that aside, moral judgments clearly require more than just understanding morally relevant acts and how they influence others. Moral judgments additionally involve an *evaluative* component wherein acts and actors are judged as good or bad; these evaluations are readily applied to actions that individuals direct toward unknown third parties, suggestive that they are not based on concerns for one's immediate self-interest. In this section, we review studies of infants' evaluations of those who have behaved prosocially versus antisocially toward third parties, continuing to focus on the domains of harm and fairness. Though we have not framed the results in this manner, evidence that infants evaluate agents who engage in help/harm and fair/unfair distributions lends convergent evidence to the conclusions about infants' understanding of third-party prosocial and antisocial action from the previous section.

28.4.1 Infants' Evaluations of Helpers Versus Harmers

The first study to explore whether infants evaluate others for their prosocial and antisocial acts presented 6- and 10-month-old infants with a version of Kuhlmeier et al.'s (2003) cartoon hill-climbing scenario in which the stimuli were 3-D and interactions were presented live (Hamlin et al., 2007). First, infants were presented with alternating helping and hindering hill events until they reached a preset habituation criterion. Following habituation, an experimenter blind to the identity of the characters presented infants with a choice between the helper and the hinderer, placed 30 cm apart on a white board. Choices were recorded as the character infants touched first via a visually guided reach. Results showed that both 6- and 10-month-olds were significantly more likely to reach for the helper than for the hinderer, even if parents' eyes were closed so that they could not influence infants' choices. These results suggest that infants prefer those who help versus hinder third parties' unfulfilled goals by 6 months of age.

Subsequent studies explored whether younger, 3-month-old infants also evaluate helpers and hinderers. Because 3-month-olds are not yet capable of reaching for objects, 3-month-olds' evaluations were measured via a preferential looking procedure in which characters were held in front of infants' faces for 30 seconds; infants' attention was captured on video and coded offline. Just like older infants who reliably reached for the helper, 3-month-olds looked significantly longer to the helper than to the hinderer (Hamlin et al., 2010). These results suggest that the tendency to prefer those who help versus hinder unknown third parties, at least within the hill paradigm, emerges within the first few months after birth.

Other studies expanded on this initial result by examining infants' preferences for characters who help versus hinder various other unfulfilled goals (Hamlin & Wynn, 2011). In the "box scenario," a hand-puppet protagonist repeatedly tries, but fails, to open the lid of a box containing a toy. The helper always assists the protagonist in lifting the lid so that he can get the toy; the hinderer always jumps and slams the lid of the box shut so that the protagonist cannot get the toy. In the "ball scenario," a protagonist plays with, and then drops, a ball toward one of two other characters. The helper always rolls the ball back to the protagonist; the hinderer always runs away with the ball. The preferential reaching procedure in these studies is similar to the one just described for simple shapes, with some differences: An experimenter presents the helper and hinderer puppets in front of infants' faces but slightly out of reach, and infants are required to look at each puppet and back to the experimenter before puppets are moved within reach. Choice is then recorded as the first puppet contacted via a visually guided reach. Using these methods, Hamlin and Wynn (2011) found that infants were significantly more likely to choose the helper than the hinderer in the box and ball shows from 5 months of age; further, infants attended significantly longer to the helper than to the hinderer in the ball show at 3 months.

These results suggest that infants prefer those who facilitate versus hinder a variety of unfulfilled goals within the first year after birth. Further, these choices have been shown to be resistant to at least some amount of self-interest. A recent study demonstrated that although 12-month-olds prefer to reach toward more versus fewer cookies (two cookies vs. one as well as eight cookies vs. one; see also Feigenson, Dehaene, & Spelke, 2004); when the cookies were offered by a helper (who offered one cookie) and a hinderer (who offered two), infants still chose the helper even though they had to give up a cookie to do so (Tasimi & Wynn, 2016). Notably however, when the hinderer offered eight cookies and the helper offered one, infants showed a (nonsignificant) preference for the hinderer. That is, infants were willing to give up one cookie to avoid interacting with a hinderer, but they were less willing to give up seven. Although infants were only willing to forego a small windfall to avoid the hinderer, these results suggest that some form of impartiality may already be operative from early in life.

Infants' preference for helpers over hinderers could reflect one or both of the following two evaluations: (1) infants positively evaluate and approach helpers and/or (2) infants negatively evaluate and avoid hinderers. These possibilities have been probed directly utilizing variations of the hill scenario, in which infants in different conditions are shown either helping or hindering events paired with neutral events. Infants' patterns of choice/attention between valenced and neutral characters in these studies have shown that at 6 and 10 months of age, infants prefer both helpers to neutral characters and neutral characters to hinderers, suggestive that both positive and negative evaluation are operative (Chae & Song, 2018; Hamlin et al., 2007). In contrast, younger, 3-month-old infants may only negatively evaluate hinderers: Although 3-month-olds in the neutral-hinderer condition selectively attended to the neutral character over the hinderer, infants in the neutral-helper condition looked equally to both (Hamlin et al., 2010; see also Chae & Song, 2018). These results suggest that negative evaluations of hinderers may emerge first, by 3 months of age.

Studies demonstrating infants' preferences for helpers over hinderers in the hill, box, and ball scenarios have been followed up in various ways. Some have explored the robustness of infants' responses, both by replicating past methods closely (Hamlin, 2013a; Salvadori et al., 2015; Woo, Steckler, Le, & Hamlin, 2017) and by adjusting them in various ways (Cowell & Decety, 2015; Hamlin, 2015; Scarf, Imute, Colombo, & Hayne, 2012; Scola, Holvoet, Arciszewski, & Picard, 2015; Shimizu, Senzaki, & Uleman, 2018; Tasimi & Wynn, 2016). Though not all attempts have replicated (see, e.g., Cowell & Decety, 2015; Salvadori et al., 2015), a recent meta-analysis of both published and unpublished results put the rate of choosing helpers over hinderers at about 2/3, even after correcting for possible publication bias (Margoni & Surian, 2018). Together, then, the extant data suggests that infants show a reliable preference for those who help, versus hinder, others' unfulfilled goals.

Related studies have examined infants' evaluations of prosocial and antisocial characters in scenarios involving physical aggression. For instance, infants appear to negatively evaluate aggressors: 10-month-olds are more likely to reach for a victim of aggression over an aggressor (Kanakogi, Okumura, Inoue, Kitazaki, & Itakura, 2013), and selectively avoid an agent who pushed another agent over one who pushed an inanimate object (Buon et al., 2014). Further, 6-month-olds have been shown to prefer an agent who intervenes to stop an aggressive interaction over an agent who fails to intervene (Kanakogi et al., 2017). Finally, a recent study demonstrated that although 21–31-month-olds will selectively reach for "winning" versus "losing" agents if winning is defined as being allowed to get by in a conflict, toddlers selectively avoid winners who won because they were physically aggressive (Thomas, Thomsen, Lukowski, Abramyan, & Sarnecka, 2018). Thus, infants appear not only to positively evaluate helpers and negatively evaluate hinderers, but also to positively evaluate protectors and negatively evaluate bullies.

28.4.2 Preferences for Fair Versus Unfair Others

Infants have also been shown to evaluate others in the domain of fairness, preferentially interacting with those who divide resources equally versus unequally. For instance, in the study described above involving cartoon agents distributing resources, 16-month-olds selectively reached for the fair over the unfair agent (though 10-month-olds did not; Geraci & Surian; 2011). In a study using human actors, 15-month-olds selectively accepted toys from, and walked toward, fair versus unfair distributors (so long as both infants and actors were of the same race; Burns & Sommerville, 2014), and in another both 13- and 17-month-old infants were more likely to approach and retrieve a toy offered by a fair versus an unfair distributor (here race was not manipulated; Lucca, Pospisil, & Sommerville, 2018; see also DesChamps, Eason, & Sommerville, 2016).

Together, these results suggest that infants evaluate others for their fair versus unfair resource distributions by the second year of life. Notably, we are aware of no evidence suggesting that infants prefer fair distributors to unfair ones prior to the second year. This is somewhat surprising, given (1) the extensive evidence that infants prefer helpers to harmers in the first year, and (2) the evidence that infants expect fair versus unfair distributions by just 4 months of age. One possibility is that the appropriate studies have not yet been run, as the work described herein is all fairly new. On the other hand, perhaps infants really do not evaluate fair and unfair distributors in the first year of life. If the latter were true, it would reveal an important dissociation between infants' assessments in the domains of harm and fairness in the first year. Specifically, it would reveal that whereas infants in the first year expect, but do not evaluate, fair distributions, they evaluate, but do not expect, helpful actions. Further probing this possibility as well as what it means for theories of moral development is a critical avenue for future study.

28.4.3 How to Make Sense of Infants' Choices

Why do infants of any age approach helpers/fair individuals and avoid harmers/unfair individuals? That infants' preferences have been demonstrated across a variety of sociomoral domains and scenarios, each with distinct low-level properties, makes it unlikely that there is something about the low-level features of prosocial and antisocial acts that infants are evaluating. Furthermore, the studies reviewed above have typically included control conditions in which infants are shown animate characters engaging in similar (or identical) physical acts to those that were prosocial and antisocial in other conditions, but toward inanimate objects incapable of possessing goals and so incapable of being helped and harmed or possessing distributed objects. Infants in these control conditions consistently choose randomly, suggestive that low-level stimulus properties are unlikely to be responsible for infants' choices (Geraci & Surian, 2011; Hamlin & Wynn, 2011; Hamlin et al., 2007, 2010; see also Buon et al., 2014; Hamlin, 2015; Scarf et al., 2012).

But what is it about prosocial and antisocial others that infants evaluate? One possibility is that infants' evaluations are based on *outcomes*; that is, perhaps infants like those who make good things happen for other agents (achieved goals, protection from harm, equal distributions), and dislike those who make bad things happen for other agents (thwarted goals, physical harm, unequal distributions). Indeed, infants may assume that those who make good things happen for other agents are likely to do the same for them. If this were the basis on which infants were evaluating prosocial and antisocial others, it would be difficult to argue that their evaluations are based on some impartial sense of right and wrong, given the importance of intent over outcome in adults' moral judgments (Cushman, 2008; Kant, [1789] 1959; Malle, 1999). Although past work has consistently shown that young children's explicit moral judgments prioritize outcome over intent (e.g., Baird & Astington, 2004; Costanzo, Coie, Grumet, & Farnill, 1973; Cushman, Sheketoff, Wharton, & Carey, 2013; Piaget, 1932), in what follows, we summarize work suggestive that mental states play a driving role in infants' evaluations of prosocial and antisocial others from late in the first year, and, critically, that outcomes never appear important.

Studies examining the role of mental states and outcomes in infants' evaluations have utilized several classic cases in which intention and outcome conflict, including failed attempts to help and harm, accidental help and harm, and ignorant help and harm. In a failed attempts design, Hamlin (2013a) used an adaptation of the box show to demonstrate that 8-month-olds prefer puppets who tried but fail to help open a box (a positive intent resulting in a negative outcome) over those who tried but failed to hinder (a negative intent resulting in a positive outcome), suggestive that intention valence is prioritized over outcome valence by 8 months of age. Notably, 8-month-olds failed to distinguish characters that were *only* distinguishable by outcome (for example, successful helpers vs. failed helpers), suggestive that they do not make outcome-based evaluations at all. Unlike 8-month-olds, 5-month-olds failed to distinguish characters in any condition involving failed attempts, only ever preferring successful helpers to successful hinderers. These results add to other evidence that young infants may struggle to interpret actions involving failed attempts as goal directed (see, e.g., Brandone & Wellman, 2009), and suggest that mentalistic evaluation may emerge between 5 and 8 months of age.

Other work has explored infants' evaluations of individuals who help or hinder others accidentally. For example, Woo et al. (2017) demonstrated that 10-month-olds prefer an intentional helper to an accidental one, but an accidental hinderer to an intentional one, consistent with the notion that helpers and hinderers should be judged based on possessing positive and negative intent, respectively. Similar results were observed in a condition within the bullying intervention paper by Kanakogi et al. (2017) described in several earlier sections. Here, 10-month-olds preferred a character who intentionally intervened on bullying over one who accidentally intervened, again suggesting that intentions and not outcomes structure infants' evaluations. Notably, 6-month-olds in this study did not distinguish between intentional and accidental interveners, consistent with how 5-month-olds failed to distinguish characters involved in failed attempts (Hamlin, 2013a). Together, these studies suggest that mentalistic evaluation is something that infants are capable of in the second half of the first year, but not in the first half.

Finally, a paper by Hamlin, Ullman, Tenenbaum, Goodman, and Baker (2013) further explored 10-month-olds' evaluations of intentions versus outcomes by holding the *local* intentionality of characters' actions constant (e.g., no cues demonstrated that any actions were accidental or otherwise not intended), while manipulating whether or not their actions should be conceived of as helping or hindering based on whether or not the helper and hinderer *knew* that what they were doing would help or hinder. Specifically, 10-month-olds saw characters intentionally unblock a protagonist's access to one of two toys, only one of which the protagonist preferred. Critically, in one condition the characters knew which toy the protagonist liked, and in another condition the characters did not know. Choice results showed that only infants in the preference-known condition reliably preferred the observer who granted access to the preferred toy, suggestive that infants' evaluations are attuned to whether or not a given intentional action was undertaken with the knowledge that it would facilitate someone's specific goal. Together with work on failed attempts and accidents, these results provide strong support for the idea that infants evaluate action mentalistically.

28.4.4 What Are Infants Evaluating? Actions in Context

Of course, possessing helpful/harmful intent is not *always* positively/negatively evaluated. Indeed, there are contexts under which evaluators positively judge those who intentionally act antisocially; for example, some individuals' goals should arguably be blocked (e.g., a small child about to touch a hot stove), and others may deserve punishment for antisocial acts they have previously performed. Here we review evidence that infants' and toddlers' evaluations of prosocial and antisocial others are sensitive to the context in which they occur.

To study this, researchers have shown infants characters who direct their positive and negative actions toward differentially deserving protagonists (Hamlin, 2014; Hamlin, Wynn, Bloom, & Mahajan, 2011). Specifically, unlike in the studies described thus far in which infants saw giving and taking directed toward someone entirely novel, here infants had previously viewed the protagonist either helping (prosocial target condition) or hindering (antisocial target condition) a different third party's goal to open a box. In these contexts, the formerly prosocial protagonist presumably deserved to be treated well, whereas the formerly antisocial protagonist presumably deserved to be treated poorly. Results demonstrated that at 19, 8, and even 4.5 months of age infants' preferences differed based on the protagonist's previous behavior: Infants in the prosocial protagonist condition preferred the giver to the taker, whereas infants in the antisocial protagonist condition preferred the taker to the giver (note that 4.5-month-olds required significantly more experience with the prosocial and antisocial acts of the protagonist in order to show this effect than did older infants). Further studies showed that infants' context-based evaluations were not based on simple valence-matching mechanisms: Infants distinguished between protagonists who had previously performed bad acts (who deserve harm) and those who had previously received them (who do not).

28.4.4.1 *Understanding Infants' Context-Based Evaluation: Is It Moral?*

But what is the nature of infants' context-based evaluation? One possibility is that infants view hindering protagonists as *deserving* to have their ball taken away, and so positively evaluate the individual who does the taking. This possibility aligns with mature moral notions that some individuals deserve punishment, and that individuals who appropriately punish should be positively evaluated (Barclay, 2006; Brown, 1991; Robinson, Kurzban, & Jones, 2007).

On the other hand, infants may simply positively evaluate those who harm someone disliked, for any reason, along the lines of "the enemy of my enemy is my friend" (e.g., Aronson & Cope, 1968; Gawronski, Walther, & Blank, 2005; Heider, 1958). That is, perhaps infants inferred that a giver to a prosocial target and a taker from an antisocial target condition share their positive evaluation of helpers and negative evaluation of hinderers, and based their choices on these shared evaluations. Notably, if infants' context-based evaluations reflect that they like anyone who harms anyone disliked for any reason, this would be importantly different from the impartiality thought to be required for mature moral judgment.

To explore whether or not infants' context-based evaluations are extended to anyone they dislike for any reason, researchers have adapted methods from work demonstrating that infants and toddlers positively evaluate those who are similar to them, preferring those who share their preference for toys and foods and who speak their language (Fawcett & Markson, 2010; Kinzler, Dupoux, & Spelke, 2007; Mahajan & Wynn, 2012; see also Gerson, Bekkering, & Hunnius, 2017; Pun, Ferrera, Diesendruck, Hamlin, & Baron, 2018). For instance, Hamlin, Mahajan, Liberman, and Wynn (2013) first exposed 9- and 14-month-old infants to two puppets, one who shared infants' food preference (e.g., the similar protagonist) and another that showed the opposite preference (the dissimilar protagonist). Infants were then habituated to either the similar or the dissimilar protagonist having his ball both given back to him and taken away, and were given the choice between the giver and taker. During choice, infants' preferences depended on whether or not the protagonist was similar to them: In the similar protagonist condition infants preferred the giver, while in the dissimilar target condition they preferred the taker. Though these results provide additional evidence that infants evaluate prosocial and antisocial acts in context, they also suggest that the tendency may be based on something like a sense that the enemy of their enemy is their friend, rather than a sense of deservingness. Although adults clearly demonstrate similar tendencies (for instance, experiencing pleasure at the pain of out-group members; e.g., Cikara, Bruneau, & Saxe, 2011), and some have argued that these tendencies are part of a "binding" or group-based morality (Haidt & Kesebir, 2010), these findings suggest that infants' evaluations may share some of adults' somewhat less praiseworthy sociomoral tendencies, ones that some would not consider moral at all (for further discussion, see Wynn, Bloom, Jordan, Marshall, & Sheskin, 2018).

28.5 How Infants' and Toddlers' Social Evaluations Influence Their Valenced Social Interactions

A remaining question concerns how infants' understanding and evaluation of prosocial and antisocial actions and individuals influences their own actions. For instance, does a tendency to evaluate certain actions and individuals not only influence who infants and toddlers choose to approach, but also their own prosocial and antisocial acts? This question is relevant both to the role that infants' evaluations might play within infants' everyday lives, as well as to theories linking morality to the evolution of cooperation. Indeed, these theories not only require individuals to evaluate others for their cooperation-relevant acts, but also to act in ways that serve to promote further prosocial acts (for example, rewarding them) and discourage antisocial ones (for example, punishing them; e.g., Axelrod & Hamilton, 1981; Bull & Rice, 1991; Fehr & Gachter, 2002; Nowak, 2006; O'Gorman, Henrich, & van Vugt, 2009). Here we review evidence suggestive that infants selectively adjust their own behaviors based on the past prosocial and antisocial acts of their interaction partners, in ways that have been theorized to support cooperative systems. Given the linguistic and behavioral capacities that these studies require, they all utilize infants late in their second year.

The first study to explore how infants behave toward prosocial and antisocial others exposed 19–23-month-old toddlers to either the box show or the ball show, and then presented them with one of two possible treat-scarcity conditions. In the giving condition, neither the prosocial nor the antisocial dog received a treat, and toddlers were asked to choose who to give one last treat to. In the taking condition, the experimenter gave both the prosocial and antisocial dog a treat, but then "found" a third, new dog who had not yet received a treat. Toddlers were asked to take a treat from one of the dogs so that the new dog could have one. Toddlers' behaviors showed a clear interaction between the valence of the action they were asked to perform (giving vs. taking) and the past behavior of the recipient they chose: Toddlers who were asked to give a treat selectively gave to the prosocial dog, but toddlers who were asked to take a treat selectively took from the antisocial dog. Notably, these results suggest that there are situations in which toddlers are willing to approach intentionally antisocial individuals; perhaps in order to mete out punishment. Related results were observed by Dahl, Schuck, and Campos (2013), who observed that 27-month-olds were more likely to help a prosocial versus antisocial human when both wanted to retrieve a toy, and by van de Vondervoort, Ahknin, Kushnir, Slevinsky, and Hamlin (2018), who showed that 20-month-olds were more selectively nice to prosocial than to antisocial individuals even when their interactions were one-on-one.

28.6 Summary, Implications, and Unanswered Questions

Within the first 2 years of life infants and toddlers understand certain prosocial and antisocial acts, evaluate the individuals who produce them, and selectively respond to them in kind. The early emergence of these abilities, at least some of which are observed prior to a time at which extensive experience and socialization are likely to be solely responsible, lends some credence both to philosophical and evolutionary theorizing that certain aspects of the human moral sense are built in.

Of course, just as Mencius argued that moral "sprouts" are not equivalent to full-fledged morality (cited in Chan, 1963, 2A6), the results discussed herein should not be taken to indicate that infants' and adults' moral senses are one and the same, nor that infants' abilities are fully developed. Indeed, throughout the chapter we have highlighted various ways that younger infants' responses are different from older infants', and different from adults'. Thus, it is imperative not to use the results reviewed herein to conclude that morality is entirely, or even largely, built in; we simply argue that the infant's moral capacities are significantly more sophisticated than previously thought, and that results from these studies should be included in discussions of moral development that occurs later in life.

But how should we conceive of these capacities? Throughout the chapter we have framed the work as reflecting precursors to a *moral* sense, as clearly abilities to understand and evaluate prosocial and antisocial actions and individuals are foundational aspects of morality, as are both intention- and context-based judgments. That said, perhaps infants actually possess surprisingly sophisticated but nevertheless rather general *social* abilities, ones that may eventually facilitate children's moral tendencies, but should not be considered moral themselves.

One way to examine whether infants' tendencies are precursors to a specifically moral versus a generally social sense would be to determine whether the results observed in these infant tasks are meaningfully linked to other aspects of social and/or moral functioning, either concurrently or later in life. Indeed, although significant numbers of infants in the studies discussed herein have shown capacities for moral understanding, evaluation, and action, not every infant has, and within a study some infants show relatively stronger tendencies than others. Do these differences relate to other aspects of social and moral functioning? To date, three studies have explored this question. Two studies suggest that distinct features of moral functioning may be related early in life. In the first, infants who were most likely to distinguish fair from unfair distributions within the looking-time paradigms detailed above (e.g., looking longer at unfair than at fair events) were also most likely to share more versus less attractive toys with an experimenter (dubbed "prosocial sharing," e.g., Schmidt & Sommerville, 2011). In the second, 16–27-month-olds who selectively helped a prosocial individual also looked longer following antisocial taking versus prosocial giving events during the familiarization period, suggestive that these infants may have been particularly sensitive to harm (Dahl et al., 2013).

A third study utilized a longitudinal approach, examining preschool social and moral functioning in children who had participated in two or more morally relevant tasks within their first 2 years (mean age = 12 months; Tan, Mikami, & Hamlin, 2018). Around children's fourth birthday, parents filled out four questionnaires measuring individual differences in social and moral development. Restricting analyses only to neurotypical children, no relation-ship between infant performance and scores on three strictly social develop-ment questionnaires was observed. However, there was a relationship with a moral development scale, specifically the Inventory of Callous-Unemotional Traits (ICU; Frick, 2003; Frick et al., 2003) that is associated with psychopathy. These results require replication and further exploration, but tentatively sug-gest that infant studies may be tapping something about moral development specifically, as opposed to social development in general. These individual-difference studies suggest that infant morality tasks may well tap moral as well as social functioning.

28.6.1 What Are the Neural Correlates of Infants' Moral Understanding and Evaluations?

Although many are in progress, only a few investigations into the neural cor-relates of infants' assessments of prosocial and antisocial events have been published to date. Those that exist have generally supported the conclusions drawn from behavioral studies. In one study utilizing electroencephalography (EEG), researchers examined 6-month-olds' event-related potentials (ERPs) in response to still images of helpers versus hinderers after they observed a car-toon version of the hill scenario (Gredebäck et al., 2015). They observed that one ERP component, the P400, was stronger in response to the helper versus the hinderer; this difference was not observed in infants who had viewed the same characters engaging in similar, but not moral, actions. Infants' P400 is thought to be localized to the superior temporal sulcus (STS; Dalrymple et al., 2011; Gredebäck, Melinder, & Daum, 2010; Itier & Taylor, 2004), an area critically implicated in mental-state processing (Decety & Howard, 2013; van Overwalle & Baetens, 2009) and that has previously been shown to be involved in infants' processing of emotional faces (Leppänen, Moulson, Vogel-Farley, & Nelson, 2007), biological motion (Reid, Hoehl, & Striano, 2006), and refer-ential actions and gaze (Gredebäck et al., 2010; Itier & Taylor, 2004). That this component also discriminated between helpers and hinderers suggests that the discriminations demonstrated in behavioral work are, at the very least, social in nature. Further, Gredebäck et al. (2015) failed to observe distinctions between helper and hinderer trials in the negative central (Nc) component, thought to reflect basic attentional processes (e.g., Courchesne, Ganz, & Norcia, 1981; Richards, 2003). This suggests that the P400 effect was likely not due to differ-ences in how much attention infants were dedicating to the characters, but to social processing in particular.

A second EEG study observed 12–24-month-olds' brain activity while they viewed a cartoon version of the hill scenario. Although they did not utilize a method that would allow them to examine ERPs in response to helpers ver-sus hinderers, they found that infants showed relatively more activity in right versus left frontal brain areas while observing hindering than while observing helping (Cowell & Decety, 2015). This pattern of asymmetric brain activation has been linked to avoidance motivation and negative affect in infants (e.g., Davidson, 1994; Hane, Fox, Henderson, & Marshall, 2008; Saby & Marshall, 2012), suggestive that infants in the second year of life do indeed dislike hindering. Thus, although the extent to which infants showed this asymmetry did not interact with infants' tendency to choose the helper (and infants rate of choosing the helper was at chance in this study) it nevertheless suggests that infants' behavioral tendency to avoid hinderers may be related to their tendency to view hindering actions as aversive. Here the authors did observe an effect of the Nc attentional component; specifically, infants who showed a stronger Nc response to dynamic pictures of various prosocial versus anti-social acts were more likely to choose the helper in the hill paradigm. These results suggest that infants who devote more attentional resources to prosocial acts will be more likely to prefer helpers. That said, given that the association between attention and choice was observed across tasks (that is, children who had a stronger Nc to prosocial pictures in one paradigm preferred the helper in a completely different paradigm) these results should be interpreted with caution until they are replicated.

28.6.2 Examining the Role of the Sociocultural Context in Infants' Capacities

It is heretofore unclear what role children's unique environments play in the emergence of sensitivity to the moral world. At a broad cultural level, the work reviewed above has almost exclusively examined infants from middle- and upper-class homes growing up in North America and Western Europe, with the exception of a few studies in Japan in which infants have responded similarly to Western infants. Furthermore, although studies have documented cross-cultural differences in some aspects of moral development (e.g., House et al., 2013), these studies have not observed differences in younger children, and we would not necessarily expect to observe cross-cultural differences in responses to the simple and straightforward moral scenarios that have been presented to infants to date. That said, even if we were to predict cross-cultural differences in certain tendencies, there is currently not enough data available from infants growing up in different cultures to effectively explore this possibility. Regardless, future work should more directly explore the development of these capacities in diverse groups of children around the world.

Similarly, to our knowledge only a few studies have explored whether any family- or parental-level variation relates to variation in infants' capacities. At a family level, it has been observed that for infants over 12 months, the presence or absence of a sibling in the home influences sensitivity to fair versus unfair distributions, with infants with siblings showing more sensitivity than those without (Ziv & Sommerville, 2017). Another paper examining infants with and without older siblings observed no relationship between sibling status and the tendency to show context-based evaluations (that is, preferring puppets who took from hinderers; Hamlin, 2014). Although these results suggested that the tendency to view punishment in one's home (which children with older siblings likely experience much more than children without) is unrelated to the capacity to evaluate individuals who perform punishment appropriately, one relatively small study is clearly insufficient to be the final word on this relationship. At the parent level, infants' tendency to prefer prosocial others has been shown to relate to both parent-reported justice sensitivity (e.g., Cowell & Decety, 2015) as well as mothers' own tendency to describe helping and hindering events using evaluative terms (Shimizu et al., 2018); the causal relationship reflected within each of these associations is as of yet unclear. Further study should continue to explore these relationships, as well as to identify other potential sources of variation in infants' responding in studies like these. One particularly informative area of future study might be to explore responding in infants at risk for abuse and/or neglect, who may be more or less sensitive to prosocial and/or antisocial acts and who may evaluate those who perform them differently than do children without these risk profiles.

28.6.3 Implications for Policy

Although the study of infants' moral capacities is relatively new, it is nevertheless possible to envision policy implications for findings suggestive that infants' moral tendencies are significantly more advanced than previously thought. In particular, given that infants' capacities appear to be related both to concurrent and subsequent moral functioning (e.g., Dahl et al., 2013; Schmidt & Sommerville, 2011; Tan et al., 2018), it might be possible to utilize studies like these to identify children at risk for atypical moral trajectories far earlier than current methods allow. Indeed, although in recent decades the early identification of children at risk for autism spectrum disorders has gained an enormous amount of attention (e.g., Barbaro & Dissanayake, 2012; Jones & Klin, 2013; Ozonoff et al., 2011), we know far less about very early warning signs of atypical moral development (but see Rhee et al., 2013). Earlier identification of children at risk for atypical moral development could then allow for earlier intervention, for example, both parent- and child-focused interventions to increase empathic responding and cultivate a stronger sense of right and wrong (see, e.g., Hoffman & Saltzstein, 1967; Ornaghi, Brockmeier, & Grazzani, 2014; Reddy et al., 2013; Schrandt, Townsend, & Poulson, 2009).

In sum, the studies reviewed herein suggest that human infants possess surprisingly sophisticated sensitivities to morally relevant events including helping, harming, fairness, and unfairness. Infants understand these events, evaluate those who perform them, and respond to their actions in kind, each of which has been hypothesized to be required for the evolution of cooperative systems. Many unanswered questions remain, particularly regarding to what extent these findings should be considered moral versus generally social, how they feed into ongoing moral developmental trajectories, and the sources and consequences of individual differences between infants growing up both within and across cultures.

References

Alexander, R. D. (1987). *The biology of moral systems*. New York, NY: Routledge.

Aronson, E., & Cope, V. (1968). My enemy's enemy is my friend. *Journal of Personality and Social Psychology*, 8, 8–12.

Axelrod, R., & Hamilton, W. D. (1981). The evolution of cooperation. *Science*, 211(4489), 390–1396.

Baird, J. A., & Astington, J. W. (2004). The role of mental state understanding in the development of moral cognition and moral action. *New Directions for Child and Adolescent Development*, 103, 37–49.

Barbaro, J., & Dissanayake, C. (2012). Developmental profiles of infants and toddlers with autism spectrum disorders identified prospectively in a community-based setting. *Journal of Autism and Developmental Disorders*, 42(9), 1939–1948.

Barclay, P. (2006). Reputational benefits for altruistic punishment. *Evolution and Human Behavior*, 27(5), 325–344.

Bian, L., Sloane, S., & Baillargeon, R. (2018). Infants expect ingroup support to override fairness when resources are limited. *Proceedings of the National Academy of Sciences*, 115(11), 2705–2710.

Bloom, P. (2013) *Just babies: The origins of good and evil*. New York, NY: Crown Publishers.

Brandone, A. C., & Wellman, H. M. (2009). You can't always get what you want: Infants understand failed goal-directed actions. *Psychological Science*, 20(1), 85–91.

Brown, D. (1991). *Human universals*. Philadelphia, PA: Temple University Press.

Bull, J. J., & Rice, W. R. (1991). Distinguishing mechanisms for the evolution of cooperation. *Journal of Theoretical Biology*, 149(1), 63–74.

Buon, M., Jacob, P., Margules, S., Brunet, I., Dutat, M., Cabrol, D., & Dupoux, E. (2014). Friend or foe? Early social evaluation of human interactions. *PLoS ONE*, 9(2), e88612.

Burns, M. P., & Sommerville, J. (2014). "I pick you": The impact of fairness and race on infants' selection of social partners. *Frontiers in Psychology*, 5, 93.

Buyukozer Dawkins, M., Sloane, S. M., & Baillargeon, R. (2019). Do infants in the first year of life expect equal resource allocations? *Frontiers in Psychology*, 10, 116.

Chae, J. J. K., & Song, H. J. (2018). Negativity bias in infants' expectations about agents' dispositions. *British Journal of Developmental Psychology*, 36(4), 620–633.

Chan, W. (1963). *A source book in Chinese philosophy*. Princeton, NJ: Princeton University Press.

Choi, Y., & Luo, Y. (2015). 13-month-olds' understanding of social interactions. *Psychological Science*, 26(3), 274–283.

Cikara, M., Bruneau, E. G., & Saxe, R. R. (2011). Us and them: Intergroup failures of empathy. *Current Directions in Psychological Science*, 20(3), 149–153.

Cosmides, L., & Tooby, J. (1992). Cognitive adaptations for social exchange. In J. Barkow, L. Cosmides, & J. Tooby (Eds.), *The adapted mind: Evolutionary psychology and the generation of culture* (pp. 163–228). New York, NY: Oxford University Press.

Costanzo, P. R., Coie, J. D., Grumet, J. F., & Farnill, D. (1973). A reexamination of the effects of intent and consequence on children's moral judgments. *Child Development, 44*(1), 154–161.

Courchesne, E., Ganz, L., & Norcia, A. M. (1981). Event-related brain potentials to human faces in infants. *Child Development, 52*(3), 804–811.

Cowell, J. M., & Decety, J. (2015). Precursors to morality in development as a complex interplay between neural, socioenvironmental, and behavioral facets. *Proceedings of the National Academy of Sciences, 112*(41), 12657–12662.

Cushman, F. (2008) Crime and punishment: Distinguishing the roles of causal and intentional analyses in moral judgment. *Cognition, 108*(2), 353–380.

Cushman, F., Sheketoff, R., Wharton, S., & Carey, S. (2013). The development of intent-based moral judgment. *Cognition, 127*(1), 6–21.

Dahl, A., Schuck, R. K., & Campos, J. J. (2013). Do young toddlers act on their social preferences? *Developmental Psychology, 49*(10), 1964–1970.

Dalrymple, K. A., Oruc, I., Duchaine, B., Pancaroglu, R., Fox, C. J., Iaria, G., … Barton, J. J. (2011). The anatomic basis of the right face-selective N170 IN acquired prosopagnosia: A combined ERP/fMRI study. *Neuropsychologia, 49*(9), 2553–2563.

Davidov, M., Vaish, A., Knafo-Noam, A., & Hastings, P. D. (2016). The motivational foundations of prosocial behavior from a developmental perspective – evolutionary roots and key psychological mechanisms: Introduction to the Special Section. *Child Development, 87*(6), 1655–1667.

Davidson, R. J. (1994). Asymmetric brain function, affective style, and psychopathology: The role of early experience and plasticity. *Development and Psychopathology, 6*(4), 741–758.

de Waal, F. (2009). *Primates and philosophers: How morality evolved.* Princeton, NJ: Princeton University Press.

Decety, J., & Howard, L. H. (2013). The role of affect in the neurodevelopment of morality. *Child Development Perspectives, 7*(1), 49–54.

DesChamps, T. D., Eason, A. E., & Sommerville, J. A. (2016). Infants associate praise and admonishment with fair and unfair individuals. *Infancy, 21*(4), 478–504.

Deutsch, M. (1975). Equity, equality, and need: What determines which value will be used as the basis of distributive justice? *Journal of Social Issues, 31*(3), 137–149.

Fawcett, C. A., & Liszkowski, U. (2012). Infants anticipate others' social preferences. *Infant and Child Development, 21*(3), 239–249.

Fawcett, C. A., & Markson, L. (2010). Children reason about shared preferences. *Developmental Psychology, 46*(2), 299–309.

Fehr, E. & Gächter, S. (2002). Altruistic punishment in humans. *Nature, 415*, 137–140.

Feigenson, L., Dehaene, S., & Spelke, E. (2004). Core systems of number. *Trends in Cognitive Sciences, 8*(7), 307–314.

Frick, P. J. (2003). *The inventory of callous-unemotional traits.* New Orleans, LA: University of New Orleans.

Frick, P. J., Cornell, A. H., Bodin, S. D., Dane, H. E., Barry, C. T., & Loney, B. R. (2003). Callous-unemotional traits and developmental pathways to severe conduct problems. *Developmental Psychology, 39*(2), 246.

Gawronski, B., Walther, E., & Blank, H. (2005). Cognitive consistency and the formation of interpersonal attitudes: Cognitive balance affects the encoding of social information. *Journal of Experimental Social Psychology*, *41*(6), 618–626.

Geraci, A., & Surian, L. (2011). The developmental roots of fairness: Infants' reactions to equal and unequal distributions of resources. *Developmental Science*, *14*(5), 1012–1020.

Gerson, S., Bekkering, H., & Hunnius, S. (2017). Do you do as I do? Young toddlers prefer and copy toy choices of similarly acting others. *Infancy*, *22*(1), 5–22.

Gredebäck, G., Kaduk, K., Bakker, M., Gottwald, J., Ekberg, T., Elsner, C., ... Kenward, B. (2015). The neuropsychology of infants' pro-social preferences. *Developmental Cognitive Neuroscience*, *12*, 106–113.

Gredebäck, G., Melinder, A. M. D., & Daum, M. M. (2010). The neural basis and development of pointing comprehension. *Social Neurosciences*, *5*(5–6), 441–450.

Haidt, J., & Graham, J. (2007). When morality opposes justice: Conservatives have moral intuitions that liberals may not recognize. *Social Justice Research*, *20*(1), 98–116.

Haidt, J., & Kesebir, S. (2010). Morality. In S. Fiske, D. Gilbert, & G. Lindzey (Eds.) *Handbook of social psychology* (5th ed., pp. 797–832). Hoboken, NJ: Wiley.

Haidt, J., Koller, S. H., & Dias, M. G. (1993). Affect, culture, and morality, or is it wrong to eat your dog? *Journal of Personality and Social Psychology*, *65*(4), 613.

Hamlin, J. K. (2013a). Failed attempts to help and harm: Intention versus outcome in preverbal infants' social evaluations. *Cognition*, *128*(3), 451–474.

(2013b). Moral judgment and action in preverbal infants and toddlers: Evidence for an innate moral core. *Current Directions in Psychological Science*, *22*(3), 186–193.

(2014). Context-dependent social evaluation in 4.5-month-old human infants: The role domain-general versus domain-specific processes in the development of evaluation. *Frontiers in Psychology*, *5*, 614.

(2015). The case for social evaluation in preverbal infants: Gazing toward one's goal drives infants' preferences for helpers over hinderers in the hill paradigm. *Frontiers in Psychology*, *5*, 1563.

Hamlin, J. K., Mahajan, N., Liberman, Z., & Wynn, K. (2013). Not like me = bad: Infants prefer those who harm dissimilar others. *Psychological Science*, *24*(4), 589–594.

Hamlin, J. K., Ullman, T., Tenenbaum, J., Goodman, N., & Baker, C. (2013). The mentalistic basis of core social cognition: Experiments in preverbal infants and a computational model. *Developmental Science*, *16*(2), 209–226.

Hamlin, J. K., & Wynn, K. (2011). Young infants prefer prosocial to antisocial others. *Cognitive Development*, *26*(1), 30–39.

Hamlin, J. K., Wynn, K., & Bloom, P. (2007). Social evaluation by preverbal infants. *Nature*, *450*, 557–559.

(2010). Three-month-olds show a negativity bias in their social evaluations. *Developmental Science*, *13*(6), 923–929.

Hamlin, J. K., Wynn, K., Bloom, P., & Mahajan, N. (2011). How infants and toddlers react to antisocial others. *Proceedings of the National Academy of Sciences*, *108*(50), 19931–19936.

Hane, A. A., Fox, N. A., Henderson, H. A., & Marshall, P. J. (2008). Behavioral reactivity and approach–withdrawal bias in infancy. *Developmental Psychology*, *44*(5), 1491.

Heider, F. (1958). *The psychology of interpersonal relations*, New York, NY: Wiley.

Henrich, N., & Henrich, J. (2007). *Why humans cooperate: A cultural and evolutionary explanation*. New York, NY: Oxford University Press.

Hoffman, M. L., & Saltzstein, H. D. (1967). Parent discipline and the child's moral development. *Journal of Personality and Social Psychology*, *5*(1), 45.

House, B. R., Silk, J. B., Henrich, J., Barrett, H. C., Scelza, B. A., Boyette, A. H., … Laurence, S. (2013). Ontogeny of prosocial behavior across diverse societies. *Proceedings of the National Academy of Sciences*, *110*(36), 14586–14591.

Itier, R. J., & Taylor, M. J. (2004). Source analysis of the N170 to faces and objects. *NeuroReport*, *15*(8), 1261–1265.

Jin, K. S., & Baillargeon, R. (2017). Infants possess an abstract expectation of ingroup support. *Proceedings of the National Academy of Sciences*, *114*(31), 8199–8204.

Jin, K. S., Houston, J. L., Baillargeon, R., Groh, A. M., & Roisman, G. I. (2018). Young infants expect an unfamiliar adult to comfort a crying baby: Evidence from a standard violation-of-expectation task and a novel infant-triggered-video task. *Cognitive Psychology*, *102*, 1–20.

Jones, W., & Klin, A. (2013). Attention to eyes is present but in decline in 2–6-month-old infants later diagnosed with autism. *Nature*, *504*(7480), 427.

Joyce, R. (2007). *The evolution of morality*. Cambridge, MA: MIT Press.

Kana, I. Henry, J. D., Slaughter, V., Selcuk, B., & Ruffman, T. (2016). Theory of mind and prosocial behavior in children. *Developmental Psychology*, *52*(8), 1192–1205.

Kanakogi, Y., Inoue, Y., Matsuda, G., Butler, D., Hiraki, K., & Myowa-Yamakoshi, M. (2017). Preverbal infants affirm third-party interventions that protect victims from aggressors. *Nature Human Behaviour*, *1*(2), 0037.

Kanakogi, Y., Okumura, Y., Inoue, Y., Kitazaki, M., & Itakura, S. (2013). Rudimentary sympathy in preverbal infants: preference for others in distress. *PloS ONE*, *8*(6), e65292.

Kant, I. (1789/1959). *Foundations of the metaphysics of morals* (L. W. Beck, Trans.). Indianapolis, IN: Bobbs-Merrill.

Katz, L. D. (Ed.). (2000). *Evolutionary origins of morality: Cross-disciplinary perspectives*. Bowling Green, OH: Imprint Academic.

Kidd, C., Piantadosi, S. T., & Aslin, R. N. (2012). The Goldilocks effect: Human infants allocate attention to visual sequences that are neither too simple nor too complex. *PloS ONE*, *7*(5), e36399.

Killen, M., & Smetana, J. (Eds.). (2006). *Handbook of moral development*. Mahwah, NJ: Lawrence Erlbaum Associates.

    (2014). *Handbook of moral development* (2nd ed.). New York, NY: Psychology Press.

Kinzler, K. D., Dupoux, E., & Spelke, E. S. (2007). The native language of social cognition. *Proceedings of the National Academy of Sciences*, *104*(30), 12577–12580.

Kohlberg, L. (1969). Stage and sequence: The cognitive developmental approach to socialization. In D. Goslin, (Ed.), *Handbook of socialization theory and research* (pp. 347–480). Chicago, IL: Rand McNally.

Kuhlmeier, V., Wynn, K., & Bloom, P. (2003). Attribution of dispositional states by 12-month-olds. *Psychological Science*, *14*(5), 402–408.

Lee, Y., Yun, J., Kim, E., & Song, H. (2015) The development of infants' sensitivity to behavioral intentions when inferring others' social preferences. *PLoS ONE*, *10*(9), e0135588.

Leppänen, J. M., Moulson, M. C., Vogel-Farley, V. K., & Nelson, C. A. (2007). An ERP study of emotional face processing in the adult and infant brain. *Child Development*, *78*(1), 232–245.

Liberman, Z., Woodward, A. L, Sullivan, K. L., & Kinzler, K. D. (2016). Early emerging system for reasoning about the social nature of food. *Proceedings of the National Academy of Sciences*, *113*(34), 9480–9485.

Lucca, K., Pospisil, J., & Sommerville, J. A. (2018). Fairness informs social decision making in infancy. *PloS ONE*, *13*(2), e0192848.

Mahajan, N., & Wynn, K. (2012). Origins of "us" versus "them": Prelinguistic infants prefer similar others. *Cognition*, *124*(2), 227–233.

Malle, B. F. (1999). How people explain behavior: A new theoretical framework. *Personality and Social Psychology Review*, *3*(1), 23–48.

Margoni, F., & Surian, L. (2018). Infants' evaluation of prosocial and antisocial agents: A meta-analysis. *Developmental Psychology*, *54*(8), 1445–1455.

Meristo, M., Strid, K., & Surian, L. (2016) Preverbal infants' ability to encode the outcome of distributive actions. *Infancy*, *21*(3), 353–372.

Meristo, M., & Surian, L. (2013). Do infants detect indirect reciprocity? *Cognition*, *129*(1), 102–13.

(2014). Infants distinguish antisocial actions directed towards fair and unfair agents. *PLoS ONE*, *9*(10), e110553.

Nowak, M. A. (2006). Five rules for the evolution of cooperation. *Science*, *314*(5805), 1560–1563.

O'Gorman, R., Henrich, J., & van Vugt, M. (2009). Constraining free riding in public goods games: Designated solitary punishers can sustain human cooperation. *Proceedings Biological Sciences B*, *276*(1655), 323–329.

Ornaghi, V., Brockmeier J., & Grazzani I. (2014). Enhancing social cognition by training children in emotion understanding: A primary school study. *Journal of Experimental Child Psychology*, *119*, 26–39.

Ozonoff, S., Young, G. S., Carter, A., Messinger, D., Yirmiya, N., Zwaigenbaum, L., … Hutman, T. (2011). Recurrence risk for autism spectrum disorders: A Baby Siblings Research Consortium study. *Pediatrics*, *128*(3), e488–e495.

Piaget, J. (1932). *The moral judgment of the child*. New York, NY: Free Press.

Powell, L. J., & Spelke, E. S. (2013). Preverbal infants expect members of social groups to act alike. *Proceedings of the National Academy of Sciences*, *110*(41), E3965–E3972.

Premack, D., & Premack, A. J. (1994). Moral belief: Form versus content. In L. A. Hirschfeld & S. A. Gelman (Eds.), *Mapping the mind: Domain specificity in cognition and culture* (pp. 149–168). Cambridge, UK: Cambridge University Press.

Premack, D., & Premack, A. (1997). Infants attribute value± to the goal-directed actions of self-propelled objects. *Journal of Cognitive Neuroscience*, *9*(6), 848–856.

Pun, A., Ferrera, M., Diesendruck, G., Hamlin, J. K. & Baron, A. S. (2018). Foundations of infants' social group evaluations. *Developmental Science, 21*(3), e12586.

Reddy, S. D., Tenzin Negy, L., Dodson-Lavelle, B., Ozawa-de Silva, B., Pace, T. W. W., Cole, S. P., ... Craighead, L. W. (2013). Cognitive-based compassion training: A promising prevention strategy for at-risk adolescents. *Journal of Child and Family Studies, 22*(2), 219–230.

Reid, V. M., Hoehl, S., & Striano, T. (2006). The perception of biological motion in infants: An event-related potential study. *Neuroscience Letters, 395*(3), 211–214.

Rhee, S. H., Friedman, N. P., Boeldt, D. L., Corley, R. P., Hewitt, J., Knafo, A., ... Zahn-Waxler, C. (2013). Early concern and disregard for others as predictors of antisocial behavior. *Journal of Child Psychology and Psychiatry, 54*, 157–166.

Rhodes, M., Hetherington, C., Brink, K., & Wellman, H. M. (2015). Infants' use of social partnerships explain behavior. *Developmental Science, 18*(6), 909–916.

Richards, J. E. (2003). Attention affects the recognition of briefly presented visual stimuli in infants: An ERP study. *Developmental Science, 6*(3), 312–328.

Robinson, P., Kurzban, R., & Jones, O. (2007). The origins of shared intuitions of justice. *Vanderbilt Law Review, 60*, 1633–1688.

Saby, J. N., & Marshall, P. J. (2012). The utility of EEG band power analysis in the study of infancy and early childhood. *Developmental Neuropsychology, 37*(3), 253–273.

Salvadori, E., Blazsekova, T., Volein, A., Karap, Z., Tatone, D., Mascaro, O., & Csibra, G. (2015). Probing the strength of infants' preference for helpers over hinderers: Two replication attempts of Hamlin and Wynn (2015). *PLoS ONE, 10*(11), e0140570.

Scarf, D., Imuta, K., Colombo, M., & Hayne, H. (2012). Social evaluation or simple association? Simple associations may explain moral reasoning in infants. *PloS ONE, 7*(8), e42698.

Schmidt, M. F. H., & Sommerville, J. A. (2011) Fairness expectation and altruistic sharing in 15-month-old human infants. *PLoS ONE, 6*(10), e23223.

Schrandt, J. A., Townsend, D. B., & Poulson, C. L. (2009). Teaching empathy skills to children with autism. *Journal of Applied Behavior Analysis, 42*(1), 17–32.

Scola, C., Holvoet, C., Arciszewski, T., & Picard, D. (2015). Further evidence for infants' preference for prosocial over antisocial behaviors. *Infancy, 20*(6), 684–692.

Shimizu, Y., Senzaki, S., & Uleman, J. S. (2018). The influence of maternal socialization on infants' social evaluation in two cultures. *Infancy, 23*(5), 748–766.

Sloane, S., Baillargeon, R., & Premack, D. (2012). Do infants have a sense of fairness? *Psychological Science, 23*(2), 196–204.

Sommerville, J. A., Schmidt, M. F., Yun, J., & Burns, M. (2013). The development of fairness expectations and prosocial behavior in the second year of life. *Infancy, 18*(1), 40–66.

Tan, E., Mikami, A. Y., & Hamlin, J. K. (2018). Do infant sociomoral evaluation and action studies predict preschool social and behavioral adjustment? *Journal of Experimental Child Psychology, 176*, 39–54.

Tasimi, A., & Wynn, K. (2016). Costly rejection of wrongdoers by infants and children. *Cognition, 151*, 76–79.

Thomas, A. J., Thomsen, L., Lukowski, A. F., Abramyan, M., & Sarnecka, B. W. (2018). Toddlers prefer those who win, but not when they win by force. *Nature Human Behaviour*, *2*, 662–669.

Turiel, E. (1983). *The development of social knowledge: Morality and convention.* Cambridge, UK: Cambridge University Press.

Vaish, A., Grossmann, T., & Woodward, A. (2008). Not all emotions are created equal: The negativity bias in social-emotional development. *Psychological Bulletin, 134*(3), 383.

van de Vondervoort, J. W., Aknin, L. B., Kushnir, T., Slevinsky, J., & Hamlin, J. K. (2018). Selectivity in toddlers' behavioral and emotional reactions to prosocial and antisocial others. *Developmental Psychology, 54*(1), 1–14.

van Overwalle, F., & Baetens, K. (2009). Understanding others' actions and goals by mirror and mentalizing systems: a meta-analysis. *Neuroimage, 48*(3), 564–584.

Wang, Y., & Henderson, A. M. E. (2018). Just rewards: 17-month-old infants expect agents to take resources according to the principles of distributive justice. *Journal of Experimental Child Psychology, 172*, 25–40.

Warneken, F. (2015). Precocious prosociality: Why do young children help? *Child Development Perspectives, 9*(1), 1–66.

Woo, B. M., Steckler, C. M., Le, D. T., & Hamlin, J. K. (2017). Social evaluation of intentional, truly accidental, and negligently accidental helpers and harmers by 10-month-old infants. *Cognition, 168*, 154–163.

Wynn, K., & Bloom, P. (2014). The moral baby. In M. Killen & J. G. Smetana (Eds.), *Handbook of moral development* (pp. 435–453). New York, NY: Psychology Press.

Wynn, K., Bloom, P., Jordan, A., Marshall, J., & Sheskin, M. (2018). Not noble savages after all: Limits to early altruism. *Current Directions in Psychological Science, 27*(1), 3–8.

Ziv, T., & Sommerville, J. A. (2017). Developmental differences in infants' fairness expectations from 6 to 15 months of age. *Child Development, 88*(6), 1930–1951.

29 Cross-Cultural Perspectives on Parent–Infant Interactions

Marc H. Bornstein and Gianluca Esposito*

29.1 Introduction

Each day more than three-quarters of a million adults around the world experience the joys and heartaches just as they do the rewards and fears of becoming parents to a newborn infant. Each infant is an individual, of course, as is each parent and each parent–infant dyad. Yet, parents and infants around the globe share a large number of commonalities. No matter their homeland, parents have the same responsibilities to guide their infants' survival and success in life, and their infants have the same biological needs and must meet and succeed at the same developmental tasks and challenges. Although infancy encompasses only a small fraction of the life span, it is a period that parents the world over attend to and invest in. Parenting an infant is a 168-hour-a-week job. With good reason: Parenting responsibilities are arguably the greatest during the time of their child's infancy because human infants are totally dependent on caregiving and their ability to cope alone is minimal. Notably, parents everywhere appear highly motivated to carry out their caregiving tasks, and reciprocally infancy is the phase of the life cycle when caregiving is thought to exert salient influences. Indeed, the opportunity of enhanced parental influence and prolonged learning may constitute evolutionary reasons for the extended duration of human infancy (Bjorklund & Myers, 2019). More specific to the charge of this chapter, on parent–infant interaction in cultural contexts, it is the continuing task of parents to enculturate their infants by preparing them for the unique physical, psychosocial, and educational situations that are characteristic of the culture in which their offspring are to adapt and develop.

* This chapter summarizes selected aspects of our research, and portions of the text have appeared in previous scientific publications cited in the references. Supported by the Intramural Research Program of the NIH/NICHD, USA, and an International Research Fellowship at the Institute for Fiscal Studies (IFS), London, UK, funded by the European Research Council (ERC) under the Horizon 2020 Research and Innovation Program (grant agreement no. 695300-HKADeC-ERC-2015-AdG) as well as the NAP-SUG Program of Nanyang Technological University. The authors also thank Dr. Andrea Bonassi for assistance.

Human beings do not grow up, and adults do not parent, in isolation, but in multiple contexts. One significant overarching context in which infants develop and parents parent is culture. Parent–infant relationships lie at the heart of a nested series of bioecological systems (Bronfenbrenner & Morris, 2006; Wachs, 2015), and they are ultimately influenced by the broader macrosystem of cultural prescriptions and proscriptions that support and encourage, or suppress and discourage, specific parenting cognitions, parenting practices, and patterns of parent–infant interaction (Bornstein, 2012).

After approximately a century of developmental study, with considerable attention paid to infants and their parents in that time, still too little is known about the activities and development, life circumstances and experiences, of infants and their parents in non-WEIRD (i.e., Western, educated, industrialized, rich, and democratic) cultural conditions. Indeed, three cultural limitations continue to constrain our understanding of parent–infant interactions: a narrow participant database, a biased sampling of world cultures in the authorship of that database, and a corresponding bias in the audience to which it is addressed (Serpell, 1990). The vast majority of the extant literature in infancy, and consequently our understanding, derives from studies conducted in WEIRD nations (Tomlinson, Bornstein, Marlow, & Swartz, 2014). As Luria (1976) observed long ago, however, infancy and parenting always need to be considered in their sociocultural context. This chapter on parent–infant interaction takes such a cross-cultural perspective. Cross-cultural developmental research has many aims, but prominent among them are to inventory and compare similarities and differences in parent–infant interactions in different cultures.

The long-standing questions surrounding parent–infant interaction in culture include: What are the universals of infant development and infant care in our species? How do infants participate in and shape their interactions with caregivers? How do parents parent infants? How does culture embed itself in infancy, parenting, and parent–infant interaction? No study of a single culture can answer these broad questions. However, it is possible to learn lessons from different cultures that may shed light on them. For example, such lessons may illuminate which presumed universals of infant development and care obtain across different settings, how infant experiences in different settings affect future child development, and how different settings shape parenting. These questions are best addressed from the coordinated perspectives of parent, infant, and culture. The parent perspective provides insight into those responsible for organizing and implementing infant care; the infant perspective offers a basis for assessing the impact of caregiving on development; and the cultural perspective informs about the caregiving and infant development cognitions and practices of a culture, how they are instantiated, and their meaning. In this chapter, addressing parent–infant interactions from a cross-cultural perspective, we first take up its main constituents of the chapter – culture, parenting, infancy, and interaction *in seriatim*. Then, we recount some prominent similarities and differences in parent–infant interactions across cultures as well as their several sources. Next, we appraise values and challenges to the cross-cultural approach to understanding parent–infant interactions. Finally, we briefly address how policy relates to parent–infant interactions across cultures and review some takeaways of what we have learned at the intersection of culture, parenting, and infancy.

29.2 Culture, Parenting, Infancy, and Interaction

Culture defies easy definition, but most scholars agree that culture embraces patterns of cognitions and practices that distinguish social groups (Boyd & Richerson, 2005). Culture is embedded in the activities of parents and infants, and for this reason many social theorists have asserted that the family generally, and the parent–infant relationship specifically, constitute the effective crucible for the early (and perhaps eventual) development of the individual. Our expectations about culture, parenting, and infancy are entwined in the specificity principle. As pertinent here, the *specificity principle* holds that specific experiences at specific times exert specific effects over specific aspects of infant growth in specific ways (Bornstein, 1989, 2002, 2015).

29.2.1 Culture

Culture is considered by some to consist of a set of separable (if related) contextual factors, and by others to constitute abstract learned meanings and shared information transmitted from one generation to the next through social interaction. Whichever, cultures consist of distinctive norms, ideas, values, and assumptions about life that are common to a people and that guide and regulate specific practices, including inculcation of valued competencies across generations. The concept of culture is frequently used as a means of understanding relations between physical and social ecologies on the one hand and individual psychologies on the other. Every psychological construct, structure, function, and process has cultural undertones or overtones. Culture is not a static entity either, but rather a dynamic that is constantly in reconstruction and renegotiation between context and individual lives.

Human cultures have different adaptive goals, and parents in different cultures have developed different institutions and structures to instantiate parental cognitions about infant care and to implement parental practices. The origins of variation in parental cognitions and practices are multivariate and extremely complex – Holden (1997) identified more than 30 variables that have been found empirically to influence parenting – but certain factors seem to be of paramount importance (Bornstein, 2016). They include, from proximal to distal, biological processes and personality attributes of parents, actual or perceived characteristics of infants, and contextual influences, including social situational factors, family background, socioeconomic status (SES), and culture. Insofar as parents belong to a culture and subscribe to particular conventions of the culture, they follow prevailing "cultural scripts" in infant rearing. Those scripts include, for example, when and how to care for infants, what infant characteristics are desirable, and which parenting practices are accepted or expected, as well as which are unacceptable and disavowed.

Some tasks of parenting are essentially universal. All infants must be fed and thermoregulated if they are to survive, and infants must be attended to emotionally and socialized if they are to thrive. Cross-cultural comparisons show too that virtually all aspects of parenting infants – whether cognitions or practices – are fashioned by culture. Inasmuch as culture is organized information, parenting consists of that information and of mechanisms for transmitting that information, and infancy consists of processing and incorporating that information. Central to a concept of culture is the expectation that different peoples possess different parenting cognitions and practices. Parenting is therefore a principal reason why individuals in different cultures are who they are and often differ so from one another. Indeed, the cultural meanings inherent in settings and activities are characterized by thematicity, in that the same cultural messages are re-stated and re-expressed at a variety of levels and in a variety of ways.

Parents in different cultures receive many different kinds of guidance about how to rear infants, whether in the form of formal sources, such as books of advice, or via informal sources, such as simply observing family examples. Parenting advice is often accepted as basic wisdom within its own cultural context. Yet cultural variation in cognitions and practices is always impressive. As illustrations throughout this chapter attest, cross-cultural comparisons show that virtually all aspects of parent–infant interactions are informed by culture. A comparative Australian investigation of expected developmental timetables in new mothers from Australia and Lebanon, for example, found that culture molded mothers' expectations of infant development much more than experiences observing their infants, directly comparing them to other infants, and receiving advice from friends and experts (Goodnow, Cashmore, Cotton, & Knight, 1984). The lives of infants born amongst nomadic hunter-gatherers who live in temporary homes and spend each day in multiage groups can be expected to differ dramatically from the lives of infants born in a modern Western setting who reside in single-family homes and come into contact with many people who show interest in the infant's welfare. In all cultures, however, enculturating infants occurs, and social controls are in place to ensure that infants are socialized – that is, brought up in such a way that each new generation acquires prescribed patterns of cognitions and practices and eschews proscribed ones.

29.2.2 Parenting

Mothers, fathers, and others guide the development of infants via direct and indirect effects of their cognitions and practices. Different cultures may distribute infant caregiving responsibilities in different ways, and infants in many cultures are also tended to by a variety of nonparental care providers, whether in family daycare or daycare centers, villages, or fields. However, mothers are unique, the role of mother is universal, and motherhood is unequivocally principal in infant development (Murray, Richards, & Nihouarn-Sigurdardottir, 2019). Cross-cultural surveys regularly attest to the primacy of biological mothers' caregiving (Leiderman, Tulkin, & Rosenfeld, 1977), even if historically fathers' social and legal claims and responsibilities on infants were preeminent (French, 2019). Around the globe, mothers spend more time with babies than do fathers (Bornstein, 2015). For this reason, this chapter emphasizes mother–infant interactions. In addition, in a larger sense parental cognitions and practices contribute to the very "continuity of culture" by helping to define culture and by sculpting the transmission of cultural mazeways across generations.

29.2.2.1 *Parental Cultural Cognitions*

Parents' cognitions – their ideas, knowledge, values, expectations, goals, attributions, and attitudes (Holden & Smith, 2019) – serve many functions. They generate and shape, mediate the effectiveness of, and organize parenting. How parents see themselves vis à-vis their infants, how parents construe infancy in general, and how parents see their own infants lead to their expressing one or another kind of infant-rearing practice. Parents who believe that they can or cannot affect their infants' temperament, intelligence, and so forth tend to modify their parenting accordingly. In investigating and understanding infant-rearing beliefs, we may come to better understand how and why parents behave in the ways they do as well as what consequences their cognitions portend.

Parenting cultural knowledge is often conceptualized as naive theories about how infants progress toward culturally idealized social roles, what influences their acquisition of those roles, and how culturally relevant skills are attained (Keller et al., 2006; Rosenthal & Roer-Strier, 2001). Cultural theorists contend that culturally distinct parenting cognitions provide parents with a framework for interpreting their infants' behaviors, guiding parents' interactions with their infants, and determining the activities and opportunities that parents supply to their infants' development.

With respect to attributions, for example, Bornstein et al. (1998) asked mothers of infants from Argentina, Belgium, Italy, Israel, Japan, and the United States about their parenting successes and failures and if being able to successfully comfort their infant when the infant cries was due to their parenting ability (e.g., "I am good at this"), effort (e.g., "I have tried hard"), mood (e.g., "I am in a good mood"), task difficulty (e.g., "This is easy to do"), or an infant characteristic (e.g., "My infant makes this easy to do"). Among many culturally differentiated patterns of findings that emerged, Japanese mothers were less likely than mothers from all other nations to attribute success to their own ability and more likely to indicate that, when they were successful, it was because of the infant's behavior. This perspective accords with the general cultural orientation of humility in Japan. Parenting practices relate differently to infants' adjustment depending on the broader cultural context. Jamaican mothers in the UK expect their infants to sit and to walk early, whereas Indian mothers living in the same city in the UK expect their infants to crawl later. In each case, infants' actual attainments of developmental milestones accorded with their mothers' expectations (Hopkins & Westra, 1989, 1990).

Parents' cultural cognitions are thought to help influence their parenting practices, and so differences in cultural ideology make for subtle, but potentially meaningful, differences in patterns of parent–infant interaction. Harwood, Levendecker, Carlson, Asencio, and Miller (2002) compared socialization goals of Puerto Rican with those of European American mothers of infants. In general, European American mothers talked most about goals for their infants related to "self-maximization" (development of talents, self-confidence, and independence) in contrast to Puerto Rican mothers who spoke most about "proper demeanor" (respectfulness and appropriate enactment of role obligations). These differences related to the mothers' actual practices. European American mothers used suggestions (rather than commands) and other indirect means of structuring their interactions, and Puerto Rican mothers used more direct means of structuring, such as commands, physical positioning, restraints, and direct attempts to channel their infants' attention. Concretely, in naturalistic mother–infant interactions European American mothers encouraged their infants to feed themselves, whereas Latina mothers held their infants close on their laps during mealtimes and controlled feeding infants from start to finish.

Cultural cognitions help to "construct" infancy and parenting. Parents sometimes act on culturally defined cognitions as much or more than on what their senses tell them about their infants. As Ochs (1982) reported, parents in Samoa reportedly think of their young infants as having an angry and willful character, and, independent of what infants might actually say, parents consensually report that their infants' first word is "tae" – Samoan for "shit."

29.2.2.2 Parental Cultural Practices

More salient in the phenomenology of parent–infant interactions are parents' practices – the actual experiences parents provide infants. Most of infants' experiences stem directly from interactions they have within the family. A small number of overarching domains of parenting interactions have been identified as a common "core" of parent–infant interaction (Bornstein, 2015). *Nurturant parenting* meets the biological, physical, and health requirements of the infant, and parents are responsible for promoting their infants' wellness and preventing their illness. *Physical parenting* promotes infants' gross and fine psychomotor development. *Social parenting* focuses on the dyad and is foundational to communication and interpersonal interaction; social parenting includes the visual, verbal, and affective practices parents deploy in engaging infants in loving interpersonal exchanges. *Didactic parenting* consists of the variety of strategies parents employ in stimulating their infants to engage and understand the environment outside the dyad. *Material parenting* includes those ways in which parents provision and organize the infant's physical world, especially the infant's home and local environment, from books to overall safety. Parents' *language* fortifies the parent–infant bond and crosses all other domains of interaction. These categories apply to the infancy period and to normal caregiving; not all forms of parenting, or parenting domains appropriate for older children (for example, punishment), are incorporated or accounted for in this taxonomy. Moreover, there is initially asymmetry in parent and infant contributions to their interactions: After infancy, children play more active and anticipatory roles in interaction, whereas initial responsibility for adaptation in infant development lies more unambiguously with parents.

The ways that parents engage in these different domains of parenting are culturally situated, and thus parenting practices reflect cultural ideologies and values. For example, Japan and the United States maintain reasonably similar levels of modernity and living standards, and both are infant-centered cultures, but the two countries differ dramatically in terms of history as well as parenting cognitions and practices. Traditional Japanese mothers expect early mastery of emotional maturity, self-control, and social courtesy even in their very young children, whereas US European American mothers expect early mastery of verbal competence and self-actualization in theirs. American mothers promote autonomy and organize social interactions with their infants to foster physical and verbal assertiveness and independence, and they cultivate children's mastery of the external ecology. Japanese mothers organize social interactions so as to consolidate and strengthen closeness and dependency within the mother–infant dyad, and they tend to indulge young infants (Bornstein, Cote, Haynes, Suwalsky, & Bakeman, 2012). US American mothers respond more to their infants' orienting to the environment relative to their infants' social orienting, whereas Japanese mothers respond more to their infants' social than environment orienting. When responding to their infants, Japanese mothers tend to direct their infants' attention to themselves, whereas American mothers tend to direct their infants' attention away from themselves and to the environment (Tamis-LeMonda, Bornstein, Cyphers, Toda, & Ogino, 1992). Culture influences when and how parents care for infants, the extent to which parents permit infants freedom to explore, how nurturant or restrictive parents are, which practices parents emphasize, and so forth (Bornstein & Lansford, 2010).

29.2.2.3 *Direct and Indirect Effects of Parents on Infants*

Biological mothers and fathers contribute directly to the genetic makeup of their infants, and parents and others directly generate infants' experiences. A host of different characteristics of offspring – height and weight, intelligence and personality – reflect genetic endowment in some degree. However, all prominent theories in developmental science put experience in the world as either the principal direct influence over individual growth or as a major contributing component (Collins, Maccoby, Steinberg, Hetherington, & Bornstein, 2000). Parents and others also influence infants indirectly by virtue of each partner's influence on the other and their associations with larger social networks (Bornstein & Sawyer, 2005). In the natural course of things, the two sorts of direct effects are confounded: The parents who endow the infant genetically also provide their infant with experiences and structure their infant's world. Parents are fundamentally invested in infants: their survival, their socialization, and their education, as appropriate to their cultural milieu.

29.2.3 Infancy

Dramatic and thoroughgoing developmental changes take place during infancy. The body, the mind, the emotions, and the ability to function meaningfully in and on the world all develop rapidly. During infancy, the child transforms from an immature being unable to move his or her limbs in a coordinated manner to one who controls complicated sequences of muscle contractions and flections in order to walk, reach, or grasp; from the child who can only babble or cry to one who makes needs and desires abundantly clear in speech. These dynamic changes, in turn, engage the world for infants do not develop in a vacuum. In infancy, we learn how to make sense of and understand objects in the world, develop rudiments of our personality, form our first social bonds, and first learn to express and read basic human emotions. Not surprisingly, all of these developmental dynamics are closely tracked by parents, all of them affect parenting, and all are, in turn, shaped by parents. Thus, as they develop, infants profoundly change their ecologies and the people in them, just as they are changed by their ecologies and those people.

Through the mechanisms and processes detailed above, culture shapes parents and parents shape their infants. Infants in different cultures quickly learn to behave in culturally sanctioned ways and come to adhere to culturally endorsed values. These processes take hold early in the life of the infant and operate at all levels of development. Packer and Cole (2015) recount the telling example of infant cultural entrainment in terms contrasting patterns of sleep in the months following birth in rural Kenyan (Kipsigis) and US American urban-dwelling children. At night, Kipsigis infants sleep with their mothers and are permitted to nurse on demand. During the day, they are strapped to their mothers' backs, accompany them on their daily rounds of farming, household chores, and social activities, and nap when they want. At 1 month of age, the longest period of sleep reported for Kipsigis babies was 3 hours, and their longest sleep episode increased little during the first 8 months of postnatal life. The course of getting on a schedule is very different for newborns in the United States who show a marked shift toward the adult day/night cycle just a few weeks after birth; by the end of the second week, they averaged about 8.5 hours of sleep at night. The cultural pressures toward infants' sleeping through the night are easy to identify. In dual-wage-earner US American urban families, the child must be ready when parents leave home in the morning, so parents push for the child to sleep when it is convenient for them. In this way, cultural variations in sleeping arrangements reflect tacit community ideals.

Infancy is the first phase of extrauterine life, and the characteristics human beings develop and acquire in their infancy may be formative and fundamental in the sense that they endure or (at least) constitute features that later developments or experiences build on or modify. Attachment theory, for example, posits that "internal working models" of people in the child's life emerge from the nature of parent–infant interactions, and going forward people use these models as referents for social relationships throughout the balance of their lifetimes (Cummings & Warmuth, 2019). Parenting is thus central to infancy and to the long-term development of the individual (Bornstein, 2015).

29.2.4 Interaction

The altricial status of the human infant guarantees necessary interaction with a caregiver. The sheer amount of interaction between parent and offspring is greatest in infancy; parents spend more than twice as much time with their infants as they do with their children in middle childhood. Moreover, parent and infant activities are characterized by intricate patterns of synchronous interactions and sensitive mutual understandings (Azhari et al., 2019; Bornstein, 1989, 2013, 2015; Bornstein, Esposito, & Motti-Stephanidi, in press). Frequently, thinking about parent–infant relationships highlights parents as active agents; to a considerable degree, however, parent–infant interaction is a two-way street. Infants cry to be fed and changed, and when they wake they "tell" parents they are ready to play and to learn. In consequence, sometimes parents' initiatives are proactive; often, however, they are reactive and, so, interactive. Some features of parenting and of parent–infant relationships are constant, but others vary insofar as they are linked to infant development or to culture. Although mothers are often thought to lead infants in interactions because they are the more mature partner in the dyad (Kochanska & Aksan, 2004; Maccoby, 1992; Vygotsky, 1978), developmental scientists recognize the influence that infants exert in mother–infant interactions, and mother–infant relationships more generally, and so infants influence their own development (Bornstein, 2015).

29.3 Similarities and Differences in Parent–Infant Interactions Across Cultures

The "story" of cross-cultural developmental science is one of cultural similarities and differences. Some characteristics of infants are structurally common or widely shared and so likely affect parents everywhere, perhaps in similar ways. Others may be idiosyncratic to specific ethnic or cultural groups. What are some similarities and differences in activities and interactions of infants and mothers across cultures?

29.3.1 Cross-Cultural Similarities: Illustrations from the Literature

By the end of the first trimester, fetuses are felt to move *in utero* ("quickening"), a significant marker in the life of the infant and in the lives and psyches of parents. Soon after birth physiognomic features of the infant (a large head dominated by a disproportionately large forehead, widely spaced sizable eyes, a small snub nose, an exaggeratedly round face, and a small chin) prompt adults to express nurturance and solicitude (Kringelbach, Stark, Alexander, Bornstein, & Stein, 2016). Moreover, many adult responses to infants are culturally common, such as the special vocal register of infant-directed speech (Soderstrom, 2007) whose characteristics vary from adult-directed speech along prosodic, simplicity, redundancy, lexical, and content dimensions.

More generally, vocal interactions are singular in early development. Nondistress vocalizations constitute a salient infant signal, and language is a primary communication mode of mothers in many (but not all) cultures, thus reinforcing the prominence of mother–infant vocal interchanges (Bornstein et al. 1992; Hsu & Fogel, 2003; Kärtner et al., 2008; van Egeren, Barratt, & Roach, 2001). Conversational turn-taking (which is what mutually contingent vocal exchanges are) is requisite for successful verbal communication and serves as a basis for the acquisition of language and social interaction (Snow, 1977; Stern, 1985). Turn-taking is a rule of language interaction. Stivers et al. (2009) examined 10 major world languages drawn from traditional indigenous cultures in an attempt to uncover shared underlying foundations in turn-taking. Speakers of all 10 languages similarly avoided overlaps in conversation and minimized silence between conversational turns, pointing to robust human universals and a single shared architecture for language use. As Wilson and Wilson (2005, p. 958) concluded, "To our knowledge, no culture or group has been found in which the fundamental features of turn-taking are absent." So, unsurprisingly, mothers and young infants respond contingently to one another's vocalizations generally, and vocal turn-taking is an early developing and culture-common phenomenon and may be a universal mechanism by which infants experience and acquire linguistic and pragmatic skills. Bornstein et al. (2015) examined contingency of timed sequences of mother and infant vocalizations in 11 cultural communities around the world (Argentina, Belgium, Brazil, Cameroon, France, Israel, Italy, Japan, Kenya, South Korea, and the United States). Timed sequential analysis complements and enriches standard statistical techniques and offers a dynamic process-oriented method to study mother–infant interactions that more closely approximates causal inference. Maternal vocalizations to infants in all cultural communities were contingent on the offsets of infants' vocalizations overall and in every community. Five-month-old infant nondistress vocalizations were contingent on the offsets of their mothers' vocalizations to them overall and in approximately half of the communities. Likewise, these investigators assessed the contingency of five maternal responses to the onset of infant cry in the same 11 cultural communities (Bornstein et al., 2017). Infant mammals, including humans, emit distress vocalizations when they are separated from their mothers, hungry, or physically ill at ease. Hearing infant cries, mothers everywhere promptly move to retrieve and establish contact and communication with their infant offspring.

29.3.2 Cross-Cultural Differences: Illustrations from the Literature

In a comparative study of parent cognitions in seven countries (Argentina, Belgium, France, Israel, Italy, Japan, and the United States), mothers evaluated their competence, satisfaction, investment, and role balance in parenting (Bornstein et al., 1998). Systematic country differences for self-evaluations emerged that were interpretable in terms of cultural proclivities and emphases. For example, Argentine mothers rated themselves relatively low in parental competence and satisfaction. Their insecurity about mothering appeared to accord with the relative lack of social and cultural support in Argentine society, particularly the help and advice about infant rearing provided to Argentine mothers. By contrast, Belgian mothers rated themselves as relatively satisfied with their parenting, which might be expected in light of the strong infant care supports provided to parents in Belgium in terms of periodicals, consultancies, home visits, health care information workshops, and parenting demonstration sessions. As another example, among European Americans self-esteem is thought to be important to healthy development in infants, but among Taiwanese self-esteem is less important or even thought to foster psychological vulnerabilities. When Miller, Wang, Sandel, and Cho (2002) compared European American and Taiwanese mothers' cognitions about infant rearing and self-esteem, unsurprisingly they found that nearly all European American mothers spontaneously invoked self-esteem and spoke about the importance of building infants' self-esteem. In contrast, few Taiwanese mothers talked about "self-respect–heart/mind" (a Chinese term that approximates self-esteem).

29.3.3 Sources of Similarities and Differences in Parent–Infant Interactions across Cultures: From Neuroscience to Ecology

What are the sources of cultural similarities and differences in parent–infant interactions? The origins and development of any construct, structure, function, or process – like parent–infant interaction – can be expected to be the product of multiple antecedents, from genetics and biology to experience and ecology. Culture looms large in shaping parent–infant interaction. Of course, these general forces of biology and experience are inextricably intertwined, ideas (among others) that are explored in this section.

The long evolutionary history of altricial human infant dependency on requisite adult caregiving suggests that some mechanisms associated with adult attentiveness and responsiveness to infants ought to be automatic and deeply ingrained in caregivers' nervous systems (Klahr & Burt, 2014). Adults already know (or think they know) something about parenting by the time they first become parents (Papoušek & Papoušek, 2002); that is, some characteristics of parenting may be "wired" into the biological makeup of the human species (Dudin, McGowan, Wu, Fleming, & Li, 2019). For example, parents regularly speak to their infants even though they know that babies cannot understand language and will not respond, and parents even speak to very young infants in that special speech register.

The expression of parenting has been linked to hormones, some of which are homologous in females and males (Bales, 2014). In animals, primiparous females are attracted to infants and care for them, whereas virgins typically avoid or reject infants, suggesting that hormonal events involved in parturition prime the brain to be sensitive to a new and unique set of stimuli (Lambert & Kinsley, 2012). The hormone oxytocin (OT) supports the parent–infant bond in mammals (MacDonald & MacDonald, 2010). An Israeli study unearthed associations between baseline OT levels in mothers and fathers and gender-specific parenting practices: Mothers' OT levels were associated with affectionate but not stimulatory infant contact, whereas fathers' OT levels were associated with stimulatory but not affectionate infant contact (Feldman, Gordon, Schneiderman, Weisman, & Zagoory-Sharon, 2010; Feldman, Gordon, & Zagoory-Sharon, 2011).

Just as genes and hormones are wrapped up in parenting, so are the structure and function of the autonomic and central nervous systems. Esposito et al. (2014) measured autonomic physiological arousal using the novel technique of infrared thermography while Italian and Japanese adults viewed infant and adult faces of in-group versus out-group members. Both Italians and Japanese showed significant physiological activation (increase of facial temperature) to both in-group and out-group infant faces. Arousal responses to infants are mediated by the autonomic nervous system. Caria et al. (2012) placed women in a magnetic resonance imaging (MRI) scanner while they viewed faces of human or animal infants or adults. The regions of people's brains concerned with empathy and speech respond in enhanced ways to human infant faces specifically. Parents have specialized hormonal and autonomic and central nervous system reactions to infants that differ from their responses to human adults and infrahuman mammal infants and adults.

In addition to these (and possibly other) biological characteristics, a variety of psychological characteristics in the parent has been identified that shape parenting. They include the gender, age and stage, health status, cognition, personality, intergenerational proclivity, family of origin, and experiences of the parent. To parent well, a parent's own needs must be met. When women are inadequately nourished, for example, their health and social development may be compromised, and their abilities to bear and rear healthy infants are jeopardized. Malnourished women fall ill more often, and they have smaller babies, whereas women whose diets are rich in protein have fewer complications during pregnancy, transit shorter labors, and bear healthier babies. Maternal deficiencies in zinc, folic acid, and protein have been linked to central nervous system dysfunction, prematurity, and low birthweight in offspring. In many regions of the developing world, malnutrition is a chronic problem (UNICEF, 2007), but this problem is not limited to poor countries.

Another prominent psychological source of parenting infants is personality. Two general orientations have guided theory and research linking personality to parenting: One concerns a factor structure thought to compose normal personality, and the other concerns more specific personality characteristics, from anxiety and stress to depression and psychopathology. Freud (1949) speculated that a parent's personality would determine the nature of parenting as well as the parent–infant relationship and the infant's development. Another consistent theme among psychoanalytic theorists is that, if parents' emotional needs are not met during the course of their own development, then their own psychological makeup would reflect in their parenting (Cohler & Paul, 2019). Personality therefore has a significant part to play in parenting. Personality is currently conceptualized as a profile of five broad-band factors (the so-called Big Five), each with lower-level facets (McAdams & Pals, 2006) that may be "universal" (Allik & McCrae, 2004; McCrae et al., 2005). Only a small number of studies has assessed all five personality factors in relation to parenting cognitions and/or parenting practices. In one cross-cultural study, mothers of first-born 20-month-olds from seven countries (Argentina, Belgium, Israel, Italy, Japan, South Korea, and the United States) completed a Big Five Inventory (Bornstein et al., 2007). The Big Five were found to relate differently to diverse parenting cognitions and practices in different cultures.

As suggested earlier, infant characteristics influence parents' cognitions and practices. In addition to biological and psychological factors in themselves and in their infants, diverse contexts condition and channel cognitions and practices of parents' interactions with their infants. Context refers to "any event or condition outside the organism that affects or is affected by a person's development" (Bronfenbrenner & Crouter, 1983, p. 359). The contexts of parent–infant interactions are themselves complex, multidimensional, and structurally organized into levels that are linked with each other. Proximal contexts include situation and demand, family structure and system, support networks, employment status, and neighborhood residence; social group contexts include SES, religion, ethnicity, and culture; and distal contexts include ecology, history, and even evolution. All these contexts encourage or discourage similar and different patterns of parenting attitudes and actions, and so all are meaningful determinants of parent–infant interactions.

Human beings acquire understandings of what it is to parent simply by living in a culture: Generational, social, and media images of parenting, infants, and family life – handed down or ready-made – play significant roles in helping people form their parenting cognitions and guide their parenting practices (Holden & Smith, 2019). Thus, parents from different cultures differ in the ages they expect infants to reach different milestones or acquire various competencies, and they differ in their opinions about the significance of specific competencies for their infants' success in social adjustment (Goodnow, 2010).

Parenting is conditioned by ethnicity and varies in meaningful ways among people from various cultures. Parenting values is one example. Tamis-LeMonda and Kahana-Kalman (2009) interviewed low-income, urban, African Americans as well as Mexican, Dominican, and Chinese immigrant mothers in maternity wards just hours after giving birth. Mothers' views were assessed using open-ended questions, and their responses coded as relevant to four main categories: infant development, parenting, family, and resources. Mothers from the four cultural groups varied in how much they spoke about each topic. Relative to the other groups, however, Chinese immigrant mothers talked more about infant development; African American and Dominican immigrant mothers talked more about resources; and Mexican immigrant mothers talked more about family. Thus, supportive parenting and its effects may look very different in different cultures.

Specific patterns of infant rearing can be expected to adapt to specific settings and needs. Thus, ecological conditions that vary with culture can be expected to play a consequential role in many aspects of parenting (Davis, Haworth, Lewis, & Plomin, 2012). Different geographic regions have different climatic, vegetative, and living conditions, and these circumstances contribute to parenting cognitions and practices (Dunn, Davies, Harris, & Gavin, 2010). Insofar as tropical areas are denser with pathogens that lead to infections and poor infant growth and mortality, for example, parents in those ecologies need to cope with greater challenges with respect to infants' health and illness. Along these same lines, father-present social systems, monogamous marriage, and wide birth spacing are all more likely among human hunter-gatherers inhabiting harsh ecologies where biparental care is substantial and important for offspring survival and reproductive success (Davis et al., 2012; Draper & Harpending, 1988; Geary, 2000; Marlowe, 2003). Thus, different ecologies give rise to divergent patterns of parent–infant interactions. In their study of the nomadic hunter-gatherer Aka and Ngandu farming cultures in central Africa, Hewlett, Lamb, Shannon, Leyendecker, and Schölmerich (1998) observed that 3- to 4-month-old Aka infants experienced more "proximal" relationships with their caregivers (i.e., they were more likely to be held and fed) than did same-age Ngandu infants, who were more likely to be left alone, fuss, smile, vocalize, and play. The Aka and Ngandu cultures have similarly high levels of infant mortality, equivalently hazardous living conditions, comparably healthy infants, and similar maternal workloads, and thus these sociodemographic factors do not explain differences in parent–infant practices of the two cultures. Hewlett et al. (1998) speculated that Aka parents stayed closer to their infants because of their frequent moves from one location to the next in search of food. Nomadic Aka parents are always less familiar with their home surroundings than are Ngandu parents, who live a comparatively sedentary existence, and thus Aka parents may feel more inclined to stay in closer proximity to their infants to better protect them in unfamiliar ecologies.

29.4 Values and Challenges to the Cross-Cultural Approach to Understanding Parent–Infant Interactions

All that has been learned from forays into understanding parent–infant interactions from the cross-cultural perspective leads to considerations of what values there may be to such an approach as well as what challenges are inherent to it. Here we address each briefly.

29.4.1 Values of the Cross-Cultural Approach to Parent–Infant Interactions

The scope of developmental science embraces both description and explanation of cognitions and practices over the life span. Among the many perspectives from which to pursue these twin charges, the cross-cultural developmental method occupies a significant position because it encompasses the full spectrum of human variation across a worldwide context and over a life-span ontogeny. Many critics today point to culture-bound assumptions and limitations of prevailing Western psychologies, and calls for more inclusive cross-cultural investigation complement increasingly strident critiques of monocultural perspectives. In response to such criticism, cultural context is achieving greater recognition, and most contemporary psychological investigators acknowledge that cross-cultural developmental inquiry is integral to understanding both substance and process in development. Cross-cultural comparisons are especially valuable because they expose and deepen understanding of processes that generalize across or are specific to disparate populations. Identifying what is culturally common and what is culturally specific biologically and psychologically is theoretically significant in neural, behavioral, and social science.

The history of investigation of infant psychomotor development provides an illustrative case study of the pitfalls of monocultural study. On the basis of extensive and painstaking observations, Arnold Gesell (America's pre-World War II pediatrician) constructed detailed cinematic atlases of "normal" infant psychomotor development (Bornstein, 2001). Universal and culture-free concerns occupied Gesell, for he worked out of a maturationist theoretical framework, with very young infants, and on behaviors thought to be almost wholly under biological control. Regularities of motor development that he observed reinforced his beliefs. Gesell and Amatruda (1945) conceived that early psychomotor development was ballistic and under unfolding genetic control. In fact, some data support a hypothesis of genetic or prenatal influences among infants. Geber and Dean (1957a, 1957b) found that 9-hour-old Gandan neonates are significantly advanced in neuromuscular standing; and Tanner (1970) found that African neonates are advanced beyond Western European neonates in skeletal maturation and ossification at birth. Although Gesell's tests, and those of other developmentalists of the same ilk (Bayley, 1969; Griffiths, 1954), were continuously refined, infant assessment did not reach beyond the confines of the Gesell Institute in New Haven, CT, and beyond the middle-class European American culture that it served until the mid-twentieth century. The results of cross-cultural surveys among native peoples in America, in Bali, and in Africa undermined Gesell's assumptions and challenged Gesell's conclusions. These studies showed that babies from different cultures deviated from the accepted "norms" for US American middle-class culture with respect to both the stages and the timing of motor development in the first years. Hopi infants begin to walk alone late (Dennis & Dennis, 1940); Balinese infants follow a different series of stages on their way to walking (Mead & MacGregor, 1951); and Ganda and Wolof infants tend to be more advanced in motor development than US age norms would predict (Ainsworth, 1967; Geber, 1956, 1958; Lusk & Lewis, 1972; Werner, 1972). In the absence of a "generalized precocity" among infants, Super (1976) was led to study Kipsigis mothers and their parenting practices: He found that over 80% of mothers deliberately taught their infants to sit, stand, and walk. Earlier, Rebelsky (1967, 1972) had found that Dutch infants, who tend to be stimulated less than American infants, scored lower than US American infants on scales of psychomotor development, and similarly Bovet, Dasen, and Inhelder (1974) accounted for sensorimotor retardation in Baoulé (Ivory Coast) infants relative to French on the fact that the African babies tend to be carried on their mothers' backs. Pertinently, Geber (1958) and Super (1976) reported that African infants (Ganda and Kipsigis, respectively) reared in the manner of European babies lose the advantage that their traditionally reared, genetically similar compatriots maintained. Cross-cultural developmental data demonstrate that psychomotor differences among infants in some substantial degree reflect the influence of parents' infant-rearing practices and that those practices vary with culture. In retrospect, the norms of psychomotor development that Gesell strived to canonize on biological bases must be viewed as plastic (within limits) to cultural parenting.

Many reasons justify cross-cultural developmental research. First, people are always curious about development in cultures not their own, and anthropologists, sociologists, and psychologists have long sought to compare and contrast parenting infants from different regions of the world. Insofar as cultural developmental descriptions of parenting and infancy attempt to encompass the widest spectrum of human variation, they are also the most comprehensive in science: They are vital to delimiting the full range of human experience, and in this sense they are also critical to establishing realistic and valid developmental norms. Psychological science has long been concerned with description in the service of defining normality and identifying abnormality. Yet "normal" for many phenomena is a relative and situation-specific concept. Studies of parenting and infancy across cultures provide a check against the uncritical adoption of ethnocentric world views and the implications that such views convey. Perhaps because the first developmental scientists were Western, because they established the subject matter, and because they trained other (even non-Western) scientists, acceptance of Western norms as norms has often been uncritical. Needless to say, awareness of alternative modes of development sharpens our perceptions and enhances our understanding of the nature of culture, our own as well as that of others.

Second, the examination of other cultures uniquely facilitates the quest to understand forces at work in parenting and infancy by exposing variables that may be influential but "invisible" in a monocultural framework. The rationale for submitting parent–infant interactions in different cultures to psychological study derives from the extraordinary and unique power cross-cultural comparisons furnish developmental science. Cross-cultural developmental study helps to explain the origins and contingent developmental course of the widest possible variety of pertinent constructs, structures, functions, or processes. This approach also helps to distinguish those phenomena that emerge and evolve in a culture-dependent fashion from those that are independent of or transcend culture. Crossing cultures can aid uniquely in the quest to understand *what* forces contribute to parenting and infancy and *how* those forces contribute to their course and outcome. In essence, then, culturally sensitive study occasions an unconfounding of variables thought to influence development, but that might be compromised by monocultural investigation. In a related way, designs of studies of parenting infants that cross cultures can provide natural tests of specific hypotheses or special circumstances that surround parent–infant interaction, and are critical to exploring their cultural uniformity versus diversity.

A third reason motivating cross-cultural parent–infant interaction study is interpretation. Understanding an activity and its meaning often depend on examining cognitions or practices in the context of culture (Bornstein, 1995). A given parenting cognition or practice can have the same meaning in different cultures, just as a parenting activity can have different meanings in different cultures. Conversely, different parenting cognitions or practices can have similar or different meanings depending on culture. Culture is a prime context for determining relations between a cognition or a practice and its meaning. The cross-cultural perspective furnishes social scientific analysis with unique and extraordinary power to unravel meaning and the association of meaning with action.

29.4.2 Challenges to the Cross-Cultural Approach on Parent–Infant Interactions

Historically, cross-cultural studies have been only marginally multicultural. Such research has usually involved the comparison of only two cultures. By adopting pairwise comparisons, however, investigators run a risk of confounding variables. To assume that a target culture lies toward the opposite pole from some other culture on a unitary dimension, and that the two are otherwise equivalent, is almost always erroneous; cultures are complex multilayered entities that differ from one another in many ways. The challenge that confronts cross-cultural developmental scientists is to understand and represent similarities and differences in and across cultural groups in ways that transcend simplistic dichotomous group comparisons. Studies of culture and parenting have developed from individual ethnographic reports to multicultural multivariate multi-age investigations that occupy an important position in developmental science. The larger the number of cultures studied, the more compelling is the conclusion that observed findings can be validly attributed to a theoretical dimension of interest. Furthermore, to be able to compare groups in a meaningful way (i.e., to know that a construct has the same meaning across groups), measurement invariance of the construct of interest should be established across those groups (Putnick & Bornstein, 2016).

Parenting is conditioned by multiple spheres of influence in which the parent is embedded, including proximal social group and distal environment. Researchers know a lot, but still not nearly enough, about the determinants of parenting. Some key questions that arise from the foregoing considerations concern the further specification of multiple processes by which parents' cognitions and practices come about and the multiple moderators that condition them (Bornstein, 2015). Not yet adequately worked out either are functional and theoretical connections among culture, parenting, and infancy. How do components of culture relate to parenting attitudes and actions? Much more work needs to be accomplished linking parenting, infancy, and culture. The result will be an enhanced understanding of the processes and contents of parenting, infancy, and parent–infant interactions in culture.

29.5 Policy and Parent–Infant Interaction Across Cultures

As it is said, infants do not come with a manual, and not all people naturally parent or know how to or can keep up with their constantly developing infants. Parenting advice dates back at least to ancient Egypt, the Code of Hammurabi, and the pre-Socratics. Many parents can use instruction. In 1914, the US Children's Bureau published the first edition of the pamphlet *Infant Care*, which advised, among other things, that "Sunshine is as necessary for the baby as for the plant" (West, 1914, p. 10). Only a fraction of new parents who could benefit from parent services receive them, however. As a result, contemporary parenting has witnessed an explosive growth in information and support programs. One implication of the increasingly sophisticated view of the origins and conduct of parenting is that many determinants of parenting cognitions and practices are modifiable; thus, what we learn about parenting holds the promise of far-reaching practical implications.

Competent parenting, crucial to infant development and well-being, can be learned. Profession-specific competencies provide motivation and direction for learning as well as a means to judge the adequacy of parenting programs (Epstein & Hundert, 2002). Interventions to promote positive parenting have been touted to offer positive outcomes for infants, but they often consume substantial resources and require rigorous appraisal.

Practically speaking, parenting has positives, such as intimacy, nurturance, and rewards, which we want to encourage, but parenting is also encumbered with negatives, such as frustration, anger, and abuse, which we want to avert. It is a sad fact of everyday life that parenting infants does not always go well or right. Although usually protected, infants are still too often exposed to relatively hostile and emotionally negative climates in the home. Infanticide was practiced historically, and although it is rare today it is not unknown (Hrdy, 1999). Vulnerable young are too commonly the victims of parenting that is neglectful or abusive. Infant cries draw a parent's solicitude but also trigger shaken baby syndrome. Every year, child protection agencies in the United States alone receive referrals for neglect and abuse involving an estimated 6 million children younger than 5 years. About 80% of the children in investigated cases are not removed from the home, although the vast majority of perpetrators are biological parents.

Strong secular and historical trends operating in modern culture – industrialization, urbanization, poverty, increasing population growth and density, and especially widespread dual-parental employment – constitute centrifugal forces on parenting. Because these culture-wide developments exert many unfortunately debilitative influences on parenthood, on parenting, and, consequently, on infants and their development, a significant proportion of parents needs assistance to identify more effective strategies to optimize infant care and to create more satisfying family relationships. For example, the modern world is characterized by immigration and mobility to a greater degree than ever before in history (Bornstein, 2017). As a consequence, cultures "mix" today in the real world and in the virtual world with increasing frequency and permanency. Cross-cultural study has additional policy implications here because the cognitions and practices of a subculture can diverge from those of the dominant culture in type, strength, degree, and pervasiveness. Parenting practices acculturate more quickly and readily than do parenting cognitions (Bornstein & Cote, 2019). Immigrant mothers' and infants' interactive play resemble the play of European Americans, for example, but cultural differences in parenting attributions, self-perceptions, and knowledge of immigrant mothers tend to reflect traditional cultural cognitions about parenting and infants.

Parents need to know how to observe infants and how to interpret and use what they learn. Informed infant watching helps to clarify an infant's development in relation to how parents want their infant to behave and what parents want their infants to learn and to accomplish. Observing also allows parents to identify potential troubles early and may help them respond to them more meaningfully. Parents benefit from knowledge of how infants develop. For example, of three cognitive measures – maternal IQ, education, and specific knowledge of infant rearing and infant development – knowledge uniquely explains age differences in mother–infant emotional relationships (Bornstein, Putnick, & Suwalsky, 2012). Therefore, the normative patterns and stages of infants' physical, verbal, cognitive, emotional, and social development should be part of the knowledge base for parenthood.

29.6 What Have We Learned at the Intersection of Culture, Parenting, and Infancy?

Although the identification of psychological universals in humans constitutes a central goal of the biological, social, and behavioral sciences, contemporary theory posits pervasive ecological moderation by physical and social circumstances as influential in the development and expression of practice. The goals of cross-cultural research in parent–infant interactions – to remedy limitations reflective of the lack of broad representativeness and the complementary need for proper tests of generalizable theory – are to identify effects that are culture common (i.e., that obtain across cultures and generalize widely) versus culture specific (i.e., that obtain only in the place they are studied) through the close observation and comparison of multiple diverse wider-world samples. In a nutshell, only the identification of similarities and differences in parenting and infancy across disparate cultures can supply unique evidence of culture-common versus culture-specific biological, social, and behavioral processes. Science can only benefit from enlarged empirical representativeness, and the cross-cultural approach affords a still-too-often underutilized opportunity to assess the specificity versus the generality of findings in infants and their caregivers across divergent cultural contexts.

Normative cultural settings include the types of dwellings and household groups infants and parents inhabit as well as the expectable activities infants and parents engage in. The everyday settings in which parents and infants find themselves define the parameters of their lived experiences, and those settings also embody important cultural meanings. Key to understanding cultural constructions of parenting and infant development are the activities that routinely take place within different settings. The cultural practices that define infant care and infant-rearing instantiate cultural themes that are important to parents, and they communicate and reinforce overarching cultural messages.

Opportunities afforded by enhanced parental influence and prolonged infancy are thought to constitute evolutionary reasons for neoteny, the extended duration of human infancy. In the view of many philosophers and theorists through the ages, in infancy we are open to expectations and influences we carry with us long after we leave our family of origin. Reciprocally, virtually all of young infants' worldly knowledge is acquired from interactions they have with their parents. Infant and parent may be separate entities, but they are inextricably dyadic. Establishing adaptive modes of mutual mother–infant interaction soon after birth is a primary task of the dyad because it is requisite to wholesome development in otherwise wholly dependent young.

Some psychological theorists seek developmental universals, whereas other theorists focus on diversity. Comparative neural, behavioral, and social science concerns the common *and* the specific as well as the complementary conditions under which culture-common mechanisms may be expressed in culture-specific ways. These two mutually interacting forces shape ontogeny and caregiving from the very start of each individual's life.

29.7 Conclusions

Can parent–infant interaction be understood apart from its cultural context? Writing in the *Handbook of Research Methods in Infant Development*, Whiting and Whiting (1960, p. 933) long ago observed that:

> If infants are studied within the confines of a single culture, many events are taken as natural, obvious, or a part of human nature and are therefore not reported and not considered as variables. It is only when it is discovered that other peoples do not follow these practices that have been attributed to human nature that they are adopted as legitimate variables.

A major task of developmental science is to explain how contexts and settings help to shape parenting and infant development. Parenting and infancy researchers need to recognize the subtleties, complexities, and unique qualities that manifestly reflect the richness of each culture they study, while simultaneously trying to determine and understand similarities and differences in cognitions and practices, activities and development, which equally clearly exist across cultures. The challenge that confronts cross-cultural developmental scientists of parenting infants is to understand and represent these similarities and differences in and across groups to transcend simplistic and dichotomous comparisons.

Cultural ideology shapes infant care patterns and infant development. It is important to keep in mind the cultural relativity of much of parents' thinking and knowledge about infants, because it may set limits on the generalizability of research. We cannot fathom parenthood or infancy fully unless we know more about the multiple ecologies in which parents and infants interact. Cultural variation in patterns of infant-rearing exert important influences on the ways in which infants are reared and what may be expected of them as they grow up. These variations merit study because they illustrate the limits of what we know about development, because they serve to highlight the narrow perspective researchers often bring to their investigations, and because they identify the importance of factors that are often discounted or overlooked completely.

References

Ainsworth, M. D. S. (1967). *Infancy in Uganda: Infant care and the growth of attachment*. Baltimore, MD: Johns Hopkins University Press.

Allik, J., & McCrae, R. R. (2004). Toward a geography of personality traits: Patterns of profiles across 36 cultures. *Journal of Cross-Cultural Psychology*, *35*, 13–28.

Azhari, A., Leck, W. Q., Gabrieli, G., Bizzego, A., Rigo, P., Setoh, P., ... Esposito, G. (2019). Parenting stress undermines mother–child brain-to-brain synchrony: A hyperscanning study. *Scientific Reports*, *9*, 11407.

Bales, K. L. (2014). Comparative and developmental perspectives on oxytocin and vasopressin. In M. Mikulincer & P. R. Shaver (Eds.), *Mechanisms of social connection: From brain to group* (pp. 15–31). Washington, DC: American Psychological Association.

Bayley, N. (1969). *Manual for the Bayley Scales of Infant Development*. San Antonio, TX: Psychological Corporation.

Bjorklund, D. F., & Myers, A. (2019). The evolution of parenting and evolutionary approaches to childrearing. In M. H. Bornstein (Ed.), *Handbook of parenting. Vol. 2: Biology and ecology of parenting* (3rd ed., pp. 3–29). New York, NY: Routledge.

Bornstein, M. H. (1989). Sensitive periods in development: Structural characteristics and causal interpretations. *Psychological Bulletin*, *105*, 179–197.

(1995). Form and function: Implications for studies of culture and human development. *Culture & Psychology*, *1*, 123–137.

(2001). Arnold Lucius Gesell. *Pediatrics and Related Topics/Pädiatrie und Grenzgebiete*, *40*, 395–409.

(Ed.). (2002). *Handbook of parenting* (2nd ed., Vols. 1–5). Mahwah, NJ: Lawrence Erlbaum Associates.

(2012). Cultural approaches to parenting. *Parenting, Science and Practice*, *12*, 212–221.

(2013). Parenting and child mental health: A cross-cultural perspective. *World Psychiatry*, *12*(3), 258–265.

(2015). Children's parents. In R. M. Lerner, M. H. Bornstein, & T. Leventhal Eds.), *Handbook of child psychology and developmental science. Vol. 4: Ecological settings and processes in developmental systems* (7th ed., pp. 55–132). Hoboken, NJ: Wiley.

(2016). Determinants of parenting. In D. Cicchetti (Ed.), *Developmental psychopathology: Risk, resilience, and intervention* (3rd ed., Vol. 4, pp. 180–270). Hoboken, NJ: Wiley.

(2017). Parenting in acculturation: Two contemporary research designs and what they tell us. *Current Opinion in Psychology*, *15*, 195–200.

Bornstein, M. H., & Cote, L. R. (2019). Immigrant parenthood. In M. H. Bornstein (Ed.), *Handbook of parenting. Vol. 4: Social conditions and applied parenting* (3rd ed., pp. 198–233). New York, NY: Routledge.

Bornstein, M. H., Cote, L. R., Haynes, O. M., Suwalsky, J. T., & Bakeman, R. (2012). Modalities of infant–mother interaction in Japanese, Japanese American immigrant, and European American dyads. *Child Development*, *83*, 2073–2088.

Bornstein, M. H., Esposito, G., & Motti-Stephanidi, F. (in press). Coregulation: A multilevel approach via biology and behavior. *Journal of Self-Regulation and Regulation.*

Bornstein, M. H., Hahn, C.-S., Haynes, O. M., Belsky, J., Azuma, H., Kwak, K., ... Galperín, C. (2007). Maternal personality and parenting cognitions in cross-cultural perspective. *International Journal of Behavioral Development, 31,* 193–209.

Bornstein, M. H., Haynes, O. M., Azuma, H., Galperín, C., Maital, S., Ogino, M., ... Wright, B. (1998). A cross-national study of self-evaluations and attributions in parenting: Argentina, Belgium, France, Israel, Italy, Japan, and the United States. *Developmental Psychology, 34,* 662–676.

Bornstein, M. H., & Lansford, J. E. (2010). Parenting. In M. H. Bornstein (Ed.), *The handbook of cultural developmental science. Part 1: Domains of development across cultures* (pp. 259–277). New York, NY: Psychology Press.

Bornstein, M. H., Putnick, D. L., Cote, L. R., Haynes, O. M. H., & Suwalsky, J. T. D. (2015). Mother–infant contingent vocalizations in 11 countries. *Psychological Science, 26,* 1272–1284.

Bornstein, M. H., Putnick, D. L., Rigo, P., Esposito, G., Swain, J. E., Suwalsky, J. T. D., ... Venuti, P. (2017). Neurobiology of culturally common maternal responses to infant cry. *Proceedings of the National Academy of Sciences of the United States of America 114*(45), E9465–E9473.

Bornstein, M. H., Putnick, D. L., & Suwalsky, J. T. D. (2012). A longitudinal process analysis of mother–child emotional relationships in a rural Appalachian European American community. *American Journal of Community Psychology, 50,* 89–100.

Bornstein, M. H., & Sawyer, J. (2005). Family systems. In K. McCartney & D. Phillips (Eds.), *The Blackwell handbook of early childhood development* (pp. 381–398). Malden, MA: Blackwell.

Bornstein, M. H., Tal, J., Rahn, C., Galperin, C. Z., Pecheux, M. G., Amour, M., ... Tamis-LeMonda, C. S. (1992). Functional analysis of the contents of maternal speech to infants of 5 and 13 months in four cultures: Argentina, France, Japan, and the United States. *Developmental Psychology, 28,* 593–603.

Bovet, M. C., Dasen, P. R., & Inhelder, B. (1974). Etapes de l'intelligence sensorimortice chez l'enfant Baoulé. *Archives de Psychologie, 41,* 363–386.

Boyd, R., & Richerson, P. J. (2005). *The origin and evolution of cultures.* Oxford: Oxford University Press.

Bronfenbrenner, U., & Crouter, A. C. (1983). The evolution of environmental models in developmental research. In P. Mussen (Ed.), *The handbook of child psychology. Vol. 1: Theories of development* (pp. 358–414). New York, NY: Wiley.

Bronfenbrenner, U., & Morris, P. A. (2006). The bioecological model of human development. In R. M. Lerner (Ed.), *Theoretical models of human development. Volume 1 of the Handbook of child psychology* (6th ed., pp. 793–828). Hoboken, NJ: Wiley.

Caria, A., de Falco, S., Venuti, P., Lee, S., Esposito, G., Rigo, P., ... Bornstein, M.H. (2012). Species-specific response to human infant faces in the premotor cortex. *NeuroImage, 60,* 884–893.

Cohler, B., & Paul, S. (2019). Psychoanalysis and parenthood. In M. H. Bornstein (Ed.), *Handbook of parenting. Vol. 3: Being and becoming a parent* (3rd ed., pp. 563–600). New York, NY: Routledge.

Collins, W. A., Maccoby, E. E., Steinberg, L., Hetherington, E. M., & Bornstein, M. H. (2000). Contemporary research on parenting: The case for nature and nurture. *American Psychologist, 55*, 218–232.

Cummings, E. E., & Warmuth, K. (2019). Parenting and attachment. In M. H. Bornstein (Ed.), *Handbook of parenting. Vol. 4: Social conditions and applied parenting* (3rd ed., pp. 374–400). New York, NY: Routledge.

Davis, O. S. P., Haworth, C. M. A., Lewis, C. M., & Plomin, R. (2012). Visual analysis of geocoded twin data puts nature and nurture on the map. *Molecular Psychiatry, 17*, 867–874.

Dennis, W., & Dennis, M. G. (1940). The effect of cradling practices upon the onset of walking in Hopi children. *Journal of Genetic Psychology, 56*, 77.

Draper, P., & Harpending, H. (1988). A sociobiological perspective on the development of human reproductive strategies. In K. B. MacDonald (Ed.), *Sociobiological perspectives on human development* (pp. 340–372). New York, NY: Springer New York.

Dudin, A., McGowan, P., Wu, R., Fleming, A. S., & Li, M. (2019). Psychobiology of maternal behavior in nonhuman mammals. In M. H. Bornstein (Ed.), *Handbook of parenting. Vol. 2: Biology and ecology of parenting* (3rd ed., pp. 30–77). New York, NY: Routledge.

Dunn, R. R., Davies, T. J., Harris, N. C., & Gavin, M. C. (2010). Global drivers of human pathogen richness and prevalence. *Proceedings of the Royal Society: Biological Sciences, 277*(1694), 2587–2595.

Epstein, R. M., & Hundert, E. M. (2002). Defining and assessing professional competence. *Journal of the American Medical Association, 287*, 226–235.

Esposito, G., Nakazawa, J., Ogawa, S., Stival, R., Kawashima, A., Putnick, D L., & Bornstein, M. H. (2014). Baby, you light-up my face: Culture-general physiological responses to infants and culture-specific cognitive judgements of adults. *PloS One, 9*, e106705.

Feldman, R., Gordon, I., Schneiderman, I., Weisman, O., & Zagoory-Sharon, O. (2010). Natural variations in maternal and paternal care are associated with systematic changes in oxytocin following parent–infant contact. *Psychoneuroendocrinology, 35*, 1133–1141.

Feldman, R., Gordon, I., & Zagoory-Sharon, O. (2011). Maternal and paternal plasma, salivary, and urinary oxytocin and parent–infant synchrony: Considering stress and affiliation components of human bonding. *Developmental Science, 14*, 752–761.

French, V. (2019). Ancient history of parenting. In M. H. Bornstein (Ed.), *Handbook of parenting. Vol. 2: Biology and ecology of parenting* (3rd ed., pp. 287–319). New York, NY: Routledge.

Freud, S. (1949). *An outline of psycho-analysis.* New York, NY: Norton.

Geary, D. C. (2000). Evolution and proximate expression of human paternal investment. *Psychological Bulletin, 126*, 55–77.

Geber, M. (1956). Développement psycho-moteur de l'enfant Africain. *Courrier, 6*, 17–29.

   (1958). The psychomotor development of African children in the first year, and the influence of maternal behavior. *Journal of Social Psychology, 47*, 185–195.

Geber, M., & Dean, R. F. (1957a). Gesell tests on African children. *Pediatrics, 20*, 1055–1065.

(1957b). The state of development of newborn African children. *Lancet, 272,* 1216–1219.

Gesell, A., & Amatruda, C. S. 1945. *The embryology of behavior.* New York, NY: Harper & Row.

Goodnow, J. J. (2010). Culture. In M. H. Bornstein (Ed.), *Handbook of cultural developmental science* (pp. 3–20). New York, NY: Psychology Press.

Goodnow, J. J., Cashmore, J., Cotton, S., & Knight, R. (1984). Mothers' developmental timetables in two cultural groups. *International Journal of Psychology, 19,* 193–205.

Griffiths, R. (1954). *The abilities of babies.* New York, NY: McGraw-Hill.

Harwood, R., Leyendecker, B., Carlson, V., Asencio, M., & Miller, A. (2002). Parenting among Latino families in the U.S. In M. H. Bornstein (Ed.), *Handbook of parenting. Vol. 4: Applied parenting* (2nd ed., pp. 21–46). Mahwah, NJ: Lawrence Erlbaum Associates.

Hewlett, B. S., Lamb, M. E., Shannon, D., Leyendecker, B., & Schölmerich, A. (1998). Culture and early infancy among Central African foragers and farmers. *Developmental Psychology, 34,* 653–661.

Holden, G. W. (1997). *Parents and the dynamics of child rearing.* New York, NY: Perseus.

Holden, G. W., & Smith, M. M. (2019). Parenting cognitions. In M. H. Bornstein (Ed.), *Handbook of parenting. Vol. 3: Being and becoming a parent* (3rd ed., pp. 681–721). New York, NY: Routledge.

Hopkins, B., & Westra, T. (1989). Maternal expectations of their infants' development: Some cultural differences. *Developmental Medicine and Child Neurology, 31,* 384–390.

(1990). Motor development, maternal expectations, and the role of handling. *Infant Behavior and Development, 13,* 117–122.

Hrdy, S. B. (1999). *Mother nature: A history of mothers, infants, and natural selection.* New York, NY: Pantheon.

Hsu, H. C., & Fogel, A. (2003). Social regulatory effects of infant nondistress vocalization on maternal behavior. *Developmental Psychology, 39,* 976–991.

Kärtner, J., Keller, H., Lamm, B., Abels, M., Yovsi, R. D., Chaudhary, N., & Su, Y. (2008). Similarities and differences in contingency experiences of 3-month-olds across sociocultural contexts. *Infant Behavior & Development, 31,* 488–500.

Keller, H., Lamm, B., Abels, M., Yovsi, R., Borke, J., Jensen, H., … Chaudhary, N. (2006). Cultural models, socialization goals, and parenting ethnotheories: A multicultural analysis. *Journal of Cross-Cultural Psychology, 37,* 155–172.

Klahr, A. M., & Burt, S. A. (2014). Elucidating the etiology of individual differences in parenting: A meta-analysis of behavioral genetic research. *Psychology Bulletin, 140,* 544–586.

Kochanska, G., & Aksan, N. (2004). Development of mutual responsiveness between parents and their young children. *Child Development, 75,* 1657–1676.

Kringelbach, M. L., Stark, E. A., Alexander, C., Bornstein, M. H., & Stein, A. (2016). On cuteness: Unlocking the parental brain and beyond. *Trends in Cognitive Sciences, 20,* 545–558.

Lambert, K. G., & Kinsley, C. H. (2012). Brain and behavioral modifications that accompany the onset of motherhood. *Parenting: Science and Practice, 12,* 74–89.

Leiderman, P. H., Tulkin, S. R., & Rosenfeld, A. H. (Eds.). (1977). *Culture and infancy*. New York, NY: Academic Press.

Luria, A. R. (1976). *Cognitive development: Its cultural and social foundations*. Cambridge, MA: Harvard University Press.

Lusk, D., & Lewis, M. (1972). Mother–infant interaction and infant development among the Wolof of Senegal. *Human Development, 15*, 58–69.

Maccoby, E. E. (1992). The role of parents in the socialization of children: An historical overview. *Developmental Psychology, 28*, 1006–1017.

MacDonald, K., & MacDonald, T. M. (2010). The peptide that binds: A systematic review of oxytocin and its prosocial effects in humans. *Harvard Review of Psychiatry, 18*, 1–21.

Marlowe, F. W. (2003). The mating system of foragers in the standard cross-cultural sample. *Cross-Cultural Research, 37*, 282–306.

McAdams, D. P., & Pals, J. L. (2006). A new Big Five: Fundamental principles for an integrative science of personality. *American Psychologist, 61*, 204–217.

McCrae, R. R., Terraciano, A., & 78 members of the Personality Profiles of Cultures Project. (2005). Universal features of personality traits from the observer's perspective: Data from 50 cultures. *Journal of Personality and Social Psychology, 88*, 547–561.

Mead, M., & MacGregor, F. C. (1951). *Growth and culture*. New York, NY: Putnam's Sons.

Miller, P. J., Wang, S. -H., Sandel, T., & Cho, G. E. (2002). Self-esteem as folk theory: A comparison of European American and Taiwanese mothers' beliefs. *Parenting, Science and Practice, 2*, 209–239.

Murray, L., Richards, M. P. M., & Nihouarn-Sigurdardottir, J. (2019). Mothering. In M. H. Bornstein (Ed.), *Handbook of parenting. Vol. 3: Being and becoming a parent* (3rd ed., pp. 36–63). New York, NY: Routledge.

Ochs, E. (1982). Talking to children in Western Samoa. *Language in Society, 11*, 77–104.

Packer, M., & Cole, M. (2015). Culture in development. In M. H. Bornstein & M. E. Lamb (Eds.), *Developmental science: An advanced textbook* (7th ed., pp. 43–111). New York, NY: Psychology Press.

Papoušek, H., & Papoušek, M. (2002). Intuitive parenting. In M. H. Bornstein (Ed.), *Handbook of parenting. Vol. 2: Biology and ecology of parenting* (2nd ed., pp. 183–203). Mahwah, NJ: Lawrence Erlbaum Associates.

Putnick, D. L., & Bornstein, M. H. (2016). Measurement invariance conventions and reporting: The state of the art and future directions for psychological research. *Developmental Review, 41*, 71–90.

Rebelsky, F. G. (1967). Infancy in two cultures. *Nederlands Tijdschrift Voor de Psychologie En Haar Grensgebieden, 22*, 379–385.

    (1972). Cross-cultural studies of mother–infant interaction. *Human Development, 15*, 128–130.

Rosenthal, M. K., & Roer-Strier, D. (2001). Cultural differences in mothers' developmental goals and ethnotheories. *International Journal of Psychology, 36*, 20–31.

Serpell, R. (1990). Audience, culture and psychological explanation: A reformulation of the emic-etic problem in cross-cultural psychology. *Quarterly Newsletter of the Laboratory of Comparative Human Cognition, 12*, 99–132.

Snow, C. E. (1977). Mothers' speech research: From input to interactions. In C. E. Snow & C. A. Ferguson (Eds.), *Talking to children: Language input and acquisition* (pp. 31–49). Cambridge, UK: Cambridge University Press.

Soderstrom, M. (2007). Beyond babytalk: Re-evaluating the nature and content of speech input to preverbal infants. *Developmental Review, 27*, 501–532.

Stern, D. N. (1985). *The interpersonal world of the infant*. New York, NY: Basic Books.

Stivers, T., Enfield, N. J., Brown, P., Englert, C., Hayashi, M., Heinemann, T., ... Levinson, S. (2009). Universals and cultural variation in turn-taking in conversation. *Proceedings of the National Academy of Sciences, 106*, 10587–10592.

Super, C. M. (1976). Environmental effects on motor development: The case of "African Infant Precocity." *Developmental Medicine and Child Neurology, 18*, 561–567.

Tamis-LeMonda, C. S., Bornstein, M. H., Cyphers, L., Toda, S., & Ogino, M. (1992). Language and play at one year: A comparison of toddlers and mothers in the United States and Japan. *International Journal of Behavioral Development, 15*, 19–42.

Tamis-LeMonda, C. S., & Kahana-Kalman, R. (2009). Mothers' views at the transition to a new baby: Variation across ethnic groups. *Parenting, Science and Practice, 9*, 36–55.

Tanner, J. M. (1970). Physical growth. In P. Mussen (Ed.), *Carmichael's manual of child psychology* (Vol. 1, pp. 77–155). New York, NY: Wiley.

Tomlinson, M., Bornstein, M. H., Marlow, M., & Swartz, L. (2014). Imbalances in the knowledge about infant mental health in rich and poor countries: Too little progress in bridging the gap. *Infant Mental Health Journal, 35*, 624–629.

UNICEF (2007). *The state of the world's children 2008: Child survival*. New York, NY: UNICEF.

van Egeren, L. A., Barratt, M. S., & Roach, M. A. (2001). Mother–infant responsiveness: Timing, mutual regulation, and interactional context. *Developmental Psychology, 37*, 684–697.

Vygotsky, L. (1978). *Mind in society*. Cambridge, MA: Harvard University Press.

Wachs, T. D. (2015). Assessing bioecological influences. In R. M. Lerner, M. H. Bornstein, & T. Leventhal (Eds.), *Handbook of child psychology and developmental science. Vol. 4: Ecological settings and processes in developmental systems* (7th ed., pp. 811–846). Hoboken, NJ: Wiley.

Werner, E. E. (1972). Infants around the world: Cross-cultural studies of psychomotor development from birth to two years. *Journal of Cross-Cultural Psychology, 3*, 111–134.

West, M. (1914). *Infant care*. Washington, DC: US Children's Bureau.

Whiting, J. W. M., & Whiting, B. B. (1960). Contributions of anthropology to the methods of studying child rearing. In P. Mussen (Ed.), *Handbook of research methods in child development* (pp. 918–944). New York, NY: Wiley.

Wilson, M., & Wilson, T. P. (2005). An oscillator model of the timing of turn-taking. *Psychonomic Bulletin & Review, 12*, 957–968.

Index